This text was created to provide you with a high-qua...
source. As a publisher specializing in college texts ... and
economics, our goal is to provide you with learning materials that will
serve you well in your college studies and throughout your career.

The educational process involves learning, retention, and the application of concepts and principles. You can accelerate your learning efforts utilizing the study guide that accompanies this text:

Workbook for use with UNDERSTANDING BUSINESS, Second Edition, by Barbara Barrett.

This learning aid is designed to improve your performance in the course by highlighting key points in the text and providing you with assistance in mastering the basic concepts.

Check your local bookstore or ask the manager to place an order for you today.

We at Irwin sincerely hope that the text and the accompanying Workbook and Study Guide will assist you in reaching your goals both now and in the future.

UNDERSTANDING BUSINESS

UNDERSTANDING BUSINESS

SECOND EDITION

William G. Nickels

University of Maryland

James M. McHugh

St. Louis Community College—Forest Park

Susan M. McHugh

Educational Learning Consultant

IRWIN

Homewood, IL 60430
Boston, MA 02116

The cover of this text is part of a total learning system that is designed to be interesting and involving. The cover illustration was commissioned by Richard D. Irwin, Inc. from Albert Lorenz, who also did the cover for the first edition of *Understanding Business*. The original concept for the cover came from a Computers—Communications advertisement for NEC which was supplied by K & L Inc. advertising agency. The theme of the cover is "The World Is Your Marketplace." It reflects the importance of international business.

How many of the landmarks can you identify? They are listed below.

■ World Trade Center, N.Y.C. ■ Pan Am Building, N.Y.C. ■ Empire State Building, N.Y.C. ■ Statue of Liberty ■ St. Peter's Church, Rome ■ Tower of Pisa ■ Guggenheim Museum, N.Y.C. ■ Lever House, N.Y.C. ■ U.S. Capitol ■ Washington Monument ■ Pyramids at Giza ■ Lincoln Memorial ■ Jefferson Memorial ■ Disney World ■ Epcot Center ■ Cape Canaveral ■ Equitable Building, Georgia ■ Raleigh Plaza, North Carolina ■ Lexington Insurance Building, Tennessee ■ Busch Memorial Stadium, St. Louis ■ St. Louis Gateway Arch ■ Wainwright Building, St. Louis ■ Lake Point Tower, Chicago ■ John Hancock Center, Chicago ■ Sears Tower, Chicago ■ Alcoa Building, Pittsburgh ■ Oral Roberts University, Tulsa ■ NCR Headquarters, Chicago ■ Dodge City Plaza, Kansas ■ Memphis State University ■ State Capitol, Austin ■ Ferris Plaza, Dallas ■ Municipal Plaza, Dallas ■ South Western Life Insurance Building, Texas ■ Post Oak Central Building, Houston ■ Thanksgiving Square, Texas ■ Pennzoil Plaza, Houston ■ Reunion Hotel, Dallas ■ Reunion Tower, Dallas ■ Peachtree Center Plaza, Atlanta ■ Eastern Building, Los Angeles ■ Caesar Pelli Tower, Atlanta ■ Century City Tower, Los Angeles ■ Sydney Opera House, Australia ■ Golden Gate Bridge, San Francisco ■ TransAmerica Pyramid, San Francisco ■ Portland Public Services Building, Oregon ■ Space Needle, Seattle ■ Buddha, China ■ Mount Rushmore, South Dakota ■ Great Wall of China ■ Big Ben, London ■ Eiffel Tower, Paris ■ Renaissance Center, Detroit

Copyright © 1987 by Times Mirror/Mosby College Publishing
© RICHARD D. IRWIN, INC., 1990

Sponsoring editor: Frank S. Burrows, Jr.
Special Projects editor: Ann M. Granacki
Project editor: Jane Lightell
Production manager: Carma W. Fazio
Designer: Tara L. Bazata
Cover illustrator: Albert Lorenz
Compositor: Better Graphics, Inc.
Typeface: 10/12 Galliard
Printer: Von Hoffmann Press, Inc.

Library of Congress Cataloging-in-Publication Data

Nickels, William G.
    Understanding business/William G. Nickels, James M. McHugh,
Susan M. McHugh.—2nd ed.
        p.   cm.
    Includes index.
    ISBN 0-256-07623-5
    ISBN 0-256-08401-7 (International Student Edition)
    1. Business. 2. Business—Vocational guidance. I. McHugh, James
M. II. McHugh, Susan M. III. Title.
    HF5351.N53   1990
    650—dc20   89-30446
                                                          CIP

Printed in the United States of America
1 2 3 4 5 6 7 8 9 0 VH 6 5 4 3 2 1 0 9

DEDICATION

To Marsha and Joel Nickels who share in the joys and frustrations of living with an author. Also to Casey Lynch and Molly and Michael McHugh who experienced greater sibling rivalry with this book than with each other. Relax kids, the book's gone off to college now!

And to the dedicated students and instructors who offered encouragement and suggestions for making this the most readable and useful text on the market.

ABOUT THE AUTHORS

Dr. William G. Nickels is an associate professor of business at the University of Maryland, College Park, Md. He has 20 years of teaching experience and has taught the introduction to business course for several years. During his teaching career, he has received many awards, including the Outstanding Teacher on Campus Award at the University of Maryland in 1985; the Teaching Excellence Award, Division of Behavioral Science, University of Maryland, 1983–1984; and the George Washington Honor Medal for Excellence in Economic Education. He has been in the top 15 percent of teachers in the College of Business for 20 years.

Dr. Nickels received his Ph.D. from The Ohio State University.

Jim McHugh is an associate professor of business at St. Louis Community College—Forest Park. Jim holds an M.B.A. and has broad experience in both education and business. In addition to teaching several sections of Introduction to Business each semester for 10 years, Jim has maintained adjunct professorships at Lindenwood College and Fontbonne College, teaching in the marketing and management areas at both the undergraduate and graduate level. Jim has conducted numerous seminars in business and maintains several consulting positions with small and large business enterprises in the St. Louis area. He is also involved in a consulting capacity in the public sector. Jim authored several textbook supplements, including study guides and test banks. He served as a reviewer and contributor to the first edition of *Understanding Business*. In partnership with his wife, Susan, Jim prepared the first edition test bank and computer simulation package.

Susan McHugh is an educational learning specialist with extensive training and experience in adult learning and curriculum development. She holds an M.Ed. and A.B.D. in education administration with a specialty in adult learning theory. As a professional curriculum developer, she has directed numerous curriculum projects and educator training programs. She coauthored the test bank and computer simulation package for the first edition of *Understanding Business*. Susan designed the second edition's instructor's manual, test bank, and computer simulation program.

PREFACE

The first edition of *Understanding Business* was the most successful new product introduced to the market in many years. It became one of the best-selling books in the field. Many instructors said that their students were never more excited by a textbook in their lives. They also said that students were coming to class prepared and eager to participate in discussions. The consensus was that the first edition was the most readable, most interesting introductory business text on the market.

Frank Falcetta at Middlesex Community College in Burlington, Maine, said: "In my 20 years of teaching I have had the opportunity to teach courses using many different textbooks; I can honestly say that I have never used a textbook that is so student oriented and engaging." Robert Stivender at Wake Technical Community College said: "Bill's first edition was a classroom triumph. Students read it! For the first time in teaching 'intro' for six years, my students were prepared to discuss beyond the basics. Bill's book had prepared them for that." Such comments give authors the motivation to do more. And we have done more! This edition is just one part of the totally integrated teaching and testing system that resulted from reviewer and user suggestions.

Understanding Business is not the number one book in sales. Other, more established books still maintain their leadership positions. They are fine books and we are proud just to be a competitor. But, like Avis, we are trying harder. We want to be number one because this course is one of the most important a student will ever take in school. We want to introduce more competition by offering a superior product. In this second edition, we set as our goal the production of the most up-to-date text, the most involving study guide, the most comprehensive test bank, the most useful and complete instructor's manual, the best color acetates, the most interesting and educational software projects (tutorials, simulations, and games), the best videotape library, and so on.

We have the pleasure of working with a new publisher because Times Mirror/Mosby bought Richard D. Irwin, Inc. and added this text to the well-established business texts at Irwin. Irwin shares our goals and promises the resources needed to make the second edition number one.

The greatest new resource is a team of coauthors—Jim and Susan McHugh. Jim McHugh is an Associate Professor of Business Administration at St. Louis Community College at Forest Park. He was an outstanding reviewer on the first edition. He uses the text in class, and his students love it. He introduced many ideas on how to improve the instructor's manual, the text, and other parts of the overall package. Susan McHugh is an Ed.D. candidate at the University of Missouri—St. Louis with a specialty in adult learning theory. She is a professional developer of educational supplements. She introduced wonderful new ideas for the test bank, the instructor's manual, the text, and more. Bill Nickels felt that such strong people would be an asset in making *Understanding Business* number one. The team was formed, and this second edition is much stronger as a result.

It still is the most readable and interesting text on the market. It also has comprehensive pedagogy that ensures that students learn the material step by step. There are progress checks along the way and getting involved sections to help students apply the material so it becomes theirs. In this new edition, we added ethics boxes to every chapter to emphasize the need to make proper decisions as well as profitable decisions. We wrote new, exciting profiles about real-life people, including 14-year-old entrepreneurs who start lawn-mowing services and mothers who start businesses at home. They are the kind of people with whom students can easily identify.

We wrote new cases illustrating the issues of the 1990s such as AIDS, the mommy track, the capitalist experiment in China and the subsequent reversals, the service revolution, the trend toward small, efficient farms, new megamalls, microwavable lunches, and more. Almost all the footnotes are from 1988 and 1989, and there are many footnotes so that students can pursue original sources if they want. We are now ready to take on the leaders with a text that is more readable, more up-to-date, more student-oriented, and gives the student more motivation to learn. We shall describe what we did in more detail below.

CONTENT DIFFERENCES

To make the text more manageable in length, two chapters were shortened and made into appendixes. The chapter on service and nonbusiness marketing is now the appendix to Part 3. It focuses on nonbusiness marketing. The marketing of services is incorporated into the text material throughout. Similarly, the chapter on personal financial planning is now an appendix.

The marketing chapters have been integrated through a discussion of all the marketing functions with one unifying example—a new high-fiber cereal called Fiberrific. Students will be able to identify with this new product because of today's emphasis on fiber. The marketing chapters are completely rewritten so that marketing research and promotion are last rather than first. Those of you who used the first edition will have no trouble with the new chapters, however. You will simply appreciate the improved flow.

Every effort was made to make this text the most up-to-date reference source on the market. To do that, the authors added material right through the final stage of production so that you have the latest material and footnotes. Some topics that were added include:

The latest in networking of computers.

A thorough discussion of the savings and loan crisis.

The recent Supreme Court decision on set-asides for minorities.
A brief look at the protests in China and the government reaction.
A discussion of perestroika in the Soviet Union.
The unification of Europe in 1992.
The history and future of agriculture and the drought of 1988/89.
The "new morality" movement against some TV shows.
The mergers and acquisitions trend, including poison pills, white knights, and hostile takeovers.
The latest in Employee Stock Ownership Plans.
The strike at Eastern airlines and other current labor issues.
Megamalls and warehouse clubs.
The merger of Federal Express with Flying Tiger to become the biggest international air freight company.
The latest in advertising.
The making of the stealth airplane in a skunkworks.
The use of cellular phones, payfax, and other high-tech office tools.
The latest in software programs to aid managers.
The Alaskan oil spill and other ecological concerns.
Dealing with AIDS among workers.
The issue of executive pay reaching over $2 million for top people.
The latest discussion of pay equity and the "mommy track."
The latest about the insurance crisis.
The new head of the Federal Reserve and his policies.
International joint ventures.
The latest trends in ethics-based management.
The recent Supreme Court decisions on affirmative action.
No other text stays as current and discusses such issues in such depth.

CONTENT SIMILARITIES

The second edition keeps the popular Prologue. Naturally the references are changed, but the content is very similar. There is a new profile and some new information about careers and salaries.

There are still two chapters on economics. More emphasis is given the newest trends in China and the Soviet Union because of perestroika and other developments. The latest economic figures are given, including the 1990 budget.

The two chapters on small business management and entrepreneurship and franchising are reversed by popular request. Now entrepreneurship is first. The idea is to present the interesting people who are the entrepreneurs of the 1980s and 1990s and then go into the details of franchising and small business management. We have the latest trends in entrepreneurship, including the trend toward having more experienced managers become entrepreneurs.

The marketing chapters are rearranged and revised. As mentioned above, they are now united by a common case. The case is about concept testing and packaging, promoting, pricing, and distributing a new cereal.

The rest of the text is in the same order with almost all new footnotes, profiles, and cases. Popular cases are retained and updated. The chapter on personal financial planning is now an appendix, but much of the content remains.

EXTENSIVE DEVELOPMENT

This edition went through several reviews. As much as possible, reviewer comments were added to the text and additional reviews were made to make sure the additions and deletions were enthusiastically endorsed by everyone.

James McHugh and William Nickels both taught the course using the old edition. They have classroom tested the color acetates, the stock market project, and other elements of the package, especially the test bank, to be sure they are useful to both students and instructors. The new materials are greatly improved as a result. Dr. Nickels now teaches the course to classes of 500 students, so he knows the problems of trying to reach large classes. This new edition, along with the study guide, makes it possible for students to study and learn the text material on their own. This frees the instructor to add new material and integrate the concepts from the book. The integrated instructor's manual introduces new lecture material, including 200 new color acetates with narrations and TV-quality videotapes.

SUPPLEMENTS

An Integrated Teaching and Testing System

Everything in the second edtion of *Understanding Business* is designed to help teachers be more effective and to help students do better in class. It all starts with learning goals. The learning goals spell out what is expected of the student in each chapter. As students read the material, periodic progress checks enable them to see whether or not they understood what they read. At the end of the chapter is a summary in a question and answer format that is tied directly to the learning goals. Students can thus use the summaries as mini quizzes and test their progress.

The text is a self-contained learning tool. The study guide reinforces what is learned in the text. Students who use the guide write down their answers so that the material becomes part of them. It is not an easy study guide; it is an effective one that demands active participation. In other words, it will help students become proficient in the text material.

The test bank is directly tied to the learning goals. There are test questions for each learning goal that are categorized by level of learning. Some questions measure the students' knowledge of basic terms and facts. Others test their ability to understand concepts and principles. The most advanced questions ask students to apply the principles they have learned. There are at least two questions in each category.

Together, the text, study guide, and test bank become an integrated teaching and testing system in that everything is tied to the learning goals. Students know right from the start what they are expected to learn and are reinforced in that goal every step of the way, including the quizzes and tests. Supplementary materials, such as the stock market project and getting involved projects, add to the learning process and the involvement in the course. No introduction to business package is as easy-to-use and fully integrated as this one. To accomplish this integration, the authors of the text wrote the instructor's manual, the test bank, and the computer simulations and games. They also prepared the new acetates. The other supplements were prepared by outstanding practitioners who used the materials in their classes.

Study Guide

A very important component of our package is the Study Guide. Ours is uniquely designed to help students become involved in the learning process. The study guide to *Understanding Business*, written by Barbara Barrett of St. Louis Community College—Meramec, is not merely a synopsis of the text. Rather, it is a learning device that requires students to write answers and to apply what they have learned. If your students use this guide, they will be fully prepared for class discussions and exams.

Computer Exercises

McNick and Company

Our research found that instructors want an interactive computer simulation and tutorial to get their students involved in business decision making. We completely revamped the first edition's software program. It is now both an interactive tutorial and a simulation program called McNick and Company. It is designed to be used on IBM and compatible computers. The student starts a canoe company. Decisions must be made about the form of the company—sole proprietorship, partnership, or corporation. Economic decisions such as competitor analysis and pricing are made. A break-even point is calculated. Business decisions regarding all phases of business then are made. The student is given feedback and can use the program's computer to make calculations. It is a fun exercise and a great learning experience. It is a tutorial in that the questions are based on material from the book and students are given rationales for correct and incorrect answers based on sections from the book.

International Trade Game

A second computer simulation and game, called International Trade Game—An Interactive Computer Simulation, is available as well. It involves the international trading of soybeans. The student gets a certain amount of money to start with and then must buy and sell soybeans as world market conditions change. They make "money" in the process and can test themselves against other players or teams. It is an interesting exercise and involves students with the terminology and practice of world trade.

Stock Market Project

A third computer disc is available with the stock market project. It is a spreadsheet program that enables students to manipulate stock and bond figures. This frees students to spend less time on calculations and more time on analysis.

Instructor's Manual

The instructor's manual is completely redeveloped. All the material is easy to use. What makes the Instructor's Manual unique is its integration with the text and the rest of the package. Each chapter opens with a description of differences between the second edition and the first edition to make conversion to the new edition as easy as possible.

After a short topic outline of the chapter and a listing of the chapter objectives and key terms, you will find a resource checklist. This chart lists all of the supplements that correspond with this chapter. There is no need to flip through half a dozen sources to find what supplementary material is available.

To make the system even easier to use, the detailed lecture outline contains marginal notes recommending where to use acetates, supplementary cases, lecture enhancers, and application exercises. When the manual is opened flat, the lecture outline and marginal notes are on the left-side page. The right-side page contains brief article summaries to help spice up the classroom dialogue. This page also contains suggested comments that you can make when using the acetates. Of course, space is available for adding personal notes of your own so that they too may be integrated into the system.

Lecture enhancers bring in the latest business and social issues from 1988 and 1989. The end of each chapter has application exercises that you can duplicate and use for homework assignments and/or classroom discussions. This is a tremendous aid to new instructors and experienced instructors who would like to get their students more involved in the learning process.

Electronic Instructor's Manual

An electronic instructor's manual is also available. That means that the outline of the text is also available on computer disks and you can add or delete material as you see fit. You can thus rewrite the instructor's manual to fit your own teaching style.

Test Bank

One part of the Integrated Teaching and Testing System always receives more attention than the rest. That is the test bank. The success of a course depends on tests that are comprehensive and fair. Tests should measure a student's ability to remember the material and use the material in real-world situations. That means that the test bank must have questions that measure both recall and the ability of students to apply the material. Furthermore, there must be enough questions to change tests each semester and still have high-quality questions.

The Nickels/McHugh/McHugh test bank is like no other on the market. There are over 4,000 test questions to choose from and they are available on an easy-to-use computer disk so you can pick and choose questions and develop tests and quizzes in a minimum of time. The test bank tests three levels of learning: *knowledge* of key terms, *understanding* of concepts and principles, and *application* of the principles. Each item has a unique rationale for the correct answer as well as the corresponding text page and identifies objective and learning level.

A new tool was added to help you develop balanced tests. Each chapter opens with a "Test Table." This chart identifies items by objective and level of learning. By simply circling the appropriate test item numbers, you can easily identify the objectives and the levels of learning you are testing.

For the ultimate in ease, each chapter concludes with a Quick Quiz. These 10-item tests are ready for reproduction and distribution for testing or for outside assignments.

The test bank also comes in a computerized version called CompuTest II. It allows you to add questions, delete questions, and edit the questions in the test bank. It is the most up-to-date computerized testing system available.

Teletest

By far the easiest way to generate an exam is to use teletest. Teletest is a service that will generate a master copy of an exam. All you have to do is call 1-800-331-5094 and ask for extension number 2742 (Debbra Wood). You can ask for specific questions, by number, on the exam or ask for questions covering various issues at different levels of learning to be randomly selected. You will get your exam within a few days.

Color Transparencies

To augment the concepts presented in the text, 200 color acetates have been prepared. These acetates enable you to illustrate your lectures with colorful visual aids. A separate booklet contains teaching suggestions for each acetate.

Transparency Masters

In addition to the acetates, every chart, graph, and table in the text is reproduced as a transparency master for your easy use in the classroom.

Business Forms

Students are often not prepared for the variety of forms they will have to fill out for job applications and then on the job. The 68 business forms supplied with the Integrated Teaching and Testing System provide you with the means to expose students to such forms in school. You can pick and choose which forms to use, but we tried to make the package as comprehensive as possible. Frank Falcetta of Middlesex Community College in Burlington, Maine, prepared these forms.

Stock Market Project

The stock market project was a success in the classroom. It was one of the highlights of Dr. Nickels' classes. Nonetheless, students recommended certain changes to make the project more useful and practical. For example, the average young investor is more likely to buy into a mutual fund than to choose individual stocks. (It helps them to diversify and get professional advice at a minimum cost.) Therefore, we added mutual funds to the stock market project so that students can learn the terminology and techniques for getting involved.

More emphasis is also placed on data analysis rather than data gathering. The idea is to have students work with the material rather than just look it up. Furthermore, as we mentioned earlier, computer disks are now available in a spreadsheet format for students to input the data and manipulate the numbers. Joyce Newton at Jackson Community College in Michigan prepared this project.

Videotapes

Adopters will have access to The Business Insight videos created by Nathan/Tyler, the producers of the *In Search of Excellence* business film series. Other videos will be available soon. Each tape is 10–15 minutes long and is produced in the VHS format. Discussion about the videos and the related cases are included in the Integrated Instructor's Manual. The videos include:

Next, Inc.   This video shows how "the entrepreneur of the 1980s," Steve Jobs, went about the development of his new computer for the education community. There is much emphasis in the text on entrepreneurship and small business management and this video sets the stage for further discussion.

Federal Express and Marriott   This tape shows students how leading firms establish and measure service standards to make them more competitive. This is critical in an age when 70–80 percent of jobs are in the service sector.

Post-It-Note®   This video is about the intrapreneuring process at the 3M Company. This is the story of innovation and the kind of corporate culture that fosters it.

First Union National Bank & LensCrafters   These two companies show the importance of service managers in today's market. The key to success in a service economy is employees who have a consumer orientation and managers who can train and support them. This video shows this dramatically.

ZapMail   This Federal Express venture was a failure, but it anticipated the success of fax machines. What students learn here is the need for cooperation and understanding between a company and its advertising agency. If the concept is not communicated, the product fails.

Esprit   This video shows how important image is to a product's success. In this case, the brand name Esprit is highlighted. A second message is the need to delegate authority while still keeping responsibility for results. This video can lead to much discussion about managerial styles.

Honeywell   This video provides an interesting link between manufacturing and marketing. It discusses how a firm goes about choosing various production processes. It also discusses how a firm selects a marketing strategy. It then explains how the marketing strategy and manufacturing strategy are interwoven. The result is a flexible manufacturing system.

Discovery Toys   This tape is great for generating discussion about the need for managers to hear their employees and to delegate authority, even though the process can be quite painful. You simply cannot run a large company by yourself. This contrasts nicely with the tape on Esprit where the top manager takes off for months each year.

U.S. Health and J.C. Penney   This tape emphasizes the need to market internally as well as to consumers. Employees must be sold on the concept of service first and then they implement the concept to customers. Emphasis is on listening and responding and rewarding employees for being responsive.

Lotus   The 1980s was a decade of the entrepreneur. One problem was that the entrepreneurs were good at starting firms, but for one reason or another were not good at keeping the firm going through growth and troubled times. This video shows one example of that. The discussion in class can thus focus on the new entrepreneurs who have managerial experience as discussed in the text.

PEDAGOGY

There are many pedagogical devices in the second edition of *Understanding Business*. We believe that the text has the most comprehensive pedagogy available in this market. That is one reason why students reacted so favorably to the first edition. Its format assists them in doing well on exams.

Learning Goals

As we already noted, one of the more helpful pedagogical devices is learning goals that are tied directly to the summaries at the end of the chapter and the test questions. Students thus have the chance to preview ahead of time what they are supposed to know after reading the chapter, and are then able to test that knowledge when reading the questions in the summary.

The *Study Guide* is also closely linked to the learning goals as part of the total integrated teaching, learning, and testing system.

Opening Profiles

Each chapter begins with a profile of a person who illustrates an important point in the chapter. Not all the personalities are famous because they represent the full gamut of businesspeople from young students starting a lawn mowing service to Lee Iacocca. These profiles provide a transition between chapters and a good introduction to the text material. Reviewers have commented very favorably on this feature.

Progress Checks

One unique feature in *Understanding Business* is the use of progress checks. After each major topic there is a progress check that asks students to remember what they have just read. If a student is not retaining the material, the progress checks will stop them before they go very far and will show them that they need to go back and review. We have all experienced times when we were studying and our minds wandered. Progress checks are a great tool to prevent that from happening for more than a page or two.

Thinking It Through

These inserts, found throughout each chapter, ask students to pause and think about how the material they are reading applies in their own lives. This device is an excellent tool for linking the text material to the student's past experience to enhance memory. It greatly increases student involvement in the text.

Interactive Summaries

By now you know that the summaries are directly tied with the learning goals and are written in a question and answer format. This allows students to test themselves. Answering the questions and getting immediate feedback helps prepare students for quizzes and exams.

Key Terms

Key terms appear in boldface in the text the first time they are introduced to the student. They are also listed at the beginning of each chapter, defined in the margin, and defined in a glossary at the end of the text. Students can thus read through the words they will encounter, spot them immediately on a page, and pause and learn them as they go along.

Getting Involved

The goal of the Progress Checks and the Thinking It Through boxes is to increase student involvement in the learning process. The same is true of the section called Getting Involved. It assigns students miniprojects that they can do to learn more about the subject. Some of it is library work, but most of it involves talking with people to obtain their reactions and advice on certain subjects. The Instructor's Manual has the Getting Involved questions one chapter earlier than the students see them in the text. In that way, the instructor can assign the work **before** students come to class. Students thus come to class better prepared to discuss the topics. Many instructors were excited by student enthusiasm and willingness to participate as a result of these homework assignments. If your students divide these assignments among themselves, they can learn much from outside sources without any one student having to do too much work.

Practice Cases

Each chapter concludes with two cases to practice managerial decision making. These are relatively short cases because they are discussion starters and do not take up the whole class. The answers to the cases are in the instructor's manual. Supplementary cases and exercises are also included in the manual for those who have small classes.

Photo and Illustration Essays

Each photo and illustration has a short paragraph that shows the relevance of the visual to the material in the text. We call them photo essays because they give the pictures much more meaning. The same is true of the various illustrations. The accompanying descriptions help the student understand what is being said in the illustration and what to look for to get the most out of each illustration.

Ethics Boxes

A major addition to the second edition is the inclusion of ethics boxes in each chapter. Furthermore, ethical decision making is woven into the material throughout. For example, in discussing managerial decision making, one step is to select the best **ethical** answer rather than just the best answer. The difference between following the law and being ethical gets much attention. Students learn that doing the proper thing is as important as doing the profitable thing.

ACKNOWLEDGMENTS

The strength of a second edition comes from the reviewers. Because they were willing to analyze and criticize openly and freely, the authors were able to respond by writing better material. We were blessed with reviewers who were serious about the course and eager for this book to serve their needs as much as possible. Their names are listed at the end of this preface but we want to thank them one more time for their dedication and assistance. We hope that their effort will be rewarded when they use the materials in the classroom.

The second most important person in developing a second edition is the Developmental Editor. We had the best Irwin has to offer in Ann Granacki. She is a Special Projects Editor who knows how to get things done. She helped in all phases of the second edition from working with some reviewers to coordinating the selection of pictures and the development of software programs that were exciting to use. She was ably assisted by Michael O'Malley who did an excellent job of doing what needed to be done and doing it on time.

Alice Fugate handled the project while it was still at Mosby. She got the ball rolling by finding excellent reviewers and handling the review process. She is staying in St. Louis, but we appreciate her efforts. Frank Burrows took over the acquisitions editor role and participated in all the developmental work to make sure the project was coordinated and integrated.

Michael Hruby is the Photo Researcher who found the excellent pictures used throughout the text. Jane Lightell was responsible for the editing process. She made the authors' jobs easier by getting things out on time and making sure that the material was readable and smoothly written. As Senior Project Editor, it is her job to coordinate the editing, indexing, and art preparation. She did an excellent job.

Tara Bazata was in charge of the overall layout of the cover and text. A brief look at the results shows you the great job she did. Part of the effectiveness of a text is the attractiveness of the layout. By that criterion, *Understanding Business* is one of the best designed business books ever.

Carma Fazio is the Senior Production Manager. It was her job to set up schedules and manage the production suppliers. This is a complex job and it was done superbly.

John Thoeming is the Senior Graphic Artist responsible for the readable and interesting acetates that are available for classroom use. His creativity is obvious by a brief glance at the acetates.

When we needed an extra pair of hands, we could always count on Jane Childers to type the manuscript for the supplements quickly and accurately. We thank her for her patience and understanding.

Special thanks also goes to the instructors who used the first edition of *Understanding Business*. They were very supportive and willing to send suggestions and comments on their own to improve the second edition. We appreciate their overwhelmingly favorable response and suggestions.

Reviewers of the Second Edition

Dennis Butler
Orange Coast Community College

Patricia Graber
Middlesex County College

William Motz
Lansing Community College

Thomas Buchl
Northern Michigan University

Bruce Charnov
Hofstra University

Nick Sarantakes
Austin Community College

Allen Kartchner
Utah State University

Alec Beaudoin
Triton College

Renee Prim
Central Piedmont Community College

Joyce Mooneyhan
Pasadena City College

Jill Chown
Mankato State University

James Cocke
Pima County Community College

Robert Stivender
Wake Technical Community College

Karl Rutkowski
Peirce Jr. College

Milton Alderfer
Miami-Dade Community College

Scott Reedy
Brookes College

Jeri Rubin
University of Alaska

Dan Anderson
Sullivan Jr. College

Paul Williams
Mott Community College

Judith Lyles
Illinois State University

Lorraine Suzuki
University of Maryland—Asian Division

John A. Knarr
University of Maryland—European Division

John Foster
Montgomery College

William Wright
Mt. Hood Community College

George Sutcliffe
Central Piedmont Community College

Ron Young
Kalamazoo Valley Community College

Richard Stanish
Tulsa Junior College

Katherine Olson
Northern Virginia Community College

Joseph Brum
Fayetteville Technical Institute

Sanford B. Helman
Middlesex Community College

Carl Sonntag
Pikes Peak Community College

Ted Erickson
Normandale Community College

Larry Saville
Des Moines Area Community College

Gene Johnson
Clark College

Diane McCann
Kentucky College of Business

Sandy Hellman
Middlesex County College

TO THE STUDENT

Before you begin reading the second edition of *Understanding Business*, you may want to know something about the book and the overall purpose of the course. First, let's explore the objectives of the text. The primary objective is to help you learn the basic fundamentals of business. That is, you will learn the basics of what people do in marketing, management, production, accounting, finance, and other business areas. You will also learn the basic terms and concepts of economics so you can better understand the business literature. When you are finished with the course, therefore, you should be able to read with comprehension all the business publications available so that you can continue your goal of truly understanding business.

In the text, you will be encouraged to read business newspapers and magazines such as *The Wall Street Journal* and *Business Week*, *Inc.*, and *Entrepreneur*. The idea is to expose you to as many information sources as possible so you can learn about business from many perspectives. You will get much more out of this class if you really immerse yourself in business by talking with businesspeople, reading the literature, and completing the Getting Involved exercises and cases at the end of each chapter.

Why should you bother spending so much time on this class? Because a second objective of the text is to help you decide what kind of career would be rewarding and interesting for you **and** to show you how to get the job you want through effective resume writing and interviewing. There are dozens of other introduction to business texts on the market, but your instructor chose the one that was designed to guide you in your own personal search to understand what business is all about so that you can become more focused on a career. Because of that orientation, this should be one of the most valuable courses you take in school.

You'll notice that we (the authors) use a conversational tone in the text. Our goal in doing so is to help you understand business by keeping the text highly readable and interesting. You should be able to retain more if you enjoy reading the text. Another feature of the text that should increase its effectiveness for you is the number of examples taken from businesses with which you are familiar.

There are many resources available to you when taking a college-level course. They include your instructor, the text, your classmates, the library, and outside experts who are working in the business world. The prologue to the text discusses these resources and outlines a strategy for getting the most out of this course. Your college and business days will be much more productive if you start a file system and follow the other advice in the prologue.

Making Learning a Game

Business is an important and serious subject. However, experience shows that you learn more when you enjoy what you are doing. So let's make the 24 chapters in this text into 24 parts of an *Understanding Business* game. You will see how well you are playing the game when you get your grades back from the various quizzes and exams you take. But the real test of your game skills will occur when you go out into the marketplace, use the skills from this text to get a good job, and then begin practicing what you learned. Several features are included in the text to help you win the game.

Learning Goals

The *Understanding Business* game looks like this. You start the game by reading a series of goals. The objective of the game is to accomplish those goals so that you can reach the final objective: a challenging and rewarding career. To play the game right, you should read the learning goals before you begin reading the chapters. Think about the goals as you read. The progress checks will help you to keep on target. The summaries will tell you whether or not you have accomplished each goal. Note that the learning goals are repeated next to the summaries so you can review them as you test your recall.

The Study Guide

Whether or not your instructor assigns it, you can get a study guide from Irwin, 1818 Ridge Road, Homewood, Illinois, 60430. You can also call the company and order the guide. The number is 1-800-634-3961. The study guide uses the learning goals as a framework to help you learn the material from the chapters. To do it right, you will have to write out the answers and spend some time with the guide. If you do, though, you will be far ahead of students who do not use the guide and, therefore, are more likely to win the testing game. If you want a structured way to study, the study guide is your answer.

Progress Checks

As you are going through the various chapters, we will stop you and ask you some questions. If you know all the answers, you are winning the game. If you don't know the answers, it is easy to go back and find the answers before you go on. These short pauses in the game are called Progress Checks because that's what they are—checks to measure your progress in understanding the material.

Thinking It Through

It is much easier to remember text material if you pause periodically and think of how the material specifically applies to you. The boxes called Thinking It Through challenge you to think about how the material you are reading applies in your own life. That way the game has more meaning to you. Together, the Progress Checks and the Thinking It Through sections will give you plenty of opportunity to test both your knowledge and your ability to apply that knowledge.

Ethics Boxes

You will be entering the business world at a time when ethics are a major concern. Businesspeople, politicians, and others in society have a whole new perspective on what is right and proper to do. Consumer protests are forcing advertisers and TV-show producers to recognize their moral and ethical feelings as well as their entertainment needs. Each chapter, therefore, has an ethics box for you to use to practice making ethical decisions. Most of the decisions are very difficult and your fellow students may react differently. Nonetheless, you can learn much from reviewing these boxes and thinking about ethics as you read each chapter.

Summaries

The summaries at the end of each chapter are written in a question and answer format. That gives you one more chance to score yourself as you play the game. Read each question and try to answer it yourself before reading the answers in the summaries. That makes the summary more like a chapter quiz and tests your knowledge. If you used the progress checks, then every summary should show you that you are winning the game and that you do understand more and more about business.

Key Terms

All games have new terms you have to learn, such as "icing the puck" in hockey, "double dribble" in basketball, and "clipping" in football. Once you know all the terms and how they fit into the game, it is much easier to watch and enjoy games on TV and in person. The same is true of the *Understanding Business* game. Therefore, key terms are listed at the beginning of each chapter. Look them over and see how many you already know. Note which ones are unfamiliar to you and make a mental note to look for them as you read. Key terms are printed in bold and the definitions are located in the margins so it is easy to spot unfamiliar terms and easy to learn their meaning in the context of the chapter. If you learn the terms as you go through each of the 24 chapters, it will be easy to remember them when the game gets even more serious—out in the business world.

Photo and Figure Essays

You will notice as you go through the text that most pictures and figures have a paragraph accompanying them. The idea is to help integrate the pictures and figures with the text so that you get more out of them. We will also be pointing out important features of the figures so that you can see their relevance. Pay some attention to these supplementary materials. Often it is true that a "picture is worth a thousand words" in showing you the latest in the business world. This is especially true of the pictures from other countries. You may not be as familiar with business in other parts of the world, and the pictures will help you see what is happening with franchises internationally and so forth.

Career Information

There are sections and boxes throughout the text describing careers, future job opportunities in those careers, and places to look to find more information. Each of those parts is highlighted by the same color background so you can search for career information at a glance. If you play the game right, one of those careers may be waiting for you when you complete your education. Be sure to spend extra time learning how to write an effective cover letter, prepare a winning resume, and get ready for job interviews. That information is in the appendix to Chapter 16.

Learning by Doing

Each chapter ends with some exercises that encourage you to go out and do some research or somehow get involved in the learning process. This text is designed to be an action course or game, not one where the instructor talks and you sit passively and listen. Rather, you are to go out into the real world and see for yourself what is going on and then report what you see to the class. If you divide the work among several classmates, together you can do all the assignments and have lively discussions in class. There are many ways to play the understanding business game, but, like all games, it is much more fun to be on the playing field than sitting on the bench. Get involved.

Practicing Management Decisions

There are two cases at the end of each chapter that enable you to think through what you have learned in a real-world situation. You may enjoy working through these cases as game practice whether or not they are assigned in class. The cases cover interesting topics such as starting a business at school, trying to make a small farm profitable, marketing breakfast cereal and coffee, playing the cola wars, and debating the merits of the "mommy track."

Practice Makes Perfect

Your instructor has access to two software packages that you can use to supplement your learning process. The first one, McNick and Company, is a simulation that asks you to start and run a canoe company. Along the way, you will be making decisions based on the knowledge you gained in *Understanding Business*. This computer simulation lets you learn the concepts of the book while having fun playing a computer game.

A second simulation is also available. It is called the International Trade Game. It is an interactive computer simulation and game designed to teach you about trading commodities on the world market. The commodity you trade is soybeans. As you play the game, you accumulate money from your trades. It is a fun and interesting way to learn about international markets. If you are interested in these supplements, ask your instructor.

You will also be able to use another computer disk that accompanies the Stock Market Project. This interesting and fun project gives you practice in buying mutual funds and choosing stocks. The computer disk has a spreadsheet format that will let you enter the data and work with the figures more easily. You will also learn to analyze the stock and bond figures.

Game Experience

In the work world, you will be expected to come in on time, to complete your work when it is due and turn it in, and to be a responsible contributor to the organization. That means that you will be expected to communicate effectively in both oral and written form. There is no better place to practice those skills than in class. Now is the time to commit yourself to being prepared when you come to class, to contribute if you are asked, and to do the assigned work on time. If you really want to be a winner, you should do more than assigned, including work on the study guide. If you do this in all your classes, you will have work habits that will serve you well all your life.

The main reason most people play games is because they are fun. We have done everything we can to make this text a rewarding experience. That is true of the Richard D. Irwin, Inc. as well. As you can see, we have chosen an attractive cover, colorful illustrations, clear and readable charts, and a very readable format. All of this was done to make the game enjoyable and a great learning experience. Good luck. We hope you win the game.

CONTENTS

PART II

BUSINESS FORMATION

PART III

FUNDAMENTALS OF MARKETING

PART IV

Management

13 PRODUCTION AND OPERATIONS MANAGEMENT, 391

14 MANAGEMENT TOOLS FOR THE INFORMATION AGE, 425

PART V

MANAGEMENT OF HUMAN RESOURCES

PART VI

ACCOUNTING AND FINANCE

PART VII

RISK MANAGEMENT, ETHICS, AND INTERNATIONAL BUSINESS

22 RISK MANAGEMENT AND INSURANCE,   703

BUSINESS TRENDS AND THE ECONOMIC ENVIRONMENT

I

CAREER AND COURSE RESOURCES

PROFILE LARRY ADLER, TEEN BUSINESSPERSON

You can identify with Larry Adler running a lemonade stand at age 5. It's also easy to picture him at 7 doing magic tricks for money. But even Alex P. Keaton (Michael J. Fox) on "Family Ties" would be surprised at the progress Larry Adler has made in the last seven years.

When Larry was 9, his stepfather gave him $19 to pay for flyers to start a lawn mowing business. Today, Larry is 14 and is grossing about $100,000 a year in revenue. He owns several businesses that are all subsidiaries of Larry Adler & Associates. The first is called Rent-A-Kid. Larry started by mowing lawns himself, but now employs some 60 people who do everything from lawn mowing to car washing, house painting, window washing, and odd jobs of all kinds.

Larry's second company, Basket Boy, started when he was in Florida. He saw 10,000 plastic hanging baskets for sale and brought them all back home to Potomac, Maryland. He filled them with candy and gifts and sold them all in a few months. From that experience, Larry became a sales agent representing 50 companies selling children's items. He also promotes and sells a day-planner for kids, *The Play Runner*. He writes monthly articles for *Young Fashions* magazine and manages a four-man band called The Mix.

Larry works from 9 A.M. to 5 P.M. and has a tutor to keep him current with his school work. He has business cards, a business manager, and a lawyer. Periodically, he drives around town in a chauffeur- driven limousine—after all, he is not yet old enough to drive.

Recently, Larry began plans to franchise his business because he says, "That's where the money is." Indeed, small businesses and franchising offer many job opportunities for people of all ages. Larry got an early start, but you, too, can become a business success. In Part 1 of this text, you will learn strategies that will prepare you for a business career. You will also explore some of the trends that are creating new business opportunities. Finally, you will read how the American system of free enterprise works.

Sources: Beth Kaiman, "14-Year-Old Presides Over Growing Md. Business Empire," *The Washington Post*, December 28, 1987, pp. B1 and B3; Felicity Feather, "Potomac Teen Rakes in $100,000 a Year," *Chronicle Express Newspapers*, November 25, 1987, pp. 3 and 20; and Pam McLintock, "14-Year-Old Carving Out His Future as a Tycoon," *The Washington Times*, November 25, 1987, pp. A1 and A4.

Larry Adler

Tell me, I'll forget. Show me, I may remember. But involve me and I'll understand.
CHINESE PROVERB

BUSINESS SKILLS CAN BE APPLIED ANYWHERE

Larry Adler is just one of thousands of small-business operators who begin their own businesses each year. He is unusual because he is so young. But each of the others has a unique story to tell as well. Some are women with children who are starting businesses in their own homes. You will read about several such women in the Profile to Chapter 1. Others are new immigrants who can barely speak English, but who are launching successful businesses. We shall explore many such stories throughout the text. The purpose of these stories is to show you that the American dream is still alive and well. Business opportunities have never been greater.

This book and this course may be the most important learning experiences of your life. They are meant to help you understand business so that you can use business principles in your own life. But you don't have to be in business to use business principles. You can use marketing principles to get a job and to sell your ideas to others. You can use your knowledge of investments to make money in the stock market. Similarly, you will be able to use the management skills and general business knowledge wherever you go and whatever career you pursue. The story of Alan Kutz illustrates that point well (see the box below).

Learning about Careers

Almost all of us want to find a rewarding career and to be successful and happy. We just find it hard to decide what that career should be. Even those who have relatively successful careers tend to look for something more fulfilling, more challenging, and more interesting. One purpose of this text is to introduce to you

---

ALAN KUTZ—FROM HISTORY MAJOR TO BUSINESS OWNER AND GOVERNMENT WORKER

Alan Kutz's story will teach you why every college student, including liberal arts majors, should take courses in business. Alan began his college career as a political science major. He became fascinated by history and decided to become a history teacher. Alan got a B.A. in history from The George Washington University and an M.A. in history from Howard University. Alan took no courses in business.

When Alan graduated, a career in government looked more attractive to him than teaching. Thus, he began his career as a research associate at the Library of Congress. Alan wanted to move into management, but found he lacked the managerial background and business education needed. He decided to drop out of government and go back to school to get an M.A. in public administration. Alan learned a little late that a knowledge of business is necessary in any organization.

Alan became a management intern for the U.S. Department of Labor. With this experience and his managerial education, Alan was able to obtain a position as coordinator of the Comprehensive Employment Training Act (CETA) program for Montgomery County, Maryland. Alan left that job to become the executive director of the Corporation for Technological Training. None of Alan's jobs was in a business yet (these were all nonprofit, government organizations), but he was certainly using his business knowledge and skills.

Eventually, Alan became part-owner of his own firm, called Career Lab. The firm tested people for specific aptitudes and skills and placed them in today's challenging new jobs. Alan still does career counseling from his home, but is now back in government doing career placement for workers who have lost their jobs.

Your career is likely to be much like Alan's in that you may have several different careers in your lifetime. We shall discuss multiple careers in more detail in Chapter 1. Meanwhile, Alan has this piece of advice for every college student: "Learn business skills while you are in school. You will need them no matter where you work, including government and nonprofit organizations. Today it is especially important to know how to work with computers and to be able to speak and write clearly."

the wide variety of careers available in business and management. You will learn about production, marketing, finance, accounting, economics, personnel, management, and more.

When you are finished, you should have a much better idea about what kind of business career would be best for you. Not only that, you will also be prepared to use basic business terms and concepts to be a success in any organization, including government agencies, charities, and social causes—or in your own small business.

This book is written in a different style from most textbooks. It is written to you and for you, the student. It is not just a text full of facts and figures; it is a guidebook for understanding business. Special attention is given to career opportunities, techniques for starting your own business or for managing a small business, and strategies for finding and getting the rewarding career that you want.

A great place to start in your career search is with a course like this one. It should be one of the most valuable courses you take, regardless of your major. Each chapter in this book will begin with a Profile of someone in the business world. The stories of Larry Adler and Alan Kutz are two examples. Many of the people you'll meet in the Profiles learned the hard way that it is easy to fail in business if you don't know what you are doing. These stories are a good way to learn from the experiences of others.

Assessing Your Skills and Personality

The earlier you can do a personal assessment of your interests, skills, and values, the better it will be for finding some career direction. In recognition of this need, many colleges have assessment programs you can take. About 300 schools use a software exercise called SIGI (System for Interactive Guidance and Information). A different version, called DISCOVER, is used at 400 other schools. Both feature self-assessment exercises, create personalized lists of occupations based on your interests and skills, and provide information about careers and the preparation required. The Strong-Campbell Interest Inventory can be used to supplement DISCOVER and reinforce the results.

Doing a self-assessment now will help you to focus more clearly on a career choice. This textbook will give you more hints so that you should complete this course with a much better idea of what career to follow.

COLLEGE IS COSTLY, BUT THE PAYOFF IS WORTH IT

The Wall Street Journal reports that college graduates begin their careers earning 55 percent more than high school graduates. The *Los Angeles Times* pointed out that the difference between a college degree and a high school diploma is $600,000 over a working lifetime. Figuring 40 years of work, that's $15,000 a year more.

Clearly the investment in college is worthwhile. It is even more worthwhile if you study your books carefully and put in extra effort. Not only are you likely to earn more, but you may enjoy art, music, languages, travel, and work much more after learning about them in college.

Source: "College Graduates," *The Wall Street Journal*, March 22, 1988, p. A1; and James Flanigan, "Colleges Must Learn the ABCs of Economics," *Los Angeles Times*, September 4, 1988, p. 1 of Part IV.

It would be helpful to use such programs early in this course so you can discover, while you are learning about the different business fields, which ones most closely fit your interests and skills. These self-assessment programs will help you assess the kind of work environment you would prefer (for example, technical, social service, or business), what values you seek to fulfill in a career (for example, security, variety, independence), what abilities you have (for example, creative/artistic, numerical, sales), and what important job characteristics you prefer (for example, income, travel, amount of pressure on the job).

Armed with such information, you are more likely to make a career choice that will be personally fulfilling. Such assessment tests are available in college placement centers, career labs, and libraries. As the box called College Is Costly, but the Payoff is Worth It indicates, you will find the time you spend in college pays off well in the long run, especially if you find the kind of career you would like.

Establishing Resource Files

One way to find and capture the job of your choice is to have a plan for how to do that. An important part of that plan would be resource files. While it is essential to read information about careers, various businesses, and useful facts and figures, one tends to forget such data. It is extremely important to keep the names of contact people at various organizations. It is also important to have access to facts and figures of all kinds about the economy and business-related subjects. That is why you need resource files.

An effective way to become an expert on almost any business subject is to set up your own information system. Eventually you may want to store data on computer disks for retrieval on your personal computer and to access professional databases. Meanwhile, it is effective to establish a comprehensive paper-filing system.

Each time you read a story about a firm that interests you, either cut it out of the magazine or photocopy it and place it in an appropriate file. You might begin with files labeled *Careers, Small business, Economics, Management,* and *Resource people.* You definitely want to have a personal data file titled *Credentials for Resume* or some similar title. In that file you will place all reference letters and other job-related information. Soon you will have a tremendous amount of information available to you. Later, you might add to these initial files so that at a minimum they would include the following topics:

Accounting.
Career Information.
Computers (applications, new capabilities, and so on).
Economics.
Government (statistics, regulations, and so on).
International Business.
Investments.
Marketing.
Resource People.
Small-Business Management.
Social Issues.

If you start now, you will have at your fingertips information that will prove invaluable for use in term papers and throughout your career. Few college students do this filing, and as a consequence lose most of the information they read in college or even after college. Keeping up-to-date files is one of the most effective ways of educating yourself and having the information available when you need it. The only space you will need to start is a 12-inch by 12-inch corner of your room to hold a portable file box. In these files you might put your course notes, the names of your professors, the books you used, and so on. You may need this information later for references. Also, be sure to keep all the notes you make when talking with people about careers, including salary information, courses needed, and contacts.

Television shows such as "Wall $treet Week" are another good way to learn about business and investments. Have you watched Adam Smith's "Money World," "Nightly Business Report," or other business shows? Try watching some of them and see which ones you like best.

To learn more about the business world and to broaden your understanding of investments, watch such television programs as "Wall $treet Week." Check your local television viewing guide to see what other business-related programs are shown in your area.

Career Opportunities Today

This is an exciting time for college students. Not since the dawn of the industrial age have there been more new career opportunities. About 700,000 new businesses were formed in the United States in 1988 and 1989, and hundreds of thousands of new businesses will be started in the 1990s. Some of these businesses are in traditional areas such as restaurants and retail stores, but many new firms are in challenging areas that are opening whole new careers for tomorrow's graduates.

The names of some of the modern firms may be familiar to you; for example, Apple Computer and Domino's Pizza. Most firms, though, are small and are in new fields such as cable television (e.g., Heritage Communications), robotics (e.g., GMF Robotics, Prab Robots, Intelledex), biotechnology (e.g., Cetus, Genentech), and electronics (e.g., Energy Conversion Devices, Healthdyne). You may never have heard of most of these firms, yet they represent the kinds of firms in which many of tomorrow's jobs will be found.

Career Preparation

STARTING SALARIES IN VARIOUS BUSINESS CAREERS, 1988

Economics, finance	$23,136
Accounting	22,838
Marketing, sales	21,472
General business	20,335
Journalism	19,843
Agriculture	19,401
Human resource administration	19,319
Advertising	18,983
Hotel, restaurant management	18,693
Retailing	17,035

Source: Various salary projections. See, for example, *U.S. News & World Report,* April 25, 1988, p. 66 and *Recruiting Trends,* Michigan State University, annual.

How does one prepare for careers in these new areas? How can students learn more about these new firms and what they do? What courses should students take to prepare themselves for the interesting new careers of tomorrow? These are the kinds of questions that this course and all the resources discussed in this Prologue will help you answer.

If you are a typical college student, you may not have any idea what you would like to do for a career. That is not necessarily a big disadvantage in today's rapidly changing job market. There is no certain way to prepare for the most interesting and challenging jobs of tomorrow; many of them have not even been created yet. Rather, you should continue your college education; learn skills such as verbal communication, writing, and math; and remain flexible while you explore the job market.

RESOURCES FOR THE COURSE

College courses are best at teaching you terms and concepts and ways of thinking about business. To learn about real-world applications, you have to go out and learn for yourself. Textbooks are like comprehensive tour guides in that they tell you what to look for and where to look, but they can never replace experience.

This text, then, is not meant to be the only resource for this class. In fact, it is not the primary resource. Your professor is much better at responding to your questions and needs. This book is just one resource he or she can use with you to satisfy your desire to fully grasp what the business world is all about. Actually, there are six basic resources for the class:

1. The professor. Your instructor is more than a teacher of facts and figures. He or she is a resource person who is there to answer questions and guide you to the answers. One of the most valuable facets of college is the chance to study with experienced professors.
2. The text, *Understanding Business,* and the *Study Guide* that comes with it. The *Study Guide* will help you review the material and give you practice answering questions; that way you can practice taking tests before you have to take actual tests for a grade (see Figure P–1).

FIGURE P–1

Resources for the course. The text is not the only resource for this course; it is not even the primary resource. You can gain knowledge and experience from everything you read and from all the people you meet.

3. Outside readings. If you are not in the habit of reading business periodicals, now is the time to start. It is impossible to ask intelligent questions and carry on a meaningful dialogue about business topics without having some knowledge about current topics and terms from the literature. You may be pleasantly surprised to find you enjoy reading *The Wall Street Journal* and watching "Wall $treet Week" and other business shows on television. You should at least give it a try.

4. Your own experience and that of your classmates. Many college students have had some experience working in a retail store, a restaurant, or some other business or nonprofit organization. Sharing those experiences exposes you to many real-life examples that are invaluable for understanding business.

5. Outside contacts. A good way to learn about business is to go out and visit businesses personally. Who can tell you more about what it's like to start a career in accounting than someone who is doing it now? The same is true of other jobs. The world will be your classroom if you let it be.

6. The library. There are newspapers and magazines in the library on all phases of business. Take a day to review what is available. You might look for *The Wall Street Journal* newspaper and *Inc., Business Week, Venture, Forbes, Entrepreneur,* and *Financial World* magazines. Also, check out the career section of the library for what is available. The library and the librarian are excellent resources.

The Professor as a Resource

It is important for you to develop a friendly relationship with your professors. One reason for this is that professors often get job leads that they can pass on to you. They are also excellent references for future jobs. But most of all, your professor is one more experienced person who can help you find materials and answer questions about business.

The Text as a Resource

There are many learning aids included throughout the text to assist you in understanding the material. A brief review of these follows.

The first learning aid is a list of Learning Goals at the beginning of each chapter. If you read through these objectives, they will help set the framework for the chapter material. Sometimes it is hard to get into studying; the Learning Goals provide an introduction to get your mind in a learning mode. Periodically in the chapter you will encounter a set-off section called a Progress Check. The purpose of these aids is to give you a chance to pause and think about what you have just read. We all have experienced having our minds wander while we read. These Progress Checks can help you realize whether you are really absorbing the material or not. They are also an excellent review device.

You may have noticed that all the key definitions in the book are highlighted in boldface type. This will help you improve your business vocabulary. The Key Terms are also defined in the margins. A full glossary is located in the back of the book. Terminology is a major part of an introductory course, and you should rely heavily on these learning aids to help you commit the terms to memory.

The sections titled Thinking It Through are designed to help you relate the material to your own experiences. They get you thinking about the meaning of what you have read beyond the course. It is much easier to retain material that you can relate to your own life.

Each chapter has boxes called Making Ethical Decisions to emphasize the need for making moral and ethical decisions in business. One purpose of this text is to teach you about careers and how to make money in business. But another, more important, objective is to teach you the proper as well as the profitable way to do business. Because we feel business ethics is so important, we have an entire chapter devoted to legal and ethical decision making in addition to the boxes in each chapter. We hope you and your classmates spend some time with this material and think over the moral and ethical implications of the various incidents we present.

The photographs, boxes, figures, and other highlighted material are designed to reinforce and highlight key concepts and to make the book a more effective learning tool as well as a pleasure to read. Great care has been used in selecting them to make sure these objectives are achieved.

The Summaries are not mere reviews of what has been said. Rather, they are written in question-and-answer form, much like a classroom dialogue. This format makes the material more lively and should help you remember it better. Furthermore, the Summaries are directly tied to the Learning Goals so that you can see whether or not you have accomplished the objectives of the chapter.

No matter how hard we try to make learning easier, the truth is that students tend to forget most of what they read and hear. To really remember something, it is best to do it. That is why there is a section called Getting Involved in each chapter.

These are not the typical textbook end-of-chapter questions. These are miniprojects that you can do now or later to reinforce what you have read by getting more involved. You may find it easiest to divide these projects among the class and come back and share what you have learned.

The Practicing Management Decisions cases are another chance to think about the material and apply it in real-life situations. Don't skip the cases even if they are not reviewed in class. They are an integral part of the learning process because they enable you to apply what you have learned.

If you use all of these learning aids plus the *Study Guide,* you will not simply "take a course in business." Instead, you will have actively participated in a learning exercise that will help you greatly in your chosen career.

Outside Readings as a Resource

We have noted that business periodicals are one of the six major resources of the course. It is recommended that you review the following magazines and newspapers, as well as other resources, during the course and throughout your career:

The Wall Street Journal
Forbes
Inc.
Business Week
Fortune
Venture
The business section of your local paper

If you are not familiar with these sources, it is time to get to know them. You don't necessarily have to become a regular subscriber, but you should learn what information is available in these sources over time, especially information that will help you get a job. All of these sources are available free of charge in your school or local library.

If you think your future holds a career in business, start reading popular business newspapers and magazines today. By reading this type of publication, you will learn about world-famous corporations and about exciting and innovative business deals.

The Wall Street Journal is an excellent way to stay current with national and international news on business and economics. By reading just the front page of *The Wall Street Journal* daily, you can keep up with national and international news as well as business and economic conditions. The editorial pages discuss current issues in depth and explain them from a businessperson's perspective.

Forbes, Fortune, Business Week, Venture, and *Inc.* magazines are excellent sources also. They have stories about various large and small firms and their strategies for competing in today's markets. For your purposes, these magazines will introduce you to the firms that will be providing the job opportunities of the future. *Inc.* magazine, for example, picks the top 500 small businesses each year and discusses them in depth. It also introduces you to other new, growing companies and who their key people are. Using that information, you can contact those firms and explore career possibilities.

Your Classmates as a Resource

It is often quite productive to interact with your classmates out of class as well as in. They know people and have had experiences that would be very beneficial for you. Don't rely totally on the professor for "answers" to the cases and other exercises in this book. Often there is no "right" answer, and your classmates may open up whole new ways of looking at things for you.

Part of being a successful businessperson is knowing how to work with others, and college classrooms are excellent places to practice this skill. Some professors will encourage their students to work together in small groups by providing opportunities for them to do so. Such exercises build teamwork as well as presentation and analytical skills. Some of the students in your class may be quite experienced in their use of these skills. We shall discuss such students in more detail in the box called The Returning Student.

THE RETURNING STUDENT

Of the 10.6 million undergraduates enrolled in U.S. colleges, it is estimated that 45 percent are older than 25. *Modern Maturity* magazine reported that one in ten college students is over 50. Furthermore, a much larger percentage of the older students are women; the number of women students over 22 years of age more than doubled in the last decade. In urban institutions, the average age of students is 28 years. More students in such schools go to school after 4:00 P.M. than before. Returning students include:

- Veterans who are upgrading their job skills.
- Women who have returned to school for various reasons.
- High school graduates who have been working for several years but need skills in computers, writing, and other areas to find better jobs.
- Full-time employees seeking to further their careers or to take courses "just for fun."

- People who have lost their jobs because of technological change (e.g., auto workers, miners, and farmers).

The University of Maryland's University College is dedicated exclusively to part-time students. It has classes in 25 different sites throughout the United States and 300 locations worldwide that serve the U.S. military.

Returning students often are more serious about college because they have experienced the need for certain skills in the real world. They may work harder and longer than traditional 18- to 22-year-old students. Returning students often are as uncertain as traditional students about career choices and strategies for finding the right job in the right firm. This book is designed for all students who want to further their careers by understanding business better.

Source: Connie Leslie, Timothy Noah, Sue Hutchison, and Karen Springen, "The Graying of the Campus," *Newsweek,* June 6, 1988, p. 56; Don Oldenburg, "Old Man on Campus," *The Washington Post,* February 10, 1989, p. D5; and a *Modern Maturity* ad in *Advertising Age,* January 23, 1989, p. 19.

As you take college courses, your classes will have people from different backgrounds and who represent diverse age groups. One of the most valuable resources you will have in your class is people who have returned to school. Their lifelong experiences will help you to see the other side of the picture.

Outside Contacts as a Resource

After you have done a personal assessment, it is a good idea to begin exploring potential career possibilities in the areas that seem to fit you best. The time to begin studying career opportunities is now, not when you are closer to graduation. As you read about the various business functions (marketing, finance, and so on), try to imagine what it would be like doing such a job. Does it sound interesting? Do you have the needed skills? This book will give you some guidance, but the best way to learn about careers is to visit various organizations and talk with people in the different occupations.

When you go shopping, for example, think about whether or not you would enjoy working in a store. Talk with the clerks and the manager and see how they feel about the job. Think about the possibilities of working for a restaurant, a body shop, an art supply store, or any other establishment you visit. If something looks interesting, talk to the employees and learn more about the job. Soon you may discover fascinating careers in places such as the zoo, theaters, amusement parks, and health clubs. Do these careers look interesting? How much do they pay? Is there a chance to advance? The only way to find out is to ask.

What is it like to be a salesperson for a sporting goods company? Call one and ask. What is it like to be an accountant in a major firm? What do stockbrokers do? Is it fun? How do people feel about selling real estate, life insurance, or computers?

What courses should a college student take to prepare for such jobs? You'll never know unless you ask people doing them. It is not enough to read about careers; articles can make jobs look more exciting and glamorous than they really are. Visit an accounting office and see about accounting for yourself. Go to an advertising agency if that's what you're interested in.

Don't make up your mind until you have investigated. In short, be constantly on the alert to find career possibilities, and do not hesitate to talk with people about their careers. They will be pleased to give you their time because they are talking about their favorite subject—themselves.

It is as important to learn which jobs you do not enjoy as it is to find those you do. Elimination of some jobs from your alternatives takes you that much closer to the best job for you.

Later in the text, after you have learned more about different career opportunities, we shall discuss a step-by-step procedure for getting a job, including writing a résumé, writing a cover letter, managing job interviews, and more. That information is in the appendix to Part 5. Before you get involved in such details, you need to become familiar with some other resources. One of those resources is the use of business periodicals. We shall look at some key periodicals right after the box that discusses what college students want today.

BUSINESS IS NUMBER ONE

The Cooperative Institutional Research Program surveyed America's young college students. It found that business has become the number one college major, while interest in English and the humanities has fallen sharply, with teaching registering the greatest decline of all. When these students were asked what their reasons for going to college were, the number one reason given was to be "very well off financially." The report was based on replies from some 290,000 freshmen at more than 500 colleges and universities. This survey has been conducted for over two decades. In 1971, making money was listed as important by

only 49.9 percent of the students. By 1988, some 75 percent were interested in financial success. In 1966, "developing a meaningful philosophy of life" was listed as important by nearly 83 percent of the students. By 1988, only 39.4 percent listed this as important.

One objective of this course is to teach you how to become "very well off financially"; but that is only one goal. Other goals include learning to be concerned about others and the environment and the importance of business morality and ethics.

Source: William Raspberry, "A Rising Tide of Materialism," *The Washington Post*, February 1, 1988, p. A 15.

The Library as a Resource

Few exercises you do in this class will be more important to you than this one. Your assignment is to do some library research to find the resources you might use to begin a successful career search. While you are in college, you may want to work as an intern in various firms to get a better feel for what people do. Here are some sources you could use for finding such jobs:

- *Summer Jobs,* 37th ed. (Princeton, N.J.: Peterson's Guides, 1988).
- *1988 Internships* (Cincinnati, Ohio: Writer's Digest Books, 1988).

What other sources are available in your library for finding internships? Write this information down and put it in your career file.

If you would like a head start in finding businesses that are looking for students, there are many sources. See if you can find the following:

- *Peterson's Business and Management Jobs 1989* (Princeton, N.J.: Peterson's Guides, 1989). This reference lists jobs in various locations, company profiles, job hints, and opportunities.
- *The American Almanac of Jobs and Salaries* (New York: Avon, 1988–1989).
- *Jobs Rated Almanac* (Chicago, Ill.: American Reference, 919 North Michigan Avenue, Chicago, Illinois 60611, 1988). This book evaluates various jobs on a dozen different criteria. It should help you pick a job that suits your needs best.
- *101 Challenging Government Jobs for College Graduates* (Englewood Cliffs, N.J.: Prentice-Hall, 1986).
- *Career Book* (Lincolnwood, Ill.: VGM Career Horizons 1988).

When you find the section where such books are kept, look at the other titles and list them along with the call letters. See if you can find books on specific careers such as the following:

- *Business and Management Jobs* (Princeton, N.J.: Peterson's Guides, 1989). This book is written especially for business, humanities, and social science majors.
- *Advertising Careers* (New York: Henry Holt) 1987.

What books are available on the careers you prefer now? Add them to your resource file.

Finally, look for books that will help you set up a successful strategy for winning the job you want. Some good ones include:

- *The 1989 What Color Is Your Parachute?* (Ten Speed Press; new additions come out annually).
- *Job Search: The Total System* (New York: John Wiley & Sons, 1988).

Look for books on how to write cover letters and résumés, dressing for success, and special strategies for women and minorities. Examples include the following:

- *The Black Woman's Career Guide* (Garden City, N.Y.: Doubleday, 1987).
- *No Nonsense Interviewing* (Stamford, Conn.: Longmeadow Press, 1988).
- *High Impact Resumes and Letters* (Marassas, Virginia: Impact Publishers, 1988).
- *How to Have a Winning Job Interview* (Lincolnwood, Ill.: National Textbook Company, 1988).
- *Dress for Success* (New York: Warner Books, 1988).

To make this assignment and all the other assignments in the book work best for you, you should (1) do careful research, (2) keep careful notes, (3) share your notes with the class, (4) discuss your findings, and (5) put your notes into your *Career* file.

What Color Is Your Parachute? is an excellent source for learning how to get more information about jobs. You should begin now to read such books so you are prepared to apply for the job you want when you graduate.

LOOKING AHEAD

At the end of each chapter, you will find a section titled Looking Ahead. The idea is to set the stage for the next chapter by relating it to what you have just read. This Prologue may be a good place to look ahead to the whole book, how it is set up, and why.

The first chapter in the text is a follow-up to this Prologue. The world is changing so rapidly that it is hard to plan a lifetime career. One year there are too many teachers and the next there is a teacher shortage. One day petroleum engineers are in great demand, and three months later the demand collapses. To stay up with such changes, it is important to follow trends and patterns. Chapter 1 reviews some trends that will have a major effect on careers and your life. The business environment is important for everyone to understand.

The rest of Part 1 reviews the fundamentals of economics. Whether or not you have ever studied economics, it is a good idea to explore economics from a business perspective. The market for goods and services is now a world market, and the world market is seriously affected by world economic conditions. There is no way to understand business today without understanding economic principles.

After reviewing economics, we shall discuss various forms of business, with special attention given to small businesses and entrepreneurs (innovators who organize, manage, and assume the risks of starting a business). This subject is fascinating because of the many new businesses that are being started today and the job opportunities they offer.

Then we shall explore the functions of business: production, marketing, management, personnel, accounting, finance, and the major business tools (for example, computers). We end the course discussing important issues such as risk management (insurance), ethics, and international business. The logic is that we should study the environment of business first (trends, economic issues), then the forms of business, and finally the functions. There are, however, good reasons to discuss ethics and international business earlier, so your instructor may assign these chapters sooner. That should not hurt the continuity of the book, because each chapter is a separate learning experience that links with the other chapters.

Good luck in the course; We hope you enjoy it.

Bill Nickels
Jim and Susan McHugh

Jacob Adam
6 lb. 7 oz.
May 16 1988

TRENDS AFFECTING BUSINESS

1

LEARNING GOALS

After you have read and studied this chapter, you should be able to:

1. Explain the need for students today to be flexible in their career plans.
2. Describe four major trends in business as outlined by Tom Peters.
3. Discuss the career opportunities available in the service sector.
4. Explain the trend to small business and describe the fast-growing career areas for college graduates in small business.
5. Relate the success of small, efficient farms to the success of small, efficient manufacturers.
6. Identify the potential marketing opportunities that are created by the population trends of today, especially the increase in older citizens.
7. Discuss the trends regarding women and minorities in business and how this has affected managerial decision making.
8. Describe the changes in the U.S. economy in the past 10 years.
9. Show how the trend toward international trade and investment is creating new growth opportunities.
10. Describe the importance of the trends in business and education regarding moral and ethical conduct.

KEY TERMS

business, *p. 18*
career, *p. 19*
demography, *p. 30*
goods-producing sector, *p. 21*
hierarchy, *p. 20*
job, *p. 19*

nonprofit organization *p. 19*
service sector, *p. 21*
small business, *p. 23*
world investment, *p. 37*
world trade, *p. 37*

Carol Lindsey and Joanne McGrew.

PROFILE   WOMEN WHO STARTED BUSINESSES AT HOME

Twenty years ago, Helen Christian, like so many of today's young women, was a mother who wanted to work. She began tailoring and dressmaking for friends and neighbors out of her home. She did an excellent job and soon was getting more and more work. Today, Helen has as many as 150 jobs in one month. She finds she has to work at least 12 hours a day to keep up with the demand. The business got to be too much for her home and Mrs. Christian expanded to a shop in a nearby town. She says, "A lot of women start businesses within the home. It helps everyone. You don't have the overhead of a separate location and you can be there for your children when they need you."

Jean Collins is a 28-year-old mother of three. She just started a business at home. Front Office, Inc., is a word processing service. Jean had a hard time at first convincing people that the work would be professional coming out of a home office, but the proof came from the work. Now Jean must manage her time to fill the orders that come flowing in.

Carol Searles Wood has a 2-year-old daughter. Carol is a horse broker. No, not a house broker, a horse broker who works out of her house. She matches people who need horses with people with horses to sell. She works hard, makes good money, and loves it.

Carol Lindsey and Joanne McGrew started a business called Special Delivery out of their homes. They rent wooden storks to announce newborns and arrange clowns for birthdays and other events. Carol has a 1-year-old daughter and Joanne has a son who is 7 months old. Both women make nearly as much at this business as they did working for others. Carol worked for a bank and Joanne was an art teacher.

We could go on talking about successful women business owners. You probably know some in your neighborhood. This chapter is about trends affecting business. One of the major trends is the flood of women entering the work force. Another trend is the number of small businesses being started in the United States every year.

Source: Jessica Johns, "Area Mothers Nurture Own Businesses," *Rockville Gazette*, April 27, 1988, pp. B1–B2.

One of the more important tasks of businesspeople is to monitor the trends in society and adjust their products to meet the changing needs of people. We begin the book by looking at some major trends so that you will have some feel for where business is heading. Then we shall explore economic trends in the United States and around the world to get a better grasp of what the future holds. After that, we shall look at small business and how you can become a small-business owner like the women in these Profiles.

PREPARING FOR A BUSINESS CAREER

business
Any activity that seeks profit by providing needed goods and services to others.

A **business** is any activity that seeks profit by providing needed goods and services to others. To run a business, you will have to learn the business concepts and skills presented in this text. If you want to work in a nonprofit organization, you will need to learn the same business skills such as management, marketing, and financial management. A **nonprofit organization** is an organization whose goals do not include making a personal profit for its owners. Nonprofit organizations *do* strive to make a profit, but such profit is used to meet the stated social or educational goals of the organization. Such organizations include the government, charities, and social causes. The knowledge and skills you will learn in this course and in other business courses will be useful for careers in any organization, including nonprofit organizations.

nonprofit organization
An organization whose goals do not include making a personal profit for its owners.

Career Flexibility

One thing you can learn from the Profiles at the beginning of this chapter is that circumstances change in your life and you will have to change along with them. The women profiled adapted to becoming mothers by starting businesses in their own homes so that they could be with their children and work at the same time. Both men and women are finding that some industries in the United States are in decline and are laying off people. Other industries are growing rapidly and seeking qualified workers. A person's career, therefore, is likely to consist of many jobs in many industries, possibly including a nonprofit organization such as a government agency.

The days when one went to school, found a good job, and then stayed on that job for 40 years are pretty much over. Today, one in five people leaves his or her job every year. Every year about half of the people who leave their jobs must move a long distance to find work.[1]

What this trend means for today's college students is that they are likely to change employers many times in their lifetime. Not only are they likely to have many different jobs; they are likely to have many different careers. A **job** is the specific assignment one has with a specific company. A **career** is a job or a series of jobs in an occupation or profession. For example, you may start off in a bank with a job as a teller and move up to various *jobs* such as loan officer and branch manager during your career in the banking profession. In the future, you are likely to have *careers* in various occupations. You may work for several years in banking, then move on to selling, and then maybe start your own business.

job
The specific assignment one has with a specific company.
career
A job or a series of jobs in an occupation or profession.

There are many factors that contribute to the need for people to change jobs over a lifetime. Two of these factors are:[2]

1. A group of fast-growing *small* companies is creating most new jobs. A group of rapidly declining *larger* companies is the source of most job losses. Generally, workers must flow from the falling to the rising companies. Today, that usually means moving from a larger firm to a smaller firm. As we shall see below, smaller firms are succeeding by being more responsive to the wants and needs of people.
2. The numbers of businesses starting up or failing continue to climb. Again, workers flow out of one and into the other.

To prepare for a varied career or careers, you must become skilled at what you do and be prepared to do it for different employers. You will also have to stay current. That may mean going back to school periodically to update your skills. No doubt you have noticed that many of the students in college today are returning students who are older than traditional students. These people are learning new skills and updating old ones so they can progress in their career paths. Lifelong learning will be a major focus of the future.

Future Trends

One way to learn more about future trends and opportunities in business is to read futurist literature. One of the most popular writers in the 1980s was Tom Peters, one of the authors of *In Search of Excellence*. As a result of his direct experience with today's dynamic corporations, Peters forecasts four major trends in the future of business:[3]

1. From the Age of the Pyramid to the Destruction of Hierarchy

hierarchy
The various levels of management in a firm.

Hierarchy refers to the various levels of management in a firm. Peters feels that as a result of the technological revolution and the uncertainty in the world economies, companies with many levels of management will not be able to stand the challenges of tomorrow. The new, more successful companies have created organizational forms to exploit information-based technologies such as the computer. For example, they have virtually no middle management and much decision making is delegated to lower-level managers and employees.

One example Peters cites is Wal-Mart, a $20 billion firm without many levels of management. This point is important enough to justify a whole chapter. Therefore, we shall devote Chapter 12 to the organization of businesses.

2. From the Age of the Machine to the Era of the Worker

After getting rid of unneeded layers of middle management, companies must necessarily give more decision-making authority to workers. Lightning-fast response to change and the improvement of everything that goes on in the firm can be achieved, Peter's feels, only through "continuous learning by everyone." Not just top management, but everyone in the firm should learn to be a strategic thinker. We shall explore how to hire, train, motivate, and adapt to the new worker in Chapters 15, 16, and 17.

3. From the Age of Standard Products to the Era of Customization

This busy street in Hong Kong represents the dynamic growth of Pacific Rim countries. They provide both a challenge and an opportunity for U.S. businesses. A major trend in business is to expand toward international markets. What are you doing to prepare yourself for such trends?

Peters notes that the successful firms of the future will adapt their products to the needs of individual buyers, not to mass markets. By using computers and advanced production techniques, most products can be adapted to individual consumers. For example, you will be able to buy custom-made shoes and clothes for about the same price as off-the-rack items. In Chapter 8, we shall explore whole new ways of thinking about products and their development. We shall explore the new production techniques in Chapter 13.

4. From the Age of the Atlantic to the Pacific Century

The shift of innovation and experimentation—and volume of business—toward the Pacific Rim is just in its infancy. That is, countries such as Japan, South Korea, Taiwan, Hong Kong, and Singapore will continue to grow and challenge American and European producers. This challenge makes international business one of the most interesting and challenging careers for tomorrow's college graduate. Because of this, you will see examples of international business applications throughout the text. We saved the last chapter for a detailed discussion of international business because we want you going away from this class knowing all the terms and concepts of business and then thinking of how you can apply them in international markets.

Peters notes that California is the heartland of biotechnology and electronics. But it is also the center for creative financing and manufacturing. The blending of California's entrepreneurial energy and fast-paced informality with Asia's approach to managing people is becoming the hallmark of pioneering firms. It may be time for you to get out your map and learn about the Pacific Rim countries and to start learning a language of that area. That is where the action is predicted to be in the 1990s and beyond.

When thinking through the predictions above, it is important to recognize the fact that the United States has become largely a service economy and much of the international trade we will be doing will be in services. We'll now explore that trend in more detail.

THE TREND TOWARD THE SERVICE SECTOR

The **goods-producing sector** of society produces tangible products (products you can see, touch, and inspect) such as automobiles, furniture, clothing, and appliances. The **service sector** provides intangible products (products that cannot be easily touched and inspected before use) such as health services, financial services, recreation services, and repair services.

A major change in the economy is the shift from manufacturing of goods to providing services. In many industries, production workers were either displaced by automation or their jobs were eliminated by a combination of competition from abroad and mismanagement at home. Over the last 25 years, the steel industry lost 500,000 jobs; the auto industry, 500,000; and textiles, 600,000. In that same approximate period, jobs in the service sector grew from 27 million employees to 55 million and from 55 percent of the work force to over 70 percent.[4]

Since 1985, services have generated all the employment increases in the nonfarm sector. Since over 70 percent of the jobs in America today are in the service sector, the chances are very high that you will be working in the service

goods-producing sector
Part of society that produces tangible products such as automobiles, furniture, and so on.

service sector
Part of society that provides intangible products such as health services, financial services, and so on.

Health clubs are part of the service sector. Over 70 percent of the jobs in America are now in the service sector and most new jobs will be there as well. Service-sector jobs can be fun, as illustrated by health clubs. They also pay well if you have the right education. This is especially true in accounting, finance, and other professional services.

sector sometime in your career. Figure 1–1 lists many of the service-sector jobs. Look it over to see where the careers of the future are likely to be. One bit of good news is that there is a bigger share of high-paying jobs in the service sector—in health care, accounting, law, software engineering, and airline piloting—than high-paying manufacturing jobs.[5] The bad news is that many service jobs are called "McJobs" because they are low-paying jobs in fast-food restaurants and other retail establishments. The difference is the level of education required. College graduates generally will find satisfying and profitable careers in the service sector.

Projections are that the service sector will grow well into the 1990s (see Figure 1–2). It is predicted that about 80 percent of the labor force will be in the service sector by the year 2000.[6] Some sectors, like telecommunications, will grow rapidly, while others may have much slower growth. Again, the strategy for college graduates in the future is to remain flexible, find where the jobs are being created, and move when appropriate.

FIGURE 1–1   What is the service sector?

There is much talk about the service sector, but few discussions actually list what it includes. Below is a representative list of services as classified by the government:

Lodging Services
Hotels, rooming houses, and other lodging places
Sporting and recreation camps
Trailering parks and camp sites for transients

Personal Services

Laundries	Child care
Linen supply	Shoe repair
Diaper service	Funeral homes
Carpet cleaning	Tax preparation
Photographic studios	Beauty shops
Health clubs	

Business Services

Accounting	Exterminating
Ad agencies	Employment agencies
Collection agencies	Computer programming
Commercial photography	Research and develop-
Commercial art	ment labs
Stenographic services	Management services
Window cleaning	Public relations
Consulting	Detective agencies
Equipment rental	Interior designing

Automotive Repair Services and Garages

Auto rental	Tire retreading
Truck rental	Exhaust system shops
Parking lots	Car washes
Paint shops	Transmission repair

Miscellaneous Repair Services

Radio and television	Welding
Watch	Sharpening
Reupholstery	Septic tank cleaning

Motion Picture Industry

Production	Theaters
Distribution	Drive-ins

Amusement and Recreation Services

Dance halls	Racetracks
Symphony orchestras	Golf courses
Pool halls	Amusement parks
Bowling alleys	Carnivals
Fairs	Ice skating rinks
Botanical gardens	Circuses

Health Services

Physicians	Nursery care
Dentists	Medical labs
Chiropractors	Dental labs

Legal Services

Educational Services

Libraries	Correspondence schools
Schools	Data processing schools

Social Services

Child care	Family services
Job training	

Noncommercial Museums, Art Galleries, and Botanical and Zoological Gardens

Selected Membership Organizations
Business associations
Civic associations

Financial Services

Banking	Investment firms
Insurance	(brokers)
	Real estate agencies

Miscellaneous Services

Architectural	Surveying
Engineering	Utilities

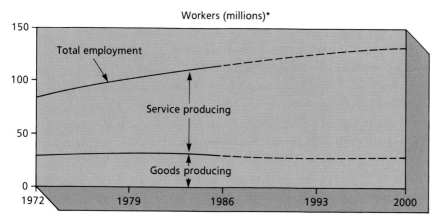

*Includes wage and salary workers, the self-employed, and unpaid family workers.

FIGURE 1–2
Future employment opportunities.
The future of American business is outlined on this chart. Note that all the growth in employment will be in the service-producing sector. The goods-producing sector will not lose many more jobs, but won't gain many either.
Source: *Occupational Outlook Handbook 1988–1989*, Department of Labor, p. 10.

There are indications that there will be no growth in goods-producing industries. This may be misleading. The fact is that some of the major manufacturers whose names are quite familiar to the general public—GM, Ford, Westinghouse—may experience slow or no growth. On the other hand, there are many smaller, more innovative manufacturers that are growing relatively rapidly. You may not recognize their names. In fact, many of them have not yet been started, but they will be offering exciting new jobs with great potential.

Finding these companies will be more difficult for college grads since they are so small. The search may be worth the effort, however, because these firms may turn out to be the IBMs and Xeroxes of the future. The major message in this discussion is that smaller and/or more innovative businesses are the future of the United States. Larger businesses can stay competitive with such firms by creating smaller units that are more flexible. That is part of what Tom Peters was saying in his first trend prediction.

THE TREND TOWARD SMALL BUSINESS

One of the more popular books of the 1980s was Naisbitt's *Megatrends*. In *Megatrends*, Naisbitt said, "The transition times between economies are the times entrepreneurship blooms. We are now in such a period."[7] New businesses were being created at a pace of about 93,000 per year in 1950, and today, as we noted earlier, over 700,000 are started each year. Most of these are small businesses. A **small business** is defined by the Small Business Administration (SBA) as one that is independently operated, is not dominant in its field of operation, and meets certain standards of size in terms of employees or annual receipts.

To learn about small businesses, interested students should read *Inc.*, *Entrepreneur*, *Venture*, or other magazines geared toward small businesses because other business publications tend to favor *big* business and government. The future of small businesses is indicated by what is popular now. The United States has already entered the transition period between old, large "smokestack" industries, for example, steel, auto, tires, chemicals, and utilities, and smaller, more efficient service and high-tech industries, including fast-food restaurants, auto rental firms, and firms producing computer chips, solar panels, and computers.

small business
A business that is independently operated, not dominant in its field, and meets certain standards of size in terms of number of employees and annual receipts.

FIGURE 1–3

Growth of industries. The businesses that are predicted to grow most rapidly in the 1990s are mostly manufacturers. Commercial savings banks will grow as savings and loan organizations fail. Note too that there will be growth in basic industries such as paper products, steel, and plastics.

RANK	TYPE OF INDUSTRY
1.	Commercial savings banks
2.	Electronic component manufacturers
3.	Paperboard container manufacturers
4.	Computer and office machine manufacturers
5.	Miscellaneous paper product manufacturers
6.	Miscellaneous plastic product manufacturers
7.	Basic steel manufacturers
8.	Pharmaceutical manufacturers
9.	Communication equipment manufacturers
10.	Partition and fixture manufacturers

Reprinted by permission, *Inc.* magazine, January 1988. Copyright © 1988 by Inc. Publishing Company, 38 Commercial Wharf, Boston, MA 02110.

Millions of small businesses are owned by women, and thousands more are being started each year. The trend is for a greater percentage of the owners and workers in America to be women. You can learn more about the opportunities of being a woman in business by talking to women who are already involved.

The figures show that Americans started some 700,000 new enterprises in 1988. Some 500,000 of these firms were sole proprietorships; that is, they are owned and managed by one person. The most frequently started firms were business services, eating and drinking establishments, miscellaneous shops selling consumer goods (e.g., women's and men's clothing stores), auto repair shops and housing construction firms. The ones most likely to grow significantly were mostly small manufacturing firms (9 of 10). Figure 1–3 lists the ones most likely to grow. Because many of the jobs in the future will be in small businesses, we shall devote two chapters to entrepreneurship, franchising, and starting and running a small business.

Women in Small Businesses

The number of businesses solely owned by women has grown to more than 3.8 million, which represents 28 percent of all privately owned businesses in the United States. It is predicted that by the year 2000 50 percent of all privately owned businesses will be owned by women.[8] The women in the Profiles give some indication of how such businesses get started.

John Naisbitt (*Megatrends*) said, "It becomes increasingly clear that women will not only join their male counterparts as equals in business, they may pass them . . . . They bring perspectives, values, talents and skills, well-suited to the new economy we are building." There is a National Association of Women Business Owners, and the Small Business Administration has an Office of Women's Business Ownership. Chapters 5 and 6 will discuss women in small business further.

THINKING IT THROUGH   Look through the list of jobs in the service sector (see Figure 1–1). Which of the jobs listed looks most appealing to you? Can you imagine starting a small business providing one of those services? What kind of educational background would you need? What do you anticipate the future growth in that business would be?

Job Opportunities for You

Over 26 million new jobs were created in the United States between 1975 and 1989. Some 13 million new jobs are expected to be added in the 1990s. Nine out of ten of those new jobs will be in service industries. Eight out of ten will be filled by women, minorities, and immigrants. Hispanic women already constitute one of the fastest-growing groups in the U.S. labor force. This does not mean that white males will be shut out from jobs; rather, it means that opportunities are growing for all segments of the population.

Tomorrow's jobs will require more education than in the past. Figure 1–4 shows the trends. Students are likely to continue their education well into their careers because of the career changes we mentioned earlier. Therefore, it would be wise for you to plan educational development along with career development. They go hand in hand.

Where will the jobs be? Figure 1–5 shows the fastest-growing business jobs for college graduates. Throughout this text, we shall be describing these jobs and growth prospects. By the end of the course, you should have a much better feel for which jobs would appeal to you most.

YEARS OF SCHOOLING NEEDED TO PERFORM JOB	CURRENT JOBS (PERCENT)	FUTURE JOBS* (PERCENT)
8 years or less	6.0%	4.0%
1–3 years of high school	12.0	10.0
4 years of high school	40.0	35.0
1–3 years of college	20.0	22.0
4 or more years of college	22.0	30.0
Median years of school	12.8	13.5

* For new jobs created between 1987 and 2000.

Source: Hudson Institute. Reprinted from August 10, 1987 issue of *Business Week*, by special permission. Copyright © 1987 by McGraw-Hill, Inc.

FIGURE 1–4

Demand for education in the future.
The jobs of the future will demand more education. While only 22 percent of the jobs in 1987 required four or more years of college, 30 percent will in the near future. Note that high school graduates will not be able to get as many jobs in the future as they could in 1987.

OCCUPATION	NUMBER OF JOBS CREATED
Retail sales	1,200,000
Accountant and auditor	882,000
Computer programmer	335,000*
Systems analyst	251,000*
Bank officer and manager	119,000
Data processing equipment repair	56,000*
Personnel specialist	39,000
Purchasing agent	36,000
Public relations specialist	30,000
Medical records technician	30,000*
Hotel manager and assistant	21,000
Economist	7,300

* These figures are for the year 2000; the rest are for 1995.

Source: Bureau of Labor Statistics, compiled from various publications, 1988.

FIGURE 1–5

Jobs of the future.
Fastest-growing business jobs in the 1990s for college grads. Note that most jobs will be in the service sector, including retailing, banking, and lodging. Note also the large number of openings for accountants and people with computer skills.

This is the information age. Over half of the workforce is involved in teaching and other aspects of the information industry. These trends are likely to continue, so you need to learn to work with computers, fax machines, and the other information technology of the 1990s.

What competition will you be facing for those jobs? Luckily for you, the baby boom generation—people born from 1946 to 1964—are having about half as many children as their parents did. This means that the number of students entering the labor force will fall in the 1990s. There will be more opportunities for traditional young students as long as they have the schooling needed. There may be fewer opportunities for the returning student hoping to move up to a managerial position because there will be fewer people to manage, but those with the most schooling will do best.

The United States has moved from an industrial society to an information society.[9] Now 60 percent of us are in the information industry, following careers in areas such as teaching, research, programming, accounting, and managing media. Does that mean that today's student should forget about careers in such areas as agriculture and manufacturing and focus only on careers in service organizations? Certainly not. Promising careers are available in both agriculture and manufacturing.

Let's explore the history of agricultural development to see what the prospects are for tomorrow's business graduates who are interested in agriculturally related careers. Pay attention to this history because it is being repeated in the industrial sector today. Just as opportunities moved from agriculture to industry in the past, the movement is now away from industry to services. First, please pause and do the Progress Check.

PROGRESS CHECK

- There were 15 broad categories listed in Figure 1–1, the chart on the service sector. Since this is where over 70 percent of the jobs will be in the future, you should be familiar with what is included. Can you name half or more of these categories and some of the jobs included in each?

- What are the kinds of small businesses most likely to grow in the future?

- What are the fastest-growing jobs for business graduates?

RELATING TRENDS IN AGRICULTURE AND INDUSTRY

To understand the agricultural situation today, you need a sense of history. The government has supported farms in the United States since the Homestead Act of 1862. From 1910 to 1920, farmers prospered. In June 1920, farm prices collapsed. From 1929 to 1932, farm prices fell 50 percent. In just one *day*, in April 1932, one quarter of the state of Mississippi went into foreclosure; that is, farms were taken over by the bank for sale to the highest bidder.

By the 1940s, the farm economy was again booming. World War II and other factors greatly increased demand. Nonetheless, some 600,000 farms disappeared in the 1940s. Smaller farms were merged into bigger farms. That trend continued into the 1960s, when another 1.5 million farms went out of business. In the 1970s, we lost 500,000 more. During the 1980s, we lost some 40,000 a year in spite of federal farm programs. As you can see, though, the decline in the number of farms has gone on for 50 years. About 30 percent of the workers in the United States worked on farms in 1920. By 1950 the figure had declined to 15 percent. Today it is only 2 percent. It is not a new phenomenon. What is new is the increased effort by the government to halt the decline.

Mechanization has enabled farmers to produce bumper crops with a minimum of labor.[10] There is little the government can do to halt that trend. A similar trend is now occurring in manufacturing as workers are being replaced by machinery. There is no reason to doubt that the results will be equally disrupting to the work force. Farmers went from the farm to the factory. This time they will go from the factory to service organizations.

Today there are only 2.2 million farms left. Most of those (about 1.6 million) are owned by people who earn most of their income elsewhere and work on the farm in their free time. Some 90 percent of total farm output comes from just 599,000 farms (27 percent of the total number). These large farms receive 82 percent of federal farm subsidies. In spite of all you read in the papers, the average farmer, from farm and off-farm income, made $36,000 in 1986, $8,000 more than the median family income.[11] Thus, farming continues to be a good occupation, but for fewer and fewer people on larger and larger farms. The drought of 1988–1989 showed how dependent farmers are on the weather and eliminated more marginal farmers.

The 1980s Farm Crisis and Opportunities

The 1980s crisis in farming may have resulted from farm prosperity, not failure. In the 1970s, for example, an Iowa farmer saw land prices increase from $250 an acre to over $2,000 an acre. Eager to profit from increasing land prices, the farmer bought 80 acres for $208,000 and borrowed $160,000 to buy another farm. Then, in the 1980s, the Third World stopped buying as much food as it once did because we had taught its citizens how to grow their own. The dollar rose, making food prices higher to overseas markets, and President Carter stopped selling grain to the Soviet Union. Farmland prices plummeted as farm crop prices fell. The land the farmer bought in Iowa for $2,600 an acre fell to $800 an acre. Farmers couldn't pay off their debts with declining farm prices and about 200 farm-lending banks failed.[12]

By 1988, however, land prices had stopped falling, farm debt was declining, and government aid helped farmers to stay in business. For future college graduates, agriculture has great potential. Land prices are likely to rise again, new technologies will make farms more productive, and there will be fewer, but larger farms producing more food. Profits will continue to be high on the better farms. This means many job opportunities for those who sell *to* farmers as well. Companies selling tractors, fertilizers, trucks, seed, and other farm materials are likely to prosper as farms regain their strength.

It is predicted that the biggest 50,000 farms will produce 63 percent of all U.S. agricultural sales in 1990. Some farmers are finding it difficult to get laborers to gather the harvest because of new immigration policies limiting who they can hire. Some are turning to machinery to do such difficult chores. Robotic fruit harvesters could slash labor costs by 75 percent. Because of such trends, fewer and fewer farmers will be producing a greater and greater volume of food.

The Success of Small, Efficient Farms

Buried under the statistics that show that farms have to be bigger and bigger is a trend that has great significance for you and others who want to understand where the United States is heading economically. That trend is toward successful *small* farms. Richard Clark has a relatively small, 80-acre farm in Bedford, New Hampshire. This is certainly small compared to some North Dakota wheat farms with thousands of acres under cultivation. Nevertheless, Mr. Clark brings in over $300,000 a year and makes a profit of at least $60,000.[13] How does he do it?

Mr. Clark represents a number of successful farmers who are using the latest in technology to produce more in smaller spaces. He lives near an urban center and noticed that the city folk were tired of the hard, tasteless tomatoes available in the supermarket. He set out to produce big, juicy, fresh, and tasty tomatoes. To do that he had to learn how to grow such tomatoes in the cold climate of New Hampshire. After much experimenting with plastic covers, greenhouses, and the like, Mr. Clark hit upon a plastic cover that worked. Along with plastic mulches,

Small specialty farms and large farms will be successful in the 1990s. Medium-sized farms may have more difficulty. The same is true in manufacturing. Small, specialized producers and large producers will prosper while medium-sized firms may not.

the system produces tomatoes just like he wanted. He followed that experiment with a similar one for growing melons. Now he sells his produce in supermarkets and at his own roadside stand.

Farmers across America near urban areas have learned that consumers will go out of their way for fresh produce. There are some 21,000 pick-your-own farms and roadside stands nationwide.[14] Farmers' markets are opening at a rapid pace. Case 2 in Chapter 6 describes in detail another successful small farm and shows how you could start one, also.

Why all this attention to farms and agriculture at this point? First, agriculture is a big business in the United States, especially when you include all the organizations involved in food processing and distribution. Second and more importantly for your understanding of business, the trends in farming reveal future trends in industry.

Just as farms were merged into larger and larger farms, industrial businesses are merging into larger and larger units. For some manufacturers, as with some farmers, bigger is better. In the 1990s, however, it is the smaller, more efficient, high-technology—using businesses that will thrive in industry and agriculture. In both manufacturing and in agriculture, therefore, it is the big and the small that will prosper. The medium-sized organizations are not expected to do as well.[15]

In the 1990s, for example, we will see new developments in *hydroponics* (growing crops in greenhouses in high-nutrient water solutions). We will also see more fish farms and high-intensity farming (growing a greater than normal volume in a small space), especially near urban areas.

The Industrial Crisis of the 1990s

What happens to farmers who are forced off the farm? In the past, most farmers went into industry and worked in mines and manufacturing plants. It is important to know the history of farms because history is now repeating itself. People who work in manufacturing are now being forced out of business as farmers were in the 1940s, 1950s, and 1960s. Where are they to go? Most are going into the service sector, but many simply cannot be retrained or are too old to switch. Nevertheless, manufacturing is following the pattern of farming in that a few large firms will survive and inefficient firms will go out of business. What is also happening today is the reemergence of smaller, more efficient manufacturers. They are small and innovative and use the latest in technology. They will be providing career opportunities for college graduates in the future, but the jobs will be a lot different from the assembly line jobs of the past. In the future, such firms will be looking for computer and robot specialists and other highly skilled workers. Society keeps evolving with one kind of industry rising to dominance and another falling. It is technological change that is shaping the business future.

TECHNOLOGICAL TRENDS

One way U.S. firms can compete with foreign firms with lower labor costs is to cut down on the need for workers by replacing them with computers, machines, and robots. One IBM plant that makes laptop computers has almost no employees. It is fully automated. One cannot function fully in the business world today without at least some knowledge of computers. You should know how to do some word processing and some analysis of business problems using computers before you leave school.

Robots like this one can replace dozens of workers in manufacturing plants. This creates new opportunities for technicians, but eliminates many factory jobs. Technological change will accelerate in the 1990s creating new opportunities on the one hand and eliminating jobs on the other. Your job is to prepare for the new jobs being created.

Tomorrow's jobs call for a more highly educated worker who knows something about the latest in technology. We shall discuss the latest in technological advances in production and other phases of business in Chapter 13.

You will want to follow developments in the high-technology areas because many career possibilities will open in areas not even discovered today. There will be wonderful new products and dynamic new firms in the biotechnology area. There could be major breakthroughs in medicine, health care, chemicals, and computers. Note in Figure 1–4 the demand for computer programmers, systems analysts, and high-tech equipment repairers.

Soon you will be reaping the advantages of new developments in supercomputers, robotics, superconductivity, lasers, biotechnology, gene splicing, and more. We shall explore the uses of such technology in business in Chapters 13 and 14.

PROGRESS CHECK

- What are the four trends in the future of business that were developed by Tom Peters of *In Search of Excellence?*

- What are the trends in farming today and what opportunities do those trends present for you?

- What do industry trends tell you about the need for higher education in the future?

DEMOGRAPHIC TRENDS

demography
The statistical study of human population to learn its size, density, and characteristics.

Demography is the statistical study of the human population to learn its size, density, and characteristics. In this book, we are particularly interested in the demographic trends that most affect businesses and career choices. We are going through a kind of social revolution in the United States that is having a dramatic impact on how we live, where we live, what we buy, and how we spend our time. Furthermore, there are tremendous population shifts that result in new opportunities for some firms and declining opportunities for others. Let's start our exploration of these trends by looking at the broader population shifts.

Population Trends

Perhaps the most dramatic population trend in the United States is the increase in older people. The fastest-growing segment of the population is people over 80 years old. That group also happens to be the one on which the government spends the most money. That amount is estimated to be $10,000 per person per year. Soon we will be spending over $100 billion on these older citizens.

Another fast-growing segment is people over 65. That group will increase in size by about 50 percent between 1990 and 2040.[16] Americans 65 and older are the second richest group in U.S. society. Only those in the 55 to 65 bracket are better off.[17] What does this mean for you and business in the future? Older citizens with money will demand more and better health care, more and better nursing homes, more recreation and travel, and new and different experiences of all kinds. They will be traveling on mass transit systems downtown to shop and find recreation. Businesses that cater to older citizens will find tremendous growth in the 1990s. Maybe you will prosper as well if you join such a firm. For example, William Texido is prospering by selling reverse mortgages. They allow senior citizens to turn the equity in their homes into a monthly check for as long as they live.[18]

The richest members of the population, as we just noted, are those 55 to 65. If we broaden that segment to include those 45 to 55, we find that the segment is expected to increase by over 23 percent from 1987 to 1997. These people are buying bigger homes; taking expensive vacations; buying new furniture, clothes, and cars; and generally keeping the economy going. Combine them with the upwardly mobile 35- to 44-year-olds, who will be increasing by over 25 percent, and you see that the next decade will be one of great growth and opportunity for retailers, recreation specialists, and others who cater to the middle-aged group.

One of the most dramatic changes in coming decades will be the increase in the number of people 65 and older. They will seek leisure activities such as golf and travel, and they will seek all kinds of services in medical care, housing, and food preparation. The opportunities will be great for those who provide care for the older members of society.

The Future Labor Pool

The growth of the teenage population from 1987 to 1997 will be about 7 percent. This slow growth will mean some difficulty for those businesses that hire teenagers and sell to teenagers. You already see the difficulty fast-food restaurants, service stations, and lawn mowing services are having in finding teenage help. Fewer teenagers may mean less teen crime (a good trend), but also declining sales of records, movies, and other teen products including, perhaps, higher education. There is actually a large decline coming in 18- to 24-year-olds, which means that competition for starter careers such as management trainees will be less. The decline in teenage workers means more opportunity for retired workers looking for part-time work. You may have noticed older people working in the local McDonalds or Burger King.

Many lower-level starter jobs will be taken by the new wave of immigrants coming to the United States. Over 600,000 immigrants came to the United States in one year toward the end of the 1980s and 75 percent intended to live in just six states: California, New York, Florida, Texas, New Jersey, and Illinois.[19] These new Americans create many job opportunities for businesses that adapt their offerings to these new groups.

SOCIAL TRENDS

Several trends in the 1970s and 1980s have had a dramatic impact on businesses. These include the number of women who entered the work force, the growth of two-income families, the trend toward fewer children, and the demand for a better, more comfortable lifestyle.

Women in the Workplace

One of the most visible trends in the business world is the surge of women joining the work force. In 1960, it was relatively rare for a married woman with a child to work outside her home; only one woman out of five did. Today about 55 percent of the mothers with children are in the labor force.[20] The largest growth in the labor force during the 1990s will be among native white females (42 percent). If you add in native nonwhite females, the total percentage comes to 55 percent of the growth.[21] One of the rapidly growing services in the United States, therefore, is child care.

In order to join the work force, women are delaying having children until later than they once did. Women in their 30s now account for one birth in four. More of their children are first-borns than at any time in the past. Married couples with children under six spend substantially above average amounts for a wide array of goods and services, including insurance, entertainment, autos, apparel, and everything for the child (bedroom furniture, toys, clothes, shoes, etc.). Working women thus create job opportunities for people in retailing, services, travel, and other industries.

Women's Pay Getting Better

Women workers, on average, earn about 69 percent of what men make. But this overall figure hides some positive trends for women. For example, among workers under 35 the ratio rises to about 78 percent. In this same age group, blue-collar women make about 89 percent of their male co-workers' income. Even more

Women in the workforce are creating many new opportunities for those who provide day care and other services. Two-income couples have little time and lots of need for services. Female professionals earn 90 percent of what their male counterparts earn, a promising figure for female college graduates.

promising for females in college is that female professionals earn 90 percent of what male professionals earn. Female administrative and technical employees earn 91 percent of what male colleagues earn. This takes on added meaning when you note that the percentage of women professionals increased from 19 to 27 percent in the decade from 1976 to 1986. In administrative jobs during that same period, the number of women rose from 19 to 35 percent, and in technical jobs from 38 to 49 percent.

Women most likely to receive pay equity, therefore, are those who go to college and major in business (administration) or in technical fields such as chemistry, computer science, and engineering. Some analysts say that women's pay will never equal men's pay because women are more likely to take off from work to have children, and that slows promotion and decreases time at work. Nonetheless, the pay gap will narrow considerably as more women go to college and enter professional and managerial jobs. It is estimated that women in general will make about 80 percent of what men make by the year 2000.[22] We'll discuss this issue further in Chapter 17.

Two-Income Families

Several factors have led to a dramatic growth in two-income families. The high cost of housing and the maintenance of a comfortable lifestyle made it difficult if not impossible for many households to live on just one income. Furthermore, many women today simply want a career outside of the home.

One result of this trend is a whole host of programs that companies are implementing to assist two-income families. IBM and Procter & Gamble, for example, have implemented pregnancy benefits, parental leaves, flexible work schedules, and eldercare programs. Some 500 companies offer referral services that provide counseling to parents in search of child care or eldercare. Such trends create many new opportunities for graduates in human resource management. We shall discuss these trends in detail in Chapters 16 and 17.

About 2,500 employers provide child-care benefits of some type; 150 of these programs are on-site.[23] Such centers are expensive to operate and often cause resentment from employees who do not use the benefits. The resentment has led companies to offer "cafeteria benefits" packages that enable families to choose from a "menu" of benefits. A couple may choose day care instead of a dental plan, for instance. Many companies are increasing the number of part-time workers to enable mothers and fathers to stay home with children and still earn some income. The net result of all these trends is increased opportunity for men and women to both enhance their standard of living and raise a family. It also creates many job opportunities in day care, counseling, and other related fields.

African-Americans* in Business

The story for African-Americans in business is a mixed one, depending on education levels. On the one hand, the news is not good. African-American median weekly salaries in 1979 were 80.2 percent of the median for whites. The latest figures show that the median for African-Americans has fallen to 78.6 percent.[24] On the other hand, the news is very good. African-American females with at least two years of college earn *more* than comparable white females.[25] Education is the key to success.

African-Americans with college degrees are doing very well in business. In 1987, there were 1.6 million African-American managers and executives. Successful African-Americans can be found in many industries. Reginald F. Lewis is president of the largest African-American–owned firm—TLC Beatrice International Holdings, Inc. This firm had $1.96 billion in revenue in 1988, close to half of the total revenue generated by the top 100 Afro-American companies combined. Johnson Publishing Company, Inc. of Chicago is the second largest Afro-American firm. It is a publisher, broadcaster, and producer of cosmetics and hair-care products. In third place is J. Bruce Llewellyn's Philadelphia Coca-Cola bottling company, Inc. Next is H.J. Russell & Co. of Atlanta, a construction, property management, and food and beverage company. Then there's Gordy Company, which was better known as Motown Records before it sold that off.[26] Clifton R. Wharton, Jr., is the chairman and chief executive of the sixth largest insurance

Dr. Clifton Wharton is one of thousands of successful African-American businesspeople. He is chairman and chief executive officer of TIAA/CREF, the company that handles the investments for college teachers. Some 340,000 U.S. businesses are owned by African-Americans.

* *Black Enterprise* magazine, April 1989, p. 22 followed Jesse Jackson's lead and called for the use of *African-American* rather than *black* in publications. We honor that preference in this text.

company in America. Thousands of other examples could be given, but you get the idea. Afro-American businesspeople are finding great success in all kinds of businesses. The U.S. Census Bureau's latest survey of minority business found that about 340,000 businesses were owned by African-Americans.

Other Minorities in Business

One does not have to go far in major cities throughout the United States to see the progress new immigrants are making in owning and managing small businesses. A *Wall Street Journal* article begins with this line, "It's rare to see a coffee shop in New York that is not owned by Greeks, a produce store that is not owned by Koreans, or a newsstand not owned by Indians."[27] The purpose of the article was to show the success of minorities in business.

Nicholaos Merges was a stowaway on a ship from Greece to the United States. He started his career as a dishwasher and advanced to short-order cook, baker, and waiter. Mr. Merges saved his money and invested $20,000 in a coffee shop called Tiffany Restaurant. He works 10 to 12 hours a day.

Kirtisingh Chudasama is from India and is one of the biggest newsstand owners. He bought a franchise for $1,800. With his profits he bought a newsstand in a building lobby for his daughter to run. Now he has 21 stands and estimates that about 60 percent of the 1,500 newsstands in New York City are owned by people from India, Pakistan, and Bangladesh. Mr. Chudasama's 14-year-old daughter does his payroll.

The Washington Post reported that 85 percent of the fresh produce markets in New York are owned by Koreans. A study of these grocers found that they work 16 to 18 hours a day, six or seven days a week. Seo Wang Won is a Korean market owner. He says, "Many times, I only wish for sleep."[28]

Hispanics are doing well in small businesses, also. Gilberto Gonzalez left behind a successful career as manager of a sugar cane farm in Cuba. He and a partner now own five stores and warehouses that serve the Hispanic population in and around Washington, D.C. He grosses some $11 million annually. Fiesta Marts, Inc. has become the fourth-largest grocer in Houston.[29] Hispanic supermarkets are doing well in a number of cities, including Dallas, Los Angeles, and Fort Worth.

Gilberto Gonzalez is one of many Hispanics who have prospered running small businesses. His grocery stores cater to a largely Hispanic customer base. Such small business owners will create most of the new jobs in the 1990s.

What can we learn from the experiences of these new entrepreneurs? We see that hard work and persistence pays off in small business. We also see that there are opportunities for all in the United States. Also apparent is the fact that small businesses often demand the involvement of whole families. Owning and managing a small business is very difficult, but the rewards are many as well. That is why we devote so much of this text to small-business ownership and management, including franchising.

Managerial Trends

The new, highly educated, highly skilled workers of the future will demand a new managerial style. Such workers don't need "bosses" as much as leaders with vision and direction. In Chapter 11 we shall explore management and leadership trends in detail.

The surge of women and minorities into the workplace has created new demands for managers in all areas of business. New hiring and firing practices have been instituted. New training programs have been started. Whole new ways of responding to employee needs are being implemented including flextime, leave time for having children, part-time work, and more. We shall explore these trends further in Chapters 16 and 17.

ECONOMIC CHANGES

The United States experienced one of its longest periods of economic growth from 1982 to 1989. Unemployment dropped to 5.0 percent, the lowest it had been for 15 years. Inflation rates were relatively low, exports to other countries were increasing, and the stock market was recovering from a deep fall that happened in October of 1987. But 1988 was an election year and there was much talk about the negatives in the economy. We had a huge national debt and our trade balance with other countries was negative. There was talk of trade protectionism and increased taxes.

All in all, one was hard pressed to know where the economy was going. Some said a recession was coming; others talked of inflation. Some said we would have both. There was no consensus as to the direction or the stability of the economy. Investors were nervous because the state of the economy has a direct bearing on the growth prospects and profits of business. In fact, it is impossible to understand business without understanding economics.

By now, you should be reading *The Wall Street Journal*. You will see terms such as *gross national product, trade deficits, productivity, unemployment,* and so on. To understand what is happening in business, you will have to learn what those terms mean and what is happening to the national and world economy. We will not try to explain all these terms in this chapter because there is simply too much to learn. Rather, we will devote the next two chapters to economics. When you are finished with those chapters, you should be able to discuss economic facts and issues with anyone. A critical element in economics is the success or failure of the United States to increase exports to other countries. We shall discuss the issue of international trade next.

INTERNATIONAL TRADE

One of the important trends of the 1980s was the move from a national economy to a world economy. No country can isolate itself economically from the rest of the world. The future prosperity and growth of the United States is directly tied to the future prosperity and growth of other countries. The reason for that interdependency is obvious when you read some key facts and figures:

- The population of the United States is about 250 million people. World population is about 5 billion. If you take out your handy-dandy calculator, you will find that about 95 percent of the market for goods and services is in other countries.

- Major companies in the United States are already doing a significant part of their business overseas. Boeing, the airplane manufacturer, gets 45 percent of its business from other countries. Caterpillar sells 28 percent of its tractors and other equipment overseas. Even film producer MGM/UA Communications gets 45 percent of its sales from exporting.

- More than 60 percent of our TV sets, radio sets, tape recorders, and phonographs come from other countries. You can tell from the names— Sony, Mitsubishi, Saab, Volkswagen, Toshiba, and so forth—that many of our cars, machinery, and other products come from foreign countries.

Many people see the invasion of foreign goods as a threat to American manufacturers and American jobs. In some industries that is true. In a world market, you must expect the most efficient producers to win the market. Thus, the United States will lose some of its domestic markets for manufactured goods to other countries. On the other hand, some of those countries that will profit by selling goods to the United States will be able to buy more U.S. goods and services that we are more efficient at producing. Thus, we may buy motorcycles and videotape recorders from a country and sell that country insurance, vacation travel, computers, farm equipment, and chemicals. Overall, the whole world can become more affluent if free trade among nations grows.

One problem in the late 1980s is that some nations are restricting what they buy from us. We are continuing to restrict what they can sell to us in return. Rather than promote free trade, we are designing legislation to restrict free trade. This is a serious situation and demands more thought and discussion. You will read more about international business in Chapter 24.

International Investment

More important than world trade in the future may be world investment. **World trade** refers to the exchange of goods and services among countries. **World investment** means buying stock in companies in other countries, buying farms and businesses in other countries, building your own plants in other countries, and joining firms from other countries in producing products for world markets. Here is how Peter Drucker, business consultant, sees the trend:[30]

> International trade has been steadily slowing down for most of the past decade. But international investment is booming as never before. It has now become the dominant factor in the world economy. Most of it is investment in securities, of course. But the growing portion—by now, a third or more—is permanent investment in manufacturing and financial services.

world trade
The exchange of goods and services among countries.

world investment
Buying stock in companies in other countries, buying farms and businesses in other countries, building your own plants in other countries, and joining firms from other countries in producing products for world markets.

U.S. firms are going international. This 7-Eleven outlet in an Asian country is just one example. In the future, a well-trained manager will be one who feels free to move in international markets. That means learning foreign languages, foreign cultures, and foreign ways of doing business.

Drucker goes on to say that about one fifth of the total capital invested in U.S. manufacturing is in facilities outside of the United States. A similar proportion of the output of U.S. manufacturing industries is being produced in other countries. Furthermore, major commercial banks and brokerage houses (firms that sell stocks and bonds) have a similar proportion of their total business through their foreign branches.[31]

Similarly, Japan, Germany, and other foreign producers are building manufacturing plants in the United States. Throughout the world, major businesses are getting together to make products that are competitive in world markets. Thus, Chevrolet joined with Toyota to make the Nova automobile. Ford and Volkswagen joined together to produce Volkswagens and Fords on the same assembly line. The plant is in South America!

In other words, many American firms are no longer American firms; they are world firms. The same is true of firms from Japan, Germany, England, France, South Korea, and so on. What does this mean for you? It means new opportunities to reach world markets with billions of people who need and want U.S. goods and services. It also means that you must learn geography, other languages, and international economics to become a successful manager in the 1990s. Future managers, according to Lester Thurow, Dean of MIT's Sloan School of Business, "must have an understanding of how to manage in an international environment. To be trained as an *American* manager is to be trained for a world that is no longer there."[32]

BUSINESS ETHICS

Television, movies, and the print media have all painted a pretty dismal picture of business ethics. Often the reality seemed to match the image. In the last few years, we have seen Hertz charged with overcharging customers by $13 million, Chrysler was caught tampering with its odometers on "new" cars, Rockwell International was indicted for defrauding the Air Force, Ivan Boesky was charged with insider trading that led to illegal profits of $50 million, Beech-Nut executives were charged with selling phony apple juice for babies, and Ocean Spray was indicted on pollution charges. Each week the public seemed to be faced with another example of questionable business ethics, not to mention the scandals among preachers and politicians.

One positive element in all this sordid behavior is that it *is* being reported and the public seems genuinely upset at the findings. The first step toward improving a negative social condition is to admit that it exists. The next step is to do something about it. The second step is now being implemented. Business schools are adding courses in ethics to their curricula. The chief executive officers of 200 major corporations (members of the Business Roundtable) have conducted a study of business ethics. They found that businesses are working hard to change their behavior in a positive way. The Roundtable called for a greater commitment by top managers to ethics programs, written codes that clearly communicate management expectations, programs to implement the guidelines, and surveys to monitor compliance.[33]

At Chemical Bank, 250 vice presidents have attended seminars on ethical issues such as loan approvals, staff reductions, branch closings, and foreign loans. Chemical Bank has fired employees for violating ethical codes even when there were no violations of the law.

Xerox Corporation has fired employees for taking bribes, for manipulating records, and for cheating on expense accounts. Johnson & Johnson has a code of ethics that sets the stage for ethical behavior. That code helped the company to gain national recognition for its ethical behavior during the Tylenol product-tampering crisis in the 1980s. Many other cases could be cited to show that business is putting much more emphasis on ethical behavior. The problem is that the behavior of businesspeople often reflects the values and morals of society as a whole. When the culture glamorizes greed, dishonesty, and corruption in all the media, one can expect such behavior to be reflected not only in businesses, but in all organizations, including churches. Unethical and immoral behavior seems to have infected our schools, our politicians, and our children.

Ethics and Education

In 1776, religion and morals accounted for more than 90 percent of the content of school readers. By 1926, this content had fallen to 6 percent and in recent times has all but disappeared. Ethical behavior is caught as much as it is taught. That is, children learn from their parents, peers, and the media what is acceptable in society and what is not. Young people listen to the lyrics of some rock songs and watch afternoon and evening TV and see that the message is not one of high moral and ethical standards. Clearly, if we want moral and ethical behavior from businesspeople, we need to instill those values in all people, and that begins with education.

MAKING ETHICAL DECISIONS

Throughout the text you will see boxes with the title, Making Ethical Decisions. The idea is for you to think about the moral and ethical dimensions of the decisions you make. If all of us practiced being more concerned and caring for others, more honest, and more reliable, the business environment would greatly improve. Don't you agree?

Soon you will be taking exams in this course. Some students will have missed several classes because of illness or other reasons. How could you and the others in the class help these students catch up on what they missed? Is that the right thing to do or should you ignore those other students and do what is best for you? What about students who "cut" class on purpose? If you don't help them, you may do better in the class than they do and get a better job when you graduate. Is it better to live in a world where

everyone competes with everyone else or one where people work together? Should people be helped even when they break the rules or act irresponsibly?

Another way to improve your grade would be to cheat on exams. How does cheating in college affect how you feel about yourself and how does it affect your success in business later? Who is really cheated when students cheat?

It is easy to criticize the ethics of businesspeople. It is more difficult to see the moral and ethical misbehavior of your own social group. The standards of ethical conduct are set when you are young. What are some of the behaviors of your friends that you find morally or ethically questionable? How could the school or society change such behaviors so that people learn to be more ethical and moral in their business decisions? Is education enough to change people's behavior?

An ethics-based program developed in San Antonio called the Character Education Curriculum is used in thousands of classrooms throughout the country. This program stresses honesty, kindness, courage, tolerance, freedom, and sound use of talents. Business leaders support such programs with time and money.

There seems to be a reaction against the moral decline of society, especially since the AIDS epidemic. Even TV ads are slowly changing from overt sexual images to more romantic themes and more programs are being devoted to raising the moral standards in the United States. One woman objected to the low moral tone of the show "Married . . . with Children" and threatened a boycott of the sponsors. Such citizen action is likely to increase. The rejection of John Tower as Secretary of Defense in 1989 for "drinking and womanizing" may have set a new moral standard for political leaders. The resignations of Tony Coehlo and Jim Wright were prompted by the application of new ethical standards. It will be interesting to follow the trend.

Social Involvement

Ethical behavior is more than not doing what society says is bad. It means getting involved in society to help improve conditions. A national poll by the Gallup organization found that half the people who responded were involved in charitable or social service activities such as helping the poor, the sick, or the elderly. This is up from only 29 percent in 1982.[34]

This is a healthy sign and indicates that people are not just talking about moral and ethical behavior; they are starting to do something about it. For example, the hot new business course at Cornell University's School of Hotel Administration is called "Housing and Feeding the Homeless."[35] Ethics has become a major part of business decision making in many firms. Because it is so important, we shall discuss ethical issues in every chapter in this text. Later in the book we shall devote a whole chapter to legal and ethical issues in business.

■ What are the trends regarding women in business? What about women's pay?

■ What are the trends for African-Americans and other minorities in business? What are the keys to success for minority students entering the business world?

■ What is the difference between world trade and world investment?

■ What are schools and businesses doing today to improve the ethical behavior of businesspeople?

SUMMARY

1. Today's business environment demands flexibility in changing jobs. There are 20 million job changes every year in the U.S.

■ What reasons can you give for people changing jobs so often during their careers?

Two factors that contribute to the need to change jobs are: (1) small companies are creating most new jobs while larger companies are tending to lose workers; and (2) as many businesses start and fail, workers shift from the failing ones to the new, start-up firms.

1. Explain the need for students today to be flexible in their career plans.

2. Tom Peters was one of the authors of *In Search of Excellence,* one of the most popular business books of the 1980s. He sees many changes coming to American business in the 1990s.

■ What are the four major trends Tom Peters forecasts about the future of business?

The four trends are: (1) From the age of the pyramid to the destruction of hierarchies—that is, businesses will get rid of most middle managers and much more responsibility will be delegated to lower-level managers and employees; (2) from the age of the machine to the era of the worker—the new high-tech firms will rely more than ever on a skilled work force that can make the machines do what they are supposed to do. Everyone must become a "continuous learner" to do a better job of serving others; (3) from the age of standard products to the era of customization—products will be designed to meet the needs of individual consumers; and (4) from the age of the Atlantic to the Pacific century—Countries along the Pacific Rim such as Japan, South Korea, and Taiwan will be the major industrial competitors in the coming years, rather than European countries.

2. Describe four major trends in business as outlined by Tom Peters.

3. Over the last 25 years, jobs in the service sector grew from 27 million to 55 million and from 55 percent of the work force to over 70 percent. It is predicted that by the year 2000 some 89 percent of jobs will be in the service sector.

■ What career opportunities will be available for you in the service sector?

During the 1990s, some areas, such as telecommunications, will grow rapidly while others, like banking, may grow slower. See Figure 1-1 to review some of the job opportunities in the service sector.

3. Discuss the career opportunities available in the service sector.

4. Explain the trend to small business and describe the fast-growing career areas for college graduates in small business.

5. Relate the success of small, efficient farms to the success of small, efficient manufacturers.

6. Identify the potential marketing opportunities that are created by the population trends of today, especially the increase in older citizens.

7. Discuss the trends regarding women and minorities in business and how this has affected managerial decision making.

8. Describe the changes in the U.S. economy in the past 10 years.

9. Show how the trend toward international trade and investment is creating new growth opportunities.

10. Describe the importance of the trends in business and education regarding moral and ethical conduct.

4. Most of the jobs in the future will be in small business.

 ▪ What are the fastest-growing business jobs for college graduates?
   See Figure 1–5 to review the areas with most of the new jobs. Remember, most of tomorrow's jobs will require more education than in the past. It is important to plan your educational development along with your career development.

5. In agriculture today, there is a trend toward successful small farms.

 ▪ How is the success of small, efficient farms related to the success of small, efficient manufacturers?
   The trends in farming reveal future trends in industry. Just as farms merged into bigger farms, manufacturers are merging into larger companies. Just as the trend in agriculture today is toward smaller, specialized farms, so, too, the trend in the 1990s will be toward smaller, more efficient, high-technology–using businesses. Manufacturing is following the pattern of farming. There is the reemergence of smaller, more efficient manufacturers that use the latest in technology.

6. The population trends are toward older, wealthier, and better educated Americans.

 ▪ How do these trends affect you and business?
   More employees will be needed in health care, nursing homes, recreation and travel, and so on. Businesses catering to older citizens will prosper in the 1990s.

7. There are more women in the work force today. The number of Hispanic and African-American workers is also increasing.

 ▪ How has the increase of female, Hispanic, and African-American workers affected managerial decision making?
   New employment policies have been introduced. Training programs have been developed. Such practices as flextime, leave for having children, and part-time work have been implemented.

8. It is impossible to understand business without understanding economics.

 ▪ How has the U.S. economy changed in the last 10 years?
   From 1982 to 1989, the United States had one of its longest periods of economic growth. Unemployment was lower than it had been for 15 years. Inflation rates were relatively low but increasing, exports were increasing, and the stock market was recovering from the plunge of October 1987. There was a huge national debt and there was no consensus on the direction or the stability of the economy.

9. Changes in the U.S. market will have profound effects on businesses and careers. But the greatest potential for business is overseas.

 ▪ Why is international trade so important?
   The United States has 250 million people, but the world market is over 5 *billion* people. Think of all the many career opportunities available in international trade and business.

10. The number of scandals among businesspeople, preachers, and politicians reported in the news media suggest that unethical and immoral behavior are a growing problem in American society.

 ▪ What steps have business and education taken to combat the apparent increase of unethical and immoral behavior?
   Many businesses are working hard to solicit the commitment of top managers to ethics programs, written codes of ethics that clearly state

management expectations, programs to implement the guidelines, and surveys to monitor compliance. School districts throughout the country are instituting ethics-based programs in their schools.

■ What can you do to become more aware of your own ethical standards? It is easy to criticize the ethical behavior of others and much more difficult to see your own ethical misbehavior. One way of becoming more concerned about our own honesty and reliability is to practice making ethical decisions. Throughout the text, boxes entitled Making Ethical Decisions will give you a chance to practice identifying ethical dilemmas, suggesting possible alternative solutions, and making decisions. Share your answers with the class; we think you will find that your class will suggest many different and interesting solutions to the problems

GETTING INVOLVED

1. Go to the library and get copies of *Inc., Venture,* and *Entrepreneur* magazines for the last couple of years. Read about the small-business people in those issues. See if you can't find some inspiration in their success stories. While there, have the librarian help you find other journals about small business and franchising. Spend half a day reading such journals to see what is available and to learn about career opportunities.

2. Read about computers in Chapter 14 and then do a thorough investigation of computer courses at your school and in your area. Talk with people about the best courses to take. Visit a local computer store and consider investing in a personal computer to practice your skills. Consider this an investment in education and your career.

3. Read current business publications to find which countries are growing the fastest economically. Read about those countries to see if you would like to work there, at least some of the time. What languages could you take in school to prepare you for working with people in these countries? Remember, no area of business has more promise for growth than international trade.

4. Review the statistics in the section titled Population Trends. Write a two-page report for your files discussing the possible effects of such trends on business and your career. Check the population shifts in your area of the country. Think of three services for the elderly that you could provide. What is the potential for profit providing those services?

5. Observe the lifestyle and personal satisfaction of workers over 40 years old. Is their emphasis on work or family? What are the consequences? Are there any signs that people in your area are shifting attention to quality-of-life issues such as health, education, the environment, personal development, ethics, morality, and family togetherness? How do your observations help in seeking balance in your life?

6. Make a plan for your educational advancement throughout your business career. Note that some fabulous careers have not been invented yet; therefore, you can only prepare for them by keeping current and going to school periodically all of your life.

CASE ONE   **LIFE IN A SERVICE ECONOMY**

PRACTICING MANAGEMENT DECISIONS

Paul and Patty Johnson are twins who live in Detroit and attend a community college near a major automobile manufacturing plant. What they read in the business section of the paper makes them nervous. One article said, "Drucker estimates by the year 2010, blue-collar jobs (e.g., working on the assembly line at an automobile factory) will be down to 12 million, compared with 18 million in 1986 and 23 million in 1975." In the same article, Drucker predicted that the auto industry would be down to one third of its blue-collar force in 25 years. Such a drop in demand for workers would devastate the community where the Johnsons live.

Another article in *The Wall Street Journal* reported that 82 percent of the non-agricultural jobs in Florida are now in the service industries. Pay in those service jobs is good. The average wage in manufacturing in Florida is $25,500, while the average for finance, insurance, and real estate is $28,125. The Johnsons figure that the economic recovery of Detroit is likely to come from two sources: (1) a strengthening of the manufacturing base through automation to keep American firms competitive, and (2) a shift in training and economic development to move blue-collar workers in manufacturing to service sector jobs in industries such as banking, insurance, education, communication, recreation, travel, health care, finance, and transportation.

DECISION QUESTIONS

1. What can the Johnsons do in college to prepare themselves for careers in the service sector? Will the twins face mostly similar career problems or is one more likely to have problems than the other? Remember, one is a male and one a female.
2. What can the economic planners in Detroit do to alleviate the disruptions caused by a changeover from an industrial to a service economy? What kind of industries should they try to bring to Detroit?
3. What can business and educators do to prepare present employees for the new knowledge and skills needed in semiautomated plants and service industries?
4. What will happen to those workers too old to be retrained or too set in their ways to move from Detroit? What can be done with such people? Is this where corporate responsibility is important?

CASE TWO   MAKING BIG PLANS IN SMALL BUSINESSES

The story of Larry Adler (see the Profile on Adler at the beginning of the Prologue) should provide some inspiration for you. Larry, you see, is the businessperson of the future. He is an entrepreneur who has started several *service* organizations to serve his community. All of them are relatively small. He does lawn mowing, car washing, window cleaning, painting, and the like. Nationwide the story of Larry Adler is being repeated hundreds of thousands of times a year. The only difference is that the new, small businesses are usually started by older people.

The figure in the margin tells the story dramatically. Between 1984 and 1987, most of the jobs created were in small firms employing from 1 to 99 people. Note that employment in larger companies (those employing from 100 to 499 people) grew slowly or declined. College students tend to think *big* business when planning their careers. They are more likely to read *Business Week* and *The Wall Street Journal* than *Inc.*, the magazine of small business.

Since future careers are more likely to be in small businesses, college may be a good place to start getting some experience. Larry Adler started at age 5. Certainly, college students could do as well. Larry Adler learned that many such job opportunities exist in franchises.

NET EMPLOYMENT GENERATED BY SIZE OF FIRM; IN THOUSANDS OF EMPLOYEES, 1984–1987

SIZE	START-UPS	EXPAN-SIONS
1–19 employees	5,180	2,171
20–99	3,129	991
100–499	44	124
500 or more	232	738
Total	8,585	2,548

Source: David Birch, ''The Hidden Economy,'' *The Wall Street Journal*, June 10, 1988, p. 23R.

DECISION QUESTIONS

1. What are some of the trends in society that are creating new opportunities for small, service-oriented firms?
2. What sources could a student explore to find ideas for starting a part-time small business during college years?
3. What franchises are already successful near the school you attend? What franchises are located near other schools that may provide opportunities for you in your area?
4. What do you perceive to be the advantages and disadvantages of working in a small business versus a large one?

To understand the language of business, you will have to understand basic economics. The language of business is largely the language of economics. Furthermore, it is important to understand the roots of the American business system. America is being challenged for the political and economic allegiance of other countries. There is a clash of values among capitalist, socialist, and communist systems. The survival of free markets may depend on knowledgeable businesspeople who understand the system and can market its benefits to the rest of the world. Chapter 2 discusses the various world economic systems and the advantages and disadvantages of each.

LOOKING AHEAD

WORLD ECONOMIC SYSTEMS

2

---

1. Define economics and explain the difference between microeconomics and macroeconomics.

2. Draw a diagram showing the circular flows of money in the international economy and discuss the increasing importance of international economic flows relative to national economics.

3. Discuss Adam Smith's strategy for wealth creation and his basic principles.

4. Outline the basic rights of capitalism.

5. Describe how free markets work, using the terms *supply, demand,* and *prices.*

6. Discuss some limitations of the free market system and what countries are doing to offset those limitations.

7. Show how socialism attempts to solve some of the limitations of capitalism, but creates new problems of its own.

8. Describe the effects of the economic system in communist countries and what that means for world economic development.

9. Examine the mixed economy in the United States and explain its strengths and weaknesses.

10. Compare and contrast capitalism, socialism, and communism and reach your own conclusions about what a successful world economy would look like.

KEY TERMS

capitalism,   *p. 54*
capitalist system,   *p. 49*
communist system,   *p. 49*
demand,   *p. 56*
demand curve,   *p. 56*
economics,   *p. 49*
equilibrium point,   *p. 57*
factors of production,   *p. 49*
free market system,   *p. 55*
macroeconomics,   *p. 50*
market price,   *p. 57*

microeconomics,   *p. 51*
mixed economy,   *p. 69*
monopolistic competition,   *p. 59*
monopoly,   *p. 60*
oligopoly,   *p. 59*
perestrioka,   *p. 66*
perfect competition,   *p. 58*
socialist system,   *p. 49*
supply,   *p. 55*
supply curve,   *p. 55*

Joseph A. Schumpter.

The ideas of economists and political philosophers, both when they are right and when they are wrong, are more powerful than is commonly understood. Indeed the world is ruled by little else.

JOHN MAYNARD KEYNES

PROFILE JOSEPH A. SCHUMPETER, ECONOMIST

Joseph A. Schumpeter (pronounced *Shoom-pater*) was one of the first economists to give a clear explanation of business profits. His doctoral dissertation, "The Theory of Economic Development," became popular and was published when Schumpeter was only 28. That was back in 1911. The year is significant, because way back then Schumpeter anticipated the rapid structural changes the economy is now experiencing; that is, the rise of innovative small businesses and service organizations.

Schumpeter felt that an expanding economy needed more and more capital investment. The source of that investment was *profit*. Schumpeter considered profit a necessary cost of doing business. He felt profits were the only way to maintain jobs and create new ones. For the first time in economic history, profit became a moral obligation and goal.

Later, Schumpeter wrote *The Tax State* to describe the government's power to redistribute income from the productive to the unproductive. He felt such power would lead to political irresponsibility and inflation.

The best-known work of Schumpeter is *Capitalism, Socialism, and Democracy*, published in 1942. In this book, he argues that capitalism would be destroyed by its own success. He felt that, to be popular, a freely elected government would cause the nation to become more and more like the "welfare state." Eventually the government burden and the inflation it caused would destroy both democracy and capitalism.

A nation that demonstrated what Schumpeter predicted was Britain. To redistribute income in Britain, tax rates on the rich were raised to 83 percent. That meant if you made an extra dollar, all you could keep was 17 cents. As a consequence, motivation and the economy collapsed. Margaret Thatcher's policies led to tax cuts that brought the top rate down from 83 percent to 40 percent. The new, lower tax rates increased incentives and the economy recently has enjoyed the highest economic growth in Europe.

Sources: For a good review of the ideas of Schumpeter, see Peter F. Drucker, "Schumpeter and Keynes," *Forbes,* May 23, 1983, pp. 124–32; and for a review of Britain's turnaround, see M. S. Forbes, "An Immense Move," *Forbes,* May 23, 1988, p. 25.

Although Schumpeter saw the trend toward a welfare state, he did not anticipate the recognition by world governments that such a trend was counterproductive and that major changes would be introduced to reverse the trend. We shall discuss economic trends throughout the world in this chapter because the nature of the economy has a direct bearing on the freedoms enjoyed by businesses and consumers.

THE IMPORTANCE OF ECONOMICS TO BUSINESS

The success of the American system is based on an economic and political climate that allows business to operate freely. Any change in the economic or political system has a major influence on the success of the business system. The *world* economic situation and world politics also have a major influence on businesses in the United States. Therefore, to understand business, one must also understand basic economics and politics. Most universities require students to take economics courses *before* they take business courses, because economic concepts are the basis for most business decision making.

For this reason, the next two chapters will be devoted to teaching you the *fundamentals* of economics. The basic objective of this section is to teach you some basic terms and concepts from economics so that when you read business periodicals you will understand what they mean when they discuss economic terms and organizations. If you have already studied economics, you will find these two chapters an excellent review of how economics affects business and learn the latest trends and statistics.

Recent studies have shown that American high school students do not understand economics. Only 34 percent knew what gross national product was. On the average, students missed 60 percent of the questions on a basic economics test.[1] It is important, therefore, to go over economic principles again to be sure that you are ready to read the business journals that use economic terms so often.

WHAT IS ECONOMICS?

Economics, says Paul Samuelson, is the study of how society chooses to employ scarce productive resources to produce various goods and services and distribute them for consumption among various competing groups and individuals. You understand what it means to "economize" in your own life. It means we have to learn to "make do" because we do not have all that we want. The world is in a similar situation. There are **factors of production** available: land and natural resources, human labor, capital (machines, tools, and buildings), and entrepreneurship (the willingness by business owners to take risks and introduce new products and services to the market). Those resources are used to produce goods and services to satisfy our need for food, shelter, and clothing, and our other needs. The economic questions are: "*Who* decides how to allocate those resources?" and "*How* should they be allocated?"

Today, resource allocation in some countries is largely government controlled. That is the nature of the **communist systems** (for example, the Soviet Union). Resource allocation may also be left to individual consumers, bargaining in the marketplace and trading goods and services. That is the nature of **capitalist systems** (for example, the United States and Hong Kong). In between are systems that are based on private exchange *and* some government ownership and allocation. That is the nature of **socialist systems** or welfare-state systems (for example, Sweden and Denmark). Even welfare-state countries such as Norway and Sweden rely mostly on *private* business for wealth. There are no pure capitalist or communist systems; all systems have some mixture of consumer choice plus government-controlled allocation. Regardless of the system used, the ultimate goal of economics is to make optimum use of resources so that people can attain a good *standard of living* (that is, have homes, cars, clothes, and other tangibles) and enjoy a good *quality of life* (that is, education, health, a clean environment, and happiness). Figure 2–1 page 50 shows the economic system and its ultimate goals.

economics
The study of how society chooses to employ scarce resources to produce various goods and services and distribute them for consumption among various competing groups and individuals.

factors of production
The basic inputs of a society: land and natural resources, human labor, capital, and entrepreneurship.

communist system
System in which resource allocation is largely government controlled.

capitalist system
System in which resources are allocated by consumers bargaining in the marketplace and trading goods and services.

socialist system
System in which allocation of resources is done partially by the market (the free trade of goods and services) and partially by the government.

FIGURE 2-1

FIGURE 2-1

The economic system. Regardless of whether resources are allocated by free markets or government forces or both, the goal is the same—a high standard of living and good quality of life. The question is: what form of allocation creates the best *overall* results?

Economic resources: land, labor, capital, and entrepreneurship . . .

are allocated by the market or the government . . .

to produce a
high standard of living
and quality of life.

THE STUDY OF ECONOMICS

If you were to go through the course list in economics at most colleges, you would find courses in both macroeconomics and microeconomics. You would likely find other courses on the history of economic thought. The following sections define some basic terms in economics and give you some feel for what is covered in various economics courses.

Macroeconomics

What causes one country to prosper and grow while other countries, with similar resources, remain poor? What causes unemployment? How much of a country's wealth should be spent on government programs such as defense, welfare, and education?

macroeconomics
The study of the nation's economy as a whole.

These and other similar questions are the subject of macroeconomics. **Macroeconomics** is the study of a nation's economy as a whole. Macroeconomics can be a fascinating subject to study, because it looks at such important issues as whether or not taxes should be raised, the problems of inflation and depression, and much more. Nearly every major social, political, or economic issue can be discussed more intelligently and objectively once one understands basic macroeconomics.

A major macroeconomic question in the United States today is how much money to spend on education. Many people feel that the future of the country is dependent upon well-educated students with a strong knowledge of math and other basic subjects. Of course, there are trade-offs among the programs competing for money: education, defense, welfare, and so on.

Microeconomics

What happens to the price of corn when there is a drought in the Midwest? What happens to the supply of farm products when the government subsidizes farmers or keeps farm prices artificially low? What is the impact of income taxes versus sales taxes on consumers? How does one determine the value of leisure time? These and other similar questions are the subject of microeconomics. **Microeconomics** is the study of the behavior of people and organizations in particular markets. It looks at how prices are determined and how people and businesses respond to changes in the market (for example, changes in the demand for and supply of products).

Microeconomics can also be challenging to study because it teaches principles that can be used in everyday buying and selling transactions with others.

microeconomics
The study of the behavior of people and organizations in particular markets.

ECONOMIC FLOWS

You and I and all the other people in the world provide businesses with the factors of production we mentioned earlier: land, labor, capital, and entrepreneurship. In return, businesses provide us with the goods and services we want and need. Businesses receive money from individuals who become owners. Profits the businesses make belong to the owners and flow back to them through dividends. Thus, there is a circular flow of inputs, outputs, and money between businesses and the public (see Figure 2–2, page 52). In addition to the circular flow between businesses and the public, there is a flow of money and other resources to the government from the public and businesses that is returned in the form of public goods and services such as roads, schools, and hospitals. The total estimated civilian payroll of the government is about $325 billion. Figure 2–2 shows these circular flows as well.

Today the U.S. economy is an integral part of the world economy. American business firms use labor from other countries, buy land in other countries for their facilities, and receive money from foreign investors. To understand events in the U.S. economy, therefore, one has to understand the world economy. Figure 2–2 also shows the circular flows between U.S. businesses and businesses of nations throughout the world.

FIGURE 2–2

The three major economic flows.
This figure shows the exchange of land, labor, capital, and entrepreneurships by the public for wages, goods, services and profits from business. Businesses also provide the government with goods and services and tax revenues in exchange for government services such as military protection, police protection, and so on. The government provides similar services to the public in exchange for taxes. U.S. businesses also trade with foreign businesses and the U.S. public also trades with foreign businesses.
Altogether there are three major economic flows: (1) business-consumer flows, (2) government trade with businesses and consumers, and (3) international trade among businesses and between businesses and the public.

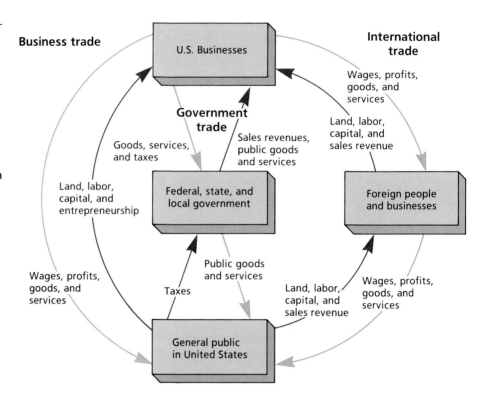

During the past five years, $800 billion in foreign capital flowed into the United States. Foreign investors have been buying companies, banks, luxury hotels, and retail chains. They have also been building new factories and financing a major portion of the national debt by buying government securities.[2]

One reason for the inflow of money is that American businesses and land are relatively inexpensive to many foreign investors. Luxury condominiums in Japan recently sold for $13 million each! That is more than 10 times what comparable luxury condos cost in Manhattan.[3] Recently Seibu Railway bought one of Hawaii's best-known resorts, the Western Mauna Kea, for $310 million—a million dollars per room. Japanese businesses and individuals are buying up property in Hawaii at unbelievable prices. Soon, Hawaii may become more Japanese than American. That is how important international exchange has become. See the box titled International Exchange Ebbs and Flows for more on this topic.

Because the world has become so interdependent, it is important for you to understand the various world economic systems and how they work. The future of the U.S. economy is directly tied to the future of economies in Japan, West Germany, the Soviet Union, South Korea, Canada, and so on. How each economy allocates scarce resources and how each views international trade will determine economic flows among nations in the future. Furthermore, the role of business in an economy is directly tied to the economic system. In some government-run systems, for example, business as we know it in the United States does not exist. They have neither the incentives we have nor the free flow of resources. To understand the differences, however, you must first understand how our economic system works, so let's begin there.

When Americans buy Japanese cars, videocassette recorders, and other products money flows out of the United States. It flows back in when Japanese businesspeople buy property much as the Westin Mauna Kea. Such international flows of money show the importance of international economics.

INTERNATIONAL EXCHANGE EBBS AND FLOWS

Throughout the 1950s and 1960s, the giant U.S. multinational corporations invested $4 or $5 abroad for every $1 that foreigners invested here. In the 1970s, the tide shifted as oil-rich nations began buying American properties. By 1986, there was close to a balance between what the United States bought overseas and what foreign investors bought here. By 1988, the balance had shifted and foreigners were investing more in the United States than the United States was investing in other countries. This caused quite a stir in the media, but the alarm was misplaced. Foreign investors control less than 5 percent of the nation's assets.

In 1987, the Japanese alone spent $5.9 billion buying American companies. In 1988, they spent some $2 billion in just one week. For example, a subsidiary of the Bank of Tokyo bought Union Bank of San Francisco and Bridgestone Corporation bought Firestone Tire & Rubber. Total foreign purchases of U.S. companies were $38 billion in 1987. Some people worry that such trends will cost U.S. jobs. Others point out that foreign owners are bringing with them new management ideas that can make U.S. firms more competitive. For example, the Japanese have been innovative in their use of quality circles and just-in-time inventory controls. Some states are beginning to monitor sales to foreign buyers to be sure that oil-rich countries, for example, do not buy up all the domestic producers and control the prices.

What all this means to you is that businesses are no longer U.S. businesses or Japanese businesses. They are world businesses. And the success of those businesses affects countries around the world. That means, in turn, that the economic success of one country is very closely related to the economic success of other countries. The flows of money among countries is almost as free as the flow within a country. As a businessperson, that means you must become skilled in international finance as well as international trade. That is the future and that is why you must understand world economic systems.

Sources: Robert Johnson, "Distant Deals," *The Wall Street Journal*, February 24, 1988, pp. 1 and 12; "Brace for More Japanese Takeovers," *Fortune*, March 14, 1988, p. 8; and "Reagan's Legacy: America for Sale," *The Wall Street Journal*, February 28, 1988, p. 1.

What is the difference between microeconomics and macroeconomics? Which would be concerned with international trade fluctuations?

What are the three major circular flows that together make up the American economic system?

Adam Smith.

capitalism
Economic system in which all or most of the means of production and distribution are privately owned and operated for profit.

CAPITALIST ECONOMICS: ALLOCATION OF SCARCE RESOURCES THROUGH A FREE MARKET SYSTEM

The year was 1776. A Scotsman named Adam Smith published his book *An Inquiry into the Nature and Causes of the Wealth of Nations*. He espoused the importance of freedom and the power of *economic* freedom.

Smith felt the freedom to compete was vital to the survival of any economy. He believed that people would work hard if they knew they would be rewarded for doing so. He made the desire for money *(capital)* the foundation of his theory. According to Smith, as long as farmers, laborers, and businesspeople could see economic reward for their efforts, they would work long hours. As a result of these efforts, the economy would prosper with plenty of food to eat and products of all kinds available to buy. Like an *invisible hand,* as people try to improve their *own* situation in life, the economy grows and prospers through the production of needed goods, services, and ideas. The invisible hand turns self-directed gain into social and economic benefits.

The name used to describe Smith's powerful economic system, based on economic freedom and incentives, was capitalism. **Capitalism** is an economic system in which all or most of the means of production and distribution (for example, land, factories, railroads, and stores) are privately owned and operated for profit. Distribution of wealth is done by the workings of the market.

A new book by Hernando DeSoto is called *The Other Path*. Like Adam Smith, DeSoto suggests that Third World countries (mostly the poor countries of the world) would benefit from capitalism. This includes countries like Peru, Mexico, and Argentina.[4] It is interesting to see that books written over 200 years apart have the same theme. What are the benefits of capitalism that these authors advocate?

Individuals living in a capitalist system have certain basic rights. These include:

The right to private property. This is the most fundamental of all rights under capitalism. It means that people can buy, sell, and use land, buildings, machinery, inventions, and other forms of property, and pass the property on to their children.

The right to keep all profits, after taxes, of a business.

The right to freedom of competition. Within certain guidelines established by the government, a company is free to compete with new products, promotions, and other strategies.

The right to freedom of choice. People are free to choose where they want to work, whether or not they will join a union, and what they want to follow. Other freedoms of choice include where to live and what to buy or sell.

One of the most important features of capitalism is free markets. Let's see why in the next section.

There are no limits to what free men and free women and free enterprise and free markets and a free society can accomplish when people are free to follow their dreams.
JACK KEMP

HOW FREE MARKETS WORK

A **free market system** is one in which decisions about what to produce and in what quantities are decided by the market, that is, by buyers and sellers negotiating prices for goods and services.

You and I and other consumers in the United States send signals to tell producers what to make, how many, in what color, and so on. The way we do that is by going to the store and buying products and services. For example, if all of us decided we wanted more fish (rather than red meat), we would signal fishermen to catch more fish. The message is sent by the *price*. As the demand for fish goes up, the price goes up as well, because people are willing to pay more. Fishermen notice this price increase and know they can make more money by catching more fish. Thus, they have the *incentive* to get up earlier and fish later. Furthermore, more people go fishing. These are people who previously could not make a profit fishing but now can because of the higher price. The kind of fish they go for depends on the kind of fish we prefer (requests in the store).

The same process occurs with all products. The *price* tells producers how much to produce. As a consequence, there is rarely a long-term shortage of goods in the United States. If anything were wanted but not available, the price would tend to go up until someone would begin making that product or sell the ones they already had, given free markets.

How Prices Are Determined

The previous discussion about supply, demand, and pricing is an important part of microeconomics. It illustrates the fact that prices are not determined by sellers. Rather, they are determined by buyers and sellers negotiating in the marketplace. A seller may want to receive $10 a pound for fish, but the quantity demanded at that price may be quite low. The lower the price the fisherman can charge, the higher the quantity demanded is likely to be. Many more people can and will buy fish at $1 a pound than at $10 a pound. How is a price determined that is acceptable to both buyers and sellers? The answer is found in the economic concepts of supply and demand.

Supply

Supply refers to the quantity of products that manufacturers or owners are willing to sell at different prices at a specific time. Generally speaking, the amount supplied will increase as the price increases. Economists usually show this relationship between quantity supplied and price on a graph. Figure 2–3 page 56 shows a simple supply curve. The price of an item in dollars is shown vertically on the left of the graph. Quantity is given horizontally at the bottom of the graph. The various points on the graph indicate how many fish a fisherman would provide at different prices. For example, at a price of $2, a fisherman would provide only two fish, but at $8, he or she would supply eight fish. The line connecting the dots is a supply line or **supply curve.*** It indicates the relationship between the price and the quantity supplied. All things being equal, the higher the price, the more fishermen will be willing to supply.

---

* Such lines are usually curved, but are shown straight to keep the example easier to understand.

free market system
System in which decisions about what to produce and in what quantities are decided by the market; that is, by buyers and sellers negotiating prices for goods and services.

supply
The quantity of products that manufacturers or owners are willing to sell at different prices at a specific time.

supply curve
Line on a graph that shows the relationship between price and the quantity supplied.

FIGURE 2–3

FIGURE 2–3

Supply line for different
quantities of fish.
A simple supply line showing
the quantity of fish supplied
at different prices. The
supply line rises from left to
right. Think it through. The
higher the price of fish goes
(the left margin), the greater
the quantity that fishermen
will be willing to supply.

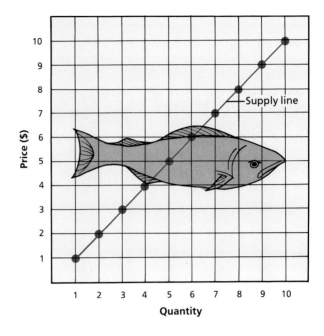

FIGURE 2–4

Demand line for different
prices.
A simple demand line
showing the quantity of fish
demanded at different
prices. The demand line falls
from left to right. It is easy
to understand why. The
higher the price of fish, the
lower the quantity
demanded. As the price falls,
the quantity demanded goes
up.

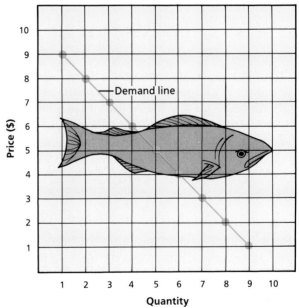

Demand

demand
The quantity of products
that people are willing to
buy at different prices at a
specific time.

demand curve
Line on a graph that shows
the relationship between
quantity demanded and
price.

Demand refers to the quantity of products that people are willing to buy at
different prices at a specific time. Generally speaking, the quantity demanded will
decrease as the price increases. Again, the relationship between price and quantity
demanded can be shown in a graph. Figure 2–4 shows a simple demand line. The
various points on the graph indicate the quantity demanded at various prices. For
example, at a price of $8, the quantity demanded is just two fish. But if the price
were $2, the quantity demanded would increase to eight. The line connecting the
dots is a **demand curve.** It shows the relationship between quantity demanded and
price.

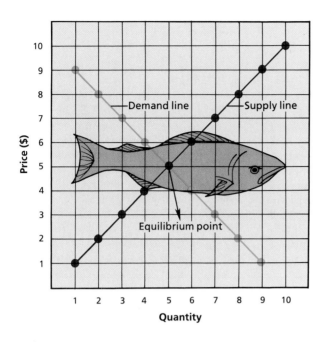

FIGURE 2-5

The equilibrium point. The interaction of quantity demanded and supplied at the equilibrium point. When we put supply and demand lines on one graph, we find that they interact at a price where the quantity supplied and the quantity demanded are equal. This is therefore called the equilibrium point. In the long run, the market price will tend toward the equilibrium point.

Equilibrium Point

It should be clear to you after reviewing the graphs that the key factor in determining supply and demand is price. Sellers prefer a high price and buyers prefer a low price, all other things being equal. If you were to lay the two graphs on top of one another, the supply line and the demand line would cross. At that crossing point, the quantity demanded and the quantity supplied would be equal. Figure 2–5 illustrates that point. At a price of $5, the quantity demanded and the quantity supplied are equal. It is known as the **equilibrium point.** That would become the market price. **Market price,** then, is determined by supply and demand.

What would happen if the seller moved his or her price up to $6? At that price, the buyer would be willing to buy only four fish, but the seller would be willing to sell six fish. Similarly, if the price were cut to $4, then buyers would be willing to buy six fish, but sellers would be willing to sell only four. In a free market, prices will always tend toward the equilibrium price.

It is the interaction between supply and demand, then, that determines the market price in the long run. Proponents of a free market would argue there is no need for government involvement or government planning. If surpluses develop, a signal is sent to sellers to lower the price. If shortages develop, a signal is sent to sellers to increase the price. Eventually, supply will again equal demand if nothing interferes with market forces.

equilibrium point
Point at which supply and demand are equal.
market price
Price determined by supply and demand.

Competition in a Free Market System

Competition is a cornerstone of the free market system. In the United States, the Justice Department's antitrust division serves as a watchdog to ensure that competition among sellers flows freely and new competitors have open access to the market. However, competition exists in different degrees ranging from being perfect to nonexistent. Economists generally agree that four different degrees of competition exist. They are called (1) perfect competition, (2) monopolistic competition, (3) oligopoly, and (4) monopoly.

WHY ARE FISH SO EXPENSIVE WHEN THEY REACH THE SCALES?

Supply and demand do not tell the whole story about the pricing of fish. The demand for fish is way up. The average person now eats over 15.4 pounds of fish a year, up from 12.2 pounds in 1975.

A cod from New England can be bought off the boat for 67 cents a pound. It costs $5.49 a pound in a Safeway store in Washington, D.C. Why is fish so expensive? A food processor takes the whole fish and cuts it into fillets. Once a fish is filleted, only about a third of its original weight remains, so the cost of the fish is now about three times its original cost. In fact, the cost is $2.23 a pound after processing. Safeway pays the processor $3.00 a pound and charges you $5.49, a good-sized 83 percent markup. Of course, Safeway cannot hold the fish too long

or it spoils and Safeway will have to absorb the cost of unsalable fish.

A Washington gourmet store buys fresh tuna for $7.25 a pound and sells it for $13.99. Such prices would not be possible, of course, if consumers would not pay those prices. Supply and demand ultimately dictate the price. If you and I and all other consumers stopped buying fish at such high prices, Safeway and the other retailers would likely cut the markup until supply again equaled demand.

By the way, fish are now traded on the Fish Exchange. The exchange is called Fishex and uses a central computer to create a network of fish buyers and sellers. This new system will make the market more efficient and able to react to supply and demand even faster.

Sources: Carole Sugerman, "From Boat to Market: The Convoluted Tail of How a Fish Lands on Your Table," *The Washington Post*, February 8, 1989, p. E1 and "Fishin' Market Theory," *Forbes*, May 2, 1988, p. 12.

The focus of supply and demand ultimately sets the price you see at the fish market. When there is a huge oil spill in Alaska, you can expect the supply of fish to fall and the price to rise. The high demand for fish today has pushed the price rather high. I'm sure you've noticed.

perfect competition
The market situation where there are many buyers and sellers and no seller is large enough to dictate the price of a product.

    Perfect competition exists when there are many buyers and sellers in a market and no seller is large enough to dictate the price of a product. Under perfect competition, sellers produce products that appear to be identical. Agricultural products are often considered to be the closest examples of perfect competition at work. For example, a buyer would be content to buy wheat from either farm A or

In competitive markets, some businesses succeed and some fail. Going-out-of-business sales are common but so are new start-ups. The market rewards those who provide the best value and ignores those who do not.

farm B since there is little or no difference between the wheat and because the prices would be the same. Why are the prices the same? Remember, no seller is large enough to dictate the price of a product. Price is determined according to the principles of supply and demand. Under perfect competition, the market is guided by Adam Smith's invisible hand theory.

Now that you know *what* perfect competition is, you should also know that there are *no* true examples of perfect competition. Today, government price supports and drastic reductions in the number of farms make it hard to argue that even farming is an example of perfect competition.

Monopolistic competition exists when a large number of sellers produce products that are very similar but are *perceived* by buyers as different. Under monopolistic competition, product differentiation (the attempt to make buyers think similar products are different in some way) is a key to success. Think about what that means for just a moment. Through tactics such as advertising, branding, and packaging, sellers try to convince buyers that *their* product is different from competitors. Actually, the competitive products may be similar or even interchangeable. Motor oil is a good example of this. One seller may inform consumers its product contains a super cleaning additive, a competitor promises more gas mileage, still another competitor offers faster acceleration. The buyer selects a particular brand as superior even though any of the three products would work in the car. Under monopolistic competition, limited barriers (such as start-up capital) exist for new firms wanting to enter the market. Prices are set by individual sellers. An **oligopoly** is a form of competition in which a market is dominated by just a few sellers. Generally, oligopolies exist in industries such as steel, automobiles, aluminum, and aircraft. One reason some industries remain in the hands of a few sellers is that the initial investment to enter an oligopolistic industry is tremendous. Think what it would cost to build a steel mill or an automobile assembly plant. In an oligopoly, prices are generally similar rather than competitive. The reason for this is simple. Intense price competition would lower profits for *all* the competitors, since a price cut on the part of one producer would most likely be matched by the others. Product differentiation rather than price differences is usually the major factor in market success.

monopolistic competition
The market situation where there are a large number of sellers that produce similar products, but the products are perceived by buyers as different.

oligopoly
A form of competition where the market is dominated by just a few sellers.

monopoly
A market in which there is only one seller.

A **monopoly** occurs when there is only one seller for a product or service. Obviously, in a monopoly situation, both the price and supply of a product are controlled by the single seller. In the United States, laws prohibit the creation of monopolies (we shall look at these in a later chapter). However, the legal system does permit approved monopolies such as public utilities that sell gas and electric power. These utilities' prices and profits are usually monitored carefully by public service commissions that protect the interest of buyers.

World Markets: Supply and Demand

Every day, billions of consumers throughout the world are sending signals to millions of producers throughout the world telling them what they want. The signal is sent by the price of various goods and services. The signals are sent very quickly, so that there should be little delay in ending surpluses and shortages. In the real world, there are many interferences to the free exchange of goods and services among countries. Consequently, some countries have surpluses (for example, the United States has a surplus of many crops) and others suffer from scarcity (many countries do not have sufficient food). A free market system would seem to be the best system for improving the world's economic condition. Given the advantages of such a system, there must be offsetting disadvantages or else the world would be joined in one, united free market.

LIMITATIONS OF THE FREE MARKET SYSTEM

The free market system, with its freedom and incentives, was a major factor in creating the wealth that some advanced countries now enjoy. Some even talk of the free market system as a true economic miracle. On the other hand, certain inequities seem to be inherent in the system. Rich people can buy almost everything that they need, and poor people often cannot. We shall explore how this happens and then we'll discuss what can be done about it.

Picture a market with buyers all willing to *buy* one unit of a commodity (for example, a large steak), but with each person willing to pay a different *price*. Picture also 10 sellers who are calling to *sell*, but at different prices. Figure 2–6 shows how this market may look.

As you can see, the price where supply equals demand (the equilibrium point) is at $6. If the steak were priced at $6, there would be no excess supply nor any excess demand. But notice this also. At the price of $6, there are some buyers who want steak, but are shut out by the market. All the buyers willing to pay from $1 to $5 (the majority) don't get what they want. Similarly, all the sellers who were willing to sell at prices from $7 to $11 are effectively shut out from the market. The market thus *excludes* buyers with too little money and sellers that cannot survive at low prices.

Thus, we have the situation in the United States where some poor people cannot afford enough food or adequate housing. The same thing is true with health care, clothing, and other goods and services. The wealthy seem to get all they need, and the poor get less than they need. Furthermore, there is much crime in the United States, including white-collar crime by business executives. There seems to be little control over pornography, prostitution, and drugs. The hunger for *economic* freedom may lead to too much tolerance for negative *social* behaviors. Many people feel that free markets do not foster moral and ethical behavior. This is not true in all capitalist countries, however. It is possible to have economic freedom and tight controls on social behavior. Such decisions are up to the public.

Freedom in the United States means freedom to succeed or to fail. It also means freedom to live on the streets if you so desire. One criticism of free markets is that they do not account for the special needs of society such as the homeless and the aged.

MAKING ETHICAL DECISIONS

In the United States, people are free to say just about anything and do just about anything except things that are illegal, and many people do illegal things as well. Some people object to the fact that freedom of expression has led to much cursing and swearing on TV and the showing during prime time of many immoral acts. The same is true of violence. Many actors are shown on TV shows drinking, smoking, taking drugs, and doing many illegal things. Many times the people being portrayed are businesspeople. This may cause much negative feeling about businesspeople among impressionable young viewers.

Bookstores and video stores in the United States sell what many consider to be pornographic magazines and videotapes. Some movie theaters also show such films. The lyrics of some rock songs are often shocking to many people.

In the United States, most people seem to accept such things as part of what it means to be free. In much of the world, however, such materials and such behaviors are totally unacceptable to the average person. Does freedom carry no responsibility for moral and ethical behavior? Who sets the moral and ethical tone for a society? Do the media have any responsibility to regulate themselves? What is the relationship between moral and ethical behavior and economic success in a country?

Do you feel that the moral standards of a society have anything to do with the economic growth and survival of that economy worldwide? Why should you act in a moral and ethical way if you can get away with not behaving that way? Why should businesspeople act in a moral and ethical way if they can get away with not behaving that way?

						Equilibrium point						FIGURE 2–6
Price	$11	$10	$9	$8	$7	$6	$5	$4	$3	$2	$1	The number of buyers and sellers at different prices. Five people are willing to buy or sell a steak for $6. Most people prefer bargain prices.
Number willing to buy a steak at this price	0	1	2	3	4	5	6	7	8	9	10	
Number willing to sell a steak at this price	10	9	8	7	6	5	4	3	2	1	0	

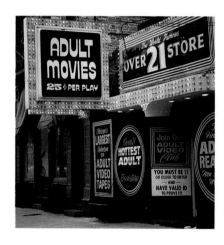

In a totally free market, people are able to purchase anything they want. That means adult movies, prostitution, automatic weapons, and more. A major issue in society is how far to take freedom or, expressed in another way, what limits to place on freedom. When do public safety and moral standards take precedence?

When people criticize the *results* of capitalism, they are saying, in effect, that they do not approve of the price mechanism (free markets) as the *only* means for allocating scarce resources and regulating the economy. Remember, economics is the study of how to allocate scarce resources. The goal is to create a high standard of living and a decent quality of life. In the pursuit of a high standard of living, people may neglect the quality of life, including the need for a clean environment and a high level of morality. Do you feel that is happening now?

Free markets brought prosperity to the United States, but also brought inequality. It is that inequality that has caused much national and world tension. In the search to create more equality in the United States, the government has intervened in the free market system to create more social fairness and a more even distribution of wealth.

The government at the state, local, and federal levels takes a large share of total national output and reallocates it to create more equality. Some money goes to schools, some goes to help those who are unemployed, some goes to the handicapped, and so on. The economic question becomes how much money should be available to the government to allocate for the defense of the country and for social welfare and how much should be left to free market forces to provide incentives for more output. If more is left to business, then the economic pie may grow and there will be more money to spread around. But if too much money is allocated by free markets, then some people may suffer.

What is the proper blend of government and free markets and freedom of behavior? That is the question. We shall discuss such issues in greater depth in Chapter 3. Before we do, let's review what other countries have done to allocate scarce resources. One alternative system is socialism. Socialism is an interesting contrast, because it is a combination of free market allocation and government allocation.

THINKING IT THROUGH	How much government involvement should there be in an economy? How important is freedom versus equality? How much control should the government have over ownership of production and distribution facilities? How much of the wealth of a nation should go to support those in need? Should government give direct aid to the poor or should it provide incentives to businesses to provide jobs or both? What should the role of government be in regulating things like pornography, music, movies, and the moral and ethical behavior of its citizens? These are the issues that businesses and government face throughout the world.

PROGRESS CHECK	What did Adam Smith believe were the two keys to economic success?
	Can you explain how supply, demand, and the price system tells producers how much to make and in what color? What happens if a producer makes too many items? What happens if a producer makes fewer items than are needed?
	What are three negative consequences of basing an economy totally on a free market system?

SOCIALISM: ALLOCATION OF SCARCE RESOURCES BY THE MARKET AND BY THE GOVERNMENT

The United States could be *the* economic model for the rest of the world. Adam Smith's free market economic principles are clearly a means to prosperity. How is it, then, that most Third World countries (mostly poor countries) have adopted socialism as their economic model? Why has the Soviet Union adopted a communist model for its economy? These are important questions, because the answers spell out the future of American businesses. If free market capitalism is to expand worldwide and create prosperity for all the world's citizens, capitalism will have to prove itself a better system *overall*.

What is capitalism's weak point in the eyes of the world? One answer is *equality*. Capitalism needs to meet the needs of *all* people, especially the poor, the sick, the old, and the unemployed, if it wants to win the hearts and the votes of citizens in other countries. Socialist systems have tried to address these problems. However, some argue they may go too far in letting government allocate resources. Let us look at a few examples.

Denmark

In Denmark, two thirds of the population were sustained by the state. A breadwinner with a meager salary paid at least 55 percent in taxes and *marginal rates* (rates for earning above a certain amount) of as much as 73 percent. A plumber who charged $20 for a job paid $4 in sales taxes, $5 in income tax, and $8 for expenses, leaving him or her $3.[5] That was perceived as unfair for the people who worked hard to make a living in Denmark. One third of the people were supporting two thirds. As a consequence, tax rates were recently lowered from a top rate of 73 percent to 68 percent. Denmark feels that certain functions such as health care are better provided by the state. Thus, the government needs more money to provide such services.

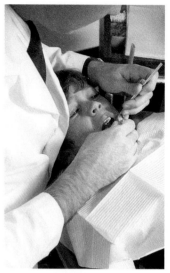

Many socialist countries provide free or very low-cost health care. Such care is provided with funds from taxes, but that often makes tax rates very high. The economic question is how high tax rates can be to provide desired social benefits without causing a lack of incentives among the more productive members of society. When taxes are too high, high wage earners may leave the country.

Denmark does not like to call its system socialist because most businesses are still privately owned. Nonetheless, the government is highly involved in allocating resources as it would under socialism. Danes prefer the term *welfare-state capitalism* to describe their system. It is basically a capitalist system with a socialist-style government. Whatever term is used, the result is a country with much more of its resources allocated by the government. This is one definition of socialism.

Holland

In Holland, there are almost as many inactive people (including retired) as there are private-sector workers. There is not much incentive to go back to work if you lose your job. An unemployed worker gets 80 percent of his or her previous salary for six months and 75 percent for the next two years. Sweden also lowered its top marginal rate recently from 82 percent to 75 percent.

Sweden

In Sweden, the government benefits seem good. To minimize unemployment, the government pays $5.25 per hour toward the wages of workers who would otherwise be laid off. Hospital care is just $4 a day. Dental care for children is free. But, as they say, "There's no such thing as a free lunch." A person who makes more than $31,000 in Sweden pays 75 cents of each additional dollar he or she earns to the government. Also, sales taxes in Sweden amount to 25 percent. (Could you imagine buying a $20 concert ticket and having to pay a $5 sales tax?) Bengt Westerberg, the head of the Swedish Liberal Party, recognizes the drawbacks of having tax rates too high and calls for a cut in tax rates. Here is what he said about the proposed cuts:[6]

> A reduction of the top rate to 50 percent . . . would greatly enhance the performance of the economy in several respects. First, we would run less risk of losing some of our most clever researchers and technicians to other countries and thereby getting behind in development. Second, we would increase the possibility of combining higher disposable income with lower nominal wage increases and thus reducing cost inflation. Third, and perhaps most important, we would increase incentives to work.

Mr. Carl Bildt, a member of the Swedish Moderate Party, says much the same. He, too, calls for tax cuts:[7]

> Unless the tax burden on the economy is lowered, the supply of knowledge, labor and capital will be withheld from the expanding part of our industry, and our growth performance will continue to decline.

You get the point. In socialist countries, the government sometimes gets the bulk of the money people make and allocates that money back to people in the form of social services. You are usually given more care by the government than under capitalism, but you have less discretion in how you spend your money. This, of course, seems like a good deal to those who make little, but is not nearly as attractive to people who make a lot of money, such as doctors and other professionals. That is one reason many professionals leave socialist countries to live in capitalist countries where they can keep more of what they earn.

Tennis players Mats Wilander, Bjorn Borg, Joakim Nystrom, Stefan Edberg, and Anders Jarryd all have moved from Sweden to London to escape Sweden's 75 percent tax rate for England's 40 percent rate.[8]

Finally, in 1988, Sweden cut its top marginal tax rate to 60 percent. For the 9 out of 10 Swedes who make $26,000 or less, the top rate was dropped from 60 percent to 30 percent.[9] As a result of such cuts, Sweden should lose fewer of its top income earners and should have greater economic growth.

The goal of socialist countries, therefore, is to provide enough freedom to keep their best workers and still provide social benefits that are more generous than capitalist countries. The problem is in finding the right balance between government and private industry.

THE RESTRUCTURING IN EUROPE

The European Economic Community is now bargaining over the dropping of all international barriers among the 12 member states. This is to take place in 1992. One of the major issues of that debate will be the nature of the new, united economy. Prime Minister Margaret Thatcher of England is arguing for capitalism. European Commission Chairman Jacques Delors says that the British model cannot be imposed on the rest of the community. He wants social safety nets and worker participation in management.[10] In other words, he leans toward a socialist model. The debate will get hotter and hotter as the deadline approaches. You will learn much about economic systems if you follow this debate in the next couple of years. Taxation in Italy amounts to 82 percent of net pay.[11] Such taxes are way out of line with England and other countries in Europe. What will be the outcome when they unite? We'll see.

THINKING IT THROUGH	Socialism depends on capitalism for wealth creation and then depends on the government to distribute the wealth more evenly. Can you explain why that eventually may cut off the source of wealth? How hard would you study in school if you knew everyone would get a C regardless of how they did on the tests? Would you give your car as much care and attention if it were owned by the state? How would you go about deciding how much of a wage earner's salary should go to the government for defense and welfare and how much should remain with the wage earner? Would your answer differ if you were suddenly fired and could not find a job and were forced to live on the street?

This highly automated farm in China is an example of how China is experimenting with capitalism. The increased output under capitalist incentives has been outstanding. The Soviet Union is now trying a similar experiment. In both countries, citizen protests are occurring to speed up the process of introducing capitalism and democracy. Government reaction may actually slow the process.

COMMUNISM: ALLOCATION OF SCARCE RESOURCES MOSTLY BY THE GOVERNMENT

Karl Marx, the 19th-century economist, wrote that capitalism would lead to the economic exploitation of the working class by an elite class. He held that the elite would control the factors of production. He forecasted a worldwide class struggle that would eventually do away with all traces of private property in an economy. The result would be all people sharing a nation's resources under the direction of strong central government. He called this system of state control of industry and resources communism.[12]

Today, many nations, including the Soviet Union and the People's Republic of China, have communist economic systems. Their governments play a major role in the planning and functioning of the economy in both these countries.

The Soviet economy has been somewhat of a disaster in recent years. Some 40 percent of the Soviet population lives in poverty, including 79 percent of its elderly. South African blacks own more cars per capita than do Soviet citizens.[13] The government has tried to give the people jobs, housing, health care, and defense from foreign invaders, but in doing so it has not created the incentives for people to create the wealth needed to fund all these projects. This has resulted in shortages of food and basic household goods. Tomatoes cost $10 a pound, and the average Soviet makes only $350 a month. There are few fruits and vegetables available to the average consumer.[14] Consumer goods simply are not available in the abundance found in noncommunist countries throughout the world. No one recognizes the poor conditions in the Soviet Union more than President Mikhail Gorbachev. Here is how he describes the state of the Soviet Union today:[15]

> The Soviet Union, the world's biggest producer of steel, raw materials, fuel and energy has shortfalls in them due to wasteful or inefficient use. . . . We have the largest number of doctors and hospital beds per thousand of population and, at the same time, there are glaring shortcomings in our health services.

* * * * *

> Decay began in public morals. Alcoholism, drug addiction, and crime were growing.

* * * * *

The theory of Communism may be summed up in one sentence: Abolish all private property.
KARL MARX AND FRIEDRICH ENGELS, 1848

But we also see that dishonest people try to exploit [the] advantages of communism; they know only their rights, but they do not want to know their duties. They work poorly, shirk and drink hard. . . . We are fully restoring the principle of socialism, "From each according to his ability, to each according to his work," and we seek to affirm social justice for all, equal rights for all, one law for all, one kind of discipline for all, and high responsibilities for each.

perestroika
Restructuring of the Soviet economy.

The name of the restructuring of the Soviet economy is **perestroika.** In the past, Soviet bureaucrats generally preferred to keep prices artificially low to show there was no inflation under communism. In fact, however, the low prices only resulted in the misallocation of resources, and inflation was reflected in shortages and lines outside the shops. Another basic problem is that without the ability to bring output and prices in line with demand, no manager had any incentive to be flexible. When asked whether most Soviets understand the link between high prices and more plentiful supply, Leonid Abalkin, the man in charge of restructuring the Soviet economy, said:[16]

No, they don't. In the coming two to three years, we will reform the entire pricing system. It will certainly involve increases in prices of meat and dairy products. There will be some confusion. We hope to convince our people of the need for price reform, but this is a problem that will take some time to resolve.

Free market forces do not operate in the Soviet Union as they do in capitalist countries, and the result is often great imbalances. It will be interesting to follow the attempts by President Gorbachev to reform his country. Much of the future of world tensions, world trade, and world prosperity and growth depends on the outcome.

Living in Communist versus Capitalist Systems

Figure 2–7 will help you compare the economic systems on several dimensions. Clearly, you would live an entirely different kind of life under a communist system. You would be assured of a job, but not necessarily the job of your choice. You would be assured of housing, but could not move from city to city or from home to home. The government selects where you will live. If you worked very hard, you would make the same as the next person who came to work drunk and didn't do much work at all. This may ruin your motivation to do a good job. You would also have less motivation to paint up and fix up your office and home because you would have no ownership investment and would be tempted to leave that responsibility to others. You would have no freedom to protest, to assemble, or to state your views in the media. The recent crackdown on student protestors in China showed this to be true.

One reason the Soviet Union normally does not allow its citizens to travel abroad is that many of the best and brightest would leave for a more open system where they could prosper. For example, some 328,000 people from Poland have remained abroad after leaving on "tourist trips." This includes some 3,500 doctors, 11,000 engineers, 4,000 scientists, and 36,000 technicians.[17] Economic conditions are not improving rapidly in most communist countries and the tension is building for social protests. The 1990s will be a real challenge to communism.

To a person raised in a free country, such a system would seem very oppressive. For a businessperson, it would be very frustrating because one could not own his or her own business and keep the profits of one's own work. As an employee, you would not have much incentive to work hard because you would make the same regardless of how hard you worked. The basic philosophy is, "From each according to his ability, to each according to his need."

Comparing economic systems.   FIGURE 2–7

	CAPITALISM	MIXED ECONOMY	SOCIALISM	COMMUNISM
Social and economic goals	Private ownership of land and business. Liberty and the pursuit of happiness. Free trade. Emphasis on freedom and the profit motive for economic growth.	Private ownership of land and business with government regulation. Government control of some institutions (e.g., mail). High taxation for defense and the common welfare. Emphasis on a balance between freedom and equality.	Public ownership of major businesses. Some private ownership of smaller businesses and shops. Government control of education, health care, utilities, mining, transportation, and media. Very high taxation. Emphasis on equality.	No private property. Public ownership of factories. Centralization of communication and transportation with the State. No rights of inheritance. Free education. Emphasis on equality.
Motivation of workers	Much incentive to work efficiently and hard because profits are retained by owners. Workers are rewarded for high productivity.	Incentives are similar to capitalism except in government-owned enterprises, which have few incentives. High marginal taxes can discourage overtime work.	Capitalist incentives exist in private businesses. Government control of wages in public institutions limits incentives.	Worker incentives come largely from within. The idea is "To each according to his or her need." Some incentives are being introduced by the state and some free enterprise is encouraged.
Control over markets	Complete freedom of trade within and among nations. No government control of markets.	Some government control of trade within and among nations (trade protectionism). Government regulation to assure fair trade within the country.	Some markets are controlled by the government and some are free. Trade restrictions among nations vary and include some free trade agreements.	Central control of markets and production.
Choices in the market	A wide variety of goods and services are available. Almost no scarcity or oversupply exists for long because supply and demand controls the market.	Similar to capitalism, but scarcity and oversupply may be caused by government involvement in the market (e.g., subsidies for farms).	Variety in the marketplace varies considerably from country to country. Choice is directly related to government involvement in markets.	Often very limited variety in the market. Scarcities common. Response to market demand and market changes very slow.
Social freedoms	Freedom of speech, press, assembly, religion, job choice, movement, and elections.	Similar to capitalism. Some restrictions on freedoms of assembly and speech. Separation of church and state may limit religious practices in schools.	Similar to mixed economy. Governments may restrict job choice, movement among countries, and who may attend upper-level schools (i.e., college).	Government control of press. Limited freedom of speech, religion, and assembly. Often difficult to emigrate or to move from one district to another—restricted travel. Almost no free elections.

On the other hand, to a person living under a communist system, life in a capitalist country seems to have some severe problems as well. You have no right to a job, so you may be unemployed for months or years. You have no right to a home, so you may have to live on the streets as some people do. You may have more drug and crime problems under a capitalist system, although communist systems, too, have problems with excessive drinking. You may not be able to afford health care and may die as a result, whereas communist systems provide relatively free health care. To a person living under a communist system, the U.S. government does not appear to take very good care of the sick, the old, and the handicapped, and communists feel that is uncaring.

Nations throughout the world are struggling to decide which economic system is the best one for growth, prosperity, peace, and a reasonable sense of freedom. All peoples of the world want a comfortable standard of living and a high quality of life. What kind of economic system is most likely to provide those results? The answer is likely to be some system with the best qualities of all systems, but the most important ingredients to Americans seem to be free markets, free elections, and freedom of worship and protest.

Capitalist Inroads

There is much discussion about applying capitalist incentives in the Soviet Union. There has even been some discussion with American advertising agencies about creating more ads for Soviet media. There were also serious trade discussions between the United States and the Soviet Union in 1988 and 1989. One reason the Soviets are looking at such changes is the success the Chinese communists have had with capitalist-type reforms. Many communist countries are experimenting with capitalism, especially the incentives of profit. In March of 1989, President Gorbachev announced a new plan for having private farms compete against collectevized farms. He called private farms "individual property," a term close to the capitalist "private property."[18] Gorbachev is following China's leadership in introducing capitalism into the system.

In China, agriculture and industry has been infused with many capitalist experiments with highly rewarding results (see Case 2 at the end of this chapter). In 1987, Premier Zhao Ziyang declared that in two to three years only about 30 percent of the country's economy will be controlled through central planning. The introduction of capitalism in China has done wonders for the economy, but it has brought problems as well. Here is how it was reported in *The Wall Street Journal:*[19]

> Mr. Deng's economic policies have brought about a considerable increase in production (especially in agriculture), in wealth, in inequality and in corruption. White-collar crime is growing. . . . The number of lawyers is increasing; in Liaoning Province alone, 2,300 lawyers have opened 122 offices. The divorce rate is also rising. Beggars and vagrants are seen more often in the streets. The decollectivization of agriculture has elevated short-term profit over long-term considerations of land use and conservation, weakened the traditional system of irrigation, canals and dikes and has exposed the countryside to new threats of soil exhaustion, erosion, pollution and flooding.

When the people in China protested to have more freedom and democracy, the government shot the protestors and arrested others. This reaction by the government is likely to slow economic gains and alienate trading partners (see Case 2 at the end of this chapter). What all countries are seeking is the right economic mix. We have seen how socialist Sweden is cutting back on government and putting in more incentives. The same is happening in communist China and the Soviet Union. The United States has also been introducing deregulation of industry and cuts in taxes. We shall discuss that next.

MIXED ECONOMIES: ALLOCATION OF SCARCE RESOURCES BY FREE MARKETS WITH GOVERNMENT REGULATION

The United States is not a purely capitalist nation. Rather, it has a **mixed economy;** that is, a combination of free markets plus government allocation of resources. As a mixed economy, the United States falls somewhere between a pure capitalist state and a socialist state. The degree of government involvement in the economy is a matter of some debate in the United States today. In 1986, the Congress proposed the largest change in the tax system since it was started. Top tax rates were lowered, and rates for some low-income families were cut to nothing. These changes were implemented to simplify the tax codes and to stimulate the economy. The new tax code was designed to discourage investments that were made to avoid taxes and encourage investments that promoted business growth.

mixed economy
An economy that combines free markets with some government allocation of resources.

The government has a great effect on the success of business in the United States and throughout the world. In Chapter 3 we shall explore many issues having to do with the government and the economy. Keep in mind as you read Chapter 3 that the foundation of the U.S. economy is capitalism. The government serves as a means to supplement that basic system and thus promote growth and greater equality. Changes in the tax codes will have a significant effect on the economy over the next few years. You will be better able to understand what is happening in the economy and how it affects business after you read the next chapter. But first, let's pause and review what we have learned so far about economics.

How high are marginal tax rates in leading socialist countries? What do such rates do to incentives for people to work harder and produce more?

PROGRESS CHECK

What are some of the potential negative social consequences of introducing freer markets into communist countries such as China and the Soviet Union?

What does perestroika mean and how is it affecting the economy of the Soviet Union?

What is a mixed economy and what are the advantages of a mixed economy over a free market economy?

---

1. Economics is the study of how society chooses the ways to use scarce resources and to distribute goods and services to competing groups and individuals.

   SUMMARY

   How do capitalist, socialist, and communist economic systems allocate resources?

   In capitalist systems, resources are allocated by individual consumers, bargaining in the marketplace. In socialist systems, the market and the government allocate resources. The government allocates the resources in communist systems.

   What is the difference between macroeconomics and microeconomics?
   Macroeconomics is the study of a nation's economy as a *whole*; whereas microeconomics is the study of the behavior of people and organizations in particular markets.

   1. Define economics and explain the difference between microeconomics and macroeconomics.

2. Draw a diagram showing the circular flows of money in the international economy and discuss the increasing importance of international economic flows relative to national economics.

3. Discuss Adam Smith's strategy for wealth creation and his basic principles.

4. Outline the basic rights of capitalism.

5. Describe how free markets work, using the terms *supply, demand,* and *prices.*

6. Discuss some limitations of the free market system and what countries are doing to offset those limitations.

7. Show how socialism attempts to solve some of the limitations of capitalism, but creates new problems of its own.

8. Describe the effects of the economic system in communist countries and what that means for world economic development.

2. There is a circular flow of inputs, outputs, and money and other resources between the U.S. economy and the economics of other nations (see p.52).
   - Why is it important for you to understand the various economic systems and how they work?
     Economic flows among nations in the future will be determined by how each economy allocates scarce resources and how they view international trade.
3. The foundation of Adam Smith's economic theory was man's desire for money.
   - Explain what Adam Smith meant by an "invisible hand."
     Adam Smith's invisible hand referred to the idea that countries would prosper as individuals within the country prosper because the way to make money is to provide needed goods and services to others through trade. The invisible hand turns self-directed gain into social benefits for all.
   - What were the two keys to economic success identified by Adam Smith?
     Smith's keys to economic success were freedom and incentives.
4. People living in capitalist systems enjoy certain basic rights.
   - What are the basic rights of capitalism?
     The basic rights of capitalism are the rights to: (1) private property, (2) keep all profits, (3) competition, and (4) choice.
5. A free market system is one in which decisions about what to produce and in what quantities are decided by the market.
   - How does supply and demand affect what kind and in what quantity products are produced in a free market system?
     The price of a product tells producers to make more or less of a product. The more money producers make from higher prices the more they are likely to produce the product. Price is determined by supply and demand. The higher the quantity demanded, the higher the price. In turn, the higher the supply, the lower the price.
6. In spite of the wealth that countries with a free market system enjoy, the system also suffers from certain inequities.
   - What are some of the limitations of the free market system?
     In countries with free market systems, the rich can buy almost everything, and the poor often cannot buy what they need. There may be much crime and, much tolerance of negative social behavior. That is, economic freedoms and social freedoms often go hand in hand.
7. Socialism attempts to avoid some of the limitations of capitalism.
   - How do socialist countries try to avoid the problems of capitalism?
     In socialist countries, the government provides many social services such as health care and care for the elderly. The government distributes the wealth more evenly.
   - What problems are created by a socialist system?
     In a socialist system, you may earn plenty, but you must give most of your salary to the government in the form of taxes in order for it to provide social services for others. Many professionals leave socialist countries for this reason.
8. The governments of countries with communist systems decide how the nation's resources will be allocated.
   - What effects have their economic system had on communist countries.
     People in communist countries have few incentives to create the wealth

needed to fund the governments' projects. As a result, there are often shortages of food and basic household goods.

9. The United States does not operate under a pure capitalist system, but is a mixed economic system.
   - What does it mean to say the United States has a "mixed economy"?
   The United States falls somewhere between a pure capitalist state and a socialist state. Its economy is a combination of free markets plus government allocation of resources.

10. There are many similarities and differences among capitalist, socialist, communist, and mixed economic systems.
   - Compare and contrast the various economic systems.
   See Figure 2–7 on page 67.

9. Examine the mixed economy in the United States and explain its strengths and weaknesses.

10. Compare and contrast capitalism, socialism, and communism and reach your own conclusions about what a successful world economy would look like.

GETTING INVOLVED

1. Go to your local or school library and find a couple of introductory Economics texts. Look through the Tables of Contents and briefly leaf through the books. What are the major topics? How hard are the books to read? Share your findings with others in the class.

2. What are some of the *disadvantages* of living in a free society? How could such disadvantages be minimized? What are the advantages? Write a short essay describing why a poor person in India might reject capitalism and prefer a socialist/communist state. How could the United States overcome this situation to broaden the base of the free market system? Perhaps two students could debate capitalist versus communist societies to further reveal the issues.

3. Democratic capitalism is said to be based on a Judeo-Christian base of ethics. Write a short essay discussing whether or not the moral and ethical foundation of our country is weakening. What would you recommend? Discuss with your class.

4. The leaders of both communist and capitalist societies feel so strongly about the benefits of their systems that they are sometimes willing to go to war to defend them. Show that such tensions are created largely by *economic* pressures, and discuss how such tensions can be minimized or eliminated. Would you support free trade with communist countries? Give arguments for both sides.

5. If you were a political leader in the United States, would you call for more government involvement in the economy, or less? Why? What percent of the total money earned in the United States would you allocate to the government? What are the benefits and drawbacks of having high taxes, as revealed in this chapter?

CASE ONE   **MIXING IN A MIXED ECONOMY**

PRACTICING MANAGEMENT DECISIONS

The United States is now a mixed economy. The major reason it is a mixed economy is that pure capitalism may have negative consequences. In the United States, those consequences included sick people who could not afford basic health care, old people who could not afford decent housing or nourishing food, unemployment, millions of illiterate citizens, and large, powerful businesses that had the power to drive out smaller firms. This led to a whole series of government agencies to assure more fairness, equality, and a high level of general welfare.

Some agencies, such as the Federal Trade Commission, encourage competition among businesses. Other agencies, such as Health and Human Services, look after the health and welfare of citizens. The Department of Education concerns itself with schooling. In spite of all these efforts, the United States still has sick people who cannot afford health care, old people who need care, millions of illiterate citizens, and so on.

DECISION QUESTIONS

1. What can be done in the United States to solve the problem of the old, the sick, the unemployed, the poor, and the illiterate? Should the government be responsible for handling such problems or are better private alternatives available? What are the latest trends?

2. Have other countries solved the problems outlined in this Case better than the United States? Can there be negative consequences from focusing on these problems? What has been the experience of other countries?

3. Why would business owners and managers be particularly concerned about how the government solves the problems in this Case?

4. One negative consequence of pure capitalism not mentioned in the Case is the potential for immoral and unethical behavior among businesspeople. Is this problem one that should involve government or some other institution or institutions?

CASE TWO   THE CAPITALIST EXPERIMENT IN CHINA

China is a land of over 1 billion people, most of whom live in poverty. There are 400,000 state-owned enterprises in China. It was and is a communist/socialist country. However, China is trying to introduce some capitalism into the system.

The announcement was made October 20, 1984. The plan was adopted by the Communist Party's Central Committee. The plan called for dismantling of the state planning system, greater freedom for business enterprises, heavier reliance on market forces to determine output, free-floating prices on certain goods, higher wages for skilled workers, and more private entrepreneurs. (This was quite a drastic change from the previous state control of wages, prices, production, and trade.)

In the past, prices were kept artificially low, subsidized by the state. Ignoring market signals, the system often had shortages of some goods and huge stockpiles of unwanted merchandise. The government was careful to retain control over some major products (steel, coal, machinery, and synthetic fibers).

The report said that, as the economy diversifies, the role of private entrepreneurs should expand and take over enterprises now run by the state. The driving force behind these changes is Deng Xiaoping. He began this move by taking the commune out of communism and restoring family farms and free market incentives. Production jumped by 89 percent. The experiment worked. The plan was to try a similar experiment in industry. It could be called market socialism. State enterprises will now function as independent companies responsible for making profits. Here are some of the results, as reported in the U.S. press:

- At the Beijing Television Factory, monthly output went up 30 percent since the managers began offering piece-rate bonuses for each set produced above target. Profits rose by $81,000.
- Bicycles, radios, and watches that once were scarce are now plentiful.
- Farmers are setting up small agribusinesses such as papaya growing and are trucking fresh vegetables to market.
- Three years ago, the people in Sha Zui village were fishermen and farmers living at a subsistence level. Today, there are 15 factories employing 2,300 people. The average income of many families is $2,700 a year, enough to buy motorcycles and trucks. "If every place in China did this, they'd all be rich" says a former fisherman who is village chief.
- Chinese factories are starting to sell large quantities of higher quality but inexpensive goods to the United States and other international markets.
- Bu Xinsheng is a national hero for raising productivity at his factory and improving quality. How did he do it? He switched from wages to piecework. Maximum wages went from $18 to $41 a month, but workers had to work harder to earn them. They did.
- In the cities, literally millions of people have set up shops or stalls where they sell just about everything. There are now a few millionaires in China.

Along with the prosperity has come some of the Western culture China's leaders had worried about. Young Chinese are listening to rock and roll music, watching TV, and wearing makeup. Western clothes are the rage. Some entrepreneurs are making huge profits by selling hard-to-get consumer goods. The old values of sharing and caring seem to be losing out to profiting and affluence.

Government involvement in agriculture has not been a big success, either. Rather than rely on free markets, the government put a low price on grain to keep prices low for those farmers who purchase grain to feed livestock. As a consequence, farmers began growing more profitable crops such as celery, which brings in twice as much profit as wheat. This led to shortages in wheat in China such that the government had to import 14 million tons in 1987 at a cost of about $1 billion.

The demand for grain goes up every year as the population in China grows by 15 million a year. To get more wheat, the government could raise the price of wheat, but it is a tradition in China to keep basic food prices such as wheat and rice low. Another alternative is to recollectivize the farms and introduce more mechanization, but farmers resist that effort as well.

Recently, the people of China took to the streets to demand more democracy and freedom and less government corruption. The government answered by calling in the military to shoot and arrest the protestors.

DECISION QUESTIONS

1. What are the capitalist principles that enabled China to raise productivity so quickly?
2. What effect has the new capitalism had on workers? Consumers? Small-business people? Farmers? Who is hurt by the new reforms?
3. What are the negatives associated with the new capitalism? Can they be minimized?
4. What would you recommend be done about the wheat shortages? Would you recommend freer markets or more government control? What would be the advantages and disadvantages of each?
5. What do you anticipate will happen to economic reform in China after the political repression of 1989?

Sources: "The Greatest Leap Yet Toward a Free Market," *Business Week,* November 5, 1984, p. 45; Amanda Bennett, "Capitalism in China," *Business Week,* January 14, 1985, pp. 53–59; Adi Ignatius, "Bitter Harvest," *The Wall Street Journal,* January 19, 1988, pp. 1 and 16; and Dori Jones Yang and Maria Shao, "China's Reformers Say: Let a Thousand Businesses Bloom," *Business Week,* April 11, 1988, pp. 70–71; and Daniel Southerland, "1 Million in Beijing Center Demand Democracy," *The Washington Post,* May 18, 1989, p. 1.

The U.S. government recognizes the inequality of a free market system. As a consequence, more and more funds are being diverted to the government for care of the aged (social security), the poor (welfare), and the sick (medicare). In spite of increased spending, the problems persist.

LOOKING AHEAD

Funds are also spent on defense, crime prevention, and regulation of business. Too much government spending may slow business growth. Too little may result in social decay.

Chapter 3 looks at economic issues affecting business. Such issues include productivity, unemployment, taxes, money creation by the government, inflation, the national debt, and trade deficits. The health of the economy is directly related to the health of business. Chapter 3 will teach you terms and concepts you can use to read and understand the business literature.

ECONOMIC ISSUES AFFECTING BUSINESS

3

James M. Buchanan.

You know, not too long ago I was asked to explain the difference between a small businessman and a big businessman. And my answer was that a big businessman is what a small businessman would be if only the government would get out of the way and leave him alone.

FORMER PRESIDENT RONALD REAGAN

PROFILE   NOBEL PRIZE WINNER IN ECONOMICS

The 1986 Nobel Prize for economics was awarded to Professor James M. Buchanan for his Public Choice doctrine. Professor Buchanan teaches at George Mason University in Virginia. He studied political decision making to see why politicians make the kind of decisions they do. What he discovered was that politicians and public administrators are much like you and me. They're human beings with limited information and with incentives to satisfy their own interests, the interests of their own groups, and their own political parties. One large incentive is to seize power and to retain power in the economic process. In short, politicians and public administrators are not always acting in what they perceive to be the best interests of the public as a whole; instead, they have their own hidden agendas and goals—just like the average citizen.

This should come as no surprise to people and, in fact, many criticized the nomination of Buchanan because they felt that all he did was state what was common sense. It is instructive, however, to notice that politicians do not have perfect knowledge and do not always follow the policies recommended by economists because they have their own goals and motives. It is important to keep this in mind as you read the economic problems facing the United States today and try to reason why the politicians are trying to solve those problems the way they do. Economists have much to teach us about the workings of the economy and how politicians can make an economy grow and prosper. Certainly Adam Smith was a major contributor to that process, as we learned in Chapter 1. You will want to learn more about economics as you study business because much of the terminology of business is economic terms. This is especially true when the media report about business. Therefore, this chapter will discuss the major economic influences on the economy and some of the economic problems facing the United States today. You may become fascinated by the subject and be a future Nobel Prize winner yourself. The terms and concepts in the two economics chapters will provide the foundation for your further study.

ECONOMICS AND BUSINESS

The strength of the economy has a tremendous effect on business. When the economy is strong and growing, most businesses prosper and almost everyone benefits through plentiful jobs, reasonably good wages, and sufficient revenues for the government to provide needed goods and services. When the economy is weak, however, businesses are weakened as well, employment and wages may fall, and government revenues may decline as a result.

Because business and the economy are so closely linked, *The Wall Street Journal, Business Week,* and the other business newspapers and magazines are full of economic terms and concepts. It is virtually impossible to read such business reports with much understanding unless you are familiar with the economic concepts and terms being used. The purpose of this chapter is to help you learn additional economic concepts, terms, and issues—the kind that you will be seeing daily if your read the business press, as we encourage you to do.

As you read the business literature, you will probably find many articles by Sylvia Porter, a well-known writer in business. One column she wrote recently was about the major economic statistics that help identify where the nation stands in relationship to the business cycle (the up and down trends of business growth and decline over time).[1]

The first figure that Sylvia Porter says to keep your eye on is gross national product. **Gross national product (GNP)** is the total value of a country's output of goods and services in a given year. It is a measure of economic growth or decline. When people discuss what share of the "economic pie" should go to government, they mean what percent of GNP should be spent on defense, welfare, education, and other government programs. Also, GNP gives business owners some measure of how the economy is functioning.

If the economy is growing too fast, it is said to be in danger of "overheating"; that is, maintaining a growth level it can't possibly sustain. This results in corrective action, such as tightening of credit by the Federal Reserve Board. We shall discuss that process briefly in this chapter and in great detail in Chapter 21. If growth of GNP slows or actually declines, there are often many negative effects on business. A **recession** is two consecutive quarters of decline in the GNP. A major influence on the growth in GNP is how productive the work force is. That is, how much output workers create with a given amount of inputs such a machinery and capital.

A second indicator of an economy's health is unemployment figures. There are two important figures to watch: (1) the monthly unemployment figure, which tells you the percentage of people seeking jobs; and (2) the percentage of the population that is employed.

A third indicator of the economy's health, according to Porter, is the consumer price index (CPI). The consumer price index consists of monthly statistics that measure the pace of inflation (consumer prices going up) or deflation (consumer prices going down). The producer price index (PPI) measures prices at the wholesale level.

In the following sections, we shall look at these figures and more. The government plays a major role in trying to maintain growth in the economy without causing prices to go up too much. How the government does that and how much of GNP the government should have to work with are two critical issues that we shall discuss later in the chapter. For now, let's look more closely at the key economic indicators: GNP, unemployment figures, and the consumer and producer price indexes.

gross national product (GNP)
The total value of a country's output of goods and services in a given year.

recession
Two consecutive quarters of decline in the GNP.

GROSS NATIONAL PRODUCT

Almost every discussion about a nation's economy is based on gross national product (GNP). The reason is obvious once you recall what GNP is—the total value of a country's output of goods and services in a given year. Earlier, we said that it was good for GNP to grow, but not too fast or too slow. From 1979 to 1988, GNP, adjusted for inflation, grew about 1.3 percent annually. That compares with 3.1 percent during the 1970s and 4.2 percent during the 1960s. Clearly, growth is slowing, but the country is at the end of one of the longest periods of economic growth in history and slower growth may be necessary as the economy prepares for a new era. Certainly, the United States remains a very strong international competitor.

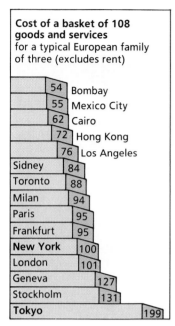

Cost of a basket of 108 goods and services
for a typical European family of three (excludes rent)

54	Bombay
55	Mexico City
62	Cairo
72	Hong Kong
76	Los Angeles
Sidney	84
Toronto	88
Milan	94
Paris	95
Frankfurt	95
New York	100
London	101
Geneva	127
Stockholm	131
Tokyo	199

Index: New York = 100, based on dollar exchange rate as of March 31, 1988

Note that living costs are about twice as high in Tokyo, Japan, as they are in New York. On the other hand, living costs in Bombay, India, and Mexico City, Mexico, are about half of New York's.

Note: Living costs are about twice as high in Tokyo, Japan, as they are in New York.

Source: Reprinted from November 7, 1988, issue of *Business Week* by special permission, copyright © 1988 by McGraw-Hill Inc.

productivity
The total output of goods and services in a given period of time divided by work hours (output per work hour).

A government big enough to give us everything we want is a government big enough to take from us everything we have.
FORMER PRESIDENT GERALD FORD

One way to compare the economic strength of countries is to compare gross national products. Using that yardstick, the United States falls slightly behind Japan and West Germany. In 1988, the GNP per person for Japan was $19,642, for West Germany, $18,449, and for the United States, $18,406. Does this mean that people in Japan and West Germany have a higher standard of living than those in the United States? No! Prices in those countries tend to be higher, so people can buy less with the money they make. In terms of purchasing power, Japan and Germany have about three fourths the American level. That is, Americans can buy about one fourth more. That means a higher standard of living in the United States.[2] We noted in Chapter 2 that a high standard of living is a major goal of economic policy.

We said that one way to increase the growth in GNP was to increase productivity. To stay competitive with other countries, U.S. workers must increase their productivity. How are they doing now? In 1988, productivity grew by 3.8 percent, the highest in four years.[3] The predicted rate of growth for the 1990s is about 1.5 percent, which is not enough to get the economy booming again. In the next section, we shall explore the concept of productivity in more depth so you can see what is happening, but first let's look at how GNP is distributed.

Distribution of GNP

The money that is earned from producing goods and services goes to the people who own businesses and to the government in the form of taxes. You learned in Chapter 2 that some countries take a much larger percentage of GNP for the government than other countries. The question in the United States each year is, "How much of GNP should go to the government and how much should go to businesses and the owners of businesses"?

In the United States, the percentage of GNP taken by the government at all levels (federal, state, and local) was about 20 percent in the early 1950s. By the late 1980s, that figure had risen to about 33 percent.[4] Some 12.2 percent of GNP went to state and local governments.[5]

Productivity

Productivity is the total output of goods and services in a given period of time divided by work hours (output per work hour). An *increase in productivity* means that the same amount of labor input is now able to produce more goods and services. The higher productivity is, the lower costs are in producing goods and services, and the lower prices can be. Therefore, businesspeople are eager to increase productivity.

Productivity is one of the major ingredients of capitalist growth. The word *capitalism* is based on the word *capital*. Capital refers to machinery and materials that are used on farms and in businesses to help workers produce more. At the beginning of the 20th century in the United States, one out of three workers was needed to produce enough food to feed everyone and create some surplus for world use. Today, less than 1 out of 20 workers can produce far greater quantities of food that contribute a much larger share of world production. What made the difference? The answer is that the use of tractors, chemical fertilizer, combines, silos, and other machines and materials (capital) raised farmers' productivity.

GOVERNMENT SHARE OF GNP IN SELECTED FOREIGN COUNTRIES

When considering whether or not the government is taking too much or too little of GNP, it is helpful to see what other countries are doing. One of our major competitors is Japan. Japan's government takes about the same as the U.S. government (33.1 percent). The socialist governments of Europe take a lot more. For example, Italy takes 50.5 percent and West Germany takes 46.6 percent. Even the United Kingdom, which has been trying to cut back on government spending, still takes 46.2 percent of GNP. By most measures, therefore, the U.S. government does not appear to be taking a disproportionate share of GNP for defense and social programs.

Source: "Has the Government Role in the U.S. Economy Been Reduced?" *Forbes,* October 31, 1988, p. 86.

Productivity of workers is greatly increased by the use of machines. This is true on the farm and true in the factory. It is less true in a service economy where machinery can improve the quality of the service provided, but not increase total output. Figure 3–1 shows that computers and other machinery have not increased productivity much in the service sector.

The increase in farm productivity was the basis for economic growth in the United States for years. The next revolution in productivity occurred in the manufacturing industry. The use of machines made mass production possible (that is, production of thousands of items such as shoes and cars by just a few workers). Again, it was capital that made such gains possible.

Now that we are in a third type of economy, a service economy, productivity is again an issue because service firms are so labor intensive. Machinery, not labor, increases productivity. Productivity in farming and manufacturing has slowed so that annual increases in productivity are low in the United States. Spurred by foreign competition, productivity in the manufacturing sector is rising at the fastest rate in decades. But manufacturing is only a fifth of the economy's output. It is the nonmanufacturing sector (the service sector) that is holding back productivity gains.[6] (See Figure 3–1, page 80.)

To give you some idea of the relationship between productivity and GNP, let's look at some statistics. If pre-1965 productivity growth had continued through 1988, the GNP would have exceeded $7 trillion instead of nearly $5 trillion. Median family income would have been $45,000 instead of $30,853.[7] Clearly, a major effort in the 1990s should be to raise productivity in the service sector.

FIGURE 3–1

FIGURE 3–1

Productivity growth in the 1980s.
This figure shows that productivity in the manufacturing sector is growing at a healthy pace. Productivity is growing in the service sector also, but it is not reflected in the figure because the government doesn't measure quality differences. We need new measures of productivity now that the United States is a service economy.

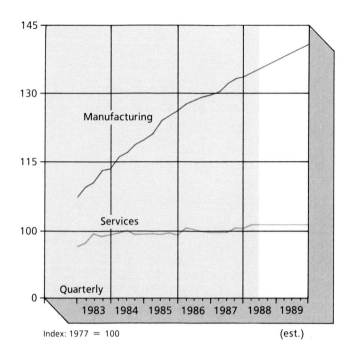

Index: 1977 = 100   (est.)

Productivity in the Service Sector

In the service sector, computers, word processors, and other machines are making service workers more productive. The United States is ahead of much of the world in service productivity, but there is much competition from Japan, South Korea, and other countries. One problem with the service industry is that an influx of machinery may add to the *quality* of the service provided, but not the output per worker (the definition of productivity).

For example, you have probably noticed how many computers are being installed on college campuses. They add to the quality of education, but not necessarily to the productivity of professors. The same is true of some new equipment in hospitals. It improves patient care, but does not necessarily increase the number of patients that can be seen. We may need to develop different measures of productivity for a service economy, measures that include quality as well as quantity of output. Adding equipment to the service sector may add to the quality of life, but not to the standard of living. New measures may be needed to recognize this improvement. Since 1979, service productivity has increased only .4 percent annually, compared to an average of 3.4 percent for manufacturing productivity. Wholesale and retail trade is the largest service-producing sector, and probably the most important. Growth in that area has been slower than in many competing countries.[8]

All in all, a major issue in the coming years will be business productivity. More money will be invested in machines such as robots, lasers, and computers to keep production high for each worker. The problem is that many workers are being replaced by machines in the quest for higher and higher productivity. This has resulted in another major economic issue: unemployment. We shall discuss this issue next.

- Can you define gross national product, net national product, and productivity?

- Why may productivity increases be slower in a service economy? What could be done to adjust the figures to show improvement in service quality rather than output?

THE ISSUE OF UNEMPLOYMENT

Any student preparing to enter the job market has to be concerned about unemployment. So much is said and written about the jobless in various cities that one could get depressed thinking about the future prospects for jobs. The fact is that, in the 1980s, the unemployment rate has varied from 5.0 to 10 percent (see Figure 3–2). This means that as many as 7 million or more people were unemployed at one time. Such figures seem overwhelming and must be put in some perspective.

We said that there were two figures to look at when discussing unemployment. One is the number of people employed. It is important to note that there were over 116,000,000 people working in the United States in 1989, more people working in America than ever before in history. That is the good news. More good news is that some 17 million new jobs were created in the 1980s.

The best news may be that the overall unemployment rate in 1989 fell to 5 percent (the lowest point in 15 years).[9] Unemployment rates in some states were spectacularly low. For example, Vermont and New Hampshire had less than 3 percent unemployed. Along the Atlantic coast in general, rates were about 3 to 4 percent. In general, there was much good news on the unemployment front.

Hidden in those statistics, however, was some bad news. The bad news is that Louisiana still had over 10 percent unemployment. West Virginia had 8.8 percent unemployment. Alaska and Mississippi also had high rates.

We have a strange situation in the United States relative to unemployment. Retailers are finding it hard to find help in places such as fast-food restaurants and department stores, especially during the holidays.[10] On the other hand, we have many workers seeking jobs who can't find anything. What is the problem? The problem is that many of today's workers are not trained for the jobs that are available and will be coming available in the 1990s. Others are simply in the wrong part of the country or city.

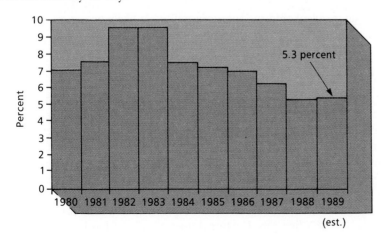

FIGURE 3–2

Unemployment rates in the 1980s.
Unemployment fell to 5.0 percent in 1989, the lowest it had been for 15 years. Note that unemployment was almost twice that high in 1981–1982. Low unemployment puts inflationary pressure on the economy because business has to pay workers more to attract them.

Many hospitals have purchased PET scanners to get clearer pictures of the brain. The machinery is very costly and improves the quality of service at hospitals. It does not necessarily increase productivity, however. We may need a new definition of productivity to reflect quality differences in services.

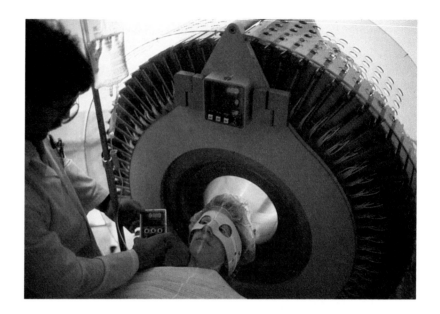

Business Week says that, "Where the jobs are is where the skills aren't." There is a critical need for schools and businesses in the United States to begin preparing students for the jobs of tomorrow. Part of the problem is that many students are dropping out of school before they finish high school. Others are simply not receiving the education they need. The unemployment problem in the United States today is largely an education problem and a relocation problem. Creating more and better jobs will not solve the problem because there simply are not the skilled workers available to fill them.[11]

The labor department doesn't consider you unemployed unless you are out of work but looking for work. In 1988, there were some 6,851,000 people who were unemployed and looking for work. There were another 910,000 "discouraged workers" who were unemployed, but not included in the unemployment figures because they were not looking for work because they felt that there were no jobs available for them. These were mostly people with not much education in depressed areas of the country. About half of the people counted as unemployed had been in that state for five weeks or less, so the problem may not be as large as the raw numbers may suggest.[12] You can see that unemployment is more a regional than a national problem, and the solutions will most likely be regional as well (see Figure 3–3).[13]

Categories of Unemployment

There are four types of unemployment: frictional, structural, cyclical, and seasonal. Each type has a different effect on the economy. New people wanting to enter the labor force are part of the frictionally unemployed. **Frictional unemployment** refers to those people who have quit work because they did not like the job, the boss, or working conditions and who have not yet found a new job. It also refers to those people who are entering the labor force for the first time (for example, new graduates) or are returning to the labor force.

There will always be some frictional unemployment, because it takes some time to find a new job or a first job. Frictional unemployment has little negative effect

frictional unemployment
Unemployment of people who have quit work and have not yet found a new job and also new entrants in the labor force.

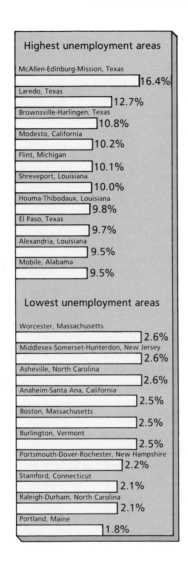

Highest unemployment areas

McAllen-Edinburg-Mission, Texas	16.4%
Laredo, Texas	12.7%
Brownsville-Harlingen, Texas	10.8%
Modesto, California	10.2%
Flint, Michigan	10.1%
Shreveport, Louisiana	10.0%
Houma-Thibodaux, Louisiana	9.8%
El Paso, Texas	9.7%
Alexandria, Louisiana	9.5%
Mobile, Alabama	9.5%

Lowest unemployment areas

Worcester, Massachusetts	2.6%
Middlesex-Somerset-Hunterdon, New Jersey	2.6%
Asheville, North Carolina	2.6%
Anaheim-Santa Ana, California	2.5%
Boston, Massachusetts	2.5%
Burlington, Vermont	2.5%
Portsmouth-Dover-Rochester, New Hampshire	2.2%
Stamford, Connecticut	2.1%
Raleigh-Durham, North Carolina	2.1%
Portland, Maine	1.8%

FIGURE 3–3

Where unemployment is highest and lowest in the United States. Although unemployment in general fell to 5.0 percent in 1989, there were cities where unemployment was three times that. On the other hand, other cities had almost no unemployment. Texas and Louisiana were hurt by low oil prices. Maine, New Hampshire, and Connecticut enjoyed the benefits of a high-tech revolution.

on the economy. About 800,000 of the unemployed in 1988 were seeking their first job, another 1.87 million had been in the labor force and had left it for some reason and had not found a new job yet, and a million more left their previous jobs for one reason or another. As you can see, therefore, a large number of the unemployed are getting their first job or are simply between jobs.[14]

There is a second important group called the structurally unemployed. **Structural unemployment** refers to that unemployment caused by a mismatch between the skills (or location) of job seekers and the requirements (or location) of available jobs. For example, one finds coal miners in an area where the mines have been closed. You have learned that a major cause of this type of unemployment is the decline of the manufacturing sector. Another cause is the replacement of workers by robots and other technology. Structural unemployment calls for industry retraining programs to move workers into growth industries.

A third kind of unemployment is **cyclical unemployment.** It occurs because of a recession or a similar downturn in the business cycle. This type of unemployment lasts until the economy recovers and businesses begin rehiring.

structural unemployment
Unemployment caused by people losing jobs because their occupation is no longer part of the main structure of the economy.

cyclical unemployment
Unemployment caused by a recession or a similar downturn in the business cycle.

seasonal unemployment
Unemployment that occurs where the demand for labor varies over the year.

The fourth type of unemployment is **seasonal unemployment.** It occurs where the demand for labor varies over the year, as with the harvesting of crops. Only about 2.6 percent of the unemployed fall into these latter two categories. This seems like a relatively low amount and historically it is very low. That doesn't mean that the United States has solved its labor problems. There are still some 5.2 million people working part-time who would like to be working full-time. The jobless rate in construction was 11 percent and in agriculture it was 11.4 percent in 1988.[15]

THINKING IT THROUGH   Would the United States be better off today if we had not introduced modern farm machinery? There *would* be more people employed on the farm if we had not. Would the world be better off in the future if we did not introduce new computers, robots, and machinery? They *do* take away jobs in the short run. What happened to the farmers who were displaced by machines? What will happen to today's workers who are being replaced by machines?

Unemployment Compensation

The government has tried to cushion the effects of unemployment by paying people *unemployment benefits* for a limited period while they seek new jobs. Such payments may affect the unemployment roles in that they lessen the incentive to hurry and find new jobs. In Florida, for example, a laid-off worker who had made $16,000 annually and has a wife and two children may find that unemployment and public assistance benefits available to the family are equal to his former take-home pay. His disposable income (that is, income after taxes) may actually *increase*.

Even with Florida's relatively low benefit levels, government programs can provide considerable inducement for staying off the job. Unemployment compensation provides as much as $537.50 a month for each unemployed worker. A family of four may be eligible for as much as $253 a month in food stamps, as much as $443 for rent and utilities assistance, about $50 in Low Income Energy Assistance, $150 in Emergency Energy Assistance, and school breakfast and lunch valued at $70.90. Two dozen other sources of "in-kind" income could also be available to them.

There are several kinds of unemployment in the United States. Many people have left one job for one reason or another and are seeking a new one. This line of workers seeking jobs represents such people. The overall unemployment rate recently hit a 15-year low of 5 percent. That rate can change quickly if the economy slows. That is one reason why economics is so important to businesspeople and workers.

The United States, in other words, is trying to protect those people who are unemployed because of factors such as recessions and industry shifts. One problem is that such payments may get high enough to further, rather than relieve, unemployment problems because they may destroy the incentive to find new work until the payments end.

Can you explain the differences between frictional, structural, and cyclical unemployment? Which is causing the largest unemployment today?

What is the effect of unemployment compensation on unemployment figures?

PROGRESS CHECK

INFLATION AND THE CONSUMER PRICE INDEX

Earlier we said that the third measure of an economy is its ability to control inflation. **Inflation** basically refers to a general rise in the price level of goods and services over time. Inflation had gone over 10 percent in the 1980s, and people were afraid it would go even higher. Figure 3–4 shows that inflation rates have come down considerably since then. There are many causes of inflation, according to economists. Two of the most important are cost-push inflation and demand-pull inflation.

inflation
A general rise in the prices of goods and services over time.

Cost-push inflation   **Cost-push inflation** refers to the fact that businesspeople raise prices when the costs of various factors of production go up. For example, increases in the cost of labor, machinery, raw materials, fuels, and credit push up prices. The push for a higher minimum wage and the lower number of unemployed people may add greatly to cost-push inflation in the 1990s.

cost-push inflation
Inflation caused by rising business costs.

Demand-pull inflation   **Demand-pull inflation** refers to a condition in which buyers want to buy more goods and services than are available at the time. The demand for goods and services is related to the amount of money in the economy.

demand-pull inflation
Inflation caused by excessive demand for goods and services.

FIGURE 3–4

Percentage change in consumer prices, 1975–1989. Consumer prices started taking off early in 1989 and are likely to go higher than this figure indicates. You can follow such data in *The Wall Street Journal* or other business periodicals. Note the large drop in price increases from 1980 to 1989 as oil prices and other prices were lowered.

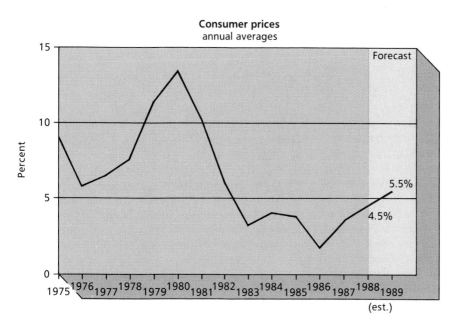

Consumer prices
annual averages

Forecast

5.5%

4.5%

1975 1976 1977 1978 1979 1980 1981 1982 1983 1984 1985 1986 1987 1988 1989

(est.)

If the supply of money increases faster than production increases, the result is inflation. This is called "too much money chasing too few goods." Later in this chapter we shall talk about how the Federal Reserve Board tries to control the money supply and interest rates to hold inflation down.

Measures of Inflation

consumer price index (CPI)
Monthly statistics that measure changes in the prices of about 400 goods and services that consumers buy.

Two of the more popular measures of price changes over time (inflation indicators) are the consumer price index (CPI) and the producer price index (PPI), also known as the wholesale price index. The **consumer price index** measures changes in the prices of about 400 goods and services that consumers buy. It measures the price of an average market basket of goods for an average family over time. Such an index gives a vivid picture of the effects of inflation on consumer prices. If the cost of the "market basket" is $1,000 one month and goes up to $1,006 the next, it is said that the inflation rate for the month was 0.6 percent or roughly 7.2 percent annually.[16] At that rate, the cost of consumer goods would double in about 10 years (see the box called Inflation and the Rule of 72).

producer price index (PPI)
Monthly statistics that measure changes in the prices businesses pay for goods and services over time.

The **producer price index** measures changes in the prices businesses pay for goods and services over time. Both the consumer price index and the producer price index are calculated monthly and are published in business periodicals. The consumer price index is the most closely followed because many companies and government programs base their salary and payment increases on it. Many people also follow the producer price index closely, because it usually indicates future consumer prices and is therefore a barometer of future inflation.

INFLATION AND THE RULE OF 72

No formula is more useful for understanding inflation than the rule of 72. Basically, the idea is to compute quickly how long it takes the cost of goods and services to double at various compounded rates of growth. For example, if houses were increasing in cost at 9 percent a year, how long would it take for the price of a home to double? The answer is easy to calculate. Simply divide the annual increase (9 percent) into 72 and you get the number of years it takes to double the price (eight years). If houses go up in price by 12 percent, it only takes 6 years to double in price (72/12 = 6), and so on. Of course, the same calculation can be used to predict how high food prices will be or the price of a car 10 years from now.

Let's go over an example of how you can use this formula. Let's say you wanted to buy a house for $100,000 but found interest rates were so high that you would end up paying almost $500,000 for the house after 30 years (assuming no money down). It sounds as if you would be paying way too much for the house, given the information so far. But if you calculate how much the house may be worth after 30 years, you may change your mind. If housing prices increase 10 percent per year, prices will double

every seven years or so (72/10 = 7.2). In 30 years, then, the price will double about four times (30/7 = 4.5). Your $100,000 house would then sell for about $1.6 million in 30 years. Since you would have paid less than $500,000, the home would be a good deal (assuming a 10 percent increase). What if the price only went up 6 percent a year? Then the price would be what after 30 years? It would double in 12 years, so it would double about 2.5 times in 30 years. In other words, it would be worth about $600,000, still more than you paid for it.

It works in reverse, too. Let's say, for example, that someone tells you to buy real estate in Florida. He says, "I bought land for $5,000 10 years ago and it's worth $10,000 today. It doubled already, isn't that great?"

Well, how did he do? If the land doubled in price in 10 years, that means the buyer made about 7.2 percent per year compounded (72/10 = 7.2). That may be less than a tax-free government bond earns. In short, that is *not* necessarily a good return, especially since the real estate salesperson takes part of the sale price.

If one year in college costs $9,000 today, how much will it cost when a 4-year-old goes to school 14 years from now, if college costs go up 10 percent a year? The answer is that college costs will quadruple. So the cost will be $36,000 a year! Are you ready for that?

THE ISSUE OF RECESSION VERSUS INFLATION

A recession was defined earlier in the chapter as two consecutive quarters of decline in the GNP. When recession occurs, prices fall and businesses begin to fail. A recession has severe consequences for an economy: high unemployment, business failures, and an overall drop in living standards. For years (since 1930 when the Great Depression occurred), the government has put much of its effort into preventing another recession or depression. A **depression** is a severe recession. Whenever business has slowed or unemployment has increased, the government has pumped money into the economy to revive it.

depression
A severe form of recession.

The U.S. government becomes concerned when inflation is in the range of 5 percent to 10 percent. However, these figures must be put in some perspective. In 1988, inflation in Brazil was 1,000 percent; in Peru, it was over 10,000 percent;[17] and in Nicaragua it was 20,000 percent.[18] Inflation rates like these can destroy an economy and business. Such rates also set the stage for major revolutions. In Germany, inflation rates in 1923 were unbelievable. The price of coffee or bread often doubled in an *hour!* At the height of the problem, a loaf of bread cost 200 *billion* marks. People had to carry baskets filled with money to buy groceries. Is it any wonder that Germany today is *very* concerned about inflation?

The longest period of growth in the U.S. economy occurred from 1961 to 1969. The average expansion period is only 33 months. From 1982 until 1989, the economy was expanding. That made it one of the longest periods of expansion in U.S. history. Toward the end of such a period, inflation tends to worsen as the economy encounters more and more constraints to growth. Productivity gains come harder or disappear and labor costs climb. If past history is a guide, that will be the situation in the United States in the early 1990s.

Stagflation in the 1980s

A rather new economic phenomenon occurred in the late 1970s and early 1980s. Inflation kept rising even though the economy was slipping into recession. This was an unexpected economic event that called for a new term. The word used was **stagflation,** or high unemployment and slow growth combined with inflation. Thus, two bad situations were occurring at once. To slow inflation, the government took money out of the economy. This slowed growth, plunging the economy into a deeper recession. Inflation finally came down, but there were still two bad situations: economic stagnation combined with high unemployment (above 10 percent).

stagflation
Stagnant (no growth) economic conditions combined with inflation.

In the middle of the 1980s, economic attention turned toward lowering the unemployment rate and getting the economy moving again. The money supply was increased and taxes were cut. By 1989, unemployment had fallen to 5.0 percent while the economy picked up. The money supply was cut late in the 1980s which may again result in stagflation in the 1990s. Supply-side economics kept the economy going through early 1989. Let's see how that happened.

Supply-Side Economics

supply-side economics
The policy of lowering taxes so that more money is available for investment in production, leading to an increase in production activity, causing a drop in unemployment.

Supply-side economics is the term used to describe the policy of lowering taxes so that more money can be invested in production. Supporters of supply-side economics believe this will lead to an increase in production activity, causing a drop in unemployment. In diagram form, supply-side economics looks like Figure 3–5. The United States tried supply-side economics during the 1980s. Here is how *Forbes* magazine reported the results:[19]

> We have achieved the highest continuous peacetime real average rate of economic growth during any five-year period in our nation's history. We now have a record number of Americans at work . . . a record rate of high- and middle-wage new job creation, a record rate of industrial output, a record rate of new business incorporations, a record rate of real per-capita personal income and the highest absolute rate of manufacturing productivity of any country in the world.

Because of the success the United States had with supply-side economics, many of the countries of the free world are trying a similar experiment. You read in Chapter 2 how many socialist countries are cutting income tax rates. Britain has

FIGURE 3–5

The theory of supply-side economics.
Lowering taxes frees money for investments. These investments increase production activity. The end result is a drop in unemployment.

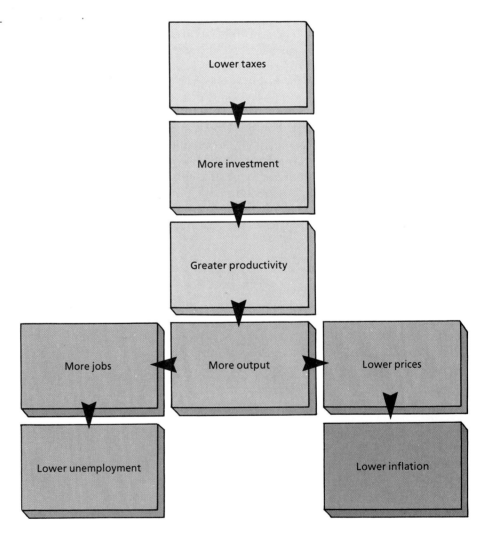

had some success already with its supply-side initiatives.[20] Tax cuts have been made in Canada, Japan, New Zealand, France and Australia based on the same supply-side theories.

One issue that has dominated discussion about supply-side economics is the fact that tax rates were cut for the rich. The promise was that the rich would then pay more in taxes because they would not use as many tax-avoidance strategies. Furthermore, the poor were expected to pay a smaller share of taxes. The results? From 1981 to 1986, the share of the tax dollar paid by the poorest half of taxpayers fell from 7.5 cents to 6.4 cents (a 15 percent drop). The share paid by the richest 5 percent rose from 34.9 cents to 44.3 cents (a 27 percent increase). The share paid by the richest 1 percent of taxpayers went from 18 cents to 26 cents. In short, supply-side economics *did* result in the rich paying a larger share of the tax burden and the poor paying a smaller share. In spite of this, the gap between the incomes of the rich and poor is not closing, although there are many more rich and fewer in the middle class as incomes rise.[21]

The election of George Bush in 1988 was partly a result of the success of supply-side economics plus the voters perceiving a relatively strong economy and relative peace among nations. Democrats were quick to point out that the growth was purchased at the cost of the highest national debt in the nation's history. There remains much debate about the future of the U.S. economy as the government tries to keep employment high, inflation low, and business growing. Government stimulation of the economy could lead to inflation again in the 1990s.

To fight inflation and recession, the government and the Federal Reserve Bank try to manage the economy. To understand the economic situation in the United States and the world today with regard to inflation, recession, unemployment, and other economic matters, you must understand the government's and the Federal Reserve Bank's roles. Two terms that are crucial to your understanding are: monetary policy and fiscal policy. We shall discuss them after you have thought about the ethics of paying taxes and have checked on your progress in learning the material in this chapter.

MAKING ETHICAL DECISIONS

Imagine that you have been out of school for a while and you and your spouse are now earning $50,000 a year. To get to that point, you both paid your way through college. You look forward to buying a home and cars and other goods and services that you have been postponing all these years to get your education.

You decide to buy a nice home. The government allows you to deduct all the interest charges on the mortgage for that home and the property taxes. That makes the payments much easier at first. In fact, almost all the money you are paying into the home the first few years goes for taxes and interest, and all of that is tax deductible. That means that you will not have to give the government as much money in taxes.

You also feel that you should give some money to charities. The money you give is also deductible from your taxes. You read in the paper that you and other people who

buy homes and give money to charity are receiving unfair tax breaks. After all, poor people cannot get deductions for the rent they pay and they can't afford to give to charity. They feel that you should not receive a "government subsidy" to buy your home. You, on the other hand, feel that you are paying enough in taxes, but you want to give your fair share.

Is it ethical for the government to give tax breaks to people who have more money than others? Such people can buy tax free bonds, get deductions for interest payments on their homes, receive deductions for money given to charity, and get tax breaks to own a *second* home. Businesses can write off some luncheon expenses, travel expenses, and more. What percent of a person's income should go to the government? Should everyone pay equally or should the rich pay more? What are the moral and ethical reasons for your position?

PROGRESS CHECK
- Can you explain cost-push versus demand-pull inflation?
- What is a recession and how does it differ from a depression?

THE ISSUE OF MONETARY POLICY

In learning about monetary policy, the first thing one must understand is the role of the Federal Reserve Bank (the Fed). The Fed is one of the sources of money; it can add or subtract money from the economy as it sees fit. For example, the Fed can simply produce more dollars or cut the amount it lends to banks, if it thinks one of those actions is warranted.

Managing the money supply is the responsibility of the Federal Reserve System. It operates independently of the president or congress and has the goal of keeping the economy growing without causing inflation. It does that by trying to manage the money supply and interest rates. This process is called monetary policy (Chapter 21 discusses this in detail).

monetary policy
The management of the amount of money placed into the economy by the government and the management of interest rates.

A nation's **monetary policy** is the management of the money placed into the economy and the management of interest rates. As you know, inflation is sometimes caused by having too much money in the economy. When that happens, the Fed cuts the money supply and increases interest rates. That makes less money available for spending and discourages businesses and consumers from borrowing money (because of high interest rates). When businesses find it hard to borrow money, they often cut back on production and lay off workers. This slows the economy and lowers inflation.

Tight versus Loose Monetary Policy

When unemployment gets too high, the Federal Reserve Bank may put more money into the economy and lower credit rates. This stimulates spending and encourages business growth, which leads to the hiring of more people.

When you read that the Fed is "loosening up on the money supply" or "lowering interest rates," it means that the Fed is trying to stimulate the economy (that is, increase consumer spending and increase business investment). A *tight monetary policy* is one in which the Fed restricts the supply of money and increases credit costs to lower inflation. (We shall discuss the Federal Reserve System in more detail when we explore money and banking.) See the box on page 92 called How Interest Rates Affect Small Business to see the effect the Fed has on businesses.

The Federal Reserve System has a great influence on the economy by controlling the money supply. Pumping money into the economy stimulates production and spending. Taking money out of the economy slows production and spending. The Federal Reserve is concerned about inflation and adjusts the money supply to control inflation, but those adjustments affect business as well.

As you can imagine, such intervention into free markets has serious consequences for businesses. They watch the Fed very closely to see what the monetary policy is now and will be in the future.

The Federal Deficit

Sometimes the Fed is forced to put more money into the economy than it planned. This happens, for example, when government spending exceeds the revenue from taxes. The **federal deficit** (the difference between government revenue from taxes and government spending) is often corrected by increasing the supply of money, and that is inflationary. There was much concern about deficit spending throughout the 1980s. For example, government spending exceeded revenue by $155 billion in 1988 (see Figure 3–6). The deficit is not just the result of tax cuts (revenues have risen continuously over time) but is also the result of increased spending. The deficit is running about 3 percent of GNP, an amount that is historically manageable. Nonetheless, the main topic of conversation in the late 1980s was, "How can we cut the budget deficit?" To understand this issue, we must turn to *fiscal* policy.

federal deficit
The difference between government revenue from taxes and government spending.

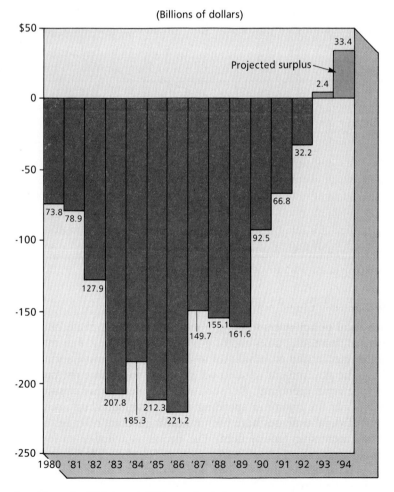

(Billions of dollars)

Note: Figures for 1989 through 1994 are estimated

FIGURE 3–6

The federal deficit.
This figure is an optimistic projection of the federal deficit. The important trend to notice is the gradual decline in the deficit from the mid-1980s. Nonetheless, the total deficit keeps increasing and those deficits must be repaid in the future.

HOW INTEREST RATES AFFECT SMALL BUSINESS

Articles from business journals tend to say things such as, "High interest rates are slowing the search by Acme-Cleveland Corporation, a machine-tool producer, for a major acquisition to help diversify the company." Another article may say, "With fixed mortgage rates dropping toward 10 percent, home builders are expected to increase production."

Such quotes are meant to show the impact of interest rates on the economy. Interest rates affect every kind of industry, from banking to farming and manufacturing. When rates are rising, business confidence and consumer confidence tend to fall because things are going to be more expensive to buy. When they fall, people get more optimistic.

The **prime rate** is the most favorable interest rate that businesses can get from banks. Small businesses and consumers like you and me must pay higher rates than the prime.

What are interest rates today? Check your local paper's business section to find out. Is business confidence high or low? Businesspeople watch interest rates very closely. You should learn to do so also if you want to understand the business environment.

FIGURE 3–7

Spending exceeds revenue leading to a deficit.
This figure shows that the total federal deficit increased throughout the 1980s. Spending always was greater than revenues. Revenue keeps going up, as the figure shows, but spending goes up equally fast or faster. The goal is to eliminate the deficit by increasing revenue (mostly taxes), cutting spending, or both.

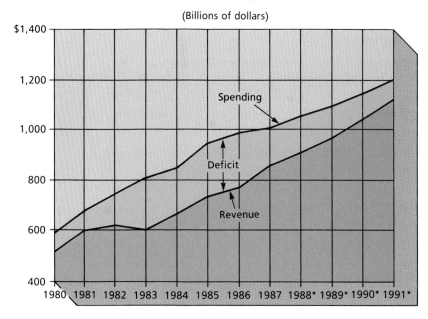

(Billions of dollars)

*Projections

THE ISSUE OF FISCAL POLICY

prime rate
The most favorable interest rate that businesses can get from banks.

fiscal policy
Government efforts to keep the economy stable by increasing or decreasing taxes or government spending.

The term **fiscal policy** refers to government efforts to keep the economy stable by increasing or decreasing taxes and/or government spending. For many years, the government has tended to raise taxes to fund more and more social and defense programs. The government tried to cut spending to balance the budget (that is, make income equal spending). But such attempts were rather unsuccessful in that they merely cut the *growth* in spending rather than spending itself. Figure 3–7 shows how federal expenses have been exceeding federal revenues for years. The result is an increasing federal debt. The debate is whether to lower the debt through more taxes or through less spending. The debate begins to sound like a beer commercial: "More taxes!" "Less spending!" The answer will likely be some combination of the two.

JOHN MAYNARD KEYNES, INTERVENTIONIST

John Maynard Keynes (pronounced *Canes*) was one of the economists who have had a great influence on U.S. economic policy. It was Keynes who advocated stabilizing the economy by the use of fiscal policy. That is, he thought that inflation could best be slowed by increasing taxes and/or lowering government spending. If unemployment got too high, he proposed cutting taxes and/or increasing government expenditures. Such a strategy is known as Keynesian economics and was a guiding philosophy in the United States for decades (and still is for many people).

Keynes' father was a lecturer in economics at Cambridge University. John Maynard began his studies at Cambridge (math and philosophy) and was encouraged to go into economics. Eventually he, too, became a lecturer at Cambridge.

He published his most famous book, *General Theory of Employment, Interest and Money,* in 1936. Until that time, American economic thinking was dominated by Adam Smith's *classical economics.* Smith felt that the economy would *automatically* function at full employment if there was minimal government intervention. The depression of the 1930s changed that view, and Keynesian economics took over.

Keynesian policies have been tried off and on since the 1930s. Some people say that supply-side economics is just one form of Keynesian involvement in markets. Recently, an article in *Business Week* said that Keynesian theory was becoming popular again. One thing is for sure: Keynes is one name from economics with which you should be familiar.

Source: Robert J. Shapero, "Look Who's Making a Comeback," *Business Week,* February, 1988, pp. 43–45.

One of the more famous economists of this century is John Maynard Keynes. He was a major influence on the government's attempts to "fine-tune" the economy with fiscal policy. You can explore more about Keynes by reading the box above that describes him.

Taxes and Spending

A major issue in the 1988 political campaign concerned fiscal policy, especially taxes. Michael Dukakis seemed to favor increasing income taxes to pay for government programs. George Bush resisted increased taxes and called for less spending instead. He said, "Read my lips; no new taxes." Still others proposed taxes on gasoline or "sin taxes," that is, higher taxes on alcohol and tobacco. George Bush's victory certainly did not assure taxpayers that no new taxes would be proposed. That will always be an issue in an economy that involves politicians. That is what Professor Buchanan was talking about (see the Profile at the beginning of this chapter).

John Maynard Keynes.

Some people felt that taxes should be raised mostly on the rich. They felt that rich people were not paying their fair share. Of course, rich people feel that 28 percent federal tax plus state and local taxes are high enough already. In fact, they want to lower capital gains taxes—the taxes on income earned from investments such as stocks and bonds and home ownership. The point is that people are divided in the United States over economic issues such as taxation and fiscal policy in general. Such issues will dominate government/business/economic thinking in the future. Business periodicals and current newspapers, TV, and radio news shows will keep you abreast of the debate.

- How does the government manage the economy using monetary policy?   **PROGRESS CHECK**

- How does the government manage the economy using fiscal policy?

TAX FREEDOM DAY COMES LATER

You and I have to pay a certain percent of our income to the government. If all of us sent our money to the government before spending it on anything else, we would be able to keep all the money earned after a certain date—the date when we paid the government all that it gets. When would we be able to keep some income for ourselves? In 1984, "tax freedom" day was April 28th. By 1988, it was May 5th. That is, all of us together worked for the government until May 5th. After that, the money we earned was ours to keep. How do you feel about that? Do you think the government should get more or less? That is the political debate that has been going on for years. Some feel we must pay more, and some people feel we are overburdened by taxes already. One thing seems sure: Either we will all have to pay more taxes or the government will have to

slow down on spending or the national debt may grow to unmanageable levels.

The problem is that government spending has exceeded government income for so long that the **national debt** (the sum of government money borrowed and not paid back) is approaching $3 trillion. That is about $12,000 for every man, woman, and child in the United States! To borrow money to pay the debt, the government goes to the same sources (banks) as businesspeople do. Government bonds may be more attractive to these sources, and this can drive businesspeople out of the credit market. Such a situation can hurt business and be inflationary. Most people feel that more must be done about the national debt before it becomes unmanageable.

FIGURE 3–8

Government spending and revenue.
Most of the government's revenue comes from you and me and other taxpayers in the form of taxes and social security payments. Corporate taxes provide a much smaller revenue source. The bulk of spending goes to individuals in the form of welfare, sound security, and related programs. Defense takes a little more than one fourth. The national debt gobbles up 15 percent in interest payments.

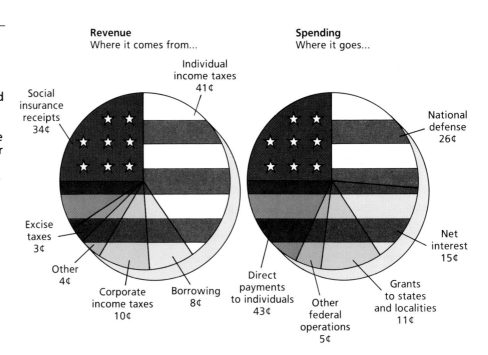

Revenue
Where it comes from...

Individual income taxes 41¢

Social insurance receipts 34¢

Excise taxes 3¢

Other 4¢

Corporate income taxes 10¢

Borrowing 8¢

Spending
Where it goes...

National defense 26¢

Net interest 15¢

Direct payments to individuals 43¢

Other federal operations 5¢

Grants to states and localities 11¢

THE ISSUE OF THE NATIONAL DEBT

national debt
The sum of money the government has borrowed and not paid back.

The **national debt** reached the $2.8 trillion level in 1988.[22] The questions are: What is the national debt? How did it get so high? What can be done about it?

First, let's look at how the national debt got so high. Figure 3–8 gives some details about the sources of government funds and the way that money is spent. The government is growing faster than the economy's ability to support its programs. Most government programs have automatic increases built into them, so government spending goes up automatically every year.

One question that economists, government officials, and ultimately, you and other taxpayers must answer is, "What are our national priorities?" Do we want a strong military capability, including nuclear weapons and a strategic defense system, and how much are we willing to pay for such a capability?

Another huge chunk of the budget goes for social security payments. Social security was not meant to be a retirement program, but a *supplement* to savings. Many people ignored that fact and rely on social security for survival. Can the government cut their benefits now? Could people retire later? This will be a major issue throughout the 1990s.

Millions of people receive medicare treatment, school lunches, medicaid, food stamps, housing subsidies, low-cost student loans, and other government-paid (taxpayer-paid) assistance. What is the national priority regarding such payments? Should the government continue such payments and expand the programs when hard times come, or should such payments be limited somehow? Are such payments more or less important than defense or social security? What should the policy be if such payments threaten the economy by siphoning too much money from business? These are the issues you should be following in the various media. They have a direct effect on you (in taxes) and on business.

> If you had a stack of $1,000 bills in your hand only four inches high, you'd be a millionaire. A trillion dollars would be a stack of $1,000 bills 67 miles high.
> **FORMER PRESIDENT RONALD REAGAN**

THE ISSUE OF TRADE DEFICITS

Historically, the United States has sold more goods and services to other nations than it has bought. Recently, however, that situation reversed, and the United States began buying more goods than it sold. The term used to describe the situation where imports (purchases from abroad) exceed exports (sales abroad) is **trade deficit.**

One reason that deficits were so high was that the U.S. dollar increased in value relative to foreign money. This made foreign goods cheaper and U.S. goods more expensive in world trade.

There were other reasons for the deficit as well. Foreign products such as Japanese cars were perceived to be of better quality. Furthermore, American labor costs were much higher than those of other countries such as South Korea, Mexico, and Brazil.

The U.S. government worked with other nations to lower the value of the dollar relative to other currencies and to improve the trade balance. The trade deficit has improved as a result (see Figure 3–9, page 96). The health of the U.S. economy affects the success of economies throughout the world. We hope you now see the relationship between the success of businesses worldwide and economics. If you study economics, you will learn more about how the system functions.

trade deficit
The situation where imports (purchases from abroad) exceed exports (sales abroad).

Where Is the Economy Going?

You may want to read the September 26, 1988 issue of *Fortune* magazine. On pages 86–96, you can read *Fortune's* predictions for the economy in the 1990s. This chapter and the previous chapter have prepared you to understand that article and most other articles about economics in business journals. Some of the predictions are:[23]

- GNP growth between 2.3 percent and 2.6 percent, slower than in the 1980s and much slower than the 1970s.
- Unemployment should run between 5 and 6 percent, a relatively low rate.

People in the United States buy more goods from foreign producers than U.S. producers sell overseas. Cars such as these are a good example. This leads to a trade deficit.

FIGURE 3-9

The trade deficit.
The trade deficit peaked in 1987 and is slowly coming down. Nonetheless, there is still a deficit. American businesses need to become more competitive through higher productivity. The government is also negotiating to have more open markets for U.S. goods and services to lower the trade deficit.

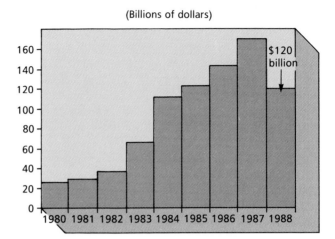

(Billions of dollars)

Productivity growth is expected in the 1.5 percent range, an increase from the overall 1 percent increase during the 1980s.

Real interest rates are expected to be about 3 percent. This is about the historical norm and below the 4 to 5 percent of the early 1980s.

The value of the dollar is expected to decline some 15 to 25 percent against its trading partners, but trade deficits are expected to continue.

All in all, the decade of the 1990s is expected to be an economically challenging one. It may not be a decade of rapid growth, but growth should be steady. There should be many opportunities for college graduates.

PROGRESS CHECK

What is the size of the national debt?

Can you list three economic forecasts for the 1990s?

SUMMARY

1. Define the three major indicators of economic health.

1. Most businesspeople feel it is important to measure the pulse of the nation's economy.

What are the three major indicators of economic health identified in this chapter?

This chapter focuses on the following economic indicators: (1) the gross national product, (2) unemployment, and (3) inflation.

2. Almost evey discussion about a nation's economy is based on a concept called gross national product (GNP). If GNP is rising, the economy is said to be strong. If GNP is stable or falling, the economy is said to be weak.

2. Describe the distribution of gross national product (GNP) in the United States and explain the role of productivity in changes in the GNP.

What is GNP?

GNP is the total value of a country's output of goods and services produced over a given period of time. It can be used to measure economic growth or decline.

How can a country increase its GNP?

To increase GNP, a country needs to be more productive. An increase of productivity means that the same amount of labor is able to produce more goods and services.

Why is productivity slowing in the United States?

At the beginning of this century, one out of three workers was a farmer. Today, less than 1 out of 20 workers is a farmer, yet we produce much more food. The reason is that farm productivity increased because of *capital* inputs (for example, tractors, plows, and fertilizer). When farm productivity leveled off, the industrial revolution began, and capital (machinery) made industrial laborers more productive. Industrial productivity leveled off as we entered a third revolution, the service revolution. Productivity in the service sector is not growing as fast as other sectors have grown and that is slowing the GNP.

■ What will increase productivity in the future?

The service sector is now introducing more capital goods (for example, robots and computers) to make white-collar (service) workers more productive.

3. When an economic system introduces new technology, temporary unemployment often occurs. Farm employment, for example, fell dramatically over the last 50 years and continues to fall.

■ What are the types of unemployment?

Frictional unemployment refers to those people just entering the labor force or who are between jobs. *Structural unemployment* refers to those who are laid off because their type of work is no longer needed in such quantity (farmers over the last 50 years are one example; today, steel workers are another). *Cyclical unemployment* is caused by ups and downs in the economy. *Seasonal unemployment* occurs where the demand for labor varies over the year.

■ How does the United States protect the unemployed?

Unemployed people get *unemployment benefits* from the government for a limited period until they can find new jobs.

3. Describe the implication of unemployment and unemployment compensation on a nation's economy and identify four types of unemployment.

4. A general rise in the price of goods and services over time is called *inflation.*

■ What are the major causes of inflation?

Cost-push inflation means that products cost more as the cost of producing them goes up. *Demand-pull inflation* is caused when the demand for goods exceeds the supply.

■ How is inflation measured?

The government measures the increase in the cost of consumer items with the consumer price index (CPI) and the cost of wholesale items with the producer price index (PPI).

4. Identify two causes of inflation and describe two major measures of inflation.

5. When real GNP declines for two quarters, an economy is said to be in a recession. A deep recession is known as a depression.

■ What happens in a recession or depression?

There is likely to be an increase in unemployment, prices fall, and businesses fail.

■ What is stagflation?

Stagflation is a combination of high unemployment and slow economic growth with inflation.

■ What is supply-side economics?

Supply-side economics is the policy of lowering taxes so that more money is available for investment in production. Supporters of such policy believe that production activity will increase and unemployment will drop.

5. Distinguish between recession, inflation, and stagflation; and explain the concept of supply-side economics.

6. In its attempt to keep the economy from going into depression or from rapid inflation, the government has two weapons: monetary policy and fiscal policy.

6. Explain monetary policy and its impact on the economy.

    What is monetary policy?

    Monetary policy refers to the manipulation of the amount of money placed into the economy and the management of interest rates.

    How does monetary policy work?

    When money is "tight" and interest rates are high, the economy slows, and there is less investment in capital equipment. When money is poured into the economy and interest rates fall, the economy picks up, capital spending increases, and employment rises. One danger of too much money being placed into the economy is inflation.

7. In addition to monitoring policy, the government can also use fiscal policy to help control the economy.

7. Explain fiscal policy and its impact on the economy.

    What is fiscal policy?

    Fiscal policy refers to government efforts to manage the economy through taxes and government spending.

    How does fiscal policy work?

    Some say the key to keeping the economy stable is to lower the federal debt by increased taxes. Others think the answer is for the government to spend less. The answer is likely to be some combination of the two.

8. Because the government is spending more than it is receiving in taxes, the national debt is going up.

8. Discuss the issues surrounding the national debt.

    What is the national debt?

    The national debt is the sum of money the government has borrowed and not paid back.

    How did the national debt get so high?

    Most government programs have automatic increases built into them, so spending goes up automatically each year. Revenues from taxes have not gone up as fast as spending; thus a deficit.

    What can be done about the national debt?

    Some people feel the government is spending too much money. They want to cut back on government programs. Others feel that taxes are too low. They want to keep or increase government programs. To increase government revenues, some people propose putting more money into the economy and lowering interest rates. That is supposed to increase production and thereby increase government income. But that could also cause inflation.

9. Recently, the United States has had *trade deficits;* that is, it buys more from other countries than it sells to them.

9. Explain the issues of trade deficits.

    How can the United States create a better balance of trade?

    The United States should be able to sell more overseas when our products are cheaper (a result of higher productivity or lower labor costs), when the quality of our products increases, and when the value of the dollar declines. We shall return to this issue in Chapter 24 when we discuss international business.

GETTING INVOLVED

1. Is the economy now experiencing inflation, recession, economic growth with little inflation, or stagflation (inflation with no economic growth)? What government policies have led to that situation? What should the policy now be? Read current business literature to get the views of others and discuss the alternatives. What economic priorities should be considered?

2. How large is the national debt today? Is it rising or falling, and at what rate? What is being done to reduce the debt? Discuss.

3. What is the situation today regarding the trade balance with other nations? Is the United States importing more than it sells, or vice versa? What is being done in this area? Is free trade being promoted or restricted? Discuss.

4. Have some fun using the rule of 72 to anticipate future prices. For example, calculate how much a new car will cost a child now 5 years old when he or she reaches age 17 if the car prices go up by 6 percent a year. Assume the cost of a new car is now $15,000. How much will a textbook cost if prices go up by 12 percent a year, and the book now costs $30? These exercises will teach you about the problems of inflation!

5. Everyone is for peace, but nobody seems to know how to create it. Discuss the proposition that some percent of the world's military expenditures should go to help develop poor countries. Would that be a step toward peace? How would you promote such a step? Discuss both sides of the issue, including a defense for high military spending in the United States, to understand both sides of the issue.

6. Discuss other current economic issues with your classmates and instructor. Pick two issues of general concern and discuss various viewpoints. Be ready to defend your position by finding facts and figures to support it. Have you set up a file system yet to keep such figures?

CASE ONE   **ECONOMIC DISTRIBUTION IN VARIOUS NATIONS**

PRACTICING
MANAGEMENT
DECISIONS

One reason the government gets involved in the economy is to create more equality by taxing those who have more and distributing that money to those who have less. Welfare spending in the United States has increased dramatically since World War II. Here are the results. In 1947, the lowest fifth of the U.S. population received 5 percent of national income, while the highest fifth received 43 percent. Since then, the tax code has been changed many times and many new welfare programs have been introduced and expanded. The result? In 1987, the lowest fifth received 5 percent and the top fifth about 42 percent. In other words, there was no appreciable change.

It is informative to see how other systems have done in the same attempt at income distribution. The Soviet Union, a communist country, has focused much of its economic plans at income distribution. The result is the lowest fifth receive 7.5 percent of the national income and the highest fifth receive 37.5 percent. Sweden is a socialist country with a similar intent toward a more equal distribution of income. In Sweden, the lowest fifth receives 7.7 percent of the national income and the highest fifth receives 35.9 percent. The percentage going to the top 5 percent in the three countries is:

United States	15.9%
Soviet Union	14.0%
Sweden	12.9%

The figures show that the top 5 percent receive a disproportional amount of income in all the countries. In the United States, only 2 percent of the families remain on welfare for more than seven years. Most families are able to work their way out of poverty. Research has shown that 25 percent of those in the lowest fifth move up to the top third in 10 years!

DECISION QUESTIONS

1. What do these figures indicate about the effort to create income equality in the world?

2. Is income equality a proper goal of society? Should recent high school and college graduates make nearly the same as someone who has worked for 40 years?

3. What significance do you give the fact that 25 percent of the people in the lowest income group move up to the top 33 percent in 10 years in the United States? Would you expect that same upward mobility in the Soviet Union?

4. Income redistribution often assumes a fixed size of the economic pie. What happens when the size of the pie doubles? Who benefits? Is it better in the long run to give a bigger piece of the pie to those in need or to make a bigger pie, or both?

Source: Walter Williams, "Economic Equality Mirage," *The Washington Times*, February 16, 1988, p. D3.

CASE TWO   EDUCATING THE PUBLIC ABOUT ECONOMICS

A recent poll showed that 57 percent of the people polled thought that defense spending took more than 20 percent of the gross national product (GNP). Twenty-three percent thought it took more than 40 percent. Only 6 percent knew that defense took less than 10 percent of GNP (the actual figure is 7 percent).

Another poll showed that the American public felt that the after-tax profits of American businesses averaged 34 percent of sales. The actual after-tax profits for nonfinancial domestic corporations averaged between 5 and 7 percent over the last three years. Mr. Richards, an economist for the National Association of Manufacturers, says, "Corporations have historically been taxed at three to four times the rate of individuals, and this notion of excessive profits only fuels the idea that they should be taxed even further."

A third area where the general public misperceives reality is in the area of tax cuts. Many feel that lowering tax rates benefits the rich and hurts the poor. Tax rates for the rich have been cut from 91 to 28 percent. The most recent cuts occurred in 1986 when rates were cut from 72 percent to 28 percent. Since then, revenues from those with income over $200,000 are up 25 percent from what was expected under the higher rates.

While the rich paid more under the new rates, the poor paid less. The newest proposal among Republicans is to cut the capital gains tax as well. It is expected that the rich would pay $13.5 billion more in taxes if such cuts were implemented. A recent poll of high school students found that they too were ignorant about economic concepts and facts. For example, only 39 percent chose the right definition of GNP and only 45 percent knew that government deficits occur when spending exceeds tax revenues.

DECISION QUESTIONS

1. How is it that the rich end up paying more taxes when the tax rates are cut?
2. What harm do you feel is caused by the general public not knowing economic facts and figures such as those quoted in the previous section of this chapter? What could be done to correct such misperceptions?
3. What rate of taxes do you feel is fair for people making over $200,000? Would you feel the same if you were making that much?
4. It has been proposed that the tax rate be 15 percent for everyone, and that there would be no deductions. That system would likely bring in more money and would eliminate the complex tax codes and the need for lawyers and accountants to figure peoples' taxes. What do you perceive as the benefits and drawbacks of such a tax rate?

Sources: "For the Record," *The Washington Post,* December 1, 1987, p. A-20; Peter LaBarbera, "Public Exaggerates Corporation Profits," *The Washington Times,* December 1, 1987, p. C-1; and "U.S. Students Score Low on Economics Test," *Los Angeles Times,* December 29, 1988, p. 2 of Part IV.

LOOKING AHEAD

Now that you are familiar with some economic terms that you should know when you read business literature, we can focus our attention on business itself. We shall start by looking at different ways of starting a business. You can start a business by yourself. You can take on one or more partners. Or, you can form a corporation or a multinational firm. Each of these forms of business has its advantages and disadvantages that we shall discuss in Chapter 4.

Many people today are interested in starting their own businesses to make a profit. Such people are called entrepreneurs and are the backbone of the American economy. In Chapter 5, we shall discuss entrepreneurs from the past and the new entrepreneurs of the 1990s. At the end of Part 2, we have an entrepreneurial quiz that will give you some feel for whether or not you are the entrepreneurial type. If you are, you may be interested in a less risky way of owning your own business. One way is through franchising. That is, owning and managing a franchise such as McDonalds or Burger King. All of that is covered in Chapter 5. If you do want to start your own business, you will need to know some very basic information such as how to write a business plan, how to get the money to start, and so on. These topics are covered in Chapter 6.

BUSINESS FORMATION

FORMS OF BUSINESS ORGANIZATION

4

Gail Borden.

If at first you don't succeed, you are running about average.
M. H. ANDERSON

PROFILE　GAIL BORDEN, FOUNDER OF BORDEN, INC.

"I tried and failed, and I tried again and succeeded" reads the tombstone of Gail Borden. The epitaph is certainly a condensed account of Borden's life story. Borden had a series of dazzling business failures, including the Terraqueous Wagon. He designed the vehicle to travel on land or water. Unfortunately it sank the first time out!

Borden tried and failed three times to get a patent on another invention. When he finally got the patent on the fourth try, he didn't have much capital and credit. The poor sales finally washed him out.

Convinced that his product had potential, Borden tried again. What was his product? It was his process for giving milk a long shelf life through vacuum condensation. Borden finally reached his first business success with his condensed milk—at age 56! In 1986, Borden, Inc. earned $223 million on sales of $6.5 billion.

Gail Borden is just one of many success stories in the United States. His company took years to build, but Borden stuck with it. He found the best way to expand was to incorporate and sell part ownership of the company to others. The founder's determination to try, try again is a common thread linking many large corporations with today's small businesses struggling to survive.

Source: Bob Gatty, "Building On Failure," *Nation's Business,* April 1987, p. 50.

FORMS OF BUSINESS OWNERSHIP

Like Gail Borden, hundreds of thousands of people start new businesses in the United States every year. Chances are you have thought of owning your own business or know someone who has. One key to success at a new business is knowing how to get the resources you need to start. You may need to take on partners or find other ways of obtaining money. To stay in business, you may need help from someone with more expertise than you in certain areas or you may need

Almost 75 percent of the businesses in the United States are sole proprietorships like this one-owner barbershop. While most businesses take this form, they do less than 10 percent of sales volume. Clearly there are advantages and disadvantages to sole proprietorships.

to raise more money to expand. How you form your business can make a tremendous difference in your long-run success. You can form a business in several ways. The three major forms of business ownership are: (1) sole proprietorships, (2) partnerships, or (3) corporations.

It is easy to get started in your own business if you want. For example, you can begin a typing service out of your home, open a car repair center, start a new restaurant, or go about meeting other wants and needs of the community on your own. An organization that is owned, and usually managed, by one person is called a **sole proprietorship.** That is the most common form of business ownership (over 12 million firms).

Many people do not have the money, time, or desire to run a business on their own. They prefer to have someone else or some group of people get together to form the business. When two or more people legally agree to become co-owners of a business, the organization is called a **partnership** (about 1.4 million firms).

Gail Borden learned that there are advantages to creating a business that is separate and distinct from the owners. A legal entity that has an existence separate from the people who own it is called a **corporation.** There are only 2.8 million corporations in the United States (17 percent of all businesses), but they do 87 percent of the business (see Figure 4–1).

As you will learn in this chapter, each form of business ownership has its advantages—and disadvantages. It is important to understand these advantages and disadvantages before starting a business. Keep in mind that just because a business starts in one form of ownership, it doesn't always stay in that form. Many companies, like Gail Borden's, started out as "one man shows," added a partner or two, and eventually became corporations.

sole proprietorship
A business that is owned, and usually managed, by one person.

partnership (general)
A legal form of business with two or more owners.

corporation
A legal entity with authority to act and have liability separate from its owners.

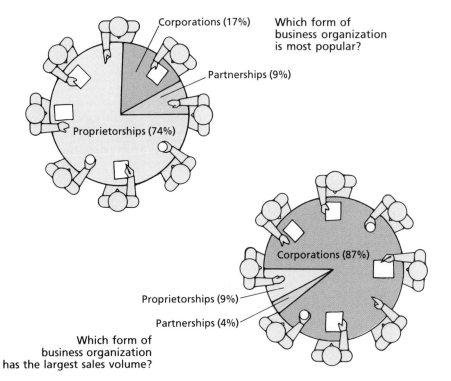

Which form of business organization is most popular?

Corporations (17%)

Partnerships (9%)

Proprietorships (74%)

Corporations (87%)

Proprietorships (9%)

Partnerships (4%)

Which form of business organization has the largest sales volume?

FIGURE 4–1

Forms of business organizations.
Although corporations make up only 17% of the total *number* of businesses, they make 87% of the sales volume. Sole proprietorships are the most common form of ownership (74%), but they make only 9% of sales volume.

SOLE PROPRIETORSHIPS

Advantages of Sole Proprietorships

There must be some major advantages to being a sole proprietor. After all, over 12 million people in the United States have formed this kind of business. Sole proprietorships are also the easiest kind of businesses for you to explore in your quest for an interesting career. Every town has some sole proprietorships that you can visit. There's the local produce stand, the beauty shop, the auto repair garage, and the liquor store. If you look closely, you'll find sole proprietors who do income taxes, repair appliances and television sets, and provide all kinds of local services. Talk with them about the joys and frustrations of being on their own. Most people will mention the benefits of being their own boss and setting their own hours. They may also mention the following advantages.

1. Ease of starting and ending the business   All you have to do to start a sole proprietorship is buy the needed equipment (for example, a saw, a word processor, a tractor, a lawn mower) and put up some announcements saying you are in business. It is just as easy to get out of business; you simply stop. There is no one to consult or to disagree with about such decisions. You may have to get a permit or license from the government, but that is usually no problem. The Profiles of the women who started sole proprietorships in their own homes (see Chapter 1) give you some feel for how such businesses can start small and grow rapidly.

2. Being your own boss   "Working for others simply does not have the same excitement as working for yourself." That's the way sole proprietors feel. You may make mistakes, but they are *your* mistakes—and so are the many small victories each day.

3. Pride of ownership   People who own and manage their own businesses are rightfully proud of their work. They deserve all the credit for taking the risks and providing needed goods or services.

4. Retention of profit   Other than the joy of being your own boss, there is nothing like the pleasure of knowing that you can make as much as you can and do not have to share that money with anyone else (except the government, in taxes). Store owners and service people are often willing to start working early in the day and stay late because the money they earn is theirs to keep.

5. No special taxes   All the profits of a sole proprietorship are taxed as the personal income of the owner, and he or she pays the normal income tax on that money. Owners *do* have to file an estimated tax return and make quarterly payments. It is wise for small-business owners to pick up a packet of information for small-business owners from the local Internal Revenue Service office to avoid any problems later.

It is for these and other reasons that there are more sole proprietorships than any other kind of business in the United States. Hundreds of thousands of new businesses are formed every year. However, thousands more fail. Many people dream of owning their own business, but there are also disadvantages to sole proprietorships.

To open a shop is easy; the difficult thing is to keep it open.
CHINESE PROVERB

Disadvantages of Sole Proprietorships

Not everyone is cut out to own and manage a business. Often it is difficult to save enough money to start a business *and* keep it going. Often the cost of inventory, supplies, insurance, advertising, rent, utilities, and other expenses is simply too much to cover alone. There are other disadvantages of owning your own business.

1. Unlimited liability—the risk of losses   When you work for others, it is their problem if the business is not profitable. When you own your own business, you and the business are considered one. You have **unlimited liability;** that is, any debts or damages incurred by the business are *your* debts and *you* must pay them, even if it means selling your home, your car, and so forth. This is a serious risk and one that requires careful thought and discussion with a lawyer, insurance agent, and others.

2. Limited financial resources   Funds available to the business are limited to the funds that the one (sole) owner can gather. Since there are serious limits to how much one person can do, partnerships and corporations have a greater probability of recruiting the needed financial backing to start a business.

3. Difficulty in management   Most businesses need some management; that is, someone must keep inventory records, accounting records, tax records, and so on. Many people who are skilled at selling things or providing a service are not so skilled in keeping records. Sole proprietors may have no one to help them. It is often difficult to find good, qualified people to help run the business. Perhaps one of *the* most common complaints among sole proprietors is the fact that good employees are hard to find.

4. Overwhelming time commitment   It is hard to own a business, manage it, train people, and have time for anything else in life. The owner must spend long hours working. The owner of a store, for example, may put in 12 hours a day, at least 6 days a week. That is almost twice the hours worked by a salaried laborer, who may make more money.

5. Few fringe benefits   If you are your own boss, you lose many of the fringe benefits that come from working for others. For example, you have no health insurance, no disability insurance, no sick leave, no vacation pay, and so on. These benefits may add up to 30 percent or more of a worker's income.

6. Limited growth   If the owner becomes incapacitated, the business often comes to a standstill. Since a sole proprietorship relies on its owner for most of its funding, expansion is often slow. This is one reason why many individuals seek partners to assist in a business.

7. Limited life span   If the sole proprietor dies, the business no longer exists unless arrangements have been made to pass the ownership/management on to others.

Talk with a few entrepreneurs about the problems they have faced in being on their own. They know more about the situation in your area than anyone else does. They are likely to have many interesting stories to tell, such as problems getting

unlimited liability
The responsibility of a business's owners for all of the debts of the business, making the personal assets of the owners vulnerable to claims against the business; sole proprietors and general partners have unlimited liability.

loans from the bank, problems with theft, and problems simply keeping up with the business. These problems are the reason that many sole proprietors discourage their children from following in their footsteps, although many would have it no other way. These problems are also reasons why many sole proprietors choose to find partners to share the load. Remember, though, partnerships have disadvantages, too.

THINKING IT THROUGH	Have you ever dreamed of opening your own business? If you did, what would it be? What talents or skills do you have that you could use? Could you start a business in your own home? About how much would it cost to start? Could you begin part-time while you worked elsewhere? What could you get from owning your own business in the way of satisfaction and profit? What would you lose?

PARTNERSHIPS

A partnership is a legal form of business with two or more owners. It is not difficult to form a partnership, but it is wise to get the counsel of a lawyer experienced with such agreements. Lawyers' services are expensive, so would-be partners should read all about partnerships and reach some basic agreements before calling in a lawyer. It is often easier to *form* a partnership agreement than to operate or end one, and many friendships have ended after friends became partners. Let's look at some of the advantages and disadvantages of partnerships.

Advantages of Partnerships

There are many advantages of having one or more Partners in a business. Often, it is much easier to own and manage a business with one or more partners. Your partner can cover for you when you are sick or go on vacation. Your partner may be skilled at inventory-keeping and accounting while you do the selling or servicing. A partner can also provide additional money, support, and expertise. Some of the people who are enjoying the advantages of partnerships today, more than ever before, are doctors, lawyers, dentists, and other professionals. They have learned that it is easier to take vacations, stay home when they are sick, or relax a little when there are others available to help take care of clients. With some care, partnerships can have the following advantages:

limited partner
Owner who invests money in the business, but does not have any management responsibility or liability for losses beyond the investment.

limited liability
The responsibility of a business's owners for losses only up to the amount they invest; limited partners and shareholders have limited liability.

1. More financial resources   Naturally, when two or more people pool their money and credit, it is easier to pay the rent, utilities, and other bills incurred by a business. There is a concept called limited partnership that is specially designed to help raise capital (money). A **limited partner** invests money in the business but cannot legally have any management responsibility, and has limited liability. **Limited liability** means that limited partners are not responsible for the debts of the business beyond the amount of their investment—their *liability* (debts they must pay) is *limited* to the amount they put into the company; their personal property is *not* at risk.

2. Shared management   It is simply much easier to manage the day-to-day activities of a business with carefully chosen partners. Partners give each other free time from the business, and provide different skills and perspectives. Many people find that the best partner is a spouse. That is why you see so many husband/wife teams managing restaurants, service shops, and other businesses.

Many of the disadvantages of owning your own business are taken care of when you find a business partner. When Bobbie is not there to manage, Brenda can take over. About 10 percent of all businesses are partnerships. Although the funding for partnerships is easier than for sole proprietorships, it is not as easy as with corporations.

3. Longer survival   A recent study reported in *Forbes* magazine found that of 2,000 businesses started since 1960, partnerships were four times as likely to succeed as sole proprietorships. Having a partner helps a businessperson to become more disciplined because someone is watching over him or her.[1]

The availability of more financial resources and ease of shared management are the primary advantages of partnerships, but let's not forget that partnerships have disadvantages as well.

Disadvantages of Partnerships

Any time two people must agree on anything, there is the possibility of conflict and tension. Partnerships have caused splits among families, friends, and marriages. Let's explore the disadvantages of partnerships.

1. Unlimited liability   Each general partner is liable for the debts of the firm, no matter who was responsible for causing those debts. Like a sole proprietor, partners can lose their homes, cars, and everything else they own if the business fails or is sued by someone. Such a risk is very serious and should be discussed with a lawyer and an insurance expert. A **general partner,** then, is an owner (partner) who has unlimited liability and is active in managing the firm. (As mentioned earlier, a limited partner risks an investment in the firm, but is not liable for the business's losses beyond that investment and cannot legally help manage the company.)

general partner
An owner (partner) who has unlimited liability and is active in managing the firm.

2. Division of profits   Sharing the risk means sharing the profit, and that can cause conflicts. For example, two people form a partnership: one puts in more money and the other puts in more hours. Each may feel justified in asking for a bigger share of the profits. Imagine the resulting conflicts.

3. Disagreements among partners   Disagreements over money are just one example of potential conflict in a partnership. Who has final authority over employees? Who hires and fires employees? Who works what hours? What if one partner wants to buy expensive equipment for the firm and the other partner disagrees? Potential conflicts are many. Because of such problems, all terms of partnership should be spelled out in writing to protect all parties and to minimize misunderstanding in the future.

4. Difficult to terminate   Once you have committed yourself to a partnership, it is not easy to get out of it. Questions about who gets what and what happens next are often very difficult to solve when the business is closed. Surprisingly, law firms often have faulty partnership agreements and find that breaking up is hard to do. How do you get rid of a partner you don't like? It is best to decide that up front—in the partnership agreement.[2]

Again, the best way to learn about the advantages and disadvantages of partnerships is to interview several people who have experience with such agreements. They will give you additional insights and hints on how to avoid problems.

How to Form a Partnership

The first step in forming a partnership is choosing the right partner. The importance of this step cannot be overemphasized. Many partnerships dissolve because of disagreements between partners. One should choose a business partner as carefully as a marriage partner.

CATEGORIES OF PARTNERS

Several different types of partners can be involved in a partnership. The most common types are the following:

- *Silent partners* are partners who take no active role in managing a partnership but their identities and involvement are known by the public.
- *Secret partners* are partners who take an active role in managing a partnership but whose identities are unknown to the public.
- *Nominal partners* are not actually involved in a partnership but lend their names to it for public relations purposes.

- *Dormant partners* are neither active in managing a partnership nor known to the public.
- *Senior partners* assume major management roles due to their long tenure or amount of investment in the partnership. They normally receive large shares of the partnership's profits.
- *Junior partners* are generally younger partners in tenure who assume a limited role in the partnership's management and receive a smaller share of the partnership's profits.

MAKING ETHICAL DECISIONS

Imagine that you and your partner own a construction company. You receive a bid from a subcontractor that you know is 20 percent too low. Such a loss to the subcontractor could put him out of business. Accepting the bid will certainly improve your chances of winning the contract for a big shopping center project. Your partner wants to take the bid and let the sub suffer the consequences of his bad estimate. What do you think you should do? What will be the consequences of your decision?

For your protection, be sure to put your partnership agreement *in writing*. The Model Business Corporation Act recommends including the following in a written **partnership agreement:**

1. The name of the business. Many states require the firm name to be registered with state and/or county officials if the firm name is different from the name of any of the partners.
2. The names and addresses of all partners.
3. The purpose and nature of the business, the location of the principal offices, and any other locations where the business will be conducted.
4. The date the partnership will start and how long it will last. Will it exist for a specific length of time or will it stop when one of the partners dies or when the partners agree to discontinue?
5. The contributions made by each partner. Will some partners contribute money, others real estate, personal property, expertise, or labor? When are the contributions due?
6. The management responsibilities. Will all partners have equal voices in management or will there be senior and junior partners?
7. The duties of each of the partners.
8. The salaries and drawing accounts of each of the partners.
9. Provision for sharing of profits or losses.
10. Provision for accounting procedures. Who will keep the accounts? What bookkeeping and accounting methods will be used? Where will the books be kept?
11. The requirements for taking in new partners.
12. Any special restrictions, rights, or duties of any partner.
13. Provision for a retiring partner.
14. Provision for the purchase of a deceased or retiring partner's share of the business.
15. Provision for how grievances will be handled.
16. Provision for how to dissolve the partnership and distribute the assets to the partners.

One of the fears of owning your own business or having a partner is the fear of losing everything you own if the business loses a significant amount of money or someone sues the business. Many businesspeople try to avoid this and the other disadvantages of sole proprietorships and partnerships by forming corporations.

partnership agreement
Legal document that specifies the rights and responsibilities of the members of a partnership.

Abraham Lincoln and a partner bought a small country store in New Salem, Illinois, in 1832. Lincoln wasn't very good at business, or his partner at staying away from whiskey. Within a year, his partner died, and Lincoln was left owing $1,100 to his creditors, a huge sum he referred to as "the National Debt."
Source: *Inc.*, May 1985, p. 18.

Most people who start a business in the United States are sole proprietors and most of them are no longer in business after 10 years. What are the advantages and disadvantages of this form of business?

What are some of advantages of partnerships over sole proprietorships?

Unlimited liability is one of the biggest drawbacks to sole proprietorships and general partnerships. Can you explain what that means?

What is the difference between a *limited* partner and a *general* partner?

PROGRESS CHECK

Size and money are just two of the advantages of corporations such as GM. They have over 85 percent of total business sales with a little over 15 percent of total businesses. Clearly corporations have many advantages over other forms of business, but there are disadvantages too.

CORPORATIONS

TOP 25 U.S. CORPORATIONS, 1988 (by sales)

1. General Motors
2. Ford Motor
3. Exxon
4. International Business Machines
5. General Electric
6. Mobil
7. Chrysler
8. Texaco
9. E. I. Du Pont De Nemours
10. Philip Morris
11. Chevron
12. Amoco
13. Shell Oil
14. Occidental Petroleum
15. Procter & Gamble
16. United Technologies
17. Atlantic Richfield
18. Eastman Kodak
19. Boeing
20. RJR Nabisco
21. Dow Chemical
22. Xerox
23. USX
24. Tenneco
25. McDonnell Douglas

Although the word *corporation* makes people think of big businesses like GM, IBM, Ford, Exxon, GE, Westinghouse, and USX (formerly U.S. Steel), it is not necessary to be big in order to *incorporate* (start a corporation). Obviously, many corporations *are* big. However, incorporating may be beneficial for small businesses, also.

A corporation is a state-chartered legal entity with authority to act and have liability separate from its owners. What this means for the corporation's owners (stockholders) is that they are not liable for the debts or any other problems of the corporation beyond the money they invest. Owners no longer must worry about losing their houses, cars, and other property because of some business problem—a very significant benefit. A corporation not only limits the liability of owners, it enables many people to share in the ownership (and profits) of a business without working there or having other commitments to it.

Advantages of Corporations

The concept of incorporation is not too difficult, even though the procedures for incorporating are often rather complex. Most people are not willing to risk everything to go into business. Yet, for businesses to grow and prosper and create abundance, many people would have to be willing to invest their money in business. The way to solve this problem was to create an artificial being, an entity that existed only in the eyes of the law. That artificial being is called a *corporation*. It is nothing more than a technique for involving people in business at a minimal risk. Let's explore the advantages of such an entity.

1. More money for investment   To raise money, a corporation sells ownership (stock) to anyone who is interested. (We shall discuss stock at length in Chapter 20.) This means that millions of people can own part of major companies like IBM, Xerox, and GM. If a company sold 10 million shares for $50 each, it would have $500 million available to build plants, buy materials, hire people, build products, and so on. Such a large amount of money would be difficult to raise any other way.

So a major advantage of corporations is their ability to raise large amounts of money, if they can sell their stock. Laws regulate how corporations can raise this money. These laws vary in different states in terms of the type of stock and the amount of debt that can be used when incorporating.

2. Limited Liability   It bears repeating that a major advantage of corporations is the limited liability of owners. Corporations in England and Canada have the letters "Ltd." after their names, as in British Motors, Ltd. The Ltd. stands for *limited liability* and is probably the most significant advantage of corporations. Remember, limited liability means that the owners of a business are responsible for losses only up to the amount they invest.

3. Size   That one word summarizes many of the advantages of corporations. Because they have large amounts of money to work with, corporations can build large, modern factories with the latest equipment. They can also hire experts or specialists in all areas of operation. Furthermore, they can buy other corporations in other fields to *diversify their risk*. (What this means is that a corporation can be involved in many businesses at once so that if one fails, the effect on the total corporation is lessened.) In short, a major advantage of corporations is that they have the size and resources to take advantage of opportunities anywhere in the world. However, corporations do not have to be large to enjoy the benefits of limited liability and more money for investment. Many doctors, lawyers, and individuals and partners in a variety of businesses have incorporated. There are many small corporations in the United States.

4. Perpetual life   Because corporations are separate from those who own them, the death of one or more owners does not terminate the corporation. This makes corporations a better risk to bankers and lenders, and makes it easier to get loans.

5. Ease of ownership change   It is easy to change the owners of a corporation. All that is necessary is to sell the stock to someone else.

6. Separation of ownership from management   Corporations are able to raise money from many different investors without getting them involved in management. The corporate hierarchy is shown in the illustration on page 114. The pyramid shows that the owners/shareholders are separate from the managers and employers. The owners elect a board of directors. The directors select the officers. They, in turn, hire managers and employees. The owners thus have some say in who runs the corporation, but no control.

NONPROFIT CORPORATIONS

A nonprofit corporation is a special type of corporation formed for charitable and other purposes. It does not seek *personal profit* for its owners. Such a corporation has many of the features of business corporations with the major exception of its tax status. Owners of a nonprofit corporation can contact the Internal Revenue Service for forms to qualify for tax-exempt status (IRS booklet number 557).

The number of nonprofit corporations is remarkable, running into the hundreds of thousands. In states such as Ohio and New York, over one third of all corporations with state charters are nonprofit. In some towns and cities, over 50 percent of the property is tax exempt because it belongs to nonprofit organizations such as churches and hospitals.

How owners affect management.
Owners have an influence on how a business is managed by electing a board of governors. The board hires the top managers (or fires them). It also sets the pay for top managers. Top managers then select other managers and employees with the help of the human resources department.

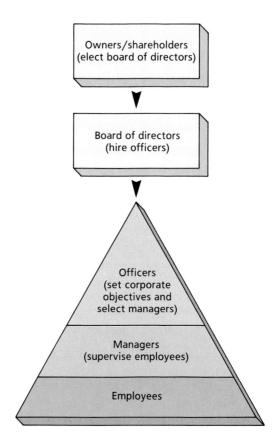

Disadvantages of Corporations

There are so many sole proprietorships and partnerships in the United States that it is clear that there are real disadvantages to incorporating. Otherwise, more people would incorporate their businesses. Here are a few of the disadvantages.

1. *Initial cost* Incorporation may cost thousands of dollars and involve expensive lawyers and accountants. There are less expensive ways of incorporating in certain states (see the subsection called Individuals Can Incorporate, later in this chapter), but most people do not have the time or confidence to go through this procedure without the help of a lawyer.

2. *Paperwork* The papers to be filed to start a corporation are just the beginning. Tax laws demand that a corporation prove all its expenses and deductions are legitimate. A corporation, therefore, must process many forms. A sole proprietor or partnership may keep rather broad accounting records; a corporation, on the other hand, must keep detailed records, the minutes of meetings, and more.

3. *Two tax returns* If an individual incorporates, he or she must file both a corporate tax return and an individual tax return. The corporate return can be quite complex.

4. Size   Size may be one advantage of corporations, but it is a disadvantage as well. Large corporations sometimes become too inflexible and too tied down in red tape to respond quickly to market changes.

5. Termination difficult   Once a corporation is started, it's relatively difficult to end.

6. Double taxation   Corporate income is taxed twice. First the corporation pays tax on income before it can distribute any to stockholders. Then the stockholders pay tax on the income (dividends) they receive from the corporation. States often tax corporations more harshly than other enterprises. Sometimes they levy special taxes that apply to corporations but not to other forms of business.

Many people are discouraged by the costs, paperwork, and special taxes corporations must pay. Partners may feel that the hassles of incorporation outweigh the advantages. Figure 4–2 on page 116 summarizes the advantages and disadvantages of the various forms of business organizations.

How to Incorporate

The process of forming a corporation varies somewhat from state to state. The **articles of incorporation** are usually filed with the secretary of state's office in the state in which the company incorporates. The articles contain the following information:

- The corporation's name.
- The names of the people who incorporated it.
- Its purpose.
- Its duration (usually perpetual).
- The number of shares that can be issued, their voting rights, and any other rights the shareholders have.
- The corporation's minimum capital.
- The address of the corporation's office.
- The name and address of the person responsible for the corporation's legal services.
- The names and addresses of the first directors.
- Any other public information the incorporators wish to include.

articles of incorporation
Filed with the secretary of state, this is a legal document listing the name and address of the corporation and who is incorporating it and responsible for its legal services; as well as the corporation's purpose, duration, number of shares, minimum capital, and first directors.

Corporate Bylaws

In addition to the articles of incorporation listed, a corporation also has *bylaws*. These describe how the firm is to be operated from both a legal and managerial point of view. The bylaws include items such as:

- How, when, and where shareholders' and directors' meetings are held, and how long directors are to serve.
- Directors' authority.
- Duties and responsibilities of officers, and the length of their service.
- How stock is issued.
- Other matters, including employment contracts.

FIGURE 4–2   Comparison of forms of business ownership.

		PARTNERSHIPS		CORPORATIONS	
	SOLE PROPRIETORSHIP	GENERAL PARTNERSHIP	LIMITED PARTNERSHIP	CONVENTIONAL CORPORATION	S CORPORATIONS
Documents needed to start business	None, may need permit or license	Partnership agreement, oral or written	Written agreement. Must file certificate of limited partnership	Articles of incorporation, bylaws	Articles of incorporation, bylaws, must meet criteria
Ease of termination	Easy to terminate, just pay debts and quit	May be difficult to terminate, depending on the partnership agreement	Same as general partnership	Difficult and expensive to terminate	Same as conventional corporation
Length of life	Terminates on the death of owner	Terminates on the death or withdrawal of partner	Same as general partnership	Perpetual life	Same as conventional corporation
Transfer of ownership	Business can be sold to qualified buyer	Must have other partner(s)' agreement	Same as general partnership	Easy to change owners, just sell stock	Can sell stock, but with restrictions
Financial resources	Limited to owner's capital and loans	Limited to partners' capital and loans	Same as general partnership	More money to start and operate, may sell stocks and bonds	Same as conventional corporation
Risk of losses	Unlimited liability	Unlimited liability	Limited liability	Limited liability	Limited liability
Taxes	Taxed as personal income	Taxed as personal income	Same as general partnership	Corporate, double taxation	Taxed as personal income
Management responsibilities	Owner manages *all* areas of the business	Partners share management	Cannot participate in management	Separate management from ownership	Same as conventional corporation
Employee benefits	Usually fewer benefits and lower wages	Often fewer benefits and lower wages; promising employee could become a partner	Same as general partnership	Usually better benefits and wages, advancement opportunities	Same as conventional corporation

---

Individuals Can Incorporate

It is important to remember that a corporation does not need to have hundreds of employees or thousands of stockholders. Individuals (for example, doctors, lawyers, movie stars, rock stars, and so forth) can also incorporate. By doing so, they may save on taxes and receive other benefits of incorporation. It is not always as difficult as it sounds to form a corporation, especially if you choose to do it in a state with less complex rules. Many firms incorporate in Delaware because it is relatively easy to do so there. A book called *How to Form Your Own Corporation*

CORPORATE TYPES

You may find some confusing terms when reading about corporations. Here are a few of the more widely used terms:

Alien corporation: Does business in the United States, but is chartered (incorporated) in another country.

Domestic corporation: Does business in the state in which it was chartered (incorporated).

Foreign corporation: Does business in one state, but is chartered in another; about one third of all corporations are chartered in Delaware because of its relatively attractive rules for incorporation. A foreign corporation must register in states where it operates.

Open corporation: Sells stock to the general public. Those corporations listed on the New York Stock Exchange are examples.

Closed corporation: One whose stock is held by a few people and is not available to the general public. The Mars candy company is an example.

Public corporation: A corporation created for governmental purposes by the federal, state, or local government. Incorporated cities are examples as are parking and housing authorities.

Quasi-public corporation: A corporation chartered by government as an approved monopoly to perform services to the general public. Public utilities are examples of quasi-public corporations.

Nonprofit corporation: One that does not seek personal profit for its owners. Charitable organizations are examples.

Multinational corporation: A firm that has operations in several countries such as IBM or Ford.

---

without a Lawyer for Under $500 by Ted S. Nicholas (Enterprise Publications, 1986) tells you the steps to take. The title gives you a good idea of the ease involved. However, it is usually wise to take the time to contact an attorney.

PROGRESS CHECK

- What are the major advantages and disadvantages of incorporating a business?

- There are 10 requirements in the articles of incorporation and 5 items in the bylaws—can you list most of them?

- What is the role of owners (stockholders) in the corporate hierarchy?

- If you buy stock in a corporation and someone gets injured by one of the corporation's products, can you be sued? Why or why not? Could you be sued if you were a general partner in a partnership?

THINKING IT THROUGH

What would the United States be like without major corporations? What products would be hard to get? What would be the benefits? Now that you've read about sole proprietorships, partnerships, and corporations, which sounds like the best place for you to work? Why? Which calls for taking the most risks? Which would be most fun? Most profitable? What part of your personality most determines where you fit in best?

CORPORATE EXPANSION: MERGERS AND HOSTILE TAKEOVERS

The 1980s was a decade of considerable corporate expansion. It seemed nearly every day you heard a new corporate merger or acquisition announced in the news. A **merger** is the result of two firms forming one company. An *acquisition* is when one company buys another company. Figure 4–3 on page 118 highlights several important corporate deals that occurred in the 80s.

merger
The result of two firms forming one company.

FIGURE 4–3

Top 10 deals.
The largest deal in history was in 1989—the KKR purchase of RJR Nabisco. KKR put a little over $15 million into the purchase. KKR borrowed $18 billion more and gave RJR Nabisco shareholders securities for the rest. The investment community was amazed to see a company control $25 billion in assets for a $15 million investment.

Source: Jerry Knight, "KKR Using Only $15 Million Of Its Own in Nabisco Buyout," *The Washington Post*, December 2, 1988, pp. A1 and A16.

FIRMS INVOLVED	COST (IN BILLIONS)	YEAR
Kohlberg Kravis Roberts (KKR) and RJR Nabisco	$25	1989
Philip Morris and Kraft	13.41	1988
Gulf and Chevron	13.3	1984
Getty and Texaco	10.1	1984
Conoco and DuPont	8.0	1981
Standard Oil and British Petroleum	7.8	1987
Marathon Oil and U.S. Steel	6.6	1982
Campeau and Federated Department Stores	6.5	1988
RCA and GE	6.0	1986
General Foods and Philip Morris	5.8	1985

Source: Various newspapers, 1989.

vertical merger
The joining of two firms involved in different stages of related businesses.

horizontal merger
The joining of two firms in the same industry.

conglomerate merger
The joining of completely unrelated firms.

There are three major types of corporate mergers: vertical, horizontal, and conglomerate. A **vertical merger** is the joining of two firms involved in different stages of related businesses. Think of a merger between a large soup company and a company that produces aluminum cans. Such a merger would ensure a constant supply of aluminum cans needed by the soup company. It could also help insure quality control of the soup company's product. A **horizontal merger** joins two firms in the same industry and allows them to diversify or expand their products. An example of a horizontal merger is the merger of a large milk company with a soft drink producer. The milk company can now supply a variety of beverage products. A **conglomerate merger** unites completely unrelated firms. The primary purpose of a conglomerate merger is to diversify business operations and investments. The acquisition of a movie studio by a soup company would be an example of a conglomerate merger. Some 2,785 mergers and acquisitions took place in 1988.[3] More such deals are expected in the 1990s.

Hostile Corporate Takeovers

hostile takeover
An unrequested acquisition of an organization through the purchase of company stock in the open market.

Not all mergers or acquisitions occur under friendly circumstances. Companies may chose to merge voluntarily or one firm may purchase the controlling interest in the other. A **hostile takeover** is the unrequested acquisition of an organization through the purchase of company stock in the open market. The acquisition of Trans World Airlines by Carl Icahn is an example of a hostile takeover.

Why would a firm resist being taken over by another firm? The main reason is that many of the top managers and employees may be fired by the new owners and be forced out of the firm to find new employment. One of the reasons one corporation would try to buy another is that the buyer thinks that it can manage the firm more effectively and make better use of the firm's assets. Naturally, the present managers of the firm disagree. Thus, the term *hostile takeover*.

tender offer
A proposal to purchase all or part of a firm's stock at a price above the current market value.

How does a hostile takeover generally develop? Most begin with what is called a tender offer. A **tender offer** is a proposal to purchase all or part of a firm's stock at a price above the current market value. Icahn's takeover of TWA occurred this way.

When such an offer is made, the management of the firm being bought often institutes antitakeover strategies to stop the purchase. Figure 4–4 illustrates several strategies used by management to avoid hostile takeovers.

FIGURE 4–4

Antitakeover strategies. When corporations face hostile takeovers, they sometimes use these antitakeover strategies to stop the purchase. You can learn more about these different strategies as you read this page.

Greenmail

Greenmail can be thought of as a type of corporate "ransom." Top management "pays off" those threatening to take over the firm by buying their stock for more than market price. (You will read more about greenmail in Chapter 21.)

Shark repellent

Think of the "shark" as the corporate raider and the "repellent" as management's policies designed to prevent hostile takeovers. There are a variety of shark repellents. Included are changing the corporation bylaws so that a greater percentage of outstanding shares is needed to call a shareholders meeting (where takeovers might be considered) and changing the rules so that a "supermajority" (75–80 percent) of the stockholders must approve a takeover bid.

Poison pills

The managers of a few companies would rather see the company greatly weakened than taken over by someone else. Such managers concoct "poison pills" that weaken the firm so it is less attractive to a raider. One way to discourage a company from buying your firm is to make the firm a poor business risk. A popular way to do that is to sell many bonds to the public and thus incur much debt. That debt becomes a "poison pill" that the purchaser would have to take to buy the firm.

Ogilvy Group, Inc., an advertising agency, used a different kind of poison pill. It gave shareholders the right to buy stock at half price under certain circumstances, such as the takeover of the firm by another firm. Fairchild Industries used a similar defense—offering shares at a discount if a takeover occurred. Borden Inc. threatened an unusual poison pill. All of the top 25 managers threatened to quit if there was a takeover that they felt was unfair, and the acquirer must pay the executives $10 to $30 million to buy out their contracts if they resign. Borden called their action "people pills." All together, some 800 companies have poison pills in place ranging from the selling of bonds to the selling of the firm to employees if a takeover is imminent.*

Golden parachutes

When a company changes hands, top managers are usually "pushed out" of the top office. To make their landing a little gentler, many companies are now including a golden parachute provision in management contracts. The parachute guarantees that the acquiring company will pay the managers cash settlements (ranging from several hundred thousand dollars to more than $5 million) when the company is taken over. More about golden parachutes in Chapter 18.

White knights

When a takeover seems inevitable, some companies turn to a "white knight" to protect them from the dreaded "black knight" corporate raider. A white knight is a company that is considered more favorable by the target company facing a hostile takeover because it may agree not to fire managers or employees after the takeover. The white knight negotiates a friendly takeover of the target company.

* Joanne Lipman, "Ogilvy Adopts Poison Pill Tactic to Ward Off Unwelcome Suitors," The Wall Street Journal, January 13, 1989, p. B3; David Field, "Fairchild Prepares 'Poison Pill' Defense," The Washington Times, January 24, 1989, p. C3; and Christopher Farrell, "First It Was Poison Pills, Now It's 'People Pills'," Business Week, January 16, 1989, pp. 33–34.

Some of the goals of any corporate merger are to expand product lines and to increase profits. So the buyer of a company is willing to pay millions of dollars to strike just the right deal.

taking a firm private
The efforts of a group of stockholders or management to obtain all of the firm's stock for themselves.

leveraged buyout (LBO)
An attempt by employees, management, or a group of investors to purchase an organization primarily through borrowing.

There is much debate about the value of such takeovers to society. In general, society benefits from such takeovers because the new management runs the firm more efficiently than the old managers and makes better use of the land and other resources. The problem is that many employees and managers lose their jobs. This, of course, causes many problems.

Other problems emerge when companies resist being taken over. Often firms will make themselves unattractive to buyers by going into debt by selling what are called "junk bonds." As you will learn in Chapter 20, junk bonds are bonds that are relatively risky to investors. Selling such bonds weakens the financial base of the corporation and could weaken the corporate base of the United States in general.[4] Therefore you may see more legislation regarding mergers and attempted mergers in the future.

Keeping Control of an Organization in a Hostile Environment

Because of the threat of hostile takeovers and other hassles with stockholders, some corporations have decided to recapture control of the firm internally. For example, Cox Communications, a large firm in the cable television industry, decided to "take the firm private" in 1987. What does this mean exactly? **Taking a firm private** involves the efforts of a group of stockholders or management to obtain all the firm's stock for themselves. In the Cox situation, the Cox family successfully gained total control of the company. The stock can no longer be purchased by investors in the open market.

Suppose the employees in an organization feel there is a good possibility they may lose their jobs. Or what if management believes that corporate performance could be enhanced if they owned the company? Do either of these groups have an opportunity of taking ownership of the company? Yes—they might attempt a leveraged buyout. A **leveraged buyout (LBO)** is an attempt by employees, management, or a group of investors to purchase an organization primarily through *borrowing* (see Figure 4–5). The funds borrowed are used to buy out the stockholders in the company. The employees, managers, or group of investors now become the owners of the firm. In 1988, the Southland Corporation underwent a $4.9 billion leveraged buyout from the firm's founding family. As in most leveraged buyouts, the agreement called for the loans to be repaid through the firm's operations or the sale of its assets.

KOHLBERG KRAVIS ROBERTS & CO. (KKR)

The kings of leveraged buyouts on Wall Street are Jerome Kohlberg, Jr., Henry R. Kravis, George R. Roberts, and Robert I. MacDonnell, the four partners of KKR. They engineered the over $25 billion leveraged buyout of RJR Nabisco, putting up only $15 million of their own money (see Figure 4–3 for more details).

Kohlberg, Kravis, and Roberts each made an estimated $50 million in 1986. McDonnell, who has a smaller stake in the firm, only made $15 million. (Don't you feel sorry for him?) In 1986, the firm managed the largest buyout before that time, the $6.2 billion deal to buy Beatrice, the food company. For managing that deal, KKR made $45 million. In 1987, it arranged a $3.6 billion leveraged buyout of Owens-Illinois. It had put together three of the largest buyouts ever before it surpassed itself with the leveraged buyout of RJR Nabisco. Firms like KKR made Wall Street look very attractive to college graduates in the 1980s. It lost some luster with the stock market crash of 1987, but may regain its luster in the 1990s.

Source: Louis Rukeyser (ed.), *Louis Rukeyser's Business Almanac* (New York: Simon and Schuster, 1988), p. 252.

How leveraged buyouts work.

FIGURE 4–5

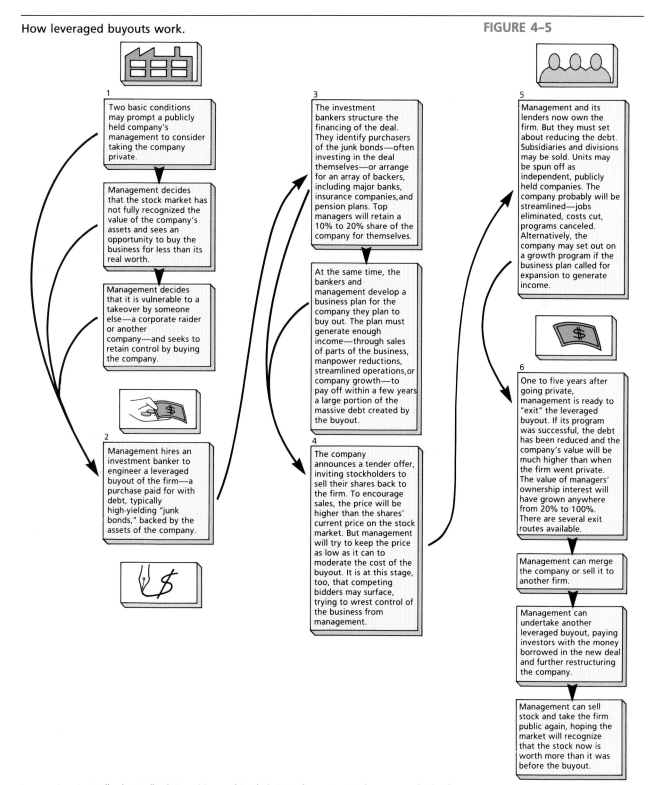

1
Two basic conditions may prompt a publicly held company's management to consider taking the company private.

Management decides that the stock market has not fully recognized the value of the company's assets and sees an opportunity to buy the business for less than its real worth.

Management decides that it is vulnerable to a takeover by someone else—a corporate raider or another company—and seeks to retain control by buying the company.

2
Management hires an investment banker to engineer a leveraged buyout of the firm—a purchase paid for with debt, typically high-yielding "junk bonds," backed by the assets of the company.

3
The investment bankers structure the financing of the deal. They identify purchasers of the junk bonds—often investing in the deal themselves—or arrange for an array of backers, including major banks, insurance companies, and pension plans. Top managers will retain a 10% to 20% share of the company for themselves.

At the same time, the bankers and management develop a business plan for the company they plan to buy out. The plan must generate enough income—through sales of parts of the business, manpower reductions, streamlined operations, or company growth—to pay off within a few years a large portion of the massive debt created by the buyout.

4
The company announces a tender offer, inviting stockholders to sell their shares back to the firm. To encourage sales, the price will be higher than the shares' current price on the stock market. But management will try to keep the price as low as it can to moderate the cost of the buyout. It is at this stage, too, that competing bidders may surface, trying to wrest control of the business from management.

5
Management and its lenders now own the firm. But they must set about reducing the debt. Subsidiaries and divisions may be sold. Units may be spun off as independent, publicly held companies. The company probably will be streamlined—jobs eliminated, costs cut, programs canceled. Alternatively, the company may set out on a growth program if the business plan called for expansion to generate income.

6
One to five years after going private, management is ready to "exit" the leveraged buyout. If its program was successful, the debt has been reduced and the company's value will be much higher than when the firm went private. The value of managers' ownership interest will have grown anywhere from 20% to 100%. There are several exit routes available.

Management can merge the company or sell it to another firm.

Management can undertake another leveraged buyout, paying investors with the money borrowed in the new deal and further restructuring the company.

Management can sell stock and take the firm public again, hoping the market will recognize that the stock now is worth more than it was before the buyout.

Source: Gary L. Wedbush, Wedbush Securities, and Frederic M. Roberts, F. M. Roberts & Co., both of Los Angeles. Jim Schachter, "How LBOs Work," *Los Angeles Times,* October 21, 1988, p. 1 of Part IV.

Again, there is much controversy about leveraged buyouts by managers. Some people feel that corporations should not go into so much debt just to avoid the probing of outside stockholders. If you go on to take finance courses, you will learn more about corporate debt and how it can weaken the firm. We shall discuss such issues again in the finance chapters later. At this point, we simply want to introduce you to the terms and concepts you will be encountering as you read the business literature.

S CORPORATIONS

S corporation
A unique government creation that looks like a corporation, but is taxed like sole proprietorships and partnerships.

One issue that has been receiving increased attention in the last couple of years is the formation of **S corporations,** formerly called Subchapter S corporations. An S corporation is a unique government creation that looks like a corporation, but is taxed like sole proprietorships and partnerships. S corporations have shareholders, directors, and employees, but the profits are taxed as the personal income of the shareholders—thus avoiding the double taxation of conventional corporations. The major advantage of S corporations is this Federal income tax break. Some 37 states now give S corporations tax breaks as well. For example, California taxes S concerns at 2.5 percent instead of the regular corporate 9.6 percent.[5]

Not all businesses can become S corporations. In order to qualify, a company must:

1. Have no more than 35 shareholders.
2. Have shareholders who are individuals or estates and are citizens or permanent residents of the United States.
3. Have only one class of outstanding stock.
4. Not own 80 percent or more of the stock of another corporation.
5. Not have more than 25 percent of income derived from passive sources (rents, royalties, interest, etc.).

Originally, S corporations had the benefit of limited liability and some real tax advantages over partnerships, including deductible fringe benefits for owners. However, the Subchapter S Revision Act of 1982 changed the rules. Now a Subchapter S corporation looks more like a partnership. It still has limited liability, stockholders, directors, and officers, but fringe benefits of owners are no longer deductible.

The S-style of corporation is gaining popularity among businesspeople. In 1982 there were only 564,219 such returns. By 1987 there were over 800,000 S corporations. The IRS expects over 1 million S returns in 1992—22 percent of all corporate returns.[6]

The paperwork and details of S corporations are similar to those of regular corporations. However, the profits of such businesses are taxed as regular personal income of the shareholders. Before 1986, this meant that owners of S corporations paid lower taxes than conventional corporations. The Tax Reform Act of 1986 changed the individual tax rate. This means that a S corporation is not *necessarily* taxed at a lower rate than conventional corporations. However, there is much talk about raising the individual tax rates again to help bring down the deficit. If that happens, S corporations would again be attractive for small businesses. As you can see, the benefits of S corporations change every time the tax rules change. The best way to learn all the benefits for a specific business is to go over the tax advantages and liability differences with a lawyer or accountant or both.

Cooperatives are important in agriculture. They enable farmers to purchase seed and equipment at reasonable prices. They also provide an outlet for farm products. Cooperatives do not pay the same taxes as corporations do and have other advantages for selected businesspeople.

COOPERATIVES

Some people dislike the notion of having owners, managers, workers, and buyers as separate individuals with separate goals. They envision a world where people cooperate with one another more fully and share the wealth more evenly. These people have formed a different kind of organization that reflects their social orientation. Such an organization is called a cooperative.

A **cooperative** is an organization that is owned by members/customers who pay an annual membership fee and share in any profits (if it is a profit-making organization). Often the members/customers work in the organization so many hours a month as part of their duties. Owners, managers, workers, and customers are all the same people. You may have a food cooperative near you. If so, stop by and chat with the people and learn more about this growing aspect of American trade.

There is another kind of cooperative in the United States, set up for different reasons. These cooperatives are formed to give members more economic power as a group than they would have as individuals. The best example of such cooperatives is a farm cooperative. The idea at first was for farmers to join together to get better prices for their food products. Eventually, however, the organization expanded so that farm cooperatives now buy and sell fertilizer, farm equipment, seed, and other products needed on the farm. This has become a multibillion dollar industry. The

cooperative
An organization owned by members/customers who pay an annual membership fee and share in any profits (if it is a profit-making organization).

JOINT VENTURES IN AUTOS

COMPANIES	AUTOS
GM/Isuzu	Spectrum
GM/Suzuki	Sprint
Chrysler/ Maserati	TC (Turbo Coupe)
Ford/Mazda	Probe
Chrysler/ Mitsubishi	Summit
Ford/Kia	Festiva
Ford/ Volkswagen	Fox
GM/Daewoo	Le Maus
GM/Toyota	Prism, Corolla

Source: Various newspapers, 1989

joint venture
An effort by two or more business firms to capture new markets through cooperation and shared investment risk.

cooperatives now own many manufacturing facilities. Farm cooperatives do not pay the same kind of taxes that corporations do, and thus have an advantage in the marketplace.

To give you some idea of the size of farm cooperatives, let's look at Farmland Industries, Inc. Recently, this cooperative merged (joined) with FAR-MAR-CO to become a $5 billion organization. Farmland Industries owns manufacturing facilities, oil wells and refineries, fertilizer plants, feed mills, and plants that produce everything from grease and paint to steel buildings. It also owns a network of warehouses plus insurance, financial and technical services for its 750,000 members. There are over 7,500 more smaller cooperatives in the country, some of which do a billion dollars of business a year. As you can see, cooperatives are a major force in agriculture today. Some top farm co-ops have familiar names such as Land O'Lakes, Sunkist, Ocean Spray, Blue Diamond, and Welch's.[7]

JOINT VENTURES

One of the latest trends in business is for two or more corporations (often from two different countries) to form strategic alliances to accomplish some objectives. A **joint venture,** then, is an effort by two or more business firms to capture new markets through cooperation and shared investment risk. This enables world markets to benefit from the expertise of all nations' businesspeople working together. For example, GM joined with Toyota to assemble Geo Prizms and Toyota Corollas in Fremont, California.[9] Such agreements are known as joint ventures or strategic alliances*, and are taking place all over the world. Britain's state-owned car company, BL, formed a joint venture with Japan's Honda to build cars in England. In 1988, Chrysler joined with Mitsubishi Motors to make a sporty car code-named X25.

In other areas, Wheeling-Pittsburgh Steel formed a joint venture with Japan's Nisshin Steel to make steel in the United States. McDonald's has a joint venture in Thailand to franchise fast-food restaurants. Walt Disney Productions and Oriental Land in Japan created Tokyo Disneyland, a theme park much like the Disney parks in America. The results were fantastic. Over 10 million visitors came to the park in the first year.

Not all joint ventures involved different countries. Borden, Inc. agreed to form a joint venture with Dairymen, Inc., a farmers' cooperative in Louisville, Kentucky. It is estimated that the joint venture will increase Borden's market share to more than 15 percent from 10 percent in the 38 states in which it operates.

WHICH FORM IS FOR YOU?

As you can see, you may participate in the business world in a variety of ways. You can start your own sole proprietorship, partnership, corporation, or cooperative. There are advantages and disadvantages to each. However, the risks are high no matter which form you choose. The miracle of free enterprise is that the freedom and incentives of capitalism make such risks acceptable to many people, who go on to create the great corporations of America. You know many of their names: J. C. Penney, Malcolm Forbes, Sears and Roebuck, Levi Strauss, Ford, Edison, and so on. They started small, accumulated capital, grew, and became industrial leaders. Could you do the same?

---

* This is one of the latest "buzzwords" in business.

BORDEN, INC.—THE CREAM OF THE DAIRY INDUSTRY

When Borden joined the Louisville, Kentucky, farmers' cooperative, Dairymen, Inc., in early 1988, it consolidated Borden's position as the first nationwide dairy. The joint venture produces and distributes dairy products in the 11 southeastern states. It combined Dairymen's 15 milk-processing plants with Borden's and Meadow Gold's 22 milk-processing plants. Borden acquired Beatrice's Meadow Gold Dairies in a $315 million transaction in 1986.

Dairymen, Inc., wanted out of the dairy processing business, which was the strong point of Borden, Inc. Now they can operate more efficiently by combining purchasing for things like packaging and by combining production and distribution systems. The agreement enables the two companies to market the national brand alongside the cooperative's brands, thus getting the advantages of regional brand loyalty and distribution. The joint venture expects sales of around $1 billion! Not bad for a company started by a man who's tombstone reads he "tried and failed, and tried again and succeeded!"

Source: Alix M. Freedman, "Borden, Inc. Agrees to Joint Venture with Dairymen," *The Wall Street Journal,* November 22, 1987, p. 25.

Tokyo Disneyland is a joint venture of Walt Disney Productions and Oriental Land in Japan. The Japanese have formed many joint ventures with U.S auto manufacturers. Such cooperation between countries fosters international trade and better relations overall.

Most students prefer to take the more cautious route of working for a corporation. The advantages are many: a fixed salary, paid vacations, health coverage, limited risk, job security, promotional possibilities, and more.

The disadvantages of working for others are also significant: limited income potential, fixed hours, repetitive work, close supervision, and limited freedom.

Going to work for a large company is like getting on a train. Are you going 60 miles an hour, or is the train going 60 miles an hour and you're just sitting still?
JOHN PAUL GETTY

Sometimes it is fun to work for others while starting your own business on the side. Apple Computer was started in a garage. Many firms were started in people's basements, garages, and attics. The point is that business offers many different opportunities for tomorrow's graduates.

PROGRESS CHECK

▪ Why would a firm resist being bought by another firm, so that they would refer to such an attempt as a "hostile takeover"?

▪ What are three of the antitakeover strategies you could use?

▪ What is the major benefit of an S corporation?

▪ Suppose you want to start a day care center where you and your friends could send your children. You do not want to make it a profit-making organization and you want all your friends to help in running the organization. What form of organization would you use? (For more on this, see Case 1 at the end of this chapter.)

SUMMARY

1. Define the three basic forms of business ownership.

1. A business can be formed in several ways.
   ▪ What are the three major forms of business ownership?
     The three major forms of business ownership are: sole proprietorships, partnerships, and corporations (including Subchapter S corporations).

2. Compare the advantages and disadvantages of:
1. Sole proprietorships.
2. Partnerships.
3. Corporations.

2. Each form of business ownership has advantages and disadvantages.
   ▪ What are the advantages and disadvantages of sole proprietorships, partnerships, and corporations? Is there some way to review them quickly?
     See Figure 4–2 on page 116.
   ▪ Which form of business is the most popular?
     About 74 percent of all businesses are sole proprietorships. Some 17 percent of businesses are corporations, and only 9 percent are partnerships.
   ▪ Which form of business sells the most?
     Corporations do 87 percent of the business in the United States. Proprietorships do 9 percent of the business and partnerships only 4 percent.
3. Not all partners have the same roles and responsibilities.

3. Explain the differences between limited and general partnerships.

   ▪ What are the main differences between general and limited partnerships?
     General partners are owners (partners) who have unlimited liability and are active in managing the company. Limited partners are owners (partners) who have limited liability and are not active in the company.
   ▪ What does unlimited liability mean?
     Unlimited liability means that sole proprietors and general partners must pay all debts and damages caused by their business. They may have to sell their houses, cars, or other personal possessions to pay business debts.
   ▪ What does limited liability mean?
     Limited liability means that corporate owners (stockholders) and limited partners are responsible for losses only up to the amount they invest. Their other personal property is not at risk.
4. The first and *most important* step in forming a partnership is choosing the right partner.

4. List the contents of a partnership agreement.

   ▪ How do you form a partnership?
     The most important step in forming a partnership is choosing a partner

wisely. Then, no matter how good friends you and your partner may be, *put your partnership agreement in writing* (see p. 111).

5. Forming a corporation is more complex than forming a partnership.
   - How do you form a corporation?
     Two major steps are needed to form a corporation. You must file articles of incorporation in the state of your choice (the articles include the name, purpose, and duration of the corporation). You must also write bylaws telling how the firm will operate (authority of directors, dates, and officers, etc.).
   - Why do people incorporate?
     Two important reasons for incorporating are special tax advantages and limited liability.

6. The 1980s seemed to be the decade of corporate mergers.
   - What is a merger?
     A merger is the result of two firms forming one company. The three major types of mergers are: vertical mergers, horizontal mergers, and conglomerate mergers.

7. All mergers are not friendly.
   - What is a hostile takeover and how can corporations prevent them?
     A hostile takeover is the unrequested purchase of a company by purchase of the company's stock in the open market. Corporations use a variety of strategies to prevent hostile takeovers including: greenmail, shark repellent, poison pills, golden parachutes, and white knights.

8. To combat the threat of hostile takeovers, some corporations recapture control of the firm internally.
   - What are leveraged buyouts and what does it mean to "take a company private"?
     Leveraged buyouts are attempts by managers and employees to borrow money and purchase the company. Individuals who, together or alone, buy all of the stock for themselves are said to "take the company private."

9. S corporations have some of the advantages of both partnerships and corporations.
   - What are the advantages of S corporations?
     S corporations have the advantages of limited liability (like a corporation) and simpler taxes (like a partnership). In order to qualify for S corporation status, a company must have fewer than 35 stockholders; its stockholders must be individuals or estates and U.S. citizens or permanent residents; the company cannot own more than 80 percent of another corporation; and the company cannot have more than 25 percent of its income derived from passive sources.

10. People who dislike organizations in which owners, managers, workers, and buyers have separate goals often form cooperatives.
    - What is the role of a cooperative?
      Cooperatives are organizations that are owned by members/customers. Some people form cooperatives (FAR-MAR-CO, for example) to give members more economic power than they would have as individuals.

11. One of the latest trends in business is for two or more companies to participate in a joint venture.
    - What is the purpose of joint ventures?
      Joint ventures enable firms to capture new markets by cooperating and sharing investment risk.

5. Describe the process of incorporation.

6. Define and give examples of three types of corporate mergers.

7. Explain how hostile takeovers develop and what strategies companies can use to defend against them.

8. Explain leveraged buyouts and what it means for a company to "go private."

9. Summarize the advantages and disadvantages of Subchapter S corporations.

10. Explain the role of cooperatives.

11. Describe the purpose of joint ventures.

1. If you look around, you will be able to find people who are involved in sole proprietorships, partnerships, and corporations in your area. Since your career depends on such information, spend some time interviewing people from each form of ownership and get their impressions, hints, and warnings. How much does it cost to start? How many hours do they work? What are the specific benefits? Share the results with your class.

2. Contact a publicly owned company (i.e. water company, electric company, or local transportation company). Ask how the manager sees the company as being different from privately owned businesses. Find out how government regulations affect the company.

3. Ever think of starting your own business? What kind of business would it be? Think of a friend(s) who you might want for a partner in the business. List the capital and personal skills you need for the business. Then make separate lists of the capital and personal skills that you might bring and those that your friend(s) might bring. What capital and personal skills do you need, but neither of you have?

4. Look in the *Yellow Pages* and find a cooperative in your community. Visit the cooperative to find out how it was formed, who may belong to it, and how it operates.

5. Get an annual report of a large corporation from the library or by writing the company. What are the firm's annual sales? Net income (profit)? Number of common shareholders? Profit shareholders receive in dividends?

6. Debate the following statement with fellow students: "It is better for a college graduate to go to work for a large corporation than to start his or her own business because the risks are less, the salary is secure, the fringe benefits are ample, and the chances for promotion are good."

PRACTICING MANAGEMENT DECISIONS

CASE ONE   SHOULD COOPERATIVES GO CORPORATE?

The idea of starting a cooperative to meet a social need is not a new one in the United States. The first formal American co-op was organized by Ben Franklin in 1752 and is still operating today. Today, cooperatives usually evolve because some need has not been met by the other three forms of business: proprietorships, partnerships, or corporations. For example, many homes in rural areas are serviced by cooperative telephone and electric co-ops. Back in the 1930s, no one else would provide those services when they were needed for farmers to enjoy the benefits of new technology.

Today, the need is for child care and care of the aged. Because such needs are not being met by traditional organizations or are being offered at too great a cost, new cooperatives are emerging. A group of agricultural leaders in Texas, for example, has started a co-op to meet the special needs of retired people who want small houses with less upkeep, greater security, easy access to health care, shops, and recreational facilities, and so forth.

Similarly, child-care cooperatives are emerging in various places to assist parents in finding a good, reliable place to leave their children as they work. In a child-care cooperative, the parents select a board of directors, help determine what kind of services will be provided, and volunteer in various ways to keep costs down.

Smaller, independent druggists and other small businesses rely on cooperatives to allow them to compete with mass merchandisers. They usually form some kind of co-op wholesale facility where they can get goods for less.

Some of the larger cooperatives, though, are in farming. Names you may be familiar with include Land O' Lakes, Sunkist, Ocean Spray, Blue Diamond, and Welch's. Ocean Spray is a farmer-owned cooperative that is now the number-three juice marketer in the United States. Because of the growth in sales of co-ops such as Ocean Spray, many of the top cooperatives are thinking of selling shares to the public. They would thus become corporations much like the big companies they compete with such as Coca Cola and Beatrice Foods.

DECISION QUESTIONS

1. What are some of the advantages and disadvantages of a cooperative changing to a corporation? What would be the major reason for them to do so?

2. What is the future of cooperatives to provide housing and other services to the elderly? What are some of the differences you would expect to see at a cooperative housing development versus a corporate one?
3. What advantages do you see in the fact that members of a cooperative often volunteer their time to help in the running of the organization?
4. Might farmers lose some control over the production and marketing of their goods if farm cooperatives began going corporate?

Sources: Corie Brown, Mary Pitzer, and Teresa Carson, "Why Farm Co-ops Need Extra Seed Money," *Business Week,* March 21, 1988, p. 96; and "Co-op Is Integral to Business Scene," *The Washington Times,* March 21, 1988, p. B6.

CASE TWO   REVERSING THE TREND: CORPORATIONS BECOME PARTNERSHIPS

One of the bigger drawbacks to the corporate form of organization is double taxation. The corporation pays up to 34 percent on the profits it earns and corporate owners (stockholders) pay taxes on those profits again when they are distributed as dividends. Many people think this is unfair. As a consequence, a new form of partnership called a *master limited partnership* is becoming very popular. A master limited partnership looks much like a corporation in that it acts like a corporation and is traded on the stock exchanges like a corporation, but is taxed like a partnership and thus avoids the corporate income tax. Some well-known names in publicly traded companies include Burger King and the Boston Celtics.

The movement toward public partnerships began in 1981 when a group of oil partnerships were combined to create Apache Petroleum, which began trading on the New York Stock Exchange. The trend grew rapidly when Congress increased the corporate tax rate and lowered the tax rate on individuals. It made sense to switch the organization of a firm from a corporate structure to a publicly traded partnership to lessen the tax rate on owners. There are now about 100 master limited partnerships listed on the major stock exchanges and it is expected that many more will be coming.

Naturally, Congress is watching this trend with interest because the government will lose a lot of revenue if corporations suddenly become partnerships and avoid the corporate tax. It could begin taxing publicly traded partnerships much the same as corporations.

Another way businesses are trying to avoid corporate taxes is by forming S corporations. An S corporation is much like a regular corporation, but profits, whether paid out or retained in the firm, are taxed at the personal rate of the owners, not the corporate rate. An S corporation has several limitations such as the fact that there can be a maximum of 35 shareholders and one common stock. Therefore, only small firms use the S corporation format. In fact, many advisers are counseling against using the S corporation format because the benefits do not outweigh the drawbacks in most cases. For example, a corporation is taxed at only 25 percent on the first $75,000 of income, but individual taxpayers may pay as much as 33 percent on that much income. If you are confused by all this, don't feel alone. Most small businesspeople are just like you and do not understand all the complexities of the income tax codes and the various ways of structuring a business to minimize taxes.

DECISION QUESTIONS

1. Is it ethical, in your view, for a company to restructure itself to become a master limited partnership or an S corporation just to avoid paying corporate income taxes?
2. Master limited partnerships cause many problems for the government because it has to collect taxes from thousands of partners instead of from one corporation; this means that the government loses some control over the process. Should the government lower corporate tax rates to the same as individual tax rates and end the problem?
3. The idea of creating S corporations was to give small-business people the benefit of limited liability as enjoyed by corporations without the corporate tax. Was this a good idea in your view? Why or why not?

4. The government needs to bring in more money to balance the budget. Businesses seem to be doing all they can to avoid paying more taxes and individuals are doing the same. If you were in charge of the government, which would you raise—corporate taxes or taxes on individuals? What if someone told you that corporations don't pay taxes anyhow; rather, we all do in the higher prices corporations charge for products to pay the higher taxes?

Sources: Alan Murray and Monica Langley, "Relatively New Form of Business Structure is Causing Controversy," *The Wall Street Journal,* June 30, 1987, pp. 1 and 14; and Kimberly S. Mahlandt, "Tax Reform and the S Corporation," *University of Baltimore Business Review,* July 1987, pp. 1-6.

LOOKING AHEAD

If you are a little excited about the idea of starting your own business someday, join the crowd. Entrepreneurship is the "in thing" for the near future. Entrepreneurs are starting the new high-tech firms that will be the IBM's and Xerox's of tomorrow. Chapter 5 will discuss such entrepreneurs. Also, you will learn about the response of large corporations to competition from small firms—intrapreneuring, or creating small entrepreneurial areas within the firm.

One area of strong interest today is franchising. Franchising is a way of getting into business with less risk and more certain managerial assistance. Chapter 5 also describes opportunities and pitfalls to watch out for in starting a franchise.

After that, the text will introduce the use of business functions in small business. Later chapters will go into much greater detail about these business functions—marketing, accounting, personnel, finance, and so forth.

ENTREPRENEURSHIP AND FRANCHISING

5

LEARNING GOALS

After you have read and studied this chapter, you should be able to:

1. Define entrepreneurship and name several of the leading entrepreneurs from the past.

2. Explain the difference between a corporate and a small-business entrepreneur.

3. Explain why people are willing to take the risks of entrepreneurship.

4. Describe the attributes needed to be a successful entrepreneur.

5. Describe the entrepreneurs emerging in the 1990s.

6. Compare the benefits of entrepreneurial teams with individual entrepreneurs.

7. Cite the reasons for the growing number of women, immigrants, young people, and minorities in entrepreneurship.

8. Describe intrapreneuring and its benefits for big businesses.

9. Compare the advantages and disadvantages of franchising.

10. Outline the areas that need to be analyzed when evaluating a franchise.

11. Describe the opportunities in franchising.

12. Examine the challenges and opportunities of international franchising.

KEY TERMS

corporate entrepreneurs *p. 135*
entrepreneur *p. 134*
entrepreneurial team *p. 139*
franchise *p. 145*
franchise agreement *p. 145*
franchisee *p. 145*
franchising *p. 145*

franchisor *p. 145*
intrapreneur *p. 143*
skunkworks *p. 143*
small-business entrepreneurs *p. 135*
subfranchising agreement *p. 154*

Joanna Doniger.

If there is one coefficient of entrepreneurial success, it is energy. You may have all the ambition in the world, gobs of capital, a gambling man's soul, and business degrees covering an entire wall, but if you are not a human dynamo, forget it.
JOSEPH R. MANCUSO, in
Have You Got What It Takes?

PROFILE   JOANNA DONIGER

Ever had an important social or business engagement that requires a touch of sophistication in your attire? For years men have enjoyed the opportunity of renting formal wear for those special occasions. Well today, thanks to Joanna Doniger, some women are taking their cues from the opposite sex. At One Night Stand, a shop opened by Doniger in New York, patrons can rent dresses for those special occasions by top designers such as Scaasi, Oscar de la Renta, and Terence Nolder that sell for as much as $5,000.

Doniger came up with the idea a few years ago when she made a dress for a friend and rented it to her. Acting on a hunch that many women don't want to plunk down big bucks for a dress they may only wear once, she decided to take a risk, invest some money, and go for the reward of entrepreneurship. Today, customers are offered a selection of 600 gowns in sizes 4 to 18 for as little as $75 plus a $200 deposit. Customers must return the dresses within three days.

How do the competing shops on fashion-conscious Madison Avenue feel about Doniger's rental bargains? According to Connie Deans, manager of Portantina, which sells handmade velvet and silk evening wear, "A different clientele shops at designer shops than those who rent dresses." "She may be right," admits financial director Stan Berg, "but an average of 150 women per week rent dresses from One Night Stand only after they have made an appointment to view the available stock." He projects annual revenues of $500,000.

As for Doniger, she plans to open five more stores in major U.S. cities in the next year. She also admits to the possibility of selling franchises in a few years.

Source: Joan Delaney, "Dresses Perfect for a One-Night Stand," *Venture,* April 1988, p. 11. Reprinted by permission.

THE IMPORTANCE OF ENTREPRENEURSHIP TO AN ECONOMY

Entrepreneurship is accepting the calculated risk of starting a business to make a profit. At one time, entrepreneurship was not included in the factors of production. Economics texts tended to focus on land, labor, and capital. It became clear over time, however, that a country that had little land and few other natural resources could prosper *if* it had brilliant entrepreneurs. The best examples today are Japan and South Korea. The United States has both natural resources and entrepreneurs, but the success of the United States is more dependent on entrepreneurs than it is on natural resources. An **entrepreneur** is an innovator who organizes, manages, and assumes the risks of starting a business to make a profit.

Entrepreneurs are special people, the driving force behind innovation and growth. Entrepreneurs are not the same as inventors. An entrepreneur *may* invent a product, but he or she also has the ability to develop that invention into a successful business product.

The history of the United States is the history of its entrepreneurs. Consider just a few of the many entrepreneurs who have helped shape the American economy:

> Du Pont was started in 1802 by Eleuthere Irenee du Pont. Some 18 shareholders provided $36,000 in start-up money.

entrepreneur
An innovator who organizes, manages, and assumes the risks of starting a business to make a profit.

- Campbell Soup began in 1869 as a partnership of Joseph Campbell and Abraham Anderson. (We could all be warming ourselves with a steamy bowl of Anderson's Soup.)
- Avon started in 1886 on $500 David McConnell borrowed from a friend.
- Kodak was launched by George Eastman in 1880 with a $3,000 investment.
- Procter & Gamble was formed in 1837 by William Procter and James Gamble with a total of $7,000 in capital.
- Ford Motor Company began with an investment of $28,000 by Henry Ford and 11 associates.

These entrepreneurs left their imprint on U.S. business. An interesting exercise would be to go to the reference section of the library and track the career of any of these successful entrepreneurs. Your research would identify characteristics in those past entrepreneurs that closely approximate modern-day entrepreneurs.

This chapter will examine the implications of entrepreneurship for you and your career. It will also explore the many possibilities of operating a franchise as a career choice. The potential in franchising is particularly impressive. In 1988, there were over 500,000 franchised outlets in the United States selling $640 billion worth of goods and services. Franchising sales accounted for 33 percent of all retail sales in the United States.[1]

When William Procter and James Gamble formed Procter & Gamble they had a single successful product, soap. As customer needs increased, these entrepreneurs grabbed the opportunity to develop other related products. As entrepreneurs, Procter and Gamble played an important role in this country's economy.

Corporate versus Small-Business Entrepreneurship

The definition of an entrepreneur given above applies to *all* people who start a business to make a profit. However, when you read articles about entrepreneurship in magazines such as *Nation's Business, Entrepreneur, Black Enterprise,* and *Inc.,* they are talking mostly about small-business owners and managers. These small-business entrepreneurs are quite different from the entrepreneurs mentioned above: Henry Ford, George Eastman, and the like.

Actually, the term *entrepreneur* has evolved to mean two rather different but related things. It is true that anyone who accepts the risk of starting a small business for profit can and must be considered an entrepreneur. But what do you call a person who has the vision and drive to start and develop a major new business that will go on to employ thousands of people and become a major influence in the economy? Today, we use the same word: *entrepreneur.* The major difference between the two groups is that one group, **small-business entrepreneurs,** is often quite content to start a small business and remain small. The other group has visions of much greater size and scope. Both groups are vital to an economy and both are fascinating to study. For purposes of clarity, however, let's give a new name to those entrepreneurs who take the risk of starting and developing major corporations. Let's call them **corporate entrepreneurs.**

Corporate entrepreneurs, past and present, seem to share characteristics that distinguish them from small-business entrepreneurs:

1. Corporate entrepreneurs may start their business as a small business, but that is not their ultimate goal.
2. Corporate entrepreneurs may begin their organizations as sole proprietorships or partnerships, but eventually most form corporations to get more capital and to expand.
3. Corporate entrepreneurs have vision and drive and are innovators with great leadership ability.

small-business entrepreneurs People who are willing to take the risk of starting small businesses for profit.

corporate entrepreneurs Those entrepreneurs who take the risk of starting and developing a major corporation.

Have you ever tasted Mrs. Fields' cookies? Debbi Fields started her business believing that her home-style cookies were just what we've been waiting for—delicious cookies straight from the oven. This entrepreneur took a risk that paid off.

THE ENTREPRENEURIAL CHALLENGE

The Internal Revenue Service reported in 1988 that 12 million Americans worked for themselves. That's over twice the number recorded in 1970. Why have we experienced such an explosion of entrepreneurs in past two decades? Baumbeck and Mancuso claimed that entrepreneurs were stimulated by achievement itself, rather than money. They felt money was the by-product and scorecard for the accomplishment of goals and achievement.[2] In actuality, it's safe to conclude that there are many reasons why people are willing to take the risks of ownership. The following are some of these reasons.

Profit   Tom Monaghan opened his first pizza store in Ypsilanti, Michigan, near the campus of Eastern Michigan University. He had a hunch that dormitory food probably had the same appeal of food he had eaten in an army mess hall. Today, he rules over Domino's Pizza, the largest pizza delivery company in the world, and has a personal net worth over $600 million. Debbi Fields borrowed money from her husband to open her first Mrs. Fields Cookies store in Palo Alto, California. Today, she has over 650 cookie stores and bakeries with annual sales of nearly $200 million.

Independence   As Baumbeck and Mancuso suggest, many entrepreneurs are not in it for the money. Rather, they simply do not enjoy working for someone else. Ten years ago, money was the lure; today, half of the new owners are more interested in the freedom of ownership.

Opportunity   Many immigrants do not have the necessary skills for working in today's complex organizations. They *do* have the initiative and drive to work the long hours demanded by entrepreneurship. To them, the opportunity to share in the American dream is a tremendous lure. They are willing to sacrifice to see that their children have a chance for a good life. The same is true of many corporate managers who leave the security of the corporate life and try running businesses of their own (see the box Leaving the Corporate Nest).

Challenge   *Venture* magazine concluded that entrepreneurs were excitement junkies who flourished when taking risks, but others disagree. Nancy Flexman and Thomas Scanlan wrote a book called *Running Your Own Business*. They contend that entrepreneurs take moderate, calculated risks; they are not just gambling. In general, though, entrepreneurs seek *achievement* more than *power*.[3]

What Does It Take to Be an Entrepreneur?

Would you succeed as an entrepreneur? You can learn the managerial and leadership skills needed to run a firm. However, you may not have the corporate entrepreneurship personality to assume the risks, take the initiative, create the vision, and rally others to follow your lead. Those traits are harder to learn or acquire. A list of attributes you would look for in yourself includes:[4]

1. *Self-directed.* You should be thoroughly comfortable and thoroughly self-disciplined even though you are your own boss. *You* will be responsible for your success or possible failure.
2. *Self-nurturing.* You must believe in your idea when no one else does, and be able to replenish your own enthusiasm. When Walt Disney suggested the

LEAVING THE CORPORATE NEST

It's safe to assume once a manager builds a niche in a major corporation he or she would never think of leaving the security of corporate life. Right? Wrong! Thousands of salaried Americans decide every year to leave the corporate nest and try running businesses of their own. In addition to these executives who volunteer to fly solo, 17 percent of the executives displaced by corporate mergers and acquisitions choose to start their own companies rather than return to corporate life. Consultant Gary Blake, who advises would-be entrepreneurs, says the principal reasons more and more corporate managers are spreading their own wings and leaving the nest are "dissatisfaction with their present prospects, a need for independence, autonomy and growth, and a feeling they would be willing to make sacrifices to build a business they could enjoy and which would reward them directly."

Dallan Peterson spent 13 years as a corporate employee, rising to head a major division of a national company before he opted for the insecurity of entrepreneurship. "It was like going from renting a house to owning your own home—all of a sudden you see the dandelions in the front yard." Dallan did know about perseverance. After leaving his corporate home as a division manager for a national food company, he had to go into business twice to find lasting success. Despite his first setback with a snack food company, he rejected a return to corporate life. "I had a taste of running my own business and I liked that feeling of 'I did it on my own.'" Peterson then started another business in a brand new field, professional home cleaning. Today, his company, Merry Maids, is the biggest operation of its kind, with franchise operations in 42 states. He also likes to point out that more than half of his 400 franchises are operated by former corporate employees who wanted to get into businesses of their own.

Source: Harry Bacas, "Leaving the Corporate Nest," *Nation's Business,* March 1987, pp. 14–22; and Amy Schulman, "Big-Company Exodus," *Inc.,* September 1988, p. 56.

possibility of a full-length, animated feature film, Snow White, the industry laughed. His personal commitment and enthusiasm caused the Bank of America to back his venture. The rest is history.

3. *Action-oriented.* Great business ideas are not enough. The most important thing is a burning desire to realize, actualize, and build your dream into reality.

4. *High energy level.* It's your business, and you must be emotionally, mentally, and physically able to work long and hard.

5. *Tolerant of uncertainty.* Successful entrepreneurs take only *calculated* risks (if they can help it). Still, they must be able to take some risks. Remember, entrepreneurship is not for the squeamish nor the person bent on security.

If you are interested in seeing if you may have the entrepreneurial spirt in your blood, there is an entrepreneurial test you can take at the end of Part 2 on page 189.

Here is more advice for would-be entrepreneurs to follow:[5]

- Research your market, but do not take too long to act.
- Work for other people first and make your mistakes on their money.
- Start out slowly. Start your business when you have a customer. Maybe try your venture as a sideline at first.
- Set specific objectives, but don't set your goals too high. Remember, there's no easy money.
- Plan your objectives within specific time frames.
- Surround yourself with people who are smarter than yourself—including an accountant and an outside board of directors who are interested in your well-being and who will give you straight answers.
- Do not be afraid to fail.

Do you know anyone who seems to have the entrepreneurial spirit? What about him or her makes you say that? Are there any similarities between the characteristics demanded of an entrepreneur and those of a professional athlete? Would an athlete be a good prospect for entrepreneurship? Why or why not? Could teamwork be important in an entrepreneurial effort?

Entrepreneurs of the 1990s

Entrepreneurship can be learned. Witness the rapid growth of entrepreneurial courses at leading colleges all across the country. Management specialist Peter Drucker feels that in the future people with college training and some corporate experience will do much better as entrepreneurs *in the long run*. Drucker feels this college and corporate training will give the new entrepreneurs certain tools (skills). The more tools you have, the greater your chance for success.

If you want to describe what the entrepreneur of the 1990s will be like, you could not do better than to write the biography of Mary Anne Jackson. Jackson is both an M.B.A. (she has a Masters degree in business) and a C.P.A. (she is certified in public accounting). For eight years, she did financial and strategic planning at Beatrice Companies. Before that, she worked at two leading accounting firms. What is most interesting about Jackson is that she is quite different from the entrepreneurs of the 1980s. They tended to be visionaries who were young, self-made, intuitive, rash, and better at starting a firm and creating excitement about a project than planning, organizing, and controlling. Jackson has strong management as well as leadership skills. (A manager is good at planning, organizing, and controlling while a leader inspires people and brings out the best in them by presenting them with a vision and being a model.)

Mary Anne Jackson used her education and managerial experience to form a successful new business, My Own Meals, Inc. This nutritious food alternative represents carefully designed and implemented research and management skills. Jackson is one of the entrepreneurs of the future.

As a result of a leveraged buyout, Jackson found herself without a job, but with excellent managerial experience. She began looking about for a market opportunity. She surveyed the market and found a great demand for nutritious, quick meals that busy active and working mothers could serve their children. After extensive market research, she determined just what those meals should look like and contracted with experienced firms to make those products. She called them My Own Meals because young people could easily identify with the plastic pouched meals that are popped into a microwave oven or boiled.

The development of My Own Meals, Inc., is a lesson in planning and careful management. Jackson broke the start-up process into 20 separate steps: setting up an office, developing the product, testing the market, and so forth. She implemented those steps in a professional and controlled manner. She also has long-range plans, and growth rates will be strictly controlled. Sales are expected to be $1 million in the first year, $10 million the second, and $60 million in the fifth year.

Entrepreneurs like Mary Anne Jackson are different than the entrepreneurs of the 1980s such as Steve Jobs (Apple Computer), Nolan Bushnell (Atari and Pizza Time), and Bill Gates (Microsoft). Some of the differences between the entrepreneur of the 1980s and the entrepreneur of the future are likely to be:[6]

   - More education. The new entrepreneur is likely to have a business degree or an M.B.A.
   - More experience. Future entrepreneurs are likely to come from major corporations where they learned managerial skills.

- Age. New entrepreneurs will be older since they will be starting their businesses later in life.
- More reliance will be placed on deliberation and considered judgment than on instinct and reflex as in the past.
- More planning, organization, and control will be used and less reliance will be placed on emotion and seat-of-the-pants decision making (that is, reacting to crises as they occur).
- New entrepreneurs will have the same enthusiasm, drive, and leadership ability, but will also have the education and managerial skills to carry out the venture for the long run.

The fact that we can name the successful corporate entrepreneurs from the past indicates that it is not easy to be such a person. It makes sense, does it not, that several people together may have a better chance of having all the skills and experience needed to start a new venture? That is what we shall discuss next.

Entrepreneurial Teams

An **entrepreneurial team** is a group of experienced people from different areas of business who join together to form a managerial team with the skills needed to develop, make, and market a new product. A team may be better than an individual entrepreneur because it combines creative skills with production and marketing skills right from the start. The team assures more cooperation and coordination among functions.

One of the exciting new companies that developed in the 1980s was Compaq Computer.[7] It was started by three senior managers at Texas Instruments: Bill Murto, Jim Harris, and Rod Canion. All three were bitten by the entrepreneurial bug, and decided to go out on their own. They debated starting a Mexican restaurant, a company to produce hard disks for computers, or a business built around a beeping device for finding car keys. However, they finally decided to build a portable personal computer compatible with the IBM PC.

The key to Compaq's success was that it was built around this "smart team" of experienced managers. The chief executive officers in such firms are not order givers, but coordinators whose main task is to tap the potential of their "teams." A study of 90 West Coast companies found that a strong management team was the top priority for success. At Compaq, the team wanted to combine the discipline of a big company with an environment where people could feel they were participating in a successful venture. The trio of corporate entrepreneurs recruited seasoned managers with similar desires. They recruited a 14-year veteran from Texas Instruments to set up a state-of-the-art accounting system. A senior vice president from Datapoint became operations manager, and an IBM veteran became the sales and resource manager.

All the managers work as a team. That is, the company's treasurer and top engineer contribute to production and marketing decisions. Everyone works together to conceive, develop, and market products. In its first year, Compaq generated $11 million in sales, the hottest performance in the history of American business. Compaq's sales soared 95 percent to $1.2 billion, and soon Compaq ranked fifth in *Fortune* magazine's list of the 25 fastest-growing U.S. corporations. The success of Compaq can be traced to its entrepreneurial team.

entrepreneurial team
A group of experienced people from different areas of business who join together to form a managerial team with the skills needed to develop, make, and market new products.

In February 1982, Compaq Computer Corporation was formed. Rod Canion is one of the managers of an entrepreneurial team responsible for forming this new venture. Using the talents of all team members, Compaq has soared to the top of its industry.

- What are the major differences between corporate entrepreneurs and small-business entrepreneurs?
- Can you give five differences between traditional entrepreneurs and those that are emerging in the 1990s?
- What are the advantages of entrepreneurial teams?

ENTREPRENEURIAL OPPORTUNITIES

In the past, small-business entrepreneurs tended to be middle-aged white males who often came from a business background and had a significant amount of capital to invest. Today, other groups have been successfully entering the field. As we noted in Chapter 1, women, minorities, immigrants, and young people have greatly changed the face of entrepreneurship.

No group has taken more advantage of the entrepreneurial spirit than women. They are not just *joining* the labor force; they are the fastest-growing segment of the nation's small-business entrepreneurial explosion. More than 90 percent of these female entrepreneurs are involved in sole proprietorships (small-business entrepreneurs). In fact, the number of female sole proprietors has increased at a rate three times that of men over the past five years.

The Small Business Administration has started an experimental program designed to give women entrepreneurial advice. The Women's Network for Entrepreneurial Training operated initially in California, Illinois, and New York. For example, in California, 12 successful women who run small businesses have volunteered to counsel 12 women who are just starting. They agree to meet once a week for a year until the new business gets started. Similar programs are being started all across the country.[8]

The New Entrepreneur

According to the Census Bureau, the last survey of minority-owned enterprises found almost 850,000 businesses owned by nonwhite persons.[9] African-Americans, Hispanics, Asian-Americans, and Native Americans are expanding their role in the U.S. economy by actively joining the entrepreneurial explosion, especially in small businesses.

Jolyn Robichaux is just one of thousands of successful African-American entrepreneurs. She is president of Baldwin Ice Cream.

ASSISTING FEMALE ENTREPRENEURS

Since 1977, Bea Fitzpatrick has been developing and polishing the skills of female entrepreneurs. Bea is the founder of the American Woman's Economic Development Corporation (AWED), which has provided training, counseling, conferences, and seminars to over 35,000 women from all 50 states and Canada.

She feels the greatest obstacles women entrepreneurs face are the attitudes instilled in them since childhood that they should serve others, not run things. "They think they're supposed to be mothers; the employees think they're supposed to be mothers!" At AWED, we stress it's your responsibility to have a successful business. If you want to make your employees happy, be sure that you can pay them on payday and that you can expand your company so they have careers they can look forward to." For more information about AWED, write AWED, The Lincoln Building, 60 E. 42nd Street, New York, N.Y. 10165

Source: Sharon Nelton, "Polishing Women Entrepreneurs," *Nation's Business*, July 1987.

Minorities like Dr. Anthony Chan are successful entrepreneurs in a variety of businesses. Dr. Chan's business is Chinese food. The name on the label is Xian.

After attaining his law degree, J. Bruce Llewellyn's primary goal was to work his way up into New York City government. Today, Bruce heads the third-largest African-American owned U.S. company, a Coca Cola bottler, Philadelphia Coca-Cola Bottling. He also owns a network-affiliated TV station. Bruce hopes to be the first black to own a major sports franchise.[10]

Hank Aguirre and Remedios Diaz-Oliver are Hispanic-Americans intent on making their mark in today's entrepreneurial-driven economy. Before Hank began pitching baseballs for the Detroit Tigers, he worked in his father's tortilla factory. Today, the ex-Tiger owns a Detroit auto supply firm with annual sales of $17 million. Ms. Diaz-Oliver is a manufacturer of glass containers for soft drinks and pharmaceuticals. She has found a niche in the packaging industry and boasts of being the largest manufacturer of packing materials in Florida.

Ucho Lee left a rather secure future in South Korea to build what he hoped was a better one in the United States. Today, after years of dedicated work, he owns five businesses and three buildings in Boston, as well as a suburban home with tennis courts.[11] He is typical of a growing number of immigrants who are arriving in the United States not to escape political or social oppression, but to fulfill their dreams of entrepreneurship. As their numbers increase, competition will intensify among entrepreneurs in the marketplace.

Like Ucho Lee, many of the new Americans are of Asian ancestry. They bring with them a strong work ethic and a sense of dedication in work endeavors. Over 70 percent of their entrepreneurial efforts are centered in service or retail businesses. More than 9 out of 10 firms operate as sole proprietorships. The Census Bureau reports that over 250,000 firms are now owned by Asian-Americans and the numbers are expected to increase in the future.

Some Native Americans are keeping up with the latest trends in entrepreneurship as well. Melody Lightfeather, for example, is a member of the Pima tribe. She learned beadwork working on moccasins. Today, everyone seems to be wearing tennis shoes, so Ms. Lightfeather began decorating Reebok tennis shoes with handsewn beadwork. Her business quickly grew to $1.5 million a year.

In the end, though, there is no such thing as a Native American entrepreneur or a female entrepreneur in America. There are only American entrepreneurs who are facing the same problems and handling them pretty much in the same way. The opportunities and challenges are about the same. In fact, the challenge is there for you to take, too. In the box called Entrepreneurship in College we discuss the possibility of taking the entrepreneurial plunge while still in school.

PROGRESS CHECK

What are four reasons why people are willing to assume entrepreneurial risks?

What attributes does it take to be an entrepreneur?

ENTREPRENEURSHIP IN COLLEGE

Youthful entrepreneurs have always been a part of the American economy, and today is no exception. All over the United States, young entrepreneurs are building enterprises ranging from line-waiting services to video game development to exporting. Doug Mellinger, national director of the Association of Collegiate Entrepreneurs, reports that entrepreneurs under the age of 30 generated more than $2.5 billion in gross revenues in 1988.

The Association of College Entrepreneurs (ACE) started with 7 member colleges in 1983 and has grown nationwide to about 300 member colleges in 1989. The association also boasts chapters in 35 countries.

Being an entrepreneur while in college is an excellent way to pay for college and begin a career. For example, Jed Roth started a car-cleaning business that earned him $15,000 in his senior year. After graduation, he stayed in the business and soon had revenues of $100,000.

Audie Cashion was typical of many young entrepreneurs who are not afraid to look beyond our national borders. After a summer visit to Japan, he decided to get involved in international trade. His firm exports everything from pickles to Arizona Indian jewelry to Japanese department stores.

Malcolm K. May began selling T-shirts that said "Black By Popular Demand" at Morehouse. He expanded his T-shirt line into other businesses and opened a store near the campus. His 1989 sales were expected to top $200,000. Malcolm is also selling his products at North Carolina A&T, Florida A&M, and Hampton University.

Is there an entrepreneurs' club on your campus? Would you like to start one? Write the Center for Entrepreneurship, Wichita State University, Wichita, Kansas 67208. It is an excellent way for students to learn the secrets of success and failure from other student entrepreneurs.

Nancy L. Croft and Dan Dickinson, "To Be Young and in Business," *Nation's Business,* March 1988; and Linda Williams, "Student Entrepreneurs on Campus," *Black Enterprise,* February 1989, pp. 169–72.

ENTREPRENEURSHIP WITHIN LARGE FIRMS

Entrepreneurship has been so successful in small firms that larger corporations are trying to imitate the results. But how do you create an atmosphere of innovation and daring in a stodgy old firm? The answer is to break away from the traditional tight organization structures and create small, creative entrepreneurial centers where innovative ideas are developed.

The name given to highly innovative, fast-moving entrepreneurial units operating at the fringes of the corporation is **skunkworks.** The term comes from the *L'il Abner* comic strip and was first used at the Lockheed California Company. A man named Clarence L. "Kelly" Johnson organized a division of the company in 1943 to design, build, and test the first tactical jet fighter in the United States—the XP 80.[12] The plane was designed, built, and flown 143 days after the project was started. Johnson's philosophy was, "Do the best possible job in the simplest way, at the cheapest cost, in the quickest time." He handpicked a few good workers, shared his vision, asked for their best, and provided the leadership needed to make the project work. Today, *skunkworks* describes any highly motivated entrepreneurial team in a large corporation that emphasizes innovation. The latest product to come from Lockheed's skunkworks is the "stealth" fighter.[13]

skunkworks
A highly innovative, fast-moving entrepreneurial unit operating at the fringes of a corporation.

Intrapreneuring

Entrepreneurship in a large organization is often reflected in the efforts and achievements of intrapreneurs. An **intrapreneur** is a person with entrepreneurial skills employed in a corporation. The idea is to use a company's existing resources—human, financial, and physical—to launch new products and generate new profits. At 3M Company, for example, managers are expected to come up with at least 25 percent new products for 3M every five years.

Have you seen those yellow Post-it note pads people use to stick messages up on a wall? That product was developed by Art Fry, a 3M employee. He needed a piece of sticky paper so he could mark the pages of a hymnal without the marker

intrapreneur
A person with entrepreneurial skills who is employed in a corporation to launch new products; such people take hands-on responsibility for creating innovation of any kind in an organization.

The Air Force's newest operational stealth fighter, the F-117A, was built by Lockheed Corporation in California. This fighter is another project developed from Lockheed's skunkworks team. The Air Force has already purchased five of these aircraft, and seven more are currently in production.

Intrapreneurs such as Art Fry develop new products for the corporations that employ them. One product, the Post-it note pads, are widely used by people in business and academic settings. The development of this product generated new profits for the 3M Company.

falling out. The 3M labs soon produced a sample, but distributors thought the product was silly, and market surveys were negative. Nonetheless, 3M kept sending samples to secretaries of top executives. Eventually, after 12 years, the orders began pouring in, and Post-its became a $12 million winner.

Hewlett-Packard calls their entrepreneurial approach the Triad Development Process. The idea is to link the design engineer, the manufacturer, and the marketer (the Triad) in a team from the design phase on. Everything, even the assembly line, shuts down if the Triad team wants to test an innovation.

Some business schools are now teaching courses on how big corporations can develop new products and adapt to changing markets by using intrapreneuring. Many of you who seek the security of a large corporation but worry about a lack of creativity might focus your future toward intrepreneurship. The first school for intrapreneurs was started in Sweden in 1980 by the Foresight Group. They now have a similar school in the United States.

Advantages of Intrapreneuring

Do the benefits of entrepreneurship outweigh the benefits of intrapreneurship? That's a decision you would have to make yourself. However, as you might suspect, there are certain advantages of working as an intrapreneur within an organization. Several advantages of intrapreneuring include:

- *Employee morale*. It is fun and exciting to be able to work on your own products with much freedom.
- *Marketing clout*. P. D. Estridge developed a good personal computer, but it was infinitely more attractive with the IBM name on it.
- *Technology base*. The research laboratories at major corporations have everything one needs to launch a product.
- *Financial backing*. An obvious point, but entrepreneurs can find much venture capital, too, *outside of major firms*.
- *People to help*. Some of the best minds are already in corporations where they can be of great help.
- *Information resources*. It is expensive to set up the complex computer systems that are already available in major firms.

Would You Make a Good Intrapreneur?

Well, would you? If you are interested in this subject, a good book to read is Gifford Pinchot's *Intrapreneuring* (New York: Harper & Row, 1985). Pinchot defines an intrapreneur as:

Any of the "dreamers who do." Those who take hands-on responsibility for creating innovation of any kind within the organization. The intrapreneur may be the creator or inventor but is always the dreamer who figures out how to turn an idea into a profitable reality.

Another interesting piece about intrapreneuring appears in the February 1989 issue of *Black Enterprise*. The author explores three forms of intrapreneuring: (1) establishing an entirely new entity to handle short-term projects, (2) stimulating and devising new services, and (3) creating an entirely new division for a new product.[14]

A familiar intrapreneur cited by Pinchot is Lee Iacocca. In the 1960s, Mr. Iacocca set his mind to producing a new, innovative car for the market. However, he knew the perfect car would not just fall in his lap. What Mr. Iacocca did was put together a team from sources both inside and outside the Ford Motor Company. His team met at a location beyond the corporate boundaries to avoid any type of interference from inside the company. The end result of this intrapreneurial venture was the development of the Ford Mustang. Of course, Iacocca went on to great success at Chrysler.

- What are skunkworks and how did they get started?   **PROGRESS CHECK**

- What are some advantages of being an entrepreneur within a large firm (intrapreneuring)?

FRANCHISING

Not everyone is cut out to be an entrepreneur, or an intrapreneur, either. The personality called for is that of a risk taker and innovator. Some people are more cautious or simply want more assurance of success. For them, there is a vastly different strategy for operating a business; that is the opportunity of franchising. Business students often mistakenly identify franchising as an industry. **Franchising** is not an industry but a method of distributing a product or service, or both, to achieve a maximum market impact with a minimum amount of investment.

Entrepreneurship and franchising are actually complementary processes. Entrepreneurs develop ideas and build a winning product that they offer to share through a franchise agreement. Basically, a **franchise agreement** is nothing more than an arrangement whereby someone with a good idea for a business (the **franchisor**) sells the rights to use the business name and sell a product or service (the **franchise**) to others (the **franchisee**) in a given territory. As you might suspect, both franchisors and franchisees have a stake in securing the success of the franchise. This mutual reliance caused the number of franchise outlets to grow to over 500,000 in 1988 with sales of over $640 billion. With about one out of every three retailers now operating as a franchise, you shouldn't have much difficulty finding places to visit where you can get more information from franchise owners/managers.

Advantages of Franchises

Franchising has penetrated every aspect of American and global business life by offering products and services that are reliable, convenient, and cost effective. Richard Ashman, chairman of the International Franchise Association headquartered in Washington, D.C., probably put it best when he commented, "You name it and there is a good chance that someone out there is franchising it."[15] Obviously, the growth experienced in franchising throughout the world could not have been accomplished by accident. Franchising clearly has many advantages. The following are some of these advantages.

franchising
A method of distributing a product or service, or both, to achieve a maximum market impact with a minimum amount of investment.

franchise agreement
An arrangement whereby someone with a good idea for a business sells the rights to use the business name and sell its products or services to others in a given territory.

franchisor
A company that develops a product concept and sells others the rights to make and sell the products.

franchise
The right to use a specific business's name and sell its products or services in a given territory.

franchisee
A person who buys a franchise.

I was 66 years old, I still had to make a living. I looked at my social security check of $105 and decided to use that to try to franchise my chicken recipe. Folks had always liked my chicken.
COLONEL HARLAND SANDERS

Management Assistance   A franchisee (the person who buys a franchise) has a much greater chance of succeeding in business because he or she has an established product (for example, McDonald's hamburgers), help with choosing a location and promotion, and assistance in all phases of operation. It is like having your own store with full-time consultants available when you need them. Furthermore, you have a whole network of peers who are facing similar problems who can share their experiences with you.

Personal Ownership   A franchise operation is still *your* store and you enjoy much of the freedom, incentives, and profit of any sole proprietor. You are still your own boss, although you must follow more rules, regulations, and procedures than you would with your own privately owned store.

Nationally Recognized Name   It is one thing to open a new hamburger outlet or ice cream store. It is quite another to open a new Burger King or a Baskin-Robbins ice cream shop. With an established franchise, you get instant recognition and support from a product group with established customers from around the world.

Financial Advice and Assistance   A major problem with small businesses is arranging financing and learning to keep good records. Franchisees get valuable assistance in these areas and periodic advice from people with expertise in these areas. In fact, some franchisors will even provide financing to potential franchisees they feel will be valuable parts of the franchise system. One quarter of *Entrepreneur* magazines's top 500 franchisers offer some sort of direct financing.[16]

Disadvantages of Franchises

It almost sounds like the potential of franchising is too good to be true. Indeed there *are* costs associated with joining a franchise that must be considered. You must be sure to check out any such arrangement with present franchisees and possibly discuss the idea with a lawyer. The following are some disadvantages of franchises.

Large Start-Up Costs   Most franchises will demand a fee to just obtain the rights to the franchise. Fees for franchises can vary considerably. See Figures 5–1 and 5–2 to get a feel for the range of investment required to involve yourself in franchising.

Shared Profit   The franchisor often demands a large share of the profits, or a percentage commission based on *sales,* not profit. This share demanded by the franchisor is generally referred to as a *royalty.* Often, the share taken by the franchisor is so high that the owner does not make a profit that matches the time and effort involved in owning and managing a business. For example, the Southland Corporation, franchisors of 7-Eleven stores, insists on a 57 percent share of the gross profit earned by its franchisees. In some areas, the expense of this royalty is causing 7-Eleven franchisees to lose their stores. The royalty demanded by a franchisor is an important factor to consider in your involvement in a franchise.

Management regulation Management assistance has a way of becoming managerial orders, directives, and limitations. Franchisees may feel burdened by the company's rules and regulations and lose the spirit and incentive of being their own boss with their own business. See Figure 5–3 below for a summary of benefits and drawbacks in franchising.

COMPANY	START-UP COST AND FRANCHISE FEE
1. Hampton Inn	$2,300,000
2. Quality Inns International	1,900,000
3. Econo Lodge	1,800,000
4. Hardee's	433,000
5. Roy Rogers	396,000
6. McDonald's	363,000
7. Ponderosa Steakhouses	342,000
8. Jack in the Box	331,000
9. Round Table Pizza	322,000
10. Super 8 Motels	320,000

Source: Harriet C. Johnson, "Special Report: Doing Business the Franchising Way," *USA Today*, February 11, 1988, p. 8B.

FIGURE 5–1

Ten most expensive franchises.
Note that they are largely fast food establishments and motels. The land and locations are the biggest expense items.

COMPANY	START-UP COST AND FRANCHISE FEE
1. Packy the Shipper	$ 995
2. Novus Windshield Repair	2,000
3. Sunshine Polishing System	2,675
4. Coverall	4,200
5. Stork News	5,000
6. Chem-Dry	9,000
7. Coustic-Glo	11,250
8. Jani-King	13,500
9. Duraclean	16,800
10. Video Data Services	16,950

Source: Harriet C. Johnson, "Special Report: Doing Business the Franchising Way," *USA Today*, February 11, 1988, p. 8B.

FIGURE 5–2

Ten least expensive franchises.
One costs less than $1,000. As you can see, virtually anyone can get into franchising if they want.

BENEFITS	DRAWBACKS
▪ Nationally recognized name and established reputation	▪ High initial franchise fee
▪ Help with finding a good location	▪ Additional fees may be charged for marketing
▪ A proven management system	▪ A monthly percentage of gross sales may go to the franchisor
▪ Tested methods for inventory and operations management	▪ Possible competition from other nearby franchisees
▪ Financial advice and assistance	▪ No freedom to select decor or other design features
▪ Training in all phases of operation	▪ Little freedom to determine management procedures
▪ Promotional assistance	▪ Many rules and regulations to follow
▪ Periodic management counseling	
▪ Proven record of success	
▪ It's your business!	

FIGURE 5–3

Additional benefits and drawbacks of franchising. The start-up fees and monthly fees can be killers. Ask around. Don't be shy. This is the time to learn about opportunities and risks.

Taco Bell is part of Pepsico. It has about 2,712 restaurants and has about 60 percent of the Mexican fast-food market. Del Taco and Naugles merged recently and hope to challenge Taco Bell for market leadership, but they have only 366 restaurants now.

Coattail effects   What happens to your franchise if fellow franchisees fail? Quite possibly you could be forced out of business even if your particular franchise were profitable. This is often referred to as a coattail effect. The actions of other franchisees clearly have an impact on your future growth and level of profitability. Remember, franchising is a team effort. If you play with a bad team, chances are you will lose.

Buying a Franchise

As we have seen, there are many advantages *and* disadvantages that need to be explored before buying a franchise. Nonetheless, it *is* an excellent way to enter business as an owner or a manager and make a nice salary plus profit.

A good source of information about franchise possibilities is available from Franchise Watchdog in Burlington, Vermont. It compares what franchisors have to offer, including fees and support services, and also rates franchisors by sampling franchisees.

Be careful of franchises that grow too fast, however. For example, Jiffy Lube opened 1,020 units in 45 states and 6 countries in just 8 years. Early in 1989, the company went into default on $125 million in loans.[17] Be sure to check out the financial strength of a company before you get involved.

There are many things to do before jumping into a franchise. The box Checklist for Evaluating a Franchise points out that you should have a lawyer evaluate the franchise. Remember, you are making a sizable financial investment. Furthermore, you have to analyze yourself, the franchise, and the market. Take some time to go over the checklist; it will help you understand many of the questions that franchisees should ask if they want a successful venture.

THINKING IT THROUGH   Is it fair to say that franchisees have the true entrepreneurial spirit? Can you think of any possible franchise opportunities that may grow in the future? What about the future of franchising? Continued growth or a gradual slow down? Could you see yourself as a franchisee or franchisor? Which one?

McDonald's is the number one food franchiser in America. About 2,000 people apply for a franchise each year, but only about 150 get one. The average sales per unit is $1,600,000. Number two, Burger King, averages just $984,000. There are about 2,000 McDonald's franchises in the United States.

CHECKLIST FOR EVALUATING A FRANCHISE

THE FRANCHISE

- Did your lawyer approve the franchise contract you are considering after he or she studied it paragraph by paragraph?
- Does the franchise give you an exclusive territory for the length of the franchise?
- Under what circumstances can you terminate the franchise contract and at what cost to you?
- If you sell your franchise, will you be compensated for your goodwill?
- If the franchisor sells the company, will your investment be protected?

THE FRANCHISOR

- How many years has the firm offering you a franchise been in operation?
- Has it a reputation for honesty and fair dealing among the local firms holding its franchise?
- Has the franchisor shown you any certified figures indicating exact net profits of one or more going firms that you personally checked yourself with the franchisee?
- Will the firm assist you with:
  A management training program?
  An employee training program?
  A public relations program?
  Capital?
  Credit?
  Merchandising ideas?
- Will the firm help you find a good location for your new business?

- Has the franchisor investigated you carefully enough to assure itself that you can successfully operate one of its franchises at a profit to both the franchisor and you?

YOU—THE FRANCHISEE

- How much equity capital will you have to have to purchase the franchise and operate it until your income equals your expenses?
- Does the franchisor offer financing for a portion of the franchising fees? On what terms?
- Are you prepared to give up some independence of action to secure the advantages offered by the franchise?
- Are you ready to spend much or all of the remainder of your business life with this franchisor, offering its product or service to your public?

YOUR MARKET

- Have you made any study to determine whether the product or service that you propose to sell under franchise has a market in your territory at the prices you will have to charge?
- Will the population in the territory given you increase, remain static, or decrease over the next five years?
- Will the product or service you are considering be in greater demand, about the same, or less demand five years from now than today?
- What competition exists in your territory already for the product or service you contemplate selling?

Source: *Franchise Opportunities Handbook*, U.S. Department of Commerce.

Franchising Opportunities

To say that opportunities abound in franchising would be an understatement. Franchisors are finding it easier to enter the market than in the past. Service and convenience have been two key buzzwords. Give people what they want *fast* and business seems to follow. Minimizing the risk of starting a small business is an important factor in attracting new franchises. After five years, 92 percent of new franchises are still in operation compared to only 23 percent of independently owned businesses. It's not surprising that according to Commerce Department figures, employment in franchising topped 7 million in 1988. That's 6.3 percent of the U.S. work force.

Who will be the new franchisees entering the market during the next 20 years? Possibly many of you reading this textbook! Also there's a strong likelihood that women and minorities will assume a much larger role in franchising than they have in the past.

Franchising of Services

You learned in Chapter 1 that future growth in business is most likely to happen in service industries. It makes sense, therefore, that many of the opportunities of the future will be in service franchising. In fact, service franchises are booming. For example, Mail Boxes ETC is a San Diego–based franchise that offers 26 different postal, business support, and communications services. It has 800 units nationwide and expects to grow quickly in international markets, especially with facsimile transmissions and telex. It had a 60 percent increase in systemwide sales in 1988 alone.

Commercial cleaners are also doing well. Jani-King from Dallas has 1,322 units in its system. Revenues rose about 23 percent in 1988. Other service franchises match buyers and sellers of services for businesses and consumers.[18]

Women in Franchising

Neither the U.S. Commerce Department nor the International Franchise Association has been able to pinpoint the exact number of women active in franchising. Estimates are that approximately 11 percent of all franchise units are owned by women. Only one thing is certain, the number is extremely low. This raises an interesting point for us to consider. As you have learned, women entrepreneurs are increasing at a rate three times faster than that of men. Why the shortage of females in franchising?

One suggestion is that most franchisors are not certain how to reach this potentially large market. Another is that women have difficulty obtaining the rather substantial start-up capital often needed to purchase a franchise. Both of these factors are expected to change as more franchises enter the market and more women enter into franchise agreements. Susan Kezios, president of Women in Franchising, Inc., estimates that potentially 80,000 women could be involved in franchising. She agrees that women have been most involved with specific types of franchises (see Figure 5-4) but expects this to change. A national seminar series entitled Franchising for Women is anticipated to bring more women into the competitive world of franchising.[19]

MAKING ETHICAL DECISIONS

You are the franchisor of a chain of Italian restaurants called The Pasta Connection. As part of the franchise agreement, you have the option of renewing the agreements with the franchisees of your restaurants every 10 years. If for some reason you feel the franchise agreement should not be renewed, your only obligation is to give six-months termination notice before the current franchise agreement expires. At one particular franchise, things have gone exceptionally well. As a matter of fact, the profits from this restaurant far exceed your other franchises. Your attorney has informed you that the franchise agreement at this operation expires in eight months. All you would have to do is inform the franchisee that you have decided not to extend the agreement for another 10 years and the franchise becomes yours alone. What would you do? How do you justify your decision? What might be the consequences of a decision to terminate the agreement?

1. 80%—Diet/figure/health	12. 6%—Clothing/shoes
2. 75%—Home furnishings	13. 5%—Printing
3. 33%—Recreation/entertain-ment/sports	14. 4%—Pizza
4. 25%—Education/personal development	15. 3%—Retail: specialty foods 3%—Miscellaneous restaurants 3%—Nonfood retail: computer/video
5. 22%—Employment/personnel	
6. 20%—Books/art services	3%—Miscellaneous retail
7. 19%—Business/financial services	16. 2%—Hamburger
8. 14%—Beauty	17. 1%—Automotive
9. 9%—Miscellaneous services	18. 1%—Construction/remodeling
10. 8%—Pastry/ice cream/yogurt	
11. 7%—Maintenance/cleaning	

FIGURE 5–4

Industry ranking of women-owned franchises.
The percentages refer to the percent of women owning such franchises. These figures are likely to change soon as more and more women discover the benefits of franchising.

Source: Reprinted with permission, *Inc.,* magazine (April 1988). Copyright © 1988 by *Inc.* Publishing Company, 38 Commercial Wharf, Boston, MA 02110.

Minority Franchising

Franchising opportunities seem perfectly attuned to the needs of aspiring minority businesspersons. As you will recall, benefits of franchising can include training, financing, and marketing expertise—all important factors that help in reducing the risk of business failure in the market. Why have minorities, like women, lagged in entering this potentially lucrative business field? That's a question that has nagged Earl Graves, editor of *Black Enterprise* magazine. "Entering the franchise arena makes perfect sense for black entrepreneurs. For one thing, more black Americans would be part of an emerging business sector as the American economy continues its shift from manufacturing to service industries."[20] As Figure 5–5 indicates, of the top 10 franchises held by African-Americans, 7 out of 10 are in fast foods. You can also see that the number of Afro-American units are a very small percentage of the total franchise units available (see page 152).

FIGURE 5–5   African-American top 17 franchises

RANK	COMPANY	LOCATION	TYPE	BLACK UNITS	TOTAL UNITS	START-UP COSTS
1.	McDonald's Corporation	Oak Brook, IL	Fast food	365	5,550	$350,000
2.	Popeye's Famous Fried Chicken and Biscuits, Inc.	Jefferson, LA	Fast food	195	650	$225,000
3.	Burger King Corporation	Miami, FL	Fast food	161	3,982	$290,000–$375,000
4.	Kentucky Fried Chicken Corporation	Louisville, KY	Fast food	96	4,700	$620,000–$820,000
5.	Wendy's International, Inc.	Dublin, OH	Fast food	59	2,434	$750,000–$1,300,000
6.	Church's Fried Chicken, Inc.	San Antonio, TX	Fast food	57	450	$300,000–$350,000
7.	Century 21 Real Estate Corporation	Irvine, CA	Real estate	50	6,200	$9,000–$15,000
8.	International Dairy Queen, Inc.	Bloomington, MN	Ice cream shop	50	4,900	$30,000
9.	Subway Sandwiches & Salads	Milford, CT	Fast food	50	1,285	$29,900–$60,000
10.	Abraham & London Ltd.	Chatsworth, CA	Personnel agency	40	400	$8,000
11.	Hallmark Cards, Inc.	Kansas City, MO	Card shop	40	7,000	$55,000
12.	Goodyear Tire & Rubber Company	Akron, OH	Tire company	35	600	$50,000–$100,000
13.	Mister Softee, Inc.	Runnemede, NJ	Ice cream shop	28	800	$22,000–$25,000
14.	Baskin-Robbins, Inc.	Glendale, CA	Ice cream shop	24	3,400	$100,000–$165,000
15.	Dollar Rent-A-Car Systems, Inc.	Los Angeles, CA	Car rental	22	450	$50,000
16.	Meineke Discount Muffler Shops, Inc.	Houston, TX	Auto care	20	860	$48,500
17.	Servpro Industries, Inc.	Rancho Cordova, CA	Cleaning and restoration	12	640	$30,000

CHINA IN THE FAST LANE

No more Peking Duck. The word is *haodao yun shouzhi*. You see Kende-ji jia-xiang-ji (Kentucky Fried Chicken) has opened China's first fast-food restaurant. "Haodao yun shouzhi" is the chinese version of "finger-licken' good." It translates into "so good you suck your fingers."

The $1.1 million, 500-seat outlet is the largest restaurant this worldwide franchise chain currently operates. Ironically, the store is located across from the mausoleum of Mao Tse-tung who scorned Western culture as dec-adent. The company estimates that it serves approximately 3,000 customers per day.

In a nation as large as China and a city as populated as Beijing, does the company run the risk of being overrun with too many customers? Not likely. A two-piece chicken meal and small soft-drink costs 7.60 Chinese yuan, or $2.05—two days' pay for restaurant workers. A Chinese factory worker could easily eat up his or her wages of $27 per month with dinner for a family of three.

Source: USA Today, "Fast Times for China," *USA Today*, November 13–15, 1987, p. 1A; Daniel Southerland, "Capitalist Chicken Goes to Beijing, *The Washington Post*, November 13, 1987, pp. F1–4; and Mario Shao, "Laying the Foundation for the Great Mall of China," *Business Week*, January 25, 1988, pp. 68–69.

One specific reason why more minorities have not entered the franchising field relates to the problem of finding access to capital. Start-up fees for many franchises can be very costly and lenders have not been too cooperative in promoting minority involvement. This concern has prompted several franchisors such as Burger King and Southland Corporation to enter into voluntary agreements to increase the number of minorities in their franchise systems. One franchisor, Jiffy Lube, established a six-person commission to identify potential minority franchisees and provide them with special financing packages. Continued efforts such as these should help increase the number of franchises owned and operated by minorities.

Franchising in International Markets

By now you are aware of the tremendous attraction the global market has exerted on business. This attraction has certainly carried over into the area of franchising. Today, American franchisors are counting their profits in pesos, lira, francs, won, deutsch marks, krona, bahts, yen, and many other global currencies. Anyone who has traveled overseas knows that large franchisors such as McDonald's, Holiday Inns, and Hertz have many franchises in foreign nations (see the box China in the Fast Lane). In fact, even if you have not traveled to foreign lands, you are probably aware of franchisors' expansion to overseas markets. According to the U.S. Department of Commerce, roughly one in four franchised businesses today has international facilities or planned to have them available by now. Which is the most popular international market for U.S. franchisors? Canada is by far the most popular target, with Japan ranking second. Today, the most dynamic area of growth for large franchisors is the region of the Pacific Rim. Even though franchisors find the costs of franchising high in these markets, the costs are counterbalanced by less competition and a rapidly expanding consumer base.[21]

Starting a franchise in a Pacific Rim country is not always as easy as it seems at first. For example, Jay Tunney was asked to be a franchisee of Hobson's ice cream in South Korea. The first rules he learned were that he had to make his ice cream in South Korea and he had to take on a Korean partner with at least a 24 percent stake in the company. He managed those rules with little problem. But the local customers found his ice cream expensive and foreigners are not terribly welcome in Korea. The drop in the value of U.S. currency made the purchase of South Korean won more expensive. One dollar only buys 670 won when two years ago it bought 890 won. Through all the trials, Jay held on and learned as much as he could about Korean culture. He encourages U.S. franchisees to learn about foreign markets and the U.S. government to do more to help.[22]

There was a big celebration when Kentucky Fried Chicken came to Beijing (Peking), China. Notice the upper floors where people can sit and eat. This restaurant was closed during the student unrest, but opened soon after.

The Challenge of International Franchising

Franchising in international markets clearly takes time. The explosive growth of franchising in the United States has not been duplicated in most overseas markets. Caution is also a keyword to keep in mind when evaluating international opportunities. Kenneth Franklin, president of Franchise Developments, Inc., advises, "A franchise concept that works well in the U.S. may not successfully transfer into another culture [see the box called The Fish that Drowned]. Keeping someone on-site is now an important part of the franchisor's effort." Therefore, to protect their interests in many overseas markets, franchisors often make use of a subfranchising agreement.

subfranchising agreement
Agreement that gives the right to a principal living in a foreign market to oversee franchise operations in that market.

A **subfranchising agreement** gives the right to a principal living in a foreign market to oversee franchise operations in that market. Can principals sell franchises or revoke franchise agreements? Yes they can! Dunkin Donuts, a franchisor with over 1,600 franchises overseas, uses a subfranchising agreement. According to the company, this type of agreement provides incentive to both sides to perform their expected roles.[23] We will discuss in more depth the challenges of the international market in Chapter 24.

Opportunities in International Franchising

Are the major opportunities in international franchising available only to large franchise systems? Absolutely not! If you travel overseas today, you will find that newer, smaller franchises are going international as well. Smaller franchises such as Postal Instant Press (PIP), Budget Rent-a-car, Servicemaster, and Duraclean have all ventured into the international market. Video Update, Inc., a franchisor of video rental stores, recently licensed a joint venture in Malaysia to open 100 Video Update stores. A similar venture is being negotiated for Singapore. What makes franchising successful in international markets is what makes it successful in the United States: convenience and a predictable level of service and quality.

Now you can go to Osaka, Japan, and visit Studebaker's, a restaurant and bar franchise that features American songs from the 1950s and 1960s. A Wurlitzer jukebox plays the "hully gully" and the "bunny hop" while waitresses in 1950s dress serve the food and beverages. There are 542 McDonald's stores in Japan as well.

Many franchises are being solicited by potential overseas franchisees. That is what lured Gymboree, a franchisor of children's gym centers, to Spain, France, Japan, and South Korea.

Remember though, franchisors must be careful to adapt to the region. In France, the people thought a furniture stripping place called Dip 'N' Strip was a bar that featured strippers. In general, however, U.S. franchises are doing well all over the world and are adapting to the local customs and desires of consumers.[24]

PROGRESS CHECK

- Which kinds of products/services have the most franchised outlets?

- This chapter lists 10 benefits of a franchise and 7 drawbacks. How many do you recall?

- What is a subfranchising agreement? Why is such an agreement often helpful in international markets?

THE FISH THAT DROWNED

Long John Silver's operates close to 1,500 seafood restaurants in the United States. The company also has franchises in Canada and Singapore. When they received an unsolicited offer from a group of Japanese businessmen to bring their concept into Japan, they jumped at the chance. However, after six long, frustrating years, the company finally pulled the plug on its operation.

The company had sold subfranchising rights to its foreign principals. Company officials admit their Japanese partners remained conscientious until the end. Nonetheless, the partnership could still not make the company competitive. What happened?

The cost of obtaining real estate is a tremendous headache in Japan. Company vice president Gene Getchell said,

"Just for the privilege of getting some land, you often have to know the right people or grease the right wheels. There's sometimes an up-front fee for merely obtaining a lease." Distribution also created a major problem. "The roads in the U.S. are fairly standardized. In Japan, the roads are like spaghetti and the distribution system has many layers. Sometimes you can reach a store by truck, other times you need to haul supplies by handcart." Local palates also didn't seem to relish the taste of the product.

"I don't get it. I suspect if we knew everything we did wrong, maybe we would still be operating in Japan," lamented Getchell.

Source: John F. Persinos, "New Worlds to Franchise," *Venture,* November 1987, pp. 50–52.

SUMMARY

1. An *entrepreneur* is an innovator who organizes, manages, and assumes the risks of starting a business to make a profit.
   - Who are some of the leading entrepreneurs of the past?
     E. I. du Pont, Henry Ford, William Procter, and Joseph Campbell were all entrepreneurs who started companies that have grown into corporate giants.

1. Define entrepreneurship and name several of the leading entrepreneurs from the past.

2. A corporate entrepreneur is one who takes the risk of starting and developing a major corporation. A small-business entrepreneur is a person who is willing to undertake the risk of starting and managing a small business, but is not necessarily aiming at expanding and growing into a major corporation.
   - How do corporate entrepreneurs differ from small-business entrepreneurs?
     They may start with small businesses, but that is not their ultimate goal; their firms usually become corporations to get more capital and expand; and they have vision, drive, and great leadership ability.

2. Explain the difference between a corporate and a small-business entrepreneur.

3. There are many reasons why people are willing to take the risks of entrepreneurship.
   - What are a few of the reasons people start their own businesses?
     Reasons include profit, independence, opportunity, and challenge.

3. Explain why people are willing to take the risks of entrepreneurship.

4. Successful entrepreneurship takes a special kind of person.
   - What does it take to be an entrepreneur?
     A person must be self-directed, self-nurtured, action-oriented, tolerant of uncertainty, and have a high energy level.

4. Describe the attributes needed to be a successful entrepreneur.

5. The emerging entrepreneurs of the 1990s share many of the attributes of past entrepreneurs, but they have additional skills as well.
   - How would you describe the entrepreneurs emerging in the 1990s?
     The emerging entrepreneurs of the 1990s are better educated, more experienced, and more deliberate. They will have the same enthusiasm, drive, and leadership ability as past entrepreneurs, but will also have more judgment and managerial skills.

5. Describe the entrepreneurs emerging in the 1990s.

6. Compare the benefits of entrepreneurial teams with individual entrepreneurs.

6. Individual entrepreneurs have sometimes failed to maintain leadership of their firms.

   ▪ What have modern entrepreneurs done to assure longer terms of management?

   They have formed *entrepreneurial teams* that have expertise in the many different skills needed to start and manage a business.

7. Cite the reasons for the growing number of women, immigrants, young people, and minorities in entrepreneurship.

7. Women, immigrants, young people, and minorities are especially attracted to entrepreneurship.

   ▪ Why these groups?

   Entrepreneurship enables a person to grow to his or her potential. Sexism, racism, and other forms of discrimination cannot hold an entrepreneur down.

8. Describe skunkworks and intrapreneuring and their benefits for big businesses.

8. *Intrapreneuring* is big business's answer to the entrepreneur.

   ▪ What is intrapreneuring?

   It is the establishment of entrepreneurial centers within a larger firm where people can innovate and develop new product ideas internally.

   ▪ Are there successful intrapreneurs?

   Sure. For example, P. O. Estridge developed the IBM Personal Computer, and Lee Iacocca was the intrapreneur behind the Ford Mustang.

9. A person can participate in the entrepreneurial age by buying the rights to market a new product innovation in his or her area.

9. Compare the advantages and disadvantages of franchising.

   ▪ What is this arrangement called?

   A franchise is an arrangement to buy the rights to use the business name and sell its products or services in a given territory.

   ▪ What is a franchisee?

   A *franchisee* is a person who buys a franchise.

   ▪ What are the benefits and drawbacks of being a franchisee?

   The benefits include a nationally recognized name and reputation, a proven management system, promotional assistance, and the pride of ownership. Drawbacks include high franchise fees, managerial regulation, shared profits, and transfer of adverse effects if other franchisees fail.

10. Outline the areas that need to be analyzed when evaluating a franchise.

10. One should not jump blindly into franchise ownership.

   ▪ What areas should be analyzed when evaluating a franchise?

   Before you buy a franchise you should analyze yourself, the franchise, the franchisor, and the market.

11. Describe the opportunities in franchising.

11. Franchises have a much higher survival rate compared to other new businesses.

   ▪ If franchises offer a reduced risk of business failure, why are there so few women and minority franchisees?

   Both women and minorities have trouble getting the large start-up capital needed to purchase a franchise. This may change as more franchises enter the market and as more franchisors actively seek women and minority franchisees.

12. Examine the challenges and opportunities of international franchising.

12. Franchises are not limited to the United States. One in four franchised businesses has international facilities.

   ▪ What is the major challenge to international franchises?

   It is often difficult to transfer an idea or product that worked well in the United States to another culture. It is essential to adapt to the region. Franchisors often use subfranchising agreements to ensure that someone is on-site to look after the franchisor's interests in foreign markets.

1. Go to the library and find past issues of *Entrepreneur, Venture,* and *Inc.* magazines. Read about the entrepreneurs who are heading today's dynamic new businesses. Have several students in the class write profiles about various entrepreneurs and report to the class. A wonderful source is David Silver's *Entrepreneurial Megabucks.* It has profiles of 100 entrepreneurs from the last 25 years.

2. While at the library, go to the reference section and find the *Franchise Opportunities Handbook* or a similar listing of franchise opportunities. Glance through the listings looking for the cost of a franchise, the variety of franchises available, and other interesting information. If several people each write down two entries, the class will have enough information to give them a good feel for franchising opportunities.

3. Visit a franchise other than a fast-food restaurant and see what the owner has to say about the benefits and drawbacks of franchising. Would they buy the franchise again if they could start all over? What mistakes did they make, if any? What advice would they give a student interested in franchising?

4. Research as many franchise possibilities as you can find and write a brief report (two pages) on the one you find most attractive. Include the cost of obtaining the franchise, the training provided, the nature of the business, and other details. Put all the reports in a binder and make it available to the class.

GETTING INVOLVED

CASE ONE   3M COMPANY, INTRAPRENEURIAL LEADER

PRACTICING MANAGEMENT DECISIONS

This year the 3M Company will sell about 90,000 different products from 45 separate divisions employing more than 5,000 engineers and scientists making $7.7 billion in sales. A $7.7 billion company hardly sounds like an entrepreneurial hideout, but it is.

Employees are encouraged to spend some 15 percent of their work time on new ideas without having to account for that time in any short-term way. In the long term, of course, the company expects results, and results they get. That's where the 90,000 products come from. Not all the discoveries are planned, however.

Patsy Sherman, for example, accidentally spilled a test chemical on her tennis shoe (people dress informally at 3M). She discovered that chemicals and dirt could not remove or stain the spot. This discovery led to the profitable Scotchgard fabric protector.

Remember those yellow Post-it notes that Art Fry developed for marking his Sunday hymnal? Well, Art started at the University of Minnesota and worked as an intern at 3M. It was 20 years later that Fry developed Post-it notes.

Fry now works with 50 or so new products a year, 99 percent of which are not salable. If a product *is* successful, Fry gets to follow it through production and marketing. Then it's back to the lab for more research.

To give you some idea of how wide the product line is at 3M, let's look at some products they are working on. One hot item is a programmable optical disk; others include bioelectronic ears and space shuttle insulation. There is an Electronic and Information Technologies Sector, a Graphics Sector, an Industrial and Consumer Sector, and a Life Sciences Sector. The company started out as Minnesota Mining and Manufacturing (3M) company. It has come a long way from the mining days. Most of its success is due to intrapreneuring.

DECISION QUESTIONS

1. Why is it important for laboratory people to follow their new product ideas through production and marketing?
2. How can a multibillion dollar corporation keep its entrepreneurial spirit alive?
3. Is it healthy for a corporation to be involved in such widely diverse industries as Scotch tape and bioelectronic ears? Doesn't that prevent the corporation from having expertise in all those areas?
4. Could 3M survive without intrapreneuring?

Source: Peter Hall, "What It's Like to Work for 3M," *Business Week's Guide to Careers.*

CASE TWO   **OPPORTUNITIES IN FRANCHISING**

In 1988, there were over 500,000 franchised businesses in the United States. One third of all retail sales are through franchises, which employ over 7 million people. The Department of Commerce reports that each year since 1971 less than 8 percent of franchise-owned outlets have discontinued organization (but many have been sold at big losses). Compare that with the failure rate of sole proprietorship (25 to 33⅓ percent in the first year), and franchises start to look rather attractive.

Hot franchises in 1988 included maintenance and cleaning services, health and fitness centers, and hair cutting. The older fields, such as restaurants and auto repair shops, are still growing with new franchises such as T. J. Cinnamons Bakeries experiencing a growth rate of 3,700 percent. Some 20 or 30 years ago, you could get a McDonald's or AAMCO transmission franchise for about $10,000. Today, a McDonald's franchise will cost from $250,000 to over $400,000 depending on the location. Nonetheless, McDonald's is still a good investment. An average McDonald's tops $1 million in revenue, and an operator may net $100,000 or more. Newer franchises cost less, but involve more risk. You can, for example, get a Novus Windshield Repair franchise for $2,000.

The success stories are many. MAACO Enterprises was founded in 1972. It specializes in auto body repair and painting. By 1988, it had over 400 units in 42 states and Canada selling close to $200 million worth of services per year. Fantastic Sam's began franchising its hair-cutting services in 1976. In a two-year period from 1985–1987, the company opened 450 new franchised stores.

Maybe you would enjoy running a Big Daddy's Lounge and Package Liquor Stores or perhaps Packy the Shipper franchises might catch your eye. If you are not sure about franchising, maybe you should contact the International Franchise Association for more information. The address is 1350 New York Avenue, N.W. (Suite 900), Washington, D.C. 20005. The phone number is (202) 628–8000. You can get the names, addresses, phone numbers, cash investment, and qualifications needed, and other data on members. The association offers several interesting publications, including *Is Franchising For You?* and *How to Be a Franchisor.*

DECISION QUESTIONS

1. What kinds of questions might you ask before buying a franchise?
2. Are the lower risks of franchise organizations worth giving up the freedom of ownership and control? How would you find information to answer such questions?
3. Look around your town and see which franchises seem successful. Is it true that the three most important promotional elements for a franchise are location, location, and location? Is there evidence of this around you?

LOOKING AHEAD

Because the great majority of businesses in the United States are sole proprietorships and partnerships, small businesses are the heart of free enterprise. Most of the *new* jobs are in this area, as are many of the exciting new industries.

Because small business is so important to America and to your future, we devote Chapter 6 to the management of such organizations. We shall explore all phases of small-business management, from starting a business to motivating employees.

Laura's Special Double Decker

Heavenly Hash

STARTING A SMALL BUSINESS

6

LEARNING GOALS

After you have read and studied this chapter, you should be able to:

1. Define small business and discuss its importance to the American economy.

2. Identify and give examples of the five categories of small business.

3. Summarize the major causes of small-business failures.

4. Explain the reasons people start small businesses even though many others have failed.

5. Identify ways you can learn about small businesses.

6. Explain what a business plan is, and outline the six general areas of information that it should include.

7. List the major sources of capital for starting small businesses. Point out the advantages and disadvantages of arranging loans from each of these sources.

8. Explain what a market is and why it is important for a businessperson to know the market.

9. Illustrate the need for effectively managing employees and identify some of the specific problems small-business owners face in this area.

10. Describe the types of outside assistance a small-business owner needs.

11. Point out the advantages and disadvantages of small businesses entering global markets.

KEY TERMS

Active Corps of Executives (ACE), *p. 181*
business plan, *p. 172*
certified public account (CPA), *p. 180*
incubators, *p. 177*

market, *p. 178*
Service Corps of Retired Executives (SCORE), *p. 181*
small business, *p. 163*
venture capitalist, *p. 176*

PROFILE   LAURA KATLEMAN

Laura Katleman.

Mmmm, the smell of sweet success! As a little girl, Laura Katleman sold her home-baked treats to her neighbors. Today, at 30, she is building an empire of "fudgy, gooey brownies." Laura offers 25 varieties of brownies, from those laced with Grand Marnier or amaretto to cake-like delicacies of white or German chocolate.

Selling 250,000 brownies a year, Laura's Boston Brownies Co. grossed $390,000 in 1986. Laura operates a retail store in Boston's prestigious Quincy Market, manages 12 to 15 employees, and collects revenue from a Minneapolis-licensed outlet. Hoping to become the "Mrs. Fields" of brownies, Laura plans to franchise Boston Brownies nationwide and to build an international company.

"I know that sounds ambitious . . . but I know I can do it," Laura asserts with the single-minded sense of purpose that is characteristic of an entrepreneur. How did Laura begin turning her dream into reality? She began by writing a business plan when she attended Pomona College in Claremont, California. After graduating in 1980, Laura started business by posting ads on telephone poles in Boston and delivering her brownies to her customers herself. She was out of business in a month! The demand was too high and Laura only made a $50 profit.

Laura didn't succeed on her next attempt either! Selling brownies wholesale, she landed Bloomingdale's as her first client. But she had to sue the company to collect $30,000 of the $50,000 it owed her.

But perseverance paid off when she persuaded the owner of a large Boston bakery to become her business partner. She opened the successful Quincy Market store and by 1983 had earned enough money to buy him out. Today, Laura Katleman owns 100 percent of Boston Brownies Co. and tomorrow—who knows?

Source: Rita Stollman, "The New Entrepreneurial Woman," *Business Week,* October 1987, p. 90.

If sailing in a big and placid lake's your style, go to work in a large corporation, but if white water canoeing is to your liking, try a small company.
FRED MURPHY

GETTING STARTED IN SMALL BUSINESS

Have you ever thought about starting your own business? Do you think it would be too hard or too risky? Are you the type who would prefer sailing on a big and placid lake, like the people mentioned in the marginal quote? Are you the "go-for-it" white-water type? Or aren't you sure?

One way to find out is to start your own business while you're in school. There is no better way to learn about business than to start one—and now is as good a time as any. But how do you *start* a business? How much paperwork is involved? That is what this chapter is about.

In Chapter 5, we looked at buying a franchise as one way of owning a business. Now we will look at how to start your own independent business. The purpose of this chapter is to explore small businesses, their role in the economy, and small-business management. It is easier to identify with a small, neighborhood business than a giant, global firm, yet the principles of management are very similar. The management of charities, government agencies, churches, schools, and unions is much the same as the management of small and large businesses. So, as you learn about small-business management, you will make a giant step toward understanding management in general. All organizations demand capital, good ideas, planning, information management, budgets (and financial management in general), accounting, marketing, good employee relations, and good overall managerial know-how. We shall explore these areas as they relate to small businesses and then, later in the book, apply the concepts to large firms, even global organizations.

SMALL VERSUS BIG BUSINESS

There is so much talk today about "big business" that one would think that small business was not important to the U.S. economy. What is a "small" business, anyway? And how does it differ from a "big" business? The Small Business Administration (SBA) defines a **small business** as one that is independently owned and operated, not dominant in its field of operation, and meets certain standards of size in terms of employees or annual receipts (for example, less than $2 million a year for service businesses). See Figure 6–1 for some guidelines on the sizes of various kinds of small businesses.

A small business is considered small only in relation to other businesses in its industry. A wholesaler may sell up to $22 million and still be considered a small business by the SBA. In manufacturing, a plant can have 1,500 employees and still be considered small. For example, before its merger with Chrysler, American Motors was considered small because it was tiny compared to Ford, General Motors, and Chrysler. Let's look at some interesting statistics about small businesses:

- There are about 17 million small businesses in the United States.
- Small businesses account for over 40 percent of the gross national product (GNP).
- The fastest-growing business magazine and the fourth-fastest-growing U.S. magazine of any type is *Entrepreneur* magazine. *Venture* is the second-fastest-growing business magazine.[1]
- Half the small businesses have sales of less than $500,000 and fewer than 10 employees.
- Of all nonfarm businesses in the United States, almost 97 percent are considered small by SBA standards. The percentage of small businesses in various categories is shown in Figure 6–2 (see page 164).

small business
Business that is independently owned and operated, not dominant in its field, and meets certain standards of size in terms of employees or annual receipts.

FASTEST-GROWING BUSINESS PUBLICATIONS: DECEMBER 1987 TO DECEMBER 1988.

MAGAZINE	% GROWTH
Entrepreneur	39.4
Venture	5.0
Business Week	2.5
Success	1.9
Inc.	0.8
Fortune	0.4
Forbes	0.2

Source: *Los Angeles Times*, March 3, 1989, p. 3 of Part IV.

SMALL BUSINESS	EMPLOYMENT SIZE	ASSET SIZE	SALES SIZE
Independent contractor	0	0	Under 100,000
Family Size	1–4	Under $100,000	$100,000–500,000
Small	5–19	$100,000–500,000	$500,000–$1 million
Medium	20–99	$500,000–5 million	$1–10 million
Large	100–499	$5–25 million	$10 million–50 million
Total small business	0–500	$0–25 million	$0–50 million
Medium business	500–999	$25–100 million	$50–250 million
Large business	1,000+	$100 million+	$250 million+
Government-size business	10,000+	$2 billion	$2 billion+

Source: Office of Economic Research, U.S. Small Business Administration, 1989.

FIGURE 6–1

Classification of small businesses.
There is no one definition of "small business," but the U.S. Small Business Administration uses these guidelines for classification.

FIGURE 6–2

Percentage of small businesses in different categories. Note the large percentage of small firms in agriculture, wholesaling, and retailing. Also note that mining and manufacturing have the lowest percentage of small businesses.
Source: Office of the President, *State of Small Business.*

Mining: 9.5%
Manufacturing: 22.1%
Transportation: 24.1%
All industries: 45.3%
Finance: 49.5%
Services: 55.1%
Retail: 65.1%
Wholesale: 73.9%
Construction: 79.8%
Agriculture: 86.7%

As you can see, small business is really a big part of the U.S. economy. How big a part? We'll explore that question next.

Importance of Small Businesses

Most people do not have any idea of the importance of small businesses in our economy. The news media devotes so much time to employment and problems in big businesses such as automobiles, steel, and textiles that we might think that the economy is dominated totally by large businesses. Yet large companies (more than 1,000 employees) created only 6 percent of the new jobs since 1975. Since 1979, large companies actually lost about 600,000 jobs. Ninety percent of the nation's new jobs in the private sector are in small businesses. More than half of the new jobs are with companies with fewer than 20 employees.[2] Dun & Bradstreet estimates that small businesses created three fourths of the 2.6 million jobs created during 1987.[3] That means there is a very good chance that you will either work in a small business someday or will start one. You can find out which industries are creating the most new jobs by studying Figure 6–3.

No doubt media coverage leads you to believe that most of the new jobs are in high-tech industries—computers, robots, and the like. The truth is that only 10 percent of the jobs created in the last 10 years were in high technology. Most of the new jobs are in low-tech industries such as women's wear manufacturers and restaurants.

It [running a small business] requires patience, commitment, and a willingness to lose money at first. If you don't have that, you'd be better off going to Las Vegas and throwing dice.
ROBERT N. LUKAT, General Manager, Atlanta Saw Co.

Another surprising statistic is that the growth in mid-size firms (sales of $25 million to $100 million) was among *manufacturing* firms, not *service* firms, as many who speak of the "rusting of America" believe. Nine out of the 10 fastest growing industries are in manufacturing.[4] Why is this? Many analysts believe that the declining value of the dollar in 1988 spurred a revival in American exports as they became less expensive in global markets. As a result, small manufacturers that supply exporting industries may be winners in the 1990s.[5]

Today most new jobs are found in small businesses. In fact, real estate is one of the fastest growing job markets in the United States. Talk to some of your classmates about their experiences with real estate agents.

	CHANGE (PERCENT)
FASTEST EMPLOYMENT GROWTH	
Freight forwarding	13.4%
Motion picture productions and services	10.0
Social services, individual and family	9.9
Real estate agents	9.4
Medical and dental laboratories	9.3
SLOWEST EMPLOYMENT GROWTH	
School-bus drivers	−10.1%
Individual builders	−6.7
Motion picture theaters	−4.8
Nonresidential building construction	−4.6
Taxicab drivers	−4.2

FIGURE 6–3

Employment change in small-business dominated industries.
What are the fastest growing businesses in the United States? You already may be planning a career in one of these industries.

Before we explore starting a small business, let's review the kinds of businesses we are talking about.

Small-Business Categories

The government tends to classify things, including small businesses. It talks about five different classes of small business: (1) service businesses, (2) retail businesses, (3) construction firms, (4) wholesalers, and (5) manufacturers. What kind of business would be the most attractive career choice for you? Let's review the industries.

1. Service Businesses   You are already familiar with the services provided by dry cleaners, travel agencies, lawn care firms, beauty parlors, and other services that cater to you and your family. In your career search, be sure to explore services such as hotels/motels, health clubs, amusement parks, income tax preparation organizations, employment agencies, accounting firms, rental firms of all kinds, management consulting, repair services (for example, computers, robots, VCRs), insurance agencies, real estate firms, stock brokers, and so on. There are many exciting careers available in such firms (see Figure 1–1 on page 22 for a list of service organizations).

2. Retail Businesses   You have only to go to a major shopping mall to see the possibilities in retailing. There are stores selling shoes, clothes, hats, skis, gloves, sporting goods, ice cream, groceries, and more. Much more. Watch the trends, and you will see new ideas like fancy popcorn stores, T-shirt shops, videotape rental stores, yogurt shops, and more. Do any of these retail stores look like interesting places to work?

3. Construction Firms   Drive through any big city and you will see huge cranes towering over an empty lot where major construction is taking place. Would you enjoy supervising such work? Visit some areas where construction firms are building bridges, roads, homes, schools, buildings, and dams. There is a feeling of power and creativity in such work that excites many observers. How about you? Talk to some of the workers and supervisors and learn about the risks and rewards of small construction firms.

4. Wholesalers   Have you ever visited a wholesale food warehouse, a wholesale jewelry center, or similar wholesale firms? If not, you are missing an important link in the small-business system, one with much potential. Wholesale representatives often make more money, have more free time, travel more, have more fringe benefits, and enjoy their jobs more than similar people in retailing. Check it out.

5. Manufacturing   Of course, manufacturing is still an attractive career for tomorrow's graduates. The figure in the margin shows that manufacturers make the most money among small-business owners. There are careers for designers, machinists, mechanics, engineers, supervisors, safety inspectors, and a host of other occupations. Visit some small manufacturers in your area and inquire about such jobs.

Naturally, there are thousands of small farmers who enjoy the rural life and the pace of farming. Small farms are usually not very profitable, but some that specialize in exotic crops do quite well (see Case 2 at the end of this chapter). Similarly, many small mining operations attract college students with a sense of adventure and daring. People who are not sure of what career they would like to follow have a busy time ahead. They need to visit service firms, construction firms, farms, mines, retailers, wholesalers, and all other kinds of small and large businesses to see the diversity and excitement available in American business.

WHERE THE MONEY IS

Owners of closely-held companies with annual revenue of between $1 million and $100 million were asked what they earn annually in salary and indirect compensation. These are the 10 highest-paying industries, ranked by median total compensation. Overall, small-business owners reported a median total compensation of $151,000.

Industry	
Primary metal industries	$264,000
Heavy construction contractors	244,000
Transportation services	221,000
Stone, clay, and glass products	215,000
Food and related products	202,000
Electric and electronic equipment	202,000
Rubber and plastics products	200,000
Apparel products	199,000
Personal services	192,000
Textile mill products	190,000

Source: *The Wall Street Journal*, May 4, 1989, p. B1.

PROGRESS CHECK

- Can you name the five different classes of small businesses?
- What factors are used to classify a firm as a "small" business?

Small-Business Success and Failure

You can't be naive about business practices, or you'll go broke. The figures support this statement. If 100 small businesses are started at any given time, the odds are that 20 of them will be gone by the end of the first year; 17 more will go out of business in the second year; and by the end of the fifth year, a total of about 67 will have failed! Only 33 percent are likely to survive! Truly, you can't be naive about business practices or you *do* go broke. As you can see in the box listing causes of business failure, many small businesses failed because of managerial incompetence and inadequate financial planning.

CAUSES OF SMALL-BUSINESS FAILURE

- Plunging in without first testing the waters on a small scale.
- Underpricing goods or services.
- Underestimating how much time it will take to build a market.
- Starting with too little capital.
- Starting with too much capital and being careless in its use.
- Going into business with little or no experience and without first learning something about business.
- Borrowing money without planning just how and when to pay it back.
- Attempting to do too much business with too little capital.
- Not allowing for setbacks and unexpected expenses.
- Buying too much on credit.
- Extending credit too freely.
- Expanding credit too rapidly.
- Failing to keep complete, accurate records, so that the proprietor drifts into trouble without realizing.
- Carrying habits of personal extravagance into the business.
- Mistaking the freedom of being in business for oneself for liberty to work or not according to whim.

Source: SCORE, the Service Corps of Retired Executives.

WOMEN IN SMALL BUSINESS

There has been a rapid growth in the number of women starting small businesses in the last decade or so. From 1980 to 1986 the number of women-owned companies jumped from 2.5 million to 4.1 million, with women starting businesses at twice the rate of men. Ownership by women of the 1.2 million small professional firms jumped from 27 percent in 1972 to 40 percent in 1985. Why the growth? John B. Parrish, professor emeritus of economics at the University of Illinois, attributes the surge to several factors:

- Women delay starting families while gathering educational and corporate experience.
- Women can borrow money on their own more easily now.
- Many women are part of two-wage–earner families.
- The shift from manufacturing to services has created new opportunities.
- New computer technologies have lowered the investment needed to start service businesses.
- Women find themselves blocked in their corporate careers.

In spite of their increased numbers in small business, women tend to make less money than male small-business owners. Full-time, self-employed women earned 37 percent of the average $15,155 that self-employed men were earning in 1984. Not only that, they earned only 53 percent of the wages earned by women working for others. Why? Probably because many women starting businesses do so in the traditional service areas such as child care and grooming. The new head of the Small Business Administration is a woman—Susan Engeleiter. No doubt women will prosper even more under her leadership.

Source: Rita Stollman, "The New Entrepreneurial Woman," *Business Week*, October 1987, pp. 84–92, and Dyan Mochan, "Taking Charge," *Forbes*, March 6, 1989, pp. 154–156.

MOST FREQUENTLY STARTED	MOST LIKELY TO SURVIVE
1. Miscellaneous business services	1. Veterinary services
2. Eating and drinking places	2. Funeral services
3. Miscellaneous shopping goods	3. Dentists' offices
4. Automotive repair shops	4. Commercial savings banks
5. Residential construction	5. Hotels and motels
6. Machinery and equipment wholesalers	6. Campground and trailer parks
7. Real estate operators	7. Physicians' offices
8. Miscellaneous retail stores	8. Barbershops
9. Furniture and furnishings retailers	9. Bowling and billiards places
10. Computer and data processing services	10. Cash grain crops

If you'd like to start a business that will be around five years from now, study Figure 6–4, which lists the businesses with the lowest failure rates. You'll see that many of the most secure businesses require advanced training to start—veterinarians, dentists, doctors, and so on.

While training and degrees may buy security, they do not tend to produce much growth. If you want to be both independent and rich, you need to go after growth. The businesses with the highest odds of significant growth are in manufacturing, as we noted earlier. But as you can guess, these are not easy businesses to start and are even more difficult to keep going.

In general it seems that the easiest businesses to start are the ones that tend to have the least growth and the greatest failure rate. The businesses most likely to survive are the difficult ones to get started. And the ones that can make you rich are the ones that are both hard to start and hard to keep going.[6]

When you decide to start your own business, you must think carefully about what kind of business you want to start. You are not likely to find everything you want in one business—easy entry, security, *and* reward. Choose those characteristics that matter the most to you, accept the absence of the others, plan, plan, plan, and then go for it!

THINKING IT THROUGH Imagine yourself starting a small business. What kind of business would it be? How much local competition is there? What could you do to make your business more attractive than competitors'? Would you be willing to work 60 to 70 hours per week in such a business?

Why Start a Business?

Given the fact that 67 percent of small businesses are doomed to fail within five years, why do so many people continue to try? First, you should understand that thousands of new businesses are started every year. Since 1985, over 650,000 new businesses were started every year—that's 12,500 per week, or five every minute of every working day.[7]

1. Pride in product/service	7. Income	
2. Control	8. Employee contact	
3. Freedom	9. Recognition	
4. Flexibility	10. Privacy	
5. Self-reliance	11. Security	
6. Customer contract	12. Status	

FIGURE 6–5

What small-business owners like about their jobs. Most small business owners value pride in their product, control, and the freedom that comes from being your own boss.

These four restaurants represent the thousands of small businesses that are run by immigrants. Some of their business comes from other immigrants from the same country looking for familiar foods (Greek, Chinese, Thai, and so forth). But most customers are people who enjoy the diversity of foods available in a country full of new entrepreneurs from other parts of the world.

Clearly, something in the American spirit motivates people to try, try again to start and run their own small businesses. What do business owners find so alluring? A recent survey of small-business owners showed that owners ranked the pride of offering a product or service as the number one source of business satisfaction. After pride, the owners were motivated by control and freedom. Income ranked only seventh and status was dead last. (See Figure 6–5.)

One of the best ways to learn retailing is to get a job at a bustling retail store and learn from the owner/manager. You can start in high school or college and work in several stores. Soon you will gather many insights about how to run a successful store.

Thus, in spite of overwhelming odds against them, entrepreneurs set out to conquer the business world, confidently and enthusiastically. How hard do they work? Most (53 percent) new owners work more than 60 hours a week. Less than 20 percent of the executives of big corporations work that many hours. In addition to the long hours working the new business, nearly 20 percent of the owners keep up full-time or part-time jobs as well. Clearly, the job of owner of a new, small business calls for considerable stamina.[8]

LEARNING ABOUT SMALL–BUSINESS OPERATIONS

Hundreds of would-be entrepreneurs of all ages have asked the same question: "How can I learn to run my own business?" Many of these people had no idea what kind of business they wanted to start; they simply wanted to be in business for themselves. That seems to be a major trend among students today. As you learned earlier in the chapter, you have to understand business practices or you'll go broke in your own business. Here are some hints for learning about small business.

Learn from Others

There are a few courses available that teach small-business management well. You might begin by investigating your local schools for such classes. The best thing about these courses is that they bring together entrepreneurs. *That* is how to learn to run a small business—talk to others who have done it.

The starting place for budding entrepreneurs is talking with small-business owners and managers. Learn from their experience, especially their mistakes. They will tell you that location is critical. They will caution you not to be under-capitalized. They will warn you about the problems of finding and retaining good employees. And, most of all, they will tell you to keep good records and hire a good accountant and lawyer before you start. Small-business owners can give you hundreds of good ideas, ranging from how to get bank loans to how to design creative advertising. This free advice is invaluable.

SITUATIONS FOR SMALL-BUSINESS SUCCESS

- When the customer requires a lot of personal attention, as in a beauty parlor.
- When the product is not easily made by mass-production techniques (for example, custom-tailored clothes or custom auto-body work).
- When sales are not large enough to appeal to a large firm (for example, a novelty shop).
- When the neighborhood is not attractive because of crime or poverty. This provides a unique opportunity for small grocery stores, liquor stores, and laundries. The risk is higher, but often so are profits.
- When a large business sells a franchise operation to local buyers. Don't forget franchising as an excellent way to enter the world of small business.

Get Some Experience

There is no better way for learning small-business management than by becoming an apprentice or working for a successful entrepreneur. In fact, 42 percent of small-business owners got the idea for their businesses from their prior jobs. The prior jobs of almost half of new business owners were in small businesses. The rule of thumb is: three years experience in a comparable business.

We noted in Chapter 5 that the new entrepreneur of the 1990s would come from corporate management. Many corporate managers are tired of the big-business life and are quitting to start small business (see the marginal quotation). They bring their managerial expertise and enthusiasm.[9]

> I decided to quit Ford and work for a small company to get out of the rat race. I found out there was another rat race.
>
> **HARRY FEATHERSTONE, CEO** of Will-Bart Co. in Orrville, Ohio, *Inc.*, February 1989, p. 82.

Take Over a Successful Firm

One thing you have learned about small-business management is that it takes long hours, dedication, and determination. Owners work long hours and rarely take vacations. After many years, they may feel stuck in their business. They may think that they can't get out because they have too much time and effort invested. In short, there are millions of small businesses out there with owner/managers eager to get away, at least for a long vacation.

This is where you come in. Find a mature businessperson (50 to 60 or more years old) who owns a small business. Tell him or her that you are eager to learn the business and would like to serve an apprenticeship, a training period. At the end of that period (one year or so), you would like to help the owner/manager by becoming assistant manager. As assistant manager, you would free the owner to take off weekends and holidays, and to take a long vacation—a good deal for him or her. For another year or so, work very hard to learn all about the business—suppliers, inventory, bookkeeping, customers, promotion, and so on. At the end of two years, make the owner this offer. He or she can retire or work only part-time, and you will take over the business. You can establish a profit-sharing plan for yourself plus a salary. Be generous with yourself; you will earn it if you manage the business. You can even ask for 40 percent or more of the profits.

The owner benefits by keeping ownership in the business and making 60 percent of what he or she earned before—without having to work. You benefit by making 40 percent of the profits of a successful firm. Believe me, this is an excellent deal for an owner about to retire who is able to keep his or her firm and a healthy profit flow. It is also a clever and successful way to share in the profits of a successful small business without any personal money investment. If the deal falls through, you can quit and start your own business fully trained.

PROGRESS CHECK

- Why do so many people continue to start new businesses when the majority of them will be out of business in five years?

- What advice would you give a friend who wanted to learn more about starting a small business?

STARTING AND RUNNING A SMALL BUSINESS

The Small Business Administration has reported that 90 percent of all failures are a result of poor management. The problem is that "poor management" covers a number of faults. It could mean poor planning, poor record-keeping, poor inventory control, poor promotion, or poor employee relations. Most likely it would include poor capitalization (that is, not enough money to operate the firm). This chapter gives us a chance to explore the functions of business in a small-business setting. Often, it is easier to picture such functions in a small firm. After we have discussed these functions in this setting, we shall explore each function more completely in later chapters. The functions we shall explore are:

- Planning your business.
- Financing your business.
- Knowing your customers (marketing).
- Managing your employees (human resource development).
- Keeping records (accounting).

Although all of the functions are important in both the start-up phase and the management phase of the business, the first two functions, planning and financing, are the primary concern when you start your business. The remaining functions are the heart of the actual running of the business once it is started.

Begin with Planning

It is amazing how many people are eager to start a small business, but have only a vague notion of what they want to do. Eventually, they come up with an idea for a business and begin discussing the idea with professors, friends, and other businesspeople. It is at this stage that the entrepreneur needs a **business plan.** A business plan is a detailed written statement that describes the nature of the business, the target market, the advantage the business will have in relation to competition, and the resources and qualifications of the owner(s). See the box Outline of a Comprehensive Business Plan for details.

A business plan forces potential owners of small businesses to be quite specific about the products or services they intend to offer. They must analyze the competition, the money needed to start, and other details of operation. A business plan is also mandatory for talking with bankers or other investors (see the box Tips from a Banker on page 174). To prepare a thorough plan, a person would most likely need the assistance of a good accountant. In general, a business plan should include the following:

1. A brief description of the industry and a detailed explanation of the products or services to be offered.
2. A thorough market analysis that discusses the size of the market, the need for the new product (service), and the nature of the competition.

business plan
A detailed written statement that describes the nature of the business, the target market, the advantages the business will have over competitors, and the resources and qualifications of the owners.

The business plan is the grammar of an entrepreneurial venture; without it you cannot construct coherent thoughts.
NED HEIZER

OUTLINE OF A COMPREHENSIVE BUSINESS PLAN

SECTION 1—INTRODUCTION

Begin with a two- or three-page management overview of the proposed venture. Include a succinct description of the business and discuss major goals and objectives.

SECTION 2—COMPANY BACKGROUND

Describe company operations to date (if any), potential legal considerations, and areas of risk and opportunity. Summarize the firm's financial condition and include past and current balance sheets, income and cash flow statements, and other relevant financial records (you will read about these financial statements in Chapter 18).

SECTION 3—MANAGEMENT TEAM

Include an organization chart, job descriptions, and detailed résumés of the current and proposed executives. Managers should have expertise in all disciplines necessary to start and run a business. If not, mention outside consultants who will serve in these roles and describe their qualifications.

SECTION 4—FINANCIAL PLAN

Provide five-year projections for income, expenses, and funding sources. Explain the rationale and assumptions used to determine the estimates. Assumptions should be reasonable and based on industry/historical trends. Make sure all totals add up and are consistent throughout the plan. If necessary, hire a professional accountant or financial analyst to prepare these statements.

Stay clear of excessively ambitious sales projections; rather, offer best-case, expected, and worst-case scenarios. These not only reveal how sensitive the bottom line is to sales fluctuations but serve as good management guides.

SECTION 5—CAPITAL REQUIRED

Indicate the amount of capital needed to commence or continue operations and describe how these funds are to be used. Make sure the totals are the same as the ones on the cash flow statement. This area will receive a great deal of review from potential investors so it must be clear and concise.

SECTION 6—MARKETING PLAN

Review industry size, trends, and the target market segment. Discuss strengths and weaknesses of the product or service and pricing compared to competition. Forecast sales in dollars and units. Outline sales, advertising, promotion and PR programs. Make sure the costs agree with those projected in the financial statements.

SECTION 7—LOCATION ANALYSIS

In retailing and certain other industries, the location of the business is one of the most important factors. Provide a comprehensive demographic analysis of consumers in the area of the proposed store as well as a traffic-pattern analysis and vehicular and pedestrian counts.

SECTION 8—MANUFACTURING PLAN

Describe minimum plant size, machinery required, production capacity, inventory and inventory control methods, quality control, plant personnel requirements, and so on. Estimates of product costs should be based on primary research.

SECTION 9—APPENDIX

Include all marketing research on the product or service (reports, article reprints, etc.) and other information about the product concept or market size. Provide a bibliography of all the reference materials you consulted. This section should demonstrate that the proposed company won't be entering a declining industry.

Source: R. Richard Bruno, "How to Write a Business Plan for a New Venture," *Marketing News,* March 15, 1985, p. 10.

3. A marketing plan that includes location, signs, advertising, and display.
4. An operating plan that includes a sales forecast, financial projections, accounting procedures, and human resource requirements.
5. A comprehensive capitalization plan describing how much money the owner(s) is committing. Few banks or investors will support a new firm unless the owner(s) has a substantial financial commitment.
6. A description of the experience and expertise of the owner(s). This may include a résumé, letters of recommendation, and financial statements.

TIPS FROM A BANKER

Michael Celello is president of the People's Commercial Bank. He says that fewer than 10 percent of prospective borrowers come to a bank adequately prepared. He offers several tips to small-business owners:

1. Pick a bank that serves businesses the size of yours and choose the bank carefully. If you are rejected by one bank, other banks can learn of your inquiry through credit bureaus and turn you down also.
2. Have a good accountant prepare a complete set of financial statements as well as a business plan and personal balance sheet. If you come to the bank with an accountant and all the necessary financial information, you increase your odds of getting a loan by 75 percent.
3. Make an appointment before going to the bank.
4. Demonstrate to the banker that you're a person of good character: civic-minded and respected in business and community circles.
5. Read *The Wall Street Journal* and other business publications so you can demonstrate industry knowledge and economic knowledge.
6. Ask for all the money you need and be specific. The banker may want to make separate loans for different needs with varying life expectancies.
7. Be prepared to personally guarantee the loan.

Adapted from Michael Celello, "Tips from a Banker," *Inc.*, November 1981, p. 44.

This man is busy planning for his future. He is working on a business plan that will be the foundation for success. It will spell out who the market will be, how much capital will be needed, and how the business will meet and beat the competition.

I've foreseen many problems in my life. Luckily many of them never turned up!
MARK TWAIN

Unless you spend adequate time and effort preparing your business plan, like thousands of others it may end up in a venture capitalist's wastebasket—unread! Of 1,200 proposals received during a several-months period, the Aegis Partners, a Boston venture capital firm, read 600, researched 45, and funded only 14.[10] Why? Because most entrepreneurs get their priorities reversed. They don't spend enough time preparing their business plan. Then they expect potential lenders to spend several hours reading it.

According to Joseph Mancuso, director of the Center for Entrepreneurial Management in New York and author of a book on how to prepare business plans, a good business plan takes a minimum of five months to write but you've got to convince your readers in five minutes not to throw the plan away.

Mr. Mancuso says there is no such thing as a perfect business plan, but he suggests some things that investors uniformly look for in a business plan:

- Brevity—12 pages is about right.
- Executive summary (introduction) is the most important component—limit it to a one- or two-page summation containing the key elements of the project.
- Management—a mediocre idea with a proven management team is funded more often than a great idea with an inexperienced team.
- Commitment—part-time entrepreneurs who try to hold down a regular job while launching a new company have a harder time attracting investors.
- Description of product—keep it short; the most important things investors want to know is what makes the product more desirable than what's already available and if the product can be patented.
- Marketing strategies—a carefully devised marketing strategy is critical; don't underestimate the competition.
- Financial section—don't assume the business will grow in a straight line; adjust your planning to allow for funding at various stages of the company's growth.
- Details—think out the smallest detail.
- Get the completed business plan in the right hands—this requires research.

One of the most common mistakes made by new small-business owners is waiting too long to talk to bankers. You would be surprised how long it takes to review and process loans. Another common mistake is to ask for too little money.

Next, we will discuss some of the many sources of money available to new business ventures. All of them call for a comprehensive business plan. The time and effort invested *before* a business is started pays off many times later. With small businesses, the big payoff is survival.

Laura Katleman wrote the business plan for her brownie business when she was still in college. Which part of the plan do you think was the most important? How long do you think it took her to prepare the plan? Was the investment in time worthwhile? Why?

THINKING IT THROUGH

Funding a Small Business

The problem with most new, small businesses is that the entrepreneurs have more enthusiasm than managerial skills and capital. The economic system in America is called capitalism for a reason. It is capital (money) that enables entrepreneurs to get started; buy needed goods, services, labor, and buildings; and keep the business going. Some of the *financial* reasons cited by the Small Business Administration for failure are:

- Starting with too little capital.
- Starting with too much capital and being careless in its use.
- Borrowing money without planning how and when to pay it back.
- Trying to do too much business with not enough capital.
- Not allowing for setbacks and unexpected expenses.
- Extending credit too freely.

Entrepreneurs, like most people, are not highly skilled at obtaining, managing, and using money. Inadequate capitalization or poor financial management can destroy a business even when the basic idea behind the business is good and the products are accepted in the marketplace. One of the secrets of finding the money to start your business is knowing where to look for it.

Venture capitalists are investors who will lend you money to finance your new venture. One such firm, Drexel Burnham Lambert, will give you cash to start your business for a share in your company. You should study closely several firms before you make an investment decision.

WE DON'T THROW THE SMALL ONES BACK.

We don't refuse Fortune 500 companies when they come to us for capital. That's unthinkable.
By the same token, we don't turn our backs on companies whose fortunes have yet to be made. For

one very good reason. Small companies have a way of turning into big companies overnight.
And, along the way, the million dollar deals become multi-million dollar deals. Or even billion dollar deals.

The way we see it, promising young firms are long on vision. They're chock full of brilliant ideas. And enthusiasm they have plenty of. All they need is someone to lend them support.
If your company

sounds like that, give us a call.
And if you're still skeptical, consider MCI, Charter Medical, Golden Nugget, or

Kinder Care. Right now, they're some of our biggest clients.
At one time, they were among our smallest.

Drexel Burnham
Drexel Burnham Lambert Incorporated

PROGRESS CHECK

▪ There were nine sections in the business plan on page 173. This plan is probably *the* most important document a small-business person will ever make. Can you describe at least five of those sections now?

▪ The U.S. Small Business Administration gives six reasons why small businesses fail financially. Can you name three?

One of the major problems of new entrepreneurs is misinformation and lack of information about capitalization and financial management. According to most sources, a new entrepreneur has several sources of capital: personal savings, relatives, former employers, banks, finance companies, venture capital organizations, government agencies such as the Small Business Administration, the Farmers Home Administration, the Economic Development Authority, and more.

Two thirds of new businesses are started with personal savings. According to a study by the National Federation of Independent Business, the average entrepreneur uses $20,000 to start a new business.[11] Many entrepreneurs turn to their families for the needed funds. Watch out if you plan to tap your relatives for a loan. Such a plan can backfire. Be sure to cover an intrafamily loan with a letter of agreement just in case a silent partner becomes outspoken.

You may want to consider borrowing from a potential supplier to your future business. Helping you get started may be in the supplier's interest if there is a chance you will be a big customer later.

Investors known as **venture capitalists** may finance your project—for a price. Venture capitalists ask for a hefty stake (frequently 60 percent) in your company in exchange for the cash to start your business. Experts recommend that you talk with at least five investment firms and their clients in order to find the right venture

venture capitalist
Individuals or organizations that invest in new businesses in exchange for partial ownership of the company.

FINANCE HINTS FROM ASIAN SMALL-BUSINESS OWNERS

Have you ever wondered how Asian businesspeople get the financing to own the thousands of small businesses they have started in the United States? The secret is an important one to know because it could be a way for African-Americans, Hispanics, and other ethnic groups to prosper and grow in business even faster than they now are.

Here is how the system works. A group of 40 or so Asians get together at a local gathering spot. Each of them puts $1,000 or so in a pot. One of the 40 bids for the pot and winner takes all. That is, the person who gets the pot takes the $40,000 and uses it to finance the start of a business. The next month the group gets together again and someone else gets the pot until all 40 participants have

$40,000 to invest. There are no written loan agreements, no deposit slips, or anything. These people trust one another and rely on one another for financing and support. Naturally, they also become customers of each other.

The system is called *kye* in Korean, *hui* in Chinese, *tanomoshi* in Japanese, and *hoi* in Vietnamese. The system worked better in the native countries where people knew each other better and had long-term commitments. Nonetheless, it is still being practiced in the United States. In fact, the Hanmi Bank in Koreatown introduced a **kye**-like program to get in on the action. Ultimately, people helping people is the secret to small business financing and success.

Source: David J. Jefferson, "Neighborhood Financing," *The Wall Street Journal Reports (Small Business)*, February 24, 1989, pp. R13–R14.

capitalist. You can get a list of venture capitalists free of charge from the Small Business Administration. Ask for the Directory of Operating Small Business Investment Companies. You can also follow the ups and downs of venture capital availability in *Inc.* and *Venture* magazines.

Two good books about finding venture capital are: Robert J. Gaston, *Finding Private Venture Capital for Your Firm* (New York: John Wiley & Sons, 605 Third Ave., N.Y., N.Y., 10158), and G. Steven Barrill and Craig T. Norback, *The Arthur Young Guide to Raising Venture Capital* (Blue Ridge Summit, Pa., Liberty House, 17294).

States are becoming stronger advocates of entrepreneurs as they create programs that invest directly in new businesses. Often, state commerce departments serve as clearinghouses for such investment programs. States are also creating incubators and technology centers to reduce start-up capital needs. **Incubators** provide low-cost offices with basic business services such as accounting, legal advice, and secretarial help. There are now some 300 incubator programs nationwide.[12]

incubators
Centers that provide "newborn" businesses (usually in technological industries) with low-cost offices and basic business services.

As you may have guessed already, the technology-minded entrepreneurs have the best shot at attracting start-up capital. Such potential businesses are not only more attractive to venture capitalists and state governments, the federal government has several grant programs that provide funds for computer-related ventures.

Other than tapping personal savings, individual investors are the primary source of capital for most entrepreneurs. They provide 6 of every 10 dollars for very small firms with less than four employees and sales of under $150,000 a year. About $56 billion in risk capital comes from these "business angels" each year.[13] How do you find such investors? Computer networks are available that link entrepreneurs with potential investors. The University of New Hampshire and the Business & Industry Association of New Hampshire launched the Venture Capital Network in 1984. In 1987, the California Technology Stock Letter in San Francisco introduced the Venture Capital Connection.

Obtaining money from banks, venture capitalists, and government sources is very difficult for most small businesses. (You will learn more about financing in Chapter 19.) The costs of drawing up documents, hiring accountants and lawyers, added to the psychological costs of being turned down by organization after organization, is sometimes too high for many entrepreneurs to bear. Those who do survive the planning and financing of their new ventures are eager to get their businesses up and running. Operating a business on a daily basis is a challenge that tests even the most capable entrepreneur. As an entrepreneur, the challenges you face in running a small business are no different from running a global corporation. Your success in running a business depends on three key factors; knowing your customers, managing employees, and keeping efficient records.

Knowing Your Customers

Over a hundred years ago, a journalist named Horace Greeley offered the unemployed of New York City the advice, "Go West." Appropriate advice to aspiring entrepreneurs today might be to "Find an unsatisfied need and fill it." It's amazing today how many people are so eager to enter business that they fail to identify the wants and needs of a critical component—their customers. How many times have you heard someone say "There's a market for this or a market for that?" Do you think most budding entrepreneurs have ever thought about what a market actually is?

market
People with unsatisfied wants and needs who have both the resources and willingness to buy.

A market is nothing more than people; people who are potential buyers for goods and services. In business, a **market** consists of people with unsatisfied wants and needs who have both the resources and willingness to buy. Consider this for a moment. We can confidently state that most of our students have the willingness to take a Caribbean cruise during their spring break. However, few of them have the resources necessary to satisfy this want. Would they be considered a good market for the local travel agency to pursue?

Businesspersons must know the market in which they compete if they hope to survive. Perhaps Professor Harold Hill, the smooth-talking salesperson in the musical *The Music Man* summed it up best when he proclaimed, "You gotta know the territory!" You will gain more insights into getting to know your territory in Chapters 7 through 10. Now let's consider the importance of effectively managing the employees that help you serve your territory.

Managing Employees

Running a small business takes an enormous amount of time and personal effort. As a business grows, it becomes impossible for an entrepreneur to oversee every single detail, even if he or she is putting in 60 hours per week. This means that hiring, training, and motivating employees becomes critical.

It is not easy to find good, qualified help when often you offer little money, skimpy benefits, and limited room for advancement! That is one reason why employee relations is such an important part of small-business management. Employees of small companies are often more satisfied with their jobs than are their counterparts in big business. Why? Quite often they find that their jobs are more challenging, their ideas are more often accepted, and their bosses more often treat them with respect.

It is also no surprise to find that over 90 percent of the top growth companies listed by *Inc.* share ownership and profits with their employees. Let's think about that for a moment. If you own your own car, you are more likely to wash it, polish

EMPLOYEE RELATIONS PLUS

Victoria Dapena de Kuscher is from Puerto Rico. She owns a Dunkin' Donuts franchise in Rockville, Maryland. It is one of the highest volume shops in the Dunkin' Donuts system.

A visit to the shop is like a tour of the United Nations. Vicki employs an Egyptian, a Thai, a Vietnamese, several Hispanics, and a black American. The Kuschers bought a house across the street from the shop, which they use as a rooming house for employees. "This way if they come off the streets they have a clean place to sleep and wash up, and that means they work better," she says.

Vicki has a family of her own (three children), but still has time to be active in the community. Most of all, she's known for saying, "I tell job-hunters my door is always open, but it opens both ways. I don't fire anyone—they fire themselves if they don't do the job."

Vicki is a model for today's modern women in business. She works hard, she's fair, she treats her employees well, and she's successful.

---

it, and perform proper maintenance. The same is true with people in companies. People tend to work harder for themselves than they work for others. Those who have an ownership or profit-sharing interest tend to be more careful, more involved, and more committed to their jobs.

Watching a small business develop is similar to watching a child grow. You beam with pride as your children mature, but you realize your ability to control their lives is declining with every year. The same is true with small-business growth. Often, entrepreneurs reluctantly face the reality that to keep growing, delegating responsibility to others is essential. However, nagging questions such as "Who should be delegated authority?" and "How much control should they have?" create perplexing problems.

This can be a particularly touchy issue in small businesses with long-term employees and in family businesses. As you might expect, entrepreneurs who have built their companies from scratch often feel compelled to promote employees who have been with them from the start—even when those employees aren't qualified to serve as managers. Common sense probably tells you this could be detrimental to the business.

The same can be true of family-run businesses that are expanding. Attitudes such as "You can't fire family" or you must promote someone because "they're family" can hinder growth. Entrepreneurs can best serve themselves and the business if they gradually recruit and groom employees for management positions. By doing this, trust and support of the manager is enhanced among other employees. It's probably fair to say that in managing employees, it's often the entrepreneur who must undergo the major change in attitude in business operations. You'll learn more about managing employees in Chapters 15 through 17.

Keeping Records

If you talk with small-business owners, they are likely to say that the most important assistance they needed in starting and managing the business involved accounting. They may call it record-keeping, for that is the foundation of accounting. A businessperson who sets up an accounting system early will save much grief later. Computers make record-keeping much easier and enable a small-business owner to follow the progress of the business (sales, expenses, profits) on a daily basis, if necessary. An inexpensive computer system can also help with inventory control, customer records, and payroll.

ONCE AN ACORN
Sometimes, to make it big you first have to make it small. Conrad Hilton started by sweeping floors in a dusty New Mexico hotel. He cleaned up as owner of a famous hotel chain. John Paul Getty started with a $500 oil lease in Oklahoma and become one of America's richest men. David Packard baked the paint onto his first product in a kitchen oven. Forty-five years later, he was running a $4.7 billion company. There are anonymous men and women starting small today whose names will be household words in 20 years. Will one of those names be yours? Get started!
Harry J. Gray, chairman and chief executive officer, United Technologies

You can't imagine the amount of paperwork generated by a small business until you get involved. By then, it is a little late to set up a control system. Experts in small-business management will help you select a computer program to help manage some of the work.

A good accountant is invaluable in setting up such systems and showing you how to keep the system operating smoothly. Many business failures are caused by poor accounting practices.

In this age of computers, it should not surprise you that there is a software package that is very helpful for those planning to start a business. *Venture, the Entrepreneurs Handbook* is a $349 software system for planning and running a business. It includes word processing and other functions needed to run a business such as accounting and access to business data sources. The system is available from Star Software Systems, 363 Van Ness Way, Torrance, California, 90501. You can draft a business plan on this software, and it includes business forms such as contracts for employees, partnership agreements, and more.[14]

Looking for Help

Small-business owners have learned, sometimes the hard way, that they need outside consulting advice early in the process. This is especially true of legal, tax, and accounting advice, but may also be true of marketing, finance, and other areas. Most small and medium-size firms cannot afford to hire such experts as employees, so they must turn to outside assistance (see Figure 6–6).

certified public accountant (CPA)
An individual who is certified by one of the states after passing a rigorous examination and meeting certain educational, moral, and job experience requirements.

A good **certified public accountant (CPA)** is invaluable to a small business. He or she can help make decisions such as whether to buy or lease equipment and whether to own or rent the building. Help may also be provided for tax planning, financial forecasting, choosing sources of financing, and writing up requests for funds. You need an experienced professional who is committed to the business and determined to play an active role in helping it grow.[15]

Other small businesses may give you an idea where to find a CPA experienced in small business. It pays to shop around for advice. CPAs provide a service and should be willing to answer questions, submit references, and otherwise show that they can help a business at a reasonable fee.

Another necessary and invaluable aid is a competent, experienced lawyer—one who knows and understands small businesses. Partners have a way of forgetting agreements unless the contract is written up by a lawyer and signed. Lawyers can help in a variety of matters including leases, contracts, protection against liabilities,

SOURCE	PERCENT USING SOURCE	IMPORTANCE RANK OF SOURCE
Accountant	78%	1
Other business owners	77	3
Friends/relatives	76	5
Bankers	72	2
Lawyers	63	6
Books/manuals	62	7
Suppliers	59	4
Trade organizations	47	9
Seminars	41	8
Government sources	33	10

FIGURE 6–6

Information sources. Small-business managers turn to accountants and bankers for important advice. They also question other business owners and friends for ideas.

and more. Again, it is wise to ask for references and interview people until a personal as well as professional fit is made. Pay your CPA and lawyer a fee rather than offering them a share of profits.

Marketing decisions should be made long before a product is produced or a store opened. An inexpensive marketing research study may help determine where to locate, what group to select as your target market, and what would be an effective strategy for reaching those people. Thus, a marketing consultant with small-business experience can be a great help to you.

Two other invaluable experts are a commercial loan officer and an insurance agent. The commercial loan officer can help you design an acceptable business plan and give you useful financial advice as well as loan you money when you need it. An insurance agent will explain all the risks associated with a small business and how to cover them most efficiently with insurance and other means (for example, safety devices and sprinkler systems).

Small-business owners tend to laugh when they hear how many consultants or "experts" they will need. They laugh because they don't have the money to hire such experts, and they wouldn't know what to ask if they could afford them. In fact, much of this expertise could come from *one* small-business consultant who knows marketing, accounting, and some law. (It is wise to seek a lawyer, however, in any case.)

The Small Business Administration (SBA)

The Small Business Administration (SBA) is a good source of expertise on starting a new business. The SBA has produced many publications to assist small-business owners in all areas of management. You can get many of its booklets at your local library.

An important source of information for small businesses is the **Service Corps of Retired Executives (SCORE).** This SBA office provides consulting services for small businesses free (except for expenses). The SBA also sponsors volunteers from industry, trade associations, and education who counsel small businesses. They are called the **Active Corps of Executives (ACE).**

The SBA also makes direct loans to *selected* small businesses (for example, handicapped owners, Vietnam veterans, and other special cases), and guaranteed loans for small businesses with special problems with the bank. Thanks to the Women's Business Ownership Act of 1988, women should find it easier to get loans for less than $50,000. Banks will make the loans, but the SBA will guarantee them.[16]

Service Corps of Retired Executives (SCORE)
Part of SBA made up of experienced businesspersons who provide consulting services to small businesses for free (except expenses).

Active Corps of Executives (ACE)
Volunteers from industry, trade associations, and education who counsel small businesses.

You may want to write or call the Department of Commerce or other federal agencies in Washington, D.C., for the latest information about such programs and report to the class. You might also go to the library and find out what SBA booklets are available.

Often a local university has business professors who will advise small-business people for a small fee. It also is wise to seek the counsel of other small-business owners. Other sources of counsel include chambers of commerce, the Better Business Bureau, and the business reference section of your library. In short, small businesses need expert, outside assistance in areas such as accounting, finance, and legal matters. Owners should obtain such assistance as soon as possible, before they make any major decisions, including whether the business should be started or not.

You know that small businesses are important to the American economy. Next, you will see that small businesses are expanding across American borders and going international.

GOING INTERNATIONAL: SMALL-BUSINESS PROSPECTS

There are only about 250 million people in the United States, but there are over 5 billion people in the world. Obviously, the world market is potentially a much larger, much more lucrative market for small businesses than the United States alone. In spite of that potential, most small businesses still do not think internationally. Only 39,000 American manufacturers—about 1 in 10—are exporting.[17] By Commerce Department estimates, there are 18,000 manufacturers (most of them small) that could export their products but don't. Figure 6–7 lists the industries with the highest potential in global markets.

Why are these companies "missing the boat" to the huge overseas markets? Primarily because the voyage involves a few major hurdles: (1) financing is often difficult to find; (2) many would-be exporters don't know how to get started; (3) potential global businesspeople do not understand the cultural differences of prospective markets; and (4) the bureaucratic paperwork can bury a small business.[18]

FIGURE 6–7

Global markets.

U.S. industries with the highest potential in international markets:

1. Computers and peripherals (hardware)
2. Telecommunications equipment and systems
3. Computer software and services
4. Medical instruments, equipment, and supplies
5. Electronic parts
6. Analytical and scientific laboratory instruments
7. Industrial process control instruments
8. Aircraft and parts and avionics and ground support equipment
9. Automotive parts and service equipment and accessories
10. Electronic production and test equipment
11. Electronic power generation and distribution systems and transmission equipment
12. Food processing and packaging equipment and machinery
13. Safety and security equipment
14. Printing and graphic arts equipment
15. Water resources equipment

Beside the fact that 95 percent of the world's population lives outside the United States, there are other good reasons for going international. For instance, exporting products can absorb excess inventory, soften downturns in the domestic market, and extend product lives. It can also spice up dull routines.

Small businesses have several advantages over large businesses in international trade.

- Overseas buyers enjoy dealing with individuals rather than large corporate bureaucracies.
- Small companies can usually begin shipping much faster.
- Small companies provide a wide variety of suppliers.
- Small companies can give more personal service and more undivided attention, because each overseas account is a major source of business to them.

There are many opportunities to start small businesses overseas. Often the competition is not nearly as stiff. This 7-Eleven store in Norway, for example, will not have many similar stores nearby. With over 5 billion people in the world market, there are many, many opportunities to take a successful concept from the United States to another country.

MAKING ETHICAL DECISIONS

You opened a small grocery store in a neighborhood where the majority of the residents are over 65. Most of the neighborhood lives on low, fixed incomes. Over two thirds don't have private transportation and must walk to buy their groceries. There are no competing grocery chains because they don't see a potential for profit in the area. You are considering charging higher than average prices for milk, bread, butter, coffee, and other products your customers buy regularly. What will you do? Is your decision ethical? What are the consequences of your decision?

The growth potential of small businesses overseas is truly phenomenal. The pioneers in overseas expansion were franchised organizations such as McDonald's, Avis, Hertz, Kentucky Fried Chicken, and Hanna car washes.[19] They were soon followed by entrepreneurs who faced too much competition in the United States and saw the opportunity to start small businesses in a foreign country. For example, John Stollenwerk found customers for his Wisconsin-made shoes in Italy and Ohio's Andrew Bohnengel opened an entire world for his tape company by adopting the metric standard. It is predicted that exports from unglamorous small businesses such as these will double in five years, having a significant impact on the balance of trade.[20] Judith Sons International Inc. is an Atlanta-based cosmetics firm. She went on a Commerce Department mission to Taiwan and ended up swamped with orders. She expects half of her 1990 sales to be exports.[21]

There is an abundance of inexpensive information about exporting. A good place to start is with the Commerce Department. Other sources of information include the SBA, banks, local freight forwarders, export management companies, and export trading companies. "Exportise," a step-by-step guide to exporting, is available from the Small Business Foundation. The most important lesson each of these sources will teach you is: Get to know your market before you commit yourself—and be prepared to be flexible. That's sound advice no matter where you do business!

PROGRESS CHECK

▪ Why do many small businesses avoid doing business overseas?

▪ What are some of the advantages small businesses have over large businesses in selling in global markets?

SUMMARY

1. Define small business and discuss its importance to the American economy.

1. Of all the nonfarm businesses in the United States, over 95 percent are considered small by the Small Business Administration.
   ▪ Why are small businesses important to the U.S. economy?
     Small business accounts for over 40 percent of GNP. Perhaps more important to tomorrow's graduates, 90 percent of the nation's new jobs in the private sector are in small businesses.
   ▪ What does the "small" in small business mean?
     The Small Business Administration defines a small business as one that is independently owned and operated, not dominant in its field of operation, and meets certain standards of size in terms of employees (less than 100) or sales (depends on the size of others in the industry, for example, American Motors was considered small in the auto industry before it merged with Chrysler).

2. Identify and give examples of the five categories of small business.

   ▪ What are the various classes of small businesses?
     There are five classes: (1) service businesses, (2) retail businesses, (3) construction firms, (4) wholesalers, and (5) manufacturers.

2. Over two thirds of the small businesses started this year will not survive to celebrate their fifth anniversary.

3. Summarize the major causes of small-business failures.

   ▪ Why do so many small businesses fail?
     Many small businesses fail because of managerial incompetence and inadequate financial planning.

- If you wanted to start a business that has a good chance of celebrating its fifth anniversary, what service or product would you offer?

    The businesses that are most likely to survive require advanced training to start—veterinarians, dentists, doctors, and so on.

3. Since so many small businesses fail, it is amazing that over 650,000 new businesses will be started this year!

    - Why do so many people start new businesses in spite of the slim odds for success?

        Owners ranked the pride of offering a product or service as the number one reason for wanting to start their own business. They ranked control and freedom next and ranked income way down in seventh place.

    4. Explain the reasons people start small businesses even though many others have failed.

4. Most people have no idea how to go about starting a small business. They have some ideas and the motivation; they simply don't have the know-how.

    - What hints would you give someone who wants to learn about starting a small business?

        First, learn from others. Take courses and talk with some small-business owners. Second, get some experience working for others. Third, take over a successful firm. Finally, study the latest in small-business management techniques, including the use of computers for things like payroll, inventory control, and mailing lists.

    5. Identify ways you can learn about small businesses.

5. Begin with a plan. The more effort you put into a business plan, the less grief you'll have later.

    - What goes into a business plan?

        See the box on p. 173.

    - Should you do it all yourself?

        Most small-business owners advise new entrepreneurs to get outside assistance in at least two areas: you need a good lawyer and a good accountant. Also, seek help from the Small Business Administration publications and any other sources you can find. The more knowledge you can gain early, the better.

    6. Explain what a business plan is, and outline the general areas of information that it should include.

    10. Describe the types of outside assistance a small-business owner needs.

6. Inadequate capitalization or poor financial management can destroy a business.

    - What sources of funds would you suggest someone wanting to start a new business consider investigating?

        A new entrepreneur has several sources of capital: personal savings, relatives, former employers, banks, finance companies, venture capital organizations, government agencies, and more. Of course, there's a price to be paid for such funds. A wise businessperson carefully considers the effect of paying the price.

    7. List the major sources of capital for starting small businesses. Point out the advantages and disadvantages of arranging loans from each of these sources.

7. It is important for a small-business person to "know the market."

    - What is a market?

        A market consists of a group of people with unsatisfied wants and needs who have both the resources and willingness to buy.

    - Why must a businessperson know the market?

        The goal of a businessperson is to find a need and fill it. In order to fill these needs, one must first identify the wants and needs of potential customers.

    8. Explain what a market is and why it is important for a businessperson to know the market.

8. Hiring, training, and motivating employees is critical to the success of a business.

    - What are some of the special problems that small-business people have in dealing with employees?

    9. Illustrate the need for effectively managing employees and identify some of the specific problems small-business owners face in this area.

Small-business owners often have difficulty finding competent employees. They also have trouble delegating authority, supervising relatives/workers, and grooming employees for management responsibilities.

9. The future growth of some small businesses is in foreign markets.

11. Point out the advantages and disadvantages of small businesses entering global markets.

Name several advantages small businesses have over large businesses in global markets?

Foreign buyers enjoy dealing with individuals rather than large corporations because (1) small companies provide a wider variety of suppliers and can ship more quickly and (2) small companies give more personal service.

Why don't more small businesses start trading internationally?

There are several reasons: (1) financing is often difficult to find; (2) many people don't know how to get started; (3) many do not understand the cultural differences of foreign markets; and (4) the bureaucratic red tape is often overwhelming.

GETTING INVOLVED

1. Write to the Small Business Administration, the Small Business Institute, the Committee for Economic Development, and the Office of Minority Business Enterprises. Find out what kinds of programs they offer and share your findings with the class. Go to the library to see what publications are available from the SBA. Bring some of the publications to class to review.

2. Select a small business that looks attractive as a career possibility for you. Talk to at least three people who manage such businesses. Ask them how they started their businesses. Ask about financing, personnel problems (hiring, firing, training, scheduling), accounting problems, and other managerial matters. Pick their brains. Let them be your instructors. Share your findings with the class, including whether or not the job was rewarding, interesting, and challenging, and why.

3. Go to the library and get *Inc., Venture,* and *Entrepreneur* magazines for the last couple of years. Look through the table of contents and briefly review several articles in each issue. What kind of information is available? Make copies of interesting articles for your career file. Share what you found with the class.

4. Do a survey of local schools and the local Chamber of Commerce. What classes are available in small-business management? What other resources are available, if any? Discuss.

5. Go to a local banker and discuss the financing of small businesses. What do they suggest? What is their experience with such loans? Share what you learn.

6. Put together a checklist of factors that might mean the difference between success and failure of a new business. Discuss the checklist in class.

PRACTICING MANAGEMENT DECISIONS

CASE ONE   **BMOC: STARTING A SMALL BUSINESS AT SCHOOL**

Many students do not wait until they complete school before they try to get their feet wet in small business management. As you remember, Laura Katleman wrote the business plan for her brownie business when she was in college. Many other students go beyond the planning stage and actually run their businesses while still in school. They look around them, see thousands of students, and try to develop small businesses that would appeal to students. For example, some students assemble and sell "Home Emergency Kits" for students returning in the fall. The kits contain items like pens, chocolate chip cookies, aspirin, and other college "necessities." The kits are sold to the parents and distributed to students the first week of class as a start-the-year-right gift from home.

Some students produce and sell calendars with pictures of beautiful women on campus or male "hunks." Others sell desk mats with advertising messages on the sides. More conservative students become salespeople for beer companies, cosmetic companies, and other traditional firms. They too feel as if they are in their own business on campus, because they have exclusive sales rights but don't have to assume as many risks.

One student makes more than his professors by selling ice cream from a truck. Others try to learn the retail business by delivering pizza or other fast foods. Others rent VCRs and microwave ovens.

Dick Gilbertson considered such options when he was a student at Indiana University. He felt students might enjoy having food other than pizza and subs delivered to the dorms. His research showed that students preferred McDonald's hamburgers and Taco Bell burritos. Students said they were willing to pay $1.00 more for a Big Mac, fries, and a Coke rather than ride the mile or so to the fast-food stores. Mr. Gilbertson's company, Fast Breaks, now serves the 13,000 students at his school. Guess who his partner is? A professor of entrepreneurship at Indiana University.

John-Lindell Pfeffer from Duke University sells candy at video stores so that customers can take home candy and eat it while watching movies, just as they do at theaters. Robert Lewis Dean II rents limosines to executives. Suzanne Duncan and Kelly Wilson are at Atlanta's Spelman College. They started a greeting card company.

Jimmy Enriquez was busy getting a degree in accounting at the University of Texas when he started two companies. One is a construction-site cleaning business that is run by his sister. It has 15 employees, grosses about $4,000 a week, and has expanded to Dallas and Houston. The other business is a vending company that leases "foosball" games.

There are now more than 350 entrepreneurship clubs on college campuses. Jimmy started an entrepreneur club at the University of Texas that has 260 members. Some 250 schools now have entrepreneurship classes. The Association of Collegiate Entrepreneurs recently published a list of the top 100 businesses started by people under 30. All are worth over $1 million. Maybe you should consider getting started now, too.

DECISION QUESTIONS

1. What are the advantages and potential problems of starting a business while in school?
2. What kinds of entrepreneurs are operating around your school? Talk to them and learn from their experiences.
3. What opportunities exist for satisfying student needs at your school? Pick one idea, write a business plan, and discuss it in class (unless it is so good you don't want to share it; in that case, good luck).

Source: Based on material from articles by Linda Williams, "Student Entrepreneurs on Campus," *Black Enterprise,* February 1989, pp. 169-172; John-Lindell Pfeffer, "Movie Time Candy," *Concepts,* 1988; Pamela Babcock, "Entrepreneur Hopes Limo-Booking Firm Will Be Smooth Ride to Success," *Washington Business,* March 28, 1988; and Suzanne Alexander, "Road to Riches on Campus," *The Wall Street Journal,* June 23, 1989, pp. B1 and B3.

CASE TWO   BOOKER WHATLEY: CAN SMALL FARMS BE PROFITABLE?

The newspapers are full of stories about the decline of the small farm. The government spends billions of dollars each year trying to save the farmer. Clearly, farming is not a business to be entering today, especially a small farm. That is what most people think. But not Booker T. Whatley.

Booker thinks he has a formula for successful small farming. His slogan: "Stay small, but get smart." Here is the formula. Find a small farm on a paved road within 50 miles of a city of at least 50,000 people. Grow about 10 different crops such as sweet potatoes, berries, and sweet corn. If one crop fails, you see, you will have nine others to sell. Completely irrigate the farm with a drip irrigation system to ensure against drought. The farm doesn't have to be much bigger than 25 acres. (The average American farm is 456 acres, which is nearly double the 1953 acreage.) The idea is to gross about $100,000 a year. You'll need a medium-size tractor, but not much else in the form of equipment.

The secret to success is not the production but the marketing function. The idea is to make this a "pick your own" farm-products place. People in town would pay you a nominal membership fee for the right to pick fresh vegetables at a cost of about 40 percent below supermarket prices. The theme is, "Eliminate the middleman for cheap, farm-fresh produce." That is why the farm is located relatively close to town. You save the time and money of harvesting; your customers do it for you.

For year-round income, you might add a place to raise rabbits, quail, or bees. Building and stocking a pond with fish provides a source of entertainment for customers and another cash crop. You may also want to lease out a nut tree or grapevine. You see the possibilities. The details depend on the location, local tastes, and competition.

Mr. Whatley's model was designed using a $250,000 grant from the Rockefeller Foundation (at Tuskegee Institute). One farmer in Alabama followed these ideas and has a 45-acre farm with 1,000 beehives that produce 17,000 pounds of honey. There are also pick-your-own blueberry patches and a plot of grapevines. Some land is leased for sheep grazing. The owner is now planning a fish pond.

One variation on Whatley's theme is growing specialty foods such as Alfalfa sprouts. Since sprouts are grown indoors, you avoid the problem of weather changes. In a 1,500 square foot shed, Bob Peer grows about 2,200 pounds of sprouts a week. The sprouts mature in just a few days and sell for about $1.00 per 6-ounce container. Indoor farming may be *the* future for small farmers.

DECISION QUESTIONS

1. Is a business plan as necessary for starting a small farm as for starting a small retail store? What are the differences, if any?
2. Could a farmer use the concepts of learning from others and taking over from others, as described in this chapter?
3. Can you anticipate any special problems a farmer might have in starting a business versus other small-business people?
4. Evaluate the Whatley formula.

Source: This case is based on Ed Bean, "Booker T. Whatley Contends His Program Will Help Small Farmers Make Big Money," *The Wall Street Journal*, October 4, 1984, p. 35; and Caroline E. Mager, "Down on the Sprout Farm," *The Washington Post*, March 23, 1988, pp. E1 and E14.

LOOKING AHEAD

It is no accident that books like *In Search of Excellence* and *A Passion for Excellence* have been best-sellers in recent years. What these books emphasized was the need for businesses to work more closely with their customers, to listen, to be more responsive, and more innovative. One reason for the growth of entrepreneurship is that smaller firms are more responsive to the market.

The key words are "responsive to the market." Business depends on customer relationships, and as with all relationships, customer relationships rely on open, two-way communication. The function responsible for market responsiveness and communication is marketing.

The next four chapters will explore all phases of marketing: product design, packaging, branding, pricing, distribution, promotion, retailing, and more. Marketing finds out what people want, and then communicates those wants to production so that the firm produces what people want. Marketing (listening) comes first. That is why it is the first function we discuss in this text. Before we get into marketing, though, take a few minutes to fill out the entrepreneurial readiness questionnaire. It will help you determine whether or not you are the entrepreneurial type.

APPENDIX TO PART TWO
ENTREPRENEURIAL READINESS
QUESTIONNAIRE*

Not everyone is cut out to be an entrepreneur. The fact is, though, that all kinds of people with all kinds of personalities have succeeded in starting small and large businesses. There are certain traits, however, that seem to separate those who will be successful as entrepreneurs and those who may not be. The following questionnaire will help you determine in which category you fit. Take a couple of minutes to answer the questions and then score yourself at the end. Making a low score doesn't mean you won't succeed as an entrepreneur. It does indicate, however, that you may be happier working for someone else.

Each of the following items describes something which you may or may not feel represents your personality or other characteristics about you. Read each item and then circle the response (1, 2, 3, 4, or 5) that most nearly reflects the extent to which you agree or disagree that the item seems to fit you.

	RESPONSE				
LOOKING AT MY OVERALL PHILOSOPHY OF LIFE AND TYPICAL BEHAVIOR, I WOULD SAY THAT . . .	AGREE COMPLETELY (1)	MOSTLY AGREE (2)	PARTIALLY AGREE (3)	MOSTLY DISAGREE (4)	DISAGREE COMPLETELY (5)
1. I am generally optimistic.	1	2	3	4	5
2. I enjoy competing and doing things better than someone else.	1	2	3	4	5
3. When solving a problem, I try to arrive at the best solution first without worry about other possibilities.	1	2	3	4	5
4. I enjoy associating with co-workers after working hours.	1	2	3	4	5
5. If betting on a horse race I would prefer to take a chance on high payoff "long shot."	1	2	3	4	5
6. I like setting my own goals and working hard to achieve them.	1	2	3	4	5
7. I am generally casual and easy going with others.	1	2	3	4	5
8. I like to know what is going on and take action to find out.	1	2	3	4	5
9. I work best when someone else is guiding me along the way.	1	2	3	4	5
10. When I am right I can convince others.	1	2	3	4	5
11. I find that other people frequently waste my valuable time.	1	2	3	4	5

* Source: Kenneth R. Van Voorhis, *Entrepreneurship and Small Business Management* (New York: Allyn and Bacon, 1980).

	RESPONSE				
LOOKING AT MY OVERALL PHILOSOPHY OF LIFE AND TYPICAL BEHAVIOR, I WOULD SAY THAT . . .	AGREE COMPLETELY (1)	MOSTLY AGREE (2)	PARTIALLY AGREE (3)	MOSTLY DISAGREE (4)	DISAGREE COMPLETELY (5)
12. I enjoy watching football, baseball, and similar sports events.	1	2	3	4	5
13. I tend to communicate about myself very openly with other people.	1	2	3	4	5
14. I don't mind following orders from superiors who have legitimate authority.	1	2	3	4	5
15. I enjoy planning things more than actually carrying out the plans.	1	2	3	4	5
16. I don't think it's much fun to bet on a "sure thing."	1	2	3	4	5
17. If faced with failure, I would shift quickly to something else rather than sticking to my guns.	1	2	3	4	5
18. Part of being successful in business is reserving adequate time for family.	1	2	3	4	5
19. Once I have earned something I feel that keeping it secure is important.	1	2	3	4	5
20. Making a lot of money is largely a matter of getting the right breaks.	1	2	3	4	5
21. Problem solving usually more effective when a number of alternatives are considered.	1	2	3	4	5
22. I enjoy impressing others with the things I am able to do.	1	2	3	4	5
23. I enjoy playing games like tennis and handball with someone who is slightly better than I am.	1	2	3	4	5
24. Sometimes moral ethics must be bent a little in business dealings.	1	2	3	4	5
25. I think that good friends would make the best subordinates in an organization.	1	2	3	4	5

Scoring: Give yourself one point for each 1 or 2 response you circled for questions 1, 2, 6, 8, 10, 11, 16, 17, 21, 22, 23, 24. Give yourself one point for each 4 or 5 response you circled for questions 3, 4, 5, 7, 9, 12, 13, 14, 15, 18, 19, 20, 25.

Add your points and see how you rate in the categories below:

21–25 Your entrepreneurial potential looks great if you have a suitable opportunity to use it. What are you waiting for?

16–20 This is close to the high entrepreneurial range. You could be quite successful if your other talents and resources are right.

11–15 Your score is in the transitional range. With some serious work you can probably develop the outlook you need for running your own business.

6–10 Things look pretty doubtful for you as an entrepreneur. It would take considerable rearranging of your life philosophy and behavior to make it.

0–5 Let's face it. Entrepreneurship is not really for you. Still, learning what it's all about won't hurt anything.

FUNDAMENTALS OF MARKETING

I'M A TOYS"R"US KID!
I'M A TOYS"R"US KID!
JE SUIS UN P'TIT ENFANT TOYS"R"US!
NIÑO
ICH BIN EIN TOYS"R"US
TOYS"R"US

MARKETING PRINCIPLES

7

Charles Lazarus.

Marketing is the whole business seen from the viewpoint of its final result, that is, from the customer's point of view.
PETER DRUCKER

PROFILE CHARLES LAZARUS OF TOYS "R" US

Charles Lazarus is the founder of the best-known toy store in the United States—Toys "R" Us. He created the company and the concept of supermarket-style toy stores from the shell of bankrupt Interstate Stores. Today, sales in his 314 stores are about $4 billion yearly. Most recently, Lazarus has branched out into children's clothing with the Kids "R" Us chain. That chain now has 112 stores, with more scheduled to open.

What makes Toys "R" Us so successful in a market with so many stores selling toys and related items? One key to the company's success is knowing precisely what customers are buying. Each product is tracked by computer and that helps the company spot hot-selling items before most competitors do. Toys "R" Us can then stock up and capture the market before others are even aware the fad had started.

Lazarus still has dreams of expansion. His next target? Foreign expansion of toy stores. Friends call Mr. Lazarus a "retail junkie." He genuinely enjoys visiting stores, talking to customers, and playing with the toys. Customers are happy with the emphasis on "selection, stock, and price." Each store has some 18,000 discounted items. The idea is to say to shoppers, "If you can't find it at Toys "R" Us, you can't find it anywhere."

Charles Lazarus succeeded by having a wide range of *products* available at a *place* away from other stores so that consumers would not be distracted. His *promotional* efforts are boosted by word of mouth because his *prices* are so low. Product, place, promotion, and price are the heart of marketing and Toys "R" Us is one store that does a great job of marketing. Chapters 7 through 10 will cover the heart of marketing, and the appendix to Part 3 will discuss how these concepts can be applied to the marketing of nonbusiness organizations.

Source: "Toys 'R' Us", *Business Week,* October 23, 1987, p. 315; Subrata N. Chakravarty, "Will Toys 'B' Great?" *Forbes,* February 22, 1988, pp. 37–39; and Joseph Pereira, "Toys 'R' Us, Big Kid on the Block, Won't Stop Growing," *The Wall Street Journal,* August 11, 1988, p. 6.

THE ROLE OF MARKETING IN SOCIETY

Charles Lazarus is successful in business because he knows what marketing is. He understands that a business succeeds or fails on its ability to *satisfy customers.* The key to success in any enterprise was summarized in the best-selling book *A Passion for Excellence.* The whole of the book is summed up in this passage:[1]

> In the private or public sector, in big business or small, we observe that there are only two ways to create and sustain superior performance over the long haul. First, take exceptional care of your customers . . . via superior service and superior quality. Second, constantly innovate. That's it.

Too many people think that marketing is little more than a combination of good selling and effective advertising. Ask people what comes to mind when they hear the word *marketing* and most will say *selling* or *advertising* or some other word having to do with *manipulating* or *persuading* consumers. Executives like Charles Lazarus realize that marketing means much more. It means paying careful attention to consumer wants and needs and then satisfying them. Effective marketing means that a business *listens* to consumers and responds to them. A popular slogan to describe marketing is this:

Find a Need and Fill It

GTE Sprint has the right idea when it comes to marketing: "Find a Need and Fill It." They know that listening to customers is as important as talking. "We hear you loud and clear" is an effective slogan if implemented properly.

That slogan appears in the ad for GTE Sprint above. It is a great way to think about marketing. A more scholarly definition—the one we will be using throughout this text—is:

> **Marketing** is the process of studying the wants and needs of others and then satisfying those wants and needs with quality goods and services (products) at competitive prices.

Marketers satisfy consumer wants and needs by assisting in the exchange of items of value. Certain conditions must be met before an exchange can take place:

1. There must be at least two participants.
2. Each participant must have something that is of value to the other participant(s).
3. Each participant can communicate with others.
4. Each participant is free to accept or reject the offer of others.
5. Participants feel that it is appropriate or desirable to exchange with others.

marketing
The process of studying the wants and needs of others and then satisfying those wants and needs with quality goods and services (products) at competitive prices.

THE IMPORTANCE OF MARKETING

A recent survey of executives from the fastest-growing 500 *small* businesses in the United States found that *marketing* was the greatest source of strength for these firms. Some 55 percent of respondents indicated that marketing strategy was their strong point.

The real competitive edge, according to 40 percent of these leading small-business executives, is gained by providing good *customer service*. Almost 30 percent felt that *quality* provided the major competitive edge. Terry Hill of the National Foundation for Independent Business summarizes the study this way:[2]

> Small businesses have to find their niche in the market. You can have some of the most innovative ideas in the world, but unless you have people who want to buy them or come back again, it will fail.

A recent poll of executives from *large* corporations found similar results. The executives selected "foreign competition" as public enemy number one. As a consequence, 54 percent said they were spending more time on marketing.[3]

Whether small or large, American businesses feel that their future success is greatly dependent on marketing. To them, that means better customer service, high-quality products, and innovation in product design.

Marketing is not limited to business firms. Nonprofit organizations such as public schools and hospitals, charities, churches, and social causes such as Save the Whales all do marketing as well. Marketing is also done by individuals. For example, athletes use marketing to win higher salaries. Job applicants use marketing to obtain a satisfying job. Marketing is the way all individuals and organizations meet some of their wants and needs by exchanging goods and services with others. We are focusing on business marketing in this text because business is the subject of the course. But if you decide to major in marketing in college, you will learn strategies for marketing in all kinds of organizations.

We need to focus on business marketing because America is losing ground in its marketing effectiveness, and that affects all of us. Here is how Leo Cherne, the executive director of the Research Institute of America, analyzed the state of marketing:[4]

> It wasn't long ago that we were the world's masters in marketing, motivation, and innovation. If any one aspect has suffered most, it has been the extent to which we have let our marketing and product design deteriorate. [Marketing, according to Cherne, means "knowing what it is that your market *needs* or *wants,* not just selling what you already have."]

THE CHANGING BUSINESS ORIENTATION

What marketers do at any particular time depends on what needs to be done to satisfy consumer wants. Consumer wants continually change. In the early 1900s, consumers primarily needed the basic necessities of life—food, clothing, and shelter. The marketing problem was getting goods from the producer to the consumer. Since the most basic need was for food, marketers concentrated on the distribution and storage of food products. Manufacturers also needed raw materials to produce various products, so the distribution of industrial goods (coal, steel, wood) was also important.

Since most of today's consumers have the basic necessities, marketers no longer consider distribution and storage as their most important functions, although they are still important. Today, marketers are most concerned with learning what consumers want and need and then providing the desired products and services. Let's look briefly at how this change of emphasis from production to marketing took place.

Marketers have changed their orientation from producing as much as possible because commodities were scarce to meeting the specific needs of selected markets. Today, for example, marketers provide all kinds of cereals to meet specific consumer wants. There are bran cereals for adults, sugared cereals for children, and so on. Learning what consumers want and providing for those wants has replaced distribution as the key marketing function.

From Production to Marketing

From the time the first settlers began their struggle to survive in America until after the Civil War, the general philosophy of business was, "Produce as much as you can because there is a limitless market." Given the limited production capability and the vast demand for products in those days, such a philosophy was both logical and profitable. Business owners were mostly farmers, carpenters, and trade workers who were catering to the public's basic needs for housing, food, and clothing. There was a need for greater and greater productive capacity, and businesses naturally had a **production orientation**—that is, the goals of business centered on production rather than marketing. This was satisfactory at that time, because most goods were bought as soon as they became available. As we noted earlier, the marketing need was for distribution and storage.

production orientation
Businesses focus on producing goods rather than marketing them.

During the period from 1890 to 1920, businesses developed mass-production techniques. Automobile assembly lines are a prime example of this development. Production capacity often exceeded the immediate market demand. The business philosophy turned in the 1920s from a production orientation to a **sales orientation.** Businesses turned their attention to promoting their products and mobilized much of the firm's resources in the sales effort.

sales orientation
Firms focus all attention on the salesperson, teaching him or her techniques for winning customers.

After World War II (1945), there was a tremendous demand for goods and services among the returning soldiers who were starting a new life with new families. These postwar years launched the baby boom (the sudden large increase in the birthrate after the war) and a boom in consumer spending. Competition for the consumer's dollar was fierce. Business owners recognized the need to be more responsive to consumers, and a new orientation emerged called the marketing concept. The **marketing concept** is a relatively new philosophy of marketing that emphasizes a consumer orientation, the training of employees, and a profit orientation.

marketing concept
Refers to a three-part business philosophy: (1) a consumer orientation, (2) training of all employees in customer service, and (3) a profit orientation.

THE MARKETING CONCEPT

The marketing concept that emerged in the 1950s and has dominated marketing thought for nearly 40 years has three parts:

1. A *consumer orientation;* that is, find out what consumers want and give it to them.
2. The *training of employees from all departments in customer service* so that everyone in the organization has the same objective—consumer satisfaction.
3. A *profit orientation;* that is, market those goods and services that will earn the firm a profit and enable it to survive and expand to serve more consumer wants and needs.

Consumer Orientation

All firms must learn to tailor their goods to meet the needs of consumers. The marketing concept calls for giving consumers what they want, training all employees in customer service, and keeping profit in mind as you select the kinds of goods and services you will offer.

Henry Ford is reported to have said, "You can have any color car as long as it's black." He seemed more interested in production than in adapting to consumer wants and needs. He felt that the best car was a good, reliable, inexpensive one. In fact, up until 1926, Ford sold half the new cars made in this country. But the people at General Motors talked with consumers and found a basic desire for individuality and status. They began making cars in all colors and shapes and eventually took away much of Ford's market. This is an example of a **consumer orientation** at work. Today, all the car companies are working harder than ever to be more responsive to consumer wants and needs. Foreign competition has become fierce, and only those firms that give consumers what they want will survive.

Training of All Employees in Customer Service

consumer orientation
Finding out what consumers want and giving it to them.

To provide optimum consumer satisfaction, all elements of marketing (product, price, place, and promotion) must be coordinated and integrated with other departments in that cause. For example, salespeople often promise delivery on a certain date, and then the delivery people fail to show up. Such lack of coordination annoys the consumer and prevents consumer satisfaction. Similarly, a salesperson may write up a sale and promise credit terms, only to find that the credit department turns down the customer's application. Again, this may cause resentment. Similar examples all show that a consumer orientation must be taught to all employees in all departments.

Profit Orientation

profit orientation
Marketing those goods and services that will earn the firm a profit.

The purpose of adopting a new business philosophy was to improve consumer relations because better relationships would also benefit the firm and increase profits. One goal of all business firms is to optimize long-term profits. This is called a **profit orientation.** Profit enables a firm to grow and hire more people, to provide even more satisfaction to consumers, and to strengthen the economy as a whole.

THINKING IT THROUGH   In much of Africa, there are few roads or inland waterways and no trains. Many of the people are starving, have few clothes, and little shelter. If you were to begin a marketing program to help these people, can you see the advantage of starting where we started in the United States—building roads, bridges, railroads, and a few storage facilities? Should businesses be production oriented rather than marketing oriented in developing Africa?

This year Americans will produce more litter and pollution than ever before.
If you don't do something about it, who will?

Give A Hoot. Don't Pollute. Forest Service-USDA

Once you acquire marketing skills, you can use them in any organization. For example, the Forest Service of the U.S. Department of Agriculture needed someone to prepare this antipollution advertisement. Other nonprofit charities, causes, and government agencies need marketers with promotion skills.

Applying a More Societal Marketing Concept in the 1990s

Is it enough to give individuals what they want? Don't firms have some obligation to society as well? There is some evidence today that organizations are adopting a broader **societal orientation** that includes a consumer orientation. For example, many large business firms and nonprofit organizations have become involved in programs designed to train the disadvantaged, improve the community, reduce the use of energy, cut back pollution, provide consumer information and consumer education, involve employees in community projects, and generally respond to the broader needs of society. A consumer orientation thus has become only one of the many social goals of today's progressive organizations and marketing managers.

societal orientation
Includes a consumer orientation, but adds programs designed to improve the community, reduce pollution, and satisfy other social goals.

Andora Freeman and Joy Ernst started a toy-recycling center to teach children the importance of conservation and to make a profit for themselves. Used toys are sold at bargain prices, and the original owners keep 50 percent of the take. The store, Toy Go Round, could earn higher profits if it carried toy guns and G.I. Joe dolls, but the owners refuse because they do not like the social effects on children of playing with war toys.

Now that the United States has become relatively affluent, people are demanding satisfaction of wants and needs that businesses often cannot and do not provide. For example, people are demanding a cleaner environment, a greater involvement with the arts, and better education programs. This has led to a whole new dimension of marketing—nonprofit organization marketing.

No longer is the objective simply to "Find individual needs and fill them." Rather, the goal is to meet the broader needs of society as well. Standard marketing practices were applied to tasks such as promoting public hospitals and universities, museums, associations, government programs, and more. But more sophisticated tools were needed to create new social attitudes and behaviors for such programs as stopping smoking, driving 55 miles per hour, wearing seat belts, picking up litter, and so on. Much future growth in marketing will be in this area. The appendix to Part 3 discusses nonbusiness marketing in more depth.

- What orientations did businesses have *before* the marketing concept was adopted?
- What are the three major elements of the marketing concept?

LEARNING ABOUT MARKETING

To help you learn about marketing, we shall first give you an overview of the marketing process by taking one product and quickly following it through the process. Remember, the basis of marketing is finding a need and filling it. So our first step is to find a need. Imagine that you and your friends do not eat big breakfasts. You want something for breakfast that is fast, nutritional, and good tasting. Some of your friends eat Quaker's 100% Natural cereal, but may not be happy with its sugar content. You ask around among your friends and acquaintances and find that there is a huge demand for a breakfast cereal that is good tasting, nutritious, high in fiber, and low in sugar. "Aha," you say to yourself—"I have found a need."

You have now completed one of the first steps in marketing. You have researched consumer wants and needs and found a need for a product that people want that is not yet available.

product
Any physical good, service, or idea that satisfies a want or need.

The next step is to develop a product to *fill that need*. A **product** is any physical good, service, or idea that satisfies a want or need. In this case, your proposed product is a multigrain cereal made with NutraSweet, an artificial sweetener.

It is a good idea at this point to do *concept testing*. That is, you develop an accurate description of your product and ask people whether or not the concept (the idea of the cereal) appeals to them. If it does, you must go to a manufacturer that has the equipment and skills to design such a cereal, and begin making prototypes. Prototypes are samples of the product that you take to consumers to test their reactions. The process of testing products among potential users is called **test marketing.**

test marketing
The process of testing products among potential users.

If consumers like the product, you may turn the production process over to an existing manufacturer or you may produce the cereal yourself. Production is *not* part of the marketing process. Marketing helps determine what products should be made, but it does not make them.

brand name
Word, letter, or groups of words or letters that differentiate the goods and services of a seller from those of competitors.

Once the product is made, you have to design a package, think up a brand name for the product, and set a price. A **brand name** is a word, letter, or group of words or letters that differentiate the goods and services of a seller from those of competitors. Cereal brand names, for example, include Cheerios, Team Flakes, and Raisin Bran. You name your cereal Fiberrific to emphasize the high fiber content and terrific taste. We shall discuss the product development process, including packaging, branding, and pricing, in detail in the next chapter. Now we are simply picturing the whole process to get an overall view of what marketing is all about.

marketing middlemen
Individuals or organizations that help distribute goods and services for the producer to the consumers.

Once the product is manufactured, you have to choose how to get it to the consumer. You may want to sell it directly to supermarkets or health food stores or you may want to sell it through organizations that specialize in distributing food products. Such organizations are called **marketing middlemen** because they are in the middle of a series of organizations that distribute goods from producers to consumers. We shall discuss middlemen and distribution in detail in Chapter 9.

Müselix was a popular cereal in Europe. Kellogg decided to try to market it here in the United States. The best way to convince people that the cereal tastes good is to have people try some. A 75¢ off coupon provides the incentive to buy and try the product.

The last step in the marketing process is to promote the product to consumers. Promotion consists of all the techniques sellers use to capture markets. They include advertising, personal selling, publicity, and various sales promotion efforts such as coupons, rebates, samples, and cents-off deals. Promotion will be discussed in detail in Chapter 10.

Fiberrific is the brand name selected for testing. Can you think of a better brand name? What kind of people would you select to test this new cereal? Can you think of other breakfast foods that people might want that you could sell along with this cereal?

THINKING IT THROUGH

The Marketing Mix

If you think through this process, you will see that managing the marketing process involves four factors after a need is discovered: (1) Design a want-satisfying *product*, (2) set a *price* for the product, (3) get the product to a *place* where people will buy it, and (4) *promote* the product. These four factors have become known as the **four Ps of marketing.**

four Ps of marketing
Product, price, place, and promotion.

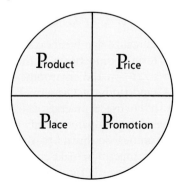

FIGURE 7–1

The four Ps and the marketing manager's role. The marketing manager chooses the proper price, promotion, and place to develop a comprehensive marketing program. In this figure, we show the mix for Fiberrific cereal. Included would be decisions about packaging, couponing, and more.

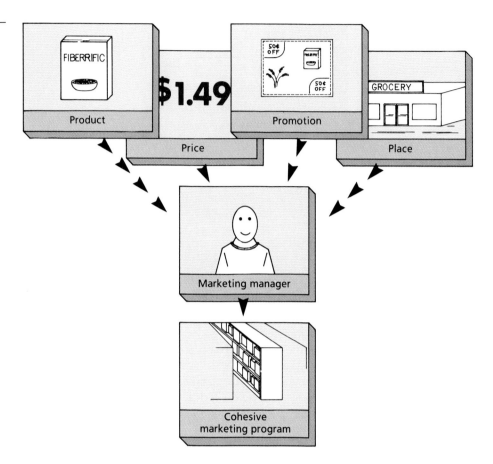

marketing mix
The strategic combination of product decisions with decisions regarding packaging, pricing, distribution, credit, branding, service, complaint handling, and other marketing activities.

marketing manager
Plans and executes the conception, pricing, promotion, and distribution of ideas, goods, and services to create exchanges that satisfy individual and organizational goals.

environmental scanning
Analysis of societal forces, economic realities, technological development and legal and regulatory conditions.

These four factors are also known as the **marketing mix** because they are the ingredients that go into a marketing program. Each of the factors of the marketing mix will be discussed in more detail in the next chapters.

A **marketing manager** designs a marketing program that effectively combines these ingredients of the marketing mix (see Figure 7–1). The American Marketing Association recently redefined the role of marketing managers as follows:[5]

> *Marketing (management)* is the process of planning and executing the conception, pricing, promotion, and distribution (place) of ideas, goods, and services (products) to create exchanges that satisfy individual and organizational goals.

SCANNING ENVIRONMENTAL FACTORS OF MARKETS

Successful marketing managers realize that business survival depends on predicting potential opportunities and future competition in their markets. Losing sight of what is going on in the market—in the environment of the business—can be disastrous (see box called Granddaddy of Diapermakers Is All Wet). Therefore, marketing managers today often use a practice called environmental scanning. **Environmental scanning** helps the company identify trends in markets and decide if the trends present opportunities or threats to the company. Today, shifting global markets and intensified competition make continuous monitoring of a firm's environment more necessary than ever before.

GRANDDADDY OF DIAPERMAKERS IS ALL WET

Procter & Gamble, a company that prides itself on leading the way in product improvement, got beaten at its own game in the Japanese disposable-diaper market. P&G lost out to Japanese competitors that designed better products and got them on the shelves faster.

Complacency was P&G's biggest problem. P&G was making diapers with old-fashioned paper pulp, when Japan's Uni-Charm Corp. introduced a highly absorbent, granulated polymer to soak up wetness and hold it in the form of a gel, keeping babies drier longer. P&G didn't introduce its polymer-packed Pampers in Japan until January 1985—three years after Uni-Charm's "superslurper" polymer product. The result: P&G's share of the market dropped to 7 percent in early 1985 from 90 percent several years before. Since the company began marketing its improved superabsorbent product, its market share has rebounded to about 15 percent.

Loss of the technological lead may have been P&G's biggest blunder, but it also fell behind the Japanese in market research. Uni-Charm spent two years studying buying habits in Europe and the United States before it came out with its superabsorbent diaper. It polled 300 Japanese mothers three times each on their opinions of foreign diapers. Using these opinions, Uni-Charm added leg gatherings and reusable adhesive closures and reshaped them for better fit long before P&G did. "P&G's product wasn't adapted for Japanese consumers," says Takasi Nomoto, an analyst with Nikko Research Center Ltd. in Toyko.

By 1990, the disposable-diaper market in Japan is expected to reach $1.3 billion. Eighty percent of all American and European babies already use disposables, but it is estimated that this figure is only 30 percent in Japan. So with 3 million Japanese babies under two years old, great marketing opportunities still exist.

Source: *Business Week*, October 13, 1986, p. 71.

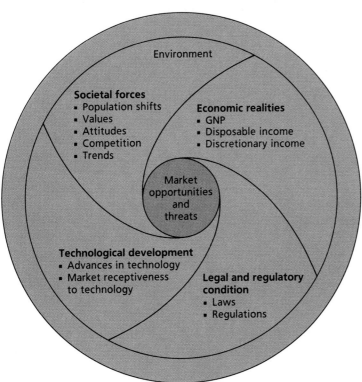

FIGURE 7–2

Environmental forces affecting marketing decisions.
A marketing manager must constantly adjust to changes in the environment. For example, people may suddenly decide that they want more rice bran in cereal rather than oat bran. The laws may change regarding what you can and must say on cereal boxes. The economy may slow making people more conscious of price. This figure shows that the environment creates both opportunities and threats to marketing managers.

An environmental scan includes a thorough analysis of four environmental factors: (1) societal forces, (2) economic realities, (3) technological development, and (4) legal and regulatory conditions (see Figure 7–2). The ability to serve a market depends on a marketer's understanding of changes in the market environment.

Societal Forces

Marketers must constantly be aware of changes in society. Often, societal shifts signal important trends that affect a company's operations by creating opportunities in a market. K mart introduced its Jaclyn Smith line of maternity clothes to meet the increasing demand of pregnant women who continued to work throughout pregnancy. The development of caffeine-free colas, low-salt food, and your own Fiberrific was in response to the increasing demands of health-conscious consumers. The progressive, forward-thinking marketer never loses touch with important societal forces in a market.

Economic Realities

disposable income
Money available after taxes for purchase of essentials.

discretionary income
Money available after taxes and essentials for purchase of nonessential items.

U.S. consumers probably find it hard to envision a market where buyers purchase items such as aspirin, cigarettes, and chewing gum one piece at a time. Yet, in such low-income markets as the Philippines, this is not uncommon. Therefore, marketers must include a careful economic analysis in the environmental scan to recognize the economic condition of a market. What do marketers look for in a market's economy? Factors such as disposable and discretionary income often indicate the potential of a market. **Disposable income** is money available after taxes for consumers to use for essentials such as food, shelter, and clothing. **Discretionary income** is money a consumer has after taxes and essentials to buy nonessential items. The People's Republic of China, with its billion-plus population, might appear to be an attractive market for products such as suntan lotion and wine coolers. But the economic realities of this market show that most consumers in China could not purchase these items because they have extremely limited discretionary income available. Do you think the economic conditions of the U.S. market can support a product like Fiberrific?

Technological Development

Advances in technology and the market's acceptance of these advances are two important factors that help us understand the opportunities in a market. Companies such as Apple Computer and Microsoft have experienced great success in the U.S. market by introducing technologically superior products. However, other markets are often less accepting of change and technology. One of the frustrations of the Peace Corps was the refusal of farmers in less-developed markets to use the modern farm equipment provided. Cultural attitudes caused them to resist using the equipment and they continued with their traditional farming methods.

As prospective producers of Fiberrific, you may be tempted to develop a product that provides daily nutritional needs in a single, time-saving capsule—just pop one in and you don't have to worry about eating the rest of the day! Keeping in mind what you know about American culture, how do you think such a product might be accepted in the U.S. market?

Legal and Regulatory Conditions

The conduct and direction of business is firmly tied to the legal and regulatory environment. Marketers must possess a clear understanding of major legislation enacted to protect the interests of consumers, competition, and society in general.

For example, zoning restrictions in cities like St. Louis limit the choice of locations for new businesses, whereas limited zoning laws in Houston allow businesses to build in residential as well as industrial areas.

In the United States, business operations are heavily impacted by various federal, state, and local laws. You will read about some of these laws in Chapter 23. Before you begin developing Fiberrific, it would be wise to review the laws that might affect you, such as restrictions on use of certain ingredients, requirements to reveal the ingredients on the package, and regulations affecting types of advertising.

WHAT MARKETERS DO: ASSISTING EXCHANGE THROUGH MARKETING FUNCTIONS

After scanning the environmental factors that affect a market, the company's marketing task begins. Keep in mind that marketing helps buyers and sellers exchange items of value. By the 1920s, marketers had expanded their efforts beyond storage and distribution of products. They were described as performing eight basic functions (see Figure 7–3):

1. Buying
2. Selling
3. Transporting
4. Storing
5. Financing
6. Standardizing (grading)
7. Risk taking
8. Research

Let's see how these eight functions apply to Fiberrific. First of all, *research* was needed to find an unmet need. Research was also needed to test the product in the market and to determine the most effective way to price, promote, and distribute the cereal. Marketing research is thus important throughout the design of the marketing mix.

To produce the cereal, one has to buy raw materials such as wheat, oats, and corn from farmers. Retail stores will buy the cereal from us and consumers will buy from the retail store. Thus, *buying and selling* are important marketing functions.

Buying and selling

Standardization and grading

Transportation and storage

Risk bearing

Credit (finance)

Marketing research

FIGURE 7–3

The traditional eight functions of marketing. Buying and selling are the heart of marketing. But buying and selling (trading) do not take place unless goods are transported to where they are wanted and stored until buyers are ready to buy (distribution). Without financing who can afford to buy a house? Marketing of farm products demanded standardization and grading of goods. Since goods are stored marketers assumed the function of taking those risks. Finally the whole process begins and ends with research knowing what the market wants.

Transportation is one of the most expensive and thus most important marketing functions. For example, grain has to be transported from the fields to the producers of Fiberrific. After the cereal is produced, it has to be shipped to wholesalers, stored, and shipped again to retailers. You then provide the final transportation to your home.

Financing (credit) was once a very important marketing function because expensive items could not be bought without credit and marketers provided the credit. Today, credit is often a separate department with separate managers, but it is still an important function to marketing managers. Many supermarkets, for example, buy cereal and other foods on credit from their suppliers.

Transportation involves moving grain from the farm to the producer and moving boxes of cereal from the producer to the retailer and other middlemen. Consumers, also perform the transportation function by bringing the cereal from the store to their homes.

The word *store* comes from the fact that retailers store items on their shelves so that consumers can buy goods whenever they want. Producers and middlemen also have *storage* facilities. Consumers may also perform the storage function by buying several boxes of cereal on sale and storing them in their homes. Whenever you buy products for resale and store them, you assume the *risk* of having them stolen or damaged or becoming obsolete. Assuming the risks of storage and distribution has traditionally been considered a marketing function. Risk management has now become a separate function, which we shall discuss in detail in Chapter 22.

The last traditional marketing function is *standardization* and *grading*. No doubt you have seen "Grade A eggs" and various classifications of beef (e.g., prime). These are forms of grading. Although cereal such as Fiberrific is not graded, its packaging does list how the product compares to certain standards—the recommended daily allowance (RDA) of vitamins and minerals.

How Marketing Adds Utility to Goods and Services

All of marketing's functions are performed to move goods from producers to consumers. The functions allow marketing to create utility. *Utility* refers to the value marketing adds to goods and services. There are five types of utility: (1) form, (2) time, (3) place, (4) possession, and (5) information. We will look briefly at each type of utility now, but you will learn more about them in Chapter 9.

A combination 7-Eleven store and Citgo gas station provides both time and place utility. Such stores may stay open long hours (time utility) and should be placed in a convenient location close to customers (place utility).

Form utility refers to the changing of raw materials to a finished product. Taking grains and turning them into our Fiberrific cereal is an example of form utility in action. Form utility is usually considered mainly a production function rather than a marketing function.

Time utility helps consumers by making products available when the consumer wishes. Supermarkets that are open 24 hours a day provide time utility for Fiberrific.

Place utility makes sure that goods and services are conveniently located to meet consumer needs. 7-Eleven stores help provide place utility for Fiberrific.

Possession utility helps make the exchange of goods between buyers and sellers easy. For example, supermarket check-cashing services make it easier for Fiberrific customers to complete their shopping. Anything that helps complete the sale—delivery, installation, warranties, credit—is considered part of possession utility.

Information utility informs buyers that the product exists, how to use it, the price, and other information. Such information is provided through advertising, salespeople, and packaging.

The word *marketing* comes from the root word *market*. A *market*, remember, is defined as people with unsatisfied wants and needs who have both the resources and the willingness to buy. Thus, if there are people who want a high fiber, low-sugar cereal like Fiberrific and have the resources and willingness to buy it, then we say that there is a market for Fiberrific. We learn whether there is a market for our cereal by studying consumer markets. We shall do that right after the Progress Check.

form utility
Changing raw materials to a finished product.

time utility
Making products available during convenient hours.

place utility
Making products and services available in convenient locations.

possession utility
Making the exchange of goods between buyers and sellers easier.

information utility
Informs buyers that the product exists, how to use it, the price, and other information.

- What are the four Ps of marketing and what else are they called?

- Can you name five of the eight traditional functions of marketing and give examples for each of them?

PROGRESS CHECK

RECOGNIZING DIFFERENT MARKETS: CONSUMER AND INDUSTRIAL

consumer market
All the individuals or households who want goods and services for personal consumption.

industrial market
Individuals and organizations that purchase goods and services to produce other goods and services or to rent, sell, or supply the goods to others.

There are two major markets in marketing, the consumer market and the industrial market. The **consumer market** consists of all the individuals or households who want goods and services for personal consumption or use. McDonald's Happy Meals, Toro lawn mowers, and Prudential health insurance policies are examples of items commonly considered consumer products.

The **industrial market** consists of all the individuals and organizations that want goods and services to produce other goods and services or to sell, rent, or supply the goods to others. Oil drilling bits, cash registers, display cases, office desks, public accounting audits, and corporate legal advice are examples of industrial goods and services.

The important thing to remember is that the buyer's reason for buying and the end use of the product is what determines whether a product is considered a consumer product or an industrial product. For example, a box of Fiberrific bought for a family's breakfast is considered a consumer product. However, if the same box of Fiberrific were purchased by Dinnie's Diner to sell to its breakfast customers, it would be considered an industrial product.

MARKETING TO CONSUMERS

The consumer market consists of the approximately 250 million people in the United States and the over 5 billion people in world markets. We learned in Chapter 1 that consumer markets are changing. The international market is growing in importance and the domestic market keeps changing as technology, the economy, and social trends change.

Who would have guessed that Tofu would become such a popular snack item? It did not happen by accident. Marketers had to explore what consumers liked. They then had to design a product that appealed to those tastes. Then the product had to be priced and promoted properly. This picture of Tofutti eaters shows how popular the uncholesterol, no butterfat product has become.

Obviously, consumers vary greatly in age, educational level, income, and taste. Because consumers differ so greatly, marketers must learn to select different consumer groups to develop products and services specially tailored to their needs. If a consumer group is large enough, a company may design a marketing program to serve that market.

Take Campbell soups, for example. You know Campbell for its line of traditional soups such as chicken noodle and tomato soup. But Campbell noticed the growth in the South and the increase in the Hispanic population and is experimenting with a Creole soup for the Southern market and a red-bean soup for the Hispanic market. In Texas and California, where they like their food with a little bit of kick, Campbell makes its nacho cheese soup spicier than in other parts of the country.

Campbell noticed that 24 percent of all U.S. households consisted of single people living alone. Most of these people are busy at work, but have money for convenience foods. Therefore, Campbell introduced many new products to appeal to singles and married young, urban professionals (yuppies) with little time to cook. Included are Le Menu frozen dinners, French Chef frozen soups, Great Starts frozen breakfasts, and Souper Combo, a frozen, microwavable soup and sandwich combination.[6] Campbell is just one company that has had great success studying the consumer market, breaking it down into categories, and then developing products for those separate groups.

The process of dividing the total market into several groups (segments) that have similar characteristics is called **market segmentation.** Usually a business cannot serve *all* of these markets. A business must decide which markets to serve. **Market targeting** is the process by which an organization decides which market segments to serve.

market segmentation
Process of dividing the total market into several submarkets (segments) that have similar characteristics.

market targeting
The process by which an organization decides which markets to serve.

Segmenting the Consumer Market

There are several ways in which a firm can segment (divide) the market for marketing purposes. Remember, the idea is to break the market down into smaller submarkets (segments) with similar characteristics (for example, all men, teenagers), and then aim the product at one or more of these groups. Let's say, for example, in trying to sell Fiberrific we begin our marketing campaign by focusing on a certain region such as the Far West, where fitness is a major issue. Dividing the market by geographic area is called **geographic segmentation** (see Figure 7–4).

geographic segmentation
Divides the market into separate geographic areas.

VARIABLE	TYPICAL SEGMENTS
Region	New England, Mideast, Great Lakes, Plains, Southeast, Southwest, Rocky Mountain, Far West
City or county size	Under 5,000; 5,000–19,999; 20,000–49,999; 50,000–99,999; and so on
Population density	Urban, suburban, rural
Zip codes	Furs and stationwagons, blue blood estates, shotguns and pickups*

FIGURE 7–4

Geographic segmentation variables.
This figure shows one way marketers use to divide the market. The aim of segmentation is to break the market into smaller units.

* See Deanne Klein, "You Are Where You Live," *Los Angeles Times,* April 16, 1989, p. 1 of Part IV.

demographic segmentation
Divides the market into groups by age, sex, income, and similar categories.

psychographic segmentation
Divides the market by values, attitudes, and interests.

benefit segmentation
Divides the market by benefits desired.

volume segmentation
Divides the market into user categories: heavy, medium, light, and nonusers.

Alternatively, we could aim our promotions toward people aged 25 to 45 who had some college training, and had high incomes—young, urban professionals, or yuppies, like Campbell soup did with its Le Menu line. Segmentation by age, income, and education level is part of **demographic segmentation** (see Figure 7–5).

We may want our ads to portray the lifestyle of this group. To do that, we could study the group's values, attitudes, and interests. This segmentation strategy is called **psychographic segmentation** (see Figure 7–6).

What benefits should we talk about? Should we emphasize high fiber, low sugar, price, health in general, or what? Determining which benefits are preferred is called **benefit segmentation** (see Figure 7–7). R. W. Frookies Inc. is hoping to capture a share of the cookie market by offering a new benefit—all-natural cookies.[7]

Who are the big eaters of cereal? Children eat cereal, but so do adults. Separating the market by usage (volume of use) is called **volume segmentation.** Most of the cereal companies seem to aim at children. Why not go for the adults, a less competitive market? (see Figure 7–8).

FIGURE 7–5

Demographic segmentation variables.
These variables divide the market into groups having similar ages and occupations. When would you use demographic information?

VARIABLE	TYPICAL SEGMENTS
Age	Under 5; 5–10; 11–18; 19–34; 35–49; 50–64; 65 and over
Education	Grade school or less; some high school; high school graduate; some college; college graduate; advanced college degree
Family size	1; 2–3; 4–5; over 6
Family life cycle	Young, single; young, married, no children; young, married, oldest child less than 6 years old; young, married, youngest child 6 or over; older, married, with children; older, married, no children; older, single; other
Income	Under $9,999; $10,000–$14,999; $15,000–$19,000; $20,000–$40,000; over $40,000
Nationality	American, Asian, British, Eastern European, French, German, Italian, Japanese, Latin American, Middle Eastern, Scandinavian, and so forth
Occupation	Professional, managerial; technical, officials, and proprietors; clerical, sales; supervisors; operatives; farmers; students; home managers; retired; unemployed
Race	White, Afro-American, Indian, Oriental, and so forth
Religion	Catholic, Protestant, Jewish, and so forth
Sex	Male, female
Social class	Lower lower, upper lower, lower middle, upper middle, lower upper, upper upper

---

FIGURE 7–6

Psychographic segmentation variables.
Using the variables in this figure would identify the lifestyles of a group of people. Can you think of an ad related to attitudes?

VARIABLE	TYPICAL SEGMENTS
Attitudes	LOV (list of values)
Behavior patterns	Self respect
Interests	Security
Lifestyles	Warm relationship with others
Opinions	Sense of accomplishment
Personality	Self-fulfillment
Self-image	Being well-respected
Values	Sense of belonging
	Fun and enjoyment in life

MAKING ETHICAL DECISIONS

Marketers have long recognized that children can be an important influence in the buying decisions of parents. In fact, many direct appeals for products are focused directly at children. At Fiberrific, we have experienced a great response to our new high-fiber, high-protein cereal among health-conscious consumers. The one important group we haven't been able to attract is children. Therefore, the product management team is considering the introduction of Fiberrific Jr to help solve this problem.

Fiberrific Jr may have strong market potential if we follow two recommendations of our research department. First, we coat the flakes generously with sugar (significantly changing its nutritional benefits). Second, we promote the product exclusively on children's programs. Such

a promotion strategy should create a strong demand for the product, especially if we offer a premium in each box. The consensus in the research department is that "kids will love the new taste," plus parents will agree to buy Fiberrific Jr because of the positive impression they have of our best-selling brand. The research director commented, "The chance of a parent actually reading our label and noting the addition of sugar is nil!"

Would you introduce Fiberrific Jr according to the recommendations of research? What are the benefits of doing this? What are the risks involved in using the recommendations? What would you do if you were the marketing manager?

VARIABLE	TYPICAL SEGMENTS
Comfort Convenience Durability Economy Health Luxury Safety Status	Benefit segmentation divides an already established market into smaller, more homogeneous segments. Those people who desire economy in a car would be an example. The benefit desired varies by product.

FIGURE 7–7

Benefit segmentation variables.
Which of these benefits are most important to you? Marketing managers need to know which variables people value.

VARIABLE	TYPICAL SEGMENTS
Usage	Heavy, light users, nonusers
Loyalty status	None; medium; strong absolute (repeat purchases)

FIGURE 7–8

Volume market segmentation.
Knowing who uses a product the most is an important consideration in marketing.

Selecting a Target Market

The best segmentation strategy is to use all the variables to come up with a consumer profile (a target market) that is clear, reachable, and sizable. Let's look more closely at procedures for selecting a target market.

Size and Growth Potential of Segment   The proper size for a market segment depends on the size of the seller and the objectives of the firm. A small business might select a small market segment that has been ignored by larger firms, but is large enough to be profitable for the small firm. The segment may be too small to attract larger competitors also, leaving that market to the smaller firm. You may have noticed the many small, ethnic grocery stores that have emerged in ethnic neighborhoods. The owners could not compete against the giant food retailers in national markets, but in those neighborhoods, the small store can be quite competitive if the size of the ethnic population is large enough and shows growth potential.

How Reachable the Segment Is   The marketer must be able to reach the target group and still make a profit. One may see the potential of selling a product in China because there are over a billion consumers there, but the cost of trying to reach those consumers may be too high.

The Nature of the Market   A marketer must look at how many competitors are already going after that market, potential new competitors, and the buying power of customers. If there are too many existing competitors or potential competitors, one may hesitate to enter certain markets. The same is true if the buying power of the target market is too low. The government has held hearings to determine if the cereal industry is so powerful that it is preventing competition from new businesses. We might want to get a copy of those hearings before we consider making and selling Fiberrific.

The Nature of the Company   Just because a market need exists and could be profitable does not mean a company should enter that market. Management must consider its present product mix, company strengths, and competence. For example, it might be a mistake for an automobile company to enter the food business. Mobil Oil was unsuccessful in running Montgomery Ward because oil executives simply do not have the expertise to run a department store even if market potential exists.

Regardless of the consumer segment a company chooses, it is important to know as much as possible about the target market. Marketers use market research to tell them what they need to know about their markets.

CONDUCTING MARKET RESEARCH

Take a moment to think about this situation. You have this terrific idea for crunching the cereal market. When friends ask you why you think you should dive into the cereal business you say you have "a gut feeling the health-conscious yuppies will love your Fiberrific." Do you immediately prepare for production and marketing of a new line of cereal to milk the market? Not unless you're flaky!

It is possible that you could be right about Fiberrific being the cream of the cereal market. However, the risk in acting on just a gut feeling is too great. It would be worthwhile to conduct some **marketing research.**

marketing research
A major function used to find needs and to determine the most effective and efficient ways to satisfy those needs.

If the goal of marketing is to find a need and fill it, then a major function must be to do research to find needs and to determine the most effective and efficient ways to satisfy those needs. Marketing research performs those tasks. You will learn about market research in Chapter 10. For now, we want you to understand that market research helps businesspeople understand how consumers are likely to act. It is important to understand consumer behavior in general. In the late 1960s, marketing scholars took a more active interest in learning how consumers think and act. Eventually, they developed textbooks in the area, and *consumer behavior* has become one of the major courses in marketing.

USING MARKET RESEARCH: UNDERSTANDING CONSUMER BEHAVIOR

Go back and review the box called Granddaddy of Diapermakers Is All Wet. Japanese producers of diapers captured the market from U.S. producers by doing better research. They talked to hundreds of consumers to learn what they wanted in a diaper. They then designed a superior diaper and won a huge market share.

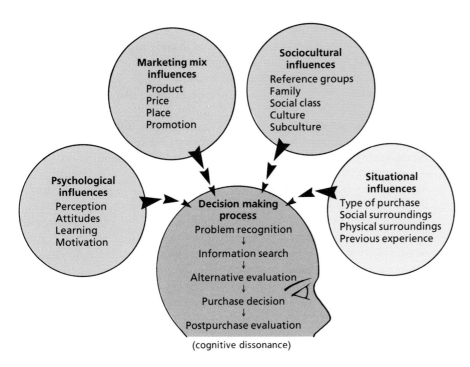

FIGURE 7-9

The consumer decision-making process and outside influences.
There are many influences on consumers as they decide which goods and services to buy. Marketers have some influence, but it is not usually as strong as sociocultural influences. Helping consumers in their information search and their evaluation of alternatives is a major function of marketing.

American manufacturers have long used marketing research, but the research process may have become too sophisticated. The secret to understanding consumers is simply to listen to consumers.[8] There are techniques for doing that, such as focus groups, that we shall discuss in Chapter 10. At this point, it is important to note that effective marketing research calls for getting out of the office and getting close to customers to find out what they want and need. Laboratory research and consumer panels can never replace going into people's homes, watching them use products, and asking them what improvements they seek. Many U.S. producers now do that, but many do not.

In international markets, the need is the same. One must learn the culture of the people and talk with them directly. What is attractive in one country may be an inconvenience in another. Marketing often is easier than some people make it. The goal, remember, is to find a need and fill it. That means listening to people constantly and adapting to what they say. It does not mean trying to sell them what they do not want.

The Consumer Decision-Making Process

Figure 7-9 illustrates the kind of subjects that are studied in a consumer behavior course. The core involves studying the consumer purchase decision process. "Problem recognition" may result from the fact that your washing machine broke down. This leads to an information search. That is, you look for ads about washing machines and begin reading brochures about them. You may even consult *Consumer Reports* and other information sources. Then you evaluate alternatives and make a purchase decision. After the purchase, you may ask others how much they paid for their machines and do other comparisons, including the performance of your new machine. Marketing researchers investigate consumer thought processes and behavior at each stage to determine the best way to facilitate marketing exchanges.

Sometimes marketing researchers must go door to door to find out what consumers want and need. That information is very helpful in designing and improving products. Be kind to researchers; they are trying to satisfy your wants and needs.

Consumer behavior researchers also study the various influences on consumer behavior. Figure 7–9 shows that such influences include the marketing mix variables, psychological influences such as perception and attitudes, situational influences such as the type of purchase and the physical surroundings, and sociocultural influences such as reference groups and culture. Some terms that may be unfamiliar to you include:

- *Culture* is the set of values, attitudes, and ways of doing things that are transmitted from one generation to another in a given society.
- *Learning* involves changes in an individual's behavior resulting from previous experiences and information.
- *Reference* group is the group that an individual uses as a reference point in the formation of his or her beliefs, attitudes, values, or behavior.
- *Subculture* is the set of values, attitudes, and ways of doing things that result from belonging to a certain nationality group, religious group, racial group, or other group with which one closely identifies, for example, teenagers.
- *Cognitive dissonance* means that consumers may have doubts after the purchase about whether or not they got the best product at the best price. That means marketers may have to reassure consumers *after* the sale if they want to establish a long-term relationship.

MARKETING TO INDUSTRY

The demand for industrial goods is a derived demand. For example, the demand for tires depends partially on the sale of new cars. The same is true of batteries, spark plugs, and other auto parts. Of course, repair parts make up a whole different market.

As consumers, we have a tendency to think of marketing as a system designed to satisfy our needs. After all, there are about 250 million consumers in the United States, and we make up a huge market. On the other hand, there is another side of marketing that we know must exist, but do not encounter as often. That market consists of all the exchanges that go on among major organizations in society. For example, somebody has to sell coal to the electric utilities that use coal. Someone else sells electricity to the major manufacturers of cars, trucks, machinery, and computers. Then someone sells these manufactured goods to farmers, government agencies, and other large organizations.

Using all the resources provided by these exchanges, producers, farmers, and government agencies begin the process of satisfying the needs of consumers. But there are still many middlemen who must be contacted before goods and services reach the final consumer. There are wholesalers who provide transportation and storage services; communications firms who keep the information flowing among the organizations (for example, ad agencies); and retailers who store the merchandise until we are ready to buy.

The marketing of goods and services to manufacturers, institutions (for example, hospitals or schools), commercial operations (retail stores), and the government is called *industrial* marketing. The basic principle of this kind of marketing is still find a need and fill it, but the strategies are different because the buyers are different. Some of the things that make industrial marketing different are:

1. The market for industrial goods is a *derived* demand; that is, the demand for consumer products such as automobiles creates the demand for industrial goods and services including tires, batteries, glass, metal, plastics, and engines.

2. The demand for industrial goods is relatively *inelastic;* that is, the quantity demanded does not always change significantly with minor changes in price. The reason for this is that industrial products are made up of so many parts that a price increase for one part is not usually a significant problem.
3. The *number of customers* in the industrial market is relatively *few;* that is, there are just a few construction firms or mining operations compared to the consumer market of 70 million or so households.
4. The *size* of industrial customers is relatively *large;* that is, a few large organizations account for most of the employment and production of various goods and services.
5. Industrial *markets* tend to be *concentrated;* for example, oil fields tend to be concentrated in areas such as the Southwest and Alaska. Consequently, marketing efforts often may be concentrated on a particular geographic area, and distribution problems are often minimized by locating warehouses near industrial "centers."
6. Industrial *buyers* generally are *more rational* in their selection of goods and services; they use specifications and carefully weigh the "total product offer" including quality, price, and service.
7. Industrial *sales* tend to be *direct.* Manufacturers will sell products such as tires directly to automobile manufacturers, but would tend to use wholesalers and retailers to sell to consumers.

Industrial markets are often more complex than consumer markets because the products are sold many times before they reach the ultimate consumer. Many universities now have courses in industrial marketing. In such courses, you would learn how to segment industrial markets using government data. You would also learn about the various kinds of industrial goods and how they are marketed. In general, industrial goods are sold through a sales force as opposed to using advertising as consumer goods are. That is because the customers tend to be large and concentrated and it is more efficient and effective to call on them with a salesperson.

Let's pause now and review marketing careers in general. You will see that few areas in business offer more variety in careers than marketing.

CAREER PROSPECTS IN MARKETING

A recent survey of 208 executives discovered that employment growth in the next five years will be led by jobs in marketing. More growth was expected in service industries than in industrial firms. Figure 7–10 shows the expected growth rates (see page 216). Some 54 percent of the executives ranked marketing jobs as the most likely to provide the most job opportunities in the next five years. (See the box that lists the many careers available in marketing on the following pages.)

- What are the three methods of targeting consumer markets?

- Can you describe the technique and give examples of how a company would use the following segmentation strategies: geographic, demographic, psychographic, benefit, and volume?

PROGRESS CHECK

SELECTED CAREERS IN MARKETING

PRODUCT MANAGEMENT

1. A product manager for consumer goods develops new products that can cost millions of dollars, with advice and consent of management—a job with great responsibility.
2. An administrative manager oversees the organization within a company that transports products to consumers and handles customer service.
3. An operations manager supervises warehousing and other physical distribution functions and often is directly involved in moving goods on the warehouse floor.
4. A traffic and transportation manager evaluates the costs and benefits of different types of transportation.
5. An inventory control manager forecasts demand for stockpiled goods, coordinates production with plant managers, and keeps track of current levels of shipments to keep customers supplied.
6. An administrative analyst/planner performs cost analyses of physical distribution systems.
7. A customer service manager maintains good relations with customers by coordinating sales staffs, marketing management, and physical distribution management.
8. A physical distribution consultant is an expert in the transportation and distribution of goods.

ADVERTISING

9. An account executive maintains contact with clients while coordinating the creative work among artists and copywriters. In full-service ad agencies, account executives are considered partners with the client in promoting the product and helping to develop marketing strategy.
10. A media buyer/analyst deals with media sales representatives in selecting advertising media and analyzes the value of media being purchased.
11. A copywriter works with art directors in conceptualizing advertisements and writes the text of print or radio ads or the storyboards of television ads.
12. An art director handles the visual component of advertisements.
13. A sales promotion manager designs promotions for consumer products and works at an ad agency or a sales promotion agency.

Source: David W. Rosenthal and Michael A. Powell, *Careers in Marketing*, 1984, pp. 352–354. Adapted by permission of Prentice-Hall, Englewood Cliffs, N.J.

FIGURE 7–10

Expected employment growth ranked by corporate divisions.
Executives rated sales, marketing, and advertising jobs as having the most employment growth during the next five years. Jobs in the field of administration show the least amount of employment growth. It makes sense to explore a career in marketing.

Source: The 1987 Dunhill Personnel System, Inc., Survey of Top Executives as reported in *Marketing News*, November 6, 1987, p. 1.

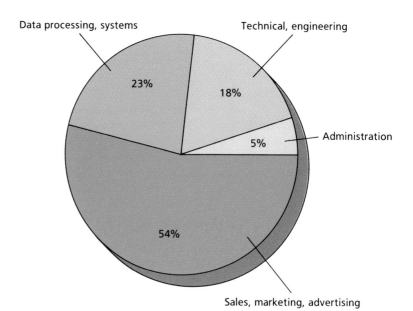

14. A public relations manager develops written or filmed messages for the public and handles contacts with the press.
15. A specialty advertising manager develops advertising for the sales staff and customers or distributors.

RETAILING

16. A buyer selects products a store sells, surveys consumer trends, and evaluates the past performance of products and suppliers.
17. A store manager oversees the staff and services at a store.

SALES

18. Door-to-door salespeople call on people at their homes or offices. They are usually paid a commission on such sales.
19. In sales to channel members, the salesperson sells to those in another step of the distribution channel (between the manufacturer and the store or customer). Compensation includes salary plus bonus.
20. An industrial or semitechnical salesperson sells supplies and services to businesses. Compensation is salary plus bonus.

21. A complex or professional salesperson sells complicated or custom-designed products to business. This requires understanding of the technology of a product. Compensation is salary plus bonus.

MARKETING RESEARCH

22. A project manager for the supplier coordinates and oversees the market studies for a client.
23. An account executive for the supplier serves as a liaison between client and market research firm, like an advertising agency account executive.
24. An in-house project director acts as project manager (see item 22) for the market studies conducted by the firm for which he or she works.
25. A marketing research specialist for an advertising agency performs or contracts for market studies for agency clients.

NONPROFIT MARKETING

26. The marketing manager for nonprofit organizations develops and directs mail campaigns, fund raising, and public relations.

SUMMARY

1. Marketing is the process of studying the wants and needs of others and then satisfying those wants and needs with quality products or services at competitive prices.
   - Why is marketing more important now?
     Overseas competition and domestic competition have made marketing the major difference among firms.

1. Describe marketing's role in society and its importance.

2. The *marketing philosophy* has changed over time. At first, emphasis was on production; then on sales. In the 1950s, the philosophy that emerged was called the *marketing concept*.
   - What is the marketing concept?
     It is (1) a consumer orientation, (2) the training of employees from all departments in customer service, and (3) a profit orientation.
   - What is the future direction of marketing?
     The aim is to satisfy all needs, including needs not met by businesses. Businesses are adopting a *societal orientation* that broadens the consumer orientation.

2. Explain the evolution of the marketing concept and describe its three parts.

3. The basis of marketing is finding a need and filling it.
   - What are the basic steps in the marketing process?
     After finding a need, the next step in the marketing process is finding a product or service to fill the need. Marketers test their ideas before developing a prototype of the proposed product and testing it in the

3. Illustrate the steps in the marketing process.

marketplace. The product development process includes packaging, branding, and pricing. Marketing middlemen distribute the product to consumers. The final step in the marketing process is promoting the product to consumers.

4. The ingredients that go into a marketing program are called the four Ps of marketing.

4. Identify the four Ps of the marketing mix.

  ⁜ What are the four Ps of marketing?
   The four Ps of marketing are: product, price, place, and promotion.

5. Business survival depends on predicting potential opportunities and future competition. Environmental scanning helps companies identify trends and decide if the trends present opportunities or threats.

5. Explain the role of an environmental scan in marketing.

  ⁜ What factors are included in an environmental scan?
   An environmental scan includes a thorough analysis of four factors: (1) societal forces, (2) economic realities, (3) technological development, and (4) legal and regulatory conditions.

6. Marketing helps buyers and sellers exchange items of value.

6. List the eight traditional functions of marketing.

  ⁜ What do marketers do?
   The eight traditional marketing functions are: buying, selling, transportation, storage, finance (credit), risk bearing, standardization, and research.

7. Utility refers to the value that marketing adds to goods and services.

7. Explain how marketing adds utility to goods and services.

  ⁜ What are the five types of utility?
   The four types of utility are: (1) form, (2) time, (3) place, (4) possession, and (5) information.

8. There are two major markets in marketing, the consumer market and the industrial market.

8. Differentiate between consumer and industrial markets.

  ⁜ How do industrial markets differ from consumer markets?
   Consumer markets consists of those who buy products for their personal consumption. Industrial markets consist of those who purchase products to produce other products or to sell, rent, or to supply products to others.

9. Because consumers differ greatly, marketers must learn to select different consumer groups for which to develop products and services.

9. Compare the various forms of market segmentation and describe how target markets are selected.

  ⁜ What is a target market?
   It is that group or groups selected for special marketing effort.
  ⁜ How are those groups chosen?
   Market segmentation breaks the total population down into segments with similar characteristics. The breakdown could be:
     Geographic: Various areas of the country are targeted.
     Demographic: Age, sex, income, religion, race, and other variables are used.
     Psychographic: Values, attitudes, and interests are some of the variables.
       Benefit: Comfort, convenience, and other benefit categories are chosen.
     Volume: Heavy, light, medium, and nonusers.

10. American companies use market research to understand consumers.

10. Discuss the process of using market research to understand consumer behavior.

  ⁜ What is the secret to understanding consumers?
   The secret to understanding consumers is *listening*—getting close to customers and finding out what they want and need.
  ⁜ What are the factors that influences buyer behavior?
   The various influences on consumer behavior include: marketing mix influences, psychological influences, sociological influences, and situational influences.

11. The marketing of goods and services to organizations is called industrial marketing.
   - How does industrial marketing differ from consumer marketing? Industrial marketing is more complex than consumer marketing. Industrial goods are more frequently sold through salespeople than through advertising as are consumer goods. See pages 214 and 215.

11. Define industrial marketing and explain how industrial markets differ from consumer markets.

12. Marketing jobs are the most likely to provide the most job opportunities in the next five years.
   - What careers are available in marketing? See the box on pages 216 and 217.

12. Discuss present and future prospects for careers in marketing.

---

1. Imagine you are the president of a small liberal arts college. Enrollment has declined dramatically. The college is in danger of closing. Show how you might revive the college by applying the marketing concept. How would you implement the three phases: (1) a consumer orientation; (2) the training of employees in all departments in customer service; and (3) a profit orientation? Would you recommend a more societal orientation as well? How would you do it?

2. It is easy to document the social ills for which marketing is partially responsible. Discuss the social benefits and social costs imposed by marketing. Take the position you have not held previously and defend it (that is, defend marketers if you have opposed them and vice versa). Discuss whether less developed countries would or would not benefit from more marketing.

3. Businesses began with a *production orientation*, producing what they wanted and selling it later. Discuss how some artists and colleges continue that orientation. What would happen if artists and colleges switched to the marketing concept? How would their interaction with consumers differ?

4. Talk to several people who work in marketing (for example, retailers, salespeople, marketing researchers, advertising people) and see how they enjoy their jobs. Which careers look best? Discuss your findings with the class.

5. Take a product and show how you would segment the market for it using the six variables listed in this chapter.

6. Go to the library and find information about SIC codes. Look through the information, take notes, and put them in a file under industrial marketing.

7. Think of a product other than cereal that your friends want but cannot get near campus. Think of a product to fill that need, do a concept test, evaluate the total market, think of a brand name and a package, develop a promotional scheme, and think of how you would distribute it to students. Begin thinking about a marketing plan for the overall business plan so you can get funding for the project later.

GETTING INVOLVED

CASE ONE CAN YOU DRAW A PICTURE OF MARKETING?

PRACTICING MANAGEMENT DECISIONS

In 1984 it was Trivial Pursuit. In that year, the U.S. producer was making 63,000 games a week and had back orders for 11 million more. The sales projection for 1985 was 20 million games. A major problem for the producer was meeting demand. When Sears ordered 100,000 sets, that took up much of the plant capacity, which meant that thousands of smaller stores couldn't get the game at all.

Now the hot game is Pictionary. In its first year, sales were $57 million. Again, supply is the problem. As you read this, sales are expected to be way above 10 million units.

Pictionary was invented by Robert Angel. In 1985, he borrowed $35,000 to produce several thousand units to sell locally. When Nordstrom department stores began selling it, sales took off. Word of mouth was the major selling tool. Pictionary is a game that the whole family can play. It is like charades except one draws a picture to elicit the right response. (Don't play it will children unless you expect to lose—they are good at it.) The game is perfect for the stay-at-home trend in family living and for parties with mixed-age groups.

DECISION QUESTIONS

1. What human need is being met by Trivial Pursuit and Pictionary? Is this an example of "Find a need and fill it?"
2. Of the four Ps of marketing, both companies producing these games had the most trouble with *place* (distribution). Actually the trouble began with insufficient production capacity. What do these examples tell you about fad marketing?
3. Is it possible to *create* a fad? If it is possible, why don't more people do it?
4. Which of the board games that are most popular in America could be adapted to markets in countries such as India and China where the market is more than a billion people?

Source: "The Gang that Got Away," *Inc.*, September 1988, p. 18, and other sources.

CASE TWO   KELLOGG: MARKETING BREAKFAST CEREAL

It all started back in the 1800s with Dr. John H. Kellogg. He was a strict vegetarian and a leader in the Seventh Day Adventist community. Dr. Kellogg noticed that the typical American breakfast consisted of salt pork, biscuits, and ham gravy or pancakes and molasses. As director of a health spa, Dr. Kellogg fed his patients corn, wheat, and oatmeal—ground and baked. No salt and no sugar.

C. W. Post was one of his patients. He decided to go into business to market what was to become Post Grape-Nuts. Post added sugar to make his cereal tastier. Dr. Kellog and his brother, Will K. Kellogg, countered by offering a sweetened cereal of their own. The breakfast battle was on.

The big Kellogg cereal in the 1800s was Corn Flakes. Guess what their number one best-seller is today? You guessed it: Corn Flakes. Number two is sugar-covered corn flakes (Frosted Flakes). All in all, Kellogg has about 41 percent of the ready-to-eat cereal market.

Let's see how Kellogg has attacked certain market segments. For adults, it has developed high-fiber cereals like Nutri-Grain, Common Sense Oat Bran, and Cracklin' Oat Bran, plus the vitamin-pill-in-a-cereal Special K. For children, it's Froot Loops, Sugar Pops, Sugar Smacks, and Apple Jacks. For traditionalists, there are Corn Flakes, Rice Krispies, and Raisin Bran.

Post Raisin Bran is now part of General Foods. It, too, has targeted certain markets. There is Grape-Nuts for the old timers. Kids can feast on sugary cereals such as Smurf-Berry Crunch, Super Sugar Crisp, and Honey-Nut Crunch Raisin Bran. Joggers might go for C. W. Post Hearty Granola or just plain Bran Flakes. All together, General Foods has about 13.2 percent of the market.

The old Cheerios is still number one for General Mills. Honey Nut Cheerios is second. Their new hot cereal product is Total Oatmeal. Anyone over 40 may remember eating graham crackers with milk. Now, General Mills makes it easy for you with Golden Grahams. Kids can sugar up on Donutz, Trix, and Lucky Charms. The General Mills market share is 21 percent or so.

A popular cereal in the Quaker Oats line is 100% Natural. Quaker Oats also makes Life, Cap'n Crunch, and Halfsies. Market share—about 7.7 percent.

We can't forget Ralston Purina with its 5.5 percent plus market share. They have given us Donkey Kong, Cookie Crisp, Waffelos, and Dinky Donuts. But their number one cereal is still Chex.

Nabisco's number one seller is Shredded Wheat. It has only about a 5.5 percent market share.

Going through the top sellers in each company is like going back to the 1940s or before. The top sellers—Corn Flakes, Cheerios, Post Raisin Bran, and Chex—are long-time favorites. Most of the best-sellers are relatively nutritious.

How far have we come from the original intent of Dr. Kellogg to give us a healthy, nutritious, sugar-free, salt-free breakfast food? Cookie Crisp is 47 percent sugar. A one-ounce serving of Mr. T's Cereal has 230 milligrams of sodium. That's 30 more milligrams than Lay's packs into an equal amount of potato chips. Other high sodium cereals include Product 19 (320), Corn Chex, Cheerios, Rice Krispies, and Kellogg's Corn Flakes. Sugar Golden Crisp is 51 percent sugar, and Honey Smacks has 57 percent refined sweetener (including honey). In fact, there is little fiber in most children-oriented cereals.

The cereal industry is now doing about $4 billion a year in sales. Some $100 million is spent on advertising.

DECISION QUESTIONS

1. Cereal makers have followed the marketing slogan of find a need and fill it by giving us any kind of cereal we want, including cereals that are mostly sugar or very high in salt content. This is definitely an example of a consumer orientation. Would the same mix of cereals be available if cereal companies adopted a more societal orientation?

2. Dropping those cereals with high sugar content would cut profits dramatically at cereal companies. Under what circumstances would a company make such cuts?

3. Cereal companies have provided us with high-fiber, high-vitamin cereals. Adults eat them, but children often choose the cereals that are half sugar. What reaction do you have to this trend?

4. In 1987, Kellogg introduced two new cereals from Europe called Muselix (muse-licks). Five-grain Muselix contains oats, wheat, corn, rice, and barley. Bran Muselix contains bran, chopped dates, figs, and almonds. These cereals have 20 percent of the total European market. How would you market them here compared to how Kellogg did it? Give brand names, markets, price, and promotional ideas. Does it sound like Kellogg has destroyed the market for Fiberrific?

Sources: Patricia Sellers, "How King Kellogg Beat the Blahs," *Fortune,* August 29, 1988, pp. 54–64; William S. Bergstrom, "Manufacturer Tries New Category in Cereal Battles." *Marketing News,* September 25, 1987; and "It's Raining Cereals," *The Washington Times,* January 4, 1989, pp. E6–E6.

In Chapter 6 on page 173 you learned that a business plan calls for a marketing plan. That plan includes a review of the industry size, trends, and the target market segment. We discussed how to do these things in Chapter 7. You may want to review segmentation strategies when writing your business plan. Chapter 8 helps you look at your product and discuss its strengths and weaknesses relative to competition. Chapter 8 will also look at the pricing information you will have to include in a business plan; for example, the number of products you will have to sell to break even.

LOOKING AHEAD

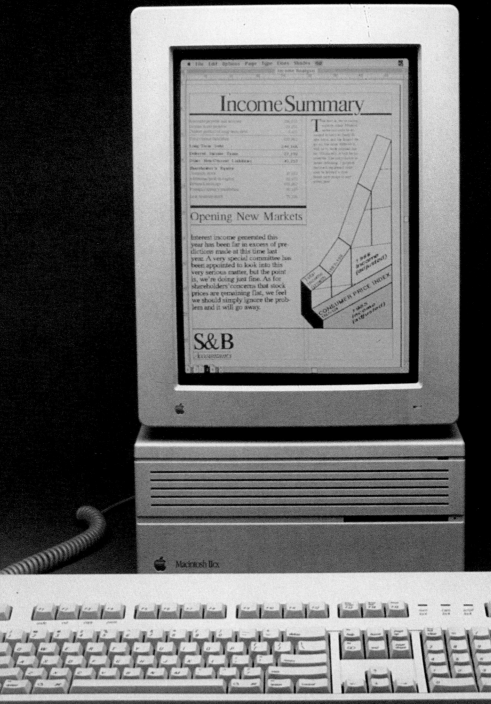

PRODUCT DEVELOPMENT AND PRICING

8

LEARNING GOALS

After you have read and studied this chapter, you should be able to:

1. Explain the difference between a product and a product offer. Define and give an example of a product mix and a product line.

2. Describe how businesses create product differentiation for their goods and services.

3. Identify the three classes of consumer products and how they are marketed.

4. Identify the two major classes of industrial goods and how they are marketed.

5. List the four functions of packaging.

6. Give examples of a brand, a brand name, and a trademark, and how to prevent a brand name from becoming generic.

7. Explain the role of a product manager.

8. Outline the five steps of the new product development process.

9. Identify and describe the stages of the product life cycle and describe marketing strategies at each stage.

10. Give examples of various pricing objectives.

11. Discuss the use of break-even analysis and calculate the break-even point.

12. Describe various pricing strategies.

KEY TERMS

brand, *p. 234*
brand name, *p. 234*
break-even analysis, *p. 246*
break-even point, *p. 246*
competition-oriented pricing, *p. 248*
convenience goods and services, *p. 229*
demand-oriented pricing, *p. 248*
generic goods, *p. 235*
generic names, *p. 235*
industrical goods, *p. 230*
knockoff brand, *p. 235*
market modification, *p. 242*
market price, *p. 248*
national brand names, *p. 235*
penetration pricing strategy, *p. 247*

price leadership, *p. 248*
private brands, *p. 235*
product differentiation, *p. 228*
product life cycle, *p. 240*
product line, *p. 226*
product manager, *p. 236*
product mix, *p. 227*
product modification, *p. 243*
product offer, *p. 225*
production goods, *p. 232*
shopping goods and services, *p. 229*
skimming pricing strategy, *p. 247*
specialty goods and services, *p. 230*
support goods, *p. 232*
trademark, *p. 234*

PROFILE   JOHN SCULLEY OF APPLE COMPUTER

John Sculley

John Sculley was once president of PepsiCo and creator of the Pepsi Generation concept. That was a surprising position to obtain for a boy who was painfully shy and had a stammer so bad he "couldn't even walk into a candy store and ask for a pack of Life Savers."

What is even more surprising, perhaps, is that John Sculley is now chief executive officer of Apple Computer, Inc. He was recruited by Steve Jobs, one of the founders of the company. A clash of personalities between Jobs and Sculley led to Jobs' resignation. Sculley was left with a company in the throes of strong competition within the personal computer industry. At first, Sculley made some major blunders; spending too much on advertising, Pepsi-style, and not enough on product development.

Sculley brought in Frenchman Jean-Louise Gassè from Paris operations to head new product development. Sculley had the skill to push the new product ideas through the corporate bureaucracy. In March of 1987, Sculley introduced two new computers for the business market: the Macintosh SE and the Macintosh II. The Mac II has 10 times the computing power of the first Mac brought out in 1984. Based on customer input, these new computers are called "open Macs" because they can use inner parts made by other companies. That lets Mac join computer networks, use bigger screens, and use software written for IBM computers and compatibles. In short, Sculley changed Apple from a computer company focused on personal computers for the *home* market to one aimed at *business* users. As a consequence, sales zoomed 40 percent to $2.7 billion and net earnings jumped 41 percent to $217 million. Nearly half the sales and most of the profit came from business users, a very small market for Apple before Sculley arrived.

We have mentioned previously in this text that the successful companies of the future will be those that are flexible and develop new products for new markets quickly and efficiently. This chapter explores product development and pricing strategies for the future.

Source: Brian O'Reilly, "Growing Apple Anew for the Business Market," *Fortune,* January 4, 1988, pp. 36–37; and "Polishing the Apple," *U.S. News and World Report,* February 8, 1988, p. 51.

If a man can . . . make a better mousetrap than his neighbor, though he builds his house in the woods the world will make a beaten path to his door.
RALPH WALDO EMERSON

PRODUCT DEVELOPMENT OVER TIME

International competition today is so strong that American businesses are losing markets to foreign producers. The only way to regain those markets is to design better products. That means products that are perceived to have high quality at a fair price. As we shall see in this chapter, whether or not a consumer perceives a product as better depends on many factors. To satisfy consumers, marketers must learn to listen better and to adapt constantly to changing market demands. A critical part of the impression consumers get about products is the price. This chapter, therefore, will explore two critical parts of the marketing mix: product development and price.

John Sculley has learned that the problem of adapting products to markets is a continuous one. An organization cannot do a one-time survey of consumer wants and needs, design a line of products to meet those needs, put them in the stores, and relax. There must be a *constant* monitoring of customer wants and needs because consumer and business needs change over time.

Nowhere is the problem of consumer choice more keenly felt than in the fast-food business. Firms such as McDonald's and Burger King are constantly monitoring consumers to detect trends, preferences, and lifestyle changes that call for new offerings. The more sophisticated firms become in marketing, the more important it becomes for others to follow. A few years ago Wendy's didn't even have a research and development staff. Today they have 42 people in that area.

The number of products in the development stage ranges from 20 or so at McDonald's to more than 50 at Wendy's. Burger King uses a computer to predict how much labor a new product will require, what effect it might have on sales of other menu items, and how much total profit it will generate.

Fast-food organizations must constantly monitor all sources of information for new product ideas. McDonald's got the idea for the Big Mac, the Filet-O-Fish sandwich and the Egg McMuffin from franchisees. Chicken McNuggets were developed when the head chef was experimenting with Onion McNuggets. McDonald's chairman suggested that the chef try chicken and after much market testing, a new product was born. Researchers also monitor grocery store shelves and cookbooks for new ideas. Product development, then, is a key activity in any modern business.

One place you may not expect to see new product development is in the produce section of the supermarket. Yet Frieda Caplan has a specialty foods company that is introducing new products every day into produce areas. For example, many grocery stores still carry only a few varieties of apples. Now growers are working on 35 types, including Northern Spys, Golden Russets, and Opalescent. The trend toward Caribbean meals has led supermarkets to sell fruits and vegetables such as yuca, malanga, boniato, and calabaza. Exotic vegetables such as osone, frisee, and tsoisin are catching on. You get the idea. There is a lot more to new product development than merely introducing new products, however. What marketers do to create excitement for those products is as important as the products themselves.

Developing a Total Product Offer

Let's review the role of products in marketing before we get too far into product concepts. We have said that marketing is the process of finding wants and needs and satisfying those wants and needs with quality goods and services (products) at competitive prices. We defined a *product* in Chapter 7 as any physical good, service, or idea that satisfies a want or need.

From a marketing management viewpoint, a product offer is more than just the physical good or service. A **product offer** consists of all the tangibles and intangibles that consumers evaluate when deciding whether or not to buy something. Thus, a product offer may be a washing machine, car, or bottle of beer, but the product offer also consists of the:

- Price.
- Package.
- Store surroundings.
- Image created by advertising.
- Guarantee.
- Reputation of the producer.
- Brand name.
- Service.
- Buyers' past experience.

product offer
Consists of all the tangibles and intangibles that consumers evaluate when deciding whether or not to buy something.

When people buy a product, they evaluate all these things and compare product offers on all these dimensions. Therefore, a successful marketer must begin to think like a consumer and evaluate the product offer as a total collection of impressions created by all the factors listed.

The marketing view demands the active recognition of a new kind of competition. This is . . . not competition between what companies produce in their factories, but between what they add to their factory output in the form of packaging, services, advertising, customer advice, financing, delivery arrangements, warehousing, and other things people value.

THEODORE LEVITT

Let's go back and look at our highly nutritious, high-fiber, low-sugar breakfast cereal, Fiberrific, for example. The product offer as perceived by the consumer is much more than the cereal itself. Anything that affects consumer perceptions about the benefits and value of the cereal may determine whether or not the cereal is purchased. The price certainly is an important part of the perception of product value. Often a high price indicates high quality. The store surroundings also are important. If the cereal is being sold in an exclusive health food store, it takes on many of the characteristics of the store (e.g., healthy and upscale). A guarantee of satisfaction can increase the product's value in the mind of consumers, as can a well-known brand name. Advertising can create an attractive image, and word of mouth can enhance the reputation. If a buyer has tried the product before, he or she has certain predispositions to buy or not. Thus, Fiberrific is more than a cereal as a product offer; it is a whole bundle of impressions in the minds of consumers.

THINKING IT THROUGH   One branch of the Chicago Public Library lends expensive power tools and such accessories as fiberglass extension ladders. At the Carnegie library, in Pittsburgh, volunteer psychologists go to the library, listen to people's troubles, and refer them to appropriate help. The Broome High School Media Center in Spartanburg, South Carolina, lends prom, wedding, and mother-of-the-bride dresses donated by members of the community. What is the product of a library? Is this a good example of find a need and fill it? What prompted libraries to be so creative in their product offers? What is the product of a college or university?

The Product Mix

product line
A group of products that are physically similar or are intended for a similar market.

Companies usually do not have just one product that they sell. Rather, they sell several different, but complementary products. Figure 8–1 shows the product lines of Procter & Gamble. A **product line** as demonstrated in Figure 8–1 is a group of products that are physically similar or are intended for a similar market. The product lines for Procter & Gamble include bar soaps, detergents, and dishwashing detergents. In one product line, there may be several competing brands. Thus, Procter & Gamble has many brands of detergent in its product line, including Bold, Cheer, Tide, and Ivory Snow. All of P&G's product lines make up its product mix.

MicroMagic has introduced a product line of microwavable snack foods that is capturing the market. It has 80 percent of the frozen microwavable milkshake

This picture features the package for MicroMagic foods. The brand name is prominent. Emphasis is on 100 percent pure ingredients and convenience. All of these things are part of the product offer.

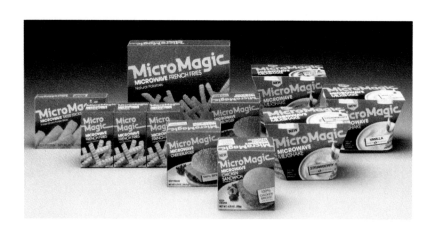

market and 45 percent of the frozen microwavable french fry market. The company hopes to add to its product line—microwavable snack foods—in coming years.[1]

Product mix is the term used to describe the *combination* of product lines offered by a manufacturer. As you can see in Figure 8-1, P&G's product mix consists of product lines of soaps, detergents, toothpastes, shampoos, and so on.

product mix
The combination of products offered by a manufacturer.

FIGURE 8-1
Procter & Gamble's product mix and product lines. Most large companies make more than one product. In this figure, you can see the various products and brands Procter & Gamble makes. Note how physically similar the products are.

	PRODUCT LINES	BRANDS
P R O D U C T M I X	Bar soaps	Camay, Coast, Ivory, Kirk's, Lava, Monchel, Safeguard, Zest
	Detergents	Bold, Cheer, Dash, Dreft, Era, Gain, Ivory Snow, Liquid Bold-3, Liquid Cheer, Liquid Tide, Oxydol, Solo, Tide
	Dishwashing detergents	Cascade, Dawn, Ivory Liquid, Joy, Liquid Cascade
	Cleaners and cleaners	Comet, Comet Liquid, Mr. Clean, Spic & Span, Spic & Span Pine Liquid, Top Job
	Shampoos	Head & Shoulders, Ivory, Lilt, Pert Plus, Prell
	Toothpastes	Crest, Denquel, Gleem
	Paper tissue products	Banner, Charmin, Puffs, White Cloud
	Disposable diapers	Luvs, Pampers
	Shortening and cooking oils	Crisco, Crisco Oil, Crisco Corn Oil, Puritan

You could plan a trip,   borrow a classic film,   get help finding a job,

learn to belly dance,   attend a concert,   get fast answers,

trace your family tree,   stay in shape,   or get your books by mail.

©Walt Disney Productions

AT THE LIBRARY? At the library.
Come see what's new besides books.
American Library Association

This ad for libraries shows that the product is much more than books. It includes films, concerts, and other consumer-satisfying offers. "Come and see what's new," is the theme. What do you suppose prompted libraries to broaden their product offering?

In the case of automobile manufacturers, the product mix consists of everything from passenger cars to small trucks, large tractor trailers, and tanks. One auto manufacturer's product line for passenger cars may include large luxury cars, midsize cars, compact cars, minivans, and station wagons.

Manufacturers must decide what product mix is best. The mix may include both goods and services to spread the risk among several industries. Companies must be careful not to diversify so widely that they lose their focus and their competitive advantage. Coca-Cola, for example, produces five of the top-selling soft drinks. When it diversified into wine companies, a movie studio, pasta manufacturing, and television shows, the results were disappointing. When it bought Columbia Pictures, it increased production from 12 movies a year to 18. This was an attempt to saturate the market with various products to get increased market share, as they did with Coca-Cola. Well, the strategy simply does not work in movies as it does in soft drinks.[2]

PRODUCT DIFFERENTIATION

Product differentiation is the attempt to create in the minds of consumers product perceptions that make one product seem superior to others. Often the *actual* product differences may be quite small, so marketers must use a clever mix of pricing, advertising, and packaging to create a unique and attractive image. One of the more successful attempts at product differentiation was accomplished by Perrier. Perrier made its sparkling water so attractive through pricing and promotion that often people ordered it by brand name instead of a Coke or Pepsi.

There is no reason why a company could not create a similar image for Fiberrific. With a high price and creative advertising, it could become the Perrier of cereals. The box called Product Differentiation—from Chicken to Sneakers gives several examples of how this has been done. The ultimate example of product differentiation would be to package and sell air. Well, guess what? The Japanese have been rather successful selling canned oxygen for $5. Michael Jackson triggered the boom by bringing his own air on his Japanese tour.[3] Would you believe that they now sell air in different "flavors" or odors? Different products call for different marketing strategies, as we'll see below. What kind of strategy would you use to sell canned air?

Products such as these could be sold as convenience goods, and the marketing emphasis would be on intensive distribution (convenient locations). Heavy brand advertising could move them up to shopping goods where consumers compare price and quality; certainly Bounty and Charmin fit that category. Some people go out of their way to buy Pampers, and that makes them a specialty good. The category is determined by consumers.

PRODUCT DIFFERENTIATION—FROM CHICKENS TO SNEAKERS

Millions of chickens are raised on Maryland's Eastern Shore. One of the most famous producers there is Frank Perdue. Perdue chickens are sold at a premium to restaurants and in supermarkets in New York City and all through the eastern United States. These chickens can be distinguished from competing chickens because they are fed "secret ingredients" that make them yellow. Furthermore, Frank Perdue promises "your money back if you don't like the chickens." Frank Perdue is proof that a homogeneous product such as chickens can be "differentiated" from competition and sold at a premium. Most producers found it difficult to create product differentiation for chicken, but Frank Perdue did not.

A similar story can be told about tennis shoes. For years, no product lacked a special identity more than did tennis shoes (sneakers). But through careful promotion and product differentiation, tennis shoes with names such as Adidas, Nike, and Reebok have captured a large share of the market—again at premium prices. Whereas plain sneakers might cost $15, these new tennis shoes may cost $50 and more. Nike products are so popular that the name Nike on a T-shirt is a status symbol in some areas. Product differentiation and promotion made Nike stand out from "ordinary" tennis shoes. Then Reebok captured the aerobics market. Keds countered in 1989 by promoting its plain canvas shoes and recaptured much of the market.

Similar stories could be told about sunglasses (Foster Grant), bananas (Chiquita), and oranges (Sunkist). Product differentiation and promotion generated special inter-

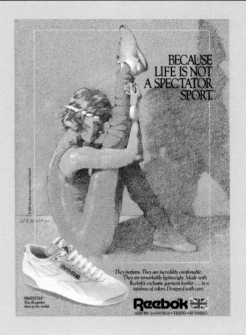

est in these products that is hard to beat. Could similar preferences be generated for other homogeneous products such as milk, cereal, eggs, butter, and gasoline? What about colleges, hospitals, movie theaters, and auto rental firms? How can you create product differentiation for Fiberrific?

Marketing Different Classes of Consumer Goods and Services

Several attempts have been made to classify consumer goods and services. One of the more traditional classifications has three general categories: convenience goods and services, shopping goods and services, and specialty goods and services. These classifications are based on consumer shopping habits and preferences.

Convenience Goods and Services   Convenience goods and services are products that the consumer wants to purchase frequently and with a minimum of effort (for example, candy, snacks, banking). Location is very important for marketers of convenience goods and services. Brand awareness and image also are important.

Shopping Goods and Services   Shopping goods and services are those products that the consumer buys only after comparing value, quality, and price from a variety of sellers. Shopping goods and services are sold largely through shopping centers where consumers can "shop around." Because consumers carefully compare such products, marketers can emphasize price differences, quality differences, or some combination of the two. Examples include clothes, shoes, appliances, and auto repair shops.

convenience goods and services
Products that the consumer wants to purchase frequently and with a minimum of effort.

shopping goods and services
Products that the consumer buys only after comparing quality and price from a variety of sellers.

Expensive specialty items are often sold through specialty magazines. For example, these Rossignol skis were sold through *Ski* Magazine. People will go out of their way to buy specialty ski products that have a popular brand name.

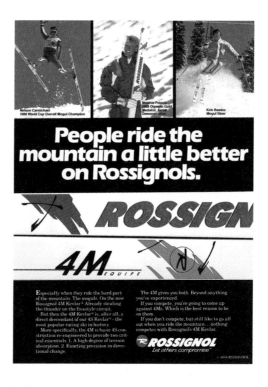

Specialty Goods and Services   Specialty goods and services are products that have a special attraction to consumers, who are willing to go out of their way to obtain them. Examples include goods such as expensive fur coats, jewelry, cars, and services provided by medical specialists or business consultants. These products are often marketed through specialty magazines. For example, specialty skis may be sold through ski magazines and specialty foods through gourmet magazines.

The marketing task varies depending on the kind of product; that is, convenience goods are marketed differently from specialty goods, and so forth. The best way to promote convenience goods is to make them readily available and to create the proper image. Price or quality are the best appeals for shopping goods, and specialty goods rely on reaching special market segments through advertising.

Whether or not a good or service falls into a particular class depends on the individual consumer. What is a shopping good for one consumer (for example, coffee) could be a specialty good for another consumer (for example, imported coffee). Some people shop around comparing different dry cleaners, so dry cleaning is a shopping service for them. Others go to the closest store, making it a convenience service. Perrier took what was basically a shopping good in the mind of the consumer (sparkling water) and tried to make it a specialty good by making it look very different and special. One could do the same for canned oxygen with the right combination of packaging, branding, pricing, and promotion.

Marketing Industrial Goods and Services

Industrial goods are products used in the production of other products. Some products can be classified as both consumer and industrial goods. For example, the Macintosh II computer pictured at the beginning of this chapter could be sold to

---

specialty goods and services
Products that have a special attraction to consumers, who are willing to go out of their way to obtain them.

industrial goods
Products used in the production of other products.

Convenience goods and services.

Shopping goods and services.

Specialty goods and services.

consumer or industrial markets. As a consumer good, the computer might be sold through computer stores like Computerland or through computer magazines. Most of the promotional task would go to advertising. As an industrial good, the Mac II is more likely to be sold by a salesperson. Advertising would be less of a factor in the promotion strategy. You can see that classifying goods by user category helps determine the proper marketing mix strategy.

production goods
Industrial goods such as grain and steel that enter into the final product.

support goods
Industrial goods such as accessory equipment and supplies that are used to assist in the production of other products.

Industrial goods are often divided into two major categories: production goods and support goods (see Figure 8–2). **Production goods** include raw materials like grain and steel that enter into the final product. Component parts such as electric motors and springs are also categorized as production goods. Producers of such goods usually sell directly to other manufacturers using salespeople as the major promotional technique. **Support goods** are purchased to assist in the production of other products. Some of the major categories and how they are promoted include:[4]

Installations such as buildings and equipment. These are usually expensive items and are sold through sales representatives. Pricing is often by competitive bid.

Accessory equipment such as tools and office equipment is often purchased in small quantities. As a consequence, they are usually sold through distributors who have many outlets and can contact many buyers.

Supplies include items like paper clips, stationery, and cleaning items. These may be purchased through distributors or may be ordered directly from the producer with little negotiating taking place over time.

Services include maintenance and repair services and professional services such as tax advice and legal counsel. Such services are sold through salespeople and through a bidding process.

In general, industrial producers rely much more heavily on salespeople than do producers of consumer goods. This means more job opportunities in sales for you in the industrial sector. The average industrial sales call costs a producer over $200, so you can see why industrial salespeople get excellent training and receive outstanding wages.

FIGURE 8–2

Types of consumer and industrial goods and services. Marketers have developed categories of goods and services to help in designing marketing strategies. A different strategy is needed for convenience goods (location) than for shopping goods (price/quality). Similarly, industrial goods and services are categorized because the marketing task for each category is different and the process of categorizing makes it clearer which strategies to use.

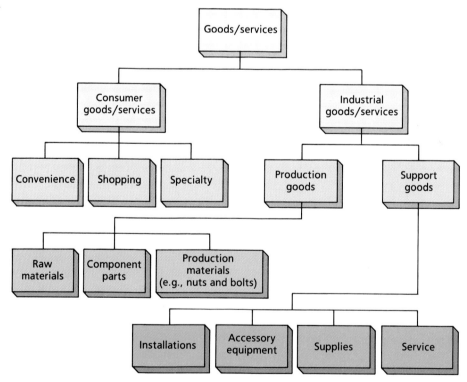

- What is the difference between a product and a product offer as viewed by a marketing manager?

- What is the difference between a product line and a product mix?

- Name the three classes of consumer goods and services, and give examples of each.

- What are the two different classes of industrial goods and how are they marketed?

PACKAGING CHANGES THE PRODUCT

We have said that consumers evaluate many aspects of the product offer, including the package and the brand. It is surprising how important packaging can be. Many years ago people had problems with table salt because it would stick together and form lumps whenever the weather was humid or damp. The Morton Salt Company solved that problem by designing a package that kept the salt dry in all kinds of weather. Thus, the slogan, "When it rains, it pours." Packaging made Morton's salt more desirable than competing products, and it is still the best-known salt in the United States.

The Morton Salt Company knew how to use packaging to change and improve its basic product—salt. Other companies have used similar techniques. Thus, we have had squeezable catsup bottles, plastic bottles for oil that eliminate the need for funnels, stackable potato chips in a can, toothpaste pumps, plastic cans for tennis balls, microwavable snack packages, dinners that can be boiled in a pouch and served immediately, whipped cream in dispenser cans, vegetables in climate-controlled packages, and so forth. In each case, the package changed the product in the minds of consumers and opened large markets. Packaging can also help make a product more attractive to retailers. For example, the Universal Product Codes on many packages make it easier to control inventory. In short, packaging changes the product by changing its visibility, usefulness, or attractiveness.

Office supplies are considered support goods. They are usually purchased through distributors or are ordered directly. Some smaller firms buy them at discount supply stores.

New, convenient forms of packaging include squeezable ketchup bottles, pourable oil bottles, and toothpaste in a pump. Can you think of other packaging that you enjoy? The new microwavable popcorn packaging, for example, has been a big hit.

The Growing Importance of Packaging

Packaging has always been an important aspect of the product offer, but today it is carrying more of the promotional burden. Many goods that were once sold by salespersons are now being sold in self-service outlets, and the package has been given more sales responsibility. As such, the package must do the following: (1) attract the buyer's attention; (2) describe the contents and give information about the contents; (3) explain the benefits of the good inside; (4) provide information on warranties, warnings, and other consumer matters; and (5) give some indication of price, value, and uses. Here is how *Marketing Communications* reported the trend:[5]

> The movement toward warehouse stores, and the lack of service people in all
> led to a demand for packaging that tells the consumer an information :
> packaging actually takes the place of the store clerk. In addition, man
> packages . . . serve as self shelves . . . eliminating expensive labor costs for

BRANDING

brand
A name, symbol, or design (or combination of these) that identifies the goods or services of one seller or group of sellers and distinguishes them from those of competitors.

brand name
That part of the brand consisting of a word, letter, or group of words or letters comprising a name that differentiates the goods or services of a seller from those of competitors.

trademark
A brand that has been given exclusive legal protection for both the brand name and pictorial design.

Closely related to packaging is branding. A **brand** is a name, symbol, or a combination of them) that identifies the goods or services of one selle of sellers and distinguishes them from those of competitors. The term *brand* is sufficiently comprehensive to include practically all means of identification of a product except perhaps the package and its shape. We learned in Chapter 7 that a **brand name** is that part of the brand consisting of a word, letter, or group of words or letters comprising a name that differentiates the goods or services of a seller from those of competitors. Brand names you may be familiar with include Chevrolet, Sony, Del Monte, Campbell, Winston, Jordache, Exxon, Borden, Michelob, and Colgate. Such brand names give products a distinction that tends to make them attractive to consumers. Those images last a long time. That's why Oldsmobile used the theme "This is not your father's Oldsmobile" in 1989. The idea was to use a good name in a new market.[6]

A **trademark** is a brand that has been given exclusive legal protection for both the brand name and the pictorial design. The trademarks shown at the top of the next page are widely recognized. So are trademarks such as McDonald's golden arches.

People are often impressed by certain brand names, even though they say they know there is no difference between brands in a given product category. For example, when someone who says that all aspirin is alike asks for an aspirin, put two bottles in front of him or her—one with the Excedrin label and one labeled with an unknown brand. See which one he or she chooses. Most people choose the brand name even when they say there is no difference. What does this indicate?

MAKING ETHICAL DECISIONS

As the developer of a new shampoo, Main Mane, you know that your formula can effectively clean hair with only one application. All of the competing shampoos recommend that users apply the shampoos twice during each washing. Should your package instruct your customers to use the product only once or should you get them to use twice as much shampoo (requiring them to buy more often) by instructing them to apply the product twice? What will be the consequences of your decision?

Do you recognize these trademarks for NBC, BMW, Shell, and 7UP? What other trademarks stand out in your mind? Certainly McDonald's golden arches could be one.

Brand Categories

Several categories of brands are familiar to you. **National brand names** are the brand names of manufacturers that distribute the product nationally. They include well-known names such as Xerox, Polaroid, Kodak, Sony, and Chevrolet. **Knockoff brands** are illegal copies of national brand name goods such as Izod shirts or Rolex watches. If you see an expensive brand name item for sale at ridiculously low prices, you can be pretty sure it's a knockoff. Counterfeiters who copy U.S. brand names steal some $20 billion in business a year.[7]

Private brands are products that do not carry the manufacturer's name, and carry the name of a distributor or retailer instead. Well-known names include Kenmore and Diehard (Sears). These brands are also known as "house" brands or "distributor" brands. Today, some distributor brands are as well known as national brand names.

What many manufacturers fear is having their brand names become generic names. **Generic names** are the names for product *categories*. Did you know that *aspirin* and *linoleum*, which are now generic names for products, were once brand names? So were *nylon, escalator, kerosene,* and *zipper.* All of those names became so popular, so identified with the product, that they lost their brand status and became *generic* (the name of the product category). The producers then had to come up with new names. The original *Aspirin*, for example, became *Bayer* aspirin. Some companies that are working hard to protect their brand names today include Xerox (one ad reads, "Don't say 'Xerox it;' say 'Copy it'") and Styrofoam.

Generic goods are nonbranded products that usually sell at a sizable discount from national or private brands, have very basic packaging, and are backed with little or no advertising. The quality varies considerably among generic goods. Some are copies of national brand names and may be close to the same quality, but others may be of minimum quality. There are generic tissues, generic cigarettes, generic peaches, and so forth. All it says on the label of the can is "Peaches," with no brand name. Consumers tend to buy generic goods when quality is not important to them or when they cannot afford brand name goods.

Brand Images

You might try an experiment for yourself. Buy an attractive but inexpensive tie and put it in a very attractive box from an exclusive store. Then buy a similar tie from the exclusive store and put it in a box from an inexpensive discount store. Tell your friends that you can't decide which tie is better and ask them to choose. If past experience is any guide, most will choose the inexpensive tie in the more expensive box. Again, laboratory experiments support these suggestions. The concept that explains such behavior is that people often cannot determine the value of products by physical inspection; they therefore turn to other indicators of quality such as labels, packaging, brand names, and price. A higher-priced, expensively packaged item is usually perceived as better regardless of its actual physical qualities.

national brand names
Brand names of manufacturers that distribute their products nationally.

knockoff brands
Illegal copies of national brand name items.

private brands
Products that do not carry the manufacturer's name, but carry the name of a distributor or retailer instead.

generic names
Names of product categories.

generic goods
Nonbranded products that usually sell at a sizable discount from national or private brands, have very basic packaging, and are backed with little or no advertising.

Generic goods have no brand names. Instead, the package says applesauce or corn flakes. Do you buy generic products sometimes? Why or why not? Often people buy generic paper products such as tissues for the nose because quality doesn't make much difference to them.

Knowing that products are perceived as better with a brand name, some companies are putting brand names where you have never seen them before. For example, the Natural Pak company has created the brand name TomAHto for its tomatoes. Packaged in an air tight package, these tomatoes stay fresh-looking red for four weeks. As a result, they can sell for 30 cents a pound more than unbranded tomatoes.

PROGRESS CHECK

- What are the five functions that packaging must perform now that retail help is declining?

- What is the difference between a brand name and a trademark?

- Can you explain the difference between a national brand, a private brand, and a generic brand?

PRODUCT MANAGEMENT

product manager
Coordinates all the marketing efforts for a particular product (or product line) or brand.

A **product manager** coordinates all marketing efforts for a particular product (product line) or brand, including the selection of a package and a brand name. The concept of product management originated over 50 years ago with Procter & Gamble, and over the last 25 years product managers have come to occupy important positions in many firms. Product management may offer a truly challenging career, if you are interested.

Product managers have direct responsibility for one brand or one product line, including all the elements of the marketing mix: product, price, place, and promotion. It's like being the president of a one-product business. You can imagine being the product manager for Fiberrific if it were purchased by a large cereal producer such as Kellogg. You would be responsible for everything having to do with that one brand. One reason companies have created this position is to have greater control over new product development and product promotion. The following material explores the success rate for new product introductions. It then outlines steps to follow in product development, including pricing strategies.

New Product Success

For many years it was commonly believed that about 90 percent of new products failed. Consequently, many firms hesitated to bring out new products. Instead, they tended to copy proven products from other companies. More recently, a study of medium- and large-size firms showed that failure rates were closer to 33 percent. One reason for the improved success rate is that firms are doing more careful consumer research and are not launching products until research shows a probable demand. (A "successful" product was one that was "sent to the market and met management's original expectations in all important respects.")[8] Some key findings from the study were:

- Firms selling mainly to industrial markets launched an average of eight major new products during the preceding five years, compared with six for consumer-oriented firms.

- Insufficient and poor market research is the leading cause of new product failure. Cited next most often as reasons for failure are technical problems in design or production and errors in timing the product's introduction.

Developing a new product includes developing an attractive brand name and package. This photo shows two women working on the label and bottle for Clorox's Hidden Valley Ranch Style salad dressing. Different samples may be tested with consumers to get their input.

The emphasis today seems to be on new product failures. A progressive firm should look to market successes. Smaller firms may experience a lower success rate, but not if they do proper product planning. We shall discuss such planning in the next section.

The New Product Development Process

Product development consists of several stages:
1. Idea generation.
2. Screening and analysis.
3. Development.
4. Testing.
5. Commercialization (bringing the product to the market).

New products continue to pour into the market every year, and the profit potential looks tremendous. Think, for example, of the potential of two-way cable TV, high definition TV sets (HDTV), cellular phones, compact video disks, hand-held video recorders and computers, and other innovations. Where do these ideas come from? How are they tested? What is the life span for an innovation? That is what the following material is all about.

Generating New Product Ideas

Figure 8–3 on page 238 gives you a good idea of where new product ideas come from. Note that 38 percent of the new product ideas for consumer goods come from analyzing competitors. This was true of 27 percent of new industrial products. Such copying of competitors in favor of discovering new products slows the introduction of new ideas.

A strong point can be made for listening to employee suggestions for new product ideas. The number one source of ideas for new industrial products was company sources other than research and development. It was also a major source for new consumer goods. Part of that is because of successful marketing communication systems that monitor suggestions from all sources.

FIGURE 8–3

Where new product ideas
come from.
This survey shows where the
ideas for new products come
from. As you know, research
plays an important role in
the development of new
products.
Reprinted by permission of the
A. C. Nielsen Company.

CONSUMER PRODUCTS (Based on a survey of 79 new products)	Percent*
Analysis of the competition	38
Company sources other than research and development	31.6
Consumer research	17.7
Research and development	13.9
Consumer suggestions	12.7
Published information	11.4
Supplier suggestions	3.8

INDUSTRIAL PRODUCTS (Based on a survey of 152 new products)	Percent*
Company sources other than research and development	36.2
Analysis of the competition	27.0
Research and development	24.3
Product users	15.8
Supplier suggestions	12.5
Product user research	10.5
Published information	7.9

* Percentages add up to more than 100 because more than one source was named for some products.

FIGURE 8–4

Some marketing
considerations for new
brands.
Ideas for new products are
carefully screened. This
screening helps the company
identify the areas where new
products are needed and
reduces the chance of a
company working on too
many ideas at a time.
Reprinted by permission of the
A. C. Nielsen Company.

Areas of company strengths and weaknesses	Consumer promotional considerations
Tie-ins with, or potential impact on, other company brands	Nature of competition
Production capabilities	Market segments
Consumer attitudes toward category Awareness Satisfaction with existing brands	Distribution channels Trade perceptions of category Turnover rates/optimum inventory allocations
Regional consumer differences	Seasonal characteristics
Advertising and merchandising norms, timing, and directions	Price margins

Look through Figure 8-3 carefully and think about the implications. Notice that more than a third of all new product ideas for industrial products came from users, user research, or supplier suggestions. This emphasizes the notion that a firm should listen to its suppliers and customers and give them what they want.

Product Screening and Analysis

Product screening is designed to reduce the number of ideas being worked on at any one time. Criteria needed for screening include whether the product fits in well with present products, profit potential, marketability, and personnel requirements (see Figure 8-4). Each of these factors may be assigned a weight and total scores computed.

Product analysis is done after product screening. It is largely a matter of making cost estimates and sales forecasts to get a feeling for profitability. Products that do not meet the established criteria are weeded from further consideration.

PRODUCT DEVELOPMENT IN HISTORY

It was, perhaps, one of the longest development efforts on record for a consumer product. Whitcomb Judson received his first patents for the zipper in the early 1890s. It took more than 15 years to perfect the product, but even then consumers weren't interested. The company suffered numerous financial setbacks, name changes, and relocations before settling in Meadville, Pennsylvania. Finally, the U.S. Navy started using Judson's zippers during World War I. Today, Talon, Inc. is the leading U.S. maker of zippers, producing some 500 million of them a year. Note, in comparison, how quickly Velcro captured market share through effective product development and marketing in general.

PRODUCT DEVELOPMENT

Identify unfilled need
Preliminary profit/payout plan for each concept
Concept test
Determine whether the product can be made
Test the concept and product (and revise as indicated)
Develop the product
Run extended product use tests

COMMUNICATION DEVELOPMENT

Select a name
Design a package and test
Create a copy theme and test
Develop complete ads and test

STRATEGY DEVELOPMENT

Set marketing goals
Establish marketing strategy
Develop marketing mix (after communication developed)
Estimate cost of marketing plan and payout (after product development)

FIGURE 8–5

Three basic elements before test marketing.
Product development, communication development, and strategy development all are used as a company develops a new product. Extensive testing is used to guarantee the success of the new product.
Reprinted by permission of the A. C. Nielsen Company.

Product Development and Testing

If a product passes the screening and analysis phase, the firm begins to develop it further. A product idea can be developed into many different product concepts (alternative product offerings based on the same product idea that have different meanings and values to consumers). For example, a firm might want to test the concept of a chicken dog—a hot dog made of chicken that tastes like an all-beef hot dog.

We noted earlier that concept testing involves taking a product idea to consumers to test their reactions (see Figure 8–5). Do they see the benefits of this new product? How frequently would they buy it? At what price? What features do they like and dislike? What changes would they make? Different samples are tested using different packaging, branding, ingredients, and so forth, until a product emerges that is desirable from both a production and a marketing perspective. Can you see the importance of concept testing for Fiberrific?

The International Challenge

John Sculley learned through experience that the secret to success in today's rapidly changing technological environment is to bring out new products and bring them out quickly. This is especially true in light of the rapid development process occurring in other countries.

Xerox executives were surprised by Japanese competitors who were developing new copier models twice as fast as Xerox and at half the cost. Xerox had to lose market share or slash its traditional four to five-year product development cycle. After millions of dollars of investment, Xerox can now produce a new copier in two years—still not as fast as the Japanese.

The big three automakers all recently formed task forces to cut product development cycles that had swollen to nearly five years. The Japanese were taking about three and a half years.

Lee Iacocca was quoted in *Fortune* magazine as saying, "If I made one mistake, it was delegating all the product development and not going to one single meeting." New product development is now high on Chrysler's priority list. It should be interesting to see the new cars in the 1990s—to find out if Chrysler was able to implement its new strategy.

PRODUCT STRATEGY AND THE PRODUCT LIFE CYCLE

product life cycle
The four-stage theoretical depiction of the process from birth to death of a product class: introduction, growth, maturity, and decline.

Once a product has been developed, tested, and placed on the market, it goes through a life cycle consisting of four stages: introduction, growth, maturity, and decline. This is called the product life cycle (see Figure 8–6). The **product life cycle** is a theoretical model of what happens to a product *class* (for example, all freeze-dried coffees) over time. Not all products follow the life cycle, and particular brands may act differently. For example, while frozen foods as a generic class may go through the entire cycle, one brand may never get beyond the introduction stage. Nonetheless, the product life cycle provides a basis for anticipating future market developments and for planning marketing strategies accordingly. Some

FIGURE 8–6

The sales and profit curves of a typical product class. Note that profit levels start to fall *before* sales reach their peak. When profits and sales start to decline, it is time to come out with a new product or to remodel the old to maintain interest and profits.

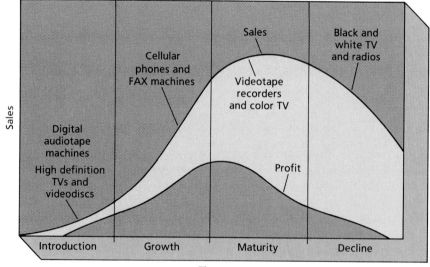

products, such as microwave ovens, stay in the introductory stage for years. Other products, such as fad clothing, may go through the entire cycle in a couple of months.

Figure 8-7 shows what happens to sales volume, competition, and profit/loss during the product life cycle. Such figures are revealing. For instance , they show that a product at the mature stage may reach the top in sales growth while profit is decreasing. At that stage, a marketing manager may decide to create a new image for the product to start a new growth cycle. Note, for example, how Arm and Hammer baking soda gets a new image every few years to generate new sales. One year it is positioned as a deodorant for refrigerators and the next as a substitute for harsh chemicals in swimming pools. Knowing what stage in the cycle a product is in helps marketing managers to decide when such strategic changes are needed.

Figure 8-8 outlines the marketing mix decisions that might be made. As you go through the table, you will see that each stage calls for multiple marketing mix changes. Next, we shall walk through the product life cycle together and discuss what happens at each stage.

LIFE CYCLE STAGE	SALES	PROFITS	COMPETITORS
Introduction	Low sales	Losses may occur	Few
Growth	Rapidly rising	Very high	Growing number
Maturity	Peak sales	Declining profits	Stable number, then declining
Decline	Falling sales	Profits may fall to losses	Declining number

FIGURE 8-7

Sales, profit, and competition at various stages in the product life cycle.
All products go through these stages at various times in their life cycle. What happens to sales as a product matures?

Strategies through the product life cycle   **FIGURE 8-8**

LIFE CYCLE STAGE	PRODUCT POLICY	MARKETING MIX ELEMENTS		
		PRICING	DISTRIBUTION	ADVERTISING
Introduction	Offer market-tested product; keep product mix small	Go after innovators with high introductory price (skimming strategy) or use penetration pricing	Use wholesalers, selective distribution	Dealer promotion and heavy investment in primary demand advertising and sales promotion to get stores to carry the product and consumers to try it
Growth	Improve product; keep product mix limited	Adjust price to meet competition	Increase distribution	Heavy competitive advertising
Maturity	Differentiate your product to satisfy different market segments	Further reduce price	Take over wholesaling function and intensify distribution	Emphasize brand name; product benefits and differences
Decline	Cut product mix; develop new product ideas	Consider price increase	Consolidate distribution; drop some outlets	Reduce advertising to only loyal customers

THINKING IT THROUGH In what stage of the product life cycle are personal computers? What does Figure 8–8 indicate firms should do at that stage? What will the next stage be? What might you do at that stage to optimize profits?

Most soft drinks are in the mature or decline stage of the product life cycle. Does that explain why Coke introduced new Coke? What other new soft drinks have been introduced in the last few years? Have any reached rapid growth?

The Product Life Cycle

We can see how the product life cycle works by looking at the introduction of instant coffee. When it was introduced, most people did not like it as well as "regular" coffee, and it took several years to gain general acceptance (introduction stage). At one point, though, instant coffee grew rapidly in popularity, and many brands were introduced (stage of rapid growth). After a while, people became attached to one brand and sales leveled off (stage of maturity). Sales went into a slight decline when freeze-dried coffees were introduced (stage of decline). At present, freeze-dried coffee is at the maturity stage. Perhaps you can think through the product life cycle of products such as hot cereals, frozen orange juice, mechanical watches, and mechanical calculators.

The importance of the product life cycle to marketers is this: Different stages in the product life cycle call for different strategies. Figure 8–8 summarizes the entire concept. It shows how a product manager changes his or her objectives and strategies over the life of a product. It is important to recognize what stage a product is in, because such an analysis leads to more intelligent marketing decisions.

Extending the Life Cycle

Most products are in the maturity stage of the product life cycle at any particular time; therefore, marketing managers deal often with mature products. The goal is to extend product life so that sales and profits do not decline. One strategy is called **market modification.** It means that marketing managers look for new users and market segments. Did you know, for example, that the backpacks that so many students carry were originally designed for the military? The search for new users led to the present-day backpack.

Market modification also means searching for increased usage among present customers. That is what Arm and Hammer does by finding new uses for baking soda over time. Many industrial firms develop products along with customers to be sure the product meets the buyers' needs.[9] Finally, a marketer may reposition the product to appeal to new market segments. Once 7-Up was considered a mix for drinks using whiskey or bourbon. It was repositioned as an alternative to colas (the UnCola) and captured whole new markets. What do you suppose we could do to extend the product life cycle if Fiberrific reaches the decline stage? Alternatives include going for a different market, such as senior citizens, or positioning it as a snack instead of a cereal. Many people already eat cereal as a snack instead of for breakfast. Cereal companies are now introducing cereal bars for breakfast (like a candy bar, but more nutritious).

market modification
Technique used to extend the life cycle of mature products by finding new users and market segments.

IMMEDIATE RELEASE

TWENTY-FIVE YEARS OF MUSTANG — Ford's legendary ponycar reaches another milestone this spring — its 25th birthday — and Mustang fans across the country will be celebrating. From the trend-setting 1965 convertible on the left, to the high-performance 1989 GT convertible on the right, the Mustang mystique continues to grow.

PUBLIC AFFAIRS, FORD DIVISION
300 RENAISSANCE CENTER, P.O. BOX 43303, DETROIT, MICHIGAN 48243

Look carefully at this photo. Can you spot the product modifications that have occurred over 25 years? This was such a popular car that most of the changes were in the engine and other not-so-visible parts. It is up to the promotion department to communicate those changes to show the improvements, especially quality improvements.

Another product extension strategy is called **product modification.** It involves changing product quality, features, or style to attract new users or more usage from present users. American auto manufacturers are using quality improvement as one way to recapture world markets. New features are keeping the sales of videotape recorders going. One can now edit tapes, receive stereo broadcasts, watch one show and have another show in the corner of the screen, and more. Style changes can also extend the life of a product. Note, for example, how auto manufacturers once changed styles dramatically from year to year to keep demand from falling. That strategy was called *planned obsolescence* because it made autos obsolete in *style* long before they were obsolete in engineering. Note, also, how some American auto manufacturers lost market share in the 1980s when style changes were slow in coming.

Different stages in the product life cycle call for different pricing strategies. We shall discuss pricing—a key management decision in product design—next.

product modification
Technique used to extend the life cycle of mature products by changing the product quality, features, or style to attract new users or more usage for present users.

- What are the five steps in the new product development process?

- Can you draw a product life cycle and label its parts? Can you give one marketing strategy in product, price, place, or promotion for each stage? (See Figure 8–8.)

- Can you explain the difference between market modification and product modification and give examples of each?

PROGRESS CHECK

PRICING

Pricing is so important to marketing that it has been singled out as one of the four Ps in the marketing mix, along with product, place, and promotion. Price is also a critical ingredient in consumer evaluations of the product. In this section, therefore, we shall explore price as both an ingredient of the product and as a strategic marketing tool.

Pricing Objectives

You can imagine that a firm may have several objectives in mind when setting a pricing strategy. When pricing Fiberrific, for example, we may want to promote the product's image. If we priced it high and used the right promotion, maybe we could make it the Perrier of cereals, as we discussed earlier. We also might price it high to achieve a certain profit objective. We could also price Fiberrific lower than competitors because we want poor people and older people to be able to afford this nutritional cereal. That is, we have some social or ethical goal in mind. Low pricing may also discourage competition because the profit potential would be less. A low price may also help us capture a larger share of the market. The point is that a firm may have several pricing strategies, and it must state these objectives clearly before developing an overall pricing strategy. The box called Popular Pricing Objectives lists some of the more popular strategies.

Another objective may be to avoid government investigation and control. Large, powerful firms cannot price their products so low that they drive out competitors, for fear of government interference. Note that a firm may have short-run objectives that differ greatly from long-run objectives. Both should be understood at the beginning and put into the strategic marketing plan. Pricing objectives should be influenced by other marketing decisions regarding product design, packaging, branding, and promotion. All these marketing decisions are interrelated.

Price Determination

We are so accustomed to thinking of pricing as something done by the seller that it is difficult to think of pricing decisions coming from anyone other than the seller. But a moment's reflection will show you that it is often the buyer who sets the price. For example, how many times have you told a seller that you would give him or her a certain amount of money for something? In the long run, as we discussed in Chapter 2, prices are determined by the *interactions* between buyers and sellers.

People feel rather intuitively that the price charged for a product must bear some relation to the cost of producing the product. In fact, we would generally agree that prices are usually set somewhere above cost. But as we shall see, prices and cost are not always related.

Cost-Based Pricing

Economists once felt there was a strong relationship between the cost of production and price. They felt that the price of a good was, and should be, based on the amount of labor needed to produce it. But it does not take much research to show this just is not so. In fact, there is often very little correlation between the price of something and its cost of production. Does a quarterback earn more than a physician because it costs more to produce a quarterback? Does a rare stamp cost a thousand times more than a regular stamp because one costs more to produce? Obviously not.

Nevertheless, producers often use cost as a primary basis for setting price. They develop elaborate cost accounting systems to measure production costs (including materials, labor, and overhead), add in some margin of profit, and come up with a satisfactory price. The question is whether the price will be satisfactory to the market as well. In the long run, the *market* determines what the price will be, not the producer.

POPULAR PRICING OBJECTIVES

ACHIEVE A TARGET PROFIT

Ultimately, the goal of marketing is to make a profit by providing goods and services to others. Naturally, one long-run pricing objective of almost all firms is to optimize profit.

BUILD TRAFFIC

Supermarkets often advertise certain products at or below cost to attract people to the store. These products are called "loss leaders." The long-run objective is to make profits by following the short-run objective of building a customer base.

ACHIEVE GREATER MARKET SHARE

The auto industry is in a fierce international battle to capture and hold marketing share. U.S. producers have lost market share to overseas producers and are offering price incentives, such as rebates, to win it back. Sears lost 33 percent of its market share in the decade before 1989. That is why it revealed its new low price strategy in March of 1989. It hopes to recapture market share from Montgomery Ward and Kmart which also have low-price strategies.[10]

INCREASE SALES

Sometimes a firm will lower prices to increase sales even though such low prices may harm short-run profits. Sometimes the very survival of the firm may rely on increased sales in the short run. Chrysler experienced such a need in the early 1980s, but brought itself back into profitability by keeping its prices low and winning new customers.

CREATE AN IMAGE

Certain watches, perfumes, and other socially visible products are priced high to give them an image of exclusivity and status. Perrier used this strategy very effectively.

SOCIAL OBJECTIVES

A firm may want to price a product low so that people with less money can afford one. Often, governments get involved in pricing farm products so that everyone can get basic products such as milk and bread at a low price.

A low-price strategy is not the only effective way to attract consumers. This ad for Bentley automobiles emphasizes a high price for people on a "higher plane" than mere "top-of-the-line" models. It may be a smaller market, but it is an attractive market.

Reprinted by permission of Rolls-Royce Motor Cars Inc.

Break-Even Analysis

Before we go into the business of producing Fiberrific cereal, it may be wise to determine how many boxes of cereal we would have to sell before we began making a profit. We would then determine whether or not we could reach such a sales goal. **Break-even analysis** is the process used to determine profitability at various levels of sales. It tells managers whether the firm will make money (or break even) at a particular price, given a certain sales volume. The **break-even point** is the quantity beyond which profits occur. The *profit equation* is as follows:

$$\text{Gross profit} = \text{Total revenue} - \text{Total cost}$$

break-even analysis
Process used to determine the profitability at various levels of sales.

break-even point
The quantity of sales beyond which profits occur.

Before we do such an analysis for our cereal company, certain terms need to be explained.

- *Gross profit (P)* is the money left after all costs are deducted and before taxes are paid.
- *Total cost (TC)* is the total cost incurred by the firm in producing and marketing a product. It is the sum of fixed costs plus variable costs.
- *Fixed cost (FC)* is the sum of the expenses of the firm that are stable and do not change with the quantity of the product that is produced and sold. Examples include rent, executive salaries, and equipment.
- *Variable cost (VC)* is the sum of the expenses that vary directly with the quantity of products produced and sold. Examples include raw materials such as wheat, oats, and rice and the direct labor used in producing the product—cereal in our case.

Using these terms and the figures that go with them, we can calculate the break-even point for our cereal. Remember, that is the point where we start making a profit! The formula is:

$$\text{Break-even point (BEP)} = \frac{\text{Fixed cost (FC)}}{\text{Price of one unit} - \text{Variable cost of one unit}}$$

Let's put some figures in the formula to see how it works. Suppose our cereal firm has a total fixed cost of $2,000. That is the total cost of the rent, equipment, and executive salaries for the firm. We price our cereal at $2.00 a box. The variable cost per box is $1.00 (for the ingredients, package, and labor). Then the break-even point (the quantity we would have to sell to just break even) would be 2,000 boxes. Here is how we reach that figure:

$$\text{BEP} = \frac{\text{FC}}{\text{Price} - \text{Unit variable cost}} = \frac{\$2,000}{\$2.00 - \$1.00} = 2,000 \text{ boxes}$$

Figure 8–9 shows how the results of the calculations look when placed on a chart.

Figure 8–9 shows that the break-even point is where the quantity is 2,000 boxes and the price is $2.00 a box. At less than 2,000 boxes, we would lose money. For example, if we sold only 1,000 boxes, we would lose $1,000. However, if we could increase sales to 5,000 boxes, we would make $3,000 profit. Figure 8–10 shows the results in an easy-to-read format.

THINKING IT THROUGH   What would the break-even point be if we were to increase the price to $3.00 a box? How would increasing the price affect the rest of the marketing effort?

Break-even analysis for Fiberrific cereal.   FIGURE 8–9

QUANTITY SOLD (Q)	PRICE PER BOX	TOTAL REVENUE (TR)	UNIT VARIABLE COST (UVC)	TOTAL VARIABLE COST (TVC)	FIXED COST (FC)	TOTAL COST (TC) (TVC + FC)	PROFIT TR − TC
0	$2	0	$1	$ 0	$2,000	$2,000	− $2,000
1,000	2	$ 2,000	1	1,000	2,000	3,000	− 1,000
2,000	2	4,000	1	2,000	2,000	4,000	0
3,000	2	6,000	1	3,000	2,000	5,000	1,000
4,000	2	8,000	1	4,000	2,000	6,000	2,000
5,000	2	10,000	1	5,000	2,000	7,000	3,000
6,000	2	12,000	1	6,000	2,000	8,000	4,000

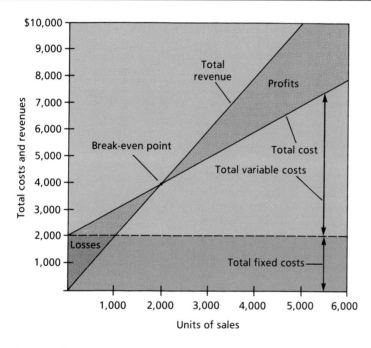

FIGURE 8–10

The break-even point. Below the break-even point, a company experiences losses. Above the break-even point, profits increase rapidly.

Pricing Strategies

Let's say a firm has just developed a new product such as video recorders. The firm has to decide how to price these recorders at the introductory stage of the product life cycle. One strategy would be to price the recorders high to recover the costs of developing the recorder and to take advantage of the fact that there are few competitors. A **skimming price strategy** is one in which the product is priced high to make optimum profit while there is little competition. Of course, those large profits will attract others to produce recorders. That is what is happening with the high-priced camcorders that were introduced recently.

A second strategy, therefore, is to price the recorders low. This would attract more buyers and discourage others from making recorders because the profit is so low. This strategy enables the firm to penetrate or capture a large share of the market quickly. A **penetration pricing strategy,** therefore, is one in which a product is priced low to attract more customers and discourage competitors. The Japanese successfully used a penetration strategy with videotape recorders. No U.S. firm could compete with the low prices the Japanese offered.

skimming price strategy
Method of pricing by which the product is priced high to make optimum profit while there is little competition.

penetration pricing strategy
Method of pricing by which a product is priced low to attract more customers and discourage competitors.

UPS promotes low prices all over the world. Service organizations have a more difficult time creating product differences that do manufacturing firms. Price is often the major difference. A theme like, "We run the tightest ship in the shipping business," is thus a good one.

market price
The price that results from the interaction of buyers and sellers in the marketplace.

demand-oriented pricing
Pricing strategy based on consumer demand.

price leadership
Procedure by which all the competitors in an industry follow the pricing practices of one or more dominant firms.

competition-oriented pricing
Pricing strategy based on all the other competitors' prices.

Ultimately, price is determined by supply and demand in the marketplace, as described in Chapter 2. For example, if we charge $2.00 for our cereal and nobody buys it at that price, we will have to lower the price until we reach a price that is acceptable to customers and to us. The price that results from the interaction of buyers and sellers in the marketplace is called the **market price.**

Recognizing the fact that different consumers may be willing to pay different prices, marketers sometimes price on the basis of consumer demand rather than cost or some other calculation. That is called **demand-oriented pricing** and is reflected by movie theaters when they charge different rates for children and by drugstores that have discount rates for senior citizens.

Another factor in the marketplace beside supply and demand forces is competition. **Price leadership** is the procedure by which all the competitors in an industry follow the pricing practices of *one or more* dominant firms. You may have noticed that practice among oil and cigarette companies. **Competition-oriented pricing** is a strategy based on what *all* the other competitors are doing. The price can be at, above, or below competitors' prices. Pricing depends on customer loyalty, perceived product differences, and the competitive climate. The box Additional Pricing Tactics lists several more pricing tactics that businesses might use to compete in the market.

Nonprice Competition

In spite of the emphasis placed on price in microeconomic theory, marketers often compete on product attributes other than price. You may have noted that price differences between products such as gasoline, cigarettes, candy bars, and even major products such as compact cars are often small, if there is any price difference

ADDITIONAL PRICING TACTICS

It is impossible to cover all pricing tactics in detail in this book. However, you should at least be familiar with the following terms:

1. *Adaptive pricing* allows an organization to vary its prices based on factors such as competition, market conditions, and resource costs. Rather than relying on one set price, the firm adjusts the price to fit different situations.
2. *Cost-oriented pricing* is the strategy of setting prices primarily on the basis of cost. For example, retailers often use cost plus a certain markup, and producers use a system of cost-plus pricing.
3. *Customary pricing* means that most sellers will adapt the product to some established, universally accepted price such as the price for gum or candy bars. Notice that when the customary price goes up, almost all producers adjust their price upward.
4. *Product-line pricing* is the procedure used to set prices for a group of products that are similar but are aimed at different market segments. For example, a beer producer might have a low-priced beer, a popular-priced beer, and a premium-priced beer.
5. *Target pricing* means that an organization will set some goal such as a certain share of the market or a certain return on investment as a basis for setting a price. Usually, market conditions prevent a firm from establishing prices this way, but such goals do give some direction to pricing policies.
6. *Uniform pricing,* also known as a *single-price policy,* means that all customers buying the product (given similar circumstances) will pay the same price. Although the most common policy in the United States, uniform pricing is unusual in many foreign markets, especially among private sellers.
7. *Odd pricing* or psychological pricing means pricing an item a few cents under a round price ($9.98 instead of $10) to make the product appear less expensive.
8. *Price lining* is the practice of offering goods at a few set prices such as $30, $40, and $50. Such a tactic makes pricing easier, it makes check-out easier, and it appeals to a market segment interested in that level of pricing.

at all. Very rarely will you see price used as a major promotional appeal on television. Instead, marketers tend to stress product images and consumer benefits such as comfort, style, convenience, and durability.

Many organizations promote the services that accompany basic products rather than price. The idea is to make a relatively homogeneous product "better." For example, airlines stress friendliness, promptness, more flights, better meals, and other such services. Motels stress "no surprises" or cable TV, swimming pools, and other extras. IBM often counters the price advantages of clones by offering better service.

Quite often the reason marketers emphasize nonprice differences is because prices are so easy to match. Few competitors can match the image of a friendly, responsive, consumer-oriented company.

PROGRESS CHECK

- Can you list two short-term and two long-term pricing objectives. Are the two compatible?
- What is wrong with using a cost-based pricing strategy?
- What is the purpose of break-even analysis?
- Can you calculate the break-even point of a product where the fixed cost of producing it is $10,000, the price of one unit is $20, and the unit variable cost is $10?

SUMMARY

1. Explain the difference between a product and a product offer.

2. Define and give an example of a product mix and a product line.

3. Describe how businesses create product differentiation for their goods and services.

4. Identify the three classes of consumer products and how they are marketed.

5. Identify the two major classes of industrial goods and how they are marketed.

6. List the four functions of packaging.

7. Give examples of a brand, a brand name, and a trademark, and how to prevent a brand name from becoming generic.

1. If the goal of marketing is to find a need and fill it, the heart of marketing is finding what products people want and seeing that they get them. Product is one of the four Ps of the marketing mix.
   ▪ What is the difference between a product and a product offer?
     A product is any physical good, service, or idea that satisfies a want or need. A product offer is much more than a physical object. A product offer involves all the tangibles and intangibles that consumers evaluate when deciding to buy. These include things like the price, the brand name, the quality, the satisfaction in use, and more.

2. Manufacturers usually produce more than one product.
   ▪ What is the difference between a product line and a product mix?
     A product line is a group of products that are physically similar (a product line of gum may include chewing gum, sugarless gum, bubble gum, etc.). A product mix is a company's combination of product lines (a manufacturer may offer lines of gum, candy bars, chewing tobacco, etc.).

3. Marketers must make their product appear to be better than the competitors'.
   ▪ How do marketers create product differentiation for their goods and services?
     Marketers use a mix of pricing, advertising, and packaging to make their products seem unique and attractive.

4. Consumer goods and services are classified according to consumer shopping habits and preferences.
   ▪ What are the three classifications of consumer goods and services?
     There are convenience goods and services (minimum shopping effort), shopping goods and services (where people compare price and quality), and specialty goods and services (where consumers will go out of their way to get them).
   ▪ Are the different classifications of consumer goods and services marketed differently?
     Yes. Convenience goods and services are best promoted by location, shopping goods and services by some price/quality appeal, and specialty goods and services by word of mouth.

5. Industrial goods are products used in the production of other products. There are two major categories of industrial goods: production goods and support goods.
   ▪ What is the difference between production goods and support goods?
     Production goods consist of raw materials (like steel or cement) that make up the final product. Support goods are the types of products that help make other products (such as, supplies and equipment).
   ▪ How are industrial goods marketed?
     Industrial goods are usually sold by salespeople in the field.

6. Packaging changes the product and is becoming more important, taking over much of the sales function for consumer goods.
   ▪ What are the functions of packaging?
     Packaging adds visibility and convenience, minimizes damage, and keeps the goods in manageable sizes.

7. Branding also changes a product.
   ▪ Can you give an example of a brand, a brand name, and a trademark?
     There are endless examples you could give. One example of a brand name of crackers is Waverly by Nabisco. The brand consists of the name *Waverly* as well as the symbol (red triangle in the corner with *Nabisco* circled in

white). The brand name and the symbol are also trademarks, since Nabisco has been given legal protection for this brand.

8. Product managers are like presidents of one-product firms.
   - What are the functions of a product manager?
     Product managers coordinate product, price, place, and promotion decisions for a particular product.

   8. Explain the role of a product manager.

9. There are many sources of new product ideas (see Figure 8-3 on page 238).
   - What are the five steps of the product development process?
     It consists of generating new product ideas, screening and analysis, development, testing, and commercialization.

   9. Outline the five steps of the new product development process.

10. Once a product is placed on the market, marketing strategy varies as the product goes through various stages of acceptance—called the product life cycle.
    - What are the stages of the product life cycle?
      They are introduction, growth, maturity, and decline.
    - How do marketing strategies change at the various stages?
      See Figure 8-8 on page 241.

    10. Identify and describe the stages of the product life cycle and describe marketing strategies at each stage.

11. Pricing is one of the four Ps of marketing. It can also be viewed as part of the product concept.
    - What are pricing objectives?
      Some objectives include achieving a target profit, building traffic, increasing market share, increasing sales, creating an image, and meeting social objectives.

    11. Give examples of various pricing objectives.

12. Break-even analysis tells a firm whether or not it would be profitable to product a product at all.
    - What is the break-even point?
      At the break-even point, total cost equals total revenue. Sales beyond that point are profitable. See pages 246 and 247.

    12. Discuss the use of break-even analysis and calculate the break-even point.

13. Marketers use a variety of strategies to determine a product's price.
    - How are prices determined?
      Some firms use cost as a basis, but ultimately prices are set by the market; that is, supply and demand and competition.
    - What strategies can marketers use to determine a product's price?
      A skimming price strategy is one in which the product is priced high to make optimum profit while there is little competition; whereas, a penetration strategy is one in which a product is priced low to attract more customers and discourage competitors. Demand-oriented pricing is based on consumer demand rather than cost. Competition-oriented pricing is based on the prices of all other competitors. Price leadership occurs when all competitors follow the pricing practice of one or more dominant companies. Please review p. 249 to be sure you understand all the terms used for other pricing tactics.

    13. Describe various pricing strategies.

---

1. Look around at the different shoes that students are wearing. What product qualities were they looking for when they chose those shoes? What was the importance of price, style, brand name, manufacturer reputation, and color? Do different students buy shoes for different reasons?

2. Discuss how packaging has changed the attractiveness of the following products:
   a. Beer.   c. Salt.
   b. Mustard.   d. Soda (pop).

GETTING INVOLVED

3. Determine where in the product life cycle you would place each of the following products and then prepare a marketing plan for each product based on the recommendations in this chapter:
   a. Alka Seltzer.   c. Electric automobiles.
   b. Cellular phones.   d. Campbell chicken noodle soup.
4. List at least seven sources of new product ideas and put them in the order you think is most important. Explain why you chose that order.
5. Discuss how the faculty at your college could increase student satisfaction by working more closely with students in developing new products (courses) and changing existing products (courses). Would it be a good idea for all marketers to work with their customers that way? Discuss.
6. Go to a shopping mall and go through several stores such as department stores, shoe stores, and clothing stores. Then go to a supermarket. Look at the prices of items that are comparable. That is, compare the price of various brands of peas and so on. What pricing strategy is being followed by the various producers? Do any patterns emerge? Which producers make several different products in the same category so that they can use multiple pricing strategies? You can do the same analysis using prices in the newspaper and bring the paper to class to discuss strategies.

PRACTICING MANAGEMENT DECISIONS

CASE ONE   PACKAGING TO REACH NEW MARKETS

Ways to extend the product life cycle of products include increasing consumption among present users and attracting new buyers. Often this can be accomplished through packaging innovation. Take products like beef stew and macaroni and beef. These products have been available for years in cans, but sales were slow. Dial Company changed the whole market around by introducing the Lunch Bucket, a shelf-stable, single-serve, microwavable product line of entrees and soups. Shelf-stable means the products can be stored on the shelf for long periods of time without losing taste or freshness.

These new products can be prepared in under two minutes in a microwave oven. Two thirds of U.S. households and about one half of offices contain microwave ovens. U.S. consumers bought 64 percent more microwave-ready food in 1987 than in 1986.

Among users of Lunch Bucket, 35 percent of their volume came from increased sales and attracting new buyers. The entrees are placed on supermarket shelves near the canned meats and the soups are placed near the canned soups to show the new product features relative to the old products.

DECISION QUESTIONS

1. What are the social and technological changes that led to the development of this new line of products? What other products or services may become more popular as a result of these social and technological changes?
2. Would you have chosen Lunch Bucket as the brand name for this new line of foods? What are the advantages and disadvantages of that name? What name do you feel might be better?
3. What other foods could be made into shelf-stable microwavable products to extend the product life cycle of those goods?
4. Can you think of other ways to increase the product life cycle of products such as soup and canned beef?

Source: "Lunch Buckets Appeal to Chord of Familiarity," *Marketing Communications*, February 1988, p. 54.

CASE TWO   COLA WARS ENTER A NEW ERA

Nothing touched off more discussion and debate in marketing in the 1980s than the introduction of new Coca-Cola (Coke). The new Coke was made sweeter, to taste more like Pepsi, and a marketing campaign was launched to sell this new taste. At first, sales were up as consumers rushed to try the new Coke. Soon the reaction became negative and people began hoarding the old Coke. Minor campaigns were started by old-Coke fans to bring back the old Coke.

A daily newspaper in Paris reported, "Coca-Cola, like the Chevrolet and Levi Strauss . . . were and are, for America, landmarks that one dare not touch. Ninety-nine years of existence, it is the equivalent of the Parthenon or the Sphinx. . . ." Articles questioned the marketing research done by Coke. They had asked people which taste they preferred, but they had failed to take into account tradition, brand loyalty, and habit.

Faced with hostile consumers from coast to coast, Coke relented and brought back old Coke under the name Coca-Cola Classic. It also kept the new Coke for those who preferred the taste. Coca-Cola Classic is doing better than new Coke thus far.

Through all of this, Coke was in the news day after day as people aired both sides of the issue. In the long run, Coke seems to be winning the marketing war because of the publicity it received and its willingness to listen to consumer protest.

Coke had a large share of the overseas market, even larger than the share it had of the U.S. market. Europeans and other foreign consumers preferred Coke—the old Coke, that is. Nevertheless, Coke decided to introduce new Coke overseas as well. Again, there was much criticism in the trade press. Again, Coke got much free publicity—this time world-wide.

Recently, *Beverage Digest* reported that Coke Classic was number one with a market share of 18.9 percent. Pepsi's market share remained about the same. It was number two at 18.5 percent of the market. Diet Coke had a 7.1 percent share and Diet Pepsi had a 4.3 percent share. New Coke had a 2.3 percent share and Cherry Coke had a 1.7 percent share. Late in 1988, Pepsi and Coke had a price war that dropped the price of a six-pack of Coke to 59 cents. The goal was market share. A 1 percent increase in market-share means $160 million in sales.

Recently, Pepsi introduced Jake's as a diet cola. Coke countered this introduction by advertising that Jake's actually contains two teaspoonfuls of sugar. Pepsi is returning to taste-test ads to show that Pepsi is "America's Choice." Nonetheless, the top three brand names in America, Japan and Western Europe are Coca-Cola, IBM, and Sony.

DECISION QUESTIONS

1. What lesson might brand name marketers learn from the Coke experience in the 1980s (that is, dropping a popular brand name for a new, untried product)? Campbell soup is thinking of changing its soup cans. Is that a good idea, given Coke's experience?

2. Pepsi decided to give its diet cola the name Jake's instead of Low-Cal Pepsi or some other name with Pepsi in it. What are the advantages and disadvantages of that strategy?

3. If you were president of Coca Cola, would you continue to market New Coke? Would you have taken New Coke overseas after what happened in the United States? Explain.

4. Explain the strategies being used at Pepsi and Coke (that is, new products being introduced and new variations of old products) in relation to the product life cycle. In what stage of the life cycle are Pepsi and Coke Classic?

Source: Betsy Morris, "Coke vs. Pepsi: Cola War Marches On," *The Wall Street Journal*, June 3, 1987, p. 33; Betsy Morris, "Coke and Pepsi Step Up Bitter Price War," *The Wall Street Journal*, October 10, 1988, p. B1; and "Top Three," *Parade*, January 22, 1989, p. 10.

A product cannot fully meet the wants and needs of consumers unless it is at the right place at the right time. Several marketing organizations have emerged to perform the functions needed to move goods from producers to consumers. Your neighborhood stores are one example. Chapter 9 looks at the distribution of products and the organizations that move and store goods on their way to your home.

LOOKING AHEAD

DISTRIBUTION: WHOLESALING AND RETAILING

9

Laura Cassagnol and
Michelle Holzman

*Distribution systems have
always been one of the
critical elements of business
success, and in my opinion,
they're getting even more
critical. That's because
customer service has, for a
variety of reasons, become
one of the important ways a
company can differentiate its
products and services.*
FREDERICK W. SMITH,
Federal Express Corporation

PROFILE   LAURA CASSAGNOL AND MICHELE HOLZMAN OF BODYWARES

There are more career opportunities in retailing than in almost any other occupation. But what if you are part of a minority and a woman? Are the opportunities as good? You bet! Take Laura Cassagnol and Michele Holzman, for example. Ms. Cassagnol is from Colombia, South America, and Mrs. Holzman is a native Hawaiian with some Chinese and French ancestry. Neither had any experience in retailing.

Mrs. Holzman learned about a line of cosmetics made by the Body Shop of Berkeley, California while still living in Hawaii. The Body Shop was started when two Berkeley housewives decided to develop a cosmetic line that had more natural ingredients and was cheaper than major brand cosmetics. The store caters largely to University of California students. The two women have refused to franchise their products, but are selling them to others who put on their own Bodywares labels.

Ms. Cassagnol and Mrs. Holzman decided that they could be successful selling the cosmetics to students at George Washington University. They bought the cosmetics, stuck on the labels, and opened a store. Because they were minority entrepreneurs, they went to the District of Columbia government to get a loan. They received $34,000 from the D.C. Office of Business and Economic Development. To get the loan, the ladies needed a detailed business plan. The plan included a second shop in Rehoboth, Maryland (at the beach).

Advertising for Bodywares products is largely by word of mouth. The partners feel that it is important to get people to try cosmetics when they are young because they tend to become very loyal over time. Is there a large student population near you? Could you prosper selling them cosmetics or other such products? Chapter 10 explores opportunities in retailing, wholesaling, and distribution. Maybe you could profit from operating a retail business while you are still in school.

Source: Pam McClintock, "2 Friends Stake Their Dream on Cosmetics," *The Washington Times*, February 17, 1988, p. c–3.

WHAT DISTRIBUTION IS

We have looked at two of the four Ps of the marketing mix—product and price. In this chapter, we shall look at the third of the four Ps—*place*. Products have to be physically moved from where they are produced to a convenient place where consumer and industrial buyers can see them and purchase them. **Physical distribution** is the movement of goods from producers to industrial and consumer users and involves functions such as transportation and storage.

A **marketing middleman** is an organization that assists in the movement of goods and services from producer to industrial and consumer users. They are called *middlemen* because they are organizations in the middle of a whole series of organizations that join together to help distribute goods from producer to consumers. It is easy to understand, therefore, why these organizations as a group are known as a channel of distribution.

A **channel of distribution** consists of marketing middlemen such as wholesalers and retailers who join together to transport and store goods in their path (channel, if you will) from producers to consumers. Figure 9–1 pictures channels of distribution for both consumer and industrial goods.

physical distribution
The movement of goods and services from producer to industrial and consumer users.

marketing middleman
An organization that assists in the movement of goods and services from producer to industrial and consumer users.

channel of distribution
Marketing middlemen such as wholesalers and retailers who join together to transport and store goods in their path (channel) from producers to consumers.

FIGURE 9-1

Channels of distribution for industrial and consumer goods.

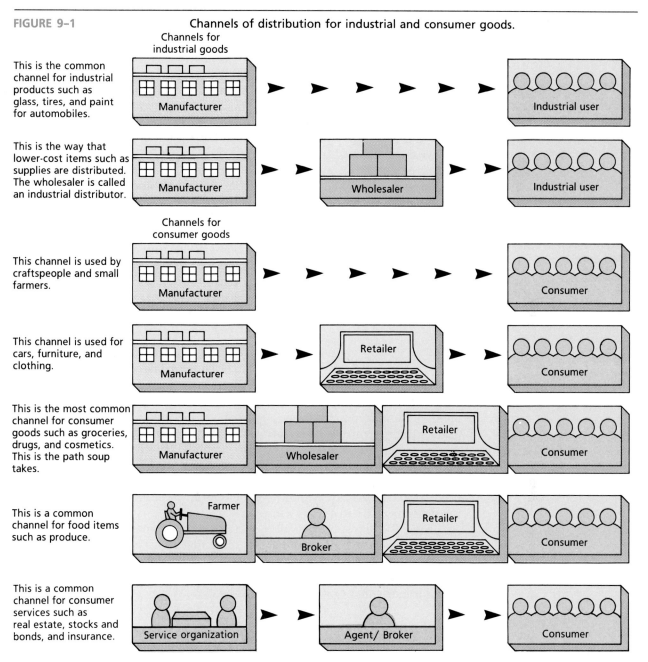

As you study the various institutions in the channel of distribution, think of them as potential employers and you will find the material more interesting. Not too many people know about all the different wholesale and retail institutions and the careers available in them. Therefore, the competition for jobs in the lesser-known institutions is not as stiff.

Our opening Profile about the women who own Bodywares shows that you can become part of a channel of distribution by finding customers (in this case students) and then contacting a distributor (wholesaler) to get products to sell to those customers. Members of a channel of distribution thus come and go as they are needed. The relationships are not permanent and change as the market changes.

DO WE NEED MIDDLEMEN?

Manufacturers do not need marketing middlemen to sell their goods to consumer and industrial markets. Figure 9–1 shows manufacturers that sell directly to buyers. So why have marketing middlemen at all? The answer is that middlemen perform certain marketing functions such as transportation, storage, selling, and advertising more effectively and efficiently than could be done by most manufacturers. A simple analogy is this: You could deliver your own packages to people anywhere in the world, but usually you do not. Why not? Because it is usually cheaper and faster to have them delivered by the post office or some private agency such as Federal Express or Emory.

Similarly, you could sell your own home or buy stock directly from other people, but most people do not. Why? Again, because there are specialists called brokers who make the process more efficient and easier. **Brokers** are marketing middlemen who bring buyers and sellers together and assist in negotiating an exchange, but do not take title to the goods. Usually, they do not carry inventory, provide credit, or assume risk. The examples with which you are likely to be most familiar include insurance brokers, real estate brokers, and stockbrokers. Figure 9–1 shows that brokers act as intermediaries in other situations as well. Food brokers, for example, sell commodities such as wheat, corn, and potatoes.

brokers
Marketing middlemen who bring buyers and sellers together and assist in negotiating an exchange.

Middlemen and Exchange Efficiency

The benefits of marketing middlemen can be illustrated rather easily. Suppose that five manufacturers of various food products tried to sell directly to five retailers. The number of exchange relationships that would have to be established is 5 times 5, or 25. But picture what happens when a wholesaler enters the system. The five manufacturers would contact one wholesaler to establish five exchange relationships. The wholesaler would have to establish contact with the five retailers. That would mean another five exchange relationships. Note that the number of exchanges is reduced from 25 to only 10 by the addition of a wholesaler. This process can be visualized as shown in Figure 9–2, where the number of exchanges is reduced from 25 to 10.

Figure 9–2 shows how middlemen create exchange efficiency by lessening the number of contacts needed to establish marketing exchanges. Not only are middlemen an efficient way to conduct exchanges, but they are often more effective as well. This means that middlemen are often better at performing their functions than a manufacturer or consumer would be.

The Value Created by Middlemen

Marketing middlemen have always been viewed by the public with some suspicion. Surveys have shown that about half the cost of the things we buy are marketing costs that are largely to pay for the work of middlemen. People reason that if we could only get rid of middlemen, we could greatly reduce the cost of everything we buy. Sounds good, but is the solution really that simple?

Let's take as an example a box of cereal such as Fiberrific. How could we, as consumers, get the cereal for less? Well, we could all drive to Michigan where some of the cereal is produced and save some shipping costs. But would that be practical? Can you imagine millions of people getting in their cars and driving to Michigan just to get some cereal? No, it doesn't make sense. It is much cheaper to have some middlemen bring the cereal to the major cities. That might involve transportation

FIGURE 9–2

How middlemen create exchange efficiency.
This figure shows that adding a wholesaler to the channel of distribution cuts
the number of contacts from 25 to 10. This makes distribution more efficient.
Source: U.S. Department of Agriculture.

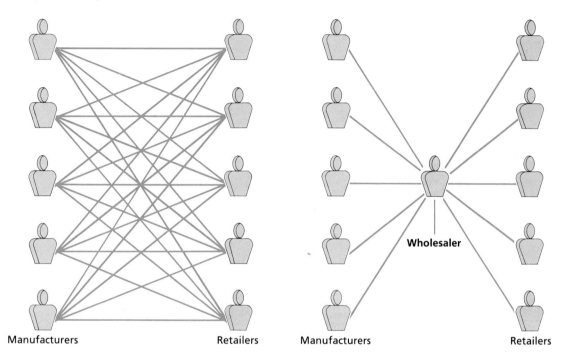

Manufacturers   Retailers   Manufacturers   Retailers

and warehousing by wholesalers. But these steps add cost, don't they? Yes, but they add value as well, the value of not having to drive to Michigan.

The cereal is now somewhere on the outskirts of the city. We could all drive down to the wholesaler's outlet store and pick up the cereal; in fact, some people do just that. But that is not really the most economical way to buy cereal. If we figure in the cost of gas and time, the cereal would be rather expensive. Instead, we prefer to have someone move the cereal from the warehouse to another truck, drive it to the corner supermarket, unload it, unpack it, stamp it with a price, put it on the shelf, and wait for us to come in to buy it. To make it even more convenient, the supermarket may stay open for 24 hours a day, 7 days a week. Think of the *costs*. Think also of the *value!* For less than $3.00 we can get a box of cereal when we want, where we want, and with little effort on our part.

If we were to get rid of the retailer, we could buy a box of cereal for a little less, but we would have to drive miles more and spend time in the warehouse looking through rows of cereals. If we got rid of the wholesaler, we could save a little more, but then we would have to drive to Michigan. But a few cents here and a few cents there add up—to the point where marketing may add up to 75 cents for every 25 cents in manufacturing costs. Figure 9–3 (see page 260) shows where your money goes in the distribution process. Notice that the largest percentage goes to people who drive trucks and work in the wholesale and retail organizations that have emerged to serve your needs. Only 3.5 cents goes to profit. Figure 9–4 (see page 260) shows the share of distribution costs that go to the various middlemen. Note that the percentages vary greatly among different products.

FIGURE 9–3

How distribution affects your food dollar. Note that the farmer gets only 25 cents of your food dollar. The bulk of your money goes to middlemen to pay distribution costs. Their biggest cost is labor (truck drivers, clerks). The next biggest costs are for warehouses and storage.

Source: Agriculture Department, 1987. Reporting on food dollars spent in stores and restaurants.

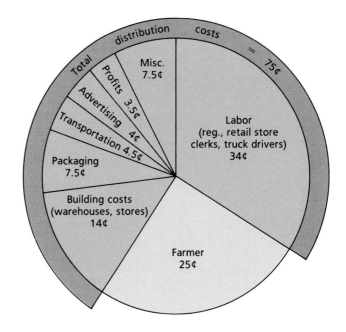

FIGURE 9–4

How middlemen share your food dollar.

ITEM	FARMER	PROCESSOR	WHOLESALER	RETAILER
1 pound choice beef	66.3%	5.4%	7.4%	20.9%
1 dozen grade A large eggs	69.7%	11.5%	5.1%	13.7%
1 half-gallon milk	50.8%	21.6%	19.8%	7.8%

This table shows that the farmer gets only 50.8 cents of the dollar you spend for milk. Some 21.6 cents goes to processors, 19.8 cents to wholesalers, and 7.8 cents to retailers. The question is, is the value added by middlemen worth the cost? Marketers say yes, as our example about Fiberrific illustrates.

Source: U.S. Department of Agriculture.

Businesses are not the only organizations in which a high proportion of costs are due to marketing middlemen. It also costs much to have several churches in one city when people "need" only one. It also is expensive to have post offices, libraries, health clinics, and other such nonbusiness middleman organizations. But again, the convenience and efficiency of having such facilities usually far outweigh the cost. Three basic points about middlemen are:

 Marketing middlemen can be eliminated, but their activities cannot be eliminated; that is, you can get rid of retailers, but then consumers or someone else would have to perform the retailer's tasks, including transportation, storage, finding suppliers, and establishing communication with suppliers.

 Middleman organizations survive because they perform marketing functions more effectively and efficiently than they could be performed by others.

 Middlemen add costs to products, but these costs are usually more than offset by the values they create.

How Middlemen Add Utility to Goods

Utility is an economic term that refers to the value or want-satisfying ability that is added to goods or services by organizations because the products are made more useful or accessible to consumers. Five utilities are mentioned in the economics literature: form, time, place, possession, and information. The first of the five, **form utility,** is performed mostly by producers. It consists of taking raw materials and changing their form so that they become useful products. Thus, a farmer who separates the wheat from the chaff and the processor who turns that wheat into flour are creating form utility. Marketers sometimes perform form utility as well. For example, a retail butcher may cut pork chops off of a larger roast and trim off the fat. Normally, however, marketers perform the other four utilities: time, place, possession, and information. Following are some examples of how they do that.

utility
Value or want-satisfying ability that is added to products by organizations because the products are made more useful or accessible to consumers.

form utility
The value added to a product by taking raw materials and changing their form so that they become useful products.

Time Utility

Rudy Lynch was watching TV with his brother when he suddenly got the urge to have a hot dog and a Coke. The problem was that there were no hot dogs or Cokes in the house. Rudy ran down to the corner delicatessen and bought some hot dogs, buns, Cokes, and potato chips. Rudy was able to get these groceries at 10 P.M. because the store was open from 7 A.M. to 11 P.M.

- Middlemen, such as retailers, add **time utility** to products by making them available *when* they are needed.

time utility
Value added to products by making them available when they are needed.

Place Utility

Mary Margaret Melchak was traveling through the badlands of South Dakota and was getting hungry and thirsty. She saw a sign saying that Wall Drug with fountain service was up ahead. She stopped at the store for some refreshments. She also bought sunglasses and souvenir items while she was there.

- Middlemen add **place utility** to products by having them *where* people want them.

place utility
Value added to products by having them where people want them.

Convenient food stores give you time utility. They stay open long hours so you can get what you want when you want it.

This ad for Gore-Tex products provides much information to consumers. Gore-Tex is a relatively expensive product, so consumers need to know that the benefits far outweigh the cost. Advertisements and salespeople are two sources of information utility.

Possession Utility

William Nathan wanted to buy a nice home in the suburbs. He found just what he wanted, but he did not have the money he needed. So he went with the real estate agent to a local savings and loan and borrowed the money to buy the home. Both the real estate broker and the savings and loan were marketing middlemen.

possession utility
Value added to products by doing whatever is necessary to transfer ownership from one party to another.

  ⬜ Middlemen add **possession utility** by doing whatever is necessary to transfer ownership from one party to another, including providing *credit*.

Information Utility

Fernando Gomez could not decide what kind of TV set to buy. He looked at various ads in the newspaper, talked to the salespersons at several stores, and read material at the library. He also got some material from the government about radiation hazards and consumer buying tips. The newspaper, salespeople, library, and government publications were all information sources made available by middlemen.

information utility
Value added to products by opening two-way flows of information between marketing participants.

  ⬜ Middlemen add **information utility** by opening two-way flows of *information* between marketing participants.

For consumers to receive the maximum benefit from marketing middlemen, the various organizations must work together to assure a smooth flow of goods and services to the consumer. Historically, there has not always been total harmony in the channel of distribution. As a result, channel members have created channel systems that make the flows more efficient. We shall discuss those systems in the next section of this chapter.

COOPERATION IN CHANNEL SYSTEMS

At one time, channel relationships were rather informal in that manufacturers, wholesalers, brokers, retailers, and other channel members were tied together only loosely by short-term agreements. Each organization remained rather independent of the other organizations in the channel, and conflict was as typical as cooperation. Many retailers were especially proud of their independence and often cooperated with manufacturers or wholesalers only when they felt that it was to their advantage. Similarly, manufacturers and wholesalers often had different philosophies of business.

Some answer had to be found to the question: How can manufacturers get wholesalers and retailers to cooperate to form an efficient distribution system? One answer was to link the firms together somehow in a formal relationship. Three systems emerged to tie firms together: corporate systems, contractual systems, and administered systems.

Corporate Distribution Systems

A **corporate distribution system** is one in which all the organizations in the channel are owned by one firm. If the manufacturer *owns* the retail firm, clearly it can exert much greater control over its operations. Sherwin Williams, for example, owns its own retail stores and thus coordinates everything: display, pricing, promotion, inventory control, and so on. Hart Schaffner & Marx owns its own clothing stores for the same reason. Other companies that have tried corporate systems include GE, Firestone, and Xerox.

corporate distribution system
Distribution system in which all the organizations in the channel are owned by one firm.

Contractual Distribution Systems

If a manufacturer cannot buy retail stores, it can try to get the retailers to sign a contract to cooperate. A **contractual distribution system** is one in which members are bound to cooperate through contractual agreements. There are three forms of contractual systems: First, there are franchise systems such as McDonald's, Kentucky Fried Chicken, Baskin-Robbins, and AAMCO. The franchisee agrees to all of the rules, regulations, and procedures established by the franchisor. This results in the consistent quality and level of service you find in most franchised organizations.

contractual distribution system
Distribution system in which members are bound to cooperate through contractual agreements.

Second, there are wholesaler-sponsored chains such as IGA food stores. Each store signs an agreement to use the same name, participate in chain promotions, and cooperate as a unified system of stores, even though each store is independently owned and managed.

A third form of contractual system is a retail cooperative. This arrangement is much like a wholesaler-sponsored chain except it is initiated by the retailers. The same cooperation is agreed to, however, and the stores remain independent.

Administered Distribution Systems

What does a producer do if it cannot buy retailers or get them to sign an agreement to cooperate? The best thing to do is to manage all the marketing functions yourself, including display, inventory, control, pricing, and promotion. The management by producers of all the marketing functions at the retail level is called an **administered distribution system.** Kraft does that for its cheeses and Scott does it for its seed and other lawn care products. Retailers cooperate with producers in such systems because they get so much help for free. All the retailer has to do is ring up the sale and make money.

administered distribution system
Distribution system in which all the marketing functions at the retail level are managed by producers.

If you want to be successful as a marketing agent, you must first determine when, where, who, and at what price consumers want your product, and then you must arrange to tell people about your product, motivate them to buy it, get it to the right parties where and when they want it and in the way they want it.
WILLIAM McINNES

channel captain
The organization in the marketing channel that gets the other members to work together in a cooperative effort.

The Channel Captain

The greatest problems in traditional independent systems are human problems. People just do not want to give up some of their freedom to benefit the system. Thus, retailers do not like to do what wholesalers want, wholesalers do not want to do what manufacturers want, and manufacturers do not always respond to the needs of their suppliers, distributors, and dealers. The channel becomes a source of conflict, antagonism, and inefficiency.

But in the wings there stands a champion of cooperation and coordination—the so-called channel captain. The channel captain's role is to somehow gain control over the channel members and get them to work together. The captain may be the manufacturer, the wholesaler, or the retailer. For example, in the automobile distribution system the manufacturer has much control over what the dealers do and when and how they do it. Retailers such as Sears have the power to control manufacturers that supply them. In other cases, it is the wholesaler who takes charge.

In each case, however, a channel captain usually has the power to get the other channel members to cooperate. A **channel captain,** therefore, is one organization in the channel of distribution that gets all the channel members to work together in a cooperative effort so that the whole channel is more efficient and more competitive with other channels in the same industry. The captain may have more financial resources, better marketing intelligence, or more managerial know-how. Regardless of the source of power, this organization maintains control. You can see how channel captains benefit all the members of the channel by motivating them to cooperate.

One of the largest costs in the channel of distribution is the actual transportation and storage of goods, especially when you factor in the labor costs, the costs of the buildings, and so on. Managing the flow of goods from producer to consumer has become a major career area in marketing. Many universities now have a major in distribution. We shall discuss that function next.

PROGRESS CHECK

- What is the relationship among middlemen, channels of distribution, and physical distribution? Why do we need middlemen?

- Can you illustrate how middlemen create exchange efficiency? How would you defend middlemen to someone who said that if we got rid of middlemen we would save millions of dollars?

- Can you give examples of the five utilities and how middlemen perform them?

- Could you tell a firm how to implement a corporate, contractual, and administered system?

PHYSICAL DISTRIBUTION

Historically, the reason for middlemen was to help perform the physical distribution function; that is, help move goods from the farm to consumer markets or move raw materials to factories and so forth. It involved the movement of goods by truck, train, and other modes, and the storage of goods in warehouses along the way. (A *mode,* in the language of distribution, refers to the various means used to

Being the transportation leader requires more than a one-track mind.

CF knows you've got to offer more to stay Miles Ahead in freight transportation. That's why CF Truckload Service delivers the advantage of both intermodal transportation as well as over-the-road truckload capabilities.

With just one call, CF Truckload Service provides single source, door-to-door responsibility to all major markets nationwide. Our professionals ensure the right equipment is always available to expedite your shipments for both prompt pickups and consistent *on-time* deliveries.

What's more, the industry's most advanced computer technology enables us to coordinate timing precisely with the railroads. It also provides rating, tracking, and tracing information to give you constant status on your shipments. CF has what it takes to move large volumes of freight for you. That's why we're the freight transportation leader— Miles Ahead on the road and on the track.

CONSOLIDATED
FREIGHTWAYS, INC.

MILES AHEAD

This ad promotes door-to-door service using trains and trucks. Emphasis is placed on consistent "on-time" delivery—customer service. Advanced computer technology is revolutionizing the distribution industry.

transport goods such as trucks, trains, planes, ships, and pipeline.) The first courses in marketing had titles such as "The Distribution of Products." Physical distribution is still the most costly marketing function. Every year, organizations in the United States spend about 20 percent of gross national product (GNP) on physical distribution, far more than for any other marketing function. This figure changes as GNP changes.

This section will introduce you to the principles of physical distribution and give you some insights into physical distribution management. If you are attracted to careers in this area, you can find courses available covering transportation, distribution management, and related topics such as carrier management. Sometimes these courses have the word *logistics* in the title. Although logistics is sometimes viewed as a slightly different concept, the course content is largely physical distribution and storage management.

One cannot overemphasize the importance of physical distribution, even in an era when the service sector is dominant. Physical distribution begins with raw materials (for example, at the mine) that have to be shipped to manufacturers who change them into useful products. Physical distribution also includes those activities involved in purchasing goods, receiving them, moving them through the plant, inventorying them, storing them, and shipping finished goods all the way to final users (including all the warehousing, reshipping, and physical movements of all kinds involved).

The Physical Distribution Manager

A smart physical distribution manager can do wonders for a firm's profitability. For example, one firm was shipping finished cabinets in carload lots to four warehouses. The traffic manager found that the company could save 40 percent by shipping the shelving separately from the bolts and nuts. This was possible because the shipping rates for components were much less than for finished parts. The increase in cost for handling and packaging the component parts was $40,000, but the savings in shipping costs was $320,000, or a net saving of $280,000. Such are the savings possible when physical distribution is carefully managed.

HOW COMPLEX IS THE DISTRIBUTION SYSTEM?

Researchers once studied the distribution system of building materials to construct a two-story, masonry dwelling with six rooms and one bath. They studied 43 different materials amounting to 186 tons of products. In traveling from place to place, these products (and their antecedents) were loaded onto carriers, moved, and unloaded 424 separate times. Some 366 business entities were involved, including 148 transportation agencies. The 217 business entities that participated in the ownership flow of materials participated in 374 transactions, including 330 purchase/sale transactions.

Physical distribution costs have been a concern of marketers for many years, but there has been more talk and theory development than action. Recently, however, the development of computers, marketing information systems, and integrated channel networks have led to a new position called **physical distribution manager.** This person is responsible for coordinating and integrating all movement of materials including transportation, internal movement (materials handling), and warehousing. Few organizations actually have such a position, but many have accepted the concept, and the process of implementing a "total systems approach" is slowly being carried out. Only very recently have firms begun to recognize the need for physical distribution management throughout the channel system, rather than just within the firm itself. That is, a department in one firm could coordinate and integrate as much of the movement of goods through the entire channel as possible. The idea is to keep distribution costs low for the whole system as well as for each individual organization in the channel.

physical distribution manager
The person responsible for coordinating and integrating all movement of materials including transportation, internal movement, and warehousing.

Transportation Modes

A primary concern of distribution managers is the selection of a transportation mode that will minimize costs and assure a certain level of service. The largest percentage of goods are shipped by rail. Railroad shipment is best for bulky items such as coal, wheat, and heavy equipment. Figure 9–5 compares the various modes on several dimensions.

For the last 20 years or so, railroads have handled about 35 to 40 percent of the total volume of goods in the United States, and this represents a decline in railroad shipping. As recently as 1950, railroads were handling up to 60 percent of volume. Today, it is just 36 percent. As you are no doubt aware, railroad lines are in a state of transition. As a result of practices such as piggyback shipments, railroads should continue to hold better than a 35 percent share of the market. (**Piggyback** means that a truck trailer is loaded onto a flatcar and taken to a destination, where it will be driven to separate plants by a truck driver.) Railroad shipment is a relatively energy-efficient way to move goods and could therefore experience significant gains if energy prices climb.

piggyback
Shipping the cargo-carrying part of a truck on a railroad car over long distances to save on transportation costs.

The second largest surface transportation mode is motor vehicles (trucks, vans, and so forth). Such vehicles handle a little over 25 percent of the volume. As shown in Figure 9–5, trucks reach more locations than railroad. Trucks can deliver almost any commodity door-to-door.

Water transportation moves a greater volume of goods than you might expect. Over the last 20 years, water transportation has carried 15 percent to 17 percent of the total. If you live near the Mississippi River, you have likely seen towboats hauling as many as 30 barges at a time with a cargo of up to 35,000 tons. On

Comparing transportation modes. FIGURE 9–5

MODE	COST	PERCENT OF DOMESTIC VOLUME*	SPEED	ON–TIME DEPENDABILITY	FLEXIBILITY HANDLING PRODUCTS	FREQUENCY OF SHIPMENTS	REACH
Railroad	Medium	35.9%	Slow	Medium	High	Low	High
Trucks	High	25.5%	Fast	High	Medium	High	Most
Pipeline	Low	23.2%	Medium	Highest	Lowest	Highest	Lowest
Ships (water)	Lowest	15.1%	Slowest	Lowest	Highest	Lowest	Low
Airplane	Highest	.3%	Fastest	Low	Low	Medium	Medium

Combining trucks with railroads lowers cost and increases locations reached. The same is true when combining trucks with ships. Combining trucks with airlines speeds goods long distances and gets them to almost any location.

*The 1988 Information Please Almanac (Boston: Houghton Mifflin, 1988), p. 73.

Distribution today combines modes to get the most efficiency with the most flexibility. Often that calls for moving truck trailers on trains across the country right to the customer's place of business. The concept is called piggyback.

smaller rivers, about eight barges can be hauled carrying up to 20,000 tons—that is the equivalent of four 100-car railroad trains. Thus, you can see the importance of river traffic. Add to that Great Lakes shipping, shipping from coast to coast and along the coasts, and international shipments, and water transportation takes on a new dimension as a key transportation mode. When truck trailers are placed on ships to travel long distances at lower rates, the process is called **fishyback.**

Another transportation mode that is not visible to the average consumer is movement by pipeline. Yet almost 25 percent of the total volume moves this way. Pipelines are used primarily for the transportation of petroleum and petroleum products. But the Cleveland Electric Illuminating Company has experimented with a coal pipeline, and several more are either planned or in operation now. In this method the coal is broken down into small pieces, mixed with water to form what is called a slurry, and piped to its destination, where it often must be dried before using. Such coal may not burn as cleanly, and there is some resistance to such pipelines by environmentalists. There have been experiments with sending other solids in pipelines, and this could be a major mode of distribution in the future.

Today, only a small part of shipping is done by air. Nonetheless, air transportation is a critical factor in many industries. Airlines carry everything from small packages to luxury cars and elephants and could expand to be a very competitive mode for other goods. Case 1 at the end of this chapter gives some interesting facts and figures about the growth of air transport in international markets.

fishyback
Shipping the cargo-carrying part of a truck on a ship over long distances to save on transportation costs.

Distribution systems have always been one of the critical elements of business success, and in my opinion, they're getting even more critical. That's because customer service has, for a variety of reasons, become one of the important ways a company can differentiate its products and services. Much has been said about America's transition to a service economy. And a lot more has been said about the add-on observation that, in this service economy, all too often, service is lousy.
FREDERICK W. SMITH, Chief Executive Officer, Federal Express Corporation

containerization
The process of packing and sealing a number of items into one unit that is easily moved and shipped.

This picture from a CSX ad is designed to show the benefits of containerization. Note the containers stacked on the ship. They can be moved by rail to major cities and moved again by truck to specific customers. The picture shows that such movement can take place internationally with no problem.

The primary benefit of air transportation is speed. No firm knows this better than Federal Express. Its theme is, "When it absolutely, positively has to be there overnight." Federal Express is just one of several competitors vying for the fast-delivery market.

Some marketers have found huge savings by switching transportation modes. For example, one firm found tremendous savings by eliminating most of its warehouses and flying goods to customers when speed was demanded. Otherwise, deliveries were made by truck. Many firms are combining distribution modes to get the advantages of several modes and minimize the disadvantages. You can see from Figure 9–5 the value of combining railroading with trucking to get less expensive transportation by railroad and more flexible distribution with trucks.

There are many trade-offs in physical distribution, such as the trade-off of increased transportation costs for lower warehouse costs.

Criteria for Selecting Distribution Systems

From a marketing perspective, two criteria dominate all thinking in physical distribution planning. One criterion is *customer service*. Customer wants and needs come first. A goal would be to serve all a firm's customers' needs with 100 percent reliability. Such a goal would be prohibitively expensive. But distribution managers do strive for an 85 to 95 percent level of customer satisfaction.

The other criterion, obviously, is *profit*. Marketing systems are designed to accomplish mutually satisfying exchanges, which means that the buyer *and* the seller must be satisfied. That means profit for the seller.

Containerization

You can imagine the problem of moving many small items from place to place in large trucks, railroad cars, or other forms of transportation. There is the danger of theft and loss, especially of small items. An effective answer is to pack and seal groups of items in one large package that can be easily moved and stored. The process of packing and sealing a number of items into one unit that is easily moved and shipped is called **containerization.** Some items are wrapped in plastic and then heated so that the plastic shrinks and holds all the items securely in place. This is called shrink wrapping. Containerization may also involve wooden boxes and other materials. As more companies use containerization techniques, shipping will become more efficient and the movement of goods will flow more smoothly.

The Storage Function

About 25 to 30 percent of the total cost of physical distribution is for storage. This includes the cost of the warehouse and its operation plus movement of goods within the warehouse. There are two kinds of warehouses: storage and distribution. A *storage warehouse* stores products for a relatively long time. Seasonal goods such as lawn mowers would be stored in such a warehouse. *Distribution warehouses* are facilities used to gather and redistribute products. You can picture a distribution warehouse for Federal Express or United Parcel Service handling thousands of packages for a very short time. Many college students work part-time in such facilities while in school and go on to be traffic managers who control the shipment of goods.

GE recently built a combination storage and distribution facility that will give you a feel for how large such buildings can be. This distribution center is 475 feet short of a half mile in length and is 465 feet wide. It is big enough to hold three Statues of Liberty, two Queen Marys, and one Empire State Building. It is located in San Gabriel Valley in California.[1]

Materials Handling

Materials handling is the movement of goods within a warehouse, factory, or store. It is instructive to go to a warehouse and watch the operations for a while. You may see forklift trucks picking up stacks of merchandise and moving them around. In more modern warehouses, computerized vehicles and robots will move the materials. Warehouse management could be an interesting career possibility for business students. Why not go to a local warehouse and see for yourself?

materials handling
The movement of goods within a warehouse, factory, or store.

You have to visit a warehouse like this to get a full appreciation of the size and the equipment used. You will learn a new appreciation for neatness and safety and the value of wholesalers and distributors.

DELIVERY BY AIR

Customer service was the primary goal of Bob Alexander, manager of international sales for Goodman Equipment. He had to deliver a 67,000-pound excavating machine to Switzerland in the fall. The customer wanted the machine as quickly as possible, because he was afraid snows would come and prevent delivery of the machine until spring. Following the buyer's specifications, Bob *flew* the machine to Switzerland, and the buyer paid the extra shipping costs. Speed, not cost, was the major consideration, because the machine was needed to help dig a railway tunnel. This is just one example of a buyer working with a small business to develop a delivery system that is satisfactory to both.

Now that we have talked about channels of distribution and physical distribution management, it is time to talk about the organizations that make up the channel. We shall begin with wholesalers. Remember that one goal of this discussion is to introduce you to the variety of career possibilities available in this area. Most college students know little or nothing about wholesaling, yet the rapid growth of warehouse clubs is providing many career possibilities. Have you ever visited one? The prices are amazingly low. If there are none in your area now, there may be soon. They are spreading rapidly across the country. The box called Warehouse Clubs, later in this chapter, gives more details. Let's look at the various kinds of wholesalers to see if you can't find one that sounds interesting to you.

PROGRESS CHECK

- What are some of the activities involved in physical distribution?
- Which of the transportation modes is fastest, cheapest, most flexible? Which modes can be combined to improve the distribution process?
- What are the two criteria for selecting a distribution system?

WHOLESALE MIDDLEMEN

wholesaler
A marketing middleman that sells to organizations and individuals, but not final consumers.

A **wholesaler** is a marketing middleman that sells to organizations and individuals, but not final consumers. For years no clear distinction was made in marketing between wholesaling and retailing. An early attempt to differentiate these two marketing middlemen occurred in 1932, when the government made a census of wholesale distributors. Today, there is still much confusion as to the difference between wholesalers and retailers. For example, many retail outlets have signs that say "wholesale distributors" or something similar.

What difference does it make whether an organization is called a wholesaler or a retailer? One difference is that many states impose a sales tax on retail sales. To collect such a tax, the state must know which sales are retail sales and which are not. Retailers are sometimes subject to other rules and regulations that do not apply to wholesalers.

For practical marketing purposes, it is helpful to distinguish wholesaling from retailing and to clearly define the functions performed so that more effective systems of distribution can be designed. Some producers will not sell directly to retailers but will deal only with wholesalers. Some producers will give wholesalers a bigger discount than retailers. What confuses the issue is that some organizations sell much of their merchandise to other middlemen (a wholesale sale) but also sell to ultimate consumers (a retail sale). The new warehouse clubs are a good example.

retailer
A marketing middleman that sells to consumers.

The issue is really rather simple: A **retailer** sells products to consumers for their own use; a wholesaler does not. *Wholesalers* sell products to businesses and institutions (e.g., hospitals) for use in the business or to wholesalers, retailers, and individuals *for resale*. It bears repeating that wholesalers *do not* sell to consumers for their own use. What is more complex is when one organization becomes both a retailer and a wholesaler. Furthermore, there are many wholesalers who specialize in just one or two marketing tasks, as we shall see below.

CAREER INFORMATION: ENTRY–LEVEL TRAFFIC AND SHIPPING JOBS

NATURE OF THE WORK

Traffic, shipping, and receiving clerks keep track of goods transferred between businesses and their customers and suppliers. In small companies, they may be assigned tasks requiring a good deal of independent judgment, such as handling problems with damaged merchandise, or supervising other workers in shipping or receiving rooms.

A job as a traffic, shipping, or receiving clerk offers a good opportunity for new workers in a firm to learn about their company's products and business practices. Some clerks may be promoted to head traffic, shipping, or receiving clerk; warehouse manager; or purchasing agent. Very experienced workers with a broad understanding of shipping and receiving may enter related fields such as industrial traffic management.

JOB OUTLOOK

Employment of traffic, shipping, and receiving clerks is expected to increase more slowly than the average for all occupations through the mid-1990s, in part because so many clerks work in manufacturing and wholesale trade, industry sectors that are expected to grow more slowly than the overall economy.

Employment growth will continue to be affected by automation, as all but the smallest firms move to hold down labor costs by using computers to store and retrieve shipping and receiving records. Methods of materials handling have changed significantly in recent years. Large warehouses are increasingly automated, using equipment such as computerized conveyor systems, robots, computer-directed trucks, and automatic storage and retrieval systems. This automation, coupled with the growing use of hand-held scanners and personal computers in receiving departments, is expected to hold down employment growth.

Shipping and receiving clerks in urban areas earned as much as the average for all nonsupervisory workers in private industry, except farming. Salaries varied substantially, however, by type of employer. Shipping and receiving clerks employed in the services industry earned less than those working for wholesale houses, who in turn made less than those employed by public utilities.

RELATED OCCUPATIONS

Traffic, shipping, and receiving clerks record, check, and often store the materials that a company receives. They also process and pack goods for shipment. Other workers who perform similar duties are stock clerks, material clerks, distributing clerks, routing clerks, and order fillers.

Source: *Occupational Outlook Handbook,* U.S. Department of Labor.

Merchant Wholesalers

Merchant wholesalers are independently owned firms that take title to goods that they handle. About 80 percent of wholesalers fall in this category. There are two types of merchant wholesalers: full-service wholesalers and limited-function wholesalers. **Full-service wholesalers** perform all eight distribution functions: transportation, storage, risk bearing, credit, market information, grading, buying, and selling (see Figure 9–6 on page 272). **Limited-function wholesalers** perform only selected functions, but do them especially well.

Full-Service Wholesalers

General merchandise wholesalers (full-service wholesalers) carry a broad assortment of merchandise. They are found in industries such as drug, hardware, and clothing.

Rack jobbers furnish racks or shelves full of merchandise to retailers, display products, and sell on consignment. This means that they keep title to the goods until they are sold, and then they share the profits with the retailer. Merchandise such as toys, hosiery, and health and beauty aids are sold by rack jobbers. (If a rack jobber does not supply credit to customers, he or she is classified as a limited-function wholesaler.)

merchant wholesaler
Independently owned wholesalers that take title to goods that they handle.

full-service wholesaler
A merchant wholesaler that performs all eight distribution functions.

limited-function wholesaler
A merchant wholesaler that performs only selected distribution functions.

general merchandise wholesaler
A merchant wholesaler that carries a broad assortment of merchandise.

rack jobber
A full-service wholesaler that furnishes racks or shelves full of merchandise to retailers, displays products, and sells on consignment.

FIGURE 9–6

Functions performed by a
full-function wholesaler.

1. *Provide a sales force* to sell the goods to retailers and other buyers
2. *Communicate* manufacturers' advertising deals and plans
3. *Maintain inventory,* thus reducing the level of the inventory suppliers have to carry
4. Arrange or undertake *transportation*
5. *Provide capital* by paying cash or quick payments for goods
6. Provide suppliers with *market information* they cannot afford or are unable to obtain themselves
7. Undertake *credit risk* by granting credit to customers and absorbing any bad debts, thus relieving the supplier of this burden
8. *Assume the risk* for the product by taking title

The wholesaler may perform the services listed below for *its customers:*

1. *Buy* goods the end market will desire and make them available to customers
2. Maintain *inventory,* thus reducing customer's costs
3. *Transport* goods to customers quickly
4. Provide *market information* and business consulting services
5. Provide *financing* through granting credit, critical to small retailers especially
6. *Order* goods in the types and quantities customers desire

Source: Thomas C. Kinnear and Kenneth L. Bernhardt, *Principles of Marketing,* 2nd ed. (Glenview, Ill.: Scott, Foresman, 1986), p. 369.

A wholesaler deals with goods in volume. This picture will give you a feel for the size of the operation and the equipment needed. When you move millions of packages, you sometimes have to move them quickly and efficiently. This is the role of wholesalers.

cash-and-carry wholesaler
A limited-function wholesaler that serves mostly smaller retailers with a limited assortment of products.

Limited-Function Wholesalers

Cash-and-carry wholesalers serve mostly smaller retailers with a limited assortment of products. Retailers go to them, pay cash, and carry the goods home; thus the term cash-and-carry wholesaler. Cash-and-carry wholesalers have begun selling to the general public in what are called warehouse clubs.

WAREHOUSE CLUBS

Warehouse clubs are a special type of cash-and-carry wholesaler that are open to members only and sell merchandise at 20 to 40 percent below supermarkets and discount stores. The primary function of such clubs is to provide small businesses (that are too small to have wholesalers service them) with merchandise and supplies at low prices. What makes these new stores different is that you and I can join these clubs for an annual fee (usually $25) and buy goods at a 5 percent markup if we belong to a credit union, are government employees, or otherwise meet the qualifications. Sam's Wholesale Clubs in the Midwest and Southwest were started by Sam Walton of Wal-Mart Stores. Kroger has started several warehouse clubs under the name Price Savers.

Source: Jack G. Kaikato, "The Boom in Warehouse Clubs," *Business Horizons,* March/April 1987, pp. 68–73.

Drop shippers solicit orders from retailers and other wholesalers and have the merchandise shipped directly from a producer to a buyer. They own the merchandise, but do not handle, stock, or deliver it. That is done by the producer. Drop shippers tend to handle bulky products such as coal, lumber, and chemicals.

Truck jobbers are small wholesalers who deliver goods by truck to retailers. They are like a cash-and-carry wholesaler on wheels. They provide no credit. They handle items like bakery goods, dairy products, and tobacco products.

In recent years, there have been many mergers among wholesalers so that there are only about 285,000 companies now versus 320,000 in 1985. Wholesalers move some $1.6 trillion worth of merchandise a year. That's a lot of merchandise and means many potential jobs for you.[2]

Perhaps the most useful marketing middlemen as far as you are concerned are retailers. They are the ones who bring goods and services to your neighborhood and make them available day and night. As we mentioned in the Profile at the beginning of this chapter, no other area of business offers more career opportunities than retailing, so let's explore what is happening in this dynamic area. Like the women in the Profile, you may want to start your own store some day.

drop shipper
A limited-function wholesaler that solicits orders from retailers and other wholesalers and has the merchandise shipped directly from a producer to a buyer.

truck jobber
A small, limited-function wholesaler that delivers goods by truck to retailers.

RETAIL MIDDLEMEN

Next time you go to the supermarket to buy groceries, stop for a minute and look at the tremendous variety of products in the store. Think of how many marketing exchanges were involved to bring you the 15,000 or so items that you see. Some products (spices, for example) may have been imported from halfway around the world. Other products have been processed and frozen so that you can eat them out of season (for example, strawberries).

A supermarket is a retailer. A retailer, remember, is a marketing middleman who sells to consumers. In the United States there are approximately 2.3 million retail stores, selling everything from soup to automobiles. Retail organizations employ more than 11 million people. They are one of the major employers of marketing graduates. There are many careers available in retailing in all kinds of firms.

Retail Store Categories

There are so many new retail establishments opening today that it is difficult to keep up. Nevertheless, some of the more important categories include the following.

Interesting fact:
R. H. Macy went broke with his first three dry-goods stores.

Department Stores

A department store has 25 or more employees, sells home furnishings, appliances, family apparel, and household linens in different departments of the store. Most large suburban malls have one or two department stores as *anchors*. An *anchor store* is one that is large enough and popular enough to attract business to a shopping center or mall. Often Sears or Montgomery Ward will be an anchor store. Major department stores such as Macy's, Saks Fifth Avenue, Nordstrom, Neiman Marcus, or I. Magnin may be anchors and draw in more affluent consumers.

Discount Stores

Discount stores are self-service outlets that sell general merchandise below department store prices. The leading discount chains (in sales volume) are K mart, Wal-Mart, Target, Gemco, and T.G.&Y. See the box The Wheel of Retailing later in this chapter for what sometimes happens to discount stores.

Specialty Stores

A specialty store sells a single category of merchandise such as shoes, cameras, flowers, or books. Some better-known names include Toys "R" Us, Hickory Farms, and Radio Shack.

TOP 10 SUPERMARKET CHAINS
1. Safeway
2. Kroger
3. American Stores
4. Lucky
5. Winn-Dixie
6. A&P
7. Albertson's
8. Supermarkets General
9. Stop & Shop
10. Grand Union

Supermarkets

A supermarket is a large, self-service store that offers a wide variety of food items (meat, produce, canned goods, etc.) and some nonfood items. The largest chains include Safeway, Kroger, Lucky Stores, Winn-Dixie, and A&P. A small version of a supermarket is called a grocery store. The latest trend in supermarkets is to install a small deli, a salad bar, a flower shop, and in-store banking. Most stores already have a small bakery shop and fresh-fish counter.[3]

Hypermarkets

A hypermarket is a giant food and general merchandise store. Such stores are popular in France and are becoming more widespread in the United States. The two Hypermarket USA stores in Dallas and the Fred Meyer stores in the Northwest are examples. A hypermarket averages about 200,000 square feet and sells about 50,000 items. This compares to the average supermarket at 39,000 square feet and 15,500 items.[4]

Convenience Stores

A convenience store is a small food store with a limited selection that emphasizes convenient locations and hours. Some popular chains are 7-Eleven, White Hen, and Open Pantry.

Catalog Stores

A catalog store sends catalogs to consumers and displays merchandise in showrooms where customers can shop and order merchandise from an attached warehouse. Examples are Best Products, Zale, Service Merchandise, Giant Stores, and Vornado.

General Stores

A general store is an early style of retail store offering a wide variety of merchandise. Many smaller towns have a general store to serve their needs.

Chain Stores

Chain stores are two or more retailers with the same name offering the same product line. Shoe stores, specialty stores, department stores, and other categories of stores can also be called chain stores if there are two or more stores. Some popular chain stores are Florsheim Shoes and Western Auto.

CAREER INFORMATION: RETAIL AND WHOLESALE BUYING

NATURE OF THE WORK

Buyers purchase, for resale, the best available merchandise at the lowest possible prices and expedite the delivery of goods from the producer to the consumer. The responsibilities of buyers vary by industry and product and range from the mundane to the glamorous. For example, wholesale grocery buyers may spend many hours deciding which brand of cereal should be promoted in the grocery stores they supply. In sharp contrast, apparel buyers in department stores may attend a fashion show in Paris and buy thousands of dollars worth of evening dresses at one time.

TRAINING, OTHER QUALIFICATIONS, AND ADVANCEMENT

Familiarity with merchandise and with wholesaling and retailing practices is important for buyers, and many persons with such experience transfer into this occupation. Marketing and distributive education programs can launch careers in wholesaling and retailing that lead eventually to a buyer's position. Vocational schools, technical institutes, and community colleges offer post-secondary training that prepares students for careers in merchandising. Many colleges and universities offer associate degree or bachelor's degree programs in marketing and purchasing. An increasing number of employers prefer applicants who have a college degree.

Courses in merchandising or marketing may help in getting started in wholesaling and retailing. However, most employers accept college graduates from any field of study for buyer trainee programs, which combine classroom instruction in merchandising and purchasing with short rotations to various jobs in the store. This training introduces the new worker to store operations and policies and to the fundamentals of merchandising and management.

JOB OUTLOOK

Employment of buyers is expected to grow about as fast as the average for all occupations through the mid-1990s, as the wholesale and retail trade industries expand in response to a growing population and higher personal incomes.

Somewhat offsetting increased demand for buyers will be productivity gains resulting from the increased use of computers to control inventory, maintain records, and to reorder merchandise. The number of qualifed jobseekers will continue to exceed the number of openings because merchandising attracts many college graduates. Prospects are likely to be best for qualified applicants who enjoy the competitive, fast-paced nature of merchandising.

A buyer's income depends on the amount and type of product purchased, the employer's sales volume, and, to some extent, the buyer's seniority. Buyers for large wholesale distributors and for mass merchandisers such as discount or large chain department stores are among the most highly paid.

RELATED OCCUPATIONS

Workers in other occupations who need a knowledge of marketing and the ability to assess consumer demand are sales managers, comparison shoppers, manufacturers' sales representatives, insurance sales agents, wholesale trade sales representatives, and travel agents.

SOURCES OF ADDITIONAL INFORMATION

General information about a career in retailing is available from: National Mass Retailing Institute, 570 Seventh Ave., New York, N.Y. 10018.

Source: *Occupational Outlook Handbook,* U.S. Department of Labor.

SUPERMARKET COMPETITION

What is it like to run a grocery store for fun and profit? Could you compete with the giants like Safeway, A&P, Kroger, and Winn-Dixie? What could you do to compete? Let's look at Gromer's supermarket in Elgin, Illinois, to see how they do it.

First of all, let's check to see how the supermarket is doing. It makes a little over 2 percent on each dollar of sales. That's better than Safeway's .99 percent, Kroger's .98 percent, or Winn-Dixie's 1.59 percent, but not as good as A&P's 3.67 percent. Most stores have about 7,500 customers a week. Gromer's has over 34,200. He grosses about $900,000 a week in sales. In other words, Gromer's is doing quite well.

How do they do it? For one thing, Gromer's tries to meet as many needs as possible. It has a magazine rack, a deli, a carryout service, a bakery on the premises, film processing, videocassette rentals, catering, and more. Gromer's listens to customers and gives them what they want. Most stores carry almost 10,500 different brands and sizes; Gromer's carries almost twice that. A typical supermarket carries 1,200 varieties of frozen food. Gromer's has 1,500. It sells 18 varieties of croutons. There are 152 barrels of bulk foods. You get the idea.

What about pricing? Well, a cup of coffee is free. Ice cream at the cone bar is 25 cents. The meat department loses money. The bakery earns just a little. The stamp-selling and utility-bill collection services lose money. Not only that, but the store stays open 24 hours a day, so the lighting bill and other such costs are high. Mind you, this is in a town of about 65,000 people where very few go shopping at night.

So where does profit come in? The salad bar is one profit center. Everything but the soup costs $2.19 a pound. Gross profit runs as high as 65 percent in season. This compares to a gross profit of 8 percent on items such as soup, sugar, and flour. Shish kebab is $4.98 a pound, and much of the weight is stick and vegetables. Fresh-squeezed orange juice goes for $2.49. All these items are highly profitable, and there are thousands more like this throughout the store, along with the great bargains.

Mr. Gromer carries a notebook and jots down consumer requests. He uses up a lot of notebooks in a year. The employees are trained to be attentive equally to customer wants and to profit. Each manager is given much responsibility for his or her area. In-store competition for profits and customers is intense. For example, the bakery competes for sales against baked goods from outside suppliers (which are sold in another department).

Of course, it is difficult to talk of small-business success without mentioning computers. Gromer's was one of the early users of checkout scanners. The scanners and an estimated quarter of a million dollars worth of computer hardware and software are the heart of Gromer's marketing intelligence system. For example, computer printouts tell Mr. Gromer which sizes of Rice Krispies sell fast and which do not. That way, unpopular sizes can be eliminated. Computer data can also tell Gromer's how to cut up a piece of meat to optimize profit. Gromer's knows how many groceries go through the lines for every 15-minute period every hour of every day. This helps immeasurably in scheduling check-out people, baggers, and so forth. The computer is an invaluable asset in inventory control and in virtually every phase of operation.

To contrast all this with the big operators, it is instructive to know that A&P once had almost 16,000 stores in 34 states, but now has some 1,088 stores in only 25 states. Small retailers can compete against the giants, if they do it right.

Gromer supermarket is unique as you'll see when you read the story about it. The outside is nothing unusual, as you can see, but the inside is different and exciting and generates much business.

MAKING ETHICAL DECISIONS

Marketers of new grocery products are finding it difficult to get shelf space in supermarkets. Grocery chains are demanding incentive money to place new goods on already-crowded shelves. The practice is known as *slotting allowances*. Stores claim that these funds are needed to add the product to the computer system, to warehouse the goods, and to promote the new products. This fee is getting higher and higher as new products enter the market. Smaller producers may eventually be forced to drop new product introductions because of these fees for shelf space.

Imagine you are a large producer of grocery products and can easily afford such fees. Would you pay them with no protest knowing that, in the long run, they will benefit you by restricting competition? Since this is a common practice, do you feel that such payments are ethical? If you had trouble with the ethics of such payments, whom would you blame, the supermarkets or the businesses that pay supermarkets for shelf space?

Source: "Industry Voices," *Advertising Age,* May 9, 1988, p. 54.

CAREER INFORMATION: RETAIL SALES

NATURE OF THE WORK

The success of any retail establishment depends largely on its sales workers. Courteous and efficient service from behind the counter or on the sales floor does much to satisfy customers and build a store's reputation.

Whether selling furniture, electrical appliances, or clothing, a sales worker's primary job is to interest customers in the merchandise. This is done by describing the product's construction, demonstrating its use, and showing various models and colors. For some jobs, particularly those selling expensive, "big ticket" items, special knowledge or skills are needed. Personal computer sales workers, for example, must have sufficient knowledge of electronics to explain to customers the features of various brands and models and the meaning of manufacturers' specifications.

In addition to selling, most retail sales workers make out sales checks, receive cash payments, and give change and receipts. More and more stores are installing point-of-sale terminals that register sales, adjust inventory figures, and perform simple calculations. This equipment increases workers' productivity—enabling them to provide better customer service. Sales workers also handle returns and exchanges of merchandise and keep their work areas neat. In addition, they may help stock shelves or racks, mark price tags, take inventory, and prepare displays.

JOB OUTLOOK

Employment of retail sales workers is expected to grow about as fast as the average for all workers through the mid-1990s. While the volume of goods sold is expected to grow rapidly, the continuation of self-service and the increase in computerized checkout systems will reduce somewhat the need for additional sales workers. However, employment in stores selling "big ticket" items will be much less affected since these items are not likely to be sold self-service.

Retail trade sales work will continue to provide more job openings than almost any other occupation through the mid-1990s. Prospects for sales jobs are good because retail selling is a large occupation and turnover is high. There will continue to be many opportunities for part-time workers, as well as for temporary workers during peak selling periods such as the Christmas season.

Some sales workers receive salary plus commissions—that is, a percentage of the sales they make. Others are paid only on a commission or salary basis. Those paid by commission may find their earnings greatly affected by ups and downs in the economy.

Sales workers in many retail stores may buy merchandise at a discount, often from 10 to 25 percent below regular prices. This privilege sometimes is extended to the employee's family. Some stores, especially the large ones, pay part or all of the cost of life insurance, health insurance, and a pension.

SOURCES OF ADDITIONAL INFORMATION

Information on careers in retail sales may be obtained from the personnel offices of local stores; from state merchants' associations; or from local unions of the United Food and Commercial Workers International Union.

Source: *Occupational Outlook Handbook,* U.S. Department of Labor.

New Retailing Megamalls

The excitement of retailing shows up best in the new megamalls coming to the United States. They are being patterned after the West Edmonton Mall in Edmonton, Canada. The mall has 800 stores and shops, including *three* McDonald's. There are 19 movie and stage theaters, a miniature golf course, an indoor water park with 20 water slides, an indoor amusement park with 28 rides, a saltwater lake, and a skating rink.[5]

Mall of America is coming to Bloomington, Minnesota, with 800 stores, a 7-acre amusement park, 18 theaters, an ice rink, miniature golf, and more. Smaller but equally impressive malls are planned for several other cities in the United States.[6]

Nonstore Retailing

For every dollar consumers spend in stores like those listed in the previous section, they spend 37.5 cents at home ordering goods and services by mail and by phone. The store figures do not include supermarkets, service stations, restaurants, and car dealerships. Still, the out-of-store shopping trend is growing. Some of the categories include the following.

Telemarketing is the sale of goods and services by telephone. Some 80,000 companies use telemarketing today to supplement or replace in-store selling. Many send a catalog to consumers and let them order by calling an 800 toll-free number. An organization called Occupational Forecasting has predicted that the number of telemarketing jobs in the year 2000 will be some 8 million workers. In other words, it will be one of the fastest-growing areas in marketing.

telemarketing
The sale of goods and services by telephone.

Vending Machines

A vending machine dispenses convenience goods when consumers deposit sufficient money in the machine. The benefit of vending machines is their convenient location in airports, office buildings, schools, service stations, and other areas where people want convenience items.

Door-to-Door Sales

Door-to-door sales involves selling to consumers in their homes. Major users of this category include encyclopedia publishers (Britannica), cosmetics producers (Avon), and vacuum cleaner manufacturers (Electrolux). The newest trend is to sell lingerie, art work, plants, and other goods at house "parties" sponsored by sellers. No doubt you have heard of Tupperware parties. Because so many women are working now and are not at home during the day, such companies are sponsoring parties at workplaces and on weekends and evenings.

Mail-Order Retailers

A mail-order retailer sends catalogs to consumers who then order goods by mail. Two popular mail-order catalogs are those for L. L. Bean and Sharper Image. Some of this business is now being shifted to telemarketing.

Even though we have covered most of the major categories of retailers, there are more that could be mentioned. Think of all the gasoline stations, restaurants,

THE WHEEL OF RETAILING

The *wheel of retailing* describes a situation that has occurred in retailing over the years. What happens is that new retailers tend to enter a market by emphasizing low price, limited service, and out-of-the-way locations. The new warehouse clubs are a good example. As business improves, they add services such as credit and get better locations. Soon prices must be raised to cover the added services and the store must now compete with traditional department stores and specialty stores. Once a store has added services, it is difficult to go back. Because the store is now competing with department stores that are more attractive, it often fails (for example, Korvette's and Robert Hall). However, new stores then enter the market at low prices and repeat the cycle. The wheel of retailing, therefore, looks like the illustration.

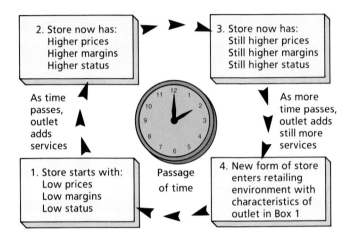

An example of this wheel of retailing is provided by discount department stores. They began by offering low prices and few services. They added services such as credit, delivery, and more to meet the competition. The new services forced them to raise prices making their products less competitive. New stores such as catalog stores and warehouse clubs entered the market with low prices. Watch for them to add services and get more expensive too.

video stores, bakeries, butcher shops, rental stores, dry cleaning establishments, and more that you see in your travels. Certainly, retailing offers a variety of careers in many different settings. There are malls that feature only outlet stores and others that sell only home-made crafts. Retailing can be an exciting career.

Home Shopping Networks

One of the newest and more popular ways of shopping at home is home shopping TV shows. These shows became very popular in 1987 and 1988. They spawned whole new shows that sell homes and automobiles on TV. For example, the new home shows feature homes in various parts of the city (inside and out) and give you a number to call for more information and directions. To learn more about home shopping networks, tune to a channel that has such a show and watch how they work. It is fascinating. You will see mostly close-out items at a bargain and lots of jewelry and household goods. No doubt you will see more of these shows as people get more comfortable with shopping at home. Employment with Home Shopping Network went from 44 employees to over 4,400 employees in just four years.[7] You can see the potential growth, therefore, in this exciting new area.

How important are middlemen such as wholesalers, retailers, trucking firms, and warehouse operators to the progress of less developed countries? What products should be distributed first? Is there a lack of middlemen in less developed countries? How do middlemen contribute to the development of a less developed country?

THINKING IT THROUGH

Scrambled Merchandising

scrambled merchandising
The strategy of adding product lines (to a retail store) that are not normally carried there.

One long-running trend that makes categorizing retailers difficult is the trend toward scrambled merchandising. **Scrambled merchandising** is the adding of product lines (to a retail store) that are not normally carried (such as auto supplies in a supermarket). A moment's reflection will remind you of how often you have seen this occur. You can buy lawn furniture and fertilizer in a drug store and drug sundries in a supermarket. Discount stores are selling food, and food stores are selling merchandise normally found in discount stores. No wonder it is called *scrambled* merchandising.

Retail Distribution Strategy

A major decision marketers must make is selecting retailers to sell their products. Different products call for different retail distribution strategies. There are three categories of retail distribution: intensive distribution, selective distribution, and exclusive distribution.

intensive distribution
The distribution strategy that puts products into as many retail outlets as possible.

Intensive distribution puts products into as many retail outlets as possible, including vending machines. Products that need intensive distribution include candy, cigarettes, gum, and popular magazines (convenience goods).

selective distribution
Distribution strategy that uses only a preferred group of the available retailers in an area.

Selective distribution is the use of only a preferred group of the available retailers in an area. Such selection helps assure the producers of quality sales and service. Manufacturers of appliances, TV sets, furniture, and clothing (shopping goods) usually use selective distribution.

exclusive distribution
The distribution strategy that uses only one retail outlet in a given geographic area.

Exclusive distribution is the use of only one retail outlet in a given geographic area. Because the retailer has exclusive rights to sell the product, he or she is more likely to carry more inventory, give better service, and pay more attention to this brand than others. Automobile manufacturers usually use exclusive distribution, as do producers of specialty goods.

Distribution in Overseas Markets

It is one thing to decide to sell a product overseas; it is something else again when you try to implement such a program. How are you going to reach the consumer? You could, of course, send people overseas to contact people directly, but that would be costly and risky. How can you get your product overseas at a minimum cost and still have wide distribution?[8]

Use Brokers   A broker is a middleman who keeps no inventory and takes no risk. A broker can find distributors for you. Brokers sell for you and make a commission on the sale. This is the least expensive way to enter foreign markets, but you still assume the risks of transportation.

Use Importers   An importer takes all the risks of business and sells your product to overseas markets. Their commission is much higher than for brokers, but they do much more for you. They will find you distributors or may do the selling to ultimate consumers themselves.

Call on Distributors Directly   You can bypass importers and brokers and call on distributors yourself. In that case, you actually become your own importer and deliver directly to distributors, but again you assume the risks of transportation.

Physical distribution often means sending goods overseas or bringing them in from other countries. Volume shipments, such as tires, often go by ship. Smaller, more expensive items are usually shipped by air. Working for international distributors can be exciting and rewarding.

Sell Direct   The most costly and risky way to sell overseas is to set up your own distribution system of wholesalers and retailers. On the other hand, this is the way to maximize profits in the long run. Many firms start out selling through importers and end up setting up their own distribution system as sales increase.

Case 1 at the end of this chapter talks about the latest strategies for shipping goods overseas. Basically, all but bulky, low-cost items are being shipped by air. International distribution will be a major new area in marketing, with many challenges and opportunities for tomorrow's college graduates. We shall talk about international business later in the book. For now, let's pause and review this chapter and look over the case on international distribution.

- Can you name six categories of retailers and describe the stores?

- What are the advantages and disadvantages, as you see them, to having an intensive distribution strategy versus an exclusive one.

- Can you explain the wheel of retailing and scrambled merchandising?

PROGRESS CHECK

---

1. Physical distribution is the movement of goods from producers to industrial and consumer users.
   - What is the role of marketing middlemen in the distribution process?
     Marketing middlemen assist in the movement of goods from producers to consumers.
   - Why do we need middlemen?
     Middlemen perform certain marketing functions (such as transportation, storage, selling, and advertising) more effectively and efficiently than most manufacturers.

SUMMARY

1. Explain why we need marketing middlemen.

2. Describe how middlemen create exchange efficiency.

2. Middlemen help make the exchange between producers and consumers more efficient.
   - How do middlemen create exchange efficiency?
     Middlemen create exchange efficiency by lessening the number of contacts needed to make a marketing exchange.

3. Middlemen add utility to goods.
   - What do we mean by utility?
     Utility refers to the value or want-satisfying ability added to products by middlemen. The products have value added in that they are made more useful or accessible to consumers by middlemen.

3. Give examples of how middlemen perform the five utilities from the economic literature.

   - What are the different types of utilities added by middlemen?
     Normally, marketing middlemen perform the following utilities: (1) time, (2) place, (3) possession, and (4) information. Sometimes middlemen also perform form utility, but that is usually done by manufacturers (pp. 261–262).

4. One way of getting manufacturers, wholesalers, and retailers to cooperate in distributing products is to form efficient distribution systems.
   - What are the three types of distribution systems?
     The three distribution systems that tie firms together are: (1) corporate systems, in which all organizations in the channel are owned by one firm; (2) contractual systems, in which members are bound to cooperate through contractual agreements; and (3) administered systems, in which all marketing functions at the retail level are managed by manufacturers.

4. Discuss how a manufacturer can get wholesalers and retailers in a channel system to cooperate by the formation of systems.

5. One of the biggest problems of independent distribution systems is getting people to work together. That's where the channel captain comes in.
   - What is a channel captain and what is its role in the distribution system?
     A channel captain can be a manufacturer, wholesaler, or retailer, whichever has power to get the other channel members to cooperate. The channel captain's role is to gain control over the channel members and get them to work together.

5. Explain the role of a channel captain.

6. Physical distribution can be a very complex process. That is why some firms are creating a new position called physical distribution manager.
   - What is the role of a physical distribution manager?
     This person is responsible for coordinating and integrating all movement of materials including transportation, internal movement, and warehousing.

6. Describe the role of a physical distribution manager.

7. Selecting transportation modes with minimum costs and assuring a certain level of service is a concern of the distribution manager.
   - What are the advantages and disadvantages of the various modes of transportation?
     See Figure 9–5.

7. Make a chart listing the various distribution modes and their advantages.

8. There are two major criteria for choosing distribution systems.
   - What are these two criteria?
     When selecting distribution systems, it is important to consider both customer service and profit.

8. Identify the criteria used to select distribution systems.

9. There are two kinds of warehouses: storage and distribution.
   - How are storage and distribution warehouses different?
     Storage warehouses store products for a long time; whereas distribution warehouses store products for only a short time until they are redistributed.

9. Explain the purpose of the two types of warehouses.

    What is materials handling?

        Materials handling is the movement of goods within a warehouse, factory, or store.

10. Wholesalers are marketing middleman who sell to businesses but not to consumers. Wholesalers may specialize in just one or two marketing tasks.

    What are some of the various categories of wholesalers?

        Merchant wholesalers own the goods they handle and include both *full-service wholesalers* (general merchandise wholesalers and rack jobbers) and *limited-function wholesalers* (cash-and-carry wholesalers, drop shippers, and truck jobbers). See pages 271 to 273.

10. Contrast the different types of wholesale middlemen and the kinds of functions they perform.

11. A retailer is a marketing middleman that sells to consumers.

    What are some of the categories of retailers?

        Retailers include retail stores and out-of-store shopping. There is a long-running trend in retailing toward scrambled merchandising (adding product lines in retail stores that are not normally carried).

11. Name the major categories of retailers and the major trends in retailing.

12. Different products call for different distribution strategies.

    What are the three categories of retail distribution strategies?

        The categories of retail distribution include: (1) *intensive distribution,* which puts products in as many retail outlets as possible; (2) *selective distribution,* which uses only a preferred group of retailers; and (3) *exclusive distribution,* which uses only one retail outlet in a given geographic area.

12. Differentiate among intensive, selective, and exclusive distribution systems.

13. Many U.S. companies are distributing their products overseas.

    How can you get your product overseas at a minimum cost and still have wide distribution?

        You can distribute your product overseas by: (1) using brokers, (2) using importers, (3) calling on distributors directly, or (4) selling directly.

13. Describe the ways producers can distribute their products overseas.

---

1. Go to the school library and look up books on physical distribution and/or logistics. What do they cover? Does it look interesting as a career?

2. Look around your community to find where the different wholesalers are located. Go visit those wholesalers and learn what they do. Look around the facilities. Are there interesting careers available?

3. When you are visiting retailers in your area, walk around the store for a while. Which stores would be the most fun to work for? Check on salaries, chances for promotion, and hours. Draw a map of a local shopping mall and show the traffic patterns to get a feel for how such malls are planned to get shoppers to buy more.

4. Visit the newest stores in your state such as the new warehouse clubs, the new hypermarkets, or the giant supermarkets. Compare their prices with the older stores. What are the trends in retailing that seem most significant to you? Be sure to watch the home shopping networks to see what they are doing.

5. Take some time to observe railroad cars as they go by. Do you see truck trailers? Have you noticed the new double-trailer trucks on the road? What seems to be the future of distribution modes? How can you take advantage of that in career preparation?

6. Go to a telemarketing center in your area and watch the operation. Ask some questions and learn all you can. This is a growing part of marketing, so you should become familiar with it.

GETTING INVOLVED

CASE ONE   INTERNATIONAL DISTRIBUTION TAKES TO THE AIR

It looks as if international distribution in the future will be dominated by the airlines. In 1987, air freight payloads jumped to 16.6 million tons. That is up 43 percent from 1982. Meanwhile, ship, truck, and train freight volumes have plateaued. Air cargo revenues have been growing 10 percent a year, nearly double the growth rate of passenger revenues.

Trucks took over the high-volume, time-sensitive products from railroads years ago. Air cargo is now taking that business from ships and trucks. What is left for ships and long-haul trucks? Largely low-value commodities. Most seaborne cargo is oil or grain selling at about 24 cents a pound. Air cargo at wholesale is about $15 a pound. Competition is now stiff in the industry and profits are rather low, but air cargo is definitely *the* international mode of the future for cargo costing over $10 a pound and packages that need to get there quickly.

One problem in the industry for U.S. airlines is perceived unfair foreign competition. Many foreign competitors are government subsidized. Others have formed powerful alliances that lock up transportation routes. Lufthansa–Cathay Pacific is one such alliance. The Germans supply prime European landing rights and Cathay Pacific supplies the contracts to get huge cargo shipments from China. American airlines can get squeezed out by such joint agreements. Federal Express recently purchased Tiger International to become the world's largest air freight company followed by Japan Air and Air France. Foreign airlines are limited in where they can land in the United States, but foreign countries are often more restrictive than the United States and dominated prime landing spots in their countries.

DECISION QUESTIONS

1. Should the U.S. government encourage free access to U.S. airports even though foreign countries do not offer such access? How could such problems be resolved?
2. Once international routes are filled with air cargo, can domestic shipping be far behind in adopting this fast mode of distribution? What may by the consequences for the other distributions modes?
3. What kinds of facilities will be needed to handle increased air cargo and how should they be linked to trucks and other ground transportation?
4. What career opportunities do you see opening as a result of increased air cargo shipments?

Source: Edwin A. Finn, Jr., "21st Century Truckers," *Forbes,* April 4, 1988, pp. 80–86; and Denise Gellene, "Consolidated Freightways to Bay Emery, Creating U.S.' Biggest Heavy Cargo Shipper," *Los Angeles Times,* February 14, 1989, pp. 1 and 13 of Part IV.

CASE TWO   SHOPPING AT RETAIL MALLS

No phenomenon better reveals the marketing habits of Americans than shopping at malls. Recently, *Shopping Center Age* found that 93 percent of the population had been to a mall at least once in the last six months. Some 78 percent of us go to a mall at least once a month. The number of shopping centers in the United States now exceeds the number of post offices or secondary schools—30,600 nationwide.

What is the attraction of a mall? Some sociologists feel that the mall has replaced the downtown plaza as a place to gather and visit. Certainly, malls have become a gathering spot for teenagers and younger "mall rats." Best of all, though, a mall is good for window-shopping.

It is no mistake that malls are called "shopping centers" by many people. The key to malls was developed by a man named Victor Gruen about 30 years ago. His goal was to change "destination shoppers" into "impulse shoppers." Here's how it works. You run to the mall to buy a pair of shoes. You go into a shoe store to get what you want, but cannot find it. You then proceed to walk through the mall to another shoe store. During that walk, you may stop for an ice cream cone, drop in to a bookstore for a paperback novel, and window-shop at several clothing stores. You went to the mall for shoes (a destination shopper) and ended up buying ice cream, books, and maybe a sweater (an impulse shopper).

Malls are ingeniously designed to foster impulse shopping. Shoe stores are usually widely separated so you have to travel the length of the mall to shop for shoes. Most malls are anchored by a couple of major department stores (e.g., Sears) that are at opposite ends, like anchors holding the mall together. Notice how the malls have spread the distance between clothing stores and other places to shop.

At Southwest Plaza in Colorado, there are 18 shoe stores. There are over two dozen women's clothing outlets and 31 eateries. In addition, there are five major department stores, five movie theaters, and 190 other retail outlets. The latest trend in malls is to have professionals such as doctors, dentists, and lawyers. Southwest Plaza has a tower with dozens of such professionals. You can go to a doctor's office in some malls and shop while you wait. You are called by a "beeper" when they are ready for you.

Countering the trend for huge malls like Southwest Plaza are smaller, more product-specific malls. Across the street from Southwest, for example, is a strip mall (stores all in a row) with seven furniture stores. This lets consumers shop for furniture conveniently, but does not lead to much impulse buying. Other shopping centers may feature several automobile dealers. Lately, a major attraction is "outlet" malls or "off-price" malls that contain many discount stores. On the other extreme are malls catering to the rich, anchored by stores such as Neiman-Marcus and filled with exclusive jewelry shops and high-fashion clothing stores.

DECISION QUESTIONS

1. Most of the new malls have no supermarkets. Why do you suppose this is?
2. Do malls sell convenience goods, shopping goods, or specialty goods (or some combination)?
3. What are the benefits and drawbacks of shopping malls in a community?
4. How can independent retailers compete with malls?

Source: "Quotables," *Marketing Communications*, September 1988, p. 7.

The last of the four Ps of marketing is promotion. We shall discuss this important function in depth in Chapter 10. All of the four Ps of marketing—product, price, place, and promotion—rely on information about markets, consumer behavior, and more. That information is obtained by conducting marketing research. We conclude Chapter 10 with an analysis of marketing communication systems and the role of research in providing marketing managers with the information they need to make decisions in today's dynamic market environment.

LOOKING AHEAD

PROMOTION AND MARKETING RESEARCH

10

LEARNING GOALS

After you have read and studied this chapter, you should be able to:

1. Define promotion and list the various elements of the promotional mix.

2. Explain how advertising differs from the other promotional tools and discuss the advantages and disadvantages of different advertising media.

3. Explain the differences among different forms of advertising such as retail and trade advertising and industrial and institutional advertising.

4. Debate the advantages of regionalism versus globalism in advertising.

5. Illustrate the seven steps of the selling process.

6. Explain the importance of word of mouth as a promotional tool.

7. Describe the functions of the public relations department and the role of publicity in that function.

8. List sales promotion tools and explain how they are used both internally with employees and externally to customers.

9. Describe the 12-step process used to conduct marketing research.

10. Differentiate between secondary and primary data and discuss the role of each in market research.

11. Explain the three parts of a marketing communication system.

KEY TERMS

advertising, *p. 289*
focus group, *p. 307*
industrial advertising, *p. 292*
institutional advertising, *p. 292*
internal marketing program, *p. 309*
marketing communication system, *p. 308*
marketing research, *p. 303*
observational method, *p. 307*
personal selling, *p. 294*
primary data, *p. 304*
promotion, *p. 289*
promotional mix, *p. 289*

prospects, *p. 296*
public relations (PR), *p. 298*
publicity, *p. 298*
pull strategy, *p. 290*
push strategy, *p. 290*
random sample, *p. 307*
retail advertising, *p. 292*
sales promotion, *p. 300*
sample, *p. 307*
secondary data, *p. 304*
survey method, *p. 307*
trade advertising, *p. 292*
word of mouth promotion, *p. 297*

PROFILE   ROBIN MILNE OF HBO COMPANY

Robin Milne

Doing business without advertising is like winking at a girl in the dark; you know what you are doing, but nobody else does.
STEWART H. BRITT

No career in marketing offers more challenges with the corresponding payoff in income and satisfaction than personal selling. Women like Robin Milne are finding that selling offers tremendous opportunities. Mrs. Milne was graduated from Arizona State University with a degree in marketing. Her first job was with American Hospital Supply. In her first year, she made $21,000 on straight commission (that was a lot back in 1978). After three years, she was promoted to sales manager, a position she won over 10 men. When the next move up meant going to an undesirable location, Mrs. Milne quit and went with Atlanta's HBO & Company.

At HBO, Mrs. Milne sold computer software to hospitals (she was vice president of Sales). She operated out of San Francisco, but was on the road so much that she didn't even keep an apartment in San Francisco. Instead she rented a room at the Westin Hotel at the airport. She flew in on weekends to be with her husband in Scottsdale, Arizona. She managed to be with him about eight days a month.

In 1987, Mrs. Milne earned $103,000. She felt she had an excellent chance of becoming a top executive at HBO. Some 28 percent of top executives do rise through marketing.

Mrs. Milne left HBO to become the branch manager for operations in Arizona and New Mexico in sales and services for Oracle Corporation, another computer software company. Mrs. Milne is no exception. The executive director of the National Association for Professional Saleswomen reports that women now comprise roughly 25 percent of the nation's sales force, up sharply in recent years. Many of those women are selling industrial goods. Women and men can find *many* rewarding careers in promotion—sales, advertising, public relations, and sales promotion—as discussed in this chapter. Effective marketing and promotion depends on effective marketing research, so we end this chapter with a discussion of research strategy.

Source: Dyan Machan, "The Life of a Saleswoman," *Forbes*, February 22, 1988, pp. 116–18; and Beth Brophy, "The Birth of a Saleswoman," *U.S. News & World Report*, February 6, 1989, pp. 40–42.

THE IMPORTANCE OF PROMOTION AND RESEARCH

No matter how much time and effort a marketer may put into product, pricing, and distribution (place) decisions, the whole process is likely to fail without good promotion. Promotion is the last, but not the least, of the four Ps of marketing. Marketers now spend over $100 billion yearly on advertising trying to convince industrial and consumer buyers to choose their products. They spend even more on sales promotion efforts such as conventions and trade shows where producers and customers meet to discuss marketing exchanges. Marketers spend the most money sending salespeople like Robin Milne out into the field to talk personally with customers. Robin works very hard at her job, and so do thousands of other skilled men and women in promotional jobs such as advertising, publicity, sales promotion, and selling.

Marketing research is a managerial tool that marketers use to improve the effectiveness of all the other marketing efforts. The marketing process begins, as we now know, by researching consumer wants and needs. Then product development calls for marketing research to test products. Research is needed to make pricing decisions and distribution decisions as well. Perhaps most importantly, research is used to make promotional efforts more effective. Research is the tool managers use to choose the best mix of all the marketing elements. We shall discuss research at the end of the chapter. Before we look at this important tool, though, let's explore promotion in detail.

WHAT IS PROMOTION?

What do you think of when you hear the word *promotion*? Most people think of advertising. But promotion is much more than just advertising, as you will see in this chapter. **Promotion** is an attempt by marketers to persuade others to participate in an exchange with them. Marketers use many different tools to promote their products and services. Besides advertising, they use personal selling, word of mouth, public relations, publicity, and sales promotion to inform potential consumers about their organization and its goods and services. This combination of promotional tools is called the company's **promotional mix** (see Figure 10–1).

Let's explore each element of the promotional mix to learn the fundamentals.

Advertising

One reason most people mistake promotion for advertising is that they do not understand the differences among promotional tools such as advertising, personal selling, publicity, and word of mouth. **Advertising** is limited to *paid, nonpersonal* communication through various *media* by organizations and individuals who are in

promotion
An attempt by marketers to persuade others to participate in an exchange with them.

promotional mix
The combination of tools marketers use to promote their products or services.

advertising
Paid, nonpersonal communication through various media by organizations and individuals who are in some way identified in the advertising message.

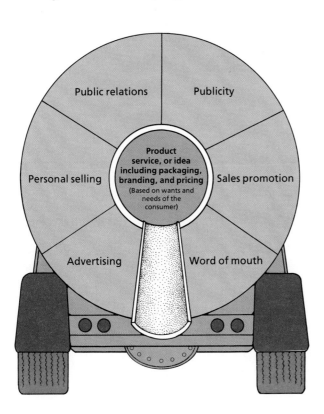

FIGURE 10–1

The promotion mix. This figure shows that the product offer is the central focus of the promotion mix. The offer is based on consumer wants and needs. All of the communication elements are designed to promote the exchange of the product offer for something of value.

some way *identified* in the advertising message. As you will see more clearly later in the chapter, word of mouth is not a form of advertising because it does not go through a medium (newspaper, TV, etc.), it is not paid for, and it is personal. Publicity is different from advertising in that media space for publicity is not paid for. Personal selling is face-to-face communication and does not go through a medium; thus, it is not advertising. The advertisement for advertising (This Ad Is Full of Lies) discusses some myths about ads.

Now that you understand what advertising is *not*, let's look at what advertising *is*. Anyone who watches television, listens to the radio, or reads magazines cannot help but notice the importance of advertising in our lives. Advertising has even become a board game. The game is called "It's Only Money" and company slogans appear on the playing cards and the spinner. The game atmosphere is said to make consumers more receptive to the ad messages. The $25 game comes with coupons worth over $250, so it's a real deal.[1]

Many people have misperceptions about advertising. They think that advertising helps sell bad products and is a waste of money. This ad for advertising addresses these issues and more.

push strategy
Use of promotional tools to convince wholesalers and retailers to stock and sell merchandise.

pull strategy
Use of promotional tools to motivate consumers to request products from stores.

PUSH STRATEGIES VERSUS PULL STRATEGIES

There are two ways to promote the movement of products from producers to consumers. The first is called a **push strategy.** In push strategy, the producer uses advertising, personal selling, sales promotion, and all other promotional tools to convince *wholesalers* and *retailers* to stock and sell merchandise. If it works, consumers will then walk into the store, see the product, and buy it. The idea is to push the product down the distribution system to the stores. One example of a push strategy is to offer dealers one free case of soda for every dozen cases they purchase.

A second strategy is called a **pull strategy.** In a pull strategy, heavy advertising and sales promotion efforts are directed toward *consumers* so that they will request the products from retailers. If it works, consumers will go to the store and order the products. Seeing the demand for the products, the store owner will then order them from the wholesaler. The wholesaler, in turn, will order them from the producer. Products are thus pulled down through the distribution system. Dr. Pepper has used television advertising in a pull strategy to increase distribution. Of course, a company could use both a push and pull strategy at the same time in a major promotional effort.

Importance of Advertising

The importance of advertising in the United States is easy to document; one need only look at the figures. The total ad volume exceeds $118 billion yearly. The number one advertising medium in terms of total dollars spent is *newspapers* (see Figure 10–2), with about 26 percent of the total. Many people erroneously think that the number one medium is TV, so take some time to look at the real figures.

> In the factory we make cosmetics; in the store we sell hope.
> CHARLES REVSON, Revlon

MEDIUM	1988 MILLIONS OF DOLLARS
Newspapers	
National	$ 3,586
Local	27,611
Total	31,197
Magazines	
Weeklies	2,646
Women's	1,504
Monthlies	1,992
Total	6,072
Farm publications	196
Television	
Network	9,172
Syndication (national)	901
Spot (national)	7,147
Spot (local)	7,270
Cable (national)	942
Local	6,514
Cable (local)	254
Total	25,686
Radio	
Network	425
Spot (national)	1,418
Spot (local)	5,955
Total	7,789
Direct mail	21,115
Yellow Pages	
National	944
Local	6,837
Total	7,781
Business papers	2,610
Outdoor	
National	628
Local	436
Total	1,064
Miscellaneous	
National	10,461
Local	4,070
Total	14,531
Total	
National	65,610
Local	52,440
Grand Total	118,050

FIGURE 10–2

Advertising expenditures by medium.
The McCann-Erickson U.S. advertising volume reports represent all expenditures by U.S. advertisers—national, local, private individuals, and so on. The expenditures, by medium, include all commissions as well as the art, mechanical, and production expenses, which are part of advertisers' budgets for each medium.

Source: "U.S. Advertising Volume," *Advertising Age,* May 15, 1989, p. 24.

LEADING U.S. AD AGENCIES
IN 1988 WORLDWIDE
GROSS INCOME

RANK	AGENCY	GROSS INCOME 1988
1.	Young & Rubicam	$758
2.	Saatchi & Saatchi Advertising Worldwide	740
3.	Backer Spielvogel Bates Worldwide	690
4.	McCann-Erickson Worldwide	657
5.	FCB-Publicis	653
6.	Ogilvy & Mather Worldwide	635
7.	BBDO Worldwide	586
8.	J. Walter Thompson Co.	559
9.	Lintas: Worldwide	538
10.	Grey Advertising	433

Source: *Advertising Age,* March 20, 1989, p. 3.

When people refer to advertising, they are usually talking about TV advertising. For example, the debate about the effect of advertising on children is really a debate about TV advertising and children. Similarly, when people talk about advertising being offensive, intrusive, manipulative, and so on, they are thinking primarily of TV advertising. But since only about 22 percent of advertising is TV advertising, there is much more to advertising than most people imagine.

Some of the leading TV ads of 1988 included those featuring the California Raisins (see opening photo) and Michael Jackson for Pepsi. Joe Isuzu was also a big hit along with the ads for Bud Light and McDonald's.[2] Such ads are memorable and tend to overpower the ads in other media.

The public benefits from advertising expenditures. First, advertising is informative. The number one medium, newspapers, is full of information about products, prices, features, and more. Does it surprise you to find that businesses spend more on direct mail than on radio and magazines? Direct mail (the use of mailing lists to reach an organization's most likely customers) is an informative shopping aid for consumers. Each day consumers receive minicatalogs in their newspapers or in the mail that tell them what is on sale, where, at what price, for how long, and more.

Advertising not only informs us about products but it also provides us with free TV and radio programs because advertisers pay for the production costs. Advertising also covers the major costs of producing newspapers and magazines. When we buy a magazine, we pay mostly for mailing costs or promotional costs.

Figure 10–3 discusses the advantages and disadvantages of various advertising media to the advertiser. Newspapers and radio are especially attractive to local advertisers. Television has many advantages to national advertisers, but it is expensive. Figure 10–4 shows how the cost of one minute of advertising during the telecast of the Super Bowl has increased to exceed $1 million. The average cost of a 30-second prime-time commercial in 1987 was $121,860.[3] How many bottles of beer or bags of dog food must a company sell to pay for such a commercial? Is it any wonder that companies are now buying 15-second commercials to save money?[4]

Most companies selling consumer goods use ad agencies to prepare their advertisements. The figure in the margin shows the top 10 agencies.

Classes of Advertising

Different kinds of advertising are used by various organizations to reach different market targets. Some major classes include:

- **Retail advertising**—advertising to consumers by various retail stores such as supermarkets and shoe stores.
- **Trade advertising**—advertising to wholesalers and retailers by manufacturers to encourage them to carry their products.
- **Industrial advertising**—advertising from manufacturers to other manufacturers. A firm selling motors to automobile companies would use industrial advertising.
- **Institutional advertising**—designed to create an attractive image for an organization rather than for a product. "We Care about You" at Giant Food is an example. "Virginia Is for Lovers" and "I (heart) New York" are two institutional campaigns by government agencies.

retail advertising
Advertising to consumers by retailers.
trade advertising
Advertising to wholesalers and retailers by manufacturers.
industrial advertising
Advertising from manufacturers to other manufacturers.
institutional advertising
Advertising by organizations designed to create an attractive image for an organization rather than for a product.

MEDIUM	ADVANTAGES	DISADVANTAGES
Newspapers	Good coverage of local markets; ads can be placed quickly; high consumer acceptance; ads can be clipped and saved	Ads compete with other features in paper; poor color; ads get thrown away with paper (short life span)
Television	Uses sight, sound, and motion; reaches all audiences; high attention with no competition from other material	High cost; short exposure time; takes time to prepare ads
Radio	Low cost; can target specific audiences; very flexible; good for local marketing	People may not listen to ad; depends on one sense (listening); short exposure time; can't keep ad
Magazines	Can target specific audiences; good use of color; long life of ad; ads can be clipped and saved	Inflexible; ads often must be placed weeks before publication; cost is relatively high
Outdoor	High visibility and repeat exposures; low cost; local market focus	Limited message; low selectivity of audience
Direct mail	Best for targeting specific markets; very flexible; ad can be saved	High cost; consumer rejection as "junk mail"

FIGURE 10–3

Advantages and disadvantages of different advertising media. The most effective media are often very expensive. The inexpensive media may not reach your market. The goal is to use the most efficient medium that can reach your desired market.

SUPER BOWL	YEAR	COST OF "60 SPOT"
I	1967	$ 80,000
II	1968	70,000
III	1969	85,000
IV	1970	200,000
V	1971	200,000
VI	1972	200,000
VII	1973	207,000
VIII	1974	214,000
IX	1975	220,000
X	1976	250,000
XI	1977	324,000
XII	1978	290,000
XIII	1979	444,000
XIV	1980	450,000
XV	1981	550,000
XVI	1982	670,000
XVII	1983	800,000
XVIII	1984	890,000
XIX	1985	1,000,000
XX	1986	1,100,000
XXI	1987	1,200,000
XXII	1988	1,300,000
XXIII	1989	1,350,000

* Now commercials are sold in 30-second spots; the first six Super Bowls had only 60-second spots.

Source: *The Washington Post*, January 20, 1989, p. G.1 and other sources.

FIGURE 10–4

Super Bowl marketing. The growth of America's premier sporting event is reflected in the rising cost of a 60-second TV commercial over the years. One minute of advertising during the Super Bowl costs over $1 million.*

Michael Jackson's Pepsi spots were considered some of the leading ads of 1988. Pepsi was trying to reach the younger generation, and Michael Jackson was an effective personality to use.

The Global Marketing and Advertising Debate

Harvard Professor Theodore Levitt is a big proponent of global marketing and advertising. His idea is to develop a product and promotional strategy that can be implemented worldwide. Certainly that would save money in research costs and in advertising design. However, other experts think that promotion targeted at specific countries may be much more successful since each country has its own culture, language, and buying habits.

The evidence supports the theory that promotional efforts specifically designed for individual countries work best. For example, commercials for Camay soap that showed men complimenting women on their appearance were jarring in cultures where men don't express themselves that way. A different campaign is needed in such countries. People in Brazil rarely eat breakfast and treat Kellogg's Corn Flakes as a dry snack like potato chips. Kellogg is trying a promotional strategy of showing people in Brazil how to eat cereal—with cold milk in the morning.[5]

Many more examples could be cited to show that international advertising calls for doing research into the wants, needs, and culture of each specific country and then designing appropriate ads and testing them.

Even in the United States, ethnic groups are large enough and different enough to call for specially designed promotions. Maybelline, Avon, and Pepsi are all targeting special promotions to Hispanics. The 1989 Grammy awards show presented an all-Spanish ad featuring Puerto Rican singer Chayanne.[6] In short, advertising today is moving from the trend toward globalism (one ad for everyone in the world) to regionalism (specific ads for each country and for specific groups within a country).

PROGRESS CHECK

- What are the six elements of the promotion mix?

- Could you describe how to implement a push strategy for Fiberrific cereal? A pull strategy?

- Can you give examples of retail, trade, industrial, and institutional advertising?

- Can you list the advertising media in order based on the total dollar amount spent by advertisers?

Personal Selling

personal selling
Face-to-face presentation and promotion of products and services plus searching out prospects and providing follow-up service.

Personal selling is the face-to-face presentation and promotion of products and services plus searching out prospects and providing follow-up service. Effective selling is not simply a matter of persuading others to buy (see Figure 10–5). In fact, it is more accurately described as helping others to satisfy their wants and needs. Selling can be an exciting, rewarding, and challenging professional career.

To illustrate the importance of personal selling in our economy and the career opportunities it provides, let us look at a few figures. First, U.S. census data show that nearly 10 percent of the total labor force is employed in personal selling. When we add those who sell for nonprofit organizations, we find that over 7 million people are employed in sales.

The cost of a single sales call to a potential industrial buyer is over $200. Surely no firm would pay that much to send out anyone but a highly skilled, professional marketer and consultant. But how does one get to be that kind of sales represen-

WHAT THE STEPS MEAN

FIGURE 10–5

Steps in the selling process.

Prospect	This first step involves researching potential buyers and choosing those most likely to buy. These people are called *prospects*. You may learn the names of prospects from present customers, from surveys, from public records, and so forth.
Preapproach	Before making a sales call, the sales representative must do further research. As much as possible should be learned about the customer and his or her wants and needs. What products are they using now? Are they satisfied? Why or why not? Before a call, a salesperson should know the customer well and have a specific objective for the call. This is probably *the* most important step in selling.
Approach	"You don't have a second chance to make a good first impression." That is why the approach is so important. It involves learning all about the prospect and his or her needs (including hobbies and so forth). Good selling begins with good research.
Make presentation	This is the actual demonstration or presentation of the product and its benefits to the prospect. This may involve audiovisual aids. Showing advantages versus competition is often included.
Answer objections	Sometimes a prospect may question facts or figures and ask for more information. Often a sales representative must come back several times. The goal is to make sure that the customer is informed and committed to the purchase.
Close sale	You have to "ask for the sale" to finalize the sales process. "Would you like the red one or the green one?" "And when would you want delivery?" are examples of questions used to close the sale.
Follow-up	The selling process isn't over until the product is delivered, installed, and working satisfactorily. The selling relationship often continues for years as the salesperson responds to customer requests and introduces new products over time. Selling is a matter of establishing relationships; not just selling goods and services.

tative? What are the steps along the way? Can women as well as men enter industrial sales? Such questions are answered in the story of Robin Milne in the Profile at the beginning of this chapter. Now let's take a closer look at the process of selling.

Steps in the Selling Process

The best way to get a feel for personal selling is to go through the selling process with a product and see what is involved. One product that you are probably familiar with is life insurance. An insurance salesperson has a difficult job persuading people to buy life insurance and an even more difficult job persuading people to buy one company's policy versus another. Let's go through the selling process with a salesperson to see what can be done to make the sale.

Insurance is one of the more difficult services to sell because so few people understand the differences among insurance policies. That is why insurance salespeople are so important—they use all the steps to satisfy the wants and needs of consumers.

prospects
People who have enough funds and are willing to discuss a potential purchase.

Prospect and Qualify   The first step in the selling process is *prospecting*. It involves researching potential buyers and choosing those most likely to buy. The choosing process is called *qualifying*. It is the market segmentation process brought down to the sales level. To qualify people means to make sure they have the ability to pay and are willing to listen to a sales message. People who have enough funds and are willing to discuss a potential purchase are called **prospects.** You may find prospects by asking present customers for names, from calling on people randomly (this is called a *cold call*), and from public records. One source of prospects for life insurance, for example, is public records of people who were recently married or had children.

Preapproach   Before making a sales call, the sales representative must do further research. As much as possible should be learned about customers and their wants and needs. Before you try to sell someone insurance, for example, you would want to know their names, whether or not they had children, and some idea of family income. Such information can be obtained when a customer refers you to another client. You can also observe the neighborhood to get an idea of family income.

Approach   "You don't have a second chance to make a good first impression." That is why the approach is so important. When you call on a customer for the first time, your appearance is very important, as are your opening comments. The idea is to create an impression of friendly professionalism. The objective of the initial sales call will probably not be to make a sale that day. Rather, the goal may be to listen to the client, learn what the insurance needs are, get some feel for the amount desired, and what kind of insurance would be appropriate. Of course, if the client seems ready to buy, an order could be taken that day.

Make Presentation   This is the actual presentation of the policy and its benefits to the prospect. This may involve audiovisual aids and flip charts. Showing the advantages of your product versus competition is often included. Since you have done your homework and know the wants and needs of the prospect, the policy will be tailored to the family's needs and be relatively easy to present.

Answer Objections   A salesperson should view questions as opportunities for creating better relationships, not as a challenge to what he or she is saying. Customers have legitimate doubts and salespeople are there to resolve those doubts. If such a dialogue were not necessary, salespeople could easily be replaced by advertising. A salesperson must be prepared to come back several times if necessary to answer any questions or bring more data. A salesperson must also be aware of when a customer is stalling or merely hesitant about making a decision. That is the time when closing is important.

Close Sale   You have to "ask for the sale" to finalize the sales process. A salesperson has limited time and cannot spend forever with one client answering questions and objections. There is a time when the salesperson should say something like this: "This policy is designed to meet your present and future insurance needs. It was designed specifically to protect your family. Sign here and you'll be covered immediately." Remember your "ABCs"—always be closing.[7]

Follow Up   The selling process isn't over until the policy is written, signed, and the customer is happy. The selling relationship often continues for years as the salesperson responds to new customer requests for information. Each time a new child is born, a client may want an insurance policy on the child or to increase the insurance coverage on the parents. Selling is a matter of establishing relationships, not just selling goods or services.

> What kind of products would you enjoy selling? Think of the customers for that product. Can you imagine yourself going through the seven-step selling process with them? Which steps would be most difficult? Which easiest? Which step could you avoid by selling in a retail store?
>
> **THINKING IT THROUGH**

Word of Mouth

Word-of-mouth promotion encourages people to tell other people about products they have enjoyed. Word of mouth is one of the most effective promotional tools, but one most marketers do not use to full effectiveness.

Anything that encourages people to talk favorably about an organization is effective word of mouth. Notice, for example, how stores use clowns, banners, music, fairs, and other attention-getting devices to create word of mouth. Clever commercials can generate much word of mouth. You can ask people to tell others about your product or even pay them to do so. Samples are another way to generate word of mouth. But the best way to generate word of mouth is to have a good product, provide good services, and keep customers happy. We consumers are happy to tell others where to get good services and reliable products. Lynn Gordon of French Meadow Bakery in Minneapolis learned about the power of word of mouth when she developed a recipe for old-fashioned bread. Word of mouth enlarged her business from 40 loaves a week at local co-ops to her own 13,500-square-foot bakery employing 15 people.[8] However, we are also quick to tell others when we are unhappy with products and services. Negative word of mouth hurts a firm badly. Taking care of consumer complaints quickly and effectively is one of the best ways to lessen negative word of mouth.

word-of-mouth promotion Consumers talking about products they have liked or disliked.

To promote positive word of mouth, advertise to people who already use your product. Yes, we said to people who already use your product. They have a commitment to that product and are more likely to read the ad. They will then go out and tell others how smart they were in buying the product. This results in positive word of mouth for you. For example, sending brochures about a beautiful vacation resort to people who have already been there gives them something to use to tell others how exciting the place was. This word-of-mouth promotion is very effective in getting others to come.

Public Relations

public relations
The management function that evaluates public attitudes, develops policies and procedures consistent with the public interest, and takes steps to earn public understanding and acceptance.

Public relations (PR) is defined by the *Public Relations News* as the management function that evaluates public attitudes, identifies the policies and procedures of an individual or an organization with the public interest, and executes a program of action to earn public understanding and acceptance.

Notice that public relations starts with good marketing research (evaluates public attitudes). Public relations is one department in an organization that has explicit responsibility for listening to the public.

The second step in a good PR program, after listening, is the development of policies and procedures that are in the public interest. One does not earn understanding by bombarding the public with propaganda; one *earns* understanding by having programs and practices in the public interest and letting people know that you have them. It is not enough to act in the public interest; you must also inform people of that fact. You might say that public relations is "good performance, publicly appreciated—with the emphasis on performance."9

Publicity

publicity
Any information about an individual, a product, or an organization that is distributed to the public through the media, that is not paid for or controlled by the sponsor.

Publicity is one of the major functions of the public relations department. Here is how it works. Suppose that when we want to introduce our new Fiberrific cereal to consumers, we have very little money to promote it. We want to get some initial sales to generate funds. One effective way to reach the public is through publicity. **Publicity** is any information about an individual, a product, or an organization that is distributed to the public through the media, and that is not paid for, or controlled by, the sponsor. We might prepare a publicity release describing Fiberrific and research findings supporting its benefits and send it to the various media.

Public relations personnel send press releases to the various media. If the stories are well prepared, the media publish the stories free and generate many favorable impressions for the organization or its products.

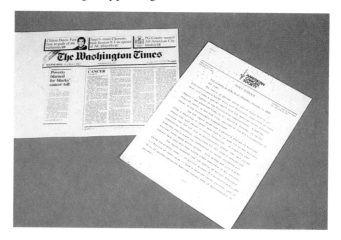

(We shall not go into detail on how this is done, but there is much skill involved in writing the story so that the media will want to publish it.) Release of the news about Fiberrific will reach many potential buyers (and investors, distributors, and dealers), and we may be on our way to becoming wealthy marketers.

The best thing about publicity is that the various media will publish publicity stories free if the material seems interesting or newsworthy The idea, then, is to write publicity that meets these criteria.

In addition to being free, publicity has several other advantages over other promotional tools such as advertising. For example, publicity may reach people who would not read an advertising message. Publicity may be placed on the front page of a newspaper or in some other very prominent position. Perhaps the greatest advantage of publicity is its believability. When a newspaper or magazine publishes a story as news, the reader treats that story as news, and news is more believable than advertising.

There are several disadvantages to publicity as well. The media do not have to publish a publicity release, and most are thrown away. Furthermore, the story may be altered so that it is not so positive. There is *good* publicity (IBM comes out with a new supercomputer) and *bad* publicity (Alar found in Apples). Once a story has run, it is not likely to be repeated. Advertising, on the other hand, can be repeated as often as needed. One way to see that publicity is handled well by the media is to establish a friendly relationship with media representatives, cooperating with them when they seek information. Then, when you want their support, they will cooperate as well.

ACTIVITIES OF THE PR DEPARTMENT

You may get a better idea of what public relations involves if we list some of the activities of PR departments:

- Establishing contact with civic groups, consumer organizations, and other concerned citizens to learn their views of the organization, to answer their questions, and to provide information (or education).
- Opening lines of communication with customers, suppliers, distributors, retailers, stockholders, government agencies, educators, and community leaders.
- Conducting studies to find the economic, environmental, and social consequences of organizational practices and to learn how to make a more positive contribution to customers, stockholders, and society.
- Providing any assistance needed to adjust the goals, policies, practices, personnel policies, products, and programs of the organization to meet the needs of changing markets.
- Assisting all members of the firm in developing effective programs of consumer information and education.
- Sending speakers to schools, clubs, and other such groups to maintain an open dialogue with students and other socially active members of society.
- Creating incentives for employees to participate in public-affairs activities such as raising funds for charitable groups, advising young people in Boy Scouts, Girl Scouts, or Junior Achievement groups, and being active in community associations.
- Answering consumer and other complaints promptly and correcting whatever it was that caused the complaint.
- Training employees or volunteers to provide prompt, friendly, courteous, and helpful service to anyone who contacts the organization in person, by phone, or by written correspondence.
- Demonstrating to society that the organization is listening, reacting, adjusting, and progressing in its attempt to satisfy its diverse publics.
- Opening two-way communications with employees to generate favorable employee opinion and to motivate employees to speak well of the organization to others.

This list is not a complete description of all the activities and responsibilities of the PR staff, but it should give you some feeling for what they do. The talking arm of the public relations function is called publicity.

Sales Promotion

Sales promotion is the promotional tool that stimulates consumer purchasing and dealer interest by means of *short-term* activities (such things as displays, shows and exhibitions, and contests—see Figure 10–6).

Those free samples of products that people get in the mail; the cents-off coupons that they clip out of the newspapers; the contests that various retail stores sponsor; the catalogs you look through; and those rebates that have been so popular in recent years all are examples of sales promotion activities. Sales promotion programs supplement personal selling, advertising, and public relations efforts by creating enthusiasm for the overall promotional program. In 1988, marketers sent out some 12 billion catalogs, or roughly 50 for every man, woman, and child in the United States.[10] You can see, therefore, how big and important sales promotion is.

Sales promotion can be both internal (within the company) and external (outside the company). It is just as important to get employees enthusiastic about a sale as it is potential customers. Often, the most important internal sales promotion efforts are directed at salespeople and other customer-contact persons such as complaint handlers and clerks. Sales promotion tries to keep the salespeople enthusiastic about the company through sales training; the development of sales aids such as flip charts, portable audiovisual displays, and movies; and participation in trade shows where salespeople can get leads. Other employees who deal with the public may also be given special training to make them more aware of company programs and a more integral part of the total promotional effort.

FIGURE 10–6

Sales promotion techniques. Spend some time with this list. Most students are not familiar with all the activities involved in sales promotion, and this is the time to learn them.

Displays (store displays)	Lotteries
Contests ("You may have won $1 million!")	Audiovisual aids
Samples (toothpaste, soap)	Catalogs
Coupons (10¢ off)	Demonstrations
Premiums (free glass when you buy a meal)	Special events
Shows (fashion shows)	Exhibits
Deals (price reductions)	Portfolios for salespersons
Trade shows	Trading stamps
Bonuses (buy one, get one free)	Conventions
Incentives (the gift in a Cracker Jack box)	Sweepstakes
Rebates (refunds from producers)	

Product samples are an effective way to promote new products. If you can get a consumer to try a superior product, the product will sell itself.

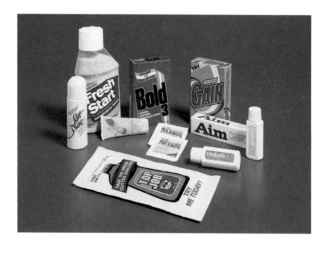

Cheerios recognized the desire for oat bran in 1989 and promoted that benefit (benefit segmentation). They also recognized that children love marshmallows, so they included them in a cereal. The use of coupons to promote these cereals is part of sales promotion.

After enthusiasm is generated internally, it is important to get distributors and dealers involved so that they, too, are enthusiastic and will cooperate by putting up signs and helping to promote the product.

After the company's employees and salespeople have been motivated with sales promotion efforts, and middlemen are involved, the next step is to promote to final consumers using samples, coupons, cents-off deals, displays, store demonstrators, premiums, and other incentives such as contests, trading stamps, and rebates. Sales promotion is an ongoing effort to maintain enthusiasm, so different strategies are used over time to keep the ideas fresh.

When thinking about a sales promotion scheme for Fiberrific, we might learn from General Food's promotion of Super Golden Crisp, Honeycomb, Fruity Pebbles, and other children's cereal. They sent a "fun book" to children featuring Sugar Bear. Cents-off coupons were placed in the book for the parents. Sales went up 80 percent. Some 90 percent of the households replying wanted more mailings.[11] Wouldn't you feel more comfortable promoting our high-fiber, low-sugar cereal to children rather than the high-sugar content cereals promoted by General Foods? Don't firms have some social responsibility in the area of nutrition?

You wouldn't believe the number of coupons sent out by marketers such as General Foods. Recently the number of coupons reached over 215 billion! *Advertising Age* reports that sales promotion is a hot area of marketing and is getting hotter.[12]

Specialty Advertising

One relatively unexplored area in promotion is specialty advertising.[13] *Specialty advertising* involves the use of specially designed products such as pens, calendars, business cards, balloons, and hundreds of other items to promote a business or a product. One of the authors of this text has used several specialty items to promote his books, including pens with the book's name on them and balloons. One year a book fair was enlivened by "jumping nickels" that explained why everyone was jumping into Nickels' book rather than the competition's. Jumping nickels ended up in people's drinks and other strange places. They caused much word of mouth for the book. The clever use of tennis ball cans, T-shirts, microwavable popcorn bags, and other items can make any other promotion come alive.

- What are the seven steps in the selling process?

- The text mentions 11 activities of a public relations department. How many can you remember?

- Promoters spend more money on sales promotion than advertising. The text lists 21 different sales promotion techniques. Do you remember most of them?

Preparing the Promotional Mix

Each target group calls for a separate promotional mix. For example, large numbers of consumers are usually most efficiently reached through advertising. Large organizations are best reached through personal selling. To motivate people to buy now rather than later, sales promotion efforts such as coupons, discounts, special displays, premiums, and so on may be used. Publicity adds support to the other efforts and can create a good impression among all publics. Word of mouth is often the most powerful promotional tool and is generated effectively by listening, being responsive, and creating an impression worth passing on to others. How do marketers decide the best promotional mix to use? They turn to marketing research for guidance.

MARKETING RESEARCH

We end our discussion of marketing by looking at one of the most important parts of marketing today—marketing research. Marketers regularly poll marketing research organizations to see what kind of research they are conducting.[14] Some 97 percent of the companies surveyed study market characteristics, market potential, and market shares held by various competitors. The marketing process begins with an analysis of the market.

It follows that the majority of companies also research new product potential and competitive products. Part of that research includes testing packaging design and physical characteristics (see Figure 10–7).

More than 80 percent of firms do pricing studies and almost 70 percent do plant and warehouse location studies. The vast majority also study promotional factors such as studies of ad effectiveness and the best media to use.

In short, marketers use research to help make decisions in all four areas of marketing: product, price, place, and promotion. In addition, marketers research business trends, the ecological impact of their decisions, international trends, and more. Businesses need information to function and marketing research is the activity that gathers that information. All the money spent on computers and information specialists is wasted, however, if the information is not used correctly.

"Finding out what people want" means more than sending out questionnaires regularly. It means getting out of the office and sitting down with people and listening to what they have to say. It also means paying attention to what shareholders, dealers, consumer advocates, and employees have to say. Managing all that information calls for a marketing communication system. We shall end this chapter by discussing such a system. First, let's look at the activity we call marketing research.

	FIRMS THAT PERFORM ACTIVITY (PERCENT)
Advertising research	
1. Motivation research	47
2. Copy research	61
3. Media research	68
4. Studies of ad effectiveness	76
5. Studies of competitive advertising	67
Business economics and corporate research	
1. Short-range forecasting (up to 1 year)	89
2. Long-range forecasting (over 1 year)	87
3. Studies of business trends	91
4. Pricing studies	83
5. Plant and warehouse location studies	68
6. Acquisition studies	73
7. Export and international studies	49
8. MIS (Management Information System)	80
9. Operations research	65
10. Internal company employees	76
Corporate responsibility research	
1. Consumers "right to know" studies	18
2. Ecological impact studies	23
3. Studies of legal constraints on advertising and promotion	46
4. Social values and policies studies	39
Product research	
1. New product acceptance and potential	76
2. Competitive product studies	87
3. Testing of existing products	80
4. Packaging research	65
Sales and market research	
1. Measurement of market potentials	97
2. Market share analysis	97
3. Determination of market characteristics	97
4. Sales analysis	92
5. Establishment of sales quotas, territories	78
6. Distribution channel studies	71
7. Test markets, store audits	59
8. Consumer panel operations	63
9. Sales compensation studies	60
10. Promotional studies	58

FIGURE 10–7

Survey of marketing research activities. Almost all organizations do research to determine market potential, to evaluate market share, and to learn more about the people in various markets. Most also do short- and long-range sales forecasting and competitor analysis.

Source: D. W. Twedt, *Survey of Marketing Research* (Chicago: American Marketing Association), Latest edition.

The Marketing Research Process

According to the American Marketing Association, **marketing research** is the systematic gathering, recording, and analyzing of data about problems relating to the marketing of goods and services. Marketing research is used both to determine what consumer and industrial clients want and need and to select the most effective way to satisfy those wants and needs. In short, marketing research provides the information needed to make intelligent marketing decisions. Although marketing research can take many forms, it is helpful to review certain steps when conducting such studies. The steps are:

marketing research
The systematic gathering, recording, and analyzing of data about problems relating to the marketing of goods and services.

1. *Study the present situation.* How does the public perceive the company and its products? What products are profitable? These are the kinds of questions that determine the present situation.
2. *Define the strengths and weaknesses of present programs.* It is as important to know what an organization does well as what it does not do well, and marketing research should report both sides.
3. *Define the problem(s) to be resolved.* Marketing researchers should be given the freedom to help discover what the problems are, what the alternatives are, what information is needed, and how to go about gathering and analyzing it.
4. *State research objectives in writing.*
5. *Determine the scope and estimated costs.* Research can get quite expensive, so some trade-off must be made between information needs and cost.
6. *Exhaust secondary data.* **Secondary data** means already published research results from journals, trade associations, the government, information services, libraries, previously published internal research reports, and other sources. There is no sense in reinventing the wheel, so find out what other research has been done first. *The Statistical Abstract of the United States* is one secondary source often used in this book. The *Occupational Outlook Handbook* is another secondary source cited. Figure 10–8 lists some of the more popular secondary sources of marketing information.
7. *Gather primary data.* **Primary data** refers to results from doing your own research. Many good books are available on research techniques. Interviews and questionnaires are two ways to gather primary data. Figure 10–8 lists some of the more widely used techniques for gathering primary data.
8. *Analyze and process the data.*
9. *Prepare a report and suggest alternative solutions,* eliminating any of questionable ethics or morality.
10. *Recommend a course of action.*
11. *Follow up on the implementation.*
12. *Redefine the situation* (that is, evaluate the strengths and weaknesses of the new situation).

secondary data
Already published research information from journals, trade associations, government, libraries, and so on.

primary data
Information resulting from original research concerning a specific problem.

Let's simplify this list by grouping the items under four major steps: (1) define the problem, (2) collect data, (3) analyze the data, and (4) make recommendations (see Figure 10–9). The following sections take a closer look at each of these steps.

Define the Problem

Problem solving is the basis of the marketing research process. Therefore, it is critical that the organization accurately defines its problem to determine the scope of the research needed. The problem may not be what it appears to be on the surface, and investigation is needed to find what the real problems are. For example, we may think that the problem is how to price Fiberrific when we introduce it when the real question is whether or not we should produce Fiberrific at all.

SECONDARY SOURCES

Government publications
  Statistical Abstract of the United States
  Survey of current business
  Census of retail trade
  Census of transportation
  Annual Survey of manufacturers

Commercial publications
  A. C. Nielsen Company studies on retailing and media
  Market Research Corporation of American studies on consumer purchases
  Selling Areas—Marketing, Inc., reports on food sales

Magazines
  Entrepreneur   *Journal of Marketing*
  Business Week   *Journal of Retailing*
  Fortune   *Journal of Consumer Research*
  Inc.   *Journal of Advertising*
  Advertising Age   *Journal of Marketing Research*
  Forbes   *Marketing News*
  Harvard Business Review   *Journal of Advertising Research*

Newspapers
  The Wall Street Journal
  Barron's

Internal sources
  Company records
  Balance sheets
  Income statements
  Prior research reports

PRIMARY SOURCES

Observation
Surveys
Experiments
Focus groups
Questionnaires

FIGURE 10–8

Selected sources of secondary and primary information. You should spend a day or two at the library becoming familiar with these sources. You can read about primary research in any marketing research text from the library.

---

1. Define the problem
2. Collect data
3. Analyze data
4. Make recommendations

FIGURE 10–9

Short version of the marketing research process.

Collect Data

Obtaining usable information is vital in the marketing research process. There are many sources of such information. The information is classified by two characteristics: (1) where it was collected (either *internally* from within the organization or *externally* from outside the organization), and (2) when and for what purpose it was collected. *Secondary* data is information already published and available whereas *primary* data is information collected for the first time for a specific project (see Figure 10–10 on page 306).

FIGURE 10–10

Marketing research data sources.
In marketing, it is best to gather as much secondary data as possible because it is relatively inexpensive to obtain. That includes internal records. Don't underestimate the value of observing people's shopping behavior too for inexpensive external data.

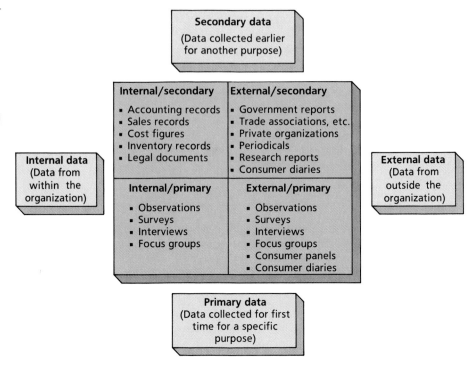

Secondary data
(Data collected earlier for another purpose)

Internal data
(Data from within the organization)

External data
(Data from outside the organization)

Internal/secondary	External/secondary
▪ Accounting records ▪ Sales records ▪ Cost figures ▪ Inventory records ▪ Legal documents	▪ Government reports ▪ Trade associations, etc. ▪ Private organizations ▪ Periodicals ▪ Research reports ▪ Consumer diaries
Internal/primary	**External/primary**
▪ Observations ▪ Surveys ▪ Interviews ▪ Focus groups	▪ Observations ▪ Surveys ▪ Interviews ▪ Focus groups ▪ Consumer panels ▪ Consumer diaries

Primary data
(Data collected for first time for a specific purpose)

Companies often use market research to gather valuable and useful data from consumers. One method a firm may use to collect information is the survey method. This popular method includes interviewing potential consumers about the product.

Remember, always use secondary data before trying to gather primary data. The information you need may already be available and, thus, save you precious time and money. Organizations usually find they need to collect both secondary and primary data before making important business decisions.

Collect Secondary Data   The amount of secondary data available is mind-boggling. Internal sources include accounting and sales records, cost figures, inventory practices, and management experience. There is a constant stream of information from many sources, many of them *unplanned*. It consists of compliments and complaints from customers, letters, comments by employees, conversations overheard in airports, and millions of other bits and pieces of information picked up by corporate executives, employees, and friends. Such information is simply there—to be used or ignored as the company wishes. If it is used, it is a powerful source of information.

External data gathering is part of the environmental scan you learned about in Chapter 7. External data is collected from trade associations, colleges and universities, libraries, and business periodicals at little or no cost. Private organizations such as A. C. Nielsen and Market Research Corporation of America collect large quantities of data that they hope to sell commercially. Did you know the largest supplier of secondary data in the world in the U.S. government?

As we prepare to market our Fiberrific, it would be important for us to look at both internal and external secondary data. Internal secondary data could answer such questions as do we have the resources to produce and market a new line of cereal? An external source such as the U.S. Census of Population could tell us the current trends in the birthrate, marriages, and shifts in population—information vital to an organization considering moving into a specialized product category.

Collect Primary Data   Usually, secondary data does not provide all of the information necessary for important business decisions. When additional, more in-depth information is needed, marketers turn to primary data. Primary data is generally collected using either the observational method or the survey method.

In the **observational method,** data is collected by observing the actions of potential buyers. One classic example of the observation technique involved Charles Parlin, often acknowledged as the founder of marketing research. He wanted to prove to Campbell Soup that the wives of blue-collar workers bought soup in a can rather than making their own. He did this by collecting garbage! He collected a scientific sample of garbage from various parts of the city, dumped the contents on an armory floor, and counted the number of soup cans. He was able to convince Campbell Soup that it should advertise in the *Saturday Evening Post* because it reached the working-class people, who were prime customers for canned soup. The garbage count was the convincing argument. Can you think of a way we could use the observational method to gather information we need to promote Fiberrific?

The **survey method** involves direct questioning of people to gather facts, opinions, or other information. The survey method is the most widely used technique for collecting primary data. Telephone surveys, mail surveys, and per-sonal interviews are the most common methods of gathering survey information. In the 1980s, focus groups became a popular method of surveying individuals. A **focus group** consists of about 8 to 12 persons who meet under the direction of a discussion leader to communicate their feelings concerning an organization, its products, or other important issues.

Realistically, it's impossible for an organization to survey all potential buyers of a product. Therefore, marketers select a sample of the target market. A **sample** is the selection of a representative group of a market population. A **random sample** means that all people have an equal chance of being selected to be part of the representative group.

Choosing Secondary or Primary Data   Both secondary and primary data have advantages and disadvantages. Secondary data offer the advantages of being rela-tively inexpensive and easy to collect. However, secondary data are often out-of-date or unsuitable to the current problem. Primary data are collected with a specific purpose in mind, which tends to make it more applicable than secondary data. However, the organization's lack of expertise in research techniques as well as cost and time involved may create problems. Collecting usable data in global markets is generally an even harder task. Problems such as unavailability, unreliability, and lack of comparability of data create difficulties with secondary data. Culture, attitudes, language, and literacy pose problems with the collection of primary data in global markets.

Analyze Research Data

Until the collected data is systematically organized and analyzed, it is of little use to an organization. A dictionary is a collection of words, but until a selection of those words is organized into meaningful sentences and paragraphs, the words do not communicate much to a reader. Likewise, the collected data communicate little until they are organized. Statistics is the tool used to reduce the collected data into useful information. If you decide to take more business courses, you will learn about what statistics mean and how they are used.

---

observational method
Method of collecting data by observing the actions of potential buyers.

survey method
Direct questioning of people to gather facts, opinions, or other information.

focus group
Group of 8 to 12 people who meet under the direction of a discussion leader to communicate their feelings concerning an organization, its products, or other important issues.

sample
A representative group of a market population.

random sample
A sample in which all people have an equal chance of being selected to be part of the representative group.

Careful and honest interpretation of data collected can provide useful alternatives to specific marketing problems. The same data can mean different things to different people. Sometimes people become so intent on a project that they are tempted to ignore or misinterpret data. For example, if our data indicate the market will not support another brand of cereal, we would do well to accept the information and drop Fiberrific rather than to slant the results as we would like to see them and go ahead with the project.

Make Recommendations

Researchers are not supposed to implement strategy based on their findings. Rather, they are to present alternative strategies to management and make recommendations as to which strategy may be best and why. It is important to include ethical and moral considerations at this point. That is, we must consider what is the right thing to do as well as the profitable thing to do. This step could add greatly to the social benefits of management decisions. The last steps in a research effort involve following up on the actions taken to see if the results were as expected. If not, corrective action can be taken and new research studies done in the ongoing attempt to provide consumer satisfaction at the lowest cost.

One problem with marketing research projects is that they are conducted periodically and take much time to complete. Meanwhile the market is changing rapidly and research data may be obsolete before they are analyzed. How can a company keep close watch on the market and be responsive to market changes as soon as they occur? The answer is to institute a formal mechanism for constantly monitoring the market and using that information to make management decisions. Such a mechanism would make it possible to collect marketing research periodically and have other information coming in daily to supplement the research information. That mechanism is called a marketing communication system. We shall discuss the concepts in detail after you pause and apply what you have learned so far.

THINKING IT THROUGH   If you conducted a focus group about your college, who would you invite to participate? How would you choose them? Would the school benefit from conducting such groups periodically? What would you say about this class and this text if you were in a focus group? Feel free to write the authors and say what you think. How would the focus group help you to design a marketing research study to supplement the information from the focus groups? Can you see the benefit of *constantly* monitoring student opinions? (That is the benefit of a marketing communication system.)

MARKETING COMMUNICATION SYSTEMS

marketing communication system
Listening to the market, responding to that information, and promoting the organization and its product.

A **marketing communication system** is a formal mechanism for making an organization responsive to its environment. It consists of three steps:
1. *Listen* constantly to the groups that are affected by the organization, including customers and potential customers.
2. *Respond* quickly to that information by adjusting company policies and practices and by designing wanted products and services for target markets.
3. *Promote* the organization and its products to let concerned groups, including customers, know that the firm is listening and responding to their needs.

MAKING ETHICAL DECISIONS

You are planning to open a business in town selling women's clothes. There is a very successful shop on the other side of town that seems to be managed well. You decide to apply for a job at that store to learn all about the business. Then you can apply what you learned at your own store. Would that be ethical? You feel it is just another form of marketing research. Is it? You hear of a similar store in another town and ask to do a term paper on that store. You don't tell the store owner that you are planning your own store. Instead, you say you are a student doing a paper for a class. Is that ethical? What is fair and what is not in gathering ideas from a competitor? When does research become corporate spying?

Listen to Various Groups Affected by the Organization

You may have noticed how often we have stressed listening as part of the marketing process. We do that because most people still think of marketing as talking; that is, promoting things to the public. Listening involves collecting consumer letters, sales reports, rumors, overheard conversations, and dozens of other sources that indicate what customers and potential customers are thinking. It is also important to know what other groups affected by or associated with the firm are thinking, including suppliers, stockholders, media people, dealers, and employees.[15]

One of the leading firms in the United States, when it comes to listening and responding, is Procter & Gamble. Every year P&G spends more than a billion dollars on advertising, making it one of the top advertisers in the United States. Therefore, most people think of P&G as a firm that promotes heavily, and believe that is how P&G became so successful. But the truth is that P&G is equally or more proficient at listening to and working with customers as it is at promoting to them.

In one year, P&G will visit some 1.5 million people as part of about 1,000 research projects designed to discover what people like and dislike about P&G's products compared to competitive products. Researchers at Procter & Gamble study how people go about basic household chores such as washing clothes, doing dishes, and so on. Any problems present an opportunity for P&G to invent new products or create new solutions to people's needs. P&G truly operates on the principle of "Find a need and fill it and your needs will be met as well."

Internal Marketing

You may think that a marketing communication system is only for listening to customers and potential customers. But successful marketers have learned that organizations have many target groups that must be satisfied in a total marketing program. An important group is the firm's employees. The marketing concept calls for training all members of the firm to provide consumer satisfaction. An **internal marketing program** is one designed to commit employees to the objectives of the firm. Like all marketing efforts, internal marketing begins with listening and being responsive to employees.

The secret of success of many marketing consultants, including marketing researchers, is: "If you want to know what is going right and wrong in a business, don't ask the managers, ask the employees. Make a list of their recommendations and insights, rewrite them, and turn them in as your consulting report." Including employees in research shows them that they are considered part of a team and that their input is considered important. The psychological effect is amazing. Not only can employees teach you much about how the business is now run, they also can

internal marketing program
Marketing program designed to commit employees to the objectives of the firm.

give you many helpful ideas for improvements. Naturally, because employees recommended them, the improvements are more easily and swiftly implemented. Can you see the benefits of listening and responding to stockholders, suppliers, dealers, community leaders, and other people that come into contact with your organization?

Respond Quickly to Wants and Needs

The second part of an effective marketing communication system, after listening, calls for *responding* to the wants and needs of various target markets. One of the most difficult marketing tasks in a firm is to convince managers that they must adapt to what various groups want and need. Most marketing organizations are so busy trying to think of ways to get consumers to buy their products that they neglect trying to get their firm to make what consumers want.

To be responsive to groups outside the firm, management must get constant reports from those in contact with outside groups. Managers must then respond promptly. Most of the time, that does not happen. Salespeople often fail to report suggestions (or complaints) by customers. When employees do report information to managers, the information is often ignored or dismissed as being foolish or irrelevant. When managers refuse to listen, employees soon learn not to pass on information. Nobody knows what's going on because everybody is afraid to speak up. We're sure you have noticed that happening in many organizations. Furthermore, there is simply too much data available today. What is needed is an effective information system that can process the data.[16]

A responsive firm adapts to changing wants and needs quickly and captures the market from other less responsive firms. That is why information is so vital to organizations today and why so much money is spent on computers to analyze data. One reason why small firms are capturing markets from large firms is that small firms tend to be better listeners, to have fewer layers of management in which information gets lost, and to be more responsive to changes in the market.[17]

Promote the Fact that You Are Responsive

When a firm is responsive, it must make that fact known to the public. That takes a variety of promotional efforts, including public relations and publicity (see Figure 10-11). Promotion is thus the third step in a marketing communication system. All employees should be encouraged to join community organizations and volunteer for charitable causes. This makes the organization more visible and gives

FIGURE 10–11

The marketing communication system. All organizations would be more effective if they listened more, were more responsive, and promoted that responsiveness.

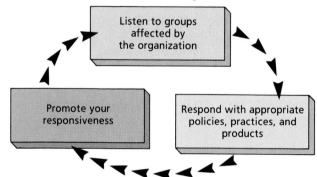

Note that a marketing communication system is a closed loop. That is, information is constantly flowing into and out of the firm as it adjusts to changing markets. Marketing research is part of the information flow, but only a part.

employees a chance to gather information from the public and to tell people about the programs and products of the firm. When an organization is responsive to the public and lets that fact be known, it will inevitably profit and grow, creating more jobs and more benefits for society. Ultimately, marketing is the way society meets its needs by exchanging goods and services. Marketing communication systems create the information flows that make such exchanges possible.

PROGRESS CHECK

- What are some examples of specialty advertising?

- What are the four major steps in the marketing research process?

- What are the three steps in a marketing communication system?

SUMMARY

1. Promotion is an attempt by marketers to persuade others to participate in exchanges with them. Marketers use many different tools to promote their products and services.
   - What are the promotional tools that make up the promotional mix?
     Promotional tools include advertising, personal selling, word of mouth, public relations, publicity, and sales promotion.

1. Define promotion and list the various elements of the promotional mix.

2. Many people mistake promotion for advertising.
   - How does advertising differ from the other promotional tools?
     Advertising is limited to *paid, nonpersonal* communication through various *media* by organizations and individuals who are in some way *identified* in the advertising message.
   - In terms of total dollars, what is the number one advertising medium?
     Many people mistakenly believe that TV is the number one medium, but it is newspapers. Review the advantages and disadvantages of the various advertising media in Figure 10–3.

2. Explain how advertising differs from the other promotional tools and discuss the advantages and disadvantages of different advertising media.

3. Different target markets are reached by different kinds of advertising.
   - What are the major classes of advertising?
     The major classes of advertising include: (1) retail advertising (from retail stores to consumers), (2) trade advertising (from wholesalers and retailers to manufacturers), (3) industrial advertising (from manufacturers to other manufacturers), and (4) institutional advertising (ads used to create a favorable image for an organization).

3. Explain the differences among different forms of advertising such as retail and trade advertising and industrial and institutional advertising.

4. Advertising is moving away from globalism to regionalism.
   - What are the advantages of regionalism versus globalism in advertising?
     Although developing a product and promotional strategy that can be implemented worldwide (globalism) can save money in research costs and in advertising design, promotion targeted at specific countries (regionalism) may be much more successful since each country has its own culture, language, and buying habits.

4. Debate the advantages of regionalism versus globalism in advertising.

5. Personal selling is the face-to-face presentation and promotion of products and services plus the searching out of prospects and follow-up service.
   - What are the seven steps of the selling process?
     The steps of the selling process are: (1) prospect and qualify, (2) preapproach, (3) approach, (4) make presentation, (5) answer objections, (6) close sale, and (7) follow up.

5. Illustrate the seven steps of the selling process.

6. Explain the importance of word of mouth as a promotional tool.

7. Describe the functions of the public relations department and the role of publicity in that function.

8. List sales promotion tools and explain how they are used both internally with employees and externally to customers.

9. Describe the 12-step process used to conduct marketing research.

10. Differentiate between secondary and primary data and discuss the role of each in market research.

11. Explain the three parts of a marketing communication system.

6. Word-of-mouth promotion encourages people to talk about an organization.
    - What is the best way to generate positive word of mouth?
      The best way to generate positive word of mouth is to have a good product, provide good services, and keep customers happy.
7. Public relations is the management function that evaluates public attitudes, identifies the policies and procedures of an organization with the public interest, and executes a program of action to earn public understanding and acceptance.
    - What are the three major steps in a good public relations program?
      The three major steps in a good public relations program are: (1) listening, (2) developing policies and procedures in the public interest, and (3) earning public understanding and acceptance. One effective way to reach the public is through publicity (information distributed by the media that is not paid for, or controlled by, the sponsor). Publicity's greatest advantage is its believability.
8. Sales promotion is the promotional tool that stimulates consumer purchasing and dealer interest by means of *short-term* activities.
    - How are sales promotion activities used both within and outside of the organization?
      Internal sales promotion efforts are directed at salespeople and other customer-contact persons to keep them enthusiastic about the company. Internal sales promotion activities include sales training, sales aids, audio-visual displays, and trade shows. External sales promotion (promotion to consumers) involves using samples, coupons, cents-off deals, displays, store demonstrators, premiums, and other incentives.
9. Marketing research is the systematic gathering, recording, and analyzing of data about problems relating to the marketing of goods and service.
    - What are the major steps of the marketing research process?
      There are 12 steps in the marketing research process (see p. 304). These steps can be condensed into four major steps: (1) defining the problem, (2) collecting data, (3) analyzing the data, and (4) making recommendations.
10. Collecting useful information is essential to marketing research.
    - What kinds of data are collected in the marketing research process?
      Research data are classified by two characteristics: (1) where they were collected (either *internally* from within the organization or *externally* from outside the organization), and (2) when and for what purpose they were collected. *Secondary data* consists of information already published and available, whereas *primary* data consists of information collected for the first time for a specific project (see Figure 10–10).
11. A marketing communication system is a formal mechanism for making an organization responsive to its environment.
    - What are the three steps in a marketing communication system?
      The marketing communication system consists of: (1) listening, (2) responding, and (3) promoting.

GETTING INVOLVED

1. Many universities have a course on promotion. Check your school library and see what is covered in such a text. You may want to use such texts for reference if you ever get involved in promotions, so write down the names and the call letters and a brief outline of what is covered and add the information to the file system you set up after reading the Prologue.

2. Give examples from your experience with businesses to prove that "the more communication with customers that occurs, the less promotion to customers is necessary." Are
   there successful firms in your area that do little promotion?
3. Explain the importance of internal marketing to a total marketing program. Give
   examples (from your experience or knowledge) of good and bad internal marketing.
   How does this differ from personnel's motivation efforts?
4. Bring in samples of advertising to show how informative consumer advertising can be.
   Bring in other ads that are not so informative. Discuss both sets of ads with the class to
   see which are more effective in attracting consumer interest.
5. Go through your paper and cut out examples of publicity (stories about new products
   you see in the paper) and sales promotion (coupons, contests, sweepstakes). Discuss the
   effectiveness of such promotional efforts with the class.
6. How would you go about generating word-of-mouth promotion for the following?
   a. An upcoming dance at school.
   b. A new restaurant in the area.
   c. A great vacation spot.
   d. A microwave oven.
7. Go to the library and look up *Advertising Age* and *Marketing Communications.* They cover
   current advertising, promotion, and sales promotion topics, including direct marketing.
   Copy and save articles you find particularly interesting and share them with the class
   before filing them.

CASE ONE   DEVELOPING EFFECTIVE SALES PROMOTION EFFORTS

PRACTICING
MANAGEMENT
DECISIONS

A recent article in *Marketing News* reported that spending on sales promotion is over $100
billion a year. In fact, spending on sales promotion activities in recent years has been about
$40 billion more than advertising. Here is the breakdown on where sales promotion dollars
were spent:

	DOLLARS SPENT (PERCENT)
Meetings and conventions	31%
Direct mail	16
Premiums and incentives (e.g., rebates)	14
Point-of-purchase displays	12
Audiovisuals and miscellaneous	8
Promotional ad space	8
Exhibits and trade shows	6
Couponing	4

   Coupons were highly accepted. When asked about their reactions to sales promotion
efforts, 83 percent of 7,554 households polled felt coupons increased the value of shopping
dollars. Some 50 percent of respondents felt rebates gave the best value. Many felt that
sweepstakes, contests, and mail-in efforts were not worth the trouble. About 40 percent
found sweepstakes and contests "too much to deal with."
   Much time, effort, and expense is spent evaluating advertising effectiveness. Not nearly
as much effort is placed on evaluating sales promotion efforts, even though more money is
spent on these promotions than advertising.

DECISION QUESTIONS

1. Meetings, conventions, exhibits, and trade shows take up some 37 percent of sales
   promotion dollars. How would you go about measuring the effectiveness of such
   meetings? Do you see any signs of wasteful spending at such events?
2. Point-of-purchase displays are an important sales promotion tool. Think about the
   displays you have seen. Which are most effective and why?
3. What is the reaction to coupons, rebates, sweepstakes, and contests in your family?
   Are your reactions similar to others in the survey? What would you recommend to
   producers given those reactions?

4. There is some debate among promotion professionals as to whether direct mail is part of advertising or sales promotion. Either way, it is a major part of promotion efforts today. Evaluate the best and worst direct mail pieces you have received. What makes them "good" or "bad"?

Source: Joe Agnew, "Burgeoning Sales Promotion Spending to Top $100 Billion," *Marketing News*, May 22, 1987; and Scott Hume, "Coupons Score with Consumers," *Advertising Age*, February 15, 1988, p. 40.

CASE TWO   WAKING UP THE COFFEE INDUSTRY

About 25 years ago, the number one drink in America was coffee. The trend is not good, however. From 1962 to 1985, the sales of coffee declined and the sales of soft drinks went up. By the end of 1985, soft drinks became the number one drink. The history of coffee sales is revealing.

The original colonists were mostly tea drinkers, bringing the habit with them from England. There were some coffee drinkers in the Dutch colony called New Amsterdam. In 1773, the colonists dumped hundreds of chests of tea into Boston harbor because of taxes, and America became a coffee-drinking nation.

By 1962, coffee sales were up to $1 billion a year and three fourths of the population drank an average of over three cups a day. The market looked so good at that time that Procter & Gamble bought Folger in 1963. From 1963 on, however, coffee sales have declined.

What happened in the 1960s to change the market? A major factor was the battle between Pepsi and Coke for the teenage drinker. Pepsi developed the theme of the "Pepsi Generation." Coke responded with themes directed toward young people as well. Coffee ads, meanwhile, were directed toward the over-35 crowd. The spokespeople for coffee were middle-aged women such as Mrs. Olsen, who promoted Folgers Coffee. Meanwhile, the Pepsi generation grew up and took their preference for soft drinks with them.

One problem with the coffee industry is that it was successful in making caffeine a "dirty" word in the 1980s by heavily advertising decaffeinated coffee. Suddenly, however, soft drinks such as Jolt became popular promoting heavy caffeine and sugar. Coffee producers were shocked—that was their market!

More recently, coffee producers have been trying to woo back younger drinkers. Nescafe Silka, for example, is a "smooth, lighter coffee" aimed at 18- to 35-year-olds. Another campaign is aimed at the new generation of college students. The Coffee Development Group has opened 50 "coffee houses" on college campuses, providing a coffee grinder, a brewer, and a cappucino machine, among other supplies. The idea is to get students back to drinking coffee. Recent studies have found that students are drinking soft drinks for breakfast. Coffee makers want to change that trend back to coffee for breakfast.

Coffee makers noticed the success of Jolt and countered with their own coffee with twice the caffeine of regular brews. It is called Buzz and is made by the Barrie House Coffee Company in Mount Vernon, New York. It is said to have twice the flavor, too. That should wake you up in the morning! A "Buzz-mobile" is cruising Manhattan streets to let people try Buzz. Coffee makers have also introduced iced coffee in a can.

DECISION QUESTIONS

1. What would you recommend to coffee producers to win the college market to coffee? Will the new iced coffee help?
2. Would you develop different strategies for regular versus decaffeinated coffee? Why or why not? Which would you emphasize for college students today or would you try to sell them both?
3. What kind of marketing research might you conduct before starting any campaign?
4. You have talked with many college students and heard what they say about coffee versus soft drinks. What has your marketing intelligence system told you? What recommendation would you make to coffee producers based on that information? Would a focus group help to confirm those impressions?

Sources: John Valentine, "While Coffee Makers Fight Loss of Younger Drinkers," *The Wall Street Journal*, March 19, 1986, p. 33; and "Selected Market Share Leaders," *Advertising Age*, September 24, 1987; and Judith A. Beltekoff, "Buzz Coffee Jolts Caffeine Freaks Into Sales Frenzy," *Advertising Age*, August 15, 1988, p. 28; and Susan Dillingham, "Coffee Goes on the Rocks," *Insight*, June 5, 1989, p. 43.

It pays to learn more about the marketing of nonprofit organizations. There are many exciting career possibilities in areas such as recreation, travel, communications, health care, and education. Nonprofit organizations such as government agencies, social causes, and charities all need experts trained in marketing. The appendix to Part 3 of this book looks at these challenging areas to help you expand your views of where the jobs are for those with a business degree.

Part 4 of the book looks at management. After a firm has surveyed the market and decided on a product mix, it must then go on to produce the product. Part 4 will look at the management and leadership principles that are needed to guide organizations in the future. We shall also look at the latest in production techniques and the use of computers and other high-tech instruments to make U.S. firms number one in the world.

LOOKING AHEAD

APPENDIX TO PART III
NONPROFIT ORGANIZATION MARKETING

Today more than ever nonprofit organizations are seeking students trained in marketing, finance, accounting personnel, and other business functions. Training in business does not mean you have to work in business. The following examples will give you some feel for marketing opportunities in the nonprofit sector:

- The Baltimore Aquarium was being built on the waterfront. It promised to be a major tourist attraction for the city. During the construction phase, the director of marketing conducted a series of focus group interviews among several potential target audiences. The information that was gathered was very helpful in designing pricing strategies, promotional programs, parking places, transportation systems, and more.

- Fred Mindlin, executive director of Opportunities Resources for the Arts, received a letter from 30 second-year Harvard M.B.A. students interested in arts administration. These students had learned that various symphony groups, ballet companies, and similar arts organizations were eager to find administrators who could conduct marketing research studies; develop a salable product offer; set a pricing policy; promote the arts to the public; raise funds from patrons, foundations, and various government agencies; and generally manage the communications function.

- The U.S. government spends millions of dollars every year for advertising. This money goes to 21 different government accounts, most of which are military recruitment programs. Other government programs that spend millions in advertising are the U.S. Postal Service, the Department of Energy (DOE), the Department of Agriculture, AMTRAK (the passenger railroad service), the U.S. Travel Service, the National Institute on Drug Abuse, the IRS, and the Office of Education.

We could go on listing programs of churches, boys' and girls' clubs, unions, charities, social causes, hospitals, foundations, and other nonprofit organizations, but the point is clear. Nonprofit organizations, which have tended to actively scorn marketing and other business functions, are now turning to business school graduates for help in soliciting more funds and better serving all their publics.

This ad for the army is a good example of the creativity that goes into nonprofit advertising. Nonprofit organizations also need people skilled in marketing research, product design, and other marketing functions.

IF YOU HAVE WHAT IT TAKES TO FLY,
WE'LL HELP YOU EARN YOUR WINGS.

ARMY
BE ALL YOU CAN BE.

JOB OPPORTUNITIES IN THE NONPROFIT SECTOR

In a new book, *The Nonprofit Economy,* University of Wisconsin economics professor Burton Weisbrod says that there are now nearly 1 million tax-exempt nonprofit institutions in the United States with the number growing by tens of thousands each year.[1] *Fortune* magazine reported in 1988 that the 10 largest charities in the United States, their annual revenues, and the number of volunteers they enlist are:

ORGANIZATION	INCOME (MILLIONS OF DOLLARS)	NUMBER OF VOLUNTEERS
1. American Red Cross	$973	1,400,000
2. Salvation Army	865	1,000,000
3. Unicef	463	N.A.
4. Goodwill	447	N.A.
5. CARE	397	N.A.
6. American Cancer Society	308	2,500,000
7. Planned Parenthood	274	18,000
8. Cerebral Palsy Association	233	2,000,000
9. Easter Seal Society	212	800,000
10. Boys Clubs of America	187	150,000

Just because an organization is tax exempt and has many volunteers does not mean that it doesn't also have a large staff of professional marketing people to do fund raising, publicity, and so on. In fact, competition for these jobs is less stiff because fewer college graduates aim for the nonprofit sector when they graduate. Pay for college graduates is often lower than in the profit sector, but there is the added benefit of being able to contribute to society. One is often able to move up faster in such organizations because of the lower competition for jobs, and once you reach the managerial level, you can live quite comfortably. It is estimated that there will be 9.3 million jobs in the nonprofit sector in 1995.[2] The box at the end of this appendix discusses careers in nonprofit organizations in more depth and gives you some sources to go to for more information.

Special Types of Nonprofit Marketing

This text cannot possibly discuss in detail the special marketing problems of all nonprofit organizations such as churches, schools, charities, foundations, social causes, unions, fraternities, politicians, youth groups, libraries, and nonprofit health care agencies. However, a brief look at some of these organizations will give you some feeling for the problems involved.

Marketing of Social Causes

Often the goals of marketing are to mobilize the public behind some cause that seems beneficial to everyone. Many of these causes develop a slogan or some basic statement that everyone can recognize and support. You are probably familiar with campaigns such as the following:

Take a bite out of crime.	Stop smoking.
Just say no.	Buy bonds.
Don't drink and drive.	Give to the college of your choice.
Give blood.	Help prevent forest fires.
Love your neighbor.	Stay in school.
Drive defensively.	Support your local police.
Fasten your seat belt.	Hire the handicapped.
See America first.	

Various religious organizations use marketing to attract new members and to promote good causes. Millions of dollars are raised for feeding the hungry and clothing the poor in this manner. The importance of God in the lives of people is promoted in this ad for the Episcopal Church.

One of the goals of social marketing is to encourage people to support a specific cause that will benefit a group of people. In Tampa, Florida, a local TV station (WXFL-TV-8), the Tampa Chamber of Commerce, and Kash-n-Karry food stores joined ranks to support the "For Kid's Sake" campaign.

The promotion of such causes is part of the area called *social marketing*. Social marketing is the marketing of social ideas, causes, or practices. Social causes that people are concerned with today include pollution control, world freedom, women's and men's liberation, racial integration, and world hunger. All these social causes must generate support among the public if they are to be successful. This calls for effective and efficient marketing programs.

Political Marketing

Politics is a very important part of American life, and marketing is becoming an increasingly important part of the political scene. Political marketing, then, is the application of marketing strategies in the political arena. Market research, market segmentation, marketing communication, and the other marketing functions are as important to politicians as they are to any other marketer. The political campaign of 1988 was particularly interesting. Senator Dole failed largely because of his marketing campaign. On the other hand, Jesse Jackson won many supporters with his message and way of delivery. Some concepts of note are:

- Mass advertising for a political candidate has the same function as national advertising for products—to establish the name and a favorable image.
- Political candidates must rely heavily on organization—getting their supporters to recruit other supporters and to keep the momentum going throughout the campaign, including getting voters to the polls.
- Political candidates need very careful market-segmentation strategies to ensure that pertinent issues will be discussed with different market segments as needed.

Politicians need marketing middlemen for the same reasons that manufacturers do. It is impossible for a candidate to contact every one of his or her constituents, and so middlemen must be organized to contact various market segments. If a candidate has 100 close political supporters and each of those supporters contacts five people each and asks those five to contact five more through five layers, then potentially 312,500 people will be personally contacted and encouraged to vote for the candidate. In the case of presidential elections, such pyramiding often takes place within each state and within each city.

Marketing for Charities

There are more than half a million charitable organizations in the United States today. Each of them is competing for the public's support. The National Center for Voluntary Action estimates that 50 to 60 million people belong to volunteer groups of some sort. In 1987, charitable giving reached over $92.5 billion in the United States.[3]

In spite of the willingness of Americans to volunteer their time and money for charitable causes, there is much discontent and hesitancy about charitable giving. One of the most damaging criticisms of charities has been their inefficiencies in one area—you guessed it, marketing. Some charities spend as much as 70 to 90 percent of their income on fund raising. There is little doubt that many charitable organizations are desperately in need of marketing assistance.

The Marketing of Cities

Many opportunities exist for college graduates trained in city management and promotion. Take Albany, New York, for example. The city suffered from a combination of plant closings, downtown blight, and the unexpected deaths of seven city officials. The Albany/ Dougherty Economic Development Commission sent out its chief official to rally the city's civic groups. "Part of our marketing strategy," he said "is to sell Albany to Albanians." Print ads invite outsiders to "Share the Vision" of Albany while radio ads are aimed at boosting local morale.[4]

We shall now discuss a strategy for mobilizing volunteers to support any cause, including the rebirth of a city. Whether the cause is to clean up the parks, fix up homes, help the aged, or whatever, the solution is the same—get people concerned and involved. Even serious problems such as crime and drugs can be lowered with Neighborhood Watch programs and other volunteer efforts. Who is responsible for solving the problems of the city, the country, and the world? You are! The job of marketers is to show people that *they* are the solution.

MARKETING TO GET VOLUNTEERS

President Bush has called for a renewed interest in voluntarism in America. He said "there needs to be a new activism—a new engagement in the lives of others." He called such volunteers "a thousand points of light."[5]

Most businesspeople today are already involved in community organizations as part of their social responsibility. One reason such people are asked to assist in these organizations is their business expertise. Without the incentive of profit and paid workers, however, it is difficult to manage a successful program. Nonetheless, business concepts can be applied effectively to such organizations. There are six elements to a strategic marketing plan for nonprofit organizations to get and hold volunteers:

1. A social catalyst or person who provides leadership.
2. Targeting volunteers.
3. Giving direction.
4. Structuring the organization.
5. Visible success and feedback.
6. Maintaining enthusiasm.

Social Catalyst

A social catalyst is a person who sees a social need and mobilizes others to support an organization to satisfy that need. Businesspeople have always provided leadership in such causes. There is a need today to find and train students for tomorrow's leadership positions. A dozen chief executive officers from America's leading firms are on the board of the National Business Consortium for Gifted and Talented. They are getting business involved in education programs for young people. Business leaders are involved in many such organizations, from Junior Achievement and United Appeal to the local boys' and girls' clubs and scouts.

Working for a nonprofit organization brings rewards beyond the salary you receive. This ad for helping the homeless is a public service ad in conjunction with the Boy Scouts. One can get tremendous satisfaction in nonprofit organizations working for good causes.

Joseph Jaworski's American Leadership Forum is an organization designed to develop local leaders to help solve community problems. Here is how *The Washington Post* describes the potential:[6]

> No amount of law-enforcement exertion . . . can solve the drug problem that plagues so many of our cities. But citizens, working together across lines of class, income and politics, can find ways to make a substantial dent in the problem.

Jaworski says, "People in general have to consider what happens in the country as their personal responsibility." It is the job of a catalyst to point out that responsibility and then mobilize people to act.

Targeting Volunteers

The segmentation variable that works best for nonprofit organizations is the degree of interest in the cause. Business coordinators for such organizations must find people who are already highly committed to participating.

The targeting strategy goes like this: Get highly committed people to contact a few other highly committed people. Usually they either know these people already or can find them easily. Each contacted person is asked to contact several more in a pyramiding scheme that generates dozens of concerned and partially committed volunteers. They then may be called together at one or several meeting places.

Politicians have used this strategy for years. Concerned businesspeople and other citizens can use similar strategies for solving problems such as neighborhood crime, hunger, drug abuse, pollution (for example, clean-up campaigns), and gaining support for organizations such as local schools, churches, charities, causes, and clubs.

Notice how many volunteers are needed for some of these organizations to function. The Red Cross alone has over 2 million volunteers. The American Cancer Society and the American Heart Association rely on over 2.5 million volunteers.

Giving Direction

Volunteers must be told what to do, when, where, and how often. Volunteering is not a priority for most people, and they need someone to guide them in what they do. Businesspeople are experienced in planning, organizing, directing, and controlling people. Volunteers need even more management control because they are not being paid and often feel less commitment.

Structuring the Organization

It is important for nonprofit organizations to have some structure; that is, a place to meet, a name, a slogan, and some clear objectives. Think of the change that has occurred because of organizations with names like Neighborhood Watch, MADD (Mothers Against Drunk Driving), and Red Cross. Businesspeople are often highly skilled at creating such organizations.

Visible Success

Few things motivate people more than seeing that their work makes a difference. To motivate volunteers, an organization must provide them with feedback about the success of each effort. Volunteers need recognition for what they do. They also must feel that the effort is accomplishing something or they will lose motivation.

Maintaining Enthusiasm

Because of the new two-career family lifestyles, volunteers are harder to find today. More flexibility is needed in scheduling times and days for people to work. To maintain enthusiasm, a volunteer job must be personally rewarding. Time must be taken to acknowledge volunteers and give them incentives, much like any worker: prizes, certificates, recognition dinners, newspaper articles, and so forth. The easier an organization can make volunteering the better.

Success So Far

There is much evidence that U.S. citizens are ready to be the "thousand points of light" President Bush has requested. About 45 percent of all adults now volunteer an average of 4.7 hours per week to teach people to read, work with AIDS patients, help out in hospitals, serve food to the hungry, and work in thousands of other charitable endeavors. In all, 80 million people now donate over 19 billion hours to causes.[7] That is strong evidence that people in the United States are generous with their time and money. What is needed is better management and marketing of nonbusinesses to put there resources to better use in combating drugs, crime, poverty, illiteracy, and the other social problems in the United States and the world. *The Wall Street Journal* reports that more volunteers are receiving training in managerial skills and nonperformers are being asked to leave.[8] The linking of businesspeople with nonprofit organizations holds much promise for raising the standard of living and quality of life in America—the goals of our economic system.

THINKING IT THROUGH	What cause most interests you? Would you like to fix up your neighborhood park, cut down on neighborhood crime, or start a neighborhood co-op? Just follow the six steps. You see, business concepts can be used for all kinds of causes.

ANALYZING MARKETING PROGRAMS IN NONPROFIT ORGANIZATIONS

All of the concepts that you have learned to market profit-making organizations apply with equal force to nonprofit organizations. Concepts such as segmentation, target marketing, and product design and development are as important to a charity or cause as a retail store selling shoes. Some marketing consultants have developed a self-assessment scale for nonbusinesses to test their marketing program (see Figure A–1).

Low scores on the Orientation section indicate that the organization is not clear about the markets (client and contributor) that it is trying to reach and the unique benefits the organization is trying to provide. Low scores on the Research section reveal the need for a marketing communication system. Low scores on the Planning questions indicate marketing deficiencies in general. Low scores on questions 18 and 19 indicate a lack of control or feedback. Again, a marketing communication system is one answer. A low score on the final question indicates that there may be an opening for you if you can prove your marketing expertise.

Overall, a score of 40–59 indicates a weak organization. A score of 60–79 suggests a good marketing orientation. A score of 80–100 indicates a smart marketing organization.

UNIVERSALLY APPLICABLE BUSINESS CONCEPTS

The growth and prosperity of business is directly tied to the growth and prosperity of the national and local economy. Businesspeople recognize this interdependency, and are active in all phases of national and local political and social organizations. Business tools (for example, computers) and business concepts (for example, planning, organizing, leading, staffing, and controlling) are equally applicable in nonprofit organizations as in business organizations.

ORIENTATION
The organization:
1. Is aware of clients needs, problems, and opportunities._____
2. Is aware of contributor needs, problems, and opportunities._____
3. Uses rational and emotional appeals to present benefits to clients and contributors._____
4. Has product/service knowledge so facts can be used to support promised benefits._____
5. Knows its competition for clients and contributors._____
6. Has developed a unique approach or distinguishing benefit compared to the competition._____
7. Targets or directs marketing efforts to a defined group of clients or contributors._____

RESEARCH
The organization:
8. Plans and conducts research to learn about clients' and contributors' needs, problems, and opportunities._____
9. Analyzes and uses research to adjust offerings to clients and contributors—their needs, problems, and opportunities._____
10. Has designated individual(s) responsible for ongoing research._____

MARKETING PLANNING
The organization:
11. Concentrates on long-term planning vs. detailed how-to lists._____
12. Develops a three-year marketing plan for the organization._____
13. Has several strategies for marketing products/services to each target market of clients and contributors._____
14. Includes product/service, price, place, and promotion in planning its marketing efforts. _____
15. Fully markets, rather than simply promotes, its products._____
16. Has designated individual(s) responsible for implementing major marketing strategies._____
17. Has fixed a time line for major marketing strategies._____

MARKETING CONTROL
The organization:
18. Uses evaluation measures to assess implementation of the plan._____
19. Uses the feedback to redirect the orientation, research, and marketing planning of the group. _____
20. Has a person designated as the head marketer._____

Source: Doris C. Van Doren and Louise W. Smith, "Self-Analysis Can Gauge Marketing Orientation," *Collegiate Edition Marketing News*, January 1986, p. 16.

FIGURE 3A–1

Nonprofit marketing analysis for organizational self-study. *Rank the organization from 5 (high) to 1 (low).*

The next several chapters will focus on management principles. Keep in mind as you read them that the same concepts can be applied in any organization. Business courses are not just for businesspeople. They are the foundation for managing all successful organizations. Note also that you can learn much about business techniques and strategies (for example, motivation, human relations skills, and marketing) by volunteering to participate in a nonprofit organization.

CAREER INFORMATION: NONPROFIT ORGANIZATIONS

NATURE OF THE WORK

A career in a nonprofit organization offers a variety of opportunities, including greater advancement for women and minorities, doing work that has direct and meaningful impact, and high levels of responsibility for young professionals. A *nonprofit organization* is one that pays no tax on the income it generates and has no private owners. Any money such an organization earns goes into expenses and salaries. The rest is used for educational programs or expansion of the organization. Careers in marketing-related areas include marketing research, promotion, public relations and publicity, advertising, fund raising (personal selling), and program design.

JOB OUTLOOK

There always seem to be new openings somewhere in nonprofit organizations. The salary level is not always comparable with profit-making organizations, but sometimes it is. Some comments about specific organizations follow.

- *Common Cause.* Recent college graduates interested in Common Cause should have strong interests in public affairs and American politics. This organization calls itself "a national nonpartisan educational organization in Washington, D.C., that informs the public about government abuses and issues facing the electorate."
- *National Student Action Center.* Working at this organization enables you to help coordinate the flow of information to hundreds of campuses on issues ranging from reproductive rights to Central America.
- *Urban Housing Assistance Board.* Would you like to help reduce bureaucratic red tape for low-income people? In New York, Andy Reicher manages 22 people who help the poor convert abandoned buildings into tenant-owned co-op housing. He looks for college grads with some background in volunteer work. One who works at such a job gets benefits more than pay and health benefits. One also gets the self-satisfaction from moving homeless families into safe, clean, and adequate shelters.
- *National Public Radio.* National Public Radio broadcasts through a network of 33 nonprofit member stations across the country. Beginners move into positions of responsibility much faster than at commercial stations. It's best to have had some experience with a campus radio station or an internship with a commercial station.

SOURCES OF ADDITIONAL INFORMATION

Nonprofit organizations also include the League of Women Voters, the American Automobile Association, local parochial schools, local and national charities and causes, and more. College students may be particularly interested in the National Association of Intercollegiate Athletics or the United Negro College Fund. For information write: "Community Jobs," 1319 18th St., N.W., Washington, D.C. 20036. This publication lists possible jobs in nonprofit organizations throughout the country. For the addresses and phone numbers of associations and foundations, write: "The National Directory of Addresses and Telephone Numbers," 14 Park Road, Tinton Falls, New Jersey 07724.

ACCESS is a databank that has a mailing list of over 350,000 not-for-profit organizations. From that databank comes a publication called "Opportunities in Non-Profit Organizations." Some 200 schools subscribe to this publication. Check around.

Source: Tony Vellela, "Profit by Association," *Business Week Careers,* April/May 1988, pp. 45–48; and Eddie David, "Doing Good and Doing Well," *CU Magazine,* February–March 1989, pp. 50–55.

MANAGEMENT

IV

Management and Leadership

11

LEARNING GOALS

After you have read and studied this chapter, you should be able to:

1. Explain how and why the role of managers is changing in the 1990s.
2. Identify the four functions of management.
3. Distinguish between goals and objectives; between strategic, tactical, and contingency planning; and explain the relationships of goals and objectives to the various types of planning.
4. Describe the significance of an organization chart and explain the role of each management level in the corporate hierarchy.
5. Summarize the five steps of the control function of management.
6. Describe the directing function of management and illustrate how the function differs at the various management levels.
7. Explain the differences between managers and leaders and compare the characteristics and use of the various leadership styles.
8. Describe the skills needed by top, middle, and first-line managers.
9. Illustrate the five skills you will need to develop your managerial potential and outline activities you could use to develop these skills.

KEY TERMS

conceptual skills, *p. 345*
contingency planning, *p. 334*
controlling, *p. 331*
delegating, *p. 346*
directing, *p. 331*
goals, *p. 332*
human relation skills, *p. 345*
leadership, *p. 341*
management, *p. 331*
management by walking around, *p. 330*
middle management, *p. 336*

objectives, *p. 332*
organizing, *p. 331*
participative management, *p. 342*
planning, *p. 331*
rational decision-making model, *p. 346*
strategic planning, *p. 333*
supervisory (first-line) management, *p. 336*
tactical planning, *p. 334*
technical skills, *p. 345*
top management, *p. 336*

Jack Welch

PROFILE   JACK WELCH OF GENERAL ELECTRIC

Recently, *Fortune* magazine ran an article called "Wanted: Leaders Who Can Make A Difference." In that article, the author said that "Consultants and academics would probably choose GE's Jack Welch as the best example of the new kind of top executive U.S. business needs." What is it that makes Jack Welch so special? Certainly it is not his humble personality or his ability to calm things down in a storm. Quite the contrary, some experts felt that Welch was too abrasive to succeed at the job. Nonetheless, Welch managed to revitalize GE by cutting out more than 100,000 jobs (1 job in 4), getting rid of low-growth businesses such as housewares and television, and moving into more promising areas such as broadcasting (RCA), investment banking, and high-tech manufacturing.

One change Welch made in GE was to change what was taught in its Management Development Institute in New York. Emphasis was switched from managerial skills like financial analysis to new ideas about risk taking, leadership, and values.

The reaction to Welch's changes has been mixed. Union workers call him "Neutron Jack," the job-killer who is demoralizing the work force. Managers also complain about the high-stress environment he has created. Some say that Welch has lost the loyalty of many managers. Admirers feel that Welch is changing GE from a plodder into a racehorse. A *Business Week* survey asking executives which colleague they most admired found Welch second only to Lee Iacocca.

Welch has spent his entire career at GE. As he rose through the ranks, he saw how too many top managers can muddy up the firm. When he reached the top, therefore, Welch cut the corporate staff from 1,700 to 1,000. More responsibility and authority were passed down to lower-level managers. Welch wants managers to feel freer to make decisions.

To survive at GE now you must be an effective manager. Since Welch took over, 11 of 14 managers of business units have been replaced. Welch has a vision for GE and he wants managers who share that vision and are capable of inspiring others to attain the vision as well. Naturally, there are older managers and workers who resent all this change. They feel overworked and are afraid of being fired. Welch feels that such reactions are normal in a changing firm and is rushing ahead to make GE into one of the top firms in the world.

What is happening in American business that makes a man like Jack Welch so popular among other executives? Is he the model for the executive of the future or merely an unusually successful manager with a unique style? How important is management to a firm anyhow, and does managerial style make much difference? These are the questions we will be exploring in the next few chapters.

Sources: Russell Mitchell and Judith H. Dobrzynski, "Jack Welch: How Good a Manager?" *Business Week*, December 14, 1987, pp. 92–103; Jeremy Main, "Wanted: Leaders Who Can Make a Difference," *Fortune*, September 28, 1987, pp. 92–102; and Mark Potts, "G.E.'s Management Mission," *The Washington Post*, May 22, 1988, pp. H1 and H4.

Leadership is the ability to inspire in others the kind of moral action that the times we live in demand: We can't stand still.
JOSEPH P. KENNEDY

THE MANAGEMENT CHALLENGE OF THE 1990s

Jack Welch is just one example of many managers who are radically changing the whole approach to corporate management in the 1990s. Why such radical changes now? *Fortune* magazine cites what it calls the four "horsemen of the corporate apocalypse: global competition, deregulation, accelerating technological change, and the threat of takeover." As a consequence, over half of the *Fortune* 500 companies are doing what Jack Welch did: laying off employees, restructuring, and cutting costs.[1]

A major factor in the reorganization of businesses is the need to respond better to customers. To respond faster to consumer demands, corporations had to give more authority and responsibility to lower-level managers who could respond to consumer requests more quickly. Foreign competitors were known for being more responsive to the market and for bringing out innovations more quickly. American firms had to restructure and change their management styles to become equally responsive and equally able to produce new products quickly.

Accelerating technological change also brought in a new breed of workers, more educated and with higher skill levels. They demanded more freedom of operation and a different managerial style as well.

Furthermore, American managers were forced to change their rather conservative style of management because of the threat of takeovers. If a company were perceived as being capable of being more efficient and more productive with new management, corporate raiders stepped in and took over the firm. This meant that many managers and employees would be fired and divisions sold. A firm had to become competitive in world markets *or else!* Jack Welch saw such trends and decided to take GE into the 21st century before some corporate raider did.

Perhaps the greatest challenge to managers in the 1980s was global competition. The major impetus behind the restructuring and refocusing of corporations in this period was the need to compete with foreign producers. Chief executives in the year 2000 will likely have experience abroad. Meanwhile, the executive of today must learn how to deal in global markets and in a global economy.[2]

In short, the end of the 1980s was an era for corporate housecleaning—time to get rid of the old divisions and managerial styles that had been accumulating in the attic and time to introduce a whole new way of operating. Naturally, this caused much disruption in business. Many managers were fired and had to find new jobs. The same was true of blue-collar workers. GE was one of hundreds of firms that went through sweeping organizational and managerial changes. Now U.S. firms are leaner and meaner and ready to take on world competition. That will call for great managers.

The Changing Role of Managers

An early management scholar, Mary Parker Follett, defined management as "the art of getting things done through people." At one time, that meant that managers were called *bosses,* and their job was to tell people what to do and watch over them to be sure they did it. Bosses tended to reprimand those who didn't do things correctly, and generally acted stern and "bossy." Many managers still behave that way. Perhaps you have witnessed such managers yelling at employees at fast-food restaurants or on shop floors.

Today, management is changing from that kind of behavior. Managers are being educated to *lead, guide* and *coach* employees rather than to boss them around. Modern managers emphasize teamwork and cooperation rather than discipline and order giving. Managers in some high-tech and progressive firms dress more casually, are more friendly, and generally treat employees as partners rather than unruly workers.

AMERICA'S MOST ADMIRED MANAGERS

Roger Enrico of Pepsi-Cola USA was one of 10 people cited by *Fortune* magazine as "America's Most Wanted Managers." Other selections included Nolan Archibald of Black & Decker, Donald Beall of Rockwell International, and Jane Evans of Monet, Crystal Brands, Incorporated. Jack Welch of GE (see the opening Profile) was number three in a more recent poll.

What these managers have in common is that they are action oriented. A manager today has to be able to effectively manage change. A second characteristic such managers have is the ability to build a sense of shared values—an ability to motivate and generate loyalty.

Nine attributes were listed by one executive recruiter: an advanced degree; profit and loss experience; steady progress through the ranks, with an occasional detour to a staff position; some background in international business; excellent communications skills; a vision that can be imparted to others; self-confidence; the ability to take risks without undue worry; and high integrity.

These are the traits that make top executives attractive to other firms. The favorites typically have a healthy ego, a fondness for competitive sports, and a lot of experience moving from city to city.

Source: Roy Rowan, "America's Most Wanted Managers," *Fortune,* February 3, 1986, pp. 18–19; and Charles A. Riley, II "The No. 1 Leader Is Peterson of Ford," *Fortune,* October 24, 1988, p. 69.

A manager needs to get out of the office periodically and circulate among the employees. This is called management by walking around. It is equally important to mingle with customers to learn their wants, needs, and suggestions.

management by walking around
Managers get out of their offices and personally interact with employees and customers.

In general, therefore, management is experiencing a revolution. Books like *The One Minute Manager* encourage supervisors to actively praise employees (see Case 2 at the end of the chapter). A concept called **management by walking around** (MBWA) encourages managers to get out of their offices and mingle with workers and customers. This does not mean that managers are becoming mere cheerleaders. It does mean, though, that managers are working more closely with employees in a joint effort to accomplish common goals.

What this means for tomorrow's graduates is that managerial careers demand a new kind of person. That person is a skilled communicator as well as a planner, coordinator, organizer, and supervisor. Many managers today believe that they are part of a team and enjoy the new responsibility and flexibility that comes with more open and casual management systems. These trends will be discussed in the next few chapters to help you decide whether or not management is the kind of thing you would like to do.

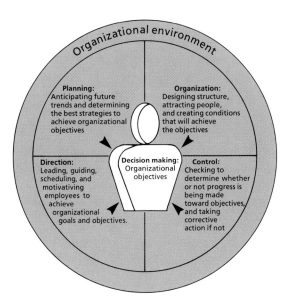

FIGURE 11–1

Management functions. The primary functions of management are planning, organization (including staffing), direction (leadership and motivation), and control. One of the more neglected functions is control.

The Definition and Functions of Management

One reason people go to college is because college prepares them to become managers. Students have told us, "I don't know *what* I want to do, really. I guess I would like to be in management." Management is attractive to students because it represents authority, money, prestige and so on. But few students are able to describe just what it is that managers do. That is what this chapter is for: It describes what managers are, what they do, and how they do it.

As we noted earlier, management could be called the art of getting things done through people and other resources. A well-known management consultant, Peter Drucker, says managers give direction to their organizations, provide leadership, and decide how to use organizational resources to accomplish goals.[3] Certainly, that describes what Jack Welch is trying to do at GE. Both definitions give you some feel for what managers do. The definition of management we will be using in this text is: **Management** is the process used to accomplish organizational goals through planning, organizing, directing, and controlling people and other organizational resources.

This definition spells out the four key functions of management: (1) planning, (2) organizing, (3) directing, and (4) controlling (see Figure 11–1).

1. **Planning** includes anticipating future trends and determining the best strategies and tactics to achieve organizational goals and objectives.
2. **Organizing** includes designing the organizational structure, attracting people to the organization (staffing), and creating conditions and systems that ensure that everyone and everything works together to achieve the goals and objectives of the organization.
3. **Directing** is guiding and motivating others to work effectively to achieve the goals and objectives of the organization.
4. **Controlling** is checking to determine whether or not an organization is progressing toward its goals and objectives, and taking corrective action if it is not.

management
The process used to accomplish organizational goals through planning, organizing, directing, and controlling organizational resources.

planning
Management function that involves anticipating future trends and determining the best strategies and tactics to achieve organizational objectives.

organizing
Management function that involves designing the organizational structure, attracting people to the organization (staffing), and creating conditions and systems that ensure that everyone and everything work together to achieve the objectives of the organization.

directing
Guiding and motivating others to achieve the goals and objectives of the organization.

controlling
Management function that involves checking to determine whether or not an organization is progressing toward its goals and objectives, and taking corrective action if it is not.

WHAT MANAGERS DO

PLANNING

- Setting organizational goals.
- Developing strategies to reach those goals.
- Determining resources needed.
- Setting standards.

ORGANIZING

- Allocating resources, assigning tasks, and establishing procedures for accomplishing goals.
- Preparing a structure (organization chart) showing lines of authority and responsibility.
- Recruiting, selecting, training, and developing employees.
- Placing employees where they will be most effective.

DIRECTING

- Leading, guiding and motivating employees to work effectively to accomplish organizational goals and objectives.
- Giving assignments.
- Explaining routines.
- Clarifying policies.
- Providing feedback on performance.

CONTROLLING

- Measuring results against corporate objectives.
- Monitoring performance relative to standards.
- Taking corrective action.

> The four most important things in running a business are management, management, management, and a superior product.
>
> DAVID MINTZ, inventor of Tofutti

You have some familiarity with management tasks already: You have *planned* to go to college to learn something about business. You have *organized* your time and materials to do that. You may also have experienced *directing* in a sports team or a social group. Periodically, you will have to evaluate and *control* your progress to decide whether or not you are meeting your objectives. You know how important it is for a manager to set goals, to inspire others, and to establish strong values that will enable the organization to succeed.

You might also know that management is much more complex than doing a few tasks. A good manager must know about the industry the firm is in and all the technological, political, competitive, and social factors affecting that industry. He or she must also understand the kind of people who work in the industry and what motivates them. Finally, a manager must be skilled in performing various managerial tasks, especially technical tasks, human relations tasks, and conceptual tasks.

The four functions listed above are the heart of management, so let's explore them in more detail. The process begins with planning.

PROGRESS CHECK

What were some of the environmental factors that forced executives like Jack Welch to change their organizations and managerial styles in the 1980s?

What is the definition of management and the four functions in that definition?

---

goals
Broad, long-term accomplishments an organization wishes to attain.

objectives
Specific, short-term tasks that must be completed to achieve the organizational goals.

PLANNING

Planning is the first managerial function used to pursue organizational goals. Planning involves the process of setting objectives. Therefore, it is important to understand what goals are and how they differ from objectives. **Goals** are the broad, long-term accomplishments an organization wishes to attain. **Objectives,** on the other hand, are specific, short-term tasks that must be completed to achieve the goals. One of your goals for reading this chapter, for example, may be to learn

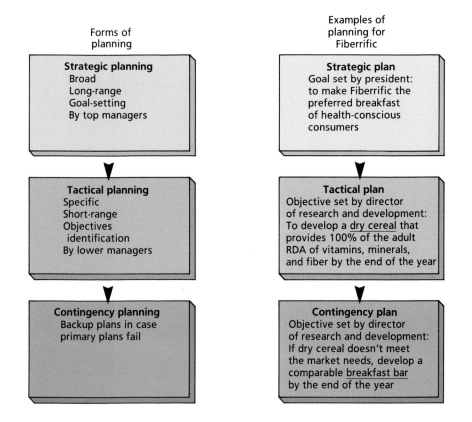

Forms of planning

Examples of planning for Fiberrific

Strategic planning
Broad
Long-range
Goal-setting
By top managers

Strategic plan
Goal set by president:
to make Fiberrific the
preferred breakfast
of health-conscious
consumers

Tactical planning
Specific
Short-range
Objectives
 identification
By lower managers

Tactical plan
Objective set by director
of research and development:
To develop a <u>dry cereal</u> that
provides 100% of the adult
RDA of vitamins, minerals,
and fiber by the end of the year

Contingency planning
Backup plans in case
primary plans fail

Contingency plan
Objective set by director
of research and development:
If dry cereal doesn't meet
the market needs, develop a
comparable <u>breakfast bar</u>
by the end of the year

FIGURE 11–2

Planning functions.
Very few firms bother to
make contingency plans. If
something changes the
market, such companies are
slow to respond. Strategic
planning and tactical
planning are practiced in
most firms.

basic concepts of management. One objective you could use to achieve this goal is to plan to answer correctly the Thinking It Through and Progress Check boxes. Another example of a goal is to make Fiberrific, our hypothetical cereal in the previous chapters, the number one cereal in America. One objective might be getting Fiberrific on the shelves of 85 percent of the supermarkets in the Midwest by the end of the year. What is important to remember is: goals are broad and long-term statements of what the organization wants to achieve, whereas objectives are specific and short-term statements of how to meet those goals.

Most planning follows a pattern. The procedure you would follow in planning your life and career is basically the same as those used by businesses for their plans. Planning answers three fundamental questions for businesses:

1. *What is the situation now?* What is the state of the economy? What opportunities exist for meeting people's needs? What products and customers are most profitable? Why do people buy (or not buy) our products? Who are our major competitors?

2. *Where do we want to go?* How much growth do we want? What is our profit goal? What are our social objectives? What are our personal development objectives for employees?

3. *How can we get there from here?* This is the most important part of planning. It takes three forms (see Figure 11–2):

    a. **Strategic** *(long-range)* **planning** determines the major goals of the organization and the policies and strategies for obtaining and using resources to achieve those goals. In this definition, *policies* are broad guides to action, and *strategies* determine the best way to use resources.

strategic planning
Process of determining
the major goals of the
organization and the
policies and strategies for
obtaining and using
resources to achieve those
goals.

At the strategic planning stage, the company decides which customers to serve, what products or services to sell, and the geographic areas in which the firm will compete.

tactical planning
Process of developing detailed, short-term decisions about what is to be done, who is to do it, and how it is to be done.

b. **Tactical** *(short-range)* **planning** is the process of developing detailed, short-term decisions about what is to be done, who is to do it, and how it is to be done. Just as objectives are *specific* plans to meet *broad* goals, tactical planning involves defining *specific* plans to achieve *broad* strategic plans. Tactical planning is normally done by managers at lower levels of the organization, whereas strategic planning is done by the top managers of the firm (for example, the president). Tactical planning involves setting annual budgets and deciding on other details of how to meet the strategic objectives.

contingency planning
Process of preparing alternative courses of action that may be used if the primary plans do not achieve the objectives of the organization.

c. **Contingency planning** is the preparation of alternative courses of action that may be used if the primary plans do not achieve the objectives of the organization. The economic and competitive environments change so rapidly that it is wise to have alternative plans of action ready in anticipation of such changes.

Planning in Action

Daniel Merkel, president of American Orthodontics, says that planning is very important to his firm. He says that both long-term (strategic) and short-term (tactical) planning play extremely important roles in the company. He believes that planning is a *continuous process:*[4]

> To take the same plan that worked yesterday and use it with any degree of success in today's market is impossible. Every two months, I meet with our entire management team specifically to address short-term planning. Some of the issues we discuss include the alignment of sales territories, production needs, pricing and other marketing strategies, and personnel requirements.
>
> In our long-range planning, we address wider issues, such as present and future competition, and tapping opportunities available to our company through penetration of new markets.

Each year, the company makes detailed long-range plans that cover the next three years and less detailed plans that look six years into the future.

Planning is a critical part of a manager's job. It consists of setting goals and objectives. Objectives are the steps one must accomplish to reach the long-term goals.

As president, Mr. Merkel focuses on strategic issues and encourages managers to come up with action plans. After planning meetings, formal plans are written down and distributed to managers. The plan acts as a reference tool (control measure) to ensure that daily activities are compatible with the general plan. This example is typical of how planning fits with a firm.

Planning versus Informed Opportunism

In 1987, Robert Waterman wrote a book to follow his best-selling *In Search of Excellence* (see Case 1 at the end of this chapter). His new book is called *The Renewal Factor: How the Best Get and Keep the Competitive Edge.* He says that leaders of renewing companies set *direction*, not detailed strategy. They are the best of strategists precisely because they are suspicious of forecasts and open to surprise. They think strategic planning is great—as long as no one takes the plans too seriously. The problem is that strategy is needed, but the future is uncertain. The answer is to stay flexible, listen for opportunities, and seize opportunities when they come whether they were *planned* or not.[5]

ORGANIZING

How often have you heard the comment, "One of these days we'll have to get organized"? Clearly, organization is an important managerial task. Basically, organizing means allocating resources, assigning tasks, and establishing procedures for accomplishing the organizational objectives. The basic concepts are rather easy to understand because you already have some experience organizing. For example, to play baseball, you have to gather together some materials: gloves, ball, bat. Then you have to find people to play the various positions. (In business, this is called *staffing*.) Then each person is assigned some task: first base, pitcher, outfield, and so on. Someone must decide who bats first, who second, and so on.

When organizing, a manager develops a structure or framework that relates all workers, tasks, and resources to each other. That framework is called the organization structure. Most organizations draw a chart showing these relationships. This is called an organization chart. A very simple chart would look like the illustration on the following page.

It is easier to understand the functions of management if you can relate them to your own experiences or observations. For example, it is easier to understand what organization is all about when you imagine this process of organizing players for a baseball game.

This is a rather standard chart with managers for major functions and supervisors reporting to the managers. Each supervisor manages three employees.

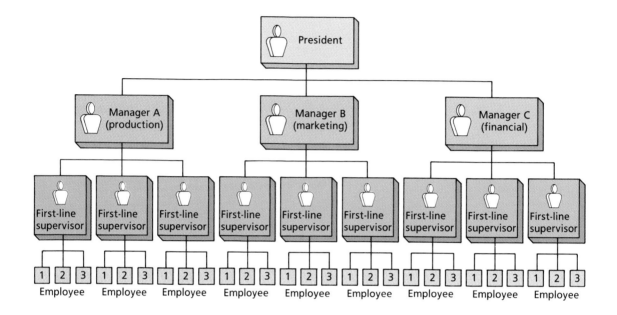

The organization chart pictures who reports to whom and who is responsible for each task. The problem of developing organization structure will be discussed in more detail in a later chapter. For now it is important to know that the corporate hierarchy illustrated on the organization chart includes top, middle, and first-line managers.

Top management is the highest level of management and consists of the president and other key company executives who develop strategic plans. Two terms you are likely to see often are chief executive officer (CEO) and chief operating officer (COO). The CEO is often the president of the firm and is responsible for all the top-level decisions in the firm. See the box titled Characteristics of Corporate America's Top Executives to see what these people are like. CEOs are responsible for introducing changes into an organization. The COO, chief operating officer, is responsible for putting those changes into effect. His or her tasks include structuring, controlling, and rewarding to ensure that people carry out the leader's vision.[6]

Middle management includes branch and plant managers, deans, and department heads who are responsible for tactical plans. **Supervisory (first-line) management** includes people directly responsible for assigning specific jobs to workers and evaluating their daily performance; they are often known as first-line managers because they are the first level above workers (see Figure 11–3).

All of this work of gathering materials and people together and assigning tasks is called organizing. If you were to draw a baseball field to show everyone where to stand, you would have an organization chart. A list of who bats in what order could be part of the chart. Managers call that scheduling. In short, organizing is a necessary part of all human effort, and is not too difficult if you know what you are doing.

top management
Highest level of management, consisting of the president and other key company executives who develop strategic plans.

middle management
Level of management that includes plant managers and department heads who are responsible for tactical plans.

supervisory (first-line) management
First level of management above employees; includes people directly responsible for assigning specific jobs to employees and evaluating their daily performance.

CHARACTERISTICS OF CORPORATE AMERICA'S TOP EXECUTIVES

What is it like to be the chief executive officer (CEO) of a top American firm? *Fortune* magazine tried to answer that question by surveying the executives from the top industrial and service companies. Some 351 respondents gave the following details. All of the respondents were men. (A few women have become top managers thus far, and there are several in the wings.) The top managers have been married only once (80 percent) and most have been married over 20 years. Over a third have four or more children. Only 4 percent have one child and 2 percent have none. Most (93 percent) do not smoke cigarettes, but most of them do drink (92 percent), the most popular drinks being wine and Scotch. About half own American cars (Cadillac, Lincoln, and Oldsmobile) and they prefer Seiko watches. Some 46 percent have gone to college, 34 percent have master's degrees, and 13 percent have their doctorate. The school of choice? Yale is number one, then Princeton, Cornell, and Wisconsin (undergraduate training). Golf is their number one hobby.

Over 86 percent work for charitable groups. The most popular are United Way, Boy Scouts, Girl Scouts, and the Salvation Army. The religious preference includes Roman Catholic (21 percent), Presbyterian (20 percent), Episcopalian (17 percent). Methodist, Congregational, or Jewish organizations had 7 percent each.

Source: "Life among the Business Elite," A Special Report on Executive Style, *Fortune*, March 20, 1987, pp. 20D–21D.

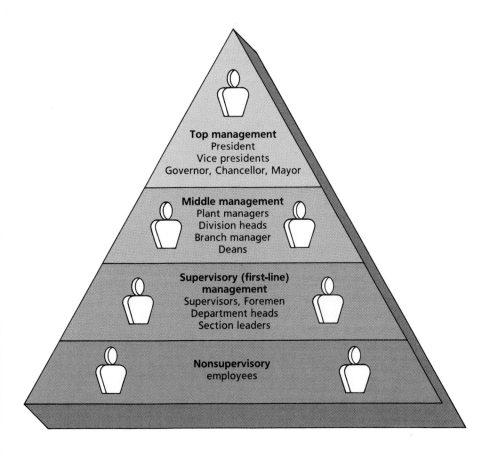

Top management
President
Vice presidents
Governor, Chancellor, Mayor

Middle management
Plant managers
Division heads
Branch manager
Deans

Supervisory (first-line) management
Supervisors, Foremen
Department heads
Section leaders

Nonsupervisory
employees

FIGURE 11–3

Levels of management. This figure shows the three levels of management. In many firms, there are several levels of middle management. Recently, however, firms have been eliminating middle-level managers in a cost-cutting attempt.

MAKING ETHICAL DECISIONS

As a first-line manager, you assist in the decisions made by your department head. The department head retains full responsibility for the decisions—if the plans succeed, it is his or her success; if the plans fail, it is his or her failure. You have new information that the department head hasn't seen. The findings in this report indicate that your manager's recent plans are sure to fail. If the plans do fail, the manager will probably be demoted and you are the most likely candidate to fill his vacancy. Will you give him the report? What will be the consequences of your decision?

An important part of organizing is staffing, getting the right people on the business team. You are probably most familiar with the term *personnel* to describe that function. Today it is called *human resource management* because it is as important to develop the potential of employees as it is to recruit good people in the first place. We will discuss human resource management in Chapter 16.

Making Organizations More Flexible

Tom Peters was a coauthor of *In Search of Excellence*. Like Robert Waterman, he, too, wrote a follow-up book called *Thriving on Chaos* (see Case 2 at the end of this chapter). He emphasized the need for organizations to become more flexible. That usually means that the organization should be smaller, have fewer levels of management, and be quicker to adapt to changes in the market, including the international market.[7] We shall talk more about organization in Chapter 12.

CONTROL

Often managers get so involved with the planning process and the day-to-day crisis management of the firm that they tend to short-change the control function. The control function involves measuring performance relative to objectives and standards and taking corrective action when necessary. The control function, therefore, is the heart of the management system because it provides the feedback that enables managers to adjust to any deviations from plans and to changes that have occurred in the environment that have affected performance (see Figure 11–4).

Controlling consists of the following steps:
1. Setting clear performance standards.
2. Monitoring and recording actual performance (results).
3. Comparing results against plans and standards.
4. Communicating results and deviations to the employees involved.
5. Taking corrective action when needed.

Setting Standards

The control system's weakest link tends to be the setting of standards. To measure results against standards, the standards must be specific, attainable, and measurable. Vague goals and standards such as "better quality," "more efficiency," and "improved performance" are not sufficient. It is also important to have a time period established when goals are to be met. Examples of goals and standards that meet these criteria include:

- Cutting the number of finished product rejects from 10 per 1,000 to 5 per 1,000 by March 31.

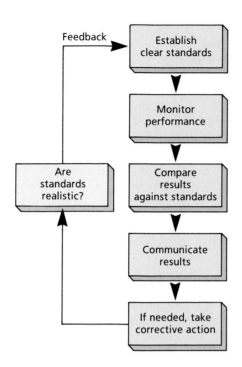

Feedback

Establish
clear standards

Monitor
performance

Compare
results
against standards

Are
standards
realistic?

Communicate
results

If needed, take
corrective action

FIGURE 11–4

The control process.
The whole control process is
based on clear standards.
Without such standards, the
other steps are difficult, if
not impossible. With clear
standards, performance
measurement is relatively
easy and the proper action
can be taken.

- Increasing the times managers praise employees from 3 times per week to 12 per week.
- Increasing the sales of product X from 10,000 in the month of July to 12,000 in that same period.

One key to making control systems work is the establishment of clear procedures for monitoring performance. Naturally, management should not be burdened with such control procedures unless the goals are important enough to justify such reporting. Most managers have seen, for example, elaborate accident reports that took hours of management time, and that reported, "All is well." To minimize paperwork, such reports could be limited to exceptions.

At The University of Maryland, to cite one example, all faculty are required to report daily on whether or not they performed their regular duties. This report is designed to measure sick leave. The paperwork could be cut by 98 percent or better if faculty merely reported sick days rather than every day. Many companies have similar examples where there is too much reporting of trivial details and too little reporting of significant performance results. To assure a free flow of communication on performance results versus standards, the number of elements measured should be kept to a minimum; those elements measured must be written; and management must provide feedback to those reporting that action is being taken on deviations.

DIRECTING

After the plans are made, the organization designed, and the standards established, managers must direct the workers in activities to meet the goals and objectives of the organization. Directing involves giving assignments, explaining routines, clarifying policies, and providing feedback on performance.

All managers, from top managers to first-line supervisors, direct employees. The process of directing is quite different, however, at the various levels of the organization. The top managers are concerned with the broad overview of where the company is heading. Their immediate subordinates are middle managers who are responsible, in turn, for directing workers to meet company objectives. The directions of top managers to subordinates, therefore, are characteristically broad and open-ended. The farther down the corporate ladder, the more specific the manager's directions become. First-line managers allocate much of their time to giving specific, detailed instructions to employees.

Getting others to achieve organizational goals and objectives requires motivating employees to do the necessary work. We will discuss various ways of motivating employees in Chapter 15. Right now, we want to look at another, related role that many managers perform—leading.

LEADERSHIP

In 1987, *Fortune* magazine said that mere management is not enough anymore. What was needed, it said, were executives who can transform organizations and create the corporate future. It called these new managers leaders because they had to do more than manage. Leaders are supposed to:[8]

1. Have a vision and rally others around that vision. Rather than manage, the leader is supposed to be openly sensitive to the concerns of followers, give them responsibility, and win their trust. Donald Povejsil, the vice president of corporate planning at Westinghouse, said this about vision:

   > Ten years ago I believed the key to strategy was tightly reasoned analysis of markets and competitors. My thinking has really been turned on its head. I have come to believe that the entrepreneurial vision, the visionary part of the process, is what's most important.[9]

2. Establish corporate values. These values include a concern for employees, for customers, and for the quality of the products the company makes. When companies set their goals today, they are going beyond just business goals and are defining the values of the company as well. Levi Strauss, for example, uses words such as empowerment, honesty, and teamwork in

The best workers in the world still need leadership to set goals and values. A brilliant orchestra leader blends the sounds of many different musicians into a beautiful concert. That is the role a top manager plays in a firm.

their goal statement. The overall goal at Levi Strauss reads, "We want satisfaction from accomplishments and friendships, balanced personal and professional lives, and to have fun in our endeavors."[10] The values expressed here are ones we can all share.

3. Emphasize corporate ethics. This means an unfailing demand for honesty and an insistence that everyone in the company get a fair shake. That is why we have stressed ethical decision making throughout this text.

4. Not fear change, but embrace it and create it. The most important job may be to transform the way the company does business so that it is more effective and efficient.

Management, as we said earlier, is the process used to accomplish organizational goals through planning, organizing, directing, and controlling people and other resources. Leadership is more than that. **Leadership** involves creating a vision for others to follow, establishing corporate values and ethics, and transforming the way the organization does business so it is more effective and efficient. Managers work within organizational boundries. Leaders set those boundries and constantly change the organization to meet new challenges.

Today's excellent corporations, more often than not, are reflections of their leaders. The leaders of successful corporations have had a vision of excellence and have led others to share that vision. Walt Disney's leadership can still be seen in Disney amusement parks and movies. J. Willard Marriott, Sr., and other Marriotts have also created a corporate culture that spells excellence in their hotels and restaurants.

leadership
Creating a vision for others to follow, establishing corporate values and ethics, and transforming the way the organization does business so it is more effective and efficient.

Leadership Styles

Nothing has challenged researchers in the area of management more than the search for the "best" leadership traits, behaviors, or styles. Thousands of studies have been made just to find leadership *traits;* that is, characteristics that make leaders different from others. Intuitively, you would conclude about the same thing that the researchers found; the research findings were neither statistically valid nor reliable. You and I know that some leaders seem to have traits such as good appearance and tact while others appear unkempt and abrasive.

Just as there is no one set of traits that can describe a leader, there is no one best style of leadership. Let's look briefly at a few of the most commonly recognized leadership styles.

Autocratic Autocratic leadership involves making managerial decisions without consulting others, and implies power over others. Many businesspeople who are sports leaders seem to use rather successfully an autocratic leadership style that consists of issuing orders and telling players what to do. Motivation comes from threats, punishment, and intimidation of all kinds. Such a style is effective in emergencies and when absolute followership is needed (for example, on army maneuvers).

Bureaucratic Bureaucratic leadership is based on inflexible routine supported by rules, regulations, and policies. Government organizations and government-like organizations seem to prosper by using bureaucratic leadership. That is, they have rules to cover almost everything, and most employees live by the rules. There is little flexibility in such organizations and unique situations often cause indecision and paralysis among the employees.

Bureaucratic leadership calls for many rules and regulations. In fact, almost all leadership calls for some rules. For example, this photo shows reminder signs for health workers to follow the rules about washing hands.

Democratic   Democratic leadership consists of managers and employees working together to make decisions. Many new, progressive organizations are highly successful at using a democratic style of leadership where traits such as flexibility, good listening skills, and empathy are dominant.

Laissez-Faire   Laissez-faire leadership involves managers setting objectives and employees being relatively free to do whatever it takes to accomplish those objectives. In certain professional organizations, where managers deal with doctors, engineers, and other professionals, the most successful leadership style is often one of laissez-faire or free-rein leadership. The traits needed by managers in such organizations include warmth, friendliness, and understanding.

Employee Controlled   Employee-controlled leadership consists of having employees set objectives, and management handling administrative matters. Organizations with highly independent professionals (such as professors in colleges and universities) often find it appropriate to use an employee-controlled leadership style in which the employees make the decisions. Managers perform administrative tasks and must demonstrate tact, adaptability, and intelligence.

Which leadership style is the best? Observation will tell you that successful leadership depends largely on who is being led and in what situations. We will discuss this further in the next section. Take a break now to answer the Progress Check questions.

PROGRESS CHECK

- What is the difference between strategic, tactical, operational, and contingency planning?

- Why would organizations today be less concerned about strategic planning? What has become of even greater concern? Could strategic planning get in the way of an organization being flexible enough to respond to market changes?

- What does *Fortune* say are some of the characteristics of leadership today that make them different from traditional managers?

- What kind of leadership style do you think you would use in a business situation?

When to Use Various Leadership Styles

participative management
Management style that involves employees in setting objectives and making decisions; democratic and laissez-faire leadership are forms of this type of management. See p. 343.

Research supports the idea that effective leadership depends on the people being led and the situation. It also supports the notion that different leadership styles, ranging from autocratic to employee controlled, may be successful depending on the people and the situation. Figure 11–5 depicts a continuum of leadership styles.

In fact, any one manager may use a variety of leadership styles depending on whom he or she is dealing with and the situation. A manager may be autocratic but friendly with a new trainee; democratic with an experienced employee who has many good ideas that can only be fostered by a manager who is a good listener and

FIGURE 11–5   A continuum of leadership styles.* Leadership styles range from manager-
                                controlled decision making to employee-controlled decision making.

AUTOCRATIC	BUREAUCRATIC	DEMOCRATIC	FREE REIN LAISSEZ-FAIRE	EMPLOYEE CONTROLLED
Issue orders Manager decides, employee follows orders	Manager decides and sets up rules to enforce decisions; employee follows rules	Employees participate in decision making. May decide by committee	Manager sets goals and employees function somewhat independently	Employees set goals and make decisions. Managers handle administrative matters

DOMINANT MANAGERIAL TRAITS

AUTOCRATIC	BUREAUCRATIC	DEMOCRATIC	FREE REIN LAISSEZ-FAIRE	EMPLOYEE CONTROLLED
Decisiveness Dominance Aggressiveness Self-assurance Intelligence Initiative	Stability Strength of conviction Deliberateness Persistence	Sociability Flexibility Cooperativeness Judgment Insight Communicativeness Openness Friendliness Empathy	Empathy Understanding Integrity Judgment Sense of direction Vision Trust Warmth Friendliness	Responsiveness High ethics Tact Popularity Adaptability Intelligence Flexibility

WHERE EFFECTIVE AT TIMES

AUTOCRATIC	BUREAUCRATIC	DEMOCRATIC	FREE REIN LAISSEZ-FAIRE	EMPLOYEE CONTROLLED
Military battlefield	Government Maximum security prison	Progressive corporations	Research labs Engineering High-tech firms	Colleges

*This table is meant to illustrate different styles and traits and is not descriptive of any particular manager. It gives you a feel for the wide range of managerial styles that may be effective in various situations.

HOW FAR CAN YOU GO WITH PARTICIPATIVE MANAGEMENT?

Participative management involves employees in setting objectives and making decisions; democratic and laissez-faire leadership are forms of participative management.

Some firms have had difficulty implementing participative management because some managers hesitate to give up what they feel are their rights. That includes, as they perceive it, the right to be bossy, to tell others what to do, and to punish them if they don't. It certainly does not mean working with people as partners. "Why call me a boss if I am just another worker?" is their attitude. Such people must be fired if the organization is to develop the teamwork that is necessary to compete in today's changing environment.

On the other hand, some managers have welcomed participative management with open arms and have gone much further than imagined in implementing the concept. For example, Frederick Schaltz, Jr., is president of Delta Land Surveying and Engineering, Inc. At least once a year, he asks his 23 employees to vote on such issues as bonuses, tardiness penalties, choice of insurance, and dress codes. One year, moonlighting was ruled out by a vote of 18 to 5. Employees are expected to ban smoking, although Shaltz is a smoker. After each vote, the decision or rule is entered in a company *Blue Book*. The *Blue Book* provides a framework for constructive decision making, fosters teamwork, and eliminates divisive complaining. Mr. Schaltz says he is intent on having his workers as involved in the business as possible.

Source: "Managing People: The Blue Book," *Inc.*, January 1988, p. 84.

RULES OF LEADERSHIP

THE 12 GOLDEN RULES OF LEADERSHIP

1. *Set a good example.* Your subordinates will take their cue from you. If your work habits are good, theirs are likely to be, too.
2. *Give your people a set of objectives and a sense of direction.* Good people seldom like to work aimlessly from day to day. They want to know not only what they're doing but why.
3. *Keep your people informed* of new developments at the company and how they'll affect them. Let people know where they stand with you. Let your close assistants in on your plans at an early stage. Let people know as early as possible of any changes that'll affect them. Let them know of changes that won't affect them but about which they may be worrying.
4. *Ask your people for advice.* Let them know that they have a say in your decisions whenever possible. Make them feel a problem is their problem, too. Encourage individual thinking.
5. *Let your people know that you support them.* There's no greater morale killer than a boss who resents a subordinate's ambition.
6. *Don't give orders.* Suggest, direct, and request.
7. *Emphasize skills, not rules.* Judge results, not methods. Give a person a job to do and let him or her do it. Let an employee improve his or her own job methods.
8. *Give credit where credit is due.* Appreciation for a job well done is the most appreciated of "fringe benefits."
9. *Praise in public.* This is where it'll do the most good.
10. *Criticize in private.*
11. *Criticize constructively.* Concentrate on correction, not blame. Allow a person to retain his or her dignity. Suggest specific steps to prevent recurrence of the mistake. Forgive and encourage desired results.
12. *Make it known that you welcome new ideas.* No idea is too small for a hearing or too wild for consideration.

Make it easy for them to communicate their ideas to you. Follow through on their ideas.

THE 7 SINS OF LEADERSHIP

On the other hand, these items can cancel any constructive image you might try to establish.

1. *Trying to be liked rather than respected.* Don't accept favors from your subordinates. Don't do special favors trying to be liked. Don't try for popular decisions. Don't be soft about discipline. Have a sense of humor. Don't give up.
2. *Failing to ask subordinates for their advice and help.*
3. *Failing to develop a sense of responsibility in subordinates.* Allow freedom of expression. Give each person a chance to learn his or her superior's job. When you give responsibility, give authority, too. Hold subordinates accountable for results.
4. *Emphasizing rules rather than skill.*
5. *Failing to keep criticism constructive.* When something goes wrong, do you tend to assume who's at fault? Do you do your best to get all the facts first? Do you control your temper? Do you praise before you criticize? Do you listen to the other side of the story?
6. *Not paying attention to employee gripes and complaints.* Make it easy for them to come to you. Get rid of red tape. Explain the grievance machinery. Help a person voice his or her complaint. Always grant a hearing. Practice patience. Ask a complainant what he or she wants you to do. Don't render a hasty or biased judgment. Get all the facts. Let the complainant know what your decision is. Double- check your results. Be concerned.
7. *Failing to keep people informed.*

Source: "To Become an 'Effective Executive,' Develop Leadership and Other Skills," *Marketing News,* April 1984, p. 1.

flexible; and laissez-faire with a trusted, long-term supervisor who probably knows more about operations than the manager does. To summarize:

- There is no such thing as leadership traits that are effective in all situations, nor are there leadership styles that always work best.
- Different styles of leadership can be used effectively, ranging from autocratic to employee controlled; which style is most effective depends on the people and the situation.
- A truly successful leader has the ability to use a leadership style most appropriate to the situation and the employee involved.

Leadership depends on followership, and followership depends on the traits and circumstances of the follower. In general, though, one could say that good leaders tend to be flexible, able to identify with the goals and values of followers, good communicators, sensitive to the needs of others, and decisive when the situation demands it. The box called Rules of Leadership discusses 12 golden rules and 7 sins of leadership. See if you agree with them.

THINKING IT THROUGH

Do you see any problems with the new, more participative managerial style? Do you think it will be adopted by football teams? It is already practiced by some baseball teams. What is the difference between football and baseball players, what they do, and how they are managed? How does that relate to the business world?

Can you see a manager getting frustrated when he or she cannot be bossy? Can someone who is trained to give orders (for example, a military sergeant) be retrained to be a participative manager? What problems may emerge? What kind of boss would you be? Do you have evidence to show that?

PROGRESS CHECK

■ Can you explain the differences between autocratic and democratic leadership styles?

■ What are the five steps in the control process?

TASKS AND SKILLS AT DIFFERENT LEVELS OF MANAGEMENT

Anyone who has ever played a sport such as basketball, football, or soccer knows there is a tremendous difference between being an excellent player and an excellent coach (manager). Often a good player will volunteer to coach the neighborhood team and is a disaster as a manager. The same thing happens in business. Few people are trained to be managers. Rather, the process of becoming a manager is similar to the sports example. A person learns how to be a skilled accountant or salesperson or production line worker, and because of his or her skill, is selected to be a manager. The tendency is for such managers to become deeply involved in showing others how to do things, helping them, supervising them, and generally being very active in the operating task.

The further up the managerial ladder a person moves, the less such skills are required. Instead, the need is for people who are good planners, organizers, coordinators, communicators, morale builders, and motivators. Figure 11–6 (see page 346) shows that a manager must have three categories of skills:

1. Technical skills.
2. Conceptual skills.
3. Human relations skills.

Let's pause here to clarify the terms:

■ **Technical skills** involve the ability to perform tasks of a specific department such as selling (marketing) or bookkeeping (accounting).

■ **Conceptual skills** refer to a manager's ability to picture the organization as a whole and the relationship of various parts to perform tasks such as planning, organizing, controlling, systems development, problem analysis, decision making, coordinating, and delegating.

■ **Human relations skills** include leadership, motivation, coaching, communication, morale building, training and development, help and supportiveness, and delegating.

technical skills
Ability to perform tasks of a specific department (such as selling or bookkeeping).

conceptual skills
Ability to picture the organization as a whole and the relationship of various parts.

human relations skills
Ability to lead, communicate, motivate, coach, build morale, train, support, and delegate.

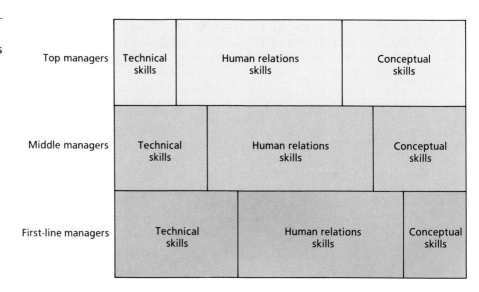

As you look at Figure 11–6, you will notice that first-level managers need to be skilled in all three areas. Most of their time is spent on technical and human relations tasks (assisting operating personnel, giving direction, and so forth). First-level managers spend little time on conceptual tasks. Top managers, on the other hand, need few technical skills. Instead, almost all their time is devoted to human relations and conceptual tasks. One who is competent at one level of management may not be competent at higher levels, and vice versa. The skills needed are different at different levels.

Spend some time reviewing the definitions of conceptual and human relations skills that are so important to top management. Note that delegating is in both conceptual and human relations definitions. Another one of the key managerial tasks is decision making. Because of their importance, we shall explore both delegating and decision making in more detail.

Delegating

delegating
Assigning authority and
accountability to others and
letting them do the job
while retaining responsibility
for results.

The most difficult task for most managers to learn is **delegating** (assigning authority and accountability to others and letting them do the job while retaining responsibility for results). Remember, managers are usually selected from those who are most skilled at doing what the people they manage are doing. The inclination is for managers to pitch in and help or do it themselves. Of course, this keeps workers from learning and having the satisfaction of doing it themselves.

Managerial skills such as decision making, motivating, and morale building are usually much more important than technical skills, but managers are not often as well trained in these important areas.

rational decision-making model
Consists of six steps:
(1) define the problem,
(2) determine and collect
needed information,
(3) develop alternatives,
(4) decide which ethical
alternative is best, (5) do
what is indicated, and
(6) determine whether the
decision was a good one and
follow up.

Decision Making

Decision making is choosing among two or more alternatives. It sounds easier than it is in practice. In fact, decision making is the heart of all the management functions: planning, organizing, controlling, and directing. The **rational decision-making model** is a series of steps managers should follow to make logical, intelligent, and well-founded decisions. These six steps are:

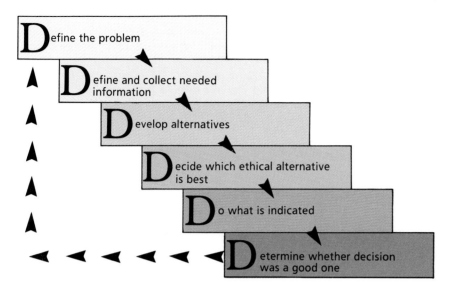

FIGURE 11–7
The rational decision-making model.
An important step in the decision-making process is to choose the best *ethical* alternative. Other alternative's may generate more money, but would be immoral or improper in some way. After an evaluation is made of the decision, the whole process begins again.

1. Define the problem.
2. Describe and collect needed information.
3. Develop alternatives.
4. Decide which ethical alternative is best.
5. Do what is indicated (implement solution).
6. Determine whether the decision was a good one and follow up (see Figure 11-7).

The best decisions are based on sound information. That is why this is known as the information age. Managers often have computer terminals at their desks so they can get internal records and external data of all kinds. But all the data in the world cannot replace a manager who is creative and makes brilliant decisions. Decision making is more an art than a science. It is the one skill most needed by managers in that all the other functions depend on it.

MANAGERS ARE NEEDED EVERYWHERE

One of the exciting things about studying management is that it prepares you for a career in any organization. Managers are needed in schools, churches, charities, government organizations, unions, associations, clubs, and all other organizations. Naturally, an important need for managers is in business.

When selecting a career in management, a student has several decisions to make:

- What kind of organization is most attractive? That is, would you like to work for government, business, or some nonprofit organization?
- What type of managerial position seems most interesting? A person may become a production manager, a sales manager, a personnel manager, an accounting manager, a traffic (distribution) manager, a credit manager, and so on. There are dozens of managerial positions from which to choose.
- What type of industry appeals to you—computer, auto, steel, railroad, or what? Would you prefer to work for a relatively new firm or an established one?
- What courses and training are needed to prepare for various managerial careers? Only careful research will answer this question.

LEARNING MANAGERIAL SKILLS

Now that you have examined what managers do and some of the new managerial styles demanded by tomorrow's organizations, we can look at the skills you will need to be a good manager. In general, it's a good idea to take as many courses as you can in speech, writing, computers, and human relations. In all managerial jobs, there are the skills that are in greatest demand. Naturally, you will also have to develop technical skills in your chosen area. Figure 11–8 lists the five skills you will need to develop your managerial potential: writing skills, verbal skills, computer skills, human relations skills, and technical skills.

Verbal Skills

The bulk of your duties as a manager will involve communicating with others. You will have to give talks, conduct meetings, make presentations, and generally communicate your ideas to others. To prepare for such tasks, you should take speech courses and become active in various student groups. Become an officer so that you are responsible for conducting meetings and giving speeches. You may want to join a choir or other group to become comfortable performing in front of others.

Half or better of communication is skilled listening. A good manager mingles with other managers, workers, and clients. He or she listens to recommendations and complaints and acts on them. Active listening requires the asking of questions and feeding back what you have heard to let others know you are truly interested in what they say.

FIGURE 11–8

Managerial potential. If you find yourself needing improvement in any of these areas, it is a good idea to take courses or read books to improve yourself. The best time to do this is *before* you go to work so you are fully prepared when you go job hunting.

Evaluating your managerial potential

Skill needed	Excellent	Good	Fair	Need work
Verbal skills				
Writing skills				
Computer skills				
Human relations skills				
Other technical skills				

Writing Skills

Managers must also be able to write clearly and precisely. Much of what you want others to do must be communicated through memos, reports, policies, and letters you must write. Organizations everywhere are complaining about the inability of many college graduates to write clearly. If you develop good writing skills, you will be miles ahead of your competition. That means you should take courses in grammar and composition. Volunteer to write term papers, even if they are not assigned. To learn to write, you must practice writing! It helps to write anything: a diary, letters, notes, and so on. With practice, you will develop the ability to write easily—just as you speak. With this skill, you will be more ready for a career in management.

Computer Skills

The office of the future will be an office full of computers. Memos, charts, letters, and most of your other communication efforts will involve the computer. When you are practicing writing, practice on a typewriter or word processor. The truly efficient manager of the future will be able to compose on a word processor and send messages electronically throughout the world. To prepare for such an environment, you can begin by taking a course or two in keyboarding. You will not need many advanced computer courses. The new software will make computer use relatively easy, but you will have to know what software is available and how to use it.

Human Relations Skills

A manager works with people, and that means that good managers know how to get along with people, motivate them, and inspire them. People skills are learned working with people. That means you should join student groups, volunteer to help at your church (temple) and local charities, and get involved in political organizations. Try to assume leadership positions where you have the responsibility for contacting others, assigning them work, and motivating them. Good leaders begin early by assuming leadership positions in sports, community groups, and so on.

One of the important skills you will need for a management position in the future is computer skills. You can learn such skills while in school by using a word processing program to prepare your papers. You may also want to take a computer course.

CAREER INFORMATION: MANAGERS

JOB OUTLOOK

Employment of salaried managers and administrators is expected to increase faster than the average for all occupations through the mid-1990s as business operations become more complex.

Employment of managers generally changes along with employment in the industries in which they work. Much faster than average growth is expected in the employment of managers in many service industries—for example, business services, including computer and data processing as well as personnel supply services; miscellaneous services, including accounting, auditing, and bookkeeping services.

Industries in which faster than average growth in the employment of managers is expected include wholesale trade in nondurable goods, food stores, electrical and electronic machinery and equipment manufacturing, and apparel and accessories stores.

EARNINGS

Managers tend to earn more than workers in other occupations. Earnings vary widely by occupation, employer, and level of responsibility. As in most fields, large employers tend to pay higher salaries than small employers, and earnings are higher in major metropolitan areas than in rural areas.

Management trainees may start at salaries not much higher than those of workers they supervise, whereas salaries of executives may be several times larger. Top-level managers in large corporations—among the highest paid workers in the country—can earn 10 times as much as their counterparts in small firms. Many corporate executives earn over $2 million a year. Most managers in the private sector receive additional compensation in the form of bonuses, stock awards, and cash-equivalent fringe benefits such as company-paid insurance premiums and use of company cars.

SOURCES OF ADDITIONAL INFORMATION

General information about managerial functions, training programs, and career development is available from: American Management Association, Management Information Service, 135 West 50th St., New York, N.Y. 10020; and National Management Association, 2210 Arbor Blvd., Dayton, Ohio 45439.

Source: *Occupational Outlook Handbook*, U.S. Department of Labor.

Be aware of how others react to you, and if you cause negative feelings or reactions, learn why. Don't be afraid to make mistakes and upset others. That is how you learn. But do learn how to work with others. Ask your friends what you could do to be a more effective and attractive leader.

In the future, managers will have to learn how to deal effectively with people from many different cultures. Many of tomorrow's workers will be Hispanic, Asian, or from some other culture. Managers will also be asked to work overseas. The more skilled you can become in other languages now and in working with diverse cultural groups, the better off you will be when you become a manager.[11]

Technical Skills

To rise up through the ranks of accounting, marketing, finance, production, or any other functional area, you will have to be proficient in that area. Therefore you should begin now to choose some area of specialization. You may start with a liberal arts education to practice your oral, written, and human relations skills. But to rise to top management, you might supplement that knowledge with an M.B.A. (Masters in Business Administration) or some similar degree in government, economics, or hospital administration. More and more students are going on to take advanced degrees. About 60 percent of top managers have taken courses beyond the bachelor's degree. The most common areas of technical expertise among top managers are marketing, finance, production, law, and engineering, in that order.

Management will be discussed in more detail in the next few chapters. Let's pause now, review, and do some exercises. Management is doing, not just reading.

PROGRESS CHECK

■ What skills do supervisors need more of than do top managers, and vice versa?

■ What are the six Ds of decision making?

■ What are the five skills you should be working on now to become a good manager later?

SUMMARY

1. Many managers are changing their approach to corporate management.
   ■ What reasons can you give to account for these changes in management?
   The four major reasons for management changes are: (1) global competition, (2) deregulation, (3) accelerating technological change, and (4) the threat of takeover.
   ■ Can you describe the changing role of managers?
   Managers are now being trained to lead, guide, and coach employees rather than boss them. The trend is toward working with employees as a team to meet organizational goals.

1. Explain how and why the role of managers is changing in the 1990s.

2. Management has been described as the art of getting things done through people.
   ■ What are the four functions of management?
   Management is the process used to pursue organizational goals through: (1) planning, (2) organizing, (3) directing, and (4) controlling.

2. Identify the four functions of management.

3. The planning function involves the process of setting objectives to meet the organizational goals.
   ■ What is the difference between goals and objectives?
   Goals are broad, long-term achievements that organizations aim to accomplish; whereas objectives are specific, short-term tasks that must be completed to reach the goals.
   ■ What are the three types of planning and how are they related to the organization's goals and objectives?
   Strategic planning is *broad, long-range* planning that outlines the *goals* of the organization. *Tactical planning*, on the other hand, is *specific, short-term* planning that lists organizational *objectives. Contingency planning* involves developing an alternative set of plans in case the first set doesn't work out.

3. Distinguish between goals and objectives; between strategic, tactical, and contingency planning; and explain the relationships of goals and objectives to the various types of planning.

4. Managers develop a framework that illustrates the relationship of workers, tasks, and resources.
   ■ What is this framework or chart called and what are the three major levels of management illustrated on the chart?
   The organization chart pictures who reports to whom and who is responsible for what task. It illustrates the top, middle, and first-line management levels.

4. Describe the significance of an organization chart and explain the role of each management level in the corporate hierarchy.

5. The control function of management involves measuring employee performance against objectives and standards and taking corrective action if necessary.
   ■ What are the five steps of the control function?
   Controlling incorporates the following: (1) setting clear standards, (2) monitoring and recording performance, (3) comparing performance with plans and standards, (4) communicating results and deviations to employees, and (5) taking corrective action if necessary.
   ■ What qualities must standards possess in order to be used to measure performance results?
   Standards must be specific, attainable, and measurable.

5. Summarize the five steps of the control function of management.

6. The directing function of management involves giving assignments, explaining routines, clarifying policies, and providing feedback on performance.
   ◾ How does the directing function vary at different levels of management?
      The farther down the corporate ladder, the more specific the managers' directions become. First-line managers spend a great deal of their time giving very specific, detailed instructions to their subordinates. On the other hand, top managers direct middle managers who require only broad, general directions.
7. Executives today must be more than just managers; they must be leaders as well.

   ◾ What is the difference between a manager and a leader?
      A manager sees that the organization runs smoothly and that order is maintained. A leader does this and more. A leader has vision and inspires others to grasp that vision, establishes corporate values, emphasizes corporate ethics, and does not fear change.
   ◾ Describe the various leadership styles.
      See Figure 11–5 for a continuum of leadership styles ranging from manager-controlled to employee-controlled decision making.
   ◾ Which leadership style is best?
      The best (most effective) leadership style depends on the people being led and the situation.
8. Managers must be good planners, organizers, coordinators, communicators, morale builders, and motivators.

   ◾ What skills must a manager have in order to be all these things?
      Managers must have three categories of skills: (1) *technical skills* (ability to perform tasks such as bookkeeping or selling), (2) *conceptual skills* (ability to see organization as a whole and how all the parts fit together), and (3) *human relations skills* (ability to communicate and motivate).
   ◾ Are these skills equally important at all management levels?
      The skills needed are different at different levels. Top managers rely heavily on human relations and conceptual skills and rarely use technical skills, while first-line supervisors need strong technical and human relations skills and use conceptual skills less often. (See Figure 11–6.)
9. Now that you have examined what managers do, you may be considering a career in management.

   ◾ What skills should you be developing now to help you become a better manager in the future?
      You will need to develop five skills to sharpen your managerial potential: (1) verbal skills, (2) writing skills, (3) computer skills, (4) human relations skills, and (5) technical skills.

GETTING INVOLVED

1. Discuss the merits of working as a manager in government, business, and nonbusiness organizations. To learn the advantages of each, talk to managers from each area and share what you learn with the class.
2. Talk with local managers and find out what they spend the most time doing. Is it planning, organizing, controlling, or directing? Or some entirely different, other task, like paperwork? Which tasks are most interesting to do; which are hardest? Which would you most enjoy? Discuss results with class.

3. Discuss the advantages of not becoming a manager. Do managers or workers seem to enjoy better lifestyles? Discuss.

4. Go through *Forbes, Fortune, Inc.*, and other business journals and read about managers. How much do they make? (See *Business Weeks* annual survey.) How many hours do they work? Do they earn their pay? Discuss.

5. Review Figure 11–5 and discuss managers you have known or read about who have practiced each style. Which did you like best? Why? Which were most effective? Why? Which would *you* most like to be? Why?

6. Recall all of the situations where you have worked under a manager. How well did he or she delegate? Did the manager assign tasks and give you freedom to work or not? How did you feel about that? Discuss those feelings and the importance of learning to delegate.

CASE ONE   IN SEARCH OF EXCELLENCE

In the 1980s, the most popular book on management was called *In Search of Excellence*. It was on the best-seller list for over a year. Clearly, managers saw in it some advice worth taking. The authors visited many of the top firms in the United States to find out what made them different; better than the other firms. They were searching for excellence. Their findings support what you have read in this book thus far. Basically, excellent organizations insisted on top quality. They cared for their customers. They listened to their employees and treated them like adults. They emphasized human creativity over analysis and high-tech tools. The following are the eight attributes of successful firms.

1. *A bias for action.* "Do it, fix it, try it" was one slogan. The idea is to get on with it and not try to analyze decisions to death. If someone has a new idea, try it and see what happens. Remain flexible. "Ready. Fire. Aim. Learn from your tries. That's enough."

2. *Close to the customer.* Excellent companies listen to their customers intently and regularly. They then provide unparalleled quality, service, and reliability. "Probably the most important management function . . . is staying close to the customer to satisfy his needs and anticipate his wants." In this text, that was called "Find a need and fill it."

3. *Autonomy and entrepreneurship.* Excellent companies encourage risk taking and support good tries. "Make sure you generate a reasonable number of mistakes." The key to remaining competitive is innovation, and the way to assure innovation is to support the creative thinkers in the firm. "No support systems, no champions. No champions, no innovations."

4. *Productivity through people.* Basically, this was support for participative management. Treat employees like adults. Seek their input. Treat them as the primary source of productivity gains. "Many of the best companies really do view themselves as an extended family."

5. *Hands on, value driven.* A belief in doing the best, in the importance of details, in superior quality and service, in the importance of informality to enhance communication, and in economic growth and profits.

6. *Stick to your knitting.* Do what you are good at. That is, don't acquire businesses that you don't know how to run. Do one thing well rather than many things in a mediocre way.

7. *Simple form, lean staff.* Keep the organization form simple. Keep staff positions to a minimum. This is the KISS formula: Keep it simple, Sam!

8. *Simultaneous loose-tight properties.* Establish a strong corporate culture emphasizing quality, service, and excellence and then delegate authority to let the people do it.

Soon after the book came out, Tom Peters wrote a new book called *Thriving on Chaos*. It emphasized the point that there is no such thing as an excellent company—there are only companies that maintain their excellence by adapting quickly to market changes. The secret to *staying* excellent is to:

1. *Become a niche-oriented market creator*, finding new, small markets and meeting their needs with short production runs. This comes very close to making custom-designed products for individual buyers.
2. *Change the structure of the organization* to have fewer layers of management. This allows the firm to adapt to consumer needs more quickly.
3. *Be responsive and adaptive* and be fast in making such changes.
4. *Be internationalist*, even if you are a small firm. The big markets are in other countries.
5. *Keep the organization small* so it can be flexible and if the organization is large, keep individual units small and semiautonomous so they can be flexible and adapt quickly.
6. *Involve employees in managerial decision making* and let them share in the profits.

DECISION QUESTIONS

1. The book *In Search of Excellence* was based on excellent companies, but some began losing market share in the 1980s and forced Tom Peters to write a new book. Given the changes he recommended, what were the problems companies were having that made them lose their excellence?
2. Almost all the changes recommended in *Thriving on Chaos* have to do with making firms faster in responding to changes in the market and more aware of international markets. What happened in the late 1980s that called for such responsiveness?
3. What managerial style or styles are advocated in these books? Why are such styles more advantageous today?
4. Most of the changes recommended *In Search of Excellence* were managerial changes. The changes recommended in *Thriving on Chaos* were mostly organizational changes. What does that tell you about the managerial needs for the 1990s?

Source: Thomas J. Peters and Robert H. Waterman, Jr., *In Search of Excellence* (New York: Harper & Row, 1982); and Thomas J. Peters, *Thriving on Chaos* (New York: Alfred A. Knopf, 1988).

CASE TWO **ONE–MINUTE MANAGING**

Many managers do not seem to have mastered the art of praising their employees so that workers feel their accomplishments are recognized. Because of this, a very popular book in the 1980s was one called *The One Minute Manager*. It was a how-to book on creating a feeling of achievement, responsibility, growth, and recognition among employees. The book was short and easy to read, but the message was strong and useful. Here is what the book said.

The way to praise employees such that they feel recognized is:
- Tell employees ahead of time that you are going to let them know how they are doing (good or bad).
- Praise employees immediately (look for a good thing to say); this only takes a minute.
- Tell them specifically what they did right.
- Tell them how good you feel about what they did and how it helps the organization.
- Encourage them to do more of the same.
- Shake hands or touch employees to show your support. (A touch on the shoulder is the idea.) The personal touch is important.

The way to instill feelings of achievement, responsibility, and growth is to encourage employees to:
- Agree on some specific goals.
- Write out the goals in less than 250 words.
- Read the goals carefully.
- Take a minute periodically to review results as compared to goals.

Clear goals give employees a feeling of responsibility, and meeting those goals creates a feeling of achievement and growth. If employees get off track, a one-minute reprimand is in order. This is, reprimand immediately; be specific about what they did wrong; tell them how you feel; touch them for reassurance; remind them of their value; tell them you know they are good workers, but not in this instance; and drop the matter (no further consequences).

DECISION QUESTIONS

1. How would you feel if at least once a day you were given one minute of praise for something you were doing well? Does that help explain the popularity of the book? Would it motivate you?
2. All of this book is really common sense. Why would managers pay to read what they already know intuitively? Is it one thing to know, another to do?
3. What is your reaction to the one-minute reprimand?
4. What is your reaction to the idea of touching employees whenever you praise or reprimand them to show support?

"One of these days we're going to have to get organized," the saying goes. True enough. Businesses today are not just "getting organized," they are going through major reorganizations. Why? Companies got so big during the 1960s, 1970s, and 1980s that management became very difficult. The idea today is to make firms smaller by breaking them up into smaller divisions. All of this and more is discussed in Chapter 12.

LOOKING AHEAD

TOTAL PERFORMANCE, BODY AND SOUL.

DODGE DAYTONA SHELBY. Its power over the road is absolute. 174 intercooled turbocharged horsepower, connected to a 5-speed Getrag gearset. Its reactions are quick, thanks to a performance suspension and vented 4-wheel disc brakes. It has our exclusive 7 year or 70,000 mile Protection Plan* and driver air-bag restraints. And with bold, all-new aerodynamic ground effects styling, it is nothing short of electrifying. The 1989 Daytona Shelby. Designed for total performance. Body. And soul. **7/70**

 Dodge

THE NEW SPIRIT OF DODGE
THE PERFORMANCE DIVISION OF CHRYSLER MOTORS

*See this powertrain limited warranty & its restrictions at dealer.   *BUCKLE UP FOR SAFETY.*

ORGANIZING A BUSINESS

12

Lee Iacocca

PROFILE   LEE IACOCCA OF CHRYSLER

When *Forbes* published the list of the 25 highest-paid executives of 1985, Lee Iacocca was number one. His compensation was over $11 million. Few would deny that Iacocca is the most controversial manager of the 1980s. His autobiography, *Iacocca,* was on the best-seller list for months. Its publisher says that it is one of the best-selling nonfiction books in history. Followers encouraged him to run for president of the United States. What made Lee Iacocca so famous?

First of all, Iacocca is known as a great manager. Lee went to Lehigh University, where he majored in engineering. Then he spent a year at Princeton working toward a master's degree. He began selling trucks for Ford. He was so good that he moved up through the sales ranks until he became marketing manager.

His biggest accomplishment at Ford was his promotion of the Ford Mustang. He made the covers of both *Time* and *Newsweek* because of his automotive marketing expertise. He became Ford's president in 1970.

On November 3, 1978, the Detroit Free Press had two headlines: "Chrysler Losses Are Worst Ever," and "Lee Iacocca Joins Chrysler." The company had lost $160 million in the third quarter. When Iacocca took over, Chrysler had 32 vice presidents and communication among them was poor. Tremendous management changes were needed fast, and financial controls were also badly needed.

Iacocca began restructuring Chrysler. He cut his salary to $1 per year. He cut executive salaries, and union workers accepted pay cuts also. Chrysler began building better cars and Iacocca appeared on Chrysler's television commercials and said, "If you can find a better car, buy it." Stressing quality, Iacocca began selling more cars, paid back the government, and earned Chrysler a $2.4 billion profit.

Basking in the light of his new-found TV fame, Iacocca let Chrysler slip in new-product development. Too much attention to cutting costs early in the 1980s and too little attention to international competition in the late 1980s forced Chrysler to restructure to become more competitive. The auto group was given *two* presidents: one for marketing and new-car design and one for production. Managers of individual car lines were given more responsibility for developing new models. In other words, restructuring is a continual process at Chrysler as it is at all modern, adaptive organizations. It is now structured to compete in the 1990s with Honda, GM, Ford, and its other competitors.

Many years from now, when people look back at the career of Lee Iacocca, what they are most likely to remember is his magnificent job of reorganizing Chrysler when many felt the company was bound to fail. It is difficult to manage a company effectively if it is not organized in a way that makes communication and cooperation possible. This chapter is about the function of organizing, which is a key management responsibility.

Sources: Kurt Andersen, "A Spunky Tycoon Turned Superstar," *Time,* April 1, 1985; and Alex Taylor III, "Iacocca's Time of Trouble," *Fortune,* March 14, 1988, pp. 79–88.

THE IMPORTANCE OF ORGANIZATIONAL DESIGN

Lee Iacocca's experience at Chrysler is being repeated in corporate offices throughout the United States. Top executives are looking at how their firms are organized and are changing their organizations to make them more efficient. One of the key questions of the 1990s is whether or not business organizations in the United

Hewlett-Packard operates smaller, people-oriented plants. That is the trend today, even for large firms. Smaller units are simply more responsive and are able to create more cohesiveness among employees.

States will be able to adapt to new international competition and become more responsive to new consumer demands.

The implication of this question is that America's huge corporations—IBM, USX (formerly U.S. Steel), General Motors, Ford, AT&T, General Electric, Westinghouse, and so on—may simply be too big and cumbersome to adapt to changing markets. Certainly, the trouble AT&T has had in adjusting to new competition from MCI and other, smaller telephone companies indicates that there may be serious problems in the near future as large organizations are challenged by newer, smaller, more flexible firms. In short, reorganization is one of the main managerial issues of this era. Generally, the move is toward smaller, more responsive units.

- General Electric's Aircraft Engine Group changed from *two* mammoth complexes to *eight* smaller "satellite" plants. You learned in Chapter 11 that, overall, the company has eliminated over 100,000 workers.
- AT&T shut down many of its large assembly lines at its Western Electric subsidiary (now called AT&T Technologies, Inc.) and put in smaller, automated facilities to make more specialized products. It has shed some 66,000 staffers in four years.[1]
- S. C. Johnson & Son, Inc. (consumer goods) divided its 1,200-person work force into four smaller groups.
- Bethlehem Steel began hacking away at its 89,000-person work force in 1980 and by the end of 1987 had chopped it in half and then some to 33,400.[2]

The problem with some large organizations is that communication among units and among managers is simply too slow and complex. Kollmorgen Corporation, for example, produces printed circuit boards, industrial motors, and other industrial goods. Its main competitors are small mom-and-pop operations. This is how John Endee, division president, described the company's situation:[3]

> The problem was that by the time our salesman in the field conferred with his regional sales manager, who would then confer with the division sales manager, who then went to manufacturing to schedule the order, "Pop" had the boards made and delivered to the customer.

To meet the efforts of smaller competitors, Kollmorgen created five separate product groups, each with a manager to oversee his or her own sales force and production capacity. Kollmorgen learned that it is difficult to get things done quickly in large organizations. This is especially true of very large organizations such as the government.

The importance of organizational design, therefore, is that the survival of many firms depends on the creation of more responsive organizations. Particular attention must be given communication, employee morale, and manageability. **Manageability** means that the organization is set up such that everyone knows who is responsible for everything that must be done, who reports to whom, what to do when problems arise, and so forth. You should be getting a feel for what organization design is, now that you know what manageability means. **Organizational design** is the establishment of manageable groups of people who have clear responsibilities and who know how to accomplish the objectives of the organization and the group.

Actually, learning about organizational design should come rather easily to you. You have been following the principles of organization all of your life. Take, for example, a game of baseball. Someone has to pitch, someone else catches, others play the bases, outfield, and so on. Each person knows what his or her function is (after some coaching), and the team works together to accomplish some goal (winning the game). As the game gets more sophisticated, you may add a first-base coach, a third-base coach, and others who advise the players on what to do.

Sometimes the organization becomes so formal, so structured, that the game is not as much fun. All the decisions are left to managers. The team may work efficiently, but it may lose the enthusiasm, the creativity, and the esprit de corps that makes winners out of even mediocre players. The questions then become, "How much structure should there be? How much decision making should be centralized with the managers? How much freedom should the players have to bat, to steal bases, and to try different positions?" What you know from experience about organizations is this:

- An organization is a group of people working together to accomplish a goal.
- The structure and formality of an organization affects the morale and enthusiasm of the people in the organization.

You may not be as familiar with the following terms, but understanding them is essential to understanding the role of managers in organizations:

- **Authority** is the right to make decisions and take action.
- **Responsibility** means that when a person is given a task to do, he or she has an obligation to do it.
- **Accountability** is the requirement that individuals in an organization, when using their authority to carry out their responsibilities, must accept the consequences of their actions (good or bad) and report those actions to their immediate supervisor.

Figure 12–1 shows the relationship of authority, responsibility, and accountability in the organizational hierarchy. Now that you understand the importance of organizational design, let's look briefly at a few of the recent organization trends.

Understanding Organizational Trends

It is easier to understand what is happening in organizations if you can relate those changes to your own life. For example, it is easier to understand why organizations are getting smaller by remembering some of your experiences with large organiza-

---

manageability
Capability of everyone in the organization to know who is responsible for what, who reports to whom, and what to do when problems arise.

organizational design
The establishment of manageable groups of people who have clear responsibilities and who know how to accomplish the objectives of the organization and the group.

authority
The right to make decisions and take actions.

responsibility
The obligation of a person to complete a given task.

accountability
Requirement that workers accept the consequences of their actions and report those actions to their immediate supervisor.

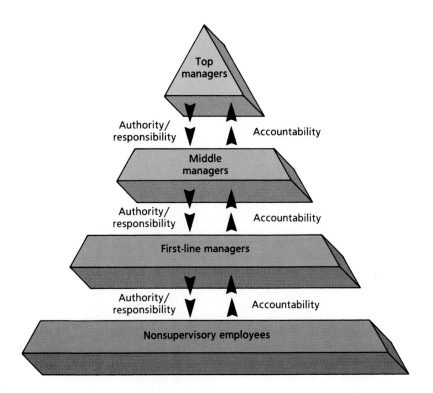

Authority/responsibility

Accountability

Authority/responsibility

Accountability

Authority/responsibility

Accountability

FIGURE 12–1

The delegation process. Along with *authority* and *responsibility* comes *accountability*. Top managers can delegate authority and responsibility to lower-level managers, but they are still accountable for results. All responsibility cannot be delegated, therefore. Similarly, nonsupervisory employees are accountable to their supervisors who, in turn, are accountable to their managers and so on up the line. Problems occur when a manager tries to delegate responsibility without delegating the needed authority.

Just as sororities create a feeling of camaraderie, involvement, and oneness, small working units in businesses create a warmer, friendlier atmosphere. Organization is the function that creates those workable units.

tions. One of the decisions high school students must make if they are going on to college is the choice between a large university or a smaller, more intimate school.

Many students prefer the smaller school, where they can get to know the other students and where they are more than just another number. They feel they would get "lost" in a big, impersonal university. On the other hand, some students choose to go to a big school. When there, they find that there are many small social groups they can join to get that feeling of being part of a small, meaningful group. They do this by joining a fraternity, sorority, professional club, political group, religious group, or whatever. The point is that often people do not feel comfortable in large, impersonal groups. They want to feel that they *belong*, and that someone knows they are there and *cares*. They get that feeling by joining small, intimate groups. Have you experienced that?

MERGER MANIA

It may seem contradictory to you to read in this book that the trend in organization design is toward smallness when you read in newspapers that big businesses are merging to become even bigger. From 1984 to 1987, there were an average of 2,733 mergers a year. That trend continued through the end of the 1980s.

The reasons for buying businesses include the need for diversification, the relatively low cost of businesses in the 1980s, the increased use of bonds as a tool for raising funds to acquire firms, and more. None of these reasons is directly related to the best size of an organization for managerial purposes. Big firms often reorganize after an acquisition to make the separate organizations more manageable. In other words, a large firm can be reorganized into a series of smaller firms. That is exactly what is happening today. Bigness is good for financial and other

reasons. Smallness is good for managerial reasons. There is no reason why a firm can't have both: a large organization and smaller, more manageable divisions.

The evidence is overwhelming, however, that restructuring unprofitable units makes them more efficient. The idea is to "Cut costs and management layers, make decisions at the bottom, get closer to customers, and help managers buy stock so they share rewards and risks." The breakup of Allied-Signal shows what happens when units of a large firm are separated and made into smaller, more focused units: Fisher moved from a $99 million loss to a $99 million profit; Wheelabrator moved from plus $10 million to plus $93 million in profit; and General Chemical from plus $4 million to plus $87 million in profit. In general, takeovers seem to cut overhead and increase profitability.

Source: Warren Brookes, "Anti-Takeover Anti-Competitiveness," *The Washington Times*, March 7, 1988, p. D4; Tom Peters, "The Key to Turnaround: Think Small!" *The Washington Times*, November 6, 1987, p. D2; and Frank R. Lichtenberg, "Takeovers Slash Corporate Overhead," *The Wall Street Journal*, February 7, 1989, p. A24.

The same feelings occur in the business world. Employees usually prefer to work in small, cohesive units where people work together, know each other, and cooperate in a common cause. The trend toward small business in many ways reflects the advantages of small units: camaraderie, involvement, flexibility, intimacy, and a feeling of oneness.[4]

Like big universities, big businesses often suffer from too much bureaucracy, too many people to manage and keep track of, and too little clear responsibility for decision making. The idea that "big is better" has shifted to "small is beautiful" in the 1990s. The idea has been to reduce the size of units to make them more responsive to the market and more motivated because of group cooperation and commitment. In other words, many businesses have created the equivalent of fraternities and sororities (that is, small homogenous units) where employees work together on projects. This is how the trend toward smallness was discussed in the business best-seller *In Search of Excellence:*[5]

> The point of smallness is that it induces manageability and, above all, commitment. A manager really can understand something that is small. . . . More important, even in institutions that employ hundreds of thousands of people, if the divisions are small enough or if there are other ways of simulating autonomy, the individual still counts and can stand out. We asserted earlier that the need to stick out, to count as an individual is vital. We simply know no other way individuals can stick out unless the size of units—divisions, plants, and teams—is of human scale. Smallness works. Smallness *is* beautiful. The economic theorists may disagree, but the excellent companies' evidence is crystal clear.

THINKING IT THROUGH   Business is finding that "Small Is Beautiful." How might this idea apply to government? Could some national government programs be handled better on a state or local basis? Is there any evidence of that happening?

Have you joined any smaller groups in your college such as a fraternity, sorority, or professional society? What has that taught you about the benefits of having small groups within large organizations?

MAKING ETHICAL DECISIONS

One of the consequences of restructuring organizations in the United States is that many people are being fired. GE alone laid off 100,000 workers. Other large firms are making similar cuts in both workers and managers (see Case 2 at the end of this chapter).

Some firms, such as IBM, are restructuring also, but top management has a commitment to employees to minimize layoffs. Therefore, IBM keeps moving people to different departments if necessary to avoid letting them go. Recently, *Business Week* wrote an article called "How IBM Cut 16,200 Employees—without an Ax." This article described how IBM used normal attrition through retirement, early retirement, and retraining to minimize the need for layoffs. Some 3,700 production workers, for example, are being trained to be programmers and 4,600 others are learning to be sales agents or customer consultants.

It is necessary to restructure American firms to make them more competitive with foreign producers, but it is not necessary to fire workers and managers whenever they do not live up to your expectations and bring in new ones. As you saw in the Profile of Jack Welch of GE, that can lower morale and create stress and fear in the organization.

What is the moral and ethical thing for a top executive to do when faced with the prospect of firing hundreds of thousands of workers? Recently, there was some debate whether or not companies should notify employees and managers 60 days before a plant closing. What is the ethical decision here and why? Do top managers have a greater responsibility to stockholders or to employees? What if the two interests conflict? Should a firm not restructure if it causes massive layoffs? What would be the long-run consequences if all firms did that?

Source: Aaron Bernstein, "How IBM Cut 16,200 Employees without an Ax," *Business Week*, February 15, 1988, p. 98; "The Battle for Corporate Control," *Business Week*, May 18, 1987, pp. 102–7; and Jesus Sanchez, "Kraft to Lay Off 250 as Result of Recent Merger," *Los Angeles Times*, January 17, 1989, p. 2 of Part IV.

No company better illustrates the need for good organization than Boeing. You can see from the picture how large the production area is. Many projects are being worked on at once, and management needs to create the right organizational design to get the projects completed on time.

Big Is Not Necessarily Bad

One should not conclude from what is happening in the business world today that big is necessarily bad. There are advantages to bigness that are important. Large firms usually have access to funds that they can allocate to the most profitable units. In an article called "Big Can Still Be Beautiful," *Fortune* magazine says this about America's successful large firms:[6]

> Such companies possess "size, scope, and management," the three qualities that Alfred Chandler, the noted business historian at the Harvard University business school, asserts were essential to the triumph of American industry in the past. They remain essential to corporate success today.

Most of the large firms in the United States are not successful just because they are large. Rather, they have reorganized so that they are made up of several smaller, more efficient units that are responsive to the market, but have the support of a large firm behind them. GE is one example of a successful large firm. Boeing is another. It is not whether a firm is large or not that counts. Rather, it is how well the firms are managed. And how well a firm is managed depends greatly on the organization structure. Theodore Levitt notes that some things can only be done by large organizations. "Who's going to be the general contractor to the moon or build a massive pipeline in Alaska?" he asks. The answer is a well-structured big corporation.[7]

The main purpose of this chapter is to discuss principles of organization such as the notion that companies function better when the operating units are small and manageable. There are other, similar organizational decisions that are just as important, for example: How many people should report to one manager? How much authority and responsibility should be delegated to lower-level managers and workers? Organizational structure is critical to the creation of morale, commitment, and overall employee/manager satisfaction. To help you understand the principles managers use to design organizations, we will begin with a brief review of the history of organizational development. Such a review will give you a better feel for the reorganization that is going on today.

ORGANIZATION THEORY

Until very recently in history, most organizations were rather small, the processes for producing goods were rather simple, and organization of workers was fairly easy to do. Not until the 20th century and the introduction of mass production did business organizations grow complex and difficult to manage. The bigger the plants, the more efficient production became, or so it seemed. The concept was called **economies of scale.** This means that the larger the plant, the more efficient it could be because all the employees could specialize in a function they could do efficiently. The problem is that managers began to think that bigger was better in all organizations. That's how some companies got too large to be efficient.

It was in this period that organization theorists emerged. In France, Henri Fayol published his book *Administration Industrielle et Générale* in 1919. It was popularized in the United States in 1949 under the title *General and Industrial Management*. Max Weber (pronounced *Vayber*) was writing organization theories in Germany about the same time Fayol was writing his books in France. Note that is was only about 40 years ago that organization theory became popular.

> **economies of scale**
> Efficiency resulting from employee specialization created in large plants.

Fayol's Principles of Organization

Fayol introduced "principles" such as:

- *Unity of command.* Each worker was to report to one, and only one, boss. The benefits of this principle are obvious. What happens if two different bosses give you two different assignments? Which one should you follow? To prevent such confusion, each person is to report to only one manager.
- *Hierarchy of authority.* Fayol suggested that each person should know to whom they should report and managers should have the right to give orders and expect others to follow.
- *Division of labor.* Functions were to be divided into areas of specialization such as production, marketing, finance, and so on.
- *Subordination of individual interests to the general interest.* Workers were to think of themselves as a coordinated team and the goals of the team were more important than the goals of individual workers.
- *Authority.* Managers have the right to give orders and the power to exact obedience. Authority and responsibility are related: Whenever authority is exercised, responsibility and accountability arises.

- *Degree of centralization.* The amount of decision-making power vested in top management should vary by circumstances. In a small organization, it is possible to centralize all decision-making power in the top manager. In a larger organization, however, decision-making power should be delegated to lower-level managers and employees on both major and minor issues.
- *Clear definition of communication channels.*
- *Order.* Materials and people should be placed and maintained in the proper location.
- *Equity.* A manager should treat employees and peers with kindness and justice.
- *Esprit de corps.* A spirit of pride and loyalty should be created among people in the firm.

Management courses in colleges throughout the world taught these principles, and they became synonymous with the concept of management. Organizations were designed so that no person had more than one boss, lines of authority were clear, and everyone knew to whom they were to report. Naturally, these principles tended to become rules and policies as organizations got larger. That led to more rigid organizations and a feeling among workers that they belonged to a *system* rather than a group of friendly, cooperative workers joined together in a common effort.

Max Weber and Organizational Theory

Weber used the term *bureaucrats* to describe middle managers whose function was to implement top management's orders. His book *The Theory of Social and Economic Organizations* was introduced to the United States in the late 1940s. Weber's concept of a **bureaucratic organization** basically consisted of three layers of authority: (1) top managers who were the decision makers, (2) middle managers (the bureaucracy) who developed rules and procedures for implementing the decisions, and (3) workers and supervisors who did the work.

It was Weber, then, who promoted the pyramid-shaped organization structure that became so popular in large firms. It is seen in Figure 12–2. Weber put great

bureaucratic organization
Organization with three layers of authority: (1) top managers who make decisions, (2) middle managers who develop procedures for implementing decisions, and (3) workers and supervisors who do the work.

FIGURE 12–2

Bureaucratic organization structure.
This chart shows Weber's concept of a bureaucratic organization, one with clear lines of authority and several layers of management.

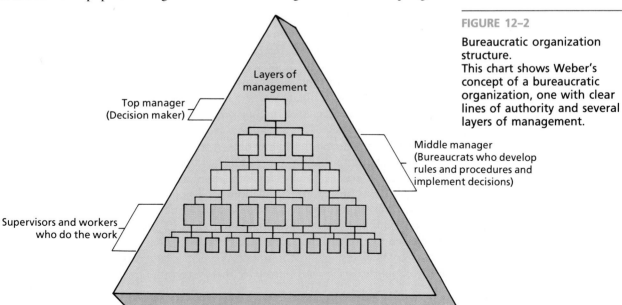

BUREAUCRACY AT UPS

United Parcel Service (UPS) is a firm that delivers small packages. It competes with firms such as Federal Express, Purolator, and the U.S. Postal Service. Competition is stiff, so UPS has to be very efficient. One way to achieve such efficiency is through bureaucracy.

UPS is run strictly, with many rules and regulations. There are safety rules for all levels of employees, and strict dress codes are enforced. Other rules cover the cleanliness of trucks and buildings. Each manager has bound copies of policy books and is expected to follow them.

UPS also keeps careful records. Daily worksheets that specify performance goals and work output are kept on every employee and department. Daily employee quotas and achievements are accumulated weekly and monthly with the help of computers.

The other half of UPS's efficiency results from automation. It has 100 mechanized hubs that can sort 40,000 packages per hour. UPS handles 6 *million* packages a day. With such precision necessary, there's little room for deviation from set practices. How could managers at UPS minimize the problems that could be caused by such a rigid work structure? Would you enjoy working in such a setting?

Source: Richard L. Daft, *Organizations: Theory and Design* (St. Paul, Minn.: West Publishing, 1983), pp. 129–49.

This UPS sorting center shows the need for rules and regulations. Safety rules and cleanliness rules must be followed or the sheer volume of business would create chaos.

trust in managers and felt that the firm would do well if employees simply did what they were told. The less decision making employees had to do, the better. Clearly, this is a reasonable way to operate if you are dealing with uneducated and untrained workers. Often, those were the only workers available at that time. Today, however, most firms feel that workers are the best source of ideas and that managers are there to facilitate workers rather than boss them around. This is not true at all firms, however (see the box on Bureaucracy at UPS).

Weber's principles of organization were similar to Fayol's. In addition, however, Weber emphasized the following:

- Job descriptions. Every job was to be outlined in detail and written down.
- Written rules, decision guidelines, and detailed records.
- Consistent procedures, regulations, and policies.
- Staffing and promotions based on qualifications.

You can thank Weber when you go to a store or government agency and have trouble getting things done because the clerk says, "That's not company policy," or "I can't do that; it's against the rules." Weber felt large organizations demanded clearly established rules and guidelines that were to be followed precisely. Overzealous enforcement led to inflexibility and insensitivity to customer needs. Although the word *bureaucrat* did not have any negative connotations as used by Weber, the *practice* of establishing rules and procedures became so rigid that *bureaucracy* has become almost a nasty name for an organization with many managers that seem to do nothing but make and enforce rules. Have you had troubles at the Bureau of Motor Vehicles or other organizations run bureaucratically?

Together, Fayol and Weber introduced organizational concepts such as (1) unity of command (one employee, one boss); (2) division of labor (specialized jobs); (3) job descriptions; (4) rules, guidelines, procedures, and policies; (5) clear lines of authority and communication; (6) placement of materials and people in some established order; (7) establishment of departments; (8) detailed record-keeping; (9) establishment of an esprit de corps or feeling of enthusiasm and devotion to the firm; and (10) assignment of a limited number of people to each manager (limited span of control). You can see the obvious benefits of such concepts. What is needed today is a way to implement those concepts while still maintaining freedom and incentives for employees to work productively on their own.

The Contributions of Joan Woodward

Managers began the process of applying the principles outlined by Fayol and Weber in their organizations, but how did the principles work in practice? One of the more important studies of that question was made by Joan Woodward and her associates. Woodward studied 100 English industrial firms between 1953 and 1971 to see if there was any relationship between how an organization was structured, the technologies it used, and its success. Success was measured by the net income of the corporation (profit) and by increases in market domination.

What Woodward found was that there is no one best way to organize a corporation. Rather, the structure depends greatly on the technical complexity of the company's production process. **Technical complexity** is the degree to which machines are used in the production process rather than people. A firm that uses a lot of labor rather than complex automated equipment (for example, the making of custom-made furniture) seemed most successful using flexible and responsive management. However, a firm using complex automated technology (for example, an automobile assembly line) was more successful with a more bureaucratic form of organization. The moral of the story is that the structure of organizations change as technologies change.

technical complexity
The degree to which machines are used in the production process rather than people.

PROGRESS CHECK

- What were some of the reasons organizations became large and what are some of the drawbacks to large firms?

- Can you name four of Fayol's principles and show how they link with Weber's principles?

- Did Woodward conclude that one organizational design was superior to others in all situations?

DESIGNING ORGANIZATIONS

Because of organizational specialists like Joan Woodward, managers have learned to adapt their organizations to meet competition and the needs of the market. At first, the division of labor led to **departmentalization** of firms. That is, firms had separate departments for manufacturing, engineering, finance, and marketing. Today, most companies use an organization chart to illustrate the relationships of departments with each other. An *organization chart* is a visual picture of an organization that shows who reports to whom. The top of the organization charts of departmentalized firms looks like the illustration below.

The tendency was to construct organization charts that looked like pyramids. Many workers reported to a group of supervisors, who reported to plant managers, who reported to regional managers, who reported to national managers, who reported to vice presidents, who reported to the president, who reported to the chairman of the board. Such a complex organization called for many rules, guidelines, and procedures. In other words, it took many years to *implement* the organizational principles outlined in the late 1940s. During the 1950s and 1960s, there was much discussion about delegating authority, developing appropriate "managerial styles," and dealing with unions and other complications in the system. The goal seemed to be to get bigger by any means, including the purchase of other firms. Organization charts grew more complicated and complex. It wasn't until the late 1970s that management began the process of *reorganizing* firms, making them smaller, less complex, and more efficient. That process continues today. National and international competition forced these changes. We shall now discuss some of the organizational issues that have resulted, including:

> An organization chart is really only a piece of paper . . . that identifies a chain of command of people and functions. True management begins only when you put all these people together, functioning together, in a vital, human interrelationship so that the company performs as a single team, driving onward toward the goals set by the chief executive.
> **HAROLD GREENE**, former president and CEO of ITT.

1. The issue of tall versus flat organizations structures.
2. The issue of span of control.
3. The issue of departmentalization.
4. The issue of centralization versus decentralization.

Tall versus Flat Organization Structures

As organizations got bigger, some began adding layer after layer of management, sometimes resulting in a dozen or more managerial steps in firms such as General Motors. Such organizations had what are called **tall organization structures.** What this means, simply, is that the organization chart would be quite tall because of the various levels of management. The organizational structure of the army is an example of how tall an organization can get. There are many layers of management

Functional organization. The top of a functionally oriented organization chart. Large organizations prospered in the past because of a division of labor. That division is reflected in departmentalization—the assigning of different functions to different departments. This chart shows a typical breakdown of functions.

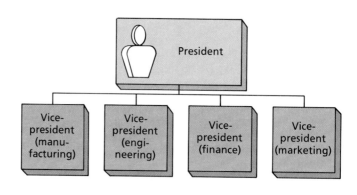

between a private and a general (e.g., sergeant, lieutenant, captain, major, colonel). You can imagine how a message may be distorted as it moves up through so many layers of management.

Business organizations tended to take on the same style of organization as the military. The organizations were divided into regions, divisions, centers, and plants. Each plant might have several layers of management. The net effect was a huge complex of managers, management assistants, secretaries, assistant secretaries, supervisors, trainers, and so on. Office workers were known as *white-collar workers*, as opposed to the *blue-collar workers* who worked on the assembly line. As you can imagine, the cost of keeping all these managers and support people was quite high. The paperwork they generated was unbelievable, and the inefficiencies in communication and decision making became intolerable.

The development of small computers is helping to bring more efficiency to white-collar operations. But, more importantly, the trend is to eliminate white-collar positions, including several layers of management:[8]

- Dana Corporation cut its corporate staff from 500 in 1970 to about 100 in the 1980s.
- Acme Cleveland Corporation cut corporate staff from 120 to 50 in just a few months.
- Ford Motor Company cut more than 26 percent of its middle-management staff and more cuts were planned—to a total of 50 percent or even 75 percent.

One reason American corporations were cutting staff is to meet the competition of foreign firms. To give you a feel for the problem, there are 5 levels of management between the chairman and first-line supervisor at Toyota, a Japanese firm. Ford has over 15 levels. Foreign firms were simply more efficient.

The trend is toward more **flat organization structures.** That is, organizations are cutting out layers of management and are expanding sideways, instead. The idea is to have many, small semiautonomous units that report to vice presidents, who report to the president. Johnson & Johnson, for example, is a $5 billion company made up of 150 independent divisions that sell over $30 million each. The divisions are called *companies*.

flat organization structures
Ones with relatively few layers of management.

One benefit of having many managers reporting to a higher-level manager is that the higher-level manager simply does not have time to get involved in the day-to-day work of the managers below. This gives lower-level managers more freedom to make changes as *they* see fit. This makes organizations more responsive and raises the morale of lower-level managers. Just how many people should report to one manager? We discuss that issue next.

Span of Control

Span of control refers to the optimum number of subordinates a manager supervises or should supervise. There are many factors to consider when determining span of control. At the lower levels, where the work is standardized, it is possible to implement a wide span of control (15 to 40 workers). However, the number should gradually narrow at higher levels of the organization because work is less standardized and there is more need for face-to-face communication. Variables in span of control include:

span of control
The optimum number of subordinates a manager should supervise.

- *Functional complexity.* The more complex the functions are, the narrower the span of control (fewer workers report to one supervisor).

Need for direction. The more subordinates need supervision, the narrower the span of control.

Need for coordination. The greater the need for coordination, the narrower the span of control.

Planning demands. The more involved the plan, the narrower the span of control.

Managerial help. The more help the superior receives, the broader the span of control (more workers can report to one supervisor).

Functional similarity. The more similar the functions, the broader the span of control.

Geographical closeness. The more concentrated the work area is, the broader the span of control.

Other factors to consider include the competence of superiors and subordinates, their degree of professionalism, and the number of new problems that occur in a day. In business, the span of control varies widely. The number of people reporting to the president may range from 1 to 80 or more.

Figure 12–3 ties together span of control and tall and flat organization structures. The tall organization with a narrow span of control might describe a lawn care service with two supervisors who manage four employees each (two of whom are more experienced). The flat structure with a wide span of control may work in a plant where all ten workers are picking crabmeat.

FIGURE 12–3
Narrow versus wide span of control.
Two ways to structure an organization with the same number of employees. The tall structure has two managers who supervise four employees each. Changing to a flat structure, the company could eliminate two managers and replace them with two more employees, but the top manager would have to supervise 10 people instead of two.

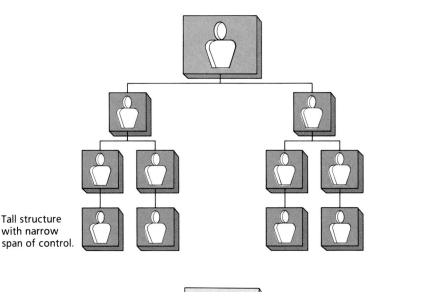

Tall structure with narrow span of control.

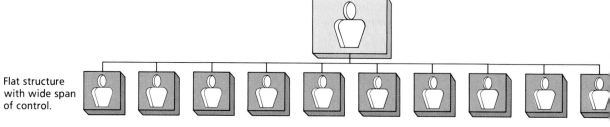

Flat structure with wide span of control.

Departmentalization

The dividing of organizational functions into separate units is called *departmentalization*. The most widely used technique for departmentalizing organization is by function. **Functional structure** is the grouping of workers into departments based on similar skills, expertise, or resource use. There might be, for example, a production department, a transportation department, a finance department, an accounting department, a marketing department, a data processing department, and so on. Such units enable employees to specialize and work together more efficiently. The advantages of such a structure include the following:

1. Skills can be developed in depth and employees can progress within a department as their skills develop.
2. It allows for economies of scale in that all the resources needed can be centralized and various experts can be located in that area.
3. There is good coordination within the function and top management can easily direct and control the activities of the various departments.

The disadvantages include:

1. The lack of communication among the different departments. For example, production may be isolated from marketing so that the people making the product do not get the proper feedback from customers.
2. Individual employees begin to identify with their department and its goals rather than the goals of the organization as a whole.
3. Response to external changes is slow.
4. People are not trained to take different managerial responsibilities; rather, they tend to become narrow specialists.

Given the limitations of this type of structure, businesses have tried various versions to overcome the limitations. Below we shall discuss some of the variations on the functional form of structure.

> **functional structure**
> Grouping of workers into departments based on similar skills, expertise, or resource use.

Different Ways to Departmentalize

Figure 12–4 (see page 372) shows five ways a firm can departmentalize. One is by *product*. A book publisher might have a trade book department, a textbook department, and a technical books department. The development and marketing processes vary greatly among such books, so each department specializes in those functions.

The most basic way to departmentalize, as we discussed above, is by *function*. This text is divided by business function because such groupings are common. Production, marketing, finance, personnel, and accounting are all distinct functions calling for separate skills.

It makes more sense in some organizations to departmentalize by *customer group*. A pharmaceutical company, for example, might have one department that focuses on the consumer market, another that called on hospitals (institutional market), and another that targets doctors.

Some firms group their units by *geographic locations*. The United States is usually considered one market area. Japan, Europe, and Korea may involve separate departments. The decision about which way to departmentalize depends greatly on the nature of the product and the customers served. A few firms departmentalize by *process* because it is more efficient to separate the activities that way. For example, a firm that makes leather coats may have one department cut the leather, another dye it, and a third sew the coat together.

FIGURE 12–4

Various ways to departmentalize.

A publisher may want to departmentalize by product, a manufacturer by function, a pharmaceutical company by customer group, and a computer company by geography (countries). A leather manufacturer may prefer departmentalization by process. In each case, the structure must fit the goals of the firm.

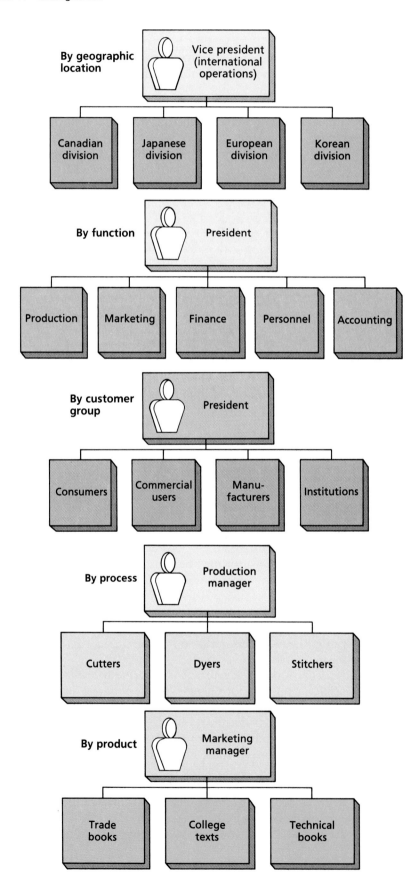

Centralization versus Decentralization of Authority

Imagine for a minute that you are a top manager for a retail company such as J. C. Penney. Your temptation may be to maintain control over all your stores to maintain a uniformity of image and merchandise. You have noticed such control works well for McDonald's; why not J. C. Penney? The degree to which an organization allows managers at the lower levels of the managerial hierarchy to make decisions determines the degree of *decentralization* that organization practices:

- **Centralized authority** means that decision-making authority is maintained at the top level of management at headquarters, or *central management*.
- **Decentralized authority** means that decision-making authority is delegated to lower-level managers who are more familiar with local conditions.

At J. C. Penney, for example, the customers in California are likely to demand clothing styles different from those in Minnesota or Maine. It makes sense, therefore, to give store managers in various cities the authority to buy, price, and promote merchandise appropriate for each area. Such a **delegation of authority** is an example of decentralized management.

On the other hand, McDonald's feels that purchasing, promotion, and other such decisions are best handled centrally. There is little need for each McDonald's store to carry different food products. McDonald's, therefore, would lean toward centralized authority.

In reality, most organizations have some degree of centralized authority and some decentralized authority. Today's rapidly changing markets, added to geographic differences in consumer tastes, tend to favor more decentralization and thus more delegation of authority. The following discussion of the Campbell Soup Company will illustrate this point.

centralized authority
Maintaining decision-making authority with the top level of management at headquarters.

decentralized authority
Delegating decision-making authority to lower-level managers who are more familiar with local conditions.

delegation of authority
Assigning part of a manager's duties to subordinates.

Organization at Campbell Soup Company

A real-life example is the best way to understand the importance of organization structure, the differences between centralized and decentralized structures, and the trend toward making firms more responsive to the market. For such an example, let's look at a company with which you are very familiar—the Campbell Soup Company. As you might imagine, Campbell was a relatively conservative company that had a few leading products. It introduced very few new products. There was almost no feeling of entrepreneurship or creativity among managers, and little freedom was allowed to explore new markets or try new ideas. Market share was declining, yet emphasis remained on production rather than marketing.[9]

In 1980, a new chief executive officer (CEO) took over. His name is Gordon McGovern. He came from Campbell's Pepperidge Farm division where he increased sales from $60 million to $300 million in five years. The previous president had an engineering background and was operations oriented. In contrast, McGovern is a progressive manager.

One of the first things McGovern did was to change the organization structure! The old structure divided the company into *two* basic groups—canned and frozen foods—based on the way the products were manufactured. Marketing, new product development, and production were all done centrally (centralized management). McGovern felt that too much power was centralized among too few people and that prevented the free flow of ideas.

Campbell makes a variety of products as this picture shows. Since the firm has decentralized, there has been more responsiveness to market changes. This means more new products designed to meet your changing needs. That includes microwavable soups.

To foster entrepreneurship and to create more incentives for creative solutions to problems, McGovern created approximately 50 *decentralized* business units (profit centers) headed by general managers, most of whom had marketing backgrounds. These managers are responsible for profits (or losses) and new product development. They also have freedom to set up marketing in their units. Internal competition among unit managers is encouraged. Each unit has its own controller and financial planning analyst. Under this *decentralized* corporate structure, each general manager acts like the president of his or her own firm. Such responsibility is accompanied by the necessary authority, freedom, and incentives to create vibrant new enterprises within the larger organization.

The overall goal of this restructuring was to make Campbell more consumer oriented, more dynamic, and more innovative. McGovern feels that the United States is not a "melting pot," but more like a stew pot in that it is a nation made up of a mixture of specialized groups that, while blended with others, still retain their own characteristics. These groups need unique marketing efforts. As you recall, this concept is called *target marketing* and is reflected in special promotions directed toward Hispanics in New York and Chicago and special promotions aimed at the upscale consumer with products like Le Menu.

The Campbell Soup Company is really an organization of organizations. There is an organization that develops and markets soups. Another organization develops frozen foods, and still others are involved with beverages, pet foods, and so forth. Each unit is like a separate team competing in a different league with different rules.

Running the organization called Soups is a general manager. Under this manager are three marketing directors: one each for condensed soups, ready-to-serve soups, and soups and special projects. Under the three directors are marketing managers and assistant marketing managers. Assisting them are advertising, accounting, finance, and manufacturing specialists. As you can see, the organization is still quite complex with many layers of management. Although Campbell retains a relatively tall organization structure, the delegation of authority has resulted in a much flatter organization structure in reality. One of the more recent structural changes has been to cut the number of staff people at headquarters.[10]

Related to the questions of tall versus flat and centralized versus decentralized organizations is the question of designing the lines of authority. Several different organization designs are possible. We shall discuss them next.

- Can you define authority, responsibility, and accountability?
- Are U.S. businesses moving toward having taller or flatter organization structures? Why?
- What are some reasons for having a narrow span of control? Is there any advantage to a wide span of control?
- What are the advantages of a centralized system of managerial decision making? What are the advantages of decentralizing decisions?

ORGANIZATIONAL TYPES

Now that we have explored the basic principles of organizational design, have learned the benefits of flat versus tall organizations, and have seen how it all comes together in the Campbell Soup example, we can explore in more depth the various ways to structure an organization to accomplish the goals we want to achieve. The three forms of organization we shall look at are: (1) line organizations, (2) line and staff organizations, and (3) matrix organizations. Figure 12–5 compares the advantages and disadvantages of each form of organization.

	ADVANTAGES	DISADVANTAGES
Line	Clearly defined responsibility and authority; Easy to understand; One supervisor for each person	Too inflexible; Few specialists to advise; Long lines of communication; Unable to handle complex questions quickly; Tons of paperwork
Line and staff	Expert advice from staff to line personnel; Establish lines of authority; Encourage cooperation and better communication at all levels	Potential overstaffing; Potential overanalyzing; Lines of communication can get blurred; Staff frustrations because of lack of authority
Matrix	Flexible; Encourages cooperation among departments; Can produce creative solutions to problems; Allows organization to take on new projects without adding to the organizational structure.	Costly and complex; Can confuse employees; Requires good interpersonal skills and cooperative managers and employees; Difficult to evaluate employees and to set up reward systems.

FIGURE 12–5

Types of organizations. Each form of organization has its own advantages and disadvantages.

Line Organizations

line organization structure
Organization in which there are direct, two-way lines of responsibility, authority, and communication running from the top to the bottom of the organization, with all employees reporting to only one supervisor.

A **line organization structure** is one in which there are direct two-way lines of responsibility, authority, and communication running from the top to the bottom of the organization, with all people reporting to only one supervisor. The most obvious example is the army, which has a clear line of authority going from general to colonel to major to lieutenant to sergeant to corporal to private. A private reports to *a* corporal, the corporal to *a* sergeant, and so on back up to the generals. A line organization has the advantages of having clearly defined responsibility and authority, of being easy to understand, and of providing one supervisor for each person. The principles of good organization design are met.

However, a line organization has the disadvantages of being too inflexible, of having few specialists or experts to advise people along the line, of having lines of communication that are too long, and of being unable to handle the complex decisions involved in an organization with thousands of sometimes unrelated products and literally tons of paperwork.

Line and Staff Systems

To minimize the disadvantages of simple line organizations, most organizations today have both *line* and *staff* personnel. A couple of definitions will help:

line personnel
Employees who perform functions that contribute directly to the primary goals of the organization.

- **Line personnel** perform functions that contribute directly to the primary goals of the organization (e.g., making the product, distributing it, and selling it).

staff personnel
Employees who perform functions that assist line personnel in achieving their goals.

- **Staff personnel** perform functions that *advise* and *assist* line personnel in performing their goals (e.g., marketing research, legal advising, and personnel). (See Figure 12–6.)

Most organizations have benefited from the expert advice of staff assistants in areas such as safety, quality control, computer technology, personnel, investing, and so forth. Such positions strengthen the line positions and are by no means inferior or lower-paid positions. It is like having well-paid consultants on the organization's payroll.

Staff usually serve an advisory function; that is, they usually cannot tell line managers *or their workers* what to do. Naturally, this can cause conflicts, in that staff experts often know more about correct procedures to follow than line managers. This can be very frustrating for staff people. In fact, different organizations handle line-staff relationships in different ways. In some organizations, line managers must *consult* with staff managers on some issues; on others, they must get staff *approval* for certain actions; and in others, staff people may actually *give orders*.

The benefits of the line and staff organization structure are rather clear. The disadvantages are not so obvious at first. Today, however, some organizations are suffering from too many staff personnel (overstaffing). To justify their existence, staff people may conduct research and generate reports that no one asks for or needs (overanalyzing). The resulting paperwork can be astounding. Lines of authority and communication can become blurred when staff people get involved in decision making (overmanaging). For example, by the time a line manager clears a decision with the legal department, the safety department, and personnel, the initial problem could have become much more serious.

As you know, the trend today is to cut staff positions or assign staff to smaller, functional units where they truly assist, rather than work independently from, line managers. Much of the attention of top managers today is focused on designing systems that enable line and staff managers to cooperate more fully and to move more quickly to respond to market changes.

Line versus line and staff organizations.   FIGURE 12–6

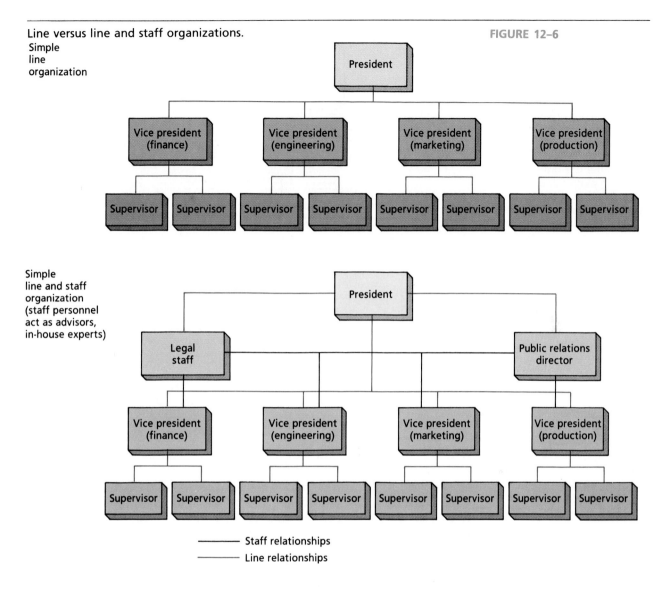

Simple
line
organization

Simple
line and staff
organization
(staff personnel
act as advisors,
in-house experts)

—————— Staff relationships
—————— Line relationships

Matrix Organizations

Both line and staff structures suffer from a certain inflexibility. Both have established lines of authority and communication and both work well in organizations with a relatively stable environment and evolutionary development (such as firms selling consumer products like toasters and refrigerators). In such firms, clear lines of authority and relatively fixed organization structures are assets that assure efficient operations.

Today's economic scene is dominated by new kinds of organizations in high-growth industries unlike anything seen in the past. These include industries such as robotics, biotechnology, and aerospace. In such industries, many new projects are developed, competition with similar projects elsewhere is stiff, and the life cycle of new ideas is very short. The economic, technological, and competitive environments are rapidly changing. In such organizations, emphasis is on new product development, creativity, special projects, rapid communication, and interdepartmental teamwork. From that environment grew the popularity of the matrix

A matrix-style organization. In a matrix-style organization, project managers are in charge of teams made up of members of several departments. In this case, project manager 2 supervises employees A, B, C, and D. These employees are accountable not only to project manager 2, but also to the head of their individual departments. For example, employee B, a market researcher, reports to project manager 2 *and* to the vice president of marketing.

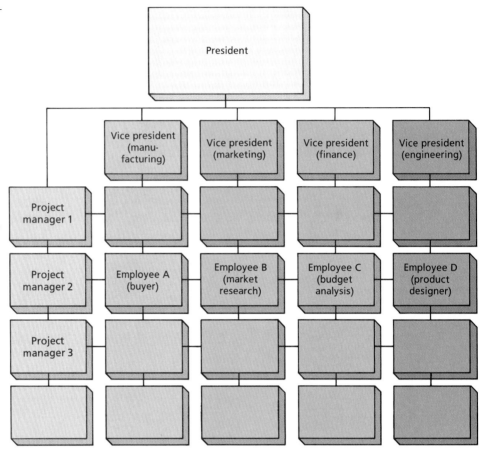

matrix organization structure
Organization in which specialists from different parts of the organization are brought together to work on specific projects but still remain part of a traditional line and staff structure.

organization. **A matrix organization** is one where specialists from different parts of the organization are brought together to work on specific projects, but still remain part of a line and staff structure (see Figure 12–7). In other words, a project manager can borrow people from different departments to help design and market new product ideas.

Matrix structures were developed in the aerospace industry at firms such as Boeing, Lockheed, and McDonnell Douglas. The structure is now used in banking, management consulting firms, accounting firms, ad agencies, and school systems. Although it works well in some organizations, it does not work in others. The advantages of a matrix structure are:

- It gives flexibility to managers in assigning people to projects.
- It encourages interorganizational cooperation and teamwork.
- It is flexible and can result in creative solutions to problems such as new product development.

The disadvantages are:

- It is complex and costly to implement.
- It can cause confusion among employees as to where their loyalty belongs—to the project manager or to their functional unit.
- It requires good interpersonal skills and cooperative employees and managers.

Departmentalization	How should departments be established—by product, by function, by customer, by process, by geographic location, or some combination of these?
Span of control	How many employees should report to each manager? (A narrow span means few people reporting; a wide span means many people reporting to one manager.)
Lines of authority	What will be the lines of authority and responsibility in the firm? What positions will be staff (support positions) and what positions will be line (directly in the chain of command)?
Delegation of authority	Should all key decisions be made by top management? What decisions should be delegated to managers and supervisors, if any?
Matrix organization formation	Who should be assigned to various committees? What authority should be given line managers to borrow employees from other areas for special committee assignments (see matrix organization discussion).
Job design	Who is responsible for doing what? How much job rotation will we have? How much specialization?
Work procedures	What are the rules and procedures of operation? What are the lines of communication?
Follow-through	Delegation without follow-through is abdication. You can never wash your hands of a task. Even if you delegate it, you are still responsible for its accomplishment.

FIGURE 12–8

Some questions to ask at various stages of organization design.

If it seems to you that matrix organizations violate some traditional managerial principles, you are right. Normally a person cannot work effectively for two bosses. (Who has the *real* authority? Which directive has the first priority—the one from the project manager or from one's immediate supervisor?) Figure 12–8 shows how decisions regarding a matrix organization fit in with other organizational decisions.

In reality, the system functions more effectively than one may imagine. Here is how it works best:

- Underlying the matrix system is traditional line and staff organization with clear and recognized lines of authority.
- To develop a new product idea, a project manager may be given *temporary* authority to "borrow" line personnel from engineering, production, marketing, and other line functions. Together, they work to complete the project and then return to their regular positions. In fact, then, they really do not report to more than one manager at a time.
- Such a system evolves easily in an organization where the informal communication system is more important than the formal organization. That is, the corporate culture encourages interaction among departments and ad hoc committees to solve problems.
- The unit of operation is small enough for such flexibility to be applied and yet everyone remains informed and clear as to relationships, goals, and procedures.

A matrix-style of organization brings together managers or employees from different functions to work on a short-term project such as a new product. Such a flexible organization style can speed up new product development.

COORDINATING WITHIN THE ORGANIZATION

One of the major goals of the matrix style of organization is to increase the communication and coordination among diverse departments. Listen to what Lee Iacocca says about the situation at Chrysler when he took over:[11]

> I couldn't believe . . . that the guy running engineering departments wasn't in constant contact with his counterpart in manufacturing. But that's how it was. Everybody worked independently.

*   *   *   *   *

> I'd call in a guy from engineering, and he'd stand there dumbfounded when I'd explain to him that we had a design problem or some other hitch in the engineering-manufacturing relationship. He might have the ability to invent a brilliant piece of engineering that would save us a lot of money. He might come up with a terrific new design. There was only one problem: he didn't know that the manufacturing people couldn't build it. Nobody at Chrysler seemed to understand that interaction among the different functions in a company is absolutely critical. People in engineering and manufacturing almost have to sleep together. These guys weren't even flirting!

If interdepartmental relationships do not appear on the organization chart, how can you be sure that communication and coordination take place? A very complex way is to set up a matrix-style organization where such interrelationships are spelled out in detail. Other, less complex ways of creating such coordination include committees, information systems, liaison people, and permanent teams.

Coordinating by Committee

One way to learn what people in other areas are doing and to communicate with them is to form a task force or committee to discuss the issues. A *task force* is the technical name given a temporary team or committee formed to solve a specific short-run problem involving several departments. The benefits of such a committee is that it can be formed relatively quickly and issues can be resolved quickly. For example, if Fiberrific experienced a problem with product tampering, a task force made up of representatives from distribution, public relations, marketing, and production could be gathered to evaluate new forms of packaging. A task force is a way of handling special projects with a wide variety of people from various areas and a way of making an organization flexible and responsive to changes.

Coordinating by Information Systems

information system
Network consisting of written and electronically based systems for sending reports, memos, bulletins, and the like.

One of the newest strategies for communicating within and among departments is to set up a computer network that links all managers. Such a network is called an **information system.** It consists of written and electronically based systems for sending reports, memos, bulletins, and the like. Such systems include electronic mail (letters sent by computer), electronic bulletin boards (notes sent by computer), and teleconferences (meetings held over two-way video networks).[12] One problem is designing software that will enable different computer systems to talk with one another. Developing such systems will be a major effort in the early 1990s. AT&T and a combination of other companies are competing to see who wins the task of networking modern firms in the future. We shall explore these systems in detail in Chapter 14.

Other Means of Coordination

Some firms have a person responsible for coordinating what goes on between or among departments. This person is called a *liaison* (pronounced lee-ay-zon). General Mills has several liaison positions at corporate headquarters to keep information flowing between headquarters and its five industry groups.

Other firms set up a permanent team made up of people from different departments who get together to solve ongoing problems. Such a team is similar to a task force or committee, but it deals with ongoing problems rather than temporary issues. Many firms use such teams to develop new products.

Remember what we are trying to accomplish with these various ways of coordinating. We want to get communication and cooperation among departments so that the whole organization can work as a unified team. If you have ever worked in a large organization, you know that often the marketing people never see, much less talk with, the people in engineering. Similarly, the people in distribution may never meet the people in marketing who are promising that they will deliver tomorrow. It doesn't take long in a large company to see how messages can get lost and that the ability to be responsive to customers can be quite difficult.

It is important for an organization to **want** to be responsive to customers and to operate as a unit. That feeling of oneness has to be established by top management. A few organizations, such as IBM and Disney, are known for their responsiveness to customers and the teamwork among employees. That teamwork (or corporate culture) is created by the top executives and may last long after the executive dies or leaves the firm. We shall discuss the creation of such a corporate culture next.

ORGANIZATIONAL CULTURE

One of the most important elements of success in any organization is the overall organizational culture (also called *organizational climate* or *corporate culture*). **Organizational culture** may be defined as widely shared values within an organization that provide coherence and cooperation to achieve common goals. Usually the culture of an organization is reflected in stories, traditions, and myths. Anyone who has been to Disneyland or Disneyworld cannot fail to be impressed by the obvious values instilled by Walt Disney that permeate the organization. One may have heard or read about the focus on cleanliness, helpfulness, and friendliness, but such stories cannot prepare you for the near-perfect implementation of those values at the parks. The workers seem to have absorbed the ideals into their very being so that they work joyfully with total attention given to the customer.

It is also obvious from visiting any McDonald's restaurant that every effort has been made to maintain a culture that emphasizes "quality, service, cleanliness, and value." Each restaurant has the same "feel," the same "look," and the same "atmosphere." In short, each has a similar organizational culture.

organizational culture
Widely shared values within an organization, reflected in stories, traditions, and myths that provide coherence and cooperation to achieve common goals.

Disney and McDonald's are two examples of corporations with favorable corporate cultures.

The corporate culture at the license bureau often seems to lack a consumer orientation. Can you think of other organizations whose corporate culture seems to create uncooperative and grumpy workers rather than friendly and helpful ones?

Disney and McDonald's are two examples of favorable corporate cultures that lead to successful operations. But an organizational culture can also be negative. Have you ever been in an organization where you feel that no one cares about service or quality? A visit to some motor vehicle licensing bureaus is often a quick lesson in negative shared values (organizational culture). The clerks may seem uniformly glum, indifferent, and testy. The mood often seems to pervade the atmosphere so that the patrons become moody and upset. There are exceptions, but you know the feeling. It gets so that one can hardly believe that an organization can be run so badly and survive, especially profit-making organizations. (Many people have written off some government agencies as hopelessly lost in bureaucratic cultures that seem anticustomer and, consequently, depressing to workers as well as customers.) Are there examples in your area?

The very best organizations have cultures that emphasize service to others, especially customers. The atmosphere is one of friendly, concerned, caring people who enjoy working together to provide a good product at a reasonable price. Those companies that have such cultures have less need for close supervision of employees, policy manuals, organization charts, and formal rules, procedures, and controls. The ideas are as follows:

- Organizational cultures are created by organizational leaders who create an atmosphere of shared values that have either a positive or negative effect on the relationships within the organization and with the various publics of the organization. A recent survey of 2,196 corporations found that 75 percent of them felt it important to redo their organizational culture.[13]
- Good organizational leaders create a culture that emphasizes cooperation and joy in serving customers, and that culture results in self-motivated employees who need minimal supervision.
- The very best companies stress high moral and ethical values such as honesty, reliability, fairness, environmental protection, and social involvement.

Thus far, we have been talking as if organizational matters were mostly controllable by management. The fact is that the *formal organization structure* is just one element of the total organizational system. To create organizational culture, the *informal organization* is of equal or greater importance. Let's explore this notion next.

What is the organizational culture at your college? Is it known for its excellence, quality, and student orientation? If not, what is it known for? How is that reflected in student attitudes, community support, and faculty attitudes? How could the culture be improved?

Informal Organization

All organizations have two organizational systems. One is the formal organization. It is the official system that details the responsibility, authority, and position of each person. Formal organization is used for baseball teams and for companies such as Campbell Soup. But there is also an informal organization. It consists of the various cliques, relationships, and lines of authority that develop outside the formal organization. The basic ideas, therefore, are these:

- A **formal organization** is the structure that details lines of responsibility, authority, and position. It is the structure that is shown on organization charts.
- The **informal organization** is the system of relationships that develop spontaneously as employees meet and form power centers. It is the human side of the organization that does not show on any organization chart.

No organization can operate effectively without both types of organization. The formal system is often too slow and bureaucratic to enable the organization to adapt quickly. However, the formal organization does provide helpful guidelines and lines of authority to follow in routine situations.

The informal organization is often too unstructured and emotional to allow careful, reasoned decision making on critical matters. It is extremely effective, however, in generating creative solutions to short-term problems and providing a feeling of camaraderie and teamwork among employees.

In any organization, it is wise to learn quickly who the important people are in the *informal* organization. There are rules and procedures to follow for using certain equipment, but those procedures often take days. Who in the organization knows how to get you the equipment immediately without following the normal procedures? Which secretaries should you see if you want your work given first priority?

There is a story about the principal of an elementary school who finds that the informal leader is the teacher of the third grade—an older, motherly, dignified professional. The principal knows the situation and doesn't make a move unless he is sure of the support of that third-grade teacher. When the principal retires and is replaced by an energetic youngster from the big city, the new principal cannot figure out why his ideas are not being implemented. He will continue to have trouble until he identifies that informal leader and learns how to enlist her support for his initiatives. That is how the informal organization works.*

The informal organization's nerve center is the *grapevine* or the system through which unofficial information flows between and among managers and employees. It consists of rumors, facts, suspicions, accusations, and all kinds of accurate and inaccurate information. The key people in the information system usually have the most influence in the organization.

formal organization
The structure that details lines of responsibility, authority, and position. It is the structure that is shown on organizational charts.

informal organization
The system of relationships and lines of authority that develop spontaneously as employees meet and form power centers; it is the human side of the organization and does not show on any formal charts.

---

* Thanks to Professor John Bowdidge of Southwest Missouri State University for this story.

In the old *we* versus *they* system of organizations, where managers and employees were often at odds, the informal system often hindered effective management. In the new, more open organizations, where managers and employees work together to set objectives and design procedures, the informal organization can be an invaluable managerial asset that often promotes harmony among workers and establishes the corporate culture. The following are some of the more important aspects of the informal organization.

1. Group Norms   Group norms are the informal rules and procedures that guide the behavior of group members. They include often unspoken but very clear guidelines regarding things like proper dress, language, work habits (e.g., how fast one works, how many breaks one takes, who one turns to for assistance, and so on), and social behavior (where one goes for recreation, with whom, how often, and more). People who deviate from the norm are often verbally abused, isolated, and harassed.

2. Group Cohesiveness   Often a work group will develop alliances and commitments over time that tie them together strongly. The term used to describe such feelings of group loyalty is *cohesiveness*. Historically, unions have been a strong cohesive force as workers united to fight management. The goal today is to generate such cohesiveness among all corporate employees to create excellence in all phases of operation. For such cohesiveness to develop, employees must feel that they are part of a total corporate team. Often, the informal network created by corporate athletic teams, unions, and other such affiliations can assist in the creation of teamwork and cooperation. In summary, the informal organization of a firm can strongly reinforce a feeling of teamwork and cooperation or can effectively prevent any such unity; managers who maintain open, honest communication with employees can create an informal atmosphere that promotes willing commitment and group cohesiveness.

As effective as the informal organization may be in creating group cooperation, it can be equally powerful in resisting management directives. Employees may form unions, go on strike together, and generally disrupt operations. Learning to create the right corporate culture and to work within the informal organization is a key to managerial success.[14]

PROGRESS CHECK

▪ What are the advantages and disadvantages of structuring an organization functionally?

▪ What are the six ways an organization can departmentalize?

▪ What are the advantages of a line and staff organization versus a pure line organization?

▪ Why would a firm use a matrix organization?

▪ What are some ways an organization can improve lateral communication and coordination?

▪ What is organizational culture? Can you cite an example?

1. Organizational design is the establishment of manageable groups of people who have clear responsibilities and who know how to accomplish the objectives of the organization and the group.

    ▪ Why is organizational design important?

    The survival of a company depends on it becoming a responsive organization. In order to be responsive it must be organized in such a way that everyone knows who is responsible for everything that must be done, who reports to whom, what to do when problems arise, and so forth.

    ▪ Explain the relationship of authority, responsibility, and accountability to the role of a manager.

    Upper-level managers pass authority (the right to make decisions and take action) and responsibility (the obligation to perform a given task) to subordinates. In turn, the subordinates are accountable to their managers. This means that they are required to accept the consequences of their actions and report those actions to their immediate supervisors.

2. One of the major movements in today's organizations, business and nonbusiness, is toward increasing efficiency and productivity. At one time, the goal was to increase organization *size*. With size came *economies of scale* and greater productivity. Over time, however, organizations in the United States tended to become too big. Communication was slow to move up and down through level after level of management. Smaller, more flexible domestic and foreign firms began to steal markets. The result was the major restructuring of organizations now occurring.

    ▪ What are some of the trends in restructuring?

    The most obvious trend is toward smallness. Large firms are breaking up into smaller, more self-sufficient (autonomous) units. Layers of middle-management positions are being eliminated. So are many staff positions (e.g., safety inspectors, advisers, analysts, etc.). This is making organization structures flatter and wider; that is, there are fewer layers of management, but more units.

3. Organization theory is the foundation for organization design. Many organizational concepts go back 40 years or more to men such as Fayol and Weber.

    ▪ What concepts did Fayol introduce?

    Fayol's principles included unity of command, division of labor, centralization of authority, and clear lines of communication.

    ▪ What was the contribution of Weber?

    Weber emphasized job descriptions, written rules, procedures, and regulations, and consistent policies. He was the father of *bureaucratic* organizations.

    ▪ What was the contribution of Joan Woodward?

    Woodward studied organizations to determine what organizational structure was most successful. She found that the kind of structure that was most effective varied by the complexity of the technology used. There was no one best way of organizing.

4. Flat organizations have certain advantages over taller organizations.

    ▪ What are flat organizations and what are their advantages compared to taller organizations?

    Flat organizations have a minimal number of management levels; thus, it is called flat since its organization chart is flat compared to organizations with many layers between the president and workers. Information flows

---

SUMMARY

1. Define organizational design and explain its importance.

2. Describe the current trends in organizational design.

3. Explain the contributions of Henri Fayol and Max Weber to organizational theory.

4. Compare the advantages and disadvantages of tall and flat organization structures.

and flexibility in tall organizations are strained. The trend is to break up firms into smaller, more autonomous, flatter units.

5. There is much discussion about the proper span of control managers should have.

5. Explain the concept of span of control.

   ▪ What does span of control mean?
   Span of control refers to the number of subordinates that report to a manager. The best number depends on the complexity of the task, the level in the organization, and other factors.

6. Departmentalization is the division of organizational functions into separate units.

6. Describe the various ways organizations can be departmentalized.

   ▪ How can organizations departmentalize?
   Companies can departmentalize by function (production, marketing, etc.), by product, by customer group, by geographic location, or by process.
   ▪ What are the advantages and disadvantages of departmentalization?
   The advantages include (1) in-depth employee skill development, (2) economies of scale, and (3) good coordination within the function. The disadvantages are (1) lack of communication between departments, (2) employees identify with department rather than with organization, (3) slow response to change, and (4) employees become narrow specialists.

7. Decision making in an organization may be centralized or decentralized.

7. Discriminate between centralized and decentralized organizations.

   ▪ What do these terms mean?
   Centralization is the extent to which decision-making power is concentrated in the hands of one or a few people. *Decentralization* means that decisions are made at lower levels of the organization. The "small is beautiful" movement not only breaks up larger corporations into smaller units, but gives those units more authority and responsibility for results.

8. There are several types of organization: line, line and staff, and matrix.

8. Compare the advantages and disadvantages of line, line and staff, and matrix organizations.

   ▪ What's the difference among systems?
   Line organizations have clear lines of authority, with each person having one boss; there are no internal staff advisers. A *line and staff organization* brings in staff personnel (advisers) in areas such as personnel, legal advising, and quality control. A *matrix organization* is one where different specialists are brought together to work on a project while maintaining positions in the line or staff. A faculty member working with a program director is an example.
   ▪ What are the advantages and disadvantages of each of these forms of organizations?
   See Figure 12–5 on page 375.

9. One of the major goals of organizations is to improve communication and coordination among diverse departments.

9. Explain the various ways organizations can coordinate activities between and among departments.

   ▪ What methods can organizations use to improve communication and coordination?
   A complex way to improve communication and coordination is to set up a matrix-style organization. Other, simpler ways include committees, information systems, liaison people, and permanent teams.

10. The key to organizational success is not just organizing, but the creation of an organizational culture that emphasizes excellence in customer service and quality.

10. Define organizational culture and describe the role of the informal organization in that culture.

   ▪ What is organizational culture?
   Organizational culture is widely shared values that help provide the coherence and cooperation needed to achieve common goals.

▪ How does a leader create such a culture?

The leader of an organization sets the tone by example. Organizational culture is then fostered through stories, traditions, and myths surrounding the leader and other top managers.

▪ What is the difference between the formal organization and the informal organization?

A *formal organization* is the structure that details lines of authority, responsibility, and position. It is what is drawn on the organization chart. The *informal organization* is the system of relationships and lines of authority that form spontaneously as employees meet and form power centers.

▪ What is the role of the informal organization?

The informal organization can create a feeling of teamwork and cooperation across departmental lines. It can also be powerful in resisting management directives. Managerial success depends on learning to create the right corporate culture and to work with the informal organization.

GETTING INVOLVED

1. There is no way to better understand the effects of having 15 layers of management on communication accuracy than to play the children's game of "Message Relay." Take 15 members of the class and have them line up. Have the first person read the following story and whisper it to number 2, who whispers it to number 3, and so on through all 15. Have number 15 tell the story out loud and compare it to the original. The distortions and mistakes are often quite humorous, but are not so funny in organizations such as Ford that *had* 15 layers of management. Here's the story:

   Dealers in the Midwest region have received over 130 complaints about steering on the new Commander and Roadhandler models of our mini-vans. Apparently, the front suspension system is weak and the ball joints are wearing too fast. This causes slippage in the linkage and results in oversteering. Mr. Berenstein has been notified, but so far only 213 out of 4,300 dealers have received repair kits.

2. Write a short description of a situation where you were frustrated because a clerk in a bank, government agency, school, or hospital followed "the rules" or "policy" to the letter and caused you much grief and lost time. Share your story with others in the class. Compare stories and then discuss strategies for minimizing such bureaucratic hassles in organizations.

3. Discuss situations in your experience either at home, at work, or in sports when you had more than one person telling you what to do and the orders conflicted. Share several such situations and discuss the principle of one employee, one boss. How many people can one person manage? Does it depend on the circumstances? Discuss.

4. Did you choose a large school or a small one for college? Why? Discuss the merits and drawbacks of being in a large organization. How does your experience apply to business?

5. No doubt you are familiar with the informal network of communication in schools, communities, and various organizations. Discuss the power of such informal groups. How can business use that power to become more productive *and* meet the needs of workers at the same time?

6. Imagine you are working for an appliance manufacturer that produces, among other things, dishwashers for the home. Imagine further that a competitor introduces a new dishwasher that uses sound waves to clean dishes. The result is a dishwasher that cleans even the worst burnt-on food and sterilizes the dishes and silverware as well. You need to develop a similar offering fast or lose the market. Discuss how a matrix form of management would help in the process.

7. If you were free to start all over, how would you organize your college or university? Would you have the same departments? What kind of staff people would you hire? How would your organization differ from the one you have? What keeps the school from adopting a more flexible, more responsive organization structure? Discuss.

CASE ONE   **READING AN ORGANIZATION CHART**

This is the organization chart for Donahue Manufacturing Company:

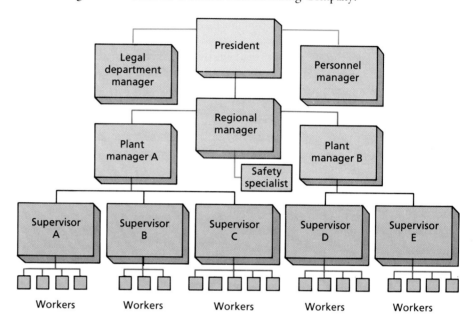

DECISION QUESTIONS

1. Which people are line managers and which are staff?
2. Which supervisor has the largest span of control? Which plant manager?
3. Would this be considered a tall or flat organization structure?
4. How many line managers are under the direct control of the personnel manager?

CASE TWO   **RESTRUCTURING HITS MANAGEMENT POSITIONS**

In the fall of 1985, AT&T announced that it was eliminating 24,000 jobs by the end of 1986. A big percentage of those jobs (30 percent) were in management. In similar fashion, United Technologies Corporation's semiconductor subsidiary laid off 2,600 of its 9,800 employees, over 20 percent of whom were managers. The list of companies with similar stories is quite long. In fact, since 1980, 89 of the 100 largest companies in the United States have reorganized to reduce the number of management levels. The result has been a loss of as many as 1.3 million middle-manager jobs since 1979. This includes a vast group of real estate managers, central purchasing agents, human resources specialists, futurologists, economists, planners, and analysts of all kinds.

W. James Fish, Ford Motor Company's personnel planning manager, says, "We're looking at a total restructuring of American business." Ford wants to cut the white-collar work force in its Ford North American Automotive Operations by 20 percent, or about 9,600 jobs, over the next five years.

Such a restructuring is inevitable in a period when competition from foreign firms is intensifying. American firms had grown fat around the middle, and needed to become "lean and mean" to be more efficient and productive. Lots of lower-level employees were being eliminated; managers logically followed.

Tom Peters, coauthor of *In Search of Excellence*, believes the staffs of the Fortune 500 companies are still hopelessly bloated despite cuts of 40 to 50 percent. Peters feels that many of those managers have their M.B.A. degree and got to top positions without ever getting real-world experience in designing, making, selling, and servicing products. They tend to rely on technology rather than people for their answers—and ignore the retraining and redeployment of the work force.

Peters recommends that managers get out of their offices and ask their workers how to make the firm more productive. Then they should visit customers to learn what they would like to see changed. Management is no longer viewed as an intellectual position involving planning, organizing, leading, and controlling. Rather it is a hands-on job where managers and employees work as a team to make the firm productive. Those who used to sit and ponder are out of there. More cuts may be coming as companies strive to become "lean and mean."

DECISION QUESTIONS

1. What does the reduction in middle-management jobs mean for tomorrow's under-graduate and graduate business students?
2. How could you, as the president of a firm, decide which managers to let go?
3. What are the advantages and disadvantages of cutting staff personnel in areas like personnel, quality control, planning, and auditing? Could there be serious consequences of rapid cutbacks in management?
4. What alternatives does a company have when it seems top heavy other than firing them all and becoming leaner and meaner in one swift action?

Sources: Cynthia Green, "Middle Managers are Sitting Ducks," *Business Week,* September 16, 1985, p. 34; Alvin P. Sanoff, "Something Is out of Whack in U.S. Business Management," *U.S. News & World Report,* July 15, 1985, p. 54; Thomas Moore, "Goodbye Corporate Staff," *Fortune,* December 21, 1987, pp. 65–72; Cindy Skrzycki, "Corporate 'Downsizing' Slows," *The Washington Post,* September 23, 1987, pp. D1 and D18; and "My Company, My Self," *Inc.,* July 1989, pp. 35–44.

So far, we have learned what customers want through *marketing*. We also know something about basic management, including how to structure organizations to accomplish our objectives. It is time, then, to begin producing products.

The problem in the past was that America's industrial base was declining. Many factories were old and obsolete, and some still are. Some foreign competitors are producing goods for less and are making high-quality goods as well. American corporations had to learn how to compete.

Chapter 13 discusses production and operations management. To regain a competitive position in manufacturing, American industry will have to improve from order processing to manufacturing, quality control, and shipping. We shall discuss how to do all that in Chapter 13. We shall discuss basic production issues first and then show how American business can recapture the industrial market.

LOOKING AHEAD

13

PRODUCTION AND OPERATIONS MANAGEMENT

LEARNING GOALS

After you have read and studied this chapter, you should be able to:

1. Describe the role of America's manufacturing base in relation to the national economy and explain the factors that are bringing renewed strength to American manufacturing.

2. Illustrate the production process and explain the importance of productivity.

3. Identify the various methods manufacturers can use to keep costs at a minimum.

4. Classify the various production processes and identify the five indicators manufacturers can use to determine the likelihood of meeting their production goals.

5. Describe the importance of materials requirement planning and discuss the benefits and problems of just-in-time inventory control.

6. Describe the changes in manufacturing processes, including the use of CAD, CAM, CAE, FMS, CIM, and enterprise networking.

7. Illustrate the use of PERT and Gantt charts in production planning.

8. Identify the steps that must occur before people and machines will be combined to revolutionize manufacturing.

9. Illustrate how today's trend toward total quality control differs from earlier attempts to control quality and relate the role of quality circles to this total quality control.

10. Suggest how the service sector might increase productivity through automation.

KEY TERMS

analytic system   p. 400
assembly process,   p. 400
computer-aided design (CAD),   p. 406
computer-aided engineering (CAE),   p. 408
computer-aided manufacturing (CAM),   p. 406
computer-integrated manufacturing (CIM),   p. 408
continuous process,   p. 400
critical path,   p. 411
flexible manufacturing systems (FMS),   p. 408
gantt chart,   p. 412
industrial park,   p. 399
intermittent process,   p. 400
just-in-time (JIT) inventory control,   p. 402

manufacturing,   p. 397
materials requirement planning (MRP),   p. 402
networking,   p. 411
open systems integration,   p. 411
PERT (program evaluation and review technique),   p. 411
process manufacturing,   p. 400
production,   p. 397
production process,   p. 396
quality circles,   p. 415
quality control,   p. 414
robot,   p. 405
synthetic systems,   p. 400
total quality control,   p. 414

J. Tracy O'Rourke

The entire industrial revolution enhanced productivity by a factor of about 100. The microelectronic revolution has already enhanced productivity in information-based technology by a factor of more than a million—and the end isn't in sight yet.
CARVER MEAD, Professor of Computer Science at California Institute of Technology

PROFILE   J. TRACY O'ROURKE, MANUFACTURING GURU

Throughout its history, the United States has had leaders in industry that kept America first in manufacturing. Henry Ford is just one example. In the early 1980s, America seemed to be losing its competitive edge. Japan's leaders were coming out with better quality cars and more attractive electronic products. New leadership was needed in the United States to show the way to success in the 1990s. One of those leaders is Tracy O'Rourke from Allen-Bradley in Milwaukee.

Allen-Bradley makes over 300,000 different items ranging in price from a few cents to a half-million dollars. As president of that firm, Mr. O'Rourke has managed to introduce the latest in high-tech equipment. Top executives from firms all over the world visit the plant to see how it is done.

What they see are polished hardwood floors. There is little dirt or noise or, more significantly, people. What there are many of are machines—machines that are run from a control room packed with computers. Mr. O'Rourke likes to point out that modern machines and computers increase productivity and that productivity leads to more jobs in distribution, sales, technological fields, and so on. The emphasis in his plants is on flexibility. Orders are placed by computer from a salesperson in the field. The machines, operating on computer instructions, make the product or part, sometimes shifting from one part to another without interrupting the production process.

Mr. O'Rourke pictures a bakery of the future as follows: There will be very few employees at the bakery. Instead, flour and other ingredients will be dumped into computerized machines at night and in the morning out will come bread, cookies, cakes, and so forth. Orders from retailers will be put into the computer, the computer will tell the mixers and ovens what to do, and the assortment of needed bakery goods will come out ready to be boxed by a robot.

Emphasis in modern plants such as Allen-Bradley is on quality and efficiency. The idea is to have no rejects and no inventory. Such plants will be able to produce products competitive with those produced anywhere in the world and will bring manufacturing leadership back to the United States. That, in turn, will create more jobs in the United States, but those jobs will be the kind that require more education than today's production workers now have. This chapter focuses on production management in the 1990s and the challenges and opportunities it presents.

Source: George Melloan, "Manufacturing's New Window of Opportunity," *The Wall Street Journal*, April 19, 1988, p. 35.

AMERICA'S MANUFACTURING BASE

The Allen-Bradley story illustrates what is happening in American industry. The changes are coming fast and furious. Some of the ideas are new and complex. Even the terminology is confusing at first. Nonetheless, this chapter is one of the more important ones in the text because it represents the future of America and, therefore, your future as well. Take some time to learn the terms and concepts. If you do not learn this base, catching up will be even harder as companies introduce new variations on the technology already here. Worldwide competition has made these changes necessary. Competition in the workplace means you have to keep up.

The heart of the free enterprise system in the United States has always been its manufacturers. Names such as General Electric, USX (formerly U.S. Steel), Westinghouse, and Navistar (formerly International Harvester) have represented the finest in production technology since the turn of the century. But, as we have learned, we are in a new era in social evolution. Today, manufacturing produces only one fourth of the U.S. gross national product. Bethlehem Steel and other manufacturing leaders from the past were in a state of decline through much of the 1980s. "The Hollow Corporation," an article in *Business Week* in 1986, said that "The U.S. is abandoning its status as an industrial power."[1] Foreign manufacturers were capturing huge chunks of the market for basic products such as steel, cement, machinery, and farm equipment.

What do those trends mean for tomorrow's college graduates? Is production and operations management a dying field? The answer is, absolutely not. Production management remains a challenging and vital element of American business. What has changed is the competitive, technological, social, and political environment. The very foundations of American business had been eroding because some manufacturers had not kept up with some foreign producers in the latest technologies. Today, all of this has changed. As you read in the Profile about Allen-Bradley, American manufacturers are now implementing the latest in technology and are competitive again with producers anywhere in the world.

The rebuilding of America's manufacturing base is likely to continue to be one of the major business issues in the near future. There will be debates about the merits of moving production facilities overseas. Serious questions will be raised about the replacement of workers with robots and other machinery. Major political decisions will be made regarding protection of American manufacturers through quotas and other free trade restrictions. Regardless of how these issues are decided, however, tomorrow's college graduates will face tremendous challenges (and opportunities) in redesigning and rebuilding America's manufacturing base. Similar changes will be occurring in the service sector.

The purpose of this chapter, therefore, is to introduce the concepts and issues in production management. You may want to visit a modern factory to experience for yourself what these new facilities look like. Would you enjoy the challenge of running such a facility? What are its advantages and disadvantages? The only way to be sure about such questions is to do your own personal research and talk to people in manufacturing. Then imagine how the same concepts can be applied in the service sector. We shall have more to say about the service sector later in the chapter.

Rebuilding the base

Even though *Business Week* published a very pessimistic article about manufacturing in 1986, by 1989 things looked much brighter. Here is how *Business Week* reported the changes:[2]

> Boosted by the depreciation of the dollar, belt-tightening from the tool room to the board room, and re-adoption of quality as a core corporate value, American manufacturing is back.

What happened to make U.S. producers stronger? Several things. Let's take them one at a time to see what it was that brought American manufacturing back to the forefront in competitiveness.

1. Dollar's Decline   *Fortune* says, "There's no question that the *dollar's decline* is the chief player in the new competitiveness drama."[3] That is, the value of the dollar relative to German marks, Japanese yen, and other foreign currencies fell dramatically during the early 1980s. That made foreign products much more expensive to American buyers and made American products much less expensive to foreign buyers. As a consequence, American producers were able to sell more overseas. American prices dropped so low that Japanese buyers were buying Japanese cars that were made in America and shipped back to Japan.

2. Productivity   A second major reason for America's renewed strength in manufacturing is its emphasis on *productivity*. Its overall factory productivity is still the highest, though Japan has passed it in such industries as autos and electronics. The United States is still the world's biggest producer in most major industries, among them aluminum, paper, aircraft, and computers.[4]

3. Lagging Labor Costs   Lagging labor costs helped regain manufacturing strength. In fact, Peter Drucker feels that low wages no longer give countries a competitive edge in winning manufacturing facilities.[5] Integrated steel mills still have blue-collar costs of 25 percent of total costs, but the "minimills" operate at blue-collar costs of 10 percent or less. This makes it possible for a manufacturer to set up production in any country, including developed countries, and still be competitive because labor makes up such a small part of the final cost of production. Thus, Japan builds manufacturing plants for autos in the United States to be close to the market and the United States does the same for other kinds of manufacturing plants.

4. Size and Efficiency   The figures in item 3 show the fourth reason why U.S. manufacturers are recovering. They are becoming *smaller and more efficient. Inc.* reports the trend as follows: "In sharp contrast to the mass-production–oriented giants of the last industrial era, the new stars of manufacturing are small, highly focused companies whose fortes are flexibility, customization, and market sensitivity. They rely neither on one product nor one customer, prefer short production runs over long, and aim for high margins rather than high volume. Productivity is invariably high."[6]

5. Restructuring   The final reason why American manufacturers are now doing well is the major *restructuring* of corporations that took place during the 1980s. Conglomerates sold off unprofitable units and began focusing more on profitable ventures. The total value of mergers in 1988 was $250 billion.[7] Those corporations that are vertically integrated—that is, they make all the parts, assemble them, and distribute them as one corporate unit—are getting rid of some functions and concentrating on the most efficient and profitable ones.[8] Firms such as automakers can now buy parts or supplies anywhere in the world and have multiple suppliers so that the most efficient suppliers can be used.

Other reasons could be cited for America's comeback in the manufacturing sector, including the increased cost of labor overseas, more effective management styles that motivate workers to be more productive, and more effective marketing internationally. What is most important for you, however, is that the U.S. remains a major industrial country and is likely to become even stronger. There are relatively few students in college today majoring in production management, inventory management, and other careers having to do with manufacturing and mining. That means more opportunities for those students who can see the future trends and have the skills (such as computer literacy) to work in tomorrow's highly automated, efficient factories and mines.

Small Is Beautiful

Remember in Chapter 1 when we talked about trends in agriculture? We noted that many farms had gone out of business over the last 80 years and now we have fewer, bigger farms. We also have some very successful high-tech small farms. Well, the same thing is happening in manufacturing. Here are some facts for you to think about.

- Between 1974 and 1984, large companies lost about 1.4 million manufacturing jobs, but during that same period 41,000 new manufacturing companies created enough new jobs to offset virtually all of those losses. As a result, companies with fewer than 250 employees now account for 46 percent of the manufacturing work force. Just as in agriculture, these small, new firms tend to use the latest in high technology.
- During the 1980s, you were able to read about large steel mills closing because they were no longer competitive with foreign producers. What was less publicized was the success of some 50 minimills (small, highly automated mills) that have increased their share of the market to 20 percent from nothing in the 1970s.
- *Inc.* magazine published 10 commandments for the new manufacturing. They are:[9]
  1. Keep production units small.
  2. Keep corporate overhead low.
  3. Keep productivity high.
  4. Keep production flexible.
  5. Remain market driven.
  6. Customize products.
  7. Strive for margins, not volume.
  8. Stress customer service.
  9. Recruit from the "new America" (that is, the new immigrant work force).
  10. Recruit a CEO with nonmanufacturing experience. (This is because managers in service firms are more consumer oriented than managers from old manufacturing firms who tended to stress cost control.)

A good example of a modern, small firm is Zero Corporation, a manufacturer of metallic packaging for industries such as aerospace, electronics, and photography. It is a small, highly focused firm whose strengths lie in flexibility, customization, and market sensitivity. Note that these are the same factors that make Allen-Bradley so successful. Zero has more than 17,000 different customers, none of whom accounts for more than 3 percent of sales. Some 40 percent of sales are specially customized products. These new firms are so automated that labor costs are no longer a major competitive factor. We shall now discuss that development.

Decreasing Importance of Labor Costs in Some Industries

Much of the automation that went on in the 1960s through the 1980s was done to high labor costs. After all, foreign labor was available for much less cost and U.S. producers simply could not become competitive without lowering labor costs.

This is a picture of the inside of a small, efficient steel mill. Such minimills are very competitive in world markets and are capturing more and more market share. You can see that such mills are highly automated. Such manufacturers are providing challenging jobs for today's college graduates.

American manufacturers were successful in that attempt. Today, automation has cut direct labor costs down to 8 to 12 percent of total production costs on average and half that much in electronics. In fact, Beckman Instruments, Inc., in Cedar Grove, California, has eliminated labor as a separate cost category because it was such a small item on the expense sheet.[10]

Peter Drucker said in *The Wall Street Journal,* "Wage levels for blue-collar workers are becoming increasingly irrelevant in world competition. Productivity still matters—indeed it matters increasingly more. Quality, design, service, innovation, marketing, all are becoming more important."[11] Competition between countries, therefore, will no longer be based on wage differentials but on managerial competence. That means that U.S. managers must learn how to be more responsive to market wants and needs, make better-quality products and make them faster, and generally become more customer oriented.

New production techniques make it possible to virtually custom make products for individual industrial buyers. The job then becomes one of getting closer to those customers to find out what the product needs are. What the future is coming down to, in other words, is effective marketing combined with effective production and management to make U.S. producers number one in the world again.

This means tremendous opportunities for careers in production management. To prepare for such a career, you will have to learn the basics of production. That is the subject of a whole course or many courses, but below we shall review some of the more fundamental things you should know.

FUNDAMENTALS OF PRODUCTION

production process
Use of basic inputs (land, labor, capital, and entrepreneurship) to produce outputs (products, services, and ideas).

Common sense and some experience have already taught you much of what you need to know about production management. You know what it takes to build a model of an airplane or make a dress. You need a place to work, you need money to buy the materials, and you need to be organized to get the task done. The same is true of the production process. It uses basic inputs to produce outputs (see Figure 13–1). The **production process** is the creation of final goods and services using the factors of production: land, labor (machinery), capital, and entrepreneurship. Production creates what is known as form utility. *Form utility* in manufacturing is the value added by the creation of finished goods and services using raw materials, components, and other inputs (see p. 207 for a more comprehensive discussion of utility).

FIGURE 13–1

The production process. The production process consists of taking the factors of production (land, etc.) and using those inputs to produce goods, services, and ideas. Planning, routing, scheduling and the other activities are the means to accomplish the objective—output.

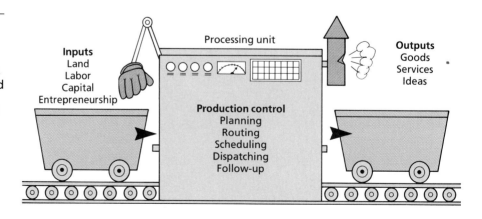

Production is a broad term that describes the creative process in all industries that produce goods and services, including mining, lumber, manufacturing, education, and health care. **Manufacturing** is one part of production. It means making goods by hand or with machinery, as opposed to extracting things from the earth (mining and fishing) or producing services.

To be competitive, manufacturers must keep the costs of inputs down. That is, the costs of workers, machinery, and so on must be kept as low as possible. Similarly, the amount of output must be relatively high. Remember, the term for output per worker is *productivity*. How does a producer keep costs low and still produce more, that is, increase productivity? This question will dominate thinking in the production sector for years to come.

production
Describes the creative process in all industries that produce goods and services, including mining, lumber, manufacturing, education, and health care.

manufacturing
Process of making goods by hand or with machinery as opposed to extracting things from the earth (mining or fishing) or producing services.

KEEPING COSTS LOW: SITE SELECTION

One of the major issues of the 1980s and 1990s is the shift of manufacturing facilities from one city or state to another in the United States or to overseas sites. Such shifts have sometimes resulted in pockets of unemployment in some parts of the country and have also led to tremendous economic growth in others.

Why would producers spend millions of dollars to move their manufacturing plants from one location to another? One major reason some producers move is the availability of the right kind of labor or cheap labor. Even though labor cost is becoming a smaller percentage of the total costs in some industries, cheap labor remains a key reason many less technologically advanced producers move their plants. For example, cheap labor is one reason why many new firms are moving to Los Angeles. Labor is provided by an enormous pool of immigrant workers, many of them recently arrived from Asia and Latin America.

Most of the labor-intensive sewing work of the garment industry is performed by "ethnic" contractors who hire workers from their native countries. Often the new immigrants seem more willing to work harder for less pay than Americans who have been here longer. New York City, too, has a huge labor pool of people willing and able to work hard. So while big businesses may pull out of major cities, smaller firms may move in to take their place.

The Southern United States has also attracted many manufacturers because the region has mostly nonunion labor. In general, such workers demand lower wages and fringe benefits. By moving South, U.S. business was able to compete more effectively with foreign producers who have much lower labor costs (see the ad for Tennessee on the following page).

Cheaper labor cost is also a major reason why many businesses shifted their production operations to Mexico, South Korea, and other overseas locations. To keep their jobs, U.S. laborers had to either become more productive or lower their demands for wages and fringe benefits. Naturally, such a suggestion caused much debate and controversy.

Businesses were said to be greedy and uncaring when they moved production facilities. But the facts were that the very survival of the U.S. manufacturing industry depended on its ability to remain competitive, and that meant either cheaper inputs or increased outputs from present inputs (increased productivity). A major controversy in 1988 was over a plant-closing provision in a trade bill. The legislation forces larger businesses to give a 60-day notice to workers before closing a plant or making significant layoffs.

Tennessee has been able to attract businesses from all over the world. Emphasis is placed on the transportation system, the school system, and the availability of good workers. Other states must design similar systems to attract business or face a declining economy.

Tennessee.
Conveniently located between Tokyo and London.

The secret is out. Tennessee is going global. Now we are not only attracting location and expansion from companies all over the United States. Companies from Japan, the United Kingdom, West Germany, Sweden, Belgium, Canada, and other countries are joining the thriving businesses of Tennessee.

Businesses have opened or expanded here *faster than one a day for the past two years.*

Certainly the interest in Tennessee is fueled by our bulls-eye location in the U.S.; our peerless travel/transport system, major airline hubs, the axis of Federal Express; our commitment to our schools, and to educating the children of today and the bright, capable work force of tomorrow.

And something else. Our government runs our state like a business. Tennessee is one of only ten states with a AAA bond rating. We have a balanced budget, mandated by state law. Governor Ned McWherter spent 14 years as Speaker of the House—the man who had the sharpest pencil on the state budget. So the ROI on tax dollars is measured in improved transportation, education and human services — not in bureaus and monuments.

But perhaps the best measure of how well business is working in Tennessee — from the newest, two-person home-grown outfit to billion-dollar giants — is that the world is beating a path to our door.

TENNESSEE
Where the world comes to work.

Contact: Department of Economic and Community Development, 320 6th Avenue North, Suite 8068, Nashville, TN 37219-5308. Or call 1-800-251-8594. Fax: 615-741-5829

Cheaper resources are another major reason for moving production facilities. Companies often need water, electricity, wood, coal, and other basic resources. By moving to areas where such resources are cheap and plentiful, costs can be lowered significantly—not only the cost of buying such resources, but the cost of shipping as well. Water shortages in the West, for example, often discourage the location of manufacturing plants there.

Locating Close to Markets

One reason businesses sometimes choose to remain in areas such as Chicago, New York, New Jersey, and California is because that's where their customers are. In spite of all the talk about the booming Southwest, much of the buying power of the United States is still centered in the Midwest, Northeast, and Far West (California). By locating close to their customers, businesses lower the costs of transportation and can be more responsive to customer needs for service. It is especially important for service organizations to be located near urban areas where they can serve their customers best. Today, the new, smaller, high-tech production firms are locating on the fringes of large cities where they can serve their customers but still find land at relatively low prices. The boom towns of the 1990s are:[12]

1. Marietta/Roswell Georgia
2. Dallas/Richardson Texas
3. Troy/Warren Michigan
4. Scottsdale/Sun City Arizona
5. Newport Beach/Laguna California
6. Herndon, Manassas Virginia
7. Santa Ana/Costa Mesa California
8. Virginia Beach/Chesapeake Virginia
9. East Brunswick New Jersey
10. Orlando/Kissimmee Florida

The bottom line is that site location has become a critical issue in production management. Companies want to be close to their markets, but also need a skilled or trainable labor supply.

Site Selection in the 1990s

The cost of land is becoming a more critical factor in choosing a plant location. Some businesses are forced to leave cities such as New York, where land is expensive, and move to rural areas where land is much, much cheaper. Some employers also enjoy living away from the noise, pollution, and traffic of big cities.

Today, another big incentive to locate or relocate in a particular city is the tax situation and government support. Some states have higher taxes than others. Some states and cities even give tax incentives and other support, such as zoning changes and financial aid, so that businesses will locate there. Some cities attract business by designing industrial parks. An **industrial park** is a planned area where businesses can find land, shipping facilities, and waste disposal outlets so they can build a manufacturing plant or storage facility.

Naturally, some places are more attractive than others because of climate, educational facilities, and other factors. The quality of life is better in some areas than others. If you have a chance to build a plant anywhere, why not choose sunny California, Florida, or Arizona? In summary, then, businesses today are trying to cut production costs and improve lifestyles by locating their plants where:

- Resources are plentiful and inexpensive.
- Skilled workers are available or trainable.
- Labor is inexpensive.
- Taxes are low and local government offers support.
- Energy and water are available.
- Land is available, inexpensive, and close to markets.
- Transportation costs are low.
- Quality of life is high.
- Quality of education is high.

Once a location is selected, production can begin. After the Progress Check, let's continue to go through the entire production process to see how it can be made more competitive.

industrial park
A planned area in a city where businesses can find land, shipping facilities, and waste disposal outlets so they can build a manufacturing plant or storage facility.

PROGRESS CHECK

- What are five reasons why the industrial base of the United States is stronger now than it was in the early 1980s?
- The text discusses 10 commandments for the new manufacturing. What are they?
- What is happening to labor costs in automated manufacturing and what does that mean for international competition?
- What are the major factors that determine where a plant locates? Which cities are winning that battle and why?

PRODUCTION PROCESSES

After a site is selected and a factory has been built, manufacturers begin the process of actually making products. There are several different processes manufacturers use. This material is probably new to you, so we will use familiar examples to help you visualize these processes.

MAKING ETHICAL DECISIONS

Depresso Industries has long been the economic mainstay of its birthplace, Hometown, U.S.A. Most of Hometown's small businesses and schools support Depresso Industries, either by supplying the materials needed for production or by training Depresso employees. Depresso has found that it can increase profits 50 percent by moving its production facilities overseas. Closing Depresso operations in Hometown will cause many of the town's businesses to fail and

schools to close, leaving a great percentage of the town unemployed with no options for reemployment. As a Depresso manager, you must help decide if the plant should be moved and, if so, when to tell the employees about closing the Hometown plant. What alternatives do you have? What are the consequences of each alternative? Which alternative will you choose?

Andrew S. Grove, chief executive officer of Intel, uses a great analogy to explain the production process:[13]

> To understand the principles of production, imagine that you're a waiter . . . and that your task is to serve a breakfast consisting of a three-minute soft-boiled egg, buttered toast, and coffee. Your job is to prepare and deliver the three items simultaneously, each of them fresh and hot.
>
> The task here encompasses the three basic requirements of production. They are to build and deliver products in response to the demands of the customer at a *scheduled* delivery time, at an *acceptable quality* level, and at the lowest possible cost.

* * * * *

> Other production principles underlie the preparation of our breakfast. In the making of it, we find present the three fundamental types of production operations: *process manufacturing,* an activity that physically or chemically changes material just as boiling changes an egg; *assembly,* in which components are put together to constitute a new entity just as the egg, the toast, and the coffee together make a breakfast; and *test,* which subjects the components or the total to an examination of its characteristics. There are, for example, visual tests.

From the breakfast example, it is easy to understand two manufacturing processes: process and assembly. In **process manufacturing,** you physically or chemically change materials. For example, boiling physically changed the egg. In **assembly process,** you put together components such as the egg, the toast, and the coffee to make a breakfast. These two processes are called synthetic systems. **Synthetic systems** either change raw materials into other products (process manufacturing) or combine raw materials or parts into a finished product (assembly process).

The reverse of a synthetic system is one called an analytic system. In an **analytic system** a raw material is broken down into components to extract other products. For example, crude oil can be reduced to gasoline, wax, and jet fuel.

A **continuous process** is one in which long production runs turn out finished goods over time. In our breakfast shop, for example, you could have eggs on a conveyor belt that lowered them into boiling water for three minutes and then lifted them out on a continuous basis. A three-minute egg would be available whenever you wanted one. An automobile factory is run on a continuous process.

It usually makes more sense when responding to specific customer orders (job-order production) to use an **intermittent process.** This is an operation where the production run is short (one or two eggs) and the machines are shut down frequently or changed to produce different products (like the oven in a bakery or

process manufacturing
Production process that physically or chemically changes materials.

assembly process
Production process that puts together components.

synthetic systems
Production processes that either change raw materials into other products or combine raw materials or parts into finished products.

analytic system
Manufacturing system that breaks down raw materials into components to extract other products.

continuous process
Production process in which long production runs turn out finished goods over time.

intermittent process
Production process in which the production run is short and the machines are shut down frequently or changed to produce different products.

This picture of an oil refinery shows the analytic system at work. Crude oil is converted to consumer and industrial products such as gasoline, wax, and jet fuel. Whereas synthetic systems combine raw materials into a finished product, analytic systems break down raw materials into useful components.

the toaster in the breakfast shop). Manufacturers of custom-designed furniture or metal railings would use an intermittent process.

Today, most new manufacturers use intermittent processes. They use computers and robots and flexible manufacturing processes that make it possible to custom make goods almost as fast as mass-produced goods were once made. We shall discuss how they do that in more detail later.

Managers use five indicators of whether or not they can meet their production goals on any given day. They are:

1. *Sales forecast.* How many breakfasts should you plan to deliver?
2. *Raw material inventory.* Do you have enough eggs, bread, butter, and coffee on hand?
3. *Equipment.* Is everything ready to produce the breakfast?
4. *Manpower.* Are there enough people available to make the sales forecasted number of breakfasts?
5. *Quality.* Are customers satisfied?

The production of breakfasts begins with the purchase of the needed food and equipment. The food and supplies must be stored in refrigerators and other storage equipment. One place we can look for production efficiency and savings, therefore, is in purchasing and storage.

Reread the story about making breakfast and imagine instead a factory producing glass that it then puts into frames for pictures. Think through how the same concepts apply.

Can you see how the picture frame plant uses both process and assembly manufacturing?

THINKING IT THROUGH

MATERIALS REQUIREMENT PLANNING (MRP)

One thing for certain about the technological changes taking place in manufacturing is that they have resulted in a whole new terminology for production and operations management. Today's students need to be familiar with this terminology before they can discuss such advances in any depth.

materials requirement planning
A computer-based operations management system that uses sales forecasts to make sure that needed parts and materials are available at the right place and time.

One of the more important terms is **materials requirement planning (MRP).** Materials requirement planning is a computer-based operations management system that uses sales forecasts to make sure that needed parts and materials are available at the right place and the right time. In our breakfast shop, for example, we could feed the sales forecast into the computer and it would specify how many of each ingredient to order, and print out the proper scheduling and routing sequence.

Holly Carburetor used MRP to solve an inventory problem. The company had too many dollars tied up in inventory and yet had problems with parts shortages. The company decided it needed a custom-designed computer program for materials requirement planning.

Using the new program, the company cut inventory costs (e.g., storage, spoilage) from $30 million to $20 million, making it well worthwhile to invest $250,000 for the computer program. In addition to cutting costs, the system enables anyone in the organization to ask the computer where the company is with respect to satisfying a customer order—where it is in the production process, the status of inventory, and what is on the order.

Home Depot introduced an advanced inventory management system recently that allowed it to turn its inventory 5.4 times a year instead of 4.5 times. That meant that Home Depot could carry $40 million less in inventory—the equivalent of 14 stores worth! When less money is tied up in inventory, the company can lower consumer prices.[14]

Just-In-Time Inventory Control

One of the major costs of production is holding parts, motors, and other items in warehouses. To cut such costs, the Japanese perfected an American idea called **just-in-time (JIT) inventory control.** The idea is to have suppliers deliver their products "just in time" to go on the assembly line. A minimum of inventory is kept anywhere on the premises. Some U.S. manufacturers have adopted the practice, and are quite happy with the results, although it is much more difficult to implement because of the greater distances involved in the United States.

just-in-time (JIT) inventory control
Arrangements for delivery of the smallest possible quantities at the latest possible time to keep inventory as low as possible

Here is how it works. A manufacturer sets a production schedule using materials requirement planning as described above, and determines what parts and supplies will be needed. It then informs its suppliers of what will be needed. The supplier must then deliver the goods just in time to go on the assembly line. Naturally, this calls for more effort on the supplier's part (and more costs). Efficiency is maintained by having the supplier linked by computer to the producer so that the supplier becomes more like another department in the firm than a separate business. The supplier delivers its materials just in time to be used in the production process, so a bare minimum must be kept in storage just in case the delivery is held up for some reason.

You can imagine how the system would work at Andrew Grove's breakfast shop. Rather than ordering enough eggs, butter, bread, and coffee for the week and storing it, he would have his suppliers deliver every morning. For another example, at the Unisys plant in Flemington, New Jersey, about 200 deliveries arrive daily. The combination of just-in-time inventory management and a faster process time has allowed Unisys to pare inventories to a 1.3-month supply from seven months. The company predicts it will cut present supplies in half again when the system is perfected.[15]

Some U.S. manufacturers have adopted just-in-time programs to cut the costs of warehousing inventory. New trucks such as those discussed in this ad make the process easier.

A moment's reflection will tell you some of the problems with just-in-time systems. What happens if the supplier doesn't deliver on time because of weather conditions or an accident? Are suppliers willing to assume the added costs of more frequent, smaller deliveries? Such questions have to be answered through planning and negotiation. The results are usually worth the effort.

Just-In-Time Supplier Relationships

For many companies, implementation of JIT methods has been rather difficult. The main problem was that producers were using JIT as a way of getting suppliers to hold inventories instead of them. This meant that the producers had no back-up inventory if the suppliers delivered the wrong parts or faulty parts, or did not deliver any parts by the time they were needed.

For the system to work well, producers have to work closely with suppliers and carefully work out details of the system, making sure that the suppliers are happy with the system, too. Xerox failed to do that when it first established its JIT system, and it caused much supplier discontent. Xerox then developed an elaborate program to develop better supplier relationships and now teaches others how to do that.

Xerox learned how to implement a JIT system from Harley-Davidson. Harley is one of the best practitioners of just-in-time inventory. The U.S. motorcycle company was about to fail because of Japanese competition. Operating costs in Japan were 30 percent lower, largely due to a JIT system and quality control procedures such as those discussed later in the chapter. Using Japanese-style techniques, Harley cut its costs for warranty repairs, scrap, and reworking of parts by 60 percent.

The ultimate in JIT systems is to locate your plant right next to a producer and then connect your plant with the other plant with a pneumatic conveying system. That is what Polycom Huntsman did. It built a plant 1,500 feet from GM's Harrison Radiator Division in Lockport, New York. Now its plastic compounds flow through the connector to GM's plant as needed.[16]

MRP and JIT systems make sure the right materials are at the right place at the right time at the cheapest cost to meet customer needs and production needs. That is the first step in modern production innovation. The next step in innovation is to change the production process itself. We shall discuss this next.

PROGRESS CHECK

　Can you explain the differences among the following production processes—process, assembly, analytic, continuous, and intermittent?

　What are five indicators of whether or not you will reach your production goals?

　What is materials requirement planning and how does it make production more efficient?

　What is just-in-time inventory control and what are the potential problems with implementing such a system?

MAKING CHANGES IN THE PRODUCTION PROCESS

Another major area for cost saving involves the design of the process used to make final products. You no doubt are familiar with the idea of a production line or assembly line. The workers are lined up on both sides of a long assembly line and perform one or more simple processes as the product goes by. For example, in making an automobile, one person puts in the seats, another installs the windows, and still others put on tires, bumpers, headlights, and so on. The process involves many, many workers doing a few not-too-complex tasks. (There are about 10,000 parts in a car.)

Recently, GM announced plans to completely redesign its production process, abandoning the assembly line. The name given the changeover was Project Saturn. The fundamental purpose of the restructuring was to dramatically cut the number of man-hours needed to build a car. It was estimated that GM intended to cut the number of man-hours per car from 175 to only 30.

The changes GM made were many, but the most dramatic was to switch to modular construction. This means that most parts will be preassembled into a few large components called *modules*. Workers are no longer strung out along miles of assembly line. Instead, they are grouped at various workstations where they put the modules together. Rather than do a few tasks, workers perform a whole cluster of tasks. Trolleys carry the partly completed car from station to station. Such a process takes up less space and calls for fewer workers—both money-saving steps. Suppliers were asked to provide a wider variety of parts and to subassemble certain parts before shipping them.

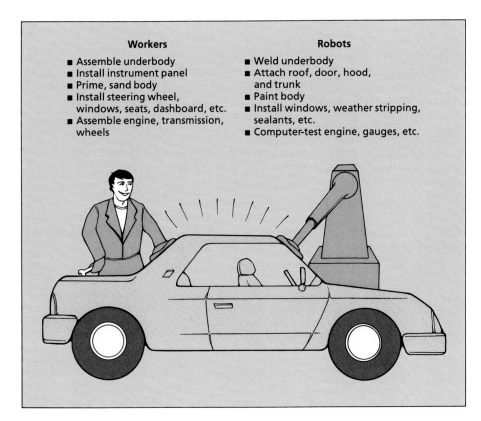

Workers
- Assemble underbody
- Install instrument panel
- Prime, sand body
- Install steering wheel, windows, seats, dashboard, etc.
- Assemble engine, transmission, wheels

Robots
- Weld underbody
- Attach roof, door, hood, and trunk
- Paint body
- Install windows, weather stripping, sealants, etc.
- Computer-test engine, gauges, etc.

FIGURE 13–2

Workers and robots assemble a car.
In the plant of tomorrow, workers and robots will work together. Robots will do much of the dirty work and repetitive work. Workers will do the more creative jobs and sensitive jobs such as sanding.

In addition to these changes, GM designed a casting process to build the engine block that uses 40 percent less machinery. This, too, saves money and time. And finally, GM greatly expanded its use of robots in the manufacturing process. A **robot** is a computer-controlled machine capable of performing many tasks requiring the use of materials and tools. Robots, for example, spray paint cars and do welding. Robots usually are fast, efficient, and accurate. However, GM had troubles implementing the whole process. Other companies have also had trouble implementing new technologies. That doesn't mean that the idea isn't good—the problem is in learning how to manage change. Because of its problems with implementing the new technology, GM switched its emphasis from robots and machinery to people management. That is, they are hiring and training workers who can make the most of the new technology.[17]

GM is just one example of how innovations are now occurring in manufacturing. In general, firms are using more robots, more computers, and less labor. Motorola produces cellular phones in a plant with only 70 employees. In a nonautomated plant, it would take almost 1,000 employees. Nabisco makes Oreos in a Garner, North Carolina plant. The cookies will be "untouched by human hands" until you take them apart to eat them. You do take them apart, don't you?

See Figure 13–2 for a look at the future of automation for the auto industry. Manufacturing plants tend to be smaller and more fuel efficient. Again, the goal is to cut costs and increase productivity to keep American business competitive. Next we shall explore the dramatic changes that are occurring that could restore American dominance in manufacturing: computer-aided design and computer-aided manufacturing (CAD/CAM).

robot

A computer-controlled machine capable of performing many tasks requiring the use of materials and tools.

COMPUTER-AIDED DESIGN AND MANUFACTURING

computer-aided design (CAD)
The integration of computers into the design of products.

computer-aided manufacturing (CAM)
The integration of computers into the manufacturing of products.

If one development in the 1980s changed production techniques and strategies more than any other, it was the integration of computers into the design and manufacturing of products. The first thing computers did was help in the design of products. The idea is called **computer-aided design (CAD).** The next step was to involve computers directly in the production process. That was called **computer-aided manufacturing (CAM).**

CAD/CAM has made it possible to design products to meet the tastes of small markets with very little increase in costs. A producer programs the computer to make a simple design change, and that change can be incorporated right into the production line. Custom products can thus be designed for narrow markets. You can no doubt identify with the following examples. Some consumers in the Midwest like hamburger on their pizza rather than pepperoni or sausage. The Pillsbury Company added a hamburger pizza to their Midwest line by making a few simple changes in the computer program for pizzas.

This picture shows tennis shoes being designed on a computer-aided design (CAD) system. Some day you will be able to buy custom-made shoes for the same price (or nearly so) as mass produced shoes because of computer-aided design and manufacturing and flexible manufacturing systems.

GM EXPERIMENTS WITH MORE AUTOMATION

In addition to the Saturn plant mentioned above, GM has built another highly automated plant to test how far automated production can go. This plant is in Saginaw, Michigan, and is called Saginaw Vanguard. In this plant, lasers inspect parts and check for wear on machine tools. Robots put together components produced using computer-aided design and manufacturing. Only two humans work there during two shifts. Eventually an overnight shift is planned with no human presence of any kind. Changeover from one product line to another is 10 minutes versus the 10 hours or 10 days needed in conventional plants. This is an experimental plant, but a model for future plants.

Source: William J. Hampton, "GM Bets an Arm and a Leg on a People-Free Plant," *Business Week*, September 12, 1988, pp. 72–73.

Another example reveals how helpful the computer can be. A Viennese architect named Josef Hoffman designed a beautiful silver-plated bowl as a gift for Albert Einstein. The original bowl has disappeared; only a photograph remains. To duplicate the bowl by hand through trial and error would have been costly and difficult. Instead, two men used the computer-aided design (CAD) process to program the dimensions of the bowl. They made 100,000 copies and sold them for $120 each. They could now make a slight change in the design on the computer and produce a new, unique design of their own.

Computer-aided manufacturing (CAM) is used to make cookies in those new, fresh-baked cookie shops. On-site, small-scale, semiautomated, sensor-controlled baking makes consistent quality easy.

Computer-aided design and manufacturing are also invading the clothing industry. A computer program establishes a pattern and cuts the cloth automatically. Soon, a person's dimensions will be programmed into the machines to create custom-cut clothing at very little additional cost.

The same flexibility is possible in large plants that produce automobiles, appliances, construction equipment, and other large, expensive items. In the past, any model change resulted in large increases in inventory and set-up costs. (All plant operations—machining, welding, assembling, and so forth—require *set-up time;* that is, time to prepare for the new process.) Today, many such changes are computerized, and the costs lowered dramatically. One manufacturer roughly tripled its number of models over a five-year period while reducing inventory by half and doubling the output per worker. How? Computer-aided manufacturing.

In summary, computer-aided design and computer-aided manufacturing (CAD/CAM) have revolutionized the production process. Now, everything from cookies to automobiles can be designed and manufactured much more cheaply. Furthermore, customized changes can be made with very little increase in cost. Think what that will mean for the clothing industry, the shoe industry, and other fashion-conscious industries. The age of custom-designed consumer and industrial goods has arrived. Figure 13–3 illustrates how consumers will be able to order custom-built cars in the future.

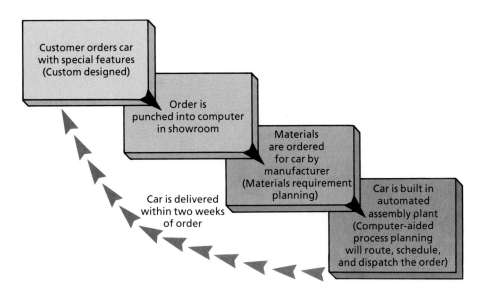

FIGURE 13–3

Custom-built cars using the latest in automation. Buying a car in the future. Note the custom features ordered by the client. Note too that the car is not produced until an order is received. That allows for custom design in just two weeks.

The Computerized Factory

Because of new ideas such as CAD/CAM, the United States is now on the brink of a whole new era in production management. No longer should the discussion be on the decline of American industry. Instead, the focus may be on the reemergence of American industry from its ashes. The force behind the change is new technology, especially computers and robots. Some terms you will be seeing over the next decade are *computer-aided engineering* and *flexible manufacturing systems*.

Computer-Aided Engineering (CAE) **Computer-aided engineering (CAE)** includes the design and analysis of products, programming of robots and machine tools, designing of molds and tools, and planning of the production process and quality control. In the past, engineering involved a lot of paperwork—blueprints, drawings, and so forth. Many inefficiencies resulted from the shuffling of such papers from desk to desk to shop floor and so on. Today, the whole engineering process from conception to production can be and is being done by computer in some firms.

Flexible Manufacturing Systems (FMS) **Flexible manufacturing systems (FMS)** are totally automated production centers that include robots, automatic materials handling equipment, and computer-controlled machine tools that can perform a variety of functions to produce different products. A recent report mentioned a Japanese manufacturer who put in a flexible manufacturing system (FMS). This enabled the plant to cut back the number of machines from 68 to 18, the number of employees from 215 to 12, and space requirements from 103,000 square feet to 30,000 square feet. Process time was cut from 35 days to a day and a half. GM's new plant uses flexible manufacturing with similar cost-saving results.

We could go on describing other systems, but the discussion would get too complex to absorb at this time. What you should learn from all this is that factories are being fully automated. Everything from customer order processing, inventory control planning, and forecasting through production, quality control, and shipping is being made more productive through the use of computers and robots.

Today this process is rather uncoordinated. Factories have computer-controlled centers performing various functions, but these centers are not linked. The goal is to integrate the whole production process. As you can guess, this is easier said than done. A few firms, however, have integrated the entire process. They call the total system computer integrated manufacturing (CIM). Let's look at how this works.

Computer-Integrated Manufacturing (CIM)

Computer-integrated manufacturing (CIM) combines computer-aided design (CAD) with computer-aided manufacturing (CAM). It then further integrates CAD/CAM with other corporate functions such as purchasing, inventory control, cost accounting, materials handling, and shipping.

The Ingersoll Milling Machine Company was an early user of CIM. This machine tool firm makes products in small lots—one or two at a time—and needed a huge amount of information processing to schedule products through design and production. Their computer-integrated manufacturing system includes scheduling, computer-aided engineering (CAE), inventory control, computer-aided design (CAD), computer-aided manufacturing (CAM), purchasing, accounts payable, cost accounting, and assembly. The system saves Ingersoll over $1 million a year, mostly in machinery design.

---

computer-aided engineering
The computer-generated design and analysis of products, programming of robots and machine tools, designing of molds and tools, and planning of the production process and quality control.

flexible manufacturing systems (FMS)
Totally automated production centers that include robots, automatic materials-handling equipment, and computer-controlled machine tools that can perform a variety of functions to produce different products.

computer-integrated manufacturing (CIM)
Computer-aided design (CAD) combined with computer-aided manufacturing (CAM); it then further integrates CAD/CAM with other corporate functions such as purchasing, inventory control, cost accounting, materials handling, and shipping.

This is the modern kind of factory that can compete in world markets. The secret is the networking of computers and the use of automated processes throughout.
Source: Reprinted from March 3, 1986 issue of *Business Week,* by special permission, copyright 1986 by McGraw-Hill, Inc.

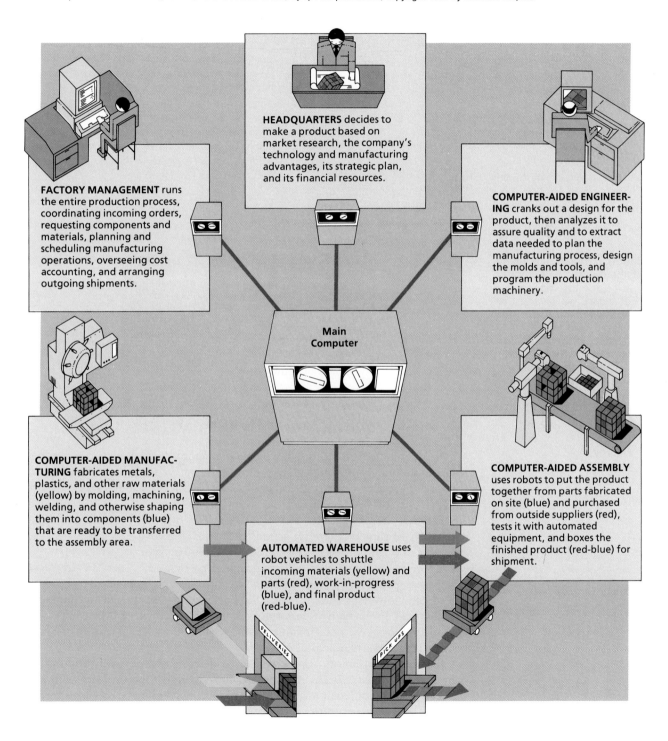

HEADQUARTERS decides to make a product based on market research, the company's technology and manufacturing advantages, its strategic plan, and its financial resources.

FACTORY MANAGEMENT runs the entire production process, coordinating incoming orders, requesting components and materials, planning and scheduling manufacturing operations, overseeing cost accounting, and arranging outgoing shipments.

COMPUTER-AIDED ENGINEER-ING cranks out a design for the product, then analyzes it to assure quality and to extract data needed to plan the manufacturing process, design the molds and tools, and program the production machinery.

Main Computer

COMPUTER-AIDED MANUFAC-TURING fabricates metals, plastics, and other raw materials (yellow) by molding, machining, welding, and otherwise shaping them into components (blue) that are ready to be transferred to the assembly area.

COMPUTER-AIDED ASSEMBLY uses robots to put the product together from parts fabricated on site (blue) and purchased from outside suppliers (red), tests it with automated equipment, and boxes the finished product (red-blue) for shipment.

AUTOMATED WAREHOUSE uses robot vehicles to shuttle incoming materials (yellow) and parts (red), work-in-progress (blue), and final product (red-blue).

DELIVERIES

PICK UPS

PROBLEMS WITH IMPLEMENTING AUTOMATION

Implementation of the new technologies into production facilities has not gone as smoothly as planned. General Motors, for example, built a $600 million assembly plant in Hamtramck, Michigan, that has 260 robots for welding, 50 automated guided vehicles to carry parts to the assembly line, and a battery of cameras and computers that use laser beams to inspect and control the production process. Some problems include:

- The automated guided vehicles sat idle for a while because of software problems.
- Robots sometimes spray paint each other instead of the cars.
- The plant was turning out only 30 to 35 cars per hour in 1986, far less than the 60 an hour for which

it was planned. Ford had similar start-up troubles making its minivan. The car arrived from the St. Louis plant seven months later than planned. At first, there were problems getting the computer-controlled machinery from various manufacturers to communicate. Then the system was too complicated even for operators with months of training.

The computer/robot age came very quickly, and it is taking time to adjust to it. Some plants tried to fully automate before the operators were sufficiently trained and the equipment was fully tested in an assembly line setting. The glitches are now being worked out, however, and computer automation is here to stay.

Source: Amal Nag, "Tricky Technology," *The Wall Street Journal,* May 13, 1986, pp. 1 and 10.

Robots can take over many of the dangerous and dirty jobs on the assembly line. That means workers of the future will need to be more educated to operate machinery rather than do production work by hand. You can see in this picture how automated the process can become.

New computer breakthroughs will make computer-integrated manufacturing a reality in thousands of manufacturing firms in the next decade. Leading firms that are developing such systems for others include IBM, GE, Schlumberger, Control Data, Xerox, and Sperry Univac.

Estimates by the National Research Council predict that organizations implementing CIM should realize reductions in engineering costs (15 percent–30 percent) and work-in-process inventory (30 percent–60 percent), as well as up to 300 percent in capital equipment operating time. Experience has shown even greater savings are possible.[18] Such advances are not easy to implement. Therefore, colleges and universities are studying the best ways to use the new technologies. Washington University in St. Louis, for example, has formed a CIM Center, which is a consortium of St. Louis manufacturers who want to stay abreast of the latest management and technological practices.

Just-in-time inventory supply systems will link suppliers with producers by computer to form networks of computer-linked firms. One problem with such integration is that different manufacturers producing computers, robots, computer software, and data transmission systems have not standardized their equipment. Thus, it has been difficult in the past to integrate systems within the firm, much less among firms. This problem introduces the concept of enterprise networking.

Enterprise Networking

For real system integration to take place, the computers of one company will have to talk to the computers of another company. This is called **networking.** That is what will occur in the 1990s, and it will revolutionize the way marketing and production are handled. Imagine a salesperson talking with a customer and learning that a slight modification in the product is needed. The salesperson could sit down with his or her laptop computer and send the modifications to the company via electronic mail (messages that are sent from computer to computer). The information is fed into a computer-aided design system that, in turn, feeds it to a computer-aided manufacturing system. The system automatically adjusts the inventory model and communicates with suppliers telling them what is needed when. The supplier's just-in-time system gets the information immediately. That is how the system of the 1990s will work.

One problem with implementing such a system is to have common standards among computer and communications industry manufacturers such that interfirm systems communication can take place. The answer is to develop an open systems interconnection (OSI) reference model that all manufacturers could use. **Open systems integration** refers to the development of standards in the computer and telecommunications industry that will allow computers to talk with one another over long distances. The problem today is that AT&T and other producers of such equipment do not agree on a common standard. That issue is now being worked out.[19] The future of manufacturing in the United States and throughout the world hangs in the balance. We shall talk more about such systems in Chapter 14. For now, you should know that great changes are occurring in manufacturing that will link suppliers, manufacturers, and business customers in one common computer system that will make the flows of goods and services much more efficient.

> **networking**
> Linking firms together by making it possible for their computers to talk to one another.

> **open systems integration**
> The ability of computers and telecommunications equipment to communicate over long distance due to the development of common standards in the computer and telecommunications industry.

CONTROL PROCEDURES: PERT AND GANTT CHARTS

Obviously, one of the important functions of a production manager is to be sure that products are manufactured and delivered *on time*. The question is, how can one be sure that all of the assembly processes will go smoothly and end up completed by the required time? One of the more popular strategies for maintaining some feel for the progress of the production process is called **PERT (program evaluation and review technique),** a process developed in the 1950s for constructing the Polaris submarines. PERT is a method for analyzing the tasks involved in completing a given project, estimating the time needed to complete each task, and identifying the minimum time needed to complete the total project.

The steps involved in using PERT include: (1) analyzing tasks that need to be done and sequencing the tasks, (2) estimating the time needed to complete each task, (3) drawing a PERT network illustrating the information from steps 1 and 2, and (4) identifying the critical path. The **critical path** is the path that takes the most time to complete. Therefore, the critical path represents the earliest time a project can be completed if all tasks along that path are completed as predicted. The critical path answers the question: "When should the project be finished?" In order for the total project to be completed on time, however, it is "critical" that tasks along the critical path be completed on schedule.

> **PERT (program evaluation and review technique)**
> A method for analyzing the tasks involved in completing a given project, estimating the time needed to complete each task, and identifying the minimum time needed to complete the total project.

> **critical path**
> The longest path a product takes from the beginning of the production process until the end.

FIGURE 13–4

Example of PERT chart for producing a music video. The minimum amount of time it will take to produce this video is 15 weeks. To get that number, you add the week it takes to pick a star and a song to the four weeks to design a set, the two weeks to purchase set materials, the six weeks to construct the set, the week before rehearsals, and the final week when the video is made. That is the critical path. Any delay in that process will delay the final video. Delays in the other processes (selecting and choreographing dancers and costume design) would not necessarily delay the video because there are more weeks in the critical path.

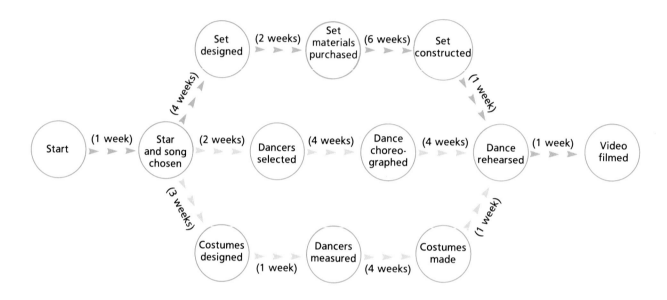

Figure 13–4 illustrates a PERT chart for producing a music video. Note that the circles on the chart indicate completed tasks and the arrows leading to the circles indicate the time needed to complete each task. The path from one completed task to the other illustrates the relationship of each task. For example, the arrow from Set designed to Set materials purchased shows that designing the set must be completed before the materials can be purchased. The critical path (indicated by the blue arrows) reflects that producing the set takes more time than auditioning dancers and choreographing dances as well as designing and making costumes. The project manager now knows that it is critical that set construction remain on schedule if the project is to be completed on time, but short delays in the dance and costume preparation should not affect the total project.

A PERT network can be made up of thousands of events over months of time. Today, this complex procedure is done by computer.

Another, more basic strategy used by manufacturers for measuring production progress is a **Gantt chart.** The Gantt chart (named after its developer, Henry L. Gantt) is a bar graph that clearly shows what projects are being worked on and how much has been completed (on a daily basis). Figure 13–5 shows a Gantt chart for a doll manufacturer. The chart shows that the dolls' heads and bodies should be

Gantt chart
Bar graph showing production managers what projects are being worked on and what stage they are in on a daily basis.

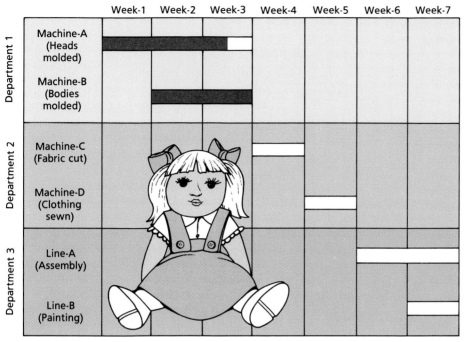

	Week-1	Week-2	Week-3	Week-4	Week-5	Week-6	Week-7
Department 1 Machine-A (Heads molded)							
Machine-B (Bodies molded)							
Department 2 Machine-C (Fabric cut)							
Machine-D (Clothing sewn)							
Department 3 Line-A (Assembly)							
Line-B (Painting)							

= Completed work

= Work to be done

FIGURE 13–5

A Gantt chart for a doll manufacturer. A Gantt chart enables a production manager to see at a glance when projects are scheduled to be completed and what the status now is. For example, the dolls' heads and bodies should be completed before the clothing is sewn, but could be a little late, as long as everything is ready for assembly in week 6. This chart shows that at the end of week 3, the dolls' bodies are ready, but the heads are about half a week behind.

completed before the clothing is sewn. It also shows that at the end of week 3, the dolls' bodies are ready, but the heads are about half a week behind. All of this was once done by hand. Now the computer has taken over, and paper Gantt charts are becoming obsolete.

PROGRESS CHECK

■ What is the difference between using a production line and producing products using modular units? Which is more flexible? Which offers more challenge to workers?

■ What is the difference between CAD/CAM and computer-integrated manufacturing (CIM)?

■ Could you draw a PERT chart for making a breakfast of three-minute eggs, buttered toast, and coffee? Which process would be the critical path, the longest process? How could you use a Gantt chart to keep track of production?

PEOPLE VERSUS MACHINES

PERT and Gantt calculations were once done slowly and carefully by skilled production managers who had years of experience. Today, production alternatives can be simulated on the computer. Calculations that once took days can now be made in minutes. Thus, it appears the future of production is secure. It seems that computers, robots, and automatic machinery will take over much of the process. The truth is that production is still dependent on people, and it will be people who will determine the success or failure of future systems. Several steps must occur before people and machines will be combined to revolutionize manufacturing:

- There is an obvious need to train future production workers in the use and repair of computers, robots, and automatic machinery.
- Today's production workers must be retrained or relocated to adapt to the new high-tech systems. Similarly, managers must be trained in how to implement the new technologies.[20]
- Major adjustments must be made in the relationships between suppliers and producers to implement concepts such as just-in-time inventory programs and enterprise networking.
- Production managers must be retrained to deal with more highly skilled workers who demand a much more participative managerial style. The box on Dave Bing dicusses how a basketball player made it big in the steel industry. His story is being repeated in thousands of small manufacturing firms every year.

QUALITY CONTROL

quality control
The measurement of products and services against set standards

total quality control
The system of planning for quality, preventing quality defects, correcting any defects that occur, and a philosophy of continuous effort to build quality into products.

Quality control is the measurement of products and services against set standards. Earlier in America, quality control was often done at the end of the production line. It was done by a quality control department. Today, things have changed. As Ford says in its ads, "Quality is Job One." **Total quality control** includes planning for quality, preventing quality defects, correcting any defects that occur, and a philosophy of continuous effort to build quality into products. Total quality control means building in and ensuring quality from product planning to production, purchasing, sales, and service.[21] Emphasis is placed on the fact that quality is everyone's concern, not just the quality control people at the end of the assembly line.

The president of Signetics (a producer of integrated circuits) reports that total quality control at his firm has resulted in $20 million in savings from 1980 to 1987. On-time deliveries have increased 50 percent and returns have decreased by 90 percent.

DAVE BING: FROM BASKETBALL STAR TO STEEL PRODUCER

Dave Bing was a star guard for the Detroit Pistons basketball team in the 1970s. He was a National Basketball Association All-Star seven times. Now Dave Bing is a star in a different field.

Former President Reagan once named Dave Bing, who is black, the National Minority Small Business Person of the Year. Mr. Bing started a steel fabricating plant soon after retiring from basketball in 1978. He is an example of today's modern production man.

Dave earned his B.A. in economics and marketing at Syracuse University. During the off-season over eight years he worked for the National Bank of Detroit and for two years as a Chrysler management trainee. When he left basketball, Mr. Bing spent two years training at Paragon Steel. Using that experience and his other managerial training, he started his own firm.

Using some of his basketball earnings to help finance the firm, Bing struggled at first. Now sales are in the $40 million range. His is the first black-owned steel company in the country. His customers include GM, Ford, and John Deere. Dave Bing's career shows that there are opportunities in production for talented people, even in declining industries such as steel.

Source: Katherine Blood, "Steel Star," *Forbes,* February 25, 1985, p. 162. Reprinted by permission of *Forbes* magazine; © *Forbes* Inc., 1985.

High-quality Japanese goods such as Toyota automobiles gave U.S. producers the incentive for quality control. Who taught Toyota about total quality control? American consultants Dr. W. Edward Deming and J. M. Juran. Deming teaches firms to (1) use statistical quality control during the process, (2) select supplies based on quality, (3) use statistical methods, not slogans, to get quality, and (4) find sources of poor quality and eliminate them. Now U.S. firms are listening to Deming and Juran and applying their strategies.

Quality Circles

Management strategies for improving quality and productivity vary depending on the latest fad. One technique that was "hot" in the mid-1980s has tended to fade. Yet the idea is so good that it deserves more attention. The concept is called quality circles. A **quality circle** consists of groups of employees who get together to develop ideas for solving problems in the workplace such as how to improve quality, increase productivity, cut back on paperwork, reduce inventory costs, or introduce new processes such as computer-integrated manufacturing.

quality circles
Groups of employees who get together to develop ideas for solving problems in the workplace such as how to improve quality, increase productivity, cut back on paperwork, reduce inventory costs, or introduce new processes such as computer-integrated manufacturing.

Quality circles are made up of a dozen or so employees, generally from the same department, who meet frequently to solve problems that occur at work. Two benefits can emerge from such programs: (1) the company learns many cost-efficient ways to operate, thus increasing productivity; and (2) employees feel that their ideas are sought and are valuable, and that increases morale. To get participation, some companies ask for volunteers; other *require* employees to participate.

Companies that have tried quality circles have found that employees often come up with answers to problems that managers knew nothing about:[22]

- At a Teledyne Semiconductor plant, employees reported that silicon wafers worth $148 each were breaking because of ill-fitting lids on storage boxes. Correcting the problem was estimated to save the company $44,000 a year.
- As a result of employee suggestions, a San Francisco public television station (KQED) reallocated space for employees, redesigned a membership form, and developed a procedures manual for accounting that significantly cut bookkeeping errors.

Hundreds of such stories could be told. The International Association of Quality Circles went from 860 members to over 5,000 members.

THE NEED FOR ZERO DEFECTS

The quality control specialists touring the country today are talking about "zero defects." You may wonder why all the fuss about zero defects. I mean, isn't 99.9 percent perfect good enough? The answer is no, and a recent article in *Inc.* magazine explained why. Do you know that if we only had 99.9 percent quality control in medicine that there would be 50 newborn babies dropped at birth by doctors every day. There would be 500 incorrect surgical procedures every week. And there would be 20,000 incorrect drug prescriptions given out every year. If the mail service had only 99.9 percent accuracy, some 16,000 pieces of mail would be lost every hour. You get the idea. We need to strive for zero defects because anything less results in tremendous harm and costs to society.

Source: Martha E. Mengelsdorf, "Why 99.9% Won't Do," *Inc.*, April 1989, p. 26.

AUTOMATING THE SERVICE SECTOR

U.S. business cannot remain competitive in world markets simply by automating production facilities in factories. The service sector will have to become more productive as well. We have already learned that 7 of 10 jobs in the United States are already in the service sector, with more to come. A truly strong America, therefore, has to be as progressive in introducing the latest technology to services as well as manufacturing.

One reason that service productivity lags behind manufacturing is because services are more labor intensive. That is, factories can more readily substitute machines for people and thus get more output from the remaining people. Traditional thinking has been that no machine can replace people in services such as banking, insurance, education, medicine, and consulting.

However, Theodore Levitt has presented a convincing argument that a production line approach can be applied to services as well as goods. He cites McDonald's as an example of this. McDonald's straddles the fine line between a retailer that offers mostly goods, such as an antique dealer, and one dealing almost exclusively in services, such as an income tax preparation service. The goods part of McDonald's was under the control of management. But the service personnel were less controllable. To gain some control, McDonald's has made almost every movement as standardized as possible:

> The tissue paper used to wrap each hamburger is color-coded to denote the mix of condiments. Heated reservoirs hold pre-prepared hamburgers for rush demand. . . . Nothing is left to chance or the employees' discretion.

> The entire system is engineered and executed according to a tight technological discipline that ensures fast, clean, reliable service in an atmosphere that gives the modestly paid employees a sense of pride and dignity.

> * * * * *

> What is important to understand about this remarkably successful organization is not only that it has created a highly sophisticated piece of technology, but also that it has done this by applying a manufacturing style of thinking to a people-intensive service situation.[23]

Most of us have been exposed to similar productivity gains in banking. For example, people in many towns no longer have to wait in long lines for harassed tellers to help them deposit and withdraw money. Instead, they use automatic tellers that take a few seconds and are available 24 hours a day.

Another service that was once annoyingly slow was the checkout counter at the grocery. The new system of marking goods with universal product codes enables computerized checkout, and allows cashiers to be much more productive when providing this service.

Airlines represent another service industry that is experiencing tremendous productivity increases through the use of computers for processing reservations, through the heavy use of prepackaged meals on board, and through more standardization of all movements of luggage, passengers, and so on.

A recent article in the *Los Angeles Times* pointed out that productivity in the service sector *is* rising, but the government simply does not have the means to measure it. The *quality* of service is greatly improving, but measuring output per employee per hour will never get at the quality differences between an hour of doctor's time today and an hour 30 years ago. Today, doctors have equipment such

Automatic teller machines make banking services more efficient. It is difficult to measure the productivity increases caused by such machines. Therefore, service productivity lags behind manufacturing productivity even though services are improving dramatically. We may need a different measure of service productivity to account for customer convenience or happiness.

as CAT and PET scanners that can tell them what is going on inside your body. Standard measures of productivity simply do not take such quality improvements into account.[24]

We learned in Chapter 2 that the goal of an economy is to provide a better standard of living *and* quality of life. Rising productivity in the service sector is providing us with a higher quality of life.

Automating the Salesperson

It takes only a little imagination and more technologically based thinking to make tremendous productivity advances in services that are now viewed as people intensive, one-on-one industries. Take life insurance sales, for example:[25]

> A life insurance agent is said to be in a service industry. Yet what does he or she really do? They research the prospect's needs by talking with them, design several policy models for them, and then "consumer-use test" these models by seeking their reactions. Then the agent redesigns the final model and delivers it for sale to the customer. This is the ultimate example of manufacturing in the field. The factory is in the customer's living room, and the producer is the insurance agent, whom we incorrectly think of as being largely a salesperson. Once we think of him or her as a manufacturer . . . we begin to think of how best to design and manufacture the product rather than how to best sell it.

The agent, for example, could be provided with a booklet of overlay sheets showing the insurance plans of people who are similar to the customer. This gives the customer a more credible and informed basis for making a choice. In time, the agent could be further supported by similar information stored in telephone-access computers.

In short, we begin to think of building a system that will allow the agent to produce his product efficiently and effectively by serving the customer's needs.

The point is that the service sector will continue to gain very slowly in productivity as long as people believe that services have to be personalized and labor intensive. But as various service industries begin to substitute machines for people, productivity will increase more quickly. Note that many of the changes will be in consumer-related areas such as personal selling (insurance), delivery (order by phone supermarkets, drugstores, and variety stores), credit (advanced credit card systems), and consumer research plus problem solving (consulting, income tax preparation, real estate, stockbroking).

Today, salespeople can carry their offices with them wherever they go. New laptop computers link them with the home office. New cellular phones the size of a cigarette pack keep them in touch. All of this adds to their productivity and effectiveness.

THINKING IT THROUGH What are some of the ways technology could affect higher education? What will be the role of videotape recorders, computers, and interactive TV? How will this affect the cost of college tuition?

What other service organizations might be changed dramatically by the new technological revolution? Think of the effect on banks, government services, health-care institutions, and hospitals.

PREPARING FOR THE FUTURE

What does all this mean to you? It means that college graduates of the future will have marvelous new technological advances available to them. It means new opportunities and a higher standard of living and quality of life. But it also means preparing for such changes. Clearly, the workplace will be dominated by computers, word processors, and other advanced machinery. Even the service sector will require the use of hand-held computers.

If all of this sounds terribly cold and impersonal, then you recognize one of the needs of the future. People will need much more contact with people outside the work environment. There will be new demands for recreation, social clubs, travel, and other diversions. The America of the next century will be radically different from the America of the 1990s. It will take both technically trained people and people skilled in human relationships to guide us through the transition.

CAREER INFORMATION: PRODUCTION SUPERVISORS

In any organization, someone has to be boss. For the millions of workers who assemble manufactured goods, service motor vehicles, lay bricks, unload ships, or perform any of thousands of other activities, a supervisor is the boss. These supervisors direct the activities of other employees and frequently ensure that millions of dollars worth of equipment and materials are used properly and efficiently. Supervisors are most commonly known as foremen or forewomen.

Supervisors make work schedules and keep production and employee records. They plan employees' activities and must allow for unforeseen problems such as absent workers and machine breakdowns. Supervisors teach employees safe work practices and enforce safety rules and regulations. They also may demonstrate timesaving or laborsaving techniques to workers and insure that new employees are properly trained.

Supervisors tell their subordinates about company plans and policies; recommend good performers for wage increases, awards, or promotions; and deal with poor performers by retraining them in proper methods, issuing warnings, or recommending that they be disciplined or fired. In companies where employees belong to labor unions, supervisors meet with union representatives to discuss work problems and grievances. They must know the provisions of labor-management contracts and run their operations according to these agreements.

Outstanding supervisors, particularly those with college education, may move up to higher management positions. In manufacturing, for example, they may advance to jobs such as department head and plant manager. Some supervisors, particularly in the construction industry, use the experience and skills they gain to go into business for themselves.

JOB OUTLOOK

Employment for supervisors is expected to increase more slowly than the average for all occupations through the year 2000. Employment in manufacturing industries will decline, due in part to increasing foreign competition. Offsetting the decline in the number of supervisors in manufacturing, however, will be an increase in jobs in nonmanufacturing industries, especially in the trade and service sectors.

SOURCES OF ADDITIONAL INFORMATION

A biography of literature on management occupations can be obtained from American Management Association, 135 West 50th Street, New York, New York 10020.

Source: *Occupations: Outlook Handbook* 1988–1989, U.S. Department of Labor.

Carnegie Mellon University now requires a course in manufacturing management for its M.S. degree. Other courses are offered in robotics and manufacturing strategy. Some students act as consultants to manufacturers in the Pittsburgh area. Stanford University has an Institute for Manufacturing and Automation. Such programs will become commonplace as other schools follow the leadership of these schools in introducing such courses at both the undergraduate and graduate levels.

Other schools are training students to manage the new high-tech managers and workers. Emphasis is on participative management and the design of attractive work environments. All of this will come together in the 1990s to mean a new era in both the manufacturing and service sectors. You have every reason to be optimistic about the future for both U.S. and world economic growth because of these changes. You can also expect to find many exciting new careers in America's new industrial boom.

- What are some of the ways corporations can improve quality control?

- Is a quality circle only a technique for improving quality?

- Why does service productivity seem to lag behind industrial productivity and what can be done to correct the problem?

PROGRESS CHECK

SUMMARY

1. Manufacturing has always been the heart of the free enterprise system. After a period of decline, manufacturing is coming back into the forefront in competitiveness.
   - What is happening in the United States that is making American manufacturing stronger?
   Several factors account for the resurgence of American manufacturing: (1) the decline of the dollar, (2) the emphasis on productivity, (3) declining labor costs, (4) improved efficiency related to smaller companies, and (5) the restructuring of corporations.

1. Describe the role of America's manufacturing base to the national economy and explain the factors that are bringing renewed strength to American manufacturing.

2. Production uses inputs to produce outputs.
   - What are these inputs and outputs?
   The inputs of the production process include land, labor, capital, and entrepreneurship. The outputs are the products and services the manipulation of these inputs produce.
   - What does form utility have to do with production?
   Production adds form utility—the value added by the creation of finished goods and services from raw materials, components, and other inputs.

2. Illustrate the production process and explain the importance of productivity.

3. Productivity requires keeping costs low and output high.
   - How can producers keep cost low?
   The first step in cutting costs is to *select a site:* near inexpensive, trained, or trainable labor; with cheap basic resources (water, electricity, etc.); close to customers; with low taxes and local government support; where land is available and inexpensive; transportation is available and costs are low; and the quality of life and education is high.

3. Identify the various methods manufacturers can use to keep costs at a minimum.

4. Manufacturers can use several different processes to make products.
   - What are these processes?
   These processes include synthetic systems (process manufacturing and assembly process) and analytic systems. The systems can be continuous or intermittent.

4. Classify the various production processes and identify the five indicators manufacturers can use to determine the likelihood of meeting their production goals.

What indicators can manufacturers use to see whether or not they can meet their goals?

The five indicators are: (1) sales forecast, (2) raw material inventory, (3) equipment, (4) manpower, and (5) quality.

5. Materials Requirement Planning (MRP) uses sales forecasts to make sure that needed parts and materials are available at the right time and place.

5. Describe the importance of materials requirement planning and discuss the benefits and problems of just-in-time inventory control.

What is just-in-time inventory?

JIT is arrangement for delivery of the smallest possible quantities at the latest possible time to keep inventory as low as possible.

What problems can develop with JIT?

The major problem for users of JIT is that they have no back-up inventory in case the suppliers can't or don't deliver the required parts on time. You can see that good relationships with reliable suppliers are essential for an efficient JIT inventory system.

6. Many new techniques are being used to make production more efficient (less expensive).

6. Describe the changes in manufacturing processes including the use of CAD, CAM, CAE, FMS, CIM, and enterprise networking.

What are some of these techniques?

New production techniques include: computer-aided design (CAD), computer-aided manufacturing (CAM), computer-aided engineering (CAE), computer-integrated manufacturing (CIM), flexible manufacturing systems (FMS), and open systems integration.

7. It is important that project managers be sure their products are produced on time.

7. Illustrate the use of PERT and Gantt charts in production planning.

What procedures can managers use to plan the timing of their projects?

Two procedures include PERT and Gantt charts. PERT is a method of analyzing what tasks need to be done, how long each task will take, and identifying the earliest date a project can be finished. The critical path indicates the longest series of steps in the process. A Gantt chart is simply a bar graph that shows the stage a project is in on a given day. Both procedures are rarely done by hand today, thanks to computers.

8. In spite of technological advances, production is still dependent on people.

8. Identify the steps that must occur before people and machines will be combined to revolutionize manufacturing.

What must happen before the combination of people and machines can revolutionize manufacturing?

Workers need to be trained to use and repair computers; suppliers and producers must develop strong relationships to implement such concepts as JIT and enterprise networking; and production managers need to develop more participative managerial styles in order to work with highly skilled workers.

9. The new orientation in production is quality control. Total quality control includes planning for quality, preventing defects, correcting sources of defects, and a philosophy of continuous effort to build quality into products, purchasing, sales, and service.

9. Illustrate how today's trend toward total quality control differs from earlier attempts to control quality and relate the role of quality circles to this total quality control.

Is that what quality circles are for?

Partly. They are also used for improving efficiency and generally to involve employees in decision making.

10. Because the United States is a service society now, automation of the service sector is extremely important.

10. Suggest how the service sector might increase productivity through automation.

Why is service productivity not increasing as rapidly as manufacturing productivity?

One important reason is that the service sector is labor intensive. Keep in mind however that productivity and quality *are* rising in the service sector, but they are more difficult to measure than the industrial sector.

1. Find the latest articles on computer-integrated manufacturing (CIM) and enterprise networking. Which companies are making the greatest advances toward having integrated networks? What companies have installed the systems? Share your articles with the class. If everyone brings in one article, you should have quite a collection for your file on the industrial sector.
2. Review all the terms in this chapter: CAD, CAM, CIM, MRP, just-in-time inventory control, FMS, and so on. These are the business terms of the 1990s. Try to use them in class so that they become familiar in different settings. Soon you will be thinking of new ways to advance business yourself, based on your understanding of these terms.
3. Have the class think of all of the applications of high technology in the service sector that have already occurred. Using this information, try to think of further uses of technology in areas such as recreation, travel, retailing, wholesaling, insurance, banking, finance, and the government.
4. Debate the following proposition: "Resolved, that the federal government should become more involved in the future of U.S. industry through a national industrial policy." Take whichever side of the issue you did not previously agree with to broaden your thinking on this issue.
5. Debate the following proposition: "Resolved, that U.S. manufacturers should halt the spread of computers and robots used in manufacturing to save jobs for U.S. workers." Again, take the other side of this issue from your normal position.

CASE ONE **THE AUTOMATION OF GENERAL MOTORS**

No firm is more committed to computerizing production than General Motors. GM paid $2.5 billion to buy Electronic Data Systems (EDS). EDS is a computer-services company that has been asked to bring its values of productivity to GM.

The model for future GM plants may be the Saturn plant in Tennessee. Saturn will cost about $5 billion to put into production, and will provide 6,000 jobs in the plant and 10,000 more in nearby facilities. Here are some of the impacts of plants such as Saturn.

Soon you will be able to go into a GM dealer and order a car, including colors, optional equipment, financing arrangements, and delivery date—all at a computer terminal. The computer will translate your order into parts orders. Radios, air conditioners, tires, and thousands of other parts will be ordered from suppliers all over the world. Computer-designed inventory control will allow just-in-time delivery to the production floor. From order to delivery could take less than two weeks.

Meanwhile, at the factory the car is being designed and built using computer-aided design and manufacturing. Robots will do much of the assembling and moving of parts. Workers will not be on assembly lines; rather, they will work in small groups (modules) to build subassemblies. Testing of parts will be done in the modules to raise quality control. The robots and computers will be able to talk to each other, and control systems will catch flaws almost immediately. Productivity in some areas will increase over present plants by 800 percent.

Workers will be paid a salary, not hourly wages. Workers as a whole will have no more than six job categories, and each worker will do a wider variety of work. Workers will have a much larger say in how jobs are performed and at what pace.

The whole plant will be virtually paperless. Everything from order forms to engineering drawings will be on computers. EDS computer specialists will link the system into computer-integrated manufacturing. When a car is ordered, computers will begin designing an inventory of spark plugs, air filters, and other parts to be sent to automobile dealerships to service the cars for the foreseeable future.

DECISION QUESTIONS

1. What will be the impact of such plants on blue-collar jobs and white-collar jobs in manufacturing? GM feels the impact on white-collar jobs will be greater. Why would that be?
2. How will such new manufacturing techniques affect the job market in the 1990s?
3. What will be the impact of such plants on suppliers, competitors, and dealers? What about unions?
4. Can you imagine GM being linked with all of its suppliers, dealers, and salespeople with one computer network that could create instant communications among all these people? What impact might that have on quality control? What other advantages do you see to such a system?

CASE TWO   QUALITY—AMERICA IS BACK

Ask any production manager in Japan what person has had the greatest influence on their tremendous increase in quality products, and they are sure to answer "W. Edwards Deming." He taught them the concepts of statistical control of quality, and they applied the principles. Japanese businesses do not need as many quality control people at the *end* of assembly lines because they test for quality all along the production line. As a consequence, many Japanese products are not only priced well, they are higher in quality as well.

Another American named Philip Crosby wrote a book called *Quality Is Free* that has had a big impact on the thinking of managers at IBM and other leading firms. He followed that successful book with two others: *Quality Without Tears* and *The Art of Getting Your Own Sweet Way*. What are all these books saying? "Why not do things right the first time?" or, "Set high standards and meet them every time."

It is no accident that Ford used the theme of "Quality is Job One" for its ad campaign. Quality will remain a major focus in the 1990s because America is starting to listen to its experts—as Japan did.

One example of the new quality approach is provided by Spectrum Control, Incorporated. The company had trouble soldering terminals to capacitors because the capacitors wouldn't accept solder. Rejects jumped from 3 percent to 32 percent and 50 percent to 75 percent of engineering time was taken up by this problem. Eventually the whole operation was shut down and Spectrum began a new quality program.

First, it had to reject the notion of acceptable quality levels (AQLs). Its customers (for example, IBM and Hewlett-Packard) were requiring something close to zero defects. Furthermore, a Japanese company (Murata Erie North American, Incorporated) was a competitor, and it was emphasizing Japanese-level quality.

Spectrum bought $15,000 worth of videotapes on quality by Deming (14 tapes, 16 hours). They also hired Philip Crosby (at $46,000 a week) to consult with them about quality.

The result? Spectrum estimates that its first year's savings on sales returns and allowances would be $767,000. Quality is now a fixture at Spectrum, and Crosby was right. Quality *is* free; in fact, it pays huge dividends.

DECISION QUESTIONS

1. How did it happen that American businesses let the quality of their products slip below that of foreign producers? Is it too late to meet the challenge?
2. How can computers and robots add to product quality? What effect does that have on labor?
3. Have you seen quality improvements in American cars in the last few years? What other products need more attention to quality?
4. What services need a quality boost in the 1990s? How would you go about implementing those changes?

Are you ready for the information age? Do you understand the language of computers? Do you understand how important robots and other high-tech machines will be in the future?

Chapter 14 will help you whether or not you are up-to-date in these areas. It is a good review of the terms and concepts from the computer area and other high-tech industries. Before we go on, however, be sure to take some time with the exercises and cases in this chapter. They set the stage for the next chapter.

LOOKING AHEAD

MANAGEMENT TOOLS FOR THE INFORMATION AGE

14

Stephen Chen

The ability of small business management to use the new computer and communication technologies to access information will determine a company's future just as much as product design or marketing savvy has in the past.

LARRY WILKE, president of International Computer Programs, Inc.

PROFILE STEVE CHEN, COMPUTER GENIUS

Steve Chen was born in China. After World War II, Steve's family moved to Taiwan. Steve obtained a degree in electrical engineering at National Taiwan University. He came to the United States in 1970 for a master's degree in electrical engineering at Villanova. After he became a U.S. citizen, Chen went on to the University of Illinois where he received his Ph.D. in computer science. He became a project engineer at Burroughs and then a project manager at Floating Point Systems. What made him most famous, however, was his job at Cray computer.

At Cray, Chen helped develop multimillion-dollar supercomputers. Chen was then put in charge of a 200-person team to develop a whole new generation of supercomputers that would be 100 times faster than any in use today. However, the project was canceled by Cray's chairman because it seemed too costly and risky.

Chen quit and took with him some 40 researchers to set up Supercomputer Systems, Inc., and continue work on the machine. Because the project was risky, it was difficult getting venture capital. IBM decided to give Chen both seed money and technical assistance because it wants to have a supercomputer to fill the upper end of its computer line. The new supercomputers use parallel processing. The idea is to have several processors working at once on the same problem. It is like having five people painting a fence instead of one. Cray's new supercomputer has eight parallel processors. Chen hopes to have 64 in his. It will be like having 64 painters working at once instead of 8. In the future, computers may have as many as 2,000 processors. Obviously the job will be done faster.

What make Steve Chen so interesting in the 1990s is that he represents the future of American business. Supercomputers, new fax machines that send messages and pictures from computer screen to computer screen, new telecommunications equipment using fiber optics, and other technological breakthroughs will revolutionize the way we do business and greatly increase productivity. This is the communications age. Businesses small and large will succeed or fail based on their ability to manage information. Computers will be a large part of that process. But so will other equipment that will enable managers to make better decisions and communicate with each other, with customers, and with other companies, including suppliers. The 1990s will be one of the most exciting decades in history in that new technological developments will be coming rapidly. The question is: Will you be able to keep up? This chapter will introduce you to the newest concepts. If you keep reading the business literature and taking courses, you will be able to take advantage of these new developments and carve out a successful career in business.

Source: Kenneth Labich, "The Shootout in Supercomputers," *Fortune*, February 29, 1988, pp. 67–70; George Melloan, "Staying Ahead of the Pack at Cray Research," *The Wall Street Journal*, February 23, 1988, p. 31; and "Is Intel About to Crunch Cray's Number-Crunchers?" *Business Week*, April 17, 1989, p. 62.

THE IMPORTANCE OF MANAGING INFORMATION

It is impossible to overemphasize the importance of information management in today's organizations. Over half of the U.S. work force is now involved in information products or services. More than 9 million business/professional PCs (personal computers) were bought in 1988. A million of them were laptop models that are more powerful than most business computers of a decade ago.[1] Now these portable computers are being linked to fax machines and cellular phones to send messages to anyone, anywhere, any time. You will learn about such developments in this chapter.

Throughout this text, we have emphasized the need for managing information flows between businesses and their employees, businesses and their customers, and so on. Those managers who try to rely on the old ways of doing things will simply not be able to compete with those who have the latest in technology *and know how to use it*. The problem today is that the technology is so new and is changing so fast that managers have not been able to keep up. This problem is going to get worse before it gets better. Computers will be able to process data 100 times faster than they can now. More and more data will be available.

What all this means to you is that you simply will not be competitive in the career marketplace unless you learn to use the latest in technology. If you have never used computers, it may seem overwhelming to you at the moment, but the process simply takes time. First, you might become familiar with computers by doing some simple word processing. Or perhaps you could begin by using the computer exercises available with this text to give you some experience in computer use as well as reinforce the content of the text. These and most other new computer programs are as user friendly as possible. That means that the designers have specifically made them easy to use. Once you learn to turn the computer on and put information in and get it out, everything else becomes easier.

Likewise, it is easy to use fax machines and the other new technologies available. Try to get down to a modern office and try some of these new products yourself. Many of them are available at your school. Your job is to be aggressive in searching out the latest technology and learning as much as possible. This is certainly possible without taking a course, but courses do help. The potential is fantastic. Some day customers will be able to order goods by computer, marketing will have instant contact with engineering and production to custom make goods, and the whole business system will become more efficient. By educating yourself, you will be one of the agents of change.

Keep in mind as you become familiar with these new machines that the goal is not to make your job easier or to help you communicate faster with others in the company. The goal is to better serve customers so your organization becomes more competitive, makes more profit, and provides more jobs in the United States.

It's Getting Easier to Be Computer Literate

The introduction of new procedures and new technology is always disruptive. People tend to be afraid of the new systems. They believe that they won't be able to learn the new skills and will appear awkward or dumb. Certainly, the introduction of computers has followed that pattern. Slowly but surely, however, computers have crept into organizations, so that the pressure on those who still are unfamiliar with computers and their uses is even greater.

To use a computer in the past, one had to learn computer languages such as FORTRAN (FORmula TRANslation) or COBOL (COmmon Business-Oriented Language). (See the box called Selected Computer Languages on page 429 to become more familiar with the language names.) The learning process was slow, errors were plentiful, and the whole process was difficult for many people.

Today's computers are much easier to use. The focus in many schools is shifting away from programming computers to using computers for managerial decision making, a more enjoyable high-level function. Of course, there will be many new jobs in computer programming, repair, and design. But more important to the majority of students, almost all jobs can be made more efficient through the use of computers. Not only are we able to buy items by using home computers, we are also able to send letters by computer (electronic mail), find information by computer (electronic library), and we are generally more connected with information resources. In other words, you will not be able to function fully in tomorrow's business or consumer world unless you learn to use the computer. It will be almost as commonplace for businesspeople to use a computer as it is to drive a car.

The main purpose of this chapter is to introduce you to some of the terms and uses of computers, robots, and other high-tech equipment in today's organizations. If you have already taken computer courses, some of this material will be a review of what you already know. If you have never touched a computer before, you will learn much about its uses in today's business. But no matter what your stage of computer literacy, we think you will find the information on the newest technology exciting.

Another goal of this chapter is to help you understand the steps for introducing computer technology into a small firm. As a potential worker in such a business, you may be the one who has to initiate such systems in the firm because veteran managers are sometimes too intimidated by the new technology to even try to use it. You should read newspapers and magazines, watch for articles on the use of fax machines, office automation, cellular phones, interactive video systems, and other high-tech developments to see what is happening in the market now. The information age is here, and it's going to be interesting and challenging.

COMPUTER HARDWARE

computer hardware
All the tangible equipment that processes and stores data.

computer software
The instructions for telling the computer what to do.

There are two major components of a computer system: hardware and software. **Computer hardware** refers to the computer equipment itself, including peripherals such as printers and modems (devices that allow computers to communicate with each other over phone lines). Computers and their peripherals are "dumb" machines—that is, they can't do anything without instructions. **Computer software** is the programs that give the computer the instructions to complete a task. Without software, the hardware will just sit there. But given the proper instructions, computers can perform great feats. The capabilities of computers are growing with each new generation, as we shall see in the next section.

Five Generations of Computers

We are now developing the so-called fifth generation of computers. It is amazing to see the progress of computers over the last 25 years or so. The first generation of computers used vacuum tubes, were very bulky, and generated much heat—like thousands of light bulbs. Such computers filled whole rooms. The second generation used smaller, cooler transistors and diodes. The third generation was the introduction of integrated circuits. An integrated circuit is a network of transistors all contained on a silicon chip about the size of the top of a pencil. The fourth generation uses very-large-scale integrated circuits (VLSI). These computers can fit on the top of a desk, but have much greater processing ability than the original room-size computers. Today's personal computers are fourth-generation computers.

SELECTED COMPUTER LANGUAGES

Wouldn't it be great if humans and computers spoke the same language? Unfortunately, even computers often can't speak to each other, much less to their users. Computers and programmers fluent in one language aren't necessarily able to use other languages since the languages are so different. The following are some of the more common computer languages.

Ada: A government (especially military) computer language.

ALGOL (*Al*g*o*rithmic *L*anguage): Math-oriented language used most often for larger computers.

APL (*A P*rogramming *L*anguage): IBM-devised language useful for math.

BASIC (*B*eginners *A*ll-purpose *S*ymbolic *I*nstructional *C*ode): Used mostly for math and statistics.

COBOL (*Co*mmon *B*usiness-*O*riented *L*anguage): Used for business applications such as billing, payroll, or inventory.

FORTRAN (*Fo*rmula *Tran*slation): Used most often for scientific problems.

LISP: Advanced artificial intelligence language for programs that deal with human languages.

LOGO: Language useful for graphics; widely used in schools.

PASCAL: Language that teaches a structured approach to programming; in the same class as Ada.

PL1 (*P*rogramming *L*anguage *1*): Similar to ALGOL, but handles business files better.

PROLOG (*Pro*gramming in *Log*ic): Basic artificial intelligence program.

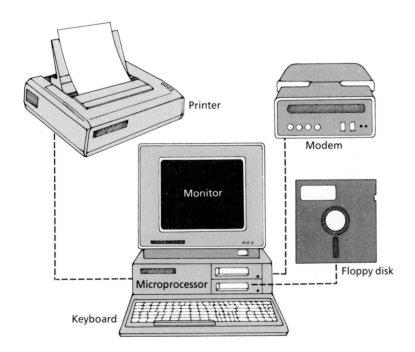

Printer

Modem

Monitor

Floppy disk

Microprocessor

Keyboard

This illustration shows the key parts of a microcomputer system. The keyboard is much like those on typewriters. The monitor is like a small TV set. The floppy disk plays like a record. The modem lets you communicate over phone lines with other computers. The printer can turn out professional-quality printing.

The fifth generation of computers is much faster. They are able to use **artificial intelligence** software. That is, the computer systems are able to "reason" and "learn" using data from their past actions. Such systems are now being used in financial management and petroleum refinery monitoring. They are also used for such things as diagnosing medical problems, providing vision systems for robots, and allowing people to use English to communicate with computers. Organizations such as NASA's Goddard Space Flight Center, GE's Space Division, and Motorola's Radar Operations Service use this new generation of computers.

artificial intelligence
The ability of computers to mimic human thought processes.

Left to right: The Compaq Deskpro 286E is a microcomputer; Digital Equipment Corporation's Micro PDP-11 is a supermicrocomputer; the Digital Vax 8974 is a superminicomputer; the IBM 3090 is a mainframe computer; the Convex C-1 is a minisupercomputer; and the CRAY is a supercomputer.

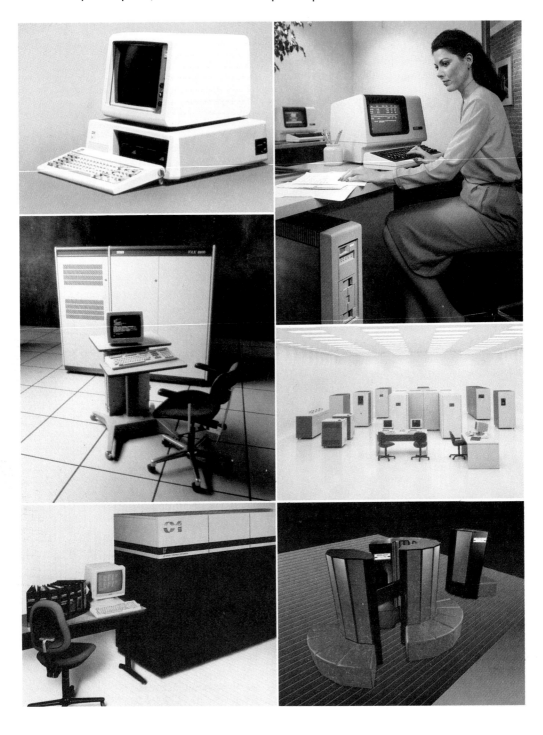

Computer manufacturers are working on new technologies that will greatly increase the speed and lower the cost of computers. How much have prices fallen for the bigger computers? How fast will innovation occur? A look back will give you some perspective. John Blankenbaker built the first personal computer in 1971.[2] It was called the Kenbak 1, and it had no keyboard or screen. About that same time, Edward Roberts introduced a computer called the Altair. Its storage capacity was about one paragraph. But it and the Kenbak 1 began the microcomputer era (the era of personal computers or PCs)—about 20 years ago. The Altair was displayed at the Homebrew Computer Club in Palo Alto, California. Two club members, Stephen Wozniak and Steven Jobs, liked the idea and proceeded to build their own similar computer in a garage. They named their product Apple 1.

Today the Apple computer is one of leading microcomputers on the market. A *microcomputer* is the smallest and least expensive class of computers. Microcomputers are used in homes, schools, and businesses. In addition to microcomputers, today's technology includes minicomputers and mainframe computers. *Minicomputers* are more powerful, more expensive, and accept more programming languages than microcomputers, but are not as large, expensive, or powerful as mainframe computers. *Mainframes* are the largest, fastest, and most expensive class of computers. (Supercomputers are the largest, fastest, and most expensive of the mainframes.) Mainframes are used for information processing in large businesses, colleges, and organizations.

In just a few years we have gone from primitive models to today's sophisticated computers, and technology is changing even faster. What will computers be like in the future? They will be as different in 20 years as they were 20 years ago. Some will be voice activated. Others will be able to read instructions written out by hand or translate such instructions into computer printing. As you'll learn later, some will be able to "think" through problems and come up with recommendations.

It is safe to say that such developments will be as significant as the industrial revolution. It is also safe to say that computers will be as common as telephones, TV sets, and radios. And that means jobs for you. Think of all the computer jobs that have been created since the very first computer was used by a business in 1954, when GE installed one at its Appliance Park in Kentucky. Think of all the jobs that will come in the next 35 years!

THINKING IT THROUGH

Imagine trying to build a house all by yourself. You would have to do one thing at a time—pouring the foundation, brick laying, plumbing, wiring, and so on. The job would go much faster if several workers were assigned jobs at the same time. You could have plumbers working at the same time as electricians, and so forth. Your problem would be to develop plans to assign all those jobs at once. Clearly, some jobs will take longer than others and other coordinating problems would arise. The same happens with parallel processing, but the job gets done much faster nonetheless. For example, a computer with parallel processing capabilities was asked to calculate the stresses and strains throughout a solid metal beam with a heavy load on it. The machine answered the question in a week. It would have taken an ordinary computer 20 years to answer the same question.

Try to imagine some uses of such a computer. The problem is that you can't. It will take many years to get used to such computing power and put it to use designing and testing products and measuring the effects of key management decisions on the whole U.S. economy, if not the world economy.

SOFTWARE APPLICATIONS IN BUSINESS MANAGEMENT

As you know, computer software (programs) provide the instructions that enable you to tell the computer what to do. At one time, computer users developed much of their own software. To do that, they had to learn a computer language.

Today it is often more important to find the right software (instructions) before finding the right hardware (the specific kind of computer to buy). The idea is to choose software that will do the jobs you want, and then find a computer that will accept that software.

Software is like a record. If you want to hear a certain singer or orchestra, you buy that particular record. The record may be an old 78 or a new laser disk. The type of records you buy dictates the kind of record player (hardware) you need.

Some software programs are easier to use than others. Some are more sophisticated and can perform more functions. A businessperson must decide what functions he or she wants performed by a computer and then choose the appropriate software. That choice will help decide what make and size computer to buy.

It is important to recognize the fact that we are still in the pioneering stage of computer software development. When selecting a computer, therefore, it is a good idea to anticipate what kind of software is likely to come out in the future. Software writers tend to develop programs that fit the most popular computers (for example, IBM, Apple). If you were to buy a record player that played the old 78s, you wouldn't be able to play the newest records when they came out. That is what happened to many people who bought certain inexpensive home computers when the company that made those computers went out of business. Nobody is writing new programs for those computers and they are rapidly becoming obsolete.

There is software available for many business applications. Even though many small businesses are not completely computerized, many use computers for accounting, inventory control, payroll, accounts receivable, accounts payable, and so on. Businesspeople most frequently use software for four major purposes: (1) writing (word processing), (2) manipulating numbers (spreadsheets), (3) filing and retrieving data (databases), (4) communicating, and (5) presenting information visually (graphics). Today's software performs all five functions in one program.

Word Processing Programs

Once you've learned to use a word processing program, you'll probably put your typewriter in the attic. When you use a word processing program you can correct errors or revise your text quickly and easily. If you consistently misspell a word, you can change the spelling one time and, with a single command, it will automatically be changed each place it occurs. You can write a report on the typewriter-like keyboard, shift sentences and paragraphs, and print the finished manuscript without worrying about spacing, paging, or margins. Word processing eliminates erasing, cutting, and pasting, allowing you to concentrate on content and style. And there are no more spelling errors! With an automated dictionary, you can check your text for spelling errors and select the correct spelling quickly.

Businesses use word processors to increase office productivity. Standardized letters can be personalized quickly, documents can be updated by changing only the outdated text and leaving the rest intact, and contract forms can be revised to meet the stipulations of specific customers.

There are many word processing software packages on the market. Some of the most popular programs include WordPerfect, PFS:Professional Write, Writing Assistant, Wordstar, and Microsoft Word. Each program has many functions. Some programs have more functions than others. Which program is right for you? It depends on what you need to do. Assess your needs and then match what you need to the available software.

Spreadsheet Programs

A spreadsheet program is simply the electronic equivalent of an accountant's worksheet. Some of the most popular programs include Lotus 1-2-3, Quattro, Surpass, Excel, and AppleWorks. A **spreadsheet** is a table made up of rows and columns that enables a manager to organize information. Using the computer's speedy calculations, managers have their questions answered almost as fast as they can ask them. For example, suppose we use a spreadsheet to figure the break-even point (Chapter 8) for our Fiberrific cereal. The spreadsheet contains the appropriate formula for calculating the break-even point. Our calculations indicate that at a price of $2 a box, we must sell 2,000 boxes to break even. We now think we can raise our price because of increased demand caused by a recent government study linking eating oat bran with lowering cholesterol levels. We can ask "What if we raise the price of Fiberrific to $2.50?" Once we insert $2.50 in the price cell (the point where columns and rows intersect), the computer will tell us instantly that we must sell 1,333 boxes to break even (see Figure 14–1).

Of course, this is a simple example. Businesses often develop very complex spreadsheets, sometimes using hundreds of columns and rows. As the complexity of the spreadsheet increases, the chance for incorporating human error increases. The information derived from spreadsheets must be reliable, though, if managers are to use it confidently to make complex decisions. Therefore, it is essential that managers and others formatting and inputting data into spreadsheets be appropriately trained.

spreadsheet
A table made up of rows and columns that enables a manager to organize information.

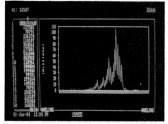

It is important to choose the software package you will be using before choosing the hardware you will use. Lotus 1-2-3 is a popular program, but many programs are written specifically for banks, small retail stores, and so forth. Check around before you buy.

FIGURE 14–1

This figure shows how a spreadsheet program works. In this case, the question is, "What would happen to the break-even point if the price of the product were raised to $2.50." You simply type $2.50 in the proper place and the program does the calculations. The answer is 1,333.

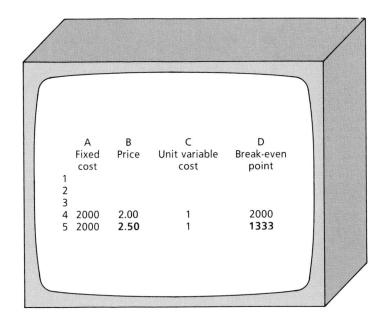

	A Fixed cost	B Price	C Unit variable cost	D Break-even point
1				
2				
3				
4	2000	2.00	1	2000
5	2000	**2.50**	1	**1333**

MAKING ETHICAL DECISIONS

Computer software, particularly the applications programs described in this text, take hundreds of hours to create. Anyone who has taken a basic programming course knows that developing such programs takes tremendous planning, effort, and tenacity. And anyone who has bought a software package knows it often takes a lot of money to buy one.

Suppose a friend of yours owns a program that you have been wanting to use for writing school term papers. Your friend offers to make a "pirate" (illegal) copy for you. What do you do? What could you have done instead? What are the consequences of your decisions?

Database Programs

Database programs allow you to work with information you normally keep in files: names and addresses, schedules, inventories, and so on. Simple commands allow you to add new information, change incorrect information, and delete out-of-date or unnecessary information. Most programs have features that let you print only certain information, arrange records in the order you want them, and change the way information is displayed. Using database programs you can create reports with exactly the information you want and the way you want the information to appear. Leading database programs include: Q & A, Rapidfile, PFS: Professional File, PC-File, dBase III Plus, R base, and HyperCard for Apple computers.

Graphics Programs

A picture is worth a thousand words. Why should we study a 1,000-line report to identify the leading Fiberrific salesperson, when a glance at a computer-generated bar graph can show us in a instant? Computer graphics programs can use data from spreadsheets to visually summarize information by drawing bar graphs, pie charts, and line charts. Do you need to change a figure or label? No need to round up the eraser, ruler, and compass. Simply insert the new data and, presto, the computer changes the lines or curves and your new chart is ready for presentation. Would you rather have a pie chart than a bar graph? No problem—for a computer with a good graphics program. Some popular graphics programs include MacDraw for Macintosh computers, Harvard Graphics, Freelance Plus, and Windows Draw.

But even the most sophisticated software is no substitute for good old human judgment. The manager must do his or her homework by selecting the most meaningful numbers to represent. In order to be useful, graphs and charts should only present essential information.

Communications Software

There are many programs that will enable a computer to exchange files with other computers, retrieve information from databases, and send and receive electronic mail (letters by computer). Two of these are Crosstalk Mk. IV and Smartcom 111. An inexpensive program is ProComm. For the Macintosh, people like Micro Phone 11.

Integrated Software

It may occur to you that having all of these different software packages might become cumbersome. It may also be difficult to integrate the information from these different software companies. One solution is an integrated software package that offers two or more applications in one package. Most such packages include word processing, database management, spreadsheet, and communications. You can switch among the programs at will with the latest programs.

The first truly integrated packages for the IBM PC were Symphony from Lotus Development and Framework from Ashton-Tate. Others include Open Access and Enable 2.0. Microsoft Word is one for Macintosh computers.

CUSTOM-MADE SOFTWARE

Ready-made software fits the needs of most users, but some businesses may find their needs are unique and unmet by existing products. They find it necessary to have their systems tailored for their specific requirements. Next we shall look at two of the largest custom-made systems used by business: management information systems (MIS) and decision support systems (DSS).

Management Information Systems

A **management information system** is a mechanism that collects, organizes, and distributes information to managers. In the past, such data were gathered and processed by an electronic data processing (EDP) department. The problem was that the reports sent to managers were often difficult to read, incomplete, and slow in coming.

The latest systems involve a network of computers that can communicate with one another internally. One manager can talk with other managers and either request information from an EDP department or call up the data on his or her own computer. Thus, all managers are able to receive data, manipulate the data at their desks, and communicate with one another if problems arise. See the illustration called Managing by Computer. Today that means that the growth in computers will be in desktop personal computers (PCs) and not in the huge, centralized mainframe computers of the past. There will still be mainframe computers, but they will be linked to desktop computers so that everyone can access data from the central source or sources.

The unified systems that tie together all the computers in a firm are called **local area networks (LANs).** Today, local area networking ties together computers within *one* firm. In the near future, enterprise networking will tie together multiple firms. Then producers will be able to share their information with suppliers as quickly as their managers get it. Similarly, manufacturers will be able to share information with distributors around the world almost instantly.[3] If you think about the implications for a minute, it will be clear to you that a major problem will involve the secrecy and protection of information. That is a problem that needs to be solved before such systems are widely implemented.

management information system
A mechanism that collects, organizes, and distributes information to managers.

local area networks (LANs)
Communications systems that link computers and other devices within a confined area such as a building.

Decision Support Systems

Decision support systems (DSS) are interactive, computer-based information systems that retrieve, manipulate, and display information for managerial decision making. Some are known as executive support systems for that reason. Such a system allows managers to ask questions and receive answers in graphic form in addition to written reports. Decision support systems are largely designed for top managers. As such, they provide data that assist in tasks such as strategic planning. The difference between a DSS and an MIS is that the DSS is used to help in unstructured decision making, as opposed to accounting systems that manage relatively structured material. A DSS gives managers the ability to ask theoretical questions and get answers.

Artificial intelligence is the science of building computer models of the human mind. Computer scientists are making some progress in that direction, but such computers are a long way from being able to compete with an average human being. Nonetheless, soon computers will be able to "see, hear, think, and talk." At least they will be able to mimic such behavior by humans.

Meanwhile, some managers have something almost as good as a computer that can think. They have a type of DSS known as an expert system. An **expert system (ES)** is a computer program that contains the expertise of human specialists (experts) in a field. For example, financial expert systems are starting to do such tasks as guide an individual's investments, warn manufacturers about foreign competition, and reject bad insurance risks.

Expert systems can store and manipulate knowledge and rules of thumb as well as data. They can "reason" by drawing inferences from stored knowledge. This is the first stage of artificial intelligence. The computer can't think for you, but it can help you formulate questions and teach you how to reach logical conclusions.

One example of expert systems at work can be seen at the Campbell Soup Company. They had an employee who worked for 44 years maintaining the cookers used to sterilize the soup. For seven months an engineer asked the worker what to do in various circumstances and all of the information was stored in the computer. Now, when a sterilizer loses power, the temperature sinks too low, or the cans come out bent, an operator simply types the problem into a computer and it answers 95 percent of the time.[4]

Is it any wonder that expert systems are some of the hottest commodities on the market? A football team can program rules such as, "If it's fourth down and more than 10 and you are further away than 50 yards from the opponents goal— punt!" What kind of investment do you recommend to a 24-year-old single woman who has $5,000 to invest? Ask the system. Stop and think for a moment of all the uses that could be made of expert systems and you could spend the rest of the day dreaming up answers. If you need someone with experience, you can use an expert system because it has such experience programmed into it.

USING COMPUTER–GENERATED INFORMATION

The problem with all the developments in computers and other technological advances is that managers have access to a tremendous amount of data, but too much data can confuse issues rather than clarify them. There is often confusion between the words *data* and *information*. Data are raw, unanalyzed, and unsummarized facts and figures. (Note that the word is plural. The singular form is *datum*.) Information is the processed and summarized data that can be used for managerial decision making.

Managing by computer.

ELECTRONIC CALENDAR

Work group

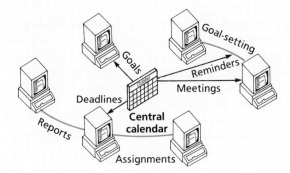

An electronic calendar keeps executives in the work group organized and on schedule. It tracks management objectives and goals, arranges meetings, sends reminders of deadlines, and warns when a project falls behind.

ELECTRONIC MAIL

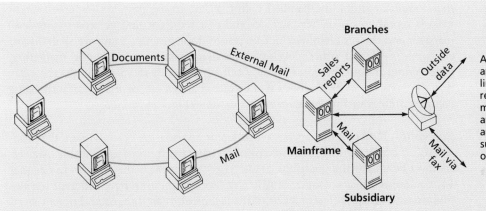

Anchored by a mainframe, an electronic mail network links the work group with remote operations. It moves messages, reports, and correspondence among headquarters, subsidiaries, branches, and overseas offices.

INFORMATION SYSTEM

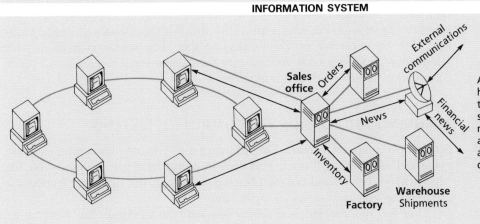

An information system handles all data relevant to the business—inventory, sales, cash flow, financial news, market reports—and makes them instantly available throughout the organization.

One role of computers today is to take raw data and translate them into useful information. For example, our cereal company may have data about sales, taxes, salaries, and movement of inventory. Those data can be analyzed by computer to give managers sales by salesperson and by region and profits per region. The usefulness of management information depends on four characteristics of that information.

Quality   Quality means that the information is accurate and reliable. When the clerk at a fast-food restaurant enters your order into the cash register, it may be automatically fed to a computer and the day's sales and profits can be calculated as soon as the store closes. The sales and expense data must be accurate or the rest of the calculations will be wrong. This can be a real problem when many calculations are based on questionable sales forecasts, for example.

Complete   There must be enough data to make a decision, but not too much to confuse the issue. Today, as we have noted, the problem is often too much data rather than too little.

Timely   Information must reach managers quickly. If a customer has a complaint, that complaint should be handled within a day. In the past, a salesperson might make a report to his or her manager and that report would go to a higher-level manager and the problem may not be resolved for months. Later we shall discuss electronic mail and other developments that make it possible for marketing, engineering, and production to hear about a problem with a product the same day that the salesperson hears about it. Product changes can be made instantly using computer-integrated manufacturing, as discussed in Chapter 13.

Relevant   Different managers have different information needs. Again, the problem today is that information systems often have too much data available. Managers must be taught the questions to ask to get the answers they desire. In Chapter 11, you learned that managers at different levels in the firm have different responsibilities and tasks. Different levels of management, therefore, need different levels of information. Lower-level managers need a system that reports to them information such as the level of inventory on hand, production schedules, and labor schedules. Middle-level managers need information about sales forecasts and problems that are occurring on the production line. Top managers need to have information about economic and industry trends, new regulations, and the profit contribution of various divisions in the firm.

PLANNING AND DESIGNING COMPUTER SYSTEMS

Setting up a computer system is like planning a trip. You must know where you are going and what you will need. You need to decide who will be responsible for which chores beforehand. Good planning will make the difference between a dream-come-true vacation and a nightmare.

Thus far, the integration of computers into the workplace has been rather disorganized and uncoordinated. One manager may order a word processor for his or her staff, another may order personal computers for workers, and so on. What results is a mishmash of machines, most of which are not compatible and many of

When choosing a computer for a business, it is important to choose the software first. Software such as shown in this picture can solve many business problems, but only if the computer can use it. In the future, software will become even more important.

which go unused. Not until the last few years has it been possible to integrate data processing, word processing, interoffice communications, external communications, printing, and other office-related functions. This was done using both new hardware and software. The manager of any organization (small or large, profit or nonprofit) should follow these 10 steps when planning office automation:

1. Identify the information needs of all the workers and managers and decide if additional computer resources are needed.
2. Involve all departments in the planning process, and consult with suppliers and distributors.
3. Seek input from the existing data processing department, if there is one.
4. Seek other expert advice.
5. Choose software first.
6. Decide whether to buy equipment or use a computer service.
7. Evaluate equipment to be purchased and possible vendors for price, quality, and service.
8. Train employees in computer use.
9. Update the system and training periodically.
10. Integrate computer communications with other communication efforts and other corporate operations.

Identify Information Needs

What a new or growing business needs is a solution to the problem of getting the right data to the right person at the right time. Owning a computer may or may not be the most cost-effective solution to such problems. To determine what system is best, the starting point is to work with managers and workers to find what their needs are. A needs-assessment program looks at information needs, equipment needs, space needs, human involvement needs, and more. Needs assessment is also the first step in buying your own home computer.

Involve All Departments, Suppliers, and Distributors

Every business or organization has some primary function such as accounting, production, marketing, or retailing. But each organization also has multiple tasks it must perform to assist in the primary function. Some obvious tasks involve payroll, inventory control, billing, employee records (for example, sick leave or vacations), and more. To design the most effective and efficient computer system, the needs of all departments must be considered. The real efficiencies in the future will come from integrated computer systems that allow managers of various departments to communicate with each other by computer and get needed data from a central information storage area.

Soon your computer system may be linked with those of your suppliers and distributors. It is important, therefore, to consult with these other organizations to make your system as compatible as possible right from the beginning.

Seek Input from the Data Processing Department

In the past, the information systems department tended to be located off by itself, and the managers and workers were treated as aliens who spoke a strange language called *computerese*. Periodically these "computer jocks" would send out reports on funny-looking computer paper that contained columns of numbers and graphs that were understood by few and used by fewer. The gulf between information systems specialists and line managers was often wide.

Today, that lack of understanding and rapport can no longer be tolerated. Computers are supposed to make management and decision making easier and more accurate, not harder and more complex. The planning phase of computer development must involve all managers, including data processing experts, from the beginning. If the needs of one group of managers are given special attention, it should be the information users, not the data processing people. Many companies now hire consultants to serve as liasions to bridge the gap between information users and the data processing staff.

Seek Other Expert Advice

The cost of hiring an outside expert to evaluate the needs of the organization and recommend a solution is usually well worth it in the long run. An inside expert may be too committed to the present system or too biased by his or her own department's needs to provide the objective analysis needed. An experienced consultant may recommend an outside computer service or some kind of time-sharing system that would prove significantly cheaper and more flexible than other options. Outside experts can also lessen the training time needed to get the system operating.

Choose Software First

Selection of software should precede any serious consideration of hardware. Too many people select the hardware first and then try to find the right software package only to find there isn't a suitable one available. It's a common mistake and a serious one. Note this step when selecting a personal computer for yourself.

Decide Whether to Buy or Use a Computer Service

Before buying equipment that could soon become obsolete or need costly servicing, an organization may consider contracting with computer service companies to perform various functions. For example, one such firm, Automatic Data Processing (ADP) of Roseland, New Jersey, handles computer problems, including payroll, of 100,000 customers averaging 70 employees each.

One type of service, called **remote processing,** works like this: An organization obtains special forms from a computer service company and fills in all the necessary information. The service company picks up the forms and processes them at its own "remote" facility (thus the term *remote processing*). The service company then provides the desired outputs—sales analyses, paychecks, bills, and so forth.

Another version of computer service is called **on-line remote processing.** A service company provides the organization with a computer terminal. The service company then trains someone at the organization to input the necessary data. The information then travels over phone lines to the service company and is sent back in processed form to the organization. Large national service firms as well as smaller regional firms provide such services.

A third option for a firm wishing to use outside services is called **time sharing.** Time sharing gives small and large firms the capability of using complex software programs and data files too expensive to be purchased by any one firm. Sometimes the data simply are not available any other way.

Individuals and smaller firms have found it valuable to use computer services that contain much information and sources. Two popular firms providing such data are The Source and CompuServe.

All of these options should be considered before equipment is purchased. Nonetheless, the new computers are so small, inexpensive, and powerful that they are affordable by individuals and very small firms. The problem may then become one of deciding which functions to do internally and which to farm out to computer-service firms.

remote processing
A computer service that processes data submitted to it on written forms in its own facilities and then returns the processed information to the client organization.

on-line remote processing
A computer service that provides the client organization with a computer terminal and training to input data; data are sent over phone lines to the service company and returned in processed form.

time sharing
A computer service that allows others to "rent" time on computers.

Evaluate Equipment and Vendors

It is not always a good idea to buy a computer from the producer. The tendency is for the producer to sell you a computer, printer, software, and other accessories all made by that firm. As with stereo systems, however, it is sometimes best to buy different components from different manufacturers. Like stereo stores, computer stores are often helpful in putting together a package system of various brand name components to form a useful (and often cheaper) computer system. Such stores may also provide helpful training and service.

The most important question to answer when selecting hardware is: Are all the pieces compatible with each other and *with your software?* What does compatible mean? Basically, it means that everything works together. Most likely you have heard of IBM compatible computers. There has been much discussion about how compatible a compatible really is. Being an IBM compatible, for example, does not mean a computer is a copy of an IBM computer. It means it can work with *some* equipment and software made to be used with IBM. Different compatibles are compatible with different equipment and software and not with others. How do you know if the equipment and software you select are compatible with each other?

Test the complete system and software yourself; don't rely entirely on vendors' recommendations.

Train Employees

Many firms have seriously neglected the task of training their employees and managers to use the new word processing and data processing equipment. It is not enough to put people through a one-week training course and assume that they are now proficient workers. Training must continue over time to help workers become familiar with all of the capabilities of the computers. Such training can be expensive, but training costs are decreasing as the new computers become more user friendly.

Often the people least skilled in the use of computers are top managers. Certainly they should leave the more time-consuming data inputting to lower-level workers, but top managers should be able to access information when needed. Productivity is an important goal of office automation, including top management productivity. And that takes training and retraining.

Update System, Including Training

It bears repeating that computer technology, software, and procedures are changing week by week. To keep up, managers must be flexible and open to new ideas, and retraining must occur regularly.

Integrate Computers with Total Communication System

The maximum benefit of computers is reached only when they become part of a total communications system or network. Remember, it is important to involve major customers, suppliers, and distributors in such plans because, in the future, computer and communications systems will be linked and you don't want to design an internal system that will be incompatible with other systems in the future.

When planning a computer system, it is important to consider the benefits of facsimile machines, copy machines, and other office machines, as well as telecommunications equipment. All of these considerations should be made at the same time to assure that the system as a whole is most efficient. After the Progress Check, we will examine several kinds of telecommunications equipment.

PROGRESS CHECK

- What are the trends occurring in business today that make the knowledge of computers and communications technology more important?

- What is artificial intelligence and how is it related to expert systems? What are the benefits of expert systems?

- What is the difference between computer software and computer hardware?

- What are the 10 steps to follow when designing a computer system for an organization? Which should you choose first, computer hardware or software?

TELECOMMUNICATIONS EQUIPMENT

What is exciting about the new enterprise networking we discussed in Chapter 13 is that it links computer technology with **telecommunications equipment** that sends data and/or information over phone lines or through satellite communication systems. This is a complicated process and not all countries are successfully introducing it. One problem the Soviet Union is having with computers is that their phone lines cannot carry data transmissions. Let's begin our look at telecommunications equipment within the firm and then move outward as we describe the best-known technologies:

Electronic Bulletin Boards   An electronic bulletin board sends messages to employees about matters such as job openings and corporate events through the company's computer system. This can cut back greatly on paperwork. It also gives the copy machine a break. Some firms also have an electronic library as part of this system so that employees can look up information using their computer terminals rather than searching in the library.

Modems   A modem is a device that converts data into a form that can be sent over phone lines so that one computer can "talk" to another. A modem allows people to stay at home and interact with a computer at work.

Voice Messaging   Using voice messaging, your computer acts like a complex phone answering machine because it will answer the manager's phone, give out prerecorded messages, and take messages. Managers can call the machines from anywhere and get their messages.

Voice Mail   Voice mail is a way of getting phone messages without buying an answering machine. Voice mail allows customers to have their phones "answered" automatically if they are out or on another call. A stuttering dial tone lets you know a message is waiting.

Electronic Mail   Electronic mail uses telecommunications equipment to send written messages to people within the organization or at other firms. It is cheaper than long-distance phoning and faster than the postal service. The message is sent to a computer terminal where it can be read at any time. It is quick and easy to send the same message to multiple people. This saves time and money. Executives no longer have to call each other by phone and hope that the person is in. Now the messages are sent instantly and the other people will get them as soon as they turn on their computers.

Computer Conferencing   Computer conferencing is an advanced form of electronic mail. Several people can sit at their computer terminals and talk with one another electronically. This is a great help when marketing people want to communicate with engineers and production people without calling a formal meeting. This saves time and money, especially when the people are scattered in different buildings.

telecommunications equipment
Equipment that uses phone lines or satellite communication systems to transfer data from one place to another.

Fax machines are showing up everywhere. Have you tried one yet?

Facsimile Machines   Can you imagine putting a piece of paper into a copy machine and having the copy turn up in an office halfway around the world? That is what facsimile (fax) machines do. A one-page letter can be sent coast to coast in 20 to 30 seconds for less than a dollar. This is probably the fastest-growing communications innovation in industry today. In 1986, only 200,000 units were sold. By 1988, sales were over 700,000.[5] Today fax machines can put you in touch with nearly 2.5 million other fax users worldwide—twice as many as in 1986 and 10 times as many as in 1984.[6] These machines enable you to send a letter or longer document to someone and have them receive it immediately. They will also act as a desktop copier. Fax machines for business cost about $2,500, but soon you will be able to buy such machines for little over $1,000. Cost still too steep for you? You can use Sir Speedy's fax machines for $12 a month if you don't want to buy one. They will even pick up and deliver free. There are also portable fax machines available for your car. PayFAX machines are like phone stations that hang on the wall. Soon you will be able to use a PayFAX like a pay phone from 20,000 units in cities around the world.[7]

Fax modems will allow you to send messages from your computer to other peoples' fax machines. Most people find it easier to use a stand-alone fax machine, however.

Cellular Phones   Cellular phone systems enable managers to dictate work to their office and conduct business by phone from anywhere. Big-city executives who spend a couple of hours commuting are able to use that time productively. Phone calls are now possible from airplanes, too, and some phones make it possible to access computer data from public areas such as airports and hotel lobbies. But salespeople have become the biggest users of cellular phones. Appointments can be made and verified over the phone (to prevent calling on someone who is not in, even though the salesperson had made an appointment). Salespeople are able to phone in orders and do all kinds of work over the phone (in the car) that once required much more time. Salespeople will also be able to receive information and messages. This will make them much more aware and in touch.

USING CELLULAR PHONES FOR SELLING

Los Angeles real estate broker Walter Sanford uses his car as a mobile office with a cellular phone system. Sanford specializes in rental properties. Using his cellular phone, he can call his office, obtain new listings, and compute projected rental earnings without leaving his car. Using a Texas Instruments 707 portable computer terminal and his phone, he can hook into a Long Beach Board of Realtors database and obtain current information on available property or tap into specially designed computer software to do computations on possible deals. In a sprawling and fast-moving real estate market such as Los Angeles, such mobility is very valuable. In fact, Sanford increased sales by 20 to 30 percent with the new cellular system. The new

cellular phones by Motorola are the size of a pack of cigarettes and are much easier to carry everywhere.

William Rorison sells annuity programs that let clients invest in six different investment funds. Before he used a laptop computer, he very rarely made a sale on the first call. Now he does about half the time. What Mr. Rorison can do is show the client what would happen if he or she switched investments from one account to another. He is able to show investors that he knows what the best investment should be and when to switch. All of that is possible with the information he can access with his laptop computer. If you'd like to try one, you can rent one for about $10 a day. Each call is about 95 cents a minute.

Source: Jonathan B. Levine and Zachary Schiller, "If Only Willy Loman Had Used a Laptop," *Business Week,* October 12, 1987, p. 137; Donald H. Dunn, "Getting a Line on the New Cellular Phones," *Business Week,* January 25, 1988, pp. 114–115; and Emily Smith, "Excuse Me, My Pocket Is Ringing," *Business Week,* May 8, 1989, p. 114.

Cellular phones can keep you in touch no matter where you go. They are handy in the city and in the country. The growth in sales has been amazing.

Video Conferencing   A video conference is a business meeting held by executives located in different rooms, in different buildings, or in different parts of the world who talk to each other while watching each other on TV screens. This is clearly much cheaper than having everyone come to a central meeting place for a conference. There are about 700 video rooms in the country now and more are added every day. Boeing has held over 9,000 meetings on such a system. Transmission costs have dropped from $2,000 an hour in 1981 to only $375 today.[8]

Videotex   Videotex, basically, is a system that allows the general public to tap into a central computer that provides a variety of services such as news, shopping hints, games, banking, advertising messages, electronic mail (sending notes to other users), and educational programs. Early attempts at such systems failed, but recently new systems have been introduced that are proving very successful. Boston Citinet, for example, provides instant access to a variety of information including

WHAT'S UP DOC?

One day 8,000 health professionals in 208 locations throughout the United States got together with eight eminent physicians a continent away. The participants in the United States were able to ask questions of the experts in Vienna, Austria. The discussion lasted about two hours and was conducted over a video conferencing system.

Can you imagine such conferences being conducted by colleges and universities throughout the world? Experts on various subjects could speak and college students from all over the world could ask questions. This could become a regular event on campuses. The technology is already here.

Source: "Point-to-Multipoint Makes Its Point," *Marketing Communications*, June 1987, pp. 75–80.

These people are attending a meeting using teleconferencing. Each person can be shown on a TV screen as they talk to people in other cities or countries. It is much cheaper than flying everyone to one place.

school menus, who won the football game, what's showing on TV tonight, and more. In three years, the system has attracted 43,000 subscribers.[9] Soon these systems will be used to review menus at restaurants, reproduce news stories on the computer screen, and help consumers purchase goods by giving them information.

Some form of interactive video will soon optimize information links among consumers and businesses. It is called *videotext*. Videotext is similar to videotex except that users can send information into the system rather than just receive information. This discussion has introduced some uses that are already available. Can you think of more? Think of electronic gambling and contests among users. What about exchanging recipes, handling license plate applications, and conducting job searches? The potential seems unlimited, and you have the opportunity to be in on the ground floor of this exciting new industry.

PROGRESS CHECK

▪ What are the four characteristics of information that make it useful?

▪ What is the difference between a management information system and a decision support system?

▪ Can you briefly describe how each of the following improves corporate communications: electronic bulletin boards, voice messaging, electronic mail, fax machines, computer conferencing, cellular phones, teleconferencing, and videotex?

STAYING CLOSE TO CUSTOMERS

An important part of marketing is follow-up service. Consumers often have questions about how to use products. GE's Answer Center can answer 750,000 questions for 8,500 models of 120 GE products. More than 1,000 calls come in every hour, and the subject of every call is recorded. From that data, GE receives feedback about its products. This is an excellent way for GE to monitor product quality, the value of instruction manuals, and more. Think of how your college could benefit from such an answering machine. The IRS could save millions if it recorded answers instead of having people provide answers that are often incorrect. The potential applications are endless.

Source: Robert H. Waterman, "The Information Edge," in an advertising supplement to *The Wall Street Journal* for Nynex, March 11, 1988, p. 15.

INTERNATIONAL COMPUTER HOOKUPS

You can imagine the problems a worldwide airline might have with coordinating reservations, flights, and luggage. American Airlines, Inc.'s SABRE reservations network links 61,026 video terminals in airports and travel agencies worldwide. This is managed with six IBM mainframe computers in Tulsa. SABRE can print tickets, reserve hotel rooms, and track luggage throughout the world.[10]

A parts dealer at a Honda dealership on Long Island can order new inventory using a computer terminal to poll the stocking systems in 10 regional warehouses in the United States. The parts dealers are linked to Honda's U.S. headquarters in California and in Tokyo.[11]

IBM has a global communications network that encompasses 145 countries. The system relies on satellites and private transmission lines leased from phone companies. One function is to interconnect IBM's 400,000 employees. In 1987, the system handled some 3 trillion characters of internal information. The electronic mail network has replaced the phone as the primary means for IBM people to communicate with one another. Wherever an IBM employee is in the world, he or she can log onto the system and retrieve "mail" that is waiting in the computer.[12]

The world has become one integrated communications network for major corporations. That makes it possible to respond to changes in world economic markets almost instantly. For example, when Westinghouse found that the prices for electronic mail in England were going up, the firm switched the routing job to Washington, D.C., and saved $250,000 in rate increases in just one year. The same kind of savings can be realized in almost all areas of business by doing jobs where it is cheapest to do so.

What are the implications for world peace and world trade given the ability to communicate instantly with firms and government organizations throughout the world?

Could the cooperation needed among telecommunications firms worldwide lead to more cooperation on other issues such as world health care and worldwide exchanges of technical information?

THINKING IT THROUGH

WHAT CAN ROBOTS DO?

- When the Nippon Hoso Kyoku Symphony Orchestra played a concert in 1985, a robot was guest organist. The robot can sight-read musical scores.
- A robot in Australia sheared a whole flock of sheep.
- A computer program named Hitech joined 765 humans as a chess master.
- Robot security guards prowl the Bayside Exposition Center in Boston.
- A Ping-Pong match was held in San Francisco between an English robot and an American one.

- A robot in Palo Alto, California, can listen to music and then print out the score.
- A patent has been issued for a robot tractor that can plant, tend, and harvest crops.
- A Japanese robot can do the work of three plasterers.
- Two robots replaced 20 humans packaging lipstick.
- The RM3 robot can wash the hulls of ships and repaint them at a rate of 1¼ acreas a day.

Source: Noel Perrin, "We Aren't Ready for Robots," *The Wall Street Journal*, February 25, 1986, p. 30; and Michael Rogers, "Robots Find Their Place," *Newsweek*, March 28, 1988, pp. 58–59.

LINKING COMPUTERS WITH ROBOTS

Thus far, we have been talking about using computers to process numbers (data processing) and words (word processing). Another major revolution is occurring in the use of computers to run machines, including robots. We have already discussed the use of computers in production firms in Chapter 13. Now we shall briefly review the consequences of such uses and discuss the linkages of computers, robots, and other high-tech equipment.

Robot technology has improved dramatically in the last few years. Today, "intelligent" robots are being used in factories. Some robots can "see" and "read" using cameras. One GE robot, for example, detects irregularities in welded seams and corrects any mistakes. Another GE robot reads identifying numbers in nuclear fuel rods. The newest robots can "feel" the difference between an egg and a piece of steel and handle each of them accordingly. Some robots even respond to voice commands.

There is a slow but sure trend toward replacing American production workers with robots. The driving force behind the automation of factories is overseas competition. In 1965, for example, almost all the clothes Americans wore were made in the United States. By 1986, half of the clothes were estimated to be foreign made. Employment in the clothing industry fell at a similar rate. One way to win back the market was to increase productivity. Manufacturers are doing just that—with robots. One machine can fold and sew pieces of fabric to make sleeves, the backs of suit coats, and vests with a speed and precision that few humans can manage. A camera "eye" can locate pieces of material and guide the sewing head to the proper position.

Here is how robots are used for the following tasks in industry, ranked by percentage of total robot use: assembly (27 percent), spot welding (23 percent), materials handling (21 percent), arc welding (11 percent), painting, coating, and finishing (8 percent), and other (including the machining mentioned above) (10 percent).[13] Note that computers largely replace workers who do difficult or repetitive jobs. In the long run, this means that workers will be free to do more creative jobs. Robots are used in nonprofit organizations as well (see the box Robots Go Nonprofit).

ROBOTS GO NONPROFIT

In Miami, Florida, the Dade County police use a robot to retrieve and disarm bombs and incendiary devices. In some cities, robots carry fire hoses into areas where no human could go.

In Japan, shoebox-size "intellibots" travel between racks of videotapes and audiotapes in the stacks of a university library. It takes only 40 seconds from the time a student requests a tape until the robot finds and loads the tape into a recorder.

Personal robots are available that can watch for burglars and get the newspaper. Others will vacuum your carpet. They will even do windows (by following magnets attached to the window sill).

A robot was even programmed to "dance" with a ballet troupe!

This is a picture of a robotic work station. Naturally there is some concern about the workers being replaced by robots. In the past farm workers were replaced by machinery and they went into industry. Now they are leaving industry and going into the service sector. Such a shift calls for retraining and more schooling.

A visit to General Electric's newly automated locomotive plant in Erie, Pennsylvania, will give you a feel for how the production plants of the 21st century will look. Running up and down a track is a robot-like vehicle carrying 2,500-pound castings to nine large "smart" machines that are computer controlled and perform dozens of operations in sequence. This job once took 70 workers 16 days to complete. Now one computer technician and two semiskilled workers complete the job, using robots, in 16 hours. This new productivity enables GE to successfully compete with foreign producers of locomotives.

Similar success stories could be told of robot efficiencies in the steel and auto industries. GM's newest auto plants are fully automated; computer-run robots make the plants more efficient than ever.

ROBOTS IN AGRICULTURE

Robots are being developed to perform all kinds of repetitive agricultural jobs that are difficult, dirty, or dangerous. For example, an orange-picking robot that was invented in Florida is now going to Sicily for commercial development.

The computer-controlled machine has a single arm tipped with a small color television camera that sees the fruit on a tree and a sonar unit that gauges its distance and direction. A commercial version would have 6 to 12 arms. An organization in Sicily has provided a $204,000 grant to complete the development of the picker. The Italian company would then produce commercial models.

Source: Paul B. Carroll, "New Products Blur Computer Categories," *The Wall Street Journal*, February 8, 1988, p. 27.

Won't machines replace workers and cause more unemployment? The answer is both *yes* and *no*. It has been estimated that 70 to 90 percent of America's industrial workers could be replaced by robots. But those workers might have lost their jobs anyway to foreign workers. By automating, American producers can remain competitive and maintain employment, but the jobs will not be on boring assembly lines. The net effect is likely to be better for workers than before robots as they move to new, more challenging jobs in the service sector.

The point is that computers linked with robots can perform dirty, difficult, repetitive tasks faster, cheaper, and better than people. To remain competitive, American industry will have to adopt the new technologies. By facing that reality now, industry can begin retraining workers, and schools can begin preparing future workers for the service-sector jobs of tomorrow.

EFFECTS OF TECHNOLOGY ON MANAGEMENT

The development of integrated computers will have a significant effect on top management in the future. Many bureaucratic functions can be replaced by technology. We talked in Chapter 12 about tall versus flat organization structures. Computers will tend to eliminate middle management functions and thus flatten organization structures.

- A sophisticated combination of word processing, electronic and voice mail, teleconferencing, and high-speed communications enabled Hercules Corporation to cut the levels of management from 12 to 6.
- Citicorp's North American Banking Group developed an information system to improve customer service and make account and market information available to clients more quickly. As a result, the staff was reduced by 500 people.

Perhaps the most revolutionary effect of computers may be the ability to allow employees to stay home and do their work from there.

- Mrs. Donna Puccini works for Continental Illinois Bank. She and three other women work at home using word processors to type letters, memos, and statistical tables. The word processing machine is in a bedroom and is linked to Continental's downtown office by a modem. Donna's work is transmitted to the office and back as easily as walking into the boss's office.
- Control Data has about 100 employees working at home or at satellite offices. Employees in the program are analysts, programmers, managers, writers, and clerks.

Naturally such work involves less travel time and costs and often increases productivity by as much as 25 percent, according to Johnson Pharmaceutical Research Institute. It enables men and women to stay home with small children and is a tremendous boon for disabled workers. Employees that can work extra hours on their home computers rather than work late at the office report less stress and improved morale.[14]

Not all of the effects of computers have been positive. One problem with computers today and in the future will be *hackers,* people who break into computer systems for illegal purposes such as transferring funds from someone's bank account to their own without authorization. There is also a problem with privacy as more and more personal information is stored in computers, and people are able to access that data illegally. The person who develops a foolproof lock for computer data will make a fortune.

There was a big scare late in 1988 when a college student infected whole computer systems with an electronic virus. An *electronic virus* is a computer program designed to spread like a contagious disease and block the functioning of a computer system. Luckily, electronic vaccines arrived just in time to prevent major harm. Nonetheless, the susceptibility of computer systems to outside tinkering is a major concern.[15]

Another danger of automating offices is that the firm may become too impersonal, too mechanical. People are often hidden in cubicles behind a computer terminal, and human contact is minimized. Such isolation can be stressful and demoralizing. Managers of such workers need to practice more management by walking around, have more social functions, and provide more opportunities for interpersonal contact during breaks, at lunch, and after work.

Electronic communication can never replace human communication for creating enthusiasm and esprit de corps. Efficiency and productivity can become so important to a firm that people are treated like robots. In the long run, that results in less efficiency and productivity. Computers are a tool, not a total replacement for managers or workers. Creativity is still a human trait. Computers should aid creativity by giving people more freedom and more time.

PROGRESS CHECK

- What affects will the computer/telecommunications link have on the way that business is conducted? What is the role of modems on that development?

- What are the major tasks that have been assigned to computers in industry?

- What affect will the growth of robots have on workers and managers?

---

1. People who rely on the old ways of managing information will not be able to compete with those who know how to use the latest technology.
   - How will this affect you?
     You will not be competitive in the job market unless you learn to use the latest technology.
2. Computers are easier to use now than several years ago.
   - What has made computers easier to use?
     Earlier you had to learn a computer language and program the computer yourself in order to use it. Now commercial software is available that

SUMMARY

1. Explain the importance of managing information and how the new technologies used to manage it will affect you.

2. Demonstrate how becoming computer literate is easier today.

makes computers more user friendly. Users can concentrate on using computers for decision making.

3. Define hardware and relate the development of computers through their five generations.

3. Computer equipment (including peripherals such as printers and modems) is referred to as hardware.
   - What are the five generations of computers?
     1. Computers used vacuum tubes and were hot and bulky.
     2. Computers used smaller, cooler transistors and diodes.
     3. Computers used integrated circuits on silicon chips.
     4. Computers used very-large-scale integrated circuits (VLSI).
     5. Computers are programmed to be a source of artificial intelligence.

4. Define software and describe the four types of computer software most frequently used by managers.

4. Computer software is the instructions that tell a computer what to do. Most software today is on disks of some kind.
   - What types of software programs are used by managers most frequently? Managers often use word processing, electronic spreadsheet, database, and graphics programs.

5. Characterize two types of custom-made software.

5. Some computer users have unique needs that are unmet by commercial software programs. They must have their programs custom made.
   - What are the two largest types of custom-made computer systems? Management information systems are networks of computers that collect, organize, and distribute information to managers. Decision support systems (including expert systems) are interactive, information systems that retrieve, manipulate, and display information that answers unstructured decision-making questions.

6. Identify the four characteristics of useful information.

6. Computers generate a tremendous amount of information, some of which is more confusing than clarifying.
   - What determines whether information is useful or not? The usefulness of management information depends on four characteristics: quality, complete, timely, and relevant.

7. Summarize the steps in planning office automation.

7. Setting up a computer system requires good planning.
   - What steps should managers follow in choosing computer hardware and software? The 10 steps recommended in this chapter are: (1) identify the information needs of all managers, (2) involve all departments in the planning process, (3) seek input from the data processing department, (4) get external advice, (5) choose software first, (6) decide whether to buy or rent equipment or use a service, (7) evaluate equipment, (8) train employees, (9) update the system periodically, and (10) integrate computer communications with other communication efforts.

8. Describe various forms of telecommunication equipment.

8. Telecommunications equipment allows data and/or information to be sent over phone lines or through satellite communication systems.
   - What types of telecommunications technology were discussed in the text? Telecommunications technology discussed include: electronic bulletin boards, modems, voice messaging, electronic mail, computer conferencing, facsimile machines, cellular phones, teleconferencing, and videotex.

9. Review the role of robots in business.

9. Robots will link with computers to do many dirty, repetitive, and skilled jobs.
   - What can robots do? They can read, play, and write music; play ping-pong; paint, weld, play chess, shear sheep, run tractors, and more.

10. Discuss the effects of computers on management.

10. Computers have a tremendous effect on the way we do business.
    - What effect have computers had on business management?

Computers eliminate some middle management functions and thus flatten organizational structures. Computers also allow workers to work from their own homes. On the negative side, computers sometimes allow information to fall into the wrong hands. Managers must find ways to prevent stealing by hackers. Computers also present the danger of making an organization too impersonal. Managers combat this by stressing social functions and providing opportunities for interpersonal contact.

---

1. Go to the local magazine stand and buy a couple of the latest magazines for computer buffs. What is the latest in hardware and software? Discuss your findings with the class.
2. Find someone who has a computer system in use at his or her business. Ask them about the problems they had in installing and using the system. What would they do differently next time? With what software are they especially pleased?
3. There are emerging careers in several high-tech industries (for example, biotechnology). Read the latest computer magazines and find out what these careers are. What career potential do you see in robotics?
4. Find a secretary who has used both a typewriter and a word processor. Ask which is easier and why. Ask for a demonstration. You can do this at a computer store. Try to get some hands-on experience doing word processing. Try to have the copy printed on a letter-quality printer.
5. If you are completely computer literate, find someone in your class or in high school who is not and teach that person how to use the computer. Nothing increases learning as much as teaching others.
6. Go to a modern office and ask to see someone use the fax machine, electronic mail, and whatever other communications equipment they have. See if you can attend a teleconference to see how it works. Then go to the library and look through the latest business magazines to learn what is happening in videotex, cellular phones, and telemarketing. Report what you learn to the class.

GETTING INVOLVED

CASE ONE   **IMPLEMENTING COMPUTER TECHNOLOGY AT GENERAL FOODS**

PRACTICING MANAGEMENT DECISIONS

Not too long ago, the managers at General Foods got their data from a central data processing department. Reports were slow in coming, and their format was inflexible. If an answer led to further questions, it often took weeks to get the desired information. The marketing people simply were not able to respond quickly enough to market conditions.

Two events changed all of this. One was the development of personal computers and software that could perform multiple functions. The second was the realization of General Foods management that they needed better decision-making tools. Now, survey results that once took five months to process, and cost $5,000, can be done in five minutes on a spreadsheet.

At first, new computer technology was not introduced in any organized manner at GF. It started when the vice president of information management bought a Radio Shack computer. A man in the tax department bought an Apple computer. In both cases the computers added to productivity and lowered costs. As more and more people brought in their own PCs, it became apparent that such machines were the wave of the future.

The firm then created a management information system group to make data available to marketing personnel. The idea was not just to bring in PCs, but to optimize data availability. Decisions had to be made about where PCs should be placed and who would be responsible for them. To answer such questions, a marketing advisory council was formed. Input was sought from information systems people as well as marketing managers. Both long-range and short-range needs were analyzed to be sure the technology would not become obsolete too quickly.

Input was sought from all departments. It was decided to introduce the program from the top down. The theory was that top managers needed to understand the system to support it. Special training programs were introduced to show top managers the technology and functions. Managers were encouraged to take computers home. Eventually, courses were offered to spouses and children.

After this training, vice presidents, directors, and functional heads were consulted, and they were trained. Finally, a training facility was set up for employees. An internal marketing campaign was launched to get employees interested and involved.

Because top management was involved from the beginning, they were more accepting of the program and flexible in allowing users to come up with new uses. Soon there were 300 personal computers in use at General Foods, and 4,000 people had been trained in their use.

Today, General Foods has a mainframe computer; a minicomputer is set up in each division; and several microcomputer systems are in use: Apple, Radio Shack, IBM, and Compaq. Wang word processors were replaced with Wang PCs for secretaries.

The biggest limitation now at General Foods is not hardware, but software. People want to do more, and the programs are simply not available. Users are responsible for getting their own funding if they want more equipment. Management wants the system to serve users, so users design the program to fit their needs. The computer center is a service department that provides training, education, research, and testing of hardware and software. It also acts as an in-house consulting group to help end users.

General Foods is linked to several external data suppliers. The divisional minicomputers store internal sales data plus data from external suppliers. The mainframe has sales data and financial data that is accessible by both minis and micros. Overall, the system is well integrated, even though many different manufacturers are involved. The future of computer systems at General Foods and all other companies will be integrated networks of computer and information systems such that all equipment will be linked.

DECISION QUESTIONS

1. Evaluate the process General Foods followed in designing and implementing its computer system. Did it use the 10 steps in the text?
2. What is your reaction to the fact that General Foods uses several different computer makers (Apple, Radio Shack, IBM, Compaq, and Wang)? Do you see advantages and disadvantages?
3. What is your reaction to the idea of introducing computers to top management first rather than give them to operating-level employees first? What will be the benefits of having integrated computer and communications systems connecting all managers?

This Case is from Virginia Dudek, "The Plugged-in Marketers at General Foods," *Marketing Communications*, March 1984, pp. C9–C13; and "Desktop Computing and Networks for Tomorrow," *Forbes*, November 28, 1988, pp. 139–58.

CASE TWO   ELECTRONIC SHOPPING—WHAT NEXT?

Picture this. You walk into one of the new, large shopping malls. Maybe it is as big as the mile-long mall in Canada with 57 entrances. You dread the idea of going from store to store on a busy Saturday shopping for gifts for the holidays. Suddenly you notice something new in the center. It is a kiosk with a video screen inside. It looks like a giant video game. It is called an *Electronistore*.

Curious, you step inside and sit down. On the screen appears a hostess who welcomes you and asks whether or not you've used the service before. You say "No" by pressing a button, and step-by-step instructions appear.

You decide to explore the household appliances listing to see what's available. A subcategory of microwave ovens appears in the list. You ask for that list and see prices and product descriptions. If you want more details, you push the "details" button and get answers to questions such as whether or not the oven has a browning element.

Fascinated by the possibilities, you push buttons for other categories such as stereo equipment, shoes, and so on. If you see what you want for yourself and for gifts, you can insert your credit card and place an order. There is no salesperson and no standing in line.

The company that makes the Electronistore (Donnelley) expected sales of $17 billion. The Electronistore has several advantages:

- It allows for quick and easy comparison shopping.
- It provides in-depth product information.
- Merchandise can be demonstrated.
- Some 500 different items can be displayed.
- Shoppers enjoy using the service.

Electronistores are just the beginning of interactive electronic shopping, however. You still have to go to the kiosk and wait if others are using it. What if you could call up all the information desired on your own TV screen using interactive cable TV? Then you could do all of your shopping at home. Your computer would be the equivalent of a giant catalog capable of demonstrating products and taking your order. That is the reality of the late 1980s. What is next? Now that consumers can interact with producers electronically, what information needs to be exchanged, with what result?

DECISION QUESTIONS

1. Which system seems to have the greater potential for success: electronic kiosks in stores or interactive TV in the home?
2. What kinds of *services* (not goods) could be sold over interactive TV systems?
3. Many people (especially those over 45) say that there is no need for a home computer. "What do you use them for, anyhow?" they say. Discuss the future of interactive TV and its uses for obtaining the latest news, banking, shopping, and more. Brainstorm all the possibilities to get a view of the future.

Computers are fine for doing many tasks, and robots are fantastic as well. Still, no machine is as creative and flexible as a human being. But human beings need motivation. They need careful attention, too. Chapter 15 explores the motivation of workers. We shall look at motivation theory and practice. This material is part of a broader topic called *human resource management*. We have learned how to select and program machines. In the following chapter, we'll learn how to select and motivate people.

LOOKING AHEAD

APPENDIX:
HELPFUL COMPUTER TERMS

One of the more intimidating parts of getting involved with computers is the terminology. People can feel so overwhelmed by the words used to explain computers that they are overly nervous about actually working with computers. Playing computer games is a good way to learn that working with a computer is easier than it may appear at first. Let's review some of the more common terms, so you are comfortable discussing computers with others:

Accessing Transferring data to or, more commonly, getting data from a storage device such as a floppy disk, to view, manipulate, and process it.

Applications Programs (software) Programs that do functions (for example, word processing, games, spreadsheet analysis, database management, accounting) that are relatively complicated and specific to one area, such as accounting or inventory control.

Artificial Intelligence The attempt to get computers to think like humans. AI programs can learn from their mistakes and correct themselves. "The computer chess programs keep getting better by using artificiial intelligence." A "smart" computer is not quite as brainy as an "intelligent" computer.

BASIC A programming language. "I programmed the computer using BASIC."

Batch Processing Data are collected for a predetermined time period before being processed and are run automatically by the computer in some priority order (that is, the user need not be there).

BDOS Pronounced *bee doss,* this means "basic disk operating system". It refers to that part of the program that customizes it to your particular system.

Binary Number The numbers that computers understand. Basically, computers use only two symbols (0 and 1) to express any number, no matter how large.

Bit Short for *binary digit,* a bit is the smallest unit of information. A bit is expressed in binary numbers as either 0 or 1.

Byte A byte is eight *bits.* This is the amount of information required to define one character (for example, one letter).

Chip Chips are the basic building blocks of computers. They are also called *integrated circuits* or *ICs.* A computer chip is smaller than a baby's fingernail and yet contains thousands of switches (transistors). The brain of a computer is a chip called the *microprocessor* or *central processing unit* (CPU). It performs all the calculations

and handles all information coming in to the computer and sends it back out.

COBOL A more advanced computer language for businesses.

Command Anything you tell a computer to do.

cps Characters per second; refers to how fast printers make words. You multiply cps by 10 to get actual words per minute.

CRT Cathode ray tube; a screen like the one on your TV set. It is an input and output device that shows users desired information.

Cursor A signal that tells you where you are on the CRT screen.

Database A large collection of data that a computer can look through to find needed information. An example would be all the names, addresses, and phone numbers of customers.

Dedicated Word Processor A computer designed to do nothing but word processing.

Disk Drive A device that writes information onto and reads information from a disk (also spelled *disc*). Disks may be floppy or hard. Floppy disks come in different sizes. Hard disks hold more data and cost more money. Disks store both the data the computer generates and computer programs (software).

DRAMs (pronounced Dee-rams). The computer's memory bank. They are used to store software programs and operating instructions.

Dvorak Keyboard A different arrangement of keys from the standard; this arrangement allows you to type faster.

EDP Electronic data processing.

Electronic Mail The sending and receiving of messages over a computer network.

Electronic Spreadsheet Program A software program that makes financial projection, budgeting, and planning easier.

FORTRAN A high-level computer language mainly for scientific and mathematical use.

Hardware The physical components of the computer system, as opposed to software (the instructions).

IBM Compatible Refers to computers that are made by competitors of IBM, but run some software designed to run on IBM equipment.

Integrated Circuit An electronic circuit that has been put on a chip.

Joystick The stick used to move objects in video games and also to move the cursor where desired.

K See *Kilobyte*.

Keyboard That part of the computer that looks like a typewriter. It is handy if it is portable or attached with a flexible cable to allow you to set it in a comfortable position. A keyboard is usually attached to a CRT (video screen).

Kilobyte 1024 bytes. This is about 170 actual words. A kilobyte takes up about two thirds of a double-spaced page (1-inch margins, pica type). The amount of memory in a computer and floppy disk capacity are often measured in kilobytes (K). "My computer has 640K of memory."

Laser Printer A high-speed printer (eight pages or more a minute) that prints in a high-resolution form comparable to typesetting.

Letter-Quality Printer A printer attached to a computer that prints out words in a form acceptable for business correspondence.

Mainframe Computer A larger capacity computer that is used when huge volumes of data need to be processed. Airlines, for example, do their reservations on mainframes. These computers are usually centrally located and can be accessed by desktop terminals.

Memory Where information and programs are stored and manipulated in the computer. *RAM* means random access memory. *ROM* stands for read-only memory. It tells the computer what to do, but you can't change what it says, like you can RAM. ROM goes away when you turn off the machine.

Menu A list of commands that you can choose from that is displayed on the screen.

Message Anything the computer tells you.

MIPS Million instructions per second.

Modem A device that converts data into a form that can be transmitted over phone lines so one computer can "talk" to another.

Mouse Like a joystick, it moves the cursor to where you want it.

Nanosecond A billionth of a second.

Network The linking of several computers or computer terminals.

Personal Computer (PC) These are usually small, desktop computers typically used for word processing, accounting, and tapping into central databases. They are also known as microcomputers. This manuscript was prepared on PCs owned by the McHugh and Nickels families.

Printer An attachment to a computer that forms words like a typewriter.

Software The instructions (programs) that tell a computer what to do.

Terminal A device that looks like a TV set attached to a typewriter that sends information to a computer and receives information from the computer.

Tutorial A training manual explaining how to use hardware and/or software.

User Friendly A computer or software that is easy to use. The ultimate would be one that could understand voice commands and respond accordingly.

Window The part of a file that is on the screen at one time. Sometimes you can have more than one window displayed at the same time (with a split screen).

Word Processing Writing (typing) and editing material on a computer. Very much like typing, but correcting or otherwise changing your work is much easier.

Workstation Basically a souped-up personal computer that is designed to do advanced work for people like engineers and scientists.

MANAGEMENT OF HUMAN RESOURCES

V

MOTIVATING EMPLOYEES

15

LEARNING GOALS

After you have read and studied this chapter, you should be able to:

1. Explain Taylor's scientific management.

2. Describe the Hawthorne studies and relate their significance to human-based management.

3. Identify the levels of Maslow's hierarchy of needs and relate the hierarchy's importance to employee motivation.

4. Differentiate between Theory X and Theory Y.

5. Describe Theory Z and its application in the United States.

6. Distinguish between motivators and hygiene factors identified by Herzberg.

7. Explain how job enrichment affects employee motivation and performance.

8. Identify the steps involved in implementing a management by objectives (MBO) program.

9. Describe the implementation of motivation theory in the 1990s.

KEY TERMS

extrinsic rewards, *p. 462*
goal-setting theory, *p. 474*
Hawthorne effect, *p. 465*
hygiene factor, *p. 472*
intrinsic rewards, *p. 462*
job enlargement, *p. 474*
job enrichment, *p. 473*
job rotation, *p. 474*
job simplification, *p. 474*
management by objectives (MBO),
    p. 474

motion economy, *p. 463*
motivators, *p. 472*
physiological needs, *p. 465*
safety needs, *p. 465*
scientific management, *p. 463*
self-actualization needs, *p. 465*
self-esteem needs, *p. 465*
social needs, *p. 465*
time-motion studies, *p. 463*

Mickey Arison

Management is nothing more than motivating other people.
LEE IACOCCA

PROFILE   MICKY ARISON OF CARNIVAL CRUISE LINES

Ever dreamt about the ultimate vacation fantasy—a floating holiday aboard a luxurious cruise ship? If you have, "Carnival's Got The Fun!" according to Micky Arison, CEO of Carnival Cruise Line, the largest and fastest growing cruise line in the Caribbean. Founded in 1972 by Mr. Arison's father, Ted, Carnival has its sights set on becoming the General Motors of the cruise industry. With a current fleet of seven ships and three more on the way (the Fantasy, the Ecstasy, and the Sensation), the company may not be far from achieving its goal.

Micky Arison grew up in the shipping industry. After graduation from the University of Miami, he worked his way through the company with stints in sales, reservations, and passenger traffic before being named president in 1979. Mr. Arison learned that satisfied passengers are the key to his cruise line's future. He also learned that the best way to satisfy passengers was to have satisfied, motivated employees. He feels the motivation of the firm's 4,000 employees is critical at every level of the organization.

One motivational tool used by Mr. Arison is the requirement that all promotions come from within the company, which encourages employees to compete for jobs. Additionally, on all cruises, the welfare of the crew is considered paramount. Specialty meals that reflect the crews' ethnic backgrounds are provided for the ship's employees. (This is no small task since as many as 35 different nationalities may work on the ship.) At all levels, employees are invited to discuss ideas and problems with their managers. It's obvious Micky Arison's efforts have paid off. Carnival thrives because its employees work hard and feel the company cares about them.

Source: Leslie Wayne, "Carnival Sets Sail on a Spending Spree," *New York Times,* August 28, 1988, p. 1.

THE IMPORTANCE OF MOTIVATION

intrinsic rewards
Reinforcement from within oneself; a feeling one has done a good job.

extrinsic rewards
Reinforcement from someone else as recognition for good work, including pay increases, praise, and promotions.

No matter where you end up being a leader—in school, in business, in sports, in the military—the key to your success will be whether or not you can motivate others to do the best they can. That is no easy job today when so many people feel bored and disinterested in work. Yet the fact is that people are willing to work and work hard *if* they feel that their work is appreciated and makes a difference. People are motivated by a variety of things, such as recognition, accomplishment, and status. **Intrinsic rewards** come from the feeling that one has done a good job and come from within a person. **Extrinsic rewards** come from someone else as recognition for good work and include pay increases, praise, and promotions. Ultimately, however, motivation comes from within, and there are ways to stimulate people that brings out that natural drive to do a good job.

The purpose of this chapter is to teach you the concepts, theories, and practice of motivation. The most important person to motivate, of course, is yourself. One way to do that is to find the right job in the right organization that enables you to reach your goals in life. The whole purpose of this book is to help you in that search and to teach you how to succeed once you get there. One secret of success is to recognize that everyone else is on a similar search. Naturally, some are more committed than others. The job of a manager is to find that commitment, encourage it, and focus it on some common goal.

This chapter will begin with a look at some of the traditional theories of motivation. We shall discuss the Hawthorne studies because they created a whole new interest in worker satisfaction and motivation. Then we'll look at some assumptions about employees: Are they basically lazy, or willing to work if given the proper incentives? We shall also explore the traditional theorists. You will see their names over and over in the business literature: Mayo, Herzberg, Maslow, and McGregor. Finally, we shall look at the modern applications of these theories and the managerial procedures for implementing them.

Early Management Studies (Taylor)

There were several books on management in the 19th century that presented management principles. For example, Charles Babbage (1792–1871) designed a mechanical computer and wrote a book on how to manage a manufacturing firm.[1] However, Frederick Taylor earned the title "father of scientific management." His book *The Principles of Scientific Management* was published in 1911. Taylor's goal was to increase worker productivity so that both the firm and the worker could benefit from higher earnings. The way to improve productivity, Taylor thought, was to scientifically study the most efficient way to do things and then teach people those methods. Three elements were basic to his approach: time, methods, and rules of work. His most important tools were observation and the stopwatch.

A classic Taylor story involves his study of men shoveling rice, coal, and iron ore with the same shovel. Taylor felt that different materials called for different shovels. He proceeded to invent a wide variety of sizes and shapes of shovels and, with stopwatch in hand, measured output over time in what were called **time-motion studies**—studies of the tasks performed to complete a job and the time needed to do each task. Sure enough, an average person could shovel more (from 25 tons to 35 tons per day) with the proper shovel using the most efficient motions. This led to time-motion studies of virtually every factory job. The most efficient way of doing things was determined and became the standard for setting goals.

time-motion studies
Study of the tasks performed to complete a job and the time needed to do each task.

Taylor's scientific management became the dominant strategy for improving productivity in the early 1900s. There were hundreds of time-motion specialists in plants throughout the country. One follower of Taylor was H. L. Gantt. He developed charts by which managers plotted the work of employees a day in advance down to the smallest detail. Frank and Lillian Gilbreth used Taylor's ideas in a three-year study of bricklaying. They developed the principle of **motion economy,** which showed that every job could be broken down into a series of elementary motions called a *therblig*—Gilbreth spelled backward. They then analyzed each motion to make it more efficient.

motion economy
Theory that every job can be broken down into a series of elementary motions.

You can imagine how workers felt having time and motion people studying their every move. **Scientific management** viewed people largely as machines that needed to be properly programmed. There was little concern for the psychological or human aspects of work. Taylor felt that workers would perform at a high level of effectiveness (that is, be motivated) if they received high enough pay because money would allow them to meet their basic needs.

scientific management
The study of workers to find the most efficient way of doing things and then teaching people those techniques.

There is much evidence today that some of Taylor's ideas are still being implemented. The difference is that machinery is being used to standardize how work is done. Nonetheless, much emphasis in some plants is still placed on conformity to work rules rather than creativity, flexibility, and responsiveness.[2] The benefits of relying on workers to come up with creative solutions to productivity problems has long been recognized as we shall discover next.

This shot of the inside of the Hawthorne plant is a classic. It is here where human-based motivational theory was born. Before then, people were programmed to work like human robots.

The Hawthorne Studies (Mayo)

One of the studies that grew out of Taylor's research was conducted at the Western Electric Company's Hawthorne plant in Cicero, Illinois. The study began in 1927 and ended six years later as one of the major studies in management literature. Let's see why.

The studies were conducted by Elton Mayo and colleagues from Harvard University. The idea was to test the degree of lighting associated with optimum productivity. In this respect, it was a traditional scientific management study: keep records of productivity performed under different levels of illumination.

The problem with the initial experiments was that the productivity of the experimental group compared to other workers doing the same job went up regardless of whether the lighting was bright or dim. This was true even when the lighting was reduced to about the level of moonlight. These results confused and frustrated the researchers.

A second series of experiments was conducted. A separate test room was set up where temperature, humidity, and other environmental factors could be manipulated. A series of 13 experimental periods were recorded and productivity went up each time. Productivity went up by 50 percent. When the experimenters repeated the original condition (expecting productivity to fall to original levels), productivity kept increasing. The experiments were a total failure at this point. No matter what the experimenters did, productivity went up. What was causing the increase?

Mayo guessed that some human or psychological factor was involved. Thus, workers were interviewed about their feelings and attitudes toward the experiment. What the researchers found was to have a profound change in management thinking that continues today. Here is what they concluded:

- The women in the test room thought of themselves as a social group. The atmosphere was informal, they could talk freely, and interacted regularly with their supervisors and the experimenters. They felt special and worked hard to stay in the group. This motivated them.

■ The women were involved in the planning of the experiments. For example, they rejected one kind of pay schedule and recommended another, which was used. The women felt that their ideas were respected and that they were involved in managerial decision making. This, too, motivated them.

■ The women enjoyed the atmosphere of their special room and the additional pay they got from more productivity. Job satisfaction increased dramatically.

Researchers now use the term the **Hawthorne effect** to refer to the tendency for people to behave differently when they know they are being studied. The results of the Hawthorne studies encouraged researchers to begin to study human motivation and the managerial styles that led to more productivity. The emphasis of research shifted away from Taylor's scientific management to Mayo's new, human-based management.

Mayo's findings led to completely new assumptions about employees. One of those assumptions, of course, was that pay was not the only motivator. In fact, money was found to be a relatively low motivator. That change in assumptions led to many theories about the human side of motivation. One of the best known motivation theorists was Abraham Maslow. We will discuss Maslow and his hierarchy of needs next.

Hawthorne effect
The tendency for people to behave differently when they know they are being studied.

MOTIVATION AND MASLOW'S NEED HIERARCHY

Abraham Maslow believed that to understand motivation at work, one must understand human motivation in general. It seemed to him that motivation arises from need; that is, one is motivated to satisfy *unmet needs;* needs that have been satisfied no longer provide motivation. He thought that needs could be placed on a hierarchy of importance.

Figure 15–1 (see page 466) shows Maslow's hierarchy of needs. The basic needs are:

Physiological needs. The need to be physically comfortable, including the need to drink, eat, and be sheltered from heat and cold.

Safety needs. The need to feel secure at work and at home.

Social needs. The need to feel loved, accepted, and part of the group.

Self-esteem needs. The need for recognition, acknowledgement, and status.

Self-actualization needs. The need to accomplish established goals and develop to your fullest potential.

When one need is satisfied, another, higher-level need emerges and motivates the person to do something to satisfy it.[3] In fact, lower-level needs (for example, hunger, thirst) may emerge at any time they are not met and take our attention away from higher-level needs such as the need for recognition or status.

Most of the world's workers struggle all day simply to meet the basic needs for food, shelter, and safety. In developed countries, such needs no longer dominate, and workers seek to satisfy growth needs (social, self-esteem, and self-actualization needs).

To compete successfully, U.S. firms must create a corporate environment that motivates the best and the brightest workers. That means establishing a corporate culture that includes goals such as social contribution, honesty, reliability, service, quality, dependability, and unity.

physiological needs
The need for basic, life-giving elements such as food, water, and shelter.

safety needs
The need for peace and security.

social needs
The need to feel loved, accepted, and part of the group.

self-esteem needs
The need for self-confidence and status.

self-actualization needs
The need for achievement and to be all you can be.

FIGURE 15–1

Maslow's need hierarchy.
Maslow's need hierarchy is
based on the idea that
motivation comes from need.
If a need is met, it no longer
is a motivator and a higher-
level need becomes the
motivator. This charts shows
the various levels of needs.

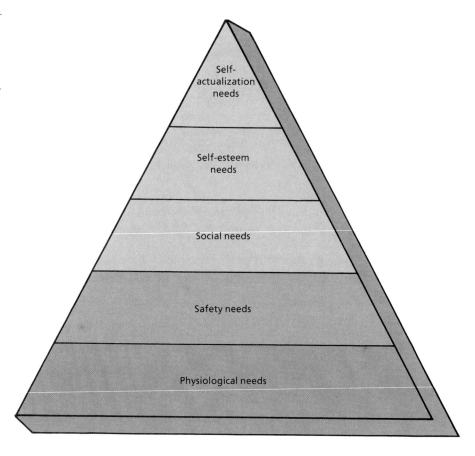

Activities such as picnics and
sports events such as this
relay race create an
atmosphere where
employees can feel part of
the group. This meets their
social needs and they can
move on to accomplish
things at work to satisfy
their self-esteem and self-
actualization needs.

MOTIVATION COMES FROM WITHIN

"When a person is not doing his or her job, there can only be two reasons for it. The person either can't do it or won't do it; he or she is either not capable or not motivated. To determine which, we can employ a simple mental test: if the person's life depended on doing the work, could he or she do it? If the answer is yes, that person is not motivated; if the answer is no, he or she is not capable.

The single most important task of a manager is to elicit peak performance from subordinates. So if two things limit high output, a manager has two ways to tackle the issue: through training and motivation, motivation has to come from within somebody. Accordingly, all a manager can do is create an environment in which motivated people can flourish."

Andrew S. Grove, *High Output Management* (New York: Random House, 1983), pp. 157–58.

When in your life have you felt strongly motivated to do something? Try to think of several different incidents. Now look at Maslow's need hierarchy to see what need was motivating you. Can you see how helpful Maslow's theory is in understanding motivation by applying it to your own life?

THINKING IT THROUGH

Applying Maslow's Theory

Andrew Grove, president of Intel, observed Maslow's concepts in action in his firm. One woman, for example, took a low-paying job, which did little for her family's standard of living. Why? Because she needed the companionship her work offered (social/affiliation need). One of Grove's friends had a mid-life crisis when he was made a vice president. This position had been a lifelong goal, and when the man reached it he had to find another way to motivate himself. People at a research and development lab were knowledge centered. They were self-actualized by the desire to know more, but they had little desire to produce results, thus little was achieved.[4] Grove had to find new people who were results oriented.

Once one understands the need level of employees, it is easier to design programs that will trigger self-motivation. Grove believes that all motivation comes from within (see the box on motivation). He believes that self-actualized persons are achievement oriented. He thus designed a managerial program that emphasized achievement. Now managers are highly motivated to achieve their objectives because they feel rewarded for doing so.

PROGRESS CHECK

- What are the similarities and differences between Taylor's scientific management and Mayo's Hawthorne studies? How did Mayo's findings influence scientific management?

- Can you draw Maslow's need hierarchy and label the parts?

- According to Andrew Grove, what is the ultimate source of all motivation?

MCGREGOR'S THEORY X AND THEORY Y

The way managers go about motivating people at work depends greatly on their attitudes toward workers. Douglas McGregor observed that managers had two different attitudes that led to entirely different managerial styles. He called the two systems *Theory X* and *Theory Y*.

Theory X

The assumptions of Theory X management are:

- The average person dislikes work and will avoid it if possible.
- Because of this dislike, the average person must be forced, controlled, directed, or threatened with punishment to motivate him or her to put forth the effort to achieve the organization's goals.
- The average worker prefers to be directed, wishes to avoid responsibility, has relatively little ambition, and wants security.

The natural consequence of such attitudes, beliefs, and assumptions is a manager who is very "busy" and who hangs over people telling them what to do and how to do it. Motivation is more likely to take the form of punishment for bad work rather than reward for good work. Workers are given little responsibility, authority, or flexibility. Those were the assumptions behind Taylor's scientific management and all the theorists who preceded him. No doubt you have seen such managers in action. How did this make you feel? Is that how you prefer to be managed? Are these assumptions accurate regarding your work attitudes?

For years, the typical manager operated from such assumptions. That is why management literature focused on time and motion studies that calculated the "one best" way to perform a task and the "optimum" time to be devoted to a task. It was assumed that workers needed to be trained and carefully watched to see that they conformed to the standards. Would you like to be told exactly how to do something in a given amount of time with no room for creativity, flexibility, or time to relax and take a breather?

Theory Y

Theory Y makes entirely different assumptions about people:

- The average person likes work; it is as natural as play or rest.
- The average person naturally works toward goals to which he or she is committed.
- The depth of a person's commitment to goals depends on the perceived rewards for achieving them.
- Under certain conditions, the average person not only accepts but seeks responsibility.
- People are capable of using a relatively high degree of imagination, creativity, and cleverness to solve problems.
- In industry, the average person's intellectual potential is only partially realized.

Rather than emphasize authority, direction, and close supervision, Theory Y emphasizes a relatively free managerial atmosphere in which workers are free to set objectives, be creative, be flexible, and go beyond the goals set by management.[5] Have you ever worked in such an atmosphere? How did that make you feel? Would you prefer to work under a Theory X or Theory Y manager? How willing would you be to be a Theory Y manager with your children or your workers?

Traditional managerial styles were based on one of two major assumptions:

- Workers are basically lazy and must be given direction, threatened, and negatively motivated (Theory X); *or*
- Workers are basically goal oriented and self-motivated, and the best managerial style is to offer them incentives and freedom (Theory Y).

APPLYING THEORY X AND THEORY Y

"The trouble with these neat theories is that no company that we know of is run in strict accordance with either Theory Y or Theory X. Not even the Army. We have known managers who prefer to be told what to do, people who do not want responsibility for making crucial decisions, and once they are given precise instructions perform their assigned tasks with care and diligence. We have also known managers who are self-starters and perform best only when they have shared in the decision-making process; in fact, they resent being given orders. Both these types of managers were working for the same company. If you were the chief executive, how would you run that company—by Theory X or Theory Y? Or, would you use your common sense and act according to the circumstances at hand? Theory G: You cannot run a business, or anything else, on a theory."

Source: Harold Geneen, *Managing* (New York: Avon Books, 1984), pp. 17–25.

Scientists are usually managed using Theory Y. The men and women are goal-oriented and motivated, and they like their work. A manager needs to give them support and encouragement, not directions and punishment for failed experiments.

It is wise for managers to be flexible in applying Theory X or Y to those they supervise. Some people do better with direction; others do better with more freedom (see the box about applying X and Y). Your natural inclination may be to choose a Theory Y–type manager as your supervisor; while your friend may prefer a Theory X–type supervisor. Case One at the end of this chapter discusses how two firms in the same industry use different approaches to management. One, Mrs. Field's Cookies, uses Theory Y techniques. The other, David's Cookies, uses Theory X. Mrs. Field's Cookies was in the news recently because of financial problems due more to management decisions other than motivational style.[6]

The trend in most U.S. businesses is toward Theory Y management. One reason for a more flexible, permissive managerial style is to meet competition from foreign firms such as those in Japan. William Ouchi, a professor of business at UCLA, wrote a bestselling book on management called *Theory Z: How American Business Can Meet the Japanese Challenge*. Next we will explore this new theory.

FIGURE 15–2 A comparison of theories X, Y, and Z.

THEORY X	THEORY Y	THEORY Z
1. Employees dislike work and will try to avoid it 2. Employees prefer to be controlled and directed 3. Employees seek security, not responsibility 4. Employees must be intimidated by managers to perform 5. Employees are motivated by financial rewards	1. Employees view work as a natural part of life 2. Employees prefer limited control and direction 3. Employees will seek responsibility under proper work conditions 4. Employees perform better in work environments that are nonintimidating 5. Employees are motivated by many different needs	1. Employee involvement is the key to increased productivity 2. Employee control is implied and informal 3. Employees prefer to share responsibility and decision making 4. Employees perform better in environments that foster trust and cooperation 5. Employees need guaranteed employment and will accept slow evaluations and promotions

THEORY Z (OUCHI)

Many organizations in Japan are run quite differently from those in the United States. Out of the Japanese system has come a concept called Theory Z. There are several major elements to this theory:[7]

- Long-term employment, virtually guaranteed, for all employees.
- Emphasis on collective decision making.
- Relatively slow evaluation and promotion.
- Creation of a sense of involvement, closeness, and cooperation in the organization (family atmosphere).
- Expectation of individual responsibility (like Theory Y).
- Trust among all managers and workers.
- Few levels of management.

Several U.S. firms are attempting to adopt this managerial style. Ouchi cites Hewlett-Packard as one such American firm. He quotes from a preamble to corporate objectives written by David Packard and William Hewlett.

The preamble begins by saying, "The achievements of an organization are the results of the combined efforts of each individual in the organization working toward common objectives." It goes on to list several requirements including (1) the most capable people should be selected for each assignment, (2) enthusiasm should exist at all levels, and (3) all levels should work in unison toward common objectives. The corporate philosophy at Hewlett-Packard is to have overall objectives that are clearly stated and agreed to and to give people the freedom to work toward those goals in ways they determine best for their own areas of responsibility.

Questioning the Team Concept

One thing American managers have learned from theory Z and the Japanese style of management is the value of work teams. The work team concept has been applied in many industries including the auto industry, food processing, paper, oil refining, steelmaking, and electrical products. There has been some criticism of such teams, saying that they are mere union-busting schemes by management.

JAPANESE FIRMS USE COMIC BOOKS TO TEACH BUSINESS BEHAVIOR

Although Japanese firms have been successful at competing with American firms, it is doubtful that American firms will learn much from their managerial style. At one firm, the personnel manager yells out "Stand!" "Bow!" "Sit" and new employees respond with military precision. Several firms use a comic book to tell new managers how to bow (15-degree bow to colleagues and a 45-degree bow to top executives). The comic book was meant to instill hard work, discipline, and polite behavior. Japanese firms operate closer to Theory X than Theory Y management. Theory Z lifetime employment cannot make up for the rigid discipline. At least, it wouldn't work as well in the United States.

Source: Margaret Shapiro, "Japan's Corporate Recruits Going Through 'Boot Camp,'" *Los Angeles Times,* May 15, 1989, p. 3 of Part IV.

When workers are given the freedom to move from job to job, it makes job classifications more difficult and lessens the power of unions.[8] Such movement also makes work more interesting and more productive.

When work teams are combined with other Japanese management techniques such as just-in-time systems and constant learning and improving, employees are often overworked. Some call this "management by stress."[9] What is needed, therefore, is for unions and management to work together to set reasonable production-line speeds and to emphasize the benefits of work teams while minimizing the stress. To make such teams work, management must give employees more recognition and make it easier for them to advance in the firm. We shall look next at what factors motivate workers the most.

MOTIVATING FACTORS: HERZBERG

Theories X, Y, and Z are concerned with styles of management. Another direction in managerial theory is to explore what managers can do with the job itself to motivate employees (a modern-day look at Taylor's research). Of all the factors controllable by managers, which are most effective in generating an enthusiastic work effort? In other words, this section is more concerned with the *content of work* than style of management.

The most discussed study in this area was conducted by Frederick Herzberg.[10] He asked workers to rank the following job-related factors in the order of importance relative to motivation. That is, what creates enthusiasm for them and makes them work to full potential? The results, in order of importance, were:

1. Sense of achievement.
2. Earned recognition.
3. Interest in the work itself.
4. Opportunity for growth.
5. Opportunity for advancement.
6. Importance of responsibility.
7. Peer and group relationships.
8. Pay.
9. Supervisor's fairness.
10. Company policies and rules.
11. Status.
12. Job security.
13. Supervisor's friendliness.
14. Working conditions.

Herzberg noted that the factors receiving the most votes were all clustered around job content. Workers like to feel that they contribute (sense of achievement was number one). They want to earn recognition (number two) and feel their jobs are important (number six). They want responsibility (which is why learning is so important), but want recognition for that responsibility by having a chance for growth and advancement. Of course, workers also want the job to be interesting.

The best motivators in business are achievement, recognition, and a chance for advancement. Reward ceremonies like this, where employees are given plaques and are praised by their bosses, are real motivators. It is not enough to reward employees at such once-a-year gatherings, however. Employees need recognition every day.

Herzberg noted further that factors having to do with the job environment were not considered motivators by workers. It was interesting to find that one of those factors was pay. Workers felt that the absence of good pay, job security, friendly supervisors, and the like could cause dissatisfaction, but the presence of those factors did not motivate them; they just provided satisfaction. John McConnell of steelmaker Worthington Industries gives employees bonuses of $10,000 or more. He realizes money is not a motivator; instead he calls it part of an overall recognition process. It is the recognition, not the money, that motivates.[11]

The conclusions of Herzberg's study were that certain factors of management did motivate employees (were **motivators**) and gave them a great deal of satisfaction (see Figure 15–3). These factors mostly had to do with job content and were grouped as follows:

motivators
Factors that provide satisfaction and motivate people to work.

Work itself.
Achievement.
Recognition.
Responsibility.
Growth and advancement.

Other factors of management were merely what Herzberg called **hygiene factors.** These had to do mostly with job environment and could cause dissatisfaction if missing but would not necessarily motivate if increased. They were:

hygiene factors
Factors that cause dissatisfaction if they are missing, but do not motivate if they are increased.

Company policy and administration.
Supervision.
Working conditions.
Interpersonal relations.
Salary

If we combined McGregor's Theory Y with Herzberg's motivating factors, we would come up with these conclusions:

Employees work best when management assumes that employees are competent and self-motivated (Theory Y). Theory Y calls for a participative style of management.

The best way to motivate employees is to make the job interesting, help them to achieve their objectives, and recognize that achievement through advancement and added responsibility.

MOTIVATORS	HYGIENE FACTORS
(These factors can be used to motivate workers.)	(These factors can cause dissatisfaction, but changing them will have little motivational effect.)
Work itself	Company policy and administration
Achievement	Supervision
Recognition	Working conditions
Responsibility	Interpersonal relations (co-workers)
Growth and advancement	Salary, status, and job security

FIGURE 15–3

Herzberg's motivators and hygiene factors. There is some controversy over Herzberg's results. For example, sales managers often use money as a motivator. Recent studies have shown that money can be a motivator if used as part of a recognition program.

Applying Herzberg's Theories to Modern Workers

Recently, *Inc.* magazine polled some 2,800 workers from the 500 fastest-growing small firms to see what motivates them. In terms of pay and benefits, these employees lagged behind the employees of larger corporations. But they felt satisfied and highly motivated nonetheless because of job-related factors, just as Herzberg predicted. Employees especially enjoyed the challenge and sense of accomplishment they felt working for smaller firms. They also enjoyed the small-business culture that values initiative and ideas.[12]

One revealing finding from the study was that about half the employees intended to leave their companies in the next few years. Why? Because they saw little chance for advancement. Remember that opportunity for advancement was high on Herzberg's list of motivators.

One conclusion of the *Inc.* study was that "large companies try to 'Taylorize' their professionals (Frederick Taylor, that is)—they worry about their productivity and try to manage them as they would manage a welder."[13] On the other hand, the new, young managers at smaller firms enjoyed the informality of beer blasts and tennis courts, the company condo in Vail, challenging work, the up-to-date equipment, and the opportunity to see their ideas implemented.

How can companies make their jobs as interesting for blue-collar workers as they do for managers? We discuss how to do that next.

JOB ENRICHMENT

Both Maslow's and Herzberg's theories were extended by job enrichment theory. **Job enrichment** is a motivational strategy that emphasizes motivating the worker through the job itself. Work is assigned to individuals so that they have the opportunity to complete an identifiable task from beginning to end. They are held responsible for successful completion of the task. The motivational effect of job enrichment can come from the opportunity for personal achievement, challenge, and recognition. Go back and review Maslow's and Herzberg's work to see how job enrichment grew out of those theories. Five characteristics of work are believed to be important in affecting individual motivation and performance.

job enrichment
Efforts to make jobs more interesting, challenging, and rewarding.

1. *Skill variety.* The extent to which a job demands different skills of the person.
2. *Task identity.* The degree to which the job requires doing a job with a visible outcome from beginning to end.
3. *Task significance.* The degree to which the job has a substantial impact on the lives or work of others in the company.

4. *Autonomy.* The degree of freedom, independence, and discretion in scheduling work and determining procedures.
5. *Feedback.* The amount of direct and clear information that is received about job performance.

Variety, identity, and significance contribute to the meaningfulness of the job. Autonomy gives employees a feeling of responsibility, and feedback contributes to feelings of achievement and recognition.

Sherwin Williams began a job enrichment program in its Richmond, Kentucky plant in the 1980s. Employees were grouped into teams and each member was trained to do all the jobs assigned the team. The teams have autonomy to decide where members work, what they do, and how they train others. The group is responsible for results. Raises are based on performance as evaluated by team leaders and peers. Employees are encouraged to feel responsible for the entire production process.

The program was quite successful. Absenteeism is much lower than at other Sherwin Williams plants. Turnover is low and productivity is higher than at other plants. Cost per gallon of paint is also much lower. Similar results were obtained at Harley-Davidson. Tom Peters uses the term *limitless* when discussing the potential of job enrichment in work teams.[14]

Job enrichment is based on Herzberg's higher motivators such as responsibility, achievement, and recognition. This is in contrast to **job simplification,** which produces task efficiency by breaking down the job into simple steps and assigning people to each of those steps. There is not much motivation in doing boring, repetitive work, but some managers still operate on the Taylor level of motivation and use job simplification. One way to increase motivation is **job enlargement,** which combines a series of tasks into one assignment that is more challenging, interesting, and motivating. For example, Maytag redesigned its work so that employees worked on an entire water pump instead of separate parts. **Job rotation** also makes work more interesting and motivating by moving employees from one job to another. You can see the problem of having to train employees to do several different operations, but usually the resulting morale building and motivation offsets the additional costs.

Job design is clearly a way to rethink jobs so that people feel responsibility and a sense of accomplishment. Another way to increase motivation is to get everyone to agree on specific corporate objectives.

GOAL–SETTING THEORY AND MANAGEMENT BY OBJECTIVES

Goal-setting theory is based on the notion that the setting of specific, ambitious but attainable goals is related to high levels of motivation and performance if the goals are accepted, are accompanied by feedback, and are facilitated by organizational conditions.[15] Nothing makes more sense intuitively than the idea that all members of an organization should have some basic agreement about the overall goals of the organization and the specific objectives to be met by each department and individual in the organization. It follows, then, that someone would develop a system to involve everyone in the organization in goal setting and implementation. Such a system is called **management by objectives (MBO).** MBO was very popular in the 1960s. Big corporations such as Ford used it. Ford executives taught the method to the U.S. Defense Department, and from there it spread to other government agencies.

job simplification
Process of producing task efficiency by breaking down the job into simple steps and assigning people to each of those steps.

job enlargement
Job enrichment strategy involving combining a series of tasks into one assignment that is more challenging and interesting.

job rotation
Job enrichment strategy involving moving employees from one job to another.

goal-setting theory
Theory that setting specific, attainable goals can motivate workers and improve performance if the goals are accepted, are accompanied by feedback, and are facilitated by organizational conditions.

management by objectives (MBO)
A system of goal setting and implementation that involves a cycle of discussion, review, and evaluation of objectives among top-level managers, middle-level managers, supervisors, and employees.

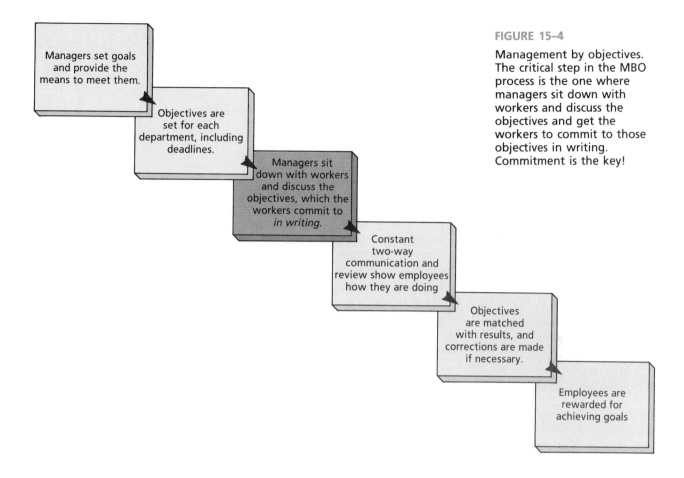

FIGURE 15–4

Management by objectives. The critical step in the MBO process is the one where managers sit down with workers and discuss the objectives and get the workers to commit to those objectives in writing. Commitment is the key!

Managers set goals and provide the means to meet them.

Objectives are set for each department, including deadlines.

Managers sit down with workers and discuss the objectives, which the workers commit to *in writing.*

Constant two-way communication and review show employees how they are doing

Objectives are matched with results, and corrections are made if necessary.

Employees are rewarded for achieving goals

Management by objectives is a system of goal setting and implementation that involves a cycle of discussion, review, and evaluation of objectives among top and middle-level managers, supervisors, and employees. It meets the criteria of goal-setting theory when implemented properly and can be quite effective.

There are six steps in the motivational MBO process (see Figure 15–4):

1. Top management consults with managers throughout the organization to set long-range goals and the means to determine whether or not those goals are being met over time.

2. Overall corporate goals are clearly formulated and subgoals are determined for each department. These subgoals are further divided into objectives for each unit and each individual within a unit. All of this is done with the full participation and cooperation of the people involved, including the means for reaching those goals and the deadlines.

3. The key to success of MBO systems is a third step where managers and workers sit down with their superiors, review the objectives and adjust them if necessary, and then commit themselves to those objectives in a written contract or agreement that states clearly the objectives, the means for reaching the objectives, and the time periods involved. The idea is that participation in goal setting involves everyone in the goals and motivates them by making them feel part of a team. This is consistent with the Hawthorne Effect, as we discussed earlier.

HELPING VERSUS COACHING

It is important for managers to understand the difference between helping and coaching subordinates. *Helping* means to work with the subordinate, doing part of the work if necessary. *Coaching* means acting as a resource—teaching, guiding, recommending—but not helping (that is, not participating actively in the task).

Helping subordinates tends to make them weak and dependent and irresponsible. Coaching subordinates tends to make them feel part of a team and capable of doing it on their own once they learn the system, and this is highly motivating.

4. Implementation of the plan calls for periodic reviews of progress, constant two-way communication among all participants, and the application of good management so that the spirit of mutual cooperation and agreed-upon goals is maintained.
5. The next step is to monitor progress by matching objectives to accomplishments, noting deviations, making needed corrections, communicating the results to all participants, and adjusting to any unanticipated situations.
6. The final step is to reward employees for achieving the desired goals or to assist employees to reach the goals in the future.

Management by objectives is most effective in relatively stable situations where long-range plans can be made and implemented with little need for major changes. Even in high-tech, rapidly changing industries such as computers and bio-technology, the concept of MBO may be effective. That is, managers should formulate plans in cooperation with everyone, commit people to those plans, monitor results, and reward accomplishment. To summarize, management by objectives is a strategy for involving all members of an organization in goal setting and implementation, and, properly conducted, generates a feeling of involvement and cooperation (motivation). MBO is also an excellent way to determine who deserves a promotion and increased pay and who does not, based on results.

Problems arise when management uses MBO as a strategy for forcing managers and workers to commit to goals that are not really mutually agreed upon but are set by top management. Care must also be taken to maintain open, two-way communication and an organizational culture that values the stated objectives. For example, all universities talk about the importance of teaching but few give full recognition to good teachers in promotion decisions. The objectives are clear, but the reward system contradicts the objectives. The same kind of conflict may occur in all organizations.

PROGRESS CHECK

▪ Briefly describe the managerial attitudes behind Theories X, Y, and Z.

▪ Employees at smaller firms seem relatively happy with their jobs, yet about half plan to leave in a few years. What is lacking in small firms that is causing employees to leave?

▪ Relate job enrichment to Herzberg's motivating factors.

▪ What are the six steps in management by objectives?

▪ What is the difference between helping and coaching and which motivates workers more?

IMPLEMENTING THE NEW CONCEPTS: MOTIVATION THROUGH COMMUNICATION

Management by objectives teaches us that one key to successful management and motivation, in any organization, is the establishment and maintenance of open, two-way communication between and among managers and workers so that everyone understands the objectives and works together effectively and efficiently to achieve them. Communication must flow two ways among all members of an organization. The problem today is that most communication flows are one way; from top management down. This communication takes the form of directives, policies, announcements, memos, rules, procedures, and the like.

The flow upward, from workers to managers, is usually severely clogged. Rarely do organizations have any formal means of upward communication (from employees to management) equivalent to directives and announcements. Instead, the burden falls on workers to initiate contact with supervisors and present their ideas and suggestions. As you know, few people in any organization tell the boss when things are not going well. Children don't tell parents when they've broken something, students don't tell teachers when someone has goofed, and employees don't tell bosses. Such a system creates an "us against them" attitude, where workers feel united in their distrust and avoidance of managers. To create an atmosphere of "us working together," managers have to become active listeners and valued assistants to workers. Such a change demands radical retraining of managers and careful creation of new attitudes and beliefs among workers.

Teamwork between and among managers and employees does not just happen. The whole organization must be structured to facilitate dialogues. Some procedures for encouraging open communication include:

- Top management must first create an organizational culture that rewards listening by being listeners themselves; by creating facilities (for example, conference rooms) for having dialogues; and by showing others that talking with superiors counts—by providing feedback, adopting employee suggestions, and rewarding upward communication, even if it is negative. Employees must feel free to say anything.
- Supervisors and managers must be trained in listening skills. Most people receive no such training in school or anywhere else, so organizations must do the training themselves or hire someone to do it.
- Barriers to open communication must be removed and facilitating mechanisms installed. Barriers include separate offices, parking spaces, bathrooms, dining rooms, and other such facilities for various levels of management and workers. Such facilities foster an "us versus them" attitude. Other barriers include different dress codes, different ways of addressing one another (for example, calling workers by their first names and managers by their last), and so on. Removing such barriers takes imagination and a willingness to give up the special privileges of management. Facilitating efforts include large lunch tables where all organizational members eat, conference rooms, organizational picnics, organizational athletic teams, and other such outings where managers mix with and socialize with each other and with workers. Note that managers in small firms mentioned such activities as very important to their motivation in the *Inc.* survey mentioned earlier.

APPLYING OPEN COMMUNICATIONS

Intel executives call their open communications policy *decision making by peers*. It has been described as "an open confrontation-oriented management style in which people go after blunt issues bluntly, straightforwardly. The main reason people need not hide is that they talk all the time. A meeting is not a rare, formal—and thus political—event."

Dana Corporation has a policy of caring, feeding, and unshackling the efforts of the average man or woman. They call it *productivity through people*.

Perhaps the best description of informal communications taking place within an organization and with custom-

ers describes the situation at the 3M Company:

> There were a score or more casual meetings in progress with salespeople, marketing people, manufacturing people, engineering people, R&D people . . . sitting around, chattering about new-product problems. We happened in on a session where a 3M customer had come to talk informally with about 15 people from 4 divisions on how better to serve his company. . . . We didn't see a single structured presentation. It went on all day—people meeting in a seemingly random way to get things done.

Source: Thomas J. Peters and Robert H. Waterman, Jr., *In Search of Excellence* (New York: Harper & Row, 1982).

Meetings that are free-wheeling and informal give employees an opportunity to contribute, and that makes them motivated. Intel calls such meetings "decision making by peers." Such meetings should not be rare events, but a normal part of the routine when problems arise.

Reinventing the Corporation

John Naisbitt and Patricia Aburdene coauthored a book they called *Re-Inventing the Corporation* (New York: Warner Books, 1985). The goal of management, according to Naisbitt and Aburdene, is to adopt "new humanistic values." Such new values enable employees to motivate themselves because they feel more a part of a unified corporate team.

Steps for creating a new, better corporate atmosphere include: calling everyone by his or her first name, eliminating executive parking spots and bathrooms, having everyone answer his or her own phone, eliminating files, doing business only with pleasant people, and throwing out the organization chart.

The authors suggest that managers also "reinvent work." This means respecting workers, providing interesting work, rewarding good work, developing workers' skills, allowing some autonomy, and decentralizing authority.

Other points include: (1) the manager's role is that of teacher, mentor, and coach; (2) the best people want ownership in the firm; (3) the best managerial style

MAKING ETHICAL DECISIONS

You work as a manager for a rather prestigious department store. Each year to offset the rush of buyers at Christmas you are required to hire temporary help. You know that *all* the temporaries will be discharged on January 10th. However, as you interview prospective temporaries, you give the impression the store will permanently hire at least two full-time retail salespeople for the coming new year. You even instruct your permanent employees to emphasize that good work over Christmas is the way to a permanent position. Is this an ethical way to try to motivate these employees? What is the danger of using this tactic?

is not top down, but a networking, people style of management; (4) quality is the new key to success; (5) successful large corporations copy the entrepreneurial flavor of small businesses; and (6) the information age enables firms to locate where there is a high quality of life since they don't have to be concerned with such industrial considerations as raw materials, and so on.

All of these ideas are derived from reading the latest in business literature. Clearly, there *is* a trend toward different management styles, as we have described earlier. What is important to learn from this chapter is that the new management styles are largely motivational tools to bring out the best in more educated, better trained workers. Those are the workers of the future and include you and me. Look through the points outlined by Naisbitt and Aburdene and see if you don't agree that it would be more fun and more productive working in such an organization and that would help motivate you to do a better job.

Changing Organizations Is Not Easy

We have come a long way from the time and motion studies of Frederick Taylor. Maslow, Mayo, Herzberg, and others have taught us to treat employees as associates and to get them more involved in decision making. This increases motivation and leads to greater productivity.

The problem is that many managers were brought up under a different system. Some were in the military and are used to telling people what to do rather than consulting with them. Others come from the football-coach school of management. They, too, tend to yell and direct rather than consult and discuss.

Furthermore, employees are often not used to participative management. The transition from Theory X to Theory Y management, from Taylor to Herzberg, is still going on. It is important, then, to have examples to follow when trying to implement the new approaches.

William Potter, the CEO of Preston Trucking Company, is one manager who has succeeded at the task of turning a disorganized, semihostile work force into a cooperative, efficient team. Let's review his story to see what lessons he can teach us.

A Model for the Future

Employees at Preston Trucking Company wear a button on their shirts that says, "Preston People: We Make a Difference." The story of Preston Trucking is a parable that illustrates management principles of the future. High-tech may bring tremendous productivity increases through robotics, computers, word processors, and the like. But the truly successful firms will be those that get the most from their people. The machinery will be much the same in all firms; the creative use of that machinery will make the difference.

Preston was not always a model company. The Teamsters Union (truck drivers) filed 723 grievances against Preston in 1978. Surveys among workers elicited 40 negative comments for every compliment.[16] Labor-management relations were the equivalent of internal warfare. Cooperation was at a minimum.

There was talk of deregulation of the trucking industry, and Preston management knew that this would make improvements in productivity and labor relations critical to the firm's survival. A whole new attitude needed to be developed among top management. The philosophy to be adopted was that people (employees) were the firm's biggest asset, and that customer service was the primary goal. The question was whether or not management could motivate the truck drivers to join in the cause.

Implementing Change

The first step Preston took was to train managers to be facilitators and listeners rather than bosses and order givers. It was not easy to get management to give up their desire for control and authority over employees. Managers were all trained together, and encouraged one another to adopt the new philosophy. Some of the changes involved terminology. Employees are now called *associates* and supervisors are called *coordinators*. The tradition in trucking firms was to record errors made by drivers and dockworkers, and management was accomplished by intimidation, threat, and negative reinforcement. Management at Preston changed that philosophy, and began keeping records of how often they complimented and encouraged employees.[17]

When deregulation became a reality, the new system was in effect; that is, management had been trained to talk with employees, listening was emphasized over order giving, employees were encouraged to become independent and responsible for their own operations, and a feeling of cooperation was established. Grievances decreased from 723 to 472 in a few years.

MANAGEMENT BY WALKING AROUND

One concept that the Preston Trucking Company adopted to improve employee relations and increase productivity is called management by walking around (MBWA). The idea is for managers to regularly wander among employees asking questions, being friendly, and being supportive:

In trying to explain the phenomenon of walk-around management, a GM manager contrasted one key aspect of the striking difference between two giant plants:

> I know this sounds like a caricature, but I guess that is how life is. At the poorly performing plant, the plant manager probably ventured out on the floor once a week, always in a suit. His comments were distant and perfunctory. At South Gate, the better plant, the plant manager was on the floor all the time. He wore a baseball cap and a UAW jacket. By the way, whose plant do you think was spotless? Whose looked like a junkyard?

The best walk-around managers are on a first-name basis with employees and stop and chat informally about family and other personal subjects. Employees are made to feel part of a team, important, and part of the corporate family. Management by walking around often goes beyond the organization. Many managers apply the same concept with suppliers, dealers, customers, and other publics. That is, they get out and visit these people, ask if they need anything, and generally behave in a friendly, supportive, helpful manner.

Mr. John Smith, a Preston terminal manager in Baltimore, Maryland, says, "We're not just a truck company anymore; we're a service company, and we want to know when the customer wants us there and when we shouldn't be there." To give an idea of how far this can go, at Activision (a videogame maker) the company telephone book is alphabetized by first names.

However, management by walking around is not effective if workers or other publics feel that the manager is there to snoop on them or to fake some camaraderie that isn't real. Managers who practice management by walking around effectively are sincere in their attempt to create a feeling of warmth and friendly cooperation—and it works.

Source: Thomas J. Peters and Robert H. Waterman, Jr., *In Search of Excellence* (New York: Harper & Row, 1982), p. 262; and David Field, "From Musclebound to Brainy, Preston Thrives on Tough Trade," *The Washington Times*, April 4, 1989, pp. C1 and C9.

The results show the benefit of a management philosophy that is people oriented. The number of trucking terminals in operation increased over 50 percent in six years. Because of better labor-management relations, it was possible to cut the number of coordinators by 4 percent (with more employees), to cut management personnel by 18 percent, and to eliminate a whole layer of management. The increase in employee morale raised productivity by 7.9 percent and resulted in a savings of $19 million.

Employees are now encouraged to buy company stock and share in the ownership and thus the profits of the firm. The attitude now is, "This is my company and I'm here to serve my customers to make a bigger profit for us." The button "Preston People: We Make a Difference" is more than a slogan. It is the reflection of a managerial philosophy.

The management team at Preston spends much of its time walking around visting the various terminals and talking with the workers. They follow the concepts of the book *In Search of Excellence* in that they believe in "management by walking around" and "keeping close to the customer."

Lessons from the Preston Experience

Will Potter, the CEO at Preston Trucking Company, believes that college students preparing for business must get involved in campus activities and learn to (1) get along with people by learning listening skills; (2) be more concise and clear writers so that they can write memos and reports that are short and readable; and (3) be public speakers by becoming officers in campus clubs and giving talks. The best way to lead is by example, and the Preston management team is a model for employees and for managers in all types of firms as well. The lessons we can learn from the Preston example include:

- The future growth of industry and business in general depends on a motivated, productive work force.
- Motivation is largely internally generated by workers themselves; the process that releases that energy includes giving employees more freedom to be creative and rewarding achievement when it occurs.
- The first step in any motivational program is to establish open communication among workers and managers so that the feeling generated is one of cooperation and teamwork, a family-type atmosphere.

William Potter is shown in this photo talking to an associate. His managers are trained to be facilitators and listeners. Mr. Potter sets the tone by being a listener himself. He believes in "management by walking around."

THINKING IT THROUGH   What do you think would have happened had top management at Preston decided to crack down on drivers and insist on better performance rather than seek their help? Would a participative managerial style work for a football team as well? What are the motivational differences, if any, between professional truck drivers and professional football players?

Motivation in the 1990s

What can we learn from all the theories and experiences discussed in this chapter? Will they work in the service economy of the 1990s as well as they did in the industrial economies of the past? The answer is "yes, if." Yes, people can be motivated much as they were in the past if managers know which technique to use and when.

Tomorrow's customers expect high-quality, customized goods and services. That means tomorrow's employees must provide extensive personal service and pay close attention to details. Employees will have to work smart as well as hard. No amount of supervision can force an employee to smile or go the extra mile to help a customer. In fact, no theory of motivation will work with *all* of tomorrow's workers.

What is the key to success in the 1990s? Michael Maccoby thinks he has the answer in his new book called *Why Work: Leading the New Generation*. The idea, he says, is to deemphasize external motivators and instead to understand people's inner drives, interests, and values. The company's goals have to be accomplished through people, and people have their own goals. The manager's problem, therefore, is to find a way to meet the company's goals by first meeting the individual employee's goals.[18]

Maccoby identifies different types of workers and shows how each needs a different type of motivational effort. For example, half of the respondents in Maccoby's study considered themselves to be "experts," or people who get their satisfaction mainly from the work itself. Experts like their independence and do not want managers to coach or cajole them. A good motivational technique for them, therefore, is to give them their freedom and recognize their achievements with rewards. "Self-developers," on the other hand, consider work as a way to develop their own knowledge and skills. Self-developers want a more collaborative relationship with managers. A good technique for them is to give them opportunities to learn new tasks and give them plenty of information about the company's goals and how each new job helps reach those goals.

Maccoby identifies other groups, which we won't go into here. The point is that employees are not alike; different employees respond to different managerial and motivational styles. Tomorrow's managers will not be able to use any one formula for all employees. Rather, they will have to get to know each worker as an individual and taylor (pun intended) the motivational effort to the individual.

In general, motivation will come from the job itself rather than from external punishments or rewards. Managers need to give workers what they need to do a good job: the right tools, the right information, and the right amount of cooperation.

You see, motivation is not so difficult. It begins with acknowledging a job well done and telling those who do such a job that you appreciate them, especially in front of others. The best motivator is often the words, "Thanks, I appreciate what you have done for me."

▪ What are several steps firms can use to increase internal communications and thus motivation?

▪ What are the six steps in "reinventing work" and how are they related to motivation?

▪ Where does management by walking around fit into Maslow's theory? Herzberg's theory?

▪ What problems may emerge when trying to implement participative management?

▪ Why is it important today to adjust motivational styles to individual employees? Are there any general principles of motivation that today's managers should follow?

1. Mickey Arison of Carnival Cruise Lines realizes that people make or break a company. This is especially true of his business, where satisfied customers are a must. Therefore, Mr. Arison works hard to see his employees are motivated to provide that "extra effort" for Carnival's passengers. Frederick Taylor was one of the first people to study motivation.

1. Explain Taylor's scientific management.

▪ Who is Frederick Taylor?

Frederick Taylor is the father of scientific management. He did time and motion studies to learn the most efficient way of doing a job and then trained workers in those procedures. He published his book on scientific management in 1911. The Gilbreths and H. L. Gantt were followers of Taylor.

2. Management theory moved away from Taylor's scientific management and toward theories that stress human factors of motivation.

2. Describe the Hawthorne studies and relate their significance to human-based management.

▪ What led to the more people-oriented managerial styles that were used to increase motivation?

The greatest impact on motivation theory was generated by the Hawthorne studies in the late 1920s and early 1930s. Elton Mayo found that human factors such as feelings of involvement and participation led to greater productivity gains than did physical changes in the workplace.

3. Maslow studied basic human motivation and found that motivation was based on need—an unfilled need motivated people to satisfy it and a satisfied need no longer motivated.

3. Identify the levels of Maslow's hierarchy of needs and relate the hierarchy's importance to employee motivation.

▪ What were the various levels of need identified by Maslow?

From the bottom of Maslow's hierarchy of needs up, the needs are physiological, safety, social, self-esteem, and self-actualization.

▪ Can managers use this theory?

Yes; they can recognize what needs a person has and have work provide the satisfaction.

4. McGregor held that managers can have two attitudes toward employees. They are called Theory X and Theory Y.

4. Differentiate between Theory X and Theory Y.

▪ What are these theories and when were they developed?

Theory X assumes that the average person dislikes work and will avoid it if possible. Therefore, people must be forced, controlled, and threatened with punishment to accomplish organizational goals. Theory Y assumes that people like working and will accept responsibility for achieving goals if rewarded for doing so. Douglas McGregor published these theories in 1970.

5. Describe Theory Z and its application in the United States.

5. In response to McGregor's Theories X and Y, Ouchi introduced Theory Z.
   ▪ What is Theory Z?
     Theory Z comes out of Japanese management and stresses long-term employment, among other factors.

6. Herzberg found that some factors are motivators and others are hygiene factors; that is, they cause job dissatisfaction if missing, but are not motivators if present.

6. Distinguish between motivators and hygiene factors identified by Herzberg.

   ▪ What are the factors called motivators?
     The work itself, achievement, recognition, responsibility, growth, and advancement.
   ▪ What are the hygiene factors?
     Company policies, supervision, working conditions, interpersonal relations, and salary.

7. Job enrichment describes efforts to make jobs more interesting.

7. Explain how job enrichment affects employee motivation and performance.

   ▪ What characteristics of work affect motivation and performance?
     The job characteristics that influence motivation are: (1) skill variety, (2) task identity, (3) task significance, (4) autonomy, and (5) feedback.
   ▪ Name two forms of job enrichment that increase motivation.
     Job enrichment strategies include job enlargement and job rotation.

8. One procedure for establishing objectives and gaining employee commitment to those objectives is called MBO (management by objectives).

8. Identify the steps involved in implementing a management by objectives (MBO) program.

   ▪ What are the steps in an MBO program?
     (1) Managers set goals, (2) objectives are established for each department, (3) workers discuss the objectives and commit themselves in writing to meeting them, (4) progress is reviewed, (5) feedback is provided and adjustments made, and (6) employees are rewarded for achieving goals or assisted in reaching goals in the future.

9. The transition from scientific management to human-based management is still going on.

9. Describe the implementation of motivation theory in the 1990s.

   ▪ What is the key to successful human-based management?
     In a word, the key to successful management is communication. That means training managers to listen and facilitating listening by removing barriers (for example, executive dining rooms) and providing necessary facilities (for example, conference rooms).

GETTING INVOLVED

1. Think of all the bosses (managers/leaders) you have had over time in sports, clubs, and so forth. Did they assume a Theory X or Y style of leadership? How did you feel about that? Would you have worked harder or less hard if they had followed the other strategy? What does this tell you about motivation? Discuss with your class.

2. Herzberg found that pay was not a motivator. If you were paid to get better grades, would you be able to get them? Have you worked harder as a result of a large raise? Discuss money as a motivator with your friends and class. Do you agree 100 percent with Herzberg?

3. Have you ever volunteered to work on a project where you felt your efforts really made a difference? How did you feel about that? If you haven't, how do you feel about that fact? Do you envy people with an obvious mission in life? How could you find a job that would satisfy your basic needs for food, shelter, safety, and esteem and feel as if you were making a difference in the world? Discuss options with classmates.

4. If you were made a manager, would you be willing to treat your employees as equals? Would you be willing to eat with them, socialize with them, and generally be their friend as well as their boss? Would it make a difference if they were from a different ethnic group, country, or social class? What kind of people do you feel need Theory X management? Discuss.

5. You have had the most experience in motivation working under various teachers in school. Which teachers got you to work hardest? How did they do it? What was their managerial style? What motivators did they use? Discuss your findings with the class.

PRACTICING
MANAGEMENT
DECISIONS

CASE ONE   THEORY X AND Y: THAT'S HOW THE COOKIE CRUMBLES

No two firms better illustrate Theory X and Theory Y than David's Cookies and Mrs. Fields Chocolate Chippery stores. You'll see what we mean.

First, let's look at David's Cookies. The owner is David Liederman. When his stores first opened, everyone criticized his cookies. However, when the *New York Times* had a cookie-tasting contest, David's won. Today, David's Cookies has 205 specialty stores, has approximately 400 compact self-contained modular stores (called kiosks), and sells frozen cookie dough and ice cream to 2,000 New York area supermarkets. David's is a big success!

How much confidence does he have in his employees? Apparently not much. David feels it's necessary to minimize employee involvement in cookie making so they can't mess things up. He does that by making all the dough in a factory and shipping it to the stores. All the employee has to do is put the dough on a tray, put it in an automatic oven, and take it out 7½ minutes later. David has hesitated to sell brownies because he feels workers can't handle the job of adding eggs. He says, "One of the reasons we do well . . . is that a chimpanzee could take cookies out of that bag and more often than not put them on the tray properly."

In contrast, let's go over to Mrs. Fields Chocolate Chippery. Debbi Fields has about 500 company-owned cookie stores in 37 states selling about $90 million a year. Not bad, either.

What does Mrs. Fields think about employees? She feels that people "will do their very best provided that they are getting proper support." Mrs. Fields says, "It's a people company. That's what it's all about. . . . What we really do is . . . we take care of people." This philosophy is reflected in how Mrs. Fields makes cookies. Store employees combine ingredients right in the store (some in proportioned containers). The ovens are not automatic. Employees put the raw dough in to bake and take out the finished cookies when it feels right. "We tell them that we want them to have fun," Mrs. Fields says. "People come to work because they need to be productive. They need to feel successful in whatever they do." Here is how Debbi sums up her job: "To make people feel important and to create an opportunity for them. That's really my role as cookie president, the cookie person."

An article in *Inc.* magazine sums it all up. It said, "Approximately 8,000 people sell Mrs. Fields' cookies over company-owned store counters. The amazing thing about them is that almost every one of them smiles at customers."

DECISION QUESTIONS

1. What motivational philosophies are in use at David's and Mrs. Fields Cookies? How do you support your conclusions?

2. Which store is more likely to build employee honesty and loyalty?

3. In which company would you rather be a manager? Employee? Investor? What are your reasons for making these decisions?

Sources: Tom Richman, "A Tale of Two Companies," *Inc.*, July 1984, pp. 37–43; "The Man Who Would Be Cookie King," *Marketing Communications*, December 1984, p. 6; Tom Richman, "Mrs. Fields' Secret Ingredient," *Inc.*, October 1987, pp. 65–72; Cheryl Turi Coutts, "David's Cookies: Taking on the Goliaths," *Restaurant Business*, May 29, 1987, pp. 134–42; and Tom Richman, "Their System Doesn't Work All the Time," *Inc.*, April 1989, p. 100.

USING COMPENSATION TO MOTIVATE

Computer Output Printing Inc. (COPI) had a real problem with profitability. Everything seemed to be geared to volume and nobody seemed to care much about quality. Salespeople earned money for bringing in new business, even if it wasn't profitable. Production people earned extra money for cranking out volume, even if the work had to be redone.

Andy Plata, the chief executive officer of COPI thought maybe profit sharing would motivate people to work smarter and generate profits but thought better of the idea because profits seemed too remote from what workers actually did on the shop floor. He then decided to try revenue sharing. All 23 employees—from secretaries and machine operators to Plata himself—receive a chunk of their income from the money that comes in from sales. There are no salespeople in the firm because everyone is now responsible for increased sales and makes more money if sales do increase.

Every employee receives a base salary about 15 percent below what others might make in similar positions elsewhere. Employees also receive semiannual bonuses based on profits and merit. But the heart of the motivational system is the monthly cut of sales revenue each employee receives. A new printer may make $1,500 in salary and $180 more for revenue sharing the first month. Over time, the salary figure will change only slowly, but the revenue-sharing portion can grow considerably. Doing a good job results in a larger share of revenues. But revenues increase only when all the employees work together to provide quality customer service. Happy customers come back. It's that simple!

Under the new revenue-sharing plan, revenues increased from $1.2 million to $5 million. There is no cap on how much an employee can earn, so monthly revenue shares averaged only $113 in 1984, but were up to $233 in 1988.

Because of the new incentives, workers are willing to stay overtime to complete a job or come in on the weekend. Now recruiting is much easier at the firm. Most new employees come recommended by present employees. The criteria used in selecting new people include whether or not they are willing to be part of a team that generates high revenues to share. Customers are excited by the concept of revenue sharing because they see the results in better and faster service.

DECISION QUESTIONS

1. What does COPI do to motivate people using money that other firms do not do? Can you see how money can be a motivator?
2. Given that there is no limit on how much an employee can make under revenue sharing, some employees can make $60,000 a year or more, way beyond normal salaries for such positions. Why do you suppose such high salaries have not hurt profits at COPI?
3. What kind of workers would enjoy working at COPI and what kind would not? Can you see how productivity at COPI would increase as certain kinds of employees would self-select themselves out of the company and others would come who fit the system better?
4. Would such a revenue sharing system work at most companies? For what kinds of companies would it work best?

Source: Bruce G. Posner, "A Company of Salespeople," *Inc.*, June 1988, pp. 123–26.

Organizations succeed or fail on the ability of the people they employ. Therefore, hiring, training, motivating, and developing human resources is a vital element in business success. This task is becoming more difficult with new hiring rules, new employee demands, and new technologies. Certainly human resource management will be an interesting and challenging career in the future. We discuss that function next in Chapter 16.

HUMAN RESOURCE MANAGEMENT

16

Scott and Cindy Keech.

Obviously the most beautiful fate, the most wonderful good fortune than can happen to any human being, is to be paid for doing that which he passionately loves.
ABRAHAM MASLOW

PROFILE   CINDY AND SCOTT KEECH OF STEELCASE, INC.

Cindy and Scott Keech are living the future everyday at Steelcase, Inc., an office-furniture company in Grand Rapids, Michigan. Cindy works as a receptionist, but only works every other week. She shares her job with another employee who works the weeks Cindy is at home. Scott upholsters chairs in the factory and earns approximately $9 per hour. However, he more than doubles his pay through profit sharing bonuses and "piecework"—incentive pay for each chair he upholsters. Every December, Scott and Cindy sit down and choose medical, dental, life insurance and disability coverage from a flexible-benefits package offered by Steelcase. Just last year, Cindy was able to earn an additional $900 in unused benefit allowances by piggybacking on Scott's coverage. How do they manage to do all this?

Steelcase, Inc., is one of a handful of companies that currently uses "flex" policies. At Steelcase, employees have a direct say in how they wish to be compensated for their work. According to James Soule, vice president for human resources, "People are becoming good at choosing what they need, as opposed to us playing God." The company also advocates flextime work schedules in addition to its cafeteria-style benefits package.

How has the experiment at Steelcase fared? Employee morale is strong and the firm has experienced significant cuts in costs. The annual rate of employee turnover is only 3 percent. Is Steelcase a forerunner of things to come? This chapter discusses the present and future challenges of human resource management, and teaches you the terms you will need to know, including piecework, flextime, and cafeteria-style benefit plans.

Source: Bob Cohn, "A Glimpse of the 'Flex' Future," *Newsweek,* August 1, 1988, pp. 38–39.

THE PERSONNEL FUNCTION

In your career search, you may be in and out of many personnel offices. While you are there, take a few minutes to observe. Talk to some of the employees and managers. Perhaps personnel is the field in which you would like to work.

There is an old story about the student who wanted to go into personnel "because I want to work with people." It is true that personnel managers work with people, but they are also deeply involved in planning, record-keeping, and other administrative duties. To begin a career in personnel, you need to develop a better reason than "I want to work with people." This chapter will discuss the personnel function, which involves recruiting, hiring, training, evaluating, and compensating people. Today, personnel management is often called human resource management. **Human resource management** is the process of evaluating human resource needs, finding people to fill those needs, and optimizing this important resource by providing the right incentives and job environment, all with the goal of meeting the objectives of the organization (see Figure 16–1). Let's explore some of the trends in the area of human resource management.

The Importance of Human Resource Management

One reason that human resource management (or personnel management) is receiving increased attention now is because of the major shift from traditional manufacturing industries to service industries and high-tech manufacturing organizations that require more technical job skills. A major problem today is retraining

human resource management
The process of evaluating human resource needs, finding people to fill those needs, and optimizing this important resource by providing the right incentives and job enrichment, all with the goal of meeting the objectives of the organization.

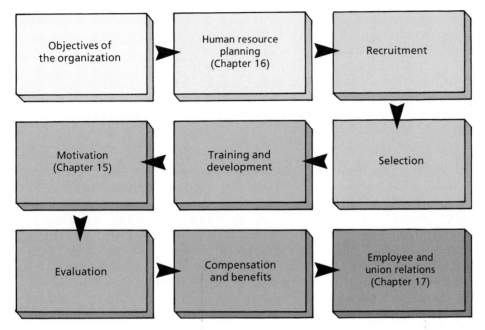

FIGURE 16–1

Human resource management. Note that human resource management includes motivation as discussed in Chapter 15 and union relations as discussed in Chapter 17. As you can see from the chart, human resource management is more than hiring and firing personnel.

workers for new, more challenging jobs. For example, when Crown Zellerbach recently modernized a Louisiana pulp mill plant, it set up a training facility nearby and paid workers full wages to learn new skills. There are also other examples:

- Hewlett-Packard spent $1 million to move 350 workers to new jobs, and Boeing enrolled laid-off electronics technicians in college to learn new microprocessor skills. The idea was to retrain their own people before going outside for skilled employees.
- At GE's Louisville dishwasher plant, assembly line workers are learning how to read computer printouts. GE has a $6 million learning center in Pennsylvania and conducts training programs worldwide.
- Motorola spends 2.6 percent of its payroll budget, or $42 million, on training blue-collar employees to use a production method called statistical-process control that employs complex mathematical guides to manage quality. The company was thus able to free its engineers to work in other essential tasks.[1]
- IBM is experimenting with a program that involves work at home for part-time employees who cannot report regularly to an IBM location.[2]

Some people have called employees the ultimate resource, and, when you think about it, nothing could be more true. People develop the ideas that eventually become the products that satisfy our wants and needs. Take away their creative minds and organizations such as IBM, GE, Hewlett-Packard, GM, and other leading firms would be nothing. The problem is that this resource has always been relatively plentiful, so there was little need to nurture and develop it. If you needed qualified people, you simply went out and hired them. If they didn't work out, you fired them and found others. Labor is more scarce today than it has been for 15 years. That makes recruiting more difficult.

Most firms assigned the job of recruiting, selecting, training, evaluating, compensating, motivating, and, yes, firing people to the various functional departments. For years, the personnel department was viewed more or less as a clerical function responsible for screening applications, keeping records, processing payroll, and finding people when necessary.

Today, the job of human resource management has taken on an entirely new role in the firm. In the future, it may become *the* most critical function in that it is responsible for the most critical resource—people. In fact, the human resource function has become so important that it is no longer the function of just one department; it is a function of all managers. Most human resource functions are shared between the professional human resource manager and the other managers. What are some of the problems in the human resource area that managers face?

The Human Resource Problem

No changes in the American business system have been more dramatic and had more impact on the future success of the free enterprise system than changes in the labor force. The ability of the U.S. business system to compete in international markets depends on an increase in new ideas, new products, and as we saw in Chapter 13, a higher level of productivity from its workers. All of these factors critically depend on the ultimate resource—people with good ideas. Some of the problems being encountered in the human resource area include:

- Shortages in people trained to work in the growth areas of the future such as computers, biotechnology, robotics, and the sciences.
- A huge population of skilled and unskilled workers from declining industries such as steel and automobiles who are unemployed or underemployed, and who need retraining.
- A growing population of blacks, Hispanics, and other minorities who are undereducated and poor and who lack adequate preparation for jobs in the contemporary business environment. (A study by the Institute of Educational Leadership indicated that 20 million new workers will be in the labor force by the year 2000, 83 per cent of whom will be women, minorities, and immigrants.
- A shift in the age composition in the work force, including many older workers.*
- A complex set of laws and regulations involving hiring, safety, unionization, and equal pay that limits organizations' freedom to create an optimum labor force; for example, it is becoming very difficult to fire an inefficient or ineffective worker (see the box called You're Fired).
- A tremendous influx of women into the labor force and the resulting demand for day care, job sharing, maternity leave programs, and special career advancement programs for women.
- A shift in employee attitudes toward work; leisure time has become a much higher priority, as have concepts such as flextime and a shorter workweek.
- A challenge from overseas labor pools available for lower wages and subject to many fewer laws and regulations; this results in many jobs being shifted overseas.
- An increased demand for benefits tailored to the individual. We shall discuss these cafeteria-style fringe benefit plans later in the chapter.
- A growing concern over such issues as health care, day-care facilities, smoking on the job, and equal pay for jobs of comparable worth (discussed in Chapter 17) and special attention given to affirmative-action programs.

Given all these issues, and others that are sure to develop, you can see why human resource management has taken a more central position in management thinking. Let's see what is involved.

---

* See Chapter 1 for a more complete coverage of demographic trends.

"YOU'RE FIRED!" OR ARE YOU?

At one time, it was relatively easy for managers to fire an employee as long as they didn't violate any laws such as the Civil Rights Act of 1964. That is no longer true. Since the 1970s, courts have chipped away at the so-called employment-at-will doctrine that declared that workers could be fired for almost any reason or in some cases for no reason. Beverly Hills attorney H. Bradley Jones proclaimed that wrongful discharge "is even more dangerous than medical malpractice . . . since few insurance companies sell insurance coverage to protect employers against wrongful discharge lawsuits."

The number of cases and the size of awards are increasing. For example, a Montana woman who was released from her job after 28 years was awarded $94,170 in economic damages, $100,000 for emotional distress, and $1.3 million in punitive damages. The Montana Supreme Court upheld a jury's judgment that declared a long-term employee has an expectation of continued employment provided the employee's work performance has been satisfactory. The average jury verdict in California unjust-dismissal cases reached $861,000 in 1987. Awards such as this are causing employers to be much more cautious about who they fire and how. Some companies are even at the point, now, of leasing rather than hiring employees.

The situation doesn't promise to get easier. Courts are asking judges and juries to decide what is "good cause" and what is "fair"—concepts that are unclear and elusive at best. In addition, several states are considering legislation that would limit instances in which an employer could fire workers. See Case One at the end of this chapter for more on this issue.

Sources: Stephen A. Ploscowe and Marvin M. Goldstein, "Trouble on the Firing Line," *Nation's Business*, March 1987, pp. 36–37; Aaron Bernstein, "More Dismissed Workers Are Telling It to the Judge," *Business Week*, October 17, 1988, pp. 68–69; and William S. Waldo, "Wrongful Dismissal Cases Will Still Have Their Day in Court," *Los Angeles Times*, January 8, 1989, p. 3 of Part IV.

Does human resource management seem like a challenging career for the 1990s? Do you see any other issues likely to affect this function? What have your experiences been in dealing with people who work in human resource management? Would you enjoy working in such an environment?

THINKING IT THROUGH

PLANNING HUMAN RESOURCES

All management, including human resource management, begins with planning. Six steps are involved in the human resource planning process. They include:

1. Preparing forecasts of future human resource needs.
2. Preparing a human resource inventory that includes ages, names, education, capabilities, training, specialized skills, and other information pertinent to the specific organization (for example, languages spoken). Such information reveals whether or not the labor force is technically up-to-date, thoroughly trained, and so forth.
3. Preparing a job analysis. A **job analysis** answers the question, "What do employees who fill various job titles do?" Such analyses are necessary in order to recruit and train employees with the necessary skills to do the job. The results of job analysis are two written statements: job descriptions and job specifications. **Job descriptions** specify the objectives of the job, the type of work to be done, the responsibilities and duties, the working conditions, and the relationship of the job to other functions. **Job specifications** specify the qualifications (education, skills, etc.) required of a worker to fill specific jobs. In short, job descriptions are statements about the *job*, whereas job specifications are statements about the *person* who does the job. Job analysis information can be obtained through observation, interviews, and diaries, or some combination of techniques. As you will see later, changes in law have made the preparation of these guidelines extremely important.

job analysis
A study of what is done by employees who fill various job titles.

job descriptions
Summaries of the objectives of a job, the type of work, the responsibilities of the job, the necessary skills, the working conditions, and the relationship of the job to other functions.

job specifications
Written summary of the qualifications required of workers to do a particular job.

FIGURE 16–2

Steps in human resource planning.
Human resource planning is a complex process involving several crucial steps. A job analyses that involves job descriptions and job specifications is an important step.

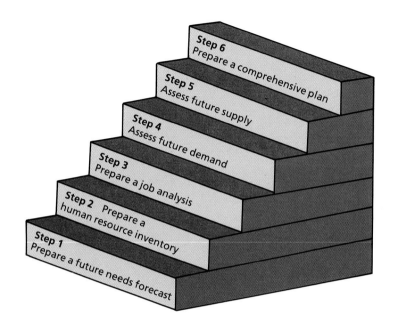

4. Assessing future demand. Changing technology often means that training programs must be started long before the need is apparent. Human resource managers that are proactive, that is, anticipate what the future of their organization will be, have the trained human resources available when needed.

5. Assessing future supply. The labor force is constantly shifting: getting older, becoming more technically oriented, attracting more women, foreign workers and so forth. There are likely to be increased shortages of some skills in the future (for example, computer and robotic repair) and oversupply of others (for example, production line workers).

6. Establishing a strategic plan for recruiting, selecting, training and developing, appraising, and scheduling the labor force, given the previous analysis. We will look at each of these elements of the strategic human resource plan in the next sections. See Figure 16–2 for an overview of the planning process.

RECRUITING EMPLOYEES

recruitment
The set of activities used to legally obtain a sufficient number of the right people at the right time to select those who best meet the needs of the organization.

Recruitment is the set of activities used to legally obtain a sufficient number of the right people at the right time to select those that best meet the needs of the organization. One would think that, with a continuous flow of new persons into the work force, that recruiting would be easy. But the truth is that recruiting has become very difficult for several reasons:

  * Legal restrictions such as the Civil Rights Act make it necessary to consider the proper mix of women, minorities, and other qualified individuals. Often people with the necessary skills are not available and must be hired and trained internally.

  * The emphasis on corporate cultures, teamwork, and participative management make it important to hire skilled people who also fit in with the culture and leadership style of the organization.

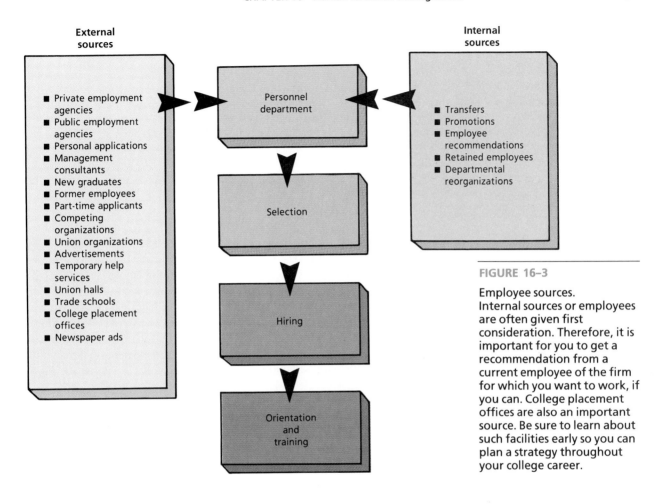

External sources

- Private employment agencies
- Public employment agencies
- Personal applications
- Management consultants
- New graduates
- Former employees
- Part-time applicants
- Competing organizations
- Union organizations
- Advertisements
- Temporary help services
- Union halls
- Trade schools
- College placement offices
- Newspaper ads

Personnel department

↓

Selection

↓

Hiring

↓

Orientation and training

Internal sources

- Transfers
- Promotions
- Employee recommendations
- Retained employees
- Departmental reorganizations

FIGURE 16–3

Employee sources. Internal sources or employees are often given first consideration. Therefore, it is important for you to get a recommendation from a current employee of the firm for which you want to work, if you can. College placement offices are also an important source. Be sure to learn about such facilities early so you can plan a strategy throughout your college career.

As we noted previously, firing unsatisfactory employees is getting more difficult to justify legally. This is especially true of discharges involving possible discrimination by age, sex, sexual preference, or race. Therefore, it is necessary to screen and evaluate employees very carefully to be sure they will be effective, long-term members of the organization.

Some organizations have unattractive workplaces, have policies that demand promotions from within, operate under union regulations, or have low wages that make recruiting and keeping employees difficult or subject to outside influence and restrictions.

Because recruiting is a difficult chore that involves finding, hiring, and training people who are an appropriate technical and social fit, human resource managers turn to many sources for assistance (see Figure 16–3). These include internal promotions, advertisements, public and private employment agencies, college placement bureaus, management consultants, professional organizations, referrals, and applicants who simply show up at the office. An interesting trend in human resource management has been the increase in the number of temporary workers. Today, temporary, part-time and contract workers make up nearly one third of the U.S. work force.[3]

Your college placement office is one of the best places to start when searching for a job. Be sure to go early to learn where it is, what information is available there, and how the interviewing process is handled. Get a head start now on the competition.

MAKING ETHICAL DECISIONS

As human resource manager for Technocrat, Inc., it is your job to recruit the best employees. You completed a human resource inventory that indicated that Technocrat currently has an abundance of qualified designers and that several lower-level workers will soon be eligible for promotions to designer positions as well. In spite of the surplus of qualified designers, you are considering offering a similar position to a designer who is now with a major competitor. Your thinking is that the new employee will be a source of information about the competition's new products. What are your ethical considerations in this case? Will you lure the employee away from the competition even though you have no need for a designer? What will be the consequences of your decision?

SELECTING EMPLOYEES

selection
The process of gathering information to decide who should be hired, under legal guidelines, for the best interests of the individual and the organization.

Selection is the process of gathering information to decide who should be hired, under legal guidelines, for the best interests of the individual and the organization. Because of high turnover, the cost of selecting and training employees has become prohibitively high in some firms. Think of the costs involved—interview time, medical exams, training costs, unproductive time spent learning the job, moving expenses, and so on. It's easy to see how such expenses can run over $50,000 for a manager. Even entry-level workers can cost thousands of dollars to recruit, process, and train. Thus, the selection process is an important element in any human resource program. A typical selection process would involve six steps (see Figure 16–4):

1. Completion of an application form. Once this was a simple procedure with few complications. Today, legal guidelines limit the kind of questions one can ask. Nonetheless, such forms help discover educational background, past work experience, career objectives, and other information directly related to the requirements of the job (see the sample application form on p. 499).

2. Initial and follow-up interviews. Applicants are often screened in a first interview by a member of the human resource department staff. If the interviewer considers the applicant a potential employee, the manager who will supervise the new employee interviews the applicant as well. Many managers and even some human resource managers are not highly skilled in conducting job interviews. However, such interviews are helpful in testing an applicant's ability to communicate clearly, to adapt to a stressful situation, and to clarify his or her goals, career objective, and background. It's important that managers prepare adequately for the interview process to avoid selection errors they may regret.

3. Employment tests. Employment tests have been severely criticized because of charges of discrimination. Nonetheless, organizations continue to use them to measure basic competencies, to test specific job skills (for example, welding, typing), and to help evaluate applicants' personalities and interests. In using employment tests, it's important that the test be directly job related. This will make the selection process more efficient and often satisfy legal requirements.

4. Background investigations. Most organizations are becoming more careful about investigating a candidate's work record, school record, and recommendations. It is simply too costly to hire, train, motivate, and lose people and then have to start the process over. Background checks help weed out candidates least likely to succeed and identify those most likely to succeed.

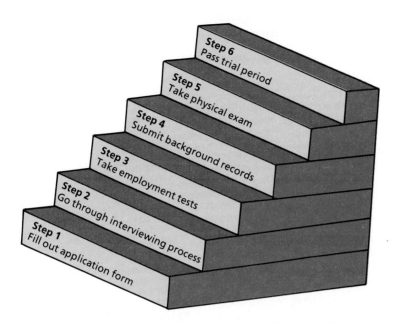

FIGURE 16–4

Steps in the selection process.
There are several steps you must take to obtain a job. First, you fill out an application blank (see page 499). Then you must go through an interviewing process and the other steps illustrated here. The goal is to find a job that is satisfying to you and to your employer.

It is not always easy to obtain this information, however. Many companies no longer provide references for fear of liability suits.

5. Physical exams. A complete medical background and checkup helps screen candidates. There are obvious benefits in hiring physically and mentally healthy people. However, medical tests cannot be given just to screen out specific applicants. If such tests are given, they must be given everyone applying for the same position. A major controversy erupted in the late 1980s related to preemployment testing to detect drug or alcohol abuse, polygraph (lie detector) testing to measure "a predisposition to dishonesty," and AIDS screening to detect carriers of the virus. Estimates are that in the 1990s over half the firms in the United States could require this mandatory type of testing of prospective workers,[4] but lie detector tests are not allowed. A *Fortune* magazine poll found that 49 percent of the top industrial and service companies tested for drugs, 24 percent for alcohol, and 11 percent used polygraphs or voice-stress analysis to test for dishonesty. Only one company tested for the AIDS antibody, but six offer the screening on a voluntary basis.[5] That was before polygraphs were outlawed.

6. Trial periods. Often an organization will hire an employee conditionally. This enables the person to prove his or her worth on the job. After a period of perhaps six months or a year, the firm has the right to discharge that employee based on evaluations from supervisors. Such systems make it easier to fire inefficient or problem employees, but do not eliminate the high cost of turnover.

The selection process is often long and difficult, but worth the effort because of the high costs of replacing workers. The process helps assure that the people an organization hires are competent in all relevant areas, including communications skills, education, technical skills, experience, social fit, and health.

Most firms recruit people who have the potential to be productive employees. They realize that potential involves effective training programs and proper managerial incentives. Carefully orienting individuals to their new environment can be an important step for the human resource manager.

PROGRESS CHECK

- What is human resource management?
- What are the six steps in human resource planning?
- What factors make it difficult to recruit qualified employees?
- What are the six steps in the selection process?

TRAINING AND DEVELOPING EMPLOYEES

New technologies such as word processors, computers, and robots have made it necessary to do more and more training, much of which is quite sophisticated. Today's forward-thinking organizations are recognizing that people are their most vital resource and an integral part for achieving increased productivity. Therefore, many firms are getting much more involved in continuing education and development programs for their employees. Career development is no longer just a haphazard system of promotions, moves, and occasional training programs. Rather, it is a long-term organizational strategy for assisting employees to optimize their skills and advance their education. **Training and development** include all attempts to improve employee performance through learning. In the next sections, we shall look at various training and development programs: employee orientation, on-the-job training, apprenticeship, off-the-job training, vestibule training, and job simulation.

training and development
All attempts to improve employee performance through learning.

Employee Orientation

Employee orientation is the activity that initiates new employees to the organization, to fellow employees, to their immediate supervisors, and to the policies, practices, and objectives of the firm. Orientation programs vary from quite informal, primarily verbal efforts, to formal schedules that have employees visit various departments for a day or more and include lengthy handouts. Formal orientation programs may cover:

employee orientation
The activity that introduces new employees to the organization, to fellow employees, to their immediate supervisors, and to the policies, practices, and objectives of the firm.

- History and general policies of the organization.
- Descriptions of products or services provided by the organization to the public.
- The organization's chain of command (organizational chart).
- Company safety measures and regulations.
- Human resources policies and practices.
- Compensation, benefits, and employee services.
- Daily routines and regulations.
- Introduction to the corporate culture—the values and orientation of the organization.
- Organizational objectives and the role of the new recruit in accomplishing those objectives.

On-the-Job Training

on-the-job training
The employee immediately begins his or her tasks and learns by doing, or watching others for a while and then imitates them, all right at the workplace.

The most fundamental training programs involve on-the-job training. **On-the-job training** means that the employee immediately begins his or her tasks and learns by doing, or watches others for a while and then imitates them, right at the workplace.

Look over the application form. Note that they ask whether you can operate word processing equipment and personal computers. They also ask for scholastic honors and scholarships. For maximum effect, you may want to attach a cover letter and a resume like the ones we suggest in the appendix to this chapter.

GENERAL DYNAMICS

GENERAL DYNAMICS IS AN EQUAL OPPORTUNITY EMPLOYER

APPLICATION FOR EMPLOYMENT

DATE		
Mo.	Day	Year

INSTRUCTIONS: FILL IN ALL INFORMATION. INCOMPLETE APPLICATIONS WILL NOT BE CONSIDERED FOR EMPLOYMENT. PRINT OR WRITE WITH BLACK INK OR TYPE IF PREFERRED. UPCOMING COLLEGE GRADUATES ATTACH A COURSE WORK TRANSCRIPT. OVERFLOW INFORMATION MAY BE PUT IN THE REMARKS SECTION.

PERSONAL

LAST NAME	FIRST NAME			MIDDLE NAME	SOCIAL SECURITY NUMBER

CURRENT ADDRESS		CITY	STATE	ZIP CODE	(A/C) TELEPHONE

PERMANENT ADDRESS		CITY	STATE	ZIP CODE	(A/C) TELEPHONE

IN CASE OF EMERGENCY NOTIFY: (A/C)   TELEPHONE

ADDRESS OF PERSON LISTED FOR EMERGENCY   CITY   STATE   ZIP CODE

ARE YOU AT LEAST 18 YEARS OF AGE?
☐ YES   ☐ NO

HOW WERE YOU REFERRED?
☐ NEWSPAPER, WHICH ONE?

IF EMPLOYED, CAN YOU PROVIDE PROOF OF UNITED STATES CITIZENSHIP?   ☐ NO ☐ YES

IF NOT A U.S. CITIZEN, SPECIFY ALIEN REGISTRATION NUMBER:

HAVE YOU EVER BEEN KNOWN BY ANY OTHER NAMES (Include Nicknames); IF SO, WHAT?

DO YOU HAVE ANY PHYSICAL OR MENTAL LIMITATIONS WHICH COULD AFFECT YOUR ABILITY TO PERFORM THE JOB OR JOBS FOR WHICH YOU ARE APPLYING? IF YES, GIVE DETAILS.
☐ NO ☐ YES ACCOMMONDATIONS REQUIRED: _____

☐ AGENCY
☐ GOVERNMENTAL EMPLOYMENT SERVICE
☐ FRIEND/EMPLOYEE
☐ COLLEGE PLACEMENT OFFICE
☐ OTHER – PLEASE SPECIFY

GEOGRAPHICAL PREFERENCE _____   RELOCATION RESTRICTIONS _____   TRAVEL RESTRICTIONS _____

EDUCATION

CIRCLE HIGHEST EDUCATION COMPLETED

		GRADE SCHOOL 1 2 3 4 5 6 7 8	HIGH SCHOOL 9 10 11 12	COLLEGE* 1 2 3 4 5		GRADUATE SCHOOL 1 2 3 4 5	

	NAME & LOCATION	DATES ATTENDED		GRADUATED	DEGREE** CERTIFICATE DIPLOMA	MAJORED IN	MINORED IN	GPA/ POSSIBLE
		MO./YR.	MO./YR.	MO./YR.				
HIGH SCHOOL								
COLLEGE(s)								
GRADUATE SCHOOL(s)								
MILITARY/ OTHER								

SCHOLASTIC HONORS, SCHOLARSHIPS, ETC. _____

LIST PUBLICATIONS, THESIS, ETC. _____

PROFESSIONAL LICENSES _____

*IF CO-OP GRADUATE, SPECIFY TOTAL WORK PERIODS .... SEMESTER _____ QUARTER _____

**SPECIFY NUMBER OF COLLEGE HOURS EARNED IF NO DEGREE OBTAINED .... SEMESTER _____ QUARTER _____

JOB INTEREST

TYPE OF WORK PREFERRED: ☐ FULL TIME ☐ PART TIME ☐ CO-OP ☐ SUMMER
☐ OTHER

HAVE YOU EVER WORKED FOR GENERAL DYNAMICS? ☐ NO ☐ YES
DIVISION: DATES:

HAVE YOU EVER BEEN GRANTED A U.S. GOVERNMENT SECURITY CLEARANCE? ☐ NO ☐ YES
TYPE/LEVEL: EMPLOYER: DATES:

HAVE YOU EVER HAD A SECURITY CLEARANCE SUSPENDED, DENIED OR REVOKED?
☐ NO ☐ YES EMPLOYER: DATE:

DO YOU HAVE RELATIVES EMPLOYED AT GD? ☐ NO ☐ YES   NAME: _____
RELATIONSHIP: GD DIVISION:

WILL YOU WORK:		DATE AVAILABLE FOR
	YES NO	EMPLOYMENT?
ANY SHIFT	☐ ☐	
OVERTIME	☐ ☐	MAY WE CONTACT
SATURDAYS	☐ ☐	YOUR PRESENT ☐ NO
SUNDAYS	☐ ☐	EMPLOYER? ☐ YES

CAN YOU OPERATE WORD PROCESSING EQUIPMENT?   CAN YOU UTILIZE PERSONAL COMPUTERS?
☐ NO ☐ YES MAKE/MODEL: ☐ NO ☐ YES MAKE/MODEL:

TYPING SPEED ____ WPM	SHORT-HAND SPEED ____ WPM

MILITARY STATUS

BRANCH OF U.S. ARMED FORCES	DATE ENTERED	DATE & TYPE OF DISCHARGE/RETIREMENT	RANK/RATE AT DISCHARGE
OTHER MILITARY SERVICE (Including Reserves)	DATE ENTERED	DATE & TYPE OF DISCHARGE/RETIREMENT	RANK/RATE AT DISCHARGE

On-the-job training means that you learn a skill while actually doing a job. You may watch other people doing similar work and ask questions as you go along. But right from the start you are being productive and learning.

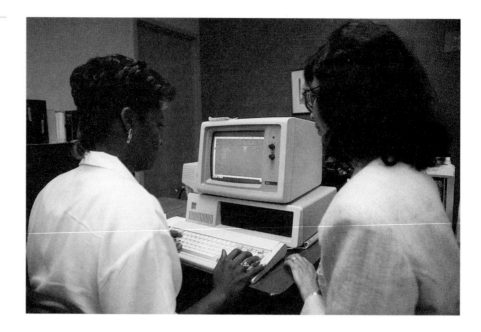

Salespeople, for example, are often trained by watching experienced salespeople perform. Naturally, this can be either quite effective or disastrous, depending on the skills and habits of the person being watched. On-the-job training is obviously the easiest kind of training to implement and can be effective where the job is easily learned, such as clerking in a store, or performing repetitive physical tasks such as collecting refuse, cleaning carpets, and mowing lawns. Training for more tedious or intricate jobs require a more intense training effort.

Apprentice Programs

apprenticeship
A time when a new worker works alongside a master technician to learn the appropriate skills and procedures.

Many skilled crafts, such as bricklaying or plumbing, require a new worker to serve several years as an apprentice. An **apprenticeship** is a period of time when a learner works alongside a skilled worker to learn the skills and procedures of a craft. Trade unions often require such periods to assure excellence among their members as well as to limit entry to the union. Workers that successfully complete an apprenticeship earn the classification of **journeyman.**

journeyman
A worker who has successfully completed an apprenticeship.

In the future, there are likely to be more but shorter apprenticeship programs to prepare people for skilled jobs in changing industries. For example, auto repair will require more intense training as new automobile models include computers and electronic advances.

Off-the-Job Training

Training is becoming more sophisticated as jobs become more sophisticated. Furthermore, training is expanding to include education (through the Ph.D.), and personal development (for example, time management, stress management, health education, wellness training, physical education, nutrition, and even classes in art and languages).

off-the-job training
Internal and external programs to develop a variety of skills and foster personal development away from the workplace.

Some firms do such training internally and have elaborate training facilities. Other firms must assign such training to outside sources. **Off-the-job training** consists of internal and external programs to develop a variety of skills and to foster personal development that occurs away from the workplace. This includes classroom, lectures, conferences, films, as well as workshops, tapes, reading programs, and the like.

Vestibule Training

Vestibule training is done in schools where employees are taught on equipment similar to that used on the job. Such schools (oddly enough called vestibule schools) enable employees to learn proper methods and safety procedures before assuming a specific job assignment in an organization. Computer and robotic training is often completed in a vestibule school.

vestibule training
Training conducted away from the workplace where employees are given instructions on equipment similar to that used on the job.

Job Simulation

One of the faster-growing aspects of training is simulation exercises. **Job simulation** is the use of equipment that duplicates job conditions and tasks so that trainees can learn skills before attempting them on the job. This is the kind of training given astronauts, airline pilots, army tank operators, ship captains, and others who must learn highly skilled jobs off the job. Astronauts, for example, must learn to work, eat, sleep, wash, and live in an environment of weightlessness. Simulation training sometimes takes place underwater (to simulate weightlessness) and in a variety of laboratories that can artificially create real-life experiences before attempting them.

Imagine the benefits of simulating the landing of an airplane in a major storm for the first time or docking a huge ocean liner in a small port facility. Such tasks are better learned in a simulator where many variables can be programmed to give people practical experience in a laboratory setting.

job simulation
The use of equipment that duplicates job conditions and tasks so that trainees can learn skills before attempting them on the job.

This is the inside of a flight simulator. It simulates the sights, sounds, and feel of actually flying a plane. Naturally, it's a lot safer to learn to fly in a simulator than in a real plane. Some simulators can create storms and other hazards to give you flight experience in all kinds of situations.

Computers can simulate the sounds, sights, smells, and emotions of the most trying circumstances (for example, fighting another jet plane in aerial combat). Given such capability, it is easy to simulate other skills, such as managing the operating room of a nuclear power plant or operating new equipment of any kind.

The damage caused by the Exxon Valdez oil tanker shows how important such training is. A Very Large Crude Carrier (VLCC), such as the Valdez, takes 6 miles to stop when running at 15 knots. By reversing the engines, you can greatly cut the stopping distance to "only" two miles! At the Seaman's Church Institute at 50 Broadway in New York, people learn how to pilot such ships on a simulator that resembles a giant video game. You can imagine piloting a ship as long as the World Trade Center is high through a narrow passage with boats all around you. Any accident can cause serious environmental damage. You don't want to learn such skills on the job.

APPRAISING EMPLOYEE PERFORMANCE

All managers must supervise employees. (Remember, that is one definition of *management*—getting work done through others.) Therefore, they must be able to determine whether or not their workers are doing an effective and efficient job, with a minimum of errors and disruptions. Such a determination is called a performance appraisal. A **performance appraisal** is an evaluation of the performance level of employees against established standards to make decisions about promotions, compensation, additional training, or firing. Performance appraisals consist of these following six steps:

performance appraisal
An evaluation of the performance level of employees against standards to make decisions about promotions, compensation, additional training, or firing.

1. *Establishing performance standards.* This is a crucial step. Standards must be understandable, subject to measurement, and reasonable.
2. *Communicating those standards.* Often, managers assume that employees know what is expected of them, but such assumptions are dangerous at best. Employees must be told clearly and precisely what the standards and expectations are and how they are to be met.
3. *Evaluating performance.* If the first two steps are done correctly, performance evaluation is relatively easy. It is a matter of evaluating the employee's behavior to see if it matches standards.
4. *Discussing results with employees.* Most people will make mistakes and fail to meet expectations at first. It takes time to learn a new job and do it well. Discussing an employee's successes and areas that need improvement is an opportunity to be understanding and helpful and to guide the employee to better performance. Additionally, the performance appraisal can be a good source of employee suggestions on how a particular task could perhaps be better performed. Employees know their jobs often better than anyone. It's important for the manager to remember that employees are not always to blame when standards are not met. An astute supervisor will learn that top management asks four questions when employees don't do well: (1) who hired them? (2) who trained them? (3) who motivates them? and (4) who should be fired if they fail? The answers make it pretty clear that supervisors are responsible for performance through others.

If you want better performance from your employees, treat them as you'd want them to treat your customers.
JOHN McCORMACK, *Inc.* magazine's "Hottest Entrepreneur of the Year.

5. *Taking corrective action.* The performance appraisal is an appropriate time for a manager to take corrective action or provide corrective feedback to help the employee perform his or her job better. Remember the keyword is *performance*. The primary purpose of conducting a performance appraisal is to increase employee performance, if possible.

1. **DON'T** attack the employee personally. Critically evaluate his or her work
2. **DO** allow sufficient time, without distractions (take the phone off the hook or close the office door) for appraisals
3. **DON'T** make the employee feel uncomfortable or uneasy. *Never* conduct an appraisal where other employees are present (such as on the shop floor)
4. **DO** include the employee in the process as much as possible. (Let the employee prepare a self-improvement program)
5. **DON'T** wait until the appraisal to raise problems about the employee's work that have been developing for some time
6. **DO** end the appraisal with positive suggestions for employee improvement

FIGURE 16–5

Making appraisals and reviews more effective.

Source: Leon C. Megginson, *Personnel Management* (Homewood, Ill.: Richard D. Irwin, 1985), p. 434.

6. *Using the results to make decisions.* Decisions about promotions, compensation, additional training, or firing are all based on performance evaluations. An effective performance appraisal system is a way of satisfying certain legal conditions concerning promotions, compensation, and firing policies.

If these steps sound like the management by objectives (MBO) you read about in Chapter 15, that is no accident. The measure of any employee's work is results. Were the objectives met or not? Management means getting results through top performance by employees. That is what performance appraisals are for—at all levels of the organization. Figure 16–5 illustrates dos and don'ts for the manager to make the performance appraisal more meaningful.

Can you name and describe four training techniques?

Why is employee orientation important? Did your college do a good job or orientating you to college life?

What is the primary purpose of a performance appraisal?

What are the six steps in a performance appraisal?

PROGRESS CHECK

COMPENSATING EMPLOYEES

Employee compensation is one of the largest operating costs for many organizations. The long-term success of a firm—perhaps even its survival—may depend on how well it can control employee costs and optimize employee efficiency. For example, service organizations such as hospitals, airlines, and banks have recently struggled with managing high employee costs. This is not unusual since these firms are considered *labor intensive;* that is, their primary cost of operations is the cost of labor. Firms in the airline, auto, and steel industry have asked employees to take reductions in wages to make the organizations more competitive or risk going out of business and losing jobs forever. In other words, the competitive environment

PAYMENT METHOD	DESCRIPTION
Straight salary	Weekly, monthly, or annual payment
Hourly wages	Number of hours worked times agreed-on hourly wage
Commission system	Sales revenue times some fixed percentage
Salary plus commission	Base salary (weekly, monthly, or annual) plus sales revenue times some fixed percentage
Piecework	Number of items produced times some agreed-on rate per unit
ADDED COMPENSATION	
Overtime	Number of hours worked beyond standard (for example, 40 hours) times hourly wages for weekdays and double time for weekends and holidays
Bonuses	Varies by company; basically, extra pay for meeting or exceeding objectives
Profit sharing	Additional payments based on company profits
Cost-of-living allowances (COLAs)	Annual increases in wages based on consumer price increases

of the 1990s is such that compensation and benefit packages are being given special attention and are likely to remain of major concern in the near future. (See Figure 16–6.)

Several objectives can be accomplished by a carefully managed compensation and benefit program. They include:

   Attracting the kind of people needed by the organization and in sufficient numbers.

   Providing employees with the incentive to work efficiently and productively.

   Keeping valued employees from leaving and going to competitors or starting competing firms.

   Maintaining a competitive position in the marketplace by keeping costs low through high productivity.

   Protecting employees from unexpected problems such as layoffs, sickness, and disability.

   Assuring employees of funds to carry them through retirement.

Pay Systems

One of the heroes in China is a man named Bu Xinsheng.[6] He runs a highly successful shirt factory. From the mid-1970s to the mid-1980s, Mr. Bu raised the factory's assets and its number of workers from $10,000 and 73, respectively, to $600,000 and 630. China is not known for its creative management techniques and highly productive work force. So, how did Mr. Bu do it? He switched his factory from straight wages to piecework. That increased the maximum possible wage from $18 a month to the equivalent of $41 a month, but workers had to work much harder to earn more. The government was thrilled with Mr. Bu's success and now supports Mr. Bu in implementing ideas such as market research, developing private brands, implementing graduated benefits for his workers, and buying equipment to expand production for export sales.

WHY ARE THESE WORKERS SMILING?

You might be smiling, too, if you just discovered you were getting a profit sharing check next month averaging $3,700. That's what approximately 160,000 hourly and salaried workers of the Ford Motor Company received on March 8, 1988. As part of an agreement with its employees, Ford agreed to share its profits with workers if pretax U.S. profits exceeded a certain percentage of the company's sales. Workers at the company said the profit sharing checks amount to approximately 10 percent of their annual wages.

What made the Ford profit sharing checks even sweeter in 1988 was that the workers at the Chrysler Corporation received only a flat $500 profit sharing check and workers at the General Motors Company did not earn any additional income from profit sharing. Ford workers plan to spend their windfall in a variety of ways. One worker at Ford's Milan Plastic Plant proudly proclaimed, "I plan to take my daughter on a senior vacation cruise—it's her graduation present." What better way to teach her that quality performance pays off?

Source: James M. Odato, "Ford Profit-Sharing up 76 percent," *USA Today,* February 22, 1988, p. 1B; and "Ford Workers to Get Profit-Sharing Checks that Average $3,700," *The Wall Street Journal,* February 22, 1988, p. 22.

It's evident from this story that the type of pay system in an organization can have a dramatic effect on efficiency and productivity. Different pay systems include the following:

- Salary systems are systems of *fixed* compensation that are computed on weekly, biweekly, or monthly pay periods (for example, $1,500 per month or $400 per week). It's probable that many of you who graduate from college will be paid a salary.
- Hourly wage or daywork is the system used for most blue-collar and clerical workers. Often employees must punch a time clock when they arrive at work and when they leave. Hourly wages vary greatly. The federal minimum wage has been raised, and top wages go as high as $20 to $30 for skilled craftspeople. This does not include benefits such as retirement systems that add 25 to 30 percent more to the total package.
- Piecework means that employees are paid according to the number of items they produce rather than by the hour or day. This system creates powerful incentives to work efficiently and productively. It was so effective for Mr. Bu that he has become a model manager in China.
- Commission plans are often used to compensate salespeople. They actually resemble a piecework system; the commission is based on some percentage of sales.
- Bonus plans are used for executives, salespeople, and other employees. They earn bonuses for accomplishing or surpassing certain objectives.
- Profit sharing plans give employees some share of profits over and above their normal pay. (See the box called Why Are These Workers Smiling?)

Fringe Benefits

Fringe benefits include sick-leave pay, vacation pay, pension plans, and health plans that provide additional compensation to employees. Fringe benefits in the 1980s grew faster than wages. According to a recent study by the U.S. Chamber of Commerce, U.S. companies now spend an average of $6,627 a year per employee for benefits. That is about 37 percent of the average worker's salary, compared with 30 percent a decade ago.[7] Many employees request more fringe benefits instead of more salary to avoid higher taxes. This has resulted in much debate and much government investigation.

fringe benefits
Benefits such as sick-leave pay, vacation pay, pension plans, and health plans that represent additional compensation to employees.

Fringe benefits include vacation time at the beach. Cafeteria plans let you choose among fringe benefits. You could choose more vacation time, a better health care program, child care, dental care, or other options. You could choose the mix of options that best meets your needs.

Fringe benefits can include everything from paid vacations to health-care programs, recreation facilities, company cars, country club memberships, day-care services, and executive dining rooms. Managing the benefit package will be a major human resource issue in the 1990s. Employees want packages to include dental care, legal counseling, eye care, and shorter workweeks.

cafeteria-style fringe benefits
Fringe benefits plan that allows employees to choose the benefits they want up to a certain dollar amount.

To counter these growing demands, many firms are offering **cafeteria-style fringe benefits** from which employees can choose the benefits they want up to a certain dollar amount. This is the kind of plan that Cindy and Scott Keech are offered at Steelcase (see the Profile at the beginning of this chapter). *Choice* is the key to flexible, cafeteria-style benefits plans. At one time, most employees' needs were similar. Today, employees are more varied and more demanding. Managers can equitably and cost-effectively meet employees' individual needs by providing benefits choices.[8]

Benefits are as important to wage negotiations now as salary. In the future, they may be more important.

SCHEDULING EMPLOYEES

By now, you are quite familiar with the trends occurring in the work force. You know, for example, that many more women are working now. You also know that managers and workers are demanding more from jobs in the way of flexibility and responsiveness. From these trends have emerged several new or renewed ideas such as job sharing, flextime, and in-home employment. Let's see how these innovations effect managing human resources.

Job-Sharing Plans

job sharing
An arrangement whereby two part-time employees share one full-time job.

Job sharing is an arrangement whereby two part-time employees share one full-time job. The concept received great attention in the 1980s as more and more women with small children entered the labor force. Job sharing enabled mothers and fathers to work part-time while the children were in school, then return to the home when the children came home. Job sharing has also proved beneficial to students, older people who want to work part-time before fully retiring, and others who can only work part-time. The following are some of the benefits of job sharing.

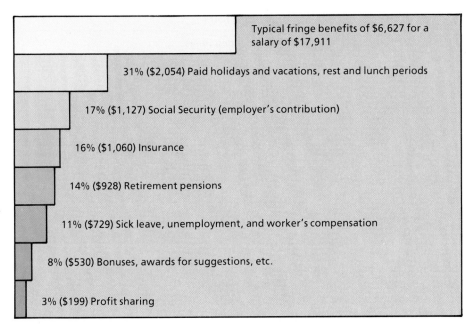

Typical fringe benefits of $6,627 for a salary of $17,911

31% ($2,054) Paid holidays and vacations, rest and lunch periods

17% ($1,127) Social Security (employer's contribution)

16% ($1,060) Insurance

14% ($928) Retirement pensions

11% ($729) Sick leave, unemployment, and worker's compensation

8% ($530) Bonuses, awards for suggestions, etc.

3% ($199) Profit sharing

Percent of fringe benefits going to various programs. The average employee receives over $6,600 in fringe benefits per year. This represents 37% of the total wage cost.
Source: U.S. Department of Commerce.

- It offers employment opportunities to those who cannot or prefer not to work full-time.
- An employee is more likely to maintain a high level of enthusiasm and productivity for four hours than eight hours; therefore, two part-time employees are often much more productive than one full-time employee.
- Problems such as absenteeism and tardiness are greatly reduced by using part-time employees. Part-time people are usually better able to handle other duties or problems in their off hours.
- Employers are better able to schedule people into peak demand periods (for example, banks on payday) when part-time people are available.

However, as you might suspect, disadvantages include having to hire, train, motivate, and supervise twice as many people and to prorate some fringe benefits. Nonetheless, most firms that were at first reluctant to try job sharing are finding the benefits outweigh the disadvantages.

Flextime Plans

Flextime plans give employees some freedom to adjust when they work as long as they work the required number of hours. The most popular plans allow employees to come to work at 7, 8, or 9 AM and leave between 4 and 6 PM. Usually flextime plans will incorporate what is called **core time.** Core time refers to particular hours of the day when all employees are expected to be at their job stations. For example, an organization may designate core time hours as between 10:00 AM and 12:00 PM and 2:00 PM and 4:00 PM. During these hours of work *all* employees are required to be there. Flextime plans, like job-sharing plans, are designed to allow employees to adjust to the new demands of the times, especially the trend toward two-income families. The federal government has experimented extensively with flextime and

flextime plans
Work schedule that gives employees some freedom to adjust when they work, within limits, as long as they work the required number of hours.

core time
The period when all employees are present in a flextime system.

A flextime chart. Employees can start any time between 6:30 and 9:30. They then take half an hour for lunch and can quit from 3:00 to 6:30. Everyone works an 8-hour day. The red arrows show a typical flextime day.

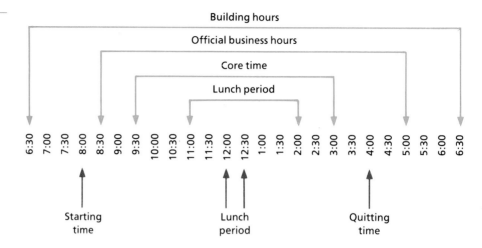

found it to be a boost to employee productivity and morale. Specific advantages of flextime include:

Working mothers and fathers can schedule their days so that someone can be home to see the children off to school and the other partner can be home soon after school.

Employees can schedule doctor's appointments and other personal tasks during working hours by coming in early and leaving at 3 or 4 PM.

Traffic congestion is greatly reduced as employees arrive over several hours instead of all at once.

Employees can work when they are most productive; some people are most alert early in the morning, while others can't get going until 9 AM.

A big psychological boost comes when an employee has some choice about sleeping late once in a while or taking off early on Friday afternoon in the spring.

There are some real disadvantages to flextime as well. Flextime is certainly not for all organizations. For example, it does not work in assembly line processes where everyone must be at work at the same time. It also is not effective for shift work.

Another disadvantage to flextime is that managers often have to work longer days to be there to assist and supervise employees. Some organizations operate from 6 AM to 6 PM under flextime, a potentially long day for supervisors. Flextime also makes communication more difficult; certain employees may not be there when others need to talk to them. Furthermore, some employees could abuse the system, if not carefully supervised, and that could cause resentment among others. You can imagine how you'd feel if half the work force left at 3 PM on Friday and you had to work until 6 PM.

In spite of the difficulties, flextime has become quite popular. It has obvious advantages for creative people who are most productive at certain times of the day. But it also is helpful for anyone who likes the flexibility of sleeping late once in a while or working long hours when a proposal is due.

compressed workweek
Work schedule made up of four 10-hour days.

Another popular option that developed in some organizations is a **compressed workweek.** That means that an employee works four 10-hour days and then enjoys a long weekend, instead of working five 8-hour days with a traditional weekend.

There are the obvious advantages of working only four days and having three days off, but some employees get tired working such long hours, and productivity could decline. Many employees find such a system of great benefit, however, and are quite enthusiastic about it.

Working in the Home

In nations such as Japan, in-home employment has traditionally been very common. These "cottage industries," as they are called, are often key suppliers to many of the large multinational firms in Japan. In the United States, the number of people working at home leaped 90 percent in just a couple of years. By now, it is estimated that 15 to 20 percent of all workers are working at home. Almost three fourths of these home-bound workers are women who want to pursue career goals and family goals at the same time.

What effect have dual-career families had on the personnel function? Have you noticed any changes in nepotism rules with so many marriages involving two professionals? (*Nepotism* means hiring relatives.) What problems can arise when family members work together in the same firm? What is your reaction to employees who date one another? Are such questions interesting enough to make you think about becoming a human resource manager?

THINKING IT THROUGH

DEVELOPING MANAGERS

In the past, employees were eager to become managers and were quite willing to make sacrifices for that honor. For example, people were willing to relocate often. (There was once a joke that *IBM* meant "I've been moved.") People were also willing to work longer hours, take on additional responsibilities, and "do what it takes" to move up the corporate ladder.

Things are different today. Moving is not only costly, but affects the employee's children, friendships, community ties, and more. Furthermore, with the growing number of dual-income families, it's difficult to convince husbands or wives to give up their careers to follow the other partner. It's safe to conclude that management responsibilities are stressful, tiring, and affect family life. For these reasons and more it is becoming more difficult to find and keep good managers. Those who are willing to be managers must be trained to assume an entirely different role: one of counselor, adviser, trainer, educator, coach, and assistant. As we have noted, managers are no longer mere bosses or rule makers and enforcers.

Managers need different training than most employees. (See the box called Wanted: Learning to Lead in the 1990s, later in this chapter.) They need to be good communicators and especially need to learn listening skills and empathy. They also need time management, planning, and human relations skills.

Management development, then, is the process of training and educating employees to become good managers and then developing managerial skills over time. Management development programs have sprung up everywhere, especially at colleges, universities, and private management development firms. Managers participate in various role-playing exercises, solve various management cases, and are exposed to films, lectures, and all kinds of management development processes.

management development
The process of training and educating employees to become good managers and then developing managerial skills over time.

Management development classes help managers in all phases of their jobs. They include courses on time management, stress management, employee relations, supervision, and many other subjects. Some programs include college courses in computers, management, and more. The idea is to keep managers up to date and effective on the job.

In some organizations managers are paid to take college level courses through the doctoral level. Most management training programs also include several of the following:

On-the-job coaching   On-the-job coaching means that a senior manager will assist a lower-level manager by teaching him or her needed skills and generally providing direction, advice, and helpful criticism. Such programs are only effective when the senior managers are skilled themselves and have the ability to educate others. This is not always the case.

Understudy Positions   Job titles such as undersecretary of . . . and assistant to . . . reveal a relatively successful way of developing managers. They work as assistants to higher-level managers and participate in planning and other managerial functions until they are ready to assume such positions themselves. Such assistants may take over when higher-level managers are on vacation or on business trips.

Job Rotation   To expose managers to different functions of the organization, they are often given assignments in a variety of departments. Top managers, of course, must have a broad picture of the organization and such rotation gives them that exposure.

Off-the-Job Courses and Training   Managers periodically go to schools or seminars for a week or more to hone their technical and human relations skills. Such courses expose them to the latest concepts and create a sense of camaraderie as the managers live, eat, and work together in a college-type atmosphere. This is often where case studies and simulation exercises of all kinds are employed.

The Importance of Networking

Over time, male managers have developed what has been called an old boy network through which certain senior managers become mentors to certain junior managers. They introduce them to the important managers, enroll them in the "right" clubs, and guide them into the "right" social groups. Young managers are thus socialized regarding proper dress, behavior, and procedures to follow to rise up the corporate hierarchy.

WANTED: LEARNING TO LEAD IN THE 1990S

Developing effective leaders has always been a key objective of American business. However, as times change, the methods of developing leaders also change. Today, for example, Apple Computer's methods of fostering leadership includes sending managers off to a resort to learn "inner tennis" and to walk the length of a high beam suspended 25 feet in the air. Managers from General Foods Corporation are challenged to work together to build a raft from 50-gallon drums, 2-by-4s and rope with the hope of paddling across a lake to seize a flag that represents new products. These methods, as strange as they may seem, are becoming popular ways of developing leaders for the 1990s. AT&T sent its product division managers to a five-day program that resembled Outward Bound wilderness training. Aetna Life & Casualty sent its employees to a sensitivity training workshop.

The methods may seem unorthodox and at times absurd, but top management and academics are not laughing. Training isn't worth much unless changes can be seen back at the office and managers see such changes. The chairman of General Foods says his managers are now more willing to take risks and less willing to accept restrictions from above. GF has also introduced new product lines and new technologies since the start of its leadership training. Apple Computer's Stefan Winsnes remarked that programs such as playing inner tennis (keeping your eye on the ball and using your instincts) "looks absolutely ridiculous." But it taught him to stop worrying about style and footwork. What does this mean at the office? You'll lose sight of what you are trying to do if you concentrate on the process too much.

What's next? The Japanese are importing to Malibu the programs from their toughest and best-known management training centers—Kanrisha Yosei. Would you like to be sent for your leadership training to this "hell camp" for 13 "fun-packed" days of hazing, calisthenics, night hikes, and action debates?

Source: Jeremy Main, "Wanted: LEADERS Who Can Make a Difference," *Fortune*, September 28, 1987, pp. 92–102; Richard Phalon, "Hell Camp, Malibu-style," *Forbes*, December 28, 1987, pp. 110–11; and Andy Skrzycki, "Shaking Up Old Ways of Training Managers," *The Washington Post*, February 26, 1989, pp. H1 and H6.

Networking, then, is the process of establishing and maintaining contacts with key managers in one's own organization and in other organizations and using those contacts to weave strong relationships that serve as informal development systems. Of equal or greater importance to potential managers is the need for **mentors,** corporate managers who supervise, coach, and guide selected lower-level employees by introducing them to the right people and groups and generally act as their organizational sponsors. In reality, an informal type of mentoring goes on in most organizations on a regular basis as older employees assist younger workers. However, many organizations such as Merrill Lynch and Federal Express use a formal system of assigning mentors to employees considered to have strong potential.

As women moved into management they also learned the importance and value of such networking and of having mentors. But since most older managers are male, women often have more difficulty attracting mentors and entering the network. Women managers recently won a major victory when the U.S. Supreme Court ruled that it was illegal to bar females from men-only clubs where business activity and contact-making flowed. More and more, women are now entering this system or, in some instances, creating their own networking systems.[9] *Black Enterprise* magazine sponsors several networking forums each year for African-American professionals. Call 1-800-54-FORUM for information.[10]

It's also important to remember that networking can go beyond the business environment. For example, your college experience is a perfect environment to begin your networking. Associations you nurture with professors, local businesspeople, and especially with your classmates might provide you with a valuable network through which you can develop for the rest of your career.

networking
The process of establishing and maintaining contacts with key managers in one's own organization and in other organizations and using those contacts to weave strong relationships that serve as informal development systems.

mentors
Experienced employees who supervise, coach, and guide lower-level employees by introducing them to the right people and groups and generally act as their organizational sponsors.

Networking can take place anywhere—on the golf course, in restaurants, and at people's homes. Men have long had "good old boy" networks. Women, blacks, and minorities of all kinds are now developing similar networks where relationships are established, job information is exchanged, and people learn how to move up the corporate ladder.

PROGRESS CHECK

Can you name and describe five alternative compensation techniques?

What advantages do compensations plans such as profit sharing offer an organization?

Can you define the terms *networking* and *mentors?*

LAWS AFFECTING HUMAN RESOURCE MANAGEMENT

The job of the human resource manager has been greatly impacted by changes in law. Legislation has made hiring, promoting, firing, and employee relations in general very complex and subject to many legal complications and challenges. Let's see how these changes in law have expanded the role and the challenge of human resource management.

The government had little to do with human resource decisions until the 1930s. Since then, though, legislation and legal decisions have greatly impacted all areas of human resource management, from hiring to training and working conditions (see Figure 16–7).

One of the most important pieces of social legislation ever passed by Congress was the Civil Rights Act of 1964. This act was passed with much debate and was actually amended 97 times before final passage. Title VII of that act brought the government directly into the operations of human resource management. Title VII prohibits discrimination in hiring, firing, compensation, apprenticeships, training, terms, conditions, or privileges of employment based on race, religion, creed, sex, or national origin. Age was later added to the conditions of the act. The Civil Rights Act of 1964 was expected to stamp out the vestiges of discrimination in the workplace. However, specific language in the legislation made its enforcement often quite difficult. With this in mind, Congress took on the task of amending the law.

National Labor Relations Act of 1935	Established collective bargaining in labor-management relations and limits management interference in the right of employees to have a collective bargaining agent.	**FIGURE 16–7** Government legislation. This figure shows some laws and decisions affecting human resource management. They were designed to protect the rights and safety of employees.
Fair Labor Standards Act of 1938	Established a minimum wage and overtime pay for employees working more than 40 hours a week.	
Manpower Development and Training Act of 1962	Provided for the training and retraining of unemployed workers.	
Equal Pay Act of 1963	Specified that men and women who are doing equal jobs must be paid the same wage.	
The Civil Rights Act of 1964	Outlawed discrimination in employment based on sex, race, color, religion, or national origin.	
Age Discrimination in Employment Act of 1967	Outlawed personnel practices that discriminate against people aged 40 to 69. An amendment outlaws company policies that require employees to retire before age 70.	
Occupational Safety and Health Act of 1970 (OSHA)	Regulated the degree to which employees can be exposed to hazardous substances and specified the safety equipment to be provided by the employer.	
Equal Employment Opportunity Act of 1972	Created the Equal Employment Opportunity Commission (EEOC) and authorized the EEOC to set guidelines for human resource management.	
The Comprehensive Employment and Training Act of 1973	Provided funds for training unemployed workers (was known as the CETA program).	
Employee Retirement Income Security Act of 1974	Regulated company retirement programs and provided a federal insurance program for bankrupt retirement plans.	
Immigration Reform and Control Act of 1986	Required employers to verify the eligibility for employment of *all* their new hires (including U.S. citizens).	
Supreme Court ruling against set aside programs (affirmative action), 1989	Declared that setting aside 30 percent of contracting jobs for minority businesses was reverse discrimination and unconstitutional.	

In 1972, the Equal Employment Opportunity Act (EEOA) was added as an amendment to Title VII. It established the Equal Employment Opportunity Commission (EEOC). Congress gave rather broad powers to the EEOC. For example, the commission was permitted to issue guidelines for acceptable employer conduct in administering equal employment opportunity. Also, specific record-keeping procedures, as set forth by the EEOC, became mandatory. In addition, the commission was vested with the power of enforcement to insure these mandates were carried out. The EEOC became a formidable regulatory force in the administration of human resource management.

affirmative action
Employment activities designed to "right past wrongs" endured by females and minorities by giving them preference in employment.

reverse discrimination
The feeling of unfairness unprotected groups may have when protected groups are given preference in hiring and promoting.

Probably the most controversial program enforced by the EEOC concerned **affirmative action.** The purpose of affirmative action was to "right past wrongs" endured by females and minorities in the administration of human resource management. Interpretation of the law eventually led employers to actively recruit and give preference to females and minority group members. As you might expect, interpretation and enforcement of the program was often difficult. Legal questions persisted about the legality of the program and the effect the program could have in creating a sort of reverse discrimination in the workplace.

Reverse discrimination refers to the feeling of unfairness unprotected groups may have when protected groups are given preference in hiring and promoting. Early in 1989, the U.S. Supreme Court ruled that a Richmond, Virginia, program setting aside 30 percent of all city contracting work for minority businesspeople amounted to unconstitutional reverse discrimination. This case may have many implications for civil rights enforcement in the 1990s and is likely to be a major issue.[11] Figure 16–8 shows the results of four other recent discrimination cases. They make it harder for employees to win discrimination cases in a move to create "color blend" hiring practices.

Laws Protecting the Disabled and Older Employees

The courts have continued their activity in issues involving human resource management. As you read above, the courts look carefully into any improprieties concerning possible discrimination in hiring, firing, training, and so on specifically related to race or sex. The Vocational Rehabilitation Act (1973) extended the same protection given minorities and women to the disabled. Today, businesses cannot discriminate against disabled persons on the basis of their physical or mental handicaps. Courts have ruled that businesses must provide reasonable accommodations for the physical and mental limitations of disabled persons. Equal opportunity for the disabled promises to be a continuing issue in the decade of the 1990s.

Older employees (between 40–69) are also guaranteed protection against discrimination in the workplace. Courts have ruled against firms in unlawful discharge suits where age appeared to be the major factor in the dismissal. Additionally, protection through the Age Discrimination in Employment Act outlawed mandatory retirement in most organizations before age 70.

Proposed Wages and Benefits Legislation

Some controversy has been raised about legislation regarding wages and employee benefits. Of major concern is the minimum wage law and mandatory health insurance protection. Good arguments abound for raising the minimum wage and providing health insurance but the question remains, "Would legislation raising the minimum wage prevent employers from hiring entry-level workers and thus cause a loss of jobs among people least able to find jobs?"

A similar argument persists concerning legislation that would require companies to give 18 weeks off without pay to new mothers and fathers. Employees taking the leave would be entitled to return to their old jobs or an equivalent job. Health benefits would continue during the period off the job. What's interesting is that all European countries have some form of parental leave. However, in Europe,

Price Waterhouse vs. Hopkins (May 1, 1989): The court decides that women and other minority plaintiffs must prove that discriminatory attitudes by management are a "substantial" reason for being denied a promotion but need not show that these attitudes "caused" it. If the plaintiff can establish that point, the burden of proof switches to the managers, who in order to avoid liability must show that promotion was denied ultimately for reasons other than sexism or other improper bias.

Wards Cove vs. Atonio (June 5, 1989): The Supreme Court reverses a unanimous 1971 ruling that had allowed aggrieved employees to sue when statistics indicated a pattern of discrimination, even if an individual could not point to specific signs of prejudice. The ruling shifts the burden of proof in certain suits from defendants to plaintiffs, making it more difficult for minorities and women to win cases based on statistics that show disparities in the number of jobs held by white men versus those held by minorities and women.

Martin vs. Wilks (June 12, 1989): The court rules that employees—usually white males—can sue to reopen affirmative action court settlements if they feel they were subject to reverse discrimination. The ruling threatens to invalidate dozens of settlements involving police, firefighters and other public employees.

Patterson vs. McLean Credit Union (June 15, 1989): The court rules that a black person who is harassed on the job because of his race cannot sue his employer for damages under the Civil Rights Act of 1866. The post-Civil War federal law, enacted after reports that newly freed slaves were being intimidated by their former masters, states that "citizens of every race and color . . . shall have the same rights" as whites to buy and sell property and "to make and enforce contracts." According to the decision, the law bars employers or schools from denying jobs, promotions or enrollment to blacks, Latinos or others because of their race, but it does not apply to general discrimination or abusive treatment once they are on the job or in school.

FIGURE 16–8

Recent affirmative action legislation.
These four controversial rulings make it more difficult to initiate affirmative action programs. Most civil rights leaders consider these rulings a setback. Others feel that they are an important first step in creating "color blend" hiring practices. These are landmark cases that you should follow closely.
Source: Jube Shiver, Jr., "Affirmative Inaction," *Los Angeles Times*, July 2, 1989, pp. 1 and 5 of Part IV.

maternity leave and parental leave are two different things. For maternity leave, a women is given four to eight weeks of partially paid leave to recuperate from childbirth. Parental leave means either parent may take additional unpaid leave— six months to two years—depending on the country. Stay tuned for developments in these important human resource management areas.

Effects of Legislation

It's very clear that legislation effects all areas of human resource management. Such legislation ranges from the Social Security Act (1935), to the Occupational Safety and Health Act (OSHA) of 1970, to the Employment Retirement Income Security Act (ERISA) of 1974. It is best to read *The Wall Street Journal, Business Week,* and other current publications to keep current with all human resource legislation and rulings.

We have devoted this much space to the legislation affecting human resource management because such decisions have had an enormous impact on human resource programs, and will continue to do so. It's apparent that a career in human resource management offers a challenge to anyone willing to put forth the effort. In summary:

  - Employers must be sensitive to the legal rights of women, minorities, disabled, and older employees or risk costly court cases.
  - Legislation affects all areas of human resource management, from hiring and training to wages and benefits.
  - Recent court cases have made it more difficult to go beyond providing equal rights for minorities to provide special employment (affirmative action) and training to correct discrimination in the past.
  - New court cases and legislation change human resource management almost daily; the only way to keep current is to read the business literature and become familiar with the issues.

PROGRESS CHECK

Can you explain what was covered by the following laws?

1. The Equal Pay Act of 1963.

2. The Civil Rights Act of 1964.

3. The Occupational Safety and Health Act (OSHA) of 1970.

SUMMARY

1. Explain the importance of human resource management and describe current issues in managing human resources.

1. *Human resource management* is the process of evaluating human resource needs, finding people to fill those needs, and optimizing this important resource by providing the right incentives and job environment, all with the goal of meeting organizational objectives.

  - What are some of the current problems in the human resource area?
    Many of the current problems revolve around the changing demographics of workers: more women, minorities, immigrants, and older workers. Other problems concern: a shortage of trained workers and an abundance of unskilled; skilled workers in declining industries requiring retraining; changing employee work attitudes; and complex laws and regulations.

2. Summarize the six steps in planning human resources.

2. As in all types of management, human resource management begins with planning.

  - What are the steps in human resource planning?
    The six steps are: (1) preparing forecasts of future human resource needs; (2) preparing human resource inventory; (3) preparing job analyses; (4) assessing future demands; (5) assessing future supply; (6) establishing a plan for recruiting, hiring, educating, and developing employees.

3. Describe methods companies use to recruit new employees and explain some of the problems that make recruitment difficult.

3. *Recruitment* is the set of activities used to legally obtain a sufficient number of the right people at the right time to select those that best meet the needs of the organization.

  - Why has recruitment become more difficult?
    Legal restrictions complicate hiring and firing practices. Finding suitable employees can also be made more difficult if companies are considered unattractive workplaces.

4. Selection is the process of gathering information to decide who should be hired.

 ▪ What are the six steps in the selection process?

 The steps are: (1) obtaining complete application forms; (2) giving initial interview and follow-up interview; (3) giving employment tests; (4) conducting background investigations; (5) giving physical exams; and (6) conducting a trial period of employment.

4. Outline the six steps in selecting employees.

5. Employee *training and development* includes all attempts to improve employee performance by increasing an employee's ability to perform through learning.

 ▪ What are some of the procedures used for training?

 They include employee orientation, on- and off-the-job training, apprentice programs, vestibule training, and job simulation.

5. Illustrate the use of various types of employee training methods.

6. A performance appraisal is an evaluation of the performance level of employees against established standards to make decisions about promotions, compensation, additional training, or firing.

 ▪ How is performance evaluated?

 The steps are: (1) establish performance standards; (2) communicate those standards; (3) evaluate performance; (4) discuss results; (5) take corrective action when needed; (6) use the results for decisions about promotions, compensation, additional training, or firing.

6. Trace the six steps in appraising employee performance.

7. Employee compensation is one of the largest operating costs for many organizations.

 ▪ What kind of compensation systems are used?

 They include salary systems, hourly wages, piecework, commission plans, bonus plans, and profit sharing plans.

 ▪ What are fringe benefits?

 Fringe benefits include sick leave, vacation pay, pension plans, and health plans that provide additional compensation to employees.

7. Summarize the objectives of employee compensation programs and describe various pay systems and fringe benefits.

8. Workers' increasing need for flexibility has generated new innovations in scheduling workers.

 ▪ What scheduling plans can be used to adjust to employees needs for flexibility?

 Such plans include: job sharing, flextime, compressed workweeks, and working at home.

8. Explain scheduling plans managers use to adjust to workers' needs.

9. *Management development* is the process of developing managerial skills over time.

 ▪ What methods are used to develop managerial skills?

 Management development methods include on-the-job coaching, understudy positions, job rotation, and off-the-job courses and training.

 ▪ How does networking fit in this process?

 Networking is the process of establishing contacts with key managers within and outside the organization to get additional development assistance.

 ▪ What are mentors?

 Mentors are experienced staff members who coach and guide selected lower-level people and act as their organizational sponsors.

9. Describe training methods used in management development programs.

10. There are many laws that affect human resource planning.

 ▪ What are those laws?

 See Figure 16–6 and review the section on laws. This is an important subject for future managers to study. See also the new rulings listed on page 515 and listen to the debate they cause during the 1990s.

10. Illustrate the effects of legislation on human resource management.

1. Visit the personnel offices of your college and of several businesses. Talk with employees and several managers. What do they do all day? Do they enjoy the work? How did it appear to you? Share your impressions with others in the class.

2. Read the current business periodicals to find the latest court rulings on issues such as pay equity, affirmative action, the minimum wage, and other personnel-related issues. What seems to be the trend? What will this mean for tomorrow's college graduates? (See p. 515.)

3. Recall the various training programs you have experienced. Think of both on-the-job and off-the-job training sessions. What is your evaluation of such programs? How would you improve them? Share your ideas with the class.

4. Look up the unemployment figures for individual states. Notice there are pockets of very high unemployment. What causes such uneven unemployment? What can be done to retrain workers who are obsolete because of a restructured economy? Is that the role of government or of business? Discuss. Could government and business cooperate in this function?

5. Find several people who work under flextime or part-time systems. Ask them their reactions. Share your findings with the class.

PRACTICING MANAGEMENT DECISIONS

CASE ONE   THE DANGERS OF FIRING EMPLOYEES

The common law has previously maintained the right of an employer to fire an employee under something called the employment-at-will doctrine. But lately this doctrine has come under attack because of recent legal rulings. Employers can still fire people, but they may incur some expensive consequences if employees sue. California employees have won jury verdicts of $10 million and more.

In recent years, state courts in some 46 states have made it legal for employees to sue their employers for wrongful discharge. This has resulted in a backlog of some 25,000 such cases. Such companies, in response, are forcing employees to sign statements saying that they can be fired at any time. Fired employees tend to sue anyway.

A different approach to such problems is to go to arbitration. In Montana, one cannot fire an employee without "just cause," and liability awards are limited. The state also requires employers to go to outside arbitration when cases arise of alleged wrongful discharge.

In the past, more than 50 percent of all discharge cases taken to arbitration are decided against the employer (80 percent in California). Corporate personnel manuals are getting more detailed to protect against legal action. For example, the Del E. Webb Corporation struck the word *permanent* from employee descriptions.

NAS Insurance Services, Inc., in California, offers insurance for companies sued for wrongful discharge. It has been estimated that only 2 out of every 1,000 employees is fired unjustly, but that amounts to some 55,000 workers a year.

DECISION QUESTIONS

1. What are the implications for the personnel department of new legal rulings against firing for unjust cause?

2. If you were an employer, would you put more effort into screening and training employees, given these rulings? Who might be hurt by such changes? Who may benefit?

3. The trend in handling wrongful discharge cases has been to call in an arbitrator such as the ones that Montana demands. What benefits do you see from arbitration versus suing employers?

Sources: "Sidestepping Wrongful Discharge Suits," *Industrial Launderer,* June 1988, pp. 99–108; "Firing Policy: There Is a Middle Ground, *Business Week,* October 17, 1988, p. 122; Aaron Bernstein, "More Dismissed Workers Are Telling It to the Judge," *Business Week,* October 17, 1988, p. 68; and William S. Waldo, "Wrongful Dismissal Cases Will Still Have Their Days in Court," *Los Angeles Times,* January 8, 1989, p. 3 of Part IV.

CASE TWO DUAL–CAREER PLANNING

Carey Moler is a 32-year-old account executive for a communications company. She is married to Mitchell Moler, a lawyer. They have one child. Carey and Mitchell had not made any definite plans about how to juggle their careers and family life until Carey reached age 30. Then she decided to have a baby, and career planning took on whole new dimensions. A company named Catalyst talked to 815 dual-career couples and found most of them, like the Molers, had not made any long-range career decisions regarding family lifestyle.

From the business perspective, such dual-career families create real concerns. There are problems with relocations, with child care, and so on that affect recruiting, productivity, morale, and promotion policies.

For a couple such as the Molers, having both career and family responsibilities is exhausting. But that is just one problem. If Carey is moving up in the firm, what happens if Mitchell gets a terrific job offer 1,500 miles away? What if Carey gets such an offer? Who is going to care for the baby? What happens if the baby gets ill? How do they plan their vacations when there are three schedules to balance? Who will do the housework?

Dual careers require careful planning and discussion, and those plans need to be reviewed over time. A couple who decide at age 22 to do certain things may change their minds at 30: whether or not to have children; where to locate; how to manage the household. All such issues and more can become major problems if not carefully planned.

The same is true for corporations. They, too, must plan for dual-career families. They must give more attention to job sharing, flextime, paternity leave policies for men, transfer policies, nepotism rules, and more.

DECISION QUESTIONS

1. What are some of the issues you can see developing because of dual-career families? How is this affecting children in such families?
2. What kind of corporate policies need changing to adapt to these new realities?
3. What can newlywed couples do to minimize the problems of dual careers? What are the advantages of dual careers? Disadvantages? How can a couple achieve the advantages with a minimum number of problems?

LOOKING AHEAD

Human resource management is an area that has been receiving more attention lately because of issues such as pay equity and executive pay. One major issue of the 1980s is the role of unions in corporations, both now and in the future. Chapter 17 will discuss these issues, with special attention to the history and future of unions. Anyone who gets involved with business today should understand union issues and other employee-management concerns.

Before we get into such issues, we will take some time to focus on a key objective of this course—helping you progress in your career. The appendix at the end of this chapter will teach you how to write a cover letter and résumé and how to prepare for job interviews.

Appendix
Getting the Job You Want

Now that we have explored human resource management from the business side, let's look at the process from your perspective. You now know that businesses are actively searching for good employees who can produce. Similarly, you are looking for an organization where your talents will be used to the fullest and where you would enjoy working. How can you find a job that will provide the optimal satisfaction for both you and the organization? That is the goal of this appendix.

If you followed the advice in the Prologue, you have done a self-assessment to determine what kind of career would be best for you. You have also gone to the library and done some background research into organizations that need people with your skills and knowledge.

If you are older and looking for a new career, your self-assessment has probably revealed that you have handicaps and blessings that younger students do not have. First of all, you may already have a full-time job. Working while going to school is exhausting. Many older students must juggle family responsibilities in addition to the responsibilities of school and work. But take heart, you have also acquired many skills from these experiences. Even if they were acquired in unrelated fields, these skills will be invaluable as you enter your new career.

Whether you are beginning your first career or your latest career, it's time to develop a strategy for finding and obtaining a personally satisfying job.

Life is a constant process of deciding what we are going to do.
JOSÉ ORTEGA Y GASSET

A FIVE–STEP JOB SEARCH STRATEGY

There are several good books available that provide guidance for finding the right job. This appendix will summarize the important steps. They are:

1. *Complete a self-analysis inventory.* A couple of such programs were discussed earlier. If you want to do an assessment on your own, see Richard Nelson Bolles, *What Color Is Your Parachute?* (Berkeley: Ten Speed Press, latest edition). See Figure 16A–1 for a sample assessment. Career Navigator is a software program that will walk you through five modules of job-seeking strategies from "Know Yourself" to "Land that Job." Call Drake Beam Morin Inc. at 1-800-345-JOBS. This program will also help you establish an interviewing strategy.
2. *Search for jobs you would enjoy.* Begin at your college placement office, if it has one. Keep interviewing people in various careers, even after you have found a job. Career progress demands continuous research.
3. *Begin the networking process as discussed in this chapter.* You can start with your family, relatives, neighbors, friends, professors, and local businesspeople. Be sure to keep a file with the names, addresses, and phone numbers of contacts, where they work, the person who recommended them to you, and the relationship between the source person and the contact.
4. *Prepare a good cover letter and résumé.* Samples are provided in this appendix.
5. *Develop interviewing skills.* We shall give you some clues as to how to do this.

A personal assessment scale.

INTERESTS

1. How do I like to spend my time?
2. Do I enjoy being with people?
3. Do I like working with mechanical things?
4. Do I enjoy working with numbers?
5. Am I a member of many organizations?
6. Do I enjoy physical activities?
7. Do I like to read?

ABILITIES

1. Am I adept at working with numbers?
2. Am I adept at working with mechanical things?
3. Do I have good verbal and written communication skills?
4. What special talents do I have?
5. In which abilities do I wish I were more adept?

EDUCATION

1. Have I taken certain courses that have prepared me for a particular job?
2. In which subjects did I perform the best? The worst?
3. Which subjects did I enjoy the most? The least?
4. How have my extracurricular activities prepared me for a particular job?
5. Is my GPA an accurate picture of my academic ability? Why?
6. Do I aspire to a graduate degree? Do I want to earn it before beginning my job?
7. Why did I choose my major?

EXPERIENCE

1. What previous jobs have I held? What were my responsibilities in each?
2. Were any of my jobs applicable to positions I may be seeking? How?
3. What did I like the most about my previous jobs? Like the least?
4. Why did I work in the jobs I did?
5. If I had it to do over again, would I work in these jobs? Why?

PERSONALITY

1. What are my good and bad traits?
2. Am I competitive?
3. Do I work well with others?
4. Am I outspoken?
5. Am I a leader or a follower?
6. Do I work well under pressure?
7. Do I work quickly, or am I methodical?
8. Do I get along well with others?
9. Am I ambitious?
10. Do I work well independently of others?

DESIRED JOB ENVIRONMENT

1. Am I willing to relocate? Why?
2. Do I have a geographic preference? Why?
3. Would I mind traveling in my job?
4. Do I have to work for a large, nationally known firm to be satisfied?
5. Must I have a job that initially offers a high salary?
6. Must the job I assume offer rapid promotion opportunities?
7. In what kind of job environment would I feel most comfortable?
8. If I could design my own job, what characteristics would it have?

PERSONAL GOALS

1. What are my short- and long- term goals? Why?
2. Am I career oriented, or do I have broader interests?
3. What are my career goals?
4. What jobs are likely to help me achieve my goals?
5. What do I hope to be doing in 5 years? In 10 years?
6. What do I want out of life?

Source: Eric N. Berkowitz, Roger A. Kerin, and William Rudelius, *Marketing* (Homewood, Ill.: Richard D. Irwin, 1989) p. 630.

The Job Search

The placement bureau at your school is a good place to begin reading about potential employers. On-campus interviewing is by far the number one source of jobs (see Figure 16A–2 on page 522).

The second most important source of jobs involves writing to companies and sending a good cover letter and résumé. You can find help identifying companies to contact in your college library. Check such sources as the *Million Dollar Directory* or the *Standard Directory of Advertisers*. Your library may also have annual reports that will give you even more information about your selected companies.

FIGURE 16A–2

Where college students find jobs.
When looking for a job, be sure to check the sources listed in the figure. Use those sources that will guarantee your success as you begin your job search.

SOURCE OF JOB	NEW EMPLOYEES (Percent)
On-campus interviewing	49.3%
Write-ins	9.8
Current employee referrals	7.2
Job listings with placement office	6.5
Responses from want ads	5.6
Walk-ins	5.5
Cooperative education programs	4.8
Summer employment	4.7
College faculty/staff referrals	4.5
Internship programs	4.5
High-demand major programs	4.4
Minority career programs	2.9
Part-time employment	2.4
Unsolicited referrals from placement	2.1
Women's career programs	2.1
Job listings with employment agencies	1.9
Referrals from campus organizations	1.8

Source: J. Singleton and P. Scheetz, *Recruiting Trends*, Michigan State University.

THE IMPORTANCE OF SCHOOL ACTIVITIES

	F	E	SB
Lettered in high school sport	71%	50%	50%
Played on college varsity team	33%	18%	15%
Belonged to college fraternity or sorority	57%	39%	28%
Served as class officer in H.S. or college	77%	46%	50%
Were suspended or expelled	8%	16%	10%

This table summarizes the school activities of some people who have gone on to become successful businesspeople. *F* = *Fortune*'s 500 executives; *E* = *Inc.*'s 500 top entrepreneurs; *SB* = Leading small business owners.

Source: Reprinted by permission of *The Wall Street Journal*, (c) Dow Jones & Company, Inc., 1985. All Rights Reserved Worldwide.

The third best source of jobs is networking; that is, finding someone in a firm to recommend you. You find those people by asking friends, neighbors, family, and others if they know anyone who knows someone, and then you track those people down, interview them, and seek their recommendation.

Other good sources of jobs include the placement center, want ads, summer and internship programs, and walking in to firms that appeal to you and asking for an interview.

The *Occupational Outlook Quarterly*, produced by the Department of Labor, says this about job hunting:

> The skills that make a person employable are not so much the ones needed on the job as the ones needed to *get* the job, skills like the ability to find a job opening, complete an application, prepare the résumé, and survive an interview.

Before you read on, check the Interview Rating Sheet in Figure 16A–3. Note what the recruiters want. Interviewers will be checking your appearance (clothes, haircut, fingernails, shoes), your attitude (friendliness is desired), your verbal ability (speak loud enough to be heard clearly), and your motivation (be enthusiastic). Note also that interviewers want you to have been active in clubs and activities and to have set goals. Have someone evaluate you on these scales now to see if you have any weak points. You can then work on those points before you have any actual job interviews.

It is never too early in your career to begin designing a résumé and thinking of cover letters. Preparing such documents reveals your strengths and weaknesses more clearly than most other techniques. Your résumé lists all your education, work experience, and activities. By preparing a résumé now, you may discover that you have not been active enough in outside activities to impress an employer. That information may prompt you to join some student groups, to become a volunteer, or to otherwise enhance your social skills. You may also discover that you are weak on experience, and seek an internship or part-time job to fill in that gap. The figure in the margin shows the importance of extracurricular activities. In any event, it is not too soon to prepare a résumé. It will certainly be helpful in deciding what you would like to see in the area marked "education" and help you to choose a major and other coursework. Given that background, let's discuss how to prepare these materials.

FIGURE 16A–3

Interview rating sheet. Some employers use an interview rating sheet like the one in this figure. When you go for a job interview you should put your best foot forward.

Candidate: "For each characteristic listed below there is a rating scale of 1 through 7, where '1' is generally the most unfavorable rating of the characteristic and '7' the most favorable. Rate each characteristic by *circling* just *one* number to represent the impression you gave in the interview that you have just completed."

NAME OF CANDIDATE _____

1. **APPEARANCE**
   Sloppy   1 2 3 4 5 6 7   Neat
2. **ATTITUDE**
   Unfriendly   1 2 3 4 5 6 7   Friendly
3. **ASSERTIVENESS/VERBAL ABILITY**
   a. Responded Completely to Questions Asked
   Poor   1 2 3 4 5 6 7   Excellent
   b. Clarified Personal Background and Related to Job Opening and Description
   Poor   1 2 3 4 5 6 7   Excellent
   c. Able to Explain and Sell Job Abilities
   Poor   1 2 3 4 5 6 7   Excellent
   d. Initiated Questions Regarding Position and Firm
   Poor   1 2 3 4 5 6 7   Excellent
   e. Expressed thorough Knowledge of Personal Goals and Abilities
   Poor   1 2 3 4 5 6 7   Excellent
4. **MOTIVATION**
   Poor   1 2 3 4 5 6 7   High
5. **SUBJECT/ACADEMIC KNOWLEDGE**
   Poor   1 2 3 4 5 6 7   Good
6. **STABILITY**
   Poor   1 2 3 4 5 6 7   Good
7. **COMPOSURE**
   Ill at Ease   1 2 3 4 5 6 7   Relaxed
8. **PERSONAL INVOLVEMENT/ACTIVITIES, CLUBS, ETC.**
   Low   1 2 3 4 5 6 7   Very high
9. **MENTAL IMPRESSION**
   Dull   1 2 3 4 5 6 7   Alert
10. **ADAPTABILITY**
    Poor   1 2 3 4 5 6 7   Good
11. **SPEECH PRONUNCIATION**
    Poor   1 2 3 4 5 6 7   Good
12. **OVERALL IMPRESSION**
    Unsatisfactory   1 2 3 4 5 6 7   Highly satisfactory
13. Would you hire this individual if you were permitted to make that decision right now?
                          Yes   No

Writing a Résumé

A *résumé* is a document that lists all the information an employer would need to evaluate you and your background. It explains your immediate goals and career objectives. This information is followed by an explanation of your educational background, experience, interests, and other relevant data.

If you have exceptional abilities and do not communicate them to the employer on the résumé, those abilities are not part of the person he or she will evaluate. You must be comprehensive and clear in your résumé if you are to communicate all your attributes.

FIGURE 16A–4

Stamp out bad résumés. A good résumé should:
1. Invite you to read it, have a clear layout, top-quality printing, and eliminate extraneous information.
2. Start sentences with action verbs such as organized, managed, and designed, rather than with lead-ins ("I was the person responsible for . . . ").
3. Highlight those accomplishments related to future work.
4. Be free of spelling, punctuation, and grammatical errors.
5. Speak the reader's language by using the vocabulary of the industry you are targeting.
6. Make a strong statement; this means using only the most relevant information–nothing less, nothing more.

Source: Special Advertising Section in *Business Week's Guide to Careers* ("The Chrysler-Plymouth Guide to Building a Resume").

Monica A. Thomas
18 Nautical Lane
Gloucester, Mass.

Age: 21
Height: 5'6"
Weight: 123 lbs.
Hair: Red
Eyes: Hazel
Marital Status: Single
Health: Good

OBJECTIVE

To apply management experience and French language skills in a corporation overseas.

EDUCATION

B.A. Management, Georgia State University, Atlanta, Ga.

Also completed a semester of study abroad in London, England (Georgia State University)

Additional Areas of Academic Competence:

8 Credit Hours in computers using FORTRAN, Small Business Counseling.

College Courses included Marketing, French, English Literature, Computer Programming, Data Processing, Statistics, Sociology, Economics.

High School Diploma: St. Agatha's High School Gloucester, MA: College Preparatory, National Honor Society, Graduated in top 25% of class.

WORK EXPERIENCE

6/84–Present

Flowers by Joann, Rockport, Mass. Responsibilities included: bookkeeping, inventory, floral design, selling merchandise, both person to person and by use of computer.

5/87–8/87

Waitress, Citronella's Taverna, London, England. Learned to work effectively with an international clientele.

5/89–9/89

Hostess, The Clam Shell, Salem, Mass.

Activities

American Marketing Association, Student Marketing Association, Fencing Club.

Your résumé is an advertisement for yourself. If your ad is better than the other person's ad, you are more likely to get the interview. In this case, "better" means that your ad highlights your attributes in an attractive way.

In discussing your education, for example, be sure to highlight your extracurricular activities such as part-time jobs, sports, clubs, and other such activities. If you did well in school, put down your grades. The idea is to make yourself look as good on paper as you are in reality.

The same is true for your job experience. Be sure to describe what you did, any special projects in which you participated, and any responsibilities you had.

Monica A. Thomas
18 Nautical Lane
Gloucester, Mass. 01930
(617) 281-0568

EDUCATION

1989	B.A. Management, GEORGIA STATE UNIVERSITY
1987	Semester, GSU-London, England
1985–86	8 Credit Hours, FORTRAN, Small Business Training-Computer Science

OBJECTIVE

To apply management experience and French language skills in a corporation overseas.

CAPABILITIES

■ Perceive motivations in others allowing them to produce results based on their goals and commitments.

■ Listen to subtle communications and convert them into active resolutions.

■ Provide spirit of trust and enthusiasm so that business transactions can occur harmoniously.

■ Handle administrative details under pressure so as to allow boss to pursue higher levels of thinking and decision making.

EXPERIENCE

■ Sold floral arrangements at $800–$1,200/month, in person and by telephone and computer.

■ Managed all administrative details of medium-size floral shop for five seasons.

■ Recognized by British restaurant manager for outstanding courtesy and efficiency.

■ Served as restaurant hostess/junior manager where patronage increased over 33% in a three month period.

1984–Present	FLOWERS BY JOANN Rockport, MA Sales Assistant
1987 (Summer)	CITRONELLA'S TAVERNA London, England Waitress
1989 (Summer)	THE CLAM SHELL Salem, MA Hostess/Junior Manager
ACTIVITIES	Member: American Marketing Association Student Marketing Association

FIGURE 16A–5

Building a résumé. Check out the new and upgraded version of Monica's résumé, and compare its impact with the former version. Things to notice:

1. You would be surprised how many people forget to include their home (permanent) phone number. You can use a second—school—number as well.
2. It is permissible to eliminate high school data if it doesn't add to the total picture. Employers will get this information on the application form anyway.
3. Use action words (see Figure 16A–6) at beginnings of sentences and paragraphs where you can.
4. Use numbers and quantities where possible.
5. It simplifies matters to eliminate month designations.
6. Rewards and citations help.
7. Note more detail on real results, and the communication of value stressed over simple "duties."
8. It is permissible to claim a piece of the overall successes.

Source: Special Advertising Section in *Business Week's Guide to Careers* ("The Chrysler-Plymouth Guide to Building a Resume").

For the "other interests" section, if you include one, do not just list your interests, but describe how deeply you were involved. If you organized the club, volunteered your time, or participated more often than usual in an organization, make sure to say so in the résumé. Figure 16A-4 shows an unedited version of a résumé. It was a part of a Guide to Building a Résumé prepared by the Chrysler-Plymouth Corporation. Look over the résumé and see what you think. Then turn to Figure 16A-5 for an improved version. Can you see how important planning and writing a résumé can be?

Managed	Wrote	Budgeted	Improved
Planned	Produced	Designed	Increased
Organized	Scheduled	Directed	Investigated
Coordinated	Operated	Developed	Sold
Supervised	Conducted	Established	Served
Trained	Administered	Implemented	Handled

Writing a Cover Letter

A cover letter is used to announce your availability and to introduce the résumé. The cover letter is probably one of the most important advertisements anyone will write in a lifetime—so it should be done right.

First, the cover letter should indicate that you have researched the organization in question and are interested in a job there. Let the organization know what sources you used and what you know about it in the first paragraph to get the attention of the reader and show your interest.

You may have heard that "It is not what you know, but whom you know that counts." This is only partly true, but it is important nonetheless. If you do not know someone, you can get to know someone. You do this by calling the organization (or better yet, visiting its offices) and talking to people who already have the kind of job you are hoping to get. Ask about training, salary, and other relevant issues. Then, in your cover letter, mention that you have talked with some of the firm's employees and that this discussion increased your interest. You thereby show the letter reader that you "know someone," if only casually, and that you are interested enough to actively pursue the organization. This is all part of networking.

Second, in the description of yourself, be sure to say how your attributes will benefit the organization. For example, do not just say, "I will be graduating with a degree in marketing." Say, "You will find that my college training in marketing and marketing research has prepared me to learn your marketing system quickly and begin making a contribution right away." The sample cover letter in Figure 16A-7 will give you a better feel for how this looks.

Third, be sure to "ask for the order." That is, say in your final paragraph that you are available for an interview at a time and place convenient for the interviewer. Again, see the sample cover letter in Figure 16A-7 for guidance. Notice in this letter how Tom subtly showed that he read business publications and drew attention to his résumé.

Some principles to follow in writing a cover letter and preparing your résumé are:

- Be self-confident. List all your good qualities and attributes.
- Do not be apologetic or negative. Write as one professional to another, not as a humble student begging for a job.
- Research every prospective employer thoroughly before writing anything. Use a rifle approach rather than a shotgun approach. That is, write effective marketing oriented letters to a few select companies rather than to a general list.
- Have your materials typed on a good typewriter or word processor by an experienced typist. For best results, have your résumé printed. (If you have access to a word processing system with a letter-quality laser printer, you could produce individualized letters efficiently.)
- Have someone edit your materials for spelling, grammar, and style. Don't be like the student who sent out a second résumé to correct "some mixtakes." Or another who said "I am acurite with numbers."
- Do not send the names of references until asked. Put "References furnished on request" at the bottom of the last page of your résumé.

Dear Mr. Franklin:

A recent article in <u>Business Week</u> mentioned that Donahue Corporation is expanding its operations into the Southwest. I have always had an interest in your firm, and so I read more about you in <u>Forbes</u> and <u>Standard & Poor's</u>. It seems as though you will be needing good salespeople to handle your expanding business. Harold Jones, your Detroit sales representative, is a neighbor of mine. He told me about your training program, compensation system, and career opportunities. He convinced me that Donahue is the place for an ambitious college graduate.

I will be graduating from State College in June with a degree in marketing. My courses in marketing management, sales management, consumer behavior, and marketing research have given me some insight into marketing for a growing organization like yours. My 3 years' experience as a salesman for Korvalis Shoes has given me valuable skills that I could apply at Donahue. You will notice when you read the attached resumé that I have always been active in the organizations I have joined. Could I do as well at Donahue?

I will be in the New York area the week of November 17–25. Please let me know which time and date would be convenient for you to discuss a future at Donahue. I am looking forward to hearing from you.

                    Sincerely,

                    Thomas J. Smith

                    Thomas J. Smith

FIGURE 16A–7

A model cover letter. Things to notice:
1. The first paragraph of the letter mentions someone in the firm (a networking strategy).
2. The second paragraph mentions specific courses and experience applicable to the job.
3. The third paragraph asks for a specific time and date for the interview.

PREPARING FOR JOB INTERVIEWS

Companies usually do not conduct job interviews unless they are somewhat certain that the candidate has the requirements for the job. The interview, therefore, is pretty much a make-or-break situation. If it goes well, you have a much greater chance of being hired. Therefore, it is critical that you are prepared for your interviews. The following are five stages of interview preparation.

1. Do Research about the Prospective Employers   Learn what industry the firm is in, its competitors, the products or services it produces and their acceptance in the market, and the title of your desired entry-level position. You can find such information in the firm's annual reports, in Standard & Poor's, Moody's manuals, and various business publications such as *Fortune, Business Week,* and *Forbes.* Ask your librarian for help. Together, you can look in the *Reader's Guide to Business Literature* and find the company name to look for articles on it. This is a very important first step. It shows you have initiative and interest in the firm.

FIGURE 16A–8

Be prepared for these
frequently asked questions.

How would you describe yourself? What are your greatest strengths and weaknesses? How did you choose this company? What do you know about the company? What are your long-range career goals? What courses did you like best? Least? What are your hobbies?	Do you prefer a specific geographic location? Are you willing to travel (or move)? Which accomplishments have given you the most satisfaction? What things are most important to you in a job? Why should I hire you? What experience have you had in this type of work? How much do you expect to earn?

FIGURE 16A–9

Sample questions to ask the
interviewer.

Who are your major competitors and how would you rate their products and marketing relative to yours?
How long does the training program last and what is included?
How soon after school would I be expected to start?
What are the advantages of working for this firm?
How much travel is normally expected?
What managerial style should I expect in my area?
How would you describe the working environment in my area?
How would I be evaluated?
What is the company's promotion policy?
What is the corporate culture?
What is the next step in the selection procedures?
How soon should I expect to hear from you?
What other information would you like about my background, experience, or education?
What is your highest priority in the next six months and how could someone like me help?

2. Practice the Interview   Figure 16A-8 (see page 528) lists some of the more frequently asked questions in an interview. Practice answering these questions and more at the placement office and with your roommate, parents, or friends. Do not memorize your answers, but be prepared—know what you are going to say. Also, develop a series of questions to ask the interviewer. Figure 16A-9 (see page 528) shows some sample questions you might ask. Be sure you know who to contact, and write down the names of everyone you meet. Review the action words in Figure 16A-6 and try to fit them into your answers.

3. Be Professional during the Interview   "You don't have a second chance to make a good first impression," the saying goes. That means that you should look and sound professional throughout the interview. Do your homework and find out how the managers dress at the firm. Then buy an appropriate outfit.

When you meet the interviewers, greet them by name, smile, and maintain good eye contact. Sit up straight in your chair and be alert and enthusiastic. If you have practiced, you should be able to relax and be confident. Other than that, be yourself, answer questions, and be friendly and responsive.

When you leave, thank the interviewers and, if you are still interested in the job, tell them so. If they don't tell you, ask them what the next step is. Maintain a positive attitude. Figure 16A-10 outlines what the interviewers will be evaluating.

Don't be concerned if upon graduation you have little understanding of your own talents or focus on your life's work. Only a minority are given such insights in their early years. Most have to find their way by diverse job experiences.
FRANK SHAKESPEARE,
president, RKO General

1. *Ability to Communicate.* Do you have the ability to organize your thoughts and ideas effectively? Can you express them clearly when speaking or writing? Can you present your ideas to others in a persuasive way?
2. *Intelligence.* Do you have the ability to understand the job assignment? Learn the details of operation? Contribute original ideas to your work?
3. *Self-Confidence.* Do you demonstrate a sense of maturity that enables you to deal positively and effectively with situations and people?
4. *Willingness to Accept Responsibility.* Are you someone who recognizes what needs to be done and is willing to do it?
5. *Initiative.* Do you have the ability to identify the purpose for work and to take action?
6. *Leadership.* Can you guide and direct others to obtain the recognized objectives?
7. *Energy Level.* Do you demonstrate a forcefulness and capacity to make things move ahead? Can you maintain your work effort at an above-average rate?
8. *Imagination.* Can you confront and deal with problems that may not have standard solutions?
9. *Flexibility.* Are you capable of changing and being receptive to new situations and ideas?
10. *Interpersonal Skills.* Can you bring out the best efforts of individuals so they become effective, enthusiastic members of a team?
11. *Self-Knowledge.* Can you realistically assess your own capabilities? See yourself as others see you? Clearly recognize your strengths and weaknesses?
12. *Ability to Handle Conflict.* Can you successfully contend with stress situations and antagonism?
13. *Competitiveness.* Do you have the capacity to compete with others and the willingness to be measured by your performance in relation to that of others?
14. *Goal Achievement.* Do you have the ability to identify and work toward specific goals? Do such goals challenge your abilities?
15. *Vocational Skills.* Do you possess the positive combination of education and skills required for the position you are seeking?
16. *Direction.* Have you defined your basic personal needs? Have you determined what type of position will satisfy your knowledge, skills, and goals?

FIGURE 16A–10

Sixteen traits recruiters seek in job prospects.

Source: "So You're Looking for a Job?" The College Placement Council.

4. Follow Up on the Interview   First, write down what you can remember from the interview: names of the interviewers and their titles, any salary figures mentioned, dates for training, and so on. Put the information in your career file. You can send a follow-up letter thanking each interviewer for his or her time. You can also send a letter of recommendation or some other piece of added information to keep their interest. "The squeaky wheel gets the grease" is the operating slogan. Your enthusiasm for working for the company could be a major factor in hiring you.

5. Be Prepared to Act   Know what you want to say if you do get a job offer. You may not want the job after hearing all the information. Do not expect to receive a job offer from everyone you meet, but do expect to learn something from every interview. With some practice and persistence, you should find a rewarding and challenging job.

FIGURE 16A–11   Government job sources. If you are interested in a government job, it helps to start by contacting directly the agency's personnel office and asking for information and assistance in preparing your résumé and interviewing process. These are the telephone numbers. The area code in Washington, D.C. is 202.

DEPARTMENTS	AGENCIES (cont.)
Agriculture—447-5626	Federal Emergency Management Agency—646-4213
Commerce—337-5438	Federal Home Loan Bank Board—377-6062
Defense—697-9205	Federal Labor Relations Authority—382-0751
Air Force (civilian)—695-4389	Federal Mediation and Conciliation Service—
Army (civilian)—695-2589	653-5260
Navy (civilian)—697-6181	Federal Reserve Board—452-3880
Defense Intelligence Agency—373-2628	Federal Trade Commission—326-2020
Defense Logistics Agency—274-7087	General Accounting Office—275-6092
Defense Mapping Agency—227-1980	General Services Administration—472-1088
Education—732-1377	Government Printing Office—275-2374
Energy—586-4494	Interstate Commerce Commission—275-7414
Health and Human Services—245-0870	Merit Systems Protection Board—653-5916
Housing and Urban Development—755-0196	National Academy of Sciences—334-3400
Interior —343-2154	National Aeronautics and Space Administration—
Justice—633-3396	453-8507
Labor—523-6677	National Archives and Records Administration—
State—235-9376	724-1513
Transportation—366-9392	National Credit Union Administration—357-1156
Treasury—566-2540	National Endowment for the Arts—682-5405
	National Endowment for the Humanities—786-0415
	National Labor Relations Board—254-9044
AGENCIES	National Mediation Board—523-5950
	National Science Foundation—357-9859
Action—634-9263	National Transportation Safety Board—382-6717
Administrative Office of the U.S. Courts—633-6116	Nuclear Regulatory Commission—492-8275
Agency for International Development—663-1406	Office of Personnel Management—632-7484
Commodity Futures Trading Commission—254-3275	Securities and Exchange Commission—272-2550
Consumer Product Safety Commission—492-6500	Small Business Administration—653-6504
Environmental Protection Agency—382-3144	Smithsonian Institution—357-2465
Equal Employment Opportunity Commission—	U.S. Arms Control and Disarmament Agency—
634-7002	647-2034
Export-Import Bank—566-8834	U.S. Information Agency—485-2617
Farm Credit Administration—883-4169	U.S. International Trade Commission—252-1651
Federal Communications Commission—632-7106	U.S. Postal Service—268-3646
Federal Deposit Insurance Corporation—898-3853	Veterans Administration—233-2495
Federal Election Commission—376-5290	

BE PREPARED TO CHANGE JOBS

If you are like most people, you will find that you will follow several different career paths over your lifetime. This is a good thing in that it enables you to try different jobs and stay fresh and enthusiastic. The key to moving forward in your career is a willingness to change jobs, always searching for the career that will bring the most personal satisfaction and growth. This means that you will have to write many cover letters and résumés and go through many interviews. Each time you change jobs, go through the steps in this appendix to be sure you are fully prepared. Good luck.

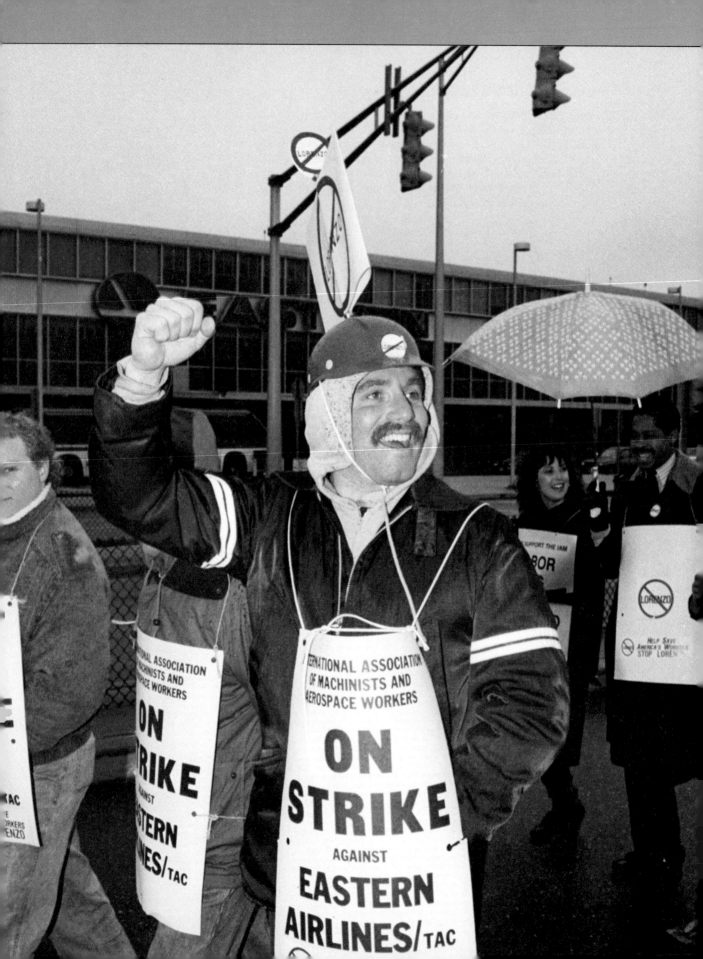

INTERNATIONAL ASSOCIATION
OF MACHINISTS AND
AEROSPACE WORKERS

**ON
STRIKE**

AGAINST

**EASTERN
AIRLINES/TAC**

EMPLOYEE MANAGEMENT ISSUES

UNIONS, EXECUTIVE COMPENSATION, COMPARABLE WORTH, AND OTHER ISSUES

LEARNING GOALS

After you have read and studied this chapter, you should be able to:

1. Trace the history of organized labor in the United States.
2. Discuss the major legislation affecting labor unions.
3. Outline the objectives of labor unions.
4. Describe the tactics used by labor and management during conflicts.
5. Discuss the role and growth of unions in the future.
6. Explain the issue of executive compensation in the 1990s.
7. Outline the issues surrounding the concept of comparable worth.
8. Explain how child care has become an employee-management issue in the 1990s.
9. Describe the concerns encompassing AIDS testing in the workplace.
10. Explain the benefits and problems of employee stock ownership programs (ESOPs).

KEY TERMS

Avis rental lot.

PROFILE   JOSEPH V. VITTORIA OF AVIS

Joseph Vittoria worked for Hertz at one time, but the chairman of Hertz demoted him twice. Vittoria left Hertz for Avis in 1982. The two companies became engaged in a price war over the nearly 70 percent of car rentals that the two firms control.

Vittoria has something on his side that Frank Olson does not have at Hertz. Avis is an employee-owned company. Some 11,000 employees bought the company through an ESOP plan (employee stock ownership plan). Avis is just one of 10,000 companies that have set up ESOP plans. There are tax benefits, financial benefits, and, best of all, the benefit of having employees work harder because they own the firm. One can truly say of Avis employees, "We're number two, but we work harder to earn your business." For example, service complaints in 1988 were down 35 percent from the year earlier.

The history of Avis is like a history of corporate takeovers. In 1983, its parent company, Norton Simon, was acquired by Esmark. In turn, Esmark was acquired by Beatrice Companies in 1984. Beatrice went private (see Chapter 4) in 1986 and sold Avis to Wesray Capital Corporation and Avis management. The ESOP bought the firm from Wesray.

Now Avis employees are caught up in a rate war that could make Avis number one. At airports today, Avis has about 28 percent of rentals and Hertz about 32 percent, down from 40 percent. ESOPs and their benefits and drawbacks for employees will be one issue of the 1990s. Other issues include mandatory drug testing, comparable worth, child care, parental leave, and more. These are interesting times in employee-management relations. Just how much say should employees have in management if they own the firm? What part should unions play in the company? Mr. Vittoria at Avis will have to face these issues, as will most other firms in the United States including thousands of smaller firms. This chapter will further discuss unions, ESOPs, comparable worth, executive pay, and many other issues that will dominate the headlines and the thoughts of business managers throughout the 1990s.

Source: Chuck Hawkins, "Is Avis Moving into the Passing Lane?" *Business Week*, May 9, 1988, pp. 100–105; and Harris Collingwood, "With Its ESOP, Avis Tries Even Harder," *Business Week*, May 15, 1989, p. 122.

By working faithfully 8 hours a day, you may eventually get to be boss and work 12 hours a day.
ROBERT FROST

EMPLOYEE-MANAGEMENT ISSUES

The relationship between owner/managers and employees has never been smooth throughout the history of business. To protect themselves from unfair managers and have some say in the operations of their jobs, workers united to form unions. This gave workers more negotiating power with managers and more political power as well. The issue of worker pay and unions has been a major one in the 1980s and will continue to be controversial in the 1990s.

A new twist has been added to the issue of pay. Women receive less pay than men overall, and jobs traditionally held by women (for example, teacher, nurse, secretary) pay less than traditional "men's jobs" (for example, truck driver, garbage collector, miner). The issue of comparable worth adds to employee-management disputes.

The pay issue reached a new intensity in the 1980s for two reasons. First, foreign labor was cheaper than U.S. labor, and jobs were being lost to foreign firms. This led workers at several firms to take pay cuts to keep their companies competitive with foreign firms. Second, executive pay was *increased* rather than decreased. This caused much debate over the issue of executive compensation.

To get a fairer share of profits, employees began asking for more equity in the firm. In fact, some companies that went bankrupt were purchased entirely by employees. Another issue, as we have seen in the Profile, is ESOPs (employee stock ownership plans)—their benefits versus their drawbacks.

Employees are also interested in other benefits we have discussed, such as flextime, part-time work, and more. Additionally, managers and employees are addressing concerns such as the need for day care and the ever-growing threats AIDS and alcohol abuse pose in the workplace. The goal of this chapter is to present and evaluate some of these issues. Like all other managerial problems, these issues must be worked out through open discussion, goodwill, and compromise. It is important to know both sides of the issues, however, to make reasoned decisions.

Any discussion of employee-management relations in the United States probably should begin with a discussion of unions. **Unions** are employee organizations that have the main goal of representing members in employee-management bargaining about job-related issues. Employees have historically turned to unions to assist in gaining specific rights and benefits. However, in the 1980s, unions lost some of the power they had achieved and certainly decreased in membership. Nonetheless, some labor analysts forecast they may gain more strength among service workers in the 1990s. There's no question that the role and positions of unions in the future will arouse emotions and opinions that contrast considerably. Let's briefly look at some contrasting viewpoints concerning labor unions.

unions
Employee organizations that have the main goal of representing members in employee-management bargaining about job-related issues.

LABOR UNIONS FROM DIFFERENT PERSPECTIVES

Are labor unions essential in the American economy today? This question is certain to evoke emotional responses from various participants in the workplace. The fisherman carrying a picket sign in Massachusetts will elaborate on the dangers to our free society if employers continue to try to bust authorized unions. The *automaker* in Detroit, the *plumber* in St. Louis, the *farmworker* in Orange County, and millions of other union sympathizers will strongly support the fisherman's contention.

A different perspective is presented by the small manufacturer who is forced to operate under union wage and benefit obligations and work rules. Such a manager argues that competition is very difficult under strict union conditions. The *automaker* in Detroit, the plumbing *contractor* in St. Louis, the large *grower* in Orange County, and millions of other small, medium, and large business enterprises may question the power of unions.

Fundamentally, most people would agree that the union movement of today is an outgrowth of the economic transition caused by the Industrial Revolution of the 19th and early 20th centuries. The workers who once toiled in the fields, dependent on the mercies of nature for survival, suddenly became dependent on the continuous roll of the factory presses and assembly lines for their living. Clearly the steps inherent in breaking away from an agrarian (farm) economy to an industrial economy were quite difficult. Nonetheless, over time workers learned that strength through unity could lead to improved job conditions, better wages,

Labor unions give workers more political clout because of the large numbers of voters in the unions. This large gathering of union members in Washington, D.C., gives you some feel for the impact of unions on the federal government. The union movement is gaining in strength as service workers demand more pay and benefits.

and job security. These issues are again in the headlines as the United States moves from an industrial to a service economy.

Today, critics of organized labor maintain that none of the inhuman conditions that once dominated U.S. industry can be found in the workplace. They charge that organized labor has in fact become a large industrial entity in itself, and the real issue of protecting workers has become secondary because the legal system and current management attitudes prohibit the reappearance of the sweatshops of the late 19th and early 20th centuries. Are these assumptions correct? Perhaps a short discussion of the history of labor unions will cast a better light on these differing positions.

The Early History of Organized Labor

The presence of formal labor organizations in the United States dates back to the time of the American Revolution. As early as 1792, cordwainers (shoemakers) in Philadelphia met to discuss the fundamental work issues of pay, hours, conditions, and job security. (Many of the same issues dominate labor negotiations today.) The cordwainers were a **craft union,** which is an organization of skilled specialists in a particular craft or trade. They were typical of the early labor organizations formed before the Civil War in that they were local or regional in membership. Also, most were established to achieve some short-range goal such as curtailing the use of convict labor as an alternative to available local labor. Often, after a specific objective was attained, the labor group disbanded. This situation changed dramatically in the late 19th century with the expansion of the Industrial Revolution.

The Industrial Revolution changed the economic structure of the United States. Enormous productivity increases gained through mass production and job specialization made the United States a true world power. However, this rapid shift in economic focus brought with it problems for workers in terms of productivity, hours of work, wages, and unemployment.

craft union
Labor organization of skilled specialists in a particular craft or trade.

Workers were faced with the reality that production was vital. If you failed to produce, you lost your job. Often, this caused workers to go to work even if they were ill or had family problems. Over time, the increased emphasis on production led firms to expand the hours of work. The average workweek in 1900 was 60 hours but 80 hours was not uncommon for some industries. Wages were low and the use of child labor was not unusual. Furthermore, periods of unemployment were severe on families who lived on subsistence wages. As you can sense, these were not short-term issues that would easily go away. The workplace was ripe for the emergence of national labor organizations.

The first truly national labor organization was the Noble Order of the Knights of Labor formed by Uriah Smith Stephens in 1869. By 1886 the **Knights of Labor** claimed a membership of 700,000 members. The Knights offered membership to all working people, including employers, and promoted social causes as well as labor and economic issues. However, their stewardship was short lived because of the rather revolutionary attitudes of their leadership. In essence, the intention of the Knights of Labor was to gain significant political power and eventually restructure the entire U.S. economy. They fell from prominence after receiving the blame for a bomb that exploded at a labor rally at Haymarket Square in Chicago, killing eight policemen.

> **Knights of Labor**
> The first national labor union (1869).

A rival group to the Knights of Labor, the **American Federation of Labor (AFL),** was formed in 1886. By 1890, the AFL, under the dynamic leadership of Samuel Gompers, had moved to the forefront of the labor movement. The AFL was an organization of craft unions that championed nuts-and-bolts labor issues. They intentionally limited membership to *skilled* workers (craftsmen) assuming they would have bargaining power in attaining concessions from some employers. However, over time an unauthorized committee in the AFL began to organize workers in **industrial unions,** which were organizations of *unskilled* workers in mass-production related industries such as automobiles and mining. This committee, called the Committee of Industrial Organization, was led by John L. Lewis, president of the United Mine Workers Union.

> **American Federation of Labor (AFL)**
> A craft union formed in 1886.

> **industrial unions**
> Labor organizations of *unskilled* workers in mass-production related industries such as automobiles and mining.

The objective of Lewis was to organize both craftspeople (craft unions) and unskilled workers (industrial unions) in particular industries. When his proposal was rejected, Lewis broke with the AFL and formed a new, rival organization called the **Congress of Industrial Organization (CIO)** in 1935. The CIO soon rivaled the AFL in membership partly because of passage of the Wagner Act the same year (see Figure 17–1). For 20 years the two organizations contested for leadership in the labor movement. It wasn't until after unfavorable legislation such as the Taft-Hartley Act (see Figure 17–1 on page 538) was passed that the two organizations saw the benefits of a merger. In 1955, under the leadership of George Meany, 16 million labor members united to form the AFL–CIO. Today, the AFL–CIO includes affiliations with over 100 labor unions including the largest of labor unions, the Teamsters, which has over 2 million members.

> **Congress of Industrial Organization (CIO)**
> Union organization of unskilled workers that broke away from the AFL in 1935 and rejoined it in 1955.

LABOR LEGISLATION AND COLLECTIVE BARGAINING

The growth and strength of organized labor has always been dependent on two major factors; the law and public opinion. Figure 17–1 outlines four major pieces of federal legislation that have had a significant impact on the rights and operations of labor unions.

FIGURE 17–1

Major legislation affecting labor-management relations.

Norris–La Guardia Act 1932 law that prohibited courts from using injunctions against nonviolent union activities and outlawed the use of yellow-dog contracts.	**Norris–La Guardia Act,** 1932	Prohibited courts from issuing injunctions against nonviolent union activities; outlawed contracts forbidding union activities; outlawed the use of yellow-dog contracts by employers. (Yellow-dog contracts were contractual agreements forced on workers by employers whereby the employee agreed not to join a union as a condition of employment.)
National Labor Relations Act (Wagner Act) 1935 law that gave employees the right to join a union, to collectively bargain, and to engage in union activities such as strikes, picketing, and boycotts.	**National Labor Relations Act (Wagner Act),** 1935	Gave employees the right to form or join labor organizations (or to refuse to form or join); the right to collectively bargain with employers through elected union representatives; and the right to engage in labor activities such as strikes, picketing, and boycotts. Prohibited certain unfair labor practices by the employer and the union, and established the National Labor Relations Board to oversee union election campaigns and investigate labor practices. This act gave great impetus to the union movement.
Labor-Management Relations Act (Taft-Hartley Act) 1947 law that permitted states to pass right-to-work laws; prohibited secondary boycotts, closed-shop agreements, and featherbedding; and set up methods to deal with strikes.	**Labor-Management Relations Act (Taft-Hartley Act),** 1947	Amended the Wagner Act; permitted states to pass laws prohibiting compulsory union membership (right-to-work laws); set up methods to deal with strikes that affect national health and safety; prohibited secondary boycotts, closed-shop agreements, and featherbedding (the requiring of wage payments for work not performed) by unions. This act gave more power to management.
Labor Management Reporting and Disclosure Act (Landrum-Griffin Act) 1959 law that gave individual rights to union members to nominate candidates, vote in union elections, attend union meetings, examine union records, and required annual financial reports from unions to be filed with the Department of Labor.	**Labor-Management Reporting and Disclosure Act (Landrum-Griffin Act),** 1959	Amended the Taft-Hartley Act and the Wagner Act; guaranteed individual rights of union members in dealing with their union, such as the right to nominate candidates for union office, vote in union elections, attend and participate in union meetings, vote on union business, and examine union records and accounts; required annual financial reports to be filed with the U.S. Department of Labor. One goal of this act was to clean up union corruption, but corruption continues today.

The Wagner Act provided labor with legal justification to pursue the issues supported by Samuel Gompers and the AFL. This act of Congress established an administrative agency, the National Labor Relations Board (NLRB), to oversee labor-management relations. It also provided guidelines and offered legal protection to workers seeking to vote on "organizing" a union to represent them in the workplace. This process of a union becoming recognized by the NLRB as the

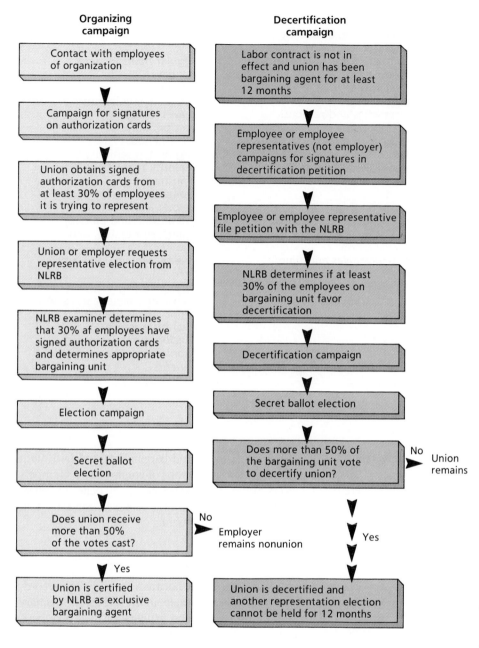

Organizing campaign

- Contact with employees of organization
- Campaign for signatures on authorization cards
- Union obtains signed authorization cards from at least 30% of employees it is trying to represent
- Union or employer requests representative election from NLRB
- NLRB examiner determines that 30% af employees have signed authorization cards and determines appropriate bargaining unit
- Election campaign
- Secret ballot election
- Does union receive more than 50% of the votes cast? — No → Employer remains nonunion
- Yes → Union is certified by NLRB as exclusive bargaining agent

Decertification campaign

- Labor contract is not in effect and union has been bargaining agent for at least 12 months
- Employee or employee representatives (not employer) campaigns for signatures in decertification petition
- Employee or employee representative file petition with the NLRB
- NLRB determines if at least 30% of the employees on bargaining unit favor decertification
- Decertification campaign
- Secret ballot election
- Does more than 50% of the bargaining unit vote to decertify union? — No → Union remains
- Yes → Union is decertified and another representation election cannot be held for 12 months

FIGURE 17–2

Note that the final vote calls for over 50 percent of the *votes cast*. Note too that the election is secret.

Source: Bureau of Labor Statistics, 1988.

certification
Process of a union becoming recognized by the NLRB as the bargaining agent for a group of employees.

decertification
Process by which workers take away a union's right to represent them.

collective bargaining
The process whereby union and management representatives reach a negotiated labor-management agreement.

bargaining agent for a group of employees is called **certification.** (Figure 17–2 describes the steps involved in a union-organizing campaign.) The act also provided management with a clear process to *decertify* a union. **Decertification** is the process by which workers take away a union's right to represent them. (Figure 17–2 also provides information on the decertification process.)

The equalization of unequals through collective bargaining was a vital issue according to Gompers. **Collective bargaining** is the process whereby union representatives sit down with management and work out a mutually agreed-upon contract for the workers. The Wagner Act made collective bargaining legal and

FIGURE 17–3

Topics covered in union-employer agreements. Labor and management often meet to discuss and clarify the terms that specify the employees' functions within the company. The topics listed in this figure are typically discussed during these meetings. Notice that the union is concerned about the employees' benefits and rights.

1. Union recognition and scope of bargaining unit
2. Management rights (management security)
3. Union security
4. Strikes and lockouts
5. Union activities and responsibilities
   a. Check-off of dues
   b. Union officers and stewards
   c. Union bulletin boards
   d. Wildcat strikes and slowdowns
6. Wages
   a. General wage adjustments
   b. Wage structure
   c. Job evaluation
   d. Wage incentives and time study
   e. Reporting and call-in pay
   f. Shift differentials
   g. Bonuses
7. Working time and time-off policies
   a. Regular hours of work
   b. Holidays
   c. Vacations
   d. Overtime regulations
   e. Leaves of absence
   f. Rest periods
   g. Meal periods
8. Job rights and seniority
   a. Seniority regulations
   b. Transfers
   c. Promotions
   d. Layoffs and recalls
   e. Job posting and bidding
9. Discipline, suspension, and discharge
10. Grievance handling and arbitration
11. Health and safety
12. Insurance and benefit programs
    a. Group life insurance
    b. Health insurance
    c. Pension programs
    d. *Supplemental unemployment benefits*

Source: Dale S. Beach, *Personnel: The Management of People at Work* (New York: Macmillan, 1985), p. 421.

negotiated labor-management agreement
Settlement that sets the tone and clarifies the terms under which management and labor agree to function over a period of time.

union security clause
Provision in a negotiated labor-management agreement that stipulates that employees who benefit from a union must either join or pay dues to the union.

closed-shop agreement
Clause in labor-management agreement that specified workers had to be members of a union before being hired (outlawed by the Taft-Hartley Act).

agency shop agreement
One where employees may hire anyone and employees do not have to join the union but must pay union fees.

obligated employers to meet at reasonable times and bargain in good faith with respect to wages, hours, and other terms and conditions of employment. Gompers and his followers were true believers in the capitalist system. They believed collective bargaining was the means to attain a fairer share of the economic pie and attain specific objectives important to the members' well-being.

Objectives of Organized Labor

As you might suspect, the objectives of organized labor frequently change according to shifts in social and economic trends. For example, in the 1970s, the primary objective of most labor unions was additional pay and benefits for their members. Throughout the 1980s, there was a significant shift toward issues related to job security and union recognition. The 1990s are certain to present new objectives. The **negotiated labor-management agreement** sets the tone and clarifies the terms and conditions under which management and labor agree to function over a specific period of time. Figure 17–3 provides a list of topics commonly appearing in labor-management agreements.

A **union security clause** stipulates that employees who reap benefits from a union must either join or pay dues to the union. After passage of the Wagner Act, labor sought security in the form of the closed shop. The **closed-shop agreement** specified that workers had to be members of a union before being hired. The Taft-Hartley Act outlawed this practice in 1947 (see Figure 17–4). Under an **agency shop agreement,** employers may hire nonunion workers who are not required to join the union but must pay a union fee.

TYPE OF CONTRACT	DESCRIPTION
Union shop	The majority of union contracts are of this type. The employer can hire anyone, but employees must join the union to keep their jobs.
Agency shop	Employers may hire anyone. Employees need not join the union, but are required to pay a union fee. Less than 10 percent of union contracts are of this nature.
Closed shop (no longer used)	The Taft-Hartley Act made this form illegal. Only union members could be hired under this system.
Open shop	Union membership is voluntary for new and existing employees. Those who do not join the union do not have to pay union dues. Few union contracts are of this type.

FIGURE 17–4

Different forms of union contracts.
Passed in 1947, the Taft-Hartley Act stated that employees do not have to be members of a union before being hired. Prior to this act union membership was a condition for employment. Now most union contracts are union shop agreements.

FIGURE 17–5

States with right-to-work laws.

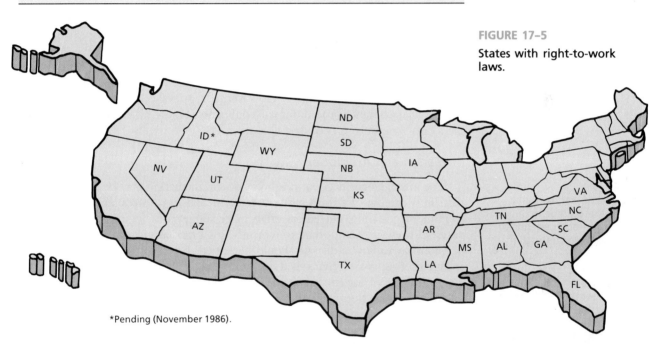

*Pending (November 1986).

union shop agreement
Clause in labor-management agreement that says workers do not have to be members of a union to be hired but must agree to join the union within a prescribed period.

right-to-work laws
Legislation that gives workers the right, under an open shop, to join a union—if it is present—or not.

open shop agreement
Agreement in right-to-work states that gives workers the option to join or not join if one exists in their workplace.

Labor today favors the union shop as the primary means for ensuring security. Under the **union shop agreement,** workers do not have to be members of a union to be hired for a job, but must agree as a condition of employment to join the union within a prescribed period (usually 30, 60, or 90 days). The Taft-Hartley Act recognizes the legality of the union shop but grants individual states the power to outlaw the union shop through passage of **right-to-work laws.** To date, 21 states have passed such legislation (see Figure 17–5). In a right-to-work state, workers under the **open shop agreement** have the option to join a union, if one is present in the workplace, or to not join.

In the future, the focus of union negotiations will no doubt shift as issues such as child care and mandatory drug and AIDS testing challenge union members.

Resolving Labor-Management Disagreements

The rights of labor and management are outlined in the negotiated labor-management agreement. On acceptance by both sides, the agreement becomes a guide to work relations between the firm's employees and managers. However, the signed agreement doesn't necessarily mean the end to employee-management negotiations. As you might suspect, there are sometimes differences concerning interpretations of the labor-management agreement. For example, managers may interpret the agreement to mean that the selection of who works overtime is their decision. The employees may interpret it to mean that managers must select employees for overtime based on employee seniority. If controversies such as this cannot be resolved among the two parties, a grievance may be filed.

A grievance is a charge by employees that management is not abiding by the terms of the negotiated labor agreement. Issues such as overtime rules, promotions, layoffs, transfers, and so on are generally sources of employee grievances. A grievance can be filed by an individual or the entire labor organization. Handling employee grievances demands a good deal of contact between labor officials and managers.

The majority of grievances are negotiated by shop stewards (labor officials that work permanently in an organization and represent employee interests on a daily basis) and supervisory managers. However, if a grievance is not resolved at this level, formal grievance procedures will commence. Figure 17–6 illustrates the steps the formal grievance procedure follows.

Mediation and Arbitration

mediation
The use of a third party, called a mediator, to encourage both parties to continue negotiating.

If labor-management negotiations break down, mediation may be necessary. **Mediation** is the use of a third party, called a mediator, to encourage both sides to continue negotiating. Mediators often make suggestions for resolving work disputes. However, it's important to remember that mediators make suggestions, not decisions, as to how a dispute should be settled. Elected officials, attorneys, and college professors are often called on to serve as mediators in a labor dispute.

arbitration
The agreement to bring in an impartial third party (an arbitrator) to render a binding decision on a labor dispute.

Another tool used to resolve labor-management conflicts is arbitration. **Arbitration** is the agreement to bring in an impartial third party (an arbitrator) to render a *binding decision* in a labor dispute. Over 90 percent of the negotiated labor-management agreements in the United States call for the use of an arbitrator to end labor disputes. The arbitrator must be acceptable to both labor and management. You probably have heard of baseball players such as Don Mattingly filing for arbitration to resolve a salary dispute. An arbitrator ruled in his case that the New York Yankees had to pay him $2 million in salary for the 1988 baseball season.

Tactics Used in Labor-Management Conflicts

When labor and management reach an impasse in their collective bargaining, and negotiations break down, either side or both sides will use specific tactics to further their objectives and perhaps sway public opinion. The primary tactics of labor are the strike and the boycott. Unions might also use pickets and work slowdowns as tactics to get desired changes. Management tactics include lockouts, injunctions, strikebreakers, and bankruptcy. Before they were outlawed by the Norris–La Guardia Act, management used yellow-dog contracts. In the following sections, we will look at each of these labor and management strategies.

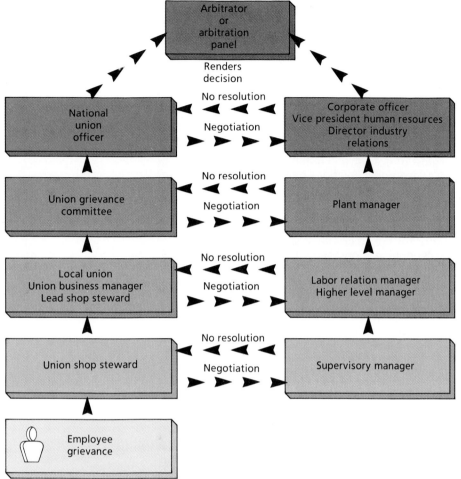

FIGURE 17-6
The grievance resolution process. The grievance process may move through several steps before the issue is resolved. At each step, the issue is negotiated between union officials and managers. If no resolution comes internally, an outside arbitrator may be mutually agreed upon. If so, the decision by the arbitrator is binding (legally enforceable).

Union Tactics

The strike has historically been the most potent union tactic. A *strike* means that workers refuse to go to work. The strike provides clear public focus on the situation and at times causes operations to totally shut done. Often strikers will also *picket* the plant. This means that they will walk around outside the organization carrying signs and talking with the public and the media about the issues. Most of you saw this happening when the NFL football players went on strike during the 1987 season. Unfortunately, strikes have often generated violence and extended bitterness because emotions on both sides frequently reach a boiling point. Today, the strike is used less often as a labor tactic. In the 1950s, there were some 400 strikes annually, on the average. In 1988, there were only 46 strikes.[1] Figure 17-7 (see page 544) identifies the major reasons why both labor and management seek to avoid strikes if at all possible. Nonetheless, as the NFL, airline, teacher, and nurses strikes in recent years have illustrated, the strike is not dead as a labor tactic.

You realize how important a worker is when he or she goes on strike. Can you imagine what an economic and social disaster it would be if doctors and nurses went on strike, or all teachers in a town left work at once? In 1989, teachers in Los

FIGURE 17–7

The growing costs of strikes. Note that there are legal expenses and costs in morale as well as profit loss and the cost of strikebreakers. After the strike, there are overtime costs and the cost of lost customers.

Prestrike costs

Legal expenses
Potential loss of orders from customers
Expense of executive negotiations
Potential slowdowns in productivity
Downturn in worker morale
Alterations in strategic planning scheme

Strike costs

Legal expenditures
Loss of profits from production stoppage or slowdown
Cost of executive negotiations
Added public relations costs
Inventory-carrying costs
Possible extra security costs
Overtime in other plants
Continuing salary expense for nonunion workers
Cost of executive strike negotiations
Continuing fringe benefits for strikers
Management cost in performing operative tasks
Potential loss of goodwill
Cost of hiring strikebreakers

Poststrike costs

Needed overtime to catch up on past orders
Loss of customers who switched allegiance
Productivity slump
Possible training of replacement workers
Chance of boycotts
Loss of consumer goodwill and loyalties

The Teamsters Union is one of the largest in the United States. When they go on strike, the impact can be tremendous. Imagine what would happen if most truckers went on strike. The whole distribution system would be affected. That is why strikes are such a potent union weapon.

primary boycott
Union encouragement of members not to buy products of a firm involved in a labor dispute.

secondary boycott
An attempt by labor to convince others to stop doing business with a firm that is the subject of a primary boycott.

Angeles went on strike and caused quite a disruption. Several cities have already experienced the smell and disruption caused when garbage collectors go on strike. How would college students react if the faculty went on strike?

Unions also use boycotts in an attempt to obtain their objectives. Boycotts can be classified as primary or secondary. A **primary boycott** occurs when labor encourages its membership, as well as the general public, not to buy the product(s) of a firm involved in a labor dispute. A **secondary boycott** is an attempt by labor to convince others to stop doing business with a firm that is the subject of a primary boycott. For example, if a union initiates a boycott against a supermarket chain because it carries the products of a target of a primary boycott, this would be considered a secondary boycott. The law permits labor to conduct authorized primary boycotts. The Taft-Hartley Act seemed to prohibit the use of secondary boycotts by labor unions.

A 1988 Supreme Court decision has again opened the door for unions to use secondary boycotts. In this case, a firm hired a contractor to build a store in a new mall. The contractor hired to build the store was the H. J. High Construction Company. The construction union thought that High was paying substandard wages and passed out handbills asking customers not to shop the mall's 85 stores. That case opened the door for unions to initiate boycotts against virtually any company that has a connection with a unionized employer. For example, one union has instituted secondary boycotts against banks that finance International Paper Co. because the union is on strike against International Paper and this puts more pressure on the company. The United Food & Commercial Workers Union began a secondary boycott against a Price Chopper supermarket that had just opened because the supermarket's low wages might cause a trend. You can see the power of such tactics. As a consumer you can also see the additional cost of food shopping. You may also sympathize with the union workers who want to maintain their income levels.

In 1989, Eastern Airline employees threatened a secondary boycott of the railroads. Through a quirk of the law, that would have been legal because airlines are under the Railway Labor Act.[2] Can you imagine what could happen to transportation in the United States if airline and railroad workers went on strike together?

Management Tactics

Management also uses specific tactics to attain its goals. Historically, management has made use of such tools as **lockouts** (putting pressure on unions by temporarily closing the business and denying employment to the worker) and **yellow-dog contracts** (in which employees had to agree as a condition of employment not to join a union) to thwart excessive labor demands. Lockouts are rarely used today and yellow-dog contracts are outlawed by the Norris–La Guardia Act. Today, management most often calls on the injunction and use of strikebreakers to stymie labor demands it sees as unreasonable.

An **injunction** is a court order directing someone to do something or refrain from doing something. Management has sought injunctions to order striking workers back to work, limit the number of pickets that can be used during a strike, or otherwise deal with issues that could be detrimental to the public welfare. For a court to issue an injunction, management must show "just cause." To stop Eastern airline employees from shutting down the railroads, local transportation agencies went to court and got an injunction preventing the shutdown.[3]

The use of strikebreakers has been a source of hostility and violence in labor relations. **Strikebreakers** (called *scabs* by unions) are workers who are hired to do the jobs of striking workers until the labor dispute is resolved. It caused quite a stir when the NFL owners went out and hired replacement players during the football strike in 1987. Several such players stayed on the teams when the strike ended.

lockouts
A management tool for putting pressure on unions by closing the business.

yellow-dog contracts
Contract agreements whereby employees agreed not to join a union as a condition of employment (outlawed by the Norris–La Guardia Act).

injunction
A court order directing someone to do something or refrain from doing something.

strikebreakers
Workers hired to do the jobs of striking workers until the labor dispute is resolved.

Certain workers have such important positions that they are not allowed to strike. For example, it would be chaotic if we allowed army or police officers or air traffic controllers to strike. Over 11,000 air traffic controllers lost their jobs when they went on strike. President Reagan enforced the law and would not let strikers return to work. Airports are still working to replace those lost workers and bring air traffic controllers up to full strength with experienced workers.[4] In 1989, the most publicized strikes involved coal miners in the United States and the Soviet Union. These disputes will have center stage in the early 1990s.

A recent tactic that management has used to combat labor unions is the use of bankruptcy laws to void union contracts (bankruptcy laws will be discussed in Chapter 23.) The U.S. Supreme Court has upheld this tactic against the opposition of the labor movement. In such cases, companies wishing to escape a labor-management agreement declare bankruptcy, thereby releasing themselves from agreements with labor unions. For example, Continental Airlines employed this tactic to escape from its union contracts.

The Future of Unions and Labor-Management Relations

Many new labor-management issues have emerged in the last decade that may encourage certain employees to join unions. Some employees feel that their pay is way below the standards in other industries. This is especially true of female employees in service industries. Nurses, teachers, secretaries, and social workers come to mind immediately. Who will fight for parental leave, child care, benefits for part-time workers, and more, if not the unions?

Consider this; since 1980, the percentage of health-care workers who have joined unions has risen from 14 percent to 20 percent.[5] Union leaders learned that organizing nurses was similar to organizing factory workers in the past. Health-care workers belong to a corporate hierarchy where they often feel they have little control and they are used to working together. They have much in common with the assembly line workers of the past. But what about home-care nurses who help the elderly eat, dress, and shop? They couldn't be organized by handing out leaflets at the hospital door. Rather, research showed that 90 percent of the workers were black women, many of whom attended church. The Service Employees International Union used 100 local black ministers and got many nurses to join.[6]

Doctors and nurses are examples of service workers who are discovering the benefits of unionization. Nurses want more pay and better treatment. Doctors are also feeling pressure from cost-cutting measures that limit how much they can charge and other freedoms they once had. Other service workers are joining unions at a record pace to win more rights and bargaining power.

Once nurses found the benefits of joining unions, doctors began to take notice. Some 200,000 doctors are salaried workers. They have suffered as hospitals have cut costs and limited the pay of doctors. The Union of American Physicians & Dentists has increased fourfold since 1982 to over 43,000 members. Doctors are now considering joining nurses in unions to increase their leverage in negotiating with management.

Other service workers cannot be far behind. Janitors will notice how effective it is to be unionized and continue joining. Secretaries, librarians, and other service workers will be added to union ranks. Professors may join the trend as they already have in many schools across the country. Note the emphasis on service workers. Union membership has fallen dramatically among industrial (manufacturing) workers and industrial workers are making up a smaller and smaller proportion of all workers.

Organized labor is at a crossroads. The unionized share of the nonfarm work force has declined from a peak of 35.5 percent in 1945 to less than 17 percent in 1987 (see Figure 17–8). The United Mine Workers alone has lost 84 percent of its membership since 1942. The United Steelworkers Union had 1.3 million workers in 1974 and now has only 572,000.[7] Additional problems include foreign competition, which has forced union workers and management to sit down and work out reasonable agreements that enable U.S. firms to stay competitive. To save jobs, many unions are granting concessions to management (see Figure 17–9 on page 548). Furthermore, public support for organized labor has drifted due to such unfavorable actions as the government attempting to take control of the Teamsters Union in 1988. Has the death knell sounded for organized labor?

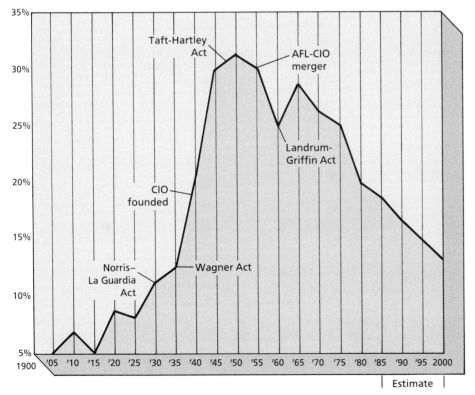

FIGURE 17–8

Percentage of union membership in the nonagricultural work force. Union membership as a percentage of the work force grew rather steadily until 1953, when it declined rather steadily. This trend has continued since then. There may be a reversal of the trend if unions are successful in recruiting service workers such as teachers, nurses, and doctors.

FIGURE 17–9

Work rule changes granted by organized labor. Unions are granting management changes in its rules. For example, because of the influence of the unions, the airline industry is eliminating unnecessary jobs and allowing the pilots more flexibility in scheduling both daily and weekly hours.

UNIONS ARE GRANTING THESE MAJOR CHANGES IN THE WORK RULES . . .		. . . IN THESE INDUSTRIES
Job assignments	Cutting size of crews; enlarging jobs by adding duties; eliminating unneeded jobs	Steel, autos, railroads, meatpacking, airlines
Skilled maintenance and construction	Combining craft jobs such as millwright, welder, rigger, and boilermaker; allowing journeymen to perform helper's duties; permitting equipment operators to run more than one machine	Autos, rubber, steel, petroleum, construction
Hours of work	Giving up relief and wash-up periods; allowing management more flexibility in scheduling daily and weekly hours; working more hours for the same pay	Autos, rubber, steel meatpacking, trucking, airlines (pilots), textile
Seniority	Restricting use of seniority in filling job vacancies, "bumping" during layoffs, and picking shifts	Autos, rubber, meatpacking, steel
Wages	Restricting pay to hours worked rather than miles traveled	Railroads, trucking
Incentive pay	Reducing incentives to reflect changing job conditions	Rubber, steel
Team work	Allowing team members to rotate jobs; permitting pay for knowledge instead of function; allowing management to change crew structure to cope with new technology	Autos, auto suppliers, steel, rubber

Source: Copyright © 1983, *Business Week* Publishing.

Definitely not. Nonetheless, to grow, unions will have to adapt to a work force that is increasingly white collar, female, and professional. The growing service sector is a major target of union organizing efforts. As Figure 17–10 highlights, the National Education Association is now one of the largest labor organization in the workplace. Additionally, unions must continue to recognize the need for changes in work rules to permit U.S. companies to compete with growing international-based firms.

MEMBERS*	UNION
974,000	Automobile, Aerospace and Agricultural Implement Workers of America, International Union, United
115,000	Bakery, Confectionary, and Tobacco Workers International Union
110,000	Boilermakers, Iron Ship Builders, Blacksmiths, Forgers and Helpers, International Brotherhood of
95,000	Bricklayers and Allied Craftsmen, International Union of
609,000	Carpenters and Joiners of America, United Brotherhood of
228,000	Clothing and Textile Workers Union, Amalgamated
524,000	Communications Workers of America
1,800,000	Education Association, National (Ind.)
200,000	Electrical, Radio and Machine Workers, International Union of
85,000	Electrical, Radio and Machine Workers of America, United (Ind.)
791,000	Electrical Workers, International Brotherhood of
142,000	Fire Fighters, International Association of
989,000	Food and Commercial Workers International Union, United
199,000	Government Employees, American Federation of
141,000	Graphic Communications Workers
327,000	Hotel and Restaurant Employees and Bartenders, International Union
140,000	Iron Workers
383,000	Laborers' International Union of North America
210,000	Ladies' Garment Workers' Union, International
186,000	Letter Carriers, National Association of
520,000	Machinists and Aerospace Workers, International Association of
230,000	Mine Workers of America, United (Ind.)
188,000	Nurses' Association; American (Ind.)
125,000	Office and Professional Employees International Union
108,000	Oil, Chemical and Atomic Workers International Union
350,000	Operating Engineers, International Union of
133,000	Painters and Allied Trades of the United States and Canada, International Brotherhood of
232,000	Paper Workers International Union, United
226,000	Plumbing and Pipe Fitting Industry of the United States and Canada, United Association of Journeyman and Apprentices of the
160,000†	Police, Fraternal Order of (Ind.)‡
232,000	Postal Workers Union, American
102,000	Railway, Airline and Steamship Clerks, Freight Handlers, Express and Station Employees, Brotherhood of
106,000	Retail, Wholesale and Department Store Union
106,000	Rubber, Cork, Linoleum and Plastic Workers of America, United
688,000	Service Employees International Union
144,000†	Sheet Metal Workers' International Association
997,000	State, County and Municipal Employees of America, American Federation of
572,000	Steelworkers of America, United
470,000	Teachers, American Federation of
1,800,000	Teamsters, Chauffeurs, Warehouseman and Helpers of America, International Brotherhood of (Ind.)
160,000	Transit Union, Amalgamated
108,000	Transportation Union, United

Note: Figures are most recent available.
*Data are for 1986.
†1982.
‡Did not reply.

FIGURE 17–10

National labor organizations with membership over 100,000.
This list of labor organizations shows you the extent of union membership in the United States. The International Brotherhood of Teamsters, Chauffeurs, Warehouseman and Helpers of America and the National Education Association top the charts in the number of members.

Source: The *Information Please Almanac* (Boston: Houghton Mufflin, 1988), p. 59.

CORPORATE RAIDERS BEWARE! HERE COME THE UNIONS

The decade of the 1980s introduced us to the likes of T. Boone Pickens, Carl Icahn, Sir Jimmy Goldsmith, and other financiers who personified the term corporate *raider*. According to Drexel Burnham Lambert, Inc., the 1990s could be the decade we are introduced to "new" corporate raiders who go by the names—Machinists, Teamsters, and Autoworkers.

Drexel Burnham Lambert believes that union buyouts are a distinct possibility in the next wave of corporate takeovers. Furthermore, they see these efforts as easier to finance than earlier takeovers involving the sale of junk bonds (these will be discussed in Chapter 21) primarily because they rely on job cutbacks and concessions rather than future asset sales. If union buyouts become a reality, the traditional focus of leaving the management of firms to managers will shift and labor will assume a more active role in running the company. The takeover trend could also induce unions to initiate a takeover move for companies where they anticipate future problems to surface. Already, moves have been made by the United Autoworkers and United Steelworkers to begin the union takeover process.

As you might suspect, some philosophical questions come into consideration here. John Peterpaul of the International Association of Machinists solidly opposes his union getting involved in the managing and decision-making processes. Eugene Keilin of Lazard Freres & Co. raises an issue that unions will have to assume the role of investors rather than job savers if these takeovers in fact occur. Another interesting question to ponder is what unions will do when they are faced with the question of cutting jobs or imposing wage cuts to stay competitive. Perhaps Ray Minella of Merrill Lynch Capital Markets raises the most direct question, "Will unions have to turn into what they have fought against?" Only time will tell.

Source: Aaron Bernstein, "Move Over Boone, Carl, and Irv—Here Comes Labor," *Business Week*, December 14, 1987, pp. 124–25.

Most importantly, labor and management must continue the retreat from the "us versus them" attitude that has historically dominated labor relations and seek to build a "we" attitude between labor and management proponents. Unions developed because the employees felt that they could not obtain what they wanted without unions. If managers are responsive to their employees' wants and needs and bring them into the decision-making process, then there is no real need for unions. This requires changes in management, but it also requires the cooperation of employees. Pay concessions and givebacks by labor in the 1980s are a step in this direction.

One issue that is likely to receive more attention in the 1990s is that of executive compensation. Union workers can hardly be expected to make all kinds of wage and work concessions when the chairman or president of the firm is making millions of dollars. If the firm is strong, labor should get its share. If the firm is weak, management should not be earning millions. Or so the debate goes. Let's look at the issue in more depth.

PROGRESS CHECK

- What kind of workers are joining unions today and why?

- What are the major pieces of legislation that affected union growth and what is covered in each?

- How have the objectives of unions changed over time and why?

- What are the major tactics used by unions and management to assert their power?

THE ISSUE OF EXECUTIVE COMPENSATION

How much should a top executive earn? In recent years, Michael Jackson sang his way to $35 million, Clint Eastwood squinted out $10 million, Martina Navratilova volleyed her way to $4 million and Dan Rather reported the news for $2.2 million. Heavyweight champion Mike Tyson earned $22 million for 91 seconds' work in his 1988 bout with Michael Spinks. Over 100 major-league baseball players make over $1 million a year.

Is it out of line, therefore, that the chairman of Walt Disney should make $40 million and that E. A. Horrigan Jr. of RJR Nabisco should make almost $22 million? The U.S. free enterprise system is built on the incentives that allow executives to make that much. Stockholders seem to support such pay; nevertheless, some people feel that executive compensation is way too high (see Figure 17–11 on page 552).

Recently it was reported that average total payment paid to top executives of the nation's top 100 industrial companies exceeded $2 million.[8] Remember Charles Lazarus from Toys "R" Us? We profiled him in Chapter 7. How much did he make in 1987? Over $60 million![9] Doesn't that encourage you to study hard to become a chief executive?

Thomas J. Peters, one of the authors of *In Search of Excellence,* feels that, "The executive-compensation system has no coherence, makes no sense, and, at a time when there's a requirement for violent restructuring in companies, has a very negative impact." He says further, "You can't say there's anything else than grotesque inequity" over the fact that workers are being forced to take pay cuts while their managers are making millions.[10] The average chief executive now makes 45 times the compensation of a middle manager, 93 times the compensation of a factory worker, and 72 times the compensation of the average teacher. *The Wall Street Journal* reports that the spectacle of lavishly compensated U.S. executives ordering cutbacks, layoffs and general corporate austerity for everyone else is beginning to rankle employees, small investors and unions. *Business Week* found the pay "difficult to justify."[11] What really annoys some people is that executive compensation does not necessarily correlate with effectiveness. Some of those making millions of dollars are losing money for their firms. Nonetheless, the feeling persists among many experts that the law of supply and demand holds and that executives are worth what they get or the market would not pay them that much.

Since firms compete globally, checking what executives in other countries make may prove revealing. In the United States, an executive of a billion-dollar firm makes $2 million on average, including salaries, bonuses, and incentives. The country that comes closest to that pay, France, averages $577,000 for a similar firm. In Switzerland, it would be $468,000, in West Germany about $403,000, and in Britain about $342,000. Our biggest competitor, Japan, pays only $330,000. In Europe, companies often have workers on their boards of directors. Since they set executive pay, the imbalance between starting pay and top pay is less (6 to 1) versus the United State's 14 to 1.[12] What do these figures say about the level of executive pay in the United States, if anything?

FIGURE 17–11   The 25 highest-paid executives.

	COMPANY	1988 SALARY AND BONUS	LONG-TERM COMPENSATION	TOTAL PAY
		(thousands of dollars)		
1. Michael D. Eisner, Chairman	Walt Disney	$ 7,506	$32,588	$40,094
2. Frank G. Wells, President	Walt Disney	3,778	28,357	32,135
3. E. A. Horrigan Jr., Former Vice-Chairman	RJR Nabisco	1,280	20,450	21,730
4. F. Ross Johnson, Former CEO	RJR Nabisco	1,836	19,235	21,071
5. Martin S. Davis, Chairman	Gulf & Western	3,673	12,577	16,250
6. Richard L. Gelb, Chairman	Bristol-Myers	1,475	12,578	14,053
7. William P. Stiritz, Chairman	Ralston Purina	1,029	11,919	12,948
8. Baine P. Kerr, Chairman, Executive Committee	Pennzoil	10,706	839	11,545
9. J. Hugh Liedtke, Chairman	Pennzoil	10,872	664	11,536
10. Paul Fireman, Chairman	Reebok Intl.	11,439	—	11,439
11. James D. Robinson III, Chairman	American Express	2,764	8,169	10,933
12. Kenneth H. Olsen, President	Digital Equipment	932	9,052	9,984
13. Donald E. Petersen, Chairman	Ford Motor	3,340	6,579	9,919
14. John Sculley, Chairman	Apple Computer	2,479	7,013	9,492
15. Dean L. Buntrock, Chairman	Waste Mgt.	1,400	7,002	8,402
16. Paul B. Rooney, President	Waste Mgt.	1,060	6,425	7,485
17. P. Roy Vagelos, Chairman	Merck	1,608	5,286	6,894
18. John H. Bryan Jr., Chairman	Sara Lee	1,367	5,396	6,763
19. Andrew S. Grove, CEO	Intel	684	5,746	6,430
20. Stephen M. Wolf, Chairman	UAL	575	5,790	6,365
21. John E. Lyons, Vice-Chairman	Merck	908	5,414	6,322
22. Joseph D. Williams, Chairman	Warner-Lambert	1,310	4,814	6,124
23. Louis V. Gerstner Jr., Former President	American Express	2,394	3,564	5,958
24. John H. Stookey, Chairman	Quantum Chemical	1,429	4,454	5,883
25. Stanton R. Cook, CEO	Tribune	1,064	4,789	5,853

The 10 largest golden parachutes.

	COMPANY	REASON FOR PAYMENT	TOTAL PACKAGE*
1. F. Ross Johnson, CEO	RJR Nabisco	Leveraged buyout	$53,800,000
2. E. A. Horrigan, Vice-Chairman	RJR Nabisco	Leveraged buyout	45,700,000
3. Gerald Tsai Jr., Chairman	Primerica	Commerical Credit takeover	46,800,000
4. Edward P. Evans, Chairman	Macmillan	Maxwell takeover	31,900,000
5. Kenneth A. Yarnell, President	Primerica	Commercial Credit takeover	18,400,000
6. John D. Martin, Executive Vice-President	RJR Nabisco	Leveraged buyout	18,200,000
7. Sanford C. Sigoloff, Chairman	Wickes	Leveraged buyout	15,900,000
8. Whitney Stevens, Chairman	J.P. Stevens	West Point-Pepperell takeover	15,700,000
9. Philip L. Smith, Chairman	Pillsbury	Grand Metropolitan takeover	11,000,000
10. Wilhelm A. Mallory, Senior Vice-President	Wickes	Leveraged buyout	7,500,000

*Includes final salary, bonus, long-term compensation, certain retirement benefits, and estimated future annuity payments as well as parachute.

Source: Reprinted from the May 1, 1989, issue of *Business Week* by special permission, © 1989 by McGraw-Hill, Inc.

It is important to recognize that most of these executives are responsible for billion-dollar corporations and work 70-plus hours a week. Many can show their stockholders that their decisions turned failure to success (Lee Iacocca at Chrysler, for example). There is no "answer" to fair compensation for executives. What's your opinion? This subject could be debated in class to get the views of a variety of people. After all, you may be one of those executives some day.

GOLDEN PARACHUTES—ANOTHER EXECUTIVE PAY ISSUE

A golden parachute is a fund set aside for corporate managers whose jobs may be threatened by a takeover by another firm. To attract an executive to a firm, the board may offer that executive a golden parachute to assure him or her that the job is a secure one—or else the golden parachute will protect against a crash. Why is this an issue? Because the golden parachutes are often huge.

The issue began when William Agee left Bendix with a $4 million golden parachute. In 1986, 30 percent of the top 250 companies had such plans, versus 15 percent five years previously, so the issue is growing in importance. So are the rewards. In 1986, Michael Bergerac got a $34 million golden parachute when he left Revlon after a takeover by Pantry Pride. William W. Granger, Jr., had been in charge of Beatrice Company less than four months when

Kohlberg Kravis Roberts began negotiations to make the company private. Mr. Granger's golden parachute was $7 million. RCA created an estimated $33 million in bailout deals for some 60 executives when General Electric came bidding to buy them out.

Do executives deserve millions of dollars for losing their jobs? Are golden parachutes fair? These are serious questions being raised today. In fact, the question is being considered by the U.S. Congress. A bill is under consideration that would allow golden parachutes *only* if they were approved by a majority vote of the company's stockholders. Figure 17–11 also shows the 10 largest golden parachutes today. Note that Ross Johnson received $53 million as a result of a takeover of RJR Nabisco. That does make leaving a little easier, you must admit.

Source: Eleanor Johnson Tracy, "Parachutes A-Popping," *Fortune,* March 31, 1986, p. 66; "Executive Pay: How the Boss Did in '85" *Business Week,* May 5, 1986, pp. 48–58; "Who Made the Most—and Why," *Business Week,* May 2, 1988, pp. 50–56; and "Anti-Chute Provision Put in Bill," *USA Today,* June 22, 1988, p. 1B; and John A. Byrne, Ronald Grover, and Todd Vogel, "Is the Boss Getting Paid Too Much?," *Business Week,* May 1, 1989, pp. 46–52.

The high pay for top executives created tremendous incentives for lower-level executives to work hard to get those jobs. The high pay also creates resentment among workers, some stockholders, and some members of the general public. What is your position on the proper level of top-executive compensation? Is there a way to make the pay more equitable?

How do you justify the fact that many sports leaders and TV stars make millions of dollars? Should top executives take a cut in pay when these people do not? What is the difference between the two groups?

THINKING IT THROUGH

THE ISSUE OF COMPARABLE WORTH

An even more pressing issue than executive pay is that of pay equity for women. This question is taking on additional importance as more and more women enter the labor force. In 1890, only 15 percent of the labor force was female. By 1950, that figure had risen, but to only 25 percent. By 1980, women made up 40 percent of the labor force, and now the figure is closer to 50 percent. More women in the labor force mean more issues: day-care centers, flextime, job sharing, and so forth. But no issue has received more attention than pay equity or comparable worth. **Comparable worth** is the demand for equal pay for jobs requiring similar levels of education, training, and skills.

Today, women earn about 70 percent of what men earn (see Figure 17–12 on page 554).[13] A partial explanation for this disparity is that women only work 50 to 60 percent of their available years once they leave school, whereas men, on the whole, work all of those years.[14] Another explanation is the idea that many women try to work as well as care for their families, and thus take more flexible jobs that pay less. But the main argument is that women make less because they are women

comparable worth
The demand for equal pay for jobs requiring similar levels of education, training, and skills.

FIGURE 17–12

Notice that there was a good increase toward pay parity from 1978 to 1988. That trend is likely to increase, but slowly, during the 1990s. One secret to pay equity is education.

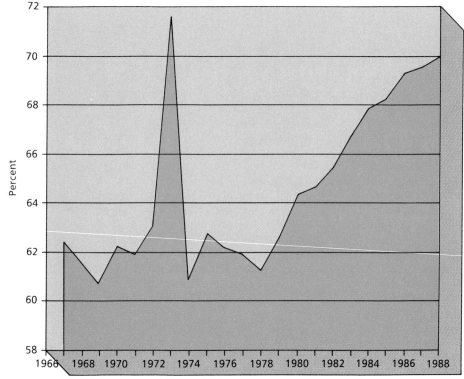

FIGURE 17–12

Notice that there was a good increase toward pay parity from 1978 to 1988. That trend is likely to increase, but slowly, during the 1990s. One secret to pay equity is education.

and are discriminated against. The idea of pay equity is to correct past discrimination by raising the pay in "women's jobs" such as nursing, secretarial work, teaching, and so forth.

Part of the problem has been understanding just what comparable worth means. It does not mean that equal wages should be paid to men and women who do the *same* job. Federal law already requires equal pay for equal work. It is against the law, for example, to pay a female nurse less than male nurse. Rather, the issue of comparable worth centers on comparing the *value* of jobs such as nurse or librarian (traditionally women's jobs) with jobs such as truck driver or plumber (traditionally men's jobs). Such a comparison shows that women's jobs pay less—much less.

As we noted earlier, one way women have fought such discrimination is to use the old tactic of forming unions. During the 1980s, for example, technical and clerical workers at Yale University formed a union. A strike in 1984 won them a 24 percent pay hike over three years. The union members are computer technicians, librarians, secretaries, hospital aides, and research assistants. They earned, on the average, $13,500. The university paid its mostly male truck drivers about 36 percent more. The union continues pushing for even higher increases to correct what they perceive as unfair differences between male and female pay.

Recent Public Sector Comparable Worth Action

The chances are good that women *will* receive adjustments in wages over time. The state of Minnesota, for example, has passed legislation requiring pay equity in public sector jobs. To compare jobs, the state used an instrument called the **Hay**

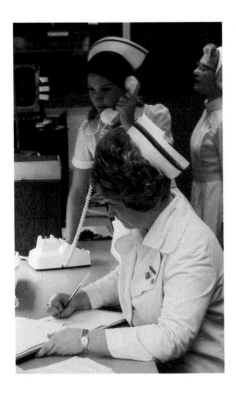

Should a a truck driver earn more than a nurse? Should a plumber make more than a librarian? These are the kinds of questions raised by the proponents of pay equity. Right now the market determines wages. Should the government have a larger role? And how can that be done? This issue will remain important throughout the 1990s.

Guide Chart Profile Method, which awards points based on the employee's knowledge, problem-solving ability, accountability, and working conditions. For example, nurses and vocational-education field instructors both earned 275 points. Yet the nurses (94 percent of whom were female) made a maximum of $1,723 a month, and the instructors, who were all male, made up to $2,260 a month. The average female state worker with *20 years* of experience made *less* than the average newly hired male worker. Minnesota is correcting such inequities and has ordered its cities, counties, and school districts to adopt similar programs, affecting 163,000 workers.

Other states including Iowa, Idaho, New Mexico, Washington, and South Dakota are also adjusting pay scales. Dozens of other states are studying the idea.

Legislation was introduced in 1988 to force companies to provide comparable pay for comparable worth.[15] Such legislation has already been passed in parts of Canada and will remain an issue in the United States for some years.

Hay Guide Chart Profile Method
A technique for measuring pay equity based on an employee's knowledge, problem-solving ability, accountability, and working conditions.

THINKING IT THROUGH

Professors in different departments of a university may make widely different wages, even though they all may have equal education and do equal work. For example, an engineering professor or business professor may make more than an English professor. Is that fair? Should English professors be paid the same using the comparable worth argument? How would that affect the supply and demand for English professors?

What role should the market play in determining wages? What about working conditions? Because a hod carrier (brick carrier) does work that is more strenuous than a bricklayer's, should he or she be paid more? Why isn't hard work rewarded more generously in the market?

Comparable Worth in Industry

Corporations see the writing on the wall, and are giving serious thought to pay equity issues. One tactic, of course, is to resist the movement. Some managers say that *the market* determines wages and that they have not discriminated. "If women want more pay," they say, "let them take jobs that pay more—truck driver, and other 'men's' jobs."

The problem becomes most acute when "the market" creates pay differences that aren't logically corrected by pay equity. For example, nurses in the state of Washington earned 573 points on their job-evaluation scale. Computer systems analysts received only 426 points. In the market, though, systems analysts make about 56 percent more than nurses. Clearly market factors (supply and demand) are a consideration when the *value* of a job is weighed; a clerical supervisor received a higher rating than a chemist, but "the market" pays a chemist 40 percent more. Trying to compare all jobs on a pay equity scale would be virtually impossible and would play havoc with market forces. Today, for example, there is a glut of Ph.D.s in English. English professors thus earn low pay because of the market. Computer software writers are in short supply and receive high wages. Should public and private organizations be forced to pay Ph.D.s in English more because they score higher on some standardized pay-equity test?

The problem seems unmanageable at the national level. This does not mean, however, that some steps toward comparable worth should not be implemented in the private sector. It does mean that the process will be quite complex and will involve much debate—much like the union negotiations of the past.

Many firms have already started comparable-worth type analyses. AT&T, for example, evaluated 20 categories of employment using 14 measurements. The results of the study are now being implemented. Other firms have also implemented changes. The public sector is ahead of private firms on this issue, but comparable worth will be a major issue in businesses now that women make up such a large percentage of the labor force.

PROGRESS CHECK

- How does top executive pay in the U.S. compare with other countries?

- What are golden parachutes and why are they so important today?

- What is the difference between comparable worth and equal pay for equal work?

- What reasons may there be for women earning less than men other than discrimination?

CONTROVERSIAL EMPLOYEE–MANAGEMENT ISSUES

This is an interesting time in the history of employee-management relations because the government is taking a much more active role in mandating what benefits businesses must provide. The proposed new legislation on comparable worth is just one example. In many instances, the government cannot afford to provide social benefits given the huge national debt, so the idea is to force businesses to provide the benefits. Let's look at a couple of growing controversial issues.

A major labor/management issue of the 1990s will be how to best handle child care for employees. Should businesses provide on-site child care centers? Should the federal government provide its own centers? Should those people who have no children subsidize those who do? Such are the issues of the 1990s.

The Issue of Child Care

One of the more important controversial issues today is child-care subsidies and programs. Between 1972 and 1988, federal child-care assistance rose from $1 billion to nearly $7 billion. Some taxpayers are asking whether or not those families that have one member stay home to take care of the children should subsidize those families that do not have anyone stay home. Furthermore, new legislation proposes no income cap on those who receive child care, so a two-income family could earn over $300,000 and receive tax credits that would have to be made up for by some families making much less. The need for child care today is obvious. Some 57 percent of women with children under six work. *The Washington Times* reports that "Only 10 percent of all families are now 'traditional' with mothers home caring for children."[16] Nearly 90 percent of the 50 million working women are likely to become pregnant during their working years, according to the U.S. Census Bureau. Two thirds of the 15 million new entrants into the job market through 1995 will be women.[17] The question is who should provide child care and who should pay for the care?

The number of corporations providing such care now numbers over 3,400. Some of the more creative child-care programs are offered at airlines, hospitals, hotels, police, and fire departments, which operate on a 24-hour basis. Since day-care centers are often geared to a more traditional workday, parents in these industries often need employer assistance. However, the strongest push for company-provided child care is primarily coming from outspoken female employees who are rapidly advancing in the management ranks. They are backed by young male executives who have been forced to bring a toddler to the office when the sitter was sick.[18] Companies have responded by providing:

- Emergency care for those days when an employee's regular arrangements go awry.
- Discount arrangements with national child-care chains.
- Vouchers that offer payments toward whatever child care the employee chooses.
- Flextime and flexible leave (see the figure in the margin).
- Referral services that help identify quality child-care facilities they recommend to employees.
- On-site child-care centers where parents can visit children at lunch or lag times during the workday.

COMPANY EFFORTS TO BALANCE WORK AND FAMILY

BENEFIT OR WORK-SCHEDULE POLICY THAT AIDS EMPLOYEE WITH CHILD CARE	% OF COMPANIES WITH 10 TO 49 EMPLOYEES THAT OFFER BENEFIT OR MAINTAIN POLICY
Flextime	45.1%
Flexible leave	43.8
Voluntary part-time	36.0
Job sharing	16.0
Work at home	9.2
Child-care information or referral services	4.3
Counseling services	3.8
Assistance with child-care expenses	2.4
Employer-sponsored day care	1.9

Source: Bureau of Labor Statistics, 1988.

MAKING ETHICAL DECISIONS

You are the owner of a small, regional brewery that serves a specialized market in three Midwest states. In the past you have considered automating one of the brewery's operations, the racking room, because it could easily be robotized. However, the employees in the racking room have been loyal and hard working. In the past they even voted down union representation, feeling it could cause your plant difficulties. Also, you are aware that the possibility of finding alternative employment for these workers is slim. However, the other day you heard that one of the employees in the racking room was diagnosed as having the AIDS antibody. You realize this person's medical bills could escalate to over $150,000 over the course of the illness, not to mention missed workdays, production slowdowns, and so on. Without a doubt, insurance premiums for your firm will increase. You are aware that legally this employee could not be dismissed because of this medical misfortune, but you could close the racking room pleading the necessity to automate. What would you do? Is your decision good for the business? Is your decision ethical?

As single parent and two-income households continue to grow in the 1990s, it will be interesting to follow this very important and controversial issue. A new twist was added to the debate over child care and other responses to women in the workforce early in 1989. An article in the *Harvard Business Review* suggested that women be given the option of competing equally with men or be put on a "mommy track" where they could balance work and home, but would sacrifice some pay and chance for promotion. This issue calls for some discussion (see Case Two at the end of the chapter).[19]

The Issue of AIDS and Drug Abuse in the Workplace

In a recent poll conducted by Roper Research, the spread of AIDS was identified as the top national concern. It easily outdistanced such issues as crime and drug abuse. By 1991, the Center for Disease Control estimates that almost 270,000 Americans will suffer from AIDS and approximately 55,000 will die. That's close to the number of people who lost their lives in the Vietnam War. These concerns are causing businesses to direct their attention to the issue of AIDS. Since no one predicts an easy solution or quick victory over AIDS, the development of clearcut policies is needed to confront this emerging issue.

One of the more controversial employee-management policies concerns the mandatory testing for the AIDS antibody. As you may recall from Chapter 16, preemployment medical testing cannot be used to intentionally screen out potential employees. If administered, the tests must be given to everyone across the board. More and more firms are insisting on mandatory AIDS testing for potential employees. One of the major reasons why is the cost to an employer that an AIDS-afflicted employee can incur in terms of insurance increases, losses in productivity, increased absenteeism, and employee turnover. However, many firms have gone beyond preemployment testing and suggested all employees be tested for the antibody. Managers argue the information gained allows for the development of a uniform and humanitarian AIDS policy at the workplace.

The grim reality of AIDS hits at the heart of the legal and ethical standards of the company. Management is faced with the challenge of how to best protect the firm without infringing on an employee's legal rights or personal privacy. Employees question the propriety and safety of such testing. The courts may be called on to resolve the controversies in question. Again, this is an issue that bears watching.

Some firms feel that alcohol abuse is an even more serious issue because so many more workers are involved. That and drug abuse are likely to be major concerns in the 1990s. Alcohol was an issue in the 1989 Exxon Valdez oil spill and in several train accidents. Many new programs will be initiated in the 1990s to assist people with drug and alcohol problems.[20]

The Issue of Employee Ownership (ESOPs)

No matter how long and hard workers fight for better pay, they will never get as wealthy as people who actually own companies. At least that is the theory behind **employee stock ownership plans (ESOPs).** As you learned in the Profile, an *ESOP* is a plan whereby employees can buy part or total ownership of the firm where they work. The idea for ESOPs was started by Louis O. Kelso about 35 years ago. His idea was to turn workers into owners by selling them stock. Using this concept, he helped the employees of a newspaper buy their company. Since then, the idea of employees taking over all or some of the ownership of their companies has gained much favor. *Business Week* has called them the "hottest thing in corporate finance since the leveraged buyout."[21] The facts are, however, that ESOPs have had mixed results.

employee stock ownership plans (ESOPs)
Plans whereby employees can buy part or total ownership of the firms where they work.

Benefits of ESOPs

First, the good news. There are now almost 10,000 businesses with ESOPs, covering some 10 million workers (see Figure 17–13: on page 560). Corey Rosen of the National Center for Employee Ownership reports that 98 percent of the firms are profitable. About 40 percent of the firms were sold to employees by owners who were ready to retire. ESOPs gave them a ready market (employees) and good tax breaks as well.[22]

During the past few years, employee participation in ownership has emerged as an important issue in just about every industry and every type of company—in die-casting shops, steel foundries, airlines, bakeries, advertising agencies, industrial equipment suppliers, publishing companies, mutual fund organizations, radio stations, and on and on. Some familiar names of organizations with ESOPs include Polaroid, U.S. West, Procter & Gamble, General Mills, Texaco, Avis, and J. C. Penney. Now ESOPs are being used as "poison pills" to avoid hostile takeovers. Employee owners are expected to vote with management to reject the takeover attempt.[23]

As might be expected, the trend is strongest in such places as California's Silicon Valley, where the passion for ownership has reached epidemic proportions. But ESOPs are popular in other regions of the country as well—even in the industrial Midwest, where basic manufacturing companies are finding it increasingly difficult to attract experienced managers without offering equity incentives.

The basic purpose of employee ownership is to give employees a share in the profits of the firm and thus increase their involvement with the firm. Some of the advantages are:

- *Higher morale* as a result of being part-owner of the firm.
- *Incentives* to produce more efficiently—any increased profits are shared by the workers.
- *Tax benefits*—ESOPs are considered as a special type of pension plan by the government; thus, there are tax breaks for employees.

FIGURE 17–13

The growth of ESOPs. It is clear from this figure that the number of ESOP plans rose dramatically throughout the 1980s. The number of employees involved more than doubled. This phenomenon is likely to continue into the 1990s as employees seek more participation in profits and managers seek lower taxes and new, creative ways of financing firms.

Source: National Center for Employee Ownership, 1989.

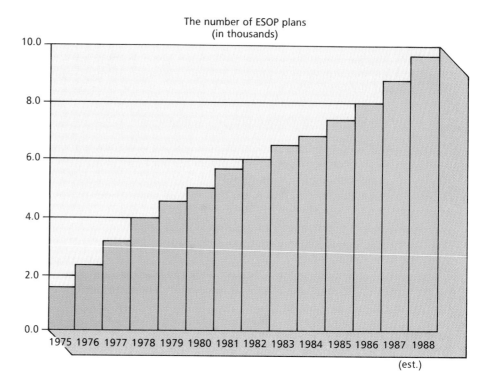

The number of ESOP plans
(in thousands)

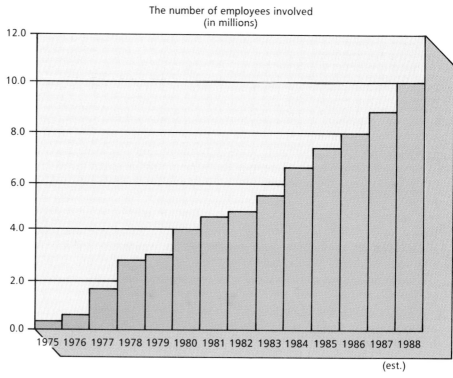

The number of employees involved
(in millions)

■ *More employee participation* in managerial decision making.

■ *More commitment* by all workers to the firm and its success.

■ *A lure* to attract highly skilled people at lower salaries with the promise that they will earn more in the long run as the *company* prospers.

■ *Feelings of cooperation and participation* are generated that cannot be matched in any other way.

These are the actual results at firms such as American West Airlines. It *requires* employees to purchase stock equal to 20 percent of their first year's base pay. Mike Ehl, a 27-year-old customer service representative, says, "Every time I go to the airport, I feel excited by what I'm part of. Equity participation creates a bond that joins people and makes us think and work harder together."[24] Similar feelings are echoed at other companies with ESOPs. It would be misleading, however, to say that ESOPs are an unqualified success. Let's look at the other side.

Problems with Employee Stock Ownership Plans (ESOPs)

Not all ESOP programs work as planned. They can be used to refinance a firm with employees' money without giving employees added participation or more job security. Employees at Dan River, Incorporated, for example, bought 70 percent of the company in a move to save jobs. Nevertheless, employment fell from 12,000 to 8,000 workers, and workers do not feel more involved in management. Employees cannot vote for directors nor on top policy matters. In short, management did very little to include employees in decision making. All employees got was ownership. Even at that, they got Class B common shares that did *not* share equally in profits with the Class A shares managers got. Quite often, it is the case that only management or financial institutions benefit by the establishment of an ESOP.

Studies show that in 85 percent of the companies with ESOPs, employees do *not* have voting rights. ESOPs are also a more risky form of pension plan for employees. Since employees do not control the price of their stock, they can become disenchanted when the market forces the stock price lower, reducing the value of the employees' stock.

At Pan American World Airways, workers took large pay cuts to get 11 percent of the company stock, but felt little was done to improve communications with management or to involve workers in solving problems. At Hyatt-Clark Industries, the leaders of the United Auto Workers Local 736 fought with management over daily operating decisions, staff appointments and salaries, and what to do with profits. At Weirton Steel, the company has been prospering since it was purchased by employees in 1984. Now management wants to cut back on pay to make the company more competitive, but the owner/workers don't want to do it. Again, employees are fighting with management.[25]

In summary, the goal of ESOPs is good—employee ownership, employee pride, and so on—but the *implementation* of such programs is often less than satisfactory. ESOPs are a relatively new managerial concept and thus have much room for improvement. Nonetheless, the good seems to outweigh the negative:

■ A survey of 360 high-tech firms found that those with ESOPs grew two to four times as fast as those where employees did not own stock.

■ A study of 52 employee-owned companies in all industries found that the best performers were those that made the large stock payments to workers' ESOP accounts.

Therefore, when used correctly, ESOPs can be a powerful strategy for improving corporate profitability and increasing employee satisfaction, participation, and *income*.[26] That is what Joseph Vittoria hopes for at Avis (see the opening Profile).

There is some concern about the competitiveness of U.S. business in the future. Firms that have healthy employee-management relations have a better chance to prosper. As managers, a proactive approach is the best strategy to ensure workable employee-management environments. The proactive manager anticipates potential problems and works toward resolving those problems before they get out of hand. Do you foresee any major issues in employee-management relations in the 1990s? Do you have possible solutions to those issues?

PROGRESS CHECK

- What are the major pieces of legislation being proposed that could be considered family issues?
- What are the benefits and drawbacks of raising the minimum wage?
- What are the issues in the recent child-care debate?
- What are the benefits and drawbacks to ESOPs?

SUMMARY

1. Trace the history of organized labor in the United States.

1. There were organized labor unions in the United States before the American Revolution.
   - What was the first union?
     The cordwainers organized a craft union of skilled specialists in 1792. The Knights of Labor, which was formed in 1869, was the first *national* labor organization.
   - How did the AFL–CIO evolve?
     The American Federation of Labor (AFL), formed in 1886, was an organization of craft unions. The Congress of Industrial Organization (CIO), a group of unskilled workers, broke off from the AFL in 1935. Over time, the two organizations saw the benefits of joining together and thus became the AFL–CIO in 1955.

2. Discuss the major legislation affecting labor unions.

2. Much legislation has been passed to balance the power of labor and management.
   - What are the provisions of the major legislation affecting labor unions?
     See Figure 17–1 on page 538.

3. Outline the objectives of labor unions.

3. The objectives of labor unions shift in response to changes in social and economic trends.
   - What topics typically appear in labor-management agreements?
     See Figure 17–3 on page 540.

4. Describe the tactics used by labor and management during conflicts.

4. Labor and management use certain tactics when they reach an impasse in collective bargaining.
   - What are the "weapons" used by unions and management in conflicts?
     Unions can use strikes and boycotts. Management can use injunctions and lockouts.

5. Union membership has dropped dramatically in the industrial sector and is increasing in the service sector.

What will unions have to do to cope with these changes?

In order to grow, unions will have to adapt to a work force that is becoming more white collar, female, and professional. To help keep American businesses competitive in international markets, unions must soften their historic "us versus them" attitude and build a new "we" attitude with management.

6. The median salary of top executives of the top 100 industrial companies exceeds $2 million a year.

What is a "fair" wage for managers?

Manager's salaries are set by the market and organizations. What is "fair" is open to debate.

7. Women want "fair" wages, too. In general, they make about 70 percent of what men make. They are asking for pay equity, or comparable worth.

What is comparable worth (pay equity)?

Comparable worth is the demand for equal pay for jobs requiring similar levels of education, training, and skills.

Why is this an issue?

Comparable worth or pay equity is an issue because "the market" has been the major factor in deciding who gets paid what, and overriding market forces is difficult.

Isn't pay inequity caused by sexism?

There is evidence on both sides of that question, but government or corporate actions would indicate that some remedial action will be taken regardless of causes.

8. With 57 percent of the women with children under six working outside the home, child care has become an important issue of the 1990s.

How are some companies addressing this issue?

Responsive companies are providing day care on the premises, emergency care when scheduled care is interrupted, discounts with child-care chains, vouchers to be used with employees' chosen care centers, and referral services.

9. One of the most recent issues emerging in the 1990s is the testing for the AIDS virus in the workplace.

What are some of the concerns surrounding AIDS and mandatory AIDS testing?

Employers want to cut the costs that an employee with AIDS can incur in terms of insurance increases, losses in productivity, increased absenteeism, and employee turnover. Employees question the accuracy of the tests and the tests' infringement on their personal right to privacy.

10. Employees today are sometimes demanding ownership in the firm.

How are employee stock ownership plans (ESOPs) working?

ESOPs have had mixed results, but the overall trend is favorable. Some 7,000 business now have ESOPs. Properly implemented, such plans can increase morale, motivation, commitment, and job satisfaction. The problem is that many firms have used ESOPs as a capital-raising scheme and have not given employees more participation in management. The issue of the *administration* of ESOPs will be a major one in the next decade.

5. Discuss the role and growth of unions in the future.

6. Explain the issue of executive compensation in the 1990s.

7. Outline the issues surrounding the concept of comparable worth.

8. Explain how child care has become a employee-management issue in the 1990s.

9. Describe the concerns encompassing AIDS testing in the workplace.

10. Explain the benefits and problems of employee stock ownership programs (ESOPs).

1. Many college faculty members do not belong to a union. Faculty pay in many disciplines has fallen way behind pay in industry. Talk with several faculty members about their feelings toward unions. What are the chances that unions will be able to recruit more faculty members? Discuss your findings with the class.

2. Debate the following in class: "Business executives receive a total compensation package that is far beyond their value." Take the opposite side of the issue from your normal stance to get a better feel for the other point of view.

3. Read both sides of the debate on pay equity in the current literature. Then debate the following: "Women's jobs must be paid more so that they are equal to the pay for men's jobs." Again, take the side you do not now support to learn more about the issue.

4. Find the latest information on legislation relative to child care, parental leave, and health insurance for employees. What are the trends? What will the cost of businesses be of these new programs? On balance, do you support or reject such legislation? Why?

5. Develop a list of three worker issues not covered in this chapter. Compare your list with others. Pick one or two popular ones and debate them in class.

CASE ONE   CLOSING UNION STORES AND FACTORIES

Mr. Arzberger worked for 37 years at a Kroger store in Pittsburgh. He lost his job recently when Kroger closed 43 Pittsburgh-area supermarkets because their 2,850 employees refused to accept pay cuts, benefit reductions, and other contract changes. With wage rates as high as they were, Kroger was simply not competitive with the other food chains. A competing food chain paid $2 an hour less, and independent supermarkets were paying $3 to $4 less per hour. Kathy Koch was the head cashier at a Kroger store in Plymouth, Michigan. She, too, managed the closing of her store as Kroger closed 70 of its 82 Michigan stores. Operating costs were simply too high, and unionized employees refused to accept contract concessions. The Michigan closings cost Kroger $10 million in severance pay and other benefits for more than 4,000 employees.

The Pittsburgh stores were purchased by Wetterau, Inc., a food wholesaler that will sell the stores to independent operators who will operate them with lower-paid help.

Other companies—Greyhound, USX, and Goodyear Tire and Rubber, to name just a few—are also saying to workers: your wages are too high. Either accept cutbacks or we may have to go out of business. The city of Dayton, Ohio, is still recovering from the closing of NCR facilities there when union workers did not accept pay cuts years ago.

Greyhound worked through many of its labor concessions by means of an old strike-breaking effort. It hired replacements for 12,000 striking drivers and resumed limited operations. Trans World Airlines is farming out some of its maintenance work to nonunion concerns. Some 3,500 employees might have to work for the new firm for less pay or quit.

United Auto Workers, faced with the choice of closing plants or taking pay cuts, chose the pay cuts but put job security clauses into new contracts. Ford has threatened to move production facilities overseas unless labor conceded to cuts in pay.

DECISION QUESTIONS

1. What would you recommend to union workers whose plants are threatening to close unless they give wage concessions? What is your reaction to the huge salaries being paid corporate executives at Kroger, Greyhound, Ford, and other companies closing down facilities?

2. Is there some alternative to cutting wages or closing down? What is it?

3. Union workers often feel that the company is bluffing when it threatens to close. How can such doubts be settled so more open negotiations can take place?

4. New plant closing laws have been passed that force businesses with a certain number of employees to give 60-day notice if the plant will be closing. Do you think such legislation will help businesses to show employees they are serious about closing a plant and could thus get concessions from labor to prevent the plant closing? Do you think such tactics are ethical?

CASE TWO   CONTROVERSY OVER THE "MOMMY TRACK"

No article in the 1990s is likely to stir up more controversy in business than the one published in the *Harvard Business Review* in the first week of January, 1989. It was written by Felice N. Schwartz and was called "Management Women and the New Facts of Life." The new facts of life are these. More women than ever are entering the workforce. Women now account for 39 percent of all new lawyers and 31 percent of all new MBAs. The problem in the past has been that such women had to choose between the fast track at work or staying home with children. Being a "super mom" and doing both was simply too stressing for most. And it was an unfair burden for women to bear.

Ms. Schwartz's proposal was to have a "mommy track" in businesses. A woman would have one of two choices. Either get on the fast track and compete equally with men and have no children, and thus be able to become partner in the law firm or chief executive officer in the firm. Or choose the "mommy track" where the options for taking extended leave or working part time would allow balancing work and family. The second choice would pretty much preclude a woman from making partner or becoming the top executive.

Many women cheered the article because it at least drew attention to a major issue in employee relations. Others were appalled by the article because it attempted to create a permanent underclass of women who would never make it to the top. What about women who have no spouse and are forced to balance work and home? They would be relegated to "second class citizens" at work because they were on the "mommy track." Over 60 percent of the members of the National Association of Female Executives who answered a survey thought the two-career track was a bad idea.

The benefit of the article is that more and more firms are designing creative ways of blending women with different needs and desires into the workplace. Whether its IBM's extended leave, North Carolina National Bank's flexible scheduling, Steelcase's job sharing, Pacific Telesis' telecommuting, or some combination of these, human resource managers are designing creative ways for women to optimize their business experience while still managing a home, if that is what they desire. As long as those women who want to compete equally with men get a chance to do so, there seems to be little harm in a "mommy track." Nonetheless, even the thought of such a tracking system causes much controversy. The debate is healthy and productive. Women can only benefit from getting this issue out into the open and thinking of creative solutions.

DECISION QUESTIONS

1. Divide the class into two groups: those who feel the "mommy track" is a good idea and those who do not. Debate the issue and see if you can't come up with some agreement on the issue. Notice that this is the same process that unions must follow when negotiating with management. Some solution must be found or arbitration would be necessary.

2. What are the benefits to women and men of a "mommy track" and what are the drawbacks? Take the position of a child of a woman who is married and one who is not: how would they feel about such a track?

3. Do you see a possibility of a woman being on a mommy track at one point in her life and then moving out of the mommy track into a fast track when she gets older or the kids grow up?

4. What about a "daddy track" for men? Are the issues the same? Should companies put more thought into "mommy and daddy tracks" rather than just "mommy tracks?"

Source: "The 'Mommy Track' Has Authorities Arguing about Women's Roles at Work," *Los Angeles Times,* March 19, 1989, p. 3 and 6 of Part IV; Elizabeth Erlich, "The Mommy Track," *Business Week,* March 20, 1989, pp. 126–134; and Beverly Beyette, "What's a Mommy Track and Why are So Many Women Upset About It?," *Los Angeles Times,* March 17, 1989, pp. 1 and 4 of Part V; and "The 'Mommy Track' Debate," *The Wall Street Journal,* May 23, 1989, p. A1.

We have now covered basic management and some of the issues involved. It is time to explore in more depth the inner workings of a firm. We shall begin with accounting. Then we shall explore finance and other important topics. You may not be as familiar with these topics as you were with management topics, so plan to spend more time learning the concepts. These subjects are not hard, but the terminology is new and you must keep up so you understand the discussions.

ACCOUNTING AND FINANCE

VI

SMITH & HAWKEN

Catalog For Gardeners

ACCOUNTING FUNDAMENTALS

18

LEARNING GOALS

After you have read and studied this chapter, you should be able to:

1. Define accounting and explain the differences between managerial accounting and financial accounting.

2. Compare accounting and bookkeeping.

3. Identify and describe the major accounts used to prepare financial statements.

4. Distinguish between an accounting journal and a ledger.

5. Prepare simple income statements and balance sheets, and explain their functions.

6. List the five steps of the accounting cycle.

7. Describe the role of computers in accounting.

8. Explain the impact of using LIFO versus FIFO inventory accounting.

9. Explain the concept of cash flow.

KEY TERMS

accounting, *p. 572*
accounting system, *p. 572*
assets, *p. 577*
balance sheet, *p. 586*
bookkeeping, *p. 575*
cash flow, *p. 592*
certified public accountant (CPA), *p. 574*
cost of goods sold, *p. 582*
current assets, *p. 578*
depreciation, *p. 591*
expenses, *p. 580*
FIFO, *p. 591*
financial accounting, *p. 574*
financial statements, *p. 582*
fixed assets, *p. 578*
fundamental accounting equation, *p. 586*
gross margin (profit), *p. 583*

income statement, *p. 582*
independent audit, *p. 575*
journals, *p. 576*
ledger, *p. 581*
liabilities, *p. 578*
LIFO, *p. 591*
liquidity, *p. 578*
managerial accounting, *p. 573*
net income, *p. 583*
net sales, *p. 583*
operating expenses, *p. 585*
other (intangible) assets, *p. 578*
owners' equity, *p. 580*
private accountant, *p. 575*
public accountant, *p. 574*
retained earnings, *p. 585*
revenue, *p. 582*
trial balance, *p. 588*

Paul Hawken.

PROFILE PAUL HAWKEN, CATALOG MERCHANDISER

Paul Hawken was much like any other beginning businessperson when he started out. He depended on his accountant to tell him how his business was doing. However, he understood little about what she was saying. Here is what Hawken says about that period: "I was operating under a thick film of ignorance that I was too embarrassed to admit. It was only later—after I got over both my ignorance and my embarrassment—that I fully appreciated the role numbers should play in the management of a small business." For seven years, he was at the mercy of his accountant.

One important concept that Hawken learned over time was financial ratios. You see, each kind of business has different costs. Usually, the industry keeps records that show the average cost of things such as inventory, labor, and so forth. Hawken's industry was catalog sales. The important statistic for that industry was that costs for goods, the catalog, and any associated advertising—excluding labor—cannot exceed 70 percent of revenue. He found that to be a very reliable guide. In order to use financial ratios, Hawken learned that he had to keep track of various categories of business himself. He did not want to rely solely on accountants or anyone else because such information was critical to the success of the firm.

Every day, for example, the firm uses a computer to keep track of orders by their source—mail, telephone, and the firm's two retail stores. At the end of the week, it totals the figures and calculates the average sale for each category. It then compares those figures to the same figures for the same week in two previous years. You can see the benefit of such information for planning, staffing, forecasting, and general managerial decision making.

Other information Mr. Hawken finds important includes payroll costs by department as compared with previous years, telephone inquiries and complaints, customer returns, the 50 best-selling products by category and price, and unfilled orders at the end of the day.

All in all, the numbers tell Mr. Hawken and the other managers in the company how well they are doing. Furthermore, the numbers tell them *why* they are doing well. They know whether the costs of doing business are lower or higher then the average firm in that business. They know whether revenues from catalogs are increasing or decreasing and how they compare with retail store sales. In short, almost every business decision Mr. Hawken makes is based on information that comes from data prepared by the accounting department.

Source: Paul Hawken, "Mastering the Numbers," *Inc.*, October 1987, pp. 19–20.

THE IMPORTANCE OF ACCOUNTING

Mr. Hawken is not the only person to discover the importance of accounting to a businessperson. Take the Stutts, for example. They learned the hard way that you'd better keep track of the figures, even if your company seems to be doing well. Brian Stutt and his wife Sharon decided to open an appliance store and began to advertise aggressively. A year and a half later, the Stutts were doing $8.5 million in business. Things were going great.

About a year later, Brian realized that the business was consistently losing money. Later, he discovered why. As long as the business was growing, cash from this month's sales had always covered the previous month's bills. "What we never realized," Sharon said, "was that we were spending $60 to make $50."

You see, Brian and Sharon knew how to sell appliances, but they knew almost nothing about accounting. Sharon had never even *seen* an income statement before. They did not pay any attention to costs because their cash revenues always covered them. Furthermore, neither their banker nor the finance company that handled their inventory demanded financial reports on a routine basis. Their accountant never told them they had a problem. "We were paying our bills," Brian said. "Who worried?"

After a few years, the firm, Warehouse Appliance, had a deficit of almost $1 million. The Stutts had to sell their BMW and Mercedes. They also put their house up for sale.

Sharon left the business for other pursuits. Brian cut back considerably. The sales force was cut from 28 to 5 people. Sales fell closer to $4.5 million. A consultant helped Brian with a five-year plan and a budget. Now, Brian is determined to keep his house. He knows now that growth for its own sake is disastrous. He has learned the value of knowing accounting and finance, no matter what business you are in or what you are most skilled at doing.[1]

Accounting Information Is the Heart of Business Management

Brian and Sharon Stutt's story is repeated hundreds of times every day throughout the country. Small businesses (and often large businesses, too) fail because they do not follow good accounting and financial procedures. Accounting is different from marketing, management, and human resource management in that we know almost nothing about accounting from experience. We have all had some experience with marketing. We have observed and understand management concepts, and human resource procedures seem relatively easy to grasp. But accounting? What is it? What do accountants do? Is it interesting?

The truth is that many people, including some business majors, are not interested in accounting at all. They would rather study marketing or management or finance—anything but accounting. The result is that there are literally thousands of businesspeople who are highly skilled in most areas of business, but relatively ignorant when it comes to accounting. The result? Like the Stutts, they plunge into the world of trade and seem to be doing well. Sales go up. Profits are high. But cash flow is poor; that is, the business simply does not have cash available to pay its bills. The net result is business failure—thousands every year.

The fact is that you will have to know something about accounting if you really want to understand business. Furthermore, accounting is not that hard. You will have to learn a few terms; that is mandatory. Then you have to understand bookkeeping and how accounts are kept. That is not too difficult, either. From the figures accountants gather and record, they prepare reports, called financial statements. It is these reports that tell a businessperson how healthy the business is. It is almost impossible to run a business effectively without being able to read, understand, and analyze accounting reports and financial statements. Accounting reports and financial statements are as revealing of the health of a business as pulse rate and blood pressure reports are in revealing the health of a person. It is up to *you*, however, to make sure your accountants give you the information you need in the form you need it. That means you must know something about accounting too.[2] That is the lesson to be learned from the Profile.

The purpose of this chapter is to introduce you to basic accounting principles. By the end of it, you should have a good idea of what accounting is, how it works, and why it is important. Spend some time learning the terms and reviewing the accounting statements. A few hours invested in learning this material will pay off repeatedly as you become more involved in business or investing, or simply in understanding what's going on out there in the world of business and finance.

WHAT IS ACCOUNTING?

accounting
The recording, classifying, summarizing, and interpreting of financial events and transactions that affect the organization. It may also be viewed as the measurement and reporting (inside and outside the organization) of financial information about the economic activities of the firm to various users.

Accounting is the recording, classifying, summarizing, and interpreting of financial events and transactions to provide management and other interested parties with the information they need to make better decisions. *Transactions* include the buying and selling of goods and services, acquiring insurance, using supplies, and paying taxes. Transactions may be recorded by hand, or they may be recorded in a computer system. As the Profile of Paul Hawken illustrated, the trend is to use computers because the process is repetitive and complex, and computers greatly simplify the task. Computers can handle large amounts of data more quickly and more accurately than manual systems.

After the transactions have been recorded, they are usually classified into groups that have common characteristics. For example, all purchases are grouped together, as are all sales transactions. The business is thus able to obtain needed information about purchases, sales, and other transactions that occur over a given period of time. The methods used to record and summarize accounting data into reports are called an **accounting system** (see Figure 18-1). Systems that use computers enable an organization to get financial reports daily if they so desire. One purpose of accounting is to help managers evaluate the financial condition and the operating performance of the firm so that they may make better decisions. Another is to report financial information to people outside the firm such as owners, lenders, suppliers, and the government (for tax purposes).

accounting system
The methods used to record and summarize accounting data into reports.

FIGURE 18-1

The accounting system. The inputs to an accounting system include sales documents and other documents. The data are recorded, classified, and summarized. They are then put into summary financial statements such as the income statement and balance sheet.

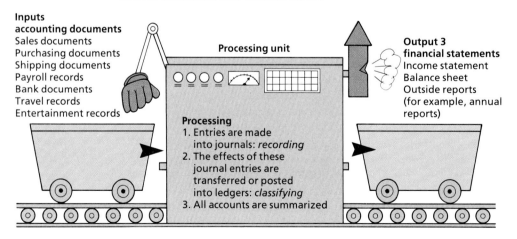

Inputs
accounting documents
Sales documents
Purchasing documents
Shipping documents
Payroll records
Bank documents
Travel records
Entertainment records

Processing unit

Processing
1. Entries are made into journals: *recording*
2. The effects of these journal entries are transferred or posted into ledgers: *classifying*
3. All accounts are summarized

Output 3
financial statements
Income statement
Balance sheet
Outside reports
(for example, annual reports)

USERS	TYPE OF REPORT
Government taxing authorities (e.g., the Internal Revenue Service)	Tax returns
Government regulatory agencies	Required reports
People interested in the income and financial position of the organization: owners, creditors, financial analyst, suppliers, others	Financial statements found in annual reports (e.g., income statement, balance sheet)
Managers of the firm	Financial statements and various internally distributed financial reports

FIGURE 18–2

Users of accounting information and the required reports.
Many different types of organizations use accounting information to make business decisions. The kinds of reports these users require vary according to the information each user requires. An accountant, then, needs to be able to prepare the appropriate forms.

One purpose of accounting is to report financial information to people outside the company. Investors (owners) and potential investors need all kinds of information, such as sales, profits, and debts. The annual report is an excellent vehicle for communicating financial information.

managerial accounting
Provides information and analyses to managers within the organization to assist them in decision making.

Accounting Is User Oriented

In more basic terms, accounting is the measurement and reporting to various users (inside and outside the organization) of financial information regarding the economic activities of the firm (see Figure 18–2). Accounting has been called the language of business, but it is also the language used to report financial information about nonprofit organizations such as churches, schools, hospitals, fraternities, and governmental units. Accounting can be divided into two major categories: managerial accounting and financial accounting. An accountant working for a firm is likely to do both.

Managerial Accounting

Managerial accounting is used to provide information and analyses to managers within the organization to assist them in decision making. Managerial accounting is concerned with measuring and reporting costs of production, marketing, and other functions (cost accounting); preparing budgets (planning); checking whether or not units are staying within their budgets (controlling); and designing strategies to minimize taxes (tax accounting).

Simple analysis of corporate figures can disclose very important information. For example, a slight month-to-month increase in payroll costs may not appear significant. But multiply that increase by 12 months and the increase in costs can be disastrous. Monitoring figures such as profit margins, unit sales, travel expenses, inventory turnover, and other such data is critical to the success of a firm. Top-management decision making is based on such data.

Some of the questions that managerial accounting reports are designed to answer include:

What goods and services are selling the most and what promotional tools are working best?

How quickly are we selling what we buy and how does that compare with other firms in the same industry?

How much profit is the firm making and does that compare favorably with other firms? If not, why not?

What are our major expenses and are they in line with what other firms spend?

How much money do we make on the investment the owners have made in the firm and does that compare favorably with other firms in the same industry? If not, why not?

How much money are we paying in taxes and how can we minimize that amount?

Will we have enough cash at the end of each month this year to pay our bills and if not, have we made arrangements to borrow that money somehow?

Are our costs of doing business in line with the costs of other firms in the industry and if not, why not?

You can see how important such information is. That is why accounting is a good subject to learn in school.

Financial Accounting

financial accounting
The preparation of financial statements for people outside of the firm (for example, investors).

Financial accounting differs from managerial accounting because the information and analyses are for people outside of the organization. This information goes to owners and prospective owners, creditors and lenders, employee unions, customers, governmental units, and the general public. These external users are interested in the organization's profits, its ability to pay its bills, and other financial information. Much of the information is contained in the annual report, a yearly statement of the financial condition and progress of the firm. Various quarterly reports keep the users more current.

Financial accounting reports answer such questions as:

Has the company's income been satisfactory? Should we invest in this company?

Should we loan money to this company? Will it be able to pay it back?

Can the company afford to raise its salaries? Is it financially strong enough to provide permanent employment?

Is the company financially strong enough to stay in business to honor product warranties?

We hope you are getting the idea that accounting is critical to business and to anyone who wants to understand business. If so, you may want to know more about accounting firms, who the people are who prepare these reports, and how you can be sure that they know what they are doing. Accounting data can be compiled by accountants who work for the firm or by outside accounting firms. We shall discuss the differences below.

Private and Public Accountants

public accountant
Accountant who provides services for a fee to a number of companies; public accountants can conduct independent audits.

certified public accountant (CPA)
An accountant who passes a series of examinations established by the American Institute of Certified Public Accountants (AICPA) and meets the state's requirements for education and experience.

Not all firms want or need a full-time accountant. There are thousands of accounting firms in the United States that will do any accounting task you want. A person who provides accounting services to individuals or firms on a fee basis is called a **public accountant.** Such accountants may help you or a business prepare taxes, do management consulting, or provide assistance in other ways. They may design an accounting system for a new business, help select the right computer hardware and software to run the system, and analyze the financial strength of the firm right from the start. Arthur Andersen, for example, earned about $1 billion in consultancy fees in fiscal 1988. Known for its accounting and auditing advice, Andersen also helps companies redesign their factories to become more efficient.[3]

The accounting profession tries to assure companies that the people they hire are as professional as doctors or lawyers. An accountant who passes a series of examinations established by the American Institute of Certified Public Accountants (AICPA) and meets the state's requirements for education and experience is called a **certified public accountant (CPA).** CPAs have much prestige among their peers and the business community as a whole.

Businesses that do need full-time accountants hire private accountants. In contrast to a public accountant, a **private accountant** works for a single business, government agency, or nonprofit organization. Private accountants may or may not be CPAs. Private accountants who pass the exams given by the National Association of Accountants are called *Certified Management Accountants (CMAs)*.

Private accountants often specialize in a particular task such as designing and installing accounting systems, budgeting, or measuring and controlling costs. Private accountants perform the same services as public accountants with one exception. Public accountants conduct independent audits of accounting and related records. An **independent audit** is an evaluation and unbiased opinion about the accuracy of company financial statements. Private accountants audit as well, but these audits are not *independent* audits because they are not prepared by someone independent of the firm.

Some people get confused about the difference between an accountant and a bookkeeper. We shall clarify that difference next.

private accountant
Accountant who works for a single company.

independent audit
An evaluation and unbiased opinion about the accuracy of company financial statements.

ACCOUNTING VERSUS BOOKKEEPING

Bookkeeping involves the recording of economic activities. It is a rather mechanical process that does not demand much creativity. We shall discuss the process in detail below. Bookkeeping is part of accounting, but accounting goes far beyond the mere recording of data. Accountants *classify* and *summarize* the data. They *interpret* the data and *report* them to management. They also *suggest strategies* for improving the financial condition and progress of the firm. Accountants are especially valuable for income tax preparation and analysis.

bookkeeping
The recording of economic activities.

Now that you understand what accountants do and who they do it for, we can get down to the fundamental aspects of bookkeeping and accounting. Accounting involves the gathering and recording of transactions (for example, the sale of merchandise, the payment of a bill, or the receipt of merchandise into storage), and the periodic preparation of financial statements that summarize those transactions.

In the following sections, you will follow the steps accountants take in their day-to-day work. When we are finished, you should have a better idea of what accountants do and how they do it. You should also be able to read and understand financial statements and discuss accounting intelligently with an accountant and others in the world of business. The goal is not to learn how to *be* an accountant, just to learn the terms and concepts. So let's begin at the beginning.

What Bookkeepers Do

If you were a bookkeeper, the first task you would perform is to divide all of the firm's paperwork into meaningful categories. Those categories would probably include the following:

- Sales documents (sales slips, cash register receipts, and invoices).
- Purchasing documents.
- Shipping documents.
- Payroll records.
- Bank documents (checks, deposit slips).
- Travel records.
- Entertainment records.

A bookkeeper gathers accounting documents, such as sales slips, bills, and travel records, and records them in journals and ledgers. These are the first steps in an accounting system that provides managers and interested outside parties with the information they need about the financial progress and condition of the firm.

journals
Recording devices used for the first recording of all transactions.

Now you would have several piles of papers, much like the piles that are generated in the preparation of income tax forms. You don't want the piles to get too high and unmanageable, so you must begin to record the data from the *original transaction documents* (the sales slips and so forth) into record books. (Thus, the term *bookkeeping*.) These books are called **journals.** They are the books where accounting data are first entered.

PROGRESS CHECK

■ Can you explain the difference between managerial and financial accounting?

■ Could you define accounting to a friend so that he or she would clearly understand what is involved?

■ What is the difference between a private and public accountant? What are certified accountants in each area called?

■ What is the difference between accounting and bookkeeping?

■ Can you name five original transaction documents that bookkeepers use to keep records?

THE "ACCOUNTS" OF ACCOUNTING

After recording the original transaction documents in a journal, the accountant or bookkeeper transfers the data to certain accounts. Hence, the term *accounting*. Accountants use five major accounts to prepare financial statements:

1. *Assets.* Economic resources owned by a firm (for example, land, buildings, machinery).
2. *Liabilities.* Amounts owed by the organization to others.
3. *Owners' equity.* Assets minus liabilities. This account shows how much money would be available to the firm's owners if all its assets were sold and all its liabilities paid off.

Trucks and buildings are called assets of the firm. Assets are tangibles and intangibles that have monetary value. That is, they can be converted to cash or have some value to the firm in other ways. Your assets include the money you have, your clothes, appliances, and other objects you own that could be sold for cash.

4. *Revenues.* The value of what is received for goods sold, services rendered, and from other sources.

5. *Expenses.* Costs incurred in operating the business, such as rent, utilities, salaries, and insurance.

6. *Cost of goods sold.* The total cost of buying goods and storing them for resale to others.

The following material will give you further insight into the accounts used by accountants.

THINKING IT THROUGH

You know how much paperwork is involved in doing your own income taxes. There are often hundreds of sales slips and other documents to sort through, add up, and so forth. Imagine having many times that paperwork every day and you'll appreciate the valuable role a bookkeeper serves. Can you see why most businesses prefer to hire someone to do this work? Would it be worth the time for an owner to do all the paperwork? Can you understand why many businesses find it easier to do this work on a computer?

The Asset Accounts

Assets are what a business owns, but they are also more than that. Assets include productive items (such as equipment, the building, land, furniture, fixtures, and motor vehicles) that contribute to income as well as intangibles such as patents or copyrights. Assets include the following:

assets
Economic resources owned by a firm, such as land, buildings, and machinery.

- Cash (cash on hand, petty cash, and deposits in banks).
- Accounts receivable (money owed to a business from customers who bought goods on credit).
- Inventory.
- Investments.
- Land.
- Equipment.
- Buildings.
- Motor vehicles.
- Patents.
- Copyrights.

FIGURE 18–3

Classifications of assets. Assets are classified by how quickly they can be turned into cash (liquidity). The most liquid are called current assets. Those that are hard to sell quickly are called fixed assets. Other assets of value include patents and copyrights.

Current assets

Fixed assets

Copyright

Other assets

liquidity
How quickly one can get back invested funds when they are desired.

current assets
Resources, including cash or noncash items, that can be converted to cash within one year.

fixed assets
Items of a permanent nature, such as land, buildings, furniture, and fixtures.

other (intangible) assets
Items that are not included in the current and fixed assets categories. This catch-all category includes items such as patents and copyrights.

liabilities
Amounts owed by the organization to others. Current liabilities are due in one year or less.

Assets, then, are things such as property and machines that have money value (see Figure 18–3). Assets are listed according to their liquidity. **Liquidity** refers to how fast an asset can be converted to cash. For example, land is considered highly nonliquid because it takes much time and paperwork to sell land. On the other hand, stock is considered highly liquid because it can be sold within minutes. Based on liquidity, assets are divided into three categories:

1. **Current assets**—items that can be converted to cash within one year.
2. **Fixed assets**—items such as land, buildings, and fixtures that are relatively permanent.
3. **Other assets**—this catch-all category includes items such as patents and copyrights.

You can see why one of the key words in accounting is *assets*. Take a few minutes to go through the list, visualizing the assets. Notice that it basically has to do with things that have value that are owned by the organization.

How accountants value assets has a big effect on investors. Some firms value their assets at original cost (for example, land and buildings) when the present value is much higher. The Financial Accounting Standards Board (FASB) is considering making firms value assets at present market rates, but is receiving much resistance from businesses. What you should learn from this is that different companies value their assets differently and you sometimes have to carefully inspect the records to see how much a company is really worth before investing.[4]

The Liabilities Account

Another important term in accounting is *liabilities*. **Liabilities** are what the business *owes* to others. As with assets, you will more easily understand what liabilities are when you review a list of some examples:

Accounts payable—money owed to others for merchandise and services purchased on credit but not paid for yet. If you have such a bill you haven't paid yet, you have an account payable.

CAREER INFORMATION: BOOKKEEPERS AND ACCOUNTING CLERKS

NATURE OF THE WORK

Every business needs systematic and up-to-date records of accounts and business transactions. Bookkeepers and accounting clerks maintain these records in journals and ledgers or in the memory of a computer. They also prepare periodic financial statements showing all money received and paid out. The duties of bookkeepers and the "tools of the trade" vary with the size of the business. However, virtually all of these workers use calculating machines and many work with computers.

In small firms, a general bookkeeper handles all the bookkeeping. He or she analyzes and records all financial transactions such as orders and cash sales. General bookkeepers also check money taken in against money paid out to be sure accounts balance, calculate the firm's payroll, and make up employee's paychecks. General bookkeepers also prepare and mail customers' bills and answer telephone requests for information about orders and bills.

In large businesses, several bookkeepers and accounting clerks work under the direction of a head bookkeeper or accountant. In these organizations, bookkeeping workers often specialize in certain types of work. Some, for example, prepare statements of a company's income from sales or its daily operating expenses. Some enter information on accounts receivable and accounts payable into a computer and review computer printouts for accuracy and completeness. Others record business transactions, including payroll deductions and bills paid and due, and compute interest, rental, and freight charges. They also may type vouchers, invoices, and other financial records.

JOB OUTLOOK

Employment of bookkeepers and accounting clerks is expected to grow more slowly than the average for all occupations through the mid-1990s. Job prospects should be good, nonetheless, in view of the large number of openings that will occur because of the need to replace workers who transfer to other occupations or stop working.

The volume of business transactions is expected to grow rapidly, with a corresponding increase in the need for financial and accounting records. However, the need for bookkeepers, who maintain these records, will not increase nearly as fast because of the increasing use of computers to record, store, and manipulate data.

EARNINGS

Accounting clerks' salaries vary by industry. They tend to be highest in public utilities and mining and lowest in finance, insurance, and real estate. Salaries are also higher for top-level accounting clerks. The more education and experience you accumulate, the more you can make. Be sure that education includes the use of computers because all accounting systems in the future will be computerized except the smallest of small firms.

RELATED OCCUPATIONS

Workers in a number of other jobs also must be good at working with figures. Among such workers are bank tellers, collection workers, insurance clerks, and statistical clerks.

SOURCES OF ADDITIONAL INFORMATION

A brochure describing a career as a bookkeeper or accounting clerk is available on request from Association of Independent Colleges and Schools, 1 Dupont Circle N.W., Suite 350, Washington, D.C. 20036.

Source: *Occupational Outlook Handbook*, U.S. Department of Labor.

- *Accrued expenses payable*—expenses the firm owes that haven't been paid. If you haven't paid the light bill or the electric bill, you have accrued expenses payable.
- *Bonds payable*—these represent money loaned to the firm that it must pay back. If you sell someone a bond, you agree to pay that person back the money lent you plus interest.
- *Notes payable*—these are short-term loans (e.g., bank loans) that must be repaid in less than a year.

Liabilities are reported on financial statements. For now, your objective is to create a mental picture of what liabilities are.

FIGURE 18–4   Sample of specific account titles in general account classifications.

FOR THE BALANCE SHEET			FOR THE INCOME STATEMENT		
ASSETS	**LIABILITIES**	**OWNERS' EQUITY**	**REVENUES**	**EXPENSES**	

Accounts
  receivable
Inventory
Investments
Equipment
Land
Buildings
Motor vehicles
Goodwill
Cash
	Accounts
	  payable
	Notes
	  payable
	Bonds
	  payable
	Taxes
	  payable
		Capital stock
		Retained earnings
			Sales revenue
			Rental revenue
			Commissions
			  revenue
			Royalty
			  revenue
				Wages
				Rent
				Repairs
				Travel
				Insurance
				Utilities
				Entertainment
				Storage
					Interest
					Donations
					Licenses
					Fees
					Supplies
					Advertising
					Taxes

The Owners' Equity Account

owners' equity
Assets minus liabilities.

Owners' equity is assets minus liabilities. For sole proprietors, owners' equity means the value of everything owned by the business minus any liabilities of the owners (for example, outstanding loans). For corporations, the owners' equity account records the owners' claims to funds they have invested in the firm (capital stock) plus earnings kept in the business and not paid out in dividends (retained earnings). The formula *assets* minus *liabilities* equals *owners' equity* is the basis for a financial statement called the *balance sheet,* which we shall discuss later.

The Revenue Account

The revenue account is where revenues from all sources are recorded. That includes sales revenues, rental revenues, commissions, royalties, and other revenue sources. Revenues are included in a financial statement called an *income statement.*

The Expense Account

expenses
Costs incurred in operating the business, such as rent, utilities, and salaries.

The expense account is where the **expenses** of running the business are recorded, including such items as wages, rent, travel, insurance, supplies, advertising, and utilities. Expenses are recorded with revenues on the income statement. A review of most of the accounts used in accounting is presented in Figure 18–4.

ACCOUNTING JOURNALS

The day-to-day accounting task is to take information from original transaction documents (sales slips, payroll statements, travel records, and so on) and record them in journals in the proper amount. A *journal* is a chronological (in order by time) record of transactions. The details of bookkeeping entries can be easily learned in a short class or on the job; for now it is important to remember that a journal is the first place transactions are recorded.

ACCOUNTING LEDGERS

Suppose that a businessperson wanted to determine how much was paid for office supplies in the first quarter of the year. That would be difficult even with accounting journals. The businessperson would have to go through every transaction seeking out those involving supplies and add them up. This is true of other categories such as inventory and accounts receivable.

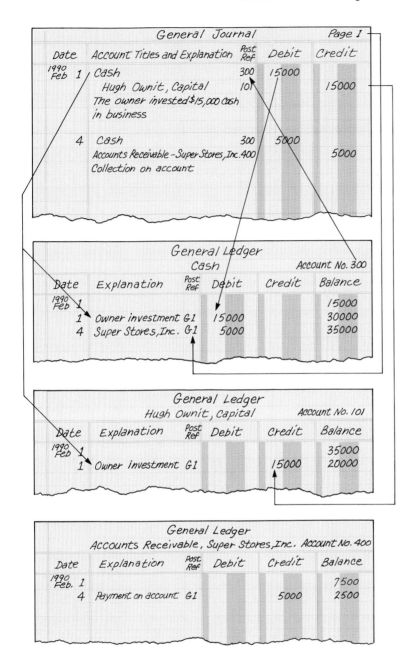

FIGURE 18–5

FIGURE 18–5

Journal entries.
This figure shows how the information from the journal is posted to various ledgers. The idea is to have all similar transactions in one place. That is, all cash transactions are recorded in one ledger, all credit transactions in another.

Clearly, what businesspeople need is another set of books that has pages labeled "Office Supplies," "Accounts Receivable," and so on. Then entries in the journal could be transferred (*posted*) to these pages, and information about various accounts can be found quickly and easily. A **ledger,** then, is a specialized accounting book in which information from accounting journals is categorized into homogeneous groups and posted so that managers can find all the information about one account in the same place. On a weekly, monthly, or quarterly basis, all the journals are totaled and posted (recorded) into ledgers (see Figure 18–5). As you can see, bookkeepers and accountants are kept busy recording data in journals and posting them in ledgers.

ledger
Recording device in which information from accounting journals is categorized into homogeneous groups and posted so that managers can find all the information about one account in the same place.

- Can you name the five "accounts" of accounting and give two examples of items that go into those accounts?
- Can you list various assets by degree of liquidity?
- What goes into the category called liabilities?
- What is the formula for owners' equity?
- What is the difference between an accounting journal and a ledger?

FINANCIAL STATEMENTS

financial statements
Report the success and position (condition) of a firm; they include the income statement and balance sheet.

The accounting process consists of two major functions: (1) recording data from transactions; and (2) preparing **financial statements**. The two most important financial statements are:

1. The *income statement* (once called the *profit and loss statement* or *P&L statement*) reports revenue and expenses for a specific period of time, showing the results of operations during that period.
2. The *balance sheet* reports the financial position of a firm on a specific date.

After taking an intensive accounting course, one reporter summarized the difference this way: "The balance sheet is a snapshot, while the income statement is a motion picture. The former tells what the company owns and owes on a certain day; the latter, what it sells its products for and what its selling costs are over a period of time."[5] These two statements are what accounting is all about.

Financial statements also provide the link between accounting and finance. An accountant's work is pretty much done when he or she prepares the financial statements, and that is where the finance person's work begins. The finance person's job is to analyze those statements and make recommendations to top management. Naturally, a good accountant may work with the finance department to help interpret the data and make recommendations. A financial statement is merely the summary of all transactions that have occurred over a particular period. Financial statements tell the health of a firm. That is why they are of interest to stockholders (the owners of the firm), banks and bondholders (people who have loaned money to the firm), investors (people who may want to own part of the firm), and, of course, the Internal Revenue Service, which wants its share of the profits.

income statement
Reports revenues and expenses for a specific period of time, showing the results of operations during that period. It summarizes all the resources that came into the firm (revenues), and all the resources that left the firm and the resulting net income.

revenue
The value of what is received for goods sold, services rendered, and other sources.

To understand accounting, you must be able to read and understand both the income statement and the balance sheet as well as understand cash flow. In the following sections, we shall explore financial statements and cash flow. If you pay attention and learn the concepts, you will know more about accounting than many small-business managers today.

The Income Statement

cost of goods sold
A particular type of expense measured by the total cost of merchandise sold (including costs associated with the acquisition, storage, transportation in, and packaging of goods).

The financial statement that shows "the bottom line," that is, profit after expenses and taxes, is the income statement or profit and loss statement. The *income statement* summarizes all the resources that come into the firm from operating activities (called **revenue**), money resources that are used up (called **cost of goods sold** and *expenses*), and what resources are left after all costs and expenses are

ARE FINANCIAL STATEMENTS TOO CONFUSING?

There are many reasons for small-business failure. One that is relatively easy to remedy is to learn how to read financial statements. According to Comprehensive Accounting Corporation, many companies fail because their owners don't understand their own financial statements. In fact, the financial bookkeeping service company says that "95 percent of small-business owners can't read their statements." The solution is now here, however. The new, user friendly computers can put statements into easily read pie charts and graphs that show visually what's going on.

Source: *The Wall Street Journal*, March 18, 1985, p. 37.

incurred (**net income** or *net loss*). It reports the results of operations over a particular period of time. The formulas for the income statement are as follows:

- Revenue *less* cost of goods sold *equals* gross profit or gross margin.
- Gross margin *less* operating expenses *equals* profit (income) before taxes.
- Income before taxes *less* taxes *equals* net profit (income) after taxes.

Let's review some of the terms used in the income statement and their significance. Naturally, stockholders and others want to know if the company is earning income or not. Also, it is instructive to note what income is made on sales and what profit is realized on the money invested by the owners (return on investment). Before we get to that, though, let's walk through the statement and learn what each step means.

net income
Revenue minus expenses.

Gross Sales, Net Sales, and Revenue

The figure that is most important at the top of the income statement is **net sales** (see Figure 18–6 on page 584). To determine net sales, a firm must add up all of its sales revenues and subtract discounts, returns, and other adjustments made for customers.

Note the terms *revenues* and *sales*. Most revenue (money coming in to the firm) comes from sales, but there are other sources of revenue such as rents received, admissions, fares, fees, money paid to the firm for use of its patents, interest earned, and so forth. The top of the income statement looks only at sales revenues. Thus, revenues and sales are synonymous at that point.

Be careful not to confuse the terms *revenue* and *income*. Some people use them as if they were synonymous. But a glance at the income statement shows that revenues are at the top of the statement and income is at the bottom: net income is *revenue minus expenses*.

net sales
Sales revenue minus discounts, returns, and other adjustments made for customers.

Cost of Goods Sold

To calculate how much money a business earned by selling merchandise over the year, you have to subtract how much it spent to buy the merchandise from the sales revenue. That cost includes the purchase price plus any freight charges paid to bring in the goods plus the costs associated with storing the goods. In other words, all the costs of buying and keeping merchandise for sale, including packaging, are included in the cost of goods sold.

When you subtract the cost of goods sold from net sales, you get what is called gross margin or *gross profit*. **Gross margin,** then, is how much the firm earned by buying and selling merchandise.

gross margin
Net sales minus cost of goods sold.

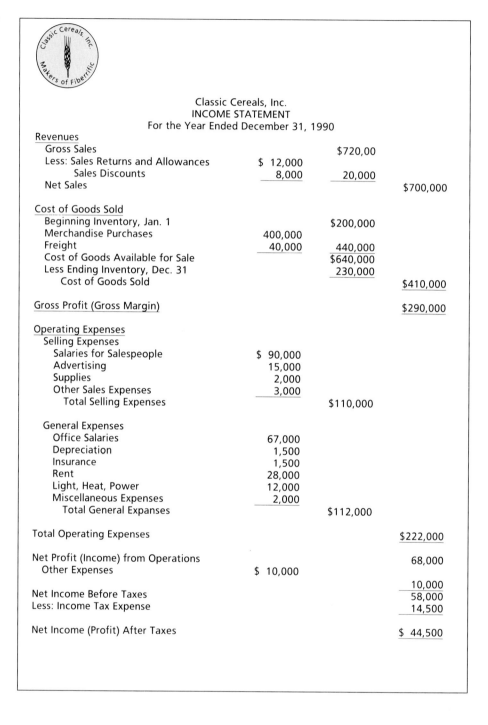

Classic Cereals, Inc.
INCOME STATEMENT
For the Year Ended December 31, 1990

Revenues			
Gross Sales		$720,00	
Less: Sales Returns and Allowances	$ 12,000		
Sales Discounts	8,000	20,000	
Net Sales			$700,000
Cost of Goods Sold			
Beginning Inventory, Jan. 1		$200,000	
Merchandise Purchases	400,000		
Freight	40,000	440,000	
Cost of Goods Available for Sale		$640,000	
Less Ending Inventory, Dec. 31		230,000	
Cost of Goods Sold			$410,000
Gross Profit (Gross Margin)			$290,000
Operating Expenses			
Selling Expenses			
Salaries for Salespeople	$ 90,000		
Advertising	15,000		
Supplies	2,000		
Other Sales Expenses	3,000		
Total Selling Expenses		$110,000	
General Expenses			
Office Salaries	67,000		
Depreciation	1,500		
Insurance	1,500		
Rent	28,000		
Light, Heat, Power	12,000		
Miscellaneous Expenses	2,000		
Total General Expanses		$112,000	
Total Operating Expenses			$222,000
Net Profit (Income) from Operations			68,000
Other Expenses	$ 10,000		
			10,000
Net Income Before Taxes			58,000
Less: Income Tax Expense			14,500
Net Income (Profit) After Taxes			$ 44,500

In a service firm, there may be no cost of goods sold; therefore, net sales equals gross margin. In either case (selling goods or services), the gross margin or gross profit figure doesn't tell you too much. What you are really interested in is net profit or net income. To get that, you must subtract expenses.

Gross margin is calculated by subtracting cost of goods sold from net sales (revenue). This picture shows huge stacks of paper. The revenue from the sale of such paper is quite high. But so is the cost of all the materials needed to make the paper. You will know how much gross profit or gross margin one can make in this business by subtracting the cost of goods sold from the sales revenue. When you subtract other expenses, you will obtain the net profit from operations.

Operating Expenses

To sell goods or services, a business has certain **operating expenses.** Obvious ones include rent, salaries, supplies, selling expenses, utilities, insurance, and depreciation of equipment. Accountants can help you deduct other expenses, including travel expenses, entertainment, and so on.

After all expenses are deducted, you get what people call "the bottom line," which is net income. It answers the questions, "How much did the business earn?" and "How much of our income will be taxed?"

operating expenses
The various costs incurred in running a business, including rent, salaries, and utilities.

Net Income

After taxes are paid, the company may want to distribute some of the income (profit) to stockholders in the form of dividends. The remainder is left in the firm to invest in a variety of other assets. This remainder is known as **retained earnings.** Keeping profits increases the value of the firm. Therefore, stockholders (owners) benefit from income whether they receive a share of it in the form of dividends or whether it is kept in the firm for reinvestment.

Pause here and review the income statement in Figure 18-6 until you feel you understand what is involved. Note that net income basically equals revenue minus expenses.

retained earnings
The amount left after a company distributes some of its net income (profit) to stockholders in the form of dividends.

CLARIFYING ACCOUNTING TERMS

- An *income statement* is sometimes called a *profit and loss statement*.
- *Income* and *profit* are synonyms. Be careful: *income* and *revenue* are *not* synonymous.
- *Gross profit* and *gross margin* are the same.
- *Net income, net profit,* and *net earnings* all refer to the same concept.

- *Revenues* and *sales* are nearly synonymous for many firms, although a firm can have revenues from services other than sales (such as rental fees).
- *Owners' equity, stockholders' equity,* and *investment* (as in "return on investment") are all the same. That is, you could say "return on equity," "return on investment," or "return on stockholders' equity" and mean the same thing.

The Balance Sheet

balance sheet
Reports the financial position of a firm at a specific date. Balance sheets are composed of assets, liabilities, and owners' equity.

A **balance sheet** is the financial statement that reports the financial position of a firm at a *specific time*. It is composed of assets, liabilities, and owners' equity. Note that the income statement reports on changes over a period of time and the balance sheet reports conditions at a specific point in time.

The words *balance sheet* imply that the report shows a balance, an equality between two figures. That is, the balance sheet shows a balance between assets and liabilities plus owners' equity. The following analogy will explain the idea of the balance sheet.

Let's say that you want to know what your financial condition is at a given point in time. Maybe you want to buy a new house or car and need to calculate the resources you have available to buy these things. First, you would add up everything you own—cash, property, money people owe you, and so forth. Subtract from that the money you owe others (for example, credit card debt, IOUs) and you have a figure that tells you that, as of today, you are worth so much. In the next section we shall discuss the same process as done by businesses.

The Fundamental Accounting Equation

fundamental accounting equation
Assets = liability + owners' equity; it is the basis for the balance sheet.

Imagine that you don't owe anybody any money. That is, you don't have any liabilities. Then the assets you have (cash and so forth) are equal to what you own (equity). Translated into business terms, you have a **fundamental accounting equation** that is rather obvious. If a firm has no debts, then:

$$\text{Assets} = \text{Owners' equity}$$

This means that the owners of a firm own everything. If a firm has debts, the owners own everything except the money due others, or:

$$\text{Assets} - \text{Liabilities} = \text{Owners' equity}$$

If you add an equal amount to both sides of the equation (you remember this operation from algebra), you get a new formula:

$$\text{Assets} = \text{Liabilities} + \text{Owners' equity}$$

This last formula is the basis for the balance sheet. On the balance sheet, you list assets in a separate column from liabilities and owners' equity. The assets are equal to or are balanced with the liabilities and owners' equity. It is that simple. The only complicated part is determining what is included in the term *assets* and what is included in the terms *liabilities* and *owners' equity*. Let's look at a balance sheet in Figure 18–7 and we'll get some clues.

Classic Cereals, Inc.
BALANCE SHEET
March 31, 1990

Assets

Current Assets
Cash	$ 15,000	
Accounts Receivable	200,000	
Notes Receivable	50,000	
Inventories At Cost	335,000	
Total Current Assets		$600,000

Fixed Assets
Land	$ 40,000	
Buildings and Improvements	200,000	
Equipment and Vehicles	120,000	
Furniture and Fixtures	26,000	
Less: Accumulated Depreciation	(180,000)	
Total Fixed Assets		$206,000

Other Assets
Goodwill	$ 20,000	
Research and Development	80,000	
Total Other Assets		$100,000
Total Assets		$906,000

Liabilities

Current Liabilities
Accounts Payable	$ 40,000	
Notes Payable	8,000	
Accrued Taxes	150,000	
Accrued Salaries	15,000	
Pension Fund	75,000	
Total Current Liabilities		$288,000

Long-Term Liabilities
Notes Payable	$ 35,000	
Bonds	290,000	
Total Long-Term Liabilities		$325,000

Owner's Equity
Common Stock	$100,000	
Retained Earnings	193,000	
Total Owner's Equity		$293,000
Total Liabilities and Owner's Equity		$906,000

FIGURE 18–7

Classic Cereals balance sheet. The fundamental accounting equation is: assets equal liabilities plus owners' equity. That is the "balance" on the balance sheet.

FIGURE 18–8   Steps in the accounting cycle.

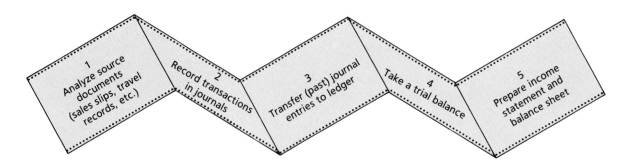

First of all, the balance sheet shows that assets are divided into three categories: (1) current assets (those that can be used or consumed in one year or less) such as cash or accounts receivable; (2) fixed assets (land, buildings, furniture); and (3) other assets, such as patents and copyrights.

Liabilities are divided into two categories: (1) current liabilities (obligations that must be paid within one year) such as accounts payable; and (2) long-term liabilities (obligations that will not be paid within one year) such as bonds.

Owners' equity consists of common stock (certificates of ownership) and retained earnings (earnings not distributed to owners). There would be no common stock for a proprietorship or partnership.

Go back to the beginning of this chapter and reread the sections on the "accounts" of accounting, the asset account, the liabilities account, and so on, and you will see that the asset, liability, and owners' equity accounts set up in the journals and ledgers are all part of the preparation for the balance sheet. Review the lists of items in these accounts and you will learn more about what is behind the figures on the balance sheet. Figure 18–8 briefly summarizes the entire accounting system. Below we shall review the steps in the accounting cycle.

The Five-Step Accounting Cycle

trial balance
Summary of all the data in the ledgers to test the accuracy of the figures.

The *accounting cycle* is a five-step procedure that results in the preparation of the two major financial statements: the income statement and the balance sheet. The first three steps are continuous: (1) analyzing documents, (2) recording the information into journals, and (3) posting that information into ledgers. The fourth step (4) involves preparing a trial balance. A **trial balance** involves summarizing all the data in the ledgers to see that the figures are correct. If they are not correct, they must be corrected before the income statement and balance sheet are prepared. The fifth step (5), then, is to prepare an income statement and balance sheet (see Figure 18–8).

Most companies also prepare a couple of other reports. One is called a statement of changes in financial position. This report is also known as a funds statement because it answers questions such as: How much income came into the business from current operations (from the income statement)? How were these funds used (purchasing of equipment, payment of dividends, etc.)? The basic question the report answers is what has happened to working capital as a result of new funds coming in and how funds were used over a given period.

Definitions for the statistics found in the Comparative Company Analysis tables in   **FIGURE 18–9**
Standard & Poor's Industry Surveys.

Operating revenues—Net sales and other operating revenues. Excludes interest income if such income is "non-operating." Includes franchise/leased department income for retailers and royalties for publishers and oil and mining companies. Excludes excise taxes for tobacco, liquor, and oil companies.

Net income—Profits derived from all sources, after deduction of expenses, taxes, and fixed charges, but before any discontinued operations, extraordinary items, and dividend payments (preferred and common).

Return on revenues (%)—Net income divided by operating revenues.

Return on assets (%)—Net income divided by average total assets. Used in industry analysis and as a measure of asset-use efficiency.

Return on equity (%)—Net income, less preferred dividend requirements, divided by average common shareholders' equity. Generally used to measure performance and to make industry comparisons.

Current ratio—Current assets divided by current liabilities. It is a measure of liquidity. *Current assets* are those assets expected to be realized in cash or used up in the production of revenue within one year. *Current liabilities* generally include all debts/obligations falling due within one year.

Debt/capital ratio—Long-term debt (excluding current portion) divided by total invested capital. It indicates how highly "leveraged" a company might be. *Long-term debt* are those debts/obligations due after one year, including bonds, notes payable, mortgages, lease obligations, and industrial revenue bonds. Other long-term debt, when reported as a separate account, is excluded; this account generally includes pension and retirement benefits. *Total invested capital* is the sum of stockholders' equity, long-term debt, capital lease obligations, deferred income taxes, investment credits, and minority interest.

Debt as a percent of net working capital—Long-term debt (excluding current portion) divided by the difference between current assets and current liabilities. It is an indicator of a company's liquidity.

Price-earnings ratio (high–low)—The ratio of market price to earnings, obtained by dividing the stock's high and low market price for the year by earnings per share (before extraordinary items). It essentially indicates the value investors place on a company's earnings.

Dividend payout ratio—This is the percentage of earnings paid out in dividends. It is calculated by dividing the annual dividend by the earnings. *Dividends* are generally total cash payments per share over a 12-month period. Although payments are usually calculated from the ex-dividend dates, they may also be reported on a declared basis where this has been established to be a company's payout policy.

Yield (high %–low %)—The total cash dividend payments divided by the annual high and low market prices for the stock.

Earnings per share—The amount a company reports as having been earned for the year (based on generally accepted accounting standards), divided by the number of shares outstanding. Amounts reported in Industry Surveys exclude extraordinary items.

Book value per share—This measure indicates the theoretical dollar amount per common share one might expect to receive from a company's tangible "book" assets should liquidation take place. Generally, book value is determined by adding the stated (or par) value of the common stock, paid-in capital, and retained earnings and then subtracting intangible assets (generally excess cost over equity of acquired companies, goodwill, and patents), preferred stock at liquidating value, and unamortized debt discount. Divide that amount by the number of outstanding shares to get book value per common share.

Share price (high–low)—This shows the calendar-year high and low of a stock's market price.

In addition to the footnotes that appear at the bottom of each page, you will notice the following notations:

NA—Not available.
NM—Not meaningful.
NR—Not reported.
AF—Annual figure. The data is presented on an annual basis.

Source: Standard & Poor's *Industry Surveys,* April 16, 1987, p. H.38.

Other reports compare results with established criteria. For example, one report might compare this year's earnings and expenses with past years. Comparisons may also be made between planned goals and the actual results. Most revealing often are comparisons of the firm's data with similar data from competing firms in the same industry. Trade associations usually have industry data of all kinds. One can compare revenues, costs, expenses, inventory turnover, and more to other firms. Figure 18–9 shows the comparison data used by Standard & Poor's when evaluating companies against other companies. Spend some time with this table until the terms become familiar to you. As you can see, other people will be carefully going over the financial statements of your firm to see if it is a good investment or not. You may also want to make such an analysis before you go to work for a firm. The terms and concepts in this chapter give you all the tools you will need to make such an analysis. If you want to learn more, you can take accounting and finance courses or read the texts on your own.

COMPUTERS IN ACCOUNTING

After reading the sections on bookkeeping, the number of accounts a firm must keep, and the reports that need to be generated, you no doubt recognize how computers can help in the process. Even relatively small retailers and other small-business owners are learning that data processing (like keeping and analyzing accounting records) is usually best done by a computer. Computers can record and analyze data and print out financial reports.

Soon it will be possible to have continuous auditing (that is, testing the accuracy and reliability of financial statements) because of computers. One auditing firm, Coopers & Lybrand, hopes to link its computers to clients' computers using Coopers' software to continuously analyze and test the correct functioning of the clients' systems. Such continuous auditing would help prevent bank failures and other business bankruptcies by spotting trouble earlier.

No computer is programmed to make good financial decisions, although they can be programmed to help in such decisions. Computers are a wonderful tool, however, in the hands of a creative accountant who can manipulate the data on a computer to see which strategy results in the best accounting procedures.

There are software programs available that allow even novices to do sophisticated analyses within days. It is important for a small business to develop its accounting system so that it works on these predesigned systems. That is one reason why we recommend that all small-business owners hire an accountant before they get started in business.

Computers are so inexpensive today that even the smallest of businesses should use them for accounting purposes. Accounting software is available that makes the task easier and more effective. Before you even start a small business, you should check out accounting software so you can begin processing your accounting documents immediately.

ACCOUNTING CREATIVITY

If accounting were nothing more than the repetitive function of gathering and recording transactions and preparing financial statements, the major functions could be assigned to computers. In fact, most medium- to large-size firms have done just that. The truth is that *how* you record and report data is critically important.

Take depreciation, for example. **Depreciation** is based on the fact that assets such as machinery lose value over time; therefore, part of the cost of the machinery is calculated as an expense each year over its useful life. Subject to certain technical rules, which are beyond the scope of this chapter, a firm may use one of several different techniques for calculating depreciation. However, once a method is chosen, it is difficult to change. Each technique results in a different bottom line; a different net income. Net incomes can change dramatically based on the specific accounting procedure that is used. Accountants can recommend ways of handling insurance, investments, and other accounts that will also affect the bottom line.

One of the more complex issues in accounting is how to handle inventory. This shows up in the cost of goods sold section of the income statement. When a firm takes merchandise from inventory and sells it, it has several different ways of calculating the cost of that item. One way is to take the oldest merchandise first, as is done in supermarkets. Clerks stack the old merchandise in front of the new merchandise so that the old stuff sells first. This is called the **FIFO** technique. FIFO stands for first in, first out. In accounting, it is not whether or not the item was really first in or not; what counts is how much the accountants say that item cost. Let's say, for example, that a company has been buying bicycles for resale. They buy a bike in 1988 for $50. Because of inflation, they buy the same bike in 1989 for $60. Now they have two bikes to sell. If the accountant used the FIFO technique, the cost of goods sold would be $50, because the bike that was bought first (in 1988) cost $50.

A second approach would be to use a technique called **LIFO**, or last in, first out. Using that strategy, a company's cost of goods sold for the bike would be $60. Can you see the difference in the two accounting approaches on the bottom line? FIFO would report $5 more of net income than LIFO (see Figure 18–10 on page 592). Sometimes firms switch from a LIFO to a FIFO system. You can see that

depreciation
Assets such as machinery lose value over time; therefore, part of the cost of the machinery is calculated as an expense each year over its useful life.

FIFO
Accounting technique for calculating cost of inventory based on first in, first out.

LIFO
Accounting technique for calculating cost of inventory based on last in, first out.

MAKING ETHICAL DECISIONS

As a full-time student majoring in accounting, you support yourself by working part time. You just started working as a bookkeeper for Cash Construction Company two weeks ago. You learned the company's accounting system and understand the internal and external reports it generates. On the 15th of the month, your boss, the sole owner, asks for the checks you received from customers. After explaining that you still need to record some of them before depositing them in the bank, your boss replies, "We don't record any revenues we get after the 15th of the month—we just record expenses. Heck, the government can't find

out about the unrecorded money because the checks are made out to 'Cash'! Shoot, the government spends too much money anyway. We're forcing some financial discipline on 'em by cutting back on the bucks they get out of us. Why, nobody reports all their income. The untaxed economy is about as much as a third of the gross national product!"

What are your alternatives in this situation? What are the likely consequences of each alternative? What will you do?

Source: Gene E. A. Johnson, *Application Exercises for Introduction to Business*, 1984.

FIGURE 18–10

Accounting using LIFO versus FIFO inventory costing. By using a LIFO strategy, the accountant can lower taxes and appear to make less profit. By switching to FIFO, the firm would show an increase in profit, but taxes would be higher. Which strategy is best depends on the goals of the firm: to lower taxes, use LIFO; to attract stockholders with profit advances, use FIFO.

	FIFO	LIFO
Revenue	$100	$100
Cost of goods sold	50	60
Income before taxes	$ 50	$ 40
Taxes of 50%	25	20
Net income	$ 25	$ 20

such a change would make it appear that the firm made more money when, in fact, nothing changed but the accounting system. Recently, small firms have been switching from FIFO to LIFO because of high inflation.[6]

This is what is meant by accounting creativity. Accountants can use many such strategies and techniques to minimize taxes, maximize net income, or create the impression that the business is doing very well or very poorly—all by using legal, established accounting procedures. So you see there is more to accounting than meets the eye. It can be fascinating. For some accounting humor, see the box called "Sometimes the Ledger of Life Doesn't Add Up." What can be even more fascinating and challenging is to understand and use both accounting and finance. We shall explore that possibility in Chapter 19.

You should be aware, however, that it is not always good to rely exclusively on your accountants for information if you are a manager. That is one of the important messages to be learned from this chapter's opening Profile. Robert Kaplan from the Harvard Business School is particularly concerned that managers design an accounting system that meets *their* information needs. Too often in the past, accountants followed their own set procedures and manipulated the numbers properly, but did not present the data in a way that optimized decision making.[7] Ultimately, top management must make key financial decisions and those decisions are most effective when the accountants, finance people, and top managers all work together to design a system that provides information that optimizes decision making.

THINKING IT THROUGH Can you see the challenge and reward of an accounting career? Do you enjoy working with figures and calculating ways to save on taxes? If so, maybe you would enjoy accounting. Have you visited an accounting firm and watched an accountant at work? What do you feel would be the advantages and disadvantages of such a career? Can you see how accounting will grow in importance as accountants work more closely with top management and the finance department?

CASH FLOW PROBLEMS

cash flow
The difference between cash receipts and cash disbursements.

If one term were selected to represent the greatest operating problem of the 1980s and 1990s, that term would likely be **cash flow.** The name of the game today is cash flow, not profit. *Profit* is an accounting term, a line on the income statement—but it is not cash. It is not always available for use. A firm can have increased sales and increased profit, and still suffer deeply from cash flow problems. That is what happened to Brian and Sharon Stutt, whom we discussed at the beginning of this chapter.

SOMETIMES THE LEDGER OF LIFE DOESN'T ADD UP

BY PAUL HELLMAN

Two accountants sit down for lunch in a fancy restaurant. One looks at the other and says:

"How're you doing? You don't look so good."

"I've depreciated terribly," says the other. "Can't get my life in balance. Nothing adds up anymore."

"Listen," says the first, "you're just having a bad quarter. You've got good assets."

"You know, you're right. It's been years since I've thought about selling the house." Suddenly, he brightens, and a malicious smile spreads across his face. "Hey, kids are assets, too—isn't that what we're told? Maybe I could sell some of mine, especially the ones that keep moving back home."

"Your work-in-progress days are over, so to speak, but your inventory of kids never quite makes it out the door, eh? But seriously, you can't sell your kids."

"I know, I know. But it doesn't seem fair, does it? My little assets have grown into big liabilities. Maybe life is just one big liability. How about you? You look cheerful—what's your secret?"

"I live according to generally accepted accounting principles. Life is a flow statement, old pal. The revenues flow in, the expenses flow out. Sometimes you profit, sometimes you don't. I take 'em as they come."

"You go with the flow."

"That's right. Take this restaurant, for example."

"Yeah? What about it?"

"See those people over there at that corner table? They were the last in, but they're already eating and they'll be the first out."

"Hey, you're right. That's not fair."

"You see. You're letting it get to you. But I look at it and say, 'That's just LIFO.'"

"Er . . ."

"Also, as another example, take the food today."

"What food? We've been sitting here for over an hour and have yet to be served. All we got was water."

"Exactly, and frankly I'm delighted. You never know when you might be poisoned."

"Oh yeah? Well it's also true that we're still hungry."

"But it's also true that we're not dead."

"I've got to get out of here. Your philosophy isn't working. I'm still depressed."

The two of them get up to leave. The cheerful accountant drops a tip of several dollars on the table.

"Hey," says the gloomy one. "Why are you doing that? All we got was water."

His friend gives him his best LIFO-is-just-a-flow-chart smile and says, "One liquid asset deserves another."

"I think you need an internal audit."

Mr. Hellman keeps his ledger in Framingham, Mass.

Cash flow is simply the difference between cash receipts and cash disbursements. You don't have to be an accountant to produce a cash flow analysis. It is just a matter of analyzing cash receipts versus cash disbursements.

Taking out a loan has no effect on profit. Similarly, repaying a loan has no effect on profit. But taking out and repaying loans has a lot to do with cash flow. This is essential to understand because the number one financial cause of small-business failure today is not unprofitability; it is inadequate cash flow.

What a business has to do to prevent cash flow problems is to prepare a simple *cash flow forecast* (also known as a *cash flow budget*). That is, predict ahead of time cash receipts versus cash disbursements. For example, over the next six months, on a month-by-month basis, what will be the net cash balance at the end of each month? Let's say that January, February, and March show slight cash surpluses, but April shows a deficit. On January 2, you might go to the bank and show your banker your yearly forecast. Explain that you are expanding so fast that your cash resources are not growing as fast as your cash needs, and that will mean a deficit for April. You ask to borrow funds for April, showing the banker that the payments you receive for April sales (a big month for you) will be made in June, and that you will be able to repay the loan then.

UNDERSTANDING CASH FLOW

Cash flow management is one of the most critical issues in operating a business successfully. Although many businesses have difficulty with it, the issue is really rather simple.

Let's say you borrow money from a friend ($10) to buy a used bike and agree to pay him back at the end of the week. You sell the used bike to someone else for $15. He agrees to pay you in a week also.

It turns out that the person who bought the bike from you doesn't have the money in a week and tells you he will pay next month sometime. Meanwhile, your friend wants his $10. Eventually, you will make a $5 profit, but right now you have a cash flow problem. You owe $10 and have no cash. What would you do if your friend insisted on

being paid? If you were a business, you might go bankrupt, even though you had the potential for profits.

Another alternative is to borrow money from the bank to pay your friend and pay the bank back when you receive the $15. That is what businesses try to do. But what if the bank refuses the loan? Then you are in trouble, just as firms get in trouble when *they* cannot get a bank loan. Clearly, one of the critical relationships a businessperson makes is with his or her banker.

Also, this example points out the importance of collecting promptly money from those who owe you funds. Most cash flow problems come from not keeping a close eye on accounts receivable—money due you from people who bought on credit.

Source: Tatiana Pouschine, "No Question It Looks Bad," *Forbes*, November 28, 1988, pp. 62–64.

The appendix to this chapter discusses several financial ratios that will help you manage cash flow problems. Be sure to spend some time learning these ratios and their uses. We know it seems like busy work now, but when you get into business, you will not have time to be learning such things along with all the other decisions you will be making. This is the time to start building the foundation of knowledge that will enable you to be successful in business right from the start.

Cash Flow and the Bank

A small firm should probably deal with a small bank and a large firm with a large bank. A large bank may not give a small firm the time and attention that a small bank might. That is why the least expensive (and often the best) consultant a small firm can find is often a local banker. If the banker is skilled in accounting and finance, he or she can provide all kinds of free financial advice. To assure that the advice comes regularly, a small-business person might visit the banker periodically, as often as once a month. By keeping a skilled banker informed about sales, profits, and cash flow, a small-business person makes sure of good financial advice and a more ready source of funds. Bankers, investment advisers, finance people, and a host of other businesspeople use the data from income statements and balance sheets to evaluate the health of firms and compare them to others.

We shall discuss the ratios they use in the appendix to this chapter. If you learn what banks are looking for, you can plan your budget such that the bank will be quite willing to lend you money. If you don't understand the ratios that banks look at, you could easily go bankrupt and never quite understand what happened.

CAREERS IN ACCOUNTING

Would accounting be a good career for you? Certain aptitudes are important for those desiring to be an accountant. They include:
- An appreciation of accuracy.
- A "feel" for figures.
- An analytical mind.
- An ability to handle masses of detail without losing perspective.
- A sense of order.

CAREER INFORMATION: ACCOUNTING AND AUDITING

NATURE OF THE WORK

Accountants and auditors prepare, analyze, and verify financial reports that furnish information to managers in all business, industrial, and government organizations.

Four major fields are public, management, and government accounting, and internal auditing. Public accountants have their own businesses or work for accounting firms. Management accountants, also called industrial or private accountants, handle the financial records of their company. Government accountants and auditors maintain and examine the records of government agencies and audit private businesses and individuals whose dealings are subject to government regulations. Internal auditors verify the accuracy of their firm's financial records and check for waste or fraud.

JOB OUTLOOK

Employment of accountants and auditors is expected to grow much faster than the average for all occupations through the mid-1990s due to the key role these workers play in the management of all types of businesses. Small businesses are expected to rely more and more on the expertise of accountants in planning and managing their operations. In addition, increases in investment and lending associated with general economic growth also should spur demand for accountants and auditors. The increasing use of computers in accounting should stimulate the demand for accountants and auditors familiar with their operation.

One of the growing areas in accounting is for information system auditors. These people examine commercial and other data stored by computer. Their objective is to protect the data from being compromised by accident or intrusion. Furthermore, internal auditors have broadened their interest beyond just studying financial compliance with accounting procedures. They now get involved in engineering, marketing, and personnel departments to be sure that the controls set up by management are being followed. As a result of these new duties, the demand for internal auditors will remain high for years to come.

RELATED OCCUPATIONS

Accountants and auditors design internal control systems and analyze financial data. Others for whom training in accounting is invaluable include appraisers, budget officers, loan officials, financial analysts, bank officers, actuaries, underwriters, tax collectors and revenue agents, FBI special agents, securities sales workers, and purchasing agents.

SOURCES OF ADDITIONAL INFORMATION

Information about careers in public accounting and about competency tests administered in colleges may be obtained from American Institute of Certified Public Accountants, 1211 Avenue of the Americas, New York, N.Y. 10036.

Information on specialized fields of accounting and auditing is available from:

National Association of Accountants, P.O. Box 433, 10 Paragon Dr., Montvale, N.J. 07645.

National Society of Public Accountants and Accreditation Council for Accountancy, 1010 North Fairfax St., Alexandria, Va. 22314.

The Institute of Internal Auditors, 249 Maitland Ave., P.O. Box 1119, Altamonte Springs, Fla. 32701.

The EDP Auditors Association, 373 South Schmale Rd., Carol Stream, Ill. 60188.

Source: *Occupational Outlook Handbook*, U.S. Department of Labor; and James H. Mannon, "Internal Auditor," *Business Week Careers*, June 1988, p. 36.

If you have not done well in math in school and don't particularly enjoy working with figures, you probably would not enjoy accounting. A good accountant must also be able to spot inaccuracies and work creatively with numbers, because he or she often works with figures prepared by others. If that sounds interesting and challenging to you, you might find accounting a rewarding career.

■ What three formulas make up the income statement? What is the difference between revenue and income on that statement?

■ What is the fundamental accounting equation that is used to make up the balance sheet? What is "balanced" on the balance sheet?

■ What is the five-step accounting cycle?

■ What is the difference between LIFO and FIFO inventory accounting?

■ What is cash flow and how can a small business protect itself against cash flow problems before they occur?

PROGRESS CHECK

SUMMARY

1. Define accounting and explain the differences between managerial accounting and financial accounting.

1. Accounting is the recording, classifying, summarizing, and interpreting of financial events and transactions that affect an organization. The methods used to record and summarize accounting data into reports are called an accounting system.
   - How does managerial accounting differ from financial accounting?
     Managerial accounting provides information and analyses to managers within the firm to assist them in decision making. Financial accounting provides information and analyses to external users of data such as creditors and lenders.
   - What is the difference between a private and a public accountant?
     Public accountants provide services for a fee to a variety of companies, whereas private accountants work for a single company. Private and public accountants do essentially the same things with the exception of independent audits. Private accountants do perform internal audits but only public accountants supply independent audits.

2. Compare accounting and bookkeeping.

2. Many people confuse bookkeeping and accounting.
   - What is the difference between bookkeeping and accounting?
     Bookkeeping is part of accounting, but only the mechanical part of recording data. Accounting also includes classifying, summarizing, interpreting, and reporting data to management.

3. Identify and describe the major accounts used to prepare financial statements.

3. There are five major accounts in accounting: assets, liabilities, owners' equity, revenues, and expenses.
   - What are assets?
     Assets are economic resources owned by the firm, such as buildings and machinery. Current assets can be converted to cash within a year while fixed assets are relatively permanent and take longer to sell. Liquidity refers to how fast an asset can be sold; the faster it can be sold, the more "liquid" it is said to be.
   - What are liabilities?
     Liabilities are money owned by the organization to others (for example, creditors, bond holders).
   - What is owners' equity?
     Owners' equity is assets minus liabilities. It tells owners how much money would be available to them if the firm sold all of its assets and paid off all its liabilities.
   - What are revenues?
     Revenues are the value of what is received from goods sold or services rendered.
   - What are expenses?
     Expenses are incurred in operating the business, including salaries, rent, and utilities.

4. Distinguish between an accounting journal and a ledger.

4. Accountants use journals and ledgers to record transactions.
   - What are journals and ledgers?
     Journals are original entry accounting documents. That means they are the first place transactions are recorded. Summaries of journal entries are recorded (posted) into ledgers. Ledgers are specialized accounting books that arrange the transactions by homogeneous groups.

5. Prepare simple income statements and balance sheets, and explain their functions.

5. The primary financial statements provided by accountants are income statements and balance sheets.
   - What is an income statement?

An income statement reports revenues and expenses for a specific period of time. The basic formula is revenue minus expenses equals gross profit (profit before taxes). (Note that income and profit mean the same thing.)

⬚ What is a balance sheet?

A balance sheet reports the financial position of a firm at a particular time. The fundamental accounting equation used to prepare the balance sheet is assets = liabilities + owners' equity.

6. The accounting cycle is a five-step procedure for preparing the income statement and the balance sheet.

⬚ What are the five steps of the accounting cycle?

The five steps of the accounting cycle are: (1) analyzing documents, (2) putting the information into journals, (3) posting that information into ledgers, (4) preparing a trial balance, and (5) preparing the income statement, balance sheet, and other reports such as the annual report.

6. List the five steps of the accounting cycle.

7. Most businesspeople realize the value of using computers to help them with their accounting activities.

⬚ How can computers help accountants?

Computers can record and analyze data and provide financial reports. Software is available that can continuously analyze and test accounting systems to be sure they are functioning correctly. Computers can help decision making by providing appropriate information, but they cannot make good financial decisions independently. Accounting creativity is still a human trait.

7. Describe the role of computers in accounting.

8. Accounting creativity makes the reporting and analysis of data a challenging occupation. Two creative accounting techniques are known as LIFO and FIFO.

⬚ What are LIFO and FIFO?

LIFO and FIFO are ways of pricing inventory. LIFO means last in, first out. FIFO means first in, first out. How you price inventory affects net income and taxes.

8. Explain the impact of using LIFO versus FIFO inventory accounting.

9. Cash flow is the difference between cash receipts and cash disbursements.

⬚ How does cash flow become a problem?

Businesses borrow money to buy products and to operate, and do not collect revenues fast enough to have cash ready when bills come due.

9. Explain the concept of cash flow.

GETTING INVOLVED

1. Go to a local business and watch the people recording data in the journals and ledgers. Look over the ledger to see what it contains. Many firms now use computers for these tasks. Visit one that does and compare its ledgers to its journals. Spend some time observing accountants at work—the surroundings, the people, and so on. Report your reactions to the class.

2. Take a sheet of paper. On every fourth line, write one of the following headings: assets, liabilities, owners' equity, expenses, and revenues. Then, list as many items as you can under each heading. When you are finished, look up the lists in the text and add to your own. Keep the lists for your notes. As you complete the lists, create a mental picture of each account so that you can understand the concepts behind accounts and accounting.

3. Prepare your own income statement. See how far you can get without looking back to Figure 18-6. Then look in the text to see what you have forgotten, if anything. Actually writing these things down does wonders for remembering the ideas later.

4. Prepare your own balance sheet. Remember the simple formula: *Assets = Liabilities + Owners' equity*. Go back and check your balance sheet against the one in Figure 18-7.

5. Write your own explanation of how small businesses get into trouble with cash flow by expanding too rapidly. Think of several ways a business could avoid such problems. Discuss your thoughts with the class.

CASE ONE **CONSTRUCTING AN INCOME STATEMENT AND A BALANCE SHEET**

Neighborhood Landscaping Service was started by Stuart Jenkins when he was in high school. As the business grew, Stu hired several of his friends and is now doing well. He is now in a position to begin keeping better records. Stu has written down some of his figures, but he doesn't know how to interpret them. He wants to take out a loan, and wants to prepare a balance sheet to calculate his financial position. These are his figures:

ASSETS		LIABILITIES	
Cash	$ 5,350	Money owed bank	$7,500
Truck	13,500	Money owed supplier	545
Accounts receivable	2,400	Money owed for equipment	500
Equipment	4,520	Total liabilities	$8,545
Office furniture	945		
Supplies	550		
Trailer	500		
Total assets	$27,765		

Some other figures Stu had hastily put together in no consistent order are:

Income from work done	$74,000
Expenses incurred for trees, shrubs, etc.	22,000
Salaries of helpers (2)	16,000
Advertising	1,360
Insurance	2,000
Office costs (phone, heat, rent, etc.)	8,400
Depreciation on truck	$ 4,000

Stu paid $1,800 for other supplies such as gravel, sand, and slate used for walkways.

DECISION QUESTIONS

1. What additional information, if any, would you need to construct a balance sheet? Is Stu in a strong or poor financial condition?
2. How much did Stu earn before taxes? Prepare an income statement to show Stu how such a financial statement looks.
3. Stu is unsure of the terminology of accounting. Study his list of figures and names and see if you can find any incorrect usage of terms.

CASE TWO **WHERE DID KATHERINE GO WRONG?**

Katherine Potter knew a good thing when she saw it. At least, it seemed so at first. She was traveling in Italy when she spotted pottery shops that made beautiful products ranging from ashtrays to lamps. Some of the pottery was stunning in design.

Katherine began importing the products to the United States, and sales took off. Customers immediately realized the quality of the items, and were willing to pay top price. Katherine decided to keep prices moderate to expand rapidly, and she did. Sales in the second three months were double those of the first few months. Sales in the second year were double those of the first year.

Every few months, Katherine had to run to the bank to borrow more money. She had no problems getting larger loans, because she always paid promptly. To save on the cost of buying goods, Katherine always took trade discounts. That is, she paid all bills within 10 days to save the 2 percent offered by her suppliers for paying so quickly.

Most customers bought Katherine's products on credit. They would buy a couple of lamps and a pot and Katherine would allow them to pay over time. Some were very slow in paying her, taking six months or more.

After three years, Katherine noticed a small drop in her business. The local economy was not doing well because many people were being laid off from their jobs. Nonetheless, Katherine's business stayed level. One day the bank called Katherine and told her she was late in her payments. She had been so busy that she didn't notice the bills. The problem was that Katherine had no cash available to pay the bank. She frantically called several customers for payment, but they were not able to pay her, either. Katherine was in a classic cash flow bind.

Katherine immediately raised her prices and refused to make sales on credit. She started delaying payment on her bills and paid the extra costs. Then she went to the bank and went over her financial condition with the banker. The banker noted her accounts receivable and assets. He then prepared a cash budget and loaned Katherine more money. Her import business grew much more slowly thereafter, but her financial condition improved greatly. Katherine had gone nearly bankrupt, but she recovered at the last minute.

DECISION QUESTIONS

1. How is it possible to have high sales and high profits and run out of cash?
2. Why did Katherine do better when she raised her prices and refused to sell on credit?
3. What was the nature of Katherine's problem? Was she correct to go to the banker for help, even though she owed the bank money?

The whole idea of accounting is to keep track of transactions, to meet the requirements of the Internal Revenue Service, and to keep management and outsiders informed as to the operations (income statement) and position (balance sheet) of the firm. Accounting's basic role ends when the financial statements are completed. At that point, finance's role begins. Finance and accounting personnel analyze the financial statements and make recommendations to management. The key to evaluating financial statements is a group of ratios that financial analysts use to compare firms. We shall look at those ratios in the appendix. They are one link between accounting and finance.

LOOKING AHEAD

Remember that accounting and finance are related so that a person cannot be fully expert in one field without understanding the other. In a firm, accounting and finance are often blended in the duties of a financial officer.

If the financial statements show that the firm needs additional funds, it is the role of the finance manager to get those funds at the lowest rates. Finance is largely about funds management. We shall discuss the function in depth in Chapter 19. Chapter 20 is about stocks and bonds—two major sources of funds for larger firms.

The financial institutions of the United States were in some difficulty in the 1980s. We shall discuss financial institutions in depth in Chapter 21. Then we shall look at your own finances and how to save and invest *your* money in the appendix to Part 6.

Appendix
Financial Ratios
The Link Between Accounting and Finance

Every person interested in finance needs to understand basic accounting. What is especially helpful to financial analysis is the use of ratios to measure a company's health. You are familiar with ratios. They are used all the time to measure the success of sports teams. For example, in basketball, the ratio of shots made from the foul line versus attempts is measured. TV announcers say, "Jones is shooting 85 percent of his foul shots, so he is not the one to foul in the final minutes." We judge basketball players by such ratios: 80 percent is good for foul shots, 65 percent is not good. We calculate similar ratios for baseball ("He's batting .300," or 30 percent), football ("He's completed 50 percent of his passes"), and so on. So ratios are not hard to understand or compute, and they give a lot of information about the relative performance of sportspeople or of businesses. Now let's look at some key ratios that businesspeople use.

HANDLING CASH FLOW PROBLEMS: AVERAGE COLLECTION PERIOD OF RECEIVABLES

We have already noted that a major financial problem of small businesses is poor liquidity or cash flow. In most cases, poor cash flow is caused by not collecting accounts receivable fast enough. Many customers do not pay their bills until they are reminded or pressured to pay. Incentives such as discounts for paying early are often mandatory for minimizing collection time. To determine whether or not a business is collecting its receivables in a reasonable period of time, an analyst calculates the average collection period. Unlike the other financial analysis calculations, this one takes two steps. The first step is to divide the annual credit sales by 365 to obtain the average daily credit sales. The second step is to divide accounts and notes receivable by the average daily credit sales (the first step) to get the average collection period in days. For example:

1. Average daily credit sales $= \dfrac{\text{Total annual credit sales}}{365 \text{ days}}$

2. Collection period in days $= \dfrac{\text{Notes and accounts receivable}}{\text{Average daily credit sales}}$

If total annual credit sales were $365,000, then the average daily credit sales would be $1,000:

$$\frac{\$365,000}{365} = \$1,000$$

If the notes and accounts receivable today were $60,000, then the collection period would be 60 days:

$$\frac{\$60,000}{\$1,000} = 60 = \text{Average collection period of receivables}$$

CASH FLOW AND CREDIT TERMS

If you collect your accounts in 60 days but pay your accounts in 10 days, you will have a cash flow problem. To encourage people to pay more quickly, most companies give credit terms such as "2/10, net 30." This means that if customers pay within 10 days, they can deduct 2 percent from the price. If they don't take advantage of a discount, the total amount is due in 30 days.

Paying within 10 days is advantageous for buyers. Here's why. A 2 percent discount for paying within 10 days means that the company saves 2 percent by paying 20 days early— because the total amount is due within 30 days. Read the last sentence again slowly to be sure you understand. Each year there are 18 20-day periods. Therefore, by paying early (within 10 days) a firm can save 36 percent annually ($2\% \times 18$). That is why most small businesses pay their bills within 10 days. It is a bargain. Now that you've learned to save money on purchases, let's look at the ratio that measures sales effectiveness.

Inventory Turnover

A business supply store once asked a consultant why its inventory turnover ratio was so low. The consultant walked through the warehouse and found box after box filled with slide rules, stacked high. These obsolete items were being carried on the books as inventory and lowering the turnover ratio. What signaled the problem was that the owner compared his turnover ratio to the average industry ratio.

A lower than average ratio indicates obsolete merchandise or poor buying practices. A higher than average ratio may indicate an understocked condition where sales are lost because of inadequate stock. The ratio to determine inventory turnover is calculated by dividing the cost of goods sold by the average inventory for the period. For example, if the cost of goods sold were $160,000 and the average inventory were $20,000, the turnover ratio would be 8. This figure by itself is rather meaningless. It has to be compared to industry figures to tell a company how it is doing in relation to competitors. The calculation looks like this:

$$\text{Turnover} = \frac{\text{Costs of goods sold}}{\dfrac{\text{Jan. 1 inventory} + \text{Dec. 31 inventory}}{2}}$$

$$\text{Turnover} = \frac{\$160,000}{\dfrac{\$23,000 + \$17,000}{2}}$$

$$\text{Turnover} = \frac{\$160,000}{\$20,000} = 8$$

MANAGERIAL INFORMATION: RETURN ON SALES

Each industry has a different rate of return on sales. Such figures are well known in the industry. Therefore, a firm can determine whether or not it is doing as well as other businesses by calculating the return on sales ratio. This involves dividing net income by net sales. If net income were $10,000 and net sales were $200,000, the return on sales ratio would be 5 percent:

$$\text{Return on sales} = \frac{\text{Net income}}{\text{Net sales}}$$

$$\text{Return on sales} = 5\% = \frac{\$10,000}{\$200,000}$$

A good example of a company that showed a poor return on sales ratio one year was Compaq Computer. It had sales of $300 million and earned only $9 million, a ratio of just over 3 percent. That was about half of IBM's return on sales ratio and 70 percent of Apple Computer's return on sales ratio. As a result, Compaq's stock fell from 11 to 3½ in that period. As you can see, investors pay attention to the return on sales ratio. One way to increase the ratio is to increase prices, but Compaq was facing a competitive market and wanted to keep its prices low. The results indicate that prices were too low. Stockholders compute ratios such as return on sales when evaluating a firm (or look up the ratios in business reports). Another ratio they look for is return on investment.

STOCKHOLDER INFORMATION: RETURN ON INVESTMENT (ROI)

Stockholders invest in a business expecting to make a greater return on their money than if they did something else with the money, such as depositing it in a bank or buying bonds. The way to calculate the return on equity (ownership) in a firm is to divide net income by the owner's equity. You are more likely to hear this formula referred to as *ROI* or *return on investment*. Investment, then, is synonymous with equity. If net income were $10,000 and stockholders' equity (investment) were $100,000, the ROI or return on investment would be 10 percent:

$$\text{ROI} = \frac{\text{Net income}}{\text{Owners' equity}}$$

$$\text{ROI} = 10\% = \frac{\$10,000}{\$100,000}$$

STOCKHOLDER INFORMATION: DEBT-TO-EQUITY RATIO

Every year, *Forbes* magazine publishes an annual report on U.S. industry. This review looks at 1,000 different corporations and ranks them by return on equity, sales growth, and earnings per share. The two ratios *Forbes* uses for comparison are return on equity (which we've discussed) and debt/equity. Debt/equity is calculated by dividing total liabilities by owners' equity. Basically, this ratio tells you how much money, relatively, the company has borrowed compared to other firms in the industry. A high ratio triggers caution among investors. But again, high or low is relatively meaningless unless compared to the average of the same industry.

In one *Forbes* edition, for example, the highest figure in the health-care industry was 1.6; that is, debt was 1.6 times equity. The median was 0.4. In heavy equipment, the median was 0.4 again, but International Harvester's figure was 5.3, Massey-Ferguson's was 6.1, and Pettibone's was 7.9. All of these firms with high figures were in deep trouble financially. The debt/equity ratio reflected that trouble. If total liabilities were $150,000 and owners' equity were $150,000, the debt/equity ratio would be 1:

$$\text{Debt/equity ratio} = \frac{\text{Total liabilities}}{\text{Owners' equity}}$$

$$\text{Debt/equity ratio} = 1 = \frac{\$150,000}{\$150,000}$$

Most consultants feel a ratio greater than 1 is not good, but again that varies by industry. Sometimes debt is a good sign if it means the company is trying to optimize the return to stockholders by assuming more risk.

INFORMATION FOR BANKERS: CAN A LOAN BE PAID?

Bankers are also interested in certain other ratios. We said earlier that a small-business person should consult with his or her banker often. One calculation that a banker is sure to make is the current ratio. The ratio is:

$$\text{Current ratio} = \frac{\text{Current assets}}{\text{Current liabilities}}$$

This ratio measures a company's ability to pay its short-term debts. A ratio of 1.5 or higher is usually desired.

If we leave inventories out of the above equation, we get a more accurate feel for whether or not a business could quickly pay its current liabilities. Thus, another test is called the *quick ratio* or *acid-test ratio*. This is the supposed acid test of whether a firm is on solid financial ground, short term or not. The formula is:

$$\text{Quick ratio} = \frac{\text{Cash} + \text{Marketable securities} + \text{Accounts receivable} + \text{Notes receivable}}{\text{Liabilities}}$$

Finance professionals use several other ratios to learn more details about the condition of a business, but this will give you an idea of what ratios are and how they are used. The point is that financial analysis begins where accounting reports end. This appendix, then, represents the transition between accounting and finance.

Get the January issue of *Forbes* magazine that compares industries and look through the various industries. Note the variance in return on equity and debt/equity ratios. Think through the importance of inventory turnover and the ability to pay off debts with liquid assets such as cash and accounts receivable. Note how obvious it is to measure a firm's return (profit) on sales compared to that of other firms in the industry. Such reflections will show you the importance of ratios to investors, financial analysts, bankers, and business managers. Could you do business effectively without understanding such ratios? It is doubtful. If the thousands of *Forbes* readers are expected to understand such ratios, certainly a business executive should, and so should you if you want to understand the financial side of business.

FINANCIAL MANAGEMENT

19

LEARNING GOALS

After you have read and studied this chapter, you should be able to:

1. Explain the role and importance of finance.

2. Describe the responsibilities of financial managers.

3. Outline the steps in financial planning by explaining the process of forecasting financial needs, developing budgets, and establishing financial controls.

4. Recognize the financial needs that must be met with available funds.

5. Distinguish between short-term and long-term financing and between debt capital and equity capital.

6. Identify and describe several sources of short-term capital.

7. Identify and describe several sources of long-term capital.

KEY TERMS

budget, *p. 610*
capital budget, *p. 610*
cash budget, *p. 611*
cash flow forecast, *p. 609*
commercial paper, *p. 618*
debt capital, *p. 614*
equity capital, *p. 614*
factoring, *p. 617*
finance, *p. 608*
financial control, *p. 611*
indenture terms, *p. 621*
inventory financing, *p. 617*

line of credit, *p. 617*
long-term financing, *p. 614*
long-term forecast, *p. 609*
master budget, *p. 611*
operating budget, *p. 610*
pledging, *p. 617*
revolving credit agreement, *p. 617*
secured loan, *p. 616*
short-term financing, *p. 614*
short-term forecast, *p. 609*
term-loan agreement, *p. 620*
trade credit, *p. 615*
unsecured loan, *p. 616*

PROFILE   REGINALD LEWIS, VENTURE CAPITAL SPECIALIST

Reginald Lewis

Imagine that a company is a car, and the role of financing becomes clear. In essence, it's fuel. In financing a company, then, the entrepreneur must answer two crucial questions: Where is the company now? and, Where do you want to take it? From there it's simply a matter of deciding when to fill up, at which station, and at what cost.

Unfortunately, many young companies sputter to a halt under a sign that says a gas station is still 35 miles away. Sometimes the entrepreneur simply underestimates the need for fuel. Other times it's the distance to the destination. The simplest mistakes overlap, snowball, and lead to disaster.

EILEEN DAVIS

Never let it be said that Reginald Lewis lacked drive or ambition. In high school and college he was an accomplished athlete. He looked forward to a career in professional sports but a shoulder injury cut short his dream. However, he took academics as seriously as athletics. He graduated from Virginia State University in 1965 and Harvard Law School in 1968. On graduation, he joined a prestigious New York law firm.

It didn't take Mr. Lewis long to realize that corporate contracts and fine print were not for him. He shifted his career from law into active investment. With a partner, he started his own firm specializing in venture capital development for small and medium-size businesses. Mr. Lewis was instrumental in assisting many minority enterprise small-business investment corporations (MESBIC's) in securing financing. Some actually credit him as being an architect of the MESBIC industry. After negotiating more than $100 million in venture capital financing, Mr. Lewis decided it was time to break out on his own.

In 1984, he launched TLC Group, his own investment firm. The knowledge he gained in finance enabled him to quickly secure $24 million in financing from First Boston Corp. for the purchase of McCall Pattern Co., a home-sewing products and publishing company. In three years, he sold McCall for $90 million. However, he set out for even bigger game: Beatrice International Foods. On August 6, 1987, Mr. Lewis outflanked potential buyers such as Citicorp and Pillsbury and gained control of Beatrice International Foods for his TLC Group through a leveraged buyout. Price tag: $985 million, financed through Kohlberg, Kravis, Roberts, & Co., Beatrice International Foods' investment bankers. TLC Group is today the nation's largest black-owned business. Maybe Reginald Lewis's shoulder injury was the luckiest thing that ever happened to him.

Reginald Lewis represents the success story of the 1980s—people who were successful in finance. Interest in finance took a tumble in the late 1980s after the Wall Street scandals and the stock market plunge. Finance will have a major comeback in the 1990s, however, because it is the key to success in starting and maintaining small businesses. In this chapter, we shall look at finance from the corporate point of view. In the next chapter, we shall explore stocks and bonds from both the corporate and investor's point of view. Your financial future could well rest on how much time and effort you put into understanding these two chapters plus the appendix to Part 6 on personal finance.

Source: Alfred Edmond, Jr., "Reginald Lewis Cuts The Big Deal," *Black Enterprise*, November 1987, pp. 43–46; "Entrepreneurs: The Best of 1987," *Business Week*, January 11, 1988, pp. 152–53; and Carol Loomis, "Buyout Kings," *Fortune*, July 4, 1988, pp. 53–60.

THE ROLE OF FINANCE

An accountant may be compared to a skilled laboratory technician who takes blood samples and other measures of a person's health and writes the findings on a health report (financial statements). A financial manager for a business is the doctor who interprets those reports and makes recommendations to the patient regarding changes that would improve health. Financial managers use the data prepared by the accountants and make recommendations to top management regarding strategies for improving the health (financial strength) of the firm.

A manager cannot be optimally effective at finance without understanding accounting. Similarly, a good accountant needs to understand finance. Accounting and finance, finance and accounting—the two go together like pizza and beer.

Venture magazine recently ran an article citing the mistakes companies make in financing. They said that "sources for this story couldn't emphasize enough that many companies' financial and money-raising woes come down to inaccurate financial reporting. Young, growing companies need to live and die by the numbers, they say."[1] The message could not be clearer—good finance begins with good accounting.

As you may remember from Chapter 6, financing a *small* business is a difficult but critical function if a firm expects to survive those important first five years. The simple reality is, the need for careful financial management is an essential, ongoing challenge a business of *any* size must endure throughout its entire life. Financial problems can arise in any type of organization. Remember when Chrysler Corporation faced extinction in the late 1970s due to severe financial problems? Had it not been for a government-backed loan of $1 billion, Chrysler may have joined the ranks of defunct auto companies such as Packard; and Lee Iacocca would not be profiled in this book.

Three of the most common ways for firms to fail *financially* are:

1. Undercapitalization (not enough funds to start with).
2. Poor cash flow.
3. Inadequate expense control.

Consider the problems encountered by a small organization called Parsley Patch. This company was started on a shoestring budget by two women. It began when Elizabeth Bertani prepared salt-free seasonings for her husband who was on a salt-free diet. Her friend Pat Sherwood felt the seasonings were good enough to sell. Ms. Bertani agreed, and Parsley Patch, Inc., was born.

The business began with an investment of $5,000. Their $5,000 was eaten up for a logo and a label design. They learned quickly the importance of capital in getting the business going. Eventually, the two women personally invested more than $100,000 to keep the business from experiencing severe undercapitalization.

Everything was going well. Hundreds of gourmet shops adopted the product line, but sales were still below expectations. Finally, the women decided the health food market offered more potential because salt-free seasonings were a natural for people with restricted diets. The choice was a good one. Sales took off and were approaching $30,000 a month. The problem was no profits. Elizabeth and Pat had not been trained in cash flow procedures nor in controlling expenses. In fact, they were told not to worry about costs, and they hadn't. They eventually hired a CPA and an experienced financial manager who taught them how to compute the costs of various blends they produced and how to control their expenses. They also offered insight into how to control cash coming in and out of the company. Today, they earn a comfortable margin on operations that run close to $1 million a year.[2] Luckily, they were able to turn things around before they went broke.

If Elizabeth and Pat had understood finance before starting their business, they may have been able to avoid many of the problems they encountered. Like all other areas we have discussed, the best way to get a true feel for finance is to visit several finance departments, observe the surroundings, watch the people at work, ask questions, get involved, and see for yourself how the financial world works. Personal interviews with owners and managers of medium-size and small businesses also provide important insights into opportunities in this important function.

One does not have to pursue finance as a career to be interested in finance. Financial understanding is important to anyone who wants to invest in stocks and bonds or plan a retirement fund. In short, finance is something everyone should study and be concerned with. In this chapter, the focus is on finance from the perspective of the businessperson. In chapter 21, an analysis of stocks and bonds as financing and investment instruments is presented. The appendix to Part 6 discusses some important *personal* finance topics so you'll be better prepared to manage your own funds. Let's first take a look at what finance is all about.

WHAT IS FINANCE?

finance
The function in a business responsible for acquiring funds for the firm, managing funds within the firm, and planning for the expenditure of funds on various assets.

Finance, basically, is the function in a business that is responsible for acquiring funds for the firm and managing funds within the firm (for example, preparing budgets, doing cash flow analyses, and planning for the expenditure of funds on such assets as plant, equipment, and machinery). As you can see, without a carefully calculated financial plan, the firm has little chance for survival regardless of its product or marketing effectiveness. Most organizations will have a manager in charge of financial operations. Generally, this chief financial officer is known as the treasurer or vice president of finance. Figure 19–1 offers a basic description of what a finance person does. As you can see, the fundamental charge is to obtain money and then plan, use, and control money effectively.

You are probably somewhat familiar with several finance functions, for example, the idea of buying merchandise on credit and collecting payment from buyers of the firm's merchandise. Both *credit* and *collections* are important responsibilities of financial managers. The finance manager must also be sure that the company does not lose too much money to bad debt losses (people or firms that don't pay). Naturally, this means that finance is further responsible for collecting overdue payments. These functions are critical to all types of businesses, but particularly important to small and medium-size businesses that typically have smaller cash or credit cushions than large corporations.

Taxes represent an outflow of cash from the business and must be paid. Therefore, they too fall under the scrutiny of finance. As tax laws and tax liabilities have changed, finance people have taken on the increasingly important responsibility of tax management. *Tax management* is the analyzing of tax implications of various managerial decisions in an attempt to minimize the taxes paid by the business (remember the discussion of LIFO/FIFO?). Businesses of all sizes must concern themselves with tax responsibilities.

Finally, often someone in the finance department serves as an internal auditor. It's the internal auditor that checks on the journals, ledgers, and financial statements prepared by the accounting department to make sure that all transactions have been treated in accordance with established accounting rules and procedures.

FIGURE 19–1

What financial managers do. All these functions depend greatly on the information provided by the accounting statements discussed earlier.

- Planning
- Budgeting
- Obtaining funds
- Controlling funds (funds management)
- Collecting funds (credit management)
- Auditing
- Managing taxes
- Advising top management on financial matters

If there were no such audits, accounting statements would be almost worthless. Therefore, it's important that the internal auditor be objective and critical of any improprieties or deficiencies he or she might note in their evaluation. Regular internal audits offer the firm assistance in the important role of financial planning, which we will look at next.

Can you see the link between accounting and finance? They are mutually supportive functions in a firm. A firm cannot get along without accounting but neither can it prosper without short- and long-term financing, managing its funds well, minimizing its taxes, and investing its funds properly. In fact, finance is so important to a firm that some finance executives go on to be presidents of firms. What would be the advantages and disadvantages of a president with a finance background versus a marketing background? Is there a danger of being too concerned with cost-cutting, budgeting, and controlling funds?

THINKING IT THROUGH

FINANCIAL PLANNING

Planning has been a continuous theme throughout this book. We have stressed the importance of planning as a managerial function and offered insights into planning your career. Financial planning involves an analysis of the short- and long-term picture of money flows to and from the firm. The overall objective of financial planning is to optimize profits and make the best use of money. It's probably safe to assume that we all could use more or better financial planning in our lives.

Financial planning involves three steps: (1) forecasting financial needs—both short- and long-term needs, (2) developing budgets to meet those needs, and (3) establishing financial control to see how well the company is following the financial plans. Let's look at the important role each step plays in the financial health of an organization.

Forecasting Financial Needs

Forecasting is an important component of financial planning. (See Figure 19–2 on page 610.) A **short-term forecast** is a prediction of revenues, costs, and expenses for a period of one year or less. This forecast is the foundation for most other financial plans, so its accuracy is critical. Part of the short-term forecast may be in the form of a **cash flow forecast** that projects the expected cash inflows and outflows in future periods, usually months or quarters. Naturally, the inflows and outflows recorded in the cash flow forecast are based on the expected sales revenues and on various costs and expenses incurred and when they will come due.

A **long-term forecast** is a prediction of revenues, costs, and expenses for a period longer than 1 year, sometimes as far as 5 or 10 years into the future. This forecast plays a crucial part in the company's long-term strategic plan. Remember, the strategic plan asks questions such as: What business are we in and should we be in five years from now? How much money should we invest in automation and new plant and equipment over the next decade? The long-term financial forecast gives top management, as well as operations managers, some feel for the income or profit potential possible with different strategic plans. Additionally, along with the short-term forecasts, long-term projections assist finance managers with the preparation of company budgets.

short-term forecast
A prediction of revenues, costs and expenses for a period of one year or less.

cash flow forecast
A prediction of cash inflows and outflows in future periods.

long-term forecast
A prediction of revenues, costs, and expenses for a period longer than 1 year, sometimes extending 5 or 10 years into the future.

Financial planning. Note the close link between financial planning and budgeting. In the appendix to Part Six, you will learn that this is important for individuals as well as firms.

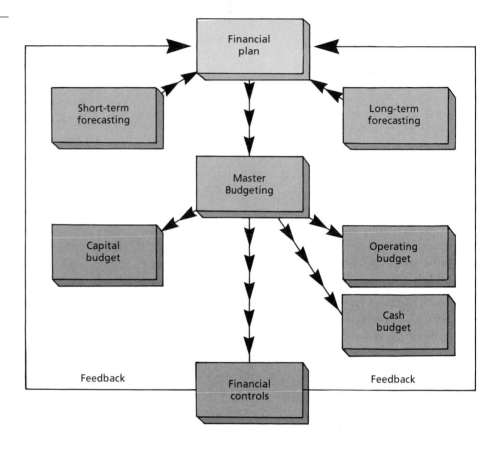

Developing Budgets

budget
A financial plan that allocates resources based on projected revenues.

A budget is itself a financial plan. Specifically, a **budget** sets forth management's expectations for revenues and, based on those financial expectations, allocates the use of specific resources throughout the firm. You may live under a carefully constructed budget of your own. A business operates in the same way. A budget becomes the primary basis and justification for financial operations in the firm.

Most firms compile yearly budgets from short- and long-term financial forecasts. There are usually several budgets established in a firm:

- An operating budget.
- A capital budget.
- A cash budget.
- A master budget.

operating budget
The projection of dollar allocations to various costs and expenses needed to operate the company, given projected revenue.

An **operating budget** is the projection of dollar allocations to various costs and expenses needed to run or operate the business, given projected revenues. How much the firm will spend on supplies, travel, rent, advertising, salaries, and so on, is determined in the operating budget.

capital budget
The spending plan for assets whose returns are expected to occur over an extended period of time (more than one year).

A **capital budget** highlights the firm's spending plans for assets whose returns are expected to occur over an extended period of time (more than one year.) The capital budget primarily concerns itself with the purchase of such assets as property, buildings, and equipment.

MAKING ETHICAL DECISIONS

You are a department manager for a major consumer products firm. Each year your supervisor asks that you prepare a short-term financial forecast and operating budget for the coming fiscal year. Your department's appropriations are determined and funds allocated from the forecast and budget you present. Preliminary analysis indicates that your department could survive the next year's operations with exactly the same budget that was allocated to you last year. The problem is, you wonder if you don't request additional funds for this year, will the firm expect you to keep your departmental costs down each and every year? You realize your supervisor would certainly approve a 10 percent increase in your budget appropriations just on the trust he has in you. You might even be able to get a 15 percent increase with little questioning of actual need. What would you do? What could be the result of your decision?

A **cash budget** is the projected cash balance at the end of a given period (for example, monthly, quarterly). Cash budgets can be important guidelines that assist managers in anticipating borrowing, debt repayment, cash disbursements, and short-term investment expectations. Cash budgets are often the last budgets that are prepared.

cash budget
The projected cash balance at the end of a given period (e.g., monthly, quarterly).

The **master budget** ties in all the above mentioned budgets and summarizes the proposed financial activities of the firm.

master budget
The financial plan that summarizes the operating, capital, and cash budgets.

At this point, it should be obvious to you that financial managers play an important role in the operations of the firm. These managers often determine what long-term investments to make, when specific funds will be needed, and how the funds will be generated. Once a company has projected its short-term and long-term financial needs and established budgets to show how funds will be allocated, the final step in financial planning is to establish financial controls.

Establishing Financial Control

Financial control means that the actual revenues, costs, and expenses (including the cash flow projections) are periodically reviewed and compared with projections. Deviations can thus be determined and corrective action taken. Such controls provide feedback to help reveal which accounts, which departments, and which people are varying from the financial plans. Such deviations may or may not be justified. In either case, some financial adjustments to the plan may be made. After the Progress Check we shall explore specific reasons why firms need to have funds readily available.

financial control
A process that periodically compares the actual revenue, costs, and expenses with projections.

■ Name three finance functions important to the firm's overall operations and performance.

■ What does an internal auditor do? Why is it important that this function remain independent?

■ What are the three primary financial problems that often cause firms to fail financially?

■ In what ways do short-term and long-term financial forecasts differ?

■ What is the organization's purpose in preparing budgets? Can you identify at least three different types of budgets?

PROGRESS CHECK

THE NEED FOR HAVING FUNDS AVAILABLE

Sound financial management is essential to businesses because the need for operating funds never seems to cease. Also, like our personal financial needs, the capital needs of a business change over time. For example, as a small business grows, its financial requirements shift considerably. (Remember the example of Parsley Patch.) The same is true with large corporations such as AT&T and PepsiCo. As they venture into new product areas or markets, their capital needs grow and intensify. It's safe to say that different firms are in need of available funds for a variety of reasons. However, in virtually all organizations, funds must be available to finance specific operational needs. Let's take a look at the financial needs that affect the operations of both the smallest and the largest of business enterprises.

Financing Daily Operations

If workers are scheduled to be paid on Friday, they don't expect to have to wait until Monday for their paychecks. If tax payments are due on the 15th of the month, the government anticipates the money will be there on time. If the interest payment on a business loan is due on the 30th, the lender doesn't mean the 1st of the next month. As you can see, funds have to be available to meet the daily operational costs of the business. The challenge of sound financial management is to see that funds are available to meet these daily cash expenditures without compromising the investment potential of the firm's money.

As you may or may not know, money has a time value. In other words, if someone offered to give you $200 today or $200 one year from today, you would benefit by taking the $200 today. Why? A very simple reason. You could start collecting interest on the $200 you receive today and over the course of a year's time, your money would grow. In business, the interest gained on the firm's investments is important in maximizing the profit the firm will gain. For this reason, financial managers often try to keep cash expenditures at a minimum, to free funds for investment in interest-bearing accounts. It's not unusual for finance managers to suggest the firm pay bills as late as possible (unless a cash discount is available) and set up collection procedures to ensure that the firm gets what's owed to it as fast as possible. This way finance managers maximize the investment potential of the firm's funds. As you might expect, efficient cash management is particulary important to small firms in conducting their daily operations.

Financing the Firm's Credit Services

The appendix to Part 6 discusses some important information on managing your personal finances. As you may suspect, establishing credit is one area covered in the personal finance section. In business, the firm knows that availability of credit helps to keep current customers happy and entices other buyers to do business with the firm. In the highly competitive business environment today, it's unlikely a firm could survive without the availability of credit purchasing.

The major problem that arises with credit purchasing is this. As much as 25 percent of the firm's assets could be tied up in accounts receivable. (To refresh your accounting memory, accounts receivable is money owed to a business from customers who bought goods or services on credit.) This means the firm needs to expend available funds to pay for the goods or services already provided purchasers who bought on credit. This outflow of funds causes financial managers to focus a

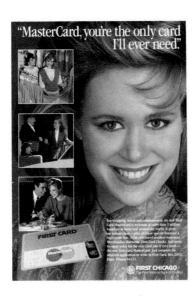

Credit cards today have many uses, both business and personal. For the business traveler, they are almost a necessity. Credit cards like First Card also offer travel insurance, merchandise discounts, checking account-type checks, and the freedom to buy what you want—up to your credit ceiling.

good part of their attention on efficient collection procedures. For example, a firm often provides cash or quantity discounts to purchasers who pay their account by a certain time. Also, finance managers carefully scrutinize old and new credit customers to see if they have a favorable history of meeting their credit obligations on time. In essence, the credit policy of the firm reflects its financial position and the desire to expand into new markets.

Financing the Purchase of Inventory

As we noted earlier in the text, the marketing concept implies a clear consumer orientation. One implication of this concept is that service and availability of goods are vital if a firm expects to prosper in today's markets. Therefore, to satisfy customers, businesses are forced to maintain inventories that involve a sizable expenditure of funds. Although it's true the firm expects to recapture its investment in inventory through sales to customers, a carefully constructed inventory policy assists in managing the use of the firm's available funds and maximizing profitability. For example, an owner of a neighborhood ice cream parlor ties up more funds in inventory (ice cream) in the summer months than in winter. It's rather obvious why. The demand for ice cream goes *up* in the summer. As you may recall from Chapter 13, innovations such as just-in-time inventory are reducing the funds the firm must maintain in inventory.

Financing the Purchase of Major Assets

In many organizations, the purchase of major assets such as land for future expansion, plants to increase production capabilities, and equipment to maintain or exceed current levels of output is essential. As you might imagine, these purchases require a huge expenditure of the organization's funds. Therefore, it's critical that the firm weigh all the possible options before it commits what may be a large portion of its available resources. (As you may remember from accounting, these purchases are often referred to as long-term or fixed assets.) For this reason, financial managers and analysts are called in to provide important insights into the appropriateness of such purchases. Let's look at an example. Suppose a firm needs to expand its production capabilities due to increases in demand. One option is to buy land and build a new plant from scratch. Another option would be to purchase an existing plant. Can you think of financial and accounting considerations that would come into play in this decision?

It's evident the firm's need for available funds raises several questions that need to be considered. How does the firm obtain funds to finance operations and other business necessities? How long will specific funds be needed by the organization? Will funds have to be repaid at a later date? What will the needed funds cost? These questions will be addressed in the next section after the Progress Check.

PROGRESS CHECK

> Money is said to have a time value. What exactly does this mean?
>
> Why are accounts receivable a financial concern to the firm?
>
> Is an efficient account collection plan more important to a small firm or a large corporation? Why?
>
> What is the major reason organizations spend a good deal of their available funds on inventory?

ALTERNATIVE SOURCES OF FUNDS

Earlier in the chapter, you learned that finance is the function in a business that is responsible for acquiring funds for the firm. The amount of money needed for various time periods and the most appropriate sources to obtain these funds from are fundamental questions in sound financial management. We will look at the different methods and sources of acquiring funds next. However, before we begin this discussion, it's important to highlight some key distinctions involved in funding the firm's operations.

Organizations typically encounter short- and long-term financing needs. **Short-term financing** refers to the need for capital that will be repaid within one year and that helps finance current operations. On the other hand, **long-term financing** refers to capital needs for major purchases that will be repaid over a specific time period longer than one year. We shall explore sources of both short- and long-term financing in the next section. The other important distinction you should familiarize yourself with involves the different *methods* of raising capital available to the firm. Specifically, a firm can seek to raise capital through debt or equity sources. **Debt capital** refers to funds raised through various forms of borrowing that must be repaid (debt). **Equity capital** is money raised from within the firm or through the sale of ownership (equity) in the firm. Again, we will discuss these two financing alternatives in depth later.

SHORT–TERM FINANCING

The bulk of a finance manager's job is *not* involved with obtaining long-term funds. The nitty-gritty, day-to-day operation of the firm calls for the careful management of short-term financial needs. Cash may be needed for additional inventory, or bills may come due unexpectedly. Much like your personal financial needs, a business sometimes needs to obtain short-term funds when other funds run out. This is particularly true of small businesses. It's rare that small businesses even attempt to

short-term financing
Money obtained to finance current operations that will be repaid in less than one year.

long-term financing
Money obtained from the owners of the firm and lenders who will be repaid over a specific time period longer than one year.

debt capital
Funds raised by borrowing money through the sale of bonds or from banks and other lending institutions.

equity capital
Funds raised within the company or from selling ownership in the firm.

find funding for long-term needs. They are concerned more with just staying afloat until they are able to build capital and creditworthiness. Short-term financing can be obtained in several different ways. Let's look at some of the options. Sources of short-term financing include:

- Trade credit.
- Family and friends.
- Commercial banks.
- Factoring.
- Commercial paper.
- Internal sources.

Trade Credit

The most widely used source of short-term funding is called **trade credit.** This means that a business is able to buy goods today and pay for them sometime in the future. When a firm buys merchandise, it receives an invoice (bill) much like the one you receive when you buy something on credit.

As discussed in the appendix to Chapter 18, a business invoice often contains terms such as "2/10, net 30." This means that the buyer can take a 2 percent discount for paying within 10 days. The total bill is due in 30 days if the discount is not taken. It is important for the finance manager to pay attention to such discounts. In fact, they are so important that the example is worth repeating here: If the discount is 2/10, net 30, the purchaser will pay 2 percent more for waiting an extra 20 days to pay the invoice. Some uninformed businesspeople feel that 2 percent is insignificant, and pay their bills after the discount period. Some quick calculations will show how costly such delay really is.

By not paying on time, the firm pays 2 percent for waiting just 20 days. If this continues over time, the firm would lose 2 percent for every 20-day period it doesn't pay its bills early. There are about 18 20-day periods in a year. Therefore, the penalty for not taking discounts is approximately 36 percent a year (18 times 2 percent). Because about 10 percent of business transactions involve trade credit, this is an important element in the daily financial management of the firm.

trade credit
The practice of buying goods now and paying for them early and getting a discount.

Family and Friends

A second source of short-term funds for most smaller firms is money lent to them by family and friends. Because short-term funds are needed for periods of less than a year, often friends are willing to help. Such loans can be dangerous if the firm does not understand cash flow. As we discussed earlier, the firm may suddenly find several bills coming due at the same time and have no other sources of funds. It is better, therefore, not to borrow from friends, but instead go to a commercial bank that understands the risk and can help analyze future financial needs. If you do borrow from family or friends, it is best to be very professional about the deal and (1) agree on terms at the beginning, (2) write an agreement, and (3) pay them back the same way you would a bank loan.

Commercial Banks

As we discussed in Chapter 18, small to medium-size businesses should have the person in charge of the finance function keep in very close touch with a local bank. It is wise to see a banker periodically (as often as once a month) and send the banker all financial statements. Remember, though, banks are not in business to lend money to risky start-up ventures. Their function, for new firms, is to provide short-term loans backed by collateral.[3]

A financial manager may obtain funds from a finance company, but the interest rates are usually higher than other lending sources. Commerical bank rates are usually lower.

Try to imagine different kinds of businesspeople going to the bank for a loan, and you'll get a better feel for the role of the financial manager. Picture, for example, a farmer going to the bank to borrow funds for seed, fertilizer, equipment, and other needs. Such supplies may be bought in the spring and paid for when the fall harvest comes in. Now picture a local toy store buying merchandise for Christmas sales. The money for such purchases might be borrowed in June and July and paid back after Christmas. A restaurant may borrow funds at the beginning of the month and pay by the end of the month. Can you see that *how much* a business borrows and for *how long* depend on the kind of business it is and how quickly the merchandise purchased with a bank loan can be resold or used to generate funds?

Have you ever found yourself going to the bank to take out funds for special emergencies such as a car accident? Sometimes such unexpected money needs arise monthly. One month it's a dentist bill, the next a need for snow tires, and so on. There are vacations to pay for, school supplies, gifts, and more. Similarly, a businessperson may have to go to the bank and borrow short-term funds often. A new shipment of goods may arrive unexpectedly, a machine may break down, an insurance bill may come due, and so forth.

Like you, a business sometimes finds itself in a position where many bills come due at once: utilities, insurance, payroll, new equipment, and more. Most times such sudden cash needs can be met; one can always ask the bank for more. But sometimes a business gets so far into debt, so far behind in its payments, that the bank refuses to lend it more. Suddenly the business is unable to pay its bills. More often than not, this results in bankruptcy or business failure, and you can chalk up another business failure to cash flow problems.

David Berch, the president of Cognetics, Inc. has this to say about cash flow:[4]

> Cash flow is a constant issue if you don't go for large outside financing, which we've chosen not to do. You've got a fixed payroll. Everything on the expense side is fixed, and everything on the revenue side is variable. Somebody gets sick and doesn't pay on his receivable, or a salesperson gets lazy and doesn't sell for a couple of months. All of a sudden your cash flow goes to (pot). You find yourself constantly managing cash flow. It's a major issue.

Can you see now how important it is for the finance or accounting person to do a cash flow forecast? By anticipating times when many bills will come due, a business can begin early to seek funds or sell other assets to prepare for the crunch. Can you see also why it is important for a businessperson to keep friendly and close relations with his or her banker? The banker may spot cash flow problems early and point out the danger. Or, the banker may be more willing to lend money in a crisis if the businessperson has established a strong, friendly relationship built on openness and trust.[5] It's always important to remember your banker wants to see you succeed almost as much as you do. Bankers can be an invaluable support to small, growing businesses.

Different Forms of Bank Loans

unsecured loan
A loan not backed by any collateral.

secured loan
Loan backed by something valuable, such as property.

The most difficult kind of loan to get from a bank or other financial institution is an **unsecured loan.** It is a loan that is not backed by any collateral. Normally, only highly regarded customers of the bank receive unsecured loans. A **secured loan** is

THE PRIME RATE

Periodically you will read that the *prime rate* has been raised or lowered. For most people, that report has little meaning. But for a financial manager, the level of the prime rate is very important. Here is why. The prime rate is the short-term interest rate that banks charge their pre-

ferred (creditworthy) customers. Most firms pay slightly more than the prime rate for a loan, but some very good credit risks can negotiate loans below prime. In either case, the prime rate is the rate from which many loan rates are calculated.

one backed by something valuable such as property. If the borrower fails to pay the loan, the lender may take possession of the collateral. That takes some of the risk out of lending money. **Pledging** is the term used for using accounts receivable as security. Some percentage of accounts receivable is accepted as collateral, and the cash received as payment for the merchandise is sent to the banker. **Inventory financing** means that inventory such as raw materials (for example, coal, steel) or other inventory is used as collateral for a loan. Other property can also be used as collateral, including buildings, machinery, and other things of value (for example, company-owned stocks and bonds).

pledging
Using accounts receivable as security

inventory financing
Financing that uses inventory such as raw materials as collateral for a loan.

If you develop a good relationship with a bank, it will open a line of credit for you. A **line of credit** means the bank will lend the business a given amount of unsecured short-term funds, provided the bank has the funds available. A line of credit is not a *guaranteed* loan, but it comes close. The purpose of a line of credit is to speed the borrowing process so that a firm does not have to go through the hassle of applying for a new loan every time it needs funds. The funds are available as long as the credit ceiling is not exceeded. As businesses mature and become more financially secure, the amount of credit often is increased. Some firms will even apply for a **revolving credit agreement**. That is a line of credit that is guaranteed. However, the bank usually charges a fee for guaranteeing the loan. A line of credit or a revolving credit agreement are particulary good ways of obtaining funds for unexpected cash needs that arise.

line of credit
The amount of unsecured, short-term credit a bank will lend a borrower that is agreed to ahead of time.

revolving credit agreement
A line of credit that is guaranteed by the bank.

Factoring

One relatively expensive source of short-term funds for a firm is called factoring. The way it works is this: as we know, a firm sells many of its products on credit to consumers and other businesses. Some of these buyers are slow in paying their bills. The company may thus have a large amount of money due in accounts receivable. A *factor* buys the accounts receivable from the firm at a discount (usually paying 50 to 70 percent of the value of the accounts receivable) for cash. The factor then collects and keeps the money that was owed the original firm. **Factoring,** then, is the process of selling accounts receivable for cash. How much this costs the firm depends on the discount rate the factor requires. The discount rate for factoring depends on the *age* of the accounts receivable, the nature of the business, and the conditions of the economy.

factoring
Selling accounts receivable for cash.

Recently, Kay Jewelers sold about $150 million in customer receivables to NCNB (National Bank of North Carolina). The company did so in order to improve its debt to equity ratio (see the appendix to the accounting chapter [18]). The bank assumed the debts at face value and will share the proceeds from the servicing of the debt.[6]

Commercial Paper

Sometimes a large corporation needs funds for a few months and wants to get lower rates than those charged by banks. One strategy is to sell commercial paper. **Commercial paper** consists of promissory notes, in amounts ranging from $25,000 up, that mature in 270 days or less. The promissory note states a fixed amount of money the business agrees to repay to the lender on a specific date. If an interest rate is involved, it is identified on the face of the promissory note. Commercial paper is unsecured, so only the more financially stable firms can sell it. It is a way to get short-term funds for less than bank rates. Since most commercial paper comes due in usually 30 to 90 days, it is also an investment opportunity where buyers of commerical paper can put cash for short periods to earn some interest. People who buy commerical paper are looking for a place to put their money for a short term without going through the hassle of dealing with banks.

Internal Sources of Funds

Just like you and me, a business is wise to get its short-term funds from internal sources as much as possible. There are several ways a firm can generate more cash internally. One way is to collect accounts receivable more quickly. Often the company accountant works with the other finance people to find such sources of funds. Inventory may also be reduced, costs may be minimized, or expenses may be cut. The healthier the balance sheet looks and the better the financial ratios are, the easier it is to borrow outside funds, if that is necessary. A wise accounting/finance team is able to save a business much money by finding internal sources of funds and freeing them, and by getting external funding at minimal rates (such as selling commercial paper). After the Progress Check, we shall look into the sources of long-term financing.

PROGRESS CHECK

- If you received terms of 3/10, net 25, exactly what would this mean?

- What is the difference between trade credit and a line of credit at a bank?

- What is meant by factoring? What are some of the considerations set in establishing a discount rate in factoring?

- How does commercial paper work and what is the main advantage of issuing commercial paper?

LONG–TERM FINANCING

Financial planning and forecasting help the firm in developing a financial plan. This plan specifies the amount of funding that the firm will need over various time periods and the most appropriate sources of those funds. In setting long-term financing objectives, the firm generally asks itself three major questions:

- What are the long-term goals and objectives of the organization?
- What are the financial requirements needed to achieve these long-term goals and objectives?
- What sources of long-term capital are available and which will best fit our needs?

MONEY DOESN'T GROW ON TREES, BUT YOU CAN PICK IT HERE!

If you are starting or running a small business, you know that one of the hardest jobs of a small-business person is to find money when it is really needed. Unless you have a rich Aunt Henrietta willing to contribute, you have to do a lot of searching for those needed funds. The text already discusses many sources of funds, but here are some other places you may want to search:

STATE FUNDS

State funding programs like the Ben Franklin Partnership in Pennsylvania will provide outright grants as well as venture capital in return for ownership in the business. The SBA has a booklet available called "Capital Formation in the States" that lists funds operated by some states. Call your Department of Commerce to ask about funds sponsored by your state. Also see *Venture* magazine, May 1989, for details about various state programs.

POTENTIAL CUSTOMER OR SUPPLIER

Companies like Du Pont have funded young companies with which it already does business and with which it plans to develop and market a product. To find this type of investor, use the *Standard Industrial Classification Manual* or Dun's Marketing Services *Million Dollar Directory* to find large companies in your industry.

SMALL–BUSINESS INVESTMENT COMPANIES (SBICs)

Most SBICs invest twice as many dollars in new businesses than venture capitalists do. The best way to find a SBIC is through the National Association of Small Business Investment Companies or the National Association of Investment Companies (which represents MESBICs—minority small-business investment companies).

COMMUNITY DEVELOPMENT FUNDS

Communities sometimes invite companies that will provide jobs for their citizens by making loans and equity investments. Ask the National Congress for Community Economic Development or your state's Department of Economic Development about community funds in your area.

ACCOUNTING FIRMS

Most large accounting firms can help small businesses in two ways: by discounting their fees in the hopes of increasing them as your company grows and by introducing you to potential investors. Call the small-business divisions of the larger firms for the names of people who work with new businesses.

ATTORNEYS

Like accountants, attorneys are interested in helping a small business that may eventually grow to be a big client. Assistance is usually through introduction to potential investors. To find a law firm willing to work with you, use your other contacts in the financial community such as accountants and informal investor groups.

SMALL–BUSINESS INCUBATORS

Incubators provide new business with shared office services and can assist in raising money from outside sources. For information, contact the National Business Incubation Association in Carlisle, Pa. Large corporations and universities also operate incubators.

SUCCESSFUL LOCAL ENTREPRENEURS

Experienced entrepreneurs may help when established sources don't. They may offer funds in exchange for equity. The only way to find such an investor is by networking—getting out and meeting people.

Source: Marie-Jeanne Juilland, "Alternatives to a Rich Uncle," *Venture*, May 1988, pp. 62–68; and Ellyn E. Spragins, "Supply-Side Financing," *Inc.* February 1989, pp. 95–96.

In business, long-term capital is used to buy fixed assets such as plant and equipment and to finance any expansions of the organization. In major corporations, decisions concerning long-term financing normally involve the board of directors and top management, as well as finance and accounting managers. In some instances even an expert like an investment banker is included in the decision making. In smaller businesses, the owner or owners of a firm are always actively involved in financing opportunities available to them.

Initial long-term financing usually comes from three sources: retained earnings, debt capital, or equity capital. We will look at these three sources of long-term funds next (see Figure 19–3 on page 620).

FIGURE 19–3

Sources of long-term funds. The three major sources of long-term funds are retained earnings, equity capital, and debt capital.

Retained Earnings
- Profits earned by the firm that are not distributed to the owners

Equity Capital
- Personal savings and second mortgages on homes
- Friends and family loans
- Partners
- Venture capital firms
- Sale of stock (equity financing)
- Retained earnings

Debt Capital
- Sale of bonds (debt financing)
- Long-term loans from banks and other financial institutions

Retained Earnings

A major source of long-term funds for a firm is income that it earns from its operations. This is especially true of small businesses since they have fewer financing alternatives available to them. However, large corporations also depend on profits assisting with long-term costs the firm expects to incur. You probably remember from Chapter 18 that the profits the company keeps and reinvests in the firm are called *retained earnings*.

Retained earnings are generally the most favored source of long-term capital in the firm. Nevertheless, many organizations do not have on hand sufficient retained earnings to finance expensive capital improvements or expansion. Think about it for a moment. If you wished to purchase an expensive personal asset such as a new car, the ideal way to do it would be to go to your personal savings and take out the necessary cash to pay for the car. No hassle! No Interest! Unfortunately, few people can do this since they rarely have such large amounts of cash available. Most businesses are no different. Even though they would like to finance long-term needs from operations, few have the resources on hand to accomplish this. Typically, this causes firms to turn to debt or equity financing to meet long-term financial needs.

Debt Financing

Long-term financing needs of a business can be achieved by securing debt capital. Debt capital is funds that come to the firm from borrowing (going into debt) through lending institutions or from the sale of bonds. With debt financing, the company has a legal obligation to repay the amount borrowed.

Once a firm is established and has developed rapport with a bank, insurance company, pension fund, or other financial institution, it can often secure a long-term loan. (For small businesses, the Small Business Administration can often be a good source of long-term loans.) Long-term loans are usually repaid within 3 to 7 years, but may extend to perhaps 15 or 20 years. For such loans, a business must sign what is called a term-loan agreement. A **term-loan agreement** is a promissory note that requires the borrower to repay the loan in specified installments (for example, monthly, yearly).

Long-term loans are often more expensive than short-term loans because larger amounts of capital are borrowed and the repayment date is less secure. Most long-

term-loan agreement
A promissory note that requires the borrower to repay the loan in installments that are specified.

IN FINANCE, IT'S OK TO BE A *SLOB*

A *SLOB* is a secured lease obligation bond; that is, a bond secured by lease payments from a utility on plants that it uses to generate electricity. Some bonds are secured by the lease and by a lien on the plant as well. That is, the bondholders would be paid off by selling the plant if the money from the lease was not sufficient. By the way, an unsecured lease obligation bond is called a LOB. You may be interested in such bonds because the return is quite good. For example, the bonds that were used to finance a coal-fueled generator in Ohio were priced to yield 11.2 percent in 1988. That's a lot better than you could do at a bank. You see, a SLOB in finance may be a good deal. If stocks and bonds interest you, stay tuned for Chapter 21 where we shall discuss them in more detail.

Source: Ben Weberman, "How Safe are SLOBs?" *Forbes,* August 8, 1988, p. 119.

A sample government treasury bond. Note that such bonds are sold in denominations of $1,000. Note too the interest rate of 11⅝ percent. Government bonds are a relatively safe investment and sometimes pay high interest.

term loans require some form of collateral, including real estate, machinery, equipment, or stock. The interest rate for such loans is based on factors such as whether or not there is adequate collateral, the firm's credit rating, and the general level of market interest rates.

If an organization is unable to attain its long-term financing needs from a lending institution, it may decide to issue bonds. To put it simply, a bond is a company IOU. It is a binding contract through which an organization agrees to specific terms with investors in return for investors lending money to the company. The terms of agreement in a bond are referred to as the **indenture terms.** We will discuss bonds in depth in the next chapter.

If you have been reading the papers, you know that businesspeople piled up a huge amount of debt in the 1980s. From 1980 to 1989, the debt increased from $1.4 trillion to nearly $3.2 trillion. The resulting debt load scares many financial experts. This is especially true when the government is in such debt also.[7]

indenture terms
The terms of agreement in a bond.

HOW TO TURN $6 MILLION INTO $480 MILLION

We said in the Profile that the 1980s was the decade of the finance professional. One story will illustrate what we meant. At the end of the decade, the stock market took a real tumble. That spelled disaster for some people not tuned into the economy. But for others it was a financial windfall.

Just before the crash on October 19, 1987, a New York investment firm agreed to buy Rexene, a producer of polyethylene, styrene, and other products that go into food packaging and disposable cups, for $456 million. After the crash, a New York bank that had agreed to finance the deal backed out. Drexel Burnham Lambert, an aggressive, innovative finance firm, stepped in to help finance the deal. Much of it was through debt financing. When the deal was completed, the investment firm and the finance firm had put up $6 million in their own money—cash. That gave them 24 million shares of stock at 25 cents each. The shares will be sold to the public for about $480 million.

These are the kinds of deals that were made in the 1980s. Similar spectacular deals will be made in the 1990s. Who will make them? People who understand finance. Will one of them be you?

Source: David A. Vise and Steve Coo, "Heavy Borrowing, Smart Timing May Turn $6 million into $500 million," *Los Angeles Times,* July 24, 1988, p. 7.

Businesses compete with the government for the sale of bonds. Some local government municipal bonds are often tax-free bonds—meaning bondholders do not have to pay taxes on any interest earned from the bond. Bonds sold by the federal government are relatively risk free, because they are backed by the power of the government to tax us. It is possible for the government to make the sale of corporate bonds more difficult by selling its own, more attractive government bonds. This is often what is referred to as "crowding out" of corporate bonds. If a firm is unable to secure a long-term loan from a lender nor issue bonds to investors, it often turns to the last alternative for long-term financing: equity capital.

Equity Financing

Equity financing comes from the owners of the firm. Therefore, equity capital is generated by selling ownership in the firm. For example, an entrepreneur who invests his or her savings in a new firm is providing equity capital. Generally, firms attempt to raise equity capital through two sources: venture capital or selling stock in the firm.

Venture Capital

The hardest time for a firm to raise money is when it is just starting. The company typically has few assets; therefore the chance of borrowing significant amounts of money from a bank are slim. The people starting the firm may be able to obtain a second mortgage on their homes, but that is usually not enough to finance a company through a year or more of operations. In Chapters 4 and 6, we talked about the advantages and disadvantages of various forms of business and small-business management. We learned that the largest single source of start-up capital is the savings of the initial owners plus those of partners, friends, and others willing to risk some money on the chance that the firm will succeed. We noted that the owners of Parsley Patch started off with investing $5,000 and eventually invested over $100,000.

The modern source of start-up capital, however, is from venture capital firms. Venture capital is money that is invested in new companies with great profit potential. The search for such funds begins with a good business plan (see Chapter

BORROWING MONEY IN INTERNATIONAL MARKETS

When you read the financial section of the newspaper, you will discover that interest rates vary for money borrowed in different countries. Often, interest rates in the United States are much higher than in Europe, Japan, or other areas of the world. Therefore, more and more U.S. corporations are seeking funds overseas. For example ITT Financial Corporation recently formed a subsidiary in the Antilles to gain access to foreign investors. A $100 million bond offering in the overseas market enabled the company to obtain funds for less than they would have cost in the United States. In fact, the bonds were originally designed to be sold in the United States but the overseas market proved better. The point is that financial officers must be able to think globally when planning to raise funds. The United States is a popular place for foreign firms to invest, and financial managers should take advantage of that desire.

6). This document must convince investors that the firm will be a success. Part of the business plan may be a financing proposal that spells out how much money is needed, how it is to be raised, and how it will be paid back.

The venture capital industry began about 50 years ago as an alternative investment vehicle for wealthy families such as the Rockefellers. They financed Sanford McDonnell, for example, when he was still operating out of a barn. That small venture grew into McDonnell Douglas, the large aerospace and defense contractor. The venture capital industry limped along for years until the early 1980s, when the new, high-tech companies were being started. Then the industry took off. It has slowed recently because high capital gains taxes makes such risky investments less attractive. Much of the gap is being filled by foreign investors from Japan and other capital-rich countries.[8]

A finance manager has to be careful in choosing a venture capital firm to help finance a new business. For one thing, the venture capital firm will want at least a one-third ownership of the business. More importantly, the venture capital firm should be able to come up with more financing if the firm needs it. The dangers of having the wrong venture capital firm are illustrated in the experience of Jon Birck.

Jon Birck started Northwest Instrument Systems with money from a venture capital firm. He worked until 11:00 or 12:00 each night to build the company. One day he was asked to leave by the venture capital firm, which wanted a more experienced chief executive officer to protect their investment. Birck had dedicated three years to the company. He had left a secure job, put his marriage on the line, taken out a second mortgage on his house, and given himself a below-average salary; and then, just when the firm was ready for rapid growth, he was asked to resign.

Ed Harris of Persoft, a computer software company, was luckier than Jon Birck. He also turned to a venture capital firm when the banks turned him down for a loan. The cost of the $2 million loan was 25 percent of the business, a new board of directors including someone from the venture capital firm, a new chief operating office, and a more structured managerial style overall. So far, Harris has prospered from the loan.[9]

Venture capital firms often invest equity funds in small to medium-size (often high-tech) firms in hopes of receiving significant financial rewards. To learn more about venture capital and new firms in general, read *Venture, Inc,* and *Black Enterprise* magazines.

Advertisements for venture capital.

Selling Stock

Regardless of whether or not a new firm can obtain venture capital funds, there usually comes a time when even more funds are required. One way to obtain needed funds is to sell ownership shares in the firm (called *stock*) to the public. If you look in the back of *The Wall Street Journal,* you will see thousands of small, medium, and large companies in every kind of industry listed, along with the current price of the firm's stock. You will learn what all this information means in the next chapter. Also, we will go into the terminology and intricacies of selling stock to raise funds. At this stage, you should have some feel for the widespread use of debt and equity financing as a way of obtaining capital. Chapter 20 will explore these sources of funding in greater depth.

PROGRESS CHECK

- What is the difference between long-term and short-term capital? Do firms actually need both types of funding?

- What are the two major forms of debt financing available to the firm?

- How does debt financing differ from equity financing?

- What are the two major forms of equity financing available to the firm?

SUMMARY

1. Explain the role and importance of finance.

1. Sound financial management is critical to the well-being of any business.
   - What are the most common ways firms fail financially?
     The most common financial problems are: (1) undercapitalization, (2) poor cash flow, and (3) inadequate expense control.

2. Describe the responsibilities of financial managers.

2. *Finance* is that function in a business responsible for acquiring funds for the firm, managing funds within the firm (for example, preparing budgets, doing cash flow analysis), and planning for the expenditure of funds on various assets.
   - What do finance managers do?
     Plan, budget, control funds, obtain funds, collect funds, audit, manage taxes, and advise top management on financial matters.

3. Outline the steps in financial planning by explaining the process of forecasting financial needs, developing budgets, and establishing financial controls.

3. Financial planning involves short- and long-term forecasting, budgeting, and financial controls.
   - What are the four budgets of finance?
     The *operating budget* is the projection of dollar allocations to various costs and expenses, given various revenues. The *capital budget* is the spending plan for assets whose returns take over a year. The *cash budget* is the projected cash balance at the end of a given period. The *master budget* summarizes the other three budgets.

4. Recognize the financial needs that must be met with available funds.

4. During the course of a business's life, its financial needs shift considerably.
   - What are the areas of financial needs?
     Businesses have financial needs in four major areas: (1) daily operations, (2) credit services, (3) inventory purchases, and (4) major assets purchases.

5. Distinguish between short-term and long-term financing and between debt capital and equity capital.

5. Businesses often have needs for short-term and long-term financing and for debt capital and equity capital.
   - What is the difference between short-term and long-term financing?
     Short-term financing refers to funds that will be repaid in less than one year, whereas long-term financing is money obtained from the owners of the firm and lenders who do not expect repayment within one year.

▪ What is the difference between debt capital and equity capital?

Debt capital refers to funds raised by borrowing (going into debt), whereas equity capital is raised from within or by selling ownership (stock) in the company.

6. There are many sources for short-term financing, including trade credit, family and friends, commerical banks, factoring, commercial paper, and internal sources.

▪ Why should businesses use trade credit?

Because even terms of 2/10, net 30 mean a savings of about 36 percent annually.

▪ What is a line of credit?

It is an agreement by a bank to loan a specified amount of money to the business at any time, if the money is available. A *revolving credit agreement* is a line of credit that *guarantees* a loan will be available—for a fee.

▪ What is the difference between a secured loan and an unsecured loan?

An *unsecured loan* has no collateral backing it. A *secured* loan is backed by accounts receivable (called *pledging*), inventory, or other property of value.

▪ Is factoring a form of secured loan?

No, *factoring* means *selling* accounts receivable at a discount.

▪ What is commercial paper?

A promissory note maturing at 270 days or less.

6. Identify and describe several sources of short-term capital.

7. One of the important functions of a finance manager is to obtain long-term capital.

▪ What are the three major sources of long-term capital?

Retained earnings: profits retained by the firm rather than paid out in dividends.

Debt capital: sale of bonds and long-term loans from banks and other financial institutions.

Equity capital: personal savings; loans from friends and family; partners; venture capital firms; sale of stock; and retained earnings.

▪ What are the two major forms of debt financing?

Debt capital comes from two sources: *selling bonds* and *borrowing* from banks and other financial institutions.

▪ What are the two types of equity capital?

Equity capital comes from two sources: *venture capital* or *selling stock in the firm.*

7. Identify and describe several sources of long-term capital.

GETTING INVOLVED

1. Obtain an annual report from a major corporation. Study the balance sheet. Which assets are fixed and what is their value? How much has the company borrowed (look under liabilities)?

2. Visit a local bank lending officer. Ask what the current interest rate is and what rate small businesses would pay for short- and long-term loans. Ask for blank forms that borrowers use to apply for loans. Share these forms with your class and explain the types of information they ask for.

3. Visit the financial manager of a furniture or appliance store. Find out how the store handles installment purchases.

4. Go to the library and look up *Venture* magazine and see what financial magazines are carried. Look through several issues of *at least* two financial journals and report what is in them to class.

5. Continue your exploration of the library by looking up the Standard & Poor's and *Value Line* reports. Ask the librarian what similar references are available. Report what you find to the class.

CASE ONE   **PLAYING THE BIGGEST GAME IN TOWN**

Timothy DeMello would be the first to tell would-be investors that Wall Street is not for the timid. Fortunes gained, fortunes lost, is the theme often played in this "greatest game in town." For those not ready, financially or emotionally, to play the "great game," DeMello offers an authentic version of the ultimate financial challenge. Wall Street Games, Inc., (WSG) offers the masses as well as the classes the opportunity to experience the thrill and challenge of Wall Street for only $99.

For this minimum investment, players receive an 800 telephone number, a stock-symbol guide, and $100,000 in bogus buying power. During each market trading day, "investors" can call for quotes, last-sale prices, and stock activity. Of course, they are also able to place orders to buy and sell in the hopes of building their "fortunes." DeMello strongly encourages competition among game players and this year anticipates more than 26,000 college students will ante up $49.95 each to participate in WSG's collegiate investing contest. What's the lure for the students? The chance to learn and experience the market plus possibly share in cash prizes and scholarships offered by AT&T, Dow Jones, and Reebok International.

Timothy DeMello founded his company six years after graduating from college with a B.S. in finance. He experienced Wall Street first hand as a stockbroker at Kidder, Peabody, and Company and L. F. Rothschild. He founded WSG with $20,000 of his own money and decided against immediately pursuing debt financing. Instead, he was able to raise $500,000 in equity financing primarily from past clients and other brokers in return for a 20 percent stake in the company. He approached bankers only after his equity financing was in place and was able to secure a $250,000 line of credit for his venture. Today, DeMello is busy pursuing the prospect of a worldwide market for a WSG game that is playable round-the-clock, trading in securities on foreign exchanges such as Japan as well as Wall Street.

DECISION QUESTIONS

1. Why do you suppose DeMello chose to seek equity financing as opposed to debt financing to fund his new company?
2. Why is a line of credit important to a new firm such as Wall Street Games, Inc.?
3. Is long-term or short-term financial planning most important to a firm such as Wall Street Games, Inc.? Why?

Source: Robert A. Mamis, "Play Money," *Inc.*, August 1988, pp. 50–55.

CASE TWO   **SEARS: THE FINANCIAL SUPERMARKET**

The chairman of Sears Roebuck and Co., Edward Brennan, believes that the company has all the parts it needs to offer a total financial package to consumers. This may be so, but the task of marketing this financial empire is yet to be completed. Sears has been called a *financial supermarket* because you can go there to buy life insurance, stocks, bonds, mutual funds, and consumer goods with Sears' own Discover credit card.

Sears is uniquely positioned to offer such services because it has such a huge customer base and is located in so many towns and cities. Furthermore, Sears has a reputation for dependability. Will Sears' reputation carry over into its financial operations? Can one company be so many things to so many people and still be effective?

DECISION QUESTIONS

1. What do you perceive as the advantages and disadvantages of having Sears as your broker?
2. Can you imagine other retail stores joining Sears in moving into financial services? Will such financial supermarkets provide a real challenge to traditional banks, brokers, and real estate firms?
3. Is it healthy for the economy to have a few, large firms dominant in both retailing and financial services? Why or why not?

The next chapter looks at stocks and bonds and other investment topics both as financing tools and as investment tools. You will learn about the stock exchanges, how to buy and sell stock, how to choose the right investment, how to read the stock and bond quotations in *The Wall Street Journal* and other newspapers, and more. Finance takes on a whole new dimension when you see how you can participate in financial markets yourself.

LOOKING AHEAD

STOCKS AND BONDS

20

Warren Buffett.

PROFILE   WARREN BUFFETT, INVESTOR

As a youngster growing up in Omaha, Warren Buffett had a fascination with numbers and money. He read his first books about the stock market at age 8 and bought his first stock at age 11. During his senior year at the University of Nebraska he read *The Intelligent Investor* written by Benjamin Graham. From this book he formulated his rules for investing: The first rule is not to lose. The second rule is not to forget the first rule. Mr. Buffett has followed his philosophy very successfully. He has turned an investment of approximately $9,800 into a personal net worth today that is close to $2 billion.

Warren Buffett's legendary success in the stock market has earned him the distinction of being called America's best investor. In 1987, the year of the stock market crash, Mr. Buffett still managed to increase his net worth by 19 percent. However, a perhaps less obvious side of Warren Buffett is his skill as a businessperson. Today, Mr. Buffett serves as chairman of Berkshire Hathaway, a conglomerate involved in such diversified businesses as insurance, home furnishings, vacuum cleaners, and candy. He credits business principles learned in college and experiences gained working in business for his great success in the market. In this chapter we shall discuss stocks and bonds as well as other investment alternatives. Who knows, maybe you are destined to become the next Warren Buffett.

Source: Carol J. Loomis, "The Inside Story of Warren Buffett," *Fortune*, April 11, 1988, pp. 26–34; and "The Business Week Corporate Elite," *Business Week*, October 21, 1988, p. 105.

SECURITIES MARKETS

The importance of a firm obtaining long-term funding cannot be overemphasized. One of the most common mistakes new companies make is starting without sufficient capital. A firm normally prefers to meet its long-term financial needs by dipping into retained earnings or getting needed capital from a lending institution such as a commercial bank or insurance company. However, if funding from these sources is not available, long-term funding often can be obtained through either debt or equity financing. As you remember from Chapter 19, debt financing is accomplished mostly through the issuing of bonds, and equity financing through the sale of stock in the corporation. In this chapter, we shall investigate these two major types of long-term financing.

We shall also become acquainted with the role securities markets play in financial operations. Securities markets, such as the New York Stock Exchange, enable businesses and individuals to buy and sell securities such as stocks and bonds. Businesses benefit from securities markets by obtaining the capital they need to begin operations, expand, and buy goods and services. It is important to understand that corporations only acquire funds the first time a particular stock is sold, not from the buying and selling of their stock between individuals. For example, if we, as the makers of Fiberrific, sell 20,000 shares of stock in our company at $15 a share, we would raise $300,000. However, if Shareholder Jones sells 100 shares of his Fiberrific stock to Investor Smith, we collect nothing. Smith bought the stock from Jones, not Fiberrific.

Securities markets offer businesses a way to earn additional funds with their income by investing in other firms. Investors also benefit from the securities market because it gives them a convenient place to buy and sell stocks and bonds. We shall look at the basics of investing in securities markets later. If you make it a habit to read *The Wall Street Journal*, *Forbes*, and other business journals over time, you can learn more about securities and find out how to invest money wisely. Each year *The Wall Street Journal* publishes an Educational Edition that explains all the various sections in the paper. It would be wise to spend some time learning the wealth of information available in *The Wall Street Journal*.

DEBT FINANCING THROUGH SELLING BONDS

Commercial banks, savings and loan associations, insurance companies, and other lending institutions provide funds to businesses to facilitate long-term operations. However, as profit-seeking businesses themselves, these lenders often will not make loans they feel are too risky and may not be repaid. Also, as their capital needs change, they may not have the loan amounts requested available. For this reason, firms often call on alternative debt financing through the issuance of corporate bonds. To put it simply, a bond is a corporate certificate indicating that a person has loaned money to a firm (see Figure 20–1). With debt financing through bonds, the company has a legal obligation to pay regular interest payments to investors and repay the entire principal at a prescribed time called the maturity date. Let's explore the terminology of bonds a bit more carefully so you clearly understand what's involved.

A sample bond certificate from IBM. This is a convertible bond, meaning that it can be converted into shares of stock at a later date. It is also a debenture bond, meaning it is backed by corporate assets not otherwise pledged. The bond will pay you 7⅞ percent interest until the year 2004 when the principle ($1,000) will be repaid.

FIGURE 20–1

The Terminology of Bonds

bond
A contract of indebtedness issued by a corporation or governmental unit that promises payment of a principal amount at a specified future time plus interest.

A **bond** is a contract of indebtedness issued by a corporation or governmental unit that promises payment of a principal amount at a specified future time plus interest. **Interest** is the payment the issuer of the bond makes to the bondholders to pay for use of the borrowed money. As you may suspect, the interest rate paid varies based on factors such as the state of the economy, the reputation of the company, and the rate being paid for government bonds. Generally, once an interest rate is set for specific bonds, it cannot be changed. **Principal** refers to the *face value* of the bond (bonds are almost always issued in multiples of $1,000).

interest
The payment the issuer of a bond makes to bondholders for the use of borrowed money.

The company is legally bound to repay the bond principal in full on the bond's maturity date. The **maturity date** refers to the date the issuer of a bond must pay the principal to the bondholder. For example, if you purchase a $1,000 bond with an interest rate of 9 percent and a maturity date of 2010, the firm is agreeing to pay you $90 in interest each year until a specified date in 2010 when it must repay you the full $1,000.

principal
The face amount of a bond.

maturity date
The date the issuer of a bond must pay the principal of the bond to the bondholder.

Advantages and Disadvantages of Selling Bonds

As a source of obtaining long-term capital needs, bonds offer advantages to an organization. The decision to issue bonds is often based on careful evaluation of these advantages. Advantages of bonds include:

- Bondholders have no vote on corporate affairs, thus management maintains control over the firm's operations. Remember, bondholders are creditors of the firm, not owners as stockholders are.
- The interest paid on bonds is a deductible expense to the firm's operations. Remember from Chapter 18, expenses help a firm to limit its tax responsibilities to the government.
- Bonds are a temporary source of funding for a firm. They are eventually repaid and the debt obligation eliminated.

However, bonds also have their drawbacks. Among the most significant are:

- Bonds are an increase in *debt* (liabilities) and may adversely affect the market's perception of the firm.
- Interest on bonds is a legal obligation. If interest is not paid, bondholders can take legal action to force payment.
- The face value of the bonds must be repaid on the maturity date. This could cause a possible cash shortage for the firm on that date.

Different Classes of Bonds

unsecured bonds
Bonds that are not backed by any collateral.

An organization can choose between two different classes of corporate bonds. The first class is called **unsecured bonds.** These are bonds that are not supported by any special type of collateral on the part of the issuing firm. In other words, the primary security the bondholder has is the reputation and credit rating of the company. Unsecured bonds are usually referred to as **debenture bonds** and are issued only by well-respected firms with excellent credit ratings. Such bonds do have the backing of all corporate assets not otherwise pledged.

debenture bonds
A bond that is unsecured, i.e., not backed with any collateral such as equipment.

The second class of bonds is referred to as **secured bonds.** These are bonds that are backed by some tangible asset that is pledged to the bondholder if interest is not paid or principal is not paid back. There are several kinds of secured bonds:

- First mortgage bonds are ensured by the company's real assets such as land and buildings. They are the most common of secured bonds and among the most desirable.
- Collateral trust bonds are backed by the stock that the company owns and that is held in trust by a commercial bank (thus the word *trust* in the title).
- Equipment trust bonds are backed by the equipment the company owns. This may include trucks, aircraft, and other equipment that is widely used in industry. A trustee often holds title to the equipment pledged until the bondholders are paid. Such items make excellent collateral since they can be taken over easily and have good resale value.
- *Zero-coupon bonds* include corporate bonds, municipal bonds, treasury bonds, and even deposit certificates from banks or savings and loans. Instead of making periodic interest payments, issuers defer the interest until maturity. Hence, these bonds are sold deeply discounted from the face value. Because they don't actually pay interest yearly, "zeros" fall more dramatically than other bonds when interest rates rise and they rise more quickly when interest rates fall.

As you can see, secured bonds are a relatively safe investment in that the risk to the bondholders are reduced. Figure 20–2 lists several kinds of bonds and their descriptions. All bonds do not include the same features. Let's look at some special features sometimes present in bonds.

secured bonds
Bonds backed by some tangible asset that is pledged to the investor if the principal is not paid back.

BOND	DESCRIPTION
Collateral trust	These bonds are secured by the general credit of the issuer as well as the specific property for which it is issued.
Convertible bond	These bonds can be exchanged for another security, usually common stock.
Coupon bond	These bonds have coupons attached; the bondholder submits the coupons to an agent for the payment of interest.
Debenture	These bonds are secured only by the general credit of the firm plus any unpledged assets.
Mortgage bond	These bonds are secured by real property (for example, buildings).
Municipal bond	A bond issued by the state or local government; interest rates are exempt from federal taxes.
Yankee bond	These bonds are issued by a foreign government and are payable in U.S. dollars.
Zero-coupon bond	These bonds pay no interest prior to maturity; the return comes from the difference between purchase price and the face (par) value.

As you can see, there are all kinds of bonds available with different risks, and bonds for every kind of investor. Zero coupon bonds are growing in popularity. Watch for stories about them in the business press.

FIGURE 20–2

Sample of different bonds available in the market.

Special Bond Features

By now you should know that bonds are issued with an interest rate, are either unsecured or secured by collateral, and must be repaid at the maturity date. This repayment requirement often induces firms to establish what is called a sinking fund to ensure the funds are available to repay bondholders on the maturity date. A **sinking fund** requires the bond issuer to pay off, on a periodic basis, some part of the bond issue before its final maturity. Sinking funds can be attractive to firms and investors for several reasons:

sinking fund
Fund that requires the issuer to retire (put in a trust fund), on a periodic basis, some part of the bond principal prior to maturity.

- They provide for an orderly retirement of a bond issue.
- Some investors like them because they reduce risk. Therefore, bonds are more attractive as an investment alternative.
- The market price of the bond is supported because the risk of the firm not being able to repay the principal on the maturity date is reduced.

Another potential feature of a bond issue is a call provision. A **call provision** permits the issuer to pay off a bond prior to its maturity date. Call provisions must be included when a bond is originally issued. Why would an organization want to repay a bond issue before its maturity date? Let's see why.

call provision
Gives the issuer of a bond the right to retire the bond before its maturity.

Call provisions give companies discretion in their long-term forecasting. Suppose a company issued $50 million in bonds in 1985 with an interest rate of 10 percent. The yearly interest expense would be $5 million. If, in 1990, the same quality bonds are yielding only 7.5 percent interest, the firm would be paying $1.5 million in excess interest yearly. It's clear it would benefit the firm to call in the bonds and perhaps reissue new bonds at the lower rate. However, one problem surfaces with call provisions. Some investors are not particularly fond of them. This often forces issuers of bonds to agree to staggered calls. For example, a 20-year issue may have staggered calls of 5 years. This means a bond issued in 1985 could not be called until 1990. This helps keep investors happy.

A last feature that can be included in bonds is convertibility. A **convertible bond** is one that can be converted into shares of common stock in the issuing company. This can be an inducement for an investor because common stock has the potential to grow over time. When we discuss common stock this advantage will become evident to you.

convertible bond
A bond that can be converted into shares of common stock.

Bonds as an Investment

As an investment, bonds are rather safe. However, two questions often bother first-time investors concerning the purchase of a corporate bond. One question is: "If I purchase a corporate bond, do I have to hold it to the maturity date?" No! You do not have to hold a bond until maturity because bonds are bought and sold daily on securities markets. However, if you sell your bond to another investor it's important to be aware that it is unlikely you will get the face value of the bond (usually $1,000). If your bond is highly valued by other investors you may have a **premium bond** (a bond that sells above its face value). But if your bond does not have specific features that make it attractive to other investors you may hold a **discount bond** (a bond that sells below its face value).

premium bond
Bond that sells above face value.

discount bond
Bond that sells below face value.

The second question on investor's minds is, "How do I know how risky a *particular* bond issue is as an investment?" Fortunately, two companies, Standard & Poor's and Moody's Investor Service, provide information that rates various corporate and government bonds as to their degree of risk to investors. Naturally, the higher the risk associated with the bond issue, the higher the interest rate the

HIGH–RISK BONDS: JUNK OR JEWELS?

As you know, we are in an age of mergers, takeovers, and leveraged buyouts. Corporate takeover artists called raiders specialize in obtaining control of companies sometimes against the will of the firm's management. Many feel these takeover bids are often inflated, so raiders actually pay too high a price for control of the company. The raiders often sell bonds to help meet the purchase price. The bonds must be offered at high interest rates to attract investors. It's not unusual for such bonds to pay interest rates 5 to 6 percent higher than treasury securities or top-grade corporate bonds. In fact, some of the more exotic and extreme junk bonds yield 18 percent or better in the market.

These high-risk, high-interest bonds are called *junk bonds*. Standard & Poor's Investment Advisory Service and Moody's Investor Services regard junk bonds as noninvest-ment-grade bonds because of their high-risk and high–interest rate features.

Why are junk bonds considered so risky and why are firms forced to pay such a high interest rate to sell them? Remember, risk and return are closely related. Plus, most junk bonds' ability to pay depends on the company's asset valuation remaining high and cash flow staying strong. In a recession or stock market collapse, both asset values and cash flow positions could suffer. This causes serious doubt about the firm's ability to pay off the junk bonds. If the company can't pay off the bond, the investor is left with a bond that isn't worth more that the paper it's written on—junk. If the company does make it and the bond is paid off, the investor collects the high interest—jewels. The 1990s will be an interesting decade for the future of junk bonds.

Source: Christopher Farrell, "Junk Bonds Finally Face the Acid Test," *Business Week,* November 16, 1987, p. 64; Rosalind Klein Berlin and Sarah Smith, "Trying Times for Junk Bonds," *Fortune,* December 7, 1987, pp. 59–60; and Bernard J. Winger and Ralph R. Frasca, *Investments: Introduction to Analysis and Planning* (Merrill Publishing Company, 1988), p. 138.

organization must offer investors. Investors will not assume high levels of risk if they don't feel the potential return is worth it. Bondholders are nervous these days because the increased use of "junk bonds" has driven down the value of regular bonds. Bondholders are forcing companies to give them more protection because of these changes.[1]

Bonds provide an excellent source of long-term financing for the firm and a good investment vehicle for investors. They are a form of debt financing as opposed to equity financing. After the Progress Check let's explore the most common form of equity financing, the issuing of corporate stock.

---

* Why are bonds considered to be a form of debt financing?

* What is meant if a firm states it is issuing a 9 percent debenture bond due in 2005?

* Explain the difference between an unsecured and a secured bond.

* Why do issuing companies typically like to include call provisions in their bonds?

* Why role do Standard & Poor's and Moody's Investor Service play in the bond market?

PROGRESS CHECK

EQUITY FINANCING THROUGH SELLING STOCK

As we noted in Chapter 19, equity financing is another form of long-term funding. *Equity financing* is the obtaining of funds through the sale of ownership in the corporation. There are two different classes of equity instruments; preferred and common stock. We will discuss them both separately after a brief look at the terminology of stock and the advantages and disadvantages of selling stock as a financing alternative.

FIGURE 20–3

Sample of different stock available in the market. Most investors deal only in common stock. Some do prefer the special rights that come with preferred stock, however.

STOCK	DESCRIPTION
Classified common stock	This stock consists of two or more classes of common stock that have different voting rights or claims on dividends. For example, class A common stock may go to the general public and class B to the original owners. Class A stock may carry no voting rights, but its holders may receive larger dividends. The owners thus retain control of the firm.
Convertible preferred (no voting rights)	This stock can be exchanged for shares of common stock at a predetermined exchange rate.
Cumulative preferred (no voting rights)	This stock pays a dividend every year. If the dividend is not paid, the amount owed accumulates and must be paid before common stockholders receive any dividends.

The Terminology of Stock

stock certificates
Tangible evidence of stock ownership.

par value
An arbitrary dollar amount printed on the front of a stock certificate (used to compute the dividends of preferred stock).

dividends
Part of the firm's profits that goes to stockholders.

Stocks are shares of ownership in a company. A **stock certificate** is evidence of ownership. It usually is a piece of paper that specifies the name of the company, the number of shares it represents, and the type of stock it is. Certificates sometimes indicate a **par value,** which is a dollar amount assigned to shares of stock by the corporation's charter. Par value of a share of stock may be nowhere near the stock's market value (the actual price at which the stock could be sold). The major use of par value today is for use in assigning the dollar value on which dividends on preferred stock are paid (this will be explained later in this chapter). **Dividends** are a part of a firm's profits that are distributed to shareholders. Dividends could be distributed in the form of cash or more shares of stock.

Advantages and Disadvantages of Issuing Stock

Securities markets contain the names of almost every large company in the United States. Evidently, companies must feel that equity financing is a good way to raise long-term funds. Some of the advantages of issuing stock are:

- Because stockholders are owners of the business, their investment never has to be repaid. Therefore, funds are available long term for acquiring land, buildings, machinery, and other assets.
- There is no legal obligation to pay dividends to stockholders. Income can be invested back in the firm for additional investment or growth.
- Selling stock can actually improve the condition of the firm's balance sheet. How? No debt is incurred and the company is stronger financially.

Nonetheless, as the saying goes, "There is no such thing as a free lunch." As you might suspect, there are disadvantages to selling equity in a firm as well. The disadvantages include:

- As owners of the firm, stockholders have the right to vote for the board of directors. As you may remember from Chapter 4, the board of directors decides who will manage the firm and what policies will be. Hence, the direction of the firm can be altered significantly through the sale of stock.

- Dividends are paid out of profit *after* taxes. Thus, it is more costly to pay dividends than interest, which is tax deductible.

- Management decision making is often tempered by the need to keep the firm's stockholders happy. This often forces managers to use short-term tactics to keep earnings up rather than strategies to keep the firm profitable in the long run. Thus the cost of equity financing may be much higher than the figures shown in the accounting records.[2]

As we noted above, there are two classes of stock: preferred and common. Let's look at each of these forms of equity funding and see how they differ.

Issuing Preferred Stock

Preferred stock gives its owners preference in the payment of dividends and an earlier claim on assets if the company is liquidated. However, it normally does not include voting rights in the firm. Preferred stock is frequently referred to as a hybrid investment in that it has characteristics of both bonds and stocks. To illustrate what we mean, consider the treatment of preferred stock dividends.

Preferred stock dividends differ from common stock dividends in several ways. Preferred stock is generally issued with a par value. The par value becomes the basis for the dividend the firm is willing to pay. For example, if a par value of $100 is attached to a share of preferred stock and a dividend rate of 8 percent is attached to the same issue, the firm is committing to an $8 dividend for each share of preferred stock the investor owns (8 percent of $100 = $8). If you own 100 shares of this preferred stock, your yearly dividend should be $800. Furthermore, this dividend is *fixed*, meaning it should not change year-by-year. Also, if any dividends are paid, the dividends on preferred stock *must* be paid in full before any common stock dividends can be distributed. Preferred stockholders normally lose their voting rights in the firm for this preferred dividend treatment.

As you can see, a similarity exists between preferred stock and bonds in that both have a face (or par value) and both have a fixed rate of return. Why not just refer to preferred stock as a form of bond? Remember, bondholders *must* receive interest and be *repaid* the face value of the bond on a maturity date. Preferred stock dividends do not legally *have* to be paid and stock *never* has to be repurchased. Remember, too, the price of the stock can go up, resulting in a higher profit than a comparable bond. On the other hand, the stock price could also go down, making it a potentially riskier investment than bonds.

> **preferred stock**
> Stock that gives owners preference in the payment of dividends and an earlier claim on assets if the business is sold but does not include voting rights.

Special Features of Preferred Stock

Because it is a hybrid investment, preferred stock can have special features not available to common stock. For example, like bonds, preferred stock could be issued with a call provision. In other words, the firm could call in the shares of preferred stock for repurchase. As an investor, you would be required to sell back your shares of preferred stock to the firm. As with bonds, the investor should be appraised of this call feature of the stock. Preferred stock could also be convertible. That is, convertible to shares of common stock. Again, the similarities between preferred stock and bonds are evident.

FIGURE 20–4

The effect of an 8 percent dividend per year, if not paid each year.
This figure shows what happens when a dividend payment is missed for different classes of stock. With cumulative preferred stock, the dividend for 1988 was 4 percent less than promised. In 1989, it was 3 percent less. That means that the bondholder would get 15 percent in 1990 if the company had the funds available. The way you figure that is 4 percent plus 3 percent plus 8 percent (the 1990 dividend).
Noncumulative preferred and common stock get only the dividends allocated. There is no cumulative provision.

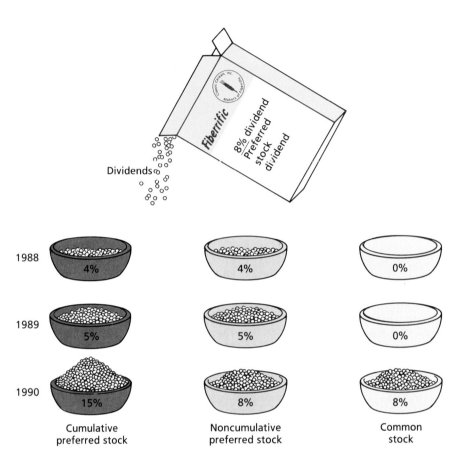

cumulative preferred stock
Preferred stock that accumulates unpaid dividends.

One of the more important features of preferred stock is that it often can be cumulative. **Cumulative preferred stock** guarantees an investor that if one or more dividends are not paid, the missed dividends will be accumulated. All the dividends, including the back dividends, must be paid in full before any common stock dividends can be given. For example, as producers of Fiberrific, we may decide not to pay our preferred stockholders the full 8 percent dividend this period in order to retain funds for further research and development. The preferred stockholders must be paid the missing amount the following period before we can pay any dividends to common stockholders. If preferred stock is noncumulative, any dividends missed are lost to the stockholder. Figure 20–4 illustrates how this process works.

If preferred stock does not meet the objectives of the firm or individual investor, the alternative of issuing or investing in common stock is available. Let's look at this interesting alternative.

Issuing Common Stock

common stock
The most basic form of ownership of firms; it includes voting rights and dividends, if dividends are offered by the firm.

Common stock represents ownership privileges in a firm. These privileges include the right to vote and the right to receive some of the firm's profits through dividends when distributed by management. By voting for the board of directors of a corporation, stockholders can influence corporate policy because the board selects the management and makes major policy decisions. In general, shareholders' voting rights are based on one vote for each share of stock held. Due to what is called a preemptive right, common stockholders have the first right to purchase any new shares of common stock the firm decides to issue to maintain a proportionate share in the company.

Common stock is considered to be more risky and speculative than either bonds or preferred stock. Remember, common stockholders receive dividends only after both bondholders and preferred stockholders receive their interest and dividends. Also, if a company is forced to cease operations, common stockholders share in the firm's assets only after bondholders and preferred stockholders recover their investments. Why, then, would investors select common stock as an investment alternative? Because the risk is often accompanied by higher returns. Several investment opportunities are available. For example, an investor may select a growth stock as a personal investment choice. **Growth stocks** are stocks of corporations whose earnings are expected to grow faster than other stocks or the overall economy. They are often quite speculative and pay rather low dividends, but the potential for growth is strong. **Income stocks** are stocks that offer investors a rather high dividend yield on their investment. Public utilities are often considered to be good income stocks as are **blue chip stocks.** Blue chip is a term often used to describe stock of a firm that is considered to be of high quality. Investors can even invest in a type of stock called a penny stock. **Penny stocks** are stocks that sell for less than $1. Such stocks frequently represent ownership in mining companies and are often highly speculative.

It's important to remember that common stock is very dependent on the performance of the corporation. Common stock is often referred to as participating stock. Stockholders participate in the success or failure of the firm. Common stock offers great opportunities but is subject to a high degree of risk as was evidenced by the stock market crash of 1987.

growth stocks
Stock of corporations whose earnings have grown rapidly in the past in comparison with the economy and are expected to continue above-average growth in the future.

income stocks
Stocks that offer a high dividend.

blue chip stocks
Stocks of high-quality companies.

penny stock
Stock that sells for less than $1

PROGRESS CHECK

- Name at least two advantages and two disadvantages of issuing stock as a form of equity financing.

- What are the major differences between preferred stock and common stock?

- In what ways are preferred stock and bonds similar? In what ways are they different?

- How does an investor benefit by owning cumulative preferred stock as opposed to noncumulative preferred?

- What is the difference between blue chip stocks and penny stocks?

How to Buy Bonds and Stock

Investing in bonds or stocks is not very difficult. First you have to decide what bond or stock you want to buy. That is perhaps the most difficult procedure. After deciding, you would call a stockbroker. A **stockbroker** is a market intermediary who buys and sells securities for clients. The broker, who is a registered representative authorized to trade in stocks and bonds, would call a member of the stock exchange who represents the firm for which the broker works. That member would go to the place where the bond or stock you want is traded and negotiate a price.

stockbroker
A middleman who buys and sells securities for clients.

Stock brokers often work in offices crammed with computers. They spend much of the day on the phone, talking with clients. The rest of the time they follow trends in the stock market and learn what the best investments are. In spite of the brokers' expertise, most people are better off buying stock in a well-managed mutual fund.

When the transaction is completed, the trade will be reported back to your broker, who will call you. The same procedure is followed if you wish to sell bonds or stocks. If you choose, the broker will keep the bond or stock certificate for you for safekeeping or so that you can sell it easily and quickly, with just a telephone call. The broker is also a valuable source of information as to what stocks or bonds would best meet your financial objectives. It is important for you to learn about stocks and bonds on your own, though, because stock analysts often give poor advice.[3] That is why the question, "If you're so smart, why aren't you rich?" applies to them so well.

Market Orders and Limit Orders

market order
Instructions to a broker to buy stock at the best price obtainable in the market now.

limit order
Instructions to a broker to purchase stock at a specific price.

Investors have several options when placing an order for stock. An investor can place a **market order** that instructs the broker to buy stock at the best price obtainable in the market at that time. This type order can be processed quickly and the trade price can be given to the investor in minutes. A **limit order,** on the other hand, tells the broker to purchase stock at a *specific price.* Let's say, for example, that a stock is selling for $40 a share, and you feel it is likely to drop a little before it goes higher. You could place a limit order at $38. The broker would purchase the stock at that amount if the stock drops. If the stock never falls to $38, no order would be processed.

Buying Stock on Margin

buying on margin
The purchase of stocks by borrowing some of the purchase cost from the broker.

Buying on margin involves the purchase of stocks by borrowing some of the purchase cost from the broker. Margin refers to the amount of money an investor must have in the stock. The Federal Reserve sets margin rates in the market. We shall discuss this in detail in Chapter 21. Thus, if the margin is 50 percent, the investor may borrow 50 percent of the stock's purchase price from a broker. Obviously, the investor's idea is to buy shares of stock that he or she believes are

THE CRASH OF 1987

October 19, 1987, started off like most other Mondays. Car pools dropped off children at the local elementary school, armchair quarterbacks conversed about how they would have handled the 3rd and 15 situation in the Redskins game on Sunday, and stockbrokers went to work hoping for an active trading day. It's doubtful any of these persons anticipated the financial shock that occurred in just six and one-half hours of security trading on that day.

On October 19th, the stock market suffered the largest one-day drop in its history. The Dow Jones Industrial Average fell *508 points*. What exactly does that mean? In just six and one-half hours of trading, a *half-trillion dollars* vanished before bewildered investors' eyes. How much is a half-trillion dollars? According to Paul Erdman, "A half-trillion dollars is more than all the people of Central America plus most of the inhabitants of Eastern Europe earn in an entire year." One investor, Sam Walton, lost over a *billion dollars* that day on his shares of Wal-Mart Stores, the discount store chain he founded. (Don't feel too bad about poor Sam—he still was left with approximately $7 billion.) The crash prompted another billionaire, Ross Perot, to

caution, "It was God tapping us on the shoulder and warning us to get our act together before we get the big shock."

What caused the crash of 1987? Ask a dozen financial analysts and you might get a dozen different responses. The simple reality is it happened and investors rightfully wonder if it could happen again. Some investing lessons that can be learned from the crash of '87 include: Be ready for volatility, it's the nature of the market; be careful of small, thinly traded stocks; look at the market globally and remember all nations' economies and markets are tied together today; be diversified in your investments; don't gamble with borrowed money; and take a long-term perspective. Never forget, investing in the stock market offers no built-in guarantees. Ask the victims of Black Monday.

Another lesson from the crash of 1987 is that investors are almost always optimistic. When the market reached precrash levels in 1989, the media were reporting more and more optimism. In fact, the financial condition of the country was still questionable and the market was just as vulnerable to another 1987-style fall.

Source: Paul Erdman, *WHAT'S NEXT? How to Prepare Yourself for the Crash of '89 and Profit in the 1990s* (Garden City, N.Y.: Doubleday, York, 1988), pp. 2–3; Jay McCormick, "What the Crash Taught Us," *USA Today,* January 4, 1988, p. 1E; and Larry Martz, Rich Thomas, Timothy Noah, and Margaret Garrard Warner, "After the Meltdown of '87," *Newsweek,* November 2, 1987, pp. 14–20; and "Dow Inches Up 0.36 to 2,239.11, a Fraction Shy of Its Pre-Crash Level," *Los Angeles Times,* January 20, 1989, p. 4 of Part IV.

going up in value. However, buying stocks on margin also has a downside. The money loaned by the broker must be repaid with interest. Additionally, if the stock's value goes down in market, the broker will issue a margin call requiring the investor to come up with more money to cover the losses. Buying on margin is more appropriate for risk takers willing to speculate than for more conservative investors.

Stock Splits

Companies and brokers prefer to have stock purchases conducted in **round lots**, that is, purchases of 100 shares at a time. The problem is that many investors cannot afford to buy 100 shares of a stock such as IBM, which may be selling for $150 or so per share. Therefore, to make it easier for investors to buy in round lots, companies often conduct **stock splits;** that is, they issue two or more shares for every share of stock outstanding. For example, if IBM stock were selling for $150 a share, it could declare a five-for-one split. Everyone who owned one share of IBM would now own five shares—but each share would now be worth only $30. A round lot would now cost $3,000 instead of $15,000 as was the case at $150 per share. In stock splits, both companies and investors win. The advantage to the company is that it may be able to sell more shares at lower prices. The advantage to shareholders is that the demand for the stock at $30 per share may be greater than the demand at $150 per share. Thus, the stock price may go up. In fact, many people buy in *odd lots;* that is, less than 100 shares. Your broker handles all the details of such purchases so that you can buy just one share if you want.

round lots
One hundred shares of stock.

stock splits
Giving stockholders two or more shares of stock for each one they own.

March 16, 1830 was the slowest day in the history of the New York Stock Exchange—only 31 shares were traded all day.

CHOOSING THE RIGHT INVESTMENT

Broadly speaking, investing means committing capital with the expectation of making a profit. The first step in an investment program is for the investor to analyze his or her specific situation. The analysis will contain specifics in terms of income desired, cash requirements, level of risk, and so on. As you might suspect, investment objectives change over the course of a person's life. A second step is to select general investment vehicles that best fit the specific needs of the investor. For example, investors should decide how much, if any, of their assets should be committed to real estate, bonds, or stocks. The third step is to select specific investments within the general areas. For example, should the investor choose common or preferred stock of Procter & Gamble? Would their objective be best served by a corporate-issued or government-issued bond? Generally, there are five criteria to use when selecting an investment vehicle: (1) investment risk, (2) yield, (3) duration, (4) liquidity, and (5) tax consequences.

1. Investment risk—the chance that an investment and all its accumulated yields will be worth less at some future time than when the investment is made.
2. Yield—the increase in the value of an investment over time, usually a year.
3. Duration—the length of time assets are committed.
4. Liquidity—how quickly one can get back invested funds when desired.
5. Tax consequences—how the investment will affect the investor's tax situation.

Diversifying Investments

diversification
Buying several different investments to spread the risk.

Diversification consists of buying several different investment vehicles to spread the risk of investing. For example, an investor may put 30 percent of his or her money into growth stocks that have a high risk. Another 30 percent may be invested in conservative government bonds, 15 percent in income stocks, and the rest placed in the bank for emergencies and possible other investment opportunities. By diversifying investments, the chance of losing everything is diminished. This type of investment strategy is often referred to as a portfolio strategy.

Investing in Mutual Funds

mutual fund
An organization that buys stocks and bonds and then sells shares in those securities to the public.

A **mutual fund** is an organization that buys stocks and bonds and then sells shares in those securities to the public. Mutual funds have the expertise to pick what they consider to be the best stocks and bonds available. The benefit to you is that you can buy shares of the mutual funds and thus share in the ownership of *many different companies* that you could not afford to invest in individually. In essence, the fund helps you to diversify and offers management of your investment, normally for a small fee. There are over 2,300 mutual funds in the market, so it is relatively easy to find one that would meet your needs.[4]

Mutual funds are probably the best way for smaller investors to begin. A variety of funds are available, ranging from very conservative funds that invest only in government securities or bonds to others that specialize in high-tech firms, foreign companies, precious metals, and other high-risk investments. A stockbroker can be helpful in assisting you to find the mutual fund that best fits your investment objectives. However, with a little research, you may be able to avoid the broker and buy some funds directly. This would save the broker's fee.

Join the team
with a track record
of success.

Success requires discipline and teamwork. That's how **Twentieth Century
Investors** has achieved the kind of
track record you look for in long-term
investing. Twentieth Century, a family
of twelve **no-load mutual funds**, has
earned its reputation by following a
disciplined investment strategy
consistently over time.
  In fact, two of our funds have out-
performed **over 90%** of all mutual funds
tracked by Lipper Analytical Services for
any given 10-year period, starting on any
calendar quarter since 1971.*

Write or call for an Information Kit
and Prospectus and find out how you
can join our team. Please read the
Prospectus carefully before investing.

For information, call toll-free:
1-800-345-2021

P.O. Box 419200
Kansas City, MO 64141-6200

*Performance data quoted represent past performance. Investment return and principal value will
fluctuate and redemption value may be more or less than original cost.*

An ad for a no load mutual fund; $10,000 invested in 1958 grew to $290,499 in 1985. That's a 13.37 percent compound return. That means you could double your money every 5-6 years.

The key point to remember is that the average small investor has a way to spread the risk of stock ownership by owning shares in many different companies through the purchase of shares in a mutual fund or some combination of funds. Most investment advisers put mutual funds high on the list of recommended investments for beginning investors. In fact, some mutual funds make it possible to buy a mutual fund that invests in other mutual funds. It is important, though, to check the costs involved in a mutual fund because these can differ. For example, a no-load (NL) fund is one that charges no commission to buy shares of the fund. A load fund would charge a commission to either buy shares in the fund or to sell shares you hold in the fund.

Mutual funds posted solid gains in 1988. The average general equity fund (stocks) rose 13.16 percent. Fixed-income funds (bonds, mostly) rose 7.73 percent.[5] In the Appendix to Part Six, we shall discuss investments earning good returns. Remember mutual funds are such investments.

What form of investment seems most appropriate to your needs now? Do you suspect your objectives and needs will change over time? Would investing other peoples' money be an interesting career to pursue? What would be some of the problems stockbrokers or mutual fund managers might undergo in the course of their jobs? Does it make sense for investors to diversify their investments or would it be more logical to put all their eggs in one basket?

THINKING IT THROUGH

STOCK EXCHANGES

As its name implies, a **stock exchange** is an organization whose members can buy and sell (exchange) securities for the public. There are stock exchanges all over the world in cities such as Paris, London, Madrid, Sydney, Buenos Aires, and Tokyo. These exchanges enable businesses and individuals to buy securities from companies almost anywhere in the world. If you hear of a foreign company that has great potential for growth, you can usually obtain shares of stock with little difficulty from a U.S. broker who has access to the foreign stock exchanges.

stock exchange
An organization whose members can buy and sell securities to the public.

U.S. Exchanges

The largest stock exchange in the United States is the New York Stock Exchange (NYSE). It does about 80 percent of all stock trading. The second-largest exchange in the United States is the American Stock Exchange (AMEX). It is also located in New York. It manages less than 10 percent of all trades. These two exchanges are called national exchanges because they handle stocks of companies from all over the United States.

In addition to the national exchanges, there are several regional exchanges in cities such as Chicago (Midwest), San Francisco (Pacific Coast), Philadelphia, Boston, Cincinnati, Spokane, and Salt Lake City. These regional exchanges deal mostly with firms in their own areas. Approximately 12 percent of all security trading done on America's organized stock exchanges occurs in these regional exchanges.

The New York Stock Exchange is the major trading center in the United States for stock. You can visit the exchange yourself and watch the action. It may inspire you to become a trader yourself or, at least, get more involved in investing.

WHO'S MINDING THE COMPUTERS?

As you know, computers are revolutionizing many industries. Trading in stocks and bonds is no exception. It is possible to obtain all kinds of stock information and actually buy and sell stocks on your personal computer, all without human contact.

You can enter trades by writing an electronic order ticket. It is transmitted by phone to your brokerage's computers and then to its trading desk. A confirmation notice appears on your computer screen.

New concerns were raised about the role of computers in stock trading on Black Monday (October 19, 1987, the day stocks crashed 508 points). Many analysts attest that "program trading" actually caused stock prices to fall to the disastrous levels they reached. In program trading, investors give their computers instructions to automatically sell if the price of their stock dips to a certain price to avoid potential losses. A threatening price automatically triggers a sell order. Assured that the computer is managing their portfolios, investors can then tend to other business. On October 19, 1988 the computers became "trigger-happy." Sell orders caused many stocks to fall to unbelievable depths.

The fear of another episode of uncontrolled computer trading provoked a Presidential Commission to suggest the creation of regulated "circuit breakers" that could temper huge market swings caused by such trading.

Source: Ruth Simon, *Forbes,* April 30, 1984, p. 130; David Pauly, "The New Invisible Hand," *Newsweek,* November 2, 1987, p. 21; and Catherine Yang, "Congress Is Taking Its Own Sweet Time on Reform," *Business Week,* April 18, 1988, p. 63.

The Over-the-Counter (OTC) Market

The **over-the-counter (OTC) market** provides a means to trade stocks not listed on the national securities exchanges. The OTC market is made up of a network of several thousand brokers. These brokers maintain contact with each other and buy and sell securities for the public. A nationwide electronic system communicates trades to the brokers. The system is known as the **National Association of Securities Dealers Automated Quotation system (NASDAQ)**—pronounced *nazz-dak*.

Originally the over-the-counter market dealt mostly with small firms that could not qualify for listing on the national exchanges or did not want to bother with the procedures. Today, however, well-known firms such as Apple, MCI, and Coors prefer to have their stock traded on the OTC market.

The over-the-counter market also handles most corporate and U.S. government bonds as well as many city and state government bonds. Common stock of most insurance companies and banks, as well as the stock of many smaller firms, is traded over-the-counter. If you look in *The Wall Street Journal* under "NASDAQ Bid and Ask Quotations," you will see that the price of over-the-counter stocks is determined by supply and demand as reflected in "bid" and "ask" prices.

over-the-counter (OTC) market
Exchange that provides a means to trade stocks not listed on the national exchanges.

National Association of Securities Dealers Automated Quotation system (NASDAQ)
A nationwide electronic system that communicates over-the-counter trades to brokers.

COMMODITY EXCHANGES

Commodities are generally considered high-risk investments for most people. However, trading in commodities can also be a vehicle for protecting businesspeople, farmers, and others from wide fluctuations in commodity prices, and thus can be a very conservative investment strategy. Let's see how this works.

The Chicago Board of Trade trades commodities. It is as hectic as it looks, but the work gets done nonetheless. Such trading is more speculative than investing in stocks or bonds.

commodity exchange
Specializes in the buying and selling of precious metals and agricultural goods such as wheat, cattle, silver, sugar, gasoline, and foreign currencies.

spot markets
The purchase and sale of commodities for immediate delivery.

futures markets
The purchase and sale of goods for delivery sometime in the future.

hedging
In its pure form, buying or selling commodities in the futures market equal and opposite to what you now have.

A **commodity exchange** specializes in the buying and selling of precious metals and agricultural goods such as wheat, cattle, sugar, silver, gasoline, and foreign currencies. The Chicago Board of Trade is the largest commodity exchange. It is involved with a wide range of commodities including corn, plywood, silver, gold, and U.S. Treasury bonds. The Chicago Mercantile Exchange is the second largest and deals in commodities such as cattle, hogs, pork bellies (bacon), potatoes, and various foreign currencies.

Commodity exchanges operate much like stock exchanges in that members of the exchange meet on the floor to exchange goods. The appearance of a commodities exchange is quite different, however, and interesting to observe. All transactions for a specific commodity take place in specific trading areas or "rings." Trades result from the meeting of a bid and offer in an open competition among exchange members. The bids and offers are made in a seemingly impossible-to-understand blending of voices, with all participants shouting at once.

Commodities trading demands much expertise and involves a high degree of risk. Unfortunately, most people who speculate in commodities lose money. The best way to get expertise and perhaps share in commodity price increases is by buying into a commodities mutual fund.

Hedging

Spot markets refer to the purchase and sale of commodities for immediate delivery. However, **future markets** involve the purchase and sale of goods for delivery some time in the future. Buying in the futures market is known as **hedging.** Hedging is an important risk-management tool for those who produce, process, market and use commodities. Take, for example, a farmer who has oats growing in the field. He or she is not sure what price the oats will sell for at harvest time. To be sure of a price, the farmer would *sell* the oats on the futures market. The price would then be fixed, and the farmer could plan accordingly. On the other hand, as producers of Fiberrific, we are worried about the possibility of oat prices rising. By hedging and *buying* the oats in the futures market, we know what we will have to pay for the oats and can plan accordingly.

Hedging, therefore, gives businesses a form of price insurance that enables them to focus on their primary function without worrying about fluctuations in commodity prices. Those who own a commodity can offset the risk of a price decline by *selling* futures contracts. Those who will need a commodity in the future can offset a price rise by *purchasing* the commodity ahead of time. All of this is possible because of commodity exchanges.

Hedging made the news in 1989 because fraud was discovered on the floor of the commodity exchange. Undercover FBI agents, posing as traders, found some incidents of fraud. This was a major issue because the margins are so small on the commodities exchange that any false reporting can cause huge losses to occur.[6] Figure 20–5 shows how such transactions are made and where the chances for fraud occur.

UNDERSTANDING INVESTMENT INFORMATION

A wealth of investment information is made available to investors in daily newspapers and various magazines. Such information is meaningless, though, until you understand what the data are all about. Look through *The Wall Street Journal,* *Barron's,* and your local newspaper's business section. Listen carefully to the business reports on radio and TV and watch a couple of business-oriented shows such as "Wall $treet Week." Listen for the terms and the different viewpoints.

How a commodity trade is made.
This figure shows where fraud can occur in commodity trading. New rules and regulations may lessen the incidents of fraud, but commodity trading will remain a high-risk investment strategy for most people. The new emphasis on ethics will not change that.

FIGURE 20–5

1. A customer places an order with a broker. The broker completes an order slip. The slip must be stamped showing the exact time the order is received from the customer.

2. The broker phones the order to a clerk or other staff person on the floor of the exchange where the trade must be executed. The clerk prepares an order slip, which must also be time-stamped.

Fraud opportunity:
The broker never executes the trade, instead pocketing the customer's money. This practice, which is rare, is known as "bucketing."

3. The clerk takes the order slip to a floor broker in a "pit" where the particular commodity or financial instrument is traded.
The floor broker executes the trade through an "open outcry" system of trading, in which the broker uses hand signals and shouts to communicate his trade. Another broker or trader willing to make that trade signals or shouts back, and the deal is made.
Once the trade is completed, the brokers must record that on their order slips. They also must signal to a price reporter at that pit, who records the trade and in turn reports that to the exchange's clearing operation. The clearing operation makes sure that all buy and sell orders are matched up. Those that aren't must be reconciled before the next day's trading.

4. The floor broker gives the order slip, with information about the completed trade, back to the clerk, who in turn calls the original broker. That broker informs the customer that the trade has been completed. The broker also may be required to report the trade to the exchange's clearing operation.

Fraud opportunity: Brokers and traders may miscommunicate in trading with each other, or may err on the terms of their trades. Because these trades still must be reconciled through the clearing process, brokers may misrepresent trades to customers to avoid eating any losses.
Brokers and traders may also collude with each other to manipulate the price of their transaction, allowing them to skim some of the customer's profits.

Fraud opportunity: The brokers may misrepresent the trade to the customer, saying they sold the commodity at a price of $5 when in fact the trade was made at $6. The broker pockets the difference. Brokers could also "replace" the customer's trade with another identical, but unprofitable, trade made for their own accounts at another time of the day. The brokers claim the more profitable trade for themselves and hit the customer with the less profitable transaction.

Investing is an inexact science, and few people are consistently right in predicting future stock and bond prices. Every time someone sells a stock believing it will go up no further, someone else is buying it, believing it will go up still higher. The following material will give you a good start toward understanding some of the information that is available.

Stock Quotations

If you look in the back of *The Wall Street Journal,* you will see stock quotations from the New York Stock Exchange, the American Stock Exchange, and the NASDAQ over-the-counter markets. Look at the top of the columns and notice the headings. Figure 20–6 describes what the various figures say for the New York Stock Exchange and the American Stock Exchange. These figures tell you what the high price over the last 52 weeks has been; the low price; the dividend paid (if

---

FIGURE 20–6

Understanding stock quotations in newspapers. Read across International Paper (Int. Paper), and you will see that the highest it sold for in the last 52 weeks was $68.50 and that the lowest was $44.25. The stock pays a dividend of $2.40 and yields 3.6%. The price divided by earnings is 20 (the PE ratio), and 567,900 shares were traded this day. The high for the day was $65.875, and the low was $64. The stock last sold for $65.875. The price went up $1.875 from the previous day's close.

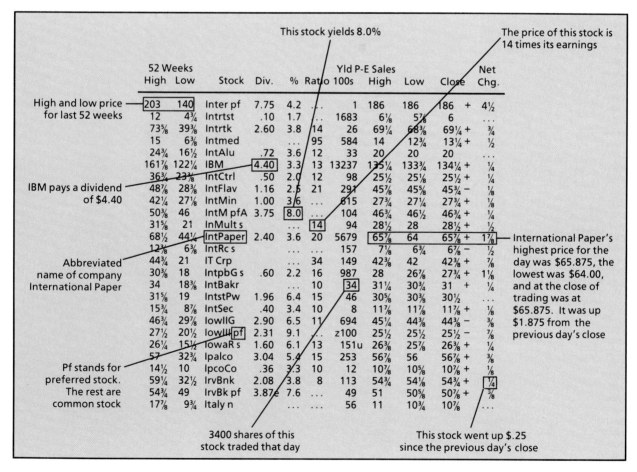

any); what the dividend yield is (the return expected); the price/earnings ratio (the price divided by the per share earnings); the number of shares traded that day; and the high, low, close, and net change in price from the previous day. Look through the columns and find the stock that pays the highest yield. Spend a little time looking through the figures until they make some sense to you.

Bond Quotations

Bonds are issued by both corporations and government units. Government issues are covered in *The Wall Street Journal* in a table called Treasury Issues. These issues are traded on the over-the-counter market. The price is quoted as a percentage of the face value. The interest rate is often followed by an *s* for easier pronunciation. For example, 9 percent bonds due in 1997 are called "nines of ninety-seven."

Figure 20–7 gives a sample of bond quotes for corporations. As you look through the sample quotes, note the variation in interest rates and the maturity dates. There are so many variables to consider in buying specific issues of stocks and bonds that most people rely on experts to help them choose the best investments. Nonetheless, the more one knows about these investments, the better one is prepared to talk intelligently with investment counselors and be sure their advice is consistent with one's best interests. It bears repeating that the easiest way to buy bonds and diversify at the same time is to buy into a bond mutual fund.

Mutual Fund Quotations

We have noted that one way to get expert investment advice, to diversify your investments among various stocks and bonds, and to purchase such securities at a minimum cost is to buy into mutual funds. Look up the listing of mutual funds in *The Wall Street Journal*. Note that some funds have the letters NL after them (in the second to the last column). This indicates the fund is a no-load fund and indicates these shares can be bought without paying a commission to a salesperson.

Understanding bond quotations in newspapers. Bonds are usually issued in $1,000 denominations, so a price of 90 is really $900. Note that some bonds yield as high as 11.7%. How does that compare to the yield from a bank account?

FIGURE 20–7

	Bonds	Cur Yld	Vol	High	Low	Close	Net Chg.
	LaQuin 10s02	cv	4	102	102	102	− 1¼
	LearS 10s04	10.0	3	100	100	100	+ 1⅝
	LearS 11½98	11.1	5	103½	103½	103½	− 1½
	LearS 11¼98	10.8	2	104¼	104¼	104¼	− ¾
	Leget 6½06	cv	36	103	102	102	...
	LipGp 8⅝01	9.4	10	92⅛	92⅛	92⅛	− 1⅞
	LincFl 8½96	8.7	5	97½	97½	97½	− 1⅜
	LomN 7s11	cv	4	104	104	104	...
	LonSl 11¾90	11.7	5	100⅜	100⅜	100⅜	− 2
	Loral 7¼10	cv	2	121	121	121	− ½
	Lorilld 6⅞93	7.6	62	90⅞	90⅜	90⅜	...
	LouGs 9¼00	9.2	10	101⅛	101	101	...
	Lowen 8½96	9.4	18	90	89	90	+ 7
	viLykes 7½94N f	...	35	19½	18	18	− 1
	viLykes 7½94f	...	79	20½	19⅞	20½	+ ⅞
	viLykes 11s00f	...	25	21	20½	20½	− ½
	MACOM 9¼06	cv	30	101	99¼	99¼	− 1¼

CV means convertible bond

These Lowen bonds are due in 1996 and originally paid 8½%. The current yield is 9.4%

500 bonds traded that day

This bond sold for a high of $900 and the low for the day was $890. It ended the day at $900, up $70 from the previous day

Remember, you do pay an annual fee for management advice, however. T. Rowe Price has a variety of funds available, including a growth fund, a high-yield fund, an international fund, and funds that yield tax-free returns. Various business periodicals will highlight the various funds available to you. You can also receive information and buy mutual funds through your broker.

The Dow Jones Average

Whether you listen to the evening news on TV or stock reports on the radio, announcers will say things like, "The Dow is up five points today in active trading." A gentleman named Charles Dow is responsible for this. Dow began the practice of measuring stock averages in 1884 when he added together the prices of 11 important stocks and dividend the total by 11 to get an average. Today, the Dow remains a barometer used to measure the direction of the market.

Dow Jones Industrial Averages

The average cost of 30 industrial stocks (used to give an indication of the direction of the market over time).

The **Dow Jones Industrial Averages** were broadened in 1982 to include 30 stocks. New stocks are substituted when deemed appropriate. The 30 stocks in the Dow Jones Industrial Average include such notables as Du Pont, Eastman Kodak, GE, IBM, Sears, Phillip Morris, and Coca Cola. McDonald's Corporation represents the first food retailing company to be included in the Dow Jones Industrial Average (see Figure 20–8). Again, the assumption is the averages give an indication of the direction of the market over time. Critics argue that the sample is too small to get a good statistical representation. Also, some feel the sample is biased in favor of stocks that are clearly blue chip and only give a reading in terms of the direction of other blue chip stocks.[7]

FIGURE 20–8

Dow Jones 30 industrial stocks.

Alcoa	Exxon	Phillip Morris
Allied Signal	General Electric	Primerica
American Express	General Motors	Procter & Gamble
AT&T	Goodyear	Sears Roebuck
Bethlehem Steel	IBM	Texaco
Boeing	International Paper	USX
Chevron	McDonald's	Union Carbide
Coca-Cola	Merck	United Technologies
Du Pont	3M Corp	Westinghouse
Eastman Kodak	Navistar	Woolworth

MAKING ETHICAL DECISIONS

Imagine that you are a reporter for a local newspaper. You are writing an article on Mega Machinery, Inc., the area's largest industrial company. In the course of your research, a disgruntled Mega employee tells you of the company's plans to take over MiniMach, a competing firm. Buying MiniMach stock now, before the takeover attempt is public knowledge, will surely reap a huge profit for you when Mega offers top dollar for the MiniMach stock. What are the ethical considerations in this situation? What are your alternatives? What are the consequences of each alternative? What will you do?

SECURITIES REGULATION

The Securities Act of 1933 protects investors by requiring full disclosure of financial information by firms selling new stocks or bonds. A registration statement with detailed economic and financial information relevant to the firm must be filed with the Securities and Exchange Commission (SEC). A condensed version of that registration document—called a **prospectus**—must be sent to purchasers.

The Securities and Exchange Act of 1934 created the **Securities and Exchange Commission (SEC).** The SEC has responsibility at the federal level for regulating the various exchanges. Those companies trading on the national exchanges must register with the SEC and provide annual updates. The act established guidelines to prevent insiders from taking advantage of their privileged information. **Insider trading** involves the use of knowledge or information that a person gains through his or her position that allows him or her to benefit from fluctuations in stock prices. Originally, *insider* was narrowly defined as a company's directors, employees, and relatives. Today, the term has been broadened to include just about anyone who has information that is not available to the general public. The Insider Trading Act of 1984 expanded the penalties that could be imposed on those found guilty of using insider information.

The Maloney Act of 1938, an amendment to the Securities Exchange Act of 1934, required any securities trade associations to register with the SEC. The National Association of Securities Dealers (NASD) was the only securities trade association formed and registered. The NASD regulates over-the-counter businesses. The NASD is also responsible for testing and licensing dealers.

The Investment Company Act of 1940 added mutual funds to the SEC's jurisdiction. Now mutual funds must also register with the SEC and provide investors with information about the company.

Most states also have laws concerning securities trading. They are called *blue-sky laws,* because one legislator remarked that promoters would sell shares of the "blue sky" if not regulated. Most state laws include penalties for fraudulent statements or actions connected with the sale of stocks or bonds. Some require that dealers register or that all new issues be registered. The first state law of this nature was passed in 1911.

prospectus
A condensed version of financial information prepared for the SEC that must be sent to purchasers.

Securities and Exchange Commission (SEC)
Federal government agency that has responsibility for regulating the various exchanges.

insider trading
Involves the use of knowledge or information that a person gains through his or her position that allows him or her to benefit from fluctuations in stock prices.

WALL STREET NICKNAMES

The ticker symbols for stocks are often the source of some humorous nicknames for corporations. For example, the nickname for McDonnell Douglas (symbol MD) is "Mad Dog." Here are a few other names from The Street:

COMPANY	NICKNAME
Champion International (CHA)	Cha Cha
Beneficial Corporation (BNL)	Big Nose Louie
McDonalds	Hamburgers
AT&T	Big Phone
Helmerick & Payne (HP)	Hot Pants
Union Carbide (UK)	Ukelele
Dayton Hudson (DH)	Dead Head
A & W Brands, Inc.	Soda
Golden Poultry Company	CHIK

Source: Beatrice E. Garcia, "If Big Nose Louie Turns You Off, Try Buying a Piece of Mad Dog," *The Wall Street Journal,* December 30, 1985, p. 15.

PROGRESS CHECK

- What does buying on margin mean? How does it work?
- What is a stock split? What advantages are there to companies splitting shares of stock?
- What exactly is a mutual fund? How do they benefit small investors?
- Why would a restaurant owner be interested in the futures market?
- What does the Dow Jones Industrial Average measure and why is it so important?
- What do the letters SEC stand for and exactly what does the SEC do?

CAREER INFORMATION: STOCKBROKER AND FINANCIAL SERVICES SALES

NATURE OF THE WORK

Securities Sales Workers. Most investors—whether they are individuals with a few hundred dollars or a large institution with millions to invest—call on securities sales workers when buying or selling stocks, bonds, shares in mutual funds, or other financial products. Securities sales workers often are called *registered representatives, account executives,* or *brokers.*

When an investor wishes to buy or sell securities, sales workers may relay the order through their firms' offices to the floor of a securities exchange such as the New York Stock Exchange. There, securities sales workers known as *brokers' floor representatives* buy and sell securities. If a security is not traded on an exchange, the sales worker sends the order to the firm's trading department, which trades it directly with a dealer in the over-the-counter market. After the transaction has been completed, the sales worker notifies the customer of the final price.

Securities sales workers also provide many related services for their customers. Depending on a customer's knowledge of the market, they may explain the meaning of stock market terms and trading practices; offer financial counseling; or devise an individual financial portfolio for the client including securities, life insurance, tax shelters, mutual funds, annuities, and other investments. Securities sales workers furnish information about the advantages and disadvantages of an investment based on each person's objectives. They also supply the latest price quotations on any security in which the investor is interested, as well as information on the activities and financial positions of the corporations issuing these securities.

Financial Services Sales Workers. Financial services sales workers call on various businesses to solicit applications for loans and new deposit accounts for banks or savings and loan associations. They also locate and contact prospective customers to present the bank's financial services and to ascertain the customer's banking needs. At most smaller and medium-size banks, branch managers and commercial loan officers are responsible for marketing the bank's financial services.

JOB OUTLOOK

The number of securities sales workers is expected to grow much faster than the average for all occupations through the mid-1990s. Most job openings, however, are expected to be created by workers who transfer to other jobs, retire, or stop working for other reasons.

Due to the highly competitive nature of securities sales work, many beginners leave the field because they are unable to establish sufficient clientele. Once established, however, securities sales workers have a relatively strong attachment to their occupation because of high earnings and the considerable investment in training.

Faster than average employment growth is expected among financial services sales workers as a result of the continued expansion in banking services and the need to finance an increasing level of commercial activity.

Financial services sales workers are paid a salary; some receive bonuses if they meet certain established goals. Average earnings of financial services sales workers are considerably less than those of securities sales workers.

RELATED OCCUPATIONS

Similar sales jobs requiring special knowledge include insurance agents and real estate agents.

SOURCES OF ADDITIONAL INFORMATION

Further information concerning a career as a securities sales worker is available for $1 from Securities Industry Association, 120 Broadway, New York, N.Y. 10271.

Source: *Occupational Outlook Handbook* (U.S. Department of Labor).

1. Companies can raise capital by debt financing, which involves issuing bonds.
   - What are the advantages and disadvantages of issuing bonds?

     The advantages of issuing bonds include: (1) management retains control since bondholders cannot vote; (2) interest paid on bonds is tax deductible, and (3) bonds are only a temporary source of finance. The disadvantage of bonds include: (1) because bonds are an increased debt, they may affect the market's perception of the company adversely; (2) interest on bonds must be paid; and (3) the face value must be repaid on the maturity date.
   - Are there different types of bonds?

     Yes. There are unsecured (debenture) and secured bonds. Unsecured bonds are not supported by collateral, whereas secured bonds are backed by tangible assets such as mortgages, stock, and equipment.

1. Compare the advantages and disadvantages of selling bonds and identify the classes and features of bonds.

2. Companies can also raise capital by equity financing, which involves selling stock.
   - What are the advantages and disadvantages of selling stock?

     The advantages of selling stock include: (1) the stock never has to be repaid since stockholders are owners in the company; (2) there is no legal obligation to pay dividends; and (3) no debt is incurred so the company is financially stronger. The disadvantages include: (1) stockholders are owners of the firm and can affect its management through the election of the board of directors; (2) it is more costly to pay dividends since they are paid after taxes; and (3) managers may be tempted to make stockholders happy in the short term rather than plan for long-term needs.
   - What are the differences between common and preferred stock?

     Common stockholders have voting rights in the company. Preferred stockholders have no voting rights. In exchange for giving up voting privileges, preferred stocks offer a *fixed* dividend that must be paid in full before common stockholders receive a dividend.

2. Compare the advantages and disadvantages of issuing stock and outline the differences between common and preferred stock.

3. To buy stock, you call a stockbroker who will arrange the deal.
   - What is a market order?

     A *market order* tells the broker to buy the stock at the best price available now. A *limit order,* on the other hand, tells the broker to buy the stock at a specific price.
   - What does buying on margin mean?

     It means that the investor borrows up to 50 percent of the cost of the stock from the broker so he or she can get more shares.
   - What does it mean when a stock splits?

     When a stock splits, stockholders receive two or more shares for each share they own. Each share is then worth half or less the original share. Therefore, while the number of the shares increases, the total value of the stockholders' holdings stays the same. The lower price per share may increase the demand for the stock, and thus the price.

3. Describe methods used to buy and sell stocks and bonds.

4. *Investing* means committing capital with the expectation of making a profit.
   - What are the criteria for selecting investments?

     They are (1) risk, (2) yield, (3) duration, (4) liquidity, and (5) tax consequences.
   - What is diversification?

     Diversification means buying several different investments to spread the risk.

4. Discuss the criteria used to select investments and describe methods of diversifying investments.

How can mutual funds help individuals diversify their investments?

A *mutual fund* is an organization that buys stocks and bonds and then sells shares in those securities to the public. Individuals who buy shares in a mutual fund are able to invest in many different companies they could not afford to invest in otherwise.

5. Stock exchanges enable businesses and investors to buy and sell stock, bonds, and mutual funds.

5. Identify the various stock exchanges.

What is a stock exchange?

An organization whose members can buy and sell securities.

What are the different exchanges?

There are stock exchanges all over the world. The largest U.S. exchange is the New York Stock Exchange (NYSE). It and the American Stock Exchange (AMEX) together are known as national exchanges because they handle stock of companies all over the country. In addition, there are several regional exchanges that deal with companies in their own areas.

What is the over-the-counter (OTC) market?

It is a system for exchanging stocks not listed on the national exchanges. It also handles bonds issued by city and state governments.

6. *Commodity exchanges* specialize in the buying and selling of precious metals and agricultural goods such as wheat, cattle, sugar, silver, gasoline, and foreign currencies.

6. Explain the role of hedging as a risk management tool for those who trade in the commodities exchange.

What are spot markets?

Buyers in spot markets purchase commodities for immediate delivery. Whereas, *futures markets* involves buying commodities for delivery some time in the future.

What is hedging and how does it help buyers and sellers of commodities decrease their risks?

Hedging is buying or selling commodities in the futures market. Hedging decreases the risks of buying and selling commodities because it fixes the price for the commodities. For example, if you have wheat growing in the field, you can sell it now in the futures market and know exactly how much money to expect at harvest time.

7. Securities quotations are given in the daily papers.

7. Explain securities quotations listed in the financial section of a newspaper.

What information do these quotations give you?

The stock quotations give you all kinds of information: the highest price in the last 52 weeks, the lowest price, the dividend yield, the price/earnings ratio, the total shares traded that day, and the high, low, close, and net change in price from the previous day. The bond quotations give you similar information regarding bonds.

What is the Dow Jones Industrial Average?

The Dow Jones Industrial Average is the average price of 30 stocks traded. There is also a utility average (15 stocks) and a transportation average (20 stocks).

8. Securities exchanges are regulated by the Securities and Exchange Commission (SEC).

8. Discuss regulation of securities trading.

What legislation gave the SEC the authority to regulate securities exchanges?

The Securities Act of 1933 and the Securities and Exchange Act of 1934 created and empowered the SEC with the authority to regulate securities exchanges. The Maloney Act of 1938 extended the SEC authority to the over-the-counter market and the Investment Company Act of 1940 added mutual funds to the SEC's jurisdiction.

1. Write the Education Department, *The Wall Street Journal*, 200 Burnett Road, Chicopee, MA 01021, and have them send you the Student Edition. Look through it at your leisure. It explains all the columns and charts. Discuss this edition with your class.

2. Read *The Wall Street Journal* daily for several months. Notice the trends in stocks and bonds and read the articles. Each day choose a particularly interesting article and share it with the class.

3. See if your professor is interested in setting up an investment game in your class. Each student should choose a few stocks and a couple of mutual funds. Each student's selections should be written in a book and the prices noted. For six weeks, you would follow the prices. The students with the largest percentage gain would win.

4. Visit a brokerage firm and watch the ticker tape that reports stock transactions. Watch the brokers in action. Talk to a broker and discuss your investment situation. Learn as much as you can about the procedures for buying stocks, bonds, and mutual funds.

5. On April 17, 1986, the price of silver closed at 544.5, or less than $5.45 per troy ounce. Look up Futures Prices in *The Wall Street Journal* to see what the price for silver is now. How much gain or loss would you have made buying 100 ounces in 1986? Also, check out the changes in gold, which closed at $339.40 on April 17; sugar, which closed at $7.98; and live cattle, which closed at $55.47.

GETTING INVOLVED

CASE ONE   HOW MUCH DEBT IS TOO MUCH DEBT?

PRACTICING MANAGEMENT DECISIONS

The number and size of corporate mergers and leveraged buyouts grew larger and larger toward the end of the 1980s. Most of those mergers and buyouts were financed through bonds, increasing corporate debt. Some experts questioned whether or not the burden of paying interest on all that debt would crush businesses in the 1990s. Corporate debt by some measures was the highest it had been since the 1920s, just before the Great Depression. On the other hand, corporate cash flow and profits required to pay off that debt were at levels normally seen during a recession.

Some academics and executives felt that corporations were borrowing beyond their means. High debt restricts the options of management, which must pay interest on the debt rather than invest in new plants and equipment. Risks of defaults and bankruptcy also increased.

Some academics and business leaders felt that the new debt was a good sign—of an expanding economy adjusting to lower inflation and lower interest rates. They did admit, however, that the percentage of debt to gross national product (36.2 percent) was the highest since WWII. Some 20 percent of cash flow was needed to pay the debt versus 12 to 15 percent during the 1970s.

Most of the debt came from issuing junk bonds. Revco was a drugstore chain that used such bonds in 1986 for a leveraged buyout. Disappointing sales led to bankrupcy proceedings. Freuhauf Corporation incurred some $1.5 billion in debt to fend off an unwanted takeover attempt, but had to sell off numerous assets to pay off the debt. There are some dangerous trends emerging. In 1984, only 51 companies faulted on some $11 billion in debt. By 1987, some 87 companies defaulted on over $21 billion in debt. Debt since then has been growing tremendously and the economy seems to be weakening. By the end of 1988, nonfinancial companies doubled their debt to $1.8 trillion.

DECISIONS QUESTIONS

1. Use all of the knowledge you have obtained in the last couple of chapters to explain why people may be concerned about companies paying for other companies using debt rather than other sources of funds.

2. What might happen if the earnings of corporations slowed and companies had difficulty paying off their bondholders? Who is more likely to be hurt—stockholders or bondholders of the corporation? Why?

3. Which kind of bondholders would be better off—those who had secured bonds or those with unsecured bonds? Explain.

4. Firms are attempting to buy other firms using junk bonds as the means of financing the purchase. Do you feel the government should do more to regulate such deals? Why or why not?

Source: Bill Sing, "Rising Corporate Debts Stir Questions—and Fears," *Los Angeles Times*, October 28, 1988, pp. 1 and 31; and Christopher Farrell, "Learning to Live with Leverage," *Business Week*, October 7, 1988, pp. 138–43.

CASE TWO INVESTING AN INHERITANCE

Jason Heimberg's grandmother died and left him $30,000. Jason needed $5,000 of the inheritance to finish his last year at County Community College. He had $25,000 left to invest. Jason investigated several stocks that he felt were likely to grow rapidly. Most were high-tech stocks in industries such as gene splicing and robotics. Jason's stockbroker was encouraging him to diversify his investments by buying stock in two mutual funds. One was a fund that specializes in smaller growth companies. Another specialized in bonds.

A broker Jason met a party suggested that he really need not use a broker at all. Her suggestion was to keep some funds in the bank for his use in an emergency. Other funds could be invested in several different mutual funds that were managed by one firm. She called them no-load mutual funds, and explained that they could be bought for no brokerage fee. She said the funds have an NL notation in the various mutual fund quotations, as found in *The Wall Street Journal*.

A financial adviser has suggested that Jason buy insurance first, even though he is not married. The idea was to buy a policy that would invest money for Jason at what looked like a reasonable return. Any excess funds would be placed in a bank (for emergencies) and in mutual funds that the adviser would recommend.

DECISION QUESTIONS

1. What are the criteria Jason should use in evaluating investment alternatives?
2. Look up no-load mutual funds in a newspaper or magazine that lists them. Do you understand what is available? What are the advantages and disadvantages of buying a mutual fund through a broker?
3. What questions does this case raise that you need to have answered before you can invest your funds more intelligently? Where could you find answers to such questions?

LOOKING AHEAD

Businesses turn to financial institutions such as banks and insurance companies to borrow funds. You and other investors often turn to banks and savings and loan corporations as a safe location to save your money. Many people, therefore, are dependent on the safety and strength of financial institutions. You will learn in Chapter 21 that some financial institutions in the United States are not doing as well as one would hope. This is a serious issue that we shall explore in depth.

Finance really comes alive when you begin using the concepts to manage your own personal finances. The appendix to Part 6 discusses ways for you to save capital to begin your own investment program. It then discusses investment alternatives, including real estate, insurance, and IRAs. Pay close attention to Chapter 21 first because you may find that putting your money in the local savings and loan may not be as safe as you thought.

HOME
SAVINGS
OF
AMERICA

AMERICA'S LARGEST

1889 1989

Amerca's largest savings and loan salutes America's most beloved parade on the mutual celebration of 100 years of service to the community and the nation.

ONE HUNDRED YEARS STRONG

An Ahmanson Company
Over $38 billion strong

FINANCIAL INSTITUTIONS

21

LEARNING GOALS

After you have read and studied this chapter, you should be able to:

1. Trace the history of banking.

2. Identify types of banking and non-bank institutions and describe the services available at each.

3. Describe the organizations created to protect your deposits in financial institutions.

4. Relate the weaknesses of the current American banking system to the conditions that led to the Great Depression.

5. Characterize the future of the American banking system.

6. Explain the functions of the Federal Reserve system and describe the tools the Fed uses to control the money supply.

7. Illustrate the role of international banking and finance in global economics.

KEY TERMS

brokerage firms, *p. 669*
certificate of deposit (CD), *p. 664*
commercial and consumer finance
  companies, *p. 669*
commercial bank, *p. 663*
credit unions, *p. 667*
currency, *p. 683*
demand deposit, *p. 663*
discount rate, *p. 681*
electronic funds transfer system
  (EFTS), *p. 677*
Federal Deposit Insurance Corporation
  (FDIC), *p. 670*
federal funds, *p. 682*
federal funds rate, *p. 682*
Federal Reserve System, *p. 679*
Federal Savings and Loan Insurance
  Corporation (FSLIC), *p. 670*

float, *p. 678*
long-term loans, *p. 665*
money supply, *p. 683*
mutual savings bank, *p. 667*
National Credit Union Administration
  (NCUA), *p. 672*
nonbanks, *p. 668*
open-market operations, *p. 680*
pension funds, *p. 669*
reserve requirement, *p. 680*
savings and loan association, *p. 665*
short-term loans, *p. 665*
superregional bank, *p. 676*
thrift institutions, *p. 665*
time deposit, *p. 663*

Alan Greenspan.

PROFILE ALAN GREENSPAN, CHAIRMAN OF THE FEDERAL RESERVE SYSTEM

Alan Greenspan was born in New York, the only son of Herbert (a broker) and Rose Greenspan. Mr. Greenspan went to George Washington High School two years behind Henry Kissinger. He went on to study music at Julliard and played the clarinet for a year or so in a jazz band.

When the attraction of music declined, Alan decided to go to New York University where he majored in economics. He received his degree summa cum laude in 1948. He went on to get his M.A. in economics at NYU and began doctoral studies under Arthur Burns at Columbia. Arthur Burns later became chairman of the Federal Reserve Board.

Greenspan began work as an economist for the Conference Board, a nonprofit research group. Later he started his own consulting frm. He went on to teach ecoomics at NYU for a couple of years, and the school granted him a doctorate later. His firm, Townsend-Greenspan, provided research, forecasts, and other economic consulting services to major firms.

As a young man, Greenspan was politically liberal. However, he became friendly with Ayn Rand, the author of very conservative books such as *Atlas Shrugged,* and she convinced him that capitalism was not only efficient and practical, but moral as well. As a consequence, he became a conservative himself.

Dr. Greenspan went to work for Richard Nixon as one of his top economic aides. He performed several duties for Nixon during his campaign for the presidency, but returned to his firm when Nixon was elected. He did work on several economic task forces for President Nixon and served as an informal adviser. He has served as a consultant to the Council of Economic Advisers, the United States Treasury, and the Federal Reserve Board. He became chairman of the Council of Economic Advisers under President Ford.

Dr. Greenspan is very much a fighter against inflation and feels that government spending must be cut. That is one reason President Reagan chose him to be chairman of the Federal Reserve (the Fed) after the powerful Paul Volker left. Greenspan had served on Reagan's 1980 transition team and chaired the National Commission of Social Security Reform.

Now Dr. Greenspan has one of the most powerful positions in the country. As chairman of the Federal Reserve, he has control over the nation's money supply. He is the one responsible for keeping the country growing without causing inflation or recession. He is also the nation's top banker.

You will hear much of Alan Greenspan as you read the business news. In this chapter, we shall talk about banks and banking and the importance of the Federal Reserve. When you are finished, you will see the importance of Alan Greenspan to the economies of the United States and the world. President Bush wants the economy to grow to pay off the national debt. Dr. Greenspan is trying to slow growth to manage inflation. This conflict should continue well into the 1990s.

Sources: Barbara Rudolph and Frederick Angeheuer, "A Conservative Who Can Compromise," *Time,* June 15, 1987, pp. 50–51; and Mickey Kaus, Rich Thomas, and Carolyn Friday, "Reagan's Man at the Fed," *Newsweek,* June 15, 1987, pp. 16–17; and John M. Berry, "Greenspan's Differences with Bush Get New Test as Fed Sets '89 Course," *The Washington Post,* February 5, 1989, pp. H1 and H16.

THE BANKING INDUSTRY

The Federal Reserve System, regular banks, and savings and loan corporations were in the news throughout the 1980s. Some banks were in the news because of the loans they made to foreign countries; loans that may not be paid back. Hundreds of savings and loan institutions were in the news because they were going bankrupt and were causing a financial "crisis." Because of deflation, land values declined, and farmers and builders could not make their mortgage payments. This put great pressure on the savings and loan institutions and banks that had loaned money to investors. Savings and loan institutions made other risky loans that turned out to be unprofitable, plunging the industry into debt.

Finally, the Federal Reserve was in the news because of its manipulation of the money supply. Alan Greenspan became a major player in the drama called "the economic policy for the late 1980s and early 1990s." Clearly, the banking industry has reached center stage going into the 1990s, and the impact of what happens in it will have a direct bearing on you. If a local savings and loan fails, it may take a long time to retrieve the money you have worked so hard to save. Therefore, you and I have a real interest in what happens to the banking and S&L industry over the next few years.

Before we discuss the present condition of the banking industry, let's review the history of banking. It is an interesting history and one that reveals much about what is happening today. It will also tell you what the Federal Reserve System is and how it came to be.

Early Banking History

The history of banking goes back thousands of years. The Babylonians performed many of the banking functions of today, taking deposits, engaging in foreign exchange, and issuing paper with the same function as checks. Over time, banks grew and prospered and became a vital part of the economy throughout the world.

In the United States, however, there were no banks at first, and strict laws limited the number of coins that could be brought to the colonies. Thus, colonists were forced to barter; that is, to trade goods for goods (for example, cotton and tobacco for shoes and lumber).

The demand for money was so great that Massachusetts issued its own paper money in 1690. Other colonies soon followed suit. Land banks were established to lend money to farmers. Britain ended both practices by 1741. Remember, we were under the rule of Britain back then. In fact, a new bank was formed in Pennsylvania during the Revolution to finance the war against England.

Alexander Hamilton persuaded Congress to form a central bank in 1781 over the objections of Thomas Jefferson and others. It closed in 1811 only to be replaced in 1816 because state-chartered banks couldn't support the War of 1812. Throughout this period, there was serious debate about the role and function of banking in this country. The battle between the Second (Central) Bank of the United States and state banks got really hot in the 1830s. Several banks in President Andrew Jackson's home state were hurt by pressure from the Central Bank. The fight ended when the Central Bank was closed in 1836.

By the time of the Civil War, the banking system was a mess. Many different banks issued different kinds of currencies. During the war, coins were hoarded because they were worth more as gold and silver than as coins. The government began printing money ("greenbacks") that was money only because the government declared it so, not because the material it was made from had any value of its own.

Eventually, the government established federally chartered and state-chartered banks. The chaos continued and reached something of a climax in 1907, when many banks failed. People got nervous about their money and went to the bank to withdraw their funds. Shortly thereafter the cash ran out and some banks had to refuse money to depositors.

The cash shortage problems of 1907 led to the formation of a bank that could lend money to banks—the Federal Reserve System. It was to be a "lender of last resort" in such emergencies. Under the Federal Reserve Act of 1913, all federally chartered banks had to join the Federal Reserve. State banks could also join. The Federal Reserve became the banker's bank. If banks had excess funds, they could deposit them in the Fed and if extra money was needed, it could be borrowed. The Federal Reserve System has been intimately related to banking ever since.

The Great Depression

The Federal Reserve was designed to prevent a repeat of the panic that occurred in 1907. In order to join the Federal Reserve System, a bank had to place a certain percentage (determined by the Fed) of its assets in "reserve." This reserve could be placed in their own vaults or deposited in the Fed in noninterest-bearing accounts. If banks were short of funds, they were able to borrow funds from the Federal Reserve and cut off any doubt that they would survive.

Nevertheless, the stock market crash of 1929 led to bank failures in the early 1930s. The stock market began tumbling and people had to rush to the bank to get money to cover their positions in the stock market. You should read about the Great Depression in some detail. The bottom line, however, was that businesses failed, jobs were lost, people went to the banks to withdraw their money, and the banks ran out of money. States were forced to close banks. President Franklin Roosevelt extended the period of the bank closings in 1933 to gain time to come up with some solution to the problem.

In 1933 and 1935, federal legislation was passed to strengthen the banking system. The most important move was to establish federal deposit insurance. You'll learn more about federal deposit insurance later in this chapter. At this point, it is important that you know that the government started an insurance program to protect us from bank failures.

During the 1960s and 1970s, many banks found that it was very costly giving up noninterest bearing reserves to the Federal Reserve System. They were attracted by the prospect of having interest-bearing reserves in state-chartered banks that were state insured. This withdrawal of reserves from the Fed left it with less money to use for fine-tuning the economy.

In the following sections, we shall discuss the differences between banks and savings and loans. We shall also discuss nonbank alternatives for placing your money. We shall examine several of the organizations created to protect the funds you deposit in banks and other financial institutions. And, finally, you will learn much more about the Federal Reserve System and its role in the economy and in banking.

THE AMERICAN BANKING SYSTEM

The American banking system consists of commercial banks, savings and loan associations, credit unions, and mutual savings banks. In addition, a variety of organizations perform several banking functions, although they are not true banks. These are *nondeposit* institutions, and are often referred to as *nonbanks*. These would include pension funds, insurance companies, commercial finance companies, consumer finance companies, and brokerage houses. We'll discuss the activities and services provided by each of these institutions, starting with commercial banks.

Commercial Banks

A **commercial bank** is a profit-making organization that receives deposits from individuals and corporations in the form of checking and savings accounts and uses some of these funds to make loans. This is the kind of institution small businesses turn to for loans. It is important to note that commerical banks have two types of customers: (1) depositors and (2) those who take out loans (borrowers). A commercial bank is equally responsible to both types of customers. Commerical banks try to make a profit by using the funds given them by depositors efficiently. In essence, a commerical bank uses customer deposits as inputs (on which the bank pays interest) to invest that money in interest-bearing loans to other customers. Commerical banks make a profit if the revenue generated by loans exceeds the interest paid to depositors plus all other operating expenses.

For legal operation, banks must be chartered by individual states or the federal government. Commerical banks chartered by states are called *state banks;* those chartered by the federal government are called *national banks.* Of approximately 14,800 commerical banks, two thirds are state banks. Nevertheless, national banks are larger since they hold about 65 percent of total commerical bank deposits.

Services Provided by Commerical Banks

Individuals and corporations that deposit money in checking accounts have the privilege of writing personal checks that can be used to pay for almost any purchase or transaction. The technical name for a checking account is a **demand deposit** because the money is available on demand from the depositor. Typically, banks charge individual consumers a service charge or demand a minimum deposit. In addition, banks might also charge a small handling fee for each check written. For corporate depositors, the amount of the service charge depends on the average daily balance in the checking account, the number of checks written, and the credit rating and the credit history of the firm.

In the past, checking accounts paid no interest to depositors, but newer interest-bearing checking accounts have experienced phenomenal growth in recent years. Most commerical banks offer NOW and super NOW accounts to their depositors. A NOW (negotiable order of withdrawal) account typically pays an annual interest rate, but requires a certain minimum balance that must be maintained in the account at all times (for example, $500) and restricts the number of checks that can be written each month.

A Super NOW account pays higher interest in order to attract larger deposits. However, Super NOW account holders are required to maintain a larger minimum balance. Super NOW accounts typically offer free and unlimited check-writing privileges. In addition to these types of checking accounts, commerical banks offer a variety of savings account options. A saving account is technically called a **time deposit** because the bank can require a prior notice before withdrawal.

commercial bank
A profit-making organization that receives deposits from individuals and corporations in the form of checking and saving accounts and uses some of these funds to make loans.

demand deposit
The technical name for a checking account; the money can be withdrawn on demand at any time by the owner.

time deposit
The technical name for a savings account for which the bank requires prior notice before withdrawal.

FIGURE 21–1

FIGURE 21–1

Some services available at some commercial banks. The number of services has expanded recently as banks seek to provide more and more assistance to consumers and businesses.

Demand deposits (checking accounts)	Traveler's checks
Time deposits (savings accounts)	Credit cards
Loans	Certificates of deposit (CDs)
Financial counseling	NOW accounts
Safe deposit boxes	Super NOW accounts
Certified checks	Telebanking
Overdraft protection	Automated teller machines (ATM.)
Insurance	Brokerage services

certificate of deposit (CD)
A note issued by a bank that earns a guaranteed interest for a fixed period of time; the CD cannot be withdrawn without penalty until the maturity date.

One common form of savings account is called a passbook savings account. Under this savings option, depositors do not have checking privileges, but can withdraw money at any time. A **certificate of deposit (CD)** is a time-deposit (savings) account that earns an interest rate, to be delivered at the end of the certificate's maturity date. The depositor agrees not to withdraw any of the funds in the account until the end of the specified period. CDs are currently available for periods of from three months to five years, and the interest rates offered vary, depending on the period of the certificate. The interest rates offered depend on economic conditions and the prime rate at the time of the deposit. In addition to the checking and savings accounts just discussed, commerical banks offer a variety of other services to their depositors. These include the following:

- Automated teller machines (ATMs) offer customers the convenience of 24-hour banking at a variety of outlets such as supermarkets, department stores, and drugstores in addition to the bank's regular branches. Depositors can now get cash, transfer funds, and make deposits at their own discretion with the use of a computer-coded personalized plastic access card.
- Commerical banks also offer credit cards to their creditworthy customers, inexpensive brokerage services, financial counseling, automatic payment of telephone bills, safe deposit boxes, tax-deferred individual retirement accounts (IRAs) for qualified individuals and couples, traveler's checks, and overdraft checking account privileges (this means preferred customers can automatically get loans at reasonable rates when they have written checks exceeding their account balance). See Figure 21–1 for a list of key banking services.

Automatic teller machines offer the convenience of 24-hour banking. They are just one of the many services offered by banks. Can you think of other services you would like to see added or improved at your local bank?

Services to Borrowers

Commercial banks offer a variety of services to individuals and corporations in need of a loan. Generally, loans are given based on the creditworthiness of the recipient. Banks want to manage their funds effectively and are supposed to carefully screen loan applicants to ensure that the loan plus interest will be paid back on time. As you will see below, some banks were not so good at screening customers and made bad loans to businesses and foreign countries.

To get a loan for a house or other large purchase in the future, it is very important for you to develop a good credit history as early as possible. Because this is easier said than done, you should carefully consider some of the tips provided in the box on developing a credit history.

Business loans are normally characterized as short-term or long-term, depending on whether they are to be repaid within one year or over a longer period of time.

HOW TO DEVELOP A GOOD CREDIT HISTORY

Small businesses often have difficulty obtaining loans at reasonable interest rates from financial institutions. Commercial banks, for example, require small-business loan applicants to provide adequate collateral—assets such as corporate stock or inventory, for instance, that the bank could assume control over in the case of delinquency. Many small businesses, especially new ones that have low equity, might not be able to fulfill collateral requirements. In such cases it is the credit rating of the individual(s) owning the business that would decide whether or not the loan was granted.

How can an individual with little credit history develop a good credit rating? Here are some tips:

- Open up a checking and savings account at a financial institution. It is important that you manage these accounts in a way that would avoid bad checks, overdrawn balances, and so forth. It is also important to keep some money in savings at all times. This could

be interpreted by prospective lenders as an indication of efficient money management.
- Establish credit with a department store or oil company. It is usually easier to get credit from such sources than from a financial institution in the form of a credit card. Pay your bills on time and avoid paying finance charges. This should enhance your credibility when you apply for a credit card.
- Pay all your rent, utility, and telephone bills promptly. If you do so, you can obtain valuable references when you need them.
- Obtain a credit card from a financial institution. No matter how small the initial credit allowance might be, a credit card is one of the best ways to develop a good credit history quickly. Remember that the more responsible you are in managing your credit card account, the more credit you will be able to obtain in the future.

Short-Term Loans **Short-term loans** are those that have to be paid within one year. Many businesses borrow on a short-term basis to obtain urgently needed cash. Businesses find it useful to establish a line of credit before they actually need money. This would involve getting approval for a specified loan amount beforehand, so that the firm can immediately borrow the money whenever it is needed.

short-term loans
Loans that have to be paid in one year or less.

Long-Term Loans **Long-term loans** are those payable in a period that exceeds 1 year. Typically, long-term loans must be repaid within 2 to 5 years but could also be extended for longer periods of time (up to 20 years). Banks give long-term loans to individuals, corporations, and domestic and foreign governments. The interest charged for most long-term loans for large corporations and governments is negotiated between the two parties. Often such loans require a long and exhausting round of bargaining before the terms of the loan (interest charged, repayment period, types and amount of collateral required, default options, and so forth) are mutually agreed upon. Most loans by law require collateral.

long-term loans
Loans that are payable in a period that exceeds one year.

Savings and Loan Associations

A **savings and loan association** (S&L) is a financial institution that accepts both savings and checking deposits and provides home mortgage loans. They are often known as **thrift institutions** since their original purpose was to promote consumer thrift and home ownership. To help them encourage home ownership, "thrifts" at one time were permitted to offer slightly higher interest rates on savings deposits to attract a larger pool of funds. These funds were then used to offer long-term, fixed-rate mortgages at whatever rate prevailed at the time. With the abrupt rise in interest rates in the late 1970s, S&Ls found themselves in deep financial trouble. The problem occurred because they were forced to pay depositors higher interest rates than before, while their revenues from the low, long-term mortgage loans

savings and loan association
A financial institution that accepts both savings and checking deposits and provides home mortgage loans.

thrift institutions
Another name for savings and loan associations.

Savings and loan associations were set up to encourage home buying? They were quite successful at that function until recently. Now the S&Ls are in deep financial trouble. Nonetheless, potential homeowners can still get loans as the S&L industry is being restructured.

A banker is a person who will loan you money only after he has determined you don't need it.
MARK TWAIN

held constant. In other words, the S&Ls' costs kept going up while their income remained the same. Unable to pay a substantially higher interest rate than their competitors (that is, commerical banks), S&Ls began to lose a large proportion of their depositors, with catastrophic results for many of them.

Between 1979 and 1983, about 20 percent of the nation's S&Ls failed because of unbearable financial pressure. Faced with this situation, the federal government permitted S&Ls to offer NOW and Super NOW accounts, to allocate up to 10 percent of their funds to commercial loans, and to offer mortgage loans with adjustable interest rates based on market conditions. In addition, S&Ls were permitted to offer a variety of other banking services, such as financial counseling to small businesses and credit cards. As a result, S&Ls became much more similar to and competitive with commerical banks.

The problem is that many savings and loan organizations began making bad loans to earn higher rates. One S&L, North America Savings & Loan of California, had 98 percent of its loans declared "bad" by the bank board.[1] Of the 3,147 S&Ls in the United States in 1988, over 500 were insolvent under generally accepted accounting principles. That is, their assets (mainly loans) were worth less than their liabilities (mainly deposits). In one Texas thrift, for example, 96 percent of its loans were delinquent. Total losses in 1987 were $13.4 billion.[2] Deposits in these S&Ls were insured by the U.S. government, but the government did not have the money to pay for such losses. In the long run, taxpayers like you and me will be bailing out failing S&Ls until the system is restructured.

Credit unions like this one pay relatively high interest rates for deposits and charge relatively low interest rates on loans. Credit unions also offer other services to members. Most accounts are insured up to $100,000, just as they are at banks and S&Ls.

Mutual Savings Banks

A **mutual savings bank** is similar to a savings and loan. However, there are fewer mutual savings banks and they are concentrated in one area of the United States. Most of the approximately 400 mutual savings banks operate in the northeastern sector of the United States, particularly in New England and New York. The range of services they provide are very similar to those offered by savings and loans.

mutual savings bank
A financial institution found mainly in the Northeast; they are very similar to S&Ls.

Credit Unions

Credit unions are nonprofit, member-owned financial cooperatives that offer basic banking services such as accepting deposits and making loans to members. Typically, credit unions offer interest-bearing checking accounts called share draft accounts at relatively high rates, short-term loans at relatively low rates, financial counseling, life insurance policies, and a limited number of home mortgage loans to their members. Credit unions may be thought of as financial cooperatives that are organized by government agencies, corporations, unions, or professional associations. Nationwide, there are now about 9,400 federally chartered credit unions with more than 32 million members. In addition, there are over 4,900 state-chartered, but federally insured credit unions. Some state-chartered credit unions, in addition, are privately insured.[3]

credit unions
Nonprofit, member-owned financial cooperatives that offer basic banking services such as accepting deposits and making loans; they may also offer life insurance and a limited number of home mortgages.

◼ Who is Alan Greenspan and what are his responsibilities?

◼ Why did the United States need a Federal Reserve System?

◼ What is the difference between a bank, a savings and loan corporation, a mutual savings bank, and a credit union?

◼ How can you establish a good credit rating?

◼ What are the services offered by a commercial bank?

PROGRESS CHECK

Banks advertise to compete against other financial institutions, such as stock brokers, S&Ls, and credit unions. The competition is likely to get stiffer in the 1990s as financial institutions step up their battle for your savings dollars.

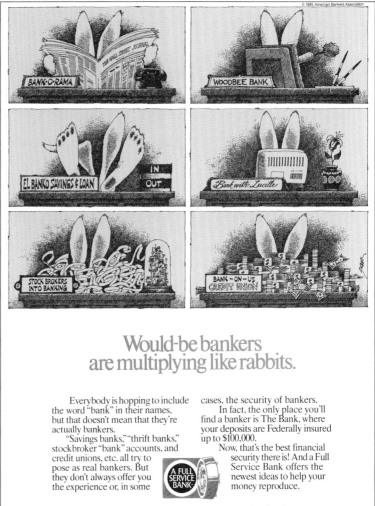

Other Financial Institutions

nonbanks
Financial organizations that accept no deposits, but offer many of the services provided by regular banks.

Nonbanks are financial organizations that accept no deposits but offer many of the services provided by regular banks (see the ad for full-service banks above). They include life insurance companies, pension funds, brokerage firms, and commerical finance companies. As competition between these organizations and banks increases, the dividing line between banks and nonbanks is becoming less and less apparent. The diversity of financial services and investment alternatives offered by nonbanks has caused banks to expand the services they offer.

You know that life insurance companies provide financial protection for policyholders who periodically pay premiums. In addition, they invest the funds they receive from policyholders in corporate and government bonds. In recent years, more insurance companies have begun to provide long-term financing for real estate development projects.

Pension funds are amounts of money designated by corporations, nonprofit organizations, or unions to cover part of the financial needs of members when they retire. Contributions to pension funds are made either by employees alone or by both the employer and employees. A member may begin to collect a monthly draw on this fund on reaching a certain retirement age. Pension funds typically invest in low return but safe corporate stocks or in other conservative investments such as government securities and corporate bonds to generate additional income.

Brokerage firms have traditionally offered services related to investments in the various stock exchanges in this country and abroad. However, brokerage houses have recently made serious inroads into the domain of regular banks by offering high-yield combination savings and checking accounts (money market accounts). Also, investors can obtain loans from their broker, using their securities as collateral. Brokerage firms experienced phenomenal growth during the past decade as more investors became aware of the options they offered. However, this interest fell off somewhat in the late 1980s because of the stock market fall. It is likely that brokerages will prove an increasingly strong challenge for regular banks and S&Ls in the future, especially if banks and S&Ls are perceived as less reliable than they are now. We shall discuss why they may be perceived that way later in this chapter.

Commerical and consumer finance companies offer short-term loans to businesses or individuals who are either unable to meet the credit requirements of regular banks or have exceeded their credit limit and are in need of more funds. The interest rates charged by these finance companies are higher than those of regular banks. The primary customers of these companies are new businesses or individuals with no credit history. In fact, college students often turn to consumer finance companies for loans necessary to pay for their education.

Let's look in more detail at the organizations that have evolved to protect your money. You should know about the agencies that insure the funds you place in financial institutions.

pension funds
Amounts of money designated by corporations, nonprofit organizations, or unions to cover part of the financial needs of members when they retire.

brokerage firms
Organizations that buy and sell securities for their clients and provide other financial services.

commercial and consumer finance companies
Financial institutions that offer short-term loans to individuals at higher interest rates than commerical banks.

Do you understand the difference between the so-called banks and nonbanks? Name a financial institution that could be called a nonbank. What are the primary functions of commercial banks? What are some of the new services offered by commerical banks? Describe the functions of credit unions.

THINKING IT THROUGH

PROTECTING YOUR FUNDS

The last thing the American economy needs is a repeat of the 1930s depression. Several organizations have evolved to protect your money in case the economy does take a turn for the worse. The three major sources of financial protection are the Federal Deposit Insurance Corporation, the Federal Savings and Loan Insurance Corporation, and the National Credit Union Share Insurance Fund. All three insure deposits in individual accounts up to $100,000. Only 85 percent of the country's credit unions have federal insurance. The rest are privately insured. Since the banking industry is relatively weak these days, it is probably best to stick with federally insured credit unions.[4]

The Federal Deposit Insurance Corporation

The **Federal Deposit Insurance Corporation (FDIC)** is an independent agency of the U.S. government that insures bank deposits. When banks fail, the FDIC arranges to have the accounts at that bank transferred to another banks or pays off depositors up to a certain amount. (This amount has increased over the years and is now at $100,000.)

To be eligible for membership in the FDIC, a bank must meet certain standards. Furthermore, approved members undergo regular examinations by federal and state agencies. Members pay semiannual insurance fees to the FDIC based on the volume of their deposits. These fees are invested in government securities and are the FDIC's deposit insurance fund. This fund is small relative to the total reserves in many of the larger banks in the United States, as is expected of an insurance fund. This has never been a problem in the past, but recently some people have questioned the ability of the FDIC to cover the losses if a large bank or two were to fail. In fact, the FDIC considered 1,400 of the nation's 14,000 banks as problems. The insurance fund lost $3 billion in 1988 and faced further loses in 1989 and into the 1990s.[5] As you shall see in the following section, the banking industry may be merged with the savings and loan industry, and neither are strong financially.

The Federal Savings and Loan Insurance Corporation

The **Federal Savings and Loan Insurance Corporation (FSLIC)**—pronounced *fizz lick*—is another independent agency of the U.S. government. It insures holders of accounts in savings and loan associations. Both the FDIC and the FSLIC were started in the 1930s. The FDIC was begun in 1933 and the FSLIC in 1934. Some 1,700 bank and thrift institutions failed during that time, and people were losing confidence in them. For some 50 years the FSLIC and the FDIC were successful in covering losses from thrift and bank institution failures.

During the 1980s, however, the thrift institutions of America began failing. Supposedly the FSLIC would be able to cover any losses and keep the system strong. The fact was, however, that the FSLIC had only $2 billion in reserves to cover $800 billion in deposits. When the thrift institutions were mostly well financed, that may have been enough, but in the 1980s it was not nearly enough. In 1988, the FSLIC paid $1.4 billion to the depositors of the American Diversified Savings Bank, which had gone bust. Think about that—over $1 billion to the depositors of one failed S&L. There were about 500 other S&Ls that were insolvent (out of a total of about 3,000). In fact, only 1,800 were in fair to good condition.[6] (See the figure in the margin called The Number of Insolvent Thrifts in the 1980s.)

The FSLIC was insolvent also. The amount owed to depositors was in the $75 to $100 billion range and growing 15 to 20 percent annually. In Texas alone, the capital of the thrift industry was a minus $11 billion. To save the industry, the Federal Home Loan Bank Board (the regulatory agency of the savings and loan industry) began merging weak thrifts with stonger ones and began selling off the assets of thrift institutions at bargain-basement prices. All in all, there was a crisis in the thrift industry that was not being handled well.

What happened to cause the crisis in the S&L industry? That is an issue that will be debated for many years to come. Certainly one aspect of the problem was the fact that deposits were guaranteed by the federal government. That made it

THE NUMBER OF INSOLVENT THRIFTS IN THE 1980s

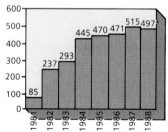

*(six months ending June 30)

Source: Federal Savings and Loan Insurance Corporation, 1988.

possible to make many high-risk loans with no fear of loss because the government would cover the deposits. Another aspect of the problem was the process of deregulation, which made it possible for the S&Ls to lend money to high-risk developers and other borrowers. Another part of the problem was fraud among the top managers of some S&Ls. Managers of some S&Ls were paying themselves huge salaries and were financing questionable operations for their friends that involved huge risks.

The government knew about the weak condition of the S&Ls early in the 1980s, but did little to stop the $6 billion or more in losses that were occurring year after year. (See the figure in the margin called How the Losses of Thrifts Increased in the 1980s.) The bulk of the losses happened among Texas thrifts and some of the blame was aimed at House Speaker Jim Wright. His involvement in the S&L crisis was part of an overall ethics investigation of Wright in 1989.[7]

Finally, the Federal Reserve System was blamed for triggering the crisis in the first place. When Paul Volker arrived at the Fed in 1979, short-term rates were 9.5 percent and 98 percent of the thrift industry was solvent. Over the next three years, the rates shot up in the 13 to 18 percent range, and 20 percent of the thrift industry became insolvent. The thrift industry was used to borrowing low in the short term and lending long. Long-term interest rates were usually higher than short-term rates and the thrifts made money. When short-term rates became higher than long-term rates (this is called an inverted yield curve), the thrifts began losing money. Rather than shut down the troubled thrifts, the government went through all kinds of maneuvers to keep them going and eventually the problem grew and grew until the losses were in the billions.

The bottom line for you and me is this: The government decided to do something about the S&L crisis in 1989. One of President Bush's first priorities was to solve the S&L problem.

Figure 21-2 (see page 672) illustrates part of the solution. It is a complex program designed to close down 350 thrift organizations that are losing the most money. The cost is $50 billion, but the cost is being spread over many years by selling bonds that will be paid back over a 30-year period. Estimates are that the total cost of the bailout will reach over $250 billion. That is about $1,000 for every man, woman, and child in the United States.[8] For a family of four, that's $4,000 you are paying so that someone else's bank deposits are secure.

The president's bailout plan includes the taking over of the Federal Home Loan Bank Board (which also charters thrifts) by the Treasury Department and renaming it the Federal Home Loan Bank System. The FDIC would take administrative control over the FSLIC and would regulate thrifts. The FDIC would also become the insurer for S&Ls, but the funds would remain separate. Banks and thrifts would also pay higher insurance premiums. Some $50 million was given the Justice Department to prosecute the illegal activities that were alleged to take place at thrifts.[9]

There are likely to be many changes occurring in the regulation and management of thrift organizations and banks in the 1990s. It will be fascinating to watch the process of the government trying to resolve this mess, and it *is* a mess. The sad part is that taxpayers will have to pay billions and billions of dollars before the clean-up is over. As many as 900 S&Ls may close and control over banks and S&Ls may be merged.[10] Some people have predicted a second crisis in the early 1990s.[11] Many people are pulling their money out of S&L institutions and putting them into government bonds or money market funds with their brokers. S&Ls lost

HOW THE LOSSES OF THRIFTS INCREASED IN THE 80s (billions of dollars)

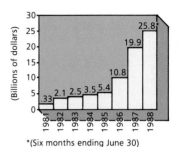

*(Six months ending June 30)

Source: Federal Savings and Loan Insurance Corporation, 1988.

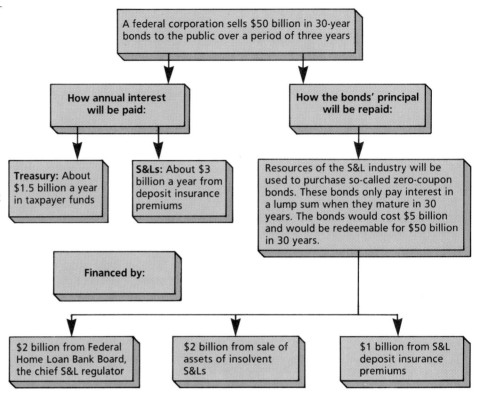

$28.5 billion in deposits in the first three months of 1989 alone. That compared with $8.6 billion in all of 1988.[12] Keep your eyes open in the 1990s. This is your money we're talking about. One thing to watch for is the fact that many savings and loan corporations are changing their names and adding the words "savings bank" to their title. Don't be fooled by the name. Just because they are called "banks" doesn't make them a bank. They do some banking functions now, but they are still S&Ls and they are still backed by the bankrupt FSLIC.[13]

The National Credit Union Administration

The **National Credit Union Administration (NCUA)** insures about 85 percent of all credit unions in the United States. The NCUA operates on the same principles as the FDIC and the FSLIC. The NCUA is the only one of the three major insurers to *not* be under the threat of running in the red. Remember, though, that some credit unions are *not* insured by the NCUA. They are not nearly as safe.

What Happens When a Federally Insured Institution Fails?

As you have learned, in spite of the efforts of federal deposit insurers, many financial institutions do fail. What happens if a bank you use fails—how do you get your money? Although bank regulators do try to avoid delays to depositors, they can legally use their right to a minimum period of "notice of withdrawal." What does that mean? It means you must give the bank 30 days notice that you want to withdraw money. Even after the 30 days, banks can delay payments further if necessary. They might even ration your withdrawals.

During times of national crisis, withdrawals can be limited by state bank regulators, the secretary of the Treasury, and the Comptroller of the Currency. Although this is rarely used, the comptroller did invoke a rationing system once in 1962.[14]

Optimally, a failed bank will close one day and reopen the next day after being merged with a healthy bank in the meantime. The Williamstown Bank in Houston, for example, closed one day at 5 P.M. as usual. At 5:30 P.M. the FDIC announced that the bank was closed and would be bought by another institution. It opened the next day as a branch of First City National Bank. The "crisis" was over before the citizens of Williamstown found out it started.

If payouts must be made, they are usually arranged in 48 hours. Insurers try to shut down a failed bank on a Friday if possible so they have the weekend to tally interest earnings and process account information for the payout on the following Monday. But as the number of failed institutions increases, the insurers no longer have the luxury of choosing the time of the final curtain call. As far as you are concerned, the chances are very high that you will get all your money back even if your local bank or S&L were to fail. You may have to wait a while, but you'd get your money.

WEAKNESSES IN THE BANKING SYSTEM

Banks were in better financial condition than S&Ls in the early 1990s, but they were also weak financially. In 1988, the FDIC handled some 190 bank failures involving institutions whose assets totaled more than $50 billion. There were about 1,434 banks on the "problem bank list" out of 14,000 commerical banks nationwide.[15] The FDIC's debts exceeded its assets by $13 billion at the end of 1987.

In summary, both the S&Ls and the commerical banks in the United States were financially weak in the early 1990s. Depositors do not have to fear losing their savings because they are insured by the federal government. The problem is that the federal government does not have the money and will have to go to taxpayers to get the billions of dollars needed to pay off depositors. This is at a time when the national debt is already sky high. You can read *The Wall Street Journal, Business Week,* and other business periodicals to see what is happening today in the banking industry. Clearly, the problem is a major one and calls for continued government action. *Business Week* has predicted that *half* of the thrifts in America could go out of business in the 1990s. Like the trends discussed in Chapter 1, the thrift industry survivors will be the very large S&Ls and the very small with selected markets.[16]

Learning the Lessons of History

Several articles have pointed out some interesting parallels between events leading to the Great Depression and now that you may find interesting, if not a little scary. For one thing, prices for farm products in the 1920s declined and farmers and retailers in rural areas could not pay off their loans. This led to many bank failures in rural parts of the country. Similar events happened from 1985 to 1989 as a result

Things were tough during the Depression. Almost one fourth of America's workers were unemployed. Buying apples for a nickel was a costly venture for many. Many economic circumstances today are similar to those of the pre-depression days, but we now have more checks and balances to prevent another depression.

of the widespread drought in the United States. As you just read, there was a financial crisis in the S&L industry in 1989. Thankfully, the agricultural sector looked a little stronger in 1989.

There had been a rapid expansion of banks in the 1920s and many were undercapitalized. This, too, happened in the 1980s. The stock market soared in the late 1920s much as it soared in the late 1980s. The stock market fall in October of 1987 was the largest fall since the Great Depression. Other events of the 1920s that are similar to today's situation are:

- There was a decline in demand for American products overseas in the 1920s. The high dollar caused a similar drop in the late 1980s. There may be another drop in 1992 when Europe unites.
- The corporate structure of the United States was rather weak in the 1920s. Trusts and holding companies were using the dividends from one company to pay the interest and dividends of other companies. If one company failed, the whole trust was in trouble. The rapid growth of mergers and acquisitions today is being financed by bonds of questionable strength. The failure of large firms could have serious consequences again.
- The stock market declined in October 1929 and rose again in the early 1930s. The passing of restrictive trade legislation was a major factor in driving the stock market lower again. The stock market declined in October 1987 and rose again early in 1989. Nobody knows where the market will go in the future, but there is some cause for concern. The economy is enjoying

one of the longest periods of growth in history. That growth could continue for years to come or not. Much of what happens depends on the actions of Congress and the Federal Reserve System.

- More than 5,500 banks failed in the nine years before the crash of 1929. Many failed in Florida because of the "collapse of the land boom." Many banks failed in Texas in 1988–1989. Why? Some say it was the "collapse of the land boom" due to lower oil prices.

- The final blow to the financial structure of the United States occurred when Congress passed the Smoot-Hawley Act, a trade protectionist act. Today, similar legislation is being proposed. The result of the events of the early 1930s resulted in the Great Depression that lasted until the 1940s. Could such an event occur again in the early 1990s? Most people doubt it. After all, we now have the Federal Reserve System and we have government agencies to protect the savings in banks. But some people feel that the potential for serious financial disorder is great. There could be a serious recession or a period of rapid inflation, or both (stagflation).

What steps are Congress and the Fed taking to strengthen the banking system? For one thing, in 1980 Congress passed the Depository Institutions Deregulation and Monetary Control Act, which required that almost all depository institutions have deposits in the Federal Reserve System. The act eliminated the ceiling on interest rates that S&Ls and banks could pay depositors and overrode state laws that limited the interest they could charge for loans. The act also gave thrift institutions the right to offer NOW accounts, which were discussed earlier in this chapter. These interest-bearing services, similar to checking accounts, were previously not allowed in most states. Banks and savings and loan institutions are now more competitive with one another. The interest-rate differential that once made thrifts more attractive is no longer there. All these steps were taken to strengthen the banking system in general. As you have read, the results were not as anticipated. In fact, they may have contributed to today's S&L crisis.

What will be the future of banks and savings and loans in the next decade? Part of the answer lies in the decisions by the Federal Reserve and the overall strength of the U.S. and world economies. One thing that is certain is that the U.S. financial community is in a rather weak state historically. Many changes are needed to further strengthen the banking system. You should know what is happening in banking today because the weakness of the banking system can cause a weakness in the whole economic system. More importantly from your individual perspective, you could find yourself short of cash if the bank or savings and loan you use suddenly goes bankrupt or closes for a few months to reorganize. Later in this chapter we shall discuss the Federal Reserve System in depth. The banking crisis has focused attention on the Federal Reserve, and you should understand how it operates.

It is impossible to predict the future of an economy. As you read this book, the economy has changed from the time it was being written. You can see for yourself what has happened over the last couple of years. One thing is for certain—the financial institutions of the United States have been going through troubled times. Much can be learned from this lesson as we learned from the lessons of the 1930s. Mistakes can become strengths if the right decisions are made and financial institutions are restructured for the future. In the next section we shall discuss some of the more recent trends in banking that may result in a much stronger financial base for the United States.

MAKING ETHICAL DECISIONS

Imagine you are one of the new financial officers sent in by the FSLIC to help bail out a S&L that is in danger of going under. One of the causes of the S&L's failure was the use of unsafe and unsound real estate acquisition practices. One of your attempts to save the S&L was to shut down its real estate development operations. This seemed like a logical move since the real estate investments were unsound. However, the real estate investments were an important source of revenue. It didn't take long to see that another problem was created by cutting off these revenues when interest payments are due each day on depositors' CDs. Your fellow managers suggest attracting new deposits by promising extremely high rates on CDs. Rather than invest the deposits, they suggest using them to pay the interest on earlier deposits and redemptions of CDs as they come due. Since the government insures deposits up to $100,000 regardless of the soundness of the institution, this strategy is legal. What would be the consequences of such plan? What ethical problems does this plan create? Would you agree to such a plan?

THE FUTURE OF BANKING IN THE UNITED STATES

From reading earlier chapters of this text, you have learned that businesses are reorganizing to become more efficient and effective. The way many businesses have become more efficient is through a whole series of mergers and acquisitions that have created larger businesses with smaller units that are more entrepreneurial in nature. That is, although the businesses are large, they give their individual units more freedom to be responsive to the market.

The same trend occurred in banking. You have learned that banks are chartered by states or the federal government. State banks have taken the lead in giving banks freedom to go into other businesses through acquisitions. Banks in Minnesota and North Carolina, for example, have been able to sell insurance for many years. In states such as Massachusetts and New Jersey, banks can engage in brokerage and underwriting, aspects of the "big three" nonbanking businesses—insurance, securities (stocks and bonds), and real estate. Today, banks may be involved in all three activities. Federal banks will likely receive the same rights if present trends continue. Here is how *Business Week* described the trend:[17]

> Is your bank starting to look more like a boutique-lined shopping mall? Do people hawking insurance, stocks, bonds, real estate, even trips to Tahiti outnumber the tellers? It isn't happenstance. Banks and thrifts want to reduce their dependence on low-margin loans and other traditional banking services to keep their customer's money out of the hands of brokers and other rivals.

As banks are taking on new roles, they are also getting larger. Many banks are acquiring the failed thrifts we mentioned earlier, and are buying them at excellent prices. The government seems to be allowing banks to grow larger and larger. We shall explore that trend next.

Superregional Banks

superregional bank
A bank that operates in several states.

As banks move into different areas of finance, they are also changing their size and power. A **superregional bank** is one that operates in several states. First Interstate Bancorp of Los Angeles, for example, operates in 21 different states. It is focusing its attention on retail and small-business lending. One of the largest superregionals is PNC Financial Corporation of Pittsburgh. Since 1983, PNC has bought several very profitable banks in Pennsylvania and in nearby states. Chemical Banking Corporation is a superregional bank with bases in Texas and the New York City area.

These new superregional banks can be run more efficiently than traditional banks, but some have had financial difficulties. For example, First Fidelity Bancorp lost over $150 million in the fourth quarter of 1988. Nonetheless, superregionals are buying many of the smaller banks that used to do business with the local retailers, farmers, and small businesses in a town. We must wait to see what the impact will be on small businesses, but the national impact may be stronger banks with less chance for failure. For one thing, the banks will be diversified into several businesses, not just banking. Furthermore, they will not be so closely tied to the economic ups and downs of a particular state. Thus, in the future, an economic collapse such as the one that occurred in Texas in the late 1980s may not force the collapse of regional banks. However, large banks have been known to be relatively impersonal and to not give full attention to smaller businesses. This will likely change in the future as big banks become more common.

In summary, two major trends are occurring in banking in the 1990s:

1. Banks are entering into new businesses such as insurance, brokering and real estate while, at the same time, brokers and insurance companies are performing several banking functions.[19]
2. Banks are buying other banks and S&Ls and merging with other banks to form superregional banks that cross state lines. These banks are much bigger and can become more efficient than banks once were. They may soon become *the* major financial institutions in the United States.[20]

PNC Financial, one of the largest interregional banks, has offices in several states. Such banks have great potential for electronic banking and better financial services. But will they be as friendly and helpful to small businesses? We shall see.

Electronic Funds Transfer Systems (EFTS)

Today, the whole banking system is on the brink of a major revolution in its day-to-day operations. The way things are done today—depositing money, writing checks, protecting against bad checks, and so on—is very expensive. You can imagine the cost of a bank approving a check, processing it through the banking system, and mailing it back to you. Something has to be done to make the system more efficient.

One step in the past was to issue credit cards. Credit cards cut down on the flow of checks, but they too, have their costs. Paper still has to be processed, and there is a chance for credit card fraud.

What all of this is leading to is a society where exchanges of money are done electronically, with no paperwork involved. The system is called an **electronic funds transfer system (EFTS).** This means that you will be given a card much like a credit card. Retailers will put that card into a slot in their cash register (which will then be called a *point-of-sale terminal*). When the sale is recorded, an electronic signal will be sent to the bank, transferring funds from your account to the store's account automatically. No paperwork will be involved. In fact, you will no longer receive a paycheck either. Rather, your employer will send the money electronically to the bank, and the bank will transfer funds from your employer's account to your account. You can see why it is called an electronic funds transfer system.

Electronic payments are gaining popularity among corporations as well as individuals. GE expects to make 40 to 50 percent of its payments electronically in 1990. Johnson & Johnson Hospital Services is starting a program to let customers pay them electronically. Growth of such systems is now 35 percent a year, but still makes up only a small percentage of overall payments.[21]

electronic funds transfer system (EFTS)
A computerized system that electronically performs financial transactions such as making purchases, paying bills, and receiving paychecks.

Naturally, such a system would be too complex if there were many banks dealing with many businesses and individuals. To make the system work, it is better to have a few, large banks that operate most efficiently. As we have already noted, this trend is already occurring. These banks would not necessarily be located in expensive urban areas. Because most transactions will be done electronically, the banks can locate in inexpensive rural areas. All in all, the system may be much more efficient, and will have many benefits for both the banks and individuals. On the other hand, there is some consumer resistance to electronic banking because consumers are worried that electronic accounts are not very private. They also could miss having paper evidence of having paid bills. And banks and consumers both would lose the benefit of **float,** the time between when a check is given to a seller and the time it is cashed at the bank.

float
The delay between the time a check is given to a seller and the time it is cashed at the bank.

On the positive side, banks will be rid of the burden of processing checks and managing credit card fraud and bad checks. Complete bank-at-home services will be available. That is, you will be able to transfer funds among accounts, make payments of various kinds (for example, utility bills and mortgage payments), and receive all kinds of information about your account. You could also buy and sell stock, get stock quotations, and more, once the system is finalized.

One function of the Federal Reserve System (the Fed) is to assure that the financial system of the United States remains secure. The role of the Federal Reserve will change as the nature of banking changes. We shall discuss how the Federal Reserve operates next. We shall also explore what the future of the Fed may be. The principle job of the Fed is to balance the need for economic growth against the pressures of inflation by regulating the growth of the nation's money supply.[22] In the future, the Fed may have much more authority over nonbanks in order to maintain its control over money.

PROGRESS CHECK

- What are the organizations that are called *nonbanks* and why are they called that?

- What similarities and differences exist between banking in the early 1930s and banking in the early 1990s?

- What is the difference between the FDIC and the FSLIC?

- What are two major trends in banking today?

- What are electronic funds transfer systems (EFTS) and what are their benefits?

THE FEDERAL RESERVE SYSTEM

Much of the future of banking will be decided by the Federal Reserve. Its guidebook states that the purpose of the Federal Reserve System "is to foster a flow of credit and money that will facilitate orderly economic growth, a stable dollar, and long-run balance in our international payments."[23] Most people know very little about the operations of the Fed, so let's spend some time reviewing its function.

As we noted at the beginning of this chapter, at the beginning of the 20th century, banks operated in a largely unstable environment. This relative freedom in banking operations created many problems for banks, their customers, states, and the federal government. Because of poor management, illegal practices, low reserves, and very little communication among banks, the American banking system operated in an environment that threatened the financial security of everyone involved in it. Furthermore, it seriously undermined the federal government's ability to regulate the money supply.

The Federal Reserve Bank was established in 1913. It now serves as the *central bank* of the United States. Its primary responsibility is to promote economic stability and growth by regulating the flow of money and credit. Some of the functions of the Federal Reserve include:

- Managing the country's money and credit.
- Providing short-term loans to banks that are temporarily short of reserves.
- Issuing currency and coins.
- Holding the reserves of commerical banks and other depository institutions.
- Providing services to banks such as checking services and wire transfer services.
- Being the government's banker by marketing its securities, paying its debts, and managing its international transactions.
- Supervising banks and other financial institutions. This role may take on much greater importance as a result of the banking crisis.

Organization of the Federal Reserve System

The **Federal Reserve System** consists of 12 Federal Reserve district banks (see Figure 21–3) located throughout the United States, and 25 branch territory banks. Each of the 12 district branches is collectively owned by member commerical

Federal Reserve System
Consists of 12 Federal Reserve District banks that serve as a deposit for excess bank funds (for members) and loan member banks money.

FIGURE 21–3

The Federal Reserve System. Note the locations of the 12 district banks.

Key
— Boundaries of Federal Reserve Districts
— Boundaries of Federal Reserve branch territories
■ Board of Governors of the Federal Reserve System
● Federal Reserve Bank cities
• Federal Reserve branch cities

banks. The Fed, however, is not controlled by the member banks. A seven-member board of governors that meets periodically in Washington, D. C., is responsible for managing the Fed. Each governor, who serves a 14-year term, is appointed by the president of the United States and is confirmed by the U.S. Senate. The chairman and vice chairman of the board are also appointed by the president.

Operations of the Federal Reserve System

All national banks are members of the Fed. State banks must also become members if they have checking accounts. The Fed's membership requirements are:
1. Member banks must purchase stock in their district reserve bank in proportion to their deposits relative to the other member banks in the district.
2. Member banks must keep funds at their district banks or in their own vaults to cover checks written by their depositors. These funds should be a certain percentage of the deposits they hold. This is called the **reserve requirement.**

On the other hand, member banks receive a number of important privileges:
1. Member banks can borrow funds from the district reserve banks.
2. Member banks use services such as check clearing provided by the Fed.
3. Member banks can obtain financial advice from the Fed.
4. Member banks are entitled to a dividend on the district reserve bank stock they own.

Regulating the Money Supply

The tools used by the Fed in its effort to regulate the money supply generally fall into three categories: reserve requirements, open-market operations, and the discount rate. Let's look at how the Fed uses these tools to perform its functions.

The Reserve Requirement

The reserve requirement is a percentage of commerical bank checking and savings accounts that must be physically retained in the bank (for example, as cash in the vault) or in a noninterest-paying deposit at the local Federal Reserve district bank. For instance, if Omaha Security Bank holds deposits of $100 million and the reserve requirement is, say, 10 percent, then the bank must retain $10 million to meet the reserve requirement. If the Fed were to increase the reserve requirement to 11 percent, then the bank would have to put an additional $1 million on reserve. This would reduce the funds available from the bank for loans. Consequently, the money supply would be reduced.

The reserve requirement is the Fed's most powerful tool. When it is increased, banks have less money for loans, fewer loans are made, money becomes more scarce, and in the long run that tends to reduce inflation. A decrease in the reserve requirement, on the other hand, increases the funds available to banks for loans, more loans are made, and money becomes more readily available. Such an increase in the money supply tends to stimulate the economy to achieve higher growth rates, but can also create inflationary pressures.

Open-Market Operations

Open-market operations is the tool most commonly used by the Fed. It involves the buying and selling of U.S. government securities by the Fed with the objective

---

reserve requirement
A percentage of member bank funds that must be deposited in the Federal Reserve Bank.

open-market operations
Tool used most commonly by the Fed to regulate the money supply; it involves the buying and selling of U.S. government securities.

WHAT DOES THE TERM *MONEY* MEAN, AS IN "MONEY SUPPLY?"

You probably think that you know what money means. After all, you have been handling money all of your life. Money consists of all those paper bills and silver coins that you carry around in your pocket, wallet, or purse, right? Wrong! That is part of what the Federal Reserve calls money, but there is more, much more. In fact, there are three categories of money recognized by the industry: M1, M2, and M3. *The Wall Street Journal* quotes variations in the three categories of money and talks about "the money supply" all the time. Federal Reserve data are reported every Friday in the *Journal*. What they are talking about is the following:

M1

M1 is the total of cash in the hands of the public (bills and coins) *plus* private checking deposits including those in interest-bearing NOW accounts. Because it represents funds readily available (highly liquid accounts), this measure, M1, is the one watched most closely as an important economic determinant. *The Wall Street Journal* prints an M1 chart every Friday.

M2

M2 is the total amount in M1 *plus* small denomination (under $100,000) time deposits (savings accounts) and retail repurchase agreements or "repos." These agreements mean that consumers in effect lend money to banks for short periods of time, and the banks put up stocks and bonds as collateral. M2 also includes money market mutual funds that service the general public.

M3

M3 is the total amount in M2 *plus* large denominations (over $100,000) time deposits and repos. It also includes money market funds set up for big institutional investors that are not counted in M2.

The reason people are interested in the money supply is that there is a large correlation between the money supply and the growth of the economy. When the money supply goes up, the economy goes up, too, and so may inflation. When the money supply goes down, so does the economy. The question is, "Which money supply are we talking about?" The answer varies among analysts, but for most purposes M1 is the one people follow. If you want to know more about this subject, you may want to take some finance courses. You are now prepared to read the business literature, however, and follow its discussions of the Federal Reserve and money supply.

---

of regulating the money supply. U.S. government securities are issued by the federal government and sold to the public. These securities pay interest to owners and are guaranteed by the federal government. Consequently, they are considered to be a stable and relatively low-risk form of investment.

How are U.S. government securities used by the Fed to control the money supply? When the Fed wants to decrease the money supply, it sells government securities. The money it obtains as payment is taken out of circulation, decreasing the money supply. If the Fed wants to increase the money supply, it buys government securities from individuals, corporations, or organizations that are willing to sell. The money paid by the Fed in return for these securities enters circulation, resulting in an increase in the money supply.

The Discount Rate

The Fed has often been called "the banker's bank." One of the reasons for this is that member banks can borrow funds from the Fed and then pass them on to their customers as loans. The **discount rate** is the interest rate that the Fed charges for loans to member banks. An increase in the discount rate by the Fed discourages banks from borrowing and consequently reduces the number of available loans, resulting in a decrease in the money supply (see Figure 21–4). On the other hand, a lowering of the discount rate encourages member bank borrowing and increases the amount of funds available for loans, resulting in an increase in the money supply.

FIGURE 21–4

The Federal Reserve System's tools for controlling the money supply.

TOOL	TO BOOST THE ECONOMY	TO COOL OFF THE ECONOMY
Reserve requirement	Decrease	Increase
Open-market operations	Buy	Sell
Discount rate	Lower	Raise

discount rate
The interest rate that the Federal Reserve System charges member banks for loans.

Federal Funds

federal funds
Short-term loans from one member bank of the Fed to another member bank that can be transferred during one business day.

Federal funds are short-term loans of funds from member bank to member bank that can be transferred during one business day. Such immediately available funds include deposits at Federal Reserve Banks. Most federal funds are considered overnight money in that the money is loaned out in one day and paid back the next morning. What happens is that a lending institution with excess reserve funds in its reserve account can authorize a transfer from its reserve account to the reserve account of the borrower. The next morning, a transfer is arranged to put the money back plus an interest payment that is based on market conditions at the time. This interest rate is known as the **federal funds rate.** Many people watch the federal funds rate because it is a key to whether or not the Fed is supplying or reducing money in the banking system. When more funds are supplied than needed, the rate declines. But when more funds are needed than supplied, the rate rises. Alan Greenspan raised the federal funds rate a full three percentage points in late 1988 and early 1989. Some felt that such an increase could cause the economy to plunge into a recession.[24] His goal, of course, was to keep inflation at a reasonable level. This management of the economy will continue throughout the 1990s and is something for you to watch closely if you want to learn more about economics.

federal funds rate
The interest rate charged for short-term (overnight) loans between Fed member banks.

Other Functions of the Fed

Checks have become the dominant medium through which payments are made in the economy. Some 95 percent of all business transactions today are paid in the form of checks. The process of handling and clearing the millions of checks written every hour would be extremely complicated and laborious if not for the Federal Reserve, which acts as a national clearinghouse for checks. The process by which a typical check is cleared through the Federal Reserve System is outlined step by step in Figure 21–5.

Setting Credit Controls

The Federal Reserve is responsible for controlling the credit practices of other financial institutions. These controls are of two major types:
1. *Enforcing credit terms* for loans involving certain consumer durables (such as cars) and real estate loans. These terms may involve the amount of down payment required and the repayment period for such loans.
2. *Setting the margin requirements* for certain transactions when buying stocks. Investors do not necessarily have to pay cash equivalent to a stock's selling price. Instead, they have the option of "buying on margin," which means that they would pay the minimum portion of the selling price that must be paid in cash at the time of the sale (this is called the *margin*) and use credit for the remainder. Since 1974, the margin requirement has been 50 percent. If an investor wants to buy $1,000 worth of XYZ Company's stock, he or she has to pay at least $500 in cash at the time of sale, while borrowing the remaining amount *"on margin."*

Issuance of Currency

The Fed is also responsible for issuing currency. All 12 Federal Reserve district banks are authorized to physically issue new money as it becomes needed. Also, the

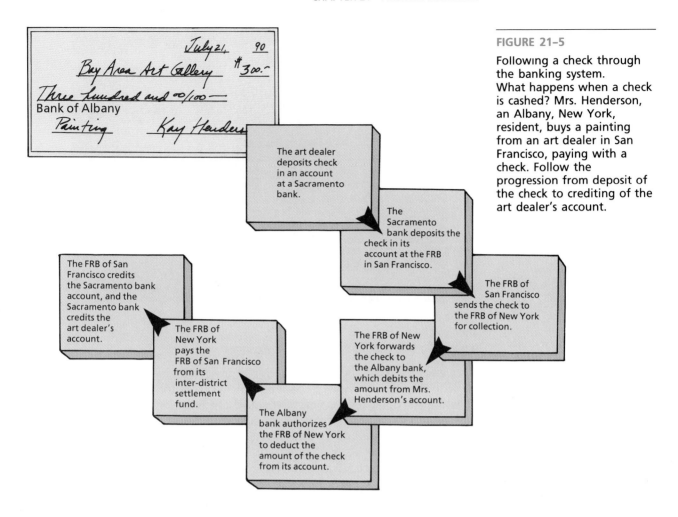

Following a check through the banking system.
What happens when a check is cashed? Mrs. Henderson, an Albany, New York, resident, buys a painting from an art dealer in San Francisco, paying with a check. Follow the progression from deposit of the check to crediting of the art dealer's account.

Fed is responsible for controlling the amount of money in circulation and for replacing worn-out bills with new ones. Given that the typical $1 bill has a life expectancy of about 18 months, you can imagine how many dollar bills have to be destroyed and replaced by newly printed ones every day.

Some terms you will have to know in order to understand what you read about the Federal Reserve and banking in general include:

- **Currency** refers to all coin and paper money issued by the Federal Reserve Banks and all gold coins. It includes all coin and paper money held by the public in the United States. It also includes cash in the vaults of commercial and savings banks and currency carried abroad by travelers.

- **Money supply** is the sum of all the funds that the public has immediately available for buying goods and services. Economists and the Federal Reserve use the money supply as a gauge for predicting and controlling U.S. economic activity. In implementing monetary policy, the Federal Reserve sets a target for money supply growth and then tries to influence bank lending and interest rates to achieve that target.

currency
All coin and paper money issued by the Federal Reserve Banks and all gold coins.

money supply
The sum of all the funds that the public has immediately available for buying goods and services.

The Federal Reserve is the source for new currency. There is more to the money supply than just currency, however. The money supply also includes money in interest-bearing NOW accounts, savings accounts, and money market accounts set up for large investors.

Expanding the Role of the Federal Reserve

The regulatory functions of the Federal Reserve are vital to the survival and prosperity of not only the U.S. banking system but of the economy as a whole. Without the Fed, the money supply would be largely out of control. Recently, the Fed has been rather successful in managing the money supply, although the ups and downs have caused some disruptions in the market.

The Fed operates as the central bank of the United States and as such it has jurisdiction over all other banks. But what about nonbanks? The ongoing revolution of the banking industry is creating a highly competitive environment. Banks are being threatened by the new generation of financial institutions. As nonbank institutions begin to control an increasing share of the banking business, it is expected that the regulatory scope of the Fed will shift to the nonbanks as well. The Fed's current organization is very similar to the way it was when the Fed was started in the early part of this century. However, the structure of the banking industry has changed tremendously since then. Many experts believe that we can expect a big shift in the Fed's organization and scope of activities within the next decade. It is argued that the mission of the reorganized Fed would include supervising the nonbank as well as banking institutions.

Given the information in this chapter, you are now prepared to read further about such decisions. Remember, the purpose of this text is to give you an introduction to business; the assumption is that you will keep up your studies. A good start is to do the exercises at the end of this chapter and to continue reading *The Wall Street Journal* and other business literature.

THINKING IT THROUGH   Talk to your friends and see how much they know about the Federal Reserve. Look over Case 2 at the end of the chapter to see how little other people know about the Fed. Do you think politicians should talk more about the Federal Reserve and who they would appoint to head that organization? Why?

This Japanese bank is located in Chicago, Illinois. There are similar banks all over the United States, and U.S. banks have offices all over the world as well. Banking has become an international business with bankers competing worldwide for funds.

INTERNATIONAL BANKING AND FINANCE

This chapter has focused on banking within the United States. In the 1990s, though, it is likely that many of the more crucial financial issues will be international in scope. The country's 20 largest banks, which are the heart of the American financial system, do nearly half of their business overseas. The federal government owes foreigners $300 billion and pays about $25 billion a year in interest to foreign creditors.

In today's financial environment, it is foolish to discuss the American economy apart from the world economy. If the Federal Reserve decides to lower interest rates, foreign investors can withdraw their money from the United States in minutes and put it in countries with higher rates. Of course, increasing interest rates can draw money to the United States equally quickly.

Today's money markets are indeed *global* markets. The United States is just a part, although a major part, of that system. International bankers tend not to be nationalistic in their dealings. That is, they tend to send money to those countries where they can get a maximum return for their money at a reasonable risk. U.S. bankers, for example, loaned billions of dollars to newly industrialized Third World countries to help them finance development of oil and other industries. When the demand for oil dropped, these countries could not repay their debts and many major U.S. banks stand to lose billions of dollars. The same is true of banks in West Germany and other countries that made similar loans. Such risky loans can greatly weaken the financial system of the world. Thus, the success of American business is directly tied to the success of businesses throughout the world.

Today's international finance markets involve holdings of almost $3 *trillion.* Just $1 trillion could buy every manufacturing corporation in the United States, as well as all the livestock, crops, buildings, and machinery of America's farms![25] Every year these banks and nonfinancial corporations lend about $300 billion to governments and nonfinancial corporations, including U.S. firms. That is, every year, international banks lend enough to purchase every new factory, railroad, port, ship, power plant, and other productive facility built in America that year plus all the machinery in them.

CAREER INFORMATION: BANKING

NATURE OF THE WORK

Practically every banking institution—whether commerical bank, savings and loan association, or personal credit institution—has one or more vice presidents acting as general managers who coordinate the activities of the institution's departments or regional offices, and financial managers who oversee the activities of their branches. Most have a controller or cashier who is an executive officer generally responsible for all bank property. Large banks may also have treasurers and other officers to oversee several departments.

Each department is headed by a highly trained and experienced manager. Risk and insurance managers establish and oversee programs to control and minimize risks and losses. Credit card operations managers establish credit rating criteria, determine credit ceilings, and monitor their institution's financial statements and direct the purchase and sale of bonds and other securities. User representatives in international accounting develop integrated international financial and accounting systems for the banking transactions of multinational organizations.

Bank officials must have a broad knowledge of business activities and also detailed knowledge of industries allied to banking, such as insurance, real estate, and securities. With growing competition, *promotion* of an expanding variety of financial services offered by banking institutions is an increasingly important function of bank managers. Beside supervising financial services, officers advise individuals and businesses and participate in community projects.

JOB OUTLOOK

Employment of bank officers was expected to increase faster than the average for all occupations through the mid-1990s. Expanded financial services offered by banks should spur demand for bank managers to provide sound management and effective quality control. The bank crisis of the early 1990s may change the demand for bank managers. Watch your papers for the latest trends.

Because of the increasing number of qualified applicants, competition for bank managerial positions is expected to stiffen. Familiarity with other financial services—for example, insurance or securities—and with computers and data processing systems may enhance one's chances for employment.

SOURCES OF ADDITIONAL INFORMATION

General information about banking occupations, training opportunities, and the banking industry itself is available from

American Bankers Association, 1120 Connecticut Ave. N.W., Washington, D.C. 20036.

Bank Administration Institute, 60 Gould Center, Rolling Meadows, Illinois 60008.

National Association of Bank Women, Inc., National Office, 500 N. Michigan Ave., Chicago, Illinois 60611.

Institute of Financial Education, 111 E. Wacker Dr., Chicago, Illinois 60601.

Information on careers with the Federal Reserve System is available from

Board of Governors, the Federal Reserve System, Personnel Division, Washington, D.C. 20551. The personnel department of the Federal Reserve bank serving each geographic area.

Who supervises all of these transactions in foreign countries? Nobody.[26] The Federal Reserve is virtually powerless in these international markets. The net result of international banking and finance is that the economies of the world have become linked into one interrelated system with no regulatory control.

American firms must compete for funds with firms all over the world. If a firm in London or Tokyo is more efficient, it is more likely to get international financing than one in Detroit or Chicago that is less efficient. Of the world's top 30 banks, only one is in the United States—Citicorp. The top five are all Japanese banks. In fact, Japan has 17 of the top 30 banks. France has five in the top 30, West Germany has two, Britain has two, Switzerland has two, and Hong Kong has one.[27] Clearly, the United States has much competition in world banking.

What all this means to you is that finance is no longer a domestic issue; it is an international issue. In order to understand the U.S. financial system, you will have to learn about the global financial system. To understand the economic condition of the United States, you will have to learn about the economic condition of countries throughout the world. It has become, basically, a world economy financed by international banks. The United States is just one more player in the game. To be a winning player, America must stay financially secure and its businesses must stay competitive in world markets. That will be the challenge of the 1990s and beyond. We shall discuss international business more in Chapter 24. Meanwhile, you should read all you can about international business and take courses if you can. You will not be living and working in a U.S. economy in the 1990s; you will be living in a world economy.

PROGRESS CHECK

- What are the major functions of the Federal Reserve? What other functions does it perform?
- How is the Federal Reserve organized?
- How does the Federal Reserve control the money supply?
- What is meant by the discount rate and the federal funds rate?
- What is M1 and its significance to monetary policy?
- What is the significance of international banking?

SUMMARY

1. Trace the history of banking.

1. There were no banks and limited coins in the American colonies at first. The colonists traded goods for goods instead of using money.
   - How did money and banking evolve in the United States?
     Massachusetts issued its own paper money in 1690, with the other colonies following suit. Britain lent money to farmers through land banks, but ended these banks by 1741. After the revolution, there was much debate about the role of banking and heated battles between the Central Bank of the United States and state banks. The banking system was a real mess by the time of the Civil War, with many banks issuing different kinds of currency. Eventually, a federally chartered and state-chartered system was established, but the chaos continued until many banks failed in 1907. The system was revived by the Federal Reserve only to fall again during the Great Depression of the 1930s. The system today is threatened by some of the same conditions that led to the Great Depression.

2. Identify types of banking institutions and describe the services available at each.

2. The U.S. banking system consists of commercial banks, savings and loan associations (thrifts), mutual savings banks, and credit unions.
   - How are savings and loans (including mutual savings banks) and commercial banks different?
     Before deregulation in 1980, commercial banks were unique in that they handled both deposits and checking accounts. At that time, savings and loans could not offer checking services; their main function was to encourage thrift and home ownership by offering high interest rates on savings accounts and providing home mortgages. Deregulation closed the gaps between banks and S&Ls so that both now offer similar services.
   - What kinds of services?
     Banks and thrifts offer such services as passbook savings accounts, NOW accounts, CDs, loans, Individual Retirement Accounts (IRAs), safe deposit boxes, traveler's checks, and more.

■ What is a credit union?

A credit union is a member-owned cooperative that operates much like a bank in that it takes deposits, allows you to write checks, and makes loans. It also may sell life insurance and make home loans. Because credit unions are member-owned cooperatives rather than profit-seeking businesses like banks, credit union interest rates are sometimes higher than those from banks and loan rates are often lower.

■ What are some of the other financial institutions that make loans and do other banklike things?

These nonbanks include life insurance companies that loan out their funds, pension funds that invest in stocks and bonds and make loans, brokerage firms that offer investment services, and commerical finance companies.

3. The government has created organizations to protect depositors from losses such as those experienced during the Great Depression.

3. Describe the organizations created to protect your deposits in financial institutions.

■ What agencies ensure that the money you put into a bank, savings and loan, or credit union is safe?

Money deposited in banks is insured by an independent government agency called the Federal Deposit Insurance Corporation (FDIC). Money in S&Ls is insured by another independent government agency called the Federal Savings and Loan Insurance Corporation (FSLIC). Money in credit unions is insured by the National Credit Union Administration (NCUA). The FDIC is assuming control over the FSLIC because of the 1989 S&L crisis. Your deposits are still backed by the federal government, but new taxes will have to be raised to cover current losses.

4. The history of banking and the Federal Reserve shows that periodically banks fail and depositors lose their money, even when the banks are insured. This has not happened under federal insurance, but it could.

4. Relate the weaknesses of the current American banking system to the conditions that led to the Great Depression.

■ How are the current economic conditions similar to those leading to the Great Depression?

The Great Depression began with lower farm profits, and more recent bank failures began in a similar way. The other parallels with the 1920s are spelled out in the chapter. Lessons from the past are valuable in preventing similar events in the present. One role of the Federal Reserve is to prevent another great depression.

5. The services of banks, S&Ls, and nonbanks have changed during the 1980s.

5. Characterize the future of the American banking system.

■ What are the major trends in banking in the 1990s?

Banking promises two major trends in the 1990s: (1) the distinctiveness of different financial institutions will fade as they continue to enter new businesses and perform many of the same functions (such as banks entering the insurance field and insurance companies performing banking functions); and (2) banks will continue to buy and merge with other banks to form superregional banks that cross state lines.

■ What does this mean to you?

In the future, you will be able to do much of your banking from home. Your paycheck can be deposited electronically at a financial institution that can offer you electronic shopping, electronic bill paying, real estate services, and more.

6. Explain the functions of the Federal Reserve system and describe the tools the Fed uses to control the money supply.

6. The Federal Reserve was designed to control the banking system and the money supply.

■ How does the Fed control the money supply?

The Fed makes financial insitutions keep funds in the Federal Reserve (reserve requirement); buys and sells government securities (open-market operations); and loans money to banks (the discount rate). It also issues money on its own.

7. Today's money markets are not national; they are global markets.

- What do we mean by global markets?

   Global markets mean that banks do not necessarily keep their money in their own countries. They send it where they get the maximum return. International finance markets hold almost $3 trillion.

- What does this mean to you?

   Since finance is now an international rather than a domestic issue, you should understand the global financial system as well as the U.S. financial system. You should learn about the economies of countries throughout the world since you will be living in a world economy.

7. Illustrate the role of international banking and finance in global economics.

---

1. Paper money is issued by the 12 Federal Reserve district banks. Try to collect $1 bills issued by as many of these Fed banks as possible. Which district bank is responsible for issuing most of the bills you have looked at? Can you explain why?

2. Go to your commercial bank or the financial institution you do business with and talk with the accounts manager about the many services that are offered.

3. This chapter ends with a discussion of international banking. Open the business section of your daily newspaper and look at the exchange rates table that lists the equivalent price of foreign currency in U.S. dollars. Run through that list and try to learn some of the foreign currencies listed. Also, observe which foreign currencies are priced less than the dollar and which cost more. This will give you a feel for foreign currency exchange rates.

4. Go to your financial institution and ask for their high-yield interest rates (time deposits). Do you think they provide a satisfactory return-on-investment (ROI)? What would be the pros and cons of such an investment opportunity?

5. Read the business section of your local paper and the front page of *The Wall Street Journal* for a week. What is being said about banking and the Federal Reserve? How important does the financial community seem to think that Federal Reserve decisions are? What decisions have been announced lately?

6. Look up the trends in M1 and other money measures in *The Wall Street Journal*. What are the trends? See if you can find articles linking money supply with economic conditions. Report what those articles say to the class and make a prediction about future economic growth given the money supply changes in the last six months.

CASE ONE   IS YOUR MONEY SAFE?

In 1983, Commonwealth Savings Company of Lincoln, Nebraska, failed. The bank was insured by a private insurance fund that was wiped out by the failure. The depositors lost their money, and they still do not know if they will ever recover it.

In 1984, Western Community Money Center in Concord, California, also failed. It was an industrial bank. The company that insured the bank, Thrift Guaranty Corporation, was hard-pressed to cover the losses to depositors.

In 1985, similar problems occurred in Ohio and Maryland. The Ohio Deposit Guarantee Fund, which insured 70 thrifts, collapsed because its largest member, Home State Savings Bank of Cincinnati, failed. (Home State was a savings and loan institution in spite of its name.) In Maryland, several S&Ls were closed and depositors could only withdraw limited funds until the organizations involved were purchased by larger, more financially secure S&Ls or federal insurance was obtained.

Even though banks and S&Ls protected by the federal government seem safe, the fact is that there is very little funding available if banks do begin to fail. Depositors may have to wait months or even years to get their funds back if their bank failed. Many depositors have spread their money among several banks to reduce the risk.

What about taking your money out of the bank and putting it into a credit union? Well, the safety may be no better. Over 3,000 of the approximately 18,000 credit unions have private insurance (over 60 have *no* insurance).

People put their money into privately insured institutions and credit unions to make a percentage point or two more interest. However, the risks associated with higher returns may be great because private insurance is not as secure as government backing. One option is to put your money into a money market fund run by a brokerage firm. Another is to buy government bonds that are backed by the federal government.

DECISION QUESTIONS

1. Do you know whether or not your money in the bank or credit union is insured by the federal government? If you don't know, you should find out.
2. What seemed to be the cause of financial failures among banks and S&Ls in the 1980s? Much of it has to do with deflation—falling housing, oil, and farm values. What else may be involved?
3. What would happen to the economy if banks and S&Ls began failing at a rapid rate? Has this happened before? What is different now?
4. What will be the effect of the new superregionals and the expansion of banking into insurance and brokering on the financial strength of banks in the future? Where would you recommend that a person put his or her savings to minimize risk today?

CASE TWO   STUDYING THE FEDERAL RESERVE SYSTEM

Unlike other cases in this chapter, the facts and figures for this case must be gathered by you. You should consult *The Wall Street Journal* or other business publications to see what the Federal Reserve is doing now to strengthen the economy. This is an important exercise because so few people know anything about the Federal Reserve.

The Coalition for Monetary Education conducted a random survey of 2,000 people to see what they knew about the Federal Reserve and monetary policy in general. Only about 1 percent (some 20 out of 2,000) understood the monetary basics.

Over 75 percent of the respondents knew that the Federal Reserve controlled the money supply; but only 9 percent of those polled were aware that the Federal Reserve's policies affected the inflation rate and only 13 percent were aware that the Fed's policies affected interest rates.

Only 31 percent of the people knew that U.S. currency is not redeemable in gold or silver. Less than 30 percent knew that bank failures were widespread and increasing! The Coalition planned to educate the public about the effect of federal policies on banking.

DECISION QUESTIONS

1. How do the Federal Reserve's policies affect interest rates and the inflation rate and why is it important for people to know that?
2. What action, if any, has the Federal Reserve taken in the last year to control the money supply and inflation? What have the results been? (The answer to this question can be found in past issues of *The Wall Street Journal*.)
3. Go back to Chapter 3 and read about fiscal and monetary policy. Which seems to be having the greater affect on the U.S. economy today, monetary or fiscal policy? Why?

After reading several chapters on finance, one cannot help but think about how to invest one's own money to optimize the return. The appendix to Part 6 looks at personal financial planning. You will learn how to save some money to invest and some strategies for investing those funds wisely. You will want to buy some insurance and think about buying a home or condo. You will also want to cover yourself with health insurance.

Insurance and risk management is important to firms as well as individuals. We shall discuss these important issues in Chapter 22. No issue is more important to the future of business than corporate ethics. We have discussed ethics throughout the book and will reemphasize the importance of moral and ethical business behavior in Chapter 23.

We end the book by looking at international business (Chapter 24). The future of business growth will be in international markets. We left international until the end of the book because you need to understand business before you can understand *international* business. We also put it last so you will remember it as you go into other business courses. It is one of *the* most important aspects of business for the future.

APPENDIX TO PART VI
PERSONAL FINANCIAL PLANNING

FINANCIAL MANAGEMENT

There are several reasons to study business subjects in college. One is to become a businessperson. Another is to understand subjects such as marketing and management so you can apply the concepts in churches, charities, social causes, unions, associations, and other nonbusiness pursuits. A third reason is to learn about subjects such as stocks, bonds, insurance, banking, credit, real estate and other topics that will help you become a better manager of your own funds (a financial manager). Did you know that the word *economist* means home manager? This chapter is designed to cover many of the topics that all people should know to be good economists—home managers.

This chapter will expose you to many subjects that will demand much further study before you feel competent dealing with them. Nonetheless, you will have a good start toward understanding personal finance—the management of your own funds.

Saving for the Future

Many people find successful careers in business and earn much money over the years but have little to show for their efforts. Making money is one thing; saving it and spending it wisely are something else. Less than 10 percent of the population has saved enough money by retirement age to live comfortably off their savings.

The essential first rule of money management: Spend less than you earn.
ANDREW TOBIAS in *Parade,* March 12, 1989.

This chapter begins with a strategy for accumulating money or capital. This money can then be invested in real estate and other investments. A careful investment plan will assure a fund for retirement purposes, so you can retire to an island if you want. The following strategy may seem radical to you. Nonetheless, read it through to get the idea, then you can apply it to your own situation in whatever way seems most appropriate.

BUILDING YOUR CAPITAL ACCOUNT

The path to success in a capitalist system is to have capital (money) to invest, yet the trend today for young graduates is to not only be capital-poor, but to be in debt. Accumulating capital takes discipline and careful planning.

The principle is simple: to accumulate capital, you have to earn more than you spend. For a young couple, that process may be easier than one might expect, given the small number of young people with significant savings. Let's assume that a couple gets married soon after college. What to do next?

The first step is to find a job for both husband and wife. Both people will want to work for several years before the couple has any children.

During those years, the couple should try to live, as much as possible, on just *one* income. The other income can then be used to generate capital. It may be invested in a mutual fund or some other relatively safe investment. Part of it could be invested in more risky investments for rapid capital accumulation.

Living on one income is extremely difficult for the average college graduate. Most graduates are eager to spend their money on a new car, a stereo, a videotape recorder, clothes, and the like. They tend to look for a fancy apartment with all the amenities. A capital-generating strategy calls for giving up most (not all) of these purchases to accumulate investment money. The living style required is close to the one adopted by most college students: a relatively inexpensive apartment furnished in hand-me-downs from parents, friends, and Goodwill. For five or six years, the couple can manage with the old stereo, used cars, and a few nice clothes. The living style desired is one of sacrifice, not luxury. It is important not to feel burdened by this plan, but happy living together frugally for a better future.*

After six years of saving one income, the savings can grow to about $90,000 (after taxes) for a college graduate (saving $15,000 per year). What to do with the money? The first investment might be a moderately priced home. This investment should be made as early as possible. The purpose of the investment is to lock in payments for shelter at a given amount. This is possible with ownership, but not by renting. Through the years, home ownership has been a wise investment.

Applying the Strategy

Some people have used the seed money from this strategy to buy duplex homes; that is, two attached homes. They lived in one of the homes and rented the other. The rent covered a good part of the payments for *both* homes, so they were able to live very cheaply while their investment in a home appreciated rapidly. They learned that it is quite possible to live comfortably, yet inexpensively, for several years. In this way they accumulated capital. When they grew older, they saw that such a strategy put them years ahead of their peers in terms of financial security. They eventually sold their duplex homes and bought single-family homes with the profits. The money saved has been invested in everything from stocks and bonds to silver, gold, insurance, additional real estate, and higher education (which is perhaps the best investment of all—an investment in yourself).

This strategy may seem too restrictive for you, but you still can apply the principles. The idea is to generate capital to invest. After all, this *is* a capitalist society, and in such a society you are lost without capital. A couple is wise to plan their financial future with the same excitement and dedication as they plan their lives together. Even a modest saving of $6,000 a year will allow a couple to buy a small home in six years and begin an investment program. Remember, money that earns 12 percent annually doubles in just 6 years! (See the rule of 72 on p. 86.) An investment of $6,000 for six years can grow to a total of over $50,000, a healthy start for any couple. (See the ad for a mutual fund on p. 643 to see how money can grow in such an investment.)

REAL ESTATE—THE NUMBER ONE INVESTMENT

As we have discussed, one of the better investments a person can make is in his or her own home. Homes grow in value each year (or have historically), and provide several other investment benefits. First of all, a home is the one investment that you can live in. Once you buy a home, the payments are relatively fixed (though taxes and utilities go up, as you'll see if you do buy). As your income rises, the house payments get easier and easier to make, but renters often find that rents tend to go up as fast or faster than income.

A home is a good way of forcing yourself to save. Every month you must make the payments. Those payments are an investment that will prove very rewarding over time for most people.

An investment in a duplex or small apartment building is also an excellent strategy. As capital accumulates and values rise, an investor can sell and buy an even larger apartment complex. Many fortunes have been made in real estate in just such a manner.

---

* An obvious alternative is to stay single and live frugally to generate capital.

Some figures will give you a better feel for the role of real estate in today's investment programs. For all people under age 45, one half of their assets are in real estate, and only $3,000 on average is invested in securities (stocks and bonds). For those over age 45, only 39 percent of assets are in real estate with $13,000 in securities.

Tax Deduction and Home Ownership

Buying a home is likely to be the largest and most important investment you will make. It is nice to know that the federal government is willing to help you with that investment. Here's how. Interest on the payments you make for a home is tax deductible. So are the real estate taxes you pay. During the first few years, almost all the payments go for interest on the loan; therefore, almost all the early payments are tax deductible. That is a tremendous benefit for homeowners. If, for example, your payments are $1,000 a month and your joint income is in the 28 percent tax bracket, then Uncle Sam will, in effect, help pay about $280 of your mortgage payment, lowering your real cost to $720. This makes the home ownership much more competitive with renting than may appear on the surface. Home ownership is one of the few tax shelters left in the new tax bill.

Real estate people will tell you that there are three keys to making the optimum return on a home; they are location, location, and location. A home in the "best part of town," near schools, shopping, and work, is the best financial investment. Most young couples tend to go further away from town where the homes are less expensive, but such homes are likely to appreciate in value much more slowly. It is better, from a financial viewpoint, to buy a smaller home in a great location.

To make payments on a home and pay the dozens of other bills a family encounters is no easy task. It takes planning and good money management. As for a businessperson, it is important for a homeowner to prepare a budget and stick to it. We'll explore this idea next.

MONEY MANAGEMENT

In hindsight, you realize that probably the silliest saying is, "Two can live as cheaply as one." Two people *eat* more than one, *wear* more than one, *drive* more than one, and *spend* more than one. In fact, the money just seems to disappear. "Where did it go?" couples ask each other. "Did *you* spend it?"

There is only one way for a couple to keep track of revenues and expenses, and it's the same way a business does: by writing it down. A couple should record *every single cent* they spend for over a year on various *accounts:* food, clothing, furniture, gas, rent, utilities, entertainment, vacations, gifts, and miscellaneous (a category that includes laundry, snacks, magazines, household items, and more). In this way they learn where the money is going, but may find it difficult to stem the flow. They learn that to become financially secure, a couple must learn to budget. Most of all, a couple must learn some discipline to live within that budget. Businesses are not alone in suffering from cash flow problems; most families have the same problem.

A budget is made by projecting revenues and expenses for the year and allocating the funds to various accounts. It is best to break down the figures to monthly revenues and expenses. At the end of the month, it is relatively easy to see if the family is living within the budget or not. The whole process is often painful, but usually is a necessary first step in getting some control over personal finances.

By keeping such a budget, you will learn the importance of setting aside money for the replacement of automobiles and appliances. If you don't add in such figures, you will find yourself suddenly in need of thousands of dollars for a replacement car—thousands of dollars you have not budgeted for.

Other items that are important in a household budget include life insurance, car insurance, and medical care costs. You will learn that running the finances of a household is very similar to running a small business. It takes the same careful record-keeping (if only for taxes), the same budgeting process and forecasting, the same control procedures, and often (sadly) the same need to periodically borrow funds. Suddenly, concepts such as *credit* and *interest rates* become only too real. This is where some knowledge of finance, investments, and budgeting pays off.

Credit Cards

Known as "plastic" to young buyers, credit cards are no doubt familiar to you. Names like Visa, MasterCard, American Express, Diners Club, and Carte Blanche are as well known to most people as Sears. In a credit card purchase, finance charges after the first 25 or 30 days usually amount to 15 to 22 percent annually. This means that a person who finances a car, home appliances, and other purchases pays much more than if he or she paid with cash. A good personal financial manager, like a good businessperson, pays on time and takes advantage of savings made possible by paying early. Those couples who have established a capital fund can tap that fund to make large purchases and *pay the fund back* (with interest if so desired) rather than a bank.

Credit cards are an important element in a personal financial system, even if they are rarely used. First of all, many merchants demand credit cards as a form of identification. It is often difficult or impossible to buy certain goods or even rent a car without owning a credit card.

Secondly, credit cards are a way to keep track of purchases. A gasoline credit card, for example, enables you to have records of purchases over time for income tax and financial planning purposes. It is sometimes easier to write one check at the end of the money for several purchases than to carry cash around. Besides, cash may be stolen or lost.

Finally, a credit card is simply more convenient. If you come upon a special sale and need more money than you usually carry, a credit card is a quick and easy way to pay. You can carry less cash and don't have to worry about keeping your checkbook balanced as often.

The danger of a credit card is the flip side of its convenience. Too often consumers buy goods and services that they would not normally buy if they had to pay cash or write a check on funds in the bank. Consumers often pile up debts using credit cards to the point where they are unable to pay. If you are not the type who has a financial plan and a household budget, it may be better not to have a credit card at all. Credit cards are a helpful tool to the *financially careful* buyer. They are a financial disaster to somebody with little financial restraint and tastes beyond income.

INSURANCE COVERAGE

One of the last things a young couple thinks about when they get married is the idea that one of them may get sick or have an accident and die. It is not a pleasant thought. Even more unpleasant, though, is the reality of thousands of young people dying every day in accidents and other unexpected ways. You have only to visit one of their families to see the emotional *and financial* havoc such a loss causes.

Today, with so many husbands and wives both working, the loss of a spouse means a sudden large drop in income. To protect each other from such devastation, a couple should invest in life insurance *for both husband and wife*. Both should be covered under the same policy, because it is cheaper that way.

Today, the preferred form of life insurance is called term insurance. *Term insurance* is pure insurance protection for a given number of years. Evey few years, you must renew the policy, and the fee usually gets higher and higher. (See Figure 6A-1 on page 696.)

A popular alternative in the past has been *whole life insurance*. This is a combination insurance plan and savings plan. The problem was that the savings portion simply was not competitive with the rates available in mutual funds and other investment alternatives.

Today, life insurance companies are becoming more aggressive in winning investment dollars. One new plan is called *variable life insurance*. This is a whole life policy whose

FIGURE 6A–1	INSURANCE NEEDS IN EARLY YEARS ARE HIGH	INSURANCE NEEDS DECLINE AS YOU GROW OLDER
Why term insurance?	1. Children are young and need money for education 2. Mortgage is high relative to income 3. Often there are auto payments and other bills to pay 4. Loss of income would be disastrous	1. Children are grown 2. Mortgage is low or completely paid off 3. Debts are paid off 4. Insurance needs are few 5. Retirement income is needed

benefits *vary* (thus the term *variable life*) based on the success of the insurance company in investing those funds. The money is placed in a portfolio that usually includes some stock, bonds, real estate, and other such investments. With such a policy, the benefits are guaranteed not to go below to certain amount. However, if the portfolio of stocks and bonds and other investments does well, the benefits will increase. Buying such a policy is a way to get insurance *and* have a diversified investment account for your family. It is also one other way that people like you and me have a vested interest in U.S. business. How much we get from insurance is tied to the success of the economy.

Another relatively new type of policy is called *universal life insurance*. It is a combination of term insurance and an accumulation fund, usually based mostly on debt instruments (bonds). Policy owners can switch funds to buy more insurance or more bonds. The interest rates earned are very close to those in the market after an initial fund of $1,000 is accumulated.

Even more creative policies are now coming on the market. They may give the policyholder the freedom to switch from whole life to term and back as life's circumstances change. This is called *adjustable life insurance*. Other policies combine the ideas from variable life, universal life, and adjustable life policies. Such policies may be considered as part of a total life savings and insurance plan. If people have the discipline to do it, though, the best option is straight term insurance with the idea that additional funds will be invested each year. That will result in the largest overall return *as long as the plan is followed*.

There are many career openings available in life insurance companies. The new policies are far superior to the old policies, and they should be relatively easy to sell. Now that so many women are working, there is a growing need to sell additional insurance to professional women. Talk to someone who sells these new policies. Are they enthusiastic? Would you enjoy such work? By now, you probably have gotten the idea that everyone you talk to is a potential source of information about careers. Right. Keep looking, and you will find hundreds of interesting and challenging careers.

Health Insurance

You are likely to have health insurance coverage through your employer. If not, you can buy insurance from a health insurance provider (for example, Blue Cross/Blue Shield) or a local health maintenance organization (HMO). Most people do not realize the benefit of having company-paid health insurance until they have to pay for the insurance on their own. The cost is quite high.

One decision you may have to make is to choose between Blue Cross/Blue Shield coverage or a HMO. For a young couple, a HMO is often an attractive alternative in that HMOs emphasive *preventive* health care. Emphasis is on checkups and the prevention of illness, although hospital care is also provided. Different plans have different policies regarding your freedom to select doctors and so on. Such a decision should not be taken lightly. Talk to people in town who have both options. Learn the advantages and disadvantages. Assess *your* family's needs, and then choose.

It is very dangerous financially not to have any health insurance. Hospital costs are simply too high to risk financial ruin by going uninsured. In fact, it is often a good idea to supplement health insurance policies with more *disability insurance* that pays part of the cost of a long-term sickness or an accident. The cost is relatively low to protect yourself from losing your livelihood for an extended period.

EDUCATION—THE BEST INVESTMENT

Throughout history, one investment strategy has paid off regardless of the state of the economy or political ups and downs. That investment is an investment in education. Everyone knows the benefits of getting graduate degrees in business and other areas. But those benefits are usually stated in terms of money or position. For example, a college graduate will earn, on the average, about $600,000 more in a lifetime than a high school graduate.[1]

Investing in areas such as art, literature, philosophy, psychology, music, and logic pays off in other ways. One can live a richer, fuller, and more enjoyable life when one fully appreciates music, drama, and knowledge for its own sake.

When planning for your financial future, it is wise to think of what you'll do when you become financially secure. Life is more than working and making money. An investment in education exposes you to other countries, other languages, new ideas, and different ways of life. If you invest in yourself, you will be making the best investment of all.

PLANNING YOUR RETIREMENT

It may seem too early to begin planning your retirement, but not to do so would be a big mistake. Successful financial planning means long-range planning, and retirement is a critical phase of life. What you do now could make a world of difference in the quality of life you will experience from age 65 to 85, and up.

Social Security

Social security is the term used to describe the Old-Age, Survivors, and Disability Insurance Program established by the Social Security Act of 1935. There is no question that by the time you retire there will be huge changes in the social security system. The problem is that the system cannot afford to pay out more than it takes in. The number of people retiring and living longer is increasing dramatically, though the number of workers paying into social security per retiree is declining. The end result is likely to be (1) a bankrupt program; (2) serious cuts in benefits, likely including much later retirement and reduced cost of living adjustments (COLAs); or (3) much higher social security taxes. What happens to social security is important to you in that you probably should not count on it to provide you with ample funds for retirement. Rather, you should plan now to save funds for your nonworking years (see Figure 6A-2: on page 698). The government has recognized the potential downfall of social security and has established incentives for you to save money now for retirement. Here are the specifics.

Individual Retirement Accounts (IRAs)

An *IRA* is a tax-deferred investment plan that enables you and your spouse to save part of your income for retirement. It is, in effect, a government-sponsored tax shelter. The money you put into the fund is not taxed, nor are the earnings taxed until you take them out when you retire. At that time, your tax rate should be lower.

FIGURE 6A–2

The fate of your social security investment. This chart shows that, at present rates, social security funds will run out in the year 2048. That is a little less than 60 years from now. Much sooner than that, the outgo will exceed revenues. It is a good idea to begin your own retirement account to supplement social security. You are likely to live a long time after retirement and will need the money.

Source: Social Security Administration data as reported in *U.S. News & World Report,* June 13, 1988, p. 71.

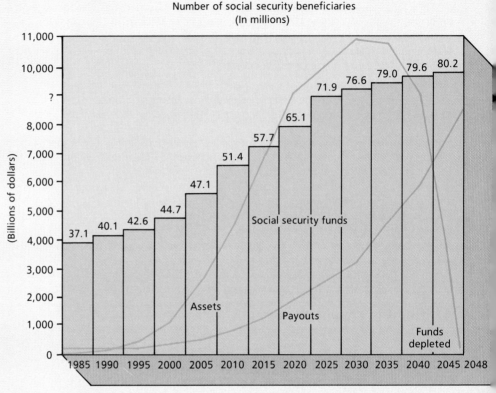

Number of social security beneficiaries
(In millions)

IRA accounts are one of the most important tax break ever made for workers. Everyone who works is eligible, even part-time workers. This includes people who are already covered by company retirement plans. However, the initial contribution is not tax free if you have a company retirement plan and make over $35,000 (see Figure 6A–3).

The amount you can put into an IRA has increased through the years. Now the dollar amount is $2,000 per year (check the latest figures). If you begin saving now, the money will compound over and over and become quite a nest egg by the time you retire. Opening an IRA account may be one of the wisest investments you can make.

A wide range of choices is available to you when you open an IRA. Your local bank, savings and loan, and credit union all have IRA savings plans available. Insurance companies offer such plans as well. You may prefer to be a little more aggressive with this money to earn a higher return. In that case, you can put your IRA funds into stocks, bonds, or mutual funds. Some mutual funds have multiple options (gold stocks, government securities, high-tech stocks, and more). You can switch from fund to fund or from investment to investment with your IRA funds. You can even open several different IRA accounts as long as the total amount invested doesn't exceed the government's limit. Talk to a broker and learn your options.

Let's see why an IRA account is such a good deal for a young investor. The tremendous benefit is the fact that the invested money is not taxed, and neither are the earnings. That means fast returns and huge returns for you. For example, say you put $2,000 a year into an IRA. Normally, you would pay taxes on that $2,000. But because you put the money into an IRA, you won't have to pay those taxes. If you're in the 28 percent tax bracket, that means you save $560 in taxes! Put another way, the $2,000 you save only costs you $1,440—a huge bargain.

If you save $2,000 a year for 20 years and earn 12 percent a year, you will accumulate savings of over $160,000 in just 20 years and over $540,000 in 30 years. If you start when

ADJUSTED GROSS INCOME	IRA TAX DEDUCTIBILITY
Under $40,000, married (Under $25,000, unmarried)	Full tax deduction
$40,000–$50,000, married ($25,000–$35,000, unmarried)	Partial deduction, reduced proportionately
Over $50,000, married (Over $35,000, unmarried)	Contributions not tax deductible

FIGURE 6A–3

Deductions for participants in employer-sponsored retirement plans.
This chart will tell you whether or not your initial contribution to an IRA is fully tax deductible or not. It is if you make under $40,000 and are married or under $25,000 and are unmarried. If you make between $40,000 and $50,000 and are married, you can still get a partial deduction. In all cases, however, the earnings are tax deductible—and that is very important to building a retirement account.

you are just out of school, you will be a millionaire by the time you retire. All you have to do is save $2,000 a year and earn 12 percent. Can you see why investment advisers often say that an IRA account is *the* best way to invest in your retirement?

You cannot take the money out until you are 59½ years old without paying a 10 percent penalty and paying taxes on the income. That is really a benefit for you, because it is less tempting to tap the fund when an emergency comes up or you see the car of your dreams. On the other hand, the money *is* there if a real emergency arises.

When you make financial plans, be sure to explore an IRA. It's a sure path to being a millionaire some day and to having the funds available to enjoy your retirement years. You might consider contributing to an IRA through payroll deductions to assure the money is invested before you are tempted to spend it.

401 (K) PLANS

Many companies now offer 401 (K) retirement plans that have three benefits: (1) the money you put in reduces your present taxable income, (2) tax is deferred on the earnings, and (3) employers often match part of your deposit—50 cents or more for every dollar deposited. You should deposit at least as much as your employer matches, often up to 6 percent of your salary. You normally can't withdraw funds from this account until you are 59½, but you can often borrow from the account. Check with your employer about the plan at your organization.

You can usually select how the money in a 401 (K) plan is invested: stocks, bonds, and in some cases, real estate. Again, plans vary so check with your employer. But financial advisers will tell you that 401 (K) plans are a wonderful investment.[2]

Keogh Plans

Millions of small-business people do not have the benefit of a corporate retirement system. Such people can contribute to an IRA account, but the amount they can invest is limited. The alternative for all those doctors, lawyers, real estate salespeople, artists, writers, small-business people, and other self-employed people is to establish their own Keogh Plan. It is like an IRA for entrepreneurs.

The advantage of Keogh Plans is that the maximum that can be invested is more than $30,000 per year. (The limit was $30,000 in 1984, and cost of living adjustments are added from 1986 on.) The original amount was much lower, but the government wanted to encourage self-employed people to build retirement funds. Both IRA and Keogh plans could be considered back-up plans to protect people against the likely declines in the value of the social security system. Even without any cuts, it looks like social security simply will not provide enough for a comfortable retirement.

Like IRA accounts, Keogh funds are not taxed nor are the returns the funds earn. Thus, a person in the 28 percent tax bracket who invests $10,000 yearly in a Keogh saves $2,800 in taxes. That means, in essence, that the government is financing 28 percent of his or her retirement fund. As with an IRA, this is a good deal; no, an excellent deal.

If a person were to put the full $30,000 a year into a Keogh plan that earns a modest 10 percent a year, he or she would have over $5 million in the account after 30 years. Remember that this same person could put another $2,000 per year into an IRA account!

As with an IRA account there is a 10 percent penalty for early withdrawal. Also like an IRA, funds may be withdrawn in a lump sum or spread out over the years. However, the key decision is the one you make now—to begin early to put funds into an IRA or Keogh plan (or both), so that the magic of compounding can turn that money into a sizable retirement fund.

Financial Planners

If the idea of developing a comprehensive financial plan for your family seems overwhelming, relax; help is available. The people who assist families in developing a comprehensive program that covers investments, taxes, insurance, and other financial matters are called *financial planners*. Be careful, though; everybody and his brother or sister are claiming to be financial planners today. Many are simply life insurance salespeople or mutual fund salespeople who call themselves financial planners.

In the last few years, there has been an explosion in the number of companies offering financial services. Such companies are sometimes called one-stop financial centers or financial supermarkets because they provide a variety of financial services ranging from banking service to mutual funds, insurance, tax assistance, stocks, bonds, and real estate. It pays to shop around for financial advice. You can go to an independent financial planner or a financial service company. In either case, ask around among your friends and family. Find someone who understands your situation and is willing to spend some time with you.

Most financial planners begin with life insurance. They feel that most people should have basic term insurance coverage. They also explore your health insurance plans. They look for both medical expense and disability coverage. They may also recommend *major medical protection* to cover catastrophic illnesses.

Financial planning covers all aspects of investing, all the way to retirement and death. (Planning for estate taxes is important early in life.) Financial planners can steer you into the proper mix of IRA investments, stocks, bonds, precious metals (for example, gold), real estate, and so on.

If all of this sounds interesting to you, maybe you would enjoy a career as a financial planner. You could work independently and be a real asset to young people in need of counsel and advice. Find a financial planner in your area. Discuss what financial planners do and what recommendations they are now making for a person in your position. This is a fascinating field to study and could be a rewarding career.

Risk Management, Ethics, and International Business

VII

RISK MANAGEMENT AND INSURANCE

22

LEARNING GOALS

After you have read and studied this chapter, you should be able to:

1. Explain the causes of the insurance crisis of the 1980s.
2. Distinguish between different kinds of risk and identify the four ways businesses manage risk.
3. Describe the guidelines used to determine insurable risks.
4. Explain the law of large numbers and other tools used by insurance companies to limit the cost of claims.
5. Distinguish between stock and mutual insurance companies.
6. Describe the various types of insurance coverage available to businesses and individuals.
7. Describe careers in risk management.

KEY TERMS

absolute liability, *p. 718*
actuaries, *p. 725*
aviation insurance, *p. 717*
coinsurance clause, *p. 713*
criminal loss protection, *p. 719*
deductible clause, *p. 713*
fidelity bond, *p. 719*
fire insurance, *p. 714*
group life policy, *p. 721*
homeowner's insurance, *p. 723*
inland marine insurance, *p. 717*
insurable risk, *p. 711*
insurance adjuster, *p. 725*
insurance policy, *p. 712*
law of large numbers, *p. 712*
multiline policies, *p. 719*
mutual insurance company, *p. 713*
nonperformance loss protection, *p. 719*

ocean marine insurance, *p. 717*
premium, *p. 712*
public liability insurance, *p. 717*
pure risk, *p. 707*
reasonable prudence, *p. 719*
rider, *p. 714*
risk, *p. 707*
risk managers, *p. 724*
rule of indemnity, *p. 713*
self-insurance, *p. 709*
speculative risk, *p. 707*
stock insurance company, *p. 713*
strict liability, *p. 718*
surety bond, *p. 720*
uninsurable risk, *p. 710*
workers' compensation insurance, *p. 717*

Heinz Popp.

PROFILE   HEINZ POPP, AUTOMOBILE DEALER

The costs of running a small business increase every year. Usually, small-business managers can adapt to such changes. In the 1980s, however, one cost of small-business management grew so fast that owners were finding it hard to adjust. Heinz Popp is one of those people. Like most of us, Mr. Popp had read about the large amounts that people were receiving from insurance companies as a result of accidents and other claims. Doctors seemed to be particularly hard hit because of the cost of malpractice insurance. But what did that have to do with Popp's auto dealership?

Mr. Popp noticed that the insurance policy for his Porsche-Audi dealership in Brooklyn was about to expire. Mr. Popp got nervous when two insurance brokers told him they could not find a company that would issue a new policy. There was a possibility that the dealership would have to close.

Mr. Popp went to an auto dealers' group and found an insurance company willing to sell him a policy. That was the good news. The bad news was that Mr. Popp would have to pay whatever the insurance company decided to charge.

Mr. Popp learned that the new policy would cost $110,000, or nearly three times his old premium of $40,000. Mr. Popp needed the insurance, though, to cover his $2.3 million worth of new cars and auto parts against loss or damage. Mr. Popp is not the only one who has had such problems recently. Across the nation, businesses of all sizes faced premium increases ranging from 25 to 1,000 percent for property and liability insurance. The reason is that insurance companies were paying out more and more each year in claims. Statistics showed that many insurance companies were paying out more than they were taking in. That was bad news for the insurance companies. More recently, insurance companies are back in the black, but that was due to the huge rate increases passed in the mid-1980s (see Figure 22–1). In fact, some insurance companies are being investigated for back-room deals and meetings to raise prices. In the long run, the people who have to pay for such increases are business owners like Mr. Popp. Ultimately, you and I pay through higher prices for automobiles and other goods and services.

This chapter is about risk management. In the past, the best way to protect against risk was to buy insurance. Today, the cost of insurance may be so high that other options besides insurance coverage must be explored, along with insurance coverage. We'll discuss all the options in this chapter.

Sources: David B. Hilden, "Small Firms Face Sharp Cost Hikes for Insurance—if they Can Get It" *The Wall Street Journal*, August 5, 1985, p. 23. © Dow Jones & Co., Inc., 1985; and Christopher Farrell, Resa W. King, Joan O'C. Hamilton, and Paula Dwyer, "An Avalanche of Lawsuits Descends on Insurers," *Business Week*, April 11, 1988, pp. 60–61.

THE INSURANCE CRISIS OF THE 1980s

The management of risk has become a major issue for businesses throughout the country. Every day you read or hear about a major earthquake, flood, fire, airplane crash, or truck accident that destroyed property or injured someone. Such reports are so much a part of the news that we tend to accept these calamitous events as part of everyday life.

Such events mean much more to the businesspeople involved. They must pay to restore the property and compensate those who are injured. In addition to the

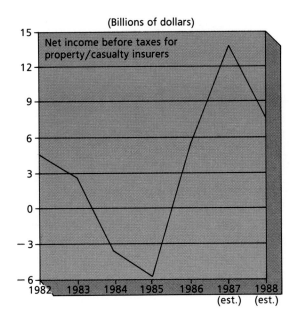

(Billions of dollars)

Net income before taxes for property/casualty insurers

FIGURE 22–1

Insurance company profits and losses in the 1980s. Note that insurance companies were losing money in 1984 and 1985. That led to huge increases in insurance rates in 1986. Profits increased in 1987 and 1988 and rates were lowered somewhat, but are still very high. Many companies cannot get insurance at all because their risk of loss is too high. One way insurance companies increase profits is by minimizing losses. They do that by refusing to insure high-risk products and/or companies. That was the case in 1989 as some companies refused to sell auto insurance in some states.

newsmaking stories, there are thousands of other incidents that might involve businesspeople in lawsuits. They include everything from job-related accidents to people being injured from using a business's products.

What businesspeople are learning is that the courts are awarding higher and higher dollar awards to people who are hurt. Often the amount paid to policyholders is very high because the court tacks on "punitive damages" to the payment. *Punitive damages* means payments in excess of the loss to warn companies not to endanger people with their products. Let us give you an example. A mechanic hurt his foot while working on a car. He was treated and released from a hospital, but his foot worsened and 12 days later his foot was amputated. The insurance company rejected his $20,000 claim, saying the amputation was due to a prior condition. The mechanic sued and won the $20,000 plus $1.6 million in punitive damages. Today, many states prohibit courts from charging punitive damages, some have caps on how much is paid, and others have passed more strict limits on when such damages can be instituted (see Figure 22–2 on page 706).

The case of the injured mechanic is not necessarily an isolated case of an unusual award. Rather, it represents the trend in litigation in the United States. In 1986, a Texas jury awarded a man $100 million in punitive damages from Ford over a defective Pinto gas tank design. The reward was reduced to $10 million on appeal. In 1987, a Delaware jury awarded three couples $75 million in punitive damages from Raymark Industries for allegedly conspiring to hide asbestos risks (under appeal). An Illinois jury punished Allied-Signal Inc. $60 million for predatory practices leading to the bankruptcy of General Poly Corp. This case is under appeal too.[1] Organizations must recognize this upward trend in insurance claims and develop strategies for dealing with it. One way to manage risk is to buy insurance, but insurance is getting very expensive. The expense makes insurance unaffordable for many businesses and created what was considered an insurance crisis in the 1980s that may last well into the 1990s.

How different states handle punitive damage.
Some states do not allow punitive damages at all. Others have limits (caps) or very high standards for applying such damages. Such efforts, in the long run, will make insurance less costly.

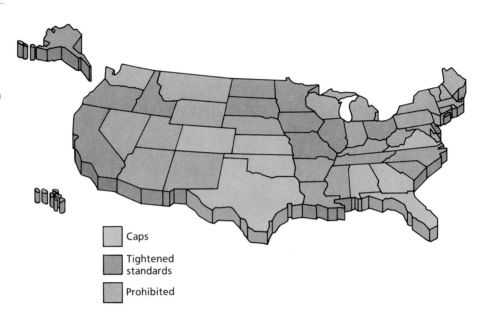

Caps

Tightened standards

Prohibited

The insurance crisis was best illustrated by this opening from a *Washington Post* article:[2]

> You cannot use a sled in Denver city parks. You cannot have a baby delivered in Monroe County, Alabama. You cannot buy any of the 58,000 published copies of Barbara Hutton's biography.
>
> If you have the stomach upset known as hyperemesis, you cannot get the pill that is certified as safe. . . . You can no longer buy the classic Jeep sedan. . . . You may not find a fireworks display next Fourth of July. You cannot set foot on dozens of the finest hiking trails in Yellowstone National Park.
>
> Each of these diverse prohibitions, and many others as well, stems from the same central problem, a problem that will be one of the preeminent legal, economic, and political issues of the 1990s: the civil liability crisis.[3]

The article went on to say that the big insurance companies couldn't or wouldn't provide all the coverage needed. Figure 22–1 tells why. Insurance losses had risen dramatically, and insurance companies were losing money in 1984 and 1985. That led to huge increases in insurance rates in 1986. The insurance companies raised premium prices high enough to cover all the risks, so coverage for day-care centers, bus lines, nurse-midwives, commercial fishing companies, and others were simply not being renewed. Many other companies could not get insurance at all because their risk of loss was also too high. One way insurance companies increase profits is by minimizing losses. They do that by refusing to insure high-risk products and/or companies.

If insurance could be found, it was at unbelievably higher prices. For example, the Southern California Rapid Transit District had *no* accidents during the year and its insurance went up from $67,000 to $3.2 million, a 4,700 percent jump in one year! The tripling of costs for Mr. Popp's Porsche-Audi dealership seems cheap by comparison.

You cannot go sledding in Denver city parks because the cost of liability insurance is too high. That is also why most city pools don't have high diving boards anymore. The cost of insurance is a serious matter for businesses today—and for municipal government too. Do you have liability insurance?

Causes of the Insurance Crisis

The insurance crisis had several causes. One, of course, was the huge increase in the number of lawsuits and the large damage awards. Another cause was the fact that people could sue organizations for injuries for which the organization was not at fault (see the discussion of absolute liability on p. 718). Yet another cause was the fact that insurance companies cut premiums in the early 1980s to compete for business when interest rates and investment earnings were high. Lower interest rates drastically cut the return on the investments, and losses occurred. In 1988, insurance companies again cut profits to capture market share. In 1989, profits fell even further. A second insurance crisis could emerge in the 1990s as a result.[4]

This chapter is concerned with managing risk. Let's begin by looking at the types of risks and how businesses try to protect themselves from the effects of risks.

MANAGING RISK

The term **risk** refers to the *chance* of loss, the degree of *probability* of loss, and the *amount* of possible loss. In business there are different kinds of risk:

- **Speculative risk** is a type of risk that involves a chance of either profit or loss. Speculative risk is the kind of risk you take when you bet on a horse race or play poker. It includes the chance a firm takes to make extra money by expanding its options, buying new machinery, acquiring more inventory, and making other decisions with which the probability of loss may be relatively low and the amount of loss is known. One takes speculative risk on the chance of making a profit. In business, building a new plant is a speculative risk in that it may result in a loss or a profit.
- **Pure risk** is defined as the threat of loss with no chance for profit. Pure risk involves the threat of fire, accident, or loss. If such events occur, a company loses money; but if the events do not occur, the company gains nothing.

risk
The *chance* of loss, the degree of *probability* of loss, and the the *amount* of possible loss.

speculative risk
A type of risk that involves a chance of either profit or loss.

pure risk
The threat of loss with no chance for profit.

The risk that is of most concern to businesspeople is *pure risk*. Pure risk threatens the very existence of some firms. Once such risks are identified, firms have several options:

1. Reduce the risk.
2. Avoid the risk.
3. Buy insurance to cover the risk.
4. Self-insure against the risk.

We will discuss the option of buying insurance in detail later in this chapter. In the next section, we will discuss each of the other alternatives for managing risk.

Reducing Risk

A firm can reduce the chance of risk occurring by establishing loss-prevention programs such as fire drills, health education, safety inspections, equipment maintenance, accident prevention programs, and so on. Many retail stores, for example, have mirrors, video cameras, and other devices to spot and prevent shoplifting. Water sprinklers are used to minimize fire loss. Most machines have safety devices to protect workers' fingers, eyes, and so on. Nonskid floors are installed to minimize falls.[5]

Employees, as well as managers, can reduce risk. For example, truck drivers can wear seat belts to minimize injuries from accidents and operators of loud machinery can wear earplugs to reduce the chance of hearing loss.

One key to good risk management, therefore, is a good loss-prevention program. High rates have also forced people to go beyond merely preventing risks to the point of *avoiding* risks—sometimes by going out of business.

One way to reduce risk is to wear protective clothing while you work. Gloves, masks, and fireproof clothing are examples. It is also important to wear earplugs at noisy work stations and to keep safety equipment repaired.

Avoiding Risk

Most risks cannot be avoided. There is always the chance of fire, theft, automobile accident, or injury. On the other hand, some companies are avoiding risk by not accepting hazardous jobs and by contracting out shipping and other functions to others. The threat of lawsuits has driven some drug companies from manufacturing vaccines and some consulting engineers refuse to work hazardous sites. Some companies are losing outside people on the board of directors for lack of liability coverage.

Recently, Cessna Aircraft Company stopped making five types of small planes because product liability premiums, which account for 30 percent of a plane's cost, had driven the price of new models beyond the reach of most customers. The city of Miami canceled plans for an experimental railbus line because it couldn't find insurance coverage. Several ice-skating rinks and ski resorts closed rather than pay sky-high insurance payments. Most manufacturers of IUD devices for birth control stopped making them because of liability risks. The *Los Angeles Times* reported that, "Fearful of lawsuits, troubled by attacks from interest groups and worried about the bottom line, all but one American drug company have stopped large-scale research into new kinds of contraception."[6] That company is Ortho Pharmaceutical Corporation of Raritan, New Jersey.

Other examples could be cited of doctors, municipalities, day-care centers, and other businesses, professionals, and nonprofit organizations avoiding risk by going out of business or ceasing services.

Self-Insuring

Many companies and municipalities have turned to **self-insurance** because they either can't find or can't afford conventional property/casualty policies. Such firms set aside money to cover routine claims, and buy only "catastrophe" policies to cover big losses. In other words, they lower the cost of insurance by paying for smaller losses and then taking out insurance for larger losses. The *amount* of loss is managed this way. Hardee's Food Systems, for example, uses that approach. It self-insures for losses up to $2 million and buys insurance against catastrophe.

Self-insurance is most appropriate when a firm has several widely distributed facilities. The risk from fire, theft, or other catastrophe is then more manageable. Firms with huge facilities, in which a major fire or earthquake could destroy the entire operation, usually turn to insurance companies to cover the risk.

One of the more risky strategies for self-insurance is for a company to "go bare," paying claims straight out of their budget. The risk here is that the whole firm could go bankrupt over one claim, if the damages are deemed high enough. A less risky alternative is the forming of "risk retention groups"—insurance pools that share similar risks. As many as 20,000 governmental entities are now self-insured, and two thirds of them have switched since 1985. In 1984, about 20 percent of U.S. insurance dollars went to "nontraditional" plans; by 1988 some 35 percent did. It is estimated that by now half the market may be self-insured.[7] See Figure 22–3 on page 710).

Once a company self-insures, if often does everything it can to eliminate risk. For example, one church camp began forbidding small children to ride large horses. Diving boards are eliminated from swimming pools in many areas across the country. As you can imagine, the real key to being successful at self-insurance is to beef up loss prevention programs substantially.

self-insurance
Putting funds away to cover routine claims, rather than buying insurance to cover them.

FIGURE 22–3

Trends in self-insurance. Nontraditional insurance (amount spent in billions of dollars). The amount spent on self-insurance almost doubled from 1984 to 1988 as a result of the insurance crisis. New pressures on risk managers are forcing them to explore all kinds of alternative ways to manage risk.

Source: *Newsweek*, March 7, 1988, p. 75.

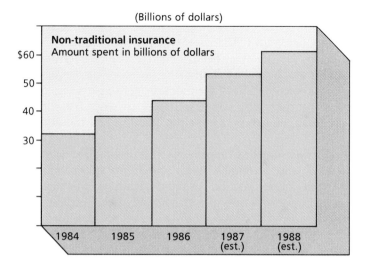

One consequence of the trend toward self insurance is the failure of many insurance companies. Some 140 companies failed from 1969 to 1986 and more have failed since. Over 500 companies are under regulatory attention, meaning that they are not strong financially. It is no wonder, therefore, that the "insurance crisis" of the 1990s is being compared to the S & L crisis.[8]

THINKING IT THROUGH	What kind of risks are you incurring every day? Which risks are you reducing through *loss prevention programs?* For example, do you lock your home and car doors? Do you eat healthy foods and exercise?
	For what risks are you self-insured? (Do you have money put away to cover such emergencies as car repairs, dental work, or loss of your job?)
	What other insurance should you have? Do you have major disability insurance for long-term illnesses? Are you insured against fire and theft? Can you see that you are a risk manager already?

BUYING INSURANCE TO COVER RISK

Although good, consistently enforced risk-prevention programs reduce the probability of claims, accidents do happen. To protect themselves from catastrophic losses, businesses turn to insurance companies for protection. We will begin our discussion of insurance by identifying the types of risks that are insurable and those that are uninsurable.

What Risks Are Uninsurable?

uninsurable risk
Risk that a typical insurance company will not cover.

One thing companies learned from the insurance crisis is that not all risks are insurable, even risks that once were covered by insurance. An **uninsurable risk** is one that no insurance company will cover. Examples of things that you cannot insure include *market risks* (e.g., losses that occur because of price changes, style changes, or new products that make your product obsolete), *political risks* (e.g., losses from war or government restrictions on trade), some *personal risks* (such as loss of a job), and some *risks of operation* (e.g., strikes or inefficient machinery). As

LLOYD'S OF LONDON INSURES WHEN OTHERS DON'T

Where can a company go to get pollution liability insurance or kidnapping insurance for its key executives? The answer: Lloyd's of London. How can an insurance company afford to assume the risks of having a satellite explode or cover a company like Union Carbide that had a chemical plant leak in Bhopal, India, that killed or injured thousands? The answer is that no one insurance company can. You see, Lloyd's is not an insurance company, but an association of some 20,000 members that buy and sell risks. These members have unlimited liability for losses. In the past, losses were anticipated well, and the company was very profitable.

Lloyd's was known as the company that insured the *Titanic*. It took a huge loss when the ship sank. It also took huge losses on ships that were sunk during the Iran/Iraq war. Lloyd's was known to insure everything from a movie star's beautiful legs to losses incurred by people exposed to asbestos.

During the 1980s, Lloyd's was struck for huge claims. For example, it lost millions of dollars on satellites that were lost. The losses on ships in the Persian Gulf and on the chemical leak at Bhopal were staggering. Now the company is reconsidering what risks it will cover. It is getting more conservative and turning down certain risks.

For example, it turned down an oil, gas, and chemical company in Texas for environmental damage insurance. Lloyd's learned that the losses from such plants can go into the billions of dollars.

How would you like to be liable for the damages caused by the Chernobyl nuclear plant disaster in the U.S.S.R., for example, or the Exxon oil spill in Alaska? Similar disasters could occur from other nuclear power plants and oil installations throughout the world. Lloyd's has learned to avoid insuring some plants with such huge risks involved.

At one time, Lloyd's was the insurer of last resort. If you were willing to pay the high costs, they were willing to sell you insurance. No more! Now there is no place to go for some kinds of loss coverage. The logical consequence is for firms to design plants that are safer and to stop certain processes that could potentially damage the environment. In other words, the insurance crisis of the 1980s hit Lloyd's too. In the long run, that could be a very positive thing because companies throughout the world are getting more serious about designing safer products, safer plants to produce those products, and safer environments for workers.

---

you now know, some risks are insurable, but at impossible prices. Some so-called uninsurable risks may be covered by insurance syndicates such as Lloyd's of London that spread the risk among several companies or individual insurers. Some insurance companies will cover almost anything if you are willing to pay the price (see the box called Lloyd's of London Insures When Others Don't).

What Risks Are Insurable?

An **insurable risk** is one that the typical insurance company will cover. Generally, insurance companies use the following guidelines when evaluating whether or not a risk is insurable:

1. *The policyholder must have an insurable interest.* You cannot, for example, buy fire insurance on your neighbor's house and collect if it burns down. You can buy life insurance on your children, however, and a business can buy insurance to cover losses if key executives die.
2. *The loss should be measurable.* Life insurance policies specify the amount to be paid in case of death because the value of a life is otherwise difficult to measure. The same may be true of health insurance. In any case, the specific amount of the loss should be possible to determine. That is the role of *insurance adjusters*. They go out to fires and other losses and calculate the loss.
3. *The chance of loss should be measurable.* Insurance companies pay actuaries to determine the degree of risk involved (see the sections on Insurance Adjusters and Actuaries on pages 725 and 727). Insurance companies, for

insurable risk
Risk that a typical insurance company will cover.

for example, estimate how many fires will occur in a given area, how many people of a given age will die, and the chances in any given year of a flood, tornado, or other disaster. If the cost of covering such losses seems too high, the company may not provide the coverage.

If the dollar amount of the potential loss is small, an insurance company may not cover the loss because the cost of processing the policy would be too high relative to the revenue. Small losses should be self-insured.

4. *The loss should be accidental.* An insurance company will not pay for fire damage if the fire was set deliberately by the insured. Similarly, it generally will not pay a life insurance policy if the insured commits suicide. Often insurance companies carefully investigate losses to be sure that the cause was accidental and not planned.

5. *The risk should be dispersed.* An insurance company tries to spread the risk among different geographical areas so that a flood or other natural disaster in one area would not bankrupt the company. The whole idea of insurance is to spread the risk so that one loss is not significant. In the next section of this chapter we shall discuss the law of large numbers to show how risk is dispersed among large populations.

6. *The insured should meet certain standards.* In some states, an insurance company may not sell life insurance to someone who has tested positive for AIDS (see Case 1). Similarly, a person may not be able to obtain health insurance if he or she has certain diseases. People who work in some high-risk occupations may not be able to obtain insurance (e.g., asbestos workers or test pilots).

PROGRESS CHECK

▪ What is the difference between pure and speculative risk, and which can be covered by insurance?

▪ What are the four options for dealing with risk? Can you give examples of each?

▪ What were some of the causes of the insurance crisis of the 1980s?

▪ What are the six criteria for making a risk insurable?

THE LAW OF LARGE NUMBERS

insurance policy
A written contract between the insured and an insurance company that promises to pay for all or part of a loss.

premium
The fee charged by an insurance company for an insurance policy.

law of large numbers
States that if a large number of people or organizations are exposed to the same risk, a predictable number of losses will occur.

An **insurance policy** is a written contract between the insured (an individual or organization) and an insurance company that promises to pay for all or part of a loss. A **premium** is the cost of the policy coverage to the insured or the fee charged by the insurance company.

As it is for all private businesses, the objective of an insurance company is to make a profit. To assure that it makes a profit, an insurance company gathers data to determine the extent of the risk. What makes the acceptance of risk possible for insurance companies is the law of large numbers.

The **law of large numbers** states that if a large number of people or organizations are exposed to the same risk, a predictable number of losses will occur during a given period of time. Once the insurance company calculates these figures, it can determine the appropriate premiums. The premium is supposed to be high enough to cover expected losses and yet earn a profit for the firm and stockholders. Today, insurance companies are charging high premiums, not for past risks, but for the anticipated costs associated with more court cases and higher damage awards.

Rule of Indemnity

The **rule of indemnity** says that an insured person or organization cannot collect more than the actual loss from an insurable risk. One cannot gain from risk management, only minimize losses. One cannot, for example, buy two insurance policies and collect from both for the same loss. If a company or person carried two policies, the two insurance companies would calculate any loss and split the reimbursement.

rule of indemnity
States that an insured person or organization cannot collect more than the actual loss from an insurable risk.

Coinsurance Clause

One way that individuals and corporations have tried to cut insurance costs is by underinsuring property. Most fires and other losses only damage part of the property, so rather than insure a building for its total worth, say $1 million, the policyholder may buy just $500,000 worth of insurance. This kind of thinking seems rational, but it throws off the calculations for the law of large numbers. Therefore, insurance companies have adopted a coinsurance clause.

A **coinsurance clause** requires businesses to carry insurance equal to a certain percentage of a building's actual value, usually 80 percent. If a firm were to buy only $500,000 worth of insurance on a $1 million property and had a $300,000 loss, the insurance company would pay only a portion of the loss. The insurance company would calculate the payment as follows:

coinsurance clause
Requires businesses to carry insurance equal to a certain percentage of a building's actual value, usually 80 percent.

$$\frac{\text{Amount of actual insurance}}{\text{Amount demanded by coinsurance}} = \frac{\$500,000}{\$800,000} = \frac{5}{8}$$

$$\text{Loss} = \$300,000 \times \frac{5}{8} = \$187,000 = \text{Insurance payment}$$

Deductible Clauses

A **deductible clause** says that the insurance company will pay only that part of a loss in excess of some figure (the deductible amount) stated in the policy. This is another way that people and businesses use to cut insurance costs. The higher the deductible amount, the lower the premium. Thus, a policy on an automobile may have a $300 deductible clause. That means the insured is responsible for the first $300 of a loss. A similar clause may be available in health insurance policies and other insurance coverages.

deductible clause
States that the insurance company will pay only that part of a loss that exceeds some figure (the deductible amount) stated in the policy.

STOCK VERSUS MUTUAL INSURANCE COMPANIES

There are two major types of insurance companies. A **stock insurance company** is owned by stockholders, just like any other investor-owned company. A **mutual insurance company** is owned by its policyholders. The largest life insurance company, Prudential, is a mutual insurance company.

A mutual insurance company issues *participating insurance*. That means that any excess profits (over losses, expenses, and growth costs) go to the policyholder/investor in the form of dividends. There are many small mutual insurance companies in the East and Midwest that provide limited coverage for fire, theft, vandalism, and natural disasters for farmers. Such companies are being established by drug, chemical, railroad, utility, hazardous waste disposal, banking, and thrift industries. Already in operation is A. C. E. Insurance Company, which was started

stock insurance company
Owned by stockholders, just like any other investor-owned company.

mutual insurance company
Insurance firm owned by its policyholders.

in 1985 by 34 major companies from a variety of industries, including auto, steel, oil, retailing, and entertainment. The rash of new mutual companies is in response to escalating insurance rates from stock insurance companies.

RISK INSURANCE

As we have discussed, risk management consists of reducing risk, avoiding risk, buying insurance, and self-insurance. In this section, we shall discuss some of the insurance policies that businesses and individuals can buy including (1) property insurance, (2) liability insurance, (3) criminal loss and nonperformance insurance, (4) health insurance, (5) life insurance, (6) farm insurance, and (7) homeowner's (or apartment) insurance. Figure 22–4 briefly reviews such policies. In the remainder of the chapter, we will discuss each of these various types of insurance in more detail.

PROPERTY INSURANCE

One of the major investments that a business needs to protect against risk is property. Types of property insurance include fire insurance, automobile insurance, and marine and aviation insurance.

fire insurance
Insurance that covers losses to buildings and their contents from fire.

rider
Addition to a fire insurance policy that covers losses from wind, hail, explosion, riot, smoke, and falling aircraft.

Fire Insurance

Fire insurance covers losses to buildings and their contents from fire. A **rider** (addition) to most policies also covers losses such as wind, hail, explosion, riot, smoke, and falling aircraft. Fire insurance is getting more expensive, along with other insurance coverage, because of the rise of arson. Each year arson destroys $3 billion worth of property and kills 1,000 people. It has been called the U.S.'s most costly crime.

When your business catches on fire, you really get nervous about starting all over again. Your nervousness may become panic if you have no insurance. Insurance protection enables businesspeople to sleep a little better, knowing they are protected from losses due to fire, theft, and other dangers.

Property	
Fire	A comprehensive policy of this type covers damage from fire, theft, windstorm, and earthquake
Automobile	Such insurance usually covers property damage, bodily injury, collision (including damage to company cars), fire, theft, vandalism, and other related vehicle losses
Marine and aviation	Covers boats and their cargo and airplanes and their cargo
Liability	This very important insurance protects against legal claims from injuries caused by the firm's products or operations. Workers' compensation that covers injuries sustained on the job is a form of liability insurance
Criminal loss and nonperformance protection	Special insurance may be needed to cover employee theft and losses from break-ins. Covers losses from failure of a contractor, supplier, or other person to fulfill an obligation, as well as losses caused by the firm being closed due to damages
Health	Usually the firm pays part of the cost of employee health insurance
Life	Firms buy life insurance to protect against the loss of key executives and workers. Small businesses are especially vulnerable to losing their owner or manager
Farm insurance	Covers property and liability risks on farms
Homeowner's	Covers home and its contents, pays for shelter if forced from home due to insured damages, third-party liability, and medical payments to others

FIGURE 22–4

Examples of risk insurance.

Automobile Insurance

Automobile insurance is the most widely purchased of all property/liability coverage. There are 10 types of coverage. Each policy pays up to the limit of the coverage.

- *Bodily injury insurance* covers bodily injury to others resulting from the ownership, maintenance, or use of a car.
- *Collision insurance* pays for damage to the insured's car as the result of collision with another car or object. The worth of the car sets a limit for the insurance.
- *Property damage insurance* covers accidental damage or destruction of property of another person.
- *Uninsured motorist insurance* pays the insured and any passengers for losses resulting from injury, sickness, disease, or death caused by the owner or operator of an *uninsured* car or a hit-and-run driver.
- *Underinsured motorist insurance* covers unpaid losses because the at-fault party's insurance was not sufficient.
- *Medical payments insurance* pays the reasonable and necessary medical expenses incurred by the insured, resident family members, and guests in the insured's car. It also covers medical expenses for injuries caused by a vehicle while the insured is walking, riding in another car, or riding a bicycle.

MAKING ETHICAL DECISIONS

Imagine that you are involved in an automobile accident. You suffer some minor injuries, but feel pretty good after a couple of days. Meanwhile, you meet a lawyer at a party who suggests that this is a great way to finance part of your college education. "All you have to do," he says, "is to claim that your back hurts and you have recurring headaches. Go to the doctor and get physical therapy treatments (a back rub). I can arrange for you to get thousands of dollars from the insurance company."

When you mention the event to a friend, she says that she has heard of many people doing that very thing. In

fact, one of her best friends did something similar a year ago. In checking around, you find that such practices are not uncommon. You certainly could use some extra money for college and your friends feel that insurance companies are "ripping students off" for outrageous car insurance bills anyhow. Why not take advantage of a bad situation? What are the ethical and social dimensions of your decision? What are the consequences of faking or not faking injuries? What will you do?

- *Personal injury protection* pays for medical expenses (in "no-fault" states), loss of income, death and/or disability, and loss of services. Coverage varies by state.
- *Auto death indemnity* provides limited life-insurance protection from death in an auto accident that is not intentional.
- *Auto disability income* provides weekly benefits in the event of total disability from an auto accident.
- *Comprehensive coverage* covers losses from theft or damage from causes other than collision, including fire, glass breakage, vandalism, falling objects, hail, windstorm, flood, or collision with an animal.

It is usually best to have one policy that covers all these risks. For collision damage, insurance is cheaper if you have a *deductible clause*. That means you pay the first $100 to $1,000 (whatever level of deductible you choose), and the insurance company pays the rest. This means you avoid going to the insurance company and getting estimates every time you have a slight bump or scrape.

Protests Over the Cost of Auto Insurance

The average auto insurance premium rose over 63 percent from 1982 to 1987. The premiums vary greatly by state. For example, the average auto insurance policy in Massachusetts costs $655 and the average policy in Iowa is less than $256. In response to high insurance rates, various states have retaliated. In California, Proposition 103 cut insurance rates by 20 percent and asked for good-driver discounts. South Carolina voted to freeze insurance rates for six months. The Ohio and New Jersey legislatures are considering Proposition 103-syle legislation.[9]

Most states have passed no-fault laws that were designed to lower court costs because drivers would accept limits on the right to sue for "pain and suffering." Rate increases have continued, nonetheless, and the dispute over auto insurance rates should continue well into the 1990s. It has been proposed that true no-fault policies with a strict verbal threshold to eliminate lawsuits for all but the most serious injuries would greatly reduce auto-insurance costs.[10] Such proposals will be a major focus of the insurance debate. Young people should be especially concerned about this issue. In 1989, a 19-year-old man driving a late-model car 18 miles to work in Philadelphia now pays $6,039 per year in insurance. If he were 45, the cost would be only $1,893.[11]

Marine and Aviation Insurance

Marine insurance is of two types: **ocean marine insurance,** which protects shippers from losses of property from damages to a ship or its cargo while at sea or in port, and **inland marine insurance,** which covers transportation-related or transportable property while goods are being transported by ship, rail, truck, or plane. *Ocean marine* insurance covers boats and cargo. *Inland marine* insurance covers virtually any transportable item from white mice used in the space program to corpses. **Aviation insurance** covers aircraft and any damage and liability from the use of aircraft.

ocean marine insurance
Insurance that protects shippers from losses of property from damage to a ship or its cargo while at sea or in port.

> What does the law of large numbers mean?

> What is the rule of indemnity?

> What is the difference between coinsurance and deductible insurance?

> What is the difference between a stock and a mutual insurance company?

PROGRESS CHECK

LIABILITY INSURANCE

In Chapter 4, we talked about the difference between a sole proprietorship, a partnership, and a corporation. As you remember, one of the major differences was that a corporation had limited liability. That means that the owners are liable for losses only up to the amount they invest in the corporation. A sole proprietor or a general partner, on the other hand, is liable for losses to the extent of almost all his or her resources, including home, car, land, and so on. It behooves such people to have a good liability insurance policy to prevent losing everything. Too many small businesses and partnerships do not have enough liability insurance and are assuming too much risk.

    Public liability insurance provides protection for businesses and individuals against losses resulting from personal injuries or damage to the property of others for which the insured is responsible. Public liability policies cover such things as a passerby's injuries on an icy sidewalk or a customer's clothing stained by a clumsy waitress. A public liability policy was once adequate but not today with lawsuits being brought from many unexpected sources. Now a firm needs *extended product liability* insurance to cover potentially *toxic substances* in products, *environmental liability,* and, for corporations, *directors and officer liability insurance.* All these new risks led to an *umbrella liability insurance* policy that covers all such risks and extends the amount of coverage to at least $1 million.

inland marine insurance
Insurance that covers transportation-related or transportable property while goods are being transported by ship, rail, truck, or plane.

aviation insurance
Insurance that covers aircraft and damage and liability from the use of aircraft.

public liability insurance
Insurance that protects against losses resulting from personal injuries or damage to the property of others for which the insured is responsible.

Workers' Compensation Insurance

All states have laws that provide compensation for workers injured on the job. Some states sell **workers' compensation insurance** themselves. Other states allow a firm to choose between private or state coverage, and still others leave coverage to private insurance companies. Regardless of the system, businesses should buy this insurance to protect themselves in case an employee is injured. The cost varies with the size of the firm's payroll and the risks involved. If a worker is injured on the job, medical and hospitalization costs are paid. The worker also receives some percentage of lost wages, usually after a short waiting period.

worker's compensation insurance
Insurance that provides compensation for workers injured on the job.

The Issue of Product Liability

strict liability
States that there is no legal defense for placing a product on the market that is dangerous to the consumer because of a known or knowable defect.

absolute liability
Responsibility of a manufacturer to cover damages caused by a product if it failed to warn of a hazard, even if the hazard was scientifically unknowable at the time of sale.

Few issues in the insurance field received more attention in the 1980s than that of product liability. Once, the standard for measuring product defects was **strict liability.** In essence, this meant that there was no legal defense for placing a product on the market that was dangerous to the consumer *because of a known or knowable defect*. This standard seemed reasonable to businesses; no one should sell a defective product. Recently, however, the courts have fashioned a new policy that extends liability in ways unexpected by producers. The new standard is called **absolute liability,** and it means a manufacturer can be held liable for failure to warn of a hazard even if the hazard was scientifically unknowable at the time of sale. Absolute liability may even be undesirable for consumers, because they ultimately must pay for the added cost of insurance through higher-priced products.

The most publicized case illustrating absolute liability involved the Manville Corporation in 1982. Manville filed for bankruptcy because it could not pay the claims made by tens of thousands of workers who had been exposed to asbestos on the job. The company denied knowing that asbestos was dangerous until recently. In the 1970s, $1 billion was spent in the United States on asbestos-exposure litigation.

The rule of absolute liability has had serious consequences for manufacturers of chemicals and drugs. A producer may place a drug or chemical on the market that everyone (including government inspectors and testers) agrees is safe. Years later, a side effect or other health problem could emerge; the drug or chemical may have caused sickness, injury, or death. Under the doctrine of absolute liability, the manufacturer is held liable. This puts much more uncertainty and risk into the business of making such products. Some notable cases will illustrate how strict the courts have become:

- International Harvester Company was held liable for the operation of a skid loader it built. The farmer who bought the machinery had the maker remove the standard protective cage so the loader could pass through his barn door. The operator was subsequently crushed by a boom arm. This could not have happened had the protective cage been attached. The product was found defective by a jury.
- The Supreme Court of Appeals of West Virginia upheld a $500,000 award against a manufacturer of radial tires for damages suffered in an accident. The driver had purchased the car used, and the previous owner had put two radials and two nonradials on the car. The radial tire maker has advertised that this shouldn't be done. The court held that the tire maker should have stamped this warning on the side of the tires so used-car buyers would be aware of the problem.
- A New Jersey Supreme Court case concerned a man who was hurt diving into a 3½- foot swimming pool, possibly from the roof of a garage. He was trespassing. He sued the pool manufacturer alleging that his hand slipped on the bottom causing him to bump his head. The court said the jury could find the pool defective, even though it had a sign on the side saying "Do Not Dive."

Other cases that could be cited reveal unexpected conclusions by the courts. Producers feel totally exposed to lawsuits for almost any accident involving almost anything, and people *will* do stupid and dangerous things with products. Several people have lost fingers by picking up electric lawn mowers to clip their bushes; the producer was held liable. As a result of absolute liability rules, many companies (one third of those surveyed) have cancelled introductions of new products because of liability worries.[12]

Recently, new legislation was proposed to introduce a new **reasonable prudence** standard for product liability. Under this bill, a product would be held to be unreasonably dangerous if "the manufacturer knew, or through the exercise of reasonable prudence, should have known about the danger that allegedly caused the claimant's harm" and if "a reasonably prudent person in the same or similar circumstances would not have manufactured the product or used the design or formulation that the manufacturer used."

Naturally, most manufacturers support such legislation because it would protect them from paying for damages that no "prudent person" could have avoided. Such legislation could do much to lower the costs of insurance to producers and to you as a customer of those firms. On the other hand, consumers would have to assume more responsibility for using products with care (or at least "reasonable prudence").

Meanwhile, many companies feel the liability crisis is far from over. Companies making everything from sporting toys to chemicals and pharmaceuticals are removing products from the market, refusing to introduce new ones, and jacking up prices on others to shield themsleves from the cost of product liability.[13]

> **reasonable prudence**
> Standard for measuring the accountability of a manufacturer for damages caused by its product; based on the question "Would a sensibly cautious (reasonably prudent) person produce and distribute the product?"

THINKING IT THROUGH

Pharmaceutical firms are being held liable for illnesses caused by shots given for childhood diseases. Diphtheria-tetanus-pertussis (DTP) vaccine saves thousands of lives each year, but a few children get sick and die from the shots. Consequently, to avoid lawsuits, many pharmaceutical companies are refusing to produce the serum. This could mean the return of certain childhood diseases if something isn't done about the problem. Who pays in the long run for huge rewards for injuries?

Physicians, especially obstetricians who deliver babies, must pay up to $60,000 a year for malpractice insurance. Is this a case of the courts being too strict, or is it merely a good example of the government (in the form of judges) protecting the consumer in a reasonable and prudent manner?

Commercial Multiline Policies

Multiline policies are insurance "packages" that include both property and liability coverage. They are specifically designed to meet the insurance needs of businesses and other organizations. Multiline policies are meant to cover virtually all of the insurance needs of the organization. The obvious advantage is having *one* policy with *one* company for everything.

> **multiline policies**
> Insurance "packages" that include both property and liability coverage.

CRIMINAL LOSS AND NONPERFORMANCE PROTECTION

Criminal loss protection is insurance against theft (stealing of unprotected property), burglary (forcible entry), or robbery (taking of property by threat of violence or actual violence). **Nonperformance loss protection** is insurance against failure of a contractor, supplier, or other person to fulfill an obligation.

A **fidelity bond** protects an employer from financial loss resulting from employee dishonesty such as theft or forgery. It is common to buy fidelity bonds for retail clerks, bank tellers, salespeople who carry expensive samples, and other employees with ready access to cash or valuable property.

> **criminal loss protection**
> Insurance against theft, burglary, or robbery.
>
> **nonperformance loss protection**
> Insurance against failure of a contractor, supplier, or other person to fulfill an obligation.
>
> **fidelity bond**
> Insurance that protects an employer for financial loss resulting from employee dishonesty such as theft or forgery.

surety bond
Insurance that protects against the failure of a second party to fulfill an obligation.

A **surety bond** protects against the failure of a second party to fulfill an obligation. In public construction projects, for example, the government requires surety bonds for every contract. Such bonds are also required for contracts on garbage collecting and snow removal. If you were to have a home built, and the bonded construction firm used improper materials or refused to finish the job, the bonding company would find another firm to correct or finish the work. Other forms of criminal and nonperformance insurance include:

- *Credit life insurance,* which guarantees the payment of the amount due on a loan if the debtor dies. It is a form of nonperformance insurance and is paid by the borrower.
- *Commercial credit insurance* protects manufacturers and wholesalers from credit losses due to insolvency or default.
- *Business interruption insurance* provides protection for a business that shuts down because of fire, storms, or other insured perils. It covers lost income, continuing expenses (for example, payroll and mortgage payments), and utility expenses.

HEALTH INSURANCE

Business and nonprofit organizations may offer their employees an array of health-care benefits to choose from. Everything from hospitalization to physician fees, eye exams, dental exams, and prescriptions can be covered. Employees often may choose between options from health-care providers (for example, Blue Cross/Blue Shield), health maintenance organizations (HMOs) that require employees to choose from a restricted list of doctors and hospitals, or preferred provider organizations (PPOs) that are like HMOs, but allow employees to choose their own physicians.

No person likes to think about being in a hospital. Nonetheless, it is important to think about such possibilities when planning insurance coverage. It is most critical to cover long-term illnesses. Major medical insurance is an important part of everyone's insurance package.

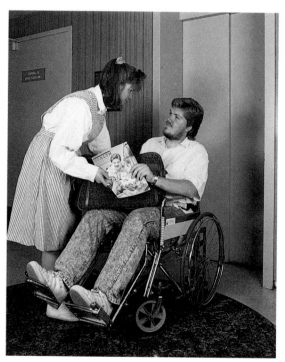

In the 1980s, HMOs became very popular with their promise of preventive health care and lower prices. Some 30 million people joined. It turns out, however, that people went more often than expected and many HMOs are not doing well financially nor are they necessarily saving money for members.[14] The quality of care has come into question because too many people are trying to see too few physicians and one often cannot choose one's own doctor. Clearly, there is room for improvement in the health insurance industry. It has been predicted that firms will be forcing employees to join HMOs because outside doctors will be too expensive. After that HMO fees may rise as well. In any case, the cost of health care is likely to go only one way—up.[15] The issue of AIDS only adds to the problem. Major medical insurance is usually available to cover major long-term illnesses. You should explore such coverage. You may also want accident insurance, cancer insurance, and other specialized health insurance policies, although they are not recommended nearly as highly.

Because of the many options available, some firms are offering flex or cafeteria plans. As you recall from Chapter 17, cafeteria plans allow employees to pick the benefits they want from a whole smorgasbord of possibilities. Options vary widely, including the choice of extra vacations rather than health insurance.

LIFE INSURANCE FOR BUSINESSES

We have already discussed life insurance in the appendix to Part 6. There, the focus was on life insurance for you and your family. Everything said there applies to life insurance for business executives as well. The best coverage for most individuals is term insurance, but dozens of new policies with interesting features have been emerging recently.

In business, risk managers are interested in life insurance for executives and employees. Some of the life insurance plans that risk managers deal with include (1) group life insurance, (2) owner or executive insurance, and (3) retirement and pension plans.

Group Life Insurance

A **group life policy** covers all the employees of a firm or members of a group. Rates for group insurance are lower than for individual policies. One reason is that insurance agents make up to 50 percent of the first year's payment, so buying in volume saves a lot of money. Usually group policies are based on the earnings of the employee. A policy may be for one or two years' salary. These are usually one-year renewable term policies. The employer often pays most of the premium.

group life policy
Insurance that covers all employees of a firm or members of a group.

LIFE INSURANCE FOR SMALL BUSINESS

More than half of the privately owned businesses in the United States would go out of business if their principal stockholder died. What's more, over half of these companies lack sufficient disability protection for their owners. One obvious answer is insurance, but there are other creative solutions. For example, the owner can leave his business to a charity and have his heirs use insurance on the owner's life to buy the company back. That way, the family gets the business, the charity gets the cash, and the estate pays no taxes.

Often you can save money by joining some group to buy group term insurance. For example, teachers, union members, and members of various organizations can buy term insurance for much less by buying it as a member of the group. A good risk manager in a firm will tell you about such options and make policies beyond the corporate coverage available to employees.

Owner or Key Executive Insurance

If a sole proprietor or a partner in a business dies, the assets may have to be sold to pay off debts, financial expenses, and taxes. An owner or key executive insurance policy would enable the firm to pay off all bills and continue operating, saving jobs for the employees. In a partnership, the beneficiary of the policy is often the other partner, who uses the funds to buy the partner's shares. A risk manager would be sure that top executives were covered by life insurance so the money would be available to hire and train or relocate another manager with no loss to the firm. Although the need is great for key executive insurance, many companies, especially the smaller entrepreneurial firms, do not have sufficient coverage.[16]

Retirement and Pension Plans

The social security system may be in financial difficulty some day in the future. It is important, therefore, that firms provide their employees with supplemental retirement and pension plans. One way of providing such a plan is for the company to pay premiums to an insurance company, which then pays benefits to the employees when they retire. If an employee should die before retirement, the benefits go to the beneficiaries much like a life insurance payment. Many different arrangements can be made relative to how much the firm contributes and how much the employee contributes. The important thing is to have some retirement plan other than social security.

FARM INSURANCE

A farm includes many pieces of property—barns, sheds, equipment, machinery, hay, and grain—that are not covered by the standard homeowner's policy. Several different kinds of policies are available to farmers to cover the risks of ownership of such property:

- *Basic coverage* covers the house and all personal property against perils such as fire, theft, windstorm or hail, explosion, riot, smoke, and vandalism.
- *Scheduled farm personal property* covers property needed for operating the farm including hay, grain, fertilizers, machinery, farm vehicles and equipment, farm records, and livestock.
- *Blanket coverage* is like scheduled farm personal property and applies to goats, horses, mules, and donkeys. (Other animals and poultry are not covered.) Some crops, including tobacco, cotton, vegetables, and fruit are not included.
- *Liability insurance* covers claims by people injured on the farm.
- *Crop-failure insurance* covers losses from fires, lightning, hail, wind, insects, excessive moisture, and drought.

HOMEOWNER'S INSURANCE (APARTMENT INSURANCE)

Homeowner's insurance protects farmers and other individuals from losses associated with residential living. With the exception of automobile insurance, there is probably no form of property-casualty insurance carried by more people. Homeowner's policies vary, but usually cover the home, other structures on the premises, home contents (furniture, stereo, TV, clothing, and so on), expenses if forced from home because of an insured peril, third-party liability, and medical payments to others.

The range of coverage is broad, including fire, smoke, theft, wind damage, water damage, vandalism, and collapse. Not covered usually are flood, earthquake, neglect, power loss, or nuclear accident.

It is usually best to buy a package that covers all the above-named risks. Different policies have different names, but it's the coverage you are looking for, not the name. Homeowner's insurance may be called apartment insurance, but regardless of the name such insurance is important to a person who has a major investment in property and clothes.

homeowner's insurance
Insurance that protects individuals from losses associated with residential living.

THE RISK OF DAMAGING THE ENVIRONMENT

Several incidents over the last few years have focused attention on a major risk that businesses face—pollution liability. One of the most publicized cases recently was the Manville Corporation's problems with asbestos. When the health hazards of asbestos were discovered, Manville was hit with 16,500 lawsuits, and the prospects were for 32,000 more lawsuits. The total cost of the lawsuits was estimated to be $2 billion. To minimize the cost of such lawsuits, Manville asked for court protection under Chapter 11 of the Federal Bankruptcy Code (we will discuss bankruptcy in Chapter 23).

The most recent concern involved the 10-million-gallon oil spill into Prince William Sound near Valdez, Alaska. Exxon was accused of being too slow in beginning the cleanup and much concern was raised over the ability of oil companies to handle such disasters.[17] The lawsuits connected with this spill will have a significant effect on insurance companies, the oil industry, and industry in general.

A continuing controversy involves the environmental threat from hazardous waste disposal. This issue reached the headlines because of the events in Times Beach, Missouri. The Northeastern Pharmaceutical Chemical Company used to manufacture a product called hexachlorophene. When the market for the product collapsed, the company hired a disposal firm to get rid of the leftover waste. An employee of the firm sprayed the waste on the dirt roads of Times Beach, not

INTERNATIONAL PERSPECTIVE ON INSURANCE

Insurance is designed to protect us from all kinds of risk. In Japan, there is a rather unique need for insurance: insurance to protect you in case you get a hole in one in golf.

Anyone who gets a hole in one is expected to have a party and send presents to friends, co-workers, and every-one who saw the event. The cost can be thousands of dollars.

The solution? Hole in one insurance. For a fee of $5 to $10 per year, a Japanese golfer is protected if such misfortune (or luck) occurs.

This shot shows dioxin-contaminated earth being trucked away from Times Beach, Missouri. The nuclear fallout from the explosion at the Chernobyl nuclear plant and the Alaskan oil spill have focused more attention on the need to protect the environment. The cost of a mistake is unbelievably high, and so are the insurance costs. That is why companies must have loss-prevention plans.

knowing that the waste contained dioxin, a deadly chemical. In 1983, the federal government stepped in to buy the whole town and evacuate the inhabitants. A federal "superfund" was established to clean up toxic waste dumps all across the United States. Meanwhile, chemical and oil companies are faced with huge damage claims from the potential harm these dumps may cause.

The risk of environmental harm reaches international proportions in issues such as acid rain. But a recent international incident that had dramatic consequences for businesses was the disaster in Bhopal, India. A chemical leak from a Union Carbide plant killed over 2,000 people and seriously injured thousands more. Public concern was raised over a similar Union Carbide plant in Institute, West Virginia.

The explosion of the Chernobyl plant in the U.S.S.R. caused much concern throughout the world. Several U.S. nuclear power plants were shut down, partially because of the proven risk of such plants because of Chernobyl. Since coal-fired plants are said to cause acid rain, there may be more research into nuclear plants to make them more safe. Clearly, this will be a public policy and risk management issue well into the 1990s.

CAREERS IN RISK MANAGEMENT

risk managers
People who do sophisticated analyses of corporate risks and design elaborate solutions to those problems.

Risk management has become one of the more dynamic functions in business in the last few years. At one time, most risks (fire, theft, environmental damage, and so on) were covered by basic *insurance* policies from one or more firms. Today, corporations have **risk managers** who do sophisticated analyses of corporate risks

INTERNATIONAL INSURANCE SALES

One bright spot in international trade for the United States is the fact that we sell more services overseas than we buy. That creates a positive trade balance in services. The United States receive nearly 40 percent of the nearly $900 billion in premiums the world's insurers collect. Many U.S. insurance companies are aggressively going after foreign insurance markets. They include Prudential, Equitable Life, and Connecticut Mutual Life. An especially interesting market is the unified Europe that is coming in 1992. Other prime markets include South Korea, Taiwan, Hong Kong, and Japan.

What this means for you is that insurance sales offers international as well as domestic opportunities for employment. Most countries now spend a lot less on insurance than U.S. citizens, but that may change as other countries become more affluent. The door to opportunity in insurance sales is opening wider. You may want to glance inside to see if you would enjoy such a career.

Source: Resa W. King, Larry Armstrong, Steven J. Dryden, and Jonathan Kapstein, "Who's That Knocking on Foreign Doors? U.S. Insurance Salesmen," *Business Week*, March 6, 1989, p. 84.

and design elaborate solutions to those problems that provide optimum coverage at a minimum cost. The growth in numbers of such managers is evidenced by the fact that there was a 67 percent increase in just two years.

Insurance Sales

Selling life insurance is one of the easier jobs to get after graduation from college. The median salary for an agent is over $22,000 and thousands of agents earn from $40,000 to $100,000, according to the Bureau of Labor Statistics. The problem is that the failure rate is unbelievable. Almost 90 percent of new agents are gone after two years. For those who persist, however, the career possibilities are good. Demographic studies show that there is a huge market for life insurance. Furthermore, because insurance companies are broadening into other financial areas, many insurance agents are calling themselves financial advisers and are selling mutual funds and other financial instruments along with insurance policies.

Other careers in insurance sales are available, including health insurance, fire and theft insurance, automobile insurance, and more. Talk to several different insurance agents and get their views of the job. Some of these agents may be quite successful. Could you be?

Insurance Adjusters and Actuaries

Another career in risk management is that of an **insurance adjuster.** When you have a loss, the insurance company sends out an insurance adjuster to calculate the extent of the loss. When a tornado hits a town, for example, insurance adjusters will be out within hours or days to estimate the losses to reimburse the insured.

The people who predict future losses based on the analysis of historical data are called **actuaries.** If you are mathematically inclined, you may enjoy such a job. By now, you know how we recommend you learn about such jobs—go out and talk with people. We know we sound repetitive in making this suggestion, but so many students fail to do this invaluable kind of career research that it bears repeating. Are you the exception? If so, you have a real head start on other students. See the box titled Career Information: Actuary for more details.

The Jobs Rated Almanac rated insurance actuaries as number one on factors such as salary, work environment, outlook, security, physical demands, and lack of stress.[18] Society can't live without actuaries. Besides keeping insurance plans

insurance adjuster
Person who calculates the extent of a loss.

actuaries
People who predict future losses based on the analysis of historical data.

solvent, actuarial calculations direct $2 billion annual expenditures of the social security system. Government regulations concerning benefit plans and a trend by companies to terminate sponsored pension plans has sharply increased the demand for actuaries. About half work for insurance companies and about a third work for independent consulting firms. The rest work in government, the academic community, and the corporate world.[19]

PROGRESS CHECK

- What does the term *punitive damages* mean, and how does it affect liability insurance?

- What are some consequences of the high cost of product liability insurance?

- What is the difference between absolute liability and reasonable prudence as measures of liability?

- How do fidelity and a surety bonds differ?

- What do PPOs offer that HMOs do not?

- What do insurance adjusters and actuaries do?

COMMUNITY LIABILITY

It is natural to think of businesses taking risks and needing insurance to protect against fire, liability, and other catastrophes. It is not so usual to think of cities and towns having the same problems, but they do.

- Plainfield, Massachusetts, had a nonalcoholic bicentennial because the town couldn't find an insurance company willing to issue liquor liability coverage.
- Columbus, Georgia, is facing an annual increase in insurance premiums from $84,000 to $213,000.

A 1978 case that went to the New York Supreme Court gave citizens the right to sue government for the negligent acts of employees. The lawsuits came roaring in. A New York State Assembly committee counted 11,296 lawsuits seeking damages of $26 *billion* from local governments in the state.

Just as in cases against businesses, the courts have been rewarding huge claims to injured parties against communities:

- Newport Beach, Rhode Island, was ordered to pay $6 million to a man who dove into water at a beach, hit a sandbar, and became paraplegic.
- Torrington, Connecticut, was ordered to pay $2.6 million because police failed to protect a woman from her estranged husband.
- A California teenager was awarded $300,000 after he fell through a skylight while he was stealing high-intensity lights!

Cities, like businesses, feel that the courts have gone out of control. If a city loses a major suit because of a bridge collapse, faulty dam, or similar problem, insurance becomes unbelievably expensive or impossible to obtain. Many cities have become self-insured.

In Los Angeles in 1987, there were almost 140,000 civil filings, compared with 80,000 in 1976. The cases are also getting more complicated and more costly. Cases are backing up in the courts and are taking years to come to justice.

The first jury verdict exceeding $1 million came in 1962; today there are more than 400 per year. The average judgment increased from $50,000 in the 1960s to more than $250,000 in the 1980s.

Can you see the potential for careers in risk management in the government? Do the courts seem out of control to you? Who ultimately pays for multimillion-dollar claims against cities? What can be done about this situation?

Source: Resa W. King, "The Coverage Crisis at Town Hall," *Business Week*, August 26, 1985, pp. 72–75; Deidre Fanning, "Justice Delayed," *Forbes*, April 4, 1988, p. 74; and Ronald Bailey, "Legal Mayhem," *Forbes*, November 14, 1988, pp. 97–98.

CAREER INFORMATION: ACTUARY

Why do young persons pay more for automobile insurance than older persons? How much should an insurance policy cost? How much should an organization contribute each year to its pension fund? Answers to these and similar questions are provided by actuaries who design insurance and pension plans and keep informed on their operation to make sure that they are maintained on a sound financial basis.

Actuaries assemble and analyze statistics to calculate probabilities of death, sickness, injury, disability, unemployment, retirement, and property loss from accident, theft, fire, and other hazards. They use this information to determine the expected insured loss. For example, they may calculate how many persons who are 21 years old today can be expected to die before age 65—the probability that an insured person might die during this period is a risk to the company. They must make sure that the price charged for the insurance will enable the company to pay all claims and expenses as they occur. Finally, this price must be profitable and yet be competitive with other insurance companies. In a similar manner, the actuary calculates premium rates and determines policy contract provisions for each type of insurance offered. Most actuaries specialize in either life and health insurance or property and liability (casualty) insurance; a growing number specialize in pension plans.

Employment of actuaries is expected to grow much faster than the average for all occupations through the mid-1990s. Job opportunities should be favorable for college graduates who have passed at least two actuarial examinations while still in school and have a strong mathematical and statistical background.

Employment in this occupation is influenced by the volume of insurance sales and pension plans, which is expected to grow over the next decade. Shifts in the age distribution of the population will result in a large increase in the number of people with established careers and family responsibilities. This is the group that traditionally has accounted for the bulk of private insurance sales.

As people live longer, they draw health and pension benefits for a longer period, and more actuaries are needed to recalculate the probabilities of such factors as death, sickness, and length of retirement. As insurance companies branch out into more than one kind of insurance coverage, more actuaries will be needed to establish rates. Growth in new forms of protection such as dental, prepaid legal, and kidnap insurance also will stimulate demand.

The liability of companies for damage resulting from their products has received much attention in recent years. Actuaries will continue to be involved in the development of product liability insurance, as well as medical malpractice and workers' compensation coverage.

For facts about actuarial qualifications and opportunities, contact:

Casualty Actuarial Society, One Penn Plaza, 250 West 34th St., New York, N.Y. 10119.

Society of Actuaries, 500 Park Blvd., Suite 440, Itasca, Illinois 60134.

American Academy of Actuaries, 1835 K St. N.W., Suite 515, Washington, D.C. 20006.

Source: *Occupational Outlook Handbook*, U.S. Department of Commerce, Bureau of Labor Statistics, pp. 72–74.

---

1. The 1980s were times of crisis in the insurance industry.
   - What caused the crisis?
     The insurance crisis was caused by more lawsuits, higher court awards, and mistakes by insurance companies.
2. The term *risk* refers to the chance of loss, the degree of probability of loss, and the amount of possible loss.
   - What are the two kinds of risks?
     Speculative risk is the risk one takes with the hope of making a profit (for example, investing in stock, buying new equipment). Pure risk is the threat of loss with no chance for profit (such as the risks of fire or theft).
   - How do organizations manage risks?
     They can either reduce risk, avoid risk, buy insurance, or self-insure against the risk. Risk reduction calls for safety programs, fire drills, and the like. Risk avoidance may mean not producing certain products, avoiding hazardous sites, and leaving certain businesses entirely. Self-insurance means setting aside funds to cover claims.

SUMMARY

1. Explain the causes of the insurance crisis of the 1980s.

2. Distinguish between different kinds of risk and identify the four ways businesses manage risk.

3. Describe the guidelines used to determine insurable risks.

3. Not all risks are insurable. In the past, Lloyd's of London insured most risks that other companies avoided if the insured were willing to pay the high price. Today, even Lloyd's will not cover certain risks.
   ■ What guidelines do insurance companies use to determine insurable risks?
     See the guidelines on pp. 710–711.

4. Explain the law of large numbers and other tools used by insurance companies to limit the cost of claims.

4. The factor that helps insurance companies predict claims and therefore limit *their* risk of covering *our* risks is the law of large numbers. It states that if a large number of people or organizations are exposed to the same risk, a predictable number of losses will occur during a given period of time.
   ■ What other tools do insurance companies use to limit claims?
     The *rule of indemnity* says an insured person cannot collect more than the actual loss. A *deductible clause* says that the insurance company will pay only the part of a loss that exceeds the deductible amount. A *coinsurance clause* requires businesses to carry insurance equal to a specified percentage of a building's value.

5. Distinguish between stock and mutual insurance companies.

5. Increasing premium costs of policies issued by stock insurance companies has led to the creation of more and more mutual insurance companies.
   ■ What is the biggest difference between stock and mutual insurance companies?
     A *mutual insurance company* is owned by its policyholders, whereas a *stock insurance company* is owned by its stockholders.

6. Describe the various types of insurance coverage available to businesses and individuals.

6. Businesses carry a variety of insurance coverages including property, liability, criminal loss and nonperformance, health, life, farm, and homeowner's.
   ■ What is property insurance?
     Property insurance includes fire insurance and its *rider*, which covers wind, hail, smoke, and other damage. It also includes auto insurance (including bodily injury, property damage, collision, and comprehensive coverage), and marine and aviation insurance.
   ■ What is liability insurance?
     Liability insurance provides protection against losses resulting from personal injuries or damage to the property of others. A variety of liability policies are available, including an *umbrella liability* policy that covers virtually everything. *Workers' compensation* is a form of liability insurance for on-the-job injuries.
   ■ Why is product liability insurance in the news so much?
     There is much discussion about a new standard of *absolute liability*, which makes firms liable for hazards even if such hazards were unknowable at the time of the sale.
   ■ What is covered by criminal loss and nonperformance insurance policies?
     Criminal loss policies cover against theft, burglary, and robbery. Nonperformance insurance covers the failure of a second party to fulfill an obligation. A *fidelity bond* covers employee dishonesty, and a *surety bond* protects against second-party nonperformance. Other coverage includes *credit life insurance* (losses if a debtor dies), *crime insurance* (nonemployee theft, burglary, or robbery), *commercial credit insurance* (losses from insolvency or default), and *business interruption insurance* (covers the operating losses from fire and other perils).

■ What other kinds of insurance coverage is available for businesses and individuals?

Health and life insurance covers illnesses and the deaths of employees and key executives. *Farm insurance* covers all farm property, including buildings, vehicles, machinery, livestock, and most crops. *Homeowner's insurance* covers homes and their contents, shelter if forced to move because of insured damage, third-party liability, and medical payments to others.

7. There are many careers in risk management including risk management, insurance sales, insurance adjustment, and actuarial work.

7. Describe careers in risk management.

1. Visit a risk manager in a major corporation and talk about what he or she does and what the challenges are. Have two or three in your class do this and report back. What is new and exciting in the field?
2. Look at any insurance policies you have. Do you understand what is covered and what is not? Should policies be clearer? Why aren't they? Bring some policies to class and discuss them.
3. Look through recent newspapers and magazines for stories about lawsuits against firms. How much was the award? What was the issue? Are the damages awarded too little, too much, or about right?
4. Debate the following statement: "Businesses are responsible for the products they make and should be liable for any and all injuries sustained by customers using them."
5. Talk to insurance salespeople in several areas: life, accident, fire and theft, auto, and so forth. How much do they earn? Do they think their work is fun? Encourage several students to do this and report back to the class. Check with your career development center and see if any insurance companies are hiring. If so, get their literature and bring it to class.
6. Find an actuary and a claims adjuster for an insurance company. Discuss their careers with them, and report your findings to class. Be sure to ask about how you can qualify for such a job.

CASE ONE   COMING TO THE AID OF AIDS VICTIMS

As you know, AIDS attacks the body's immune system, leaving victims susceptible to a wide range of life-threatening diseases. Some 1.5 million people are known to carry the virus so that diagnosed cases are expected to be about 324,000 by 1991. This fatal disease has no known cure and thus poses a real threat to its victims—and to the insurance industry.

According to the American Council of Life Insurance, in 1987 the industry paid out about $200 million in AIDS claims. Lincoln National alone paid out some $10 million, about half in death and half in health-related claims.

By the year 2000, the claims are estimated to reach some $50 billion, according to insurance actuaries, on policies currently in force. AIDs-related claims could amount to 20 percent of the total claims for some companies. Eventually the costs could drive some insurance companies out of business.

Insurers have sought the right to screen insurance applicants through the use of testing to identify those at risk for developing the disease. Some states allow such testing; others do not, including California and New York, where the number of cases are high. Opponents of testing are concerned about false results and possible disclosure and discrimination that may result.

It has been suggested that the industry form a pool of money to help AIDS victims. As it now stands, insurers are not allowed to ask prospective buyers about their sexual preferences. Some feel that the cost of life and health insurance will skyrocket for all of us if AIDS victims are part of the actuarial pool.

DECISION QUESTIONS

1. What would you recommend to your state officials that they do about AIDS testing for life and health insurance applicants?
2. What can the insurance industry do to protect itself against huge losses from AIDS victims other than testing?
3. Should employers have the right to do AIDS testing so that they can keep the cost of group insurance lower?

Source: *Industry Surveys,* Standard & Poors, January 1988, p. I-23.

CASE TWO   LIABILITY INSURANCE COSTS

Some 57 conferences were held in preparation for a White House Conference on Small Businesses. One of the major issues resulting from those conferences was the high cost of liability insurance. Liability insurance premiums soared in the 1980s, burdening some small businesses with up to four times the insurance expense they had been paying. Suggestions included limiting attorney fees, putting a ceiling on liability settlements, and replacing state regulation of insurance rates with federal regulation. Some worried that the whole liability insurance system would collapse because of enormous liability awards.

Small businesses are not the only organizations suffering from the skyrocketing cost of insurance. The problem is just as acute for big businesses and nonprofit organizations such as schools, churches, and local government agencies.

Now some government officials are proposing to make it mandatory to have health insurance for all employees. Small businesses are very worried about the cost of insurance and certainly cannot afford self-insurance when one loss would likely put them out of business.

DECISION QUESTIONS

1. If you were a government official, which of the recommendations made by small-business owners given above would you adopt?
2. Can you think of other ways for small businesses to survive the insurance crisis they are facing?
3. Some people have hinted that the cost of insurance is so high because there are so many lawyers and the court system is way out of touch with reality. Do you agree? If so, what can be done about such a situation? If you don't agree with this explanation of the high cost of insurance, what other causes can you cite for the situation?

LOOKING AHEAD

In the next chapter, we shall further discuss business and the law. We shall look at laws affecting contracts, sales, negotiable instruments (checks), and more. We will learn about laws that promote competition and fair trade. In addition, we will explore the whole area of business ethics and morality, including consumerism and the social responsibility of business. As you have read, ethics has been a major focus of this text. Moral and ethical behavior is the foundation for sound business practices. When that foundation weakens, the whole economic system weakens.

23

LEGALISTIC VERSUS ETHICS–BASED MANAGEMENT

LEARNING GOALS

After you have read and studied this chapter, you should be able to:

1. Explain the difference between legalistic and ethics-based business decisions and be able to use ethics check questions to determine when a decision is ethical.

2. Distinguish between statutory and common law.

3. Describe warranties and negotiable instruments as covered in the Uniform Commercial Code.

4. List and describe the conditions necessary to make a legally enforceable contract and describe the possible consequences if such a contract is violated.

5. Identify the purposes and conditions of patents and copyrights.

6. Distinguish among the four types of bankruptcy as outlined by the Bankruptcy Code.

7. Explain the tort system.

8. Summarize several laws that regulate competition in the United States.

9. Outline corporate social responsibility and social auditing.

10. Describe different views toward corporate responsibility and how these views impact the ethical standards a company may set.

11. Describe the role of corporate culture in determining business ethics and describe the practices corporations can use to foster ethical behavior.

KEY TERMS

bankruptcy, *p. 740*
breach of contract, *p. 739*
business law, *p. 735*
Clayton Act, *p. 744*
common law, *p. 736*
consideration, *p. 738*
consumerism, *p. 747*
contract, *p. 738*
contract law, *p. 738*
copyright, *p. 740*
corporate philanthropy, *p. 751*
corporate policy, *p. 751*
corporate responsibility, *p. 751*
damages, *p. 739*
deregulation, *p. 750*
express warranties, *p. 737*

Fair Packaging and Labeling Act, *p. 746*
Federal Trade Commission Act, *p. 745*
implied warranties, *p. 737*
involuntary bankruptcy, *p. 740*
negotiable instruments, *p. 737*
patent, *p. 739*
Robinson-Patman Act, *p. 745*
Sherman Antitrust Act, *p. 744*
social audit, *p. 752*
statutory law, *p. 736*
tort, *p. 743*
Uniform Commerical Code (UCC), *p. 737*
voluntary bankruptcy, *p. 740*

PROFILE   WILLIE CAM NIMMONS, SOCIALLY ACTIVE ENTREPRENEUR

Willie Cam Nimmons.

The performance of the corporation must be not only legal but ethical, fair, open, and considerate; it must accord with the total well-being requirements set by society.

COY G. ECKLAND, CEO of Equitable Life Assurance

Willie Cam Nimmons was a math professor at a college in Denmark, South Carolina. She was very concerned about the high level of unemployment in her area and was determined to do something about it. She began by forming a nonprofit quilting group for the unemployed welfare mothers and senior citizens in her area. She discovered that customers didn't take her group—or her prices—seriously. They seemed to think that because the group was nonprofit they were doing the work for fun.

To show potential customers that she was serious about helping people to pull themselves up, Nimmons decided to start a profit-making business called Infinite Creations, Inc. She hired more of the same kind of people to make cloth bags for major stores like K mart. Competition forced her to diversify into making pouches and tool bags for the military. Today, the company has some 125 employees working in a 32,000 square foot facility and has sales of some $3.3 million a year.

What makes Infinite Creations stand out from other firms is the value system of its founder. Willie Cam Nimmons did not go into business to make a lot of money. She started a business to provide employment opportunities for the people she knew. She is particularly proud of her training program that makes productive workers out of welfare mothers and senior citizens who had little chance of employment elsewhere.

Today the media seem to be full of stories about corrupt businesspeople who seem to have no value system. What these stories tend to ignore is that most businesspeople are honest. For every corrupt businessperson reported in the media there are dozens of Willie Cam Nimmonses somewhere providing jobs for others and operating in a moral and ethical manner.

Source: Martin E. Mengelsdorf, "Nimmons to Boesky: Drop Dead," *Inc.*, April, 1988, p. 15; and Frederick Wackerle, "Morality Tales and Corporate Managers," a letter to the editor in *Business Week*, March 14, 1988, pp. 8 and 12.

MOVING FROM A LEGALISTIC TO AN ETHICS-BASED MANAGERIAL STYLE

This chapter is based on the ethical code of businesspeople like Willie Cam Nimmons. We combined legal and ethical decisions in this chapter to show that moral and ethical behavior are *not* the same as following the dictates of the law, but following the law is an important first step. Social responsibility and moral and ethical behavior call for actions that go beyond the law.

As you know, we placed boxes called Making Ethical Decisions throughout the text. The purpose of those boxes was to demonstrate to you that it is important to keep ethics in mind whenever you are making a business decision. Blanchard and Peale suggest three "ethics check questions" that can help individuals and organizations be sure their decisions are ethical. A "no" answer to any one of these questions means your decision is probably not ethical:[1]

- *Is it legal?* Am I violating any law or company policy? Whether you are gathering marketing intelligence, designing a product, hiring or firing employees, or planning on how to get rid of waste, it is necessary to think of the legal implications of what you do. This is the most basic step in an ethics-based management system, but ethics go way beyond legality. (See the box titled The Lowest Ethical Standard Is Legality on page 736).

- *Is it balanced?* Is it fair or will I win everything at the expense of another party? Win-lose situations often end up as lose-lose situations. There is nothing like a major loss to generate retaliation from the loser. This can eventually lead to using your limited resources to combat the competition in the "backroom" rather than using them to compete in the marketplace. Every situation cannot be completely balanced, but it is important to the health of our relationships that we avoid major imbalances over time. An ethics-based manager has a win-win attitude.
- *How will it make me feel about myself?* Will I feel proud if my family learned of my decision? How would I feel if my decision were announced on the evening news? Decisions that go against our sense of right and wrong make us feel bad—they corrode our self-esteem. That is why an ethics-based manager does what is proper as well as what is profitable.

If there is to be trust and cooperation between workers and managers, that trust must be based on a foundation of fairness, honesty, openness, kindness, and moral integrity. The same can be said about relationships among businesses and among countries. President Bush, for example, has pledged to generate "a kinder, gentler" nation. In many dealings, the saying, "Do unto others as you would have them do unto you" is about as good a guideline as any.

What has been happening in the world of business lately is that the government has been stepping in to make more laws to govern behavior because businesspeople have not taken sufficient steps to make moral and ethical decisions on their own. Thus, you see more regulations regarding sexual harassment on the job, more laws regarding the hiring and firing of employees, and more strict enforcement of environmental and safety laws. If this continues, there will be still more laws and regulations and less freedom for businesspeople to make prudent decisions themselves. Businesspeople greatly prefer to set their own standards of behavior, but have not been perceived as implementing such practices fast enough.

To hasten the process, the judges of America are giving harsher penalties for misbehavior, including punitive damages, as we discussed in Chapter 22. Business has heard the message and is acting now to establish more formal moral and ethical guidelines. Meanwhile, the government is keeping a watchful eye on business and is ready and willing to make more laws and regulations if necessary. It is our hope that a new ethics-based management system will make such actions unnecessary.

Let's begin this chapter by looking at some of the laws and regulations now in place. One cannot obey the law unless one knows what the law is. Then, later in the chapter, we can explore more fully what it means to make moral and ethical decisions in business and what steps can be taken to make business more socially responsive and responsible.

BUSINESS LAW

Business law refers to rules, statutes, codes, and regulations established to provide a legal framework within which business may be conducted and which are enforceable by court action. In the United States, there are more than 700,000 lawyers, that is, one for every 384 people. In Washington, D.C., there is a lawyer for every 17 people! For every 1,000 people, the United States has 3 times as many lawyers as Germany, 10 times as many as Sweden, and 20 times as many as Japan. Lawyers outnumber physicians almost two to one. There are also more lawyers than teachers.[2] Clearly, the law is a critical component of business decision making.

business law
Rules, statutes, codes, and regulations established to provide a legal framework within which business may be conducted and that are enforceable in court.

THE LOWEST ETHICAL STANDARD IS LEGALITY

An editorial in *The Washington Times* discussed some questionable ethical decisions by people connected with the government. The article said that to be ethical in Washington these days means no more than having escaped conviction. The *ethical* question has become, "Was it legal?" Here is how the author feels about the situation:

> When a society equates "ethics" and "legality," it's in trouble. Beginning philosophy and law students can tell you that ethics and law are two dramatically different things. "Ethics" ponders people's proper relations with one another: . . . How should they treat others? What responsibility should they feel for others?
>
> "Legality" confines itself to a much smaller arena. It refers to laws we have written to protect ourselves from fraud, theft and violence. Many immoral and ethical acts fall well within our laws.

Many people feel that the United States is slipping into lower and lower standards when it comes to moral and ethical behavior. One of the *lowest* standards is that of legality. Nonetheless, it is important to operate within the law. Keep in mind as you read this chapter that law and ethics are related, but that ethics is far more important to the conduct of business and personal relations. Another author states the present situation this way:

> Our national "litigation binge" has caused the culture to shift from a moral standard to a legal standard. It becomes not what you should or should not do, but what your lawyer can find a loophole for. Of course, such an attitude strips moral behavior of its ethical content. It sends people through life as moral neuters.

Source: Tony Snow, "Ethics, Schmethics," *The Washington Times*, June 16, 1988, p. F2; and Al Thomas, *The Death of Ethics in America* (Waco, Texas: World Books, 1988), p. 54.

Corporations hire many lawyers. AT&T, for example, employs 905 attorneys; Exxon has 551, GE 415, and Ford 210. With that many lawyers around, there may be a tendency toward a legalistic approach to problems and decision making.

There are many reasons for a business today to be very legalistic in its managerial decision making. Several topics we have covered in this text have indicated the importance of law to businesspeople. We learned, for example, that a major benefit of incorporating is that it gave investors limited liability from lawsuits. The discussion of risk management showed that lawsuits today resulting from product injuries or other liability suits may be so costly that insurance is difficult, if not impossible, to buy. In addition to the laws regarding liability, a businessperson should be familiar with the laws regarding contracts, negotiable instruments (for example, checks), and bankruptcy. Let us begin at the beginning, therefore, and discuss the foundations of the law.

Statutory and Common Law

There are two major kinds of law: statutory law and common law. Both are important for businesspeople.

statutory law
State and federal constitutions, legislative enactments, treaties, and ordinances (written laws).

Statutory law includes state and federal constitutions, legislative enactments, treaties of the federal government, and ordinances (written laws). You can read these laws, but many are written in such a form that their meaning must be determined in court. That is one reason why there are so many lawyers.

common law
The body of law that comes from judges' decisions; also known as unwritten law.

Common law is the body of law that comes from decisions handed down by judges. Common law is often referred to as unwritten law because it does not appear in any legislative enactments, treaties, and so forth. In law classes, therefore, students study case after case to learn about common law as well as statutory law. What judges have decided in previous cases is very important to today's cases. Such decisions are called *precedent,* and guide judges in their handling of new cases.

In the next few sections, we shall look at some of the most important laws affecting business. Because the Uniform Commerical Code affects every state, we shall look at it first.

THE UNIFORM COMMERCIAL CODE

At one time, laws involving businesses varied from state to state, making interstate trade extremely complicated. Today, the **Uniform Commerical Code (UCC) has** been adopted by all the states except Louisiana, which uses only part of it. The UCC simplifies trading across state lines. The UCC has 11 articles that contain laws covering sales; commerical paper; bank deposits and collections; letters of credit; bulk transfers; warehouse receipts, bills of lading, and other documents of title; investment securities; and secured transactions. We do not have space to discuss all of these articles, but we would like to tell you about two of them— Article 2, which contains laws regarding warranties, and Article 3, which covers negotiable instruments.

Uniform Commercial Code (UCC)
A comprehensive commerical law adopted by every state that covers sales laws and other commercial law.

Sales Law

One of the items under Article 2 of the Uniform Commercial Code is warranties. **Express warranties** are specific representations by the seller and relied on by the buyer regarding goods. The warranty you receive in the box with a clock or toaster is the express warranty. It spells out the seller's warranty agreement. **Implied warranties** are legally imposed on the seller. It is implied, for example, that the product will conform to the customary standards of the trade in which it passes. Many of the rights of buyers, including the acceptance and rejection of goods, are spelled out in Article 2 of the Uniform Commerical Code. Both buyers and sellers should become familiar with the Code. You can read more about it in business law books in the library.

express warranties
Specific representations by the seller reaardina aoods.

implied warranties
Guarantees legally imposed on the seller.

Negotiable Instruments

Negotiable instruments are forms of commercial paper (such as checks) that are transferable among businesses and individuals. Article 3 of the Uniform Commercial Code states that a negotiable instrument must be written and (1) signed by the maker, (2) made payable on demand at a certain time, (3) made payable to the bearer or to order, and (4) contain an unconditional promise to pay a specified amount of money.

negotiable instruments
Forms of commerical paper (such as checks) that are transferable among businesses and individuals.

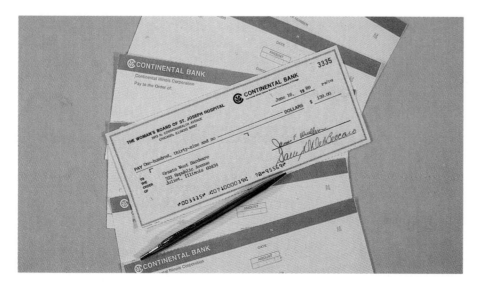

Look over this check. It is a legal negotiable instrument because it is signed by the maker, made payable to a certain person, and specifies a certain amount to be paid. It is important to learn how to endorse checks as well because there are new rules for such endorsements.

When you think about whether or not to do something questionable, what keeps you from doing it? The fact that the behavior is illegal, the fact that it is morally or ethically wrong, or the fact that you might get caught? What are some illegal things that people you know do? Why do they not obey the law? Can you see them continuing to break the law when they go into business? If not, what will change in the interim to make them different? How do you perceive the moral and ethical behavior of students at your school? Do you feel it has gone up or down or stayed about the same in the last few years? How do you feel about that?

CONTRACT LAW

If I offer to sell you my bike for $35 and later change my mind, can you force me to sell the bike, saying we had a contract? If I lose $120 to you in a poker game, can you sue in court to get your money? If I agree to sing at your wedding for free and back out at the last minute, can you claim we had a contract? These are the kinds of questions that contract law answers.

A **contract** is a legally enforceable agreement between two or more parties. **Contract law** specifies what a legally enforceable agreement is. Basically, a contract is legally binding if the following conditions are met:

contract
A legally enforceable agreement between two or more parties.

contract law
Law that specifies what constitutes a legally enforceable agreement.

consideration
Something of value; it is one of the requirements of a legal contract.

1. *An offer is made.* An offer to do something or sell something can be oral or written. If I agree to sell you my bike for $35, I have made an *offer*. That offer is not legally binding, however, until other conditions are met.
2. *There must be voluntary acceptance of the offer.* If I use "duress or undue influence" to get you to agree to buy my bike, the contract would not be legal. The *principle of mutual acceptance* means that both parties to a contract must agree on the terms. You couldn't use duress to get me to sell, either. Even if we both agree, though, the contract is still not legally binding without the following.
3. *Both parties must give consideration.* **Consideration** means something of value. If I agree to sell you my bike for $35 and you give me $5 to hold it until you earn the rest, the $5 is *consideration,* and we have a legally binding contract. If I agree to sing at your wedding and you do not give me anything in return, we have no contract.
4. *Both parties must be competent.* A drunk, drug addict, or an insane person (one who has been legally declared incompetent), for example, cannot be held to a contract. In many cases, a minor may not be held to a contract, either. For example, if a 15-year-old agrees to pay $10,000 for a car, the seller may not be able to enforce the contract.
5. *The contract must be legal.* Gambling losses are not legally collectible. If I lose money to you in poker, you cannot legally collect. The sale of illegal drugs is another example of an unenforceable contract.
6. *The contract must be in proper form.* An agreement for the sale of goods worth $500 or more must be in writing. Contracts that cannot be fulfilled within one year also must be put in writing. Contracts regarding real property (land and everything attached to it) must be in writing.

Breach of Contract

Breach of contract means that one party fails to follow the terms of the contract. Both parties may agree to end a contract, but if just one person violates the contract, the following may occur:

1. *Specific performance.* The person who violated the contract may be required to live up to the agreement if no money damages would be adequate. For example, if I offered to sell you a rare painting, I would have to sell you that painting.
2. *Payment of damages.* **Damages** is the monetary settlement awarded to a person who is injured by a breach of contract. If I fail to live up to a contract, you can sue me for damages, usually the amount you would lose from my nonperformance. If we had a legally binding contract for me to sing at your wedding, for example, and I failed to come, you could sue me for the cost of a new singer.
3. *Discharge of obligation.* If I fail to live up to my end of a contract, you could agree to drop the matter, and then you would not have to live up to your agreement, either.

Lawyers would not make so much money if the law were as simple as implied in these rules of contract. In fact, it is always best to have a contract *in writing*. The offer and consideration should be clearly specified, and the contract should be signed and dated. A contract does not have to be long and complicated, as long as it has these elements: (1) it is in writing, (2) the consideration is specified, and (3) there is a clear offer and agreement.

breach of contract
Violation when one party fails to follow the terms of a contract.

damages
The monetary settlement awarded to a person who is injured by a breach of contract.

- What is the difference between statutory and common law?

- What is covered in the Universal Commercial Code? What are express warranties, as opposed to implied warranties?

- What are the four elements of a negotiable instrument, according to the UCC?

- What are the six conditions for making a contract legally binding? What could happen if a contract is broken?

PROGRESS CHECK

PATENT LAW

Many students invent products that they feel are of commerical value, and then they wonder what to do next. One step may be to apply for a patent. A **patent** gives inventors exclusive rights to their inventions for 17 years. Patent owners may sell or license the use of the patent to others. Filing a patent with the U.S. Patent Office requires a search to make sure the patent is truly unique, followed by the filing of forms, and the payment of fees ($170). Some 700,000 patents are filed each year.[3] The advice of a lawyer is usually recommended. See Figure 23-1 (page 740) for a review of patent laws. Penalties for violating a patent can be very severe. Polaroid was able to force Kodak to recall all of its instant cameras because Polaroid had several patents that Kodak violated. Kodak lost millions of dollars, and Polaroid maintained market leadership in instant cameras.

patent
Exclusive rights for inventors to their inventions for 17 years.

FIGURE 23–1

Patent law: In a nutshell, here's the law as it stands today.

- A U.S. patent is enforceable for 17 years from its issue date. An issued patent excludes others from making, using, or selling a patented product or using a patented process
- A patent defines its protected product or process in claims that set forth the required elements and features of that product or process. An unauthorized product or process that incorporates *all* of the claimed elements and features typically infringes the patent—even if the product or process utilizes additional elements or features not set forth in the claims
- A patent must be issued before it can be infringed, which means that a patent pending has no legal effect—it serves only as an advance warning
- A patent application generally takes from six months to about four years to issue as a patent, and is kept secret by the Patent & Trademark Office up until the time the patent is issued
- If the Patent & Trademark Office, or a court, determines that a claimed invention has been marketed for more than a year before a patent application is filed, the patent will be rejected or declared invalid

Reprinted with permission, *Inc.* magazine (July 1988). Copyright © 1988 by *Inc.* Publishing Company, 38 Commercial Wharf, Boston, MA 02110.

copyright
Protects an individuals' rights to materials such as books, articles, photos, and cartoons.

A **copyright** protects an individual's rights to materials such as books, articles, photos, and cartoons. Copyrights are filed with the Library of Congress and involve a minimum of paperwork. You may charge a fee to allow someone to use copyrighted material.

BANKRUPTCY LAWS

bankruptcy
The legal process by which a person or business, unable to meet financial obligations, is relieved of those debts by having the court divide any assets among creditors, freeing the debtor to begin anew.

Bankruptcy is the legal process by which a person or business that is unable to meet financial obligations is relieved of those debts by the court. The court divides any assets among creditors, allowing creditors to get at least part of their money and freeing the debtor to begin anew. The U.S. Constitution gives Congress the power to establish bankruptcy laws. There has been bankruptcy legislation since the 1890s, but the Bankruptcy Code was amended by the Bankruptcy Amendments and Federal Judgeships Act of 1984. This act allows a person who is bankrupt to keep part of the equity in a house, $1,200 in a car, and some other personal property. Exemptions vary by state.

voluntary bankruptcy
Legal procedures filed by a debtor.

involuntary bankruptcy
Bankruptcy procedures initiated by a debtor's creditors.

Bankruptcy can be either voluntary or involuntary. In **voluntary bankruptcy** cases, the debtor applies for bankruptcy; whereas in **involuntary bankruptcy** cases, the creditors start legal procedures against the debtor. Most bankruptcies today are voluntary because creditors usually want to wait in the hope that they will be paid *all* of the money due them rather than settle for only part of it.

Bankruptcy procedures begin when a petition is filed with the court under one of the following sections of the Bankruptcy Code:

- Chapter 7—straight bankruptcy or liquidation (used by businesses and individuals).
- Chapter 11—reorganization (used by businesses).
- Chapter 12—reorganization (used by farmers).
- Chapter 13—repayment (used by individuals).

Chapter 7   Chapter 7 calls for "straight bankruptcy," which requires the sale of nonexempt assets of debtors. When the sale of assets is over, the resulting cash is divided among creditors, including the government. Almost 70 percent of bankruptcies follow these procedures.

AFRO-AMERICAN PATENTS

History often ignores the contributions of African-Americans to business. No doubt you can name a couple of famous Afro-American contributors, but that would be just the surface. A book called *The Afro-American Inventor* by Carroll Gibbs lists many inventors. Dexter and Robert Akinsheye have developed a series of drawings of Afro-American patents along with the picture of the inventor. Three Dimensional Publishing in Silver Spring, Maryland, sells them. Some popular drawings include:

- Frederick M. Jones, who invented the first automatic refrigeration system for long-haul trucks and railroads. He received patents for these in 1944 and 1954, respectively.
- George Carruthers, who in 1969 patented an image converter for detecting electromagnetic radiation.
- Garrett Morgan, who patented an automatic traffic signal in 1923.

- Lewis H. Latimer, who worked with Thomas Edison and patented a light bulb filament in 1881.
- Jack Johnson, a champion boxer who patented a monkey wrench in 1922.
- Elijah McCoy, son of a runaway slave, who earned a mechanical engineering degree in Scotland. He created an automatic lubricator that oiled machinery while it moved, and patented it in 1898. The expression "the real McCoy" was derived from his name, according to Mr. Akinsheye.
- Miriam E. Benjamin, who created a gong signal chair to ask for assistance, used in Congress, hotels and hospitals. The chair was patented in 1888.

Today's students, including Afro-American students, need to know patent law so that they too can have their inventions patented. The payoffs are often quite high.

Source: Stephen Goldstein, "Black Inventors' Story Told with Patent Prints," *The Washington Times*, March 28, 1989, p. C3.

Chapter 7 stipulates the order in which the assets are to be distributed among the creditors. First, the creditors with *secured* claims receive the collateral for their claims or repossess the claimed asset. Then the *unsecured* claims are paid in this order:

1. Costs involved in the bankruptcy case.
2. Any business costs incurred after bankruptcy was filed.
3. Wages, salaries, or commissions (limited to $2,000 per person).
4. Employee benefit plans contributions.
5. Refunds to consumers who paid for products that weren't delivered (limited to $900 per claimant).
6. Federal and state taxes.
7. Remainder (if any) is divided among unsecured creditors in proportion to their claims.

See Figure 23–2 (page 742) for the steps used in liquidating assets under Chapter 7.

Chapter 11   Chapter 11 allows a company to reorganize and continue operations while paying only a limited proportion of its debts. Chapter 11 applies only to businesses, not individuals. Less than 5 percent of all bankruptcies are handled this way. Under some conditions, the company can sell assets, borrow money, and change officers to strengthen its position. All such matters usually are supervised by a trustee appointed by the court to protect the interests of creditors. Chapter 11 is designed to help both debtors and creditors find the best solution.

Under Chapter 11, a company continues to operate, but has court protection against creditors' lawsuits while it tries to work out a plan for paying off its debts. For example, Allegheny International, Inc., maker of Sunbeam and Oster appliances, filed for protection from creditors under Chapter 11. The company had been plagued by severe debt since its purchase of Sunbeam for $543 million.

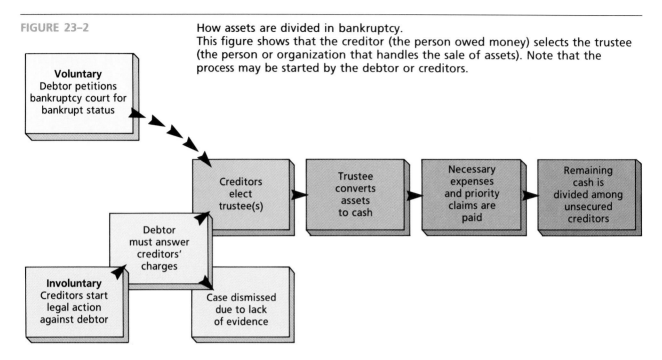

FIGURE 23–2

How assets are divided in bankruptcy.
This figure shows that the creditor (the person owed money) selects the trustee (the person or organization that handles the sale of assets). Note that the process may be started by the debtor or creditors.

Remember in Chapter 19 when we talked about cash flow problems? Allegheny had liabilities of $845 million and assets of only $735 million. But it was a "cash crunch" that ultimately did them in. Allegheny needed $75 million in working capital to get through April. It had been shipping lawn furniture and gas grills, but hadn't yet received payment from customers. Its lead bank wouldn't give it the terms it wanted, so the managers decided to use Chapter 11 to get back on a firm financial footing.[4] It is now trying to work out new debt and credit arrangements and is restructuring. Eventually, Allegheny's creditors will be paid off. It has already sold some of its units to reduce bank debt from $664 million to $221 million.

Chapter 11 bankruptcy was in the headlines recently when Eastern Airlines used Chapter 11 to try to break the hold of its unions. Rather than settle an airline strike costing him $4 million a day, Eastern's Chairman Frank Lorenzo filed Chapter 11 proceedings. Texaco also made the front page by using Chapter 11 to avoid paying billions of dollars in fines to Pennzoil. The number two steel maker, LTV, also made headlines when it filed to pay more than $2 billion in debt and used Chapter 11 to rebuild.[5] Clearly, Chapter 11 has become a managerial tool that has implications way beyond mere bankruptcy.

Chapter 13   Chapter 13 permits individuals, including small-business owners, to pay back creditors over a three- to- five-year period. It is less complicated and less expensive than Chapter 7 proceedings. The debtor files a proposed plan for paying off debts to the court. If the plan is approved, the debtor pays a court-appointed trustee in monthly installments as agreed upon in the repayment plan. The trustee, then, pays each creditor. About 25 percent of all bankruptcies take this form.

Chapter 12   Chapter 12 was passed in 1986 to give farmers a fighting chance to reorganize their debts and keep their land. Originally, farmers had too much debt to qualify for Chapter 13, and Chapter 11 was too complicated, time-consuming,

This farmer has had his farm auctioned off because he couldn't make the payments. Chapter 12 bankruptcy proceedings give such farmers a chance to regroup and bring in another crop to make the payments. Businesses of all kinds use bankruptcy as a way to hold off creditors until the business is financially fit again.

and expensive. Chapter 12 was modeled after Chapter 13 with special provisions making it easier for farmers to follow. Basically, though, farmers have the same three to five years to pay back creditors. Since this was new legislation designed for a specific group, legislators were not certain how long to keep the law in effect. Therefore, this Chapter will be reevaluated in 1993.

There are many thousands of business bankruptcies each year in the United States. Most are of small businesses. As you learned in Chapter 6, many small businesses simply do not make it past five years of operation.

THE TORT SYSTEM

Wrongful conduct that causes injury to another person's body, property, or reputation is called a **tort.** What constitutes wrongful conduct is not spelled out in laws. Rather, it has emerged from court decisions over time (common law). A major issue of the early 1990s, as you learned in reading about risk management, is that more and more people are suing businesses for wrongful conduct, and the rewards for such litigation are very high.

tort
Wrongful conduct that causes injury to another person's body, property, or reputation.

Because there is so much uncertainty regarding the nature of torts and the likely cost if injury is found, state and federal government agencies are beginning to pass new legislation that spells out more clearly the limits of such suits. The tort system is likely to go through a major revision in the early 1990s. You may be interested in following these changes as they occur, because they will have a significant impact on the cost of doing business.

LAWS TO PROMOTE FAIR AND COMPETITIVE PRACTICES

One objective of legislators and judges is to pass laws that will maintain a competitive atmosphere among businesses and promote fair business practices. There was a time when businesses operated under relatively free market conditions. Business leaders became very powerful and were able to drive smaller competitors out of business. The following discussion shows what the government response was to this situation.

The Sherman Antitrust Act of 1890

In the late 19th century, big oil companies, big railroads, big steel companies, and other large firms dominated the U.S. economy. People were afraid that such large and powerful companies would crush any competitors and would therefore be able to charge high prices. It was in that atmosphere that Congress passed the Sherman Antitrust Act in 1890.

Sherman Antitrust Act
Law that forbids contracts, combinations, or conspiracies in restraint of trade and actual monopolies or attempts to monopolize any part of trade or commerce.

The **Sherman Antitrust Act** was designed to prevent large organizations from stifling the competition of smaller or newer firms. The Sherman Act forbids the following: (1) contracts, combinations, or conspiracies in restraint of trade, and (2) actual monopolies or attempts to monopolize any part of trade or commerce.

The Sherman Act and the laws that followed it are most effective, not because the government has been so diligent in enforcing them, but because businesses are forced to make decisions knowing that the threat of legal action exists. Government thus becomes a pervasive force in business decision making.

Periodically, the government gives businesspeople a stiff reminder that the law is not to be ignored. One such reminder was the "electrical equipment" cases of the 1960s. Several producers of electrical equipment were charged with violating one section of the Sherman Act by conspiring (1) to fix and maintain prices, terms, and conditions for the sale of specified products; (2) to allocate among themselves the business in heavy electrical equipment; (3) to submit noncompetitive bids for supplying specified equipment to various organizations; and (4) to refrain from selling certain types of equipment to other manufacturers of electrical equipment.

As a consequence of this case, some top managers of several electrical equipment companies were given prison sentences. Several served time in prison, and others were given suspended sentences. Furthermore, some companies were charged with triple damage claims for alleged overcharges on various pieces of equipment, with penalties reaching as much as $16 million. Such actions by the government force businesses to be very concerned about any actions that might be construed as violating the Sherman Act or any of the other laws affecting businesses.

The Clayton Act of 1914

Clayton Act
Law that prohibits practices whose effect will be to substantially lessen competition or to create a monopoly.

There was some doubt about just what practices were prohibited under the Sherman Antitrust Act of 1890. The **Clayton Act** of 1914 was an attempt to clarify some of the legal concepts in the Sherman Act. Various practices are prohibited "where the effect will be to substantially lessen competition or to create a monopoly." This language is also unclear and open to much interpretation. For example, it will be interesting to see if Atari Corporation is successful in its suit against Nintendo for monopolizing the market by barring software firms from making games for other video systems.[6]

The act prohibits organizations from selling or leasing goods with the condition or agreement that the "buyer" will not deal in goods supplied by a competitor (when the effect lessens competition). This is called *exclusive dealing*. The law also prohibits *interlocking directorates* (where a member of the board of directors is on a competitor's board) in competing corporations (except banks and common carriers) where one of the corporations has capital and surplus of more than $1 million and where the elimination of competition between them would constitute a violation of any of the provisions of the antitrust laws. The law also prohibits any corporation engaged in commerce from acquiring the shares of a competing corporation or from purchasing the stocks of two or more competitors. Notice that the Clayton Act is concerned with the *prevention* of practices that would lessen competition.

The government continued its actions to minimize restraint of trade with the Celler-Kefauver Act of 1950. It was an amendment to the Clayton Act and prohibited the acquisition of stocks or assets where in any line of commerce, in any section of the country, the effect of such an acquisition may be substantially to lessen competition, or to tend to create a monopoly. The government has kept a watchful eye on businesses throughout the last 100 years or so and has progressively cleared up the language of legislation regarding competitive practices. Only common law, that is, court cases, will really clarify the extent of such laws.

The Federal Trade Commission Act of 1914

Like the Clayton Act, the Federal Trade Commission Act supplements the Sherman Act with additional prohibitions and makes the provisions clearer. The Federal Trade Commission (FTC) is an independent regulatory agency with enforcement responsibility. The **Federal Trade Commission Act** prohibits unfair methods of competition in commerce.* Note the words *in commerce:* it was not until 1938 that the *Wheeler-Lea Act* gave the FTC power to prevent practices that injure *the public.*

Federal Trade Commission Act
Law that prohibits unfair methods of competition in commerce.

Of most interest to the public in the last decade or so have been the FTC's actions against deceptive advertising. The FTC has a group of lawyers who screen national ads and process complaints from the public. The FTC may force an advertiser to cease and desist deceptive advertising and may even force an advertiser to place "corrective ads" that explain past deceptive actions. For example, Listerine had to spend $10.2 million on advertisements to correct prior messages claiming that the product was an effective cold remedy. The FTC is now exploring whether or not Campbell soup should disclose the high salt content of the soups it advertises as "low in fat and cholesterol."[7]

Such corrective actions have been taken in only a few cases, but the threat is there. Most advertisers have learned to avoid creating advertisements that would come under FTC investigation. Obviously, this has not made ads any more informative or interesting—it has only made them less blatantly deceptive.

The Robinson-Patman Act of 1936

The **Robinson-Patman Act** expanded federal regulation of businesses even further than previous laws. This act had four basic purposes: (1) to make it unlawful for any person engaged in interstate commerce to discriminate in price between purchasers of commodities of like grade and quality; (2) to prohibit the granting of brokerage fees to large buyers who purchase directly from producers or through "dummy" brokerage houses manned by regular employees of the purchasing organization; (3) to prohibit any payment to a customer unless such payment is made on proportionally equal terms to all other competing customers (for example, special advertising allowances); and (4) to protect independent merchants, the public, and manufacturers from unfair competition.

Robinson-Patman Act
Law that makes it unlawful to discriminate in price, to grant false brokerage fees, or to make disproportionate payments to buyers; protects merchants, the public, and manufacturers from unfair competition.

---

* *Unfair competition* includes individual practices against a competitor involving misrepresentation, deception, and fraud, and methods of competition having a tendency to unduly hinder competition or to create a monopoly.

The photo shows a modern food-processing plant. It is clean and inspected regularly. It makes hamburger meat. You can imagine what went into such meat before regulations limited what was allowed. Even today, consumers are amazed to learn how many insect parts and other foreign substances are allowed in peanut butter and other foods.

One interesting aspect of the Robinson-Patman Act is that it applies to both sellers *and buyers* who "knowingly" induce or receive an unlawful discrimination in price. It also stipulates that certain types of price cutting shall be criminal offenses punishable by fine and imprisonment. As you can see, the laws have grown more precise and the punishment more definite as the years have passed. Congress is continuing to monitor business practices and to pass laws to regulate those practices when necessary.

The Pure Food and Drug Act of 1906

Anyone who watches cowboy movies on television is familiar with the fast-talking salesman who sold snake oil and other all-purpose medicines off the back of a horse-drawn wagon. During the 1800s, sanitary conditions in food plants were deplorable. There was special concern about the sale of contaminated meat. There where many questionable business practices associated with the sale of food and drugs in that period. Nevertheless, it took 10 years of debate in Congress to get final passage of the Pure Food and Drug Act in 1906.

The Pure Food and Drug Act stopped people from selling questionable drugs to the public.

Now known as the Food, Drug, and Cosmetic Act, a 1938 law requires the truthful disclosure of ingredients on certain products. Before such laws were passed, some businesses were putting impurities like sawdust into ground meat products. Consumers were almost totally unaware of what they were eating, or putting on their skin with cosmetics. The law also prohibits false labeling and packaging of foods, drugs, cosmetics, and certain devices. Examples of mislabeling included using unnecessarily large containers and untruthful claims on labels.

The Fair Packaging and Labeling Act of 1966

When you go shopping now, you can read what the ingredients are on the foods you buy. Because the ingredients are listed in order, with the primary ingredient listed first and the others listed in descending order, you can get an idea of how much of each ingredient is in the product. Notice, for example, how much sugar goes into the cereals we eat. Note, too, all the artificial coloring and flavoring that is used. This labeling is especially important for people who must be careful how much salt they eat or who are allergic to certain foods such as eggs or wheat. The **Fair Packaging and Labeling Act** of 1966 gave the Food and Drug Administration authority to *require* information on labels. That is one reason why you see so much information on labels today.

Congress passed the Drug Listing Act in 1972. This act gives the Food and Drug Administration (FDA) a comprehensive list by established name and by

Fair Packaging and Labeling Act
Law that gave the Food and Drug Administration authority to require information on labels.

VITAMIN A	*	2
VITAMIN C	*	2
THIAMINE (VITAMIN B₁)	25	30
RIBOFLAVIN (VITAMIN B₂)	15	25
NIACIN	25	25
CALCIUM	*	15
IRON	25	25
VITAMIN B₆	25	25
FOLIC ACID	25	25
VITAMIN B₁₂	15	20
ZINC	15	15
PANTOTHENIC ACID	20	20

*CONTAINS LESS THAN 2 PERCENT OF THE U.S. RDA OF THESE NUTRIENTS.

INGREDIENTS
SUGAR, MARSHMALLOWS (SUGAR, MODIFIED FOOD STARCH, CORN SYRUP, DEXTROSE, GELATIN, ARTIFICIAL AND NATURAL FLAVORS, SODIUM HEXAMETAPHOSPHATE AND ARTIFICIAL COLORS), WHEAT FLOUR, CORN FLOUR, OAT FLOUR RICE FLOUR, COCONUT OIL, SALT, ARTIFICIAL COLOR, REDUCED IRON, NIACINAMIDE, CALCIUM PANTOTHENATE, NATURAL FLAVORS, ZINC OXIDE, THIAMINE MONONITRATE (VITAMIN B₁), BHT (A PRESERVATIVE), PYRIDOXINE HYDROCHLORIDE (VITAMIN B₆), RIBOFLAVIN (VITAMIN B₂), FOLIC ACID AND VITAMIN B₁₂.

MADE BY:
RALSTON PURINA COMPANY
CHECKERBOARD SQUARE
ST. LOUIS, MO 63164 U.S.A.
®

NIACIN	25	25
CALCIUM	**	15
IRON	6	6
VITAMIN D	10	25
VITAMIN E	25	25
VITAMIN B₆	25	25
FOLIC ACID	25	25
VITAMIN B₁₂	25	35
PHOSPHORUS	10	20
MAGNESIUM	8	10
ZINC	25	30
COPPER	6	8

*WHOLE MILK SUPPLIES AN ADDITIONAL 30 CALORIES, 4 g FAT, AND 15 mg CHOLESTEROL.
**CONTAINS LESS THAN 2% OF THE U.S. RDA OF THIS NUTRIENT.

INGREDIENTS: WHOLE WHEAT KERNELS, MALT FLAVORING, SALT,
VITAMINS AND ZINC: VITAMIN C (SODIUM ASCORBATE AND ASCORBIC ACID), VITAMIN E (ACETATE), VITAMIN B₃ (NIACINAMIDE), ZINC (ZINC OXIDE), VITAMIN A (PALMITATE), VITAMIN B₆ (PYRIDOXINE HYDROCHLORIDE), VITAMIN B₂ (RIBOFLAVIN), VITAMIN B₁ (THIAMIN HYDROCHLORIDE), FOLIC ACID, VITAMIN B₁₂, AND VITAMIN D.

MADE BY KELLOGG CO.
BATTLE CREEK, MICH. 49016, U.S.A.
©1983 BY KELLOGG CO.
®KELLOGG COMPANY
CARBOHYDRATE INFORMATION

	CEREAL	WITH SKIM MILK
COMPLEX CARBOHYDRATES	20 g	20 g
MALTOSE & OTHER SUGARS†	2 g	8 g
DIETARY FIBER	2 g	2 g
TOTAL CARBOHYDRATES	24 g	30 g

†NO SUGAR ADDED. ALL SUGARS IN NUTRI-GRAIN CEREAL OCCUR NATURALLY IN THE WHEAT AND MALT FLAVORING.

Ingredients labels provide helpful information for consumers. Look at your own cereal boxes at home. Is sugar a leading ingredient? What other ingredients are in the cereal that might not be good for you, if any? Labels help you learn such information before you buy.

proprietary name of all drugs sold. The FDA is concerned about drug safety in light of the harmful effects certain drugs have caused. The Tylenol poisoning problem, in which people died when someone put poison into Tylenol capsules, led to new packaging rules that tried to prevent such tampering. Nonetheless, the problem recurred in 1986, and Tylenol scrapped the production of capsules (see case 1).

The government has been very closely involved in the monitoring and testing of foods, drugs, and cosmetics over time. There is some debate today whether the Food and Drug Administration is demanding *too much* testing of drugs. Critics argue that overtesting keeps lifesaving drugs off the market that are available in other countries. "Better safe than sorry" has been the rule, but too much restriction can also be detrimental. Because of such legislation, though, you can be assured of the quality and safety of the food and drugs you buy. You are also much better informed because of the new labeling requirements.

Consumerism

Consumerism is defined as a social movement that seeks to increase and strengthen the rights and powers of buyers in relation to sellers. President John F. Kennedy proposed four basic rights of consumers: (1) the right to safety, (2) the right to be informed, (3) the right to choose, and (4) the right to be heard. These rights will not be gained if consumers passively wait for organizations to recognize

consumerism
A social movement that tries to increase the rights and powers of buyers in relation to sellers.

	LEGISLATION	PURPOSE
FIGURE 23–3 Consumer protection laws.	Pure Food and Drug Act (1906)	Protects against the adulteration and mis-branding of foods and drugs sold in interstate commerce
	Food, Drug, and Cosmetic Act (1938)	Protects against the adulteration and sale of foods, drugs, cosmetics or therapeutic devices and allows the Food and Drug Administration to set minimum standards and guidelines for food products
	Wool Products Labeling Act (1940)	Protects manufacturers, distributors, and con-sumers from undisclosed substitutes and mixtures in manufactured wool products
	Fur Products Labeling Act (1951)	Protects consumers from misbranding, false ad-vertising, and false invoicing of furs and fur products
	Flammable Fabrics Act (1953)	Prohibits the interstate transportation of dan-gerously flammable wearing apparel and fabrics
	Automobile information Disclosure Act (1958)	Requires automobile manufacturers to put sug-gested retail prices on all new passenger vehicles
	Textile Fiber Products Identification Act (1958)	Protects producers and consumers against mis-branding and false advertising of fiber content of textile fiber products
	Cigarette Labeling Act (1965)	Requires cigarette manufacturers to label ciga-rettes as potentially hazardous to health
	Fair Packaging and Label-ing Act (1966)	Makes unfair or deceptive packaging or label-ing of certain consumer commodities illegal
	Child Protection Act (1966)	Removes from sale potentially harmful toys and allows the FDA to pull dangerous prod-ucts from the market
	Truth-in-Lending Act (1968)	Requires full disclosure of all finance charges on consumer credit agreements and in adver-tisements of credit plans
	Child Protection and Toy Safety Act (1969)	Protects children from toys and other products that contain thermal, electrical, or mechnical hazards
	Fair Credit Reporting Act (1970)	Requires that consumer credit reports contain only accurate, relevant, and recent informa-tion and are confidential unless a proper party requests them for an appropriate rea-son
	Consumer Product Safety Act (1972)	Created an independent agency to protect consumers from unreasonable risk of injury arising from consumer products and to set safety standards
	Magnuson-Moss War-ranty-Federal Trade Commission Improve-ment Act (1975)	Provides for minimum disclosure standards for written consumer product warranties and al-lows the FTC to prescribe interpretive rules and policy statements regarding unfair or de-ceptive practices
	Alcohol Labeling Legisla-tion (1988)	Provides for warning labels on liquor saying women should not drink when pregnant and alcohol impairs your abilities.

them; they will come partially from consumer action in the marketplace. Consumerism is the people's way of getting a fair share in marketing exchanges. Although consumerism is not a new movement, it has taken on new vigor and direction in the last decade or so. Figure 23–3 lists the major consumer protection laws.

Recent Legislation

Businesspeople have gotten the message that Congress is going to force them to be more socially responsive and responsible if businesses do not regulate themselves more closely. In 1966, for example, Congress passed the National Traffic and Safety Act to create compulsory safety standards for automobiles and tires, something the automobile industry could have done on its own. The Child Protection Act was also passed in 1966. It banned the sale of hazardous toys and articles, certainly something that industry should have been careful to do.

In 1967, the U.S. government required that cigarette packs have a label that said, "Warning: The Surgeon General Has Determined that Cigarette Smoking Is Dangerous to Your Health." The Environmental Protection Agency was created in 1970. The Consumer Product Safety Commission was formed in 1972.

By 1980, there were laws and regulations covering almost every aspect of business. There was concern that there were too many laws and regulations, and that these laws and regulations were costing the public money (see Figure 23–4).

Hamburger regulations. Does this amount of regulation seem just right, too little, or too much to you?   FIGURE 23–4

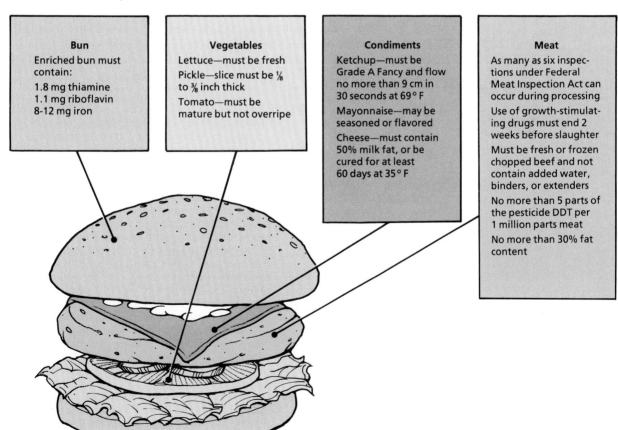

Bun
Enriched bun must contain:
1.8 mg thiamine
1.1 mg riboflavin
8-12 mg iron

Vegetables
Lettuce—must be fresh
Pickle—slice must be ⅛ to ⅜ inch thick
Tomato—must be mature but not overripe

Condiments
Ketchup—must be Grade A Fancy and flow no more than 9 cm in 30 seconds at 69° F
Mayonnaise—may be seasoned or flavored
Cheese—must contain 50% milk fat, or be cured for at least 60 days at 35° F

Meat
As many as six inspections under Federal Meat Inspection Act can occur during processing
Use of growth-stimulating drugs must end 2 weeks before slaughter
Must be fresh or frozen chopped beef and not contain added water, binders, or extenders
No more than 5 parts of the pesticide DDT per 1 million parts meat
No more than 30% fat content

deregulation
Government withdrawal of certain laws and regulations that seem to hinder competition (for example, airline regulations).

Thus began the movement toward deregulation. **Deregulation** means that the government withdraws certain laws and regulations that seem to hinder competition. Perhaps the most publicized example is the deregulation of the airlines. At one time, airlines were restricted by the government as to where they could land and fly. When such restrictions were lifted, the airlines began competing for different routes and charging lower prices. This was a clear benefit to consumers, but it put tremendous pressure on the airlines to be more competitive. New airlines were born to take advantage of the opportunities.[8] Similar deregulation of the trucking industry has made it more competitive as well.

Today, there is some call for reregulation of the airlines because they are not serving smaller cities as well as some would like and prices are going up. There is also a call for new regulations for the banking industry as a result of the S&L crisis we discussed earlier. Banks and S&Ls seem to have taken too much liberty in their unregulated state. Some regulation of business seems necessary to assure fair and honest dealings with the public. Of course, that would be less important if businesses took on moral social responsibility themselves.

There now appears to be more dialogue and more cooperation between business and government than in the past. Businesses have adapted to the laws and regulations, and have done much toward producing safer, more effective products (see Figure 23–5). Competition is getting fierce, as many small and innovative firms have been started to capture selected markets. Overseas competition is also increasing. Business and government need to continue to work together to create a competitive environment that is fair and open. If businesses do not want additional regulation, they must accept and respond to the responsibilities they have to society.[9] The next section will discuss business's social responsibility more fully. The goal is to establish a base for an ethics-based management system that is less concerned about obeying laws and more concerned about creating a moral and ethical corporate culture that will result in a better society for all.

FIGURE 23–5

Federal regulatory agencies. The FCC is just one federal agency that regulates, enforces, and develops guidelines for businesses.

AGENCY	FUNCTION
Federal Trade Commission (FTC)	Enforces laws and guidelines regarding unfair business practices and acts to stop false and deceptive advertising and labeling
Food and Drug Administration (FDA)	Enforces laws and regulations to prevent distribution of adulterated or misbranded foods, drugs, medical devices, cosmetics, veterinary products, and hazardous consumer products
Consumer Products Safety Commission	Ensures compliance with the Consumer Product Safety Act and seeks to protect the public from unreasonable risk of injury from any consumer product not covered by other regulatory agencies
Interstate Commerce Commission (ICC)	Regulates rates, finances, and franchises of interstate rail, bus, truck, and water carriers
Federal Communications Commission (FCC)	Regulates wire, radio, and television communication in interstate and foreign commerce
Environmental Protection Agency (EPA)	Develops and enforces environmental protection standards and researches the effects of pollution
Federal Power Commission (FPC)	Regulates rates and sales of natural gas producers, wholesale rates for electricity and gas, pipline construction, and imports and exports of natural gas and electricity to and from the United States

▪ How long is a patent enforceable? How long does it take to get one?

▪ Can you briefly describe bankruptcy under Chapters 7, 11, 12 and 13 and give examples?

▪ What are four provisions of the Sherman Antitrust Act?

▪ What is covered in the Clayton Act, the Federal Trade Commission Act, and the Robinson-Patman Act? Which agency has the responsibility of monitoring deceptive advertising?

CORPORATE SOCIAL RESPONSIBILITY

John Filer, chairman of Aetna Life & Casualty, says this about corporate social responsibility:[10]

> Justice, equality, recognition, freedom, mobility, and self-determination are unevenly distributed in the United States today, and corporate America can either do something about the inequities or be required to do something. . . . I suggest that each corporation give attention to the social consequences of each of its activities and, further, that each corporation examine its own special characteristics, strengths, and particular areas of interest and plan how it may best contribute to the fulfillment of one or more unmet public needs.

Harvey Kapnick, former chairman of Arthur Andersen & Co. says, "Part of the price we pay to maintain our free society is to accept voluntarily the necessity of self-regulation and self-discipline in the public interest in order to keep the role of government limited." He recommends a four-step social responsibility program:[11]

1. Specifically assign executive responsibility for the program.
2. Develop a plan that will ensure maximum benefits to society consistent with the company's particular goals, capabilities, earning capacity, and available resources.
3. Establish clear-cut priorities.
4. Communicate the results, including cost-benefit data, in a specific and meaningful way to those parts of the business that are actively engaged.

Dozens of other top executives who could be quoted agree that business has a social responsibility and needs to accept that responsibility in a structured way. The social performance of a company has several dimensions:

▪ **Corporate philanthropy** includes charitable donations to nonprofit groups of all kinds. Corporate giving to charity has risen at a 21 percent annual rate since 1970. Total giving to charities by businesses reached about $4.6 billion in 1987 and 1988.[12]

▪ **Corporate responsibility** includes everything from minority hiring practices to the making of safe products, minimization of pollution, wise energy use, provision of a safe work environment, and more.

▪ **Corporate policy** refers to the position a firm takes on issues that affect the firm and society, including political issues.

Corporations are less likely to give to other organizations (charities) than they are to start their own programs of social responsibility. It would be instructive for you to read about the thousands of programs sponsored by leading U.S. firms. So much news coverage is devoted to the social *problems* caused by corporations that

corporate philanthropy
Charitable donations made by the corporation to nonprofit groups of all kinds.

corporate responsibility
Issues such as setting minority hiring practices, manufacturing safe products, and minimizing pollution.

corporate policy
The position a firm takes on issues that affect the corporation as well as society.

people tend to get a one-sided view of the social impact of companies. In fact, many corporations are publishing reports that document their net social contribution. To do that, a company must measure its social contributions and subtract its negative social impacts. We shall discuss that process next.

Social Auditing

It is nice to talk about having organizations become more socially responsible. It is also hopeful to see some efforts made toward creating safer products, more honest advertising, and so forth. But is there any indication that organizations are making social responsiveness an integral part of top management's decision making? The answer is yes, and the term that represents that effort is *social auditing*.

A **social audit** is a systematic evaluation of an organization's progress toward implementing programs that are socially responsible and responsive. One of the more difficult problems with social auditing is how to define what is meant exactly by "socially responsible and responsive." Is it being socially responsible to delay putting in the latest technology (for example, robots and computers) to save jobs, even if that makes the firm less competitive? There are literally hundreds of such questions that make the design of social audits difficult.

Another major problem is establishing procedures for measuring a firm's activities and their effects on society. What should be measured? Business activities that could be considered socially responsible include the following:

- Community-related activities such as participating in local fund-raising campaigns, donating executive time to various nonprofit organizations (including local government), and participating in urban planning and development. For example, Dollar General Corporation (a discount store) has helped 10,000 people get their high school equivalency degrees.[13]
- Employee-related activities such as equal opportunity programs, flextime, improved benefits, job enrichment, job safety, and employee development programs.
- Political activities such as taking a position on issues such as nuclear safety, gun control, pollution control, and consumer protection; and working more closely with local, state, and federal government officials.
- Support for higher education, the arts, and other nonprofit social agencies.
- Consumer activities such as product safety, honest advertising, prompt complaint handling, honest pricing policies, and extensive consumer education programs.

There is some question whether positive actions such as these should be added up and then negative effects subtracted (for example, pollution, lay-offs) to get a *net social contribution*. Or should just positive actions be recorded?

In general, social auditing has become a concern of business. It is becoming one of the aspects of corporate success that business evaluates, measures, and develops.

social audit

A systematic evaluation of an organization's progress toward implementing programs that are socially responsible and responsive.

PROGRESS CHECK

- What are the four consumer rights outlined by President Kennedy?
- What are four steps to follow in developing a social responsibility program?
- What is a social audit and what kinds of activities are monitored in such a program?

SETTING ETHICAL STANDARDS

What should be the guiding philosophy for business in the 21st century? For most of the 20th century, there has been uncertainty regarding the position top managers should take. Three different views of corporate responsibility have been presented.[14]

1. The Invisible Hand   Under this philosophy: "the true and only social responsibilities of business organizations are to make profits and obey the laws . . . the common good is best served when each of us and our economic institutions pursue not the common good or moral purpose . . . but competitive advantage. Morality, responsibility, and conscience reside in the invisible hand of the free market system, not in the hands of the organizations within the system, much less the hands of managers within the system." (This approach is based on the theories of Adam Smith, as discussed in Chapter 2.)

2. The Hand of Government   Under this philosophy: "the corporation would have no moral responsibility beyond political and legal obedience . . . corporations are to seek objectives that are rational and purely economic. The regulatory hands of the law and the political process rather than the invisible hand of the marketplace turn these objectives to the common good."

3. The Hand of Management   This philosophy: "encourages corporations to exercise independent, noneconomic judgment over matters [of morals and ethics] that face them in their short-and long-term plans and operations." It [seeks] "moral reasoning and intent" from the corporation, and for managers to apply individual morality to corporate decisions.

In corporations today, you can find examples of all three philosophies in action. Some organizations are totally profit oriented and leave social results to the marketplace. Others operate within the letter of the law, but provide no moral or ethical leadership. Managers at companies such as Johnson & Johnson and Du Pont, however, are going far beyond the narrow goals of profit to act as social citizens and ethical leaders (see Case 1).

The trend today is for society to demand moral and ethical leadership from business. Few business leaders are taking a public stand on such issues, but many are doing so in their own firms. The American Marketing Association published a Code of Ethics in 1986 (see Figure 23–6 on page 754). It is just one example of many similar codes being proposed by business organizations. Notice that it goes beyond being honest and calls for active efforts to satisfy consumer rights to safety, to be informed, to choose among competing goods, and to be heard. Before we go further in this discussion, we need to clarify some terms:

Ethics is the study of morality.

Morality refers to the attempt to live by certain values and standards of conduct accepted by society as right and wrong.

Integrity refers to the honesty, sincerity, and morality of a person.

A rise in ethics and morality begins with each person living a life of integrity. We teach others a higher level of ethics and morality through example. Strong ethical *leadership* from corporate executives may be the best source for maintaining America's "goodness."

Honesty is the cornerstone of character. The honest man or woman seeks not merely to avoid criminal or illegal acts, but to be scrupulously fair, upright, fearless in both action and expression. Honesty pays dividends both in dollars and in peace of mind.

B.C. FORBES

FIGURE 23–6

American Marketing
Association Code of Ethics.

Honesty and fairness

Marketers shall uphold and advance the integrity, honor, and dignity of
the marketing profession by:

1. Being honest and impartial in serving the public, employers, suppliers,
   and clients
2. Communications that are truthful and avoid misleading omissions of
   pertinent details
3. Avoiding any conflict of interest and avoiding being a party to bribery

Rights of the consumer

In March 1962, President John F. Kennedy presented his now famous
Consumer Bill of Rights: (1) the right to safety, (2) the right to be
informed, (3) the right to choose, and (4) the right to be heard. To meet
these objectives, the AMA encourages adherence to the following:

1. Communications should be clear so that the recipient can understand
   the message
2. Risks connected with products and services should be fully disclosed
3. No attempt should be made to disparage or maintain a limited stock or
   availability of an advertised product or service in an attempt to switch a
   customer to a more expensive one
4. Those products or services which do not perform as advertised or
   represented should be subject to a refund or allowance
5. Added features at extra cost must not be included without the
   customer's specific approval
6. Attempts to sell or to raise funds must not be carried out under the
   guise of marketing research
7. Customers have the right to have their names deleted from lists used or
   sold for further marketing efforts
8. Names obtained during the course of marketing research studies must
   not be used for purposes other than research

Source: Draft proposal (abbreviated) in *Marketing News*, May 9, 1986, pp. 1 and 11.

BUSINESS ETHICS BEGIN AT THE TOP

Ethics are caught more than taught. That is, people learn their standards and values
from observing what others do, not what they say. This is as true in business as it is
at home. Corporate values are instilled by the leadership and example of strong top
managers. The result is what we have called *corporate culture*.

Companies such as IBM, Xerox, McDonald's, Disney, Marriott, and dozens of
others are known to have strong, effective, and ethical leadership. Within these
firms, a high value system has become pervasive, and employees feel part of a
corporate mission that is socially beneficial. On the other hand, *The Wall Street
Journal* recently reported a study that showed that corporate culture can work the
other way, too. Managers with strong personal values may compromise those
values if they feel that the corporation's profits are compromised. The study
concluded that "People's personal values are getting blocked by the needs of the
company."[15] One problem is that most company ethics codes leave out any
mention of ethical matters regarding product quality, product safety, environmental affairs, or civic and community affairs.[16]

Without the civilizing force
of universal moral standards,
particularly honesty, trust,
self-respect, integrity, and
loyalty, the marketplace
quickly degenerates.
WARREN BROOKS in
Goodness and the GNP

MAKING ETHICAL DECISIONS: THE INFANT FORMULA CASE

In 1988, Third World nations were still trying to enforce a 1981 decision by the World Health Organization to adopt a worldwide code to restrict the marketing of infant formula. This issue goes back to the 1950s, 1960s, and 1970s, when health authorities had identified bottle feeding as a source of infant diarrhea, malnutrition, and death. The cause of the sickness and death was traced to the fact that mothers in poor countries were mixing polluted water with the formula or using too much water to make it cheaper, and they were using nonsterile bottles.

The Nestlé company was targeted as the main culprit in the problem because it was promoting the infant formula to illiterate and poverty-stricken mothers. "Mothercraft nurses," who distributed free infant formula samples in hospitals, were found not to be nurses, but saleswomen in costume. Pediatricians were given gifts, travel, and so forth to promote the formulas. Nestlé's advertisements said that formula was better than mother's milk. Efforts to end these practices failed until 1981 when the World Health Organization passed a code governing industry marketing practices that were "detrimental to breast-feeding." Most companies complied, and Nestlé got a new leader who promised to comply with the new code. A boycott called against Nestlé products was then lifted.

This problem persisted and received much media attention because the firms involved, especially Nestlé, did not react as soon as problems were discovered. Rather, the situation had to become a worldwide issue before action was taken. In fact, an advocacy group threatened a new boycott on Nestlé products in 1988 because Nestlé continued to give free samples of its products to hospitals in Third World countries so that mothers would be exposed to the product.

Clearly, the people of the world are concerned about the marketing practices of businesses. Such people are also concerned about U.S. firms that sell drugs that are banned in the United States to other countries. The same questions have been raised about sales of banned pesticides and other such products in less developed countries.

What obligation would you feel as a businessperson to protect people in other countries who were ignorant of the potential harm of your products? It is *not* illegal to sell products such as baby's formula and certain dangerous pesticides overseas. In fact, you can make a lot of money doing so. What are the long-run consequences of using legality as your guide to proper international relations versus high moral and ethical standards?

Source: Joe Davidson and Alix M. Freedman, "Nestlé Faces New Boycott Threat in Distribution of Infant Formula," *The Wall Street Journal*, June 29, 1988, p. 28.

In the United States, it is usually healthful to give a baby milk in a bottle. But in some countries, the milk is spoiled by polluted water. What happens if a mother is too sick to breastfeed her baby and the water is contaminated? Such are the legal and ethical questions surrounding the Nestlé case.

When Profits Become More Important than Ethics

Recently, the executives of Beech-Nut Nutrition Corp. learned the consequences of not behaving ethically. Here is the story. The director of research at Beech-Nut sent senior management a memo saying he thought a supplier was selling Beech-Nut a fake apple juice formula. The formula was used to make apple juice for infants. Management paid little attention to the memo. Later, a private investigator came to the same conclusions. Did Beech-Nut management then pull the product off the shelves and apologize for being fooled by a supplier? They did not. Instead, they hurried the sale of the remaining inventory by using price-cutting tactics to get rid of the products. Had the company recalled the inventory, it may have successfully proven itself the victim of a supplier. It also would have lost some $3.5 million in inventory of its best-selling apple juice.[17] As a result of their actions, two Beech-Nut executives were given prison sentences of a year and a day. Justice Department and Food and Drug Administration officials said the prison terms would be a powerful deterrent to business executives who would sacrifice ethics and the public interest in pursuing careers and profits. Subsequently, the executives were freed on a technicality, but the message to executives was clear. Follow ethical and legal rules or risk jail.[18]

The State of Business Ethics Today

If the Beech-Nut case were an isolated incident, we would not have to spend so much time on ethics throughout the text. But the truth is that the Beech-Nut case is not unique. In the 1980s, Wall Street was hit by the news of insider trading cases (that is, people making profit in the stock market by illegally obtaining knowledge about companies from insiders who gave them the information). Ivan Boesky had to pay a $100 million Security and Exchange Commission penalty for making huge profits on insider knowledge, which is against the law. Although the Boesky case was the most publicized, *The Wall Street Journal* recently reported on 50 such cases.[19]

Beech-Nut makes good products for babies. That is why mothers trust the brand. That is also why people were shocked and dismayed over the charge that executives were knowingly selling fake apple juice. The cost of pulling the apple juice off the shelves seemed too much, and the managers made a legal and ethical blunder as a result.

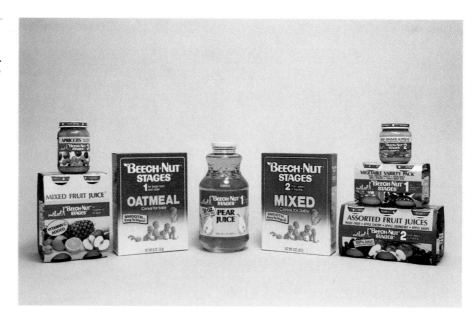

A DynCorp subsidiary was found guilty in two bid-rigging cases and faces criminal fines that could exceed $7.5 million, $4 million more than the firm had reserved to cover its potential liabilities. Nothing so stunned the business world as the judgment against Texaco in favor of Pennzoil Co. Texaco was to pay $10.3 *billion* for interfering with Pennzoil's 1984 agreement to buy part of Getty Oil Company. Texaco took the case to the Supreme Court, but after much legal wrangling and accusations concerning improprieties on both sides, Texaco agreed to pay Pennzoil $3 billion dollars to settle the lawsuit out of court.

Most recently, there has been much written about scandals in the defense industry.[20] Again, the charge was inside information that affected bidding on government contracts. This is in spite of the fact that most defense contractors have ethics codes. At General Dynamics alone, ethics officials received some 5,000 calls and visits from employees resulting in 27 employee dismissals and 29 temporary suspensions of employees who violated the program.[21]

Hertz has been charged with making fictitious auto damage estimates. The car rental firm will now have to pay $22.5 million in fines and restitution.[22] Norelco was charged with selling water filters after learning they may contain carcinogens.[23] In industry after industry, companies are doing things that are ethically and morally questionable. One has only to watch TV for a full day to see that the level of morality on TV has slipped tremendously. One wonders what is being done to correct the situation today. Much of the movement against immorality has come from individuals. For example, Ms. Terry Rakolta of Bloomfield Hills, Michigan, complained about the immorality in the TV series "Married . . . With children." She threated boycotts against the advertisers. That received much publicity and led to many advertisers boycotting "trash TV." Shows such as "Geraldo" and "Morton Downey Jr. Show" were also targeted. The movement was called "The New Puritanism" by *Advertising Age*. It was a major effort by consumers to restore ethics and morality to TV.[24] The Morton Downey show has since been canceled.

Corporate Ethical Codes

A survey of 1,000 corporate executives found that nearly one in four executives believed that living up to ethical standards can impede successful careers. That is, they felt that to be ethical would impede their progress in the firm. Furthermore, 68 percent agree that younger executives are driven to compromise their ethics "by

---

EXECUTIVE PAY AS AN ETHICS ISSUE

In Chapter 17, we discussed executive pay as an employee/management issue. The issue has become so dominant that it has become an ethics issue. The center of attention is Michael Milken of Drexel Burnham Lambert. They paid him $550 million in 1987 alone. He made over $1 billion in a four-year period. The questions were: Is anyone worth that much? How much pay is too much?

Economist Milton Friedman thought that his pay was simply compensation for a job well done. He said most of it will go to taxes and a foundation anyhow. Economist John Kenneth Galbraith found it "excessive."

Others argued that if Millken were an owner, he could have made billions and no one would have objected. He earned it. A union economist found the pay "atrocious."

It will always be an issue under a capitalist system that some people will be paid more than others. Where do you draw the line? Is $550 million too much? What are the ethical guidelines? What if the money is donated to charity? There are no "answers" to such ethical questions. But it is good to raise the issue so that alternatives can be explored.

Source: "How Much Pay Is Too Much?," *Los Angeles Times*, April 9, 1989, p. 3 of Part IV.

MORAL QUALITY CIRCLES

You learned in Chapter 13 that a quality circle was a group of employees that get together to develop ideas for solving quality problems and other problems in the workplace. A *moral quality circle* would assess whether what the company is doing is right or wrong or neutral. Should the problem be brought to higher management? Could the problem in time produce a subtle erosion of employee commitment to the decent purposes of the organization?

The idea of moral quality circles was presented in a *Wall Street Journal* article. The article says that, "The moral quality circle should institutionalize the possibility that members of work groups operate at their moral best—not their compromising worst. If an organization's leaders broadcast the implicit message that they are concerned with the organization's ethical as well as economic health, they can mobilize forces of citizenship and commitment, which are also necessary to an organization's general effectiveness . . . Economics and ethics are not mutually exclusive."

Source: Lionel Tiger, "Stone Age Provides Model for Instilling Business Ethics," *The Wall Street Journal*, January 11, 1988, p. 22.

FIGURE 23–7

Who writes ethics codes? This figure shows that top management is largely responsible for writing ethics codes. The legal department is often involved, but it is important to separate doing what is ethical from doing what is merely legal. Ethics goes far beyond legality.
Source: Reprinted by permission of *The Wall Street Journal*, July 15, 1988. © Dow Jones & Company Inc., 1988. All Rights Reserved Worldwide.

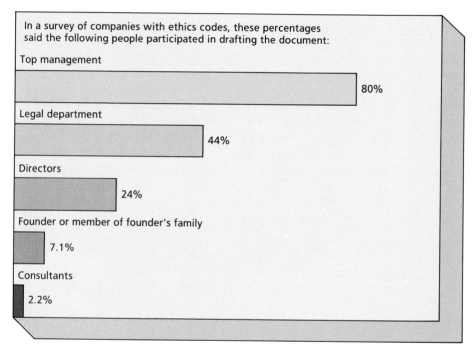

In a survey of companies with ethics codes, these percentages said the following people participated in drafting the document:

Top management — 80%
Legal department — 44%
Directors — 24%
Founder or member of founder's family — 7.1%
Consultants — 2.2%

the desire for wealth and material things."[25] This means that executives feel pressure *not* to do the right thing, *not* to follow their own ethical standards. The only way to counter such feelings is to have a strong corporate culture that emphasizes ethical behavior plus a strong ethics code.

The Wall Street Journal reports that "formal ethics codes are hot these days. Companies without them are scrambling to commit corporate values to paper. Companies that already have codes are rushing to update, disseminate and interpret them."[26] Figure 23–7 shows who participates in preparing ethics codes. Note that it is mostly top management and the legal department. To be effective, the

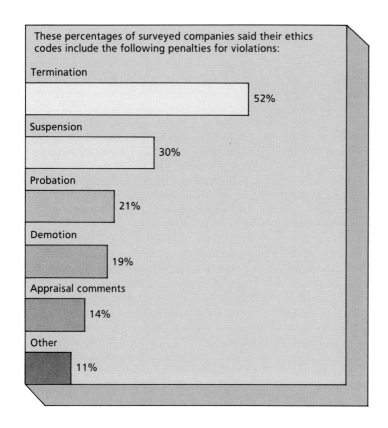

These percentages of surveyed companies said their ethics codes include the following penalties for violations:

Termination — 52%
Suspension — 30%
Probation — 21%
Demotion — 19%
Appraisal comments — 14%
Other — 11%

FIGURE 23–8
What are the penalties for ethics violations?
This figure shows that many companies are very serious about ethics violations. More than half may fire violators. Some 70 percent will suspend employees, put them on probation, or demote them.

Source: Reprinted by permission of *The Wall Street Journal,* July 15, 1988. © Dow Jones & Company Inc., 1988. All Rights Reserved Worldiwde.

codes must be enforced and employees held responsible for their behavior. Figure 23-8 shows the typical penalties for violating the codes.

Ethical codes are meaningless, however, unless the company itself abides by them—and this is not always the case. For example, when Security Pacific Corp. drafted the bank's first ethics code, they tried it out on their employees in focus groups. Point by point, the employees disputed the code's precepts. For example, the employees did not agree that "The company assesses the moral fitness of clients before we do business with them." The employees believed that the company took "business where they could get it."[27] If the company is not abiding by the ethical code, what message is being sent to lower-level employees?

Developing an ethical code and living by that code are two different things. How can you behave ethically when there are so many pressures not to? Blanchard and Peale suggest that individuals and organizations can build inner strength to resist external pressure and do what is right by practicing what they call the five Ps of ethical power: purpose, pride, patience, persistence, and perspective.[28]

Purpose. The mission of the organization is communicated from the top down. The organization is guided by the values, hopes, and vision that help to determine what is acceptable and unacceptable behavior.

Pride. Employees feel pride in themselves and in their organization. Pride helps us resist temptations to behave unethically.

Patience. Holding to ethical values will lead to success in the long term. Balance must be maintained between obtaining results and caring about how the results are achieved.

INTERNATIONAL ETHICAL DECISIONS

The one situation in the 1980s that perhaps best illustrates ethical decision making on an international level is that of South Africa. The government of South Africa has long practiced apartheid, separation of the races. The blacks in South Africa protested apartheid throughout the 1980s, and many people were killed in clashes between blacks who had differences of opinion about the apartheid system and between blacks and the white ruling government.

Virtually all nations, including the government of South Africa, felt that something had to be done about the system of apartheid. Some small steps were made to change some of the rules, but the changes were few and slow. Protesters in the United States demanded that American organizations, such as universities, stop investing in firms that did business in South Africa. The idea was to pressure the South African government to end apartheid more quickly. The protests grew more insistent when increased violence erupted in South Africa. Soon, protesters called for U.S. firms to pull out of South Africa entirely.

In 1986, an advertisement sponsored by 80 American companies operating in South Africa, including Citibank, IBM, Coca-Cola, and Union Carbide, called for a complete end of all forms of apartheid. One possibility is that all such U.S. firms would pull their subsidiaries out of South Africa. Many people proposed that very solution.

The problem is that U.S. firms employ many black employees and are some of the fairest and most liberal employers in the country. If they were to pull out, it would hurt the economy of South Africa badly. That means both whites and blacks would suffer, and other nations would be less likely to lend money to businesses in the area. The government might fall, but what would remain would be a country with a weaker business base to build on. This would hurt blacks more than whites in the long run, because blacks are in the majority.

American businesses with subsidiaries in South Africa faced a serious ethical problem. Should they stay in South Africa and try to influence the government to be more liberal with blacks? They do have a significant influence. Or should they pull out in protest and potentially hasten the end of apartheid, but increase black unemployment and remove a source of pressure on other businesses to be as fair as U.S. businesses are with blacks? American businesses have subsidiaries in many countries with poor race relations or suppressive governments. Should they pull out of *all* such countries or stay and try to promote change? What is the moral and ethical position for businesses to take relative to other governments? These are the kinds of international ethical questions that will have to be answered in the next decade.

Source: "Steven Mufson," South Africa Regime Is Confident Sanctions Could be Circumvented," *The Wall Street Journal*, June 20, 1986, p. 23; and Arnold Beichman, "Selective Prison of Sociology." *The Washington Times*, January 4, 1989, p. F3.

- *Persistence*. The company is committed to living by ethical principles. Actions are consistent with the organization's purpose.
- *Perspective*. Managers and employees take time to stop and think about where they are, evaluate where they want to go, and figure out how they are going to get there.

There are no easy solutions to ethical problems. Companies that develop strong ethical codes, that put their decisions through the ethics check described at the start of this chapter, and that practice the five Ps of ethical power have a better chance than most of behaving ethically. These steps are the foundations of "ethics-based management" that forms the title of this chapter.

INTERNATIONAL ETHICS

Ethical problems are not unique to the United States. Top business and government leaders in Japan recently were caught in a major "influence peddling" (read bribery) scheme in Japan. Similar charges have been brought against top officials in South Korea and the People's Republic of China.[29]

What is new about these changes to the new moral and ethical standards by which farmers and government leaders are being judged? They are much more strict than in previous years. In the United States, Gary Hart, John Tower, Tony Coelho, and Jim Wright are all politicians caught up by the new standards. In other countries, similar top leaders are being held to a new, higher standard. The 1990s may be the era when a new morality is recognized worldwide. Will you do your part?

- What are three different views of corporate responsibility?

- What is the difference between ethics, integrity, and morality?

- What are the major issues in the infant formula case?

- What was the issue in the Beech-Nut case?

- What is a moral quality circle?

SUMMARY

1. Some people think behaving ethically means no more than obeying the laws.
   - What is the difference between "legalistic" and "ethics-based" decision making?
     Ethics go beyond obeying laws. They also involves abiding by the moral standards accepted by society.
   - How can we tell if our business decisions are ethical?
     Blanchard and Peale suggest putting our business decisions through an ethics check by asking three questions: (1) Is it legal? (2) Is it balanced? and (3) How will it make me feel?

1. Explain the difference between legalistic and ethics-based business decisions and be able to use the ethics check questions to determine when a decision is ethical.

2. Business law refers to rules, statutes, codes, and regulations established to provide a legal framework within which business may be conducted that is enforceable by court action.
   - What is the difference between statutory law and common law?
     Statutory law is the written law contained in legislative enactments, treaties, and ordinances. Common law is the unwritten law derived from judges' decisions.

2. Distinguish between statutory and common law.

3. The Uniform Commerical Code (UCC) is the law that covers sales law and other commercial law in all states except Louisiana (which uses part of it).
   - What does Article 2 of the UCC cover?
     It covers warranties. *Express warranties* are guarantees made by the seller, whereas *implied warranties* are guarantees imposed on the seller by law.
   - What does Article 3 of the UCC cover?
     It covers negotiable instruments (such as checks). It states that a negotiable instrument must be written and (1) signed by the maker, (2) made payable on demand at a certain time, (3) made payable to the bearer or to order, and (4) contain an unconditional promise to pay a specified amount of money.

3. Describe warranties and negotiable instruments as covered in the Uniform Commerical Code.

4. Contract law specifies what a legally enforceable agreement is.
   - What makes a contract enforceable under the law?
     It must meet six conditions: (1) an offer must be made, (2) the offer must be voluntarily accepted, (3) both parties must give consideration, (4) both parties must be competent, (5) the contract must be legal, and (6) the contract must be in proper form.
   - What are the possible consequences if a contract is violated?
     If a contract is violated, one of the following may be required: (1) specific performance, (2) payment of damages, or (3) discharge of obligation.

4. List and describe the conditions necessary to make a legally enforceable contract and describe the possible consequences if such a contract is violated.

5. Patents and copyrights protect the rights of inventors, writers, and other developers of original products.
   - What are patents and copyrights?
     Patents are exclusive rights to inventions for 17 years. A search is required to be sure the product is unique. *Copyrights* protect rights to materials such as books, articles, photos, and cartoons.

5. Identify the purposes and conditions of patents and copyrights.

6. Distinguish between the four types of bankruptcy as outlined by the Bankruptcy Code.

6. When businesses or individuals become buried in debt, they can file for bankruptcy.
   - What are the bankruptcy laws?
     The Bankruptcy Code was amended in 1984. *Chapter 7* of the Code calls for straight bankruptcy, in which all of the assets are divided among creditors after exemptions. *Chapter 11* is for businesses; it allows a firm to reorganize and continue operation after paying only a limited portion of its debts. *Chapter 13* is for individuals; it allows individuals to pay their creditors over an extended period of time. *Chapter 12* is much like Chapter 13, but covers farmers who often have more debt than the consumers covered in Chapter 13.

7. Explain the tort system.

7. A *tort* is wrongful conduct that causes injury to another person's body, property, or reputation.
   - Is "wrongful injury" defined by law?
     No, the meaning of wrongful injury has evolved from court decisions over time (common law).

8. Summarize several laws that regulate competition in the United States.

8. Several laws were passed to promote fair and competitive practices.
   - What does the Sherman Act cover?
     It forbids contracts, combinations, or conspiracies in restraint of trade and actual monopolies or attempts to monopolize any part of trade or commerce. Note that this language is indefinite.
   - What does the Clayton Act add?
     It prohibits practices that will "substantially lessen competition," such as selling or leasing goods with the condition that the buyer will not deal in goods supplied by a competitor (exclusive dealing). It also prohibits *interlocking directorates*—serving on a competitor's board of directors.
   - Which act regulates false and deceptive advertising?
     The Federal Trade Commission Act.
   - Which act prohibits price discrimination and demands proportional promotional allowances?
     The Robinson-Patman Act.
   - Which laws made producers put ingredients on labels?
     The Food, Drug, and Cosmetic Act and the Fair Packaging and Labeling Act (1966).

9. Outline corporate social responsibility and social auditing.

9. Organizations have social responsibilities beyond merely obeying laws and following regulations.
   - How are such efforts measured?
     A *corporate social audit* measures the effects of positive social programs and subtracts the negative effects of business (for example, pollution) to get a net social benefit.

10. Describe different views toward corporate responsibility and how these views impact the ethical standards a company may set.

10. There is uncertainty among top managers concerning a corporation's responsibility in setting ethical standards.
    - What are the three major viewpoints concerning corporate responsibility for ethical standards?
      Those holding the *invisible hand* philosophy contend that businesses should abide by the laws and let ethics be regulated by the invisible hand of the free market system. The *hand of government* philosophy holds that the law and the political process should regulate ethical objectives. The *hand of management* philosophy encourages corporations to apply ethics to corporate decisions and managers to apply ethics in implementing corporate decisions.

11. Corporate values are instilled by the leadership and example of strong top managers. These values become part of the corporate culture.

   ■ How can businesses communicate their values to employees?

   Many companies have developed ethical codes that outline their moral expectations. In order to be effective, the codes must be enforced and employees must be held accountable if they violate them.

   ■ How can companies and individuals live by these ethical codes when there are so many pressures not to?

   Blanchard and Peale recommend building inner strength to resist such pressure by practicing what they call the five Ps of ethical power: purpose, pride, patience, persistence, and perspective. These are the steps one must take to have an "ethics-based management" system as discussed in the chapter title.

11. Describe the role of corporate culture in determining business ethics and describe the practices corporations can use to foster ethical behavior.

GETTING INVOLVED

1. Go to the library and look up the Uniform Commercial Code. Take a few minutes to review what it covers, and report your findings back to class.
2. While at the library, check to see if there are any books on business law. Go through a business law book and read some of the cases cited. Get a feel for both statutory law and common law. Does the subject seem interesting enough to take a course in it? You should in any case, because the law is extremely important to business.
3. Discuss the merits of increased legislation versus self-regulation to prevent deceptive business practices. Which is better for society and business in the long run? Defend your answer.
4. Where do you see leadership emerging to improve the moral standards of the United States? What could you do to support such leadership?

CASE ONE   **JOHNSON & JOHNSON AND DU PONT DO WHAT IS RIGHT**

PRACTICING MANAGEMENT DECISIONS

One company that has demonstrated its social responsiveness and social responsibility is Johnson & Johnson. Its troubles began in 1982, when seven Chicagoans died after taking poisoned Tylenol capsules. It cost Johnson & Johnson and its McNeil Laboratories subsidiary $100 million to pull Tylenol capsules off the shelf and reintroduce a new package. The new package had three tamper-resistant features—a sealed carton, a shrink-wrapped seal over the bottle cap, and a foil seal under the cap. Johnson & Johnson received much favorable publicity for its quick action, and sales of Tylenol went back up.

In 1986, a 23-year-old woman died from another poisoned Tylenol capsule. A second tainted bottle was found in a store nearby. Johnson & Johnson again responded by pulling all the product off the shelves and replacing them with "caplets," or capsule-shaped tablets. The cost was estimated to be $150 million this time. Johnson & Johnson has said it will not return Tylenol capsules to the market. The Tylenol brand is a $525 million product for the company. It hopes consumers will adapt to the new "caplets" that are tamper resistant, but not tamper proof. Johnson & Johnson did what they felt was the right thing to do even though the decision cost them millions of dollars.

Du Pont is another company that is willing to take losses to do what is right. In this case, we are talking about a $2.7 *billion* market for chlorofluorocarbons (CFCs). Why is Du Pont concerned about CFCs? Because they contribute to the harm of the earth's ozone layer. Du Pont has called for the end of production of these chemicals that are so important in the making of refrigerators, air conditioners, and many other products. The task will require worldwide cooperation and good substitutes. It will cost hundreds of millions of dollars in research and new plant construction. Nonetheless, Du Pont feels the survival of the planet is more important than a few million dollars spent on research and development to make a substitute product. Again, Du Pont is doing what is right.

DECISION QUESTIONS

1. There is no way to make products on the shelves completely tamper proof. Was Tylenol wise to cease production of capsules while other companies continue selling them?

2. It is not against the law to sell over-the-counter drugs in capsules. Is it ethical? What obligation do producers of such capsules have to the public, if any?

3. Johnson & Johnson and Du Pont decided to do what was right and to do it as quickly as possible. That could have cost both firms much money, but that was not the criterion for making the decision. The criterion was, "Is it the right thing to do?" How can a business know what is the right thing to do? Should an executive have the right to make such decisions when the effect on stockholders may be negative? How would you go about resolving such issues in businesses in general?

Source: "Two-Time Loser," *Advertising Age,* February 17, 1986, pp. 1 ff; Bill Powell and Marton Kasindorf, "The Tylenol Rescue," *Newsweek,* March 3, 1986, pp. 52–53; Laurie Hays, "CFC Curb to Save Ozone Will Be Costly," *The Wall Street Journal,* March 28, 1988, p. 6; and Michael Weisskopf and Malcolm Gladwell, "Du Pont Taking Big Risk with CFC Phase-Out," *The Washington Post,* March 23, 1988, pp. B1 and B4.

CASE TWO   THE PROFIT OBJECTIVE AND SOCIAL RESPONSIBILITY

Milton Friedman, an economist from the University of Chicago, has argued that "Few trends could throughly undermine the very foundation of our free society as the acceptance by corporate officials of a social responsibility other than to make as much money for stockholders as possible." Basically, Friedman's argument for this position goes like this:

1. Business exists to make a profit.
2. When a business makes a profit, it uses scarce resources efficiently, provides desired products and services, creates jobs, and serves society.
3. Business involvement in the social/political process will only increase the political influence of business. Because big business has more to spend, influence will be concentrated in big business.
4. The business of business is business.
5. Business profits belong to stockholders, not the public.

On the other hand, there is a sizable body of literature that says that business has a social responsibility beyond profit. Some points of this argument include the following:

1. As part of society, business should be involved in solving society's problems.
2. It is in the self-interest of business to help solve society's problems.
3. Results have not come from leaving social problems to government.
4. Everyone has a responsibility to help his fellow citizen, including businesspeople.
5. Business has plenty of money to spend on social programs if it wanted.

DECISION QUESTIONS

1. Does the president of a firm have a right and obligation to use corporate profits for social programs? To whom do the profits belong?
2. Does a business executive have the same social responsibility as any other citizen, or is his or her responsibility greater? Why?
3. What socially responsible behavior could be profitable as well as socially beneficial?

Source: Milton Friedman, *Capitalism and Freedom* (Chicago: University of Chicago Press, 1963), p. 133.

The business world extends beyond the borders of the United States. The future of American business is directly tied to the future of world business. Environmental issues such as acid rain are *world* problems. International trade directly affects the economies of individual nations. This book ends by looking at international business. People over much of the world go to bed hungry; poverty and disease still exist in the world (including in the United States). One approach to such world problems is free world trade conducted by compassionate, honest, and committed businesspeople. We shall explore the fascinating subject of international business next.

INTERNATIONAL BUSINESS

24

LEARNING GOALS

After you have read and studied this chapter, you should be able to:

1. Discuss the increasing importance of the international market and the roles of comparative advantage and absolute advantage in international trade.

2. Explain how the marketing motto "Find a need and fill it" applies to international business.

3. Apply the terminology used in international business.

4. Describe the status of the United States in international business.

5. Illustrate the strategies used in reaching global markets.

6. Discuss the hurdles of trading in world markets.

7. Debate the advantages and disadvantages of trade protectionism.

8. Describe the role of multinational corporations.

9. Identify and describe international trade organizations and trade agreements.

10. Discuss the future of international trade.

KEY TERMS

absolute advantage, *p. 770*
balance of payments, *p.774*
balance of trade, *p. 774*
bartering, *p. 782*
common market, *p. 792*
comparative advantage theory, *p. 769*
countertrading, *p. 782*
debtor nation, *p. 777*
dumping, *p. 774*
embargo, *p. 787*
exchange rate, *p. 774*
exporting, *p. 772*
export trading companies, *p. 778*
Foreign Corrupt Practices Act of 1978, *p. 785*
foreign subsidiary, *p. 779*

General Agreement on Tariffs and Trade (GATT), *p. 792*
importing, *p. 772*
import quota, *p. 787*
international joint venture, *p. 780*
International Monetary Fund (IMF), *p. 791*
licensing, *p. 779*
mercantilism, *p. 787*
multinational corporation (MNC), *p. 789*
producers' cartels, *p. 792*
protective tariffs, *p. 787*
revenue tariffs, *p. 787*
trade protectionism, *p. 774*
World Bank, *p. 792*

Virginia Kamsky.

PROFILE   VIRGINIA KAMSKY, CHINA TRADER

The road to international trade is not always obvious, even to the most successful. Take Virginia Kamsky, for example. When Virginia was 10, she read a book about China called *The Good Earth* by Pearl Buck. She decided to learn Chinese, so at 11 she signed up for an introductory course in Chinese at the China Institute in New York City. At 13, she enrolled in a State Department program that trained high school students in Chinese. At 17, Ms. Kamsky spent her senior year at Fujen Catholic University in Taiwan and became fluent in Chinese.

Ms. Kamsky went on to Princeton to study Japanese and classical Chinese. She took graduate courses in the Woodrow Wilson School of Public and International Affairs. That summer, Virginia took her first macroeconomics course and became fascinated by economics as well as China and Japan.

A year later, she was an economic analyst for the U.S. embassy in Singapore when Chase Manhattan Bank lured her away to join their global credit training program. She went to Tokyo to be assistant treasurer of Chase. Kamsky became the first and only woman bank officer in Japan at age 23. Handling credit transactions at the bank, Ms. Kamsky became interested in world trade. That led her back to New York where she was able to learn more about trade as a lending officer.

One day, Chase's president had to go to China. He took Ms. Kamsky along because of her language skills and knowledge. She loved it and has been part of Chinese trade ever since. She became vice president in charge of the bank's corporate division in China. She spent much of her time helping the bank's clients get through the bureaucracy, paperwork, and cultural details involved in negotiating real estate projects and trading contracts of all kinds. Eventually, Ms. Kamsky left Chase to start her own firm called Kamsky Associates.

Kamsky Associates has been responsible for helping U.S. and foreign firms sign more than a billion dollars in joint ventures and trade agreements with China. That represents more than 100 projects in different industries—40,000 tons of zinc concentrate from Germany, and the technology to build a chocolate factory in China. Virginia Kamsky is one of the most successful traders in the world.

Ms. Kamksy represents the successful international businessperson of the future. That is, one who knows several languages and goes into countries where trade is minimal and creates huge trade agreements that affect the whole world. Who would have guessed 20 years ago that China would become such a large trading partner? Europe is joining together to become a trading unit that will rival the United States in size and power. The future of U.S. growth is directly tied to this growth in world trade. That is what this chapter is all about.

Source: Susan Hazen-Hammond, "One Smart Cookie," *Business Week Careers*, June 1988, pp. 15–21; and Pranay Bupta, "Man in the Middle," *Forbes*, April 25, 1988, p. 132.

THE INTERNATIONAL MARKET

Throughout this book we have been talking about opportunities in various careers. There is no question that there will be many challenging careers available in high-tech industries, in the service sector in general, and in small businesses. What doesn't show up as clearly in most projections of future careers is the potential for careers in international business, especially international marketing.

Have you stopped to think about the possibilities of a career in international business? Maybe a few statistics will awaken more interest:

- There are about 250 *million* people in the United States, but there are about 5.5 *billion* potential customers in the world market.
- Every year, the world's population increases by some 90 million people. That means as many people as live in all of England, Wales, Scotland, Ireland, Sweden, and Norway are added to world markets *every year*. Think of all those potential customers.
- Combined world exports and imports exceed $4 *trillion* per year!
- The United States is the largest importer and exporter in the world.
- The 1989 Pontiac Le Mans was designed in West Germany, the engines were produced in South Korea and Australia, the radio was from Singapore, and the sheet metal from Japan; South Korea also produced the tires, the electrical wiring harness, the battery, and rear axle components. The transmissions came from the United States and Canada. The fuel pump and fuel injection systems were from the United States, but final assembly took place in South Korea—all this for an American car![1]

These figures show that international trade is big business today and will be even more important in the coming decades. Will you be ready? Are you studying a foreign language in school? Have you talked with anyone about the excitement and rewards of traveling to and trading with other countries?

The purpose of this chapter is to expose you to international business, including its potential and problems. Because most career advisers do not say much about international business, there are not many students preparing for such a career. That means that the demand for students with such training is likely to exceed the supply as international trade grows. Maybe you will be one of the lucky ones to find a challenging and rewarding career in international business.

WHY TRADE WITH OTHER NATIONS?

There are several reasons why one country would trade with other countries. First, no nation, even a technologically advanced one, can produce all the products that its people want and need. Second, even if a country became self-sufficient, other nations would demand trade with that country to meet the needs of their people. Third, some nations have an abundance of natural resources and lack of technological know-how. Other countries (for example, Japan) have sophisticated technology, but few natural resources. Trade relations enable each nation to produce what it is most capable of producing and to buy what it needs in a mutually beneficial exchange relationship.

The Theories of Comparative and Absolute Advantage

International trade is the exchange of goods and services across national borders. Exchanges between and among countries involve more than goods and services, however. Countries also exchange art, athletes (for international competition and friendly relations), cultural events (plays, dance performances), medical advances, space exploration (for example, the U.S.-Soviet space programs), and labor. The guiding principle behind international economic exchanges is the economic **comparative advantage theory.** This theory states that a country should produce and sell to other countries those products that it produces most effectively and efficiently and should buy from other countries those products it cannot produce as effectively or efficiently.

comparative advantage theory
Theory that asserts that a country should produce and sell to other countries those products that it produces most efficiently and effectively and should buy from other countries those products it cannot produce as effectively or efficiently.

770 PART VII Risk Management, Ethics, and International Business

FIGURE 24–1

The most successful exporters. Boeing makes airplanes. MGM makes movies that are popular overseas. The rest of the major exporters make products such as computers, machinery, coal, and tobacco.

COMPANY*	EXPORTS AS PERCENT OF TOTAL SALES
Boeing	45%
MGM/UA Communications	38
Advanced Micro Devices	37
Pittston	36
Teradyne	34
Computervision	30
Caterpillar	28
Universal Leaf Tobacco	26
Cray Research	24
McDonnell Douglas	22

* Chosen from *Business Week,* top 1,000 companies with exports of $100 million or more. Excludes shipping companies and sales by companies to their overseas affiliates.

Source: Reprinted from the November 16, 1987 issue of *Business Week,* by special permission, copyright © 1987 by McGraw-Hill, Inc.

FIGURE 24–2

Leading U.S. imports and exports.

LEADING IMPORTS	LEADING EXPORTS
Machinery and transportation equipment	Aircraft and transportation equipment
Oil and oil products	Office machines and computers
Apparel	Professional and scientific instruments
Telecommunications equipment	Specialized machinery
Chemicals	
Crude materials such as rubber, wood, and paper	

Source: Government reports, 1988.

The United States has a comparative advantage in producing many goods and services such as those in high-tech fields. Figure 24–1 lists the most successful exporters selling over $100 million or more. On the other hand, the United States does not have a comparative advantage in producing some shoes, clothes, videotape recorders, and other products that it imports. Figure 24–2 lists some of the leading import and export products for the United States.

absolute advantage
When a country has a monopoly on producing a product or is able to produce it at a cost below that of all other countries.

A country has an **absolute advantage** if it has a monopoly on the production of a specific product or is able to produce it more cheaply than all other countries. For instance, South Africa dominates diamond production. There are very few instances of absolute advantage in today's competitive economy.

GETTING INVOLVED IN INTERNATIONAL TRADE

Students often wonder which U.S. firms are best for finding a job in international business. Naturally, the discussion focuses on *large* multinational firms (for example, GM, Ford, GE, IBM, Du Pont, and Kodak) that have large overseas accounts. But the real secret to success in overseas business may be with *small* businesses. Getting started is often a matter of observation, determination, and risk. What does that mean? First of all, it is important to travel overseas to get some feel for the culture and lifestyles of various countries to see if you really want to work and trade

INTERNATIONAL TRADE IN FARM PRODUCTS

One area of promise in the international trade of goods is in farm commodities. To see where the U.S. is going in this area, let's look at California, which is the leader in agricultural production (beating Iowa by $14.5 billion to $9.1 billion). California is also the country's largest exporter. In 1987, such exports reached $3.3 billion and included everything from asparagus to raisins.

More and more foreign countries have learned to become self-sufficient in basic crops such as rice, wheat, and corn. That leaves the market for high-value farm commodities such as soybean oil, flour, and fresh fruits and vegetables. Such products make up about half of California's foreign sales. Almost 60 percent of California's crops go to the Pacific Rim countries, half of them to Japan. The state offers matching funds to growers who promote their products in foreign lands. Many farmers are finding new opportunities overseas through federal and state programs and through their own initiatives. It is helpful to learn about foreign tastes and legal restrictions. For example, Japan limits beef imports, but allows imports of cattle. One rancher took advantage of that loophole and sold $11 million of cattle to Japan.

Washington, Oregon, and Florida are also starting to benefit from the demand for high-value crops. Other states are likely to follow. The bottom line is that farmers, like all other businesspeople in the United States, are learning that the growth market is overseas. With the government's help and some lifting of import restrictions by foreign countries, farmers will see new prosperity in international trade.

Source: "California's Classy Crop Cornucopia," *Fortune,* June 6, 1988, p. 91.

This photo shows a soybean farmer. Soybeans are an important crop in international markets. You might enjoy a computer simulation/game that lets you practice trading soybeans on the international commodity exchanges. Such a game is available free to your instructor from the publisher of this text.

overseas. When you are in foreign countries you will notice that most have few of the material advantages (goods and services) that are widely available in the United States.

For example, a traveler in one part of Africa noticed that there was no ice available for drinks, for keeping foods fresh, and so on. Further research showed that, in fact, there was no ice factory for hundreds of miles, yet the market seemed huge. The man returned to the United States, found some venture capital, and returned to Africa to build an ice-making plant. Much negotiation was necessary with the authorities (negotiation best done by locals who know the system), and the plant was built. Now the man is indeed wealthy.

Lyle Fox was in Japan working as a journalist. He discovered that there were no bagels in the part of Japan in which he lived. Using an old family recipe, Mr. Fox and his Japanese wife began producing bagels and selling them in the local market.

Mike Solomko bought a franchise to sell West Bend Cookware in Japan. Today, his company has 400 salespeople selling pots and pans door-to-door in Japan. Mike appears on Japanese TV as "Super Solomko." You can see that international business is something like domestic business in that the goal is to find a need and fill it. The difference is that one has to do much more preparation to buy and sell in foreign markets.

KEN HAKUTA'S WACKY WALLWALKER

One day, 3½-year-old Kenzo Hakuta received a present from his grandparents in Tokyo. It was a plastic toy that looked like a giant spider. You threw the toy against the wall. It stuck there briefly, and then began flipping over and creeping down the wall in a twitching motion. The toy was great fun to watch. It was called a WallWalker. Kenzo's father, Ken, a Harvard graduate, thought the toy had great potential. He learned that nobody had bought the North American rights to the toy, and so he acquired them and began selling the toys himself. He began with an order of 300,000. Soon, he had orders for 15 million WallWalkers from stores like Woolworth's, Kmart, and Revco.

Eventually, Mr. Hakuta built a WallWalker plant in Korea and began promoting the toy as a premium to be given away with other products. Soon Ken had sold over 27 million WallWalkers and was going strong. Mr. Hakuta believes the potential for this toy is fantastic.

Mr. Hakuta kept his eyes open and found a product overseas that he felt could be popular in the United States, and made a fortune. His story is just one of hundreds, or even thousands, that describe the success of importing foreign goods to the United States.

Source: Robert B. Harrow, Jr., "D.C. Entrepreneur Sticks With Wacky WallWalker Idea," *The Washington Post*, February 4, 1985, p. 7 of Washington Business, © *The Washington Post*, 1985.

Importing Goods and Services

importing
Buying products from another country.

Importing is *buying* products from another country. Students often find that importing goods into the United States can be quite profitable. Foreign students attending U.S. universities often notice that some products widely available in their countries are not available in the United States, or are more costly here. Such products include food (witness the growth of Vietnamese restaurants in large American cities), household goods (including furniture, art, rugs, lamps, tile, and pottery), and manufactured goods (motorcycles, watches, cameras, videotape recorders, autos, and TV sets). By working with foreign producers and finding some working capital, these students have become major importers.

Executives from Minnetonka, Inc., of Chaska, Minnesota, were browsing in a West German supermarket when they noticed a fascinating new product—toothpaste in a pump dispenser. The company contacted Henkel, the German manufacturer, and together they introduced the product into the United States as Check-Up toothpaste. It was so popular that Colgate, Crest, and other brands soon followed with their own versions of the pump. Maybe you, too, could find such products to bring back to the United States (see the box called Ken Hakuta's Wacky Wallwalker).

Exporting Goods and Services

exporting
Selling products to another country.

Exporting is *selling* products to another country. Once you decide to get into international trade, you would be surprised at what you can sell overseas. Who would think, for example, that a U.S. firm could sell beer in West Germany where so many good beers come from? Yet right around the corner from a famous beer hall in Munich one can purchase Samuel Adam's Boston Lager. Some 16,000 cases have been sold, and a local licensing agreement will assure more sales to come. You no doubt have heard that the Italians make the best shoes. Yet the Allen-Edmonds

One way to participate in international exchange is to import fine products from other countries. This picture shows the Tullycross Fine Irish Imports store in Philadelphia, which sells quality goods from Ireland. No doubt you have seen similar stores selling shoes from Italy, small appliances from all over Europe, and so on. If not, shop around and see if such stores might be an interesting career possibility.

Shoe Corporation of Wisconsin sells high-quality shoes to the Italians. But you haven't heard anything yet. Can you imagine selling sand to the Middle East? Meridan Group sells a special kind of sand used in swimming pool filters. How about starting a laundry in China? Fred Chao of San Francisco has 24 SuperKleen shops in China. Lakewood Industries sells disposable chopsticks to Japan and a Rhode Island fishery sells sushi to Japan.[2]

So what can you sell to other countries? You can sell them just about anything of quality you can sell in the United States. You can sell snow plows to the Saudi Arabians. Why? They use them to plow sand off their driveways. All kinds of franchises are doing well in other countries. There are 7-Eleven stores in Japan that sell Pepperidge Farm cookies. Just about any good or service that is used in the United States is needed in other countries and the competition is not nearly as stiff for most of them. That is not to say that selling overseas is easy, as we shall see next.

To get started in exporting, write for "The Basic Guide to Exporting," Government Printing Office, Superintendent of Documents, Washington, D.C. 20402. More advice can be found in *Business America*, a trade magazine published by Commerce's International Trade Administration. You order it from the Government Printing Office as well. You can also call the Small Business Administration at (617) 350–5096 and ask for a copy of *Exportise*.

TERMS OF INTERNATIONAL TRADE

When you read business periodicals or listen to news reports, you will see and hear terms relating to international business. Many of these terms may be familiar to you, but it will be helpful to review them before we discuss international business in more detail.

FIGURE 24-3

Balance of trade in the 1980s.
Although export sales are rising, imports are rising faster, leaving the United States with a negative balance of trade. Balance can be restored by increasing exports, cutting back on imports, or by doing both.

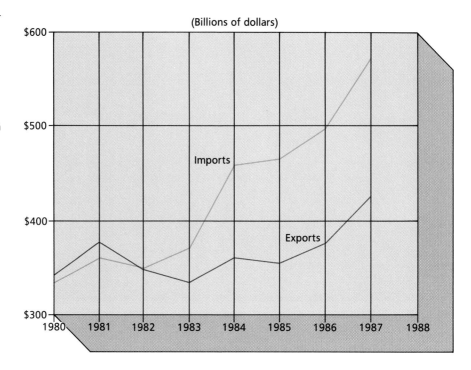

balance of trade
The relationship of exports to imports.

Balance of Trade   The **balance of trade** is the relationship of exports to imports. A *favorable balance of trade* occurs when the value of exports exceeds imports. An *unfavorable balance of trade* or trade deficit occurs when the value of imports exceeds exports (see Figure 24–3). It is easy to understand why countries prefer to export more than they import. If I sell you $200 worth of goods and buy only $100 worth, I have an extra $100 available to buy other things. However, I'm in an *unfavorable* position if I buy $200 worth of goods and sell only $100.

balance of payments
The difference between money coming into a country (from exports) and money leaving the country (for imports) *plus* money flows from other factors such as tourism, foreign aid, and military expenditures.

Balance of Payments   The **balance of payments** is the difference between money coming into a country (from exports) and money leaving the country (for imports) *plus* money flows from other factors such as tourism, foreign aid, and military expenditures. The amount of money flowing into or out of a country for tourism and other reasons may offset a trade imbalance. The goal is always to have more money flowing into the country than flowing out of the country. This is called a *favorable balance of payments*. In 1987, the United States had an *unfavorable balance of payments* of about $161 billion—that is, the amount of money flowing out of the U.S. was about $161 billion more than the money flowing into the country (see Figure 24–4).

dumping
Selling products for less in a foreign country than is charged in the producing country.

Dumping   **Dumping** is the practice of selling products in foreign countries for less than you charge for the same products in your own country. South Korea, for example, has been accused of such dumping practices. The United States has laws against dumping, specifying that foreign firms must price their products to include 10 percent overhead costs plus 8 percent profit margin. Dumping is hard to prove, however. Charges of dumping have been made against manufacturers of several products, including steel, motorcycles and microwave ovens.

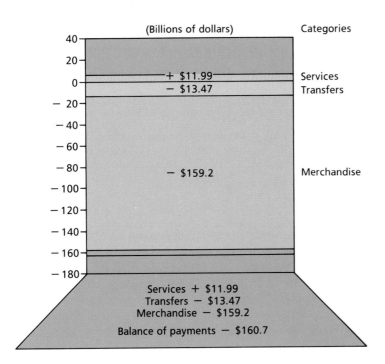

(Billions of dollars)

40
20
0
− 20
− 40
− 60
− 80
− 100
− 120
− 140
− 160
− 180

Categories

+ $11.99   Services
− $13.47   Transfers

− $159.2   Merchandise

Services + $11.99
Transfers − $13.47
Merchandise − $159.2
Balance of payments − $160.7

FIGURE 24–4

Balance of payments. This figure shows that the service sector is a positive factor in the balance of payments. However, it is far outweighed by the negative flows in merchandise trade and transfers.

Trade Protectionism   **Trade protectionism** is the use of government regulations to limit the import of goods and services. Countries often use trade protectionism measures to protect their industries against dumping and foreign competition that hurts domestic industry. Protectionism is based on the theory that such practices will help domestic producers survive and grow, producing more jobs. We shall discuss trade protectionism in detail later.

trade protectionism
The use of government regulations to limit the import of goods and services, based on the theory that domestic producers can survive and grow, producing more jobs.

Exchange Rate   The **exchange rate** is the value of one currency relative to the currencies of other countries. *High value of the dollar* means that a dollar would buy more foreign goods (or would be traded for more foreign currency) than normal. *Lowering the value of the dollar* means that a dollar can buy less overseas than it once did. That makes foreign goods more expensive because it takes more dollars to buy them. It also makes American goods cheaper to foreign buyers because it takes less foreign currency to buy American goods. The net effect is to sell more overseas and buy less foreign products, lessening the trade deficit.

exchange rate
The value of one currency relative to the currencies of other countries.

Much has been said in the business journals about the exchange rate of the dollar against foreign currencies all through the 1980s. The reason for the discussion is that the value of the dollar was so high in the early 1980s that foreign goods were cheaper to buy. U.S. citizens began buying more overseas, which hurt the U.S. balance of trade. A "group of five" countries (U.S., Britain, France, West Germany, and Japan) banded together to lower the value of the dollar and thus (1) increase the export market for U.S. goods and (2) decrease imports. That effort was successful. At the same time, exports increased so that the trade deficit came down some. At the end of the decade, the value of the dollar rose again, threatening to increase the trade deficit.

Now that you understand some terms, we can begin discussing international trade in more depth. The first question to address is how the United States is doing in world trade. First let's check your progress.

PROGRESS CHECK

- Can you cite statistics to show why international trade is the future for U.S. business (world population, size of market, growth of market)?

- What is the difference between comparative advantage and absolute advantage?

- What is the difference between balance of trade and balance of payments?

- Can you explain how changes in the value of the dollar affect imports and exports?

TRADING IN WORLD MARKETS: THE U.S. EXPERIENCE

Fully 95 percent of the world's population lies outside the United States and is growing 70 percent faster than the American population. However, the United States in general has never been very good at exporting. America's exports in 1988 were only 6.6 percent of its GNP. This compares with 26 percent in West Germany, 25 percent in Canada, and 10.5 percent in Japan.[3]

Although the United States does not export a great deal compared to other countries, for many years the United States exported more goods and services than it imported. In 1985, however, the United States bought more goods from other nations than it sold to other nations. Remember, this is called a trade deficit or unfavorable balance of trade. Figure 24–5 shows the countries with which the United States had such deficits in 1986 and 1987. The highest trade deficit is with Japan. For that reason, the U.S. and the Japanese governments are trying to devise strategies to make the trade balance more even.

In 1988, the trade deficit for goods reached over $137 billion. However, the United States has a surplus of trading in the service sector. In 1985, the United States sold over $35 billion more services than it purchased from other nations.

FIGURE 24–5

Countries with which the United States has trade deficits.
Note that the newly industrialized countries (NICs) have taken the lead from Western Europe led by Taiwan and South Korea. Note too that the largest deficit is with Japan.

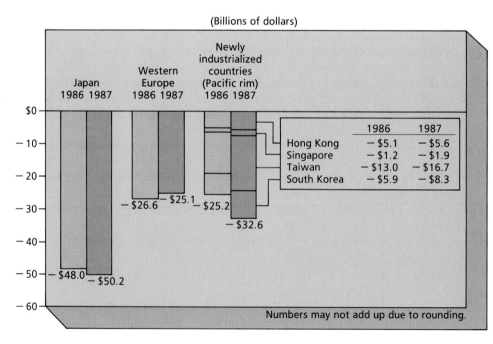

(Billions of dollars)

	1986	1987
Hong Kong	− $5.1	− $5.6
Singapore	− $1.2	− $1.9
Taiwan	− $13.0	− $16.7
South Korea	− $5.9	− $8.3

Numbers may not add up due to rounding.

The balance of payments is the broadest measure of foreign trade in goods, services, and investments. As you know, it measures the net flow of money between a country and other countries with which it trades. In 1986, the United States had a balance of payments deficit of about $138 billion. In 1987, the deficit was about $154 billion. It fell in 1988 to just over $135 billion. In fact, the United States has now become a **debtor nation.** That is, a country that owes more money to foreign creditors than foreign debtors owe to it and that owns fewer assets in foreign countries than foreigners own in it. This was the first time since 1914 that the United States has been a debtor nation.

In fact, the United States has become the world's *largest* debtor nation. U.S. debt was $269.2 billion in 1986 and went up by another $99 billion in 1987 (see Figure 24-6). The total figure is more than the debt of the next three debtor nations—Canada, Brazil, and Mexico—combined.[4] Paying off just the interest on such a debt could lower GNP by as much as 2 percent a year if such debt continues. This is quite a turnaround for the United States because in 1981 we were a creditor nation with other nations owing us some $14 billion. What happened?

What has been happening is that the devalued dollar lowered the cost of buying American assets. In addition to the devalued dollar, Black Monday's stock market crash lowered the price of many stocks, allowing foreign investors to buy stock in American companies at "bargain basement" prices. Stock prices have since risen to precrash levels. In short, foreign firms are buying office buildings and other assets in the United States faster than U.S. firms are buying similar assets in other countries. Some people see this as a sign of weakness, while others see it as a sign of strength.

Some Americans view the foreign purchase of American assets as the "selling of America." Warren Buffett, a prominent investor from Omaha, puts it this way: "We are much like a wealthy family that annually sells acreage so that it can sustain a lifestyle unwarranted by its current output. Until the plantation is gone, it's all pleasure and no pain. In the end, however, the family will have traded the life of an owner for the life of a tenant farmer."[5] Eventually, the family's standard of living

debtor nation
Country that owes more money to other nations than they owe it.

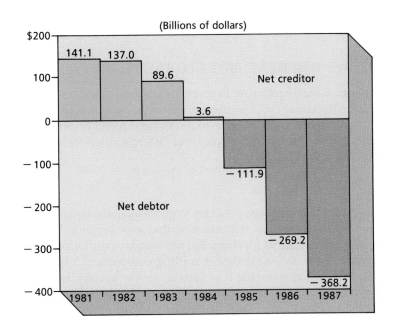

(Billions of dollars)

FIGURE 24–6

The growth in U.S. debt to other countries. This figure shows that the United States has become a debtor nation, according to Commerce Department figures. The way the figures are calculated is being questioned, however, because U.S. firms own much property overseas that is valued at cost rather than true value. The adjusted figures show more of a balance.

declines. Consider that in 1988 the United States paid more than $24 billion in interest alone to foreigners—that's more than the federal government spent on our schools. It is feared that foreigners will gain greater control of the American economy as their U.S. assets increase.

Those who view foreign investment in the United States as a sign of strength contend that foreign firms are investing in the United States because the U.S. economy over the last several years has been very strong. Such assets as buildings and such investments as stock in U.S. firms are more attractive than in other countries. When a British or Japanese firm buys a U.S. firm, that increases our national debt on the records, but to optimists that is not really a debt: it is an investment in America.[6]

Contrary to what some people imply, it may not necessarily be a good sign if the nation's debt swings back and we become a creditor nation again. It may mean that the United States is no longer perceived as the strong economic leader it is now and nations are no longer investing in our businesses' stock or building new plants here.[7] If you are getting the idea that the national income accounting that determines a nation's debt status is confusing, you are right. You may need to take a course in international economics or international accounting if you plan to get involved in international trade. This will help you to better understand what is behind the statistics.

THINKING IT THROUGH   You have read that some 95 percent of the world's population lives outside the United States, but only a small percentage of U.S. companies engage in world trade. Why is that? What do such figures indicate about the future potential for increasing U.S. exports? What do they say about future careers in international business?

In which countries would you enjoy living other than the United States? What languages do they speak? What are the trade possibilities? Are you missing out on an opportunity by failing to take other languages in school and courses in international business?

STRATEGIES FOR REACHING GLOBAL MARKETS

An organization may participate in international trade in many ways, including exporting and importing, joint venturing, licensing, creating subsidiaries, franchising, and countertrading. Pay close attention to these topics because they represent future careers that will be both challenging and rewarding for the savvy college graduate.

Exporting

Because so many U.S. firms are reluctant to go through the trouble of establishing trading relationships overseas, it makes sense that some organization would step in to negotiate such exchanges for them. In fact, Congress authorized such organizations in 1982. They are called **export trading companies.** A good place to get experience in international trade is at such an export house. Their function is to match buyers and sellers from different countries. Although the idea sounds great, the implementation of such trades has been less than expected. *The Wall Street*

export trading companies
Companies that attempt to match buyers and sellers from different countries.

Journal reported that, "A principal problem of U.S. export trading companies is that they tend to lack experience and expertise." International trade is so new to most U.S. firms that hardly anyone knows how to do it well.

Some companies handle exporting functions internally in the form of an export department or an export section in marketing. GE has 60 bilingual workers with M.B.A.s (Masters of Business Administration) in its trading department, and 70 percent of them are foreign born. Students *who learn foreign languages in school* and enter international trade have an opportunity to improve the status of export trading firms and make good money besides. By the time you graduate from college, firms such as GE Trading may be doing billions of dollars worth of foreign trade. The opportunities are there for those who prepare. Opportunities also exist for smaller entrepreneurs who are internationally oriented.

Licensing

A firm may decide to service a growing overseas market by **licensing** the manufacture of its product by a foreign producer on a royalty basis. The company sends representatives to the foreign producer to help set up the production process and may provide a variety of services such as marketing advice.

A licensing agreement can be beneficial to a firm in several different ways. Through licensing, an organization can gain additional revenues from a product that it would not have normally generated domestically. In addition, foreign licensees often must purchase start-up supplies, component materials, and consulting services from the licensing firm. In some instances, these services extend beyond the start-up stage and become an ongoing source of additional revenue. Coke and Pepsi often enter foreign markets through licensing agreements that typically extend into long-term service contracts. One final advantage of licensing worth noting is that licensors spend little or no money to produce and market the product. These costs come from the licensee's pocket. Therefore, licensees generally work very hard to see that the product succeeds in their market. The more sales, the more royalties.

Unfortunately, licensing agreements may provide some disadvantages to a company. One major problem is that often a firm must grant licensing rights to its product for an extended period, maybe as long as 20 years. If a product experiences remarkable growth in the foreign market, the bulk of the revenues go to the licensee. Perhaps even more threatening is the fact that a licensing firm is actually selling *its* expertise in a product area. If a foreign licensor learns the technology, it may break the agreement and begin to produce a similar product on its own. If legal remedies are not available, the licensing firm loses its trade secrets, not to mention the agreed upon royalties.

Creating Subsidiaries

As the size of a foreign market expands, a firm may want to establish a foreign subsidiary. A **foreign subsidiary** is a company that is owned by another company (parent company) in a foreign country. Such a subsidiary would operate much like a domestic firm with production, distribution, promotion, pricing, and other business functions under the control of the foreign subsidiary's management. Of course, the legal requirements of both the home and host country would have to be observed. As you might suspect, the primary advantage of a subsidiary is that the

licensing
Agreement in which a producer allows a foreign company to produce its product in exchange for royalties.

Coke has licensing agreements in several countries. This is a Coke can as sold in China. It is sometimes amusing to see American products overseas with pictures of Mickey Mouse or other well-known U.S. characters. Foreign companies buy the rights to use such images on their products.

foreign subsidiary
A company owned by another company (parent company) in a foreign country.

You will see American franchises everywhere you go in the world. This McDonald's franchise is in Paris. You may enjoy visiting other countries and imagining yourself owning an ice cream franchise or a car rental firm. The opportunities are great for those seeking world travel and international living.

company maintains complete control over any technology or expertise it may possess. Additionally, after tax obligations are paid, profits generated belong exclusively to the parent firm.

The major shortcoming associated with creating a subsidiary is that the company is committing a large amount of funds and technology within foreign boundaries. Should relations with the host country falter, the firm's assets could be taken over by the foreign government.

Franchising

Franchising is popular both domestically and in international markets. Firms such as McDonald's, 7-Eleven, Ramada Inn, Avis, Hertz, Travelodge, and Dunkin' Donuts have many overseas units operated by franchisees. For example, PepsiCo's Kentucky Fried Chicken has more than 2,700 units in 56 nations.[8] In all, U.S. franchisers operated 31,626 foreign outlets in 1986.[9]

Franchisers have to be careful to adapt in the countries they serve. For example, Kentucky Fried Chicken's first 11 Hong Kong outlets failed within two years. Apparently, the chicken was too greasy and messy to be eaten with fingers by the fastidious people of Hong Kong. McDonald's also made a mistake when entering the Amsterdam market. It originally set up operations in the suburbs, as it does in the United States, but soon learned that Europeans mostly live in the cities. Therefore, McDonald's began to open outlets downtown. There are now thousands of franchises operating internationally. McDonald's franchises now serve beer in Germany and wine in France. Other franchises are doing well also. Have you ever thought of opening a yogurt or ice cream franchise in one of the warm, exotic places where balmy breezes blow and life is relatively easy? The opportunities are there for the internationally minded businessperson.

Joint Ventures

international joint venture
A partnership in which companies from two or more different countries join to undertake a major project.

An **international joint venture** is a partnership in which companies from two different countries join to undertake a major project. News reports of such alliances have increased 47 percent annually in the past decade. A survey of affiliations by U.S.-based companies reported about 12,000 in which the American company owned a 10–50 percent equity position in a foreign firm.[10] It is often hard to gain entry into a communist country like China, whose economy is centrally planned.

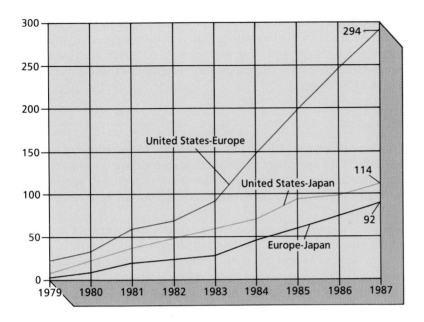

FIGURE 24–7

The trend in international joint ventures.
Joint ventures became very popular in the 1980s, as the figure shows. Such ventures leaped from less than 50 to almost 300 per year. The upward trend is likely to continue into the 1990s as businesses learn to think internationally.

Joint ventures often help. For example, Otis Elevator has a joint venture with Tianjin Lifts to make elevators for China. Alsthom of France makes the high-speed trains that go from Paris to Marseilles at speeds exceeding 180 miles per hour. That firm combined with Bombardier of Montreal (which has factories in the U.S.) to produce subway cars for New York. Figure 24–7 shows the trend toward more and more such joint ventures. In 1987, there were 294 new joint ventures between U.S. and European firms. There were 92 such agreements between U.S. and Japanese firms. Over 900 joint ventures between the United States and the Soviet Union were registered in 1989.[11]

Two of the more heavily publicized international joint ventures in the 1980s were the GM-Toyota plant in California and the Ford-Toyo Kogyo (Mazda) plant in Mexico. Both GM and Ford needed a small car to compete with the small Japanese cars. What better place to find the technology and experience than Japan? The GM-Toyota plant is equally owned by the two companies. The plant is called NUMMI for New United Motor Manufacturing, Inc., and makes the Chevy Nova Twin Cam with 16–valve engine.[12] Ford owns the assembly plant in Mexico, but the car is one designed by Japan's Toyo Kogyo.

These auto company ventures are merely the most *publicized* cooperative efforts. Joint ventures are nothing new in international trade. Perhaps the most visible example is the cooperation between major department stores and foreign producers of TV sets, videotape recorders, and other such goods (especially Japan). The foreign company produces the goods, and U.S. corporations provide the distribution and promotion expertise. In the United States, names such as Panasonic and Sony are as familiar as GE and Westinghouse because of joint ventures.

The benefits of international joint ventures are clear—shared technology, shared marketing expertise, entry into markets where foreign goods are not allowed unless produced locally, and shared risk. The drawbacks are not so obvious. One important one is that the partner can learn your technology and practices and go off on its own as a competitor—a rather common practice. Over time, the technology may become obsolete or the partnership may be too large to be as flexible as needed. Because of these drawbacks, such agreements need to include some provision for shared information, shared management, and procedures for evaluating the agreement and potential separation. Given such arrangements, cooperative ventures promise to be a growing phenomenon as business firms seek to expand markets overseas.

Countertrading

bartering
The exchange of merchandise for merchandise.

countertrading
Bartering among several countries.

One of the oldest forms of trade is called **bartering,** the exchange of merchandise for merchandise with no money involved. **Countertrading** is more complex than bartering in that several countries may be involved, each trading goods for goods. It has been estimated that countertrading accounts for 25 percent of all international exchanges.[13]

Examples of countertrade and bartering agreements are many. Chrysler traded its vehicles in Jamaica for bauxite. McDonnell Douglas traded jets in Yugoslavia for canned hams. General Motors has traded vehicles with China for industrial gloves and cutting tools. Telelex Media has traded television shows for advertising time in several foreign countries. Westinghouse sold a $100 million air defense radar system to Jordan in trade for phosphate.[14]

Barter is especially important to poor countries that have little cash available for trade. Such countries may barter with all kinds of raw materials, food, or whatever resources they have. Colombia has traded coffee for buses. Romania traded cement for steam engines. The Sudan pays for Pepsi concentrate with sesame seeds. Tanzania uses sisal, and Nicaragua uses sesame seeds and molasses.

With many world economies still in a state of flux, there is no question that countertrading will grow in importance in the 1990s. Trading products for products helps avoid some of the problems and hurdles experienced in global markets. After the Progress Check, we'll look at some of the major hurdles in world markets.

PROGRESS CHECK

- What does a trade deficit mean and what does it mean to be a debtor nation?
- Can you name four ways to enter foreign markets?
- What are the major benefits a firm may gain from licensing its products in foreign markets? What are the primary drawbacks?
- What are the major benefits of a joint venture in global markets? Can you name two important joint ventures that occurred in the 1980s?
- How does countertrading work? Who generally gains the most from countertrades in global markets?

HURDLES OF TRADING IN WORLD MARKETS

By now, you must be aware that succeeding in *any* business takes work and effort due to the many hurdles you encounter. Unfortunately, the hurdles get higher and more complex in world markets. This is particularly true in dealing with differences in cultural perspectives, societies and economies, laws and regulations, and fluctuations in currencies. Let's take a look at each of these hurdles.

Cultural Differences

If you hope to get involved in international trade, one thing you will have to learn is the cultural differences among nations. Different nations have very different ways of conducting business and American businesspeople are notoriously bad at adapting. In fact, American businesspeople have consistently been accused of *ethnocentricity*. This means they feel our culture is superior to all others and our job is to teach others the *American Way* to do things. On the other hand, foreign businesspeople are very good at adapting to the U.S. culture. Let us give you a couple of examples to show how American businesses have difficulty in adapting to important cultural differences.

Religion is an important part of any society's culture and can have a significant impact on business operations. For example, in Islamic countries, dawn-to-dusk fasting during the month of Ramadan causes workers' output to drop considerably. Also, the requirement to pray five times daily can affect output. For example, an American manager in Islamic Pakistan toured a new plant under his control in full operation. He went to his office to make some preliminary forecasts of production. As he was working, suddenly all the machinery in the plant stopped. He rushed out expecting a possible power failure and instead found his production workers on their prayer rugs. He returned to his office and lowered his production estimates.[15]

Cultural differences can also have an impact on such important business factors as human resource management. In Latin American countries, managers are looked on by workers as authoritarian figures responsible for their well-being. Consider what happened to one participative American manager who neglected this important cultural characteristic. This manager was convinced he could motivate his workers in Peru to higher levels of productivity by instituting a more democratic decision-making style. He even brought in trainers from the United States to teach his supervisors to solicit suggestions and feedback from workers. Shortly after his new style was put in place, workers began quitting their jobs in droves. When asked why, Peruvian workers said the new production manager and supervisors did not know their jobs and were asking the workers what to do. All stated they wanted to quit and find new jobs, since obviously this company was doomed because of incompetent managers.[16]

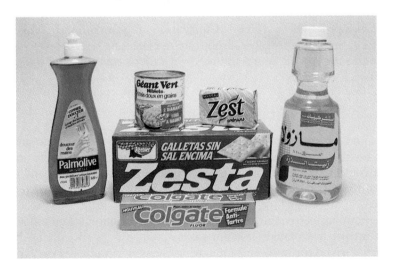

These popular American products are packaged for overseas markets. U.S. producers must learn the cultures of other nations so that the design of products and packages and the selection of distribution channels match the needs of different countries. Each country poses a different challenge calling for a different marketing strategy.

Without question, culture presents a significant hurdle for global managers. Learning about important cultural perspectives toward time, change, competition, natural resources, achievement, even work itself can be a great assistance. Today, firms often provide classes and training for managers and their families on how to adapt to different cultures and avoid culture shock. Your involvement in courses in cultural variations and anthropology can assist you in your career in global business.

Cultural differences affect not only management behaviors but international marketing strategies as well. As you recall, *global marketing* is the term used to describe selling the same product in essentially the same way everywhere in the world. The growth of satellite systems will soon make it possible to have world-wide promotions. Rupert Murdoch, for example, has a satellite based in the United Kingdom that transmits to nearly 2.5 million homes in Norway, Finland, Switzerland, Austria, West Germany, and the United Kingdom itself. Many U.S. programs reach Canada, of course. The question is whether or not international promotions will be successful given the problems we have already discussed. Some companies *have* developed universal appeals. Sky Channel, Murdoch's European system, successfully promotes Coca-Cola, Wrigley, Ford, Polaroid, Kodak, and other companies whose products have wide appeal. Others, unfortunately, have hit the hurdles and failed. Some past experiences are revealing of the problems of global marketing. For example, translating a theme into a different langauge can be disastrous:

- "Body by Fisher" became "Corpse by Fisher."
- The Chevrolet Nova had little appeal in Spanish-speaking countries because "no va" in Spanish means "it doesn't go."
- Campbell soup failed in Brazil because housewives felt they were not fulfilling their role by serving ready-made soup. They preferred dehydrated products that they could use as a soup starter, to which they could then add their own creative touch.

Thousands of similar stories could be told. The truth is that most U.S. manufacturers simply do not *think* globally yet. For example, they don't adapt automobiles to drive on the left side of the road as is done in many countries. They often print instructions only in English. Parts can be hard to get. Some electrical outlets can't handle American-style plugs. The problems go on and on. Only when U.S. producers begin to thoroughly research foreign markets before attempting sales will such problems be solved.[17] Global marketing works only in limited cases. International marketing usually calls for careful marketing research (listening) and adaptation to the specific wants and needs of various countries and to the differences between countries.

Societal and Economic Differences

Certain social and economic realities are often overlooked by American businesses. General Foods squandered millions of dollars in a fruitless effort to introduce Japanese consumers to the joys of packaged cake mixes. The company failed to note, among other factors, that only 3 percent of Japanese homes were equipped with ovens.[18] Since Japan is such an important trading partner, you would think that American businesspeople would know such important information about the Japanese market, but often that is not so.

Surely it's hard for us to imagine buying chewing gum by the stick instead of by the package. However, in economically oppressed nations like the Philippines, this buying behavior is commonplace because consumers have only enough money to buy small quantities. Remember, factors such as disposable and discretionary income (see Chapter 7) can be critical in evaluating the potential of a market. What might seem like an opportunity of a lifetime may in fact be unreachable due to economic conditions.

Technological constraints may also make it difficult or impossible to carry on effective trade. For example, some less developed countries have such primitive transportation and storage systems that international food exchanges are ineffective because the food is spoiled by the time it reaches those in need. These constraints are further complicated by the tremendous geographic distances that separate some countries.

American exporters must also be aware that certain technological differences affect the nature of exportable products. For example, how would the differences in electricity available (110 versus 220 volts) affect an American appliance manufacturer wishing to export? How would the European use of the metric system affect an American exporter?

Legal and Regulatory Differences

In any economy, the conduct and direction of business is firmly tied to the legal and regulatory environment. As we know, in the United States, business operations are heavily impacted by various federal, state, and local laws and regulations. In global markets, no one group of laws and regulations dominates. This makes the task of conducting world business even tougher.

What businesspersons find in global markets is a myriad of laws and regulations that are often inconsistent. Important legal questions related to antitrust, labor relations, patents, copyrights, trade practices, taxes, product liability, and other issues are written and interpreted differently country by country. To compound problems, American businesspeople are bound to follow U.S. laws and regulations in conducting business affairs. For example, some legislation such as the **Foreign Corrupt Practices Act of 1978,** can create hardships for American businesspersons in competing with other foreign competitors. This law specifically prohibits "questionable" or "dubious" payments to foreign officials to secure

Foreign Corrupt Practices Act of 1978
Law that prohibits "questionable" or "dubious" payments to foreign officials to secure business contracts.

Hong Kong is obviously a growing city with many successful businesses. It is not always easy to become established in such markets, but there are people who can help in every country. Businesspeople are a little cautious about doing business in Hong Kong today because of the unrest in China and the upcoming takeover of Hong Kong by China.

MAKING ETHICAL DECISIONS

As a top manager of Nightie Nite, a maker of children's sleepwear, you are required to be aware of all the new government regulations that affect your industry. A recently passed safety regulation prohibits the use of the fabric that you have been using for girl's nightgowns for the past 15 years. Apparently the fabric does not have sufficient flame retardant capabilities to meet government standards. In fact, last week Nightie Nite lost a lawsuit brought against it by the parents of a young child severely burned because the nightgown she was wearing burst into flames when she ventured too close to a gas stove. Not only did you lose the law suit, but you may lose your nightshirt if you don't find another market for the warehouse full of nightgowns you have in inventory. You realize that there are other countries that do not have such restrictive laws concerning products sold in their borders. You are considering exporting your products to these countries. What are your alternatives? What are the consequences of each alternative? What will you do?

business contracts. In many countries, corporate bribery is acceptable and perhaps the only way to secure a lucrative contract. How do you think American business and government leaders should handle this ethical dilemma?

To be a successful trader in foreign countries, one might choose to begin by contacting local businesspeople and gaining their cooperation and sponsorship. The problem is that foreign bureaucracies are often stumbling blocks to successful foreign trade; to penetrate those barriers, often one must find a local sponsor who can pay the necessary fees to gain government permission. One of Ms. Kamsky's jobs in China is to smooth the way toward trade with China. This is one of the more difficult international jobs because of the bureaucracy in China (see the Profile at the beginning of this chapter).

Problems with Currency Shifts

As you are probably aware, the global market does not have a universal currency. Mexicans shop with pesos, West Germans with deutsche marks, South Koreans with won, the British with pounds, and Americans with dollars. One thing that makes world trade difficult today is the widely fluctuating values these currencies undergo. For example, on one day a dollar may be exchanged for 3 deutsche marks, but on the next you may only get 2.5 deutsche marks for your dollar. These changes cause many problems. Consider the H. B. Fuller Company. The company has 43 plants in 27 foreign countries making paints, adhesives, and coatings. Mr. Fuller feels that the most dramatic problem he faces is in the currency area. He has an adhesive plant in Japan where the yen's value went from 260 yen to an American dollar to just 137. Since you can't control the currency, you must learn to control your business. Mr. Fuller uses currency fluctuations to his advantage now by buying raw materials from sources with relatively weak currencies.[19]

Understanding currency fluctuations and financing opportunities is vital to success in the global market. It is not surprising that Virginia Kamsky started out in banking. Banks traditionally have led the way in financing export operations in the United States. Recently, however, banks have cut back on export financing and U.S. exporters have had to turn to foreign banks for financing. But foreign banks pick and choose who they will finance and this leaves out most small and medium-size firms that are the future of the United States.[20] What this means for you is that there will be a tremendous opportunity in banking for those people who are knowledgeable about the global market and willing to make loans for international trade.

TRADE PROTECTIONISM

As we said in the previous section, dealing with cultural differences, societal and economic factors, legal and regulatory requirements, and currency shifts are all hurdles to those wishing to trade globally. What is often a much greater barrier to international trade is the overall political atmosphere between nations. This barrier is best understood through a review of some economic history of world trade.

Business, economics, and politics have always been closely linked. In fact, economics was once referred to as "political economy" indicating the close ties between politics (government) and economics. For centuries, businesspeople have tried to influence economists and government officials. Back in the 16th, 17th, and 18th centuries, nations were trading goods (mostly farm products) with one another. Businesspeople at that time advocated an economic principle called **mercantilism.** Basically, the idea of mercantilism was to sell more goods to other nations than you bought from them; that is, to have a favorable balance of trade. This results in a flow of money to the country that sells the most. Governments assisted in this process by charging a tariff (basically a tax) on imports, making them more expensive.

There are two different kinds of tariffs: revenue and protective. **Protective tariffs** are designed to raise the retail price of imported products so that domestic products will be more competitive. These tariffs are meant to save jobs for domestic workers and to keep industries from closing down entirely because of foreign competition. Without such a protective tariff, the U.S. shoe industry, for example, would have been almost totally taken over by imports. **Revenue tariffs,** on the other hand, are designed to raise money for the government. Revenue tariffs are commonly used by developing countries.

Today, there is still much debate about the degree of protectionism a government should practice. For example, the U.S. government is concerned about protecting domestic auto producers and workers from Japanese producers. The government convinced Japanese producers to voluntarily limit the number of Japanese cars sold here.

The term that describes limiting the number of products in certain categories that can be imported is **import quota.** The United States has import quotas on a number of products such as beef and steel. Over the last eight years, the U.S.' share of imports subject to quotas or official restraint has grown from 12 percent to 18 percent.[21] Again, the goal is to protect industry to preserve jobs. An **embargo** is a complete ban on the import or export of certain products. The ban on the sale of Cuban cigars in the United States is one example. The United States also prohibits the export of some products. For example, the Trans-Alaskan Pipeline Authorization Act prohibits the export of oil from North Slope fields in Alaska. Another law bans the export of timber from federal lands. The Export Administration Act prohibits exporting goods that would endanger national security (for example, military hardware to the U.S.S.R.). Political considerations have caused many countries to establish embargoes. For example, the United States placed an embargo on grain sales to the U.S.S.R. for a while after it invaded Afghanistan.

James Thwaits, president of international operations of the 3M Company, says that as much as *half* of all trade is limited by *nontariff* barriers. In other words, countries have established many strategies to prevent foreign competition that go beyond tariffs. For example, France tried to protect its videotape recorder industry by requiring that all imported recorders be sent through an undermanned customs post that was 100 miles from the nearest port. Denmark requires that beverages be

mercantilism
The economic principle advocating the selling of more goods to other nations than a country buys.

protective tariffs
Import taxes designed to raise the price of imported products so that domestic products are more competitive.

revenue tariffs
Import taxes designed to raise money for the government.

import quota
The number of products in certain categories that can be imported.

embargo
A complete ban on the import or export of certain products.

Few measures that we could take would do more to promote the cause of freedom at home and abroad than complete free trade.
MILTON FRIEDMAN

sold in returnable bottles; this effectively cut off French mineral water producers who found the cost of returning bottles prohibitive. Margarine must be sold in cubes in Belgium, closing the market to countries that sell margarine in tubs.

Such constraints on world trade could be viewed as good reasons to *avoid* world trade. In fact, most companies in the United States do just that. But such constraints could also be viewed as a tremendous opportunity. Learn to hurdle such barriers, and you will have access to markets of billions of people!

Consequences of Protectionism

Today, nations throughout the world are debating how much protectionism they should use to keep foreign competition from driving their firms out of business. You can read about this trend in current business periodicals. As you do, keep in mind that the severity of the Great Depression of the 1930s was attributed by some people to the passage of the highly protectionist Smoot-Hawley Tariff Act of 1930. Economists were almost unanimous in opposing the bill. Nonetheless, to protect American business, the government put tariffs on goods from England, France, and other foreign nations. The result was that other countries raised tariffs in return. This hurt U.S. businesses badly.

By 1932, exports to England were at one third the 1929 level, exports to France were only one fourth of 1929, and exports to Australia were one fifth of 1929. Wheat exports fell from $200 million to $5 million, and auto exports fell from $541 million to $76 million. In short, some economic theorists contend that protectionist policies of the government (based on old mercantilist thinking)

TWO SIDES OF THE TARIFF ISSUE

Some people feel that tariffs are necessary to protect national markets from foreign competition. Some of the arguments they use include:
- *Tariffs save jobs.* Tariffs should be used to keep cheap foreign labor from taking over American jobs, thus increasing employment in the United States.
- *Tariffs are imposed on the United States by its competitors.* It is generally accepted that the United States has consistently followed a policy favoring open trade. Other countries such as Japan have nevertheless imposed severe tariffs on our products. To make competition fair we have to take reciprocal measures.
- *Tariffs protect industries vital to American security.* The U.S. government has been protecting certain industries that are sensitive for our defense, such as the automobile, aerospace, and shipbuilding industries.
- *Tariffs are needed to protect new domestic industries from established foreign competitors.* The so-called infant-industry argument supports tariffs for new industries until they can compete with foreign competitors.

The opponents of tariffs counterargue by presenting the following negative effects tariffs can have:
- *Tariffs reduce competition.* Any tool used to restrain international trade in effect reduces competition, with all the negative implications this has on the economy.
- *Tariffs tend to increase inflationary pressure.* Tariffs raise consumer prices and as such act as a stimulant for inflation.
- *Tariffs tend to support special interest groups.* Tariffs in general benefit special interest groups such as local manufacturers but overall hurt the public, who are forced to pay higher prices for imported products.
- *Tariffs can lead to foreign retaliation and subsequently to trade wars.* If the United States imposes tariffs on products imported from certain countries, this might result in reciprocal tariffs on the part of the affected countries, which would escalate trade wars.

Debate over trade restrictions will be a major part of international politics for the next decade. You may want to stay current with such discussions because the future of world growth depends on open trade.

helped create the greatest depression in the history of the United States. Unemployment reached 24 percent. You can see the need for care when such policies are proposed. (See the box on tariffs for both sides of the tariff issue.)

In 1989, President Bush declared Japan, Brazil, and India as "unfair traders" whose barriers to U.S. goods would be subject to retaliation. This move was part of something called the Super 301 trade retaliation list.[22] We don't have enough feedback yet on the effect of this declaration, but, if the past is any guide, the results will not be good. The countries listed could counter our retaliation with more protectionist moves of their own, triggering another global trade war. The timing is awkward for the United States in that Europe is planning to loosen its trade restrictions as it forms something like a United States of Europe. Europe may respond to Super 301 by demanding that the United States drop all of its restrictive trade policies or face retaliation. Certainly the decade of the 1990s will be a critical one for world trade. You know the consequences of the Smoot-Hawley trade protection legislation. You can now watch the results of the latest such measure. We can all hope the results will be better for all the nations of the world.

PROGRESS CHECK

- What are the major hurdles to successful international trade?

- American businesspeople are often said to suffer from ethnocentricity. What exactly is meant by ethnocentricity?

- Identify at least two cultural and societal difference that can affect global trade efforts?

- What is the Foreign Corrupt Practices Act of 1978? How does it affect the conduct of an American involved in global trade?

- What are the advantages and disadvantages of trade protectionism? Tariffs?

- What is mercantilism and how do tariffs and embargoes fit into the theory?

MULTINATIONAL CORPORATIONS

There has been much discussion recently about the power of multinational corporations. It is helpful to first understand what they are and what they mean for international business. A **multinational corporation (MNC)** is an organization that does manufacturing and marketing in many different countries; it has multinational stock ownership and multinational management. The more multinational a company is, the more it attempts to operate without being influenced by restrictions from various governments.

As you probably suspect, multinational corporations are typically extremely large corporations. In fact, Barnett and Muller, in their best-selling book *Global Reach,* point out that:

> If we compare the annual sales of [multinational] corporations with the gross national product of countries . . . we discover that GM is bigger than Switzerland, Pakistan and South Africa, that Royal Dutch Shell is bigger than Iran, Venezuela and Turkey and that Goodyear tire is bigger than Saudi Arabia.

multinational corporation (MNC)
An organization that does manufacturing and marketing in many different countries; it has multinational stock ownership and multinational management.

FIGURE 24–8

The top 40 U.S. multinational corporations. Note that IBM, Mobil, and Exxon sell over half of their goods overseas. Look over the list of companies. Do you see any that you would enjoy working for in overseas markets? Notice that service organizations such as JP Morgan (banking) and Bankers Trust do over half their business overseas as well.

1987 RANK	COMPANY	FOREIGN REVENUE (Millions of Dollars)	TOTAL REVENUE (Millions of Dollars)	FOREIGN REVENUE AS PERCENTAGE OF TOTAL
1.	Exxon	$57,375	$76,416	75.1%
2.	Mobil	31,633*	52,256*	60.5
3.	IBM	29,280	54,217	54.0
4.	General Motors	24,091	101,782	23.7
5.	Ford Motor†	23,955	73,145	32.8
6.	Texaco	17,120	34,372	49.8
7.	Citicorp	13,314	27,519	48.4
8.	E. I. du Pont de Nemours	11,651‡	30,468‡	38.2
9.	Dow Chemical	7,431	13,377	55.6
10.	Chevron	5,905	26,015	22.7
11.	Procter & Gamble	5,524	17,000	32.5
12.	Eastman Kodak	5,265	13,305	39.6
13.	Chase Manhattan	5,021	10,745	46.7
14.	ITT†	4,891	19,525	25.0
15.	Xerox†	4,852†	15,125*	32.1
16.	United Technologies	4,713	17,170	27.4
17.	Philip Morris	4,544	22,279	20.4
18.	Amoco	4,400*	20,477*	21.5
19.	Digital Equipment	4,373	9,389	46.6
20.	Unisys	4,237	9,713	43.6
21.	Coca-Cola	4,185	7,644	54.7
22.	RJR Nabisco	4,045	15,766	25.7
23.	Goodyear	3,997	9,905	40.4
24.	Hewlett-Packard	3,968	8,090	49.0
25.	American Intl Group	3,875	11,278	34.4
26.	Johnson & Johnson	3,845	8,012	48.0
27.	Tenneco	3,834	14,790	25.9
28.	General Electric	3,799*	40,515*	9.4
29.	3M	3,616§	9,429	38.3
30.	JP Morgan	3,590	6,834	52.5
31.	American Express	3,525	17,768	19.8
32.	Sears Roebuck	3,180	48,440	6.6
33.	Colgate-Palmolive	3,161	5,647	56.0
34.	Bankers Trust New York	3,156	5,693	55.4
35.	NCR	3,081	5,641	54.6
36.	BankAmerica	3,051	9,753	31.3
37.	FW Woolworth	3,037	7,134	42.6
38.	Motorola	2,937	6,707	43.8
39.	American Brands†	2,835	6,029	47.0
40.	Monsanto	2,756	7,639	36.1

* includes other income.
† includes proportionate interest in unconsolidated subsidiaries and affiliates.
‡ includes excise taxes   § includes export sales.

Source: By permission of Forbes magazine, July 25, 1988. © Forbes Inc., 1988.

The multinational corporation is constantly checking opportunities for expansion all over the globe. It aggressively markets its products, capitalizing on its technological and managerial expertise. Companies such as IBM, Procter & Gamble, Du Pont, Shell, Exxon, Mobil, Toyota, Coca-Cola, and Nestlé are examples of multinational corporations (see Figure 24–8). Caution should be exercised, however, before calling a company multinational. Not all firms involved in international business are multinationals. A company may be exporting its entire product,

Multinational companies operate in many different countries. It is not surprising to see a Ford van in Germany, just as it is common to see Hondas in the United States. Multinational corporations provide commercial and economic links among countries, which may lead to more open trade and more peaceful relations.

thus deriving 100 percent of its sales and profits overseas, but that alone would not make it a multinational. Only firms that have manufacturing capacity or other physical presence in various nations can be called multinational.

Part of the trade deficit is due to multinationals such as the U.S. automakers. The Big Three automakers alone were net importers of about $6 billion in 1988.[23] That is partially due to the practice of building cars or parts of cars in other countries and importing them to the United States. Now that U.S. manufacturing is getting more competitive, the trend may shift. In fact, many foreign firms already have plants in the United States and are increasing our exports by shipping goods made here to other countries. One secret, then, to improving our trade balance is to continue the trend toward making U.S. workers and plants more productive so that U.S. and foreign firms will want to produce goods here. The trend is for U.S. firms to open offices all over the world to take advantage of cheap labor. For example, the U.S. giant insurance company, Agna Corporation, opened a claims processing center in Ireland. Texas Instruments has a software development facility in India. The legal research service Lexis flies documents to overseas units where key-punch operators type them into computers. Many firms send their data processing to Barbados where some 1,000 workers earn $10 million in foreign currency.[24] There is even some joking about putting such operations on ships and moving the ships to where labor is cheapest and taxes are lowest.

INTERNATIONAL TRADE ORGANIZATIONS

Most nations recognize the need to expand world trade. Consequently, some nations have joined together to form trading partnerships and to write up trade agreements that facilitate open trade. For example, after World War II, a spirit of intergovernmental cooperation emerged to encourage international trade. The **International Monetary Fund (IMF)** was signed into existence by 44 nations at Bretton Woods, New Hampshire, in 1944. The IMF is an international bank that usually makes *short-term* loans to countries experiencing problems with their balance of trade. Its basic objectives are to promote exchange stability, maintain orderly exchange arrangements, avoid competitive currency depreciation, establish

International Monetary Fund (IMF)
An international bank that makes short-term loans to countries experiencing problems with their balance of trade.

a multilateral system of payments, eliminate exchange restrictions, and create standby reserves. Recently, the IMF set aside over $8 billion for *long-term* loans at interest rates of just .5 percent to the world's most destitute nations to help them strengthen their economies.[25] This makes the function of the IMF very similar to that of the World Bank.

The **World Bank** (the International Bank for Reconstruction and Development), an autonomous United Nations agency, is concerned with the development of the infrastructure (roads, schools, hospitals, power plants) in less-developed countries. The World Bank borrows from the more prosperous countries and lends at favorable rates to less developed countries.

In 1948, the **General Agreement on Tariffs and Trade (GATT)** was established. This agreement among 23 countries provided a forum for negotiating mutual reductions in trade restrictions. In short, government leaders from nations throughout the world have cooperated to create monetary and trade agreements that facilitate the exchange of goods, services, ideas, and cultural programs. (See Figure 24–9 for other examples.) A recent GATT meeting was held in Geneva, Switzerland, to discuss farm subsidies and their effect on world trade.[26] Such meetings take place periodically.

Some countries felt that their economies would be strengthened if they were to establish more detailed trade agreements with other countries in the same region. Some of these agreements involved forming producers' cartels and common markets.

World Bank
An autonomous United Nations agency that borrows money from the more prosperous countries and lends it at favorable rates to less-developed countries.

General Agreement on Tariffs and Trade (GATT)
Agreement among 23 countries that provided a forum for negotiating mutual reductions in trade restrictions.

Producers' Cartels

Producers' cartels are organizations of commodity-producing countries. They are formed to stabilize or increase prices, optimizing overall profits in the long run. The most obvious example today is OPEC (the Organization of Petroleum Exporting Countries). The end of the Iraq/Iran war may strengthen OPEC again and oil prices may rise. Similar arrangements have been made to manage prices for copper, iron ore, bauxite, bananas, tungsten, and rubber.

producers' cartels
Organizations of commodity-producing countries that are formed to stabilize or increase prices to optimize overall profits in the long run. (An example is OPEC, the Organization of Petroleum-Exporting Countries.)

Common Markets

A **common market** is a regional group of countries that have no internal tariffs. Common markets have a common external tariff and a coordination of laws to facilitate exchange. Notable are the European Economic Community (EEC), the Central American Common Market (CACM), and the Caribbean Common Market (CCM).

There are many more such arrangements including *negotiating groups* (such as the Special Coordinating Committee for Latin America) that join together to negotiate trade agreements; *commodity associations* that bring together countries that are concerned with specific commodities (the group gathers statistics, does research, and provides forums for buyers and sellers of products such as cotton and wool); *commodity agreements*, which are multilateral agreements among buyers and sellers to stabilize prices and earnings (such as for cocoa, sugar, tea, and coffee); and more.

common market
A regional group of countries that have no internal tariffs, a common external tariff, and a coordination of laws to facilitate exchange. (An example is the European Economic Community.)

ORGANIZATION	OBJECTIVE
The Export-Import Bank	Government bank designed to reduce domestic unemployment. It makes loans to exporters who cannot secure financing through private sources and to foreign countries who use the funds to buy American goods
Foreign Trade Zones	Places where goods can be imported without being subject to customs duties or quotas. The imported materials are then manufactured into finished products. If reexported, they are not subject to any tariffs, but if they enter into domestic commerce, they are subject to regular tariffs
The International Finance Corporation (IFC)	This organization makes loans to private businesses when they cannot obtain loans from more conventional sources (affiliated with the World Bank)
The International Development Association (IDA)	This organization makes loans to private businesses and to member countries of the World Bank
Domestic International Sales Corporation (DISC)	U.S. firms can form tax-sheltered subsidiaries (DISCs) to handle their export sales. The purpose is to encourage exports and get American firms to enter the export market
Overseas Private Investment Corporation (OPIC)	Sells insurance to U.S. firms that operate overseas. Covers damages caused by war, revolution, or insurrection, inability to convert local currencies into U.S. dollars, and expropriation (take-over by foreign governments)
The Foreign Credit Insurance Association (FCIA)	Sells insurance to cover political risk (e.g., expropriation). Comprehensive coverage can cover business risks (e.g., credit default). The company also sells insurance coverage on credit sales to foreign customers

FIGURE 24–9

Other organizations that assist in foreign trade.

You are likely to see more such agreements in the future. For example, the United States is negotiating better trade relations with China; the less-developed countries of the world are starting to join together to become more powerful traders; and the world community in general is becoming more aware of the need for further agreements covering fishing rights, the mining of ore from the ocean bottom, international pollution control, and more open trade agreements to minimize international tensions.

FIGURE 24–10

The 12 countries in the
European trade community.

West Germany	Spain
France	The Netherlands
Portugal	Italy
Greece	Denmark
Britain	Belgium
Ireland	Luxembourg

A United Europe

On December 31, 1992, 12 nations of the European community are supposed to dissolve their economic borders (see Figure 24–10). Europe could become one vast market of some 320 million people who will trade freely and live and work where they please. Europe sees such integration as the only way to compete with Japan and the United States for world markets.

The path to such unification may be more difficult than imagined, but the goal is there. The idea of free movement of labor, shared social programs, new and strange tax systems, and shared professional standards is rather scary to countries that are more used to fighting with one another than working as a economic unit. You can imagine the struggles that will emerge over a community language, just for starters. But many people are committed to this happening and the wheels are in motion. One of the more interesting international developments to follow over the next couple of years will be this effort to unite Europe. When it takes place the GNP of the area will be about $4.2 trillion and the population about 322 million. This compares with a U.S. population of 350 million and a GNP of $5 trillion.[27] The two units, the United States of America and the United States of Europe, would be quite comparable and quite competitive.

THINKING IT THROUGH   Many countries in the world are called less-developed countries. Why are they less developed? Is it the lack of natural resources? Then how do you explain the success of Japan, which has few natural resources? Does lack of free markets keep countries from developing? Why would a government restrict free trade? What could happen to the world's standard of living and quality of life if all countries engaged in free trade? What is keeping that from happening? What would it take to eliminate such barriers?

THE FUTURE OF INTERNATIONAL TRADE

The future of world trade is getting brighter every day. One of the most significant developments is the proposed unification of 12 European countries into one trading block, as just mentioned. More important for the United States is the agreement with Canada to form a similar trading partnership. Early in the 1990s, the United States and Canada will become a common market where goods will flow between the borders duty free, with some exceptions to be phased in over time. This unification of the two countries is expected to increase the number of jobs in the United States by 750,000 and the number of jobs in Canada by 150,000. More than half of Chrysler's light trucks and 20 percent of Oldsmobile cars are already made in Canada. When the duties and paperwork of trading between the countries are eliminated, many small businesses are expected to begin trading across the borders. That will increase our trading power with other nations, including the new European economic community.[28]

It will not take long for the rest of the world to recognize the advantages of common markets without trade restrictions such as those now being formed in Europe and in North America. That will force similar arrangements elsewhere. For example, Third World countries in various regions may form similar common markets. One can picture a common market in Central and South America, for example. Similar agreements may be reached in Asia, Africa, and other regions. These agreements will not take place in the immediate future, but the trends are there. (See Case One at the end of this chapter.) The biggest thing holding back Third World growth was the cutback of loans by U.S. banks. If these countries become sound financially again, the loans will flow freely again and growth will resume.[29]

As China and the U.S.S.R. open their markets to trade, the whole world will become a more free and open market that will create jobs everywhere. Free trade will likely lead to a lessening of international tensions so that less money need be spent on the military in all countries. This may free money for investment in business and create new prosperity, especially in a nation such as the U.S.S.R. where a significant proportion of the national budget goes for the military. The 1989 demonstrations by over a million students and supporters in China called for more freedom and democracy. More freedom and democracy would likely mean more free trade as well.[30] We will have to wait to see what the government crackdown on dissenters will mean for trade with China.

Corporations will have to begin thinking globally when making decisions about where to manufacture and where to market goods and services. One could call this the Fourth Wave of change to sweep the United States. The First Wave was the agricultural revolution. The Second Wave was the industrial revolution. The Third Wave was the service revolution. The Fourth Wave will be the international revolution. It will be as disruptive as the first three economic revolutions. Many jobs will be lost to foreign producers, but many other jobs will be created as new markets open. The world market, remember, is some 5.5 billion people. That is a huge market and one that *must* be pursued with the same attention to detail and segmentation that one uses in the U.S. market. Read carefully the box called Careers in International Business, paying special attention to the sources listed for more information. The time to begin studying international markets is now, and the place to begin is learning other languages and becoming familiar with other cultures. The time to do that is while you are still in school and can take courses about other countries. The Peace Corps and other nonprofit groups can give you international experience while you earn money or, at least, spend little of your own.

- What exactly is a multinational corporation (MNC)? Can you name at least three multinational corporations?

- What is the primary purpose of the International Monetary Fund (IMF) and the General Agreement of Tariffs and Trade (GATT)?

- How does a common market work? Why do countries enter into common market agreements?

- How does the future for international trade appear? What might be some important factors that will have an impact on future global trading?

PROGRESS CHECK

CAREERS IN INTERNATIONAL BUSINESS

NATURE OF THE WORK

There are a variety of careers available in international business ranging from running your own importing or exporting firm to working for a large bank that finances international ventures. Throughout this chapter, we have been emphasizing the opportunities available in international business. If you are interested, you should begin now by taking foreign languages. Most schools are now teaching languages that were important 40 or more years ago—French, German, Spanish, and so on. To prepare for international trade in the future, you may also want to consider studying the languages of the countries where more trade will be in the future such as China, Japan, Korea, Russia, the Philippines, Thailand, Malaysia, and other developing countries. Like Virginia Kamsky in the Profile, you may want to start off in the international section of a bank and then move to the country of choice. But remember, she knew the languages first.

JOB OUTLOOK

The job outlook for those skilled in international trade is wide open. No field in business offers more opportunity for growth and financial return than this area. This is true for people trained in many areas of business, especially marketing, financing, and distribution. The most impor- ant thing for you to know at this point is where to go to get more information.

SOURCES OF ADDITIONAL INFORMATION

The place to start to prepare yourself for international business is where Virginia Kamsky started—learning the language of the countries that interest you most. Of course, you may not have to go any further than your local community college or university. Many colleges and universities offer courses in international business. Some other sources include:

Middlebury Language Schools, Middlebury College, Middlebury, Vt. 05753. This is a seven- to nine-week summer program for intensive language study and includes Chinese, Japanese, and Russian.

Monterey Institute of International Studies, 425 Van Buren St., Monterey, Calif. 93940. An intensive eight-week summer program in language development and cultural orientation.

You may want to try living in a country for a while to see if you would enjoy that. Some programs are designed for that purpose.

Experiment in International Living, Kipling Road, Brattleboro, Vt. 05301. Places students for six weeks in countries in South America, Australia, China, and Europe.

IAESTE Trainee Program, C/O AIPT, 217 American City Building, Columbia, Md. 21044. The International Association for Exchange of Students for Technical Experience has reciprocal arrangements for work in 46 countries for 8 to 12 weeks.

Volunteers for Peace, Tiffany Rd., Belmont, Vt., 05730. Workcamps in 36 countries give you a chance to live in a country for two to three weeks cheaply.

For more general information about large firms operating abroad and related material:

Directory of American Firms Operating in Foreign Countries, World Trade Academy Press, 50 E. 42nd St., New York, N.Y. 10017.

Employment Abroad: Facts and Fallacies, Publications Fulfillment, Chamber of Commerce of the United States, 1615 H. Street, N.E., Washington, D.C. 20062. This publication lists 25 other sources of information for employment overseas.

International Directory for Youth Internships, Learning Resources in International Studies, Suite 9A, United Nations Plaza, New York, N.Y. 10017. Lists over 400 intern positions.

PROGRESS CHECK

> What are the limitations to using a global marketing strategy?

> What is a joint venture and its advantages?

> What is countertrading?

> What is the difference between a multinational and a global corporation?

> Can you name five organizations that assist in international trade?

1. The world market for trade is huge. Some 95 percent of the people in the world live outside the United States.
    - Why should nations trade with other nations?

        (1) No country is self-sufficient, (2) other countries need products that prosperous countries produce, and (3) there is a world imbalance of natural resources and technological skills.
    - What is the theory of comparative advantage?

        The theory of comparative advantage contends that a country should produce and sell those products it produces most efficiently and buy those it cannot produce as efficiently.
    - What is absolute advantage?

        Absolute advantage means that a country has a monopoly on a certain product or can produce the product more efficiently than any other country. There are few examples of absolute advantage.

2. Students can get involved in world trade through importing and exporting. They do not have to work for big multinational corporations.
    - What kinds of products can be imported and exported?

        Just about any kind of product can be imported and exported. The most important thing for a potential importer or exporter to remember is to find a need and fill it.

3. In order to understand international business, you must first understand the terminology.
    - What terms are important in understanding world trade?

        Exporting is selling products to other countries.

        Importing is buying products from other countries.

        Balance of trade is the relationship of export to imports.

        Balance of payments is balance of trade plus other money flows such as tourism and foreign aid.

        Dumping is selling products for less in a foreign country than in your own country.

        Trade protectionism is the use of government regulations to limit the importation of products. See other terms in the Key Terms section to be sure you know the important ones.

4. Until recently, the United States was a *creditor* nation, meaning other nations owed us more than we owed other nations and we owned more assets in other countries than foreign countries owned in us. However, the United States is now a *debtor* nation.
    - What happened to make us the world's largest debtor nation?

        The devalued dollar and the October 1987 stock market crash lowered the cost of buying American assets. Foreign investors rushed to take advantage of the bargains.

5. A company can participate in world trade in a number of ways.
    - What are some ways that a company can get involved in international business?

        Ways of entering world trade include exporting and importing, joint venturing, licensing, creating subsidiaries, franchising, and countertrading.

SUMMARY

1. Discuss the increasing importance of the international market and the roles of comparative advantage and absolute advantage in international trade.

2. Explain how the marketing motto "Find a need and fill it" applies to international business.

3. Apply the terminology used in international business.

4. Describe the status of the United States in international business.

5. Illustrate the strategies used in reaching global markets.

6. Discuss the hurdles of trading in world markets.

6. There are many restrictions on foreign trade.

   What are some of the hurdles that can discourage participation in international business?

   Potential stumbling blocks to world trade include cultural differences, societal and economic differences, legal and regulatory differences, and fluctuations in different currencies.

7. Political differences are often the most difficult hurdles to international trade.

7. Debate the advantages and disadvantages of trade protectionism.

   What is trade protectionism?

   Trade protectionism is the use of government regulations to limit the import of goods and services, based on the theory that domestic producers can survive and grow, producing more jobs. The tools of protectionism are tariffs and embargoes.

   What are tariffs?

   Tariffs are taxes on foreign products. There are two kinds of tariffs: protective tariffs, which are used to raise the price of foreign products; and revenue tariffs, which are used to raise money for the government.

   How does an embargo differ from a tariff?

   An embargo *prohibits* the importing or exporting of certain products.

   Is trade protectionism good for domestic producers?

   That is debatable. Trade protectionism hurt the United States badly during the Great Depression because other countries responded to U.S. tariffs with tariffs of their own.

   Why do governments continue such practices?

   The theory of mercantilism started the practice of trade protectionism and it has persisted, in a lesser form, ever since.

8. Multinational corporations have a huge impact on world trade.

8. Describe the role of multinational corporations.

   How do multinational corporations differ from other companies that participate in international business?

   Unlike other companies that are involved in exporting or importing, multinational corporations also have manufacturing facilities or other types of physical presence in various nations.

9. There are many organizations and trade agreements that facilitate world trade.

9. Identify and describe international trade organizations and trade agreements.

   What are some of these organizations and trade agreements?

   Organizations and trade agreements that facilitate world trade include the World Bank, the International Monetary Fund (IMF), the General Agreement on Tariffs and Trade (GATT), common markets, and producers' cartels.

10. One of the most significant developments for the future of the world trade is the unification of 12 European countries into one trading block.

10. Discuss the future of international trade.

   What trading partnership is more important to the U.S. than a united Europe?

   Early in the 1990s, the U.S. and Canada will become a common market where goods will flow freely between the borders.

   Will future growth in world trade be with large, developed nations?

   No, more growth will likely be in less-developed countries such as China, India, Mexico, South Korea, Taiwan, Hong Kong, and Singapore.

   Can you believe this is the end of your reading of the text material?

   No, it is not the end. This book is meant to be a resource for your life and career. We hope you keep the book and read and reread it many times until you truly *understand* business.

1. Visit an Oriental rug dealer or some other importer of foreign goods. Talk with the owner/manager about the problems and joys of being involved in international trade. Visit several such organizations and compile a list of advantages and disadvantages. Then get together with others in the class and compare notes.

2. Let's dream for a minute. Imagine yourself living in an exotic country where the weather is great, the living easy, and the people friendly. Have you ever visited such a place? Well, picture yourself living there. What language would you have to learn, if any? What could you import there that would be fun to sell? Share your vision with others. What's keeping you from having that dream come true?

3. Presently, we have a world where some countries are rich and have an overabundance of food. Some countries are poor and people are starving. Some countries have few natural resources, but are prosperous (for example, Japan, Singapore). Others are relatively rich in natural resources, but are poor (for example, Ghana). What trade barriers cause such disparities to continue? Is the problem economic, social, political, or some combination? Discuss.

4. Write a short essay describing the benefits and disadvantages of trade protectionism. Have your class divide into two sides and debate this issue: "Resolved that the United States should increase trade protection to save American jobs and American companies."

5. Many U.S. firms have made embarrassing mistakes selling overseas. Sometimes the product is not adapted to the needs of the country, sometimes the advertising makes no sense, sometimes the color is wrong, and so forth. Discuss the steps U.S. businesses should follow to be more responsive to the needs of foreign markets. Discuss your list with others, and together form a plan for improving U.S. trade overseas.

CASE ONE   **THE GHOSTS OF SMOOT-HAWLEY**

No subject of this chapter has received more interest in the 1980s than that of trade protectionism. In 1985, there were 400 bills before Congress calling for some form or other of trade protection. Everywhere headlines referred to "Smoot-Hawley." Some history may help clarify the issue.

The date: June 13, 1930 (Friday the 13th). The time: 2:13 P.M. The place: the U.S. Senate. The Great Depression had started and the air was full of talk about trade protection. Over 1,000 economists warned the government that protectionism was dangerous and petitioned it not to pass the Smoot-Hawley Act. But, by a vote of 44 to 42, the bill passed. It was an act conceived by Republican congressmen, passed by a Republican Congress, and signed into law by conservative President Herbert Hoover.

The bill imposed duties of up to 60 percent on almost everything imported into the United States. World trade fell by one third, and a globel trade war started. The concept was to protect the Western beet sugar farmer by raising the duty for sugar; protect the Northwestern wheat farmer by raising the duty on wheat; and protect the Imperial Valley cotton farmer by raising the duty on cotton from Egypt. The list went on: cattle and dairy products, hides, shoes, velvet, silk, china, pocket knives, watch parts, and so on.

Exports dropped from $4.8 billion to $1.7 billion from 1929 to 1932. Imports dropped from $5.4 billion to $2.4 billion. Other countries were plunged into depression also as world trade fell.

Hawley was a professor of economics at Willamette University. Smoot was a banker and wool manufacturer. Both men lost in the 1932 election (after a combined 56 years in Congress) when Franklin Roosevelt was elected president. That was the end of Republican dominance in the Senate for a long time to come. In 1934, Congress passed the Reciprocal Trade Agreement Act to reduce tariffs, but it was too little too late.

In 1989, Congress again passed protectionist legislation (Super 301) to correct trade imbalances with nations such as Japan and India. This time the legislators said that the goal is to free up trade with these nations, not restrict it. Nonetheless, the legislation would restrict trade with nations that had serious trade imbalances with the United States. Could this be Smoot-Hawley all over again? "The current trade bill will not have a cosmic impact on world trade," according to Julie Sedky, vice president of Washington Analysis Corp./Country Securities, U.S.A., but Ms. Sedky believes that if some compromise is not reached between the executive branch and Congress, "we will get a more protectionist trade bill."

In response to protectionist legislation throughout the world, three trading blocks are emerging: the United States of North America, led by the United States of America, the United States of Europe (in 1992), and the United States of Asia (led by Japan). These trading blocs may lead to even greater protectionist legislation and less free trade among nations.

DECISION QUESTIONS

1. Why do you suppose some politicians are pushing for trade protection? What are the economic conditions that would call for such protection?
2. Has Congress learned the lessons of the early 1930s such that we will never again make the mistake of passing overly restrictive legislation on world trade? What is happening now in Congress on this issue?
3. What should the role of the U.S. government be in regard to world trade? How much effort should be made to protect American workers from foreign competition? What can the United States do to open trade among the three major trading blocs?

Source: The 100 Largest U.S. Multinationals, *Forbes*, July 25, 1988, p. 247; and Edwin A. Finn, Jr., "Sons of Smoot-Hawley," *Forbes*, February 6, 1989, pp. 38–40.

CASE TWO   ENTERING THE IMPORT/EXPORT BUSINESS

Gordon and Carole Segal went to the Caribbean on their honeymoon. While there, they were fascinated by the variety of elegant, functional housewares they saw: French copper, German cutlery, and so on. A few months later, Gordon was doing the dishes (Arzberg dinnerware) when he got the inspiration to start an importing firm. He had experience in restaurants and real estate. Carole was a teacher. Neither had any experience in retailing.

With $17,000 in capital and one employee, the couple opened the first Crate & Barrel store in an old elevator factory in Chicago's Old Town district. It took a while to learn the business. In fact, the couple forgot to buy a cash register, and went several days without one. This was in 1962.

At first, the Segals and their company, Euromarket Designs, Inc., imported only quality items they had seen and used themselves. Eventually, they toured the continent searching for more items. They learned that European tradespeople were often reluctant to sell to Americans because of past bad experiences with department store buyers. For example, these buyers would place large orders; the manufacturers would expand to fill the orders; and then, when there were no reorders, the manufacturers were stuck. Often, the Segals had to spend days negotiating to buy goods.

When the store opened, sales were $8,000 the first month. The second month they fell to $4,000, the third month to $2,000. About half the initial inventory was sold at cost due to ignorance, not charity. Eventually things got straightened out, and the Segals opened a second store in 1968 in suburban Wilmette, Illinois (outside Chicago). A third store opened in 1971.

The Segals now have 17 stores. They were the ones who set the image for new houseware stores. Glassware, dinnerware, flatware, and cookware are piled floor to ceiling on open shelves. Emphasis is on the product, not the display case.

The honeymoon shopping trip in the Caribbean led to a major retail chain in the United States. Total revenue in 1984: $46 million.

DECISION QUESTIONS

1. How much thought have you given to the import/export business as a career? The Segals imported European goods to America. Would you enjoy selling American goods in Europe?

2. What are some of the successful stores you have seen that sell imported goods? Have you ever talked to the owners about their experiences? Do so and report back to the class.

3. Why is the world market an attractive career possibility for tomorrow's college graduates relative to the U.S. market?

Source: Joseph P. Kahn, "On Display," *Inc.*, November 1985, pp. 110–22.

GLOSSARY

absolute advantage (770) When a country has a monopoly on producing a product or is able to produce it at a low cost below that of all other countries.

absolute liability (718) Responsibility of a manufacturer to cover damages caused by a product if it failed to warn of a hazard, even if the hazard was scientifically unknowable at the time of sale.

accountability (360) Requirement that workers accept the consequences of their actions and report those actions to their immediate supervisor.

accounting (572) The recording, classifying, summarizing, and interpreting of financial events and transactions that affect the organization. It may also be viewed as the measurement and reporting (inside and outside the organization) of financial information about the economic activities of the firm to various users.

accounting system (572) The methods used to record and summarize accounting data into reports.

Active Corps of Executives (181) Volunteers from industry, trade associations, and education who counsel small businesses.

actuaries (725) People who predict future losses based on the analysis of historical data.

administered distribution system (263) Distribution system in which all the marketing functions at the retail level are managed by producers.

advertising (289) Paid, nonpersonal communication through various media by organizations and individuals who are in some way identified in the advertising message.

affirmative action (514) Employment activities designed to "right past wrongs" endured by females and minorities by giving them preference in employment.

agency shop agreement (540) One where employers may hire anyone and employees do not have to join the union but must pay union fees.

American Federation of Labor (AFL) (537) A craft union formed in 1886.

analytic systems (400) Manufacturing system that breaks down raw materials into components to extract other products.

apprenticeship (500) A time when a new worker works alongside a master technician to learn the appropriate skills and procedures.

arbitration (542) The agreement to bring in an impartial third party (an arbitrator) to render a binding decision on a labor dispute.

articles of incorporation (115) Filed with the secretary of state, this is a legal document listing the name and address of the corporation and who is incorporating it and responsible for its legal services; as well as the corporation's purpose, duration, number of shares, minimum capital, and first directors.

artificial intelligence (429) The ability of computers to mimic human thought processes.

assembly process (400) Production process that puts together components.

assets (577) Economic resources owned by a firm, such as land, buildings, and machinery.

authority (360) The right to make decisions and take actions.

aviation insurance (717) Insurance that covers aircraft and damage and liability from the use of aircraft.

balance of merchandise trade (774) The relationship of exports to imports.

balance of payments (774) The difference between money coming into a country (from exports) and money leaving the country (for imports) plus money flows from other factors such as tourism, foreign aid, and military expenditures.

balance sheet (586) Reports the financial position of a firm at a specific date. Balance sheets are composed of assets, liability, and owners' equity.

bankruptcy (740) The legal process by which a person or business, unable to meet financial obligations, is relieved of those debts by having the court divide any assets among creditors, freeing the debtor to begin anew.

bartering (782) The exchange of merchandise for merchandise.

benefit segmentation (210) Divides the market by benefits desired.

blue chip stocks (639) Stocks of high-quality companies.

bond (632) A contract of indebtedness issued by a corporation or governmental unit that promises payment of a principal amount at a specified future time plus interest.

bookkeeping (575) The recording of economic activities.

brand (234) A name, symbol, or design (or combination of these) that identifies the goods or services of one seller or group of sellers and distinguishes them from those of competitors.

brand name (200) Word, letter, or groups of words or letters that differentiate the goods and services of a seller from those of competitors.

breach of contract (739) Violation when one party fails to follow the terms of a contract.

break-even analysis (246) Process used to determine profitability at various levels of sales.

break-even point (246) The quantity of sales beyond which profits occur.

brokers (258) Marketing middlemen who bring buyers and sellers together and assist in negotiating an exchange.

brokerage firms (669) Organizations that buy and sell securities for their customers and provide other financial services.

budget (610) A financial plan that allocates resources based on projected revenues.

bureaucratic organization (365) Organization with three layers of authority; (1) top managers who make decisions, (2) middle managers who develop procedures for implementing decisions, and (3) workers and supervisors who do the work.

business (18) Any organization that seeks profit by providing needed goods and services.

business law (735) Rules, statutes, codes, and regulations established to provide a legal framework within which business may be conducted and that is enforceable in court.

business plan (172) A detailed written statement that describes the nature of the business, the target market, the advantages the business will have over competitors, and the resources and qualifications of the owners.

buying on margin (640) The purchase of stocks by borrowing some of the purchase cost from the broker.

cafeteria-style fringe benefits (506) Fringe benefits plan that allows employees to choose the benefits they want up to a certain dollar amount.

call provision (634) Gives the issuer of a bond the right to retire the bond before its maturity.

capital budget (610) The spending plan for assets whose returns are expected to occur over an extended period of time (more than one year).

capitalism (54) An economic system in which all or most of the means of production and distribution are privately owned and operated for profit.

capitalist system (49) System in which resources are allocated by consumers bargaining in the marketplace and trading goods and services.

cash-and-carry wholesalers (272) A limited function wholesaler that serves mostly smaller retailers with a limited assortment of products they sell for cash.

cash budget (611) The predicted cash balance at the end of a given period (e.g., monthly, quarterly).

cash flow (592) The difference between cash receipts and cash disbursements.

cash flow forecast (609) A prediction of cash inflows and outflows in future periods.

centralized authority (373) Maintaining decision making authority with the top level of management at headquarters.

certificate of deposit (CD) (664) A note issued by a bank that earns a guaranteed interest for a fixed period of time; the CD cannot be withdrawn without penalty until the maturity date.

certification (539) Process of a union becoming recognized by the NLRB as the bargaining agent for a group of employees.

certified public accountant (CPA) (574) An accountant who passes a series of examinations established by the American Institute of Certified Public Accountants and meets the state's requirements for education and experience.

channel captain (264) The organization in the channel that gets the other members to work together in a cooperative effort.

channel of distribution (256) Marketing middlemen such as wholesalers and retailers who join together to transport and store goods in their path (channel) from producers to consumers.

Clayton Act (744) Law that prohibits practices whose effect will be to substantially lesson competition or to create a monopoly.

closed-shop agreement (540) Clause in labor-management agreement that specified that workers had to be members of a union before being hired (outlawed by the Taft-Hartly Act).

coinsurance clause (713) Requires businesses to carry insurance equal to a certain percentage of a building's actual value, usually 80 percent.

collective bargaining (539) The process whereby union and management representatives reach a negotiated labor-management agreement.

commercial and consumer finance companies (669) Financial institutions that offer short-term loans to individuals at higher interest rates than commercial banks.

commercial bank (663) A profit-making organization that receives deposits from individuals and corporations in the form of checking and saving accounts and uses some of these funds to make loans.

commercial paper (618) A short-term corporate equivalent of an IOU that is sold in the marketplace by a firm. They mature in 270 days or less.

commodity exchange (646) Specializes in the buying and selling of goods such as wheat, cattle, silver, sugar, gasoline, and foreign currencies.

common law (736) The body of law that comes from judges' decisions; also known as "unwritten law."

common market (792) A regional group of countries that have no internal tariffs, a common external tariff, and a coordination of laws to facilitate exchange. (An example is the European Economic Community.)

common stock (638) The most basic form of ownership of

firms; it includes voting rights and dividends, if dividends are offered by the firm.

communist system (49) System in which resource allocation is largely government controlled.

comparable worth (553) The demand for equal pay for jobs requiring similar levels of education, training, and skills.

comparative advantage theory (769) Theory which asserts that a country should produce and sell to other countries those products that it produces most efficiently and effectively and should buy from other countries those products it cannot produce as effectively or efficiently.

competition-oriented pricing (248) Pricing strategy based on all the other competitors' prices.

compressed work week (508) Work schedule made up of four 10-hour days.

computer-aided design (CAD) (406) The integration of computers into the design of products.

computer-aided engineering (408) The computer-generated design and analysis of products, programming of robots and machine tools, designing of molds and tools, and planning of the production process and quality control.

computer-aided manufacturing (CAM) (406) The integration of computers into the manufacturing of products.

computer hardware (428) All the tangible equipment that processes and stores data.

computer-integrated manufacturing (CIM) (408) Computer-aided design (CAD) combined with computer-aided manufacturing (CAM); it then further integrates CAD/CAM with other corporate functions such as purchasing, inventory, control, cost accounting, materials handling and shipping.

computer software (428) The instructions for telling the computer what to do.

conceptual skills (345) Ability to picture the organization as a whole and the relationship of various parts.

conglomerate merger (118) The joining of completely unrelated firms.

Congress of Industrial Organization (CIO) (537) Union organization of unskilled workers that broke away from the AFL in 1935 and rejoined it in 1955.

consideration (738) Something of value; it is one of the requirements of a legal contract.

consumerism (747) A social movement that tries to increase the rights and powers of buyers in relation to sellers.

consumer market (208) All the individuals or households who want goods and services for personal consumption.

consumer orientation (198) Finding out what consumers want and giving it to them.

consumer price index (CPI) (86) Monthly statistic that measures changes in the prices of about 400 goods and services that consumers buy.

containerization (268) The process of packing and sealing a number of items into one unit that is easily moved and shipped.

contingency planning (334) Process of preparing alternative courses of action that may be used if the primary plans are not achieving the objectives.

continuous process (408) Production process in which long production runs turn out finished goods over time.

contract (738) A legally enforceable agreement between two or more parties.

contract law (738) Law that specifies what constitutes a legally enforceable agreement.

contractual distribution system (263) Distribution system in which members are bound to cooperate through contractual agreements.

controlling (331) Management function that involves checking to determine whether or not an organization is progressing toward its objectives and taking corrective action if it is not.

convenience goods and services (229) Products that the consumer wants to purchase frequently and with a minimum of effort.

convertible bond (634) A bond that can be converted into shares of common stock.

cooperative (123) An organization owned by members/ customers who pay an annual membership fee and share in any profits, if it is a profit making organization.

copyright (740) Exclusive rights to materials such as books, articles, photos, and cartoons.

core time (507) The time when all employees are present in a flextime system.

corporate distribution system (263) Distribution system in which all the organizations in this channel are owned by one firm.

corporate entrepreneur (135) Those entrepreneurs who take the risk of starting and developing a major corporation.

corporate philanthropy (751) Charitable donations made by the corporation to nonprofit groups of all kinds.

corporate policy (751) The position a firm takes on issues that affect the corporation as well as society.

corporate responsibility (751) Issues such as setting minority hiring practices, manufacturing safe products, and minimizing pollution.

corporation (105) A legal entity with authority to act and have liability separate from its owners.

cost of goods sold (582) A particular type of expense measured by the total cost of merchandise sold (including costs associated with the acquisition, storage, transportation in, and packaging of goods).

cost-push inflation (85) Inflation caused by rising business costs.

countertrading (782) Bartering among several countries.

craft union (536) Labor organization of skilled specialists in a particular craft or trade.

credit unions (667) Nonprofit, member-owned financial

cooperatives that offer basic banking services such as accepting deposits and making loans; they may also offer life insurance and a limited number of home mortgages.

criminal loss protection (719) Insurance against theft, burglary, or robbery.

critical path (411) The longest path a product takes from the beginning of the production process until the end.

cumulative preferred stock (638) Preferred stock that accumulates unpaid dividends.

currency (683) All coin and paper money issued by the Federal Reserve Banks and all gold coins.

current assets (578) Resources, including cash or noncash items, that can be converted to cash within 1 year.

cyclical unemployment (83) Unemployment caused by a recession or a similar downturn in the business cycle.

damages (739) The monetary settlement awarded to a person who is injured by a breach of contract.

debenture bonds (632) A bond that is unsecured, i.e., not backed with any collateral such as equipment.

debt capital (614) Funds raised by borrowing money through the sale of bonds or from banks and other lending institutions.

debtor nation (777) Country that owes more money to other nations than they owe it.

decentralized authority (373) Delegating decision-making authority to lower-level managers who are more familiar with local conditions.

decertification (539) Process by which workers take away a union's right to represent them.

decision support systems (436) Interactive information systems that retrieve, manipulate, and display information that answers unstructured decision making questions.

deductible clause (713) States that the insurance company will pay only that part of a loss that exceeds some figure (the deductible amount) stated in the policy.

delegating (346) Assigning authority and accountability to others while retaining responsibility for results.

delegation of authority (373) Assigning part of a manager's duties to subordinates.

demand (56) The quantity of products that people are willing to buy at different prices at a specific time.

demand curve (56) Line on a graph that shows the relationship between quantity demanded and price.

demand deposit (663) The technical name for a checking account because the money is available on demand from the depositor.

demand-oriented pricing (248) Pricing strategy based on consumer demand.

demand-pull inflation (85) Inflation caused by excessive demand for goods and services.

demographic segmentation (210) Divides the market into groups by age, sex, income, and similar categories.

demography (30) The statistical study of the human population to learn its size, density, and characteristics.

departmentalization (568) Dividing tasks into

homogeneous departments such as manufacturing and marketing.

depreciation (591) Assets such as machinery lose value over time; therefore, part of the cost of the machinery is calculated as an expense each year over its useful life.

depression (87) A severe form of recession (see recession).

deregulation (750) Government withdrawal of certain laws and regulations that seem to hinder competition (for example, airline regulations).

directing (331) Guiding and motivating others to achieve the goals and objectives of the organization.

discount bonds (634) Bonds that sell below face value.

discount rate (681) The interest rate that the Federal Reserve Bank charges other banks for loans.

discretionary income (204) Money available after taxes and essentials for purchase of nonessential items.

disposable income (204) Money available after taxes for purchase of essentials.

diversification (642) Buying several different general investment vehicles to spread the risk.

dividend (636) Part of the firm's profits that goes to stockbrokers.

Dow Jones Industrial Averages (650) The average cost of 30 industrial stocks.

drop shippers (273) A limited-function wholesaler that solicits orders from retailers and other wholesalers and has the merchandise shipped directly from a producer to a buyer.

dumping (774) Selling products for less in a foreign country than is charged in the producing country.

economics (49) The study of how society chooses to employ scarce resources to produce various goods and services and distribute them for consumption among various competing groups and individuals.

economies of scale (364) Efficiency resulting from employee specialization created in large plants.

electronic funds transfer system (EFTS) (677) A computerized system that electronically performs financial transactions such as making purchases, paying bills, and receiving paychecks.

embargo (787) A complete ban on the import or export of certain products.

employee orientation (498) The activity that introduces new employees to the organization, to fellow employees, to their immediate supervisors, and to the policies, practices, and objectives of the firm.

employee stock ownership plan (ESOP) (559) Plans whereby employees can buy part or total ownership of the firm where they work.

entrepreneur (134) An innovator who organizes, manages, and assumes the risks of starting a business to make a profit.

entrepreneurial team (139) A group of experienced people from different areas of business who join together to form a managerial team with the skills needed to develop, make, and market new products.

environmental scanning (202) Analysis of societal forces, economic realities, technological development and legal and regulatory conditions.

equilibrium point (57) Point at which supply and demand are equal.

equity capital (614) Funds raised within the company or from selling ownership in the firm.

exchange rate (775) The value of one currency relative to the currencies of other countries.

exclusive distribution (280) The distribution strategy that uses only one retail outlet in a given geographic area.

expenses (580) Costs incurred in operating the business, such as rent, utilities, and salaries.

expert system (436) Decision support system that stores and manipulates knowledge and rules of thumb as well as data.

exporting (772) Selling products to another country.

export trading companies (778) Companies that attempt to match buyers and sellers from different countries.

express warranties (737) Specific representations by the seller regarding goods.

extrinsic rewards (462) Reinforcement from someone else as recognition for good work, including pay increases, praise, and promotions.

factoring (617) Selling accounts receivable for cash.

factors of production (49) The basic inputs of a society: land and natural resources, human labor, capital, and entrepreneurship.

Fair Packaging and Labeling Act (746) Law that gave the Food and Drug Administration authority to require information on labels.

federal deficit (91) The difference between government revenue from taxes and government spending.

Federal Deposit Insurance Corporation (FDIC) (670) Independent government agency that insures accounts in some banks against bank failures (up to a limit of $100,000 per account) and establishes banking standards.

federal funds (682) Short-term loans from one member bank of the Fed to another member bank that can be transferred during one business day.

federal funds rate (682) The interest rate charged for short-term (overnight) loans between Fed member banks.

Federal Reserve System (679) Consists of 12 Federal Reserve District banks that serve as a deposit for excess bank funds (for members) and loan member banks money.

Federal Savings and Loan Insurance Corporation (FSLIC) (670) Independent government agency that insures accounts in savings and loan associations against failures (up to a limit of $100,000 per account) and determines regulations for S&Ls.

Federal Trade Commission Act (745) Law that prohibits unfair methods of competition in commerce.

fidelity bond (719) Insurance that protects an employer from financial loss resulting from employee dishonesty such as theft or forgery.

FIFO (591) Accounting technique for calculating cost of inventory based on first in, first out.

finance (608) The function in a business responsible for acquiring funds for the firm, managing funds within the firm, and planning for the expenditure of funds on various assets.

financial accounting (574) The preparation of financial statements for people outside of the firm (for example, investors).

financial control (611) A process that periodically compares the actual revenue, costs, and expenses with projections.

financial statements (582) Report the success and position (condition) of a firm; they include the income statement and balance sheet.

fire insurance (714) Insurance that covers losses to buildings and their contents from fire.

fiscal policy (92) Government efforts to keep the economy stable by increasing or decreasing taxes or government spending.

fishyback (267) Shipping the cargo-carrying part of a truck on a ship over long distances to save on transportation costs.

fixed assets (578) Items of a permanent nature, such as land, buildings, furniture, and fixtures.

flat organization structures (369) Ones with relatively few layers of management.

flextime plans (507) Work schedules that gives employees some freedom to adjust when they work, within limits, as long as they work the required number of hours.

float (678) The delay between the time a check is given to a seller and the time it is cashed at the bank.

FMS (flexible manufacturing systems) (408) Totally automated production centers that include robots, automated materials-handling equipment, and computer-controlled machine tools that can perform a variety of functions to produce different products.

focus group (307) Group of 8 to 12 people who meet under the direction of a discussion leader to communicate their feelings concerning an organization, its products, or other important issues.

Foreign Corrupt Practices Act (785) Law that prohibits "questionable" or "dubious" payments to foreign officials to secure business contracts.

foreign subsidiary (779) A company owned by another company (parent company) in a foreign country.

formal organization (383) The structure that details lines of responsibility, authority, and position; it is the structure that is shown on organizational charts.

form utility (207) Changing raw materials to a finished product.

four Ps of marketing (201) Product, price, place, and promotion.

franchise (145) The right to use a specific business's name and sell its products or services in a given territory.

franchise agreement (145) An arrangement whereby someone with a good idea for a business sells the rights to use the business name and sell its products or services to others in a given territory.

franchisee (145) A person who buys a franchise (see franchise).

franchisor (145) A company that develops a product concept and sells others the rights to make and sell the products.

free market system (55) System in which decisions about what to produce and in what quantities are decided by the market; that is, by buyers and sellers negotiating prices for goods and services.

frictional unemployment (82) Unemployment of people who have quit work and have not yet found a new job and also new entrants in the labor force.

fringe benefits (505) Benefits such as sick-leave pay, vacation pay, pension plans, and health plans that represent additional compensation to employees.

full-service wholesalers (271) A merchant wholesaler that performs all eight distribution functions (see merchant wholesaler).

functional structure (371) Grouping of workers into departments based on similar skills, expertise, or resource use.

fundamental accounting equation (586) Assets = liability + owners' equity; it is the basis for the balance sheet.

futures markets (646) The purchase and sale of goods for delivery some time in the future.

Gantt chart (412) Bar graph showing production managers what projects are being worked on and what stage they are in on a daily basis.

General Agreement on Tariffs and Trade (GATT) (792) Agreement among 23 countries that provided a forum for negotiating mutual reductions in trade restrictions.

general merchandise wholesaler (271) A merchant wholesaler that carries a broad assortment of merchandise.

general partner (109) An owner (partner) who has unlimited liability and is active in managing the firm.

generic goods (235) Nonbranded products that usually sell at a sizable discount from national or private brands, have very basic packaging, and are backed with little or no advertising.

generic name (235) The name of a product category.

geographic segmentation (209) Divides the market into separate geographic areas.

goals (332) Broad, long-term accomplishments an organization wishes to attain.

goal setting theory (474) Theory that setting specific, attainable goals can motivate workers and improve performance if the goals are accepted, are accompanied by feedback, and are facilitated by organizational conditions.

goods producing sector (21) Part of society that produces tangible products such as automobiles, furniture, and so on.

gross margin (583) Net sales minus cost of goods sold.

gross national product (GNP) (77) The total value of a country's output of goods and services in a given year.

group life policy (721) Insurance that covers all employees of a firm or members of a group.

growth stocks (639) Stock of corporations whose earnings have grown rapidly in the past in comparison with the economy and are expected to continue above-average growth in the future.

Hawthorne effect (465) The tendency for people to behave differently when they know they are being studied.

Hay Guide Chart Profile Method (555) A technique for measuring pay equity based on an employee's knowledge, problem-solving ability, accountability, and working conditions.

hedging (646) In its pure form, buying or selling commodities in the futures market equal and opposite to what you now have.

hierarchy (20) The various levels of management in a firm.

homeowner's insurance (723) Insurance that protects farmers and other individuals from losses associated with residential living.

horizontal merger (118) The joining of two firms in the same industry.

hostile takeover (118) An unrequested acquisition of an organization through the purchase of company stock in the open market.

human relations skills (345) Ability to lead, communicate, motivate, coach, build morale, train, support, and delegate.

human resource management (490) The process of evaluating human resource needs, finding people to fill those needs, and optimizing this important resource by providing the right incentives and job enrichment, all with the goal of meeting the objectives of the organization.

implied warranties (737) Guarantees legally imposed on the seller.

importing (772) Buying products from another country.

import quota (787) The number of products in certain categories that can be imported.

income statement (582) Reports revenues and expenses for a specific period of time, showing the results of operations during that period. It summarizes all the resources that came into the firm (revenues), and all the resources that left the firm and the resulting net income.

income stocks (639) Stocks that offer a high dividend.

incubators (177) Centers that provide "newborn" businesses with low-cost offices and basic business services.

indenture terms (621) The terms of agreement in a bond.

independent audit (575) An evaluation and unbiased opinion about the accuracy of company financial statements.

industrial advertising (292) Advertising from manufacturers to other manufacturers.

industrial goods (230) Products used in the production of other products.

industrial market (208) Individuals and organizations that purchase goods and services to produce other goods and services or to rent, sell, or supply the goods to others.

industrial park (399) A planned area in a city where businesses can find land, shipping facilities, and waste disposal outlets so they can build a manufacturing plant or storage facility.

industrial unions (537) Labor organizations of *unskilled* workers in mass-production related industries such as automobiles and mining.

inflation (85) A general rise in the prices of goods and services over time.

informal organization (383) The system of relationships and lines of authority that develops spontaneously as employees meet and form power centers. It is the human side of the organization and does not show on any formal charts.

information system (380) Network consisting of written and electronically based systems for sending reports, memos, bulletins, and the like.

information utility (207) Informs buyers that the product exists, how to use it, the price and other information.

injunction (545) A court order directing someone to do something or refrain from doing something.

inland marine insurance (717) Insurance that covers transportation-related or transportable property while goods are being transported by ship, rail, truck, or plane.

insider trading (651) Involves the use of information that a person gains through his or her position that allows him or her to benefit from fluctuations in stock prices.

institutional advertising (292) Advertising by organizations designed to create an attractive image for an organization rather than for a product.

insurable risk (711) Risk that a typical insurance company will cover.

insurance adjuster (725) Person who calculates the extent of a loss.

insurance policy (712) A written contract between the insured and an insurance company that promises to pay for all or part of a loss.

intensive distribution (280) The distribution strategy that puts products into as many retail outlets as possible.

interest (632) The payment the issuer of a bond makes to bondholders for the use of borrowed money.

intermittent process (400) Production process in which the production run is short and the machines are shut down frequently or changed to produce different products.

internal marketing program (309) Marketing program designed to commit employees to the objectives of a firm.

international joint venture (780) A partnership in which companies from two different countries join to undertake a major project.

international monetary fund (791) An international bank that makes short-term loans to countries experiencing problems with their balance of trade.

intrapreneur (143) A person with entrepreneurial skills who is employed in a corporation to launch new products; such people take hands-on responsibility for creating innovation of any kind in an organization.

intrinsic rewards (462) Reinforcement from within oneself; a feeling one has done a good job.

inventory financing (617) Financing that uses inventory such as raw materials as collateral for a loan.

involuntary bankruptcy (740) Bankruptcy procedures initiated by a debtor's creditors.

job analysis (493) A study of what is done by employees who fill various job titles.

job descriptions (493) Summaries of the objectives of a job, the type of work, the responsibilities of the job, the necessary skills, the working conditions, and the relationship of the job to other functions.

job enlargement (474) Job enrichment strategy involving combining a series of tasks into one assignment that is more challenging and interesting.

job enrichment (473) Efforts to make jobs more interesting, challenging, and rewarding.

job rotation (474) Job enrichment strategy involving moving employees from one job to another.

job sharing (506) An arrangement whereby two part-time employees share one full-time job.

job simplification (474) Process of producing task efficiency by breaking down the job into simple steps and assigning people to each of those steps.

job simulation (501) A training method that uses equipment that duplicates job conditions and tasks so that trainees can learn skills before attempting them on the job.

job specifications (493) Written descriptions of the qualifications required of workers to do a particular job.

joint venture (129) An effort by two or more business firms to capture new markets through cooperation and shared investment risk.

journals (576) Recording devices used for the first recording of all transactions.

journeyman (500) A worker who has successfully completed an apprenticeship.

just-in-time (JIT) inventory control (402) Arrangements for delivery of the smallest possible quantities at the latest possible time to keep inventory as low as possible.

Knights of Labor (537) The first national labor union (1869).

knockoff brands (235) Illegal copies of national brand name items.

Labor-Management Relations Act (Taft-Hartley Act) (538) 1974 law that permitted states to pass right-to-work laws; prohibited secondary boycotts, closed-shop agreements, and featherbedding; and set up methods to deal with strikes.

Labor Management Reporting and Disclosure Act (Landrum-Griffen Act) (538) 1959 law that gave individual rights to union members to nominate candidates, vote in union elections, attend union meetings, examine union records, and required annual financial reports from unions to be filed with the Department of Labor.

law of large numbers (712) States that if a large number of people or organizations are exposed to the same risk, a predictable number of losses will occur.

leadership (341) Creating a vision for others to follow, establishing corporate values and ethics, and transforming the way the organization does business so it is more effective and efficient.

ledger (581) Recording device in which information from accounting journals is categorized into homogeneous groups and posted so that managers can find all the information about one account in the same place.

leveraged buyout (120) An attempt by employees, management, or a group of investors to purchase an organization primarily through borrowing.

liabilities (578) Amounts owed by the organization to others. Current liabilities are due in 1 year or less.

licensing (779) Agreement in which a producer allows a foreign company to produce its product in exchange for royalties.

LIFO (591) Accounting technique for calculating costs of inventory based on last in, first out.

limit order (840) Instructions to a broker to purchase stock at a specific price.

limited-function wholesaler (271) A merchant wholesaler that performs only selected distribution functions.

limited liability (108) The responsibility of a business's owners for losses only up to the amount they invest; limited partners and shareholders have limited liability.

limited partner (108) Owner who invests money in the business, but does not have any management responsibility or liability for losses beyond the investment.

line of credit (617) The amount of unsecured short-term credit a bank will lend a borrower that is agreed to ahead of time.

line organization structure (376) Organization in which there are direct two-way lines of responsibility, authority, and communication running from the top to the bottom of the organization, with all employees reporting to only one supervisor.

line personnel (376) Employees who perform functions that contribute directly to the primary goals of the organization.

liquidity (578) How quickly one can get back invested funds when they are desired.

local area networks (435) Communications systems that link computers and other devices within a confined area such as a building.

lockouts (545) A management tool for putting pressure on unions by closing the business.

long-term financing (614) Money obtained from the owners of the firm and lenders who do not expect repayment within 2 or more years.

long-term forecast (609) A prediction of revenues, costs, and expenses for a period longer than 1 year, sometimes extending 5 or 10 years into the future.

long-term loans (665) Loans that are payable in a period that exceeds 1 year.

macroeconomics (50) The study of the nation's economy as a whole.

manageability (360) Capability of everyone in the organization to know who is responsible for what, who reports to whom, what to do when problems arise, and so forth.

management (331) The process used to accomplish organizational goals through planning, organizing, directing, and controlling organizational resources.

management by objectives (MBO) (474) A system of goal setting and implementation that involves a cycle of discussion, review, and evaluation of objectives among top level managers, middle level managers, supervisors, and employees.

management by walking around (330) Managers get out of their offices and personally interact with employees and customers.

management development (509) The process of training and educating employees to become good managers and then developing managerial skills over time.

management information system (435) A system that collects, organizes, and distributes information to managers.

managerial accounting (573) Provides information and analyses to managers within the organization to assist them in decision making.

manufacturing (397) Process of making goods by hand or with machinery as opposed to extracting things from the earth (mining or fishing) or producing services.

market (178) People with unsatisfied wants and needs who have both the resources and willingness to buy.

market modification (242) Technique used to extend the life cycle of mature products by finding new users and market segments.

market order (640) Instructions to a broker to buy stock at the best price obtainable in the market now.

market price (57) Price determined by supply and demand.

market segmentation (209) Process of dividing the total market into several submarkets (segments) that have similar characteristics.

market targeting (209) The process by which an organization decides which markets to serve.

marketing (195) The process of studying the wants and needs of others and then satisfying those wants and needs with quality goods and services (products) at competitive prices.

marketing communication system (308) Listening to the market, responding to that information, and promoting the organization and its products.

marketing concept (197) Refers to a three-part business philosophy: (1) a consumer orientation, (2) training of all employees in customer service, and (3) a profit orientation.

marketing manager (202) Plans and executes the conception, pricing, promotion, and distribution of ideas, goods, and services to create exchanges that satisfy individual and organizational goals.

marketing middlemen (200) Individuals or organizations that help distribute goods and services from the producer to consumer.

marketing mix (202) The strategic combination of product decisions with decisions regarding packaging, pricing, distribution, credit, branding, service, complaint handling, and other marketing activities.

marketing research (212) A major function used to find needs and to determine the most effective and efficient ways to satisfy those needs.

master budget (611) The financial plan that summarizes the operating, capital, and cash budgets.

materials handling (269) The movement of goods within a warehouse, factory, or store.

materials requirement planning (402) A computer-based operations management system that uses sales forecasts to make sure that needed parts and materials are available at the right place and time.

matrix organization structure (378) Organization in which specialists from different parts of the organization are brought together to work on specific projects, but still remain part of a traditional line and staff structure.

maturity date (632) The date the issuer of a bond must pay the principal of the bond to the bondholder.

mediation (542) The use of a third party, called a mediator, to encourage both parties to continue negotiating.

mentors (511) Experienced employees who supervise, coach, and guide lower level people by introducing them to the right people and groups and generally act as their organizational sponsors.

mercantilism (787) The economic principle advocating the selling of more goods to other nations than a country buys.

merchant wholesalers (271) Independently owned wholesalers that take title to goods that they handle.

merger (117) The result of two firms forming one company.

microeconomics (51) The study of the behavior of people and organizations in particular markets.

middle management (336) Level of management that includes plant managers and department heads who are responsible for tactical plans.

mixed economy (69) An economy that combines free markets with some government allocation of resources.

monetary policy (90) The management of the amount of money placed into the economy by the government and the management of interest rates.

money supply (683) The sum of all the funds that the public has immediately available for buying goods and services.

monopolistic competition (59) The market situation where there are a large number of sellers that produce similar products, but the products are perceived by buyers as different.

monopoly (60) A market in which there is only one seller.

motion economy (463) Theory that every job can be broken down into a series of elementary motions.

multiline policies (719) Insurance "packages" that include both property and liability coverage.

multinational corporation (789) An organization that does manufacturing and marketing in many different countries; it has multinational stock ownership and multinational management.

mutual fund (642) An organization that buys stocks and bonds and then sells shares in those securities to the public.

mutual insurance company (713) Insurance firm owned by its policyholders.

mutual savings bank (667) A financial institution found mainly in the northeast; they are very similar to S&Ls.

NASDAQ (645) National Association of Securities Dealers Automated Quotation system. A nationwide electronic system that communicates over-the-counter trades to brokers.

national brand (235) Brand names of manufacturers that distribute their products nationally.

National Credit Union Administration (672) A government agency that insures the deposits made in credit unions against failures (up to a limit of $100,000 per account).

national debt (94) The sum of money the government has borrowed and not paid back.

National Labor Relations Act (Wagner Act) (538) 1935 law that gave employees the right to join a union, to collectively bargain, and to engage in union activities such as strikes, picketing, and boycotts.

negotiable instruments (737) Forms of commercial paper (such as checks) that are transferrable among businesses and individuals.

negotiated labor-management agreement (540) Settlement that sets the tone and clarifies the terms under which management and labor agree to function over a period of time.

net income (583) Revenue minus expenses.

net sales (583) Sales revenue minus discounts, returns, and other adjustments made for customers.

networking (511) (1) The process of establishing and maintaining contacts with key managers in one's own organization and in other organizations and using those contacts to weave strong relationships that serve as informal development systems, (2) a business relationship where a small central organization relies on other companies and suppliers to perform manufacturing, marketing, or other crucial business functions on a contractual basis, (3) **(411)** linking firms together by making it possible for their computers to talk with one another.

nonbanks (668) Financial organizations that accept no deposits, but offer many of the services provided by regular banks.

nonperformance loss protection (719) Insurance against failure of a contractor, supplier, or other person to fulfill an obligation.

Norris—La Guardia Act (538) 1932 law that prohibited courts from using injunctions against nonviolent union activities and outlawed the use of yellow-dog contracts.

objectives (332) Specific short-term tasks that must be completed to achieve the organizational goals.

observational method (307) Method of collecting data by observing the actions of potential buyers.

ocean marine insurance (717) Insurance that protects shippers from losses of property from damage to a ship or its cargo while at sea or in port.

off-the-job-training (500) Internal and external programs to develop a variety of skills and faster personal development away from the workplace.

oligopoly (59) A form of competition where the market is dominated by just a few sellers.

on-line remote processing (441) A computer service that provides the client organization with a computer terminal and training to input data; data are sent over phone lines to the service company and returned in processed form.

on-the-job training (498) The employee immediately begins his or her tasks and learns by doing or watching others for a while and then imitates them, all right at the workplace.

open-market operations (680) Tool used most commonly by the Fed to regulate the money supply; it involves the buying and selling of U.S. government securities.

open shop agreement (541) Agreement in right-to-work states that gives workers the option to join or not join a union if one exists in their workplace.

open system integration (411) The ability of computers and telecommunications equipment to communicate over long distance due to the development of common standards in the computer and telecommunications industries.

operating budget (610) The projection of dollar allocations to various costs and expenses needed to operate the company given projected revenue.

operating expenses (585) The various costs incurred in running a business, including rent, salaries, and utilities.

organizational culture (381) Widely shared values within an organization, reflected in stories, traditions, and myths, that provide coherence and cooperation to achieve common goals.

organizational design (360) The establishment of manageable groups of people who have clear responsibilities and who know how to accomplish the objectives of the organization and the group.

organizing (331) Management function that involves designing the organizational structure, attracting people to the organization (staffing) and creating conditions and systems that ensure that everyone and everything work together to achieve the objectives of the organization.

other (intangible) assets (578) Items that are not included in the current and fixed assets catagories. This catch-all category includes items such as patents and copyrights.

over-the-counter-market (645) Exchange that provides a means to trade stocks not listed on the national exchanges.

owner's equity (580) Assets minus liabilities.

participative management (343) Management style that involves employees in setting objectives and making decisions; democratic and laissez-faire leadership are forms of this type of management.

partnership agreement (111) Legal document that specifies the rights and responsibilities of the members of a partnership.

partnership (general) (105) A legal form of business with two or more owners.

par value (636) An arbitrary dollar amount printed on the front of a stock certificate.

patent (739) Exclusive rights for inventors to their inventions for 17 years.

penetration strategy (247) Method of pricing by which a product is priced low to attract more customers and discourage competitors.

penny stock (639) A stock that sells for less than $1.00.

pension funds (669) Amounts of money designated by corporations, nonprofit organizations, or unions to cover part of the financial needs of members when they retire.

perestroika (66) Restructuring of the Soviet economy.

perfect competition (58) The market situation where

there are many buyers and sellers and no seller is large enough to dictate the price of a product.

performance appraisal (502) An evaluation of the performance level of employees against standards to make decisions about promotions, compensation, additional training, or firing.

personal selling (294) The face-to-face presentation and promotion of products and services plus the searching out of prospects and follow-up service.

PERT (program evaluation and review technique) (411) A method for analyzing the tasks involved in completing a given project, estimating the time needed to complete each task, and identifying the minimum time needed to complete the project.

physical distribution (256) The movement of goods and services from producer to industrial and consumer users.

physical distribution manager (266) The person responsible for coordinating and integrating all movement of materials, including transportation, internal movement, and warehousing.

physiological needs (465) The needs for basic life-giving elements such as food, water, and shelter.

piggyback (266) Shipping the cargo-carrying part of a truck on a railroad car over long distances to save on transportation costs.

place utility (207) Making products and services available in convenient locations.

planning (331) Management function that involves anticipating future trends and determining the best strategies and tactics to achieve organizational objectives.

pledging (617) Using accounts receivable as security.

possession utility (207) Makes the exchange of goods between buyers and sellers easier.

preferred stock (637) Stock that gives owners preferences in the payment of dividends and an earlier claim on assets if the business is sold but does not include voting rights.

premium (712) The fee charged by an insurance company for an insurance policy.

premium bonds (634) Bonds that sell above face value.

price leadership (248) Procedure by which all the competitors in the industry follow the pricing practices of one or more dominant firms.

primary boycott (544) Union encouragement of members not to buy products of a firm involved in a labor dispute.

primary data (304) Information resulting from original research concerning a specific problem.

prime rate (92) The most favorable interest rate that businesses can get from banks.

principal (632) The face amount of a bond.

private accountant (575) Accountant who works for a single company.

private brand (235) Products that do not carry the manufacturer's name, but carry the name of a distributor or retailer instead.

process manufacturing (400) Production process that physically or chemically changes materials.

producer price index (86) Monthly statistics that measure changes in the prices businesses pay for goods and services over time.

producers' cartels (792) Organizations of commodity-producing countries that are formed to stabilize or increase prices to optimize overall profits in the long run. (An example is OPEC, the Organization of Petroleum-Exporting Countries.)

product (200) Any physical good, service, or idea that satisfies a want or need.

product differentiation (228) The attempt to create product perceptions in the minds of consumers that one product seems superior to others.

product life cycle (240) The four-stage theoretical depiction of the process from birth to death of a product class: introduction, rapid growth, maturity, and decline.

product line (226) A group of products that are physically similar or are intended for a similar market.

product manager (236) Coordinates all the marketing efforts for a particular product (or product line) or brand.

product mix (227) The combination of products offered by a manufacturer.

product modification (242) Technique used to extend the life cycle of mature products by changing the product quality, features, or style to attract new users or more usage from present users.

product offer (225) Consists of all the tangibles and intangibles that consumers evaluate when deciding whether or not to buy something.

production (397) Describes the creative process in all industries that produce goods and services.

production goods (232) Industrial goods such as grain and steel that enter into the final product.

production orientation (197) Business focuses on producing goods rather than marketing them.

production process (396) Uses basic inputs (land, labor, capital and entrepreneurship) to produce outputs (products, services, ideas).

productivity (78) The total output of goods and services in a given period of time divided by work hours (output per work hour).

profit orientation (198) Marketing those goods and services that will earn the firm a profit.

promotion (289) An attempt by marketers to persuade others to participate in an exchange relationship with them.

promotional mix (289) The combination of tools marketers use to promote their products or services.

prospects (296) People who have enough funds and are willing to discuss a potential purchase.

prospectus (651) A condensed, printed version of material submitted to the Securities and Exchange Commission that is sent to prospective purchasers to enable them to evaluate a stock offering.

protective tariff (787) Import taxes designed to raise the price of imported products so that domestic products are more competitive.

psychographic segmentation (210) Divides the market by values, attitudes, and interests.

public accountants (574) Accountant who provides services for a fee to a number of companies.

publicity (298) Any information about an individual, a product, or an organization that is distributed to the public through the media and that is not paid for or controlled by the sponsor.

public liability insurance (717) Insurance that protects against losses resulting from personal injuries or damage to the property of others for which the insured is responsible.

public relations (298) The management function that evaluates public attitudes, identifies the policies and procedures of an individual or an organization with the public interest, and executes a program of action to earn public understanding and acceptance.

pull strategy (290) Use of promotional tools to motivate consumers to request products from stores.

pure risk (707) The threat of loss with no chance for profit.

push strategy (290) Use of promotional tools to convince wholesalers and retailers to stock and sell merchandise.

quality circles (415) Groups of employees who get together to develop ideas for solving problems such as how to improve quality, increase productivity, cut back on paperwork, reduce inventory costs, or introduce new processes such as computer-integrated manufacturing.

quality control (414) The measurement of products and services against set standards.

rack jobber (271) A full-service wholesaler that furnishes racks or shelves full of merchandise to retailers, displays products, and sells on consignment.

random sample (307) A sample in which all people have an equal chance of being selected to be part of the representative group.

rational decision-making model (346) Consists of six steps: (1) define the problem, (2) determine and collect needed information, (3) develop alternatives, (4) decide which ethical alternative is best, (5) do what is indicated, and (6) determine whether the decision was a good one and follow up.

reasonable prudence (779) Standard for measuring the accountability of a manufacturer for damages caused by its products; based on the question, "Would a sensibly cautious (reasonably prudent) person produce and distribute the product?"

recession (77) Two consecutive quarters of negative growth in real GNP (GNP adjusted for inflation).

recruitment (494) The set of activities used to legally obtain a sufficient number of the right people at the right time to select those who best meet the needs of the organization.

remote processing (441) A computer service that processes data submitted to it on written forms in its own facilities and then returns the processed information to the client organization.

reserve requirement (680) A percentage of member-bank funds that must be deposited in the Federal Reserve Bank.

responsibility (360) The obligation of a person to complete a given task.

retail advertising (292) Advertising to consumers by retailers.

retailer (270) A marketing middleman that sells to consumers.

retained earnings (585) The amount left after a company distributes some of its net income (profit) to stockholders in the form of dividends.

revenue (582) The value of what is received for goods sold, services rendered, and other sources.

reverse discrimination (514) The feeling of unfairness unprotected groups may have when protected groups are given preference in hiring and promoting.

revolving credit agreement (617) A line of credit that is guaranteed by the bank.

rider (714) Addition to a fire insurance policy that covers losses from wind, hail, explosion, riot, smoke, and falling aircraft.

right-to-work laws (54) Legislation that gives workers the right, under an open shop, to join a union—if it is present—or not.

risk (707) The chance of loss, the degree of probability of loss, and the amount of possible loss.

risk managers (724) People who do sophisticated analysis of corporate risks and design elaborate solutions to those problems.

Robinson-Patman Act (745) Law that makes it unlawful to discriminate in price, to grant false brokerage fees, or to make disproportional payments to buyers; protects merchants, the public, and manufacturers from unfair competition.

robot (405) A computer-controlled machine capable of performing many tasks that require the use of materials and tools.

round lots (641) 100 shares of stock.

rule of indemnity (713) States that an insured person or organization cannot collect more than the actual loss from an insurable risk.

S corporation (122) A unique government creation that looks like a corporation, but is taxed like sole proprietorships and partnerships.

safety needs (465) The need for peace and security.

sales orientation (197) Firms focus all attention on the salesperson, teaching him or her techniques for winning customers.

sales promotion (300) The promotional tool that stimulates consumer purchasing and dealer interest by means of short-term activities (displays, shows, exhibitions, and contests, etc.).

sample (307) A representative group of a market population.

savings and loan associations (665) A financial institution that accepts both savings and checking deposits and provides home mortgage loans.

scientific management (463) The study of workers to find the most efficient way of doing things and then teaching people those techniques.

scrambled merchandising (280) The strategy of adding product lines (to a retail store) that are not normally carried there.

seasonal unemployment (84) Unemployment that occurs where the demand for labor varies over the year.

secondary boycott (544) An attempt by labor to force an employer to stop doing business with a firm that is the subject of a primary boycott.

secondary data (304) Already published research information from journals, trade associations, the government, information services, libraries, and other sources.

secured bonds (633) Bonds backed by some tangible asset that is pledged to the investor of the principal is not paid back.

secured loan (616) Loan backed by something valuable, such as property.

Securities and Exchange Commission (SEC) (651) Federal government agency that has responsibility for regulating the various exchanges.

selection (496) The process of gathering information to decide who should be hired, under legal guidelines, for the best interests of the individual and the organization.

selective distribution (280) Distribution strategy that uses only a preferred group of the available retailers in an area.

self-actualization needs (465) The needs for achievement and to be all you can be.

self-esteem needs (465) The need for self confidence and status.

self insurance (709) Putting funds away to cover routine claims, rather than buying insurance to cover them.

Service Corps of Retired Executives (SCORE) (181) Part of SBA made up of experienced businesspersons who provide consulting services to small businesses for free (except expenses).

service sector (21) Industries such as transportation and utilities, wholesale trade, retail trade, real estate, consumer services, health and education, and the government.

Sherman Antitrust Act (744) Law that forbids contracts, combinations, or conspiracies in restraint of trade, monopolies or attempts to monopolize any part of trade or commerce.

shopping goods and services (229) Products or services that the consumer buys only after comparing quality and price from a variety of sellers.

short-term financing (614) Money obtained to finance current operations that will be repaid in less than one year.

short-term forecast (609) A prediction of revenues, costs, and expenses for a period of 1 year or less.

short-term loans (665) Loans that have to be paid in 1 year or less.

sinking fund (634) Fund that requires the issuer to retire, on a periodic basis, some part of the bond issue prior to maturity.

skimming price strategy (247) Method of pricing by which the product is priced high to make optimum profit while there is little competition.

skunkworks (143) A highly innovative, fast-moving entrepreneurial unit operating at the fringes of a corporation.

small business (23) Business that is independently owned and operated, is not dominant in its field of operation, and meets certain standards of size in terms of employees (less than 100) or annual receipts.

small-business entrepreneurs (135) People who are willing to take the risk of starting a small business for profit.

social audit (752) A systematic evaluation of an organization's progress toward implementing programs that are socially responsible and responsive.

social needs (465) The need to feel loved, accepted, and part of the group.

socialist system (49) System in which allocation of resources is done partially by the market and partially by the government.

societal orientation (199) Includes a consumer orientation, but adds programs designed to improve the community, reduce pollution, and satisfy other social goals.

sole proprietorship (105) A business that is owned, and usually managed by one person.

span of control (369) The optimum number of subordinates a manager should supervise.

speciality goods and services (230) Products that have a special attraction to consumers, who are willing to go out of their way to obtain them.

speculative risk (707) A type of risk that involves a chance of either profit or loss.

spot markets (646) The purchase and sale of goods for immediate delivery.

spreadsheet (433) A table made up of rows and columns that enables a manager to organize information.

staff personnel (376) Employees who perform functions that assist line personnel in performing their goals.

stagflation (87) Stagnant economic conditions (no growth) combined with inflation.

statutory law (736) State and federal constitutions, legislative enactments, treaties, and ordinances (written laws).

stockbroker (639) A middleman who buys and sells securities for clients.

stock certificate (636) Tangible evidence of stock ownership.

stock exchange (643) An organization whose members can buy and sell securities to the public.

stock insurance company (713) Owned by stockholders, just like any other investor-owned company.

stock splits (641) Giving stockholders two or more shares of stock for each one they own.

strategic planning (333) Process of determining the major goals of the organization and the policies and strategies for obtaining and using resources to achieve those goals.

strict liability (718) States that there is no legal defense for placing a product on the market that is dangerous to the consumer because of a known or knowable defect.

strikebreakers (545) Workers hired to do the jobs of striking workers until the labor dispute is resolved.

structural unemployment (83) That unemployment caused by people losing jobs because their occupation is no longer part of the main structure of the economy.

subfranchising agreement (154) Agreement that gives the right to a principal living in a foreign market to oversee franchise operations in that market.

superregional bank (676) A bank that operates in several states.

supervisory (first-line) management (336) First level of management above employees; includes people directly responsible for assigning specific jobs to employees and evaluating their daily performance.

supply (55) The quantity of products that manufacturers or owners are willing to sell at different prices at a specific time.

supply curve (55) Line on a graph that shows the relationship between price and quantity supplied.

supply-side economics (88) The policy of lowering taxes so that more money is invested in production, leading to an increase in production activity, causing a drop in unemployment.

support goods (232) Industrial goods such as accessory equipment and supplies that are used to assist in the production of other products.

surety bond (720) Insurance that protects against the failure of a second party to fulfill an obligation.

survey method (307) Direct questioning of people to gather facts, opinions, or other information.

synthetic systems (400) Production processes that either change raw materials into other products or combine raw materials or parts into finished products.

tactical planning (334) Process of developing detailed short-term decisions about what is to be done, who is to do it, and how it is to be done.

taking a firm private (120) The efforts of a group of stockholders or management to obtain all of the firm's stock by themselves.

tall organization structure (368) Organizations with many levels of management.

technical complexity (367) The degree to which machines are used in the production process rather than people.

technical skills (395) Ability to perform tasks of a specific department (such as selling or bookkeeping).

telecommunications equipment (443) Equipment that uses phone lines or satellite communication systems to transfer data from one place to another.

telemarketing (278) The sale of goods and services by telephone.

tender offer (118) A proposal to purchase all or part of a firm's stock at a price above the current market value.

term loan agreement (620) A promissory note that requires the borrower to repay the loan in installments that are specified.

test marketing (200) The process of testing products among potential users.

thrift institutions (665) Another name for savings and loan associations.

time deposit (663) The technical name for a savings account, because the bank can require prior notice before withdrawal.

time-motion studies (463) Study of the tasks performed to complete a job and the time needed to do each task.

time sharing (441) A computer service that allows others to "rent" time on computers.

time utility (207) Making products available during convenient hours.

top management (336) Highest level of management, consisting of the president and other key company executives who develop strategic plans.

tort (743) Wrongful conduct that causes injury to another person's body, property, or reputation.

total quality control (414) The system of planning for quality, preventing quality defects, correcting any defects that occur, and a philosophy of continuous effort to build quality into products.

trade advertising (292) Advertising to wholesalers and retailers by manufacturers.

trade credit (615) The practice of buying goods now and paying for them early and getting a discount.

trade deficit (95) The situation where imports (purchases from abroad) exceed exports (sales abroad).

trademark (234) A brand that has been given exclusive legal protection for both the brand name and pictorial design.

trade protectionism (775) The use of government regulations to limit the import of goods and services so that domestic producers can survive and grow, producing more jobs—in theory.

training and development (498) All attempts to improve employee performance through learning.

trial balance (588) Summary of all the data in the ledgers to test the accuracy of the figures.

truck jobber (273) A small, limited function wholesaler that delivers goods by truck to retailers.

Uniform Commercial Code (737) A comprehensive commercial law adopted by every state that covers sales laws and other commercial law.

unions (535) Employee organizations that have the main goal of representing members in employee-management bargaining about job-related issues.

union security clause (540) Provision in a negotiated labor-management agreement that stipulates that employees who benefit from a union must either join or pay dues to the union.

union shop agreement (541) Clause in labor-management agreement that says workers do not have to be members of a union to be hired, but must agree to join the union within a prescribed period.

uninsurable risk (710) Risk that a typical insurance company will not cover.

unlimited liability (107) The responsibility of a business's owners for all of the debts of the business, making the personal assets of the owners vulnerable to claims against the business; sole proprietors and general partners have unlimited liability.

unsecured bonds (632) Bonds that are not backed by any collateral.

unsecured loan (616) A loan not backed by any collateral.

utility (261) Value or want-satisfying ability that is added to products by organizations because the products are made more useful or accessible to consumers.

venture capitalist (176) Individuals or organizations that invest in new businesses in exchange for partial ownership of the company.

vertical merger (118) The joining of two firms involved in different stages of related businesses.

vestibule training (501) Training conducted away from the workplace where employees are given instructions on equipment similar to that used on the job.

volume segmentation (210) Divides the market into user categories: heavy, medium, light, and nonusers.

voluntary bankruptcy (740) Bankruptcy procedures filed by a debtor.

wholesaler (270) A marketing middleman who sells to organizations and individuals, but not to final customers.

word-of-mouth promotion (297) Consumers talking about products they have liked or disliked.

workers' compensation insurance (717) Insurance that provides compensation for workers injured on the job.

World Bank (792) An autonomous United Nations agency that borrows money from the more prosperous countries and lends it at favorable rates to less-developed countries.

world investment (37) Buying stock in companies in other countries, buying farms and businesses in other countries, building your own plants in other countries, and joining firms from other countries in producing products for world markets.

world trade (37) The exchange of goods and services among countries.

yellow-dog contract (545) Contract agreements whereby employees agreed not to join a union as a condition of employment (outlawed by the Norris-La Guardia Act).

CHAPTER NOTES

CHAPTER 1

1. David L. Birch, "Musical Jobs," *Inc.,* November 1987, p. 18.
2. Ibid.
3. Tom Peters, "Thinking about the 2,000 Revolution," *The Washington Times,* August 8, 1988, p. B6.
4. John W. Wright, *The American Almanac of Jobs and Salaries* (New York: Avon Books, 1987–1988 edition), p. xxii.
5. Tom Peters, "A Sampling of Popular Misconceptions," *The Washington Times,* September 8, 1988, p. C2.
6. Marvin Cetron, "Long-Term Trends Affecting the Institute of Industrial Launderers into the 21st Century," *Industrial Launderer,* January 1989, p. 36.
7. John Naisbitt, *Megatrends* (New York: Warner Books, 1982).
8. Sylvia Porter, "Women Run 28% of Firms in Nation," *The Washington Times,* September 9, 1988, p. C2.
9. Naisbitt, *Megatrends.*
10. Kenneth Eskey, "Only 2% in U.S. Still Live on Farms," *The Washington Times,* July 20, 1988, p. B7.
11. Donald Lambro, "Separating Facts from Farm Fiction," *The Washington Times,* April 16, 1987, p. 30.
12. "Boom to Bust to Bailout," *Insight,* December 7, 1987, pp. 18–19.
13. Greg Crittser, "Small Potatoes," *Inc.,* June 1985, pp. 85–88.
14. Ibid.
15. Marvin J. Cetron, Wanda Rocha, and Rebecca Luckens, "Think Big or Think Small," *The Futurist,* October 1988, pp. 9–16.
16. "Aging Baby Boomers Will Swell Elderly Ranks," *The Wall Street Journal,* February 7, 1989, p. B1.
17. "Difficulty in Caring for the 'Oldest Old,'" *The Wall Street Journal,* March 29, 1988, p. 33.
18. "On the House," *Inc.,* March 1989, p. 22.
19. "Immigration Makes a New Wave in 1986," *Insight,* April 11, 1988, p. 24.
20. Susan Schiffer Stautberg, "Corporate Baby Sitting," *The Wall Street Journal,* February 8, 1988, p. 23.
21. Jolie Solomon, "Firms Address Workers' Cultural Variety," *The Wall Street Journal,* February 10, 1989, p. B1.
22. Jim Schachter, "Women Seen Closing the Wage Gap," *Los Angeles Times,* February 8, 1989, p. 3 of Part IV.
23. Barbara Kantrowitz and Karen Springen, "A Tenuous Bond from 9 to 5." *Newsweek,* March 7, 1988, pp. 24–25.
24. Stephen Thernstrom, "Black Progress Is Difficult to Measure," *The Wall Street Journal,* March 28, 1988, letter to the editor.
25. Kantrowitz and Springen, "A Tenuous Bond."
26. Peter Coy, "Revenue of Major Black-Owned Businesses Up 14.4 Percent in '88," *The Washington Post,* May 10, 1989, p. F1.
27. Trish Hall, "The Old Country Network," *The Wall Street Journal,* May 20, 1985, p. 51C of a special section on Small-Business Marketing.
28. John Mintz and Peter Pae, "The High Price of Success," *The Washington Post,* September 7, 1988, p. A22.
29. Alfredo Cochado, "Hispanic Supermarkets Are Blossoming," *The Wall Street Journal,* January 23, 1989, p. B1.
30. Peter F. Drucker, "From World Trade to World Investment," *The Wall Street Journal,* May 26, 1987, editorial page.
31. Ibid.
32. "The 21st Century Executive," *U.S. News & World Report,* March 7, 1988, pp. 48–51.
33. John A. Byrne, "Businesses Are Signing Up for Ethics 101," *Business Week,* February 15, 1988, pp. 56–57.
34. "Down With Greed," *Newsweek,* January 4, 1988, p. 46.
35. "These Students Love Down-And-Out 101," *Business Week,* February 29, 1988, p. 38.

CHAPTER 2

1. "Questioning Economic Literacy," *The Wall Street Journal,* January 12, 1989, p. A15.
2. John Burgess, "As Foreign Investment Increases, So Do Concerns About Its Impact," *The Washington Post,* February 21, 1988, pp. H1 and H6.
3. Andrew Tanzer, "These Prices are Really Insane," *Forbes,* December 14, 1987, pp. 76–78.
4. Ronald Bailey, "The Right Path," *Forbes,* January 23, 1989, pp. 80–81.
5. Ove Guldberg, "What's Rotten in Denmark?" *The Wall Street Journal,* April 23, 1986, p. 31.
6. Bengt Westerberg, "A Liberal Leader's Tax Strategy for Sweden," *The Wall Street Journal,* November 11, 1987, p. 27.
7. Carl Bildt, "Swedes Steel Themselves for a Tax Battle," *The Wall Street Journal,* July 23, 1987, p. 30.
8. John Moynihan, "Tennis Plays the Tax Game: Advantage, Monaco," *The Wall Street Journal,* August 2, 1988, p. 20.
9. "Supply-Side Sweden," *The Wall Street Journal,* November 30, 1988, p. A20.
10. Jim Hoagland, "A Capitalist Scandal in Socialist France," *The Washington Post,* February 7, 1989, p. A25.
11. Antonio Martino, "Unions Join Italy's Tax Revolt," *The Wall Street Journal,* August 1, 1988, p. 17.
12. Karl Marx, *The Communist Manifesto* (Chicago: Henry Regnery Company, 1954).
13. Ken Adelman, "Waiting for the Wake," *The Washington Times,* March 1, 1989, p. F1.
14. David Remmick, "What Soviet Shoppers Could Have Told the CIA," *The Washington Post,* April 26, 1988, A1 & A22.
15. Mikhail Gorbachev, "Gorbachev Speaks Out on the Roots of Perestroika," *The Washington Post,* December 6, 1987, pp. D1–D2.
16. Peter Fuhrman, "The Soviet Economy Is in a Grave State," *Forbes,* October 19, 1987, p. 10.
17. "Flows From Unrest," *Insight,* June 20, 1988, p. 41.

18. Michael Dobbs, "Gorbachev Sets Sweeping Agricultural Reforms," *The Washington Post,* March 16, 1989, pp. A1 and A47.
19. Arthur Schlesinger, Jr., "At Last: Capitalistic Communism," *The Wall Street Journal,* August 4, 1987, editorial page.
20. Arthur Shenfield, "The Mirage of the Mixed Economy," *USD-SBA Newsletter,* Spring 1989, p. 1 (A publication from the School of Business at the University of San Diego).

CHAPTER 3

1. Sylvia Porter, "Keep Your Eye on These Statistics," *The Washington Times,* October 10, 1988, p. B6 and Andrew Leckey, "Figures Chart Course of the Economy," *The Washington Times,* December 12, 1988, p. B8.
2. "Who's on First?" *The Washington Post,* March 20, 1988, p. C7.
3. Oswald Johnston, "GNP Grows 3.8% in '88, a 4-Year High; Rise only 2% in Quarter," *Los Angeles Times,* January 28, 1989, p. 2 of Part IV.
4. Howard Banks, "What's Ahead for Business," *Forbes,* May 1, 1989, p. 35.
5. Janet Novack, "But Don't Make Them Hiss," *Forbes,* November 14, 1988, pp. 159-160.
6. Robert J. Samuelson, "Beyond the Budget Fuss," *The Washington Post,* November 23, 1988, p. A21.
7. Ibid.
8. A. Gary Shilling, "Boost in Services Productivity," *Los Angeles Times,* February 12, 1989, p. 2 of Part IV.
9. "Has Unemployment Finally Hit Its Low?" *The Wall Street Journal,* August 22, 1988, p. 1.
10. George White, "Retailers Shopping for Holiday Help," *Los Angeles Times,* October 29, 1988, pp. 1 and 10 in Part 4.
11. "Needed: Human Capital," *Business Week,* September 19, 1988, pp. 100-124.
12. Figures are from John M. Barry, "Nation's Low Jobless Rate Belies Regional, Occupational Wastelands," *The Washington Post,* September 4, 1988, p. H4.
13. Hilary Stout, "Jobless Aren't Moving to Boom Areas," *The Wall Street Journal,* February 21, 1989, p. B1.
14. Ibid.
15. Ibid.
16. Alan S. Blinder, "Right Now, An Ounce of Prevention Is All Inflation Needs," *Business Week,* March 20, 1989, p. 22.
17. Felipe Ortez de Zevallos, "Peruvian Democracy on Brink," *The Wall Street Journal,* January 6, 1989, p. A11.
18. William Murchison, "Whatever Happened to . . . ?," *The Washington Times,* January 11, 1989, p. F3.
19. Malcolm S. Forbes, "Now Brits, French, Soviets and Chinese Are Supply-Siders Too," *Forbes,* May 2, 1988, p. 17.
20. James Morrison, "Supply-Side Economics Proves Its Worth—In Booming Britain," *The Washington Times,* March 22, 1988, pp. A1/A12.
21. Michael Kinsley, "A Taxing Time to Be Rich?," *The Washington Post,* April 21, 1988, p. A23.
22. "Ex-Presidents: 'Time to Begin to Put the U.S. Fiscal House in Order,'" *The Washington Post,* November 23, 1988, p. A19.
23. Sylvia Nasar, "Preparing for a New Economy," *Fortune,* September 26, 1988, pp. 86-96.

CHAPTER 4

1. Srully Blotnick, "Two for the Money," *Forbes,* February 23, 1987, p. 166.

2. Christi Harlan, "Lawyers Find It Difficult to Break Up Partnerships," *The Wall Street Journal,* October 6, 1988, pp. B1 and B7.
3. Randall Smith, "Merger Boom Defies Expectations," *The Wall Street Journal,* January 3, 1989, p. 8R.
4. Mathew Winkler and Tom Herman, "Takeover Fears Rack Corporate Bonds," *The Wall Street Journal,* October 25, 1988, pp. C1 and C3.
5. "S Corporations Get Tax Breaks in More States," *The Wall Street Journal,* February 15, 1989, p. A1.
6. " 'S' Corporations," *The Wall Street Journal,* March 23, 1988, p. A1.
7. Corie Brown, Mary Pitzer, and Teresa Carson, "Why Farm Co-ops Need Extra Seed Money," *Business Week,* March 21, 1988, p. 96.
8. Warren Brown, "It's All Done with Prisms," *The Washington Post Weekend,* February 17, 1989, p. 63.

CHAPTER 5

1. U.S. Department of Commerce, 1988.
2. C. M. Baumbeck and J. Mancuso, *Entrepreneurship and Venture Management* (Englewood Cliffs, N.J.: Prentice-Hall, 1987).
3. This section is based on John Naisbitt and Patricia Aburdene, *Re-inventing the Corporation* (New York: Warner Books, 1985.)
4. Ibid., pp. 110-11.
5. Ibid.
6. Tom Richman, "The New American Start-Up," *Inc.,* September 1988, pp. 54-66.
7. This section is based on Joel Kotkin, "The Smart Team at Compaq Computer," *Inc.,* February 1986, pp. 48-56; and Stuart Gannes, "America's Fastest-Growing Companies," *Fortune,* May 23, 1988, pp. 28-40.
8. "SBA Starts Pilot Programs for Women Entrepreneurs," *The Wall Street Journal,* October 17, 1988, p. B2.
9. Roger Thompson, "Small Business Report," *Nation's Business,* February 1988, p. 10.
10. Frank McCoy, "A Trailblazer's Trip to the Top," *Business Week,* November 16, 1987, pp. 129-30.
11. Leslie H. Whitson, "Taking a Chance in a New Country," *Nation's Business,* March 1987, p. 59.
12. This and other interesting stories about skunkworkers can be found in Tom Peters and Nancy Austin, *A Passion for Excellence* (New York: Random House, 1985).
13. George Wilson, "Secrecy's Veil Lifted from 'Stealth' Jet," *Washington Post,* November 11, 1988, p. A3.
14. Pamela Watkins, "Making Entrepreneurship an Inside Job," *Black Enterprise,* February 1989, pp. 136-42.
15. Meg Whittemore, "Franchising Options for Opportunity," *Forbes,* August 24, 1987, pp. 83-87.
16. "Franchises Now Offer Direct Financial Aid," *The Wall Street Journal,* February 6, 1989, p. B1.
17. Joseph Weber, "The Grease Guns at Jiffy Lube Are Squirting Red Ink," *Business Week,* February 27, 1989, pp. 42-43.
18. "Business Booms in Services Franchises," *Venture,* February 1989, pp. 65-67.
19. Whittemore, "Franchising Options," pp. 122-24.
20. Earl G. Graves, "Finding Fortunes in Franchising," *Black Enterprise,* September 1987, p. 9.
21. Whittemore, "Franchising Options," pp. 116-21.
22. Jay R. Tunney, "So You Want to Set Up a Business in Korea," *The Wall Street Journal,* March 1, 1989, p. A15.

23. John F. Persinos, "New Worlds to Franchise," *Venture,* November 1987, pp. 50–52.
24. Steven P. Galante, "Small Franchisers Put Accent of Growth in Markets Abroad," *The Wall Street Journal,* April 14, 1986, p. 31.

CHAPTER 6

1. Jane Applegate, "Catching Up on Executive Reading," *Los Angeles Times,* March 3, 1989, p. 3 of Part IV.
2. Warren Brookes, "Beating Up on Small Business," *The Wall Street Journal,* June 1, 1987, p. 1.
3. Roger Thompson and Joan C. Szabo, "Cooling but Still Favorable," *Nation's Business,* January 1988, p. 19.
4. David L. Birch, "The Truth about Start-Ups," *Inc.,* January 1988, p. 15.
5. Thompson and Szabo, "Cooling."
6. David Birch, "The Truth."
7. Michael Novak, "Profit Motive Not at the Top," *The Washington Times,* January 22, 1988, p. F3.
8. "Like 60-Hour Weeks? Try Your Own Business," *Business Week,* August 10, 1987, p. 75.
9. Roger Ricklefs, "Making the Transition to Small Business," *The Wall Street Journal,* February 28, 1989, p. B1.
10. Douglas R. Sease, "Entrepreneurship 101," *The Wall Street Journal,* May 15, 1987, pp. 32–35D.
11. Jill Rachlin, "Starting Up a Business in 1988: A Postcrash Course," *U.S. News & World Report,* December 21, 1987, pp. 70–72.
12. Clay Chandler, "Hatching Baby Businesses," *The Washington Post's Washington Business,* August 29, 1988, pp. 1 and 24.
13. Jane Applegate, "Looking for Pennies from Heaven? Search for an 'Angel,'" *Los Angeles Times,* April 14, 1989, p. 3 of Part IV.
14. Richard O'Reilly, "Don't Start a Venture Without It," *Los Angeles Times,* March 2, 1989, p. 3 of Part IV.
15. Mark Stevens, "Here's a Survival Kit for Business," *The Washington Times,* March 16, 1988, p. C2.
16. Martha E. Manglesdorf, "Hotline," *Inc.,* February 1989, p. 20.
17. William J. Hampton, Zachary Schiller, Resa King, Rick Melcher, and Frank Comes, "The Long Arm of Small Business," *Business Week,* February 29, 1988, pp. 63–66.
18. Michael Allen, "The Foreign Connection," *The Wall Street Journal,* May 15, 1987, pp. 16–18D.
19. William Holstein and Brian Bremmer, "The Little Guys Are Making It Big Overseas," *Business Week,* February 27, 1989, pp. 94–96.
20. William J. Hampton et al., "The Long Arm."
21. James R. Schiffman, "Venturing Abroad," *The Wall Street Journal Small Business* section, February 24, 1989, p. R30.

CHAPTER 7

1. Tom Peters and Nancy Austin, *A Passion for Excellence* (New York: Random House, 1985), p. 7.
2. Laura Litvan, "Marketing Holds Key to Firms' Success," *The Washington Times,* March 3, 1988, p. C5.
3. Ben Wattenberg, "The Competitive Edge," *The Washington Times,* March 3, 1988, p. F3.
4. "Has America Lost Its Competitive Edge?" *Marketing Communications,* February 1988, p. 13.
5. Definition is from the American Marketing Association, Chicago Illinois.
6. Janet Novack, "We're Not Running the Company for the Stock Price," *Forbes,* September 19, 1988, pp. 41–52.

7. Paul B. Brown, "Cookie Monsters," *Inc.,* February 1989, pp. 55–59.
8. John Lynker, "U.S. Suffers from Lack of Listening," *The Washington Times,* February 10, 1989, p. 63.

CHAPTER 8

1. "The MicroMagic Show," *Marketing Communications,* February 1989, p. 36.
2. John H. Taylor, "Some Things Don't Go Better with Coke," *Forbes,* March 21, 1988, pp. 34–35.
3. Yumiko Ono, " 'Waiter, We'll Have Two Coffees and a Couple of Orders of Oxygen,'" *The Wall Street Journal,* March 23, 1988, p. 29.
4. Eric N. Berkowitz, Roger A. Kerin, and William Rudelius, *Marketing* (Homewood, Ill.: Richard D. Irwin, 1989).
5. "Responding to the Changing Retail Store," *Marketing Communications,* February 1988, pp. 48–49.
6. Jerry Flint, "A Brand Is Like a Friend," *Forbes,* November 14, 1988, pp. 267–270.
7. Pete Engardio, Todd Vogel, and Dinah Lee, "Some Companies Are Knocking Off The Knockoff Outfits," *Business Week,* September 26, 1988, pp. 86–88.
8. "Survey Finds 67% of New Products Succeed," *Marketing News,* February 8, 1980, p. 1.
9. Michael Schrage, "Customers May Be Your Best Collaborators," *The Wall Street Journal,* February 27, 1989, p. A10.
10. James E. Ellis, Brian Bremmer, and Michael Oneal, "Will the Big Markdown Get the Big Store Moving Again?," *Business Week,* March 13, 1989, pp. 110–114.

CHAPTER 9

1. Dick Turpin, "Big Landmarks Could Fit Into G.E.'s Building," *Los Angeles Times,* July 24, 1988, p. 1 of Part IV.
2. Joseph Weber, "Mom and Pop Move Out of Wholesaling," *Business Week,* January 9, 1989, p. 91.
3. John Schwartz, Judith Crown, Lisa Drew, and Ted Kenney, "Super-Duper Supermarkets," *Newsweek,* June 27, 1988, pp. 40–41.
4. Bill Saporito, "Retailers Fly Into Hyperspace," *Fortune,* October 24, 1988, pp. 148–52.
5. Bill Hughes, "The Mature Traveler," *Los Angeles Times,* August 28, 1988, p. 24 of Part IV.
6. Steve Weiner, "No More Plastic Plants," *Forbes,* March 20, 1989, pp. 107–8.
7. "Career Futures 100," *Career Futures,* Spring/Summer 1989, p. 50.
8. These concepts are based on Jack Nadel, "Cracking the Global Market," *Management Review,* September 1987, pp. 40–43.

CHAPTER 10

1. "Fun with Advertising on a $25 Board Game," *Insight,* March 20, 1989, p. 93.
2. Ronald Alsop, "Best Campaigns Were Revivals of Past Themes," *The Wall Street Journal,* February 23, 1989, p. B1.
3. Verne Gay, "Time Is Money to Nets: $121,860 per :30 Spot," *Advertising Age,* January 4, 1988, p. 3.
4. Verne Gay, "Price Hikes Loom for TV's Hot :15s," *Advertising Age,* August 29, 1988, p. 1.
5. Julie Skur Hill and Joseph M. Winski, "Goodbye Global Ads," *Advertising Age,* November 16, 1987, pp. 22 and 36.

6. Bruce Horovitz, "Pepsi Adds a Latin Flavor," *Los Angeles Times,* February 22, 1989, p. 1 of Part IV.
7. "Selling Tips," *Personal Selling Power,* January-February 1989, p. 7.
8. "Word of Mouth," *Inc.,* December 1988, p. 18.
9. Paul S. Forbes, "Influence-Peddling, Press Agentry and Huckstering Are Not PR," *The Washington Post,* March 5, 1989, p. A21.
10. Paul Farhi, "Shop-by-Mail Industry Is Facing a Shakeout," *The Washington Post,* November 4, 1988, p. F1.
11. "Direct Marketing," *Marketing Communications,* November-December 1988, p. 34.
12. Kenneth Wylie, "Marketing's Rising Star," *Advertising Age,* May 1, 1989, p. S1.
13. John R. Wilson, Jr., "Specialty Advertising: The College Connection," *The Counselor,* June 1988, pp. 83-86.
14. Dik Warren Twedt (ed.), *Annual Survey of Marketing Research* (Chicago: American Marketing Association).
15. John Lynker, "U.S. Suffers from Lack of Listening," *The Washington Times,* February 10, 1989, p. G3.
16. Joel Harnett, "Filling the Black Holes in the MIS Chain," *Marketing Communications,* February 1989, pp. 54-56.
17. Tom Peters, "Doubting Thomas," *Inc.,* April 1989, pp. 82-92.

APPENDIX TO PART 3

1. Susan Dentzer, "Putting Money Ahead of Mission?," *U.S. News & World Report,* May 16, 1988, p. 25.
2. Amy Saltzman, "You Don't Have to Be Poor to Do Good," *U.S. News & World Report,* July 25, 1988, p. 64.
3. Bruce Sievers, "Toward a More Generous Nation," *Los Angeles Times,* December 25, 1988, p. 1 of Part V.
4. Anetta Miller, Andrew Murr, Michael Lerner, and Dody Tsiantar, "How Cities Beat the Rap," *Newsweek,* January 25, 1988, p. 48.
5. James M. Perry and Michel McQueen, "Bush's Thousand Points of Light are Flickering with Doubts about Role in Providing Service," *The Washington Post,* February 14, 1989, p. A16.
6. William Raspberry, "In Search of Local Leaders," *The Washington Post,* December 23, 1988, p. A15.
7. Bruce Sievers, "Toward a More Generous Nation."
8. Peter F. Drucker, "The Non-Profit Quiet Revolution," *The Wall Street Journal,* September 8, 1988, editorial page.

CHAPTER 11

1. Walter Kiechel III, "Corporate Strategy in the 1990s," *Fortune,* February 29, 1988, pp. 34-42.
2. Amanda Bennett, "Going Global," *The Wall Street Journal,* February 27, 1989, pp. A1 and A9.
3. Peter Drucker, *Management: Tasks, Responsibilities, Practices* (New York: Harper & Row, 1974).
4. "Presidential Forum," *Small Business Report,* August 1984, pp. 44-45.
5. John A. Byrne, "How the Best Get Better," *Business Week,* September 14, 1987, pp. 98-120.
6. David A. Nadler and Michael Tushman, "What Makes for Magic Leadership?," *Fortune,* June 6, 1988, p. 262.
7. Thomas J. Peters, *Thriving on Chaos* (New York: Alfred A. Knopf, 1988).
8. Jeremy Main, "Wanted: Leaders Who Can Make a Difference," *Fortune,* September 28, 1987, pp. 92-102.
9. "Donald Provejsil," *Inc.,* April 1989, p. 42.
10. "Defining Values, Not Just Goal," *The Wall Street Journal,* January 30, 1989, p. B1.
11. Carol Hymowitz, "Day in the Life of Tomorrow's Manager," *The Wall Street Journal,* March 20, 1989, p. B1.

CHAPTER 12

1. Anne B. Fisher, "The Downside of Downsizing," *Fortune,* May 23, 1988, pp. 42-52.
2. Ibid.
3. Thomas J. Peters and Robert H. Waterman, Jr., *In Search of Excellence* (New York: Harper & Row, 1982), p. 353.
4. John A. Byrne, "Is Your Company Too Big?" *Business Week,* March 27, 1989, pp. 84-94.
5. Peters and Waterman, *In Search of Excellence,* pp. 271-272.
6. Walter Guzzardi, "Big Can Still Be Beautiful," *Fortune,* April 25, 1988, pp. 50-64.
7. "The Goliaths Meet the Davids: Big Company Muscle vs. Entrepreneurial Agility?" *Business Week,* March 27, 1989, p. 86.
8. Peters and Waterman, *In Search of Excellence,* Chapter 11, "Simple Form, Lean Staff."
9. Aimee Stern, "The New . . . Souped Up Campbell," *Marketing Communications,* February 1984, pp. 29-54.
10. Janet Novack, "We're Not Running the Company for the Stock Price," *Forbes,* September 19, 1988, pp. 41-52.
11. Lee Iacocca with William Novak, *Iacocca: An Autobiography* (New York: Phantom Books, 1984), pp. 152-153.
12. "Information Networks: Linking Computers and Communications," *Forbes,* April 3, 1989, pp. 133-144.
13. "Corporate 'Cultures' Must Change to Meet Business Goals Firms Say," *The Wall Street Journal,* August 16, 1988, p. A1.
14. "Spread the Word: Gossip Is Good," *The Wall Street Journal,* October 4, 1988, p. B1.

CHAPTER 13

1. Norman Jonas, "The Hollow Corporation," *Business Week,* March 3, 1986, pp. 57-59.
2. Jo Isenberg-O'Loughlin, "Poised for the '90s," *Business Week,* March 27, 1989, pp. 123-134.
3. Sylvia Nasar, "America's Competitive Revival," *Fortune,* January 4, 1988, pp. 44-52.
4. Ibid., p. 46.
5. Peter F. Drucker, "Low Wages No Longer Give Competitive Edge," *The Wall Street Journal,* March 16, 1988, editorial page.
6. Joel Kotkin, "The Great American Revival," *Inc.,* February 1988, pp. 52-63.
7. "Then and Now," *Inc.,* April 1989, p. 220.
8. Kotkin, "The Great American Revival."
9. Ibid., p. 54.
10. Otis Port, Resa King, and William J. Hampton, "How the New Math of Productivity Adds Up," *Business Week,* June 6, 1988, pp. 103-114.
11. Drucker, "Low Wages."
12. Bernard Wysocki, Jr., "The New Boom Towns," *The Wall Street Journal,* March 27, 1989, p. B1.
13. Andrew S. Grove, *High Output Management* (New York: Random House, 1983).
14. Bill Saporito, "The Fix Is in at Home Depot," *Fortune,* February 29, 1988, pp. 73-79.
15. Ralph E. Winter, "How Unisys and Huffy Do It," *The Wall Street Journal,* November 30, 1987, pp. 1 and 8.
16. Martha E. Mengelsdorf, "Beyond Just-In-Time," *Inc.,* February 1989, p. 21.
17. Alex Taylor III, "Back to the Future at Saturn," *Fortune,* August 1, 1988, pp. 63-72.

18. C. Robert Farwell and Bradley A. Rosencrans, "Computer Integrated Manufacturing, Boon or Boondoggle?" *St. Louis Commerce*, March 1988, pp. 23–26.
19. For details on this, see "Enterprise Networking," a special advertising section in *Business Week*, April 11, 1988, pp. 29ff.
20. Merrill Goozner, "U.S. Manufacturers in No Rush to Modernize," *The Washington Post*, February 12, 1989, p. H2.
21. Ross, Johnson, and William O. Winchell, *Business and Quality Circles* (Milwaukee, Wisc.: American Society for Quality Control, 1989).
22. Robert C. Wood, "Squaring Off on Quality Circles," *Inc.*, August 1982, p. 98.
23. Theodore Levitt, "Production-Line Approach to Service," *Harvard Business Review*, September-October 1972, pp. 41–52.
24. Oswald Johnston, "Service Sector Goes High Tech to Stay Ahead of Global Rivals," *Los Angeles Times*, February 26, 1989, pp. 1 & 4 of Part IV.
25. Levitt, "Product Line Approach to Service."

CHAPTER 14

1. "Information Networks: Linking Computers and Communications," *Forbes*, April 3, 1989, pp. 133–44.
2. William M. Bulkeley, "Who Built the First PC? Hint: His Name Isn't Wozniak or Jobs," *The Wall Street Journal*, May 14, 1986, p. 33.
3. Michael Gianturco, "The Supernets Are Coming," *Forbes*, February 20, 1989, pp. 112–18.
4. Richard Lipkin, "Artificial Intelligence," *The Washington Times*, February 19, 1988, p. F6.
5. Judith Graham, "Xerox Directs Its Fax Efforts," *Advertising Age*, June 6, 1988, p. 56.
6. "Harnessing Information Technologies," *Fortune*, July 4, 1988, pp. 15–30.
7. "Fax on the Run," *Marketing Communications*, October 1988, p. 41.
8. John Burgess, "Video Conferencing Gains Popularity in Helping Firms See Eye to Eye," *The Washington Post*, January 24, 1989, pp. C1 and C2.
9. Keith H. Hammonds, "Suddenly, Videotex Is Finding an Audience," *Business Week*, October 10, 1988, pp. 92–94.
10. Kevin Kelley, "Going Global? You'll Need Lawyers, Lobbyists—and Luck," *Business Week*, March 21, 1988, p. 146.
11. John J. Keller, Thane Peterson, Mark Maremont, Katherine M. Hafner, and Matt Rothman, "A Scramble for Global Networks," *Business Week*, March 21, 1988, pp. 140–48.
12. Ibid., p. 142.
13. Hank Gilman, "The Age of Caution," *The Wall Street Journal*, A special report on Technology in the Workplace, June 12, 1987, p. 23D.
14. Geoff Lewis, "The Portable Executive," *Business Week*, October 10, 1988, pp. 102–12.
15. Barton Gellman, "Electronic Vaccines Arrived in Nick of Computer Time," *The Washington Post*, November 9, 1988, pp. A1 and A6.

CHAPTER 15

1. Richard L. Daft, *Management* (Hinsdale, Ill.: The Dryden Press, 1988), p. 39.
2. David A. Houndshell, "The Same Old Principles in New Manufacturing," *Harvard Business Review*, November-December 1988, pp. 54–61.

3. Abraham H. Maslow, *Motivation and Personality* (New York: Harper & Brothers, 1954).
4. Andrew Grove, *High Output Management* (New York: Random House, 1983), pp. 157–80.
5. For more on Theory Y, see Douglas McGregor, *The Human Side of Enterprise* (New York: McGraw-Hill, 1970).
6. Buck Brown, "How the Cookie Crumbled at Mrs. Fields'," *The Wall Street Journal*, January 26, 1989, p. B1.
7. William G. Ouchi, *Theory Z: How American Business Can Meet the Japanese Challenge* (Reading, Mass.: Addison-Wesley Publishing, 1981).
8. John Hoerr, "Is Teamwork a Management Plot? Mostly Not," *Business Week*, February 20, 1989, p. 70.
9. Mike Parker and Jane Slaughter, "The Factory that Runs on Anxiety," *The Washington Post*, October 9, 1988, p. D3.
10. Frederick Herzberg, *Work and the Nature of Man* (World Publishers, 1966).
11. Tom Peters, "Workers' Esteem Tied to Authority," *The Washington Times*, October 25, 1988, p. C2.
12. "The Joy of Working," *Inc.*, November 1987, pp. 61–67.
13. Ibid., p. 66.
14. Tom Peters, "Work Teams Shatter Old Ideas," *The Washington Times*, June 23, 1988, p. C2.
15. Martin J. Gannon, *Management* (Boston, Mass.: Allyn & Bacon, 1988), pp. 256–57.
16. "Letting Labor Share the Driver's Seat," *Business Week*, February 13, 1984, p. 110.
17. David Field, "From Musclebound to Brainy, Preston Thrives in Tough Trade," *The Washington Times*, April 4, 1989, pp. C1 and C9.
18. This section is based on John Case, "Why Work?," *Inc.*, June 19, 1988, pp. 25–28.

CHAPTER 16

1. These illustrations come from "Obsolete Workers Are More Often Retrained than Replaced by Their Firms," *The Wall Street Journal*, May 9, 1984, p. 1; and Keith H. Hammonds, "Help Wanted," *Business Week*, August 10, 1987, pp. 48–53.
2. Frank Swoboda, "IBM Sets Flexible Work Rules to Ease Home Office Strains," *The Washington Post*, October 19, 1988, pp. A1 and A17.
3. Michael J. McCarthy, "Managers Face Dilemma with 'Temps'," *The Wall Street Journal*, April 5, 1988, p. 39.
4. Tom Otwell, "Trend toward Employee Testing May Alter Workplace Expectations," *Outlook*, University of Maryland College Park, February 15, 1988, p. 6.
5. Judy Olian, "Survey Reveals Increased Use of Drug-Screening," *Maryland Today*, Summer 1988, p. 13.
6. Amanda Bennett, "Bu Xinsheng: China's Model Manager," *The Wall Street Journal*, May 30, 1984, p. 36.
7. James R. Morris, "Those Burgeoning Worker Benefits," *Nation's Business*, February 1987, p. 53.
8. Elizabeth Spayd, "The Latest in Bartering: Benefits," *The Washington Post*, April 23, 1989, p. H3.
9. Jeffrey Goldberg, "An 'Old Girls' Network Aids Female Entrepreneurs," The *Washington Business* section of *The Washington Post*, July 11, 1988, pp. 1 and 32–33.
10. "B.E. Forums Back in '89," *Black Enterprise*, March 1989, p. 27.
11. Ron Stodghill III and Paula Dwyer, "A Negative on Affirmative Action," *Business Week*, February 6, 1989, p. 40; and "Assessing Impact of Case on Race Quotas," *The Wall Street Journal*, January 25, 1989, p. B.

CHAPTER 17

1. "Union Suicide," *The Washington Times,* March 9, 1989, p. F2.
2. Lindley H. Clark Jr., "Airlines and Railroads: A Weird Marriage," *The Wall Street Journal,* March 15, 1989, p. A18.
3. Raymond Price, "Revival of Union Warfare," *The Washington Times,* March 10, 1989, p. F3.
4. James J. Kilpatrick, "Don't Rehire the Controllers," *The Washington Post,* April 7, 1988, p. A23.
5. Kevin Kelly and Hazel Bradford, "Labor May Have Found an Rx for Growth," *Business Week,* February 22, 1988, pp. 162–166.
6. Ibid.
7. Spencer Rich, "Economic Fortunes Fading for America's Less Educated," *The Washington Post,* June 2, 1988, pp. A1 and A18.
8. John A. Byrne, Ronald Grover, and Todd Vogel, "Is the Boss Getting Paid Too Much?" *Business Week,* May 1, 1989, pp. 46–52.
9. John A. Byrne, "The $60 Million Chairman," *Business Week,* May 16, 1988, p. 42.
10. Amanda Bennett, "Top Dollar," *The Wall Street Journal,* March 28, 1988, pp. 1 and 8.
11. "Bring CEO Pay Back Down to Earth," *Business Week,* May 1, 1989, p. 146.
12. "Abroad, It's Another World," *Fortune,* June 6, 1988, p. 78.
13. Aaron Bernstein, "So You Think You've Come a Long Way, Baby?," *Business Week,* February 29, 1988, pp. 48–52.
14. Report from June O'Neill of the Urban Institute in "It's Not Worth It," *The Wall Street Journal,* February 7, 1984.
15. Willis Witter and Karen Riley, "New Social Strategy: Make Businesses Pay," *The Washington Times,* March 9, 1988, pp. C1 and C4.
16. Warren Brookes, "Day Care Crises or Turf War?," *The Washington Times,* April 20, 1988, pp. F1 and F4.
17. Fern Schumer Chapman, "Making Time Out to Have a Baby," *Washington Post Health,* September 22, 1987, pp. 13–15.
18. Jane Bryant Quinn, "A Crisis in Child Care," *Newsweek,* February 15, 1988, p. 57.
19. "The Mommy Track, A Question of Choice," *Business Week,* March 20, 1989, p. 178.
20. Amanda Bennett, Jolie Solomon and Allanna Sullivan, "Firms Debate Hard Line on Alcoholics," *The Wall Street Journal,* April 13, 1989, p. B1.
21. "Lest We Forget, ESOPs Are for Employees," *Business Week,* May 15, 1989, p. 166.
22. "ESOP's Offer Way to Sell Stakes in Small Firms," *The Wall Street Journal,* May 3, 1988, p. 33.
23. Christopher Farrell, Tim Smart, and Keith H. Hammonds, "Suddenly, Blue Chips Are Red for ESOPs," *Business Week,* March 20, 1989, p. 144.
24. Bruce G. Posner, "In Search of Equity," *Inc.,* April 1985, p. 27.
25. Michael Schroeder and John Hoerr, "Has Weirton's ESOP Worked Too Well?" *Business Week,* January 23, 1989, pp. 66–67.
26. James P. Miller, "Joining the Game," *The Wall Street Journal,* December 12, 1988, pp. A1 and A7.

CHAPTER 18

1. "Through the Wringer," *Inc.,* December 1984, pp. 95–96.
2. Charles J. Bodenstab, "Flying Blind," *Inc.,* May 1988, pp. 141–44.

3. George Melloan, "Making Gizmos in Arthur Andersen's Factory," *The Wall Street Journal,* August 23, 1988, p. 27.
4. Penelope Wang, "Will the Truth Hurt?," *Forbes,* September 19, 1988, p. 138.
5. Lee Berton, "Last In, First Out, And Keep the Flies Off the Lemonade," *The Wall Street Journal,* May 13, 1988, pp. 1 and 9.
6. "Business Bulletin," *The Wall Street Journal,* April 27, 1989, p. A1.
7. Robert Kaplan, "Because of the Conventions of Accounting, Most Companies Don't Really Know What Their Products Cost or How to Go About Trimming Expenses," *Inc.,* April 1988, pp. 55–67.

CHAPTER 19

1. Eileen Davis, "The Root of All Evil," *Venture,* December 1988, pp. 77–78.
2. Sanford L. Jacobs, "A Dash of Cost-Control Savvy Help Turn Spice Firm Around," *The Wall Street Journal,* March 26, 1984, p. 31.
3. Robert Letovsky, "Why Bankers and Business Owners Fight," *Inc.,* February 1989, p. 16.
4. "David L. Birch," *Inc.,* April 1989, pp. 38–39.
5. Ellyne E. Spragins, "Courting Your Banker," *Inc.,* May 1989, p. 129.
6. David R. Sands, "Kay Jeweler Sells Receivable Accounts to Bank," *The Washington Times,* June 28, 1988, p. C3.
7. Robert J. Samuelson, "Does Business Borrow Too Much?" *The Washington Post,* January 25, 1989, p. A21.
8. Michael Shrage, "Venture Capital's New Look," *The Wall Street Journal,* May 20, 1988, editorial page.
9. Doug Garr, "Will Outside Capital Disrupt the Family?" *Venture,* December 1988, pp. 82–84.

CHAPTER 20

1. Christopher Farrell, Leah Nathans, Joan O'C. Hamilton, and Leslie Helm, "Finance," *Business Week,* February 6, 1989, pp. 82–83.
2. Jeffrey M. Laderman, "What Does Equity Financing Really Cost?" *Business Week,* November 7, 1988, pp. 196–198.
3. Kevin G. Salwen, "Wrong Calls by Analysts Leave Investors Wary," *The Wall Street Journal,* January 24, 1989, p. C1.
4. Louis Rukeyser (ed.), *Louis Rukeyser's Business Almanac* (New York: Simon and Schuster, 1988), p. 327.
5. Michael Siconolfi, "Mutual Funds," *The Wall Street Journal,* January 3, 1989, p. 6R.
6. James Flanagan, "Futures Pits Too Important Not to Reform," *Los Angeles Times,* January 20, 1989, pp. 1 and 5 of Part IV.
7. Bernard J. Winger and Ralph R. Frasca, *Investments: Introduction to Analysis and Planning* (Columbus, Ohio: Merrill Publishing Co., 1988), p. 59.

CHAPTER 21

1. David Pauly, Mark Miller, Carolyn Friday, and Harry Hurt III "Going for Broke," *Newsweek,* June 20, 1988, pp. 40–41.
2. Robert Samuelson, "Bailing Out the Thrifts," *Newsweek,* May 2, 1988, p. 52.
3. Albert B. Crenshaw, "Showdown Looms as Credit Unions Hit the Big Time," *The Washington Post,* July 31, 1988, p. H3.
4. "Credit Unions—Calm Amid Chaos," *U.S. News & World Report,* July 4, 1988, p. 64.

5. James Flanigan, "Bank Bailouts a Sure Draw for Smart Money," *Los Angeles Times*, January 8, 1989, p. 1 of Part IV.
6. Christopher Elias, "Thrifts Face Uncertain Future as Buoy-Up Costs Keep Rising," *Insight*, January 2, 1989, pp. 36-38.
7. Warren Brookes, "The Unindicted Co-Conspirator," *The Washington Times*, April 25, 1989, p. F1.
8. "The Seamless Web," *The Wall Street Journal*, May 26, 1989, p. A10.
9. David Hoffman and Kathleen Day, "Bush Unveils S&L Rescue Plan; Cost to Public Put at $40 Billion," *The Washington Post*, February 7, 1989, pp. A1 and A12.
10. Robert A. Rosenblatt, "200 Insolvent S&Ls Expected to Fail in Next 2 Years," *Los Angeles Times*, March 3, 1989, pp. 1 and 11 of Part IV.
11. Art Pine, "Thrift Crisis Could Produce a Sequel," *Los Angeles Times*, February 18, 1989, pp. 1 and 4 of Part IV.
12. Jerry Knight, "A 'Grim Report Card' for the Shrinking Savings and Loan Industry," *The Washington Post*, May 16, 1989, p. D3.
13. David Sands, "S&Ls Drop Moniker to Shake Bad Associations," *The Washington Times*, April 26, 1989, pp. C1 and C10.
14. "How Safe Are Your Deposits?" *Consumer Reports*, August 1988, pp. 502-503.
15. James Flanigan, "Bank Bailouts."
16. Catherine Yang and David Zigas, "Only the Strong Will Survive the Thrift Rescue," *Business Week*, May 8, 1969, pp. 122-123.
17. Frederick A. Miller and Jonathan B. Levine, "A Bank Line That's Getting a Lot Longer," *Business Week*, March 28, 1988, pp. 80-81.
18. Gary Hector, "How Banking Will Shake Out," *Fortune*, April 25, 1988, pp. 207-224.
19. Vicky Cahan, "Banks Are on the Brink of Breaking Loose," *Business Week*, March 7, 1989, pp. 99-100.
20. "Business Bulletin," *The Wall Street Journal*, October 6, 1988, p. A1.
21. Frederic A. Miller, "The Giants Retrench," *Business Week*, April 3, 1989, pp. 94-95.
22. Robert E. Norton, "The Fed Heads into No Man's Land," *Fortune*, April 25, 1988, pp. 121-136.
23. James E. Lebherz, "How the Federal Reserve System 'Nudges' the Nation's Economy," *The Wasington Post*, May 29, 1988, p. H8.
24. Edwin A. Finn, Jr., "How Clear Is That Rearview Mirror?," *Forbes*, April 3, 1989, p. 40.
25. Jeffrey A. Frieden, *Banking on the World* (New York: Harper & Row, 1987), p. 79.
26. Ibid., p. 81.
27. William Glasgall, "The World's Top 50 Banks: It's Official—Japan Is Way Out Front," *Business Week*, June 27, 1988, pp. 76-78.

APPENDIX TO PART 6

1. James Flanigan, "Colleges Must Learn the ABCs of Economics," *Los Angeles Times*, September 4, 1988, p. 1 of Part IV.
2. "Strategies for a Nation of Spenders," *U.S. News & World Report*, August 15, 1988, pp. 70-77.

CHAPTER 22

1. Elizabeth Grillo Olson, "Punitive Damages: How Much Is Too Much?," *Business Week*, March 27, 1989, pp. 54-56.
2. T. R. Reid, "Insurance Famine Plagues Nation," *The Washington Post*, January 23, 1986, pp. 1 and 6.
3. Ronald Bailey, "Legal Mayhem," *Forbes*, November 14, 1988, pp. 97-98.
4. Christopher Farrell and Resa King, "Insurers Are Arming for Another Rate War," *Business Week*, January 9, 1989, pp. 108-109.
5. Christopher Farrell, Resa King, and Joan O'C. Hamilton, "The Crisis Is Over—But Insurance Will Never Be the Same," *Business Week*, May 25, 1987, pp. 122-123.
6. Michael M. Phillips, "Contraception R&D Falls Out of Favor," *Los Angeles Times*, February 6, 1989, p. 3 of Part IV.
7. Steve Waldman, Daniel Shapiro, and Tom Schmitz, "The Surge in Self Insurance," *Newsweek*, March 7, 1988, pp. 74-75.
8. Lyda Phillips, "Insurance Group Warns of Crisis in Industry," *The Washington Post*, November 20, 1988, pp. F1 and F4.
9. LaBarbara Bowman, "Car Owners Rev Up Revolt on Insurance," *USA Today*, February 1, 1989, pp. A1 and A2.
10. J. David Cummins, "What's Driving Auto Insurance Up?," *The Wall Street Journal*, January 5, 1989, editorial page.
11. Christopher Elias, "Insurers Begin to Take Heed of Growing Consumer Anger," *Insight*, May 8, 1989, pp. 40-43.
12. Carolyn Lochhead, "Strict Liability Causing Some Firms to Give Up on Promising Ideas," *The Washington Times*, August 22, 1988, pp. B1 and B6.
13. Carolyn Lochhead, "All Are Liable in Product Liability," *Insight*, February 15, 1988, pp. 46-47.
14. David Holzman, "Medicine Minus a Cost Tourniquet," *Insight*, August 8, 1988, pp. 9-16.
15. Jane Bryant Quinn, "Forcing You into an HMO," *Newsweek*, September 12, 1988, p. 51.
16. Amanda Bennett, "Many Companies Aren't Prepared to Deal with Sudden Death of Chief Executive," *The Wall Street Journal*, April 29, 1988, p. 25.
17. Ken Wells and Charles McCoy, "Out of Control," *The Wall Street Journal*, April 3, 1989, pp. A1 and A4.
18. David Landis, "Best Jobs 'Pampered'," *USA Today*, May 19, 1988, p. 1.
19. William P. Barrett, "Boring All the Way to the Bank," *Forbes*, March 7, 1988, pp. 168-169.

CHAPTER 23

1. Kenneth Blanchard and Norman Vincent Peale, *The Power of Ethical Management* (New York: William Morrow, 1988).
2. Ferdinand F. Mauser and David J. Schwartz, *American Business*, 6th ed. (New York: Harcourt Brace Jovanovich, 1986), p. 594.
3. Charles Register, "Lost in Paper," *The Wall Street Journal*, February 24, 1989, pp. R5 and R8.
4. Clare Ansberry, "Allegheny International Seeks Protection Under Bankruptcy Law in Surprise Move," *The Wall Street Journal*, February 22, 1988, p. 2.
5. Malcolm Gladwell and Steven Pearlstein, "Eastern Gambles to Buy Time," *The Washington Post*, March 10, 1989, pp. D1 and D3.
6. Maria Shao, Amy Dunkin, and Patrick Cole, "There's a Rumble in the Video Arcade," *Business Week*, February 20, 1989, p. 37.
7. "FTCs Welcome Return," *Advertising Age*, February 6, 1989, p. 16.
8. Charles Register, "Airline Deregulation after 10 Years," *Business Review*, November/December 1988, pp. 1-7.
9. Tim Smart and Leah J. Nathans, "A Backlash Against Business," *Business Week*, February 6, 1989, pp. 30-31.

10. John H. Filer, "The Social Goals of a Corporation," in *Corporations and Their Critics*, ed. Thomas Bradshaw and David Vogel (New York: McGraw-Hill, 1981), p. 271.
11. Ibid., pp. 245–247.
12. Meg Cox, "Corporate Giving Is Flat, and the Future Looks Bleaker," *The Wall Street Journal*, October 17, 1988, p. B1.
13. Trevor Armbrister, "When Companies Care," *Reader's Digest*, April 1989, pp. 25–32.
14. Kenneth E. Goodpaster and John B. Mathews, Jr., "Can a Corporation Have a Conscience?" *Harvard Business Review*, January/February 1982, pp. 132–141.
15. Rick Wartzman, "Nature or Nurture? Study Blames Ethical Lapses on Corporate Goals," *The Wall Street Journal*, October 9, 1987, p. 27.
16. Ibid.
17. "Stonewalling at Beech-Nut," *Business Week*, February 22, 1988, p. 174.
18. "Conviction in Beech-Nut Case Reversed," *Los Angeles Times*, March 31, 1989, p. 5 of Part IV.
19. "What Happened to 50 People Involved in Insider-Trading Cases," *The Wall Street Journal*, November 18, 1987, p. 22.
20. John M. Broder, "1st Defense Fraud Indictments Made," *Los Angeles Times*, January 7, 1989, pp. 1 and 18 of Part 1.
21. Eileen White Read, "Defense Contractor's Ethics Programs Get Scrutinized," *The Wall Street Journal*, July 21, 1988, p. 4.
22. George Melloan, "Business Ethics and the Competitive Urge," *The Wall Street Journal*, August 9, 1988, p. 27.
23. Mike McClintock, "Norelco's Troubled Waters," *Washington Home*, February 9, 1989, p. 5.
24. Wayne Walley, "Advertisers 'Up in Arms'" *Advertising Age*, March 27, 1989, pp. 1 and 68; and Wayne Walley, "Decency Debate," *Advertising Age*, March 6, 1989, pp. 1 and 74.
25. Timothy D. Schellhardt, "What Bosses Think about Corporate Ethics," *The Wall Street Journal*, April 6, 1988, p. 27.
26. Amanda Bennett, "Ethics Codes Spread Despite Criticism," *The Wall Street Journal*, July 15, 1988, p. 17.
27. Ibid.
28. Blanchard and Peale, *The Power of Ethical Management*.
29. Danielle Pletka, "Firms Gifting Along to Get Along," *Insight*, January 23, 1989, pp. 34–35.

CHAPTER 24

1. James Risen, "The New International Auto," *Los Angeles Times*, February 12, 1989, pp. 1 and 4 of Part IV.
2. John Schwartz, Mark Starr, Stephanie Russell, and Tom Schmitz, "Selling Coals to Newcastle," *Newsweek*, January 4, 1988, pp. 37–38.
3. Paul W. McCracken, "Why U.S. Exports Are a Casualty," *The Wall Street Journal*, March 3, 1989, p. A12.
4. Stuart Auerbach, "Current Account Deficit in 1987 Hit $160 Billion," *The Washington Post*, March 16, 1988, pp. F1 and F5.
5. Jaclyn Fierman, "The Selling of American (Cont'd)," *Fortune*, May 23, 1988, p. 64.
6. Karen Riley, "U.S. Piles Up $99 Billion of Global Red Ink," *The Washington Times*, July 1, 1988, pp. C1 and C2.

7. Warren Brookes, "Black Cloud or Silver Lining?" *The Washington Times*, October 19, 1987, pp. D1 and D2.
8. Nathaniel Gilbert, "The Ten Commandments of Global Management," *Newsweek*, June 27, 1988, an advertising supplement.
9. Francis C. Brown III, "Franchising Abroad Is Hot—Perhaps Too Hot," *The Wall Street Journal*, April 25, 1988, p. 29.
10. "Business without Borders," *U.S. News & World Report*, June 20, 1988, pp. 48–53.
11. Karen Riley, "Joint Ventures with Soviet Expected to Multiply," *The Washington Times*, March 29, 1989, p. C3.
12. Mark Tapscott, "Chevrolet and Toyota Teamwork Pays Off in Nova," *The Washington Times*, February 26, 1988, p. E9.
13. "Bypassing Sanctions with Countertrade," *Insight*, February 8, 1988, p. 38.
14. Matt Schaffer, "Barter for Exports," *The Washington Post*, January 8, 1989, p. C2.
15. Donald A. Ball and Wendell H. McCullock, Jr., *International Business*, 3rd ed. (Homewood, Ill.: BPI/Irwin, 1988), p. 279.
16. Ibid.
17. Thomas Burdick and Charlene Mitchell, "Ignore Global Protocols at Your Peril," *The Washington Times*, April 18, 1989, p. C2.
18. Charles C. Smith, "A Yen for Japan," *Contact* (University of Massachusetts at Amherst), Winter 1986, p. 3.
19. Mary J. Pitzer, "Fuller's Worldwide Strategy: Think Local," *Business Week*, November 16, 1987, p. 169.
20. Peter Truell, "Financing for Exports Grows Harder to Find for All but Big Firms," *The Wall Street Journal*, May 14, 1987, pp. 1 and 19.
21. Edwin A. Finn Jr., "Sons of Smoot-Hawley," *Forbes*, February 6, 1989, pp. 38–40.
22. Jim Powell, "Super-301: The Economic Equivalent of Civilian Bombing," *The Wall Street Journal*, May 30, 1989, editorial page; and Warren Brookes, "Treacherous Trade Move?," *The Washington Times*, May 30, 1989, p. C1.
23. Bruce Nussbaum, Dori Jones Young, Gregory Miles, Russell Mitchell, and Lois Therrien, "Help Wanted from the Multinationals," *Business Week*, February 29, 1988, pp. 68–70.
24. John Burgess, " 'Global Offices' on Rise as Firms Shift Service Jobs Abroad," *The Washington Post*, April 20, 1989, pp. E1 and E2.
25. David G. Pearson and Eduardo Lachica, "IMF Creates $8.4 Billion Facility for Poorest Nations, Marking Shift," *The Wall Street Journal*, December 30, 1987, p. 14.
26. Howard Banks, "GATT—Almost Back on Track," *Forbes*, March 20, 1989, p. 33.
27. Casper W. Weinberger, " '1992' Is Closer than We Think," *Forbes*, April 17, 1989, p. 33.
28. Edith Terry, William J. Holstein, Wendy Zellner, and Zachary Schiller, "Getting Ready for the Great North American Shakeout," *Business Week*, April 4, 1988, pp. 44–46.
29. Warren Brookes, "Mistaking Cause for Effect," *The Washington Times*, May 11, 1987, p. D1.
30. "China Globalized," *The Wall Street Journal*, May 22, 1989, p. A14.

NAME INDEX

COMPANY AND PRODUCT INDEX

GENERAL INDEX

CREDITS

CONTENTS

PROLOGUE

CHAPTER 1

CHAPTER 2

CHAPTER 3

CHAPTER 4

CHAPTER 5

CHAPTER 6

CHAPTER 7

CHAPTER 8

CHAPTER 9

CHAPTER 10

APPENDIX TO PART 3

MN. p. 318, Courtesy Media General. p. 320, Boy Scout Council of Greater St. Louis/Centra Advertising Company. p. 321, American Cancer Society.

CHAPTER 11

p. 326, Courtesy of General Electric. p. 328, Courtesy of General Electric. p. 330, Courtesy of International Business Machines Corporation. p. 334, Gill Copeland/Journalism Services. p. 335, Stephen Green/Journalism Services. p. 340, Brownie Harris/The Stock Market. p. 341, Scott Wanner/Journalism Services. p. 349, Photo courtesy of Hewlett-Packard.

CHAPTER 12

p. 356, Courtesy Chrysler Corporation. p. 358, Courtesy Chrysler Corporation. p. 359, Photo courtesy Hewlett-Packard Company. p. 361, Photo courtesy of Anchora of Delta Gamma. p. 363, Courtesy The Boeing Company. p. 366, Photo by Dana Duke. p. 374, Courtesy of Campbell Soup Company. p. 379, Scott Witte/Third Coast. p. 382, Photography by Voyles.

CHAPTER 13

p. 390, Courtesy Allen-Bradley Co. p. 392, Courtesy Allen-Bradley Co. p. 395, Paul E. Burd/Journalism Services. p. 398, Courtesy Tennessee Department of Economic and Community Development/Advertising Agency: Eric Ericson and Associates, Nashville, Tennessee. p. 401, Courtesy Union Electric Co. p. 403, Photo courtesy Leaseway, Inc. p. 406, Courtesy of Converse, Inc. p. 410, Courtesy Union Electric Co. p. 416, Fingertip Banking ®, Mercantile Bancorporation, St. Louis, MO. p. 417, Photo courtesy of Hewlett-Packard Company.

CHAPTER 14

p. 424, Reproduced with the permission of AT&T. p. 426, Courtesy Supercomputer Systems Inc. p. 430, Courtesy of Compaq Computer Corporation; Photos courtesy of Digital Equipment Corporation; Courtesy of International Business Machines Corporation; Graphics courtesy of Convex Computer Corporation; Courtesy of Cray Research, Inc. p. 433, Lotus Development Corporation. p. 438, Photography by Voyles. p. 444, Reprinted with permission: Tribune Media Services. p. 445, Reprinted with permission of BellSouth Corporation. p. 446,

Brownie Harris/The Stock Market. p. 449, Photo reprinted with the permission of General Motors Corporation.

CHAPTER 15

p. 460, Courtesy Carnival Cruise Lines. p. 462, Courtesy Carnival Cruise Lines. p. 464, Reproduced with the permission of AT&T Corporate Archive. p. 466, Photo courtesy Southwestern Bell Corporation. p. 469, Photo courtesy Hewlett-Packard Company. p. 472, Courtesy The Limited Stores. p. 478, Courtesy of Apple Computer, Inc. p. 481, Courtesy of Preston Company, Inc.

CHAPTER 16

p. 488, Courtesy Amigo Mobility International. p. 490, James Schnepf. p. 495, Courtesy College of Lake County Placement Office/Patricia R. Kirrchherr Director/Bill Kniest Photographer. p. 499, Courtesy General Dynamics. p. 500, Courtesy College of Lake County Placement Office/ Patricia R. Kirrchherr Director/Bill Kniest Photographer. p. 501, Courtesy of American Airlines. p. 506, Dirk Gallian/Journalism Services. p. 510, Tom Tracy/The Stock Market. p. 512, Rich Clark/Journalism Services.

CHAPTER 17

p. 532, Wide World Photos, Inc. p. 534, Cynthia Mathews/The Stock Market. p. 536, © Joan Liftin. p. 544, Joseph Jacobson/Journalism Services. p. 546, John Patsch/Journalism Services. p. 555, Studio 7L Ltd. Dick Luria, Medichrome, Div./The Stock Shop, Inc. p. 557, Photography by Voyles.

CHAPTER 18

p. 568, Courtesy Smith & Hawken. p. 570, Courtesy Smith & Hawken. p. 573, Photo courtesy of Hewlett-Packard Company. p. 576, Photography by Voyles. p. 577, Joseph Jacobson/Journalism Services. p. 585, Gregory Murphey/Journalism Services. p. 590, Melanie Carr/Journalism Services.

CHAPTER 19

p. 604, Paul F. Gero/Journalism Services. p. 606, Lawrence Barns. p. 613, First Chicago. p. 621, Courtesy of The Department of the Treasury Fiscal Service.

CHAPTER 20

p. 628, Gregory Murphey/Journalism Services. p. 630, ©1989 Louie Psihoyos/Matrix. p. 640, Jon Riley/The Stock Shop. p. 643, Courtesy Twentieth Century Investors. P. 644, Journalism Services. p. 645, Courtesy the Chicago Board of Trade. p. 647, Bill Crofton/Journalism Services; Mike Kidulich/Journalism Services.

CHAPTER 21

p. 658, Courtesy Home Savings of America. p. 660, Courtesy of the Board of Governors, Federal Reserve System. p. 664, Scott Wanner/ Journalism Services. p. 666, The Stock Shop. p. 667, Joseph Jacobson/Journalism Services. p. 668, © American Bankers Association. Reprinted with permission. All rights reserved. p. 674, Bettmann, Newsphotos. p. 677, Courtesy PNC Financial Corp. p. 684, Courtesy of U.S. Department of the Treasury. p. 685, Joseph Jacobson/Journalism Services.

CHAPTER 22

p. 702, Michael J. Hruby. p. 704, Courtesy of Heinz Popp. p. 707, John Patsch/Journalism Services. p. 708, Oscar Williams/Journalism Services. p. 714, Joseph Jacobson/Journalism Services. p. 720, Joseph Jacobson/Journalism Services. p. 724, St. Louis *Globe-Dispatch*.

CHAPTER 23

p. 732, Everett C. Johnson/Folio, Inc. p. 734, Courtesy Infinite Creations, Inc. p. 737, Scott Wanner/Journalism Services. p. 743, Brent Nicastro/Third Coast, p. 746, The Bettmann Archive. p. 747, Scott J. Witte/Third Coast; Photography by Voyles. p. 755, Harvey Moshman/Journalism Services. p. 756, Joseph Jacobson/Journalism Services.

CHAPTER 24

p. 766, Courtesy Ford Motor Company. p. 768, © 1990 Steven Begleiter. p. 771, Tim McCabe/ Journalism Services. p. 799, Dave Brown/Journalism Services. p. 780, N'Diaye/Journalism Services. p. 783, Scott Wanner/Journalism Services. p. 785, Mark Snyder/Journalism Services. p. 791, Courtesy Ford Motor Company.